Lecture Notes in Artificial Intelligence 12713

Subseries of Lecture Notes in Computer Science

Series Editors

Randy Goebel
University of Alberta, Edmonton, Canada
Yuzuru Tanaka
Hokkaido University, Sapporo, Japan
Wolfgang Wahlster
DFKI and Saarland University, Saarbrücken, Germany

Founding Editor

Jörg Siekmann
DFKI and Saarland University, Saarbrücken, Germany

More information about this subseries at http://www.springer.com/series/1244

Kamal Karlapalem · Hong Cheng ·
Naren Ramakrishnan · R. K. Agrawal ·
P. Krishna Reddy · Jaideep Srivastava ·
Tanmoy Chakraborty (Eds.)

Advances in Knowledge Discovery and Data Mining

25th Pacific-Asia Conference, PAKDD 2021
Virtual Event, May 11–14, 2021
Proceedings, Part II

 Springer

Editors
Kamal Karlapalem ⓘ
IIIT, Hyderabad
Hyderabad, India

Naren Ramakrishnan
Virginia Tech
Arlington, VA, USA

P. Krishna Reddy ⓘ
IIIT Hyderabad
Hyderabad, India

Tanmoy Chakraborty ⓘ
IIIT Delhi
New Delhi, India

Hong Cheng
Chinese University of Hong Kong
Shatin, Hong Kong

R. K. Agrawal
Jawaharlal Nehru University
New Delhi, India

Jaideep Srivastava
University of Minnesota
Minneapolis, MN, USA

ISSN 0302-9743   ISSN 1611-3349   (electronic)
Lecture Notes in Artificial Intelligence
ISBN 978-3-030-75764-9   ISBN 978-3-030-75765-6   (eBook)
https://doi.org/10.1007/978-3-030-75765-6

LNCS Sublibrary: SL7 – Artificial Intelligence

© Springer Nature Switzerland AG 2021
This work is subject to copyright. All rights are reserved by the Publisher, whether the whole or part of the material is concerned, specifically the rights of translation, reprinting, reuse of illustrations, recitation, broadcasting, reproduction on microfilms or in any other physical way, and transmission or information storage and retrieval, electronic adaptation, computer software, or by similar or dissimilar methodology now known or hereafter developed.
The use of general descriptive names, registered names, trademarks, service marks, etc. in this publication does not imply, even in the absence of a specific statement, that such names are exempt from the relevant protective laws and regulations and therefore free for general use.
The publisher, the authors and the editors are safe to assume that the advice and information in this book are believed to be true and accurate at the date of publication. Neither the publisher nor the authors or the editors give a warranty, expressed or implied, with respect to the material contained herein or for any errors or omissions that may have been made. The publisher remains neutral with regard to jurisdictional claims in published maps and institutional affiliations.

This Springer imprint is published by the registered company Springer Nature Switzerland AG
The registered company address is: Gewerbestrasse 11, 6330 Cham, Switzerland

General Chairs' Preface

On behalf of the Organizing Committee, it is our great pleasure to welcome you to the 25th Pacific-Asia Conference on Knowledge Discovery and Data Mining (PAKDD 2021). Starting in 1997, PAKDD has long established itself as one of the leading international conferences in data mining and knowledge discovery. Held during May 11–14, 2021, PAKDD returned to India for the second time, after a gap of 11 years, moving from Hyderabad in 2010 to New Delhi in 2021. Due to the unexpected COVID-19 epidemic, the conference was held fully online, and we made all the conference sessions accessible online to participants around the world.

Our gratitude goes first and foremost to the researchers, who submitted their work to the PAKDD 2021 main conference, workshops, and data mining contest. We thank them for the efforts in research, as well as in preparing high-quality online presentations videos. It is our distinct honor that five eminent keynote speakers graced the conference: Professor Anil Jain of the Michigan State University, USA, Professor Masaru Kitsuregawa of the Tokyo University, and also the National Institute of Informatics, Japan, Dr. Lada Adamic of Facebook, Prof. Fabrizio Sebastiani of ISTI-CNR, Italy, and Professor Sunita Sarawagi of IIT-Mumbai, India. Each of them is a leader of international renown in their respective areas, and we look forward to their participation.

Given the importance of data science, not just to academia but also to industry, we are pleased to have two distinguished industry speakers. The conference program was further enriched with three high-quality tutorials, eight workshops on cutting-edge topics, and one data mining contest on the prediction of memory failures.

We would like to express our sincere gratitude to the contributions of the Senior Program Committee (SPC) members, Program Committee (PC) members, and anonymous reviewers, led by the PC co-chairs, Kamal Karlapalem (IIIT, Hyderabad), Hong Cheng (CUHK), Naren Ramakrishnan (Virginia Tech). It is through their untiring efforts that the conference have an excellent technical program. We are also thankful to the other Organizing Committee members: industry co-chairs, Gautam Shroff (TCS) and Srikanta Bedathur (IIT Delhi); workshop co-chairs, Ganesh Ramakrishnan (IIT Mumbai) and Manish Gupta (Microsoft); tutorial co-chairs, B. Ravindran (IIT Chennai) and Naresh Manwani (IIIT Hyderabad); Publicity Co-Chairs, Sonali Agrawal (IIIT Allahabad), R. Uday Kiran (University of Aizu), and Jerry C-W Lin (WNU of Applied Sciences); competitions chair, Mengling Feng (NUS); Proceedings Chair, Tanmoy Chakraborthy (IIIT Delhi); and registration/local arrangement co-chairs, Vasudha Bhatnagar (University of Delhi), Vikram Goel (IIIT Delhi), Naveen Kumar (University of Delhi), Rajiv Ratn Shah (IIIT Delhi), Arvind Agarwal (IBM), Aditi Sharan (JNU), Mukesh Giluka (JNU) and Dhirendra Kumar (DTU).

We appreciate the hosting organizations IIIT Hyderabad and the JNU, Delhi, and all our sponsors for their institutional and financial support of PAKDD 2021. We also appreciate Alibaba for sponsoring the data mining contest. We feel indebted to the

PAKDD Steering Committee for its continuing guidance and sponsorship of the paper and student travel awards.

Finally, our sincere thanks go to all the participants and volunteers. There would be no conference without you. We hope all of you enjoy PAKDD 2021.

May 2021

R. K. Agrawal
P. Krishna Reddy
Jaideep Srivastava

PC Chairs' Preface

It is our great pleasure to present the 25th Pacific-Asia Conference on Knowledge Discovery and Data Mining (PAKDD 2021). PAKDD is a premier international forum for exchanging original research results and practical developments in the space of KDD-related areas, including data science, machine learning, and emerging applications.

We received 768 submissions from across the world. We performed an initial screening of all submissions, leading to the desk rejection of 89 submissions due to violations of double-blind and page limit guidelines. Six papers were also withdrawn by authors during the review period. For submissions entering the double-blind review process, each paper received at least three reviews from PC members. Further, an assigned SPC member also led a discussion of the paper and reviews with the PC members. The PC co-chairs then considered the recommendations and meta-reviews from SPC members in making the final decision. As a result, 157 papers were accepted, yielding an acceptance rate of 20.4%. The COVID-19 pandemic caused several challenges to the reviewing process, and we appreciate the diligence of all reviewers, PC members, and SPC members to ensure a quality PAKDD 2021 program.

The conference was conducted in an online environment, with accepted papers presented via a pre-recorded video presentation with a live Q/A session. The conference program also featured five keynotes from distinguished researchers in the community, one most influential paper talk, two invited industrial talks, eight cutting-edge workshops, three comprehensive tutorials, and one dedicated data mining competition session.

We wish to sincerely thank all SPC members, PC members, and external reviewers for their invaluable efforts in ensuring a timely, fair, and highly effective PAKDD 2021 program.

May 2021

Hong Cheng
Kamal Karlapalem
Naren Ramakrishnan

Organization

Organization Committee

General Co-chairs

R. K. Agrawal	Jawaharlal Nehru University, India
P. Krishna Reddy	IIIT Hyderabad, India
Jaideep Srivastava	University of Minnesota, USA

Program Co-chairs

Kamal Karlapalem	IIIT Hyderabad, India
Hong Cheng	The Chinese University of Hong Kong, China
Naren Ramakrishnan	Virginia Tech, USA

Industry Co-chairs

Gautam Shroff	TCS Research, India
Srikanta Bedathur	IIT Delhi, India

Workshop Co-chairs

Ganesh Ramakrishnan	IIT Bombay, India
Manish Gupta	Microsoft Research, India

Tutorial Co-chairs

B. Ravindran	IIT Madras, India
Naresh Manwani	IIIT Hyderabad, India

Publicity Co-chairs

Sonali Agarwal	IIIT Allahabad, India
R. Uday Kiran	The University of Aizu, Japan
Jerry Chau-Wei Lin	Western Norway University of Applied Sciences, Norway

Sponsorship Chair

P. Krishna Reddy	IIIT Hyderabad, India

Competitions Chair

Mengling Feng	National University of Singapore, Singapore

Proceedings Chair

Tanmoy Chakraborty	IIIT Delhi, India

Registration/Local Arrangement Co-chairs

Vasudha Bhatnagar	University of Delhi, India
Vikram Goyal	IIIT Delhi, India
Naveen Kumar	University of Delhi, India
Arvind Agarwal	IBM Research, India
Rajiv Ratn Shah	IIIT Delhi, India
Aditi Sharan	Jawaharlal Nehru University, India
Mukesh Kumar Giluka	Jawaharlal Nehru University, India
Dhirendra Kumar	Delhi Technological University, India

Steering Committee

Longbing Cao	University of Technology Sydney, Australia
Ming-Syan Chen	National Taiwan University, Taiwan, ROC
David Cheung	University of Hong Kong, China
Gill Dobbie	The University of Auckland, New Zealand
Joao Gama	University of Porto, Portugal
Zhiguo Gong	University of Macau, Macau
Tu Bao Ho	Japan Advanced Institute of Science and Technology, Japan
Joshua Z. Huang	Shenzhen Institutes of Advanced Technology, Chinese Academy of Sciences, China
Masaru Kitsuregawa	Tokyo University, Japan
Rao Kotagiri	University of Melbourne, Australia
Jae-Gil Lee	Korea Advanced Institute of Science and Technology, South Korea
Ee-Peng Lim	Singapore Management University, Singapore
Huan Liu	Arizona State University, USA
Hiroshi Motoda	AFOSR/AOARD and Osaka University, Japan
Jian Pei	Simon Fraser University, Canada
Dinh Phung	Monash University, Australia
P. Krishna Reddy	International Institute of Information Technology, Hyderabad (IIIT-H), India
Kyuseok Shim	Seoul National University, South Korea
Jaideep Srivastava	University of Minnesota, USA
Thanaruk Theeramunkong	Thammasat University, Thailand
Vincent S. Tseng	National Chiao Tung University, Taiwan, ROC
Takashi Washio	Osaka University, Japan
Geoff Webb	Monash University, Australia
Kyu-Young Whang	Korea Advanced Institute of Science and Technology, South Korea
Graham Williams	Australian National University, Australia
Min-Ling Zhang	Southeast University, China
Chengqi Zhang	University of Technology Sydney, Australia

Ning Zhong   Maebashi Institute of Technology, Japan
Zhi-Hua Zhou   Nanjing University, China

Senior Program Committee

Fei Wang   Cornell University, USA
Albert Bifet   Universite Paris-Saclay, France
Alexandros Ntoulas   University of Athens, Greece
Anirban Dasgupta   IIT Gandhinagar, India
Arnab Bhattacharya   IIT Kanpur, India
B. Aditya Prakash   Georgia Institute of Technology, USA
Bart Goethals   Universiteit Antwerpen, Belgium
Benjamin C. M. Fung   McGill University, Canada
Bin Cui   Peking University, China
Byung Suk Lee   University of Vermont, USA
Chandan K. Reddy   Virginia Tech, USA
Chang-Tien Lu   Virginia Tech, USA
Fuzhen Zhuang   Institute of Computing Technology, Chinese Academy
                            of Sciences, China
Gang Li   Deakin University, Australia
Gao Cong   Nanyang Technological University, Singapore
Guozhu Dong   Wright State University, USA
Hady Lauw   Singapore Management University, Singapore
Hanghang Tong   University of Illinois at Urbana-Champaign, USA
Hongyan Liu   Tsinghua University, China
Hui Xiong   Rutgers University, USA
Huzefa Rangwala   George Mason University, USA
Jae-Gil Lee   KAIST, South Korea
Jaideep Srivastava   University of Minnesota, USA
Jia Wu   Macquarie University, Australia
Jian Pei   Simon Fraser University, Canada
Jianyong Wang   Tsinghua University, China
Jiuyong Li   University of South Australia, Australia
Kai Ming Ting   Federation University, Australia
Kamalakar Karlapalem   IIIT Hyderabad, India
Krishna Reddy P.   International Institute of Information Technology,
                            Hyderabad, India
Lei Chen   Hong Kong University of Science and Technology,
                            China
Longbing Cao   University of Technology Sydney, Australia
Manish Marwah   Micro Focus, USA
Masashi Sugiyama   RIKEN, The University of Tokyo, Japan
Ming Li   Nanjing University, China
Nikos Mamoulis   University of Ioannina, Greece
Peter Christen   The Australian National University, Australia
Qinghua Hu   Tianjin University, China

Rajeev Raman	University of Leicester, UK
Raymond Chi-Wing Wong	Hong Kong University of Science and Technology, China
Sang-Wook Kim	Hanyang University, South Korea
Sheng-Jun Huang	Nanjing University of Aeronautics and Astronautics, China
Shou-De Lin	Nanyang Technological University, Singapore
Shuigeng Zhou	Fudan University, China
Shuiwang Ji	Texas A&M University, USA
Takashi Washio	The Institute of Scientific and Industrial Research, Osaka University, Japan
Tru Hoang Cao	UTHealth, USA
Victor S. Sheng	Texas Tech University, USA
Vincent Tseng	National Chiao Tung University, Taiwan, ROC
Wee Keong Ng	Nanyang Technological University, Singapore
Weiwei Liu	Wuhan University, China
Wu Xindong	Mininglamp Academy of Sciences, China
Xia Hu	Texas A&M University, USA
Xiaofang Zhou	University of Queensland, Australia
Xing Xie	Microsoft Research Asia, China
Xintao Wu	University of Arkansas, USA
Yanchun Zhang	Victoria University, Australia
Ying Li	ACM SIGKDD Seattle, USA
Yue Xu	Queensland University of Technology, Australia
Yu-Feng Li	Nanjing University, China
Zhao Zhang	Hefei University of Technology, China

Program Committee

Akihiro Inokuchi	Kwansei Gakuin University, Japan
Alex Memory	Leidos, USA
Andreas Züfle	George Mason University, USA
Andrzej Skowron	University of Warsaw, Poland
Animesh Mukherjee	IIT Kharagpur, India
Anirban Mondal	Ashoka University, India
Arnaud Soulet	University of Tours, France
Arun Reddy	Arizona State University, USA
Biao Qin	Renmin University of China, China
Bing Xue	Victoria University of Wellington, New Zealand
Bo Jin	Dalian University of Technology, China
Bo Tang	Southern University of Science and Technology, China
Bolin Ding	Data Analytics and Intelligence Lab, Alibaba Group, USA
Brendon J. Woodford	University of Otago, New Zealand
Bruno Cremilleux	Université de Caen Normandie, France
Byron Choi	Hong Kong Baptist University, Hong Kong, China

Cam-Tu Nguyen Nanjing University, China
Canh Hao Nguyen Kyoto University, Japan
Carson K. Leung University of Manitoba, Canada
Chao Huang University of Notre Dame, USA
Chao Lan University of Wyoming, USA
Chedy Raissi Inria, France
Cheng Long Nanyang Technological University, Singapore
Chengzhang Zhu University of Technology Sydney, Australia
Chi-Yin Chow City University of Hong Kong, China
Chuan Shi Beijing University of Posts and Telecommunications,
China
Chunbin Lin Amazon AWS, USA
Da Yan University of Alabama at Birmingham, USA
David C Anastasiu Santa Clara University, USA
David Taniar Monash University, Australia
David Tse Jung Huang The University of Auckland, New Zealand
Deepak P. Queen's University Belfast, UK
De-Nian Yang Academia Sinica, Taiwan, ROC
Dhaval Patel IBM TJ Watson Research Center, USA
Dik Lee HKUST, China
Dinesh Garg IIT Gandhinagar, India
Dinusha Vatsalan Data61, CSIRO, Australia
Divyesh Jadav IBM Research, USA
Dong-Wan Choi Inha University, South Korea
Dongxiang Zhang University of Electronic Science and Technology
of China, China
Duc-Trong Le University of Engineering and Technology, Vietnam
National University, Hanoi, Vietnam
Dung D. Le Singapore Management University, Singapore
Durga Toshniwal IIT Roorkee, India
Ernestina Menasalvas Universidad Politécnica de Madrid, Spain
Fangzhao Wu Microsoft Research Asia, China
Fanhua Shang Xidian University, China
Feng Chen UT Dallas, USA
Florent Masseglia Inria, France
Fusheng Wang Stony Brook University, USA
Gillian Dobbie The University of Auckland, New Zealand
Girish Palshikar Tata Research Development and Design Centre, India
Giuseppe Manco ICAR-CNR, Italy
Guandong Xu University of Technology Sydney, Australia
Guangyan Huang Deakin University, Australia
Guangzhong Sun School of Computer Science and Technology,
University of Science and Technology of China,
China
Guansong Pang University of Adelaide, Australia
Guolei Yang Facebook, USA

Guoxian Yu	Shandong University, China
Guruprasad Nayak	University of Minnesota, USA
Haibo Hu	Hong Kong Polytechnic University, China
Heitor M Gomes	Télécom ParisTech, France
Hiroaki Shiokawa	University of Tsukuba, Japan
Hong Shen	Adelaide University, Australia
Honghua Dai	Zhengzhu University, China
Hongtao Wang	North China Electric Power University, China
Hongzhi Yin	The University of Queensland, Australia
Huasong Shan	JD.com, USA
Hui Xue	Southeast University, China
Huifang Ma	Northwest Normal University, China
Huiyuan Chen	Case Western Reserve University, USA
Hung-Yu Kao	National Cheng Kung University, Taiwan, ROC
Ickjai J. Lee	James Cook University, Australia
Jaegul Choo	KAIST, South Korea
Jean Paul Barddal	PUCPR, Brazil
Jeffrey Ullman	Stanford University, USA
Jen-Wei Huang	National Cheng Kung University, Taiwan, ROC
Jeremiah Deng	University of Otago, New Zealand
Jerry Chun-Wei Lin	Western Norway University of Applied Sciences, Norway
Ji Zhang	University of Southern Queensland, Australia
Jiajie Xu	Soochow University, China
Jiamou Liu	The University of Auckland, New Zealand
Jianhua Yin	Shandong University, China
Jianmin Li	Tsinghua University, China
Jianxin Li	Deakin University, Australia
Jianzhong Qi	University of Melbourne, Australia
Jie Liu	Nankai University, China
Jiefeng Cheng	Tencent, China
Jieming Shi	The Hong Kong Polytechnic University, China
Jing Zhang	Nanjing University of Science and Technology, China
Jingwei Xu	Nanjing University, China
João Vinagre	LIAAD, INESC TEC, Portugal
Jörg Wicker	The University of Auckland, New Zealand
Jun Luo	Machine Intelligence Lab, Lenovo Group Limited, China
Jundong Li	Arizona State University, USA
Jungeun Kim	ETRI, South Korea
Jun-Ki Min	Korea University of Technology and Education, South Korea
K. Selçuk Candan	Arizona State University, USA
Kai Zheng	University of Electronic Science and Technology of China, China
Kaiqi Zhao	The University of Auckland, New Zealand

Kaiyu Feng	Nanyang Technological University, Singapore
Kangfei Zhao	The Chinese University of Hong Kong, China
Karan Aggarwal	University of Minnesota, USA
Ken-ichi Fukui	Osaka University, Japan
Khoat Than	Hanoi University of Science and Technology, Vietnam
Ki Yong Lee	Sookmyung Women's University, South Korea
Ki-Hoon Lee	Kwangwoon University, South Korea
Kok-Leong Ong	La Trobe University, Australia
Kouzou Ohara	Aoyama Gakuin University, Japan
Krisztian Buza	Budapest University of Technology and Economics, Hungary
Kui Yu	School of Computer and Information, Hefei University of Technology, China
Kun-Ta Chuang	National Cheng Kung University, China
Kyoung-Sook Kim	Artificial Intelligence Research Center, Japan
L Venkata Subramaniam	IBM Research, India
Lan Du	Monash University, Canada
Lazhar Labiod	LIPADE, France
Leandro Minku	University of Birmingham, UK
Lei Chen	Nanjing University of Posts and Telecommunications, China
Lei Duan	Sichuan University, China
Lei Gu	Nanjing University of Posts and Telecommunications, China
Leong Hou U	University of Macau, Macau
Leopoldo Bertossi	Universidad Adolfo Ibañez, Chile
Liang Hu	University of Technology Sydney, Australia
Liang Wu	Airbnb, USA
Lin Liu	University of South Australia, Australia
Lina Yao	University of New South Wales, Australia
Lini Thomas	IIIT Hyderabad, India
Liu Yang	Beijing Jiaotong University, China
Long Lan	National University of Defense Technology, China
Long Yuan	Nanjing University of Science and Technology, China
Lu Chen	Aalborg University, Denmark
Maciej Grzenda	Warsaw University of Technology, Poland
Maguelonne Teisseire	Irstea, France
Maksim Tkachenko	Singapore Management University, Singapore
Marco Maggini	University of Siena, Italy
Marzena Kryszkiewicz	Warsaw University of Technology, Poland
Maya Ramanath	IIT Delhi, India
Mengjie Zhang	Victoria University of Wellington, New Zealand
Miao Xu	RIKEN, Japan
Minghao Yin	Northeast Normal University, China
Mirco Nanni	ISTI-CNR Pisa, Italy
Motoki Shiga	Gifu University, Japan

Nam Huynh   Japan Advanced Institute of Science and Technology, Japan
Naresh Manwani   International Institute of Information Technology, Hyderabad, India
Nayyar Zaidi   Monash University, Australia
Nguyen Le Minh   JAIST, Japan
Nishtha Madan   IBM Research, India
Ou Wu   Tianjin University, China
P. Radha Krishna   National Institute of Technology, Warangal, India
Pabitra Mitra   Indian Institute of Technology Kharagpur, India
Panagiotis Liakos   University of Athens, Greece
Peipei Li   Hefei University of Technology, China
Peng Peng   inspir.ai, China
Peng Wang   Southeast University, China
Pengpeng Zhao   Soochow University, China
Petros Zerfos   IBM T.J Watson Research Center, USA
Philippe Fournier-Viger   Harbin Institute of Technology, China
Pigi Kouki   Relational AI, USA
Pravallika Devineni   Oak Ridge National Laboratory, USA
Qi Li   Iowa State University, USA
Qi Qian   Alibaba Group, China
Qian Li   University of Technology Sydney, Australia
Qiang Tang   Luxembourg Institute of Science and Technology, Luxembourg
Qing Wang   Australian National University, Australia
Quangui Zhang   Liaoning Technical University, China
Qun Liu   Louisiana State University, USA
Raymond Ng   UBC, Canada
Reza Zafarani   Syracuse University, USA
Rong-Hua Li   Beijing Institute of Technology, China
Roy Ka-Wei Lee   Singapore University of Technology and Design, Singapore
Rui Chen   Samsung Research, USA
Sangkeun Lee   Korea University, South Korea
Santu Rana   Deakin University, Australia
Sebastien Gaboury   Université du Québec à Chicoutimi, Canada
Shafiq Alam   The University of Auckland, New Zealand
Shama Chakravarthy   The University of Texas at Arlington, USA
Shan Xue   Macquarie University, Australia
Shanika Karunasekera   University of Melbourne, Australia
Shaowu Liu   University of Technology Sydney, Australia
Sharanya Eswaran   Games24x7, India
Shen Gao   Peking University, China
Shiyu Yang   East China Normal University, China
Shoji Hirano   Biomedical Systems, Applications in Medicine – Shimane University, Japan

Shoujin Wang	Macquarie University, Australia
Shu Wu	NLPR, China
Shuhan Yuan	Utah State University, USA
Sibo Wang	The Chinese University of Hong Kong, China
Silvia Chiusano	Politecnico di Torino, Italy
Songcan Chen	Nanjing University of Aeronautics and Astronautics, China
Steven H. H. Ding	Queen's University, Canada
Suhang Wang	Pennsylvania State University, USA
Sungsu Lim	Chungnam National University, South Korea
Sunil Aryal	Deakin University, Australia
Tadashi Nomoto	National Institute of Japanese Literature, Japan
Tanmoy Chakraborty	IIIT Delhi, India
Tetsuya Yoshida	Nara Women's University, Japan
Thanh-Son Nguyen	Agency for Science, Technology and Research, Singapore
Thilina N. Ranbaduge	The Australian National University, Australia
Tho Quan	John Von Neumann Institute, Germany
Tianlin Zhang	University of Chinese Academy of Sciences, China
Tianqing Zhu	University of Technology Sydney, Australia
Toshihiro Kamishima	National Institute of Advanced Industrial Science and Technology, Japan
Trong Dinh Thac Do	University of Technology Sydney, Australia
Tuan Le	Oakland University, USA
Tuan-Anh Hoang	L3S Research Center, Leibniz University of Hanover, Germany
Turki Turki	King Abdulaziz University, Saudi Arabia
Tzung-Pei Hong	National University of Kaohsiung, Taiwan, ROC
Uday Kiran Rage	University of Tokyo, Japan
Vahid Taslimitehrani	PhysioSigns Inc., USA
Victor Junqiu Wei	Huawei Technologies, China
Vladimir Estivill-Castro	Griffith University, Australia
Wang Lizhen	Yunnan University, China
Wang-Chien Lee	Pennsylvania State University, USA
Wang-Zhou Dai	Imperial College London, UK
Wei Liu	University of Western Australia, Australia
Wei Luo	Deakin University, Australia
Wei Shen	Nankai University, China
Wei Wang	University of New South Wales, Australia
Wei Zhang	East China Normal University, China
Wei Emma Zhang	The University of Adelaide, Australia
Weiguo Zheng	Fudan University, China
Wendy Hui Wang	Stevens Institute of Technology, USA
Wenjie Zhang	University of New South Wales, Australia
Wenpeng Lu	Qilu University of Technology (Shandong Academy of Sciences), China

Wenyuan Li	University of California, Los Angeles, USA
Wilfred Ng	HKUST, China
Xiang Ao	Institute of Computing Technology, CAS, China
Xiangliang Zhang	King Abdullah University of Science and Technology, Saudi Arabia
Xiangmin Zhou	RMIT University, Australia
Xiangyu Ke	Nanyang Technological University, Singapore
Xiao Wang	Beijing University of Posts and Telecommunications, China
Xiaodong Yue	Shanghai University, China
Xiaohui (Daniel) Tao	The University of Southern Queensland, Australia
Xiaojie Jin	National University of Singapore, Singapore
Xiaoyang Wang	Zhejiang Gongshang University, China
Xiaoying Gao	Victoria University of Wellington, New Zealand
Xin Huang	Hong Kong Baptist University, China
Xin Wang	University of Calgary, Canada
Xingquan Zhu	Florida Atlantic University, USA
Xiucheng Li	Nanyang Technological University, Singapore
Xiuzhen Zhang	RMIT University, Australia
Xuan-Hong Dang	IBM T.J Watson Research Center, USA
Yanchang Zhao	CSIRO, Australia
Yang Wang	Dalian University of Technology, China
Yang Yu	Nanjing University, China
Yang-Sae Moon	Kangwon National University, South Korea
Yanhao Wang	University of Helsinki, Finland
Yanjie Fu	Missouri University of Science and Technology, USA
Yao Zhou	UIUC, USA
Yashaswi Verma	IIT Jodhpur, India
Ye Zhu	Deakin University, Australia
Yiding Liu	Nanyang Technological University, Singapore
Yidong Li	Beijing Jiaotong University, China
Yifeng Zeng	Northumbria University, UK
Yingfan Liu	Xidian University, China
Yingyi Bu	Google, USA
Yi-Shin Chen	National Tsing Hua University, Taiwan, ROC
Yiyang Yang	Guangdong University of Technology, China
Yong Guan	Iowa State University, USA
Yu Rong	Tencent AI Lab, China
Yu Yang	City University of Hong Kong, China
Yuan Yao	Nanjing University, China
Yuanyuan Zhu	Wuhan University, China
Yudong Zhang	University of Leicester, UK
Yue Ning	Stevens Institute of Technology, USA
Yue Ning	Stevens Institute of Technology, USA
Yue-Shi Lee	Ming Chuan University, China
Yun Sing Koh	The University of Auckland, New Zealand

Yunjun Gao	Zhejiang University, China
Yuqing Sun	Shandong University, China
Yurong Cheng	Beijing Institute of Technology, China
Yuxiang Wang	Hangzhou Dianzi University, China
Zemin Liu	Singapore Management University, Singapore
Zhang Lei	Anhui University, China
Zhaohong Deng	Jiangnan University, China
Zheng Liu	Nanjing University of Posts and Telecommunications, China
Zheng Zhang	Harbin Institute of Technology, China
Zhengyang Wang	Texas A&M University, USA
Zhewei Wei	Renmin University of China, China
Zhiwei Zhang	Beijing Institute of Technology, China
Zhiyuan Chen	University of Maryland Baltimore County, USA
Zhongying Zhao	Shandong University of Science and Technology, China
Zhou Zhao	Zhejiang University, China
Zili Zhang	Southwest University, China

Competition Sponsor

Alibaba Cloud

Host Institutes

Jawaharlal Nehru University

INTERNATIONAL INSTITUTE OF INFORMATION TECHNOLOGY

HYDERABAD

Contents – Part II

Data Mining Theory and Principles

Recommender Systems

Text Analytics

Classical Data Mining

Mining Frequent Patterns
from Hypergraph Databases

Md. Tanvir Alam[1][iD], Chowdhury Farhan Ahmed[1(✉)][iD], Md. Samiullah[1],
and Carson K. Leung[2][iD]

[1] Department of Computer Science and Engineering, University of Dhaka,
Dhaka, Bangladesh
{farhan,samiullah}@du.ac.bd
[2] Department of Computer Science, University of Manitoba, Winnipeg, MB, Canada
kleung@cs.umanitoba.ca

Abstract. Hypergraph is a complex data structure capable of expressing associations among any number of data entities. Overcoming the limitations of traditional graphs, hypergraphs are useful to model real-life problems. Frequent pattern mining is one of the most popular problems in data mining with a lot of applications. To the best of our knowledge, there exists no flexible frequent pattern mining framework for hypergraph databases decomposing associations among data entities. In this work, we propose a flexible and complete framework for mining frequent patterns from a collection of hypergraphs. We also develop an algorithm for mining frequent subhypergraphs by introducing a canonical labeling technique for isomorphic subhypergraphs. Experiments conducted on real-life hypergraph databases demonstrate both the efficiency of the algorithm and the effectiveness of the proposed framework.

Keywords: Frequent pattern mining · Graph mining · Hypergraphs

1 Introduction

Graphs are being widely used to represent complex structures such as social network, web, protein structures, chemical compounds, etc. It has the ability to model complex pairwise relationships among various types of data entities. However, in many real-life problems, relationships among data entities go beyond pairs. Graphs fail to preserve any kind of associations involving more than two entities. To illustrate this limitation, let us consider a problem of presenting collaborations of authors in a bibliography of a paper. A naive solution can be using a graph where each vertex represents an author and vertices representing authors collaborating in a paper are connected by edges. But from such a representation, it cannot be determined whether a paper has contributions from any three or more given authors. Hypergraph is a flexible data structure that overcomes this limitation. A hypergraph consists of a set of vertices and a set of hyperedges where a hyperedge can associate any number of vertices. In Fig. 1(a), we show

© Springer Nature Switzerland AG 2021
K. Karlapalem et al. (Eds.): PAKDD 2021, LNAI 12713, pp. 3–15, 2021.
https://doi.org/10.1007/978-3-030-75765-6_1

a hypergraph presenting collaborations of authors in a bibliography of a paper. Here the vertices v_1, v_2, v_3, v_4, v_5 and v_6 refers to six authors and hyperedges e_1, e_2 and e_3 refers to three papers. For example, authors referred by vertices v_1, v_2 and v_3 has collaborated in the paper referred by e_1. Hypergraphs are being used in various data mining and machine learning tasks as classification and clustering [1,11,13].

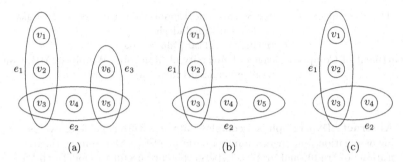

Fig. 1. (a) A hypergraph, (b) A subhypergraph pattern, (c) Another subhypergraph pattern.

Extracting interesting patterns from a collection of data is a core problem of data mining. Frequency is one of the mostly used parameters in pattern mining. Frequent pattern mining can be applied to many real-life applications such as clustering, classification, outlier analysis, etc. Various algorithms have been proposed for mining frequent patterns from transactional itemset databases [2,9], sequential databases [6,8] and graph databases [4,5,12]. A framework for frequent hypergraph mining has been proposed in [3]. However, the proposed framework is rigid as it avoids decomposing associations presented by any hyperedge. Let us consider a hypergraph H, presented in Fig. 1(a); a subhypergraph pattern h_1, presented in Fig. 1(b); and another subhypergraph pattern h_2, presented in Fig. 1(c). Let each hyperedge represent a research paper containing vertices corresponding to authors collaborating in the paper. For example, the hyperedge e_1 in hypergraph H expressed the collaborations of authors corresponding to vertices v_1, v_2 and v_3 in a paper. According to the framework in [3], h_1 is considered only as a candidate pattern or subhypergraph of H but not h_2 as the hyperedge e_2 has been decomposed in h_2. But the collaborations in h_2 of authors v_1, v_2 and v_3 in paper e_1; v_3 and v_4 in paper e_2 is also expressed by H. Thus h_2 is a potential interesting pattern for H and inflexible definition of subhypergraph without decomposing hyperedges leads to loss of many interesting patterns.

In the current work, we establish a complete and flexible framework for mining frequent patterns from a collection of hypergraphs. In our framework, the definition of subhypergraph decomposes each hyperedge considering all the subsets of vertices contained by it. This provides flexibility in the framework and results in mining more useful patterns for real-life applications. We also propose an efficient algorithm named FHGM (Frequent HyperGraph Miner) for mining frequent hypergraphs from a vertex and edge labeled hypergraph database. The major challenge in frequent pattern mining is the explosion of candidate pattern search space especially for complex types of data. Mining frequent patterns from graph databases is more costly than sequential databases. For hypergraphs, the search space explodes even more. Besides, finding subhypergraph isomorphism is an NP-complete problem and so testing false candidates are costly. To cope with these challenges, our algorithm constructs the search space in a depth first search manner unlike Apriori [9] based algorithms. It helps to avoid costly level-wise candidate generation process and minimizes false candidates. Another major challenge of frequent hypergraph mining is the generation of isomorphic sub-hypergraph candidates. To avoid testing and expanding duplicate isomorphic subhypergraphs, we introduce canonical labeling of subhypergraph candidates. Testing and expanding candidates associated with canonical label only helps to skip redundant subhypergraph isomorphism tests. Furthermore, following the widely used downward closure property to prune the search space, our algorithm does not expand any infrequent candidates as any hypergraph extended from an infrequent hypergraph will also be infrequent.

Our key contributions can be summarized as:

- We propose a flexible framework for frequent hypergraph mining.
- We develop an efficient algorithm named FHGM for extracting frequent hypergraphs that constructs the search space avoiding level-wise candidate generation.
- We devise a canonical labeling technique for hypergraph to define the representative of the whole isomorphism class of a hypergraph to prune duplicate isomorphic candidates.

The rest of the paper is organized as follows: Sect. 2 defines the proposed framework. In Sect. 3, we present our proposed methods. Section 4 contains the details of experiments and we conclude the paper in Sect. 5.

2   Proposed Framework

Let D be a set of labeled hypergraphs and L be the set of labels. A hypergraph H can be represented with a 3-tuple, $< V_H, E_H, l_H >$, where V_H is a set of vertices, E_H is a set of hyperedges each containing the vertices that it connects, $l_H :$ $V_H \cup E_H \rightarrow L_H$ is a function that labels the vertices and hyperedges. In Fig. 2, we show an example database of hypergraphs containing three hypergraphs H_1, H_2 and H_3 with labeled vertices and hyperedges. For example, the vertex v_1 and the hyperedge e_1 in H_1 are labeled as a and p respectively. A subhypergraph isomorphism from a subhypergraph h $= < V_h, E_h, l_h >$ to a hypergraph H $=$ $< V_H, E_H, l_H >$ holds if there exists a function $\phi : V_h \cup E_h \rightarrow V_H \cup E_H$, such that,

1. $\forall v \in V_h, l_h(v) = l_H(\phi(v))$.
2. $\forall e \in E_h, l_h(e) = l_H(\phi(e))$ and $e \subseteq \phi(e)$.

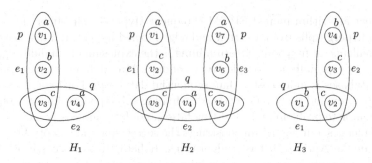

Fig. 2. A hypergraph database D

In Fig. 3, we present a subhypergraph h'. In Table 1, we show two subhypergraph isomorphism from h', ϕ_1 and ϕ_2, to hypergraphs H_1 and H_2 respectively. There exists no subhypergraph isomorphism from h' to hypergraph H_3.

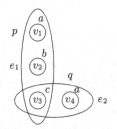

Fig. 3. A subhypergraph h'

Table 1. Subhypergraph isomorphisms

Vertex/Hyperedge	ϕ_1(in H_1)	ϕ_2(in H_2)
v_1	v_1	v_7
v_2	v_2	v_6
v_3	v_3	v_5
v_4	v_4	v_4
e_1	e_1	e_3
e_2	e_2	e_2

Let $\Phi(h, H)$ be the set of all subhypergraph isomorphism from a subhypergraph h to a hypergraph H. The frequency support of a subhypergraph h in a hypergraph H can be defined as,

$$sup(h, H) = \begin{cases} 1, & \text{if } |\Phi(h, H)| \geq 1 \\ 0, & \text{otherwise} \end{cases} \tag{1}$$

In our example database, the frequency support of a subhypergraph h in a hypergraph H, $sup(h', H_1) = 1$ as there is a subhypergraph isomorphism from h' to hypergraph H_1. Similarly, $sup(h', H_2) = 1$. But $sup(h', H_3) = 0$ as there exists no subhypergraph isomorphism from h' to hypergraph H_3.

The frequency support of a subhypergraph h in a hypergraph database D can be defined as

$$sup(h, D) = \sum_{H \in D} sup(h, H) \tag{2}$$

For example, the frequency support of the subhypergraph h' of Fig. 3 in the hypergraph database D of Fig. 2, $sup(h', D) = sup(h', H_1) + sup(h', H_2) + sup(h', H_3) = 1 + 1 + 0 = 2$.

Frequent Hypergraph Mining Problem: Given a set of labeled hypergraphs D and a user defined threshold δ, frequent subhypergraph mining discovers all subhypergraphs h, such that $sup(h, D) \geq minsup$ where $minsup = |D| \times \delta$. For our example database D, if δ is $\frac{2}{3}$, then $minsup = 3 \times \frac{2}{3} = 2$. Now h' is a frequent subhypergraph as $sup(h', D) \geq minsup$.

3   Proposed Methods

In this section, we present our proposed algorithm named FHGM. To discover all the frequent subhypergraphs, we have to develop a search space of candidate subhypergraphs in such a way that all frequent subhypergraphs are enumerated. For generating candidate subhypergraphs, starting from an empty hypergraph, we extend each candidate subhypergraph in a depth first search fashion rather than level-wise candidate generation which have been proven to be expensive in terms of both runtime and memory for itemset, sequence and graph mining. A naive way of extending a candidate can be adding vertex or a new hyperedge to the existing subhypergraph in every possible way but it will generate large number of duplicate subhypergraphs. In our algorithm, we identify each vertex and hyperedge of all candidates with a unique discovery time value that is assigned according to the order in which they have been added to the candidate. We define the vertex and hyperedge with maximum discovery time value as last vertex and last hyperedge respectively. For a candidate subhypergraph h, we can denote them as $last_v(h)$ and $last_e(h)$ respectively. To minimize duplicate subhypergraphs generation, FHGM extends the candidates in any of the following ways possible:

- **Hyperedge-extension:** Adding a vertex to the last hyperedge. This vertex can be a new vertex or one the the vertices that already exists in the candidate.
- **Hyperedge-append:** Adding a new hyperedge containing only one of the existing vertices.

We can present an extension using a 4-tuple <type, vertex, vertex label, edge label>. For example, <e, 1, a, -> represents hyperedge-extension by adding a vertex with label "a" and discovery time 1. On the contrary, <a, 0, b, p> represents hyperedge-append by adding a new hyperedge with label "p" that contains only one vertex with label "b" and discovery time 0. Now, we can present each candidate subhypergraph with a sequence of extension tuples. In Algorithm 1, we present the pseudocode for finding all possible extensions of a candidate in a hypergraph database.

However, extending this manner can still generate duplicate isomorphic candidates. A solution to this problem can be keeping a list of candidates generated.

Algorithm 1: Find Extensions

    Input : h : a candidate subhypergraph, D: a set of hypergraphs
    Output: E: the set of possible extensions

1 **begin**
2    $E \leftarrow \emptyset$;
3   **for** $H \in D$ **do**
4   **if** $h = \emptyset$ **then**
5   **for** $e \in E_H$ **do**
6   **for** $v \in e$ **do**
7                $E \leftarrow E \cup \{<a, 0, l(v), l(e)>\}$;
8   **else**
9   **for** $\phi \in \Phi(h, H)$ **do**
10   **for** $e \in E_H$ **do**
11   **for** $v \in e$ **do**
12   **if** $e \notin \phi^{-1}$ *and* $v \notin \phi^{-1}$ **then**
13                     $E \leftarrow E \cup \{<a, discovery(\phi^{-1}(v)), l(v), l(e)>\}$;
14   **for** $v \in \phi(last_e(h))$ **do**
15   **if** $v \notin \phi^{-1}$ **then**
16                  $E \leftarrow E \cup \{<e, discovery(last_v(h)) + 1, l(v), ->\}$;
17   **else if** $\phi^{-1}(v) \notin last_e(h)$ **then**
18                  $E \leftarrow E \cup \{<e, discovery(\phi^{-1}(v)), l(v), ->\}$;

Whenever a new candidate is generated, it can be discarded if any isomorphic candidate already exist in the list. But it requires a lot of hypergraph isomorphism tests which is costly. To solve this problem, we introduce canonical labeling to candidates. We define a partial order among the isomorphic candidate and extended the minimum isomorphic candidate as a representative of the whole isomorphism class.

Given two extensions $ext_1 = <t_1, d_1, l_{v_1}, l_{e_1}>$ and $ext_2 = <t_2, d_2, l_{v_2}, l_{e_2}>$, let us define a partial order among extensions such that $ext_1 < ext_2$ if and only if one of the followings holds,

- $t_1 = e$ and $t_2 = a$.
- $t_1 = a$ and $t_2 = a$ and $d_1 < d_2$.
- $t_1 = a$ and $t_2 = a$ and $d_1 = d_2$ and $l_{e_1} < l_{e_2}$.
- $t_1 = a$ and $t_2 = a$ and $d_1 = d_2$ and $l_{e_1} = l_{e_2}$ and $l_{v_1} < l_{v_2}$.
- $t_1 = e$ and $t_2 = e$ and $d_1 < d_2$.
- $t_1 = e$ and $t_2 = e$ and $d_1 = d_2$ and $l_{v_1} < l_{v_2}$.

Given two candidate subhypergraphs, we can define a partial order between them by comparing their extension tuple by tuple according to the sequence. Based on this order, we define the minimum sequence of extension tuples as the canonical representative. FHGM extends a candidate if it is canonical and discards others as they are isomorphic form of the canonical one. Algorithm 2 shows how to determine whether a candidate is canonical or not. Finally, we utilize downward closure property by not extending any infrequent candidates as any candidate extended from an infrequent candidate will also be infrequent. Pruning the search space using downward closure property helps to eliminate many false candidates. We present the pseudocode of FHGM for mining frequent subhypergraph in Algorithm 3.

Algorithm 2: Check Canonical

Input : C : a sequence of extension tuples

```
1 begin
2     h ← GetHypergraph(C) // converts extensions to hypergraph
3     C_t ← ∅;
4     for i ← 1 to —C— do
5         E ← FindExtensions(GetHypergraph(C_t), {h});
6         if C[i] ≠ min(E) then
7             return False;
8         C_t.insert(C[i]);
9     return True;
```

Algorithm 3: FHGM

Input : h : a subhypergraph, D: a set of hypergraphs,
$minsup$: a support threshold // Initially h ← ∅

```
1 begin
2     E ← FindExtensions(h, D);
3     for e ∈ E do
4         h_t ← extend(h, e);
5         if CheckCanonical(h_t) = true and sup(h_t, D) ≥ minsup then
6             h_t is a frequent subhypergraph;
7             FHGM(h_t, D, minsup);
```

In Fig. 4, we present a simulation of our proposed FHGM algorithm on database D of Fig. 2. For the convenience of presentation, we have taken a high value of $\delta = 1$ to limit candidate generation. For $\delta = 1$, $minsup = 3 \times 1 = 3$. Starting from an empty subhypergraph candidate C_0, we have extended each candidate using Algorithm 1. We have presented each candidates in the search tree using a sequence of extension tuples. We have skipped extending any non-canonical candidates which are presented by dashed boxes. For example, we have not extended candidate C_{13} as it is a non canonical representation. However, the candidate C_{10} represents an isomorphic subhypergraph of the subhypergraph presented by C_{13} and C_{10} has been extended for being the canonical representation. The infrequent candidates are shown in dotted boxes. For example, the candidate C_{17} is a canonical representation. But it has not been extended as the frequency of C_{17} in D is 1 which fails to satisfy the $minsup$ threshold. The frequent candidates are shown in solid box. That means the subhypergraphs corresponding to C_2, C_3, C_5, C_7, C_{10} and C_{16} are frequent in D with respect to $\delta = 1$.

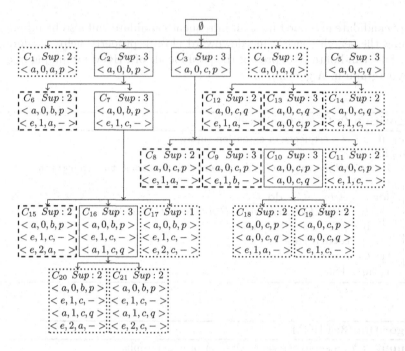

Fig. 4. Simulation of frequent hypergraph mining algorithm

4 Experiments

To evaluate the effectiveness and efficiency of our proposed algorithm, we have conducted experiments. In this section, we discuss the experimental settings and result analysis. We present the details of dataset extraction process in Sect. 4.1, experimental result analysis in Sect. 4.2. To evaluate the framework, we analyze hypergraph classification performance using frequent patterns in Sect. 4.3.

4.1 Dataset Description

We have extracted academic social networks data provided by ArnetMiner [10] to build hypergraph databases. The ArnetMiner [10] dataset provides details of research articles such as authors, domain, bibliography, and etc. We have built six databases using papers from six different domains. From each domain, we have randomly selected 1000 papers. For each paper, we have created a hypergraph where the hyperedges represent the papers that have been cited and contains vertices corresponding to the authors of the cited paper. In Table 2, we present the statistical description of the databases.

Table 2. Statistical description of databases

Domain	No. of hypergraphs	Average no. of vertices	Average no. of hyperedges	Average hyperedge length	No. of vertex labels
Data mining	1000	15.865	5.884	3.095	107
Machine learning	1000	11.895	5.146	2.653	96
Computer security	1000	17.051	6.488	3.053	92
Computer network	1000	17.048	5.852	3.227	110
Bioinformatics	1000	19.16	4.688	4.428	263
Distributed computing	1000	14.584	5.013	3.275	127

4.2 Results and Discussions

For analyzing the performance of our proposed algorithm, we have conducted experiments on our collected real-life datasets. We have implemented the FHGM algorithm using Python 3.7 programming language. We have utilized an Intel Core i7-6700k CPU @ 4.00 GHz with 16 GB RAM to conduct all the experiments. As a baseline for comparison, we have considered a naive version of FHGM that mines frequent subhypergraphs without pruning the search space using canonical labeling. For performance evaluation metrics, we have included runtime and the number of candidates generated. Higher number of candidates generation indicates higher number of false candidates generation as well as weaker search space pruning ability.

In Fig. 5, we present the runtime of FHGM both with and without pruning using canonical labeling on six real-life hypergraph databases. It is evident that pruning using canonical labeling reduces the runtime substantially. The runtime increases as the frequency threshold decreases. The increment in runtime is less significant when pruning using canonical labeling is performed which results in higher performance gap for lower frequency thresholds. For example, the runtime increases by 53.91 s when the frequency threshold reduces from 1.0% to 0.6% on database Data Mining without pruning whereas the increment with pruning is only 12.54 s. In Table 3, we present the number of candidates generated and the number of frequent patterns. The number of candidates generated is higher without pruning which is the reason behind longer runtime. The number of frequent patterns also increases as the frequency threshold decreases.

4.3 Hypergraph Classification Using Frequent Patterns

To evaluate the effectiveness of our proposed frequent pattern mining framework, we have implemented a hypergraph classification algorithm. The task is to predict the domain of a paper given the hypergraph representation of the bibliography. For feature extraction, we have mined frequent subhypergraphs from the six databases separately. We have followed elbow method on the number of frequent patterns [7] to determine the frequency thresholds. Finally, we build a feature vector for each hypergraph of size equal to the number of total mined

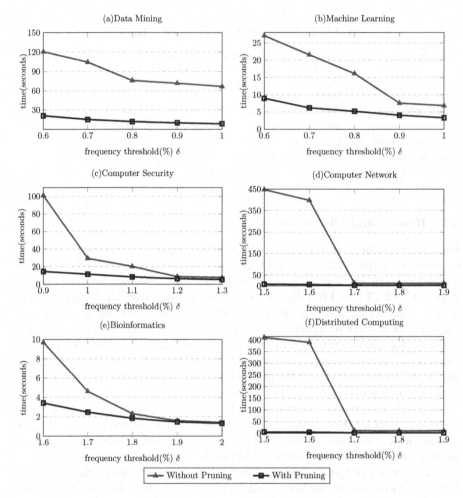

Fig. 5. Runtime analysis of FHGM

frequent patterns. The i-th element of the vector is 1 if there exists a subhypergraph isomorphism from the i-th pattern to the hypergraph, and 0 otherwise. We have utilized an ensemble classifier of Multi-layer Perceptron classifier (Neural Network), SupportVector Machine, Decision Tree classifier, Naive Bayes classifier, and K-NearestNeighbour classifier with max voting strategy. To split the train set and test set, we have followed K-Fold stratified cross-validation technique(Nine folds for training and one fold for testing). For comparison, we have considered another classifier that uses frequent patterns mined without decomposing hyperedges as proposed in [3] to build the feature vector. In Table 4, we present the classification accuracy for both the methods along with standard deviation. Significantly higher accuracy indicates the effectiveness of our proposed framework to mine interesting patterns from hypegraphs.

Table 3. Runtime and patterns statistics of FHGM

(a) Data mining

δ	Without pruning		With pruning		Frequent patterns
	Runtime(sec.)	Candidates	Runtime(sec.)	Candidates	
0.9%	71.626	19985	10.034	13155	371
0.8%	75.742	21574	11.920	13911	445
0.7%	104.241	29440	15.185	15514	629
0.6%	120.555	34968	21.081	17243	813

(b) Machine learning

0.9%	7.562	9347	4.072	8867	171
0.8%	16.16	10540	5.204	9249	231
0.7%	21.562	11846	6.188	9826	294
0.6%	27.110	12961	8.962	10518	424

(c) Computer security

1.2%	8.715	12916	6.464	12223	237
1.1%	20.112	14549	8.209	12951	318
1.0%	29.329	18366	11.380	14122	411
0.9%	101.041	51535	14.532	16154	603

(d) Computer network

1.8%	11.345	13623	2.990	11372	93
1.7%	11.836	13908	3.273	11554	104
1.6%	397.913	84111	6.012	12205	203
1.5%	447.722	13830	7.888	12311	213

(e) Bioinformatics

1.9%	1.586	12130	1.468	11862	32
1.8%	2.305	13176	1.829	12289	46
1.7%	4.614	17252	2.467	13134	63
1.6%	9.693	21952	3.420	14014	93

(f) Distributed computing

1.8%	10.154	12637	2.114	10405	60
1.7%	10.526	12783	2.339	10501	67
1.6%	389.831	94635	4.554	11112	158
1.5%	410.713	94730	4.754	11202	162

Table 4. Classification accuracy

Features	Without decomposing hyperedges	FHGM framework
Accuracy(%)	33.15 ± 1.80	51.55 ± 1.57

5 Conclusions

In this paper, we have proposed a complete framework for mining frequent patterns from hypergraph databases that decomposes hyperedges to build patterns. We have also developed an efficient algorithm named FHGM for mining frequent patterns from a collection of hypergraphs. To cope with the exploding search space, we have adopted search space pruning techniques in the algorithm. We have introduced a canonical labeling technique for the whole isomorphic class of a hypergraph for search space reduction. We have conducted experiments on real-life datasets. Significantly lower runtime and reduced search space demonstrates the efficiency of our algorithm whereas higher classification accuracy obtained by using frequent patterns as features indicates the effectiveness of the framework to mine interesting patterns. More efficient methods for mining using parallel processing, approximate methods can be considered as future work.

Acknowledgement. This work is partially funded by (a) ICT Division, Government of People's Republic of Bangladesh; (b) NSERC (Canada); and (c) University of Manitoba.

References

1. Feng, Y., You, H., Zhang, Z., Ji, R., Gao, Y.: Hypergraph neural networks. In: AAAI 2019, pp. 3558–3565 (2019)
2. Han, J., Pei, J., Yin, Y.: Mining frequent patterns without candidate generation. In: ACM SIGMOD 2000, pp. 1–12. ACM (2000)
3. Horváth, T., Bringmann, B., De Raedt, L.: Frequent hypergraph mining. In: Muggleton, S., Otero, R., Tamaddoni-Nezhad, A. (eds.) ILP 2006. LNCS (LNAI), vol. 4455, pp. 244–259. Springer, Heidelberg (2007). https://doi.org/10.1007/978-3-540-73847-3_26
4. Inokuchi, A., Washio, T., Motoda, H.: An Apriori-based algorithm for mining frequent substructures from graph data. In: Zighed, D.A., Komorowski, J., Żytkow, J. (eds.) PKDD 2000. LNCS (LNAI), vol. 1910, pp. 13–23. Springer, Heidelberg (2000). https://doi.org/10.1007/3-540-45372-5_2
5. Kuramochi, M., Karypis, G.: Frequent subgraph discovery. In: IEEE ICDM 2001, pp. 313–320. IEEE (2001)
6. Pei, J., et al.: PrefixSpan: mining sequential patterns efficiently by prefix-projected pattern growth. In: ICDE 2001, pp. 215–224. IEEE (2001)
7. Rousseau, F., Kiagias, E., Vazirgiannis, M.: Text categorization as a graph classification problem. In: ACL-IJCNLP 2015, pp. 1702–1712 (2015)
8. Srikant, R., Agrawal, R.: Mining sequential patterns: generalizations and performance improvements. In: Apers, P., Bouzeghoub, M., Gardarin, G. (eds.) EDBT 1996. LNCS, vol. 1057, pp. 1–17. Springer, Heidelberg (1996). https://doi.org/10.1007/BFb0014140
9. Srikant, R., Vu, Q., Agrawal, R.: Mining association rules with item constraints. In: KDD 1997, pp. 67–73 (1997)
10. Tang, J., Zhang, J., Yao, L., Li, J., Zhang, L., Su, Z.: ArnetMiner: extraction and mining of academic social networks. In: KDD 2008, pp. 990–998 (2008)

11. Yadati, N., Nimishakavi, M., Yadav, P., Nitin, V., Louis, A., Talukdar, P.: Hyper-GCN: a new method for training graph convolutional networks on hypergraphs. In: NeurIPS 2019, pp. 1511–1522 (2019)
12. Yan, X., Han, J.: gSpan: Graph-based substructure pattern mining. In: IEEE ICDM 2002, pp. 721–724 (2002)
13. Zhou, D., Huang, J., Schölkopf, B.: Learning with hypergraphs: clustering, classification, and embedding. In: NIPS 2006, pp. 1601–1608 (2006)

Discriminating Frequent Pattern Based Supervised Graph Embedding for Classification

Md. Tanvir Alam[1] , Chowdhury Farhan Ahmed[1(✉)] , Md. Samiullah[1],
and Carson K. Leung[2]

[1] Department of Computer Science and Engineering, University of Dhaka,
Dhaka, Bangladesh
{farhan,samiullah}@du.ac.bd
[2] Department of Computer Science, University of Manitoba, Winnipeg, MB, Canada
kleung@cs.umanitoba.ca

Abstract. Graph is used to represent various complex relationships among objects and data entities. One of the emerging and important problems is graph classification that has tremendous impacts on various real-life applications. A good number of approaches have been proposed for graph classification using various techniques where graph embedding is one of them. Here we propose an approach for classifying graphs by mining discriminating frequent patterns from graphs to learn vector representation of the graphs. The proposed supervised embedding technique produces high-quality entire graph embedding for classification utilizing the knowledge from the labeled examples available. The experimental analyses, conducted on various real-life benchmark datasets, found that the proposed approach is significantly better in terms of accuracy in comparison to the state-of-the-art techniques.

Keywords: Pattern mining · Graph mining · Frequent pattern mining · Discriminating pattern mining · Graph classification

1 Introduction

Graph is a widely used data structure for many domains such as social network analysis, bioinformatics, and chemo-informatics. It has gained popularity due to its ability to represent a variety of data types and complex relationships between data entities. Graphs can also be used to represent sequences and trees. With the colossal amount of graph data being accumulated worldwide from various sources, graph classification has become an important problem in the domain of Knowledge Discovery and Data Mining. It can be applied to many real-world problems, namely predicting property of chemical compounds, detecting anomalous activity in social networks, etc. However, many of the existing classification algorithms consider vector representation of data entities that

© Springer Nature Switzerland AG 2021
K. Karlapalem et al. (Eds.): PAKDD 2021, LNAI 12713, pp. 16–28, 2021.
https://doi.org/10.1007/978-3-030-75765-6_2

encodes descriptive, discriminating features. The accuracy of any classification algorithm depends primarily on the discriminating power of the features used.

Graph kernel-based approaches [13,14,19] have been proposed for accomplishing above mentioned or various data analytical tasks on graph dataset. A graph kernel is a function that captures the similarity between two objects or entities represented by graphs. The similarity is defined generally based on the similarity between the elementary fragments of the objects such as random walks or paths, fixed-sized sub-graphs, or rooted sub-trees. The kernel-based approaches have some major limitations: (i) the fragments used as features are not often discriminating as randomly sampled fragments are used as features; (ii) these methods scale poorly to large datasets or large graphs as the number of fragments escalates highly; and finally, (iii) the generated fragments are often not large enough to distinguish between graphs well due to loss of connectivity information.

Inspired by the success of word and document embedding techniques [6,8], methods for embedding of substructures within a graph such as nodes, edges [5] have been proposed. The approaches are effective for tasks like node classification, link prediction, etc. For graph analysis tasks, such as graph classification and clustering, simple aggregate functions like average is used on the embeddings of the substructures within a graph to obtain the entire graph embedding which results in loss of structural information. To address the limitation, various attempts have been made to obtain entire graph embedding directly. One such approach is, Graph2vec [9], an unsupervised approach to learn graph embedding from rooted sub-trees. GE-FSG [10], another similar unsupervised approach, employs frequent subgraphs to learn entire graph embedding. A major drawback of using Graph2vec and GE-FSG for graph classification is that they follow unsupervised approaches without exploiting the knowledge of ground truths (labeled examples) available while learning the embedding. As a result, it becomes hard to determine the class from the embedding. Besides, in the case of GE-FSG, frequent subgraphs may not be contained in many of the graphs as frequent subgraphs mining with a significantly lower threshold is prohibited due to computational complexity. For example, 191 graphs of 1000 graphs from benchmark graph dataset IMDB-B do not contain any of the frequent subgraphs mined with 20% frequency threshold. In consequence, these graphs are characterized in the embedding only by the absence of all feature subgraphs and such characterization fails to help determine the class properly as these graphs belong to different classes (123:68 in IMDB-B).

In the current paper, we propose a supervised entire graph embedding technique dedicated to graph classification. We develop an algorithm for extracting discriminating frequent subgraphs as features. To ensure that each graph contains a significant amount of feature subgraphs while overcoming the computational complexity, we adopt multi-phase frequent subgraph mining. We also propose a measure for filtering non-discriminating candidate feature subgraphs which utilizes the given classes of the labeled graphs. Then we employ the discriminating subgraphs to learn graph embeddings which have turned out to be effective for classification even though we have used simple and shallow neural network to learn the embeddings. Substantial improvement from other existing approaches in classification accuracy along with visualization of the embeddings demonstrate the effectiveness of our proposed feature extraction, representation learning and classification methods for graphs. Our key contributions in this work can be summarized as:

- We propose a supervised embedding method that produces entire graph embedding for classification.
- We develop an algorithm for extracting discriminating feature subgraphs from a graph dataset.
- We conduct extensive experiments on benchmark graph datasets and achieved significant improvement in graph classification accuracy.

The rest of the paper is organized as follows: Sect. 2 describes the neural word and document embedding methods related to our approach. In Sect. 3, we propose our graph embedding method in detail. Section 4 contains details about experimental setup, results and analysis. In Sect. 5, we discuss the future research scopes and summarize our methods and analysis.

2   Background

In this section, we review two popular approaches for neural embedding of words and documents respectively. These approaches are successfully being applied to many natural language processing (NLP) tasks such as document classification, word clustering, and etc. Continuous bag of words (CBOW) and Skip-gram model [8] attempt to produce high-quality dense vector representation of words that are able to capture semantic properties of a word. In both approaches, the embedding of a target word is learned from the context. The context is defined by the encompassing words. This model takes a corpus of sentences as sequences of words. Given such a sequence $\{w_1, w_2,..., w_t,..., w_T\}$, the m-length context of a target word w_t is defined by the words $w_{t-m},..., w_{t-1}, w_{t+1},..., w_{t+m}$. CBOW model tries to predict the target word given the context. Mathematically, for each target word w_t in a sequence, it maximizes the log-likelihood $\log Pr(w_t|w_{t-m}, ..., w_{t-1}, w_{t+1}, ..., w_{t+m})$. However, Skip-gram model adopts a somewhat different approach. It tries to predict the context words given the target word. That is, it maximizes $\log Pr(w_{t-m}, ..., w_{t-1}, w_{t+1}, ..., w_{t+m}|w_t)$.

PV-DBOW [6] is an approach for learning vector representation of entire document from the words contained. The proposed model is an extension of Skip-gram model. Here, the entire document is comparable to the target word, and the words in the document is used as the context. Given a set of documents $D = \{d_1, d_2,..., d_n\}$, where each $d \in D$ is a sequence of words $\{w_1, w_2,.., w_l\}$, PV-DBOW outputs the embeddings of the documents in D. For each document $d \in D$, it maximises the following log likelihood $\sum_{j=1}^{l} \log Pr(w_j|d)$.

3   The Proposed Method

This section presents the proposed graph classification method. After defining the framework, we present the candidate feature subgraphs mining process in Sect. 3.1, non-discriminating feature filtering process in Sect. 3.2 and Sect. 3.3 explains the graph embedding learning technique.

Definition 1 Supervised Graph Embedding Learning Framework: *Let D be a set of labeled graphs and L be a set of labels for nodes and edges in D. A labeled graph $G \in D$ can be represented by 3-tuple $< V, E, l >$ where V is a set of vertices; $E \subseteq V \times V$ is a set of edges; l: $V \cup E \rightarrow L$, is a function that labels vertices and edges. The graphs in D can be divided into mutually exclusive sets D_t and D_p where for each graph in D_t class labels are known and $D = D_t \cup D_p$. A function c: $D_t \rightarrow C$ is given where C is the set of class labels. Given this information, we have to learn a function f: $D \rightarrow R^m$ that maps each graph $G \in D$ to a fixed m-length vector. Finally, we have to predict the class label of each graph $G_p \in D_p$, that is, learning a function c_p: $D_p \rightarrow C$.*

3.1   Candidate Feature Subgraphs Mining

For extracting feature subgraphs to characterize the graphs, we have employed frequent subgraph mining techniques. To enforce the constraint of coverage, we define a minimum coverage threshold, min_cov. A graph is covered by a subgraph if there exists at least one subgraph isomorphism from the subgraph to the graph. Our goal is to find a set of feature subgraphs so that for each graph $G \in D$, the number of subgraphs that covers G is at least min_cov. Initially, we have mined frequent subgraphs in multiple phases (k phases where k $\geq$ 1). In each phase, frequent subgraphs are mined from those graphs with min_cov threshold yet to be fulfilled with a frequency threshold lower than the previous phase. We have used gSpan [18] algorithm to mine frequent subgraphs. However, frequent subgraph mining is expensive and not reasonable for executing a higher number of phases. On the other hand, with a lower number of phases, it is likely that min_cov threshold of many graphs may not be satisfied. Hence, in the next step, we have mined the smallest subgraphs from those graphs by the number of edges until their min_cov threshold is satisfied. The reason behind mining smallest subgraphs is that their frequency will always be higher than the larger subgraphs.

3.2   Filtering Candidate Feature Subgraphs

The number of candidate feature subgraphs extracted by frequent subgraph mining and smallest subgraphs mining is often enormous. Using all these subgraphs to learn embedding leads to higher computation cost. Note that all of the mined subgraphs are not effective for learning embeddings, especially for classification. To filter-out such non-discriminating subgraphs, we propose a feature selection measure for subgraphs inspired by information-gain measure. The entropy value of the set of graphs D_t is defined as follows:

$$H(D_t) = -\sum_{i \in C} \frac{N_i}{|D_t|} \log_2 \frac{N_i}{|D_t|} \qquad (1)$$

Here, N_i is the number of graph $G \in D_t$ such that $c(G) = i$. Let g be a subgraph and $D_t^g \in D_t$ be a set of graphs such that each $G_t \in D_t$ is covered by g. Now, we define the gain of a subgraph g in D_t as,

$$Gain_g(D_t) = \frac{\frac{|D_t^g|}{|D|} \times H(D_t^g) + \frac{|D-D_t^g|}{|D|} \times H(D - D_t^g)}{\frac{|D_t^g|}{|D|} \times \log_2 \frac{|D_t^g|}{|D|} + \frac{|D-D_t^g|}{|D|} \times \log_2 \frac{|D-D_t^g|}{|D|}} \qquad (2)$$

Algorithm 1: Feature Subgraphs Extraction

Input   : $D = D_t \cup D_p$: a set of graphs, k: number of phases, *min_cov*: minimum coverage threshold, δ: frequency threshold, Δ: frequency threshold discount

Output: D_f: a set of feature subgraphs

1 **begin**
2 $\quad$ $D_f \leftarrow \emptyset$;
3 $\quad$ Candidates $\leftarrow \emptyset$;
4 $\quad$ **for** $i \leftarrow 1$ **to** k **do**
5 $\quad\quad$ temp $\leftarrow \emptyset$;
6 $\quad\quad$ **for** $G \in D$ **do**
7 $\quad\quad\quad$ **if** *Coverage(G, Candidates)*$< min\_cov$ **then**
8 $\quad\quad\quad\quad$ temp $\leftarrow$ temp $\cup \{G\}$;
9 $\quad\quad$ **if** *temp.length()* ≤ 1 **then**
10 $\quad\quad\quad$ Break;
11 $\quad\quad$ FSGs $\leftarrow$ FindFSG(temp, δ) // FindFSG mines frequent subgraphs from temp with a frequency threshold δ
12 $\quad\quad$ Candidates $\leftarrow$ Candidates $\cup$ FSGs;
13 $\quad\quad$ $\delta \leftarrow \delta - \Delta$;
14 $\quad$ **for** $G \in D$ **do**
15 $\quad\quad$ **while** *Coverage(G, Candidates)*$< min\_cov$ **do**
16 $\quad\quad\quad$ g = Find smallest subgraph by edge number in G which is not in Candidates;
17 $\quad\quad\quad$ Candidates $\leftarrow$ Candidates $\cup \{g\}$;
18 $\quad$ **while** *True* **do**
19 $\quad\quad$ **if** *Candidates* $= \emptyset$ **then**
20 $\quad\quad\quad$ Break;
21 $\quad\quad$ g = Find subgraph in Candidates with maximum $Gain_g(D_t)$ value ;
22 $\quad\quad$ **for** $G \in D$ **do**
23 $\quad\quad\quad$ **if** *Coverage(G, D_f)*$< min\_cov$ **and** $g \in G$ **then**
24 $\quad\quad\quad\quad$ $D_f \leftarrow D_f \cup \{g\}$;
25 $\quad\quad\quad\quad$ Break;
26 $\quad\quad$ Candidates $\leftarrow$ Candidates - $\{g\}$;
27 **end**

To obtain the final set of feature subgraphs, we start with an empty set of subgraphs D_f. We pick each candidate feature subgraphs in descending order of gain value. The subgraph is added to D_f if it covers a graph whose coverage threshold is not satisfied by the subgraphs in D_f.

Algorithm 1 presents a pseudo-code of our feature subgraphs extraction process. At first, we generate candidate subgraphs by mining frequent subgraphs in multiple phases (lines 4–13) and then the smallest subgraphs (lines 14–17). Next, we pick subgraphs from candidates, based on the order of their gain value, that covers any graph whose coverage falls below the threshold (lines 18–26).

3.3 Learning Embedding from Feature Subgraphs

Our graph embedding method is inspired by PV-DBOW [6] but we have followed CBOW model rather than Skip-gram. We have designed a model that attempts to predict the graph given the feature subgraphs covering it to learn the graph embeddings. We define a partial ordering among the graphs in D and another among the subgraphs in D_f. Let G_t be the t-th graph in D, g_j be the j-th subgraph in D_f and $g_{t_1}, g_{t_2}, ..., g_{t_n}$ be the subgraphs in D_f that cover G_t. For each $G_t \in D$, we maximize $\log Pr(G_t | g_{t_1}, g_{t_2}, ..., g_{t_n})$. Let $W \in R^{|D_f| \times m}$ and $W' \in R^{m \times |D|}$ be two matrices. The i-th row of W corresponds to the vector embedding of i-th subgraph in D_f and j-th column of W' corresponds to the vector embedding of j-th graph in D. We learn W and W' using back-propagation algorithm. Our model is similar to the neural network model proposed in CBOW model as shown in Fig. 1. It is a 3-layer neural network with a hidden layer.

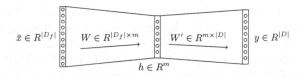

Fig. 1. Graph embedding model

Let $x_i \in R^{|D_f|}$ be a vector where the i-th element is 1 and all other elements are 0. For each $G_t \in D$, $\bar{x} = \frac{1}{n} \sum_{i=1}^{n} x_{t_i}$ is the input vector of the model. The values of the hidden layer is calculated as, $h = W^T \bar{x}$. The output layer is computed as $y = \text{Softmax}(u)$ where $u = W'^T h$. Here, y_i represents the probability of the predicted graph to be the G_i. We can define the loss function to minimize as follows,

$$L(W, W') = - \sum_{G_t \in D} \log Pr(G_t | g_{t_1}, g_{t_2}, ..., g_{t_n}) = - \sum_{G_t \in D} \log(y_t) \qquad (3)$$

In this model, W and W' are the parameters to optimize. We have used Stochastic Gradient Descent algorithm for optimizing Eq. (3). Vector embedding of graph G_t can be obtained as, $f(G_t) = w'_t$, the t-th column of W'. Finally, the vector embeddings of the graphs in D_t can be directly used to train a classifier model and vector embeddings of the graphs in D_p can be used to predict their classes.

4   Experiments

In this section, we describe the experiments conducted for evaluating the proposed graph classification technique. Details and characteristics of the datasets are presented in Sect. 4.1. We define our evaluation criteria and experimental settings in Sect. 4.2. Experimental results and comparative analyses are presented in Sect. 4.3. In Sect. 4.4, we examine the sensitivity of the algorithm performance towards parameter values. Section 4.5 shows the runtime analysis of our algorithm. Finally, in Sect. 4.6, we analyze the effectiveness of our method using visualization techniques.

4.1   Datasets

We have conducted our experiments on eight benchmark real-life datasets. These datasets cover chemoinformatics, bioinformatics and social network domains. D&D [4] is a graph dataset of protein structures divided into two classes: enzymes or non-enzymes. The nodes represent amino acids and edges denote spatial closeness. ENZYMES [1] is a dataset obtained from the BRENDA enzyme database in which the graphs correspond to protein tertiary structures. IMDB-B [19] is a dataset from social network domain. Here, the nodes indicate actors/actresses and edges represent their co-appearance in the same movie. The graphs are labeled with two classes of genre (Action or Romance). Mutag [3] is a graph dataset containing chemical compounds associated with class labels according to their mutagenic effect on a specific bacteria. NCI1 and NCI109 [17] are two chemical compound datasets screened for activity against ovarian cancer and lung cancer cell lines. PROTEINS [1] contains graphs with nodes indicating secondary structure elements and edges indicating neighborhood in amino-acid sequence. PTC [16] is another chemical compound dataset with class labels denoting carcinogenicity on rats.

4.2   Experimental Setup

To evaluate the effectiveness of the proposed algorithm, we have performed graph classification on the aforementioned benchmark datasets. As a classifier, an ensemble classifier of Multi-layer Perceptron classifier (Neural Network), Support Vector Machine, Decision Tree classifier, Naive Bayes classifier, and K-Nearest Neighbour classifier have been employed. We have adopted max voting strategy to combine their votes. K-Fold stratified cross-validation method is employed with nine folds for training and one fold for testing. For each dataset, the experiment is repeated five times then the average accuracy is taken and the standard deviation is noted. All the experiments have been conducted on an Intel Core i7-6700k CPU @ 4.00 GHz with 16 GB RAM and our algorithm is implemented using Python 3.7 programming language. The major parameters in our model are k: the number of phases, min_cov: minimum coverage threshold, δ: frequency threshold, Δ: frequency threshold discount and m: length of embedding vector. We have determined δ, the frequency threshold using elbow method on the number of frequent subgraphs as proposed in [12]. This base frequency threshold value for each dataset is presented in Table 1. We have examined with parameter values of $min\_cov \in \{10, 15, 20, 25, 30\}$ and m $\in \{2, 4, 8,..., 256\}$. Empirically, we have derived that the parameter values: $min\_cov = 10$, m = 64, k = 5, Δ = 0.025 works well across all the datasets. We present the parameter sensitivity analysis of the algorithm later in Sect. 4.4.

Table 1. Classification accuracy of our method and state-of-the-art methods on benchmark datasets.

Method	D&D	Enzymes	IMDB-B	Mutag	NCI1	NCI109	Proteins	PTC
GK	78.45	26.61	65.87	81.66	62.28	62.60	71.67	57.26
	(0.26)	(0.99)	(0.98)	(2.11)	(0.29)	(0.19)	(0.55)	(1.41)
Deep GK	73.50	27.08	66.96	82.66	62.48	62.69	71.68	57.32
	(1.01)	(0.79)	(0.56)	(1.45)	(0.25)	(0.23)	(0.50)	(1.13)
WL	77.95	53.15	72.86	80.72	80.13	80.22	72.92	56.97
	(0.70)	(1.14)	(0.76)	(3.00)	(0.50)	(0.34)	(0.56)	(2.01)
PSCN	77.12	–	71.00	92.63	78.59	–	75.89	–
	(2.41)	–	(2.29)	(4.21)	(1.89)	–	(2.76)	–
ECC	73.65	50.00	–	89.44	83.80	81.87	–	–
	–	–	–	–	–	–	–	–
SAGPool	76.45	–	78.10	90.42	74.18	74.06	71.86	–
	(0.97)	–	(4.20)	(7.78)	(1.20)	(0.78)	(0.97)	–
Graph2Vec	58.64	44.33	63.10	83.15	73.22	74.26	73.30	60.17
	(0.01)	(0.09)	(0.03)	(9.25)	(1.81)	(1.47)	(2.05)	(6.86)
GE-FSG	91.69	49.33	73.00	84.74	84.36	85.59	81.79	62.57
	(0.02)	(0.07)	(0.04)	(0.07)	(0.02)	(0.01)	(0.04)	(0.09)
GSSNN	80.26	–	80.10	96.77	80.75	–	79.73	–
	(2.50)	–	(3.25)	(4.68)	(4.07)	–	(3.31)	–
GAT-GC	–	58.45	–	90.44	–	–	76.81	–
	–	(6.35)	–	(6.44)	–	–	(3.77)	–
GCKN	–	–	77.8	**97.2**	83.9	–	76.4	70.8
	–	–	(2.6)	(2.8)	(1.6)	–	(3.9)	(4.6)
Ours	**93.46**	**59.82**	**88.56**	97.00	**94.92**	**97.40**	**83.44**	**84.94**
	(0.54)	(0.16)	(0.34)	(0.53)	(0.21)	(0.12)	(0.67)	(0.50)
δ	0.30	0.70	0.20	0.30	0.20	0.20	0.50	0.20

4.3 Results and Discussions

We have compared the performance of our algorithm with several baseline methods: Graphlet kernel (GK) [14], Deep GK [19], Weisfeiler-Lehman kernel (WL) [13], PSCN [11], ECC [15], SAGPool [7], Graph2Vec [9], GE-FSG [10], GSSNN [21], GAT-GC [20], and GCKN [2]. In Table 1, we have presented the accuracy (with standard deviation) of our model and other state-of-the-art methods. Accuracies of the baseline methods have been collected as reported in the papers. The best accuracy achieved by the methods in consideration is marked in bold. We can observe notable improvement in accuracy. Our method has outperformed other approaches on seven datasets D&D, Enzymes, IMDB-B, NCI1, NCI109, Proteins and PTC with significant gain. Despite, on dataset Mutag, our model has been outperformed by GCKN on a small margin, small standard deviation indicates our model to be more robust. This robustness is also visible for other datasets.

4.4 Parameter Sensitivity

In this section, we explore how the accuracy of our algorithm is affected by different choices of parameters. In Fig. 2, we demonstrate how classification accuracy gets affected by different choices of frequency threshold. For both the datasets, PTC and Enzymes, the accuracy is higher for lower frequency threshold. In our algorithm, high frequency threshold leads to fewer large subgraphs mined for feature subgraph candidates as large subgraphs tend to have a lower frequency than small ones. So, the increment in accuracy with lower frequency threshold shows the importance of capturing large structural information in embedding for better graph classification. In Fig. 3, we present the classification accuracy of our algorithm on datasets: PTC, Enzymes and IMDB-B for different choices of embedding vector length while keeping values of other parameters fixed. For relatively lower values of m (embedding vector length), with increment of vector length, accuracy gets better. This is a reflection of the fact that with very low vector size it is hard to capture effective feature representation. However, for relatively higher values of m, we can observe that increment of vector length results in worse accuracy for Enzymes which is due to over-fitting in embedding learning step. Figure 4 shows classification accuracy for different values of min_cov (Minimum coverage threshold). As the value of min_cov increases, less patterns are filtered out and the accuracy decreases for datasets PTC and Enzymes. This demonstrates the effectiveness of our proposed feature selection technique to filter out the non-discriminating subgraphs. However, for dataset IMDB-B, we can observe that lower value of min_cov may filter out too many patterns and result in low classification accuracy.

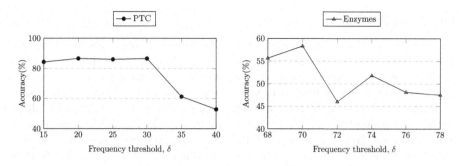

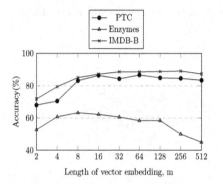

Fig. 2. Classification accuracy vs frequency threshold on PTC and Enzymes

Fig. 3. Classification accuracy vs length of vector embedding

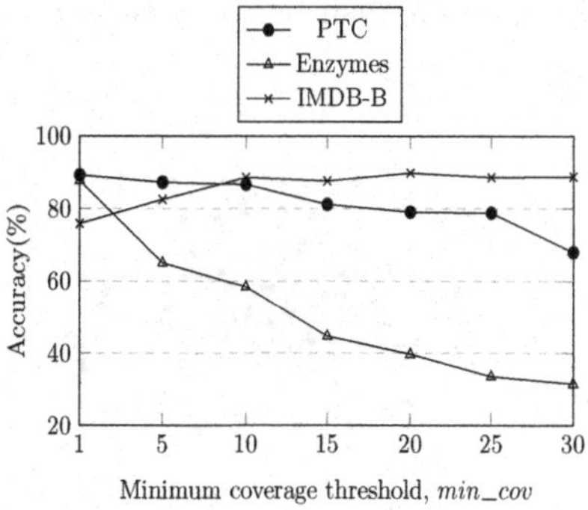

Fig. 4. Classification accuracy vs minimum coverage threshold

4.5   Runtime Analysis

For analyzing the runtime of the proposed algorithm we divide the algorithm in three phases: Feature Mining, Filtering and Embedding as described in Sects. 3.1, 3.2 and 3.3 respectively. Runtime for each of these phases on benchmark datasets is presented in Table 2. Across all datasets, feature mining phase takes significantly more time than the other two phases.

Table 2. Runtime(in minutes) for different phases on benchmark datasets.

Phase	D&D	Enzymes	IMDB-B	Mutag	NCI1	NCI109	Proteins	PTC
Feature mining	28.13	61.88	1132.08	230.36	24.66	22.58	403.26	8.68
Filtering	0.74	0.04	0.05	0.03	0.63	0.61	0.30	0.02
Embedding	0.26	0.37	0.12	0.01	2.13	2.12	0.27	0.53

4.6   Visualization

To demonstrate how using discriminating subgraphs only improves the classification accuracy, in this section, we present visualization of the graph embeddings produced by the proposed method. We have used principal component analysis for dimensionality reduction to visualize the vectors in $\mathbb{R}^2$. For comparison, we have produced visualization for embeddings both with and without filtering non-discriminating candidate feature subgraphs. In Fig. 5, visualizations of embeddings for dataset PTC and NC109 have been presented. Data points associated with different classes are displayed in different colors. From Fig. 5, it is evident that embeddings produced using discriminating subgraphs only tend to cluster better according to their classes. These well separable clusters make it easy to distinguish between classes and result in better classification accuracy.

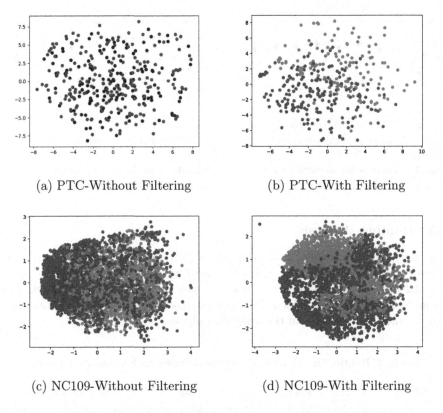

(a) PTC-Without Filtering   (b) PTC-With Filtering

(c) NC109-Without Filtering   (d) NC109-With Filtering

Fig. 5. Visualization of embedding for datasets PTC and NC109

5   Conclusions

In this paper, we have proposed a supervised neural embedding-based graph classification algorithm. We have developed an algorithm for mining discriminating frequent subgraphs from a collection of graphs using our proposed feature selection measure. Utilizing the discriminating subgraphs, our proposed algorithm produces entire graph embeddings that are easily separable between classes as demonstrated through embedding visualization. We have conducted experiments on benchmark graph datasets. Comprehensive analysis, comparing our method against baseline methods, shows that our algorithm has outperformed others with remarkable improvement in accuracy for graph classification. For future work, developing efficient methods for mining discriminating feature subgraphs faster, using deep neural network architecture can be considered.

Acknowledgement. This work is partially funded by (a) ICT Division, Government of People's Republic of Bangladesh; (b) NSERC (Canada); and (c) University of Manitoba.

References

1. Borgwardt, K.M., Ong, C.S., Schönauer, S., Vishwanathan, S., Smola, A.J., Kriegel, H.P.: Protein function prediction via graph kernels. Bioinformatics, **21**(suppl 1), i47–i56 (2005)
2. Chen, D., Jacob, L., Mairal, J.: Convolutional kernel networks for graph-structured data. In: ICML, pp. 1576–1586 (2020)
3. Debnath, A.K., Lopez de Compadre, R.L., Debnath, G., Shusterman, A.J., Hansch, C.: Structure-activity relationship of mutagenic aromatic and heteroaromatic nitro compounds. correlation with molecular orbital energies and hydrophobicity. J. Med. Chem. **34**(2), 786–797 (1991)
4. Dobson, P.D., Doig, A.J.: Distinguishing enzyme structures from non-enzymes without alignments. J. Mol. Biol. **330**(4), 771–783 (2003)
5. Grover, A., Leskovec, J.: Node2vec: scalable feature learning for networks. In: ACM SIGKDD, pp. 855–864 (2016)
6. Le, Q., Mikolov, T.: Distributed representations of sentences and documents. In: ICML, pp. 1188–1196 (2014)
7. Lee, J., Lee, I., Kang, J.: Self-attention graph pooling. In: ICML, pp. 3734–3743 (2019)
8. Mikolov, T., Sutskever, I., Chen, K., Corrado, G.S., Dean, J.: Distributed representations of words and phrases and their compositionality. In: NIPS, pp. 3111–3119 (2013)
9. Narayanan, A., Chandramohan, M., Venkatesan, R., Chen, L., Liu, Y., Jaiswal, S.: graph2vec: Learning distributed representations of graphs. In: MLG (2017)
10. Nguyen, D., Luo, W., Nguyen, T.D., Venkatesh, S., Phung, D.: Learning graph representation via frequent subgraphs. In: SDM, pp. 306–314 (2018)
11. Niepert, M., Ahmed, M., Kutzkov, K.: Learning convolutional neural networks for graphs. In: ICML, pp. 2014–2023 (2016)
12. Rousseau, F., Kiagias, E., Vazirgiannis, M.: Text categorization as a graph classification problem. In: ACL-IJCNLP, pp. 1702–1712 (2015)
13. Shervashidze, N., Schweitzer, P., Van Leeuwen, E.J., Mehlhorn, K., Borgwardt, K.M.: Weisfeiler-lehman graph kernels. JMLR **12**(77), 2539–2561 (2011)
14. Shervashidze, N., Vishwanathan, S., Petri, T., Mehlhorn, K., Borgwardt, K.: Efficient graphlet kernels for large graph comparison. In: AISTATS, pp. 488–495 (2009)

15. Simonovsky, M., Komodakis, N.: Dynamic edge-conditioned filters in convolutional neural networks on graphs. In: IEEE CVPR, pp. 3693–3702 (2017)
16. Toivonen, H., Srinivasan, A., King, R.D., Kramer, S., Helma, C.: Statistical evaluation of the predictive toxicology challenge 2000–2001. Bioinformatics **19**(10), 1183–1193 (2003)
17. Wale, N., Watson, I.A., Karypis, G.: Comparison of descriptor spaces for chemical compound retrieval and classification. Know. Inf. Syst. **14**(3), 347–375 (2008)
18. Yan, X., Han, J.: gSpan: Graph-based substructure pattern mining. In: IEEE ICDM, pp. 721–724 (2002)
19. Yanardag, P., Vishwanathan, S.: Deep graph kernels. In: ACM SIGKDD, pp. 1365–1374 (2015)
20. Zhang, S., Xie, L.: Improving attention mechanism in graph neural networks via cardinality preservation. In: IJCAI, pp. 1395–1402 (2020)
21. Zhu, S., Zhou, L., Pan, S., Zhou, C., Yan, G., Wang, B.: GSSNN: graph smoothing splines neural networks. In: AAAI, pp. 7007–7014 (2020)

Mining Sequential Patterns in Uncertain Databases Using Hierarchical Index Structure

Kashob Kumar Roy[1], Md Hasibul Haque Moon[1],
Md Mahmudur Rahman[1], Chowdhury Farhan Ahmed[1]([✉]),
and Carson K. Leung[2]

[1] Department of Computer Science and Engineering, University of Dhaka,
Dhaka, Bangladesh
{mahmudur,farhan}@du.ac.bd
[2] Department of Computer Science, University of Manitoba, Winnipeg, MB, Canada
kleung@cs.umanitoba.ca

Abstract. In this uncertain world, data uncertainty is inherent in many applications and its importance is growing drastically due to the rapid development of modern technologies. Nowadays, researchers have paid more attention to mine patterns in uncertain databases. A few recent works attempt to mine frequent uncertain sequential patterns. Despite their success, they are incompetent to reduce the number of false-positive pattern generation in their mining process and maintain the patterns efficiently. In this paper, we propose multiple theoretically tightened pruning upper bounds that remarkably reduce the mining space. A novel hierarchical structure is introduced to maintain the patterns in a space-efficient way. Afterward, we develop a versatile framework for mining uncertain sequential patterns that can effectively handle weight constraints as well. Besides, with the advent of incremental uncertain databases, existing works are not scalable. There exist several incremental sequential pattern mining algorithms, but they are limited to mine in precise databases. Therefore, we propose a new technique to adapt our framework to mine patterns when the database is incremental. Finally, we conduct extensive experiments on several real-life datasets and show the efficacy of our framework in different applications.

Keywords: Sequential pattern mining · Uncertain database ·
Weighted sequential patterns · Incremental database

1 Introduction

Sequential Pattern Mining is an important and challenging data mining problem [11,13] with broad applications where the order of the itemsets or events in a sequence is important. There are many applications such as environmental surveillance, medical diagnosis, security, and manufacturing systems etc.,

© Springer Nature Switzerland AG 2021
K. Karlapalem et al. (Eds.): PAKDD 2021, LNAI 12713, pp. 29–41, 2021.
https://doi.org/10.1007/978-3-030-75765-6_3

where uncertainty is inherent in nature due to several limitations: (i) our limited understanding of reality; (ii) limitations of the observation equipment; or (iii) limitations of available resources for the analysis of data, etc. A large number of approaches have been introduced in [1,5,7,8] to mine frequent itemsets from uncertain databases. Algorithms proposed in [3,15] mine sequential patterns in uncertain databases. However, in the real world, not all items are equally important. For example, in biomedical data analysis, some genes are more vital than others in causing a particular disease. Weighted pattern mining methods are proposed in [6,14] for this task. Rahman et al. [12] handle weight constraints in mining uncertain sequential patterns by maintaining weight and expected support threshold separately. Thus, it can efficiently mine sequences having high frequencies with high weights but incompetent to mine sequences which have low frequencies with high weights or high frequencies with low weights. Besides, existing uncertain sequential pattern mining methods have some vital limitations such as: (i) generation of a huge number of false-positive patterns due to the pruning upper bounds; (ii) inefficient maintenance of candidate patterns, which results in costly support computation; and (iii) lack of a sophisticated weight upper bound to mine weighted patterns efficiently while maintaining anti-monotone property. To address these limitations, we propose multiple novel pruning upper bounds that are theoretically tightened than respective upper bounds already introduced in the literature and utilize a hierarchical index structure to maintain potential candidate patterns in a space-efficient way.

Moreover, with the advent of modern technologies, most databases are dynamic and incremental in nature. A large number of researches [2,4,9] have been successful in incremental pattern mining. But none of the existing uncertain sequential pattern mining algorithms are effective in handling the dynamic nature because running batch algorithms from scratch after each increment is not a feasible solution in the sense of time. To the best of our knowledge, our proposed technique is the first work to mine sequential patterns in incremental uncertain databases. In summary, our contributions in this work are as follows,

1. Three theoretically tightened upper bounds: $expSup^{cap}$, wgt^{cap}, $wExpSup^{cap}$ to reduce the search space of mining potential candidate patterns.
2. A novel hierarchical index structure, $USeq\text{-}Trie$, to maintain the patterns.
3. A faster method, $SupCalc$, to compute expected support of patterns.
4. An efficient algorithm, $FUSP$, to mine sequential patterns in uncertain database.
5. An approach $InUSP$ for incremental mining of uncertain sequential patterns.

Extensive experimental analysis validates the efficacy of our proposed methods and shows that our methods consistently outperform other baseline approaches.

2   Background Study

Related Works. Among a plethora of research on sequential pattern mining, GSP [13] works based on candidate generation and testing paradigm whereas

Table 1. Initial database, DB

Id	Uncertain sequence
1	(a:0.9, c:0.6) (a:0.7) (b:0.3)(d:0.7)
2	(a:0.6, c:0.4) (a:0.5) (a:0.4, b:0.3)
3	(a:0.3) (a:0.2, b:0.2) (a:0.4, b:0.3, g:0.5)
4	(a:0.1, c:0.1) (a:0.3, b:0.1, c:0.4)
5	(d:0.1) (a:0.4) (d:0.1) (a:0.5, c:0.6)
6	(b:0.3) (b:0.4) (a:0.1) (a:0.1, b:0.2)

Table 2. Weight table

Item	Weight	Item	Weight
a	0.8	b	1.0
c	0.9	d	0.9
e	0.7	f	0.9
g	0.8		

PrefixSpan [11] follows the divide-and-conquer approach to mine frequent sequences in precise databases. *PrefixSpan* [11] expands patterns by recursively projecting the database into smaller parts and mining local patterns in those prefix-projected databases. Uncertain data has gained great attention in recent years [1,6,10,12,15]. Inspired by *PrefixSpan*, *U-PrefixSpan* [10] mines probabilistic frequent sequences whereas *uWSequence* [12] mines expected support-based frequent sequences with weight constraints in uncertain databases. *uWSequence* [12] uses $expSupport^{top}$ upper-bound to prune the mining space of patterns. They use weight threshold as an extra level of filtering which is not aligned with the concept of weighted support defined in [14] for precise databases. Following [14], we introduce the concept of weighted expected support in uncertain sequential pattern mining that considers both expected support and weight of patterns simultaneously.Further, researchers proposed various algorithms in [2,4,9] to handle increments in databases. *IncSpan* [2] introduces the concept of buffering semi-frequent sequences *(SFS)* mined from initial databases which may become frequent after future increments. *WIncSpan* [4] finds weighted sequential patterns in incremental precise databases. Despite the promising significance of incremental uncertain sequential pattern mining in different applications, existing works are not capable to mine patterns efficiently. Hence, we introduce a new concept of promising frequent sequences *(PFS)* to improve the efficiency

Preliminaries. Let $I = \{i_1, i_2,..., i_n\}$ be the set of all items in a database. An event $e_i = (i_1, i_2,...,i_k)$ is a subset of I. A sequence is an ordered set of events. For example, $\alpha = <(i_2), (i_1,i_5), (i_1)>$ consists of 3 consecutive events. In uncertain sequences, items in each event are assigned with their existential probabilities such as $\alpha = <(i_2: P_{i_2}), (i_1: P_{i_1}, i_5: P_{i_5}), (i_1: P_{i_1})>$. An uncertain sequential database is a collection of uncertain sequences shown in Table 1. Support of a sequence α in a database is the number of data tuples that contain α as a subsequence. In this paper, we follow the definition of expected support *(expSup)* for a sequence (items within the sequence are independent) which is defined in [12] as the sum of the maximum possible probabilities of that sequence in each data tuple where the probability of a sequence is computed simply by multiplying the uncertainty value of its all items. A sequence α can be extended with an item i in two ways: i) *i-extension*, insert i to the last event of α, and ii) *s-extension*, add i to α as a new event. Weight of a sequence *(sWeight)* is the sum of its each individual item's weight divided by the length of the sequence [14] i.e., the total number of items in the sequence. According to Table 1 and Table 2, for sequence $\alpha = \; <(a)(b)>$, support of α is 5, $expSup(\alpha) = max(0.9 \times 0.3, 0.7 \times 0.3) + max(0.6 \times 0.3, 0.5 \times 0.3) + max(0.3 \times 0.2, 0.3 \times 0.3, 0.2 \times 0.3) + (0.1 \times 0.1) + 0 + (0.1 \times 0.2) = 0.57$, and $sWeight(\alpha) = (0.8 + 1.0)/2 = 0.9$ as per the definitions.

3   A Framework for Mining Uncertain Sequential Patterns

In this section, we propose a new framework for mining sequential patterns in uncertain databases efficiently with/without the weight constraints in mining patterns followed by discussing the incremental mining approach when the database would be of dynamic nature.

Definitions. $maxPr$ is the maximum possible probability of a sequence $\alpha = \; < (i_1)(i_2)...(i_{|\alpha|}) >$ in the whole database [12],

$$maxPr(\alpha) = \prod_{k=1}^{|\alpha|} (\widehat{P}_{DB|\alpha_{k-1}}(i_k)) \; where \; \alpha_{k-1} = \; < (i_1)...(i_{k-1}) > \qquad (1)$$

where $\widehat{P}_{DB|\alpha}(i)$ = maximum possible probability of item i in a database $DB \mid \alpha$ that is the projection of original database with α as current prefix [11]. Moreover, [12] shows that the $maxPr$ measure holds anti-monotone property. Similar to $maxPr$, we define another measure $maxPr_S(\alpha)$ as the maximum probability of a pattern α in a single data sequence S. According to Table 1, the $maxPr(<(c)(a)>) = 0.6 \times 0.7 = 0.54$ and $maxPr(<(ac)>) = 0.9 \times 0.6 = 0.54$; where for the 1st data sequence, $maxPr_S(<(a)(b)>) = max(0.9 \times 0.3, \; 0.7 \times 0.3) = 0.27$. We define an upper bound of expected support of a sequence α of length m as,

$$expSup^{cap}(\alpha_m) = maxPr(\alpha_{m-1}) \times \sum_{\forall S \in (DB|\alpha_{m-1})} maxPr_S(i_m) \qquad (2)$$

Lemma 1. *For a sequence α, $expSup^{cap}(\alpha) \geq expSup(\alpha)$ and $expSup(\alpha) \geq expSup(\alpha')$, where $\alpha \subseteq \alpha'$; $\therefore expSup^{cap}(\alpha) \geq expSup(\alpha')$. If $expSup^{cap}(\alpha) < a$ minimum threshold γ holds, then $expSup(\alpha) < \gamma$ and $expSup(\alpha') < \gamma, \forall \alpha' \supseteq \alpha$ must be true. Thus it satisfies the anti-monotonicity constraints.*

Lemma 2. *For a sequence α, $expSup^{cap}(\alpha) \leq expSupport^{top}(\alpha)$[1] always holds. Hence, $expSup^{cap}(\alpha)$ significantly reduces the search space in mining patterns and leads to a smaller number of false positive patterns than $expSupport^{top}(\alpha)$.*

---

[1] uWSequence[12] defines the upper bound of expected support as $expSupport^{top}(\alpha) = maxPr(\alpha_{m-1}) \times maxPr(i_m) \times sup_{i_m}$ where sup_{i_m} is the support count of i_m.

Later on, we define few more definitions where each item has a weight to indicate its importance. We will be consistent with weighted pattern mining in following sections. Note that our framework is easily adaptable to mine patterns without weight constraints that is discussed in the experiments section. Following the concept of *weighted support* for precise database in [14], we define *weighted expected support* of a sequence α as $WES(\alpha) = expSup(\alpha) \times sWeight(\alpha)$. According to Tables 1 and 2, $WES(<(a)(b)>) = 0.57 \times 0.9 = 0.513$. A sequence α is called *weighted sequential pattern* if $WES(\alpha)$ meets a minimum threshold. This threshold is defined to be $minWES = min\_sup \times (size\ of\ the\ whole\ database) \times WAM \times wgtFct$. Here, min_sup is user given value in range [0,1] related to a sequence's frequency, WAM is weighted arithmetic mean of all item-weights present in the database and defined as $WAM = (\sum_{i \in I} w_i \times f_i)/\sum_{i \in I} f_i$, where w_i and f_i are the weight and frequency of item i in current database. Hence, the value of WAM changes after each increment in the database. $wgtFct$ is a user-given positive value chosen to tune the mining of weighted sequential patterns. Choice of min_sup and $wgtFct$ depends on how much frequent and weighted patterns are required in the respective applications.

However, the measure WES does not hold anti-monotone property as any item with higher weight can be appended to a weighted-infrequent sequence and the resulting super-sequence may become weighted-frequent. So, to employ anti-monotone property in mining weighted frequent patterns, we propose two other upper bound measures, wgt^{cap} and $wExpSup^{cap}$, which are used as upper bound of *weight* and *weighted expected support* respectively. Upper bound of weight of a sequence α, $wgt^{cap}(\alpha)$ is defined as,

$$wgt^{cap}(\alpha) = \max(mxW_{DB}(DB|\alpha), mxW_s(\alpha)) \tag{3}$$

where $mxW_{DB}(DB|\alpha)$ is the *maximum weight of all frequent items in the α-projected database* and $mxW_s(\alpha)$ is the *maximum weight of all items in the sequence α*. To enforce the anti-monotone property of weighted frequent patterns in precise databases, authors in [4,14] make an attempt to use the maximal weight of all items in database as upper bound of weight of a sequence. It is obvious to see that wgt^{cap} of a sequence is always less than or equal to the maximal weight of all items in database. As wgt^{cap} becomes tighter, it generates fewer false positive patterns compared to the existing methods.

Lemma 3. *For any sequence α, $wgt^{cap}(\alpha)$ is at least equal to the $sWeight$ value of α and all of its supersequences, α'. Because, $wgt^{cap}(\alpha) \geq sWeight(\alpha)$ and $wgt^{cap}(\alpha) \geq wgt^{cap}(\alpha')$, where $\alpha \subseteq \alpha'$; $\therefore wgt^{cap}(\alpha) \geq sWeight(\alpha')$.*

The proposed upper bound of weighted expected support is defined as,

$$wExpSup^{cap}(\alpha) = expSup^{cap}(\alpha) \times wgt^{cap}(\alpha) \tag{4}$$

Lemma 4. *For a sequence α, if $wExpSup^{cap}(\alpha) < minWES$, then none of α and its supersequences can be weighted frequent. Because, $wExpSup^{cap}(\alpha) \geq WES(\alpha)$, and $wExpSup^{cap}(\alpha) \geq WES(\alpha')$, for all $\alpha \subseteq \alpha'$.*

According to Lemma 4, we can safely define our pruning condition to reduce the search space of patterns in pattern-growth based mining as follows:

If for any k-sequence α, $wExpSup^{cap}(\alpha) < minWES$, then searching possible extension of α to (k+1)-sequence can be pruned, i.e., neither α nor any super sequences of α would be frequent at all.

Moreover, Lemma 4 ensures that our proposed algorithms do not generate any false negative patterns. However, as $wExpSup^{cap}(\alpha) \geq WES(\alpha)$, some patterns may be discovered with $wExpSup^{cap}(\alpha) \geq minWES$ but $WES(\alpha) < minWES$. An extra scan of the database is required to remove them. We have omitted proof of the lemmas due to space limitation.

3.1   USeq-Trie: Maintenance of Patterns

We use a hierarchical data structure, named as *USeq-Trie*, to store uncertain sequences and update their weighted expected support efficiently. Each node in the *USeq-Trie* represents an item in a sequence and will be created as either *s-extension* or *i-extension* from its parent node. Recall that a sequence is an ordered set of events, and an event is a set of items. In *s-extension*, the edge label is added as a different event. In *i-extension*, it is added in the same event as its parent. Each edge is labeled by an item. The edge labels in a path to a node from the root form a pattern. For example, $<(a)>$, $<(b)>$, $<(ab)>$, $<(c)>$, $<(b)(c)>$, $<(d)>$, $<(cd)>$ and $<(c)(d)>$ are sequential patterns which are stored into *USeq-Trie* shown in Fig. 1. In this figure, the *s-extensions* are denoted by the *solid lines* and *i-extensions* by *dashed lines*. For simplicity of the figure, we are not showing edge labels here. Each node represents a (weighted) frequent uncertain sequence and stores its (weighted) expected support. Now, we present an efficient method, *SupCalc*, to calculate *expSup* or *WES* for each candidate pattern stored in a *USeq-Trie*.

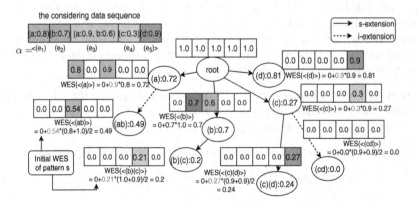

Fig. 1. An efficient way to compute *WES* of patterns stored into *USeq-Trie*

Support Calculation, SupCalc. It reads sequences from the dataset one by one and updates the support of all patterns in *USeq-Trie* against them. For a sequence $\alpha = <e_1 e_2..e_n>$ (where e_i is an event/itemset), the steps are following,

1. Define an array of size n at each node. For the root node, all values are 1.0. At a particular node, the maximum expected support of pattern s from root to that node is stored at proper indices of the node's array - are the ending positions of s as a sub-sequence in α. The values at other indices are 0.0.

2. While traversing the *USeq-Trie* in depth-first order: (i) For a node created by a *s-extension* with an item i_k, iterate over all events in α and calculate the support of the current pattern s (ends with i_k in a new event) by multiplying the probability of item i_k in current event e_m with the maximum probability in the parent node's array up to the event e_{m-1}. The resulting support is stored at position m in the following node's array. (ii) For *i-extension*, the support will be calculated by multiplying the probability of the item i_k in e_m with the value at position m in the parent node's array and stored at position m in the following child node's array. After that, the maximum value in the resulting array multiplied by its weight will be added to the weighted expected support of the current pattern at the corresponding node.

3. Use the resultant array to calculate the weighted expected support of all super patterns while traversing the next child nodes.

Figure 1 shows the resulting *USeq-Trie* after updating *WES* for all the stored patterns against a sequence, $\alpha = <(a:0.8)(b:0.7)(a:0.9,b:0.6)(c:0.3)(d:0.9)>$.

Complexity of *SupCalc*. It takes $O(N \times |\alpha|)$ for updating N number of nodes against the sequence α. Therefore, the total time complexity of actual support calculation is $O(|DB| \times N \times k)$ where k is the maximum sequence length in the dataset. It outperforms the procedure used in *uWSequence* [12] which needs $O(|DB| \times N \times k^2)$ to calculate a sequence's actual expected support. Moreover, we can remove false-positive patterns and find frequent ones from the *USeq-Trie* in $O(N)$. Thus, the use of *USeq-Trie* has made our method efficient.

3.2 FUSP: Faster Mining of Uncertain Sequential Patterns

Inspired by *PrefixSpan* [11], we propose *FUSP* to mine weighted sequential patterns in an uncertain database. It uses the $wExpSup^{cap}$ measure and *SupCalc* method to reduce the search space and improve the efficiency. The sketch of *FUSP* algorithm is as follows.

1. Process the database such that the existential probability of an item in a sequence is replaced with the maximum probability of all of its next occurrences in this sequence. This idea is similar to the *preprocess* function of *uWSequence* [12]. This preprocessed database will be used to run the *PrefixSpan*-like mining approach to find the candidates for frequent sequences. While processing, sort the items in an event/itemset in lexicographical order.

2. Calculate *WAM* of all items present in the current database and calculate the threshold of weighted expected support, *minWES*.

3. Find length-1 frequent items and for each item, project the preprocessed database into smaller parts and expand longer patterns recursively. Store the potential candidates patterns into a *USeq-Trie*.
4. While growing longer patterns, extend current prefix α to α' with an item β as *s-extension* or *i-extension* according to the pruning condition.
5. Use of $wExpSup^{cap}$ value instead of actual support generates few false-positive candidates. Scan the whole actual database, update weighted expected supports and prune false-positive candidates based on their *WES*.

3.3   InUSP: Incremental Mining of Uncertain Sequential Patterns

Existing incremental works [2,4] follow the technique to lower the minimum support threshold by a user-given buffer ratio, $\mu \in [0,1]$, and find *almost frequent* sequences called *SFS* - stating that most of the frequent patterns in the appended database will either come from *SFS* or already frequent sequences (*FS*) in the initial database. Inspired by this concept, we use $minWES' = minWES \times \mu$ to find *SFS* where $minWES' \leq WES < minWES$, along with *FS* where $WES \geq minWES$. However, we argue that *SFS* is not necessarily enough to capture new frequent patterns in future increments. Let us consider some cases: (a) an increment to the database may introduce a new sequence which was initially absent in both *FS* and *SFS* but frequently appeared in later increments; (b) a sequence had become infrequent after an increment but could have become semi-frequent or even frequent again after next few increments. There are many real-life cases where new frequent patterns might appear in future increments due to its seasonal behavior or different other characteristics. Existing approaches do not handle these cases. To address these cases, we propose to maintain another set of sequences denoted as *Promising Frequent Sequences (PFS)* which are neither globally frequent nor semi-frequent after each increment ΔDB introduced into *DB* but their *WES* satisfy a user-specified threshold that can be defined as $LWES = \gamma \times \mu \times min\_sup \times |\Delta DB| \times WAM \times wgtFct$ where γ is a constant factor, to find locally frequent patterns in ΔDB at a particular point. Here, the globally frequent or semi-frequent implies when considering the size of the entire database, and locally frequent when using the size of only one increment. Intuitively, we can say that locally frequent patterns may become globally frequent or semi-frequent after next few increments. The patterns whose *WES* values do not meet the local threshold *LWES*, are very unlikely to become globally frequent or semi-frequents. Thus maintaining *PFS* may significantly increase the performance of an algorithm in finding the almost complete set of frequent patterns after each increment. Therefore, we devise *InUSP* to incorporate the concept of *PFS* in mining patterns. Instead of performing *FUSP* from scratch after each increment, *InUSP* works only on ΔDB. Initially, it runs *FUSP* once to find out *FS* and *SFS* from initial database and uses *USeq-Trie* to store *FS* and *SFS*. In addition, a different *USeq-Trie*, which is initially empty, is used to store *PFS*.

After each increment ΔDB, the steps of *InUSP* algorithm are as follows:

1. Update the values of *database size*, *WAM*, *minWES*, and $minWES'$.

2. Run *FUWS* only in ΔDB to find locally frequent sequences (*LFS*) against a local threshold, *LWES*, and store them into *USeq-Trie*. Users can choose *LWES* based on the aspects of application.
3. For all α in *FS*, *SFS* and *PFS*, update WES_α using the *SupCalc* method.
   - if $WES_\alpha < LWES$, delete α's information.
   - else if $WES_\alpha < minWES'$, move α to PFS'.
   - else if $WES_\alpha < minWES$, move α to SFS'.
   - else move α to FS'.
4. Move new patterns α from *LFS* to PFS' or SFS' or FS' based on WES_α.
5. Use FS', SFS', and PFS' as *FS*, *SFS*, and *PFS* respectively for the next increment.

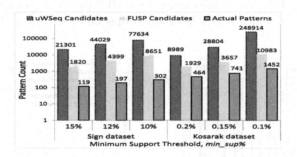

Fig. 2. *FUSP* outperforms *uWSequence* in candidate pattern generation

Table 3. Runtime (seconds) comparison between *uWSequence* and *FUSP*

Sign dataset			Kosarak dataset			Fifa dataset		
min_sup	uWSeq	FUSP	*min_sup*	uWSeq	FUSP	*min_sup*	uWSeq	FUSP
20%	717.69	10.64	*0.25%*	5942.06	348.32	*20%*	1615.50	12.73
18%	1116.75	18.34	*0.22%*	7102.27	443.13	*18%*	2943.45	25.85
15%	2052.04	32.64	*0.2%*	8581.56	475.12	*17%*	4003.97	34.79
12%	4316.43	72.39	*0.18%*	14622.38	659.30	*16%*	6114.34	56.05
10%	7275.41	122.94	*0.15%*	33864.18	1029.70	*15%*	9033.86	74.95

4 Experimental Results

We have evaluated our algorithms using several real-life and popular datasets such as *Sign, Kosarak, Fifa, Leviathan, Retail, Foodmart, Chainstore,* and *Online Retail* from *SPMF*[2] data repository. We assigned probability and weight values

---

[2] http://www.philippe-fournier-viger.com/spmf/index.php?link=datasets.php.

to the items of these datasets as all of them were precise and none of them contained weight information. We followed normal distribution with *mean* of *0.5* and *standard deviation* of *0.25 (for probabilities)* or *0.125 (for weights)* to generate these values. We implemented our algorithms in *Python* programming language and a machine with $Core^{TM}$ *i5-9600U 2.90GHz CPU* and *8GB RAM*.

Performance of *FUSP*. We have compared with the recent algorithm, *uWSequence* [12], which proposed a framework where the definition of weighted sequential pattern in uncertain databases is different from ours. Furthermore, *uWSequence* [12] outperforms existing methods for mining sequential patterns also without weight constraints in uncertain databases. So, to show the efficiency of *FUSP* in mining uncertain sequential patterns without weight constraints, we have compared *FUSP* with the current best *uWSequence* by setting the weights of all items to 1.0 which brings both algorithms under a unifying framework.

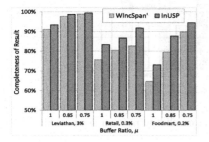
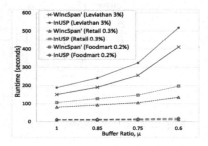

Fig. 3. Completeness comparison between *WIncSpan′* and *InUSP*

Fig. 4. Runtime comparison between *WIncSpan′* and proposed *InUSP*

(a) False Candidate Generation: Recall that both *FUSP* and *uWSequence* work like *PrefixSpan* using some upper bound of actual expected support value and thus, generate some false positive candidates. From Fig. 2, we can see that *FUSP* generates a smaller number of false candidates for any support threshold as it uses a tighter upper bound. For example, in the *Sign* (dense) dataset with 15% minimum support threshold, it generates 11 times fewer candidates compared to *uWSequence*. In *Kosarak* (sparse) with 0.15% support threshold, *FUSP* generates only 79.7% false candidates where for *uWSequence*, it is 97.4%.

(b) Runtime Analysis: *FUSP* needs to maintain a smaller number of candidate patterns in its mining process and uses a faster method to calculate expected support of a pattern. Thus, it is a way faster than the *uWSequence* for any support threshold. Results shown in Table 3 validates this claim. We can see *FUSP* is 50–70 times faster in *Sign* dataset for different thresholds. Interestingly, the difference in their runtime increases with the decrease in the threshold parameter. We have found similar results also in other datasets.

Performance of the Incremental Technique, *InUSP*. We have modified the current best incremental solution, *WIncSpan* [4] to work in uncertain data by replacing the core PrefixSpan-like algorithm by *FUSP* so that both the proposed *InUSP* and modified *WIncSpan'* mine weighted sequential patterns from uncertain database. The baseline approach is running *FUSP* from scratch in the whole updated database after each increment. We define completeness of the result from an incremental solution to be the percentage of patterns found with respect to the result of the baseline. To use the datasets as incremental ones, we used the first 50% of the dataset to be the initial part and then introduced 5 increments of random sizes[3], unless mentioned otherwise.

(a) Analysis with respect to buffer ratio: Buffer ratio, $\mu = 1.0$ means no buffer and lower values mean larger buffers to store semi-frequent sequences. Thus, with lower μ, incremental approaches generate and maintain more patterns which help to increase the completeness of their result. However, due to local mining in incremented portions and maintaining additional promising sequences, *InUSP* always achieves more completeness than *WIncSpan'*. For the same reason, it also requires slightly more time than *WIncSpan'*. From Fig. 3 and Fig. 4, we can see the trade-off between completeness and runtime. We observe that difference in completeness is larger in datasets like *Retail* and *Foodmart* (market-basket) where increments contain frequent items or introduce new items frequently than datasets like *Leviathan* (word sequences) where the initial database contains almost all of the frequent sequences. By repeating this experiment in other datasets and by varying the support threshold, we find that though *InUSP* consumes slightly more time, it outperforms *WIncSpan'* in terms of completeness of result in every dataset for any combination of μ and min_sup.

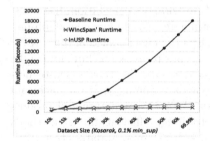

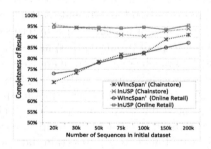

Fig. 5. Comparison of scalability using *Kosarak* dataset

Fig. 6. Change in completeness for different initial sizes of a dataset

(b) Scalability Analysis: To test scalability we have run *InUSP*, *WIncSpan'* and the baseline approach in several large datasets introducing several increments. Figure 5 shows the result for *Kosarak* dataset with $min\_sup = 0.1\%$.

---

[3] For the *Retail* market-basket dataset, we used the first one-fifth transactions (1st month) as the initial portion and then 4 increments to represent the next 4 months.

InUSP and *WIncSpan'* requires slightly more time at the initial point as they have to find and buffer the semi-frequent patterns for future use. After that, at any point of dataset increment, both of them take significantly less time to find the updated set of frequent sequences. Our proposed technique outperforms the baseline approach in terms of scalability and although it takes slightly more time than *WIncSpan'*, the difference is negligible as *InUSP* provides better completeness.

(c) **Varying Initial Size of Datasets:** We considered different initial sizes for this analysis and introduced required number of increments (each sized 50–80% of the initial size) to use the full dataset. Figure 6 shows the result in *Chainstore* and *Online Retail dataset* with $min\_sup = 0.05\%$ for both. We have found that the smaller the initial dataset, the more are the sequences to be found as new patterns after the increments. The completeness of incremental approaches also depends on the distribution of items among the increments. As a result, the completeness of *WIncSpan'* is competitive only if the initial dataset contains sufficient sequences compared to the total size of all future increments. However, the completeness of *InUSP* is less affected by initial size as it also mines in the incremented portions.

5   Conclusions

In this work, our proposed *FUSP* algorithm can mine sequential patterns in uncertain databases with or without weight constraints. It uses multiple theoretically tightened upper bounds in pruning technique and hence, generates a smaller number of false-positive patterns compared to the state-of-the-art works. Furthermore, the use of a space-efficient data structure *USeq-Trie* for pattern maintenance and an efficient method *SupCalc* for support calculation, has made *FUSP* superior to other works in terms of runtime. In case of incremental mining, the concept of promising frequent sequences lifts the effectiveness of our *InUSP* algorithm. The experimental analysis shows that our proposed techniques can be great tools for a lot of real-life applications such as medical records, sensor network, user behavior analysis, privacy-preserving data mining, that use uncertain sequential data. We hope that the concept of *USeq-Trie* structure and promising frequent sequences will help researchers to design efficient mining methods in related fields (e.g., uncertain data streams, spatio-temporal data, etc.).

Acknowledgement. This work is partially supported by NSERC (Canada) and University of Manitoba.

References

1. Ahmed, A.U., Ahmed, C.F., Samiullah, M., Adnan, N., Leung, C.K.S.: Mining interesting patterns from uncertain databases. Inf. Sci. **354**, 60–85 (2016)
2. Cheng, H., Yan, X., Han, J.: IncSpan: incremental mining of sequential patterns in large database. In: ACM SIGKDD, pp. 527–532 (2004)

3. Ge, J., Xia, Y., Wang, J.: Mining uncertain sequential patterns in iterative MapReduce. In: Cao, T., et al. (eds.) PAKDD 2015, Part II. LNCS (LNAI), vol. 9078, pp. 243–254. Springer, Cham (2015). https://doi.org/10.1007/978-3-319-18032-8_19
4. Ishita, S.Z., Noor, F., Ahmed, C.F.: An efficient approach for mining weighted sequential patterns in dynamic databases. In: Perner, P. (ed.) ICDM 2018. LNCS (LNAI), vol. 10933, pp. 215–229. Springer, Cham (2018). https://doi.org/10.1007/978-3-319-95786-9_16
5. Le, T., Vo, B., Huynh, V.N., Nguyen, N.T., Baik, S.W.: Mining top-k frequent patterns from uncertain databases. Appl. Intell. **50**, 1487–1497 (2020). https://doi.org/10.1007/s10489-019-01622-1
6. Li, Z., Chen, F., Wu, J., Liu, Z., Liu, W.: Efficient weighted probabilistic frequent itemset mining in uncertain databases. Expert Syst. e12551 (2020)
7. Lin, C.W., Hong, T.P.: A new mining approach for uncertain databases using CUFP trees. Expert Syst. Appl. **39**(4), 4084–4093 (2012)
8. Lin, J.C.-W., Gan, W., Fournier-Viger, P., Hong, T.-P., Tseng, V.S.: Weighted frequent itemset mining over uncertain databases. Appl. Intell. **44**(1), 232–250 (2015). https://doi.org/10.1007/s10489-015-0703-9
9. Lyu, X., Ma, H.: An efficient incremental mining algorithm for discovering sequential pattern in wireless sensor network environments. Sensors **19**(1), 29 (2019)
10. Muzammal, M., Raman, R.: Mining sequential patterns from probabilistic databases. In: Huang, J.Z., Cao, L., Srivastava, J. (eds.) PAKDD 2011, Part II. LNCS (LNAI), vol. 6635, pp. 210–221. Springer, Heidelberg (2011). https://doi.org/10.1007/978-3-642-20847-8_18
11. Pei, J., et al.: Mining sequential patterns by pattern-growth: the PrefixSpan approach. IEEE TKDE **16**(11), 1424–1440 (2004)
12. Rahman, M.M., Ahmed, C.F., Leung, C.K.S.: Mining weighted frequent sequences in uncertain databases. Inf. Sci. **479**, 76–100 (2019)
13. Srikant, R., Agrawal, R.: Mining sequential patterns: generalizations and performance improvements. In: Apers, P., Bouzeghoub, M., Gardarin, G. (eds.) EDBT 1996. LNCS, vol. 1057, pp. 1–17. Springer, Heidelberg (1996). https://doi.org/10.1007/BFb0014140
14. Yun, U.: A new framework for detecting weighted sequential patterns in large sequence databases. Knowl.-Based Syst. **21**(2), 110–122 (2008)
15. Zhao, Z., Yan, D., Ng, W.: Mining probabilistically frequent sequential patterns in large uncertain databases. IEEE TKDE **26**(5), 1171–1184 (2013)

Similarity Forests Revisited: A Swiss Army Knife for Machine Learning

Stanisław Czekalski and Mikołaj Morzy[✉] [iD]

Poznan University of Technology, Piotrowo 2, 60-965 Poznań, Poland
{Stanislaw.Czekalski,Mikolaj.Morzy}@put.poznan.pl

Abstract. Random Forests are one of the most reliable and robust general-purpose machine learning algorithms. They provide very competitive baselines for more complex algorithms. Recently, a new algorithm has been introduced into the family of decision tree learners – Similarity Forests, aiming at mitigating some of the well-known deficiencies of Random Forests. In this paper we extend the originally proposed Similarity Forests algorithm to one-class classification, multi-class classification, regression and metric learning tasks. We also introduce two new criteria for split evaluation in regression learning. The results of conducted experiments show that Similarity Forests can be a competitive alternative to Random Forests, in particular, when high quality data representation is difficult to obtain.

Keywords: Decision trees · Random forests · Similarity forests

1 Introduction

Despite current enchantment with deep neural networks, many traditional classification and regression algorithms can compete successfully with neural models. Random Forests [6] stand out as an example of such methods. Over the years, Random Forests have consistently outperformed other learners on a wide spectrum of datasets [10][1]. One of the most notable features of Random Forests is their resistance to over-fitting. Random Forests avoid over-fitting by combining answers from many independently induced decision trees, and each individual decision tree is built based on a subset of input features, thus forcing the model to search for multiple relationships between input features and the target feature. Another advantage of Random Forests (especially when compared with neural models) is the ability of the algorithm to produce a strong learner even in the case of data scarcity. Random Forests can be built using relatively small training sets, which makes them a perfect tool for tasks where the curating of large quantities of labeled data is prohibitively expensive.

A feature of Random Forests which is often praised by machine learning practitioners, is their versatility. The basic formulation of the algorithm can

---

[1] Although it should be noted that methodological objections have been raised [22] regarding this often cited study.

© Springer Nature Switzerland AG 2021
K. Karlapalem et al. (Eds.): PAKDD 2021, LNAI 12713, pp. 42–53, 2021.
https://doi.org/10.1007/978-3-030-75765-6_4

be readily applied to classification and regression tasks [16], but a straightforward modification turns Random Forests into Isolation Forests, a simple yet effective outlier detection mechanism [17]. Finally, Random Forests are among few machine learning algorithms which are inherently interpretable [13]. Today, when algorithmic fairness and machine learning interpretability are becoming indispensable elements of machine learning workflows, this property of Random Forests makes them the go-to algorithm for machine learning tasks.

However, Random Forests also suffer from certain deficiencies. First and foremost, the algorithm is fully dependent on the tabular representation of the training data. This makes the algorithm unsuitable for tasks in which input data structures are complex. This is not to say that Random Forests cannot be applied to time-series forecasting [21], text classification [23], or genomics data [8], but these applications require purposeful feature engineering to align the data representation with Random Forests requirements.

Recently, a new decision tree induction algorithm has been proposed, which addresses some of the deficiencies of Random Forests. Similarity Forests [19] can be readily applied to any data, irrespective of its representation. More surprisingly, the algorithm does not need to know this representation, as it utilizes only pairwise object similarity. So, Similarity Forests can be used to perform classification, regression, or metric learning tasks with any kernel similarity function.

The original paper introducing Similarity Forests focused only on binary classification tasks. In this paper we present extensions of the original framework for one-class and multi-class classification. We also introduce two new inequality-based metrics that can be used to perform regression tasks with Similarity Forests. Last, but not least, we introduce a new metric learning method based on Similarity Forests and we test this method on a clustering task. For each task we perform extensive experimental evaluation. We manage to reproduce the original results of Sathe and Aggarwal to a certain degree, but we also point out to scenarios where the authors have chosen a weaker baseline, thus producing a misleadingly optimistic impression of Similarity Forests effectiveness.

The original contribution of this paper includes:

- the extension of Similarity Forests to one-class and multi-class classification,
- the extension of Similarity Forests to regression,
- the introduction of a new metric learning method,
- the critical experimental comparison of Similarity Forests and Random Forests on diverse datasets.

The code required to reproduce all experiments and the full implementation of Similarity Forests compatible with the `scikit-learn` interface is available in the GitHub repository[2].

2   Related Work

Since their introduction [6], Random Forests have attracted intense attention from the scientific community [4]. Much work has been directed at the evalu-

---

[2] www.github.com/anonymous: anonymized for blind review.

ation of the consistency of Random Forests [9], at the analysis of the bias in Random Forests [2], at the analysis of feature importance measures for Random Forests [1], and at the extension of the original algorithm to new domains.

Ishwaran and Lu develop a modification of Random Forests for survival analysis [15]. Isolation Forests, a version of Random Forests for one-class classification, are introduced in [17]. In [18] Lucas *et al.* present Proximity Forests, distance-based Random Forests designed for the classification of time-series data. Yet another version of the original algorithm, called Extremely Randomized Trees [11], proposes to increase the generalizability of the algorithm by randomizing both feature- and cut-point choice when constructing the tree. Random Forests have even inspired the design of neural networks, leading to the concept of a Neural Random Forest [5], a multi-layer neural network which reconstructs a given ensemble of regression trees.

Comparison-based Random Forests [12] are an algorithm very similar to Similarity Forests. The main concept is identical: to define an internal splitting node of a tree by a pair of objects which belong to different classes, and to partition the remaining objects based on pairwise similarities to splitting objects. The authors start with the Classification and Regression Tree (CART) algorithm [7] and develop a procedure of branch splitting based on comparisons between objects. This procedure is less efficient than the 1-D projection proposed for Similarity Forests. Also, our extension of Similarity Forests to regression tasks includes efficient measures of split impurity, which is missing from [12].

3   Methods

3.1   Original Similarity Forests

Similarity Forests algorithm has been introduced by Sathe and Aggarwal in [19]. It is a decision tree induction algorithm, in which splitting points are based on pairwise similarities of randomly selected objects. The algorithm begins with all objects in a single partition and proceeds to recursively split partitions until the stopping criteria are met. Below we present the description of the algorithm, following the original notation presented in [19].

Consider a set of objects $O_1, O_2, \ldots, O_n$ that can be represented in some multidimensional space as vectors $\bar{X}_1, \bar{X}_2, \ldots, \bar{X}_n$. The exact representation of objects in this multidimensional space does not need to be known, only a similarity measure is required. Selecting any two objects O_i and O_j defines a vector pointing in space from $\bar{X}_i$ to $\bar{X}_j$, and each hyper-plane perpendicular to this vector defines a split of the space into two partitions. The impurity of partitions can be evaluated using traditional measures, such as the Gini index, the information gain, or the gain ratio. For a given pair of objects (O_i, O_j) which defines the current split, the hyper-plane moves along the vector of unit direction equal to $\frac{\bar{X}_j - \bar{X}_i}{\|\bar{X}_j - \bar{X}_i\|}$ and evaluates the impurity of the splitting at each point. All remaining objects O_k are projected on this unit direction by the dot product of $\bar{X}_k - \bar{X}_i$ and the unit direction. The projection is defined as:

$$P(\bar{X}_k) = (\bar{X}_k - \bar{X}_i) \cdot \frac{\bar{X}_j - \bar{X}_i}{\|\bar{X}_j - \bar{X}_i\|}$$
$$= \frac{\bar{X}_k \cdot \bar{X}_j - \bar{X}_k \cdot \bar{X}_i - \bar{X}_i \cdot \bar{X}_j + \bar{X}_i \cdot \bar{X}_i}{\|\bar{X}_j - \bar{X}_i\|} = \frac{S_{kj} - S_{ki} - S_{ij} + S_{ii}}{\|\bar{X}_j - \bar{X}_i\|}$$

where S_{ij} denotes the similarity between objects O_i and O_j. The denominator can also be expressed in terms of object similarities using

$$\|\bar{X}_j - \bar{X}_i\| = \sqrt{\|X_j\|^2 + \|X_i\|^2 - 2\bar{X}_i \cdot \bar{X}_j} = \sqrt{S_{ii} + S_{jj} - 2S_{ij}}$$

but Sathe and Aggarwal notice that the value of the denominator is independent of the object O_k being projected, so it only re-scales the position of $P(\bar{X}_k)$ on the 1-dimensional line between O_i and O_j, but it does not change the relative ordering of the projected points. So, the projection $P(\bar{X}_k)$ is proportional only to four similarities: $P(\bar{X}_k) \propto S_{kj} - S_{ki} - S_{ij} + S_{ii}$, and since S_{ij} and S_{ii} are constant for a given splitting point, the only values required to compute the projection $P(\bar{X}_k)$ are S_{kj} and S_{ki}. The authors refer to $S_{kj} - S_{ki}$ as the scaled and translated proxy for the projection $P(\bar{X}_k)$. When evaluating a splitting point for the current partition, the algorithm randomly selects two objects O_i and O_j, and sorts the remaining objects $O_k\{^n_{k=1}\}$ in the order of $(S_{kj} - S_{ki})$, computing the weighted Gini index at each of the possible $n + 1$ splitting points. After establishing the splitting point, the objects are partitioned by the hyper-plane defined by the splitting point and the procedure continues recursively until the desired depth of the tree is reached, or the size of the partition is too small to consider splitting, or the partition is pure (i.e., consists of objects of the same class). In the original paper the authors also experiment with a slightly modified splitting procedure when, at each stage, instead of selecting random objects, the pairs are always selected such that O_i and O_j belong to different classes. As the authors note, this procedure leads to more discriminative splits.

Similarity Forests have several interesting properties, which make this method an attractive alternative to Random Forests. Firstly, it is characterized by low computational complexity. Construction of a single split is linear in the number of objects in the split. If the original dataset consists of n points, and assuming that the height of the tree is of the order of $\mathcal{O}(n \log n)$ (i.e., the tree is approximately balanced), the construction time of the Similarity Forests is also of the order of $\mathcal{O}(n \log n)$. At inference, each object is compared against $\mathcal{O}(\log n)$ pairs of objects defining splitting points.

Another advantage of Similarity Forests is the fact that the representation $\bar{X}_i$ of O_i does not have to be known in advance. Also, if similarity metric is not available, the algorithm can use distances instead of similarities. Sathe and Aggarwal propose to either use exact translation of distances to similarities using the cosine law transformation (which is computationally expensive), or to approximate similarities by squared distances. Furthermore, the algorithm uses only pairwise comparisons between objects, thus allowing for the application of the kernel trick [20].

3.2   One-Class Classification

For the one-class classification problem (also known as the outlier detection problem) the adaptation of the original Similarity Forests algorithm is inspired by the Isolation Forests algorithm [17] and its extensions [14]. We build a Similarity Forests ensemble consisting of hundreds of independently induced trees. For each object in the training set we record the level (i.e. distance from the root of the tree) of the leaf into which the object has been separated. The intuition is that if an object is *typical*, it should not be separated early during the tree induction process. Similarly, if an object is an *outlier*, in many random splits the object will be projected to one of the extremes on the 1-dimensional line defining the split, thus becoming a part of a leaf node early in the induction process. In other words, if few random hyper-planes are sufficient to isolate an object, it can be considered an outlier.

3.3   Multi-class Classification

The original paper presented only the binary classification variant of Similarity Forests. Obviously, this binary classifier can be trivially adapted to multi-class setting using many techniques, such as Error Correcting Output Codes, or training a 1-versus-1 or 1-versus-all ensembles. Here we present a simple modification of Similarity Forests which adapts this method to multi-class classification. The algorithm proceeds as in the binary classification, but at each split only the first object is chosen randomly. The second object is chosen from a different class, and the best splitting point is determined based on the selected impurity metric. The selection of the second object is then repeated for all remaining classes, searching for the class which minimizes the impurity metric.

3.4   Regression

In addition to extending Similarity Forests for one-class and multi-class classification, we propose a simple modification which allows to use the algorithm for regression. The only thing that has to change is the evaluation procedure for potential splitting points. When we process a partition, as the first step we compute the standard deviation of the target value within the partition. Then, we randomly select the first object, and the second object is drawn only from objects which differ from the first object's target value by at least one standard deviation.

Again, let us consider the set of objects $O_1, O_2, \ldots, O_n$, and let $y_1, y_2, \ldots, y_n$ denote the numerical target value associated with every object. Let us further assume that the splitting point is defined by two objects O_i and O_j, and the remaining objects are projected onto the 1-dimensional line connecting O_i and O_j. Let the projection $P(\bar{X}_k)$ of the object O_k define the partitioning of the set of objects into two partitions $\mathcal{Q}_K^- = \{O_1, O_2, \ldots O_k\}$ and $\mathcal{Q}_K^+ = \{O_{k+1}, O_{k+2}, \ldots O_n\}$ laying on the 1-dimensional line to the left and to the right of $P(\bar{X}_k)$, respectively. We propose the following metrics to evaluate the quality of splitting objects into partitions $\mathcal{Q}_K^-$ and $\mathcal{Q}_K^+$:

- *weighted variance*: defined as $\text{Var}(\mathcal{Q}) = \sum_{i:O_i \in \mathcal{Q}} (y_i - \bar{y})^2$, where $\bar{y} = \frac{1}{|\mathcal{Q}|} \sum_{i:O_i \in \mathcal{Q}} y_i$ is the average label value of objects in the partition. We are minimizing the weighted variance of the split, i.e., $\arg\min_k (\frac{k}{n}\text{Var}(\mathcal{Q}_K^-) + \frac{n-k}{n}\text{Var}(\mathcal{Q}_K^+))$.

- *Thiel index*: defined as $T(\mathcal{Q}) = \frac{1}{|\mathcal{Q}|} \sum_{i:O_i \in \mathcal{Q}} \frac{y_i}{\bar{y}} ln \frac{y_i}{\bar{y}}$, where $\bar{y}$ is the average label value of objects in the partition. The Thiel index measures the difference between the maximum possible entropy of the partition and the observed entropy of the partition. As in the case of variance, we are minimizing the average Thiel index of normalized by the size of partitions, i.e., we are looking for $\arg\min_k (\frac{k}{n}T(\mathcal{Q}_K^-) + \frac{n-k}{n}T(\mathcal{Q}_K^+))$.

- *Atkinson index* [3]: defined as $A(\mathcal{Q}) = 1 - \frac{1}{\bar{y}}(\frac{1}{|\mathcal{Q}|} \sum_{i:O_i \in \mathcal{Q}} \sqrt{y_i}^{(1-\epsilon)})^{\frac{1}{(1-\epsilon)}}$ measures not only the degree of inequality in the distribution, but it also indicates which side of the distribution skews the distribution more. In this research we are setting the inequality aversion parameter ϵ of the original index to 0.5. As with the Thiel index we are minimizing $\arg\min_k (\frac{k}{n}A(\mathcal{Q}_K^-) + \frac{n-k}{n}A(\mathcal{Q}_K^+))$.

3.5 Metric Learning

Another interesting application of Similarity Forests is the ability to model the structure of the dataset in an unsupervised manner in order to learn a distance metric in the data manifold. The method is straightforward and resembles the approach used in one-class classification. An ensemble of trees is built, and all training objects are partitioned by each tree. After Similarity Forests construction, for each pair of objects (O_i, O_j) the depth $d_t(O_i, O_j)$ at which objects are split between partitions in the tree t is recorded. This procedure is repeated for all T trees. The distance between objects is then calculated as follows:

$$d(O_i, O_j) = \frac{1}{\frac{1}{T}\sum_{t=1}^{T} d_t(O_i, O_j)} = \frac{T}{\sum_{t=1}^{T} d_t(O_i, O_j)}$$

The maximum distance $d(O_i, O_j) = 1$ is obtained if objects O_i and O_j always split at the root of the tree. The distance is symmetrical, however, it does not satisfy either the identity axiom ($d(O_i, O_i) \neq 0$) or the triangle inequality, so, strictly speaking, this measure is not a proper metric.

4 Results

Table 1 presents the set of benchmark datasets used to evaluate Similarity Forests. We use the same datasets as [19] with the goal of reproducing their results, and we add several new datasets to test Similarity Forests in more challenging classification tasks (high dimensional data, multi-class classification) as well as to verify the usability of Similarity Forests in regression tasks.

Table 1. Datasets used in the experiments

Name	Task	Rows	Features	Name	Task	Rows	Features
Heart	Binary	270	13	Asian religions	Multi-class	590	1023
Ionosphere scale	Binary	352	34	Glass	Multi-class	214	9
Breast cancer	Binary	683	10	Seed	Multi-class	210	7
German numer	Binary	1000	24	Wine	Multi-class	177	13
Madelon	Binary	2000	500	Dna	Multi-class	2000	180
Diabetes	Binary	768	8	Segment	Multi-class	2310	19
Australian	Binary	690	14	Boston	Regression	506	13
Splice	Binary	1000	60	Mpg	Regression	392	7
a1a	Binary	1605	119	Comp. hard	Regression	209	8
Svmguide3	Binary	1234	22	Space ga	Regression	3107	6
Liver disorders	Binary	345	5	Eunite2001	Regression	336	16
Fourclass	Binary	862	2	Wine quality	Regression	4898	11
Leukemia	High dim	72	7129	Abalone	Regression	4177	8
Duke	High dim	44	7129	Concrete flow	Regression	103	8
Colon cancer	High dim	62	2000	kdd 99 http	One-class	58725	3
Arcene	High dim	200	10000	kdd 99 sf	One-class	73237	21
Shuttle	One-class	4909	9	kdd 99 sa	One-class	100655	99

4.1 Classification

We split the presentation of results between four types of classification tasks: one-class classification, binary classification, classification of high dimensional data, and multi-class classification. We use boldface to denote cases when an algorithm attains better results at the statistical significance level $\alpha = 0.05$. We compare Similarity Forests and Random Forests using accuracy, F_1 score, and the area under the ROC curve (AUROC). For each test of statistical significance of the difference of averages we report the p-value of the Student's t-test performed over 20 repetitions of each algorithm.

4.2 One-Class Classification

We test the effectiveness of Similarity Forests in the one-class classification task by comparing it to a standard implementation of Isolation Forests algorithm. Both methods use the same principle for classifying objects as outliers (the average height at which an object is assigned to a leaf node), so the only difference between the algorithms is the splitting procedure. The results of the comparison are presented in Table 2. The results are equivocal, both algorithms perform very similarly. Isolation Forests tend to achieve better accuracy and AUROC, while Similarity Forests result in better recall and F_1 score. Although the comparison is far from conclusive, it is safe to assume that Similarity Forests present a viable alternative to Isolation Forests in one-class classification.

Table 2. Outlier detection results

Dataset	Precision		Recall		F_1		AUROC		p-val			
	SF	IF	SF	IF	SF	IF	SF	IF	Precision	Recall	F_1	AUROC
kdd 99 http	1.00	1.00	**0.94**	0.91	**0.97**	0.95	0.99	**0.99**	0.333	4.70e−20	6.95e−20	1.23e−13
kdd 99 sf	0.99	**1.00**	**0.92**	0.88	**0.96**	0.93	**0.94**	0.93	7.44e−14	6.71e−19	8.60e−18	1.69e−07
kdd 99 sa	0.98	**0.99**	**0.96**	0.93	**0.97**	0.96	0.94	**0.96**	1.01e−06	2.62e−11	9.92e−03	1.05e−03
Shuttle	0.99	**0.99**	0.92	**0.95**	0.96	**0.97**	0.98	**0.99**	4.71e−23	2.99e−12	7.45e−13	1.54e−23

Table 3. Binary classification results

Dataset	acc		F1		AUROC		p-val		
	SF	RF	SF	RF	SF	RF	acc	F1	AUROC
Heart	**0.89**	0.85	0.89	0.85	**0.94**	0.91	9.02e−06	5.95e−06	5.09e−14
Ionoshphere scale	**0.96**	0.94	0.96	0.93	**1.00**	0.99	1.49e−07	2.46e−07	2.21e−08
Breast cancer	**0.97**	0.96	0.97	0.96	**1.00**	1.00	1.17e−2	1.19e−02	2.82e−09
German numer	0.75	**0.79**	0.71	**0.77**	0.77	**0.82**	1.24e−11	2.26e-14	4.73e−12
Madelon	0.56	**0.65**	0.56	**0.65**	0.59	**0.72**	6.97e−17	9.47e−17	1.73e−22
Diabetes	0.74	0.74	0.74	0.75	0.80	**0.83**	0.841	0.258	6.27e−15
Australian	0.85	**0.87**	0.85	**0.87**	0.90	**0.92**	2.18e−05	1.78e−05	5.00e−09
Splice	0.83	**0.94**	0.83	**0.94**	0.92	**0.98**	1.71e−28	1.61e−28	1.16e−30
a1a	0.81	**0.83**	0.77	**0.81**	0.88	0.88	7.95e−08	1.25e−13	0.179
svmguide3	0.80	**0.83**	0.76	**0.81**	0.78	**0.86**	2.15e−14	9.78e−20	3.71e−20
Liver disorders	0.64	**0.67**	0.63	**0.67**	0.64	**0.69**	1.54e−04	9.78e−05	5.99e−09

4.3   Binary Classification

Table 3 presents the results for binary classification. We use the same datasets as the authors of the original publication, with the exclusion of the *Mushroom* dataset (as this dataset is trivial for classification). We manage to reproduce the results reported in [19] only partially. For instance, we obtain better accuracy for Random Forests on the *Heart* dataset (85% vs 79% reported by Sathe and Aggarwal), the *German numer* dataset (79% vs 77%), but we also do not manage to obtain 90% accuracy on the *svmguide3* dataset. More disturbingly, though, Random Forests outperform Similarity Forests on all datasets that we add beyond the datasets used in the original publication. Thus, our evaluation paints a less optimistic view of the efficacy of Similarity Forests. While it may be competitive with SVM, it is usually outperformed by Random Forests as measured by all scores.

4.4   High-Dimensional Classification

We have hypothesized that Similarity Forests may perform better for datasets with a large number of features, where simple splits on single features performed by Random Forests might be insufficient to discover the decision boundaries in high dimensional space. However, the results presented in Table 4 do not support

Table 4. High dimensional classification results

Dataset	acc		F1		AUROC		p-val		
	SF	RF	SF	RF	SF	RF	acc	F1	AUROC
Leukemia	0.85	**0.95**	0.84	**0.85**	0.97	**1.00**	1.77e–10	2.19e–10	2.09e–12
Duke	0.87	0.90	0.88	0.87	0.91	**1.00**	0.138	0.138	6.76e–14
Colon cancer	0.68	**0.79**	0.68	**0.69**	0.75	**0.80**	2.18e–05	2.35e–05	2.58e–02
Arcene	0.78	**0.82**	0.78	**0.78**	0.85	**0.89**	1.76e–04	1.65e–04	2.51e–07
Fourclass	0.99	0.99	0.99	0.99	1.00	1.00	0.713	0.714	0.713
Asian religions	0.68	**0.70**	0.65	**0.68**	**0.94**	0.93	0.0062	0.003	8.67e–14

Table 5. Multi-class classification results

Dataset	acc		F1		AUROC		p-val		
	SF	RF	SF	RF	SF	RF	acc	F1	AUROC
Glass	0.78	**0.84**	0.76	**0.84**	0.93	**0.96**	1.14e–06	2.87e–08	1.15e–14
Seed	**0.90**	0.87	**0.90**	0.87	0.98	0.98	3.22e–05	3.60e–05	0.314
Wine	**0.96**	0.94	**0.96**	0.94	**0.99**	0.99	3.97e–02	3.96e–02	6.84e–08
dna	0.81	**0.93**	0.80	**0.93**	0.97	**0.99**	7.72e–34	1.59e–33	2.17e–28
Segment	0.96	**0.97**	0.96	**0.97**	0.99	**0.99**	3.43e–10	2.21e–10	4.28e–11

this hypothesis. Random Forests outperform Similarity Forests on all scores and almost all examined datasets.

4.5 Multi-class Classification

Finally, we evaluate Similarity Forests on the multi-class classification task (Table 5). Although Random Forests still present a very strong baseline, the results are less equivocal than in the case of binary or high dimensional classification. Even for datasets where Random Forests achieve better scores, the differences are not large, and for some datasets Similarity Forests outperform Random Forests on the accuracy, the F_1 score, and the AUROC. This result strengthens, in our opinion, the claim that Similarity Forests are a viable alternative to Random Forests and should be considered as a go-to classification algorithm.

4.6 Regression

In Table 6 we compare the effectiveness of Similarity Forests with Random Forests using the root mean squared error (RMSE) score. Both Similarity Forests and Random Forests underwent a similar grid search optimization of hyperparameters. The maximum depth range was $[8, 10, 12, 14, None]$, the splitting criteria were variance minimization, Theil index, and Atkinson index, the similarity kernel for Similarity Forests was either dot product or radial basis function. Ensembles consisted of 25, 50, and 100 estimators. The Similarity Forests γ parameter range was $[0.0001, 0.001, 0.01, 0.1]$.

Random Forests outperform Similarity Forests on almost all datasets, the differences might not be large, but are statistically significant. It may be that the advantage of having a single multi-task algorithm outweighs the loss of predictive power, but we do not find sufficient evidence to claim that Similarity Forests present a viable alternative to Random Forests with respect to regression.

4.7   Metric Learning

Table 6. Regression results

Dataset	RMSE		p-val
	SF	RF	
Boston	3.860	**2.966**	2.64e–34
mpg	2.429	2.396	0.119
Computer hardware	0.180	**0.150**	6.24e–18
Space ga	0.123	**0.122**	7.67e–04
Eunite2001	24.719	**23.535**	2.69e–06
Wine quality	**0.587**	0.589	3.51e–02
Abalone	2.241	**2.225**	2.68e–08
Concrete flow	12.182	**11.528**	5.42e–03

Table 7. Datasets (metric learning)

Name	Rows	Features
Glass	214	9
iris	150	4
cpu	209	6
e.coli	336	7
Segment	2000	19
Vehicle	846	18
Wine	178	13
Zoo	101	16

To check how well Similarity Forests can learn a meaningful structure of a dataset, we use the learned distance metric to perform clustering using HDB-SCAN, comparing the results to the traditional Euclidean distance. We use the Clustering Benchmark datasets[3] described in Table 7. To assess the quality of clustering, Silhouette and Davies-Bouldin scores are recorded. We also present a 2D PCA projection of obtained clusters for visual inspection (see Fig. 1, best viewed in color). Similarity Trees are constructed using the linear dot product kernel. The results reported in Table 8 are averaged over 20 runs over each dataset. Similarity Forests distance usually produces better silhouette score, but results in a worse Davies-Bouldain value. Best results were obtained when the maximum depth of Similarity Forests has been constrained (which is reasonable, usually only a few splits are required to separate main clusters in the data manifold). In general, distance metric learned using Similarity Forests works well and introduces non-linearity which results in better and more meaningful clusters.

---

[3] https://github.com/deric/clustering-benchmark.

Table 8. Clustering results

Dataset	SF silhouette	Eucl. Silhouette	SF Davies-Bouldain	Eucl. Davies-Bouldain
Glass	**0.509**	0.436	**3.156**	4.241
iris	**0.556**	0.525	3.118	**0.481**
cpu	**0.382**	0.280	**1.507**	1.872
e.coli	0.194	**0.414**	5.514	**3.388**
Segment	**0.590**	−0.038	**0.674**	1.464
Vehicle	0.097	**0.218**	6.162	**3.199**
Wine	0.197	0.142	2.660	**1.361**
Zoo	**0.575**	0.424	**1.088**	1.410

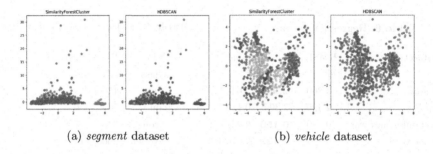

(a) *segment* dataset   (b) *vehicle* dataset

Fig. 1. Visualization of clusters

5 Conclusions

Random Forests remain one of the most robust and efficient algorithms for classification and regression tasks. They provide a hard-to-beat baseline in many practical applications. Despite their popularity and widespread use, they suffer from strong dependence on the particularities of input representation. In this paper we have advocated in favor of Similarity Forests, a recently proposed decision tree induction algorithm which addresses some of the aforementioned deficiencies. We describe the method, we present simple extensions which allow to apply Similarity Forests to one-class, binary, and multi-class classification, as well as regression. We perform an extensive comparison of Similarity Forests and Random Forests for one-class, binary, high dimensional, and multi-class classification. Finally, we show how Similarity Forests can be used for unsupervised metric learning. We believe that Similarity Forests present a viable alternative to Random Forests and should become one of the default baseline algorithms in every machine learning toolbox.

Acknowledgements. This work is supported by the National Science Center, Poland, decision no. DEC-2016/23/B/ST6/03962.

References

1. Archer, K.J., Kimes, R.V.: Empirical characterization of random forest variable importance measures. Comp. Stat. Data Anal. **52**(4), 2249–2260 (2008)
2. Arlot, S., Genuer, R.: Analysis of purely Random Forests bias. arXiv:1407.3939 (2014)
3. Atkinson, A.B., et al.: On the measurement of inequality. J. Econ. Theory **2**(3), 244–263 (1970)
4. Biau, G.: Analysis of a random forests model. J. Mach. Learn. Res. **13**, 1063–1095 (2012)
5. Biau, G., Scornet, E., Welbl, J.: Neural random forests. Sankhya **81**(2), 347–386 (2019)
6. Breiman, L.: Random forests. Mach. Learn. **45**(1), 5–32 (2001)
7. Breiman, L., Friedman, J., Stone, C.J., Olshen, R.A.: Classification and Regression Trees. CRC Press, Boca Raton (1984)
8. Chen, X., Ishwaran, H.: Random forests for genomic data analysis. Genomics, **99**(6), 323–329 (2012)
9. Denil, M., Matheson, D.: Consistency of online random forests. Tech. rep. (2013)
10. Fernández-Delgado, M., Cernadas, E., Barro, S., Amorim, D., Fernández-Delgado, A.: Do we need hundreds of classifiers to solve real world classification problems?. J. Mach. Learn. Res. **15**, 3133–3181 (2014)
11. Geurts, P., Ernst, D., Wehenkel, L.: Extremely randomized trees. Mach. Learn. **63**(1), 3–42 (2006)
12. Haghiri, S., Ghoshdastidar, D., von Luxburg, U.: Comparison Based Nearest Neighbor Search. arXiv:1704.01460 (4 2017)
13. Hara, S., Hayashi, K.: Making Tree Ensembles Interpretable. arXiv:1606.05390 (2016). http://arxiv.org/abs/1606.05390
14. Hariri, S., Kind, M.C.: Extended isolation forest. arXiv:1811.02141 (2018)
15. Ishwaran, H., Lu, M.: Random survival forests. In: Wiley StatsRef: Statistics Reference Online, pp. 1–13. John Wiley & Sons Ltd, Chichester, UK (2 2019)
16. Liaw, A.: Classification and regression by random forests. Tech. rep. (2002)
17. Liu, F.T., Ting, K.M., Zhou, Z.H.: Isolation forest. In: 2008 Eighth IEEE International Conference on Data Mining, pp. 413–422. IEEE (2008)
18. Lucas, B., et al.: Proximity forest: an effective and scalable distance-based classifier for time series. Data Mining Knowl. Discov. **33**(3), 607–635 (2019)
19. Sathe, S., Aggarwal, C.C.: Similarity forests. In: Proceedings of the ACM SIGKDD International Conference on Knowledge Discovery and Data Mining. vol. Part F1296, pp. 395–403 (2017)
20. Schölkopf, B.: The kernel trick for distances. Adv. Neural Inf. Process. Syst. 301–307 (2001)
21. Tyralis, H., Papacharalampous, G.: Variable selection in time series forecasting using random forests. Algorithms, **10**(4), 114 (2017)
22. Wainberg, M., Alipanahi, B., Frey, B.J.: Are random forests truly the best classifiers? J. Mach. Learn. Res. **17**, 1–5 (2016)
23. Xu, B., Guo, X., Ye, Y., Cheng, J.: An improved random forest classifier for text categorization. J. Comput. (2012)

Discriminative Representation Learning for Cross-Domain Sentiment Classification

Shaokang Zhang[1,2], Lei Jiang[1,2], Huailiang Peng[1,2(✉)], Qiong Dai[1,2], and Jianlong Tan[1,2]

[1] Institute of Information Engineering, Chinese Academy of Sciences, Beijing, China
{zhangshaokang,jianglei,penghuailiang,daiqiong,tanjianlong}@iie.ac.cn
[2] School of Cyber Security, University of Chinese Academy of Sciences, Beijing, China

Abstract. Cross-domain sentiment classification aims to solve the lack of labeled data in the target domain by using the knowledge of the source domain. Most existing approaches mainly focus on learning transferable feature representations for knowledge transfer across domains. Few of them pay attention to the feature discriminability, which contributes to distinguish different sentiment polarity and improves the classification accuracy. In this work, we propose discriminative representation learning, which extracts transferable and discriminative features. Specifically, we use spectral clustering to reduce the negative effect of low prediction accuracy on the target domain. Centroid alignment enforces samples of the same polarity with smaller distance in the feature space and enlarges the difference between samples of different polarities. Then intra-class compactness benefits true centroid by reducing samples distributed at the edges of the clusters. Experiments on the multiple public datasets demonstrate that discriminative representation learning outperforms state-of-the-art methods.

Keywords: Discriminative representation learning · Cross-domain sentiment classification · Domain adaptation · Clustering

1 Introduction

Sentiment classification, which aims to automatically identify the sentiment polarity (e.g., positive or negative) of a document, has attracted more and more research attention [8]. Traditional methods have been explored to learn good feature representations of sample and achieve outstanding effect [13]. However, these works are highly dependent on sufficient labeled data which needs time-consuming and expensive manual annotation.

To solve the problem, cross-domain sentiment classification has been proposed as a promising direction. Blitzer et al. [1] aims to find out the correlation between pivots (domain-shared sentiment words) and non-pivots (domain-specific sentiment words). However, these methods are complicated and the classification accuracy is low. Recently, deep neural networks are explored to automatically obtain shared sentiment features across domains. Typically, adversarial

© Springer Nature Switzerland AG 2021
K. Karlapalem et al. (Eds.): PAKDD 2021, LNAI 12713, pp. 54–66, 2021.
https://doi.org/10.1007/978-3-030-75765-6_5

learning methods [6] focus on extracting domain-invariant features whose distribution is similar in the source and target domains. It introduces a domain classifier which can minimize the discrepancy between the source and target domains by reversing the gradient direction of the neural network. This method merely extracts the transferable features (domain-invariant features) and ignores the feature discriminability which indicates the ability of separating different sentiment polarity by a classifier trained over labeled dataset. Some methods align the same polarity from different domains by assigning pseudo-labels to target samples, to increase the feature discriminability. Nevertheless, the falsely-pseudo-labeled samples can lead to serious bias that the centroid easily deviates from the true position in mini-batch, especially for the low prediction accuracy on the target samples.

In this paper, we propose discriminative representation learning (DRL) model for cross-domain sentiment classification. DRL considers the feature discriminability by aligning centroid and making intra-class distance more compact in the source and target domains. Specifically, we cluster features of target samples in mini-batch because of unlabeled data in the target domain. The cluster sentiment polarity is judged according to the centroid of source domain. Centroid alignment of the same polarity achieves the level of sentiment polarity alignment by minimizing the centroid distance. Centroid alignment of different polarities make samples more separable by maximizing the centroid distance. However, samples distributed at the edges of the clusters, or far from the high density regions are easily misclassified. To solve this issue, we make each polarity more compact by reducing the intra-class distance. In this way, the number of samples that are far from each centroid will be greatly decreased. The main contributions of our work are summarized as follows:

- As far as we know, we are the first to simultaneously learn transferable and discriminative features in cross-domain sentiment classification.
- We propose the discriminative representation learning which produces transferable and distinguishable features. After clustering the unlabeled data on target domain, it uses the centroid alignment and intra-class compactness to learn better features for sentiment classification tasks.
- We conducted the comparative experiments on Amazon, IMDB, Yelp and Airline datasets. Our method outperforms other state-of-the-art methods.

2 Related Work

Domain adaptation such as cross-domain sentiment classification has attracted more and more research attention over the past decades. In supervised domain adaptation, the training data consists of labeled source samples and a small number of target domain samples. A common method is training the classifier with labeled source samples and fine-tuning the classifier with labeled target domain samples. Some unsupervised domain adaptation methods are proposed to learning the domain-invariant features. The Structural Correspondence Learning

(SCL) [1] is proposed to produce correspondences among the features across domains. Using domain-independent words as a bridge, the Spectral Feature Alignment (SFA) [12] solves the feature mismatch problem by aligning domain-specific words. Unfortunately, the steps of these methods are cumbersome and the domain-shared features is bad.

Recently, deep learning methods have obtained better feature representations for cross-domain sentiment classification. The Stacked Denoising Auto-encoders (SDA) [7] successfully learns hidden representations from different domains. The Marginalized Stacked Denoising Autoencoder (mSDA) [3] addresses the problem of high computational cost and lack of scalability to high-dimensional features. The Domain-Adversarial training of Neural Networks (DANN) [6] which leverages the adversarial mechanism to mix the source and target domains. The Hierarchical Attention Transfer Network (HATN) [9] which transfers word-level and sentence-level attentions. But these methods only focus on extracting the transferable information, which can lead to poorly separable features across domains. To solve the above problem, we propose to produce more discriminative features by aligning centroid and making intra-class distance more compact. In computer vision applications, there are also some works which learn more discriminative features [2].

3   Approach

In this section, we first illustrate the problem definition and overall framework, followed by an overview of the domain adversarial network. Finally we introduce the details of discriminative representation learning.

3.1   Problem Definition and Overall Framework

We assume that there are two domains D_s and D_t which denote the source and the target domain, respectively. We further suppose that we give a set of labeled training data $\mathbf{X_s^l} = \{x_s^i, y_s^i\}_{i=1}^{N_s^l}$, where N_s^l is the number of labeled data. Besides, we give a set of unlabeled training data $\mathbf{X_t} = \{x_t^j\}_{j=1}^{N_t}$ from the target domain, where N_t is the number of unlabeled data. N indicates the batch size during the training stage and L is the feature dimension. The goal of cross-domain sentiment classification is building a classifier based on labeled data in the source domain and unlabeled data in the target domain.

We present an overview of the DRL model in Fig. 1 and describe the details of the model. We first introduce general adversarial domain network which reduces discrepancy between the source and target domains. However, this method does not take the feature distinguishability into account. Thus we propose the discriminative representation learning (DRL) which includes three parts, i.e., clustering, centroid alignment and intra-class compactness. The first part clusters the unlabeled data on target domain to calculate the centroid and intra-class distance. The second part makes centroid distance of the same polarity samples closer and enlarges the centroid distance between different polarities. The third part not

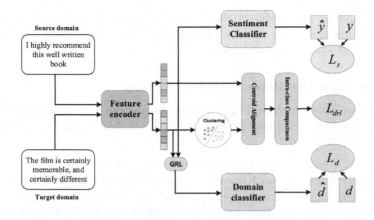

Fig. 1. The architecture of the DRL, where $\widehat{y}$ is the predicted sentiment label and $\widehat{d}$ is the predicted domain label. y and d are the ground truth. GRL stands for the Gradient Reversal Layer. L_s, L_d and L_{drl} are losses.

only reduces the number of samples that are far from the high density region but also obtains smaller intra-class distance for each polarity. In this way, we can obtain transferable and discriminative features.

3.2 Domain Adversarial Network

Domain adversarial network [6] has been successfully applied to transfer learning and the basic idea is to learn domain-invariant features. The adversarial learning procedure contains two parts, i.e., a domain classifier $d = D(f)$ is trained to correctly distinguish the source domain from the target domain and a feature encoder $f = F(x)$ is trained to fool the domain classifier. The parameters of domain classifier are updated by minimizing the loss of the domain classifier, while the parameters of the feature encoder are updated by maximizing the loss of domain classifier. To achieve this goal, the common method is Gradient Reversal Layer (GRL) [6] which reverses the gradient in the training process. The definition is $R(f) = f$, $\frac{\partial R(f)}{\partial f} = -\lambda I$. In addition, the feature encoder $f = F(x)$ and the sentiment classifier $y = G(f)$ are simultaneously learned by minimizing the loss of the category classifier. The objective function of domain adversarial network is as follows:

$$L_s = \frac{1}{N_s^l} \sum_{i=1}^{N_s^l} L(G_y(G_f(x_s^i)), y_s^i) \tag{1}$$

$$L_d = -\frac{1}{N_s^l + N_t} \sum_{i=1}^{N_s^l + N_t} L(G_d(G_f(x_i)), d_i) \tag{2}$$

where L_s and L_d the sentiment classification loss and the domain loss, respectively. The loss uses cross-entropy loss functions. d_i is the domain label (0 and 1 indicate the source and target domains).

3.3 Discriminative Representation Learning

To learn the discriminative deep features, we propose the discriminative representation learning method. In the following, we describe the details of this method successively.

Clustering: We cluster the unlabeled data on target domain. Because general clustering methods such as K-means are suitable for low-dimensional features and poor clustering effect in high-dimensional space, we select the spectral clustering [11]. However, we don't know the sentiment polarity of the cluster. The decision method can be formulated as follows:

$$
\| \mathbf{c}_{sp} - \mathbf{c}_1 \| < \| \mathbf{c}_{sp} - \mathbf{c}_2 \|, \| \mathbf{c}_{sn} - \mathbf{c}_1 \| > \| \mathbf{c}_{sn} - \mathbf{c}_2 \|
$$
$$
\Rightarrow \mathbf{c}_1 \text{ is positive centroid}, \mathbf{c}_2 \text{ is negative centroid}
$$
$$
\| \mathbf{c}_{sp} - \mathbf{c}_1 \| > \| \mathbf{c}_{sp} - \mathbf{c}_2 \|, \| \mathbf{c}_{sn} - \mathbf{c}_1 \| < \| \mathbf{c}_{sn} - \mathbf{c}_2 \|
$$
$$
\Rightarrow \mathbf{c}_1 \text{ is negative centroid}, \mathbf{c}_2 \text{ is positive centroid}
$$

(3)

where $\mathbf{c}_1, \mathbf{c}_2$ are cluster centroids of target domain and the $\mathbf{c}_{sp}$, $\mathbf{c}_{sn}$ are the positive and negative centroids of source domain. If the $\mathbf{c}_{sp}$ gives a closer distance with $\mathbf{c}_1$ than $\mathbf{c}_2$ and $\mathbf{c}_{sn}$ gives a closer distance with $\mathbf{c}_2$ than $\mathbf{c}_1$, the decision method assigns the positive centroid to $\mathbf{c}_1$ and the negative centroid to $\mathbf{c}_2$. It is similar when the $\mathbf{c}_{sp}$ gives a closer distance with $\mathbf{c}_2$ than $\mathbf{c}_1$ and the $\mathbf{c}_{sn}$ gives a closer distance with $\mathbf{c}_1$ than $\mathbf{c}_2$. If cluster centroids does not satisfy the above formula, the model will not be updated. To verify the performance of spectral clustering, we compare with BERT-DRL^p (assign pseudo labels to target samples).

Centroid Alignment: The motivation of the centroid alignment is that the samples from the same polarity should be mapped nearby in the feature space, and the samples from the different polarities should stay as far away from each other as possible. The centroid effectively represents a set of samples [10]. The centroid distance can be formulated as follows:

$$
d_c = \sum_{i=1}^{c} \| \mathbf{c}_s^i - \mathbf{c}_t^i \|_2
$$

(4)

$$
d_u = \{ \sum_{i,j=1,i\neq j}^{c} \| \mathbf{c}_s^i - \mathbf{c}_t^j \|_2 + \sum_{i,j=1,i\neq j}^{c} \| \mathbf{c}_d^i - \mathbf{c}_d^j \|_2 /2 \}
$$

(5)

where $\mathbf{c}_s^i$ and $\mathbf{c}_t^i$ are the i-th polarity centroid in the source and target domains, respectively. $c \in \{positive, negative\}$ and $\mathbf{c}_d^i$ denotes the i-th polarity centroid in d domain, $d \in \{s, t\}$. The centroid alignment loss L_{ca} can be formulated as:

$$
L_{ca} = d_c + (m - d_u)
$$

(6)

The centroid alignment loss minimizes the centroid distance of same polarity and enforces the centroid distance of different polarities at least m, where m is the constraint boundary. Note that centroid alignment is similar with moving average centroid alignment [15]. Both of them reduce the centroid distance of the same polarity. The difference is that we also enlarge the difference across different polarities.

Intra-class Compactness: Although centroid alignment produces more distinguishing features, samples distributed at the edges of the clusters are not reduced and easily lead to the deviation of centroid. So we introduce the intra-class compactness which makes each polarity more compact. The intra-class compactness loss L_{ic} can be formulated as follows:

$$L_{ic} = d_s + d_t = \frac{1}{n_s} \sum_{i=1}^{n_s} \| \mathbf{f}_s^i - \mathbf{c}_s^{y_i} \|_2 + \frac{1}{n_t} \sum_{i=1}^{n_t} \| \mathbf{f}_t^i - \mathbf{c}_t^{y_i} \|_2 \qquad (7)$$

where $f_s^i, f_t^i \in \mathbf{R}^L$ denotes the i-th deep feature in the source and target domains, respectively. $\mathbf{c}_t^{y_i}$ is the y_i-th polarity centroid of the deep features, $y_i \in \{positive, negative\}$. Finally, we propose the discriminative representation learning loss as below:

$$L_{drl} = L_{ic} + L_{ca} \qquad (8)$$

Our method can be easily implemented and embedded into modern deep learning frameworks. Algorithm 1 describes the training procedure of DRL. Different from discriminative feature learning [2], which only utilizes the source domain samples because of the unlableled target samples. We utilize the unlabeled data by spectral clustering which avoids the negative effects of falsely-pseudo-labeled samples.

Algorithm 1. Training procedure of DRL

Input: Labeled source domain S, unlabeled target domain T, N is the batch size, M is the total number of iterations, F is feature encoder, G is sentiment classifier.

1: Let $t = 0$.
2: **while** t $<$M **do**
3:    $t = t + 1$.
4:    $S_t = \text{RandomSelect}(S,N), T_t = \text{RandomSelect}(T,N)$.
5:    Cluster target features $f = F(T_t)$.
6:    Compute the current centroid c_{sp}, c_{sn} on S_t.
7:    Determine the polarity of the cluster center c_1, c_2.
8:    Compute the centroid alignment loss L_{ca}
9:    Compute the intra-class compactness loss L_{ic}
10:    Compute the discriminative representation learning loss L_{drl}
11:    Update the model parameters by minimizing L_{drl}
12: **end while**

Training Strategy: Our totally objective can be written as follows:

$$L = L_s + L_d + \beta L_{drl} + \rho L_{reg} \qquad (9)$$

where β is trade-off parameter to balance the discriminative representation learning loss. ρ is the regularization parameter. The regularization term L_{reg} prevents the overfitting. DRL model minimize L except the GRL training part which will be maximized. Additionally, all parameters are optimized by the adaptive momentum algorithm.

4   Experiment

4.1   Dataset Preparation

We use Amazon reviews dataset [1] with same origin to evaluate the effectiveness of our method. We select the data from five domains: Books (B), Dvd (D), Electronics (E) and Kitchen (K), Video (V). Each domain contains 6000 labeled reviews with 3000 positive reviews (higher than 3 stars) and 3000 negative reviews (lower than 3 stars). We conduct 20 cross-domain sentiment classification tasks: B → D, B → E, B → K, B → V, D → B, D → E, D → K, D → V, E → B, E → D, E → K, E → V, K → B, K → D, K → E, K → V, V → B, V → D, V → E, V → K. Furthermore, we randomly select 2800 positive and 2800 negative samples from the source domain as the training data, the rest from the source domain as the validation data, and all samples from the target domain for testing.

Moreover, to investigate the performance in different domains with the different origins. We randomly select samples from the IMDB (I), Yelp (Y) [14] and Airline (A) datasets[1]. The number of positive and negative samples is equal in the training and testing data. We construct 6 cross-domain sentiment classification tasks: I → Y, I → A, Y → I, Y → A, A → I, A → Y. One issue is that Yelp, IMDB and Airline datasets have 5, 10 and 2 sentiment labels, respectively. To align the space of sentiment labels for domain adaptation, we select positive reviews (higher than 3 stars for Yelp and 6 stars for IMDB) and negative reviews (lower than 3 stars for Yelp and 6 stars for IMDB). Table 1 summarizes the all datasets.

Table 1. Statistics of the experimental datasets

Domain	Books	Dvd	Kitchen	Electronics	Video	IMDB	Yelp	Airline
Train	5600	5600	5600	5600	5600	5600	5600	5600
Test	400	400	400	400	400	400	400	400

---

[1]   https://github.com/quankiquanki/skytrax-reviews-dataset.

4.2   Implementation Details

BERT is a large-scale language model with multiple layers of transformers and can learn bidirectional representations [5]. In our experiment, we adopt the $BERT_{base}$(uncased) to extract features. The maximum sequence length, batch size, epoch and dropout is 256, 20 ,10 and 0.1 respectively. The learning rate is 2e–5. The adaptation rate is increased as $\lambda = \frac{2}{1+exp(-10p)-1}$, where $p = \frac{t}{T}$. The t and T are current epoch and the maximum epoch, respectively. For the hyper-parameter β , we select the optimal parameters on the experiments B $\rightarrow$ K and K $\rightarrow$ B (Fig. 3). Finally, We set $\beta = 0.01$ in all our experiments. The average and the standard error of the accuracy are calculated over 5 runs with different random seeds on each transfer task.

4.3   Benchmark Methods

We consider the following approaches for comparisons:

Table 2. Classification accuracy (%) on the Amazon reviews dataset.

S T	DANN	HATN^h	BERT	BERT-JDDA	BERT-DRL^p	BERT-DRL
B D	81.2±0.4	87.1±0.1	88.6±0.3	89.5±0.5	89.9±0.3	**90.2±0.2**
B E	76.5±0.7	84.4±0.3	89.4±1.3	90.4±1.4	90.6±0.7	**90.9±0.4**
B K	80.3±0.2	86.4±0.4	90.5±0.4	91.4±0.6	92.3±0.3	**92.5±0.2**
B V	81.7±0.8	87.0±0.6	88.9±0.2	90.3±0.6	90.6±0.4	**91.1±0.4**
D B	81.6±0.6	87.6±0.6	90.3±0.5	91.4±0.2	91.0±0.4	**91.5±0.2**
D E	76.9±0.4	85.2±0.5	88.5±1.0	89.5±0.6	89.7±0.7	**90.7±0.5**
D K	77.6±0.6	87.0±0.7	90.9±0.2	91.6±0.7	**92.2±0.5**	92.1±0.1
D V	85.4±0.7	88.2±0.1	90.8±0.8	91.7±0.6	91.9±0.7	**92.4±0.3**
E B	77.7±0.2	81.9±0.2	88.7±0.2	88.6±0.2	89.1±0.5	**89.2±0.3**
E D	75.5±0.3	81.8±0.5	86.4±0.6	87.1±0.6	87.5±0.4	**87.8±0.3**
E K	85.0±0.6	89.5±0.3	92.8±0.6	93.4±1.0	**94.1±0.3**	94.0±0.1
E V	76.1±1.0	80.8±0.2	87.3±0.5	87.6±0.7	87.9±0.3	**88.7±0.2**
K B	79.0±0.5	83.8±0.4	89.2±0.3	89.9±0.3	89.7±0.6	**90.0±0.5**
K D	78.3±0.4	82.3±0.2	87.9±0.4	87.9±0.7	88.1±0.2	**88.2±0.4**
K E	84.6±0.2	87.5±0.3	92.5±0.2	92.9±0.6	92.8±0.6	**93.5±0.2**
K V	76.4±0.1	81.9±0.2	88.1±0.8	88.8±0.4	88.4±0.3	**89.0±0.5**
V B	79.9±0.7	86.6±0.4	88.7±0.7	89.8±0.6	90.5±0.3	**91.1±0.3**
V D	83.3±0.3	86.8±0.3	89.7±0.5	90.4±0.4	89.7±0.3	**90.9±0.2**
V E	74.7±0.3	81.5±0.2	89.4±0.7	90.7±0.3	90.7±0.5	**91.2±0.3**
V K	74.3±0.4	84.4±0.3	91.1±0.5	91.6±0.3	91.7±0.4	**92.1±0.1**
Avg	79.3	85.1	89.5	90.2	90.4	**90.9**

DANN: it performs domain adaptation with the representation encoded in a 5000-dimension feature vector [6].

HATN[h]: it extracts pivots and non-pivots by the hierarchical attention network across domains [9].

BERT: it fine-tunes vanilla BERT by source domain labeled data.

BERT-JDDA: JDDA [2] model based on BERT.

BERT-DRL[p]: it assigns pseudo labels to target samples and uses all losses on vanilla BERT.

BERT-DRL: it utilizes spectral clustering for target samples and uses all losses on vanilla BERT.

Table 3. Classification accuracy (%) on the IMDB, Yelp and Airline datasets.

S T	DANN	HATN[h]	BERT	BERT-JDDA	BERT-DRL[p]	BERT-DRL
I Y	72.4 ± 2.1	75.9 ± 1.1	80.8 ± 1.7	81.6 ± 1.5	82.1 ± 1.8	$\mathbf{82.8 \pm 1.1}$
I A	74.6 ± 1.8	77.1 ± 0.9	80.1 ± 2.1	80.6 ± 1.8	81.2 ± 2.3	$\mathbf{82.7 \pm 0.9}$
Y I	69.5 ± 1.5	71.0 ± 0.8	72.1 ± 1.3	75.3 ± 2.6	73.8 ± 1.8	$\mathbf{76.5 \pm 1.2}$
Y A	74.2 ± 2.2	78.5 ± 1.2	83.8 ± 1.6	82.7 ± 2.3	84.4 ± 2.1	$\mathbf{85.2 \pm 1.4}$
A I	63.7 ± 1.9	65.7 ± 1.1	70.6 ± 1.5	72.3 ± 2.4	73.1 ± 1.4	$\mathbf{74.3 \pm 0.8}$
A Y	73.9 ± 1.3	75.7 ± 0.8	81.0 ± 1.3	81.1 ± 1.8	82.5 ± 1.1	$\mathbf{83.2 \pm 0.9}$
Avg	71.4	74.0	78.1	78.9	79.5	**80.6**

We compare our method with other state-of-the-art methods on the Amazon reviews dataset and the experimental results are shown in Table 2. As can be seen, BERT-DRL has achieved the best performances on most tasks. HATN[h] achieves great improvements compared with traditional methods, which come to 85.1% on average. The vanilla BERT has achieved 89.5% on average by training the source domain samples. It shows that bert model can produce good word embedding vectors. The prediction accuracy on the target domain is high, so the quality of pseudo labels is good. The performance of BERT-DRL[p] exceeds BERT-DRL on some tasks (D → K, E → K). Comparing with BERT, BERT-DRL exceeds 1.4% on average. It proves that discriminative representation learning loss can produce more distinguishing features. The BERT-DRL improves the classification accuracy by 0.7% than BERT-JDDA. We cluster target domain samples and calculate the DRL loss is very necessary.

However, the cross-domain sentiment classification tasks are same origin in Table 2. To verify the effectiveness of our method on different origins, we construct 6 new tasks. The classification accuracy on the IMDB, Yelp and Airline datasets are shown in Table 3. The DANN and HATN[p] without BERT achieve 71.4% and 74.0% on average, respectively. the performance of BERT-DRL still outperforms BERT-JDDA and achieve 80.6% on average. The BERT-DRL and BERT-DRL[p] improve the classification accuracy by 2.5% and 1.4% than BERT, respectively. Comparing with BERT-DRL^p, BERT-DRL improves the classification accuracy substantially on hard transfer tasks. Since the discriminative representation learning loss does not depend on the prediction accuracy of target domain samples but features of target domain samples generated by feature encoder. We can train the model more effectively when features are easy to be distinguished.

4.4 Feature Visualization

For more intuitive understanding our approach, we select all samples in the source and target domains and visualize the feature of last layer as shown in Fig. 2. We perform the visualization on B → D and K → V tasks by t-SNE. The samples of different polarities in source domain are well separated in vanilla BERT (Fig. 2b and Fig. 2d). While the target domain samples with different polarities are mixed together. It shows that the source domain samples are not satisfy with the target domain classification. The samples from different domains are mixed together through discriminative representation learning loss (Fig. 2a and Fig. 2c). The boundary of sentiment polarity classification is very clear. We also quantitatively analyzed separability and compactness in Table 4. The intra-class distance (d_s and d_t) and centroid distance of the same polarity (d_c) are reduced and the centroid distance of the different polarities (d_u) is increased. For compactness, the decrease is small for one sample, but the effect is obvious when all samples are accumulated. All of the above observations can demonstrate that BERT-DRL model is able to simultaneously learn more transferable and more discriminative features.

Table 4. Separability and compactness on B → D and K → V tasks. Separability is calculated by centroid distance. Compactness is represented by the average of intra-class distances.

		Separability		Compactness	
		d_c	d_u	d_s	d_t
B D	BERT	0.878	26.175	0.898	3.721
	BERT-DRL	0.475	30.059	0.846	3.638
K V	BERT	1.625	28.794	1.188	4.053
	BERT-DRL	0.592	30.595	1.038	3.832

4.5 Parameter Sensitivity

We investigate the effects of the parameter β which balances the contributions of discriminative representation learning in Fig. 3. The average is calculated over 5 runs with different random seeds. We find that the accuracy curve increases first and then decreases as β increases. It shows that our proposed loss can improve the performance of the model through appropriate parameters to obtain more distinguished features.

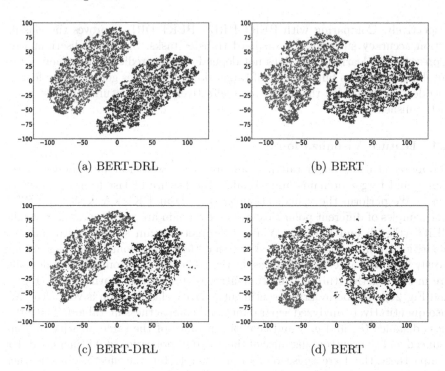

(a) BERT-DRL   (b) BERT

(c) BERT-DRL   (d) BERT

Fig. 2. The t-SNE visualization of the B → D task (a) (b) and K → V task (c) (d). The red, blue, purple and green points denote the source positive, source negative, target positive and target negative examples correspondingly. (Color figure online)

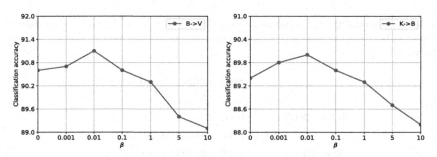

Fig. 3. Parameter sensitivity analysis of our approach on B → V task and K → B task.

4.6   Ablation Studies

To analyze the effect of Domain-Adversarial training of Neural Networks (DANN) [6], centroid alignment (CA) and intra-class compactness (IC), we conduct the ablation experiments on task B → D, E → V, V → D, I → A, Y → I and A → I in Table 5. The experimental results show that DANN, CA and IC are both beneficial to cross-domain sentiment classification.

Table 5. Results of ablation study.

Model	B → D	E → V	V → D	I → A	Y → I	A → I
BERT-DANN	89.4± 0.4	87.8 ± 0.4	90.1 ± 0.4	80.8 ± 2.5	73.7 ± 2.8	72.7 ± 1.3
BERT-DANN-IC	89.8 ± 0.6	88.3 ± 0.3	90.4 ± 0.5	81.7 ± 1.6	76.2 ± 1.1	73.2 ± 2.3
BERT-DANN-CA	90.1 ± 0.5	88.5 ± 0.6	90.6 ± 0.4	82.1 ± 1.4	75.0 ± 2.0	73.4 ± 1.5
BERT-DRL	**90.2 ± 0.2**	**88.7± 0.2**	**90.9±0.2**	**82.7 ± 0.9**	**76.5 ± 1.2**	**74.3 ± 0.8**

5 Conclusion

In this paper, we propose to improve the transfer performance by discriminative representation learning for cross-domain sentiment classfication. It uses spectral clustering to avoid the harmful effect of low prediction accuracy on the target domain. Centroid alignment can map the sampels of same polarity to the neighborhood in feature space and enforces the samples of the different polarities with greater distance. Besides, the samples distributed at the edges of the clusters are reduced and classification accuracy is improved by intra-class compactness. In this way, we can product transferable and distinguishable features by introducing our discriminative loss. Experiments on the Amazon, IMDB, Yelp and Airline datasets demonstrate that DRL significantly outperforms the state-of-the-art methods.

Acknowledgments. This paper is Supported by National Key Research and Development Program of China under Grant No. 2017YFB0803003 and National Science Foundation for Young Scientists of China (Grant No. 61702507).

References

1. Blitzer, J., McDonald, R., Pereira, F.: Domain adaptation with structural correspondence learning. In: Proceedings of the 2006 Conference on Empirical Methods in Natural Language Processing. Association for Computational Linguistics, pp. 120–128 (2006)
2. Chen, C., Chen, Z., Jiang, B., Jin, X.: Joint domain alignment and discriminative feature learning for unsupervised deep domain adaptation. In: Proceedings of the AAAI Conference on Artificial Intelligence. vol. 33, pp. 3296–3303 (2019)
3. Chen, M., Xu, Z., Weinberger, K., Sha, F.: Marginalized denoising autoencoders for domain adaptation. arXiv preprint arXiv:1206.4683 (2012)
4. Chen, X., Wang, S., Long, M., Wang, J.: Transferability vs. discriminability: batch spectral penalization for adversarial domain adaptation. In: International Conference on Machine Learning, pp. 1081–1090 (2019)
5. Devlin, J., Chang, M.W., Lee, K., Toutanova, K.: Bert: pre-training of deep bidirectional transformers for language understanding. arXiv preprint arXiv:1810.04805 (2018)
6. Ganin, Y., et al.: Domain-adversarial training of neural networks. J. Mach. Learn. Res. **17**(1), 2096–2030 (2016)

7. Glorot, X., Bordes, A., Bengio, Y.: Domain adaptation for large-scale sentiment classification: a deep learning approach. In: Proceedings of the 28th International Conference on Machine Learning (ICML-11), pp. 513–520 (2011)
8. Hu, M., Liu, B.: Mining and summarizing customer reviews. In: Proceedings of the Tenth ACM SIGKDD International Conference on Knowledge Discovery and Data Mining, pp. 168–177. ACM (2004)
9. Li, Z., Wei, Y., Zhang, Y., Yang, Q.: Hierarchical attention transfer network for cross-domain sentiment classification. In: Thirty-Second AAAI Conference on Artificial Intelligence (2018)
10. Luo, Z., Zou, Y., Hoffman, J., Fei-Fei, L.F.: Label efficient learning of transferable representations a crosss domains and tasks. In: Advances in Neural Information Processing Systems, pp. 165–177 (2017)
11. Luxburg, U.V.: A tutorial on spectral clustering. Stat. Comput. **17**(4), 395–416 (2007)
12. Pan, S.J., Ni, X., Sun, J.T., Yang, Q., Chen, Z.: Cross-domain sentiment classification via spectral feature alignment. In: Proceedings of the 19th International Conference on World Wide Web, pp. 751–760. ACM (2010)
13. Tang, D., Qin, B., Feng, X., Liu, T.: Target-dependent sentiment classification with long short term memory. arXiv preprint arXiv:1512.01100 (2015)
14. Tang, D., Qin, B., Liu, T.: Learning semantic representations of users and products for document level sentiment classification. In: Proceedings of the 53rd Annual Meeting of the Association for Computational Linguistics, pp. 1014–1023 (2015)
15. Xie, S., Zheng, Z., Chen, L., Chen, C.: Learning semantic representations for unsupervised domain adaptation. In: International Conference on Machine Learning, pp. 5419–5428 (2018)
16. Zhang, K., Zhang, H., Liu, Q., Zhao, H., Zhu, H., Chen, E.: Interactive attention transfer network for cross-domain sentiment classification (2019)

SAGCN: Towards Structure-Aware Deep Graph Convolutional Networks on Node Classification

Ming He$^{(\boxtimes)}$, Tianyu Ding, and Tianshuo Han

Faculty of Information Technology, Beijing University of Technology, Beijing, China
heming@bjut.edu.cn, {dingtianyu,hants}@emails.bjut.edu.cn

Abstract. Graph Convolutional Networks (GCNs) have recently achiev-ed impressive performance in different classification tasks. However, over-smoothing remains a fundamental burden to achieve deep GCNs for node classification. This paper proposes Structure-Aware Deep Graph Convolutional Networks (SAGCN), a novel model to overcome this burden. At its core, SAGCN separates the initial node features from propagation and directly maps them to the output at each layer. Furthermore, SAGCN selectively aggregates the information from different propagation layers to generate structure-aware node representations, where the attention mechanism is exploited to adaptively balance the information from local and global neighborhoods for each node. Our experiments verify that the SAGCN model achieves state-of-the-art performance in various semi-supervised and full-supervised node classification tasks. More importantly, it outperforms many other backbone models, by using half the number of layers, or even fewer layers.

Keywords: Deep learning · Graph Convolutional Networks · Node classification · Attention mechanism

1 Introduction

Graph Convolutional Networks (GCNs) [6] are an efficient variant of Convolutional Neural Networks (CNNs) on graphs. A GCN learns representation for a node by aggregating representations of its neighbors iteratively. In recent years, GCNs and their variants have been successfully applied to a wide range of applications, including node classification [25], social analysis [8,15], biology [3,19], recommender systems [4], and computer vision [11,24].

Despite their enormous success, most of the current GCN models are shallow. Numerous recent models, such as GCN [6], GAT [21], and APPNP [7], achieve their best performance with two-layer models. Such shallow architectures limit their ability to extract information from high-order neighbors. Moreover, the performance of these models degrades significantly when stacking multiple layers. This phenomenon, called over-smoothing [9], states that representations from different classes become inseparable due to repeated propagation.

© Springer Nature Switzerland AG 2021
K. Karlapalem et al. (Eds.): PAKDD 2021, LNAI 12713, pp. 67–78, 2021.
https://doi.org/10.1007/978-3-030-75765-6_6

Recently, several works have tried to tackle over-smoothing problem. The JKNet model [22] uses dense skip connections combining the output of each layer to preserve the locality of the node representations. A further model, GCNII [1] suggests that by utilizing residual connection to carry information about the initial layer and the previous layer, one can relieve the impact of over-smoothing. Most existing methods, however, still face two problems. *First, these models do not consider how to adequately preserve initial node features, which can lead to the loss of information that is crucial for node classification. Second, they lack the capability of adapting neighborhood ranges to nodes individually, which may not dynamically aggregate neighborhood information with different weights.*

In this paper, SAGCN, a structure-aware deep GCN model is proposed to address the aforementioned issues and relieve over-smoothing. Unlike GCNII, which combines information about the initial layer with propagation to achieve this task, information from propagation is separated, and mapped directly to the output at each layer. In this manner, SAGCN can both reduce the loss of important information and alleviate over-smoothing. Furthermore, all layers are stacked and an attention mechanism is applied to selectively aggregate the information from different neighborhood ranges for each node. Extensive computational experiments show that our model outperforms other state-of-the-art models on both semi-supervised and full-supervised node classification tasks.

The key contributions of the present work are summarized as follows:

- A novel model named SAGCN is proposed to help improve classification accuracy, which can fully preserve initial node features by separating them from propagation. Different from recent models, SAGCN adequately keeps the feature information that is critical for node classification.
- An attention mechanism is utilized, that can adaptively leverage the information from local and global neighborhoods for each node, thus obtaining structure-aware node representations. Compared to existing works, SAGCN flexibly aggregates information from different neighborhood ranges for each node rather than a fixed receptive field.
- Extensive experiments of both semi-supervised and full-supervised node classification tasks are conducted on real-world datasets. Results reveal that our model significantly outperforms baseline models.

2   Related Work

2.1   Deep GCNs

In spite of fruitful progress in this field, most previous studies only focus on shallow GCNs, while the deeper extension is seldom discussed. The first attempt to build deep GCNs is dated back to the GCN paper [6], where the residual mechanism is applied. The follow-up study PPNP [7] employs the relationship between GCNs and PageRank to derive an improved propagation scheme. Oono [13] generalizes the forward propagation of a GCN as a specific dynamical system, and theoretically proves that the node features of deep GCNs will converge to a subspace and incur information loss. Over-smoothing is solved in DropEdge [16] by randomly removing a certain number of edges from the input graph at each training epoch. A recent method GCNII [1] incorporates initial residual and identity mapping into GCN to facilitate the development of deep architectures. *The major difference between previous work and the present model is that we apply an attention mechanism to flexibly leverage different neighborhood ranges for each node, rather than aggregating information from a fixed receptive field.*

2.2 Attention-Based GCNs

A separate line of techniques target the attention-based GCN model. For example, GAT [21] utilizes attention mechanisms to learn the edge weights at each layer based on node features. The method by Thekumparampil [20] replaces the propagation layers with attention mechanisms to learn a dynamic and adaptive local summary of the neighborhood. Jumping Knowledge Networks [22] employ LSTM-attention to obtain adaptive node representations. Recently, DAGNN [10] introduced an attention mechanism after the propagation to derive more discriminative node embeddings. *Compared with previous studies, not only do we additionally introduce a smoothed representation of this layer, but also include a large number of initial node representations in each layer of our model to get better node embeddings for classification.*

3   Preliminaries

3.1   Notations

A graph is formally defined as $\mathcal{G} = (\mathcal{V}, \mathcal{E})$, where $\mathcal{V}$ is the set of nodes (vertices) indexed from 1 to n, and $\mathcal{E} \subseteq \mathcal{V} \times \mathcal{V}$ is the set of edges between nodes in $\mathcal{V}$. The numbers of nodes and edges are $n = |\mathcal{V}|$ and $m = |\mathcal{E}|$, respectively. In this paper, we consider unweighted and undirected graphs. Topology information for the whole graph is described by the adjacency matrix $\mathbf{A} \in \mathbb{R}^{n \times n}$, where $\mathbf{A}_{(i,j)} = 1$ if an edge exists between node i and node j, otherwise it is 0. The diagonal matrix of node degrees is denoted as $\mathbf{D} \in \mathbb{R}^{n \times n}$, where $\mathbf{D}_{(i,i)} = \sum_j \mathbf{A}_{(i,j)}$. $\mathcal{N}_i$ denotes the neighboring nodes set of node i. A graph has a initial node feature matrix $\mathbf{h}^{(0)} \in \mathbb{R}^{n \times d}$, where each row $\mathbf{h}_i^{(0)} \in \mathbb{R}^d$ represents the feature vector of node i and d is the dimension of node features.

3.2   Graph Convolutional Network (GCN)

The GCN was originally developed by Kipf & Welling [6]. The feed forward propagation in GCN is recursively conducted as

$$\mathbf{H}^{(l+1)} = \sigma \left(\hat{\mathbf{A}} \mathbf{H}^{(l)} \mathbf{W}^{(l)} \right), \tag{1}$$

where $\mathbf{H}^{(l)} \in \mathbb{R}^{n \times d^{(l)}}$ and $\mathbf{H}^{(l+1)} \in \mathbb{R}^{n \times d^{(l+1)}}$ are the input and output node representation matrices of layer $(l+1)$. $\hat{\mathbf{A}} = \hat{\mathbf{D}}^{-1/2} \tilde{\mathbf{A}} \hat{\mathbf{D}}^{-1/2}$ is the re-normalization of the adjacency matrix, where $\tilde{\mathbf{A}} = \mathbf{A} + \mathbf{I}$ is the adjacency matrix with added self-connections and $\hat{\mathbf{D}}$ indicates the corresponding degree matrix of $\tilde{\mathbf{A}}$. Adding an extra self-loop, however, makes the features indistinguishable and hurt the classification accuracy according to another study [9]. In this paper, we use original adjacency matrix $\mathbf{A}$ and the corresponding degree matrix $\mathbf{D}$. $\mathbf{W}^{(l)} \in \mathbb{R}^{d^{(l)} \times d^{(l+1)}}$ is a layer-specific trainable weight matrix and σ is a non-linear activation function, such as ReLU [12]. It was originally applied for semi-supervised classification tasks, where only partial nodes have training labels in a graph. Owing to the propagation process, the representation of a labeled node carries information from its neighbors that are usually unlabeled, thus training signals can be propagated to the unlabeled nodes.

4   Proposed Model

This section shows the proposed model, with its architecture of as illustrated in Fig. 1. Two components in the framework are described: (1) information propagation and (2) layer aggregation.

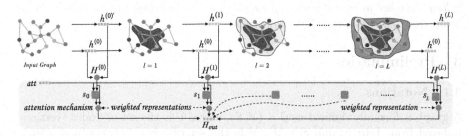

Fig. 1. The overall architecture of our proposed model. It contains two major components: information propagation and layer aggregation. In the figure, *att* is the attention vector, which computes retainment scores for representation generating from various receptive fields, and s_0, s_1, s_L represent the retainment scores of $H^{(0)}$, $H^{(1)}$ and $H^{(L)}$, respectively.

4.1   Information Propagation

In this iterative process, each iteration indicates that an additional hop of information has been propagated on the graph. Due to the shallow architecture of GCNs, the nodes on the graph cannot capture sufficient neighborhood information. Nevertheless, the performance degrades greatly when multiple layers are applied to leverage more neighborhood information. Several recent works attribute this performance degradation to the over-smoothing issue. Over-smoothing is indeed a challenging problem, however our model effectively relieves it by two modifications: 1) The initial features $\mathbf{h}^{(0)}$ are separated from propagation; 2) A smoothed representation $\hat{\mathbf{A}}\mathbf{H}^{(l)}$ of this layer is additionally introduced.

Formally, the l-th layer of SAGCN is defined as

$$\mathbf{H}^{(l+1)} = \sigma\left(\left(\delta\hat{\mathbf{A}}\mathbf{H}^{(l)}\mathbf{W}^{(l)} + (1-\delta)\,\hat{\mathbf{A}}\mathbf{H}^{(l)}\right) + \eta\mathbf{h}^{(0)}\right), \tag{2}$$

where δ and η are two hyper-parameters. The symmetrical normalization propagation mechanism $\hat{\mathbf{A}} = \mathbf{D}^{-1/2}\mathbf{A}\mathbf{D}^{-1/2}$ is employed. It is important to note that original adjacency matrix $\mathbf{A}$ is used instead of $\tilde{\mathbf{A}}$. Most of the previous studies add a self-connection to retain its information during layer-wise propagation. However, it is stated in other works [9,25] that a self-connection is meaningless and may even introduce extra noises. Correspondingly, the original node degree matrix $\mathbf{D}$ is used instead of $\hat{\mathbf{D}}$ in the present work. σ is an activation function, for which ReLU is used.

As mentioned above, initial node embeddings play an important role in the classification task. A recent study [10] verifies that the exclusive application of a Multi-Layer Perceptron to the original feature matrix $\mathbf{h}^{(0)}$ performs well without using any graph structure information. This shows that the original structure of data is important for classification, thereby this work aims to fully preserve it. Moreover, it has been observed that frequent interaction between different dimensions of the feature matrix [7] degrades the performance of the model. Unlike GCNII, which combines $\mathbf{h}^{(0)}$ with propagation, our model reduces such interactions by separating $\mathbf{h}^{(0)}$ from propagation and mapping it directly to the output. In this manner, SAGCN is capable of making full use of $\mathbf{h}^{(0)}$ to improve classification accuracy, and relieve the over-smoothing problem.

Furthermore, the additional introduction of smoothed representation $\hat{\mathbf{A}}\mathbf{H}^{(l)}$ assures that a deep model achieves at least the same performance as a shallow one, facilitating its implementation. The principle of setting δ is to ensure that the decay of weight matrix $\mathbf{W}^{(l)}$ adaptively increases as we stack more layers. Notably, SAGCN ignores the weight matrix $\mathbf{W}^{(l)}$ by setting sufficiently small δ. In our experiments, we set δ following the design of GCNII (i.e., $\delta = \log\left(\frac{\lambda}{l}+1\right)$, where λ is a hyper-parameter).

4.2   Layer Aggregation

The hidden representation of the layers (e.g., $\mathbf{H}^{(0)}$, $\mathbf{H}^{(1)}$) is obtained through information propagation. Many existing models aggregate information from a fixed range of neighbors. Nevertheless, JKNet [22] shows that the same number of iterations (i.e., layers) can lead to very different effects for different nodes in the same graph and the range of effective information obtained by each node is heavily affected by the graph structure. In order to get structure-aware node representations for classification, we employ an attention mechanism to flexibly leverage the information from different neighborhood ranges for each node. The mathematical expression of this subsection is defined as

$$\mathbf{H} = stack\left(\mathbf{H}^{(0)}, \mathbf{H}^{(1)}, \cdots, \mathbf{H}^{(L)}\right) \quad \in \mathbb{R}^{n\times(L+1)\times d}, \tag{3}$$

$$\mathbf{S} = \sigma\left(softmax\left(\mathbf{Hatt}\right)\right) \quad \in \mathbb{R}^{n\times(L+1)\times 1}, \tag{4}$$

$$\hat{\mathbf{S}} = reshape\,(\mathbf{S}) \quad \in \mathbb{R}^{n \times 1 \times (L+1)}, \tag{5}$$

$$\mathbf{H}_{out} = squeeze\left(\hat{\mathbf{S}}\mathbf{H}\right) \quad \in \mathbb{R}^{n \times d}, \tag{6}$$

where $\mathbf{att} \in \mathbb{R}^{d \times 1}$ is a trainable attention vector; σ is an activation function, for which sigmoid is used; *stack*, *reshape* and *squeeze* are used to adjust the data dimension, so it can be matched during computation.

As mentioned in Sect. 4.1, $\mathbf{H}^{(l)}$ denotes the hidden representations derived by extracting information from nodes that are l-hop away, thus $\mathbf{H}^{(l)}$ captures the information from the sub-tree of height l with the target node as the root. As the number of layers l increase, more global information is propagated in $\mathbf{H}^{(l)}$ because the corresponding sub-tree is deeper. However, it is difficult to determine an appropriate l. A small l may fail to extract sufficient high-order neighborhood features, while a large l may bring too much global information leading to a dilution of essential local information. Furthermore, each node has a different sub-tree structure rooted at this node (e.g., tree-like, expansion-like) and the most appropriate receptive field for each node should be different. For this reason, an attention mechanism is applied after the information propagation. A trainable attention vector $\mathbf{att}$ is employed, which is shared by all nodes to generate retainment scores. These retainment scores measure how much information of the corresponding representations obtained by different propagation layers should be retained to generate the final representation for each node. By using this attention mechanism, SAGCN selectively aggregates different propagation layers according to their importance to generate an adaptive structure-aware representation for each node.

5   Experiments

In this section, extensive experiments are conducted on both semi-supervised and full-supervised tasks to evaluate the performance of the proposed SAGCN.

Table 1. Statistics of the datasets.

Dataset	Classes	Nodes	Edges	Features
Cora	7	2708	5429	1433
Citeseer	6	3327	4732	3703
Pubmed	3	19717	44338	500
Chameleon	4	2277	36101	2325
Cornell	5	183	295	1703
Texas	5	183	309	1703
Wisconsin	5	251	499	1703

5.1 Datasets

Following previous pieces of work [18,21,23], we use three standard citation network datasets Cora, Citeseer, and Pubmed for semi-supervised node classification. In these citation datasets, nodes and edges represent documents and citation relations, respectively, between documents. The Chameleon [17], Cornell, Texas, and Wisconsin [14] datasets are also included for full-supervised node classification. These datasets are web networks, where nodes and edges represent web pages and hyperlinks, respectively. The feature of each node is the bag-of-words representation of the corresponding page. Some statistics of these datasets are provided in Table 1.

5.2 Semi-supervised Node Classification

Experimental Settings. To ensure a fair comparison, the standard fixed training/validation/testing split [23] is utilized for the semi-supervised node classification task on three datasets: Cora, Citeseer and Pubmed, with 20 nodes per class for training, 500 nodes for validation and 1,000 nodes for testing. We use the Adam SGD optimizer [5] and early stopping with a patience of 100 epochs to train SAGCN.

Baselines. The following state-of-the-art models are used as baselines in our experiments:

- **GCN** [6] is an efficient variant of convolutional neural networks which operates directly on graph-structured data.
- **GAT** [21] leverages masked self-attentional layers instead of a symmetrically normalized adjacency matrix in the GCN model.
- **APPNP** [7] utilizes the relationship between GCN and PageRank to derive an improved propagation scheme based on personalized PageRank.
- **JKNet** [22] is the first deep GCN model employing dense skip connections to combine the output of each layer, preserving the locality of the node representations.
- **JKNet(Drop)** [16] is an improved version of JKNet, which randomly removes some edges from the graph to retard convergence speed of oversmoothing.
- **Incep(Drop)** [16] is an improved version of IncepGCN that randomly removes a certain number of edges to relieve the information loss caused by over-smoothing.
- **GCNII** [1] is a state-of-the-art deep GCN model with initial residual and identity mapping, which effectively relieves the problem of over-smoothing.

Hyper-parameter Settings. In our model, we set $\eta = 0.7$ and $\lambda = 2.0$ on all datasets. We tune the following hyper-parameters: (1) layers $\in \{8, 16, 32\}$, (2) learning rate $\in \{0.001, 0.003, 0.004\}$, (3) hidden layer dimensions $\in \{64, 256\}$, (4) dropout rate $\in \{0.5, 0.8\}$, (5) weight decay for convolutional layers $\in \{0.01, 0.02, 0.15\}$, and (6) weight decay for dense layers $\in \{0.02, 0.005, 0.01\}$.

Performance Comparison. The mean classification accuracy after 100 runs for three citation datasets are summarized in Table 2. We reuse the metrics already reported in [2] for GCN, GAT, and APPNP, the best metrics reported in [16] for JKNet, JKNet(Drop), Incep(Drop), and the metrics reported in [1] for GCNII. As shown in Table 2, our results successfully demonstrate that SAGCN achieves new state-of-the-art performance across all three datasets. Notably, the fact that deep models (e.g., GCNII) always work better than shallow models (e.g., GCN and GAT) indicates that global and local information together help boost performance. It is also worthwhile to note that we use half the number of layers to achieve even better results than the deep GCN model GCNII, which benefits from the ability of our model to flexibly utilize local and global information.

Table 2. Mean classification accuracy (%) of semi-supervised node classification. The number in parentheses corresponds to the number of layers in the model.

Model	Cora	Citeseer	Pubmed
GCN	81.5	71.1	79.0
GAT	83.1	70.8	78.5
APPNP	83.3	71.8	80.1
JKNet	81.1 (4)	69.8 (16)	78.1 (32)
JKNet(Drop)	83.3 (4)	72.6 (16)	79.2 (32)
Incep(Drop)	83.5 (64)	72.7 (4)	79.5 (4)
GCNII	85.5 (64)	73.4 (32)	80.3 (16)
SAGCN	**86.3** (32)	**73.6** (16)	**80.9** (8)

A Detailed Comparison with Other Deep Models. Table 3 summarizes the results for the deep models with various numbers of layers. We reuse the best-reported results for JKNet, JKNet(Drop), Incep(Drop) and GCNII. It can be observed that on three datasets, the performance of SAGCN consistently improves as the number of layers are increased. Notably, SAGCN achieves state-of-the-art results with half the number of layers than deep model GCNII. This suggests that too many layers may lead to a dilution of local information that is important for node classification.

5.3   Full-Supervised Node Classification

Experimental Settings. Following the setting in [14], 7 datasets are used: Cora, Citeseer, Pubmed, Chameleon, Cornell, Texas, and Wisconsin. For each dataset, nodes of each class are randomly split into 60%, 20%, and 20% for training, validation and testing, respectively, and the performance of all models on the test sets are measured over 10 random splits, as suggested in [14].

Table 3. Summary of classification accuracy (%) results with various depths.

Dataset	Method	Layers					
		2	4	8	16	32	64
Cora	GCN	81.1	80.4	69.5	64.9	60.3	28.7
	GCN(Drop)	82.8	82.0	75.8	75.7	62.5	49.5
	JKNet	-	80.2	80.7	80.2	81.1	71.5
	JKNet(Drop)	-	83.3	82.6	83.0	82.5	83.2
	Incep	-	77.6	76.5	81.7	81.7	80.0
	Incep(Drop)	-	82.9	82.5	83.1	83.1	83.5
	GCNII	82.2	82.6	84.2	84.6	85.4	85.5
	SAGCN	74.5	80.3	82.6	83.8	**86.3**	-
Citeseer	GCN	70.8	67.6	30.2	18.3	25.0	20.0
	GCN(Drop)	72.3	70.6	61.4	57.2	41.6	34.4
	JKNet	-	68.7	67.7	69.8	68.2	63.4
	JKNet(Drop)	-	72.6	71.8	72.6	70.8	72.2
	Incep	-	69.3	68.4	70.2	68.0	67.5
	Incep(Drop)	-	72.7	71.4	72.5	72.6	71.0
	GCNII	68.2	68.9	70.6	72.9	73.4	73.4
	SAGCN	64.0	66.2	70.2	**73.6**	-	-
Pubmed	GCN	79.0	76.5	61.2	40.9	22.4	35.3
	GCN(Drop)	79.6	79.4	78.1	78.5	77.0	61.5
	JKNet	-	78.0	78.1	72.6	72.4	74.5
	JKNet(Drop)	-	78.7	78.7	79.1	79.2	78.9
	Incep	-	77.7	77.9	74.9	-	-
	Incep(Drop)	-	79.5	78.6	79.0	-	-
	GCNII	77.7	78.2	78.8	80.3	79.8	80.1
	SAGCN	77.8	80.0	**80.9**	-	-	-

Baselines. In addition to the previously mentioned baselines, three variants of the state-of-the-art Geom-GCN model [14] are included on these datasets.

- **Geom-GCN**: This is a geometric aggregation scheme for graph neural networks, which can extract the discriminative structures and long-range dependencies. Geom-GCN-I, Geom-GCN-P, and Geom-GCN-S are three variants of Geom-GCN.

Hyper-parameter Settings. In SAGCN, we fix the η to 0.7 on all datasets. We tune the following hyper-parameters: (1) layers $\in \{8, 16, 32\}$, (2) learning rate $\in \{0.005, 0.01, 0.03\}$, (3) hidden layer dimensions $\in \{64, 128\}$, (4) dropout rate $\in \{0.4, 0.5\}$, (5) L_2 regularization $\in \{0.0002, 0.001, 0.005, 0.01\}$, and (6) λ $\in \{2.0, 2.5\}$.

Performance Comparison. Table 4 reports the mean classification accuracy of each model. The metrics already reported in [1] are reused for GCN, GAT, Geom-GCN, and GCNII. Notably, it is observed that SAGCN achieves better performance over the current state-of-the-art models by significant margins of 0.8%, 1.6%, 5.7%, and 1.6% on the Chameleon, Cornell, Texas, and Wisconsin, respectively.

Table 4. Mean classification accuracy (%) of full-supervised node classification.

Model	Cora	Cite.	Pumb.	Cham.	Corn.	Texa.	Wisc.
GCN	85.77	73.68	88.13	28.18	52.70	52.16	45.88
GAT	86.37	74.32	87.62	42.93	54.32	58.38	49.41
Geom-GCN-I	85.19	**77.99**	90.05	60.31	56.76	57.58	58.24
Geom-GCN-P	84.93	75.14	88.09	60.90	60.81	67.57	64.12
Gcom-GCN S	85.27	74.71	84.75	59.06	55.68	59.73	56.67
APPNP	87.87	76.53	89.40	54.30	73.51	65.41	69.02
JKNet	85.25	75.85	88.94	60.07	57.30	56.49	48.82
JKNet(Drop)	87.46	75.96	89.45	62.08	61.08	57.30	50.59
Incep(Drop)	86.86	76.83	89.18	61.71	61.62	57.84	50.20
GCNII	88.49	77.13	90.30	62.48	76.49	77.84	81.57
SAGCN	**88.71**	77.29	**90.82**	**63.33**	**78.11**	**83.51**	**83.14**

5.4   Ablation Study

The results of an ablation study are shown in Fig. 2. We remove the attention from SAGCN (denoted by "SAGCN-A") and initial node features separating from SAGCN (denoted by "SAGCN-S"), respectively, to see how its performance changes. We make four observations from Fig. 2: 1) Applying an attention

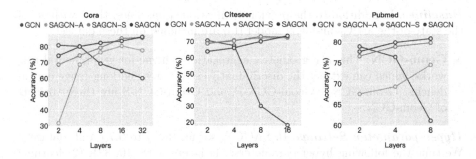

Fig. 2. Ablation study on initial node features separating and attention.

mechanism significantly improves the performance of the model. 2) Separating initial node features from propagation increases the performance of the model to varying degrees. 3) Employing both techniques simultaneously achieves the best results on the three different datasets.

6   Conclusion

In this paper, we propose SAGCN, a novel deep GCN model that relieves the over-smoothing problem. Differently from previous deep models like GCNII, we separate initial node features from propagation to fully preserve the original information that is important for node classification. We further employ an attention mechanism that flexibly leverages different neighborhood ranges for each node, leading to structure-aware node representations for classification. Experiments show that our model can achieve new state-of-the-art performance with half the number of layers, or even less, on various semi-supervised and full-supervised node classification tasks.

Acknowledgements. This work is supported by the Beijing Natural Science Foundation under grant 4192008.

References

1. Chen, M., Wei, Z., Huang, Z., Ding, B., Li, Y.: Simple and deep graph convolutional networks. arXiv preprint arXiv:2007.02133 (2020)
2. Fey, M., Lenssen, J.E.: Fast graph representation learning with PyTorch geometric. arXiv preprint arXiv:1903.02428 (2019)
3. Fout, A., Byrd, J., Shariat, B., Ben-Hur, A.: Protein interface prediction using graph convolutional networks. In: Proceedings of the 31th Advances in Neural Information Processing Systems, pp. 6530–6539 (2017)
4. He, X., Deng, K., Wang, X., Li, Y., Zhang, Y., Wang, M.: LightGCN: simplifying and powering graph convolution network for recommendation. arXiv preprint arXiv:2002.02126 (2020)
5. Kingma, D.P., Ba, J.: Adam: a method for stochastic optimization. arXiv preprint arXiv:1412.6980 (2014)
6. Kipf, T.N., Welling, M.: Semi-supervised classification with graph convolutional networks. In: Proceedings of the 6th International Conference on Learning Representations (2017)
7. Klicpera, J., Bojchevski, A., Günnemann, S.: Predict then propagate: graph neural networks meet personalized pagerank. arXiv preprint arXiv:1810.05997 (2018)
8. Li, C., Goldwasser, D.: Encoding social information with graph convolutional networks forpolitical perspective detection in news media. In: Proceedings of the 57th Annual Meeting of the Association for Computational Linguistics, pp. 2594–2604 (2019)
9. Li, Q., Han, Z., Wu, X.-M.: Deeper insights into graph convolutional networks for semi-supervised learning. arXiv preprint arXiv:1801.07606 (2018)
10. Liu, M., Gao, H., Ji, S.: Towards deeper graph neural networks. In: Proceedings of the 26th International Conference on Knowledge Discovery & Data Mining, pp.338–348 (2020)

11. Ma, J., Wen, J., Zhong, M., Chen, W., Zhou, X., Indulska, J.: Multi-source multi-net micro-video recommendation with hidden item category discovery. In: Li, G., Yang, J., Gama, J., Natwichai, J., Tong, Y. (eds.) DASFAA 2019. LNCS, vol. 11447, pp. 384–400. Springer, Cham (2019). https://doi.org/10.1007/978-3-030-18579-4_23

12. Nair, V., Hinton, G.E.: Rectified linear units improve restricted Boltzmann machines. In: International Conference on Machine Learning (2010)

13. Oono, K., Suzuki, T.: On asymptotic behaviors of graph cnns from dynamical systems perspective. arXiv preprint arXiv:1905.10947 (2019)

14. Pei, H., Wei, B., Chang, K.C.C., Lei, Y., Yang, B.: Geom-GCN: geometric graph convolutional networks. arXiv preprint arXiv:2002.05287 (2020)

15. Qiu, J., Tang, J., Ma, H., Dong, Y., Wang, K., Tang, J.: DeepInf: social influence prediction with deep learning. In: Proceedings of the 24th International Conference on Knowledge Discovery & Data Mining, pp. 2110–2119 (2018)

16. Rong, Y., Huang, W., Xu, T., Huang, J.: DropEdge: towards deep graph convolutional networks on node classification. In: International Conference on Learning Representations (2019)

17. Rozemberczki, B., Allen, C., Sarkar, R.: Multi-scale attributed node embedding. arXiv preprint arXiv:1909.13021 (2019)

18. Sen, P., Namata, G., Bilgic, M., Getoor, L., Galligher, B., Eliassi-Rad, T.: Collective classification in network data. AI Mag. **29**(3), 93–93 (2008)

19. Shang, J., Xiao, C., Ma, T., Li, H., Sun, J.: GAMNet: graph augmented memory networks for recommending medication combination. In: Proceedings of the 33rd AAAI Conference on Artificial Intelligence, vol. 33, pp. 1126–1133 (2019)

20. Thekumparampil, K.K., Wang, C., Oh, S., Li, L.J.: Attention-based graph neural network for semi-supervised learning. arXiv preprint arXiv:1803.03735 (2018)

21. Veličković, P., Cucurull, G., Casanova, A., Romero, A., Lio, P., Bengio, Y.: Graph attention networks. In: Proceedings of the 7th International Conference on Learning Representations (2018)

22. Xu, K., Li, C., Tian, Y., Sonobe, T., Kawarabayashi, K., Jegelka, S.: Representation learning on graphs with jumping knowledge networks. arXiv preprint arXiv:1806.03536 (2018)

23. Yang, Z., Cohen, W., Salakhudinov, R.: Revisiting semi-supervised learning with graph embeddings. In: International Conference on Machine Learning, pp. 40–48. PMLR (2016)

24. Zhao, L., Peng, X., Tian, Y., Kapadia, M., Metaxas, D.N.: Semantic graph convolutional networks for 3d human pose regression. In: Proceedings of the IEEE Conference on Computer Vision and Pattern Recognition, pp. 3425–3435 (2019)

25. Zhu, H., et al.: Bilinear graph neural network with neighbor interactions. In: Proceedings of the 29th International Joint Conference on Artificial Intelligence, vol. 5 (2020)

Hierarchical Learning of Dependent Concepts for Human Activity Recognition

Aomar Osmani[1], Massinissa Hamidi[1(✉)], and Pegah Alizadeh[2]

[1] LIPN-UMR CNRS 7030, Univ. Sorbonne Paris Nord, Villetaneuse, France
{ao,hamidi}@lipn.univ-paris13.fr
[2] Léonard de Vinci Pôle Universitaire, Research Center,
92 916 Paris, La Défense, France
pegah.alizadeh@devinci.fr

Abstract. In multi-class classification tasks, like human activity recognition, it is often assumed that classes are separable. In real applications, this assumption becomes strong and generates inconsistencies. Besides, the most commonly used approach is to learn classes one-by-one against the others. This computational simplification principle introduces strong inductive biases on the learned theories. In fact, the natural connections among some classes, and not others, deserve to be taken into account. In this paper, we show that the organization of overlapping classes (multiple inheritances) into hierarchies considerably improves classification performances. This is particularly true in the case of activity recognition tasks featured in the SHL dataset. After theoretically showing the exponential complexity of possible class hierarchies, we propose an approach based on transfer affinity among the classes to determine an optimal hierarchy for the learning process. Extensive experiments show improved performances and a reduction in the number of examples needed to learn.

Keywords: Activity recognition · Dependent concepts · Meta-modeling

1 Introduction

Many real-world applications considered in machine learning exhibit dependencies among the various to-be-learned concepts (or classes) [6,17]. This is particularly the case in human activity recognition from wearable sensor deployments which constitutes the main focus of our paper. This problem is two-folds: the high volume of accumulated data and the criteria selection optimization. For instance, are the criteria used to distinguish between the activities (concepts) *running* and *walking* the same as those used to distinguish between *driving a car* and *being in a bus*? what about distinguishing each individual activity against the remaining ones taken as a whole? Similarly, during the annotation process, when should someone consider that *walking* at a higher pace corresponds actually to *running*? These questions naturally arise in the case of the SHL dataset [7] which

© Springer Nature Switzerland AG 2021
K. Karlapalem et al. (Eds.): PAKDD 2021, LNAI 12713, pp. 79–92, 2021.
https://doi.org/10.1007/978-3-030-75765-6_7

exhibits such dependencies. The considered activities in this dataset are difficult to separate due to the existence of many overlaps among certain activities. Some of the important causes for these overlaps are: (1) the on-body sensors deployments featured by this dataset, due to sensors coverage overlaps, tend to capture movements that are not necessarily related to a unique activity. Authors in [8], for example, have exhibited such overlaps; (2) The difficulty of data annotation during data collection conducted in real-world conditions. For instance, the annotation issues can include the time-shift of a label with respect to the activity [19], as well as wrong or missing labels [13]. Similarly, long lines of research in computer vision [20] and time-series analysis [13,19] raised these issues which hinder the development and large-scale adoption of these applications.

To solve these problems, we propose an original approach for structuring the considered concepts into hierarchies in a way that very similar concepts are grouped together and tackled by specialized classifiers. The idea is that classifications at different levels of the hierarchy may rely on different features, or different combinations of the same features [27]. Indeed, many real-world classification problems are naturally cast as hierarchical classification problems [1,24,25,27]. A work on the semantic relationships among the categories in a hierarchical structure shows that they are usually of the type *generalization-specialization* [27]. In other words, the lower-level categories are supposed to have the same general properties as the higher-level categories plus additional more specific properties. The problem at hand is twice difficult as we have to, first, find the most appropriate hierarchical structure and, second, find optimal learners assigned to the nodes of the hierarchical structure.

We propose a data-driven approach to structure the considered concepts in a bottom-up approach. We start by computing the affinities and dependencies that exist among the concepts and fuse hierarchically the closest concepts with each other. We leverage for this a powerful technique based on transfer which showed interesting empirical properties in various domains [14,26]. Taking a bottom-up approach allows us to leverage learning the complete hierarchy (including the classifiers assigned to each non-leaf node) incrementally by reusing what was learned on the way. Our contributions are as follows: (1) we propose a theoretical calculation for computing the total number of tree hierarchical combinations (the search space for the optimal solution) based on the given number of concepts; (2) we propose an approach based on transfer affinity to determine an optimal organization of the concepts that improves both learning performances and accelerates the learning process; (3) extensive experiments show the effectiveness of organizing the learning process. We noticeably get a substantial improvement of recognition performances over a baseline which uses a flat classification setting; (4) we perform a comprehensive comparative analysis of the various stages of our approach which raises interesting questions about concept dependencies and the required amount of supervision.

2   Problem Statement

In this section, we briefly review the problem of hierarchical structuring of the concepts in terms of formulation and background. We then provide a complexity analysis of the problem size and its search space.

2.1   Problem Formulation and Background

Let $\mathcal{X} \subset \mathbb{R}^n$ be the inputs vector[1] and let $\mathcal{C}$ be the set of atomic concepts (or labels) to learn. The main idea of this paper comes from the fact that the concepts to be learned are not totally independent, thus grouping some concepts to learn them against the others using implicit biases considerably improves the quality of learning for each concept. The main problem is to find the best structure of concepts groups to be learned in order to optimize the learning of each atomic concept. For this we follow the three dimensions setting defined in [10], and we consider: (1) single-label classification as opposed to multi-label classification; (2) the type of hierarchy (or structure) to be trees as opposed to directed acyclic graphs; (3) instances that have to be classified into leafs, i.e. mandatory leaf node prediction [17], as opposed to the setting where instances can be classified into any node of the hierarchy (early stopping).

A tree hierarchy organizes the class labels into a tree-like structure to represent a kind of "IS-A" relationship between labels. Specifically, [10] points out that the properties of the "IS-A" relationship can be described as asymmetry, anti-reflexivity and transitivity [17]. We define a tree as a pair $(\mathcal{C}, \prec)$, where $\mathcal{C}$ is the set of class labels and "$\prec$" denotes the "IS-A" relationship.

Let $\{(x_1, c_1), \ldots, (x_N, c_N)\} \overset{i.i.d.}{\sim} X, C$ be a set of training examples, where X and C are two random variables taking values in $\mathcal{X} \times \mathcal{C}$, respectively. Each $x_k \in \mathcal{X}$ and each $c_k \in \mathcal{C}$. Our goal is to learn a classification function $f : \mathcal{X} \to \mathcal{C}$ that attains a small classification error. In this paper, we associate each node i with a classifier $\mathcal{M}_i$, and focus on classifiers $f(x)$ that are parameterized by $\mathcal{M}_1, \ldots, \mathcal{M}_m$ through the following recursive procedure [27] (check Fig. 2):

$$f(x) = \begin{cases} \textbf{initialize } i := 0 \\ \textbf{while } (Child(i) \text{ is not empty}) \quad i := \text{argmax}_{j \in Child(i)} \mathcal{M}_j(x) \\ \textbf{return } i \quad \%Child(i) \text{ is the set of children for the node } i \end{cases} \quad (1)$$

In the case of the SHL dataset, for instance, learning *train* and *subway* or *car* and *bus* before learning each concept alone gives better results. As an advantage, considering these classes paired together as opposed to the flat classification setting leads to significant degradation of recognition performances as demonstrated in some works around the SHL dataset [23]. In contrast, organizing the various concepts into a tree-like structure, inspired by domain expertise, demonstrated

---

[1] In our case, we select several body-motion modalities to be included in our experiments, among the 16 input modalities of the original dataset: *accelerometer, gyroscope*, etc. Segmentation and processing details are detailed in experimental part.

significant gains in terms of recognition performances in the context of the SHL challenge [12] and activity recognition in general [15,16].

Designing such structures is of utmost importance but hard because it involves optimizing the structure as well as learning the weights of the classifiers attached to the nodes of that structure (see Sect. 2.2). Our goal is then to determine an optimal structure of classes that can facilitate (improve and accelerate) learning of the whole concepts.

2.2 Search Space Size: Complexity Analysis

A naive approach is to generate the lattice structure of concepts groups and to choose the tree hierarchies which give the best accuracy of atomic concepts. In practice, this is not doable because of the exponential (in the number of leaf nodes) number of possible trees. We propose a recurrence relation involving binomial coefficients for calculating the total number of tree hierarchies for K different concepts (class labels).

Example 1. Assume we have 3 various concepts, and we are interested in counting the total number of hierarchies for classifying these concepts. We consider that we have three classes namely c_1, c_2 and c_3, there exist 4 different tree hierarchies for learning the classification problem as following: (1) $(c_1c_2c_3)$ the tree has one level and the learning process takes one step. Three concepts are learned while each concept is learned separately from the others (flat classification), (2) $((c_1c_2)c_3)$ the tree has two levels and the learning process takes two steps: at the first level, it learns two concepts (atomic c_3 and two atomics c_1 and c_2 together). At the second level it learns separately the two joined concepts c_1 and c_2 of the first level, etc. and (3) $(c_1(c_2\ c_3))$ and (4) $((c_1c_3)c_2)$.

Theorem 1. *Let $L(K)$ be the total number of trees for the given K number of concepts. The total number of trees for $K+1$ concepts satisfies the following recurrence relation:* $L(K+1) = \binom{K}{K-1}L(K)L(1) + 2\sum_{i=0}^{K-2}\binom{K}{i}L(i+1)L(K-i)$. *(See Appendix A in the supplementary material for complete proof).*

3 Proposed Approach

Our goals are to: (i) organize the considered concepts into hierarchies such that the learning process accounts for the dependencies existed among these concepts; (ii) characterize optimal classifiers that are associated to each non-leaf node of the hierarchies. Structuring the concepts can be performed using two different approaches: a **top-down** approach where we seek to decompose the learning process; and a **bottom-up** approach where the specialized models are grouped together based on their affinities. Our approach takes the latter direction and constructs hierarchies based on the similarities between concepts. This is because, an hierarchical approach as a bottom-up method is efficient in the case of high volume SHL data-sets. In this section, we detail the different parts of our approach which are illustrated in Fig. 1. In the rest of this section, we introduce the three stages of our approach in detail: *Concept similarity analysis, Hierarchy derivation,* and *Hierarchy refinement.*

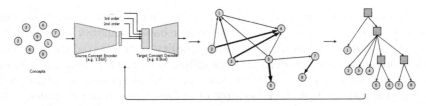

Fig. 1. Our solution involves several repetitions of 3 main steps: (1) Concept similarity analysis: encoders are trained to output, for each source concept, an appropriate representation which is then fine-tuned to serve target concepts. Affinity scores are depicted by the arrows between concepts (the thicker the arrow, the higher the affinity score). (2) Hierarchy derivation: based on the obtained affinity scores, a hierarchy is derived using an agglomerate approach. (3) Hierarchy refinement: each non-leaf node of the derived hierarchy is assigned with a model that encompasses the appropriate representation as well as an ERM which is optimized to separate the considered concepts.

3.1   Concept Similarity (Affinity) Analysis

In our **bottom-up** approach we leverage transferability and dependency among concepts as a measure of similarity. Besides the nice empirical properties of this measure (explained in the *Properties* paragraph below), the argument behind it is reuse what has been learned so far at the lower levels of the hierarchies. Indeed, we leverage the models that we learned during this step and use them with few additional adjustments in the final hierarchical learning setting.

Transfer-Based Affinity. Given the set of concepts $\mathcal{C}$, we compute during this step an affinity matrix that captures the notion of transferability and similarity, among the concepts. For this, we first compute for each concept $c_i \in \mathcal{C}$ an encoder $f_\theta^{c_i}$ (parameterized by θ) that learns to map the c_i labeled inputs, to $\mathcal{Z}_{c_i}$. Learning the encoder's parameters consists in minimizing the reconstruction error, satisfying the following optimization [22]: $\operatorname{argmin}_{\theta,\theta'} \mathbb{E}_{x,c \sim X, C|c=c_i} \mathcal{L}(g_{\theta'}^{c_i}(f_\theta^{c_i}(x)), x)$, where $g_{\theta'}^{c_i}$ is a decoder (parameterized by θ') which maps back the learned representation into the original inputs space. We propose to leverage the learned encoder, for a given concept c_i, to compute affinities with other concepts via fine-tuning of the learned representation. Precisely, we fine-tune the encoder $f_{c_i}^\theta$ to account for a target concept $c_j \in \mathcal{C}$. This process consists, similarly, in minimizing the reconstruction error, however rather than using the decoder $g_{\theta'}^{c_i}$ learned above, we design a genuine decoder $g_{\theta'}^{c_j}$ that we learn from the scratch. The corresponding objective function is $\operatorname{argmin}_{\theta,\theta'} \mathbb{E}_{x,c \sim X, C|c=c_j} \mathcal{L}(g_{\theta'}^{c_j}(f_\theta^{c_i}(x)), x)$. We use the performance of this step as a *similarity score* from c_i to c_j which we denote by $p_{c_i \to c_j} \in [0,1]$. We refer to the number of examples belonging to the concept c_j used during fine-tuning as the *supervision budget*, denoted as b, which is used to index a given measure of similarity. It allows us to have an additional indicator as to the similarity between the considered concepts. The final similarity score is computed as $\frac{\alpha \cdot p_{c_i \to c_j} + \beta \cdot b}{\alpha + \beta}$. We set α and β to be equal to $\frac{1}{2}$.

Properties. In many applications, e.g. computer-vision [26] and natural language processing [14], several variants of the transfer-based similarity measure have been shown empirically to improve (i) the **quality** of transferred models (wins against fully supervised models), (ii) the **gains**, i.e. win rate against a network trained from scratch using the same training data as transfer networks', and more importantly (iii) the **universality** of the resulting structure. Indeed, the affinities based on transferability are stable despite the variations of a big corpus of hyperparameters. We provide empirical evidence (Sect. 4.2) of the appropriateness of the transfer-based affinity measure for the separability of the similar concepts and the difficulty to separate concepts that exhibit low similarity scores.

3.2   Hierarchy Derivation

Given the set of *affinity scores* obtained previously, we derive the most appropriate hierarchy, following an agglomerative clustering method combined with some additional constraints. The agglomerative clustering method proceeds by a series of successive fusions of the concepts into groups and results in a structure represented by a two-dimensional diagram known as a dendrogram. It works by (1) forming groups of concepts that are close enough and (2) updating the affinity scores based on the newly formed groups. This process is defined by the recurrence formula proposed by [11]. If defines a distance between a group of concepts (k) and a group formed by fusing i and j groups (ij) as $d_{k(ij)} = \alpha_i d_{ki} + \alpha_j d_{kj} + \beta d_{ij} + \gamma |d_{ki} - d_{kj}|$, where d_{ij} is the distance between two groups i and j. By varying the parameter values $\alpha_i, \alpha_j, \beta$, and γ, we expect to get clustering schemes with various characteristics.

In addition to the above updating process, we propose additional constraints to refine further the hierarchy derivation stage. Given the dendrogram produced by the agglomerative method above, we define an *affinity threshold* τ such that if the distance at a given node is $d_{ij} \geq \tau$, then we merge the nodes to form a unique subtree. In addition, as we keep track of the quantities of data used to train and fine-tune the encoders during the transfer-based affinity analysis stage, this indicator is exploited to inform us as to which nodes to merge. Let $\mathcal{T}$ be the derived hierarchy (tree) and let t indexes the non-leaf or internal nodes. The leafs of the hierarchy correspond to the considered concepts. For any non-leaf node t, we associate a model $\mathcal{M}_t$ that encompasses (1) an encoder (denoted in the following simply by $\mathcal{Z}_t$ in order to focus on the representation) that maps inputs X to representations $\mathcal{Z}_t$ and (2) an ERM (Empirical Risk Minimizer) [21] f_t (such as support vector machines SVMs) that outputs decision boundaries based on the representations produced by the encoder.

3.3   Hierarchy Refinement

After explaining the hierarchy derivation process, we will discuss: (1) which representations are used in each individual model; and (2) how each individual model (including the representation and the ERM weights) is adjusted to account for both the local errors and also those of the hierarchy as a whole.

Which Representations to Use? The question discussed here is related to the encoders to be used in each non-leaf node. For any non-leaf node t we distinguish two cases: (i) all its children are leafs; (ii) it has at least one non-leaf node. In the first case, the final considered ERM representation, associated with the non-leaf node, is the representation learned in the concept affinity analysis step (first-order transfer-based affinity). In the second case, we can either fuse the nodes (for example, in a case of classification between 3 concepts, we get all 3 together rather than, first $\{1\}$ vs. $\{2,3\}$, then $\{2\}$ vs. $\{3\}$), or keep them as they are and leverage the affinities based on higher-order transfer where, rather than accounting for a unique target concept, the representation is then fine-tuned. Figure 2 illustrates how transfers are performed between non-leaf nodes models. We index the models with the encoder $\mathcal{M}_{[z_i]}$. In the case of higher-order transfer, the models are indexed using all concepts involved in the transfer, i.e. $\mathcal{M}_{[z_{i,j,\dots}]}$.

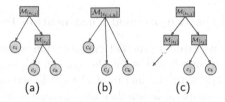

(a)   (b)   (c)

Fig. 2. Transfers are performed between non-leaf nodes models. The hierarchy in (a) can be kept as they are merged to form the hierarchy in (b). (b): a high-order transfer between the concepts c_i, c_j, and c_k is performed. (c): no transfers can be made.

Adjusting Models Weights. Classifiers are trained to output a hypothesis based on the most appropriate representations learned earlier. Given the encoder (representation) assigned to any non-leaf node t, we select a classifier $\hat{f} := \operatorname{argmin}_{f \in \mathcal{H}} \hat{R}(f, \mathcal{Z}_t)$ where $\hat{R}(f, \mathcal{Z}_t) := \frac{1}{M} \sum_{x,c \sim X, C | c \in Child(t)} \mathbb{E}_{z \sim \mathcal{Z}_t | x} [\mathcal{L}(c, f(z))]$ and $\mathcal{H}$ is the hypothesis space. Models are adjusted to account for local errors as well as for global errors related to the hierarchy as a whole. In the first case, the loss is defined as the traditional hinge loss used in SVMs which is intended to adjust the weights of the classifiers that have only children leaves. In the second case, we use a loss that encourages the models to leverage orthogonal representations (between children and parent nodes) [27].

4   Experiments and Results

Empirical evaluation of our approach are performed on three steps: we evaluate classification performances in the hierarchical setting (Sect. 4.1); then, we evaluate the transfer-based affinity analysis step and the properties related to the separability of the considered concepts (Sect. 4.2); finally, we evaluate the derived hierarchies in terms of stability, performance, and agreement with their counterparts defined by domain experts (Sect. 4.3)[2]. Training details can be found in Appendix B and evaluation metrics are detailed in Appendix C.

SHL Dataset [7]. It is a highly versatile and precisely annotated dataset dedicated to mobility-related human activity recognition. In contrast to related representative datasets like [2], the SHL dataset (26.43 GB) provides , simultaneously, multimodal and multilocation locomotion data recorded in real-life settings. Among the 16 modalities of the original dataset, we select the body-motion modalities including: *accelerometer, gyroscope, magnetometer, linear acceleration, orientation, gravity,* and *ambient pressure*. This makes the data set suitable for a wide range of applications and in particular transportation recognition concerned with this paper. From the 8 primary categories of transportation, we are selected: *1:Still, 2:Walk, 3:Run, 4:Bike, 5:Car, 6:Bus, 7:Train,* and *8:Subway (Tube)*.

4.1 Evaluation of the Hierarchical Classification Performances

In these experiments, we evaluate the flat classification setting using neural networks which constitute our baseline for the rest of the empirical evaluations. To compare our baseline with the hierarchical models, we make sure to get the same complexity, i.e. comparable number of parameters as the largest hierarchies including the weights of the encoders and those of the ERMs. We also use Bayesian optimization based on Gaussian processes as surrogate models to select the optimal hyperparameters of the baseline model [9,18]. More details about the baseline and its hyperparameters are available in the code repository [9].

Per-Node Performances. Figure 3 shows the resulting per-node performances, i.e. how accurately the models associated with the non-leaf nodes can predict the correct subcategory averaged over the entire derived hierarchies. The nodes are ranked according to the obtained per-node performance (top 10 nodes are shown) and accompanied by their appearance frequency. It is worth noticing that the concept 1:*still* learned alone against the rest of the concepts (first bar) achieves the highest gains in terms of recognition performances while the appearance frequency of this learning configuration is high (more than 60 times). We see also that the concepts 4:*bike*, 5:*car*, and 6:*bus* grouped together (5th bar) occur very often in the derived hierarchies (80 times) which is accompanied by fairly significant performance gains ($5.09 \pm 0.3\%$). At the same time, as expected, we see that the appearance frequency gets into a plateau starting from the 6th bar (which lasts after the 10th bar). This suggests that the most influential nodes are often exhibited by our approach.

Per-Concept Performances. We further ensure that the performance improvements we get at the node levels are reflected at the concept level. Experimental

---

[2] Software package and code to reproduce empirical results are publicly available at https://github.com/sensor-rich/hierarchicalSHL.

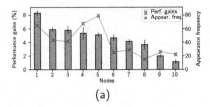
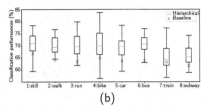

(a)   (b)

Fig. 3. (a) Per-node performance gains, averaged over the entire derived architectures (similar nodes are grouped and their performances are averaged). The appearance frequency of the nodes is also illustrated. Each bar represents the gained accuracy of each node in our hierarchical approach. For example, the 8th bar corresponds to the concepts 2:*walk*-3:*run*-4:*bike* grouped together. (b) Recognition performances of each individual concept, averaged over the entire derived hierarchies. For reference, the recognition performances of the baseline model are also shown.

results show the recognition performances of each concept, averaged over the whole hierarchies derived using our proposed approach. We indeed observe that there are significant improvements for each individual concept over the baseline (flat classification setting). We observe that again 1:*still* has the highest classification rate ($72.32 \pm 3.45\%$) and an improvement of 5 points over the baseline. Concept 6:*bus* also exhibits a roughly similar trend. On the other hand, concept 7:*train* has the least gains ($64.43 \pm 4.45\%$) with no significant improvement over the baseline. Concept 8:*subway* exhibits the same behavior suggesting that there are undesirable effects that stem from the definition of these two concepts.

4.2 Evaluation of the Affinity Analysis Stage

These experiments evaluate the proposed transfer-based affinity measure. We assess, the separability of the concepts depending on their similarity score (for both the transfer-affinity and supervision budget) and the learned representation.

Appropriateness of the Transfer-Based Affinity Measure. We reviewed above the nice properties of the transfer-based measure especially the universality and stability of the resulting affinity structure. The question that arises is related to the separability of the concepts that are grouped together. Are the obtained representations, are optimal for the final ERMs used for the classification? This is what we investigate here. Figure 4b shows the decision boundaries generated by the considered ERMs which are provided with the learned representations of two concepts. The first case (top right), exhibits a low-affinity score, and the second case (bottom right) shows a high-affinity score. In the first case, the boundaries are unable to separate the two concepts while it gets a fairly distinct frontier.

Impact on the ERMs' Decision Boundaries. We train different models with various learned representations in order to investigate the effect of the initial affinities

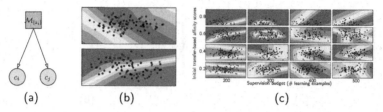

(a)   (b)   (c)

Fig. 4. (a) Non-leaf node grouping concepts c_i and c_j. (b) Decision boundaries generated by the ERM of the non-leaf node using an encoder (representation) fine-tuned to account for (top) the case where c_i and c_j are dissimilar (low-affinity score) and (bottom) the case where c_i and c_j are similar (high-affinity score). (c) Decision boundaries obtained by SVM-based classifiers trained on the representations $\mathcal{Z}_t$ as a function of the distance between the concepts (y-axis) and the supervision budget (x-axis).

(obtained solely with a set of 100 learning examples) and the supervision budget (additional learning examples used to fine-tune the obtained representation) on the classification performances of the ERMs associated with the non-leaf nodes of our hierarchies. Figure 4c shows the decision boundaries generated by various models as a function of the distance between the concepts (y-axis) and the supervision budget (x-axis). Increasing the supervision budget to some larger extents (more than ∼300 examples) results in a substantial decrease in classification performances of the ERMs. This suggests that, although our initial affinity scores are decisive (e.g. 0.8), the supervision budget is tightly linked to generalization. This shows that a trade-off (controlled by the supervision budget) between separability and initial affinities arises when we seek to group concepts together. In other words, the important question is whether to increase the supervision budget indefinitely (in the limits of available learning examples) in order to find the most appropriate concepts to fuse with, while expecting good separability.

4.3   Universality and Stability

We demonstrated in the previous section the appropriateness of the transfer-based affinity measure to provide distance between concepts as well as the existence of a trade-off between concepts separability and their initial affinities. Here we evaluate the **universality** of the derived hierarchies as well as their **stability** during adaptation with respect to our hyperparameters (affinity threshold and supervision budget). We compare the derived hierarchies with their domain experts-defined counterparts, as well as those obtained via a random sampling process. Figure 5 shows some of the hierarchies defined by the domain experts (first row) and sampled using the random sampling process. For example, the hierarchy depicted in Fig. 5d corresponds to a split between static (1:*still*, 5:*car*, 6:*bus*, 7:*train*, 8:*subway*) and dynamic (2:*walk*, 3:*run*, 4:*bike*) activities. The difference between the hierarchies depicted in Fig. 5a and 5b is related to 4:*bike* activity which is linked first to 2:*walk* and 3:*run* then to 5:*car* and 6:*bus*. A possible interpretation is that in the first case, biking is considered as "on feet"

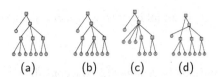

(a)   (b)   (c)   (d)

Fig. 5. Examples of hierarchies: (a) defined via domain expertise, (b-c) derived using our approach, and (d) randomly sampled. Concepts 1—8 from left to right.

Table 1. Summary of the recognition performances obtained with our proposed approach compared to randomly sampled and expert-defined hierarchies.

Method	Agree	Perf. avg.± std.
Expertise	–	72.32 ± 0.17
Random	0.32	48.17 ± 5.76
Proposed	0.77	75.92 ± 1.13

activity while in the second case as "on wheels" activity. What we observed is that the derived hierarchies tend to converge towards the expert-defined ones.

We compare the derived hierarchies in terms of their level of agreement. We use for this assessment, the Cohen's kappa coefficient [4] which measures the agreement between two raters. The first column of Table 1 provides the obtained coefficients. We also compare the average recognition performance of the derived hierarchies (second column of Table 1). In terms of stability, as we vary the design choices (hyperparameters), defined in our approach, we found that the affinity threshold has a substantial impact on our results with many adjustments involved (12 hierarchy adjustments on avg.) whereas the supervision budget has a slight effect, which confirms the observations in Sect. 4.2.

5   Conclusion and Future Work

This paper proposes an approach for organizing the learning process of dependent concepts in the case of human activity recognition. We first determine a suitable structure for the concepts according to a transfer affinity-based measure. We then characterize optimal representations and classifiers which are then refined to account for both local and global errors. We provide theoretical bounds for the problem and empirically show that using our approach we are able to improve the performances and robustness of activity recognition models over a flat classification baseline. In addition to supporting the necessity of organizing concepts learning, our experiments raise interesting questions for future work. Noticeably, Sect. 4.2 asks what is the optimal amount of supervision for deriving the hierarchies. Another future work is to study different approaches for searching and exploring the search space of different hierarchical types (lattices, etc.).

Appendix A

Proof. Theorem 1. It can be explained by observing that, for $K + 1$ concepts containing K existed concepts $c_1, \cdots c_K$ and a new added concept γ, we can produce the first level trees combinations as below. Notice that each atomic element o can be one of the $c_1, \cdots c_K$ concepts. In order to compute the total number of trees combinations, we show what is the number of tree combinations by assigning the K concepts to each item:

- $(\gamma(\overbrace{o \cdots o}^{K\text{concepts}}))$: the number of trees combinations by taking the concept labels into the account are: $\binom{K}{0}L(1) \times 2 \times L(K)$; the reason for multiplying the number of trees combinations for K concepts to 2 is because while the left side contains an atomic γ concept, there are two choices for the right side of the tree in the first level: either we compute the total number of trees for K concepts from the first level or we keep the first level as a $\overbrace{o \cdots o}^{K\text{concepts}}$ atomics and keep all K concepts together, then continue the number of K trees combinations from the second level of the tree.

- $((\gamma o)(\overbrace{o \cdots o}^{K-1\text{concepts}}))$: similar to the previous part we have $\binom{K}{1}L(2) \times 2 \times L(K-1)$ trees combinations by taking the concepts labels into the account. $\binom{K}{1}$ indicates the number of combinations for choosing a concept from the K concept and put it with the new concept separately. While $L(2)$ is the number of trees combinations for the left side of tree separated with the new concept γ.

- $((\gamma oo)(\overbrace{o \cdots o}^{K-2\text{concepts}})), \cdots$

- $((\gamma \overbrace{o \cdots o}^{K-1\text{concepts}})o)$: $\binom{K}{K-1}L(K)L(1)$ in this special part, we follow the same formula except the single concept in the right side has only one possible combination in the first level equal to $L(1)$.

All in all, the sum of these items calculates the total number of tree hierarchies for $K+1$ concepts.

The first few number of total number of trees combinations for $1, 2, 3, 4, 5, 6, 7, 8, 9, 10, \cdots$ concepts are: 1, 1, 4, 26, 236, 2752, 39208, 660032, 12818912, 282137824, $\cdots$. In the case of the SHL dataset that we use in the empirical evaluation, we have 8 different concepts and thus, the number of different types of hierarchies for this case is $L(8) = 660,032$.

Appendix B Training Details

We use Tensorflow for building the encoders/decoders. We construct encoders by stacking Conv1d/ReLU/MaxPool blocks. These blocks are followed by a Fully Connected/ReLU layers. Encoders performance estimation is based on the validation loss and is framed as a sequence classification problem. As a preprocessing step, annotated input streams from the huge SHL dataset are segmented into sequences of 6000 samples which correspond to a duration of 1 min. given a sampling rate 100 Hz. For weight optimization, we use stochastic gradient descent with Nesterov momentum of 0.9 and a learning-rate of 0.1 for a minimum of 12 epochs (we stop training if there is no improvement). Weight decay is set to 0.0001. Furthermore, to make the neural networks more stable, we use batch normalization on top of each convolutional layer. We use SVMs as our ERMs in the derived hierarchies.

Appendix C Evaluation Metrics

In hierarchical classification settings, the hierarchical structure is important and should be taken into account during model evaluation [17]. Various measures that account for the hierarchical structure of the learning process have been studied in the literature. They can be categorized into: distance-based; depth-dependent; semantics-based; and hierarchy-based measures. Each one is displaying advantages and disadvantages depending on the characteristics of the considered structure [5]. In our experiments, we use the *H-loss*, a hierarchy-based measure defined in [3]. This measure captures the intuition that *"whenever a classification mistake is made on a node of the taxonomy, then no loss should be charged for any additional mistake occurring in the sub-tree of that node."* $\ell_H(\hat{y}, y) = \sum_{i=1}^{N} \{\hat{y}_i \neq y_i \wedge \hat{y}_j = y_j, j \in Anc(i)\}$, where $\hat{y} = (\hat{y}_1, \cdots \hat{y}_N)$ is the predicted labels, $y = (y_1, \cdots y_N)$ is the true labels, and $Anc(i)$ is the set of ancestors for the node i.

References

1. Cai, L., Hofmann, T.: Hierarchical document categorization with support vector machines. In: CIKM, pp. 78–87 (2004)
2. Carpineti, C., et al.: Custom dual transportation mode detection by smartphone devices exploiting sensor diversity. In: PerCom wksh, pp. 367–372. IEEE (2018)
3. Cesa-Bianchi, N., Gentile, C., Zaniboni, L.: Incremental algorithms for hierarchical classification. JMLR **7**, 31–54 (2006)
4. Cohen, J.: A coefficient of agreement for nominal scales. Educ. Psychol. Measur. **20**(1), 37–46 (1960)
5. Costa, E., Lorena, A., Carvalho, A., Freitas, A.: A review of performance evaluation measures for hierarchical classifiers. In: Evaluation Methods for machine Learning II: papers from the AAAI-2007 Workshop, pp. 1–6 (2007)
6. Essaidi, M., Osmani, A., Rouveirol, C.: Learning dependent-concepts in ilp: Application to model-driven data warehouses. In: ILP, pp. 151–172 (2015)
7. Gjoreski, H., et al.: The university of sussex-huawei locomotion and transportation dataset for multimodal analytics with mobile devices. IEEE Access **6**, 42592-42604 (2018)
8. Hamidi, M., Osmani, A.: Data generation process modeling for activity recognition. In: ECML-PKDD. Springer (2020)
9. Hamidi, M., Osmani, A., Alizadeh, P.: A multi-view architecture for the shl challenge. In: UbiComp/ISWC Adjunct, pp. 317–322 (2020)
10. Kosmopoulos, A., Partalas, I., Gaussier, E., Paliouras, G., Androutsopoulos, I.: Evaluation measures for hierarchical classification: a unified view and novel approaches. Data Min. Knowl. Disc. **29**(3), 820–865 (2014). https://doi.org/10.1007/s10618-014-0382-x

11. Lance, G.N., Williams, W.T.: A general theory of classificatory sorting strategies: 1. hierarchical systems. Comput. J. **9**(4), 373–380 (1967)
12. Nakamura, Y., et al.: Multi-stage activity inference for locomotion and transportation analytics of mobile users. In: UbiComp/ISWC, pp. 1579–1588 (2018)
13. Nguyen-Dinh, L.V., Calatroni, A., Tröster, G.: Robust online gesture recognition with crowdsourced annotations. JMLR **15**(1), 3187–3220 (2014)
14. Peters, M.E., Ruder, S., Smith, N.A.: To tune or not to tune? adapting pretrained representations to diverse tasks. arXiv preprint arXiv:1903.05987 (2019)
15. Samie, F., Bauer, L., Henkel, J.: Hierarchical classification for constrained IoT devices: a case study on human activity recognition. IEEE IoT J. **7**(9), 8287-8295 (2020)
16. Scheurer, S., et al.: Using domain knowledge for interpretable and competitive multi-class human activity recognition. Sensors **20**(4), 1208 (2020)
17. Silla, C.N., Freitas, A.A.: A survey of hierarchical classification across different application domains. Data Min. Knowl. Disc. **22**(1–2), 31–72 (2011)
18. Snoek, J., Larochelle, H., Adams, R.P.: Practical bayesian optimization of machine learning algorithms. In: NIPS, pp. 2951–2959 (2012)
19. Stikic, M., Schiele, B.: Activity recognition from sparsely labeled data using multi-instance learning. In: Choudhury, T., Quigley, A., Strang, T., Suginuma, K. (eds.) LoCA 2009. LNCS, vol. 5561, pp. 156–173. Springer, Heidelberg (2009). https://doi.org/10.1007/978-3-642-01721-6_10
20. Taran, V., Gordienko, Y., Rokovyi, A., Alienin, O., Stirenko, S.: Impact of ground truth annotation quality on performance of semantic image segmentation of traffic conditions. In: Hu, Z., Petoukhov, S., Dychka, I., He, M. (eds.) ICCSEEA 2019. AISC, vol. 938, pp. 183–193. Springer, Cham (2020). https://doi.org/10.1007/978-3-030-16621-2_17
21. Vapnik, V.: Principles of risk minimization for learning theory. In: NIPS (1992)
22. Vincent, P., et al.: Stacked denoising autoencoders: Learning useful representations in a deep network with a local denoising criterion. JMLR **11**(12), (2010)
23. Wang, L., et al.: Summary of the sussex-huawei locomotion-transportation recognition challenge. In: UbiComp/ISWC, pp. 1521–1530 (2018)
24. Wehrmann, J., Cerri, R., Barros, R.: Hierarchical multi-label classification networks. In: ICML, pp. 5075–5084 (2018)
25. Yao, H., Wei, Y., Huang, J., Li, Z.: Hierarchically structured meta-learning. In: ICML, pp. 7045–7054 (2019)
26. Zamir, A.R., Sax, A., Shen, W., Guibas, L.J., Malik, J., Savarese, S.: Taskonomy: Disentangling task transfer learning. In: CVPR, pp. 3712–3722 (2018)
27. Zhou, D., Xiao, L., Wu, M.: Hierarchical classification via orthogonal transfer. In: ICML, pp. 801–808 (2011)

Improving Short Text Classification Using Context-Sensitive Representations and Content-Aware Extended Topic Knowledge

Zhihao Ye[1], Rui Wen[2], Xi Chen[2], Ye Liu[3], Ziheng Zhang[2], Zhiyong Li[1(✉)], Ke Nai[1], and Yefeng Zheng[2]

[1] Hunan University, Changsha, China
zhiyong.li@hnu.edu.cn
[2] Tencent, Jarvis Lab, Shenzhen, China
{ruiwen,jasonxchen,zihengzhang,yefengzheng}@tencent.com
[3] Sun Yat-sen University, Guangzhou, China

Abstract. Most existing short text classification models suffer from poor performance because of the information sparsity of short texts and the polysemous class-bearing words. To alleviate these issues, we propose a context-sensitive topic memory network (**cs-TMN**) by learning context-sensitive text representations and content-aware extended topic knowledge. Different from TMN that utilizes context-independent word embedding and extended topic knowledge, we further employ context-sensitive word embedding, comprised of local context representation and global context representation to alleviate the polysemous issue. Besides, extended topic knowledge matched by context-sensitive word embedding is proven content-aware in comparison with previous works. Empirical results demonstrate the effectiveness of our **cs-TMN**, outperforming state-of-the-art models on short text classification on four public datasets.

Keywords: Short text classification · Context-sensitive text representations · Topic knowledge

1 Introduction

Short text classification, widely applied to question answering, dialogue systems, sentiment analysis and others, is one of the most important tasks in natural language processing. Many models designed for text classification, like support vector machines (SVM) [27] and neural networks [10,11,29], have been proposed and achieved promising results, but these models inevitably underperform when being directly applied to the short text classification due to the information sparsity.

Recently, many novel methods have been proposed to classify short texts. On one hand, to alleviate the problem of polysemy, some researchers [20,21]

© Springer Nature Switzerland AG 2021
K. Karlapalem et al. (Eds.): PAKDD 2021, LNAI 12713, pp. 93–105, 2021.
https://doi.org/10.1007/978-3-030-75765-6_8

proposed to learn context-sensitive word embedding by leveraging local contextual information or global topic information. Nonetheless, these models are incapable of representing the interactions among the words, topics and contexts clearly, thereby under-utilizing topic knowledge. On the other hand, in order to solve the information sparsity of short text, some researchers [4,19] applied topic models to derive latent topics, and then employed topic knowledge as features to enrich the representations of short texts from extra large corpora.

More recently, topic memory network (TMN), proposed by [31], jointly explored topic inference and text classification with memory networks in an end-to-end manner. Their model achieved the state-of-the-art results on different short text datasets. This model, however, has two limitations. Firstly, it utilizes the context-independent word representation, leading to the issue of polysemous word confusion. Moreover, due to the polysemy of class-bearing words, the topic memory mechanism sometimes cannot match to the extended latent topic knowledge accurately.

In this paper, to address the aforementioned limitations of TMN, we develop a context-sensitive topic memory network (cs-TMN) and demonstrate that significant improvements can be achieved by using context-sensitive word representations. It can not only effectively address the polysemy of class-bearing words, but also help to match content-aware extended topic knowledge. Our cs-TMN first encodes the short text into local context representations via a self-attention mechanism [25] or bidirectional encoder representation from Transformers (BERT) [5]. Inspired by the success of neural topic model (NTM) [16], we employ it to capture the co-occurrence of words and text topic representation, thereby discovering latent topics. The context-sensitive word representations are then obtained by leveraging local context representation and the relevant global topic information mapping using a word-topic attention mechanism. Finally, cs-TMN employs context-sensitive text representation and a topic memory mechanism to match the content-aware extended topic knowledge. In other words, topic information is applied to cs-TMN in two aspects. One is to apply global topic information of text to help establish context-sensitive word embedding; the other is to apply content-aware topic knowledge as extended features of classification. The contributions of this paper can be summarized as follows:

(1) We propose a novel short text classification model that employs context-sensitive word embedding comprised of local context and global context representation.

(2) We demonstrate that context-sensitive word embeddings can alleviate the polysemy issue effectively and gain better extended topic knowledge for short texts.

(3) Our cs-TMN achieves state-of-the-art performance on four commonly used short text datasets and shows robustness across languages.

2   Framework Overview

In real-world scenarios, short texts suffer from information sparsity, and many class-bearing words being polysemous or ambiguous. For instance, in the

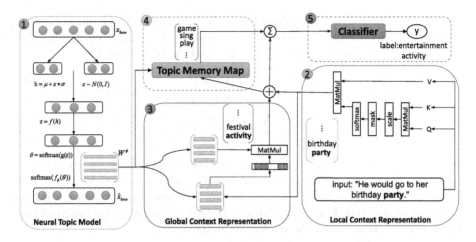

Fig. 1. Overview of cs-TMN consisting of five modules: 1) neural topic model, 2) local context representation, 3) global context representation, 4) extended topic memory map, and 5) the classifier.

sentence "He would go to her birthday party.", the word "party" may refer to a social event under the topic "activity", or a political organization under the topic "politics". In short text classification, due to the problem of polysemy and information sparsity, previous methods may classify this sentence as relating to political events rather than relating to entertainment activities. To address those issues, our cs-TMN firstly generates the context-sensitive word embedding which can express the specific meaning of polysemous words in a sentence more accurately. Moreover, cs-TMN matches the content-aware topic knowledge features with context-sensitive word embeddings. The overall framework is illustrated in Fig. 1.

2.1 Neural Topic Model

In cs-TMN, we utilize topic information from two aspects: the global topic information of words, which represents the global semantic information, and the extended features of texts, such as other topic words that are not in the original text but play an important role in the classification task. Specifically, following TMN, we employ a neural topic model (NTM) [16,22] to induce latent topics.

Different from the TMN, inspired by NTM-R [6], which achieves substantially higher topic coherence, the objective function of our NTM is defined as:

$$L_{NTM-R} = L_{NTM} + \lambda C \tag{1}$$

where L_{NTM} is the loss function of NTM and C is topic coherence regularization. Specifically, L_{NTM} is defined as:

$$L_{NTM} = D_{KL}(q(z)||p(z|x)) - E_{q(z)}[p(x|z)] \tag{2}$$

where $q(z)$ denotes a standard normal prior $N(0; I)$. Here, $p(z|x)$ and $p(x|z)$ are probabilities describing the encoding and decoding processes, respectively. The $D_{KL}(\cdot||\cdot)$ is the Kullback–Leibler divergence and the C is defined as:

$$F = (W^\phi E)^T \tag{3}$$

$$S = EF \tag{4}$$

$$C = \sum_i (S^T \odot W^\phi)_i \tag{5}$$

where $E \in \mathbb{R}^{|V| \times d}$ is the pre-trained word embedding matrix for the vocabulary, $F \in \mathbb{R}^{d \times T}$ is the W^ϕ-weighted centroid (topic) vector, and $S \in \mathbb{R}^{|V| \times T}$ is the cosine similarity matrix between word vectors and topic vectors. Here, d is the dimension of the embedding space. Due to the space limitation, we leave out the derivation details and refer the readers to [6,16].

2.2   Local Context Representation

We evaluate and compare two local context representations within the cs-TMN framework: the self-attention mechanism vs. BERT.

We apply self-attention [25] to obtain the local context representations of the input sentence. Formally, given an input text $X = x_0, x_1, ..., x_n$, where n is the text length, each hidden state in the r-th layer is constructed by attending to the states in the $(r-1)$-th layer, where the first layer is the word embedding layer. Specifically, the $(r-1)$-th layer $H^{r-1} \in \mathbb{R}^{n \times d}$ is first transformed into the queries $Q \in \mathbb{R}^{n \times d}$, the keys $K \in \mathbb{R}^{n \times d}$, and the values $A \in \mathbb{R}^{n \times d}$ with three separate weight matrices. The r-th layer is calculated as:

$$H^r = Attention(Q, K, A) = ATT(Q, K)A \tag{6}$$

where $ATT()$ is a dot-product attention model, defined as:

$$ATT(Q, K) = softmax(\frac{QK^T}{\sqrt{d}}) \tag{7}$$

where $\sqrt{d}$ is the scaling factor.

In addition, we also attempt to experiment with the state-of-the-art BERT model [5], to generate word vectors since BERT representation is expected to further enhance the performance of our cs-TMN. Specifically, we employ a pre-trained BERT model to predict text category, and we take the word vectors obtained by all BERT hidden layers as local context representation $L = l_0, l_1, ..., l_n$, which are taken as the context-sensitive representations.

2.3   Global Context Representation and Context-Sensitive Word Embedding

In order to take advantage of global topic information, which could disambiguate polysemous words, we employ a word-topic attention mechanism to match related topics. Specifically, we assume that after the local context representation module, we will obtain the local context representation of all n words, where n equals the length of the short text. For the global context g_i of each word, we have:

$$g_i = \sum_{k=1}^{T} \alpha_{ik} t_k \tag{8}$$

$$\alpha_{ik} = softmax(t_k l_i) \tag{9}$$

where t_k is vector representation of the k-th topic, i.e., the k-th row of topic-word weight matrix W^ϕ. The α_{ij} is the similarity of local context representation l_i and each latent topic.

After obtaining the global information of n words, we add the local context vector of word l_i and the global topic vector of word g_i:

$$c_i = l_i + g_i \tag{10}$$

where c_i is the context-sensitive word embedding of the word i.

2.4 Exploiting Content-Aware Topic Knowledge

We apply a topic memory mechanism [23,28] to map the content-aware topic knowledge as the extended features for classification. Specifically, after obtaining the topical-word weight matrix W^ϕ using NTM, we input this matrix into two ReLU-activated neural perceptrons and output two memory matrices, a source memory O and a target memory M. We first compute the match score between the k-th topic of source memory and the context-sensitive embedding of the i-th word as:

$$P_{k,i} = sigmoid(W^s con(O_k; U_i) + b^s) \tag{11}$$

where the $con(\cdot; \cdot)$ operation [4,8] denotes the concatenation of two matrices, $U = [c_0...c_i...c_n]$ is the embedded sentence X (in the word sequences form), and W^s and b^s are parameters to be learned. Then, we design the integrated memory weights as:

$$\varphi_k = \theta_k + \gamma \sum_i P_{k,i} \tag{12}$$

where γ is the pre-defined coefficient. Finally, we obtain the output representation $R_k = \varphi_k M_k$ of the topic memory mechanism and $R \in \mathbb{R}^{n \times d}$ can represent other topic words which are beneficial to text classification. The concatenation of R and U, i.e., the context-sensitive word sequence, further serves as classification features.

2.5   Classifier and Training

We use the convolutional neural network (CNN) as the final classifier. Specifically, after exploiting extended topic knowledge, the concatenation of topic knowledge R and context-sensitive word sequences U further serves as feature inputs to the CNN to obtain the final text category. Topic discovery is induced jointly with text classification in an end-to-end manner, and the loss function of the overall framework to combine the two effects is defined as:

$$L_{loss} = L_{NTM-R} + \lambda L_{CLS} \tag{13}$$

where L_{NTM-R} denotes the loss of NTM-R in Eq. (6), L_{CLS} represents the cross-entropy to reflect classification loss, and λ is the trade-off parameter to control the balance between topic model and classification.

3   Experiments

3.1   Datasets

We conduct experiments on four different short text datasets: SearchSnippets, StackOverflow, Biomedical, and Weibo. The dataset details are described as follows:

SearchSnippets. This dataset contains Google search snippets released by [19]. There is a total of eight ground-truth labels, e.g., business, engineering, and sport.

StackOverflow. This dataset is extracted from competition data released by Kaggle. Following [30], in our experiment, we randomly sample 18,000 question titles from 20 different tags, e.g., excel, svn, and ajax.

Biomedical. We use the challenge data related to biomedicine released on BioASQ, an internationally renowned biomedical platform. Following [30], we randomly select 18,000 paper titles from 20 different MeSH5 major topics, e.g., chemistry, cats, and lung.

Weibo. To evaluate cs-TMN on a different language other than English, we use Chinese microblog (Weibo) data to conduct the experiment. We experiment with the raw dataset [9] with 50 distinct categories in total.

Table 1 lists the statistics information of these four datasets. Since Search-Snippets, StackOverflow and Biomedical were already preprocessed by [19] and [30], we did not process these datasets further. For Weibo data, short texts were converted into sequences of words using the Jieba Chinese word segmentation module.[1] It should be noted that the average length of Weibo is the number of words in Chinese.

---

[1] https://github.com/fxsjy/jieba.

Table 1. Statistics of the experimental datasets. EN denotes English and ZH denotes simplified Chinese.

Dataset	#Docs	#Classes	Average length	Vocabulary size
SearchSnippets (EN)	12,332	8	17.0	7,334
StackOverflow (EN)	18,000	20	7.3	6,123
Biomedical (EN)	18,000	20	16.1	5,722
Weibo (ZH)	30,000	50	7.3	10,001

3.2 Experimental Methods

We compare our approach with five widely used short text classification methods. The comparative baseline models along with cs-TMN are described as follows:

SVM-based methods. We use the popular baseline SVM+BOW proposed by [27].

AttBiLSTM. The model is a widely used neural classifier from [32].

CNN-based models. CNN [11] is another widely used neural classifier. We employ the pre-trained CNN+ELMo [18] and CNN+NTM as two different baselines.

TMN. The TMN [31] jointly learns the topic inducing module and classification module, and it is a state-of-the-art model on short text classification, acting as a strong baseline in our comparison.

BERT. We fine-tune BERT on each of our datasets with a small learning rate and its output is considered as the text category.

cs-TMN. Our proposed model uses context-sensitive word embeddings and the content-aware topic knowledge as extended features. In our experiments, we apply the self-attention mechanism (cs-TMN-Self shown in Table 2) and BERT (cs-TMN-BERT shown in Table 2) to generate the local context representation respectively.

3.3 Experiment Settings

In our experiment, we randomly select 90% of the samples as the training set and the remaining 10% as the test set for all the datasets. We use pre-trained embeddings to initialize all word embeddings. Specifically, for datasets Search-Snippets, StackOverflow, and Biomedical, we use pre-trained GloVe embeddings [17] with a dimension of 200. For Weibo, we use pre-trained word2vec embeddings obtained from large Chinese corpora [13] with a dimension of 300. For the final classifier, we employ a one-layer CNN with three kernels. The kernel sizes of CNN layer are set to d, $2d$, and $3d$, respectively, where d is the word embedding dimension. The number of feature maps of the CNN is set to 500. In the training process, we train cs-TMN for at most 800 epochs, and an early-stop strategy is adopted to avoid overfitting [2]. For the BERT model, we adopt a pre-trained uncased BERT Base model for English datasets, while for the Chinese Weibo dataset, we apply a pre-trained BERT-Base Chinese model.[2]

3.4   Experimental Results

As can be seen from the experimental results in Table 2, both cs-TMN-Self (self-attention based local embeddings) and cs-TMN-BERT (BERT based local embeddings) perform better than all other models in these four short text datasets.

Our cs-TMN gains significant improvements in short text classification. According to Table 2, we can conclude that compared with TMN, cs-TMN yields a significant improvement of about 2% on F1 and accuracy on English dataset Biomedical, and Chinese dataset Weibo. In particular, for StackOverflow, the improvement is up to 7%. The experimental results fully show that the ability of cs-TMN to classify short texts has been greatly improved due to the context-sensitive word embedding, which can not only solve the problem of the polysemy of class-bearing words in the text but also improve the matching effect of relevant extended topic knowledge features. In addition, it also proves that cs-TMN makes more comprehensive use of the latent topic information than TMN. The specific ablation study is shown in Sect. 3.5.

Context-sensitive word representation and content-aware topic knowledge can improve the classification accuracy. We can find that for four experimental datasets (especially for Weibo), cs-TMN outperforms CNN+ELMo and BERT. This suggests that compared with existing multi-sense word embedding approaches, the proposed context-sensitive word embedding comprised of global topic information and local context representation is more effective.

Table 2. The comparison of different models w.r.t accuracy (Acc) and weighted average F1.

Models	SearchSnippets		StackOverflow		Biomedical		Weibo	
	Acc	F1	Acc	F1	Acc	F1	Acc	F1
SVM+BOW	0.210	0.080	0.232	0.231	0.202	0.200	0.102	0.039
AttBiLSTM	0.943	0.943	0.801	0.801	0.698	0.699	0.547	0.547
CNN+NTM	0.945	0.945	0.816	0.817	0.713	0.715	0.556	0.556
CNN+ELMo	0.937	0.940	0.825	0.828	0.714	0.719	0.553	0.558
BERT	0.964	0.967	0.903	0.903	0.742	0.742	0.602	0.602
TMN	0.964	0.964	0.830	0.831	0.724	0.723	0.595	0.586
cs-TMN-Self	**0.967**	0.967	0.841	0.841	0.734	0.734	0.611	0.601
cs-TMN-BERT	**0.967**	**0.968**	**0.908**	**0.908**	**0.745**	**0.745**	**0.624**	**0.624**

---

[2] https://github.com/google-research/bert.

It also proves that content-aware topic features can improve the classification accuracy of short text. In addition, cs-TMN jointly generates context-sensitive word embedding and text classification with neural networks in an end-to-end manner, which is more efficient and effective.

Local context representation generated by pre-trained BERT improves the model. From Table 2, we see that local context representation generated by pre-trained BERT word vectors is more effective and greatly improves the classification ability of cs-TMN, especially in the StackOverflow dataset.

3.5 Ablation Study

In order to explore the influence of different components of our cs-TMN, we perform corresponding ablation experiments and the results are shown in Table 3. Specifically, "cs-TMN w/o local" indicates that when constructing context-sensitive word embedding, only global context representation is employed, and the local context representation is removed. "cs-TMN w/o global" indicates that when constructing context-sensitive word embedding, only local context representation is employed. From Table 3, both modules are demonstrated to be necessary and removing any module deteriorates the performance as cs-TMN without local representation shows similar performance as TMN. Specifically, on dataset SearchSnippets, cs-TMN w/o local even perform worse than TMN, and the possible reason could be that there are fewer labels and the dataset is relatively simple. Finally, cs-TMN_CI represents extended topic knowledge matching in the same way as TMN, that is, using context-independent word embedding to match the corresponding extended topic knowledge. It can be found that using context-sensitive as opposed to context-independent word embedding gains better extended topic knowledge for short text. In addition, for "cs-TMN w/o global", cs-TMN_CI, and cs-TMN, we employ the self-attention mechanism and BERT to generate the local context representation, respectively.

Table 3. Experimental results of the ablation study w.r.t. accuracy.

Models	SearchSnippets		StackOverflow		Biomedical		Weibo	
TMN	0.964		0.830		0.724		0.595	
cs-TMN w/o local	0.957		0.839		0.721		0.602	
cs-TMN w/o global	$0.956^\dagger$	$0.958^\ddagger$	$0.833^\dagger$	$0.905^\ddagger$	$0.727^\dagger$	$0.739^\ddagger$	$0.602^\dagger$	$0.615^\ddagger$
cs-TMN_CI	$0.965^\dagger$	$0.961^\ddagger$	$0.841^\dagger$	$0.905^\ddagger$	$0.726^\dagger$	$0.740^\ddagger$	$0.605^\dagger$	$0.617^\ddagger$
cs-TMN	$\mathbf{0.967^\dagger}$	$\mathbf{0.967^\ddagger}$	$\mathbf{0.841^\dagger}$	$\mathbf{0.908^\ddagger}$	$\mathbf{0.734^\dagger}$	$\mathbf{0.745^\ddagger}$	$\mathbf{0.611^\dagger}$	$\mathbf{0.624^\ddagger}$

Self-attention based and BERT based local embeddings are denoted as † and ‡ respectively.

3.6 Visualization of Matching Mechanism for Content-Aware Topic Knowledge

In order to understand the matching mechanism of our cs-TMN and TMN in an intuitive way, we create heat maps of the weight matrix (Fig. 2) and top-5 words of some selected topics (Table 4). From Fig. 2, it shows that the matching mechanisms of cs-TMN and TMN can match the corresponding topic information effectively. However, for cs-TMN, the context-sensitive word embedding of polysemous words can match to the content-aware topic knowledge, while context-independent word embedding of TMN cannot. For example, from Fig. 2 and Table 4, we can find that for cs-TMN, the polysemous word "party" is matched with *topic 6* of "entertainment activity" and not matched with *topic 4* of "politics". On the contrary, for TMN, the polysemous word "party" is matched *topic 4* and not matched with *topic 6*, which causes extra noises.

Table 4. Top-5 words of some selected topics corresponding to Fig. 2.

Topic 1	Topic 2	Topic 3	Topic 4	Topic 5	Topic 6	Topic 7	Topic 8	Topic 9
e-business	Application	Welfare	Labour	Fracking	Athletics	Civilised	Club	Arty
Client	Load	Attachment	Policy	Coal	Game	Facility	Party	Culture
Churn	Programming	Shape	Independent	Mining	Play	Service	Activity	Soul

4 Related Work

Recently, many researchers employed deep learning methods for short text classification [7,12,26] which achieved promising performance. Some previous works further applied topic representation [4,19,21] to improve the classification of short text. Besides, pre-trained topic mixtures [4,19] learned by latent dirichlet allocation (LDA) were leveraged as part of features to alleviate data sparsity issues. Combining word embedding and the neural topic model, TMN [31] achieved state-of-the-art performance on short text classification. However, with context-independent word embedding, it suffers from the polysemy issue of class-bearing keywords. Although cs-TMN is largely inspired by TMN, it differs in the following respects. First, cs-TMN generates context-sensitive representation by local context representation and global topic information while TMN employs context-independent word embedding. Second, we not only use global topic information to help establish context-sensitive word representation but also apply content-aware topic knowledge as extended features for classification.

In order to obtain the context-sensitive word embedding, [1] represented each word with a Gaussian mixture density, where the mean of a mixture component is given by the sum of n-grams. [24] proposed to learn multiple embedding vectors for polysemous words from a probabilistic perspective, by designing an expectation-maximization algorithm. [21] proposed a model to learn topic-enriched multiprototype. Some researchers [14,15] combined topic vectors and word vectors via a neural network, and concatenated pre-trained topic vectors with the word vectors to represent word prototypes. More recently, BERT proposed by [5], achieved state-of-the-art performance in a series of NLP tasks. We also try to apply the vectors obtained by BERT's hidden layers as local context representation. Different from previous models, cs-TMN applies both local context representation and global topic information to obtain context-sensitive word embedding. Finally, unlike approaches that are dependent on external knowledge bases [3, 26], cs-TMN does not require additional knowledge, and topic information is extracted through the task-specific dataset.

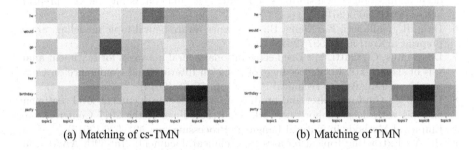

(a) Matching of cs-TMN   (b) Matching of TMN

Fig. 2. Visualization of attention weights for one selected example.

5 Conclusions and Future Work

In this paper, we have proposed a novel context-sensitive Topic Memory Network (cs-TMN), which utilizes the latent topic knowledge discovered by neural topic networks. The model applies context-sensitive embedding and extends the features with content-aware topic knowledge to improve short text classification accuracy. In future work, we will try to address multi-label classification tasks and test larger datasets to further verify the robustness of the model.

Acknowledgements. This work was partially supported by National Key Research and Development Program of China (No. 2018YFB1308604), National Natural Science Foundation of China (No. 61672215, No. 61976086), Hunan Innovation Technology Investment Project (No. -2019GK5061), Special Project of Foshan Science and Technology Innovation Team (No. FS0AA-KJ919-4402-0069), and the Foundation of Guangdong Provincial Key Laboratory of Big Data Analysis and Processing (2017017, 201805), the Research Project Foundation in the Data Center of Flamingo Network Co., Ltd.

References

1. Athiwaratkun, B., Wilson, A.G., Anandkumar, A.: Probabilistic FastText for multi-sense word embeddings. arXiv preprint arXiv:1806.02901 (2018)

2. Caruana, R., Lawrence, S., Giles, C.L.: Overfitting in neural nets: backpropagation, conjugate gradient, and early stopping. In: Advances in Neural Information Processing Systems, pp. 402–408 (2001)
3. Chen, J., Hu, Y., Liu, J., Xiao, Y., Jiang, H.: Deep short text classification with knowledge powered attention. In: 33rd Proceedings of the AAAI Conference on Artificial Intelligence, pp. 6252–6259 (2019)
4. Chen, P., Sun, Z., Bing, L., Yang, W.: Recurrent attention network on memory for aspect sentiment analysis. In: Proceedings of the 2017 Conference on Empirical Methods in Natural Language Processing, pp. 452–461 (2017)
5. Devlin, J., Chang, M.W., Lee, K., Toutanova, K.: BERT: pre-training of deep bidirectional transformers for language understanding. arXiv preprint arXiv:1810.04805 (2018)
6. Ding, R., Nallapati, R., Xiang, B.: Coherence-aware neural topic modeling. arXiv preprint arXiv:1809.02687 (2018)
7. Dos Santos, C., Gatti, M.: Deep convolutional neural networks for sentiment analysis of short texts. In: Proceedings of the 25th International Conference on Computational Linguistics: Technical Papers, pp. 69–78 (2014)
8. Dou, Z.Y.: Capturing user and product information for document level sentiment analysis with deep memory network. In: Proceedings of the 2017 Conference on Empirical Methods in Natural Language Processing, pp. 521–526 (2017)
9. He, Y.: Extracting topical phrases from clinical documents. In: 30th AAAI Conference on Artificial Intelligence (2016)
10. Joulin, A., Grave, E., Bojanowski, P., Mikolov, T.: Bag of tricks for efficient text classification. arXiv preprint arXiv:1607.01759 (2016)
11. Kim, Y.: Convolutional neural networks for sentence classification. arXiv preprint arXiv:1408.5882 (2014)
12. Lee, J.Y., Dernoncourt, F.: Sequential short-text classification with recurrent and convolutional neural networks. arXiv preprint arXiv:1603.03827 (2016)
13. Li, S., Zhao, Z., Hu, R., Li, W., Liu, T., Du, X.: Analogical reasoning on Chinese morphological and semantic relations. arXiv preprint arXiv:1805.06504 (2018)
14. Liu, P., Qiu, X., Huang, X.: Learning context-sensitive word embeddings with neural tensor skip-gram model. In: 24th International Joint Conference on Artificial Intelligence (2015)
15. Liu, Y., Liu, Z., Chua, T.S., Sun, M.: Topical word embeddings. In: 29th AAAI Conference on Artificial Intelligence (2015)
16. Miao, Y., Grefenstette, E., Blunsom, P.: Discovering discrete latent topics with neural variational inference. In: Proceedings of the 34th International Conference on Machine Learning, vol. 70, pp. 2410–2419. JMLR. org (2017)
17. Pennington, J., Socher, R., Manning, C.: GloVe: global vectors for word representation. In: Proceedings of the 2014 Conference on Empirical Methods in Natural Language Processing (EMNLP), pp. 1532–1543 (2014)
18. Peters, M.E., Neumann, M., Iyyer, M., Gardner, M., Clark, C., Lee, K., Zettlemoyer, L.: Deep contextualized word representations. arXiv preprint arXiv:1802.05365 (2018)
19. Phan, X.H., Nguyen, L.M., Horiguchi, S.: Learning to classify short and sparse text & web with hidden topics from large-scale data collections. In: Proceedings of the 17th International Conference on World Wide Web, pp. 91–100. ACM (2008)
20. Reisinger, J., Mooney, R.J.: Multi-prototype vector-space models of word meaning. In: The 2010 Annual Conference of the North American Chapter of the Association for Computational Linguistics, pp. 109–117. Association for Computational Linguistics (2010)

21. Ren, Y., Zhang, Y., Zhang, M., Ji, D.: Improving Twitter sentiment classification using topic-enriched multi-prototype word embeddings. In: 30th AAAI Conference on Artificial Intelligence (2016)
22. Srivastava, A., Sutton, C.: Autoencoding variational inference for topic models. arXiv preprint arXiv:1703.01488 (2017)
23. Sukhbaatar, S., Szlam, A., Weston, J., Fergus, R.: End-to-end memory networks. In: Advances in Neural Information Processing Systems, pp. 2440–2448 (2015)
24. Tian, F., et al.: A probabilistic model for learning multi-prototype word embeddings. In: Proceedings of the 25th International Conference on Computational Linguistics, pp. 151–160 (2014)
25. Vaswani, A., et al.: Attention is all you need. In: Neural Information Processing Systems, pp. 5998–6008 (2017)
26. Wang, J., Wang, Z., Zhang, D., Yan, J.: Combining knowledge with deep convolutional neural networks for short text classification. In: International Joint Conference on Artificial Intelligence, pp. 2915–2921 (2017)
27. Wang, S., Manning, C.D.: Baselines and bigrams: simple, good sentiment and topic classification. In: Proceedings of the 50th Annual Meeting of the Association for Computational Linguistics, pp. 90–94. Association for Computational Linguistics (2012)
28. Weston, J., Chopra, S., Bordes, A.: Memory networks. arXiv preprint arXiv:1410.3916 (2014)
29. Xiao, Y., Cho, K.: Efficient character-level document classification by combining convolution and recurrent layers. arXiv preprint arXiv:1602.00367 (2016)
30. Xu, J., Xu, B., Wang, P., Zheng, S., Tian, G., Zhao, J.: Self-taught convolutional neural networks for short text clustering. Neural Net. **88**, 22–31 (2017)
31. Zeng, J., Li, J., Song, Y., Gao, C., Lyu, M.R., King, I.: Topic memory networks for short text classification. arXiv preprint arXiv:1809.03664 (2018)
32. Zhang, S., Zheng, D., Hu, X., Yang, M.: Bidirectional long short-term memory networks for relation classification. In: Proceedings of the 29th Pacific Asia Conference on Language, Information and Computation, pp. 73–78 (2015)

A Novel Method for Offline Handwritten Chinese Character Recognition Under the Guidance of Print

Keping Yan[1], Jun Guo[1(✉)], and Weiqing Zhou[2]

[1] School of Data Science and Engineering, East China Normal University, Shanghai, China
51194507015@stu.ecnu.edu.cn, jguo@cc.ecnu.edu.cn
[2] DongQi AI Co., Ltd., Nanjing, China
zhouweiqing@dqaitech.net

Abstract. In this paper, we present a new method that views offline handwritten chinese character recognition (HCCR) as a Re-identification (ReID) task. We introduce a print dataset as the target that needs to be retrieved, and make the test set of offline HCCR as the object of interest. According to ReID's scene, the goal is to find the most similar print sample as the prediction result for each object of interest. We also employ triplet loss for metric learning, and train model together with cross-entropy loss, which has a good effect on improving performance. Compared with the classification model, the experimental results show that our method achieves much better results in few-shot learning, whose dataset is randomly selected from overall datasets. When the training set used is 5% of HWDB1.1, the gap between them even reached 9.8%. At the same time, it also obtains an accuracy of 97.69% on ICDAR-2013 offline HCCR competition dataset.

Keywords: HCCR · Few-shot learning · ReID · Metric Learning · ResNet

1 Introduction

Handwritten Chinese character recognition (HCCR) has received extensive research and attention in recent decades. With the development of deep learning, this task has made breakthrough progress in method and performance. HCCR is divided into online HCCR and offline HCCR according to the dataset collection method. The handwritten text processed by offline HCCR is two-dimensional pictures of the handwritten text collected by image capture devices such as scanners or cameras, while the handwritten text processed by online HCCR is text signal obtained by using physical devices such as digital handwriting pad. The former is still hard to identify because of the following reasons, and some samples of different writing styles and indistinguishable samples are shown in Fig. 1.

© Springer Nature Switzerland AG 2021
K. Karlapalem et al. (Eds.): PAKDD 2021, LNAI 12713, pp. 106–117, 2021.
https://doi.org/10.1007/978-3-030-75765-6_9

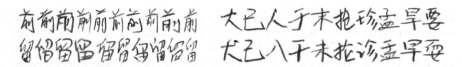

Fig. 1. Samples of different writing styles (left part) and several pairs of indistinguishable samples (right part).

1. Handwritten writing is random and irregular, and everyone has a different writing style, which can't meet the requirements of print.
2. Many Chinese characters are hard to distinguish because the majority of the Chinese are similar in appearance.
3. Online HCCR can obtain the writing track information through timing sampling, but the offline HCCR samples are only two-dimensional images, so it is more difficult to achieve good performance.

In order to address these problems, we propose a method, which establishes a relationship between handwriting and print with the thought of Re-identification (ReID). ReID is widely regarded as a sub-problem of image retrieval. It's a task that uses computer vision technology to determine whether there is specific pedestrian in an image or video sequence. For example, given a monitored pedestrian image, retrieve the pedestrian image under cross-devices. It hasn't yet been used in HCCR, previous attempts [3,12,27,29] either only consider the loss function and template separately, or have not obtained particularly good result on the overall datasets. Moreover, they regard offline HCCR as a classification task and only use a multi-classification model to train them, which requires a large number of image samples for Chinese characters with many categories.

Our method introduces the print, and establishes a relationship with handwritten through the ReID thought. We view print as the gallery in ReID and handwritten as the query in ReID. For each query object, find the most similar object in gallery. Cross-entropy loss [18] and triplet loss [19] are both adopted to train the model. We also show the few-shot learning performance of our proposed method, and the shot percentages are 5%, 10% 30% and 60%. In the following, we'll call these shots small-scale datasets. Experiments show that our method is much better than classification method that just use cross-entropy loss. The model is evaluated on ICDAR-2013 offline HCCR competition dataset. And the results also illustrate the robustness of our method.

The rest of this paper is organized as follows. Related works are reviewed in Sect. 2. Section 3 are the details of our proposed method. Experiments are described in Sect. 4, and Sect. 5 gives the conclusion of our work.

2   Related Work

2.1   Re-identification

Re-identification is a retrieval task, which is to find the same person images from a dataset collected by different cameras for each query pedestrian image

[2,24,31,32,35]. Many deep learning methods have been proposed in ReID which can be divided into two major directions. Some works [21,25,33] extract features on entire images by using classification models. They treat each person ID as a category and train the ReID model as image classification. These works usually use the pre-trained parameters on ImageNet [11] to initialize their models. There are also some works focus on local features and divide the whole image into several parts (by Hand-crafted Splitting [26], Semantic Segmentation [10], etc.), and extract features for each part separately. Obviously, the former method which we select is more suitable for offline HCCR, because the class can only be recognized from the information of an entire image. Hermans et al. [9] finds that triplet loss significantly increases the performance of ReID, so we have a try to apply it in our method.

Most of the datasets of ReID such as DukeMTMC-reID [17] and Market-1501 [31] include three parts: train, query and gallery. Correspondingly, we use the train dataset of HCCR datasets and the print, the test dataset of HCCR datasets, the print. And the print are the images that generated by font files. The dataset will be described in detail in Sect. 4.1.

2.2   Offline HCCR

HCCR has been studied in the past fifty years, and a large number of methods have been proposed to improve the accuracy of recognition. Traditional methods for offline HCCR are often based on three steps: shape normalization [1], feature extraction [13] and classification [14]. With the rapid development of deep learning, it has played an important role in HCCR. It has also proved that deep learning methods far surpass traditional methods. Multi-column Deep Neural Network (MCDNN) [4] is the first method of deep learning for HCCR, which obtains an error rate of 4.21% on the ICDAR-2013 dataset (the same dataset as below works). The GoogLeNet [36] is the first model beyond human-level, and the accuracy of ensemble model reached 96.74%. The difference between inter-class and intra-class of the samples is considered in [3,29], where Cheng et al. [3] introduces the triplet ranking into deep learning, which achieves an accuracy of 97.07%. And Zhang et al. [29] achieves an accuracy of 97.03% by using center loss in deep network. Zhang et al. [30] obtains a new highest accuracy of 97.37% by integrating the traditional normalized cooperative direction decomposition feature map (directMap) with the deep convolutional neural network (convNet), and adding an adaptation layer. Template images are introduced in [12], this paper proposes a method for training Siamese neural network and gets an accuracy of 92.31%. Wang et al. [22] uses the radical-level composition of Chinese characters and get an accuracy of 96.97%.

According to the above descriptions, most of the previous works consider HCCR as a multi-classification task, so they only design a multi-class classifier to solve it. But this approach requires a large number of data samples to get good results. In other methods, either only add template images, or just the loss function is considered. There isn't a way to combine them to achieve better results. Therefore, with the help of ReID's thought, we establish a relationship between handwritten and print, and introduce cross-entropy loss and triplet loss functions to learn more accurate features. This method achieves a higher accuracy than previous related methods.

3 Method Description

3.1 Proposed Architecture

We select the ResNet-50 [7] as backbone because of its outstanding performance on ImageNet, and take handwritten images and print images together as the input of the network. According to [16], we add a batch normalization layer (BN) before the last fully connected layer (FC), and set the last stride of ResNet-50 to 1, which achieves better results. The final model architecture is shown in Fig. 2, and only cross-entropy loss is employed in classification model. In training phrase of overall network, cross-entropy loss and triplet loss are both employed. One of the differences of them is that the features triplet loss uses are from the last pooling layer, while cross-entropy loss's features are from the last fully connected layer. In evaluation phrase, we also use the features which are extracted from the last pooling layer. In order to obtain the results, distance metric learning methods, Euclidean and cosine measures, are employed to calculate the distance between handwritten features and print features. More details can be seen in next subsection.

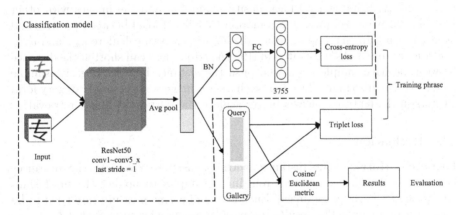

Fig. 2. Overall network

3.2 Loss Function

Our method applies two different loss functions, which have different effective effects on the performance of the model. The total loss is defined as Eq. 1, where $\mathcal{L}_{cl}$ and $\mathcal{L}_{tl}$ wil be introduced below.

$$\mathcal{L}_{total} = \mathcal{L}_{cl} + \mathcal{L}_{tl} \tag{1}$$

Cross-Entropy Loss. Cross-entropy loss measures the performance of classification tasks whose output is a probability value between 0 and 1. It increases as the predicted probability deviates from the actual label. In multi-class classification tasks, it can be defined as Eq. 2.

$$\mathcal{L}_{cl} = \sum_{c=1}^{C} -y_{o,c} \log\left(p_{o,c}\right) \tag{2}$$

where C is the number of classes, p is predicted probability that observed sample o belongs to the category. y is the indicator variable (0 or 1), if the category is same as the sample o's category, it is 1, otherwise it is 0. By applying cross-entropy loss to train the model, it will tend to make the predicted output better fit to the ground truth.

Triplet Loss. Unlike the classification loss, the triplet loss requires three input samples, and an input triple includes a pair of positive samples and a pair of negative samples. It is expressed as Eq. 3.

$$\mathcal{L}_{tl} = d_{a,p} - d_{a,n} + \alpha \tag{3}$$

where $d_{a,p}$ represents the distance between the anchor sample a of a specific class and a positive sample p of the same class, and $d_{a,n}$ is the distance between the anchor sample a and a negative sample n of any other classes. Each image and the images with its own ID form positive samples, and the images with other IDs form negative samples. α is a margin that is enforced between positive and negative pairs. In this paper, cosine distance is used to calculate $d_{a,p}$ and $d_{a,n}$, and α is set to 0.3. As illustrated in [19], the triplet loss can shorten the distance between positive sample pairs, and push the distance between negative sample pairs, so it can also make the Chinese character images of the same category form clusters in the feature space to better achieve the purpose of image retrieval.

3.3 Evaluation

Distance Metric. The distance metric is used to calculate the distances between the features extracted from input samples to predict the most similar sample for each query image. Euclidean and cosine measures are tried to be used in experiments. The results comparison can be viewed in Sect. 4.3.

Evaluation Metric. Cumulative matching characteristics (CMC) [23] is the most widely used measurements in ReID evaluation. Only Rank-1 in CMC is selected in our experiments because the main factor is the accuracy of the classification results for HCCR. Rank-1 represents the accuracy of the first retrieved target of query images, it can be represented as follows Eq. 4 and 5.

$$\text{Rank-1} = \frac{1}{\|Q\|} \sum_{q \in Q} R\left(L_q, L_q^1\right) \tag{4}$$

$$R(L_q, L_q^i) = \begin{cases} 1, & L_q = L_q^i \\ 0, & L_q \neq L_q^i \end{cases} \tag{5}$$

where Q is the query images, L_q is the label for a query image q, and L_q^i represents the class of the image ranked i-th in similarity to q in its query results (for example, L_q^1 is the class of the most similar image to q in its query results).

4   Experiments

In this section, we show that our proposed method achieves competitive results compared to other methods on HWDB datasets. We have also verified that this method is more robust than the model only uses classification, and it has a strong performance on few-shot learning. Finally, we provide an ablation result of image preprocessing, loss function, distance metrics and other settings.

Fig. 3. Samples of the print.

4.1   Datasets

We use the datasets HWDB1.0-1.1 [15] to train the model, which is collected by National Laboratory of Pattern Recognition(NLPR) and Institute of Automation of Chinese Academy of Sciences(CASIA). ICDAR-2013 offline HCCR competition dataset [28], the most common benchmark for offline HCCR, is used to evaluate the model. We merge HWDB1.0 and HWDB1.1 according to the classes of HWDB1.1 to ensure that the merged dataset and ICDAR-2013 have the same class labels.

The dataset of ReID is divided into three parts, including train, query and gallery, so we first generate a print dataset (corresponding to 3755 classes) that consists of 10 fonts every class (stzhongs.ttf, stxinwei.ttf, stxingka.ttf, stxihei.ttf, stsong.ttf, stliti.ttf, stkaiti.ttf, sthupo.ttf, stfangso.ttf, dengl.ttf). Examples of print are shown in Fig. 3. Then put them into train and gallery. At the same time, the train set of HWDB is also added in train, and the test set of HWDB (training phrase) or ICDAR-2013 (evaluation) is put in query. Our goal is to find the most similar sample in the gallery as the prediction result for each query sample.

When we conduct few-shot learning experiments on small-scale datasets, we randomly select several proportion of datasets in train and test of the HWDB1.1. For example, when the proportion is 5%, the train datasets is composed by randomly selecting 12 samples from each class of HWDB1.1 training set. And the sub test dataset is always the same (randomly select 10 samples from each class of HWDB1.1 test dataset). The number of class is always 3755, which is the level-1 set of GB2312-80. More detailed information is showed in Table 1.

Table 1. Offline Handwritten Chinese character recognition datasets.

Dataset	Writers	Total	Train/Test	Class
HWDB1.0	420	1,556,675	1,246,991/309,684	3740
HWDB1.1	300	1,121,749	897,758/223,991	3755
ICDAR-2013	60	224,419	n/a	3755
5% sub HWDB1.1	300	82,610	45,060/37,550	3755
10% sub HWDB1.1	300	127,670	90,120/37,550	3755
30% sub HWDB1.1	300	307,910	270,360/37,550	3755
60% sub HWDB1.1	300	578,270	540,720/37,550	3755
Print	n/a	37,550	n/a	3755

4.2 Training Strategy

We implement the proposed models using Pytorch and conduct all experiments on GeForce GTX 1080 Ti. The classification model and our proposed model are trained separately, but they have the same backbone.

Classification Model. We resize the images to 64×64, and we use stochastic gradient descent (SGD) with the momentum of 0.9 for training. The learning rate is set to 0.01 and the batch size is 128. In order to deal with the overfitting of this model, we add dropout with the 0.5 probability before the last fully connected layer. The model is initialized with pre-trained parameters on ImageNet [5]. We also find if we initialize the model with the trained parameter of our proposed model, the performance can get better.

Our Proposed Model. We resize the images to 128×128. As used in many ReID papers [6,8,16,20], we also apply random padding with 10 pixels on each border and random erasing with 0.5 probability in the image preprocessing for training and only image resize is employed in the test phase. Experiments show that they all have a positive influence on the results. The optimizer this model uses is Adam, and its batch size is set to 1024. For triplet loss, we select 4 samples for each class, so it will have 256 classes and 4 images per class in every batch. The learning rate adjustment strategies we use include warm up and

MultiStepLR [16]. During the first 10 epochs, the learning rate will gradually increase from 3.5×10^{-5} to 3.5×10^{-4}, and then it will become 3.5×10^{-5} and 3.5×10^{-6} in steps 40 and 90 respectively. By the way, the model is always initialized with pre-trained parameters on ImageNet [5].

4.3 Results

We first evaluate our method by comparing the results on small-scale datasets. As mentioned above, for classification model, the sub train dataset is randomly selected from HWDB1.1 train dataset according to a specific ratio, and the test dataset is composed by randomly selecting 10 samples from each class of HWDB1.1 test dataset. For our proposed model, the print is the gallery and it is also put into the train dataset. And ICDAR-2013 is always used to evaluate their performance. As the Table 2 shows that our method has better performance than classification method. And when the size of training set is smaller, the gap between these two methods gets bigger. Their accuracy differs by about 9.8% when the ratio is 5%. The experimental results demonstrate that our method has better robustness.

Table 2. Results of our method and classification model on small-scale datasets.

Dataset	Classification Acc (%)	Our method Acc (%)
5% sub HWDB1.1	85.82	95.63
10% sub HWDB1.1	90.84	96.33
30% sub HWDB1.1	94.50	97.05
60% sub HWDB1.1	95.68	97.39
100% HWDB1.1	96.19	97.55

Fig. 4. Result samples

The experiments on total dataset are also conducted. We use the HWDB1.0 and HWDB1.1 for training, and ICDAR-2013 for evaluation. Similar to small-scale datasets' experiments, the print is still used as gallery and put in train dataset. Examples of evaluation result are shown in Fig. 4. It shows the top 10 results of each query sample. The first row is an example of wrong results and the others are correct examples. From the first row of Fig. 4, we can see that the handwritten sample is hard to distinguish, which leads to multiple prediction results. Although these results are incorrect, they all look similar to the sample. Table 3 shows the results and the comparison with other models' performances. As we can see, the accuracy of our proposed work is 97.55% when the training data is HWDB1.1, and it is 97.69% when training data is HWDB1.0+1.1. Some works [12,27] also introduce extra dataset as template. The method Xiao et al. [27] proposed is to calculate template feature distance by using template dataset which is different from our method. Li et al. [12] is to predict the similarity between handwritten and print, and their work get a good result on new classes that don't appear in training set, while the performance on total dataset is 92.31%. Similar to our work, Cheng et al. [3], Zhang et al. [29] respectively use triplet loss and center loss to distinguish the learning of inter-class and intra-class information. The difference between our methods is that they still use classification prediction in the testing phase. And compared to other ResNet-based models, we add a batch normalization (BN) layer between the final fully connected layer and the last pooling layer, which has a positive effect on results.

Table 3. Results on ICDAR-2013 Offline HCCR competition Dataset. * indicates whether extra data samples are added during the experiment, such as the print.

Method	Acc (%)	Training Data	Ensemble	Extra*
Human Performance [28]	96.13	n/a	n/a	n/a
HCCR-Gabor-GoogLeNet [36]	96.35	HWDB1.0+1.1	No	No
HCCR-Gabor-GoogLeNet-Ensemble [36]	96.74	HWDB1.0+1.1	Yes	No
STN-Residual-34 [34]	97.37	HWDB1.0+1.1	No	No
DCNN-Similarity ranking [3]	96.44	HWDB1.1	No	No
DCNN-Similarity ranking [3]	97.07	HWDB1.0+1.1	No	No
DirectMap+ConvNet+Adaptation [30]	97.37	HWDB1.0+1.1	No	No
ResNet+Center loss [29]	97.03	HWDB1.0+1.1	No	No
Deep Template Matching [12]	92.31	HWDB1.0+1.1	No	Yes
Template-Instance loss [27]	97.45	HWDB1.0+1.1	No	Yes
Our Method	97.55	HWDB1.1	No	Yes
Our Mthod	**97.69**	**HWDB1.0+1.1**	**No**	**Yes**

4.4 Ablation Experiment

In order to demonstrate the influences of different model settings and modules, we also conduct ablation experiments on image preprocessing, distance metric, loss function and whether to add the BN layer. A comparison of these methods on 5% sub HWDB1.1 dataset is shown in Table 4. The first line of Table 4 is the optimal setting of the model parameters, and the ablation experiments is performed by changing a single parameter and comparing their results. As Table 4 shows, we can know that cosine distance metric is better than Euclidean, this might because cosine distance pays more attention to the relative differences between dimensions and is more suitable for distinguishing the similarity between the Chinese character features, while the Euclidean distance mainly measures the differences in values. The BN layer added before the last fully connected layer also plays an important role, and the difference is nearly 1%. The effects of these two loss functions are almost the same, but they can get better results by using together. Triplet loss better constrains the distance between intra-class and inter-class, while cross-entropy loss pays more attention to whether the results of each class classification is close to the ground truth. Random erasing and Random padding all have good performance, probably because they have a good effect on alleviating overfitting caused by so many classes.

Table 4. Ablation experiment results for parameters.

Random erasing	Random padding	Cosine	Euclidean	Add BN	Cross-entropy	Triplet	Acc (%)
✓	✓	✓		✓	✓	✓	95.63
✓	✓	✓		✓		✓	95.58
✓	✓	✓		✓	✓		95.48
✓	✓		✓	✓	✓	✓	95.27
✓		✓		✓	✓	✓	94.89
✓	✓	✓			✓	✓	94.69
	✓	✓		✓	✓	✓	94.59

5 Conclusion

In this paper, we propose a new method for offline handwritten Chinese character recognition by learning from Re-identification's method, and achieve a good performance. We generate print as the gallery dataset, and find the most similar gallery image for each handwritten test sample, so the relationship is established between the handwritten and the print. We also use triplet loss for metric learning, and train the network together with cross-entropy loss. Experiments show that the performance of our proposed method on few-shot learning is significantly improved compared to the classification model. Moreover, the result on the ICDAR-2013 exceeds the previous related works, the highest is 97.69%.

References

1. Casey, R., Nagy, G.: Recognition of printed Chinese characters. IEEE Trans. Electron. Comput. **1**, 91–101 (1966)
2. Chang, X., Hospedales, T.M., Xiang, T.: Multi-level factorisation net for person re-identification. In: Proceedings of the IEEE Conference on Computer Vision and Pattern Recognition, pp. 2109–2118 (2018)

3. Cheng, C., Zhang, X.Y., Shao, X.H., Zhou, X.D.: Handwritten Chinese character recognition by joint classification and similarity ranking. In: 2016 15th International Conference on Frontiers in Handwriting Recognition (ICFHR), pp. 507–511. IEEE (2016)
4. Cireşan, D., Meier, U.: Multi-column deep neural networks for offline handwritten Chinese character classification. In: 2015 International Joint Conference on Neural Networks (IJCNN), pp. 1–6. IEEE (2015)
5. Deng, J., et al.: ImageNet: a large-scale hierarchical image database. In: 2009 IEEE Conference on Computer Vision and Pattern Recognition, pp. 248–255. IEEE (2009)
6. Guo, J., Yuan, Y., Huang, L., Zhang, C., Yao, J.G., Han, K.: Beyond human parts: dual part-aligned representations for person re-identification. In: Proceedings of the IEEE International Conference on Computer Vision, pp. 3642–3651 (2019)
7. He, K., Zhang, X., Ren, S., Sun, J.: Deep residual learning for image recognition. In: Proceedings of the IEEE Conference on Computer Vision and Pattern Recognition, pp. 770–778 (2016)
8. He, L., Liao, X., Liu, W., Liu, X., Cheng, P., Mei, T.: FastReID: a Pytorch toolbox for general instance re-identification. arXiv preprint arXiv:2006.02631 (2020)
9. Hermans, A., Beyer, L., Leibe, B.: In defense of the triplet loss for person re-identification. arXiv preprint arXiv:1703.07737 (2017)
10. Kalayeh, M.M., Basaran, E., Gökmen, M., Kamasak, M.E., Shah, M.: Human semantic parsing for person re-identification. In: Proceedings of the IEEE Conference on Computer Vision and Pattern Recognition, pp. 1062–1071 (2018)
11. Krizhevsky, A., Sutskever, I., Hinton, G.E.: ImageNet classification with deep convolutional neural networks. In: NIPS (2012)
12. Li, Z., Xiao, Y., Wu, Q., Jin, M., Lu, H.: Deep template matching for offline handwritten Chinese character recognition. J. Eng. 2020(4), 120–124 (2020)
13. Liu, C.L.: Normalization-cooperated gradient feature extraction for handwritten character recognition. IEEE Trans. Pattern Anal. Mach. Intell. 29(8), 1465–1469 (2007)
14. Liu, C.L., Sako, H., Fujisawa, H.: Discriminative learning quadratic discriminant function for handwriting recognition. IEEE Trans. Neural Netw. 15(2), 430–444 (2004)
15. Liu, C.L., Yin, F., Wang, D.H., Wang, Q.F.: CASIA online and offline Chinese handwriting databases. In: 2011 International Conference on Document Analysis and Recognition, pp. 37–41. IEEE (2011)
16. Luo, H., Gu, Y., Liao, X., Lai, S., Jiang, W.: Bag of tricks and a strong baseline for deep person re-identification. In: Proceedings of the IEEE Conference on Computer Vision and Pattern Recognition Workshops (2019)
17. Ristani, E., Solera, F., Zou, R., Cucchiara, R., Tomasi, C.: Performance measures and a data set for multi-target, multi-camera tracking. In: Hua, G., Jégou, H. (eds.) ECCV 2016. LNCS, vol. 9914, pp. 17–35. Springer, Cham (2016). https://doi.org/10.1007/978-3-319-48881-3_2
18. Rubinstein, R.: The cross-entropy method for combinatorial and continuous optimization. Methodol. Comput. Appl. Probab. 1(2), 127–190 (1999)
19. Schroff, F., Kalenichenko, D., Philbin, J.: FaceNet: a unified embedding for face recognition and clustering. In: Proceedings of the IEEE Conference on Computer Vision and Pattern Recognition, pp. 815–823 (2015)
20. Wang, D., Zhang, S.: Unsupervised person re-identification via multi-label classification. In: Proceedings of the IEEE/CVF Conference on Computer Vision and Pattern Recognition, pp. 10981–10990 (2020)

21. Wang, F., Zuo, W., Lin, L., Zhang, D., Zhang, L.: Joint learning of single-image and cross-image representations for person re-identification. In: Proceedings of the IEEE Conference on Computer Vision and Pattern Recognition, pp. 1288–1296 (2016)
22. Wang, T., Xie, Z., Li, Z., Jin, L., Chen, X.: Radical aggregation network for few-shot offline handwritten Chinese character recognition. Pattern Recogn. Lett. **125**, 821–827 (2019)
23. Wang, X., Doretto, G., Sebastian, T., Rittscher, J., Tu, P.: Shape and appearance context modeling. In: 2007 IEEE 11th International Conference on Computer Vision, pp. 1–8. IEEE (2007)
24. Wei, L., Zhang, S., Gao, W., Tian, Q.: Person transfer GAN to bridge domain gap for person re-identification. In: Proceedings of the IEEE Conference on Computer Vision and Pattern Recognition, pp. 79–88 (2018)
25. Wu, L., Shen, C., van den Hengel, A.: PersonNet: person re-identification with deep convolutional neural networks. arXiv preprint arXiv:1601.07255 (2016)
26. Wu, S., Chen, Y.C., Li, X., Wu, A.C., You, J.J., Zheng, W.S.: An enhanced deep feature representation for person re-identification. In: 2016 IEEE Winter Conference on Applications of Computer Vision (WACV), pp. 1–8. IEEE (2016)
27. Xiao, Y., Meng, D., Lu, C., Tang, C.K.: Template-instance loss for offline handwritten Chinese character recognition. In: 2019 International Conference on Document Analysis and Recognition (ICDAR), pp. 315–322. IEEE (2019)
28. Yin, F., Wang, Q.F., Zhang, X.Y., Liu, C.L.: ICDAR 2013 Chinese handwriting recognition competition. In: 2013 12th International Conference on Document Analysis and Recognition, pp. 1464–1470. IEEE (2013)
29. Zhang, R., Wang, Q., Lu, Y.: Combination of ResNet and center loss based metric learning for handwritten Chinese character recognition. In: 2017 14th IAPR International Conference on Document Analysis and Recognition (ICDAR), vol. 5, pp. 25–29. IEEE (2017)
30. Zhang, X.Y., Bengio, Y., Liu, C.L.: Online and offline handwritten Chinese character recognition: a comprehensive study and new benchmark. Pattern Recogn. **61**, 348–360 (2017)
31. Zheng, L., Shen, L., Tian, L., Wang, S., Wang, J., Tian, Q.: Scalable person re-identification: a benchmark. In: Proceedings of the IEEE International Conference on Computer Vision, pp. 1116–1124 (2015)
32. Zheng, L., Yang, Y., Hauptmann, A.G.: Person re-identification: past, present and future. arXiv preprint arXiv:1610.02984 (2016)
33. Zheng, L., Zhang, H., Sun, S., Chandraker, M., Yang, Y., Tian, Q.: Person re-identification in the wild. In: Proceedings of the IEEE Conference on Computer Vision and Pattern Recognition, pp. 1367–1376 (2017)
34. Zhong, Z., Zhang, X.Y., Yin, F., Liu, C.L.: Handwritten Chinese character recognition with spatial transformer and deep residual networks. In: 2016 23rd International Conference on Pattern Recognition (ICPR), pp. 3440–3445. IEEE (2016)
35. Zhong, Z., Zheng, L., Zheng, Z., Li, S., Yang, Y.: Camera style adaptation for person re-identification. In: Proceedings of the IEEE Conference on Computer Vision and Pattern Recognition, pp. 5157–5166 (2018)
36. Zhong, Z., Jin, L., Xie, Z.: High performance offline handwritten Chinese character recognition using GoogLeNet and directional feature maps. In: 2015 13th International Conference on Document Analysis and Recognition (ICDAR), pp. 846–850. IEEE (2015)

Upgraded Attention-Based Local Feature Learning Block for Speech Emotion Recognition

Huan Zhao$^{(\boxtimes)}$, Yingxue Gao, and Yufeng Xiao

College of Computer Science and Electronic Engineering, Hunan University,
Changsha 410082, China
hzhao@hnu.edu.cn

Abstract. Speech emotion recognition (SER) plays a vital role in natural interaction between humans and machines. However, due to the complexity of human emotions, the features learned in existing researches contain a large amount of redundant information that has nothing to do with emotions, which reduces the performance of SER. To alleviate the problem, in this paper we propose a novel model, named as Upgraded Attention-based Local Feature Learning Block (UA-LFLB). Concretely, the LFLB is used to extract deep local sequence features and as input to the UA mechanism to capture the salient features of the discourse level with contextual information. In doing this, more accurate and discriminative features can be learned, which greatly reduces redundant information in the features. To evaluate the feasibility of the proposed model, We conduct experiments on a widely used emotional database. Experimental results show that the proposed model outperforms the state-of-the-art methods on the IEMOCAP database and achieving 9% improvement in terms of average accuracy.

Keywords: Speech emotion recognition · Convolutional neural network · Bidirectional long short-term memory · 3D attention mechanism

1 Introduction

SER plays an important role in human-computer interaction (HCI) [5,19,20], which can help computers perceive human purpose and make users feel a natural interactive experience. It has been applied in many real-world scenarios [17], such as psychology, robotics engineering, automotive systems, and call centers [1,3,7,13,15]. In recent years, deep neural networks (DNN) has been widely used in SER. For example, Mao *et al.* [10] used convolutional neural networks (CNN) to extract salient features of emotions for SER and achieved good performance on several public corpora. The CNN model has two training processes. First, the model is trained to learn local invariant features with unlabeled data. Second, the learned local invariant features are fed into the feature extractor to learn salient

© Springer Nature Switzerland AG 2021
K. Karlapalem et al. (Eds.): PAKDD 2021, LNAI 12713, pp. 118–130, 2021.
https://doi.org/10.1007/978-3-030-75765-6_10

features. Chen *et al.* [4] proposed a 3D convolutional recurrent neural network (CRNN) based on the attention mechanism for SER. The log-Mel spectrogram and the deltas and delta-deltas of the spectrogram are used as input to the model to reduce the influence of speaker-related features. Overall, the high-level features captured by deep learning are better than the results obtained by traditional low-level features. Haomeng *et al.* [11] proposed the dilated CNN with residual block and BiLSTM based on the attention mechanism to capture significant emotional features.

Since the features captured in the above researches contain a large number of redundant features that are not related to emotions, the performance of SER is reduced. In this paper, we propose an UA-LFLB model. The model can not only reduce the interference of redundant features, but also capture the contextual salient features. Concretely, the LFLB composed of Convolutional layers, Batch Normalization (BN) layers, and Leaky-Relu activation functions learns local sequence features from the input signal. Then, the UA composed of bidirectional long short-term memory (BiLSTM) and 3D attention obtains salient features with contextual information by calculating the weight values of the features. Hence, the UA-LFLB network can learn discriminative features from the input signal for SER.

The contributions of this paper can be summarized as below.

* We propose a novel model: UA-LFLB. It can be divided into two main modules, one is the segment-level local feature learning block, and the other is the discourse-level salient feature learning block. Combining these two modules for SER can enhance the discrimination of features.
* We utilize the UA mechanism that can learn significant features with context relevance and ignore the interference of irrelevant emotional information. This mechanism combines the BiLSTM layer and 3D Attention. The BiLSTM obtains past and future information and captures contextual relevance. Then, the 3D Attention focuses attention on significant emotional features by calculating the weight values of features.
* We evaluate our method on the public dataset IEMOCAP. The results show that the performance of our proposed model has been significantly improved compared with the state-of-the-art models.

The structure of this paper is organized as follows: Sect. 2 briefly discusses the previous work of SER. Section 3 details our approach. Section 4 presents the visualization of our experimental results. Section 5 summarizes the paper.

2   Related Work

In recent years, SER has become one of the hot topics of researchers in the field of signal processing [8,18,21]. Researchers are gradually paying attention to how to extract salient features from speech and use these features to improve recognition performance. Nowadays, with the rapid development of DNN, researchers have attempted to use DNN to learn deep emotional features for SER. Compared with traditional machine learning methods, deep learning can learn more discriminative features.

Huang et al. [6] used semi-CNN to learn salient features. This method includes two stages. One was to use unlabeled samples to learn candidate features. The other was to use objective functions to enhance feature saliency, orthogonality, and discrimination. Mirasamadi et al. [12] combined DNN and recurrent neural network (RNN) with local attention. By calculating the weight coefficients of different features, the model can automatically focus on the parts of prominent emotional features. Schmidt et al. [16] used a deep belief network to learn emotional features from the magnitude spectra. Experimental results show that compared with traditional acoustic features, it has better recognition performance. The deep belief network is very useful for identifying music emotions. Mustaqeem et al. [14] designed a framework that using a key sequence segment selection based on redial based function network (RBFN). They used the short time fourier transform (STFT) algorithm to convert the selected sequence into a spectrogram and passed it to the CNN model to extract discriminative salient features from the speech spectrogram. Zhao et al. [22] investigated that the overall performance of the 2D CNN network is better than the 1D CNN network. Zheng et al. [24] established a CNN model to process labeled data. Experimental results show that the method is better than support vector machine (SVM) classification. Zhao et al. [23] proposed attention-based BiLSTM+RNN and full convolutional network to solve the problem of speech emotion feature extraction to automatically learn the best spatio-temporal representation of speech signals. Finally, input the learned features into the DNN for emotion prediction. To reduce the interference of redundant information in the features on classification results. We use the LFLB to extract local sequence features and use the UA mechanism to capture salient discourse-level features.

3   Methodology

In this section, we introduce the UA-LFLB model for SER. First, we generate 3D static data as the input of UA-LFLB model. Then, we introduce the architecture of UA-LFLB, followed by a dropout layer, a dense layer, and a softmax classifier. The overall framework of our model is shown in Fig. 1.

3.1   3D Static Data

We extract 3D static representations from speech raw signal as the input of the model to reduce the impact of speaker-related information (e.g. speaking styles). It is composed of the Log-Mel spectrum, the deltas and delta-deltas of the spectrogram. The deltas and delta-deltas can not only reduce the interference of irrelevant information, but also perceive emotional changes to capture more emotional information. The waveform and spectrogram of speech are shown in Fig. 2.

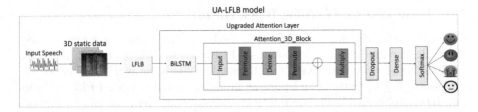

Fig. 1. Framework of upgraded attention-based local feature learning block (UA-LFLB).

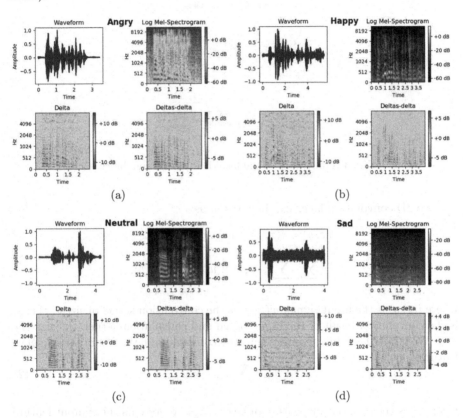

Fig. 2. Voice waveform and spectrogram of the *Angry, Happy, Neutral*, and *Sad* emotional state in IEMOCAP database.

The spectrogram represents the short-term power spectrum of an audio clip, which has been proven to be an effective distinguishing feature in emotion recognition. It can be observed from Fig. 2 that the signal strength of different frequency bands of the voice changes along the time axis. The horizontal stripes in the figure reflect the strong energy in the voice. We also find that the frequency of *happy* emotion and *neutral* emotion 8192 Hz at the same time distribution. Their emotional signal intensity distribution is similar.

3.2   Local Feature Learning Block (LFLB)

Given the 3D static data, the LFLB is used to extract local sequence features for SER. The module mainly contains 6 LFLBs of size 32, 32, 64, 64, 128, 128, and one 2D Max-Pooling layer. The 2D max-Pooling layer is used to reduce the dimensionality of features and prevent model overfitting. Each LFLB includes one 2D convolutional layer, one BN layer, and one leaky-relu activation function. The model is shown in Fig. 3.

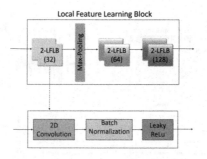

Fig. 3. Framework of the local feature learning block

The 2D convolution layer can be written as:

$$z(x,y) = i(x,y) \times w(x,y)$$
$$= \sum_{a=-c}^{c} \sum_{b=-d}^{d} i(a,b) \times w(x-a, y-b), \tag{1}$$

where $i(x,y)$ is the input signal, $w(x,y)$ is the convolution kernel of size c, $z(x,y)$ is the convolution result of the input signal and convolution kernel, the size is $c \times d$. We input the value of $z(x,y)$ into the convolution layer to obtain sequence features:

$$z_x^l = b_x^l + \sum_y z_x^{l-1} \times w_{xy}^l, \tag{2}$$

where z_x^l is the x-th output feature of layer l, z_x^{l-1} represents the x input feature of layer $l-1$, w_{xy}^l represents the convolution kernel between the x-th feature and the y-th feature of the l-layer. The convolutional layer can be used as a local feature extractor. Then, we input the output z_x^l of the convolution layer into the BN layer to standardize the activation of each batch of convolution layers. The BN layer can be defined as:

$$Z_x^l = BN(z_x^l) = \gamma(\frac{z_x^l - \mu}{\sqrt{\sigma^2 + \varepsilon}}) + \beta, \tag{3}$$

where μ and σ^2 represent the mean value and variance of the x-th output value in the l layer, respectively. The ε and β represent the parameters that can be adjusted in the training process. Then, we input the value processed by the BN layer into the leaky-relu activation function. The leaky-relu function can be expressed as:

$$p_x = \begin{cases} q_x, & q_x \geq 0 \\ \frac{q_x}{a_x}, & q_x < 0 \end{cases}.$$

(4)

The leaky-relu solves the situation where the input value of relu is negative and the first derivative is zero, avoiding the phenomenon that neurons may die. In the end, we can obtain the 128-dimensional frame-level local feature sequence.

3.3   Upgrade Attention Mechanism (UA)

To focus attention on useful features, in this paper, we use the UA mechanism to learn salient and discriminative features that contain context information. The UA mechanism includes the BiLSTM layer and 3D attention mechanism. The structure of the UA mechanism is shown in Fig. 4. First, we use the BiLSTM layer to associate context information. So far, the features learned are still segment level. It is more useful to obtain the speaker's emotional state according to the utterance. Then, we input the obtained segment-level features into the 3D attention mechanism and combine the time step information to calculate the attention value of each feature to obtain the discourse-level salient features. Finally, we pass the salient features into a Dropout layer to prevent over fitting and a Dense layer with a size of 4 units.

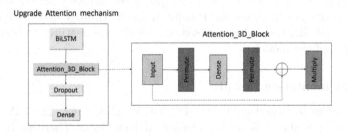

Fig. 4. Framework of the upgrade attention mechanism

The BiLSTM layer obtains the past and future information by hiding the connections between the layers in reverse order and automatically ignores irrelevant information. The calculation process of the BiLSTM layer is as follows:

$$\overrightarrow{h_i} = f_a(\overrightarrow{h_{i-1}}, \overrightarrow{x_i}) + \overrightarrow{x_i},$$

(5)

$$\overleftarrow{h_i} = f'_a(\overleftarrow{h_{i+1}}, \overleftarrow{x_i}) + \overleftarrow{x_i},$$

(6)

$$h_i = (\overrightarrow{h_i} + \overleftarrow{h_i}),$$

(7)

where f_a and f_a' are LSTMs with parameter α forward and backward, h_i represents the hidden state of time step i, x_i represents the i-th spectral feature in the audio signal, $\overrightarrow{h_i}$ means forward propagation, $\overleftarrow{h_i}$ means backward propagation, $(\overrightarrow{h_i} + \overleftarrow{h_i})$ is the hidden representation of the forward and backward LSTM.

The 3D attention learns significant features by calculating and comparing the attention values of the features. First, the input is a three-dimensional array including BatchSize, TimeStep, and HiddenVector. Second, we use the permutation function to transpose the input features to get the required dimensions. Third, we connect a Dense layer, which includes a softmax activation function. It can calculate the weight value of each dimension of HiddenVector in each TimeStep. Each feature has its attention weight value. The core of the Dense layer is to select the vector dimension that has the greatest impact on the final classification result. Fourth, we get the weight matrix through the permutation function. Finally, the original input of the model is multiplied with the obtained weight matrix to complete the distribution of the feature attention weight value. Different from the traditional Attention mechanism that directly performs weighted summation to obtain features. We use transposition, softmax, and flatten to filter features based on the degree of contribution to the model.

4   Experiments

In this section, we evaluate the UA-LFLB model on IEMOCAP dataset. First, we briefly introduce the details of the experimental implementation. Then, the parameters of the UA-LFLB model are optimized and we compare the performance with the previous models. Finally, the t-distributed stochastic neighbor embedding (t-SNE) technology is used to visualize the features to evaluate the performance of the model.

4.1   Implementation Details

The experiment is carried out on the IEMOCAP [2] dataset. The IEMOCAP is a dataset composed of a male and a female dialogue form. There are five groups of conversations. During the conversation, the motion capture equipment will be worn to record facial expressions and head Data on posture and hand movements. To be consistent with the previous research [4], we only consider four emotions: 1) *angry*, 2) *happy*, 3) *neutral*, and 4) *sad*. We use the 10-fold cross-validation technique and split the dataset into a training set, validation set, and test set to perform the model.

To verify the performance of the model, we choose unweighted accuracy rate (UAR), *Precision*, *Recall*, and $F1$ score as the evaluation measure. The UAR is the unweighted average of recalls for a specific category. The *Precision* represents how many of the samples predicted to be positive are true positive samples. In this paper, it is abbreviated as *Pre*. The *Recall* refers to the proportion of positive examples that have been correctly determined to the total positive examples. The $F1$ score is a harmonic average of model precision and recall.

We set the sampling rate of the sound wave 16000 Hz. The signal is divided into the same length of 3 s for better parallel acceleration. The utterance of less than 3 s is filled with zeros. Based on suggestions from previous work [4], we use openEAR toolkit to extract log-Mels from the audio signal and we set the window size to 25 ms and the offset to 10 ms. The number of CNN layers is set as 6. The first CNN layer has 32 filters and the input size is (100, 34, 1). Our input consists of data processed by 34 filter banks, which are replaced with 100-point height and width. This means that the data will be convolved with the convolution kernel in the input volume. The remaining CNN layers have 32, 64, 64, 128, and 128 filters respectively. The kernel size of each CNN layer is 3×3, and the step size is (1, 1). The model is implemented with Keras toolkit and Adam optimizer.

4.2   Parameter Optimization

We choose different batch-size and learning rates for experiments. We mainly optimize the parameters of the two sets of experiments, the difference is whether the model has 3D attention and BiLSTM. The optimization result is shown in Table 1.

Table 1. The performance of the model was evaluated on the IEMOCAP dataset with different batch-size, learning rates. Notes: BS stands for batch-size, LR stands for learning rates.

Model	BS	LR (%)	UAR (%)	Pre (%)	F1 (%)
Proposed model (with 3D attention + BiLSTM)	32	0.001	74.18	73.63	72.60
		0.0001	**84.25**	**83.88**	**83.35**
		0.00001	80.08	80.15	79.15
	64	0.001	73.50	73.59	72.58
		0.0001	83.95	83.82	83.30
		0.00001	77.8	76.95	77.10
Proposed model (without 3D attention + BiLSTM)	32	0.001	74.02	73.35	72.17
		0.0001	**82.83**	**82.53**	**82.40**
		0.00001	79.03	79.08	78.45
	64	0.001	73.16	73.24	71.78
		0.0001	82.80	82.50	81.85
		0.00001	76.43	76.78	76.70

From Table 1, we can observe that when the learning rate is 0.0001 and the batch size is 32, the model with 3D attention and BiLSTM has better performance. Compared with the model without 3D Attention and BiLSTM, the *UAR*, *Precision*, and *F1* scores are improved by 1.42%, 1.35%, and 0.95%, respectively. The reason is that the 3D attention mechanism based on BiLSTM can learn salient features with contextual information for SER.

Since when the model contains 3D attention and BiLSTM, and the learning rate and batch size are 0.0001 and 32 respectively, the model performs better.

To verify the model's ability to correctly recognize emotions, we show the recognition rate of the model in terms of emotion. As shown in Table 2.

Table 2. Emotion recognition result in IEMOCAP dataset

Emotion	Recall	Pre	F1
Angry	0.91	0.89	0.90
Happy	0.69	0.68	0.69
Neutral	0.86	0.91	0.88
Sad	0.90	0.84	0.87
Average	0.84	0.83	0.84

It can be seen from Table 2, the average recognition rate of emotion is around 84%. To further verify the recognition performance of the model, we generate a confusion matrix of emotions. The confusion matrix shows the correct prediction rate and false mixing rate of different emotions, as shown in Fig. 5.

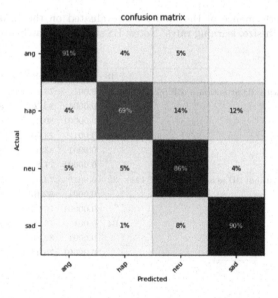

Fig. 5. The confusion matrix of the model on the IEMOCAP dataset. The experimental parameters are set to the batch size is 32 and the learning rate is 0.0001.

From Fig. 5, we can observe that the recognition rates of angry, neutral, and sad emotions are higher, reaching 91%, 86%, and 90%, respectively. The recognition rate of happy emotion is 69%, which is low compared with the other three emotions. It is observed that happy emotion is easily confused with other emotions such as neutral emotion. The reason may be that the signal strengths of happy emotions and neutral emotions reach similar frequencies at the same time.

4.3 Performance Comparison

To verify the performance of the UA-LFLB model, we selected several representative works with similar structures to the proposed model. The results are shown in Table 3.

Table 3. The recognition rate of IEMOCAP dataset is compared with the existing models using the 10 fold cross-validation. Notes: \ indicates that the evaluation index has not been used in previous work.

Network	$UAR_{(\%)}$	$F1_{(\%)}$	$Pre_{(\%)}$
3D ACRNN [4] (2018)	64.74	\	\
3Dilated CNN [11] (2019)	69.32	\	\
RBFN+BiLSTM [14] (2020)	72.25	74.00	74.00
UA-LFLB (ours)	**84.25**	**83.35**	**83.88**

From Table 3, we can observe that the average recognition rate of the proposed UA-LFLB model is improved by 9% compared with the previous models. The improvement of recognition performance is attributed to the model proposed in this paper that can capture the salient features with context relevance. To alleviate the problem of a low recognition rate caused by a large amount of irrelevant information in the extracted features, we propose a UA-LFLB model based on [4]. The comparative experiment is shown in Table 4.

Table 4. Compare the proposed model and [4] with the 10-fold cross-validation on the IEMOCAP dataset to compare the recognition accuracy.

Model	$Hap_{(\%)}$	$Ang_{(\%)}$	$Neu_{(\%)}$	$Sad_{(\%)}$
3D ACRNN [4] (2018)	29.95	70.47	66.52	84.32
UA-LFLB (ours)	**69.00**	**91.00**	**86.00**	**90.00**

From Table 4 we can observe that the identification performance of the proposed model is better than the 3D attention-based convolutional recurrent neural networks (ACRNN) [4] model. The recognition rates of *angry, happy, natural,* and *sad* emotions increased by 20.53%, 39.05%, 19.48%, and 5.68%, respectively. The recognition rate of happy emotion has been greatly improved. This indicates that the LFLB can extract deep local sequence features. Then, the obtained local features are used as the input of the UA mechanism. This mechanism can capture the contextual relevance of the features and learn the salient features of the discourse level by calculating the weight of the features.

4.4 Feature Visualization

The t-SNE [9] is mainly used for the visualization of high-dimensional data to evaluate the algorithm performance or verify the effectiveness of algorithms through visual observation. The visualization of emotional features on the IEMO-CAP dataset is shown in Fig. 6.

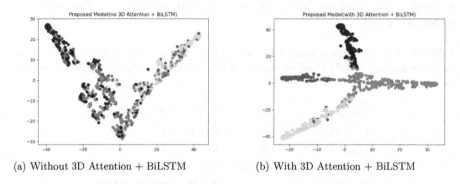

(a) Without 3D Attention + BiLSTM   (b) With 3D Attention + BiLSTM

Fig. 6. t-SNE visualization of features on IEMOCAP dataset

As can be seen from Fig. 6, there are four different color coordinate points distributed in the two-dimensional map, which represent four different emotional characteristics. When the proposed model without 3D Attention and BiLSTM, there is a large amount of overlap in the distribution of clustering features, resulting in fuzzy emotional features, as shown in Fig. 6(a). When the proposed model includes 3D Attention and BiLSTM, the overlap of features is significantly reduced, shown in Fig. 6(b). The experimental result shows that the UA mechanism composed of 3D Attention and BiLSTM can make the features more prominent and improve the recognition performance of the model.

5   Conclusion

In this paper, we propose a UA-LFLB model to learn context-related salient features to reduce the interference of irrelevant emotional information in the features. The LFLB can extract deep local sequence features. The UA is composed of BiLSTM and 3D attention. Based on local features, the BiLSTM can capture context information, while 3D attention can focus attention on salient features by calculating the weight value of features. The experimental results show that compared with the baseline methods, the average accuracy rate is increased by 9%. In the future, we will extract features from multiple modalities to increase the diversity and completeness of features. We will also improve the loss function to make the distance between the same features more concentrated, and the distance between the different features more scattered. This will greatly reduce the overlap of features and enhance the discrimination of features.

References

1. Basu, S., Bag, A., Mahadevappa, M., Mukherjee, J., Guha, R.: Affect detection in normal groups with the help of biological markers. In: 2015 Annual IEEE India Conference (INDICON), pp. 1–6 (2015)
2. Busso, C., et al.: IEMOCAP: interactive emotional dyadic motion capture database. Lang. Resour. Eval. **42**, 335–359 (2008)
3. Chen, L.F., Su, W., Feng, Y., Wu, M., She, J., Hirota, K.: Two-layer fuzzy multiple random forest for speech emotion recognition in human-robot interaction. Inf. Sci. **509**, 150–163 (2020)
4. Chen, M., He, X., Yang, J., Zhang, H.: 3-d convolutional recurrent neural networks with attention model for speech emotion recognition. IEEE Sig. Process. Lett. **25**(10), 1440–1444 (2018)
5. Han, J., Zhang, Z., Cummins, N., Schuller, B.: Adversarial training in affective computing and sentiment analysis: Recent advances and perspectives [review article]. IEEE Comput. Intell. Mag. **14**, 68–81 (2019)
6. Huang, Z., Dong, M., Mao, Q., Zhan, Y.: Speech emotion recognition using CNN. In: MM 2014, pp. 801–804 (2014)
7. Landau, M.J.: Acoustical properties of speech as indicators of depression and suicidal risk. Vanderbilt Undergraduate Res. J. **4** (2008)
8. Li, Y., Baidoo, C., Cai, T., Kusi, G.A.: Speech emotion recognition using 1d cnn with no attention. In: International Computer Science and Engineering Conference (ICSEC), pp. 351–356 (2019)
9. Maaten, L.V.D., Hinton, G.E.: Visualizing data using t-SNE. J. Mach. Learn. Res. **9**, 2579–2605 (2008)
10. Mao, Q., Dong, M., Huang, Z., Zhan, Y.: Learning salient features for speech emotion recognition using convolutional neural networks. IEEE Trans. Multimedia **16**(8), 2203–2213 (2014)
11. Meng, H., Yan, T., Yuan, F., Wei, H.: Speech emotion recognition from 3d log-mel spectrograms with deep learning network. IEEE Access **7**, 125868–125881 (2019)
12. Mirsamadi, S., Barsoum, E., Zhang, C.: Automatic speech emotion recognition using recurrent neural networks with local attention. In: ICASSP, pp. 2227–2231 (2017)
13. Mishra, S., Mandal, B., Puhan, N.B.: Multi-level dual-attention based CNN for macular optical coherence tomography classification. IEEE Sig. Process. Lett. **26**, 1793–1797 (2019)
14. Sajjad, M., Kwon, S.: Clustering-based speech emotion recognition by incorporating learned features and deep BiLSTM. IEEE Access **8**, 79861–79875 (2020)
15. Park, J.S., Kim, J., Oh, Y.: Feature vector classification based speech emotion recognition for service robots. IEEE Trans. Consum. Electron. **55**, 1590–1596 (2009)
16. Schmidt, E.M., Kim, Y.E.: Learning emotion-based acoustic features with deep belief networks. In: IEEE WASPAA, pp. 65–68 (2011)
17. Swain, M., Routray, A., Kabisatpathy, P.: Databases, features and classifiers for speech emotion recognition: a review. Int. J. Speech Technol. **21**(1), 93–120 (2018)
18. Xia, G., Li, F., Zhao, D.D., Zhang, Q., Yang, S.: Fi-net: a speech emotion recognition framework with feature integration and data augmentation. In: 2019 5th International Conference on Big Data Computing and Communications (BIGCOM), pp. 195–203 (2019)

19. Zeng, Z., Pantic, M., Roisman, G., Huang, T.: A survey of affect recognition methods: audio, visual, and spontaneous expressions. IEEE Trans. Pattern Anal. Mach. Intell. **31**(1), 39–58 (2009)
20. Zhang, Z., Cummins, N., Schuller, B.: Advanced data exploitation in speech analysis: an overview. IEEE Sig. Process. Mag. **34**, 107–129 (2017)
21. Zhao, H., Xiao, Y., Han, J., Zhang, Z.: Compact convolutional recurrent neural networks via binarization for speech emotion recognition. In: 2019 IEEE International Conference on Acoustics, Speech and Signal Processing (ICASSP), ICASSP 2019, pp. 6690–6694 (2019)
22. Zhao, J., Mao, X., Chen, L.: Speech emotion recognition using deep 1D & 2D CNN LSTM networks. Biomed. Sign. Process. Control **47**, 312–323 (2019)
23. Zhao, Z., Zheng, Y., Zhang, Z., Wang, H., Zhao, Y., Li, C.: Exploring spatiotemporal representations by integrating attention-based bidirectional-LSTM-RNNs and FCNs for speech emotion recognition. In: INTERSPEECH, pp. 272–276 (2018)
24. Zheng, W., Yu, J., Zou, Y.: An experimental study of speech emotion recognition based on deep convolutional neural networks. In: 2015 International Conference on Affective Computing and Intelligent Interaction (ACII), pp. 827–831 (2015)

Memorization in Deep Neural Networks: Does the Loss Function Matter?

Deep Patel$^{(\boxtimes)}$ and P. S. Sastry

Indian Institute of Science, Bangalore 560012, India
{deeppatel,sastry}@iisc.ac.in

Abstract. Deep Neural Networks, often owing to the overparameterization, are shown to be capable of exactly memorizing even randomly labelled data. Empirical studies have also shown that none of the standard regularization techniques mitigate such overfitting. We investigate whether choice of loss function can affect this memorization. We empirically show, with benchmark data sets MNIST and CIFAR-10, that a symmetric loss function as opposed to either cross entropy or squared error loss results in significant improvement in the ability of the network to resist such overfitting. We then provide a formal definition for robustness to memorization and provide theoretical explanation as to why the symmetric losses provide this robustness. Our results clearly bring out the role loss functions alone can play in this phenomenon of memorization.

Keywords: Memorization · Deep networks · Random labels · Symmetric losses

1 Introduction

Deep Neural Networks have been remarkably successful in a variety of classification problems involving image, text or speech data [12,18,20,21,24]. This is remarkable because these networks often have a large number of parameters and are trained on data sets that are not large enough for the sizes of these networks. This raises many questions about the (unreasonable) effectiveness of deep networks in applications and whether they can go wrong on some kind of data sets.

In an interesting recent study, [25] showed that standard deep network architectures are highly susceptible to extreme overfitting. They show that when one randomly alters class labels in the training data, these networks can learn the random labels almost exactly (with the gradient based learning algorithm driving the training error to near zero). It is seen that this memorization of the training examples cannot be mitigated through any of the standard regularization techniques such as weight decay or dropout. These results seem to imply that the usual complexity measures of statistical learning theory are inadequate to understand the learning dynamics of deep neural networks. In a further study,

© Springer Nature Switzerland AG 2021
K. Karlapalem et al. (Eds.): PAKDD 2021, LNAI 12713, pp. 131–142, 2021.
https://doi.org/10.1007/978-3-030-75765-6_11

[1] investigates this phenomenon more closely. While their study also confirms this memorization, they formulate some characterizations under which the learning dynamics of a network differ for the two cases of learning from real data and random data. Their study suggests that the data may be playing a vital role in resisting brute-force memorization by a network. While these studies experiment with many scenarios of regularization techniques and randomization of data, the role that the loss function itself can play in this has not been investigated. Motivated by this, here we present some experiments to show that a loss function can also play a significant role in preventing a network from memorizing data.

Neural networks are universal approximators [8] and networks with sufficient parameters have the capacity to exactly represent any finite amount of data [25]. Such results show that there exist parameter values that can represent any arbitrary function. However, as discussed in [1], what a network learns depends on the parameter values that a gradient-based learning algorithm can reach starting from some random initial parameter values. This learning dynamics is certainly affected, among other factors, by the loss function because the loss function determines the topography of the empirical risk, which is minimized by the learning algorithm. Hence, it would be interesting to investigate whether it is possible to have loss functions that can inherently resist (to some degree) the memorization of data by a network.

Here we present some experimental results for benchmark datasets, MNIST [14] and CIFAR-10 [11], with labels randomly changed with different probabilities. We see that for varying probabilities of random labelling, networks trained with standard loss functions such as categorical cross entropy (CCE) or mean square error (MSE) exhibit memorization by reaching close to zero training error. Then, we investigate learning these same networks using a special class of loss functions – *symmetric loss functions*. We specifically use the so-called *robust log loss* (RLL) [13] – which is obtained by modifying CCE – though we also comment on other similar loss functions. We show that keeping everything else in the training algorithm same but changing the loss function alone results in the network significantly resisting overfitting. With these loss functions the training error saturates at a level much above zero (depending on the amount of random label flipping). We also see that the learning dynamics with these symmetric loss functions resembles more of what one expects with the clean, real data. It was suggested in [1] that, with real data, the networks try to fit the patterns in the data rather than memorizing the data, while with randomly flipped labels the networks seem to be using brute-force memorization. We show that with fairly high (though less than 100%) randomization of labels in training data, networks trained with CCE or MSE loss seem to be using brute-force memorization while the same networks trained with the symmetric loss, RLL, seem to be resisting such memorization by trying to fit mainly the clean part of the data. This adequately demonstrates that the loss function also has an important role to play in resisting this type of memorization of data.

We also present some theoretical justification (using the known properties of these symmetric losses) for the ability of these loss functions to resist overfitting.

For the case of random label flipping, we formally define what can be called *resisting of overfitting* or *memorization*. Using this, we explain why symmetric loss functions can resist brute-force memorization in these scenarios. The analysis we present provides some theoretical justification for the empirically observed performance with RLL. We discuss the implications of this and speculate on how loss functions may be crucial in realizing better learning dynamics.

1.1 Related Work

Memorization in deep networks got a lot of attention recently due to [25] which showed that SGD-based training of neural networks drives the training set accuracy to 100% even in case of randomly labelled data with none of the standard regularization methods being helpful for avoiding this memorization. They speculate on the implications of this for characterizing the generalization abilities of networks. In further studies, [1,7] characterize the behaviour of neural networks on real and randomly-labelled data experimentally and find that deep networks learn simpler patterns first before starting to memorize the data. They also claim that explicit regularization such as dropout can actually help resist memorization to some extent. [3] shows that memorization is necessary for generalization for some types of distributions which has been tested empirically by [4]. However, none of these studies investigate whether the loss function has a role in memorization and that is what is explored in this paper

There are many works that attempt comparative study of loss functions for classification tasks. [9] shows, with extensive empirical experiments on a variety of data sets, that MSE performs better than CCE thus challenging the conventional wisdom of the superiority of CCE loss for classification tasks. [2] argue that CCE is favourable (compared to MSE) for multi-class settings but propose a technique that makes performance of MSE comparable to that of CCE. [19,22] find MSE has comparable or better performance than hinge loss for several tasks. [16] show that minimizers of risk obtained in case of MSE and hinge loss are the same for overparameterized linear models under certain conditions. These and other similar works compare different loss functions for classification and regression tasks from the point of view of generalization whereas our work looks at the role loss functions can play in affecting the degree of memorization in overparameterized networks.

The problem of learning under label noise, that is, learning when training data has random labeling errors, has also been extensively studied in recent years. (See, e.g., [5,6,15,17,23]). In tackling label noise the focus is mostly on algorithms that deliver good performance by, e.g., sample reweighting, label cleaning, loss correction, etc. In this work our focus is on the inherent robustness of a loss function and not on any algorithmic modifications to take care of label noise.

The main contributions of the paper are as follows: We consider some scenarios of network architectures and randomization of training labels under which deep networks are earlier demonstrated to be susceptible to memorization.

We show through empirical studies that training the same network with a different loss function, namely, RLL, can significantly resist this memorization as compared to training with standard CCE or MSE. Our experiments adequately demonstrate that the loss function has a crucial role and supports our viewpoint that it is important to study such properties of loss functions. We propose a formal definition for the ability of a network to resist overfitting of the kind studied [1,25]. Using this definition, for these scenarios of random label flipping on training data, we provide theoretical justification for the observed performance with the symmetric loss functions.

The rest of the paper is organized as follows: In Sect. 2, we present our empirical studies with the CCE, MSE, & RLL loss functions. Section 3 presents our theoretical analysis. Conclusions are presented in Sect. 4.

2   Role of Loss Function in Resisting Memorization

We experiment with two network architectures. One is an Inception-like network architecture (referred to as Inception-Lite in this paper) which is same as that used in [25] for demonstrating memorization in deep networks. The second is ResNet-32 (and ResNet-18 for MNIST) architecture as used in [23].

In this section we present results with three loss functions. Two are the standard loss functions used with neural networks, namely, CCE and MSE, and the third is a symmetric loss, viz. RLL. Since we are considering classification problems, for all the networks we assume a softmax output layer. For an input, $\mathbf{x}$, let $\mathbf{g}(\mathbf{x})$ denote the vector output of the network with components $g_i(\mathbf{x})$. When $\mathbf{x}$ belongs to class k, the label would be the one-hot vector $\mathbf{e}^k$ where $e_k^k = 1$ and $e_j^k = 0$, $\forall j \neq k$. Let K denote the number of classes. With this notation, the three loss functions can be defined as follows:

$$\mathcal{L}_{CCE}(\mathbf{g}(\mathbf{x}), \mathbf{e}^k) = -\sum_i e_i^k \log\left(g_i(\mathbf{x})\right) = -\log(g_k(\mathbf{x}))$$

$$\mathcal{L}_{MSE}(\mathbf{g}(\mathbf{x}), \mathbf{e}^k) = \sum_i \left(g_i(\mathbf{x}) - e_i^k\right)^2$$

$$\mathcal{L}_{RLL}(\mathbf{g}(\mathbf{x}), \mathbf{e}^k) = \log\left(\frac{\alpha + 1}{\alpha}\right) - \log(\alpha + g_k(\mathbf{x})) + \sum_{j \neq k} \frac{1}{K-1} \log(\alpha + g_j(\mathbf{x}))$$

where $\alpha > 0$ is a parameter of the RLL.

We can get some insights on behaviour of RLL versus CCE as follows: When $\mathbf{x}$ is in class-k, $g_k(\mathbf{x})$ is the posterior probability assigned to class-k by the network. If this is high, then the CCE loss, which is $-\log(g_k(\mathbf{x}))$, is low. However, the CCE loss is unbounded because, in principle, $g_k(x)$ can be arbitrarily small. Disregarding the constant term, the RLL takes $-\log(\alpha + g_k(\mathbf{x})) + \sum_{j \neq k} \frac{1}{K-1} \log(\alpha + g_j(\mathbf{x}))$ as its value. Since we are using $\log(\alpha + g_j(\mathbf{x}))$ rather than $\log(g_j(\mathbf{x}))$, the loss is now bounded. More importantly, the loss is essentially determined through a kind of comparison of the posterior probability assigned to class-k by the network against the average probability assigned to all other classes. (The constant term in RLL is there only to ensure that the loss is non-negative). As we shall see, this gives some amount of robustness in the risk minimization resulting in RLL exhibiting good resistance to memorization.

We train all the networks to minimize empirical risk (with each of the loss functions). We employ mini-batch based stochastic gradient descent (SGD) for Inception-Lite & ResNet-32 (for CIFAR-10) and Adam [10] for ResNet-18 (for MNIST). For Inception-Lite, we use a constant step-size of 0.01 in each epoch which is reduced by a factor of 0.95 after each epoch for 100 epochs whereas a constant step-size of 0.1 is used for ResNet-32 which is reduced by a factor of 0.1 after 100 and 150 epochs. ResNet-32 & ResNet-18 are trained for 200 epochs. The ResNet-18 is trained with a step-size of 0.001. Inception-Lite is trained for 100 epochs because the training accuracies saturate by then. Inception-Lite and ResNet-18 are trained without weight decay whereas ResNet-32 is trained with a weight decay of 0.0001.

CIFAR-10 and MNIST benchmark datasets are used for the experiments. As explained earlier, we study the memorization by the networks through randomly altering the class labels in the training set. For this, independently for each example, we retain the original label with probability $(1 - \eta)$ and change it with probability η. When the label is changed, it is changed to one of the other classes with equal probability. We experiment with $\eta = 0, 0.2, 0.4$, and 0.6. (Note that $\eta = 0$ corresponds to the clean or original training data). By varying η we can change the amount of pattern information present in training data and hence can study whether a loss function can result in learning this information. Here, we are considering 10-class classification task. Our randomization of labels is such that up to $\eta < 0.9$, in an expectation sense, for any class-j, the number of data points in the training set that are correctly labelled as class-j would be more than the number of data points of a class-i, $i \neq j$, incorrectly labelled as class-j. Hence, at η well below 0.9 there should be scope for learning the underlying patterns and not overfitting the randomized training data.

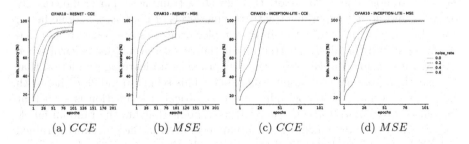

(a) *CCE*   (b) *MSE*   (c) *CCE*   (d) *MSE*

Fig. 1. Training set accuracies for ResNet-32 ((a) & (b)) & Inception-Lite ((c) & (d)) trained on CIFAR-10 with CCE and MSE losses for for $\eta \in \{0., 0.2, 0.4, 0.6\}$

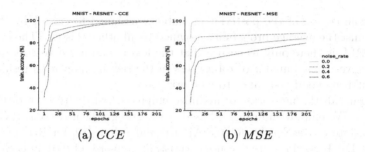

Fig. 2. Training set accuracies for ResNet-18 trained on MNIST with CCE and MSE losses for different levels of label noise

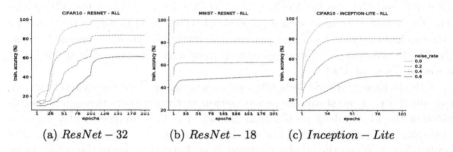

Fig. 3. Training set accuracies for networks trained on CIFAR-10 ((a) & (c)) & MNIST ((b)) with RLL for $\eta \in \{0., 0.2, 0.4, 0.6\}$

Figure 1 shows the training accuracies achieved with ResNet-32 and InceptionLite when we train the network with CCE & MSE for various values of η on CIFAR-10 while Fig. 2 shows training accuracies of ResNet-18 with CCE and MSE for MNIST. As can be seen from the figures, for all values of η the training error goes down close to zero though it takes a few epochs more with higher values of η. The only exception is when ResNet-18 is trained on MNIST with MSE; but even here the training accuracy reaches a high value. This is consistent with the results reported in [1,25]. (Note that [25] show training set performances only for $\eta = 1$ and do not experiment with varying levels of noise as was done here.) Note that at $\eta = 0.2$, 80% of training samples of a class are correctly labelled and hence would contain the patterns that the network would have learnt when trained with clean data. However, the network ends up learning a function that can exactly reproduce the training set labels. This seems to indicate that with these loss functions the topography of the empirical risk function is such that the learning dynamics takes the network to a point that fits the random labels exactly. The brute-force memorization manifests itself in these networks trained with CCE even at moderate levels of label randomization.

These results may be contrasted with those presented in Fig. 3 which are obtained when the same networks are trained with RLL for different values of η on MNIST & CIFAR-10. As can be seen from the figures, the training set accuracy achieved by RLL for non-zero values of η is always well below that achieved on clean data. This shows that the network does not blindly learn to reproduce the training set labels. This is significant because this shows that when we keep everything else same and change only the loss function, the learning dynamics now seem to be able to resist brute-force memorization. Also, for $\eta = 0.2$ and $\eta = 0.4$ the difference in training-accuracy on clean and noisy data is almost equal to the noise-rate thus suggesting that this loss function seems to be able to disregard data that are wrongly labelled.

We now take a closer look to understand the kind of classifier learnt by RLL under noisy data. Let $\{X_i, y_i\}_{i=1}^{\ell}$ denote the original training data and let $\{X_i, \tilde{y}_i\}_{i=1}^{\ell}$ denote the noisy or randomly-labelled data given to the learning algorithm. Let $h(X)$ denote the actual class label predicted by the network for X (which is determined by $\max(g_i(X))$ where $g(X)$ is the output of softmax layer). Then the training accuracy, say J_1, is defined by

$$J_1 = \frac{1}{\ell} \sum_{i=1}^{\ell} I_{[h(X_i)=\tilde{y}_i)]}$$

where I_A is indicator of A. This is the accuracy defined with respect to the labels as given in the training set. We define another accuracy, J_2, by

$$J_2 = \frac{1}{\ell} \sum_{i=1}^{\ell} I_{[h(X_i)=y_i)]}$$

J_2 is the accuracy with respect to original, uncorrupted training set. This accuracy indicates how well the network, learned with randomly-altered labels, would be able to reproduce the original clean labels of the training data.

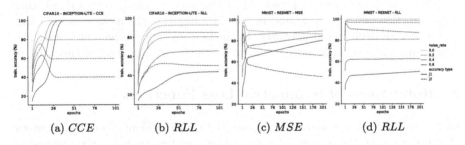

Fig. 4. J_1 and J_2 accuracies for Inception-Lite ((a) & (b)) & ResNet-18 ((c) & (d)) trained on CIFAR-10 and MNIST resp. for $\eta \in \{0., 0.2, 0.4, 0.6\}$ (Solid lines show J_1 accuracy; dashed lines show J_2 accuracy)

We show in Fig. 4 the accuracies J_1 and J_2 for networks learned with the different loss functions for different values of η. As can be seen from Figs. 4a & 4c for networks trained with CCE and MSE losses, the J_2 accuracy (dashed line) is always well below the J_1 accuracy (solid line). This is as expected because, as

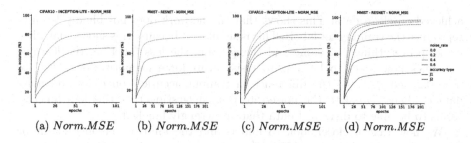

(a) $Norm.MSE$ (b) $Norm.MSE$ (c) $Norm.MSE$ (d) $Norm.MSE$

Fig. 5. Train. accuracy and J_1 & J_2 accuracies for Inception-Lite ((a) & (c)) & ResNet-18 ((b) & (d)) trained on CIFAR-10 and MNIST resp. for $\eta \in \{0., 0.2, 0.4, 0.6\}$ (Solid lines show J_1 accuracy; dashed lines show J_2 accuracy)

seen earlier, the training accuracy, which is equal to J_1, is close to 100%. However, for networks learned with RLL (Fig. 4b & 4d), it is the J_2 (dashed line) accuracy that is always higher than the J_1 accuracy (solid line). As a matter of fact, for $\eta = 0.2, 0.4$, the J_2 accuracy of the networks learned using RLL is close to the training accuracy achieved with clean data. This suggests that this loss function is able to disregard the randomly altered labels and help the network learn a classifier that it would have learned with clean data.

There is another interesting point about this figure. The figure shows how the J_1 and J_2 accuracies evolve with epochs. As can be seen from the figure, the networks learned using CCE with noisy data seemed to have initially tried to learn the patterns and thus the J_2 accuracy is higher in the early epochs. But eventually the network 'flips' and overfits to the random labels in training data. However, this 'flip' never happens for networks trained using RLL; through all the epochs, the J_2 accuracy stays higher.

All the empirical results presented in this section amply demonstrate that a loss function can play a significant role in mitigating the memorization effect observed with deep neural networks. In the next section, we present some theoretical analysis that explains, to some extent, the results presented in this section.

3   Robustness of Symmetric Loss Functions

In [25], for networks learned using training data with random labels, the accuracy obtained on part of the original data is taken as test error for the purpose of discussing the generalization abilities. However, this may be somewhat of an inaccurate nomenclature. Normally the test error is error on new data but drawn from the same distribution as that from which training data is drawn.

We will now present another way of formalizing this. For this section we assume class labels, y_i, take values in $\mathcal{Y} = \{1, \cdots, K\}$ rather than being one-hot vectors. Let $S = \{X_i, y_i\}_{i=1}^{\ell}$ be the original training data and we assume it is drawn *iid* according to a distribution $\mathcal{D}$. The training data with randomly altered labels is denoted by $S_\eta = \{X_i, \tilde{y}_i\}_{i=1}^\ell$, where, for each i,

$$\tilde{y}_i = \begin{cases} y_i & \text{with probability } 1 - \eta \\ j \in \mathcal{Y} - \{y_i\} & \text{with probability } \frac{\eta}{K-1} \end{cases}$$

That is, $\tilde{y}_i$ is same as y_i with probability $(1 - \eta)$ and takes each of the other possible labels with equal probability. We denote the distribution from which S_η is drawn as $\mathcal{D}_\eta$ and it is related to $\mathcal{D}$ as given above.

When one is empirically investigating memorization of random labels, one is using training data drawn according to distribution $\mathcal{D}_\eta$ but is interested in test error according to distribution $\mathcal{D}$. Because of the special relationship between the two distributions, we are asking whether it is possible for the network learned using data drawn from $\mathcal{D}_\eta$ to do well on data drawn from $\mathcal{D}$. As a matter of fact, we want it to do well on data only from $\mathcal{D}$; we do not want it to learn distribution $\mathcal{D}_\eta$.

Let h and h_η denote the classifier function (network) learned by an algorithm when given S and S_η as training data, respectively. We can say that an algorithm **resists memorization** if

$$\text{Prob}_{(X,y)\sim\mathcal{D}}[h(X) = y] = \text{Prob}_{(X,y)\sim\mathcal{D}}[h_\eta(X) = y]$$

What this means is that the accuracy on the original data achieved by the network learnt with noisy data is same as that of network learnt with original clean data. This is the ideal case where random altering of labels would have no effect on the classifier learnt. Note that the RHS above is what we called J_2 accuracy in the previous section.

The standard algorithm employed for training all networks is empirical risk minimization. The above property can be established for risk minimization if the loss function satisfies a special property called symmetry [6].

Definition: A loss function L is called **symmetric** if it satisfies

$$\sum_{j=1}^K L(g(X), j) = C, \quad \forall g, X$$

where C is a finite constant. That is, given any network (or function) g and any input X, if we sum the loss values over all class labels, it should give the same constant.

Theorem 1. Let $\mathcal{L}$ be a symmetric loss, $\mathcal{D}$ and $\mathcal{D}^\eta$ be as defined above. Assume $\eta < \frac{K-1}{K}$. Let y_x and $\tilde{y}_x$ denote the original and noisy label corresponding to a pattern X. The risk of h over $\mathcal{D}$ and over $\mathcal{D}^\eta$ is $R_{\mathcal{L}}(h) = \mathbb{E}_{\mathcal{D}}[\mathcal{L}(h(X), y_x)]$ and $R_{\mathcal{L}}^\eta(h) = \mathbb{E}_{\mathcal{D}^\eta}[\mathcal{L}(h(X), \tilde{y}_x)]$ respectively. Then, given any two classifiers h_1 and h_2, if $R_{\mathcal{L}}(h_1) < R_{\mathcal{L}}(h_2)$, then $R_{\mathcal{L}}^\eta(h_1) < R_{\mathcal{L}}^\eta(h_2)$ and vice versa.

Proof. (This follows easily from the proof of Theorem 1 in [6].) Given the way the randomized labels are generated, we have

$$R_{\mathcal{L}}^{\eta}(h) = \mathbb{E}_{X,\tilde{y}_x}\mathcal{L}(h(X),\tilde{y}_x)$$
$$= \mathbb{E}_X\mathbb{E}_{y_x|X}\mathbb{E}_{\tilde{y}_x|X,y_x}\mathcal{L}(h(X),\tilde{y}_x)$$
$$= \mathbb{E}_X\mathbb{E}_{y_x|X}\left[(1-\eta)\mathcal{L}(h(X),y_x) + \frac{\eta}{K-1}\sum_{i\neq y_x}\mathcal{L}(h(X),i)\right]$$
$$= (1-\eta)R_{\mathcal{L}}(h) + \frac{\eta}{K-1}(C - R_{\mathcal{L}}(h))$$
$$= \frac{C\eta}{K-1} + \left(1 - \frac{\eta K}{K-1}\right)R_{\mathcal{L}}(h)$$

where C is the constant in the symmetry condition on the loss function and K is the number of classes. Since $\eta < \frac{K-1}{K}$, we have $(1 - \frac{\eta K}{K-1}) > 0$. Hence, the above shows that whenever $R_{\mathcal{L}}(h_1) < R_{\mathcal{L}}(h_2)$, we get $R_{\mathcal{L}}^{\eta}(h_1) < R_{\mathcal{L}}^{\eta}(h_2)$ and vice versa. This completes the proof.

Theorem 1 shows that the symmetric loss maintains the risk ranking of different networks regardless of random flipping of labels (as long as $\eta < \frac{K-1}{K}$). This implies that any local minimum of risk under randomly flipped labels would also be a local minimum of risk under original labels if the loss function is symmetric.

The loss function RLL satisfies the symmetry condition [13]. Thus, if we are using RLL, then any local minimum of risk under $\mathcal{D}_\eta$ would also be a local minimum of risk under $\mathcal{D}$. Even though this result is only for minima of risk, one can expect local minima of empirical risk under random label flips to be good approximators of local minima of empirical risk with clean, original samples. This explains the empirical results presented in the previous section regarding the ability of RLL to resist memorization.

There are other losses that satisfy the symmetry condition, e.g., 0–1 loss, mean absolute value of error (MAE), etc.

It is easy to verify that neither CCE nor MSE satisfy the symmetry condition. Though the symmetry of loss is only a sufficient condition for robustness, this may provide an explanation of the overfitting observed with these loss functions when the labels are randomly flipped.

As is easy to see, the symmetry condition implies that the loss function is bounded. Given a bounded loss function we can satisfy the symmetry condition by 'normalizing' it. Given a bounded loss L, define $\bar{L}$ by

$$\bar{L}(g(X),j) = \frac{L(g(X),j)}{\sum_s L(g(X),s)}$$

It is easy to see that $\bar{L}$ satisfies the symmetry condition. As mentioned earlier, CCE loss is unbounded and hence normalization would not turn it into a symmetric loss. However, we can normalize MSE loss.

In Fig. 5 we show results obtained using normalized MSE. Once we normalize MSE, it no longer fits the data with random labels perfectly; the training accuracy now saturates at a value below 100% and thus it behaves more like RLL now.

The empirical results presented in the previous section adequately demonstrate that the loss function can play a crucial role in mitigating the tendency of deep networks to memorize the training examples. The analysis presented here provides an explanation for this ability of RLL to resist such memorization. As a mater of fact, if the loss function is symmetric it would have such robustness and we can normalize a bounded loss to have such robustness.

4 Conclusions

Many recent studies have shown that overparameterized deep networks seem to be capable of perfectly fitting even randomly-labelled data. This phenomenon of memorization in deep networks has received a lot of attention because it raises important questions on how to understand generalization abilities of deep networks. In this paper we have shown through empirical studies that changing the loss function alone can significantly change the memorization in such deep networks. We showed this with the symmetric loss functions and we have provided some theoretical analysis to explain the empirical results. The results presented here suggest that choice of loss function can play a critical role in overfitting by deep networks. We feel it is important to further investigate the nature of different loss functions for a better understanding of generalization abilities of deep networks.

References

1. Arpit, D., et al.: A closer look at memorization in deep networks. In: ICML (2017)
2. Demirkaya, A., Chen, J., Oymak, S.: Exploring the role of loss functions in multi-class classification. In: 2020 54th Annual Conference on Information Sciences and Systems (CISS), pp. 1–5 (2020)
3. Feldman, V.: Does learning require memorization? a short tale about a long tail. In: Proceedings of the 52nd Annual ACM SIGACT Symposium on Theory of Computing, pp. 954–959 (2020)
4. Feldman, V., Zhang, C.: What neural networks memorize and why: discovering the long tail via influence estimation. In: Advances in Neural Information Processing Systems, vol. 33 (2020)
5. Frenay, B., Verleysen, M.: Classification in the presence of label noise: a survey. IEEE Trans. Neural Netw. Learn. Syst. 25(5), 845–869 (2014)
6. Ghosh, A., Kumar, H., Sastry, P.: Robust loss functions under label noise for deep neural networks. In: Proceedings of the Thirty-First AAAI Conference on Artificial Intelligence, pp. 1919–1925 (2017)
7. Gu, J., Tresp, V.: Neural network memorization dissection (2019)
8. Hornik, K., Stinchcombe, M., White, H., et al.: Multilayer feedforward networks are universal approximators. Neural Netw. 2(5), 359–366 (1989)
9. Hui, L., Belkin, M.: Evaluation of neural architectures trained with square loss vs cross-entropy in classification tasks (2020)

10. Kingma, D.P., Ba, J.: Adam: a method for stochastic optimization. arXiv preprint arXiv:1412.6980 (2014)
11. Krizhevsky, A.: Learning Multiple Layers of Features from Tiny Images. Ph.D. thesis, University of Toronto (2009)
12. Krizhevsky, A., Sutskever, I., Hinton, G.E.: Imagenet classification with deep convolutional neural networks. Commun. ACM **60**(6), 84–90 (2017)
13. Kumar, H., Sastry, P.S.: Robust loss functions for learning multi-class classifiers. In: 2018 IEEE International Conference on Systems, Man, and Cybernetics (SMC), pp. 687–692 (2018)
14. LeCun, Y., Bottou, L., Bengio, Y., Haffner, P.: Gradient-based learning applied to document recognition. Proc. IEEE **86**(11), 2278–2324 (1998)
15. Manwani, N., Sastry, P.S.: Noise tolerance under risk minimization. IEEE Trans. Cybern. **43**(3), 1146–1151 (2013)
16. Muthukumar, V., Narang, A., Subramanian, V., Belkin, M., Hsu, D., Sahai, A.: Classification vs regression in overparameterized regimes: Does the loss function matter? (2020)
17. Patrini, G., Rozza, A., Krishna Menon, A., Nock, R., Qu, L.: Making deep neural networks robust to label noise: a loss correction approach. In: Proceedings of the IEEE Conference on Computer Vision and Pattern Recognition (CVPR) (2017)
18. Peters, M.E., et al.: Deep contextualized word representations. In: Proceedings of NAACL (2018)
19. Que, Q., Belkin, M.: Back to the future: radial basis function networks revisited. In: Proceedings of the 19th International Conference on Artificial Intelligence and Statistics, Proceedings of Machine Learning Research, vol. 51, pp. 1375–1383. PMLR, Cadiz (2016)
20. Raffel, C., et al.: Exploring the limits of transfer learning with a unified text-to-text transformer. J. Mach. Learn. Res. **21**(140), 1–67 (2020)
21. Redmon, J., Divvala, S., Girshick, R., Farhadi, A.: You only look once: unified, real-time object detection. In: Proceedings of the IEEE Conference on Computer Vision and Pattern Recognition, pp. 779–788 (2016)
22. Rifkin, R.M.: Everything old is new again: a fresh look at historical approaches in machine learning. Ph.D. thesis, Massachussets Insitute of Technology (2002)
23. Shu, J., et al.: Meta-weight-net: Learning an explicit mapping for sample weighting. In: Advances in Neural Information Processing Systems, pp. 1919–1930 (2019)
24. Wang, W., et al.: StructBERT: incorporating language structures into pre-training for deep language understanding (2019)
25. Zhang, C., Bengio, S., Hardt, M., Recht, B., Vinyals, O.: Understanding deep learning requires rethinking generalization (2017)

Gaussian Soft Decision Trees for Interpretable Feature-Based Classification

Jaemin Yoo[1] and Lee Sael[2(✉)]

[1] Seoul National University, Seoul, South Korea
jaeminyoo@snu.ac.kr
[2] Ajou University, Suwon, South Korea
sael@ajou.ac.kr

Abstract. How can we accurately classify feature-based data such that the learned model and results are more interpretable? Interpretability is beneficial in various perspectives, such as in checking for compliance with exiting knowledge and gaining insights from decision processes. To gain in both accuracy and interpretability, we propose a novel tree-structured classifier called Gaussian Soft Decision Trees (GSDT). GSDT is characterized by multi-branched structures, Gaussian mixture-based decisions, and a hinge loss with path regularization. The three key features make it learn short trees where the weight vector of each node is a prototype for data that mapped to the node. We show that GSDT results in the best average accuracy compared to eight baselines. We also perform an ablation study of the various structures of covariance matrix in the Gaussian mixture nodes in GSDT and demonstrate the interpretability of GSDT in a case study of classification in a breast cancer dataset.

Keywords: Gaussian Soft Decision Trees · Interpretable machine learning · Feature-based classification · Tabular data · Gaussian mixtures

1 Introduction

The interpretability of a model and its predictions is often an important factor in choosing machine learning models in various domains. Interpretable machine learning allows us to understand a decision process or the cause of a decision that can advance our understanding of the problem at hand [13,18]. Furthermore, in specific domains such as biology and medicine, there are numerous feature-based data where each feature is meaningful and conveys unique information. These data require interpretable models, which is why less accurate models with interpretable structures such as decision trees are still being widely used.

Decision trees and linear models are representative models where the decision process and the importance of features are intrinsically human-understandable, but have limited representation power. Recent advancement of decision trees is

© Springer Nature Switzerland AG 2021
K. Karlapalem et al. (Eds.): PAKDD 2021, LNAI 12713, pp. 143–155, 2021.
https://doi.org/10.1007/978-3-030-75765-6_12

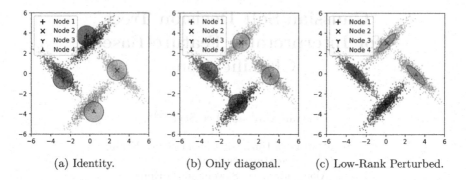

(a) Identity.   (b) Only diagonal.   (c) Low-Rank Perturbed.

Fig. 1. Comparison of Gaussian covariances of various structures on a synthetic dataset. Each point represents a data example with its label as a color, and each ellipse represents a leaf distribution learned by GSDT. The diagonal covariance with low-rank perturbations in (c) matches the true distribution better than the (a) identity and (b) diagonal covariances, resulting in higher accuracy. (Color figure online)

soft decision trees (SDT) [6] that improve the representation power of decision trees by performing soft decisions using all input features at each node. However, the interpretability of an SDT is limited, because it requires a large depth to learn complex decision rules, involving many branches for interpreting each prediction. Unlike decision trees that use only one feature at each branch with a hard threshold, the large depth of SDTs leads to a complex decision process that is difficult to interpret even with the tree structure.

In this work, we propose Gaussian Soft Decision Trees (GSDT), our novel tree model that parameterizes each tree node as a Gaussian mixture, boosting the limited accuracy of previous tree-structured models without sacrificing the interpretability. Each edge in GSDT represents a multivariate Gaussian distribution parameterized by the learnable mean and covariance, which summarizes the examples that pass through it as an interpretable prototype. This makes it possible for GSDT to naturally adopt a multi-branched structure where each edge is learned and interpreted independently of the other edges in the branch. As a result, GSDT shows at least 4.8% higher average accuracy and 4× smaller depth compared to SDT-based models in six feature-based datasets. GSDT outperforms even black box models such as random forests and multilayer perceptrons that are not interpretable but have large representation power.

The contributions of this work are summarized as follows:

- **Model:** We propose GSDT, our novel tree-structured model that supports high interpretability as well as high accuracy by modeling the internal nodes as Gaussian mixtures. We propose various options of modeling the Gaussian covariance and compare them as in Fig. 1.
- **Experiments:** We demonstrate the superior performance of GSDT by extensive experiments on six feature-based datasets, where both interpretability and classification accuracy are important.

– **Case study:** We analyze the structure and learned parameters of GSDT and shows its superior interpretability by demonstrating the decision process on an actual example on a breast cancer dataset with visualizations.

The rest of this paper is organized as follows. We introduce related works in Sect. 2. We propose GSDT in Sect. 3 with theoretical analysis in Sect. 4. We show experimental results in Sect. 5 and conclude at Sect. 6. The codes and datasets are publicly available at https://github.com/leesael/GSDT.

2   Related Works

Soft Decision Trees. Soft decision trees (SDT) [11] are tree-structured models that perform soft decisions. The internal nodes of SDTs are generalized linear classifiers [12] that pass input features through the tree structure, and the leaves learn fixed distributions over classes. With the improved representation power and interpretable nature, SDTs have been applied for various applications such as generative learning [10] and distilling the knowledge of deep neural networks [6]. EDiT [21] is a variant of SDTs, which improves the interpretability of SDTs by imposing sparsity on tree nodes and weight vectors.

Hierarchical Gaussian Mixture Models. Hierarchical Gaussian mixture models (HGMM) [5,15,19] are Gaussian mixture models (GMM) structured as a tree. HGMMs improve the efficiency of GMMs by stacking multiple layers of Gaussian components, instead of increasing the number of components horizontally. However, such models use all Gaussian components for the prediction of each example $\mathbf{x}$, making it difficult to interpret the decision process; it is required to examine all components in the model for explaining each decision.

Kernel Methods. Various machine learning algorithms adopt kernel functions to generalize linear decisions by mapping input features to another space where clear separations of classes are possible [1,9]. SVM with the radial basis function (RBF) kernel [2] is one of the most famous kernel methods, which learns a decision boundary based on the Euclidean distance between features. Kernel logistic regression [22] generalizes logistic regression by applying kernel functions to the weight vectors instead of examples. Kernel methods improve the accuracy of linear models, but degrade the interpretability due to the nonlinearity.

3   Proposed Approach

We introduce Gaussian Soft Decision Trees (GSDT), our novel tree model that makes Gaussian mixture-based decisions at the internal nodes to maximize the accuracy while gaining in interpretability.

3.1   Overview

GSDT is represented as a multi-branched tree of depth d, where each node has b children. Each internal node i computes the probability of passing a feature $\mathbf{x}$ to its child node j as a function f_{ij} such that the sum of outgoing probabilities is one. GSDT passes $\mathbf{x}$ through all branches in the tree until it reaches the b^{d-1} leaf nodes where the arrival probability vector $\mathbf{r}(\mathbf{x})$ is computed. In other words, $r_j(\mathbf{x})$ represents the probability of $\mathbf{x}$ arriving at leaf node j and is computed as the multiplication of all decision probabilities in the path from the root.

Each leaf node j has a probability distribution $\mathbf{q}_j \in \mathbb{R}^{|\mathcal{Y}|}$, where $\mathcal{Y}$ is the set of target classes, which does not change for the input $\mathbf{x}$ once it is learned. The k-th element of $\mathbf{q}_j$, which is the prediction for class $k \in \mathcal{Y}$, is defined as

$$q_{jk} = \frac{\exp(u_{jk})}{\sum_{l\in\mathcal{Y}} \exp(u_{jl})}, \tag{1}$$

where $\mathbf{u}_j$ is a parameter vector that represents an unnormalized probability. In other words, each leaf learns fixed knowledge as a result of training based on the examples that are passed to that leaf with high arrival probabilities.

The parameters in all internal and leaf nodes are learned by a gradient-based approach for minimizing the following loss function:

$$l_M(\mathbf{x}, y) = \sum_{j\in\mathcal{N}_d} r_j(\mathbf{x})l_{\mathrm{cls}}(\mathbf{u}_j, y), \tag{2}$$

where $\mathcal{N}_d$ is the set of all leaf nodes, and $l_{\mathrm{cls}}(\mathbf{u}_j, y)$ is a loss function that measures the difference between the prediction at node j and the true label y.

In the inference phase, GSDT chooses the path that leads to the leaf node j having the maximum arrival probability $r_j(\mathbf{x})$ and returns the distribution $\mathbf{q}_j$ it has learned during the training. Interpreting the single most probable path is more straightforward than interpreting all possible paths at each prediction. The complexity of the inference is also reduced from $O(b^d)$ (considering all branches) to $O(d)$. This is the main difference from HGMM [5,15,19] and ensemble models [12] that involve all experts in a tree or a forest at every prediction to boost the performance, making the decision processes not interpretable.

3.2   Gaussian Decisions

The main characteristic of GSDT is the modeling of decisions as Gaussian mixtures. Each node i models its child j as a Gaussian distribution $\mathcal{N}(\boldsymbol{\mu}_j, \boldsymbol{\Sigma}_j)$, where $\boldsymbol{\mu}_j$ and $\boldsymbol{\Sigma}_j$ are learnable mean and covariance, respectively. It then computes the likelihood of $\mathbf{x}$ being sampled from the distribution $\mathcal{N}_j$ of each child j and passes $\mathbf{x}$ to the next layer following the computed likelihoods.

In other words, the probability f_{ij} of passing $\mathbf{x}$ to node j from node i is

$$f_{ij}(\mathbf{x}) = \frac{\exp(\mathcal{L}(\theta_j \mid \mathbf{x}))}{\sum_k \exp(\mathcal{L}(\theta_k \mid \mathbf{x}))}, \tag{3}$$

where $\mathcal{L}(\theta_j \mid \mathbf{x})$ is the log likelihood of $\mathbf{x}$ being generated from $\mathcal{N}(\boldsymbol{\mu}_j, \boldsymbol{\Sigma}_j)$, which is defined as follows:

$$\mathcal{L}(\theta_j \mid \mathbf{x}) = -\frac{1}{2}\left((\mathbf{x} - \boldsymbol{\mu}_j)^\top \boldsymbol{\Sigma}_j^{-1}(\mathbf{x} - \boldsymbol{\mu}_j) + \log\det(\boldsymbol{\Sigma}_j) + d\log(2\pi)\right). \quad (4)$$

However, it is computationally expensive to learn the full covariance matrix $\boldsymbol{\Sigma}_j$ for all nodes due to the inverse and determinant operations in Eq. (4), as $\boldsymbol{\Sigma}_j$ is a $m \times m$ matrix where m is the number of features. Thus, we introduce two simpler structures for learning the covariance matrices.

Diagonal Covariance. A naive approach is to assume a diagonal covariance for every node and determine its elements by a vector $\boldsymbol{\sigma}_j$ such that $\sigma_{jt} = \Sigma_{jtt}$ for all t. Since $\boldsymbol{\sigma}_j$ should contain only positive values, we introduce a free parameter $\bar{\boldsymbol{\sigma}}_j$ and apply the softplus function [4] as follows:

$$\boldsymbol{\Sigma}_j^{(\text{diagonal})} = \text{diag}(\boldsymbol{\sigma}_j), \quad (5)$$

where $\boldsymbol{\sigma}_j = \log(1 + \exp(\bar{\boldsymbol{\sigma}}_j))$, and $\text{diag}(\cdot)$ makes a diagonal matrix from a vector. This approach is the simplest but neglects the correlations between features.

Diagonal Covariance with Low-Rank Perturbations. A more principled approach is to generalize the diagonal covariances by adding low-rank perturbations [17] with a small number of parameters by the choice of a rank k:

$$\boldsymbol{\Sigma}_j^{(\text{perturbed})} = \text{diag}(\boldsymbol{\sigma}_j) + \mathbf{U}\mathbf{U}^\top, \quad (6)$$

where $\mathbf{U} \in \mathbb{R}^{m \times k}$ is a rectangular matrix learned as a free parameter, k is given as a hyperparameter, and $\boldsymbol{\sigma}_j$ is the same as in Eq. (5). It efficiently makes the covariance matrix have non-diagonal entries for feature correlations only by the additional mk parameters included in the $\mathbf{U}$ matrix.

$\log\det(\boldsymbol{\Sigma}_j)$ and the inverse $\boldsymbol{\Sigma}_j^{-1}$ are computed efficiently thanks to the matrix determinant lemma and the Woodbury matrix identity, respectively [7]:

$$\log\det(\boldsymbol{\Sigma}_j) = \log\det(\mathbf{I}_m + \mathbf{U}^\top \mathbf{A}^{-1}\mathbf{U}) + \log\det(\mathbf{A}), \quad (7)$$

$$\boldsymbol{\Sigma}_j^{-1} = \mathbf{A}^{-1} - \mathbf{A}^{-1}\mathbf{U}(\mathbf{I}_k + \mathbf{U}^\top \mathbf{A}^{-1}\mathbf{U})^{-1}\mathbf{U}^\top \mathbf{A}^{-1}, \quad (8)$$

where $\mathbf{A} = \text{diag}(\boldsymbol{\sigma}_j)$, and $\mathbf{I}_m \in \mathbb{R}^{m \times m}$ and $\mathbf{I}_k \in \mathbb{R}^{k \times k}$ are identity matrices with different sizes. Equations (7) and (8) are easily differentiable with respect to both $\mathbf{A}$ and $\mathbf{U}$, allowing the updates of parameters in gradient-based optimization.

3.3   Training with Path Regularization

The training process of GSDT consists as three parts: parameter initialization, a loss function for each leaf node, and regularization for better performance.

Initialization. We initialize the leaf and internal nodes with different strategies considering the property of GSDT. For the leaf nodes, we randomly initialize the logit $\mathbf{u}_i$ of every node i following the standard normal distribution $\mathcal{N}(0, 1)$. For the internal nodes, we set the Gaussian mean $\boldsymbol{\mu}_i$ of every node i to zero to allow examples to be equally distributed to all leaf nodes at the early iterations of training. This allows the predictions of leaf nodes to have a sufficient variance needed to guide the training of internal nodes while minimizing the randomness of internal nodes whose parameters should be tuned carefully.

Loss Function. We use the hinge loss [3] as the function l_{cls} of Eq. (2), which is typically used by maximum-margin classifers, as follows:

$$l_{\text{cls}}(\mathbf{u}_j, y) = \sum_{k \in \mathcal{Y} \backslash \{y\}} \max(0, 1 + u_{jk} - u_{jy}), \tag{9}$$

where $\mathcal{Y}$ is the set of labels. The hinge loss gives a zero if $u_{jk} + 1 < u_{jy}$. In other words, it maximizes the score u_{jy} for the target class y, but stops the training if it reaches a reasonably good performance. Unlike the cross entropy loss [8], the hinge loss improves the robustness by allowing GSDT to focus on learning the leaf nodes whose predictions are inaccurate.

Path Regularization. We propose to add *path regularization* to encourage GSDT to utilize more leaf nodes instead of a few dominant ones. The regularizer measures the negative entropy of the arrival probability vector $\mathbf{r}(\mathcal{B})$ as

$$l_{\text{lr}}(\mathcal{B}) = \sum_{j \in \mathcal{N}_d} r_j(\mathcal{B}) \log r_j(\mathcal{B}) \text{ where } \mathbf{r}(\mathcal{B}) = \frac{1}{|\mathcal{B}|} \sum_{\mathbf{x} \in \mathcal{B}} \mathbf{r}(\mathbf{x}), \tag{10}$$

where $\mathbf{r}(\mathbf{x})$ is the vector representation of arrival probabilities of $\mathbf{x}$, and $\mathcal{B}$ is a training batch. The regularizer $l_{\text{lr}}(\mathcal{B})$ forces GSDT to distribute the examples in each batch equally to all leaves to minimize the negative entropy. We add $l_{\text{lr}}(\mathcal{B})$ to the overall objective function of GSDT with a regularization strength λ.

Post-optimization of Leaf Nodes. GSDT uses gradient-based optimization to minimize the objective function, instead of the EM algorithm commonly used with the Gaussian mixture models. To accommodate for possible weaknesses in the gradient-based approach, we apply additional post-optimization at each leaf as described in Algorithm 1. This step allows the leaf Gaussians to be closer to the examples that they represent, with respect to both mean and covariance. All parameters of GSDT are fine-tuned according to the change of leaf nodes.

4   Theoretical Analysis

We compare our GSDT with previous tree models, especially soft decision trees (SDT) that adopt the binary structure with linear decisions, with respect to the multi-branched structure and the nonlinearity of decisions.

Algorithm 1: Post-optimization of the leaf Gaussians of GSDT.

Input: A trained GSDT M, a set $\mathcal{D}$ of training features, a learning rate α for the covariances, and the number n of iterations

1: **for** leaf node j in M **do**
2:    $\mathcal{X}_j \leftarrow \{\mathbf{x} \in \mathcal{D} \mid \arg\max_k r_k(\mathbf{x}) = j\}$
3:    $\boldsymbol{\mu}_j \leftarrow \sum_{\mathbf{x} \in \mathcal{X}_j} \mathbf{x}$
4:    **for** $i \in [1, n]$ **do**
5:       $l \leftarrow \mathrm{sum}((\boldsymbol{\Sigma}_j - \mathrm{cov}(\mathcal{X}_j))^2)$
6:       $\boldsymbol{\Sigma}_j \leftarrow \boldsymbol{\Sigma}_j - \alpha \cdot \partial l / \partial \boldsymbol{\Sigma}_j$
7:    **end for**
8: **end for**
9: Fine-tune the whole parameters of M for a fixed number of epochs

---

Multiple Branches. Our Gaussian decisions make it possible to adopt multiple branches at each node without affecting the interpretability of the decision tree structure. This is because the learned distribution $\mathcal{N}(\boldsymbol{\mu}_j, \boldsymbol{\Sigma}_j)$ of each node j is itself interpretable regardless of the other children in the same branch. Specifically, $\boldsymbol{\mu}_j$ summarizes the examples that pass through node j as an interpretable prototype, while $\boldsymbol{\Sigma}_j$ takes into account the different effect of each feature in the split; small σ_{jk} represents that the k-th feature is dominant in determining the score, as a small change of x_k can change the score greatly.

The main advantage of such multi-branched structures is that one can reduce the depth of a tree while maintaining a similar number of leaf nodes, improving the interpretability of individual decisions; a tree depth directly tells the number of decisions that need to be interpreted to explain each prediction. However, such generalization to multi-branched structures is not straightforward in linear tree models such as SDTs. Consider a linear decision function f_{ij} that is represented as a multinomial logistic classifier:

$$f_{ij}(\mathbf{x}) = \frac{\exp(\mathbf{x}^\top \mathbf{w}_{ij} + b_{ij})}{\sum_k \exp(\mathbf{x}^\top \mathbf{w}_{ik} + b_{ik})}, \tag{11}$$

where $\mathbf{w}_{ij}$ and b_{ij} are the weight and bias for path (i, j), respectively. This is a direct extension of SDTs into the multi-branched structure.

The main limitation of this approach is that the weight $\mathbf{w}_{ij}$ for each child j should be interpreted in relation to the other weights, unlike the binary version where a single weight $\mathbf{w}_i$ is a complete explanation for node i. In other words, a positive weight $\mathbf{w}_{ij} > \mathbf{0}$ does not guarantee the positive correlation between $\mathbf{x}$ and $f_{ij}(\mathbf{x})$, since the other weights in the branch can have more strong weights; what matters is the relative size compared to the other children in that branch. Thus, one needs to examine all weights in that branch for interpreting a decision, which significantly drops the interpretability of the model.

Table 1. Classification accuracy for feature-based classification. The best performances are in bold, and the second-best ones are underlined. GSDT shows the highest accuracies in five datasets compared with eight strong baselines.

Model	Brain	Breast	Breast-wis	Diabetes	Heart	Hepatitis
LR	63.4 ± 0.0	65.5 ± 0.0	97.1 ± 0.0	76.0 ± 0.0	86.9 ± 0.0	77.4 ± 0.0
SVM-lin	61.0 ± 0.0	62.1 ± 0.0	97.1 ± 0.0	76.6 ± 0.0	83.6 ± 0.0	77.4 ± 0.0
SVM-rbf	58.5 ± 0.0	70.7 ± 0.0	97.1 ± 0.0	76.0 ± 0.0	86.9 ± 0.0	77.4 ± 0.0
DT	70.5 ± 0.7	68.8 ± 1.6	96.0 ± 0.9	69.7 ± 1.6	67.2 ± 1.6	70.0 ± 6.9
SDT	66.8 ± 5.0	73.3 ± 5.2	97.9 ± 0.0	76.0 ± 0.7	80.7 ± 2.7	67.3 ± 4.7
EDiT	58.5 ± 0.0	75.0 ± 2.6	97.1 ± 0.2	74.6 ± 1.5	85.2 ± 2.3	77.8 ± 3.8
MLP	73.4 ± 1.7	73.3 ± 2.3	98.6 ± 0.2	75.0 ± 0.8	80.5 ± 1.5	64.2 ± 3.0
RF	68.0 ± 2.3	76.6 ± 0.8	98.1 ± 0.3	73.4 ± 0.7	84.8 ± 0.8	70.3 ± 2.4
GSDT	**73.5 ± 1.5**	**77.2 ± 1.7**	**98.8 ± 0.6**	76.0 ± 0.9	**86.9 ± 1.2**	**78.2 ± 3.1**

Number of Parameters. GSDT has a similar number of parameters to a binary SDT assuming the same number of leaf nodes, when the rank k of low-rank Gaussian covariances is fixed as a small constant. An SDT has $O(n(m+y))$ parameters, where n is the number of leaf nodes, m is the number of features, and y is the number of classes, respectively. The number of parameters in GSDT is given formally as Lemma 1.

Lemma 1. *The number of parameters of* GSDT *is* $O(n(mk+y))$, *where* m, n, *and* y *are the numbers of features, leaf nodes, and classes, respectively, assuming that every node has the same number of children, and* k *is the rank of low-rank perturbations of Gaussian covariances.*

Proof. Let d be the depth of GSDT. Each internal node has $n^{1/d}$ children, and the overall number of branches in the tree is $\sum_{i=1}^{d} n^{i/d} = (n-1)/(1-n^{-1/d})$, which is $O(n)$. Since each branch involves $m(k+1)$ parameters in the mean and covariance, the number of parameters in all internal decisions is $O(nmk)$.

This shows that GSDT efficiently models the decision process by hierarchical Gaussian mixtures with a few additional parameters from SDTs. The rank k is set to 1 or 2 in our experiments, since small k is sufficient to model the relations between features for learning non-diagonal covariance matrices.

5   Experiments

We compare GSDT with baseline models for feature-based classification on six datasets. We also demonstrate the interpretability of GSDT in a case study and compare the different approaches for modeling Gaussian covariances.

5.1 Experimental Settings

Datasets. We use six public feature-based datasets that are generated from the bio and medical domains, where interpretability is a crucial factor. Brain-tumor[1] is used to find a brain tumor from the information of a patient. Breast-cancer[2] and Breast-cancer-wisconsin[3] are used to predict breast cancers from clinical cases. Diabetes[4] is used to predict the status of a patient from diabetes. Heart-disease[5] is used to find the presence of heart disease in a patient. Hepatitis[6] is used to predict whether a patient lives or dies from the hepatitis disease.

Baselines. We compare GSDT with baseline models that have been used widely for classification tasks. Our main competitors are models that provide direct interpretability. Logistic regression (LR), support vector machines (SVM), and decision trees (DT) make interpretable decisions but have low accuracy in overall [1]. We implement two kinds of SVMs with the linear and RBF kernels, respectively. Soft decision trees (SDT) [11] and EDiT [21] improve decision trees by adopting soft decisions at internal branches, but weaken the interpretability. We also consider popular black box models that are not interpretable such as random forests (RF) and multilayer perceptrons (MLP) for completeness.

Implementation. We split each dataset randomly into training and testing by the 8:2 ratio. We run eight experiments for each model and report the average and standard deviation of classification accuracy on the test data. Some models have zero standard deviations as they are learned to find the global optima.

We use Scikit-learn implementations [20] of most baselines except SDTs and EDiT that we have implemented by PyTorch along with GSDT. We set the tree depth of SDTs and EDiT to 8 as in their original papers. On the other hand, we set the tree depth and the number of children of GSDT to 2 and 6, respectively. We set the strength λ of path regularization to 0.001 and the number n of post-optimization updates to 10. We set the rank k of Gaussian covariances to 1 or 2 based on the datasets. We use the Adam optimizer [14] for training.

5.2 Classification Accuracy

Table 1 compares the accuracies of GSDT and the baselines on the six datasets. GSDT achieves at least the second-best accuracy in all datasets, outperforming all baselines and even the black box models by the average accuracy: the accuracy of GSDT is 4.1 and 5.5 points higher than that of the RF and MLP, respectively. This shows the effectiveness of GSDT for feature-based classification, which can

---

[1] https://www.kaggle.com/pranavraikokte/braintumorfeaturesextracted.

[2] https://archive.ics.uci.edu/ml/datasets/Breast+Cancer.

[3] https://archive.ics.uci.edu/ml/datasets/breast+cancer+wisconsin+(original).

[4] https://www.kaggle.com/uciml/pima-indians-diabetes-database.

[5] https://archive.ics.uci.edu/ml/datasets/Heart+Disease.

[6] https://archive.ics.uci.edu/ml/datasets/Hepatitis.

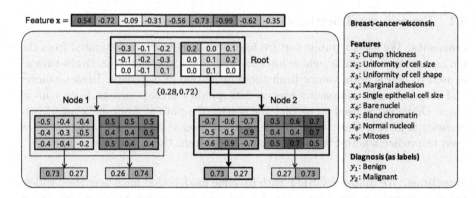

Fig. 2. The structure of simple GSDT trained for the Breast-cancer-wisconsin dataset having nine features and two labels. Each node is a Gaussian mixture that contains two Gaussian distributions with separate mean and covariance, but we represent only the mean vectors for simplicity. GSDT passes the example **x** to the third leaf through two Gaussian mixtures, classifying it as *benign*.

avoid overfitting by our regularized training while having enough representation power for learning complex decision rules even with a few tree layers.

We compare the SDT-based models from the result: SDT, EDiT, and GSDT. The accuracy of EDiT is similar to that of SDTs, as it focuses on improving the interpretability of SDTs rather than its representation power; an SDT is better at Brain-tumor, while EDiT is better at Heart-disease and Hepatitis. The core structure of EDiT is the same as SDTs, and thus it shares the same limitations that we aim to address in this work. GSDT achieves the highest accuracy among the three models, effectively improving the performance of SDTs.

5.3   Interpretability

Figure 2 shows the learned structure of GSDT of depth two, having two children at each branch, trained for the Breast-cancer-wisconsin dataset. The dataset has nine features that represent the cell characteristics of tissue images extracted from breast cancer patients to classify them into benign or malignant. The root node softly passes **x** to the right child by the probability of 72%, and the arrived node passes **x** again to the left leaf node, classifying it as benign. Since examples take a single path during inference, which is represented by a Gaussian node, it is straightforward to interpret both the structure and decisions.

Figure 3 illustrates the learned distributions and decisions of GSDT as 2D scatter plots. The same Breast-cancer-wisconsin dataset is used, but we run the t-SNE algorithm [16] before the training for clear visualization. Figure 3a shows test examples that are categorized into two classes. The root node first divides the examples into two clusters based on the Gaussian likelihoods in Fig. 3b. The distribution of the right child of the root has the largest covariance in the figures,

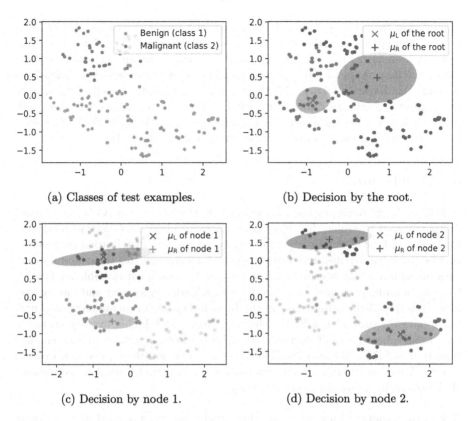

(a) Classes of test examples.   (b) Decision by the root.

(c) Decision by node 1.   (d) Decision by node 2.

Fig. 3. Gaussian distributions learned by GSDT for the Breast-cancer-wisconsin dataset. The test examples are divided first by the root and then by the internal nodes, based on the likelihoods of Gaussian distributions. The ellipses represent the covariance matrices, and the blurry points represent examples that reach at each node only at the training time, not at the inference time. (Color figure online)

reflecting the uncertainty of the decision. In Figs. 3c and 3d, each of the internal nodes splits examples to the leaf nodes for the final prediction.

Each distribution reflects the property of a decision in its mean vector and covariance matrix. Specifically, the mean vector works as an interpretable prototype that summarizes the examples that pass through that node, which is itself interpretable regardless of the other nodes. The blue and red distributions (and the orange and green distributions) have similar roles at the different branches, which is to classify the examples as benign (and malignant).

5.4 Ablation Study

We compare various options of modeling the Gaussian covariance in Fig. 1 by generating a synthetic dataset consisting of two-dimensional features. GSDT with the identity covariance works well in Fig. 1a, but the centers of Gaussians are different from those of true data because the covariance cannot be changed during training; the distributions have moved due to the bias of data. The diagonal covariance in Fig. 1b works also well, but the covariance matrices cannot reflect the long shape of true clusters. Our choice of the covariance, which is to combine the diagonal entries with the low-rank perturbations, reflect accurately the property of original data. Moreover, the diagonal covariance with low-rank perturbations is able to capture both positive and negative correlations as seen by the yellow and green clusters, respectively, without limitations.

6 Conclusion

In this work, we have proposed Gaussian Soft Decision Trees (GSDT), a novel tree-structured classifier that models the internal nodes as Gaussian mixtures. Each edge in GSDT represents a multivariate Gaussian distribution parameterized by the learnable mean and covariance, which summarizes the examples that pass through it as an interpretable prototype. This makes it possible for GSDT to adopt a multi-branched structure where each edge is learned and interpreted independently of the other edges in the branch. Our experiments on six feature-based datasets show that GSDT achieves at least 4.8% higher average accuracy than models based on soft decision tree (SDT), while having a depth 4× smaller than that of SDTs. We also visualize the learned structure and decision process of GSDT to demonstrate its interpretability on an actual feature-based dataset of the biomedical domain as a case study.

Acknowledgments. Publication of this article has been funded by the Basic Science Research Program through the National Research Foundation of Korea (2018R1A1A3A0407953, 2018R1A5A1060031).

References

1. Bishop, C.M.: Pattern Recognition and Machine Learning. Springer, Heidelberg (2006)
2. Chang, Y., Hsieh, C., Chang, K., Ringgaard, M., Lin, C.: Training and testing low-degree polynomial data mappings via linear SVM. J. Mach. Learn. Res. **11**, 1471–1490 (2010)
3. Dogan, Ü., Glasmachers, T., Igel, C.: A unified view on multi-class support vector classification. J. Mach. Learn. Res. **17**, 45:1–45:32 (2016)
4. Dugas, C., Bengio, Y., Bélisle, F., Nadeau, C., Garcia, R.: Incorporating second-order functional knowledge for better option pricing. In: NIPS, pp. 472–478. MIT Press (2000)
5. Eckart, B., Kim, K., Kautz, J.: HGMR: hierarchical gaussian mixtures for adaptive 3D registration. In: Ferrari, V., Hebert, M., Sminchisescu, C., Weiss, Y. (eds.) ECCV 2018. LNCS, vol. 11219, pp. 730–746. Springer, Cham (2018). https://doi.org/10.1007/978-3-030-01267-0_43
6. Frosst, N., Hinton, G.E.: Distilling a neural network into a soft decision tree. In: AI*IA. CEUR Workshop Proceedings, vol. 2071. CEUR-WS.org (2017)

7. Harville, D.A.: Matrix algebra from a statistician's perspective (1998)
8. Hinton, G.E., Vinyals, O., Dean, J.: Distilling the knowledge in a neural network (2015). CoRR abs/1503.02531
9. Hofmann, T., Schölkopf, B., Smola, A.J.: Kernel methods in machine learning. Ann. Statistics **36**, 1171–1220 (2008)
10. Irsoy, O., Alpaydin, E.: Autoencoder trees. In: ACML, vol. 45, pp. 378–390 (2015)
11. Irsoy, O., Yildiz, O.T., Alpaydin, E.: Soft decision trees. In: ICPR (2012)
12. Jordan, M.I., Jacobs, R.A.: Hierarchical mixtures of experts and the EM algorithm. Neural Comput. **6**(2), 181–214 (1994)
13. Kim, B., Khanna, R., Koyejo, O.: Examples are not enough, learn to criticize! criticism for interpretability. In: NIPS (2016)
14. Kingma, D.P., Ba, J.: Adam: a method for stochastic optimization. In: ICLR (2015)
15. Liu, M., Chang, E., Dai, B.Q.: Hierarchical Gaussian mixture model for speaker verification. In: Seventh International Conference on Spoken Language Processing (2002)
16. Maaten, L.V.D., Hinton, G.: Visualizing data using t-sne. J. Mach. Learn. Res. **9**(Nov), 2579–2605 (2008)
17. Magdon-Ismail, M., Purnell, J.T.: Approximating the covariance matrix of gmms with low-rank perturbations. Int. J. Data Min. Model. Manag. **4**(2), 107–122 (2012)
18. Miller, T.: Explanation in artificial intelligence: insights from the social sciences. Artif. Intell **267**, 1–38 (2018)
19. Olech, L.P., Paradowski, M.: Hierarchical gaussian mixture model with objects attached to terminal and non-terminal dendrogram nodes. In: CORES (2015)
20. Pedregosa, F., et al.: Scikit-learn: machine learning in python. J. Mach. Learn. Res. **12**, 2825–2830 (2011)
21. Yoo, J., Sael, L.: Edit: interpreting ensemble models via compact soft decision trees. In: ICDM, pp. 1438–1443 (2019)
22. Zhu, J., Hastie, T.: Kernel logistic regression and the import vector machine. In: NIPS, pp. 1081–1088 (2001)

Efficient Nodes Representation Learning with Residual Feature Propagation

Fan Wu[1], Duantengchuan Li[2(✉)], Ke Lin[3], and Huawei Zhang[1]

[1] School of Computer Science and Technology, Wuhan University of Technology,
Wuhan 430070, China
[2] National Engineering Research Center for E-Learning,
Central China Normal University, Wuhan 430079, China
[3] Department of Control Science and Engineering,
Harbin Institute of Technology Shenzhen, Shenzhen 518055, China

Abstract. Graph Convolutional Networks (GCN) and their variants have achieved brilliant results in graph representation learning. However, most existing methods cannot be utilized for deep architectures and can only capture the low order proximity in networks. In this paper, we have proposed a Residual Simple Graph Convolutional Network (RSGCN), which can aggregate information from distant neighbor node features without over-smoothing and vanishing gradients. Given that node features of the same class have certain similarity, a weighted feature propagation is considered to ensure effective information aggregation by giving higher weights to similar neighbor nodes. Experimental results on several datasets of node classification demonstrate the proposed methods outperform the state-of-the-art methods in terms of effectiveness and efficiency.

Keywords: Graph convolutional networks · Graph representation learning · Feature propagation · Node classification

1 Introduction

The goal of graph representation learning is to represent nodes on the graph by low-dimensional dense vectors while maintaining the property characteristics of nodes and the structural features of graphs. Graph convolutional networks (GCN) [5], a variant of Convolutional Neural Networks (CNNs), have shown efficacious performance in graph representation learning. GCN can learn appropriate node representation by aggregating neighbor node information. Moreover, in order to capture the high-order similarity of nodes, a non-linear transformation is introduced in each layer of GCN propagation [8,17]. Recently, GCN have been widely utilized in graph structure data researches, such as node classification [9], node clustering [21], graph classification [10], and link prediction [6]. In addition, researchers have successfully applied GCN and subsequent variants to their application areas, such as knowledge graph [13], computer vision [11], natural language processing [18], and recommendation system [19].

© Springer Nature Switzerland AG 2021
K. Karlapalem et al. (Eds.): PAKDD 2021, LNAI 12713, pp. 156–167, 2021.
https://doi.org/10.1007/978-3-030-75765-6_13

In GCN, because each layer of graph convolution needs to aggregate features from the connected node, the dependence relationship between nodes should be known before model training. This makes the optimization method of min-batch no longer applicable to GCN, which will make GCN training very difficult.

Considering these limitations of GCN, many researchers have made some improvements to solve the above problems. In [2], the authors introduced Graph-SAGE, a general inductive manner for learning node representation on large graph structure data. This method randomly sampled a fix-sized neighborhood for each node and aggregated node features from this neighborhood by a specific aggregator. Moreover, in order to resolving dependence relationship between nodes, Zeng et al. [20] constructed mini-batch by sampling the training graph and built a complete GCN on the sampled subgraph for each iteration. Although the large graph structure data can be processed by these methods, it is hard to stack more layers to obtain high-order node information.

Inspired by the great success of residual connections, dense connections and dilated convolution in deep learning, Li et al. [7] adapted these ideas into GCN to solve the vanishing gradients problem and proposed Deep Graph Convolutional Networks (DeepGCNs). Although DeepGCNs can extract deeper node information in the graph and have several advantages over previous methods. Unfortunately, it consumes bulky computing resources and prodigious time in the inference process, which means its application to large graph structure data would be difficult. The large graph structure data are very common in practical applications. However, previous works fail to efficiently aggregate deeper node information and separate dependence relationship between nodes during training processes in large graph structure data.

To build a high-efficiency graph representation learning model and separate dependence of nodes during training processes, a Residual Simple Graph Convolutional NetWork (RSGCN) by removing the non-linear activation function of DeepGCNs is proposed. In RSGCN, residual feature propagation enables the model to learn higher order node information and restrain the over-smoothing of the graph. Furthermore, as average aggregation confuses the importance of different classes to nodes itself, we propose a weighted feature propagation model RSGCN+ to learn the important information from similar nodes. RSGCN+ ensures effective information aggregation by giving higher weights to similar neighbor nodes, which is measured by the cosine similarity between node features. Finally, our models can learn accurate node representation. The major contributions of this paper are summarized as follows.

- A Residual Simple Graph Convolutional Network (RSGCN) is proposed by removing the non-linear activation function of DeepGCNs. With the residual feature propagation, RSGCN can aggregate information from distant neighbor node features without over-smoothing and vanishing gradients. More importantly, RSGCN can achieve high effectiveness and efficiency during training process.
- Given that node features of the same class have certain similarity, we propose a weighted feature propagation model RSGCN+ to ensure effective

information aggregation by giving higher weights to similar neighbor nodes, which further improves the node representation and the robustness of the model.

– To verify the performance of the proposed methods, three standard benchmark datasets for citation networks are taken as the comparing experiments. The results demonstrate that our models obtain significant improvements for the semi-supervised node classification tasks in the terms of both prediction accuracy and the training efficiency.

2   Preliminaries and Related Work

2.1   Primary Definition

Given an undirected attributed graph $\mathcal{G} = (\mathcal{V}, \mathbf{A})$, where $\mathcal{V} = \{v_i\}_{i=1,...,n}$ represents the nodes and $\mathbf{A} = \{a_{ij}\} \in \mathbb{R}^{n \times n}$ is the adjacency matrix of the graph $\mathcal{G}$. If there is an edge between node v_i and node v_j, then $a_{ij} = 1$, otherwise it equals to 0. For ease of notation, the neighbor set of node v_i can be denoted as $\mathcal{A}_i = [j|a_{ij} = 1]$. Note that $\tilde{\mathbf{A}} = \mathbf{A} + \mathbf{I}$ denotes the adjacency matrix $\mathbf{A}$ with self-loops and the degree matrix $\tilde{\mathbf{D}} = \text{diag}\{d_1, d_2, ..., d_n\} \in \mathbb{R}^{n \times n}$ is a diagonal matrix where the i-th value on the diagonal $d_i = \sum_j \tilde{a}_{ij}$ is equal to the degree of the i-th node of matrix $\tilde{\mathbf{A}}$. For the semi-supervised node classification tasks, we observe the labels of a subset of the nodes in the graph $\mathcal{G}$. The goal of node classification is to predict the unknown node labels based on the graph structure and node features we known the labels.

2.2   Graph Convolutional Network

For each node $v_i \in \mathcal{V}$, h_i^0 represents initial node representation, which is d-dimensional feature vector $x_i \in \mathbb{R}^d$. Then, GCN can learn node representation for each node based on node initial features and graph structure. Specifically, for each node v_i in the graph convolution layer, the node representation is updated recursively with the following three steps: feature propagation, linear transformation, and non-linear activation.

Feature Propagation. For each node v_i, the feature propagation step aggregates the node information from node itself representation h_i^k at previous layer k and graph neighbors $\mathcal{A}_i$,

$$h_i^{(k+1)} = \frac{1}{d_i + 1} h_i^{(k)} + \sum_{j=1}^{n} \frac{a_{ij}}{\sqrt{(d_i + 1)(d_j + 1)}} h_j^{(k)} \tag{1}$$

where d_i denotes the degree of node v_i. Besides, the update of entire graph can be expressed as a simple matrix operation. The symbol $\mathbf{S} = \tilde{\mathbf{D}}^{-\frac{1}{2}} \tilde{\mathbf{A}} \tilde{\mathbf{D}}^{-\frac{1}{2}}$

represents the "normalized" adjacency matrix with added self-loops. Thus, the update process in Eq. (1) for all nodes can be expressed as,

$$\bar{\mathbf{H}}^{(k+1)} = \mathbf{S}\mathbf{H}^{(k)} \tag{2}$$

Intuitively, this step makes each node aggregate information from connected node and eventually has a positive influence on node classification tasks. Theoretically, feature propagation output layer is regarded as the Laplacian smoothing of the node features at the previous layer [8,15].

Linear Transformation and Non-linear Activation. After feature propagation, linear transformation and non-linear activation is identical to a standard multilayer perceptron. In a GCN layer, there is a learned weight $\mathbf{W}^k$ as linear transformation after the feature propagation, which can transform node representation linearly. Finally, a non-linear activation produces the node representation of the $(k+1)$-th layer as,

$$\mathbf{H}^{(k+1)} = \sigma\left(\bar{\mathbf{H}}^{(k+1)}\mathbf{W}^k\right) \tag{3}$$

where $\sigma(\cdot)$ is a non-linear activation function.

2.3 Simplifying Graph Convolutional Network

Recently, considerable literature has grown up around the theme of simplifying GCN in order to reduce training time and memory. A Simple Graph Convolutional Network (SGCN) is proposed [16], which removes the non-linear activation function in Eq. (3) as,

$$\mathbf{H}^{(k)} = \mathbf{S}\mathbf{S}\ldots\mathbf{S}\mathbf{H}^{(0)}\mathbf{W}^0\mathbf{W}^1\ldots\mathbf{W}^k \tag{4}$$

where $\mathbf{W}^0\mathbf{W}^1\ldots\mathbf{W}^k$ can be rewritten as a single matrix $\mathbf{W}$ and the repeated multiplication with the matrix $\mathbf{S}$ can be simplified to a single matrix $\mathbf{S}^k$. The above linear matrix multiplication turns to,

$$\mathbf{H}^{(k)} = \mathbf{S}^k\mathbf{H}^{(0)}\mathbf{W} \tag{5}$$

With the simplification of SGCN, k times feature propagation $\mathbf{S}^k$ can be calculated before training, and the parameters are much less than GCN, which makes it easy to apply SGCN to large graph structure data. Many experiments show that removing the non-linear activation function in GCN does not have a negative impact on performance in many graph tasks. However, [16] shows that SGCN has the best node classification performance at feature propagation depth of 2 or 3. When feature propagates for too many times, the node representation information propagated to well-connected node rapidly increase. This leads to the over-smoothing issue, which means the features of each node are mixed by too many neighbors and lose locality.

2.4   Deep Graph Convolutional Networks

In GCN, the depth has a crucial function: after k layers each node can aggregate feature information from the nodes that are k-hops away in the graph. However, GCN with deep layers will lead to vanishing gradients, which makes accuracy drop sharply in classification tasks. Inspired by the success of the Deep CNNs technology, DeepGCNs [7] employed residual/dense connections to solve the above problem.

ResNet [3] can alleviate the problems of vanishing gradients and network degradation caused by increasing depth in deep neural networks. The node representation of the $(k + 1)$-th layer in ResGCN can be defined as:

$$\mathbf{H}_{res}^{k+1} = \sigma \left(\mathbf{SH}^{(k)} \mathbf{W}^k \right) + \mathbf{H}^{(k)} \tag{6}$$

where $\mathbf{W}^k$ has the same dimension as $\mathbf{H}^{(0)}$. Although DeepGCNs can effectively stack more layers, and the performance does not decline severely with depth increasing like GCN, it consumes abundant computing resources and prodigious time in the training process. Thus, it is difficult to apply it to large graph structure data.

3   Our Proposed Methods

In this section, we propose Residual Simple Graph Convolutional Network (RSGCN), a model of node representation learning that extracts deep node information. The overall architecture of the proposed models is shown in Fig. 1, which can be summed as two processes: (1) For mitigating over-smoothing, we propose residual feature propagation RSGCN (dashed-blue) to retain more node itself information. (2) On the basis of residual feature propagation, we adjust the final node features by adding weighted feature propagation RSGCN+ (dashed-red).

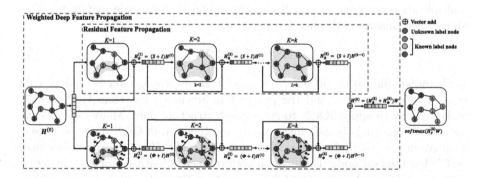

Fig. 1. Outline of our models framework.

3.1 Residual Feature Propagation

Considering that non-linear activation functions have almost no benefit in the node representation, we can simplify ResGCN by removing the non-linear activation functions. Hence, Eq. (6) can become as follows:

$$\mathbf{H}_R^{(k+1)} = \mathbf{S}\mathbf{H}_R^{(k)}\mathbf{W}^k + \mathbf{H}_R^{(k)} \tag{7}$$

In order to better mine the node feature information and simplify the model, we move the linear transformation to the end of each layer, so Eq. (7) could be changed to Eq. (8).

$$\mathbf{H}_R^{(k+1)} = (\mathbf{S} + \mathbf{I})\,\mathbf{H}_R^{(k)}\mathbf{W}^{k'} \tag{8}$$

where $\mathbf{I} \in \mathbb{R}^{n \times n}$ denotes the identity matrix. The node representation of the k-th layer can be defined as:

$$\mathbf{H}_R^{(k)} = (\mathbf{S} + \mathbf{I})\,(\mathbf{S} + \mathbf{I})\dots(\mathbf{S} + \mathbf{I})\,\mathbf{H}^{(0)}\mathbf{W}^{0'}\mathbf{W}^{1'}\dots\mathbf{W}^{k'} \tag{9}$$

where $\mathbf{W}^{0'}\mathbf{W}^{1'}\dots\mathbf{W}^{k'}$ can be rewritten as a single matrix W and the repetitive multiplication operation of the matrix $\mathbf{S} + \mathbf{I}$ can be simplified to a single matrix $(\mathbf{S} + \mathbf{I})^k$. The node representation of residual feature propagation can be defined as:

$$\mathbf{H}_R^{(k)} = (\mathbf{S} + \mathbf{I})^k \, \mathbf{H}^{(0)}\mathbf{W} \tag{10}$$

In residual feature propagation, their node features of inputs are added to the inputs of the next feature propagation, which means that node features can be well preserved. In this way, RSGCN enables more feature propagation, which can aggregate information from more distant neighbor nodes with weaker over-smoothing impact. In addition, as residual feature propagation can be calculated before training, the scale of parameters in RSGCN is lessened and the training efficiency is raised vastly. Thus, the matrix $\mathbf{H}_R^{(k)}$ can be expanded as:

$$\mathbf{H}_R^{(k)} = \left(\mathbf{S}^k + C_k^1\mathbf{S}^{k-1} + \dots + \mathbf{I}\right)\mathbf{H}^{(0)}\mathbf{W} \tag{11}$$

In general, lower order neighbor nodes contain more important information, whereas higher order neighbor nodes may contain some noisy information. In addition, $\mathbf{S}^i\mathbf{H}^{(0)}$ contains the information about the 1 to i-hop neighbors node features and initial node features. Equation (11) represents that the more distant neighbor node features are given smaller weights, which enables the node to aggregate less noisy information.

3.2 Weighted Feature Propagation

Currently, most graph neural networks use mean aggregation to learn node representation. Valid information and noise are treated equally, which may hurt the performance of models. The graph attention network [14] introduces the attention mechanism into the GCN by assigning a learned weight parameter for neighbor nodes of each node. The huge performance improvement in node classification tasks illustrates that assigning a suitable weight to neighbor node is a better way of feature propagation. However, the attention mechanism significantly increases parameters of model, thus it is difficult to apply it to large graph structure data. Therefore, we can change our mind to consider assigning a weight to neighbor nodes based on their initial features before training.

On condition that the node features of the same class have more similarity, cosine similarity is utilized as a criterion for determining the similarity of two node features. The cosine similarity matrix Θ can be defined as:

$$\Theta_{ij} = a_{ij} \cdot \frac{\sqrt{\sum_{p=1}^{d} x_p y_p}}{\sqrt{\sum_{p=1}^{d} x_p} \sqrt{\sum_{p=1}^{d} y_p}} \tag{12}$$

where x_p is the p-th feature of v_i and y is the p-th feature of v_j. In order to balance the cosine similarity scale, we normalize them by using the softmax function by row. Hence, the node weight matrix can be defined as:

$$\Phi_{ij} = \frac{\exp(\Theta_{ij})}{\sum_{j=1}^{n} \exp(\Theta_{ij})} \tag{13}$$

In order to retain more information from the node itself features, we borrowed the idea of residual feature propagation into the weighted feature propagation. The weighted feature propagation can be defined as:

$$\mathbf{H}_\Phi^{(k)} = (\mathbf{\Phi} + \mathbf{I})^k \, \mathbf{H}^{(0)} \mathbf{W} \tag{14}$$

By using residual feature propagation to obtain the final node features, RSGCN can learn part of the useful information from the node features and the graph structure. In addition, weighted feature propagation can extract further useful information about neighbor nodes and reduce the influence of irrelevant neighbor node. This information may contain some information that is not contained in the residual feature propagation. In order to preserve the useful features of both two feature propagation, we merge them in a stacked manner. Therefore, the final weighted feature propagation can be defined as:

$$\mathbf{H}_F^{(k)} = \mathbf{H}_R^{(k)} + \mathbf{H}_\Phi^{(k)} \tag{15}$$

The weighted feature propagation can assign a weight to neighbor node based on their similarity to node itself features. Although weighted feature propagation increases some memory to some extent, the neighbor node features can be aggregated more efficiently and rationally. In addition, weight feature propagation can be completed before training, and weighted feature propagation can be performed separately for each node, which is ideal for large graph structure data.

3.3   Classifier

Similar to common classification tasks, we can use a *softmax* function as a classifier after feature propagation and linear transformation. For a node classification task with C classes, the class prediction $\hat{\mathbf{Y}} \in \mathbb{R}^{n \times C}$ in RSGCN of k times feature propagation can be defined as:

$$\hat{\mathbf{Y}} = \text{softmax}\left(\mathbf{H}_F^{(k)}\right) \qquad (16)$$

where $\text{softmax}(x) = \exp(x)/\sum_{c=1}^{C} \exp(x_c)$. For multi-class node classification tasks, we generally take cross entropy as the loss function.

4 Experiments and Discussions

4.1 General Setting

Datasets. Cora, Citeseer, and Pubmed [5] are employed to evaluate the semi-supervised node classification task, which are the standard benchmark datasets for citation networks. The statistics of datasets are summarized in Table 1. The above dataset composed of diverse scientific publications are classified into different classes. Each publication in the dataset is described by a 0/1-valued word vector indicating the absence/presence of the corresponding word from the dictionary. And the edges in the datasets represent the citation relationship between articles. In order to obtain unbiased and objective results, we have leveraged 10%–20%–70% train-validation-test settings.

Comparison Algorithms. We compared the proposed RSGCN and RSGCN+ with many state-of-the-art methods, including DeepWalk [12], GCN [5], SGCN [16], FastGCN [1], GraphSAGE [2], and DeepGCNs [7]. Since GraphSAGE and DeepGCNs have a variety of models, we choose GraphSAGE-mean and ResGCN with good effects as representatives.

Experimental Implementation. The parameters of compared methods are adjusted as the suitable ones according to their papers. On all citation networks datasets, RSGCN is trained for 200 epochs using Adam optimizer [4] with learning rate 0.2. And the setting of hyper parameters like the feature propagation depth and weight decay are manually adjusted according to the validation set results. We select the model with the best performance of validation sets during the training to test the performance of test sets. RSGCN+ has the same parameters setting as RSGCN.

Table 1. Dataset statistics of the citation networks

Dataset	Cora	Citeseer	Pubmed
#Nodes	2708	3327	19717
#Edges	5429	4732	44338
#Features	1433	3703	500
#Classes	7	6	3

Table 2. Test Micro-F1 Score (%) averaged over 10 runs. The best and second values are marked by the bold font and underlines.

Method	Cora	Citeseer	Pubmed
DeepWalk [12]	73.51	55.06	79.36
GCN [5]	83.01	72.03	86.41
SGCN [16]	83.35	71.71	85.60
FastGCN [1]	80.36	70.15	85.42
GraphSAGE [2]	81.26	71.30	85.63
ResGCN [7]	82.85	71.94	86.30
RSGCN	84.06	73.06	86.33
RSGCN+	**85.10**	**74.06**	**86.95**

4.2   Results and Discussion

Performance. For accuracy comparison of DeepWalk, GCN, SGCN, FastGCN, GraphSAGE, ResGCN, RSGCN on all three datasets, the highest Micro-F1 of each model are summarized in Table 2. Table 2 shows that the performance of RSGCN is superior to GCN and its variants on the citation networks. In particular, on the Cora and Citeseer datasets, RSGCN has 1% improvement in Micro-F1 score than GCN. On the Pubmed dataset, RSGCN has similar performance to GCN result. The improvement of RSGCN performance comes from two aspects. On the one hand, RSGCN can propagate feature more times than GCN, which allows each node to aggregate feature information from more distant neighbor nodes. On the other hand, RSGCN has fewer parameters compared to GCN. This means that RSGCN has a strong generalization capability and suffers less from overfitting. Furthermore, RSGCN+ achieve the higher Micro-F1 score than RSGCN on the citation datasets. It proves that the RSGCN+ is a high-performance graph model and has the capability to enhance model effectiveness by weighted feature propagation.

Efficiency. In Table 3, we show the time to train comparison methods and our models for 200 epochs on the citation networks and the number of layers is set to be 2 for all models. In particular, RSGCN and RSGCN+ take into account the time of residual feature propagation and weighted feature propagation. The training time is measured by a PC Server equipped with an Intel(R) Xeon(R) CPU E5-2620 V4 @2.10GHz, NVIDIA TITAN V, and 64 GB RAM.

Table 3 shows RSGCN is faster than comparison methods. RSGCN achieves 80.2%/75.9%/78.3% improvement of time in training of the Cora/Citeseer/Pubmed dataset than GCN. As for other methods besides SGCN, feature propagation in each epoch with enormous parameters make training inefficient. Since SGCN with only one learned parameter matrix performs less than satisfactory, the providing source code uses two learned parameters matrix to obtain accurate classification performance. However, our models perform well

Table 3. Training time (seconds) on citation networks averaged over 10 runs. The values of brackets represent performance improvement compared to GCN method.

Method	Cora	Citeseer	Pubmed
GCN [5]	3.99	4.15	4.51
SGCN [16]	1.24	1.73	1.74
FastGCN [1]	2.15	2.32	2.63
GraphSAGE [2]	8.35	8.79	9.12
ResGCN [7]	12.64	46.15	21.78
RSGCN	0.79 (↑ 80.2%)	1.00 (↑ 75.9%)	0.98 (↑ 78.3%)
RSGCN+	2.07 (↑ 52.0%)	3.15 (↑ 24.1%)	4.08 (↑ 9.5%)

using one learned matrix and therefore faster than SGCN. RSGCN+ consumes more time due to calculating cosine similarity, which is still faster than GCN.

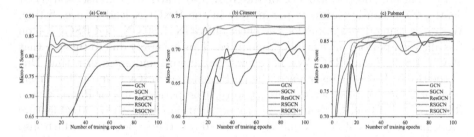

Fig. 2. Training processes of all models compared with Micro-F1 score on (a) Core, (b) Citeseer, and (c) Pubmed.

Because FastGCN and GraphSAGE will be affected by random sampling, the training has greater volatility, so they are not recorded in Fig. 2 and Fig. 3. The Micro-F1 score at a training process is depicted in Fig. 2. Figure 2 illustrates the relationship between the Micro-F1 score and the epoch on the Cora, Citeseer, and Pubmedand datasets. One can see that the proposed RGSCN and RSGCN+ not only achieve the highest Micro-F1 score in the validation set, but also require fewer epochs to converge than traditional GCN. During the training process, RSGCN and RSGCN+ demonstrate high efficiency, which shows good industrial conversion application prospects.

Training Depth Analysis. Figure 3 shows the performance in test sets of GCN, SGCN, ResGCN, RSGCN, RSGCN+ measured by Micro-F1 score with different depth on three citation datasets. For the case of 1 to 3 depth, the Micro-F1 score of above methods increases with more layers added, which suggests that deeper feature propagation may be useful. From Fig. 3, RSGCN achieve the

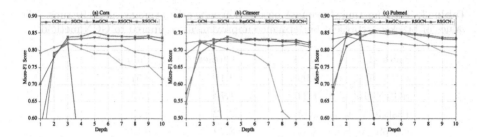

Fig. 3. Performance in test sets of five models measured by Micro-F1 score with different depth on (a) Core, (b) Citeseer, and (c) Pubmed.

best classification performance at depth between 4 and 6, while others achieves the best classification performance at depth between 2 and 3. Due to gradient vanishing problem caused by the deep network and the over-smoothing caused by the feature propagation, GCN performance decreases sharply at depth of 4. In addition, the performance of ResGCN also starts to decrease sharply at depth of 7 because enormous parameters in the ResGCN lead to over-fitting. With increasing depth of model, the effect of SGCN, RSGCN, and RSGCN+ on classification performance is less pronounced. This is largely due to the fact that SGCN, RSGCN, and RSGCN+ have fewer parameters and not over-fitting. Due to the slower feature convergence, the performance of RSGCN in shallow layers is slightly inferior to other models. However, the performance of RSGCN, and RSGCN+ is still better than SGCN. An explanation is that the residual feature propagation in RSGCN can effectively slow down the smoothness, which also gives RSGCN some edge in depth.

5   Conclusion

In this paper, we have proposed a Residual Simple Graph Convolutional Network (RSGCN), which can aggregate information from distant neighbor node features without over-smoothing and vanishing gradients. Given that node features of the same class have certain similarity, a weighted feature propagation is considered to ensure effective information aggregation by giving higher weights to similar neighbor nodes. Experimental results indicate that the proposed method performs better than compared methods on both accuracy and training efficiency in terms of quantitative assessments.

References

1. Chen, J., Ma, T., Xiao, C.: Fastgcn: fast learning with graph convolutional networks via importance sampling. In: International Conference on Learning Representations (2018)

2. Hamilton, W., Ying, Z., Leskovec, J.: Inductive representation learning on large graphs. In: Advances in Neural Information Processing Systems, pp. 1024–1034 (2017)
3. He, K., Zhang, X., Ren, S., Sun, J.: Deep residual learning for image recognition. In: IEEE Conference on Computer Vision and Pattern Recognition, pp. 770–778 (2016)
4. Kingma, D., Ba, J.: Adam: a method for stochastic optimization. In: International Conference on Learning Representations (2014)
5. Kipf, T.N., Welling, M.: Semi-supervised classification with graph convolutional networks. arXiv preprint arXiv:1609.02907 (2016)
6. Kipf, T.N., Welling, M.: Variational graph auto-encoders. arXiv preprint arXiv:1611.07308 (2016)
7. Li, G., Muller, M., Thabet, A., Ghanem, B.: Deepgcns: can gcns go as deep as cnns? In: IEEE International Conference on Computer Vision, pp. 9267–9276 (2019)
8. Li, Q., Han, Z., Wu, X.M.: Deeper insights into graph convolutional networks for semi-supervised learning. In: AAAI Conference on Artificial Intelligence (2018)
9. Li, R., Wang, S.: Adaptive graph convolutional neural networks. In: AAAI Conference on Artificial Intelligence (2018)
10. Ma, Y., Wang, S., Aggarwal, C.C., Tang, J.: Graph convolutional networks with eigenpooling. In: Proceedings of the 25th ACM SIGKDD International Conference on Knowledge Discovery & Data Mining, pp. 723–731 (2019)
11. Monfardini, G., Di Massa, V., Scarselli, F., Gori, M.: Graph neural networks for object localization. Frontiers in Artificial Intelligence and Applications. pp. 665–669 (2006)
12. Perozzi, B., Al-Rfou, R., Skiena, S.: Deepwalk: online learning of social representations. In: Proceedings of the 20th ACM SIGKDD International Conference on Knowledge Discovery and Data Mining, pp. 701–710 (2014)
13. Shang, C., Tang, Y., Huang, J., Bi, J., He, X., Zhou, B.: End-to-end structure-aware convolutional networks for knowledge base completion. In: AAAI Conference on Artificial Intelligence (2019)
14. Velickovic, P., Cucurull, G., Casanova, A., et al.: Graph attention networks. In: International Conference on Learning Representations (2018)
15. Wang, X., He, X., Wang, M., Feng, F., Chua, T.S.: Neural graph collaborative filtering. In: Proceedings of the 42nd international ACM SIGIR conference on Research and development in Information Retrieval, pp. 165–174 (2019)
16. Wu, F., Souza, A., Zhang, T., Fifty, C., Yu, T., Weinberger, K.: Simplifying graph convolutional networks. In: International Conference on Machine Learning, pp. 6861–6871 (2019)
17. Xu, K., Hu, W., Leskovec, J., Jegelka, S.: How powerful are graph neural networks? In: International Conference on Learning Representations (2018)
18. Yao, L., Mao, C., Luo, Y.: Graph convolutional networks for text classification. In: AAAI Conference on Artificial Intelligence, pp. 7370–7377 (2019)
19. Ying, R., He, R., Chen, K., Eksombatchai, P., Hamilton, W.L., Leskovec, J.: Graph convolutional neural networks for web-scale recommender systems. In: Proceedings of the 24th ACM SIGKDD International Conference on Knowledge Discovery & Data Mining, pp. 974–983 (2018)
20. Zeng, H., Zhou, H., Srivastava, A., Kannan, R., Prasanna, V.: Graphsaint: graph sampling based inductive learning method. In: International Conference on Learning Representations (2019)
21. Zhang, X., Liu, H., Li, Q., Wu, X.M.: Attributed graph clustering via adaptive graph convolution. In: AAAI Conference on Artificial Intelligence (2019)

Progressive AutoSpeech: An Efficient and General Framework for Automatic Speech Classification

Guanghui Zhu, Feng Cheng, Mengchuan Qiu, Zhuoer Xu, Wenjie Wang, Chunfeng Yuan, and Yihua Huang[(✉)]

National Key Laboratory for Novel Software Technology, Nanjing University, Nanjing 210023, China
{chengfeng,mengchuan.qiu,zhuoer.xu, wenjie.wang}@smail.nju.edu.cn,{zgh,cfyuan,yhuang}@nju.edu.cn

Abstract. Speech classification has been widely used in many speech-related applications. However, the complexity of speech classification tasks often exceeds the scope of non-experts, the off-the-shelf speech classification methods are urgently needed. Recently, the automatic speech classification (AutoSpeech) without any human intervention has attracted more and more attention. The practical AutoSpeech solution should be general and can automatically handle classification tasks from different domains. Moreover, AutoSpeech should improve not only the final performance but also the any-time performance especially when the time budget is limited. To address these issues, we propose a three-stage any-time learning algorithm framework called Progressive AutoSpeech for automatic speech classification under a given time budget. Progressive AutoSpeech consists of the fast stage, enhancement stage, and exploration stage. Each stage uses different models and features to ensure generalization. Additionally, we automatically construct ensembles of top-k prediction results to improve the robustness. The experimental results reveal that Progressive AutoSpeech is effective and efficient for a wide range of speech classification tasks and can achieve the best ALC score.

Keywords: Automatic speech classification · Deep learning · Any-time learning

1 Introduction

Deep learning has achieved great success in speech-related applications such as speaker verification, language identification, and emotion classification. Since the complexity of these tasks often exceeds the scope of non-experts, it leads to an ever-growing demand for off-the-shelf speech classification methods that can be easily used without expert knowledge.

Automatic machine learning (AutoML) aims at automating the process of applying machine learning to real-life problems [8]. Meanwhile, the automatic

© Springer Nature Switzerland AG 2021
K. Karlapalem et al. (Eds.): PAKDD 2021, LNAI 12713, pp. 168–180, 2021.
https://doi.org/10.1007/978-3-030-75765-6_14

speech classification (AutoSpeech) without any human intervention has attracted more and more attention from both academic researchers and industrial practitioners. In practice, AutoSpeech solutions should fulfill following requirements:

1. **Strong anytime performance:** In practical application scenarios, the available time budget is always limited. Thus, the AutoSpeech method should be able to yield good models with a small time budget.
2. **Strong final performance:** As the time budget increases, the AutoSpeech method should be able to yield better prediction performance.
3. **Generalization ability:** Speech-related classification tasks may come from different domains. There is no single model that can solve all tasks. The AutoSpeech strategy should be able to deal with different speech classification tasks in a unified framework.

According to these requirements, a novel metric called ALC (Area under Learning Curve) was proposed [13,24]. ALC considers the whole learning trajectory, instead of the traditional metric that focuses on the converged performance only. Both the NeurIPS 2019 AutoSpeech challenge and the InterSpeech 2020 AutoSpeech challenge adopt the ALC metric. Formally, the ALC metric of the AutoSpeech problem can be stated as follows:

Definition 1. *Given a training dataset D_{train} and a test dataset D_{test}, at each timestamp t, let $s(t)$ denote the normalized AUC (i.e., 2*AUC-1) of the most recent prediction on D_{test}. To normalize time to the $[0,1]$ interval, the time t is transformed by $\tilde{t}(t) = \frac{1+t/t_0}{1+T/t_0}$, where T is the time budget and t_0 is a reference time amount. The AutoSpeech problem aims to maximize the area under the learning curve using the formula:*

$$
ALC = \int_0^1 s(t)d\tilde{t}(t) = \int_0^T s(t)\tilde{t}'(t)dt
$$
$$
= \frac{1}{\log(1 + T/t_0)} \int_0^T \frac{s(t)}{t + t_0}dt
$$
(1)

Figure 1 shows an example of the ALC learning curve. According to Definition 1, we can see that $s(t)$ is weighted by $1/(t + t_0)$, giving stronger importance to predictions made at the beginning of the learning curve. Thus, it is encouraged to train a model with good any-time performance.

In this paper, we propose a three-stage progressive AutoSpeech framework[1] to maximum the ALC metric under a given time budget. Progressive AutoSpeech consists of the fast stage, enhancement stage, and exploration stage. The fast stage encourages any-time learning and aims to generate good prediction results as early as possible. Thus, the traditional machine learning model is employed in the fast stage. Next, the enhancement stage that contains a complex neural network model is responsible for quick performance boosting. To ensure the

---

[1] Progressive AutoSpeech won the first place in the NeurIPS 2019 AutoSpeech challenge and the second place in the Interspeech 2020 AutoSpeech challenge.

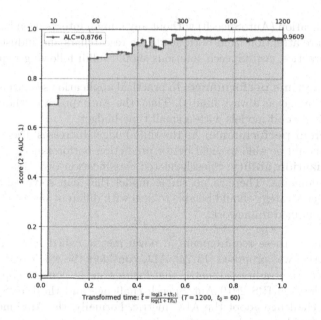

Fig. 1. An example of the ALC learning curve

generalization ability for different speech classification tasks, we employ multiple other deep neural network models that differ from the enhancement stage. Once the enhancement stage is ineffective for a specific task, the exploration stage can be used to improve the performance. Thus, as the training process progresses, the prediction performance can be continuously improved. Moreover, we leverage meta-learning to select suitable models for each stage.

Additionally, we dynamically construct an ensemble of top-k prediction results to further improve the final performance and robustness. The experimental results reveal that Progressive AutoSpeech is effective and efficient for a wide range of speech classification tasks and can achieve the best ALC score.

2   Related Work

Researchers have been working in the area of speech classification for many years. Traditional ML approaches including Gaussian Mixture Model [22] and Support Vector Machine [11] are widely used in speech classification tasks. With the rise of deep learning in recent years, deep neural networks have been applied to process speech classification tasks. The commonly-used features in the deep learning based approaches are the low-dimensional representations extracted from the raw audio such as Mel-spectrogram (Mel) [23], Mel Frequency Cepstrum Coefficients (MFCCs) [17], and Short Time Fourier Transform (STFT) [20].

Due to the short-term and long-term temporal relationship in the speech data, the Recurrent Neural Network (RNN) has received much attention in many speech classification tasks such as emotion classification [14] and audiobook genre classification [4]. The Long Short-Term Memory (LSTM) model has also been proposed to address speech recognition [12] and music genre classification [9]. The LSTM model can be combined with the attention mechanism to handle the language recognition task. The attention mechanism assigns a higher weight to the important part of speech [9,18].

Another commonly-used deep learning model for speech classification is the Convolutional Neural Network (CNN). Due to the great success achieved by CNNs on image classification, many image processing models and methods have been applied to speech classification tasks such as tone classification [10] and urban sound classification [5]. The Convolutional Recurrent Neural Network (CRNN) models have been proposed for sound event detection [2], bird audio classification [1], and music emotion recognition [15]. Moreover, the popular ResNet model can also be used for speech classification and has achieved excellent performance on many tasks [16].

Although RNN and CNN models can be used in speech classification, they usually perform well on the tasks from specific domains, lacking the generalization for cross-domain speech classification. Moreover, the existing models only focus on the final performance without considering the time cost.

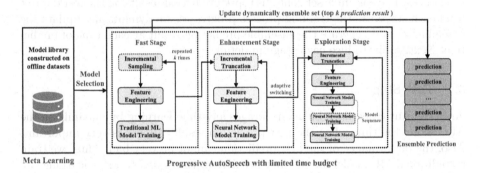

Fig. 2. Workflow of progressive AutoSpeech

3   Progressive AutoSpeech

In this section, we propose a general algorithm framework called Progressive AutoSpeech for automatic speech classification with limited time budget, which can achieve good any-time and final performance simultaneously. As shown in Fig. 2, the workflow of Progressive AutoSpeech consists of three stages: fast stage, enhancement stage, and exploration stage.

According to the definition of the ALC metric, the predictions made at the beginning of the learning curve play an important role. Training deep learning models is often time-consuming. Thus, the fast stage employs a traditional ML model along with the sampling technique to produce prediction results as early as possible. The following enhancement stage aims to achieve performance boosting by using the deep neural network model. To speed up the training process, the incremental speech truncation technique is proposed. The exploration stage uses multiple other deep neural network models that differ from the enhancement stage to improve the upper bound of the prediction performance. Additionally, if the model in the enhancement stage is ineffective for a specific task, the exploration stage can improve the prediction performance by exploring more models. The switching between different stages is adaptively determined.

Moreover, we leverage meta-learning [3] to select suitable models for each stage. Specifically, we first calculate the average rank for all available models including traditional ML models and complex deep neural network models over all offline datasets. Then, the traditional ML model that ranks first among all traditional ML models is selected as the model in the fast stage. Moreover, the deep neural network model that achieves better performance on most of the offline datasets is employed in the enhancement stage for fast performance boosting. The model sequence in the exploration stage contains other neural networks whose average ranks are close to the model in the enhancement stage.

Furthermore, we employ the ensemble technique to further improve the robustness. The ensemble set contains top-k prediction results on the test dataset from each stage. As the training process progresses, we dynamically update the ensemble set and generate the ensemble prediction result at each time of prediction. Next, we introduce each stage in detail.

3.1   Fast Stage

Since the AutoSpeech problem encourages any-time learning by maximizing the ALC score, the time when the first prediction results appear is very important. Also, the performance of the first prediction cannot be very bad. Thus, we train a traditional ML model for the first prediction. According to meat-learning, we select the linear regression model in the fast stage.

Incremental Sampling: To speed up the training process, we sample from the training set without replacement. The sample size n_{sample} can be calculated by Eq. 2, where n_{class} denotes the number of classes, k the sample size for each class, and n_{min} the minimum sample size for each training of LR. We set $k = 3$ and $n_{min} = 200$ respectively.

$$n_{sample} = max(n_{class} * k, n_{min}) \tag{2}$$

Since the sampling process is incremental, we do not put the sampled data back into the training set. Each time we train the LR model, we use both the newly sampled data and the last sampled data.

Feature Engineering: Because we need the first prediction results as early as possible, we only truncate at most the first five seconds of the raw audio to extract features. In this stage, we extract Mel-spectrogram [23] from the raw speech. The Mel-spectrogram is a spectrogram where the frequencies are converted to the mel scale. Each Mel-spectrogram extracted from a single speech sample is a two-dimensional array. Since the LR model only supports a one-dimensional array as input, we need to transform the 2-D Mel-spectrogram array into a 1-D array. Specifically, we first calculate the mean value and the standard deviation of each row in the 2-D Mel-spectrogram array, then we concatenate these mean values and standard deviations as a 1-D array. Finally, the 1-D array is standardized as the input feature of the LR model. Since the Mel-spectrogram features of the last sampled data have been extracted, we only need to extract features for the newly sampled data.

Once the number of LR models trained in the fast stage reaches the given value, we switch to the enhancement stage.

3.2 Enhancement Stage

From the enhancement stage, we focus on improving the prediction accuracy as much as possible by employing the deep neural network models. As shown in Sect. 4.3, the Thin-Resnet model can achieve better performance on most of the offline datasets. Thus, in the enhancement stage, we select the Thin-Resnet model [25] with meta-learning.

Incremental Truncation: As can be seen in Sect. 4.1, the length of raw audio usually differs a lot and the length of each raw audio in the same dataset also varies greatly. In the fast stage, we just truncate up to the first five seconds of raw audio. This is very fast and convenient. However, it will drop too much information from raw audio and cannot utilize the whole raw audio. To make full use of raw audio, we perform incremental data truncation in the enhancement stage. At the beginning of the enhancement stage, we truncate raw audio from a shorter length, and as the training progresses, we truncate longer and longer raw audio in each epoch. In our experiments, we truncate the raw audio from 5 s to 35 s. If the truncation length is longer than that of the raw audio, we simply copy the raw audio to meet the truncation requirements. If the short audio is effective for classification, then we can get good prediction results in the early stage of training. Otherwise, we can use more and more information in the raw audio as the truncation length continues to increase.

Feature Engineering: In this stage, we extract STFT [20] from the original audio. STFT represents a signal in the time-frequency domain by computing Discrete Fourier transforms (DFT) over short overlapping windows. We separate a complex-valued spectrogram D into magnitude S and phase P. Thus, $D = S \times P$. The phase component is dropped and the magnitude component is standardized as the input features for the thin-Resnet model. Additionally, to make the training process faster, we do not use all STFT features of the truncated speech data as the input of the model. We randomly intercept the STFT features for at most 2.5 s. Moreover, we reverse the STFT features with a 30% probability. These data augmentation strategies can not only speed up the training process but also greatly improve data utilization and randomness, leading to better generalization.

Adaptive Termination: The termination of the enhancement stage should satisfy one of the following conditions:

1. Although thin-Resnet performs well on most datasets, it may perform poorly on the datasets from specific domains. If this situation occurs, we need to terminate this stage as early as possible. Specifically, after several consecutive training processes, if the prediction performance of the thin-Resnet model cannot exceed that of the LR model, we directly switch to the next stage.
2. When the thin-Resnet model converges, continuing training may lead to overfitting. Thus, we need to stop training timely. The convergence condition is that there is no significant performance gain for multiple consecutive times of training processes.

3.3   Exploration Stage

When the enhancement stage is terminated, we enter the exploration stage, where we use a sequence of deep neural networks to further strengthen the final performance for different types of speech classification tasks. The model sequence that contains LSTM, Bi-directional LSTM, and CRNN is trained repeatedly until the time budget is reached. Similar to the enhancement stage, we also adopt the incremental enhancement technique.

In this stage, we extract MFCCs from the raw audio. MFCCs are commonly used as features in speech recognition systems [7], such as the systems which can automatically recognize numbers spoken into a telephone. MFCCs are also increasingly finding uses in music information retrieval applications such as genre classification, audio similarity measures. Moreover, MFCCs are the most popular acoustic features used in speaker identification [17]. MFCCs take into account human perception for sensitivity at appropriate frequencies by converting the conventional frequency to Mel Scale.

When the AUC of one model on the validation set is not rising for three consecutive times, we will switch to the next model.

3.4   Dynamic Result Ensemble

Each stage may train multiple models with different training sets or different network architectures. To further improve robustness and avoid overfitting, we adopt a simple and fast ensemble method. Specifically, during the training process of each stage, if one model can achieve better prediction performance on the validation dataset, then we use that model to predict the test dataset and add the prediction results into the ensemble set. Thus, the ensemble set that contains the top-k prediction results is dynamically updated. Every time the prediction on the test dataset is required, we access the ensemble set and calculate the average ensemble prediction.

4   Experiments

4.1   Datasets

We evaluated the performance of Progressive AutoSpeech on 10 speech datasets from different domains. The meta-features of these datasets are shown in Table 1. From Table 1, we can see that the meta-features such as the number of classes, the number of instances, maximum length, and minimum length differ a lot.

All the audios are first converted to single-channel, 16-bit streams at a 16 kHz sampling rate for consistency, then they are loaded by librosa and dumped to pickle format. Also, the speech datasets contain both long audios and short audios without padding.

Table 1. Meta-features of speech datasets from different domains

Dataset name	Domain	Source	Train/Test number	Class number	Maximum/Minimum class number	Maximum length(s)	Minimum length(s)	95% Length(s)
data01	Speaker	VoxCeleb [16]	1650/3300	330	5/5	1.00	1.00	1.00
data02	Emotion	Berlin emotional speech (see footnote 1)	346/162	7	50/7	8.98	1.23	5.16
data03	Accent	Speech sccent archive[2]	164/308	11	20/10	55.00	18.45	45.00
data04	Genre	Uspop2002 [6]	343/739	20	20/12	30.00	30.00	30.00
data05	Language	CSS10 [21]	132/151	10	23/5	2.00	2.00	2.00
data06	Speaker	Librispeech [19]	3000/3000	100	115/7	73.16	3.96	19.08
data07	Emotion	Berlin emotional speech[2]	428/107	7	81/37	6.79	1.23	4.52
data08	Accent	Speech accent archive[3]	796/200	3	407/104	91.33	16.46	40.63
data09	Genre	Uspop2002 [6]	939/474	20	49/28	5.00	5.00	5.00
data10	Language	CSS10 [21]	199/597	10	25/16	16.39	2.08	10.05

[2] http://www.expressive-speech.net/.

[3] http://accent.gmu.edu.

Table 2. Performance comparison with the ALC and accuracy metric

Method	data01		data02		data03		data04		data05	
	ALC	ACC	ALC	ACC	ALC	ACC	ALC	ACC	ALC	ACC
LR+Mel	0.7015	0.0198	0.8429	0.4838	0.156	0.1179	0.5944	0.1738	0.9366	0.4537
CNN2D+MFCCs	0.4473	0.0292	0.8452	0.6827	0.0432	0.0998	0.4807	0.2335	0.7374	0.3805
CRNN2D+MFCCs	0.4677	0.0613	0.8571	0.7603	0.0659	0.1121	0.5749	0.3831	0.8666	0.7248
BiLSTM+MFCCs	0.5604	0.1218	0.7718	0.6418	0.0136	0.0967	0.6338	0.4456	0.8928	0.785
LSTM+MFCCs	0.558	0.1144	0.8147	0.656	0.0616	0.1106	0.6528	0.4886	0.9057	0.8318
ThinResnet+STFT	0.5735	**0.2102**	0.8099	0.8914	0.2106	**0.1929**	0.6238	0.7189	0.8844	0.9404
ProgressiveAutoSpeech	**0.8237**	0.2082	**0.9579**	**0.8928**	**0.2447**	0.1893	**0.7973**	**0.7215**	**0.9829**	**0.9426**
Method	data06		data07		data08		data09		data10	
	ALC	ACC	ALC	ACC	ALC	ACC	ALC	ACC	ALC	ACC
LR+Mel	0.7943	0.2493	0.7405	0.4581	0.4371	0.5325	0.6016	0.2057	0.9723	0.7091
CNN2D+MFCCs	0.5895	0.219	0.7962	0.5342	0.3887	0.5436	0.4309	0.1831	0.8885	0.7804
CRNN2D+MFCCs	0.6462	0.5016	0.8128	0.7174	0.5878	0.705	0.5021	0.2724	0.8798	0.9897
BiLSTM+MFCCs	0.6786	0.4654	0.7199	0.5271	0.4475	0.6013	0.5319	0.3174	0.8909	0.992
LSTM+MFCCs	0.7198	0.6203	0.7489	0.5662	0.4729	0.6151	0.5575	0.3421	0.8964	0.9921
ThinResnet+STFT	0.6788	0.8704	0.8317	**0.8094**	0.6636	**0.8206**	0.618	**0.5178**	0.8563	0.9927
ProgressiveAutoSpeech	**0.9388**	**0.8747**	**0.924**	0.8044	**0.7516**	0.8153	**0.7456**	0.5163	**0.9847**	**0.9928**

4.2 Experimental Setting

We employed the ALC and accuracy metrics to evaluate all speech classification models. We sampled 20% of the training set as the validation set. We used sklearn to implement the Logistic Regression model. Moreover, we used TensorFlow to implement all deep neural network models. For all deep learning models, the loss function is the cross-entropy. The learning rate of the Adam optimizer is 0.001. The batch size is 32. We trained deep learning models on a Tesla K80 GPU and the time budget is set to 1800 s. Each experiment is run three times and the average result is calculated.

4.3 Comparison with Baselines

The commonly-used baselines for the speech classification task are as follows.

- **LR+Mel:** We extracted Mel-spectrogram as features and ran the Logistic Regression model with the max iteration of 1000.
- **LstmAttention+MFCCs:** LstmAttention model consists of an LSTM layer, an Attention layer, and two dense layers. We extracted MFCCs as features.
- **BiLstmAttention+MFCCs:** BiLstmAttention model consists of a bidirectional LSTM layer, an Attention layer, and two dense layers. We extracted MFCCs as features.
- **CRNN+MFCCs:** CRNN model consists of four conv blocks, two GRU layers, and a dense layer. We extracted MFCCs as features.
- **CNN+MFCCs:** CNN model consists of five conv blocks, and two dense layers. We extracted MFCCs as features.

- **ThinResnet+STFT:** ThinResnet model consists of ConvBlock and Identi-
tyBlock [25]. We extracted STFT as features.

These baselines represent the models employed in each stage of Progressive AutoSpeech. Moreover, these baselines and Progressive AutoSpeech use the
same speech truncation and data augmentation techniques. We evaluated all
methods in terms of both the ALC and the accuracy metrics. Table 2 shows the
experimental results. Progressive AutoSpeech can achieve the best ALC score in
all datasets due to its strong any-time performance and generalization ability.
Moreover, Progressive AutoSpeech outperforms other methods in terms of accuracy. Note that the ThinResnet+STFT method also has excellent accuracy in
most datasets. Because of this, we selected the ThinResnet+STFT model in the
enhancement stage. Due to the instability of the result ensemble, the accuracy
performance of Progressive AutoSpeech may worse than the ThinResnet+STFT
method. But, the performance gap is very small.

4.4   Ablation Study

Performance of Each Stage: For comparison, we further evaluated the performance of each single stage of Progressive AutoSpeech. In fact, each single
stage can be equivalent to a specific speech classification model. Table 3 shows
the ALC score of the fast stage, enhancement stage, and exploration stage. Progressive AutoSpeech combines the advantage of each stage and thus achieves the
best ALC score in all datasets. The fast stage can get the prediction results as
early as possible. The enhancement stage and exploration stage are responsible

Table 3. Ablation study

Method	data01	data02	data03	data04	data05
EnhancementStage	0.6734	0.8823	0.2223	0.6589	0.9174
ExplorationStage	0.5492	0.8571	0.0782	0.6019	0.906
FastStage	0.7189	0.8119	0.1369	0.5483	0.9312
ProgressiveAutoSpeech-Truncate5s	0.8167	0.957	0.217	0.7476	**0.9831**
ProgressiveAutoSpeech-Truncate15s	0.7948	0.9517	0.1951	0.7452	0.981
ProgressiveAutoSpeech-Truncate10s	0.8051	0.9572	0.181	0.7501	0.9823
ProgressiveAutoSpeech	**0.8237**	**0.9579**	**0.2447**	**0.7973**	0.9829
Method	data06	data07	data08	data09	data10
EnhancementStage	0.7567	0.865	0.6865	0.6607	0.8922
ExplorationStage	0.7127	0.8201	0.4722	0.5517	0.8938
FastStage	0.9063	0.6038	0.4395	0.6039	0.9821
ProgressiveAutoSpeech-Truncate5s	0.9315	0.9169	0.7377	**0.7469**	0.9825
ProgressiveAutoSpeech-Truncate15s	0.9292	0.9135	0.7406	0.7413	0.9833
ProgressiveAutoSpeech-Truncate10s	0.9349	0.9208	0.7349	0.7448	0.9845
ProgressiveAutoSpeech	**0.9388**	**0.924**	**0.7516**	0.7456	**0.9847**

for improving the prediction performance as much as possible. Therefore, combining all stages not only produces prediction results faster but also achieves better any-time performance and final performance for different cross-domain speech classification tasks.

Evaluation of Incremental Truncation: We disabled the incremental data truncation technique and truncated the raw audio for 5 s, 10 s, and 15 s respectively. From Table 3, we can see that Progressive AutoSpeech outperforms the fixed truncation methods in most datasets except for data05 and data09. In these two datasets, the length of each raw audio is less than or equal to 5 s. Thus, the ProgressiveAutoSpeech-Truncate5s method can capture all information of the two datasets without overfitting.

4.5   Scalability of Time Budget

We further evaluated the scalability of time budget. Because the gap between some ALC scores is too small, we performed Min-Max scaling for ALC scores under different time budgets on each dataset to better show the trend of change. From Fig. 3, we can see that the performance of Progressive AutoSpeech is getting better and better with the continuous increase of time budget, which indicates that Progressive AutoSpeech has good scalability of time budget.

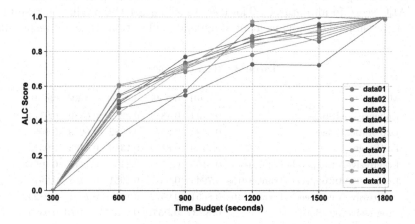

Fig. 3. Scalability of time budget

5   Conclusion and Future Work

In this paper, we proposed a general, three-stage AutoSpeech framework called Progressive AutoSpeech to maximum the ALC metric under a given time budget. Progressive AutoSpeech consists of the fast stage, enhancement stage, and exploration stage. Moreover, we leveraged meta-learning to select suitable models for each stage. The experimental results reveal that Progressive AutoSpeech is effective and efficient for a wide range of speech classification tasks and can achieve the best ALC score.

In the future, we plan to integrate more models and features for AutoSpeech and further perform automatic data argumentation for speech-related tasks.

Acknowledgments. This work was supported by the National Natural Science Foundation of China (U1811461), National Key R&D Program of China (2019YFC1711000), and Collaborative Innovation Center of Novel Software Technology and Industrialization.

References

1. Adavanne, S., Drossos, K., Çakir, E., Virtanen, T.: Stacked convolutional and recurrent neural networks for bird audio detection. In: Proceedings of the European Signal Processing Conference (EUSIPCO), pp. 1729–1733 (2017)
2. Adavanne, S., Virtanen, T.: Sound event detection using weakly labeled dataset with stacked convolutional and recurrent neural network. arXiv preprint arXiv:1710.02998 (2017)
3. Brazdil, P., Giraud-Carrier, C.: Metalearning and algorithm selection: progress, state of the art and introduction to the 2018 special issue. Mach. Learn. **107**(1), 1–14 (2018)
4. Carmi, N., Cohen, A., Avigal, M., Lerner, A.: A storyteller's tale: literature audiobooks genre classification using CNN and RNN architectures. In: Proceedings of Interspeech 2019, pp. 3387–3390 (2019)
5. Dai, W., Dai, C., Qu, S., Li, J., Das, S.: Very deep convolutional neural networks for raw waveforms. In: Proceedings of the International Conference on Acoustics, Speech and Signal Processing (ICASSP), pp. 421–425 (2017)
6. Ellis, D.P.W.: Classifying music audio with timbral and chroma features. In: Proceedings of the International Conference on Music Information Retrieval, pp. 339–340 (2007)
7. Ganchev, T., Fakotakis, N., Kokkinakis, G.: Comparative evaluation of various mfcc implementations on the speaker verification task. In: Proceedings of the International Conference on Speech and Computer, pp. 191–194 (2005)
8. Hutter, F., Kotthoff, L., Vanschoren, J. (eds.): Automated Machine Learning. TSSCML. Springer, Cham (2019). https://doi.org/10.1007/978-3-030-05318-5
9. Irvin, J., Chartock, E., Hollander, N.: Recurrent neural networks with attention for genre classification (2016)
10. Kim, T., Lee, J., Nam, J.: Comparison and analysis of sample cnn architectures for audio classification. IEEE J. Sel. Topics Signal Process. **13**(2), 285–297 (2019)
11. Lin, Y.L., Wei, G.: Speech emotion recognition based on HMM and SVM. In: Proceedings of the International Conference on Machine Learning and Cybernetics, pp. 4898–4901 (2005)
12. Liu, C., Wang, Y., Kumar, K., Gong, Y.: Investigations on speaker adaptation of LSTM RNN models for speech recognition. In: Proceedings of the International Conference on Acoustics, Speech and Signal Processing (ICASSP), pp. 5020–5024 (2016)

13. Liu, Z., et al.: Autocv challenge design and baseline results. In: CAp 2019 - Conférence sur l'Apprentissage Automatique. Toulouse, France (2019)
14. Majumder, N., Poria, S., Hazarika, D., Mihalcea, R., Gelbukh, A., Cambria, E.: Dialoguernn: an attentive RNN for emotion detection in conversations. In: Proceedings of the AAAI Conference on Artificial Intelligence, vol. 33, pp. 6818–6825 (2019)
15. Malik, M., Adavanne, S., Drossos, K., Virtanen, T., Ticha, D., Jarina, R.: Stacked convolutional and recurrent neural networks for music emotion recognition. arXiv preprint arXiv:1706.02292 (2017)
16. Nagrani, A., Chung, J.S., Zisserman, A.: Voxceleb: a large-scale speaker identification dataset. arXiv preprint arXiv:1706.08612 (2017)
17. Nakagawa, S., Wang, L., Ohtsuka, S.: Speaker identification and verification by combining MFCC and phase information. IEEE Trans. Audio Speech Lang. Process. **20**(4), 1085–1095 (2011)
18. Padi, B., Mohan, A., Ganapathy, S.: Attention based hybrid i-vector BLSTM model for language recognition. In: Proceedings of Interspeech 2019, pp. 1263–1267 (2019)
19. Panayotov, V., Chen, G., Povey, D., Khudanpur, S.: Librispeech: an ASR corpus based on public domain audio books. In: Proceedings of the International Conference on Acoustics, Speech and Signal Processing (ICASSP), pp. 5206–5210 (2015)
20. Parchami, M., Zhu, W.P., Champagne, B., Plourde, E.: Recent developments in speech enhancement in the short-time fourier transform domain. IEEE Circ. Syst. Mag. **16**(3), 45–77 (2016)
21. Park, K., Mulc, T.: Css10: a collection of single speaker speech datasets for 10 languages. arXiv preprint arXiv:1903.11269 (2019)
22. Reynolds, D.A., Quatieri, T.F., Dunn, R.B.: Speaker verification using adapted gaussian mixture models. Dig. Signal Process. **10**(1–3), 19–41 (2000)
23. Shen, J., et al.: Natural TTS synthesis by conditioning wavenet on mel spectrogram predictions. In: 2018 IEEE International Conference on Acoustics, Speech and Signal Processing (ICASSP), pp. 4779–4783. IEEE (2018)
24. Wang, J., et al.: Autospeech 2020: the second automated machine learning challenge for speech classification. In: Interspeech 2020, pp. 1967–1971 (2020)
25. Xie, W., Nagrani, A., Chung, J.S., Zisserman, A.: Utterance-level aggregation for speaker recognition in the wild. In: Proceedings of the International Conference on Acoustics, Speech and Signal Processing (ICASSP), pp. 5791–5795 (2019)

CrowdTeacher: Robust Co-teaching with Noisy Answers and Sample-Specific Perturbations for Tabular Data

Mani Sotoodeh[(⊠)], Li Xiong, and Joyce Ho

Emory University, Atlanta, GA, USA
{msotood,lxiong,jho31}@emory.edu

Abstract. Samples with ground truth labels may not always be available in numerous domains. While learning from crowdsourcing labels has been explored, existing models can still fail in the presence of sparse, unreliable, or differing annotations. Co-teaching methods have shown promising improvements for computer vision problems with noisy labels by employing two classifiers trained on each others' confident samples in each batch. Inspired by the idea of separating confident and uncertain samples during the training process, we extend it for the crowdsourcing problem. Our model, CrowdTeacher, uses the idea that perturbation in the input space model can improve the robustness of the classifier for noisy labels. Treating crowdsourcing annotations as a source of noisy labeling, we perturb samples based on the certainty from the aggregated annotations. The perturbed samples are fed to a Co-teaching algorithm tuned to also accommodate smaller tabular data. We showcase the boost in predictive power attained using CrowdTeacher for both synthetic and real datasets across various label density settings. Our experiments reveal that our proposed approach beats baselines modeling individual annotations and then combining them, methods simultaneously learning a classifier and inferring truth labels, and the Co-teaching algorithm with aggregated labels through common truth inference methods.

Keywords: Crowdsourcing · Noisy labels · Input space perturbation

1 Introduction and Background

Labeled data is essential to guarantee the success of increasingly more complex classifiers. Unfortunately obtaining large quantities of high-quality labels can be cost-prohibitive for several fields. For example, in the medical domains, it may take a clinician several hours to annotate the health records of hundreds of patients. One alternative is to gather labels using crowdsourcing, where remotely located workers are utilized to perform the task of labeling the data. Although these crowdworkers individually may not be as accurate as an expert, constructing the true label from their aggregated opinions can approximate the accuracy of an expert. However, the subjectivity of annotators and their different qualifications introduce noise to the labeling process. To model this noise, most studies

© Springer Nature Switzerland AG 2021
K. Karlapalem et al. (Eds.): PAKDD 2021, LNAI 12713, pp. 181–193, 2021.
https://doi.org/10.1007/978-3-030-75765-6_15

either focus on modeling the reliability of annotators and their correlation and reflecting it in the label aggregation phase or combining classifier training with learning the annotators' trust parameters. Yet, learning through crowdsourcing-based models can still fail in the presence of differing annotations and unreliable users [13].

A promising direction for dealing with noisy labels for training complex classifiers is Co-teaching [5]. Under the Co-teaching paradigm, two peer neural networks are trained separately and specific samples are exchanged between the networks to reduce the error of the two models and yield a more accurate model. As a result, Co-teaching methods have shown great promise for computer vision problems with noisy labels. Co-teaching can naturally counteract crowdsourcing noise since it filters out noisy samples in the beginning and only adds them at later training stages when they will be valuable. However, Co-teaching treats each sample with the same weight. This can cause the classifier to incorrectly learn from samples that may have fewer annotations or diverging human labels.

To address this limitation, we propose to leverage the certainty of samples from the label aggregation phase to inform the selection process of Co-teaching, which has not been studied before. Our model, CrowdTeacher, uses a perturbation scheme based on the uncertainty of the samples to improve the robustness of the Co-teaching framework. Given the availability of samples' uncertainty from the label aggregation step, our model uses this information to counter the inherent noise by perturbing the input space. In addition, the framework prioritizes the more confident samples of the classifier during the learning process. Thus, we tackle the problem of classification with features and crowdsourcing labels using three mechanisms:

- Estimation of the features' distributions to generate synthetic data which is then used to perturb each sample in an additive manner, proportional to its estimated label's uncertainty.
- Enhancing Co-teaching by knowledge distillation, i.e. a student-teacher model of a simple and a complex network to accommodate smaller tabular data.
- Utilization of the perturbed samples as input to the above classifier to further differentiate uncertain and certain training points based on their loss in each epoch

Next, we formally define the problem and summarize and delineate where and how CrowdTeacher ties into the relevant literature in crowdsourcing, data augmentation, and learning with noisy labels.

1.1 Problem Definition: Classification with Crowdsourcing Annotations

In practice, there are numerous applications in which the ground truth of a classification task is not available, or disputed. For instance in medicine, multiple pathologists do not always necessarily agree on the malignancy status of a tumor in an image [8], or multiple nurses do not all agree on the presence of

Table 1. Summary of notations.

Symbol	Description
N	Number of samples
R	Number of annotators
K	Number of classes
α	Perturbation lction
$\mathbf{X}_{tr}$	Training feature matrix
$\mathbf{A}$	Answer matrix of all annotators
$\mathbf{S}$	Synthetic feature matrix
$\widetilde{\mathbf{X}_{tr}}$	Perturbed training samples feature matrix
F_c	Set of continuous features
F_d	Set of all discrete features
$\mathbf{P}$	Class probability matrix
c_i	Certainty of i-th

hospital-acquired bedsores for a patient given their charts [15]. Similarly, obtaining ground truth from experts to train reliable classifiers can be expensive, as in the case of content filtering and regulation of posts on social media, which are distributed among multiple non-expert annotators to obtain some good quality labels [9]. Formally, we define learning with crowdsourcing labels as follows:

Definition 1. *(Classification with Crowdsourcing Annotations) Consider a set of R annotators labeling N samples with K possible classes. Given an answer matrix $\mathbf{A} \in \mathbb{R}^{N \times R}$ where each element a_{nr} indicates the label for sample n provided by annotator r, and the training feature matrix $\mathbf{X}_{tr} \in \mathbb{R}^{N \times M}$, the goal is to train a classifier that accurately predicts the true labels for the test data using only its feature matrix $\mathbf{X}_{ts}$.*

We use K to denote number of classes. Simulated data from the synthesizer used for perturbation is shown by $\mathbf{S}$ and the perturbed samples are denoted with $\widetilde{\mathbf{X}_{tr}}$. The set of continuous and discrete features are shown by F_c and F_d respectively. Table 1 summarizes the notations used throughout this paper.

1.2 Related Works

Classification with noisy answers or multiple crowdsourced labels overlaps with three other areas: learning with crowdsourcing labels, data augmentation and synthetic data generation for robust learning, and selective gradient propagation.

Learning with Crowdsourcing Labels. Here we summarize the three main high-level approaches for learning with multiple annotations.

Sequential. This approach first uses a truth inference method to estimate the ground truth for training samples. The estimated label is then used to train a classifier. A recent survey extensively comparing these models has shown the overall efficiency and utility of the D&S method [14]. Our proposed model falls into this category, however, we introduce ideas from the two other overlapping areas to further improve the predictive performance of this basic classifier.

Simultaneous. The second perspective jointly tackles the problem of learning classifier parameters and the estimated ground truth of the samples. Albarqouni et al. uses the Expectation-Maximization (EM) algorithm and Maximum a posteriori estimation to iteratively compute these two sets of parameters until convergence [1]. Yet, this method is computationally challenging especially for more complex classifiers.

Individual Annotator's Label Modeling. The last set of research works entail learning a model for each individual labeler. Dr. Net was proposed to learn a classifier to reproduce the labels of each annotator and is composed of two phases, individual annotator modeling and learning labelers' averaging weights for the final prediction [4]. To overcome the computational challenge of simultaneous learning and Dr. Net, multiple crowd-layer variants were introduced to remove the computational burden of the EM loop [11], by first estimating the ground truth of samples and then attempting to replicate the individual annotator's labels using a very simple neural network. Unfortunately, such models require significant samples to properly learn a robust classifier.

Data Augmentation and Synthetic Data Generation for Robust Learning. To overcome the obstacle of noisy labels or features, perturbation schemes and data augmentations have been investigated. In computer vision, data augmentation is done by applying operations like cropping and rotation to combat potential mislabelled training data [2,12,17]. Another line of work achieves robustness against noisy data by generating data synthesizers that achieves the same predictive performance as using the real data. Xu et al. have extended data augmentations to tabular data with heterogeneous feature types using Generative Adversarial Networks and Variational Autoencoders [16]. However, such synthesizers are modeled independent of the labels or the conflicting annotations.

Selective Gradient Propagation. To counter noisy labels and memorization effects in neural networks, the Co-teaching algorithm adaptively changes both the number of and the set of participating samples used in stochastic gradient descent epochs for two differently-initialized classifiers [5]. For each epoch, Co-teaching chooses a different number of samples with the lowest loss (as a proxy for clean data) and updates each classifier using the clean samples of the other network. This is in contrast to using all the samples or the clean samples of the classifier itself that may result in memorization and early overfitting which prohibits learning a generalizable classifier. A parallel can be drawn to similarly

---

Algorithm 1. CrowdTeacher.

Input: Training Features $\mathbf{X}_{tr}$, Answer matrix $\mathbf{A}$, Perturbation Fraction α
Output: *Model*
Train synthesizer to generate synthetic data:
$Data\_sampler \leftarrow Synthesizer(\mathbf{X}_{tr})$
Generate N samples from resulting sampler: $\mathbf{S} \leftarrow Data\_sampler(N)$
Run truth inference method to get class probabilities:
$\mathbf{P} \leftarrow D\&S\_Algorithm(\mathbf{A})$
/* Generate perturbed samples $\widetilde{\mathbf{X}_{tr}}$ */
for $i = 1, \cdots, N$ **do**

    Set sample's certainty using Eq. (1)
    Sample s_i from 10% closest samples of synthetic samples $\mathbf{S}$ to x_i using KNN
    /* Generate continuous features */
    for $j \in F_c$ **do**
        Generate feature $\widetilde{x}_{ij}$ according to Eq. (2)
    /*Generate discrete features*/
    Calculate f_d^i using Eq. (3)
    Sample discrete features to perturb: $F_{d_p}^i$ from F_d such that $|F_{d_p}^i| = f_d^i$
    for $j \in F_{d_p}^i$ **do**
        Generate single feature value $\widetilde{x}_{ij}$ according to Eq. (4)

Train Co-teaching Algorithm on Perturbed Samples:
$Model \leftarrow Co\_teaching(\widetilde{\mathbf{X}_{tr}})$

---

deal with the inherent noisiness of aggregated crowdsourcing labels. Co-teaching mechanism of prioritizing a smaller set of confident samples in the initial stages of learning, and gradually incorporating more of the uncertain samples in later epochs can be leveraged for problem of classification with crowdsourcing labels.

2   Methodology

Our idea is to enhance the Co-teaching framework to account for the uncertainty associated with the estimated truth label of the sample. We introduce a perturbation-based scheme to the Co-teaching framework so the trained model will be more robust to sparsity and unreliability in the annotations. For each mini-batch update of Co-teaching, synthetic samples are generated and used to perturb each sample *dependent* on the uncertainty of the estimated truth label. Thus a sample that has more certainty in the label will be perturbed more whereas a sample that has fewer annotations is likely to have less perturbation. The perturbed sample is then used to train the classifier.

2.1   Generating Synthetic Samples

To improve the robustness of the Co-teaching framework, CrowdTeacher generates synthetic samples of the data which are then used to perturb the samples to train the classifier. Any data synthesizer with reasonable data generation performance can be used. For the purpose of our paper, we focus on three data synthesizers: Conditional GAN (CTGAN) [16], TVAE [16] and Gaussian copula [10]. CTGAN can handle mixed feature types (discrete and continuous) and has been shown to perform competitively with other GAN-based, VAE-based, and Bayesian network-based data synthesizer for vision benchmark datasets [10]. It is worthwhile to note that the data synthesizer is not tied to the learning task and can be used as a stand-alone tool.

To generate synthetic data within CrowdTeacher, the training feature matrix $\mathbf{X}_{tr}$ is fed to the synthesizer. For CTGAN synthesizer, the discrete features F_d are specified explicitly since they are modeled differently compared to the continuous features F_c. Once the synthesizer has estimated the data distribution, any number of samples can be drawn. For CrowdTeacher, we generate the synthetic set $\mathbf{S} \in \mathbb{R}^{N \times M}$ with N synthetic samples once and assume each synthetic sample can serve as a unique perturbation source. Although $\mathbf{S}$ is drawn once and is the same size as our training data to minimize the computational footprint of our model, the synthetic set can be re-drawn at each mini-batch of the Co-teaching framework with a larger number of samples.

2.2   Sample-Specific Perturbations

The generated synthetic samples, $\mathbf{S}$, fail to account for the uncertainty associated with the estimated sample label as the synthetic samples are only dependent on original training data. Thus, we introduce a mechanism to leverage the uncertainty that arises from the truth inference method to individually perturb each sample. For the purpose of illustration and experimentation, we focus on the D&S algorithm [3], but note that CrowdTeacher can be used with any robust truth inference method that quantifies the label uncertainty for each sample. The D&S algorithm takes as an input the matrix of annotations ($\mathbf{A}$) and models annotators by a confusion matrix to capture their chance of mistaking one class for another or correctly reporting them in addition to the class priors. D&S outputs a matrix $\mathbf{P} \in \mathbb{R}^{N \times K}$, where the P_{ik} element denotes the probability that sample i is of class k. The certainty of each sample, c_i, is then defined as the maximum probability across all the classes:

$$c_i = \max_{k \in K} (P_{ik}) \quad \forall i \in N \tag{1}$$

Choosing an Appropriate Simulated Sample for Perturbation. Given the data synthesizer can generate synthetic samples that are quite different from the original data point and can lead to more uncertainty with respect to the truth label, we use k-nearest neighbors (KNN) to identify reasonable close samples from S. For each sample, KNN is run to find the top 10% closely simulated samples. A simulated data point, s_i, is then randomly chosen from this top 10% and used to perturb the original point.

Perturbation. Each sample x_i is perturbed using the simulated data point s_i according to the uncertainty, c_i and a user-specified perturbation fraction

$\alpha \in [0, 1]$ to obtain the perturbed sample $\tilde{x}_i$. Let s_{ij} represent the jth feature of sample s_i. If the jth feature is continuous, the value for the synthetic, perturbed sample $\tilde{x}_{ij}$ is a convex combination of the original and simulated sample:

$$\tilde{x}_{ij} = (1 - \alpha c_i)x_{ij} + (\alpha c_i)s_{ij}, \quad \forall i \in N, \quad \forall j \in F_c \quad (2)$$

For the discrete features, we use c_i and α to calculate the number of discrete features to swap. Let $|F_d|$ denote the number of discrete features in the dataset, then the number of discrete features to swap for each sample x_i, f_d^i is calculated as:

$$f_d^i = round(\alpha c_i |F_d|) \quad (3)$$

Then f_d^i features are randomly selected for perturbation from the original discrete feature set and denoted as $F_{d_p}^i$. For each feature, j in this perturbation set, the feature values are replaced with the synthetic sample value s_{ij}.

$$\tilde{x}_{ij} = s_{ij}, \quad \forall i \in N, \quad \forall j \in F_{d_p}^i \quad (4)$$

2.3 Knowledge Distillation-Based Co-teaching for Smaller Tabular Data

To combat the large performance variations associated with running the Co-teaching algorithm on smaller-sized tabular data, we incorporated the student-teacher idea from knowledge distillation [6]. Thus instead of two peer networks with the same architecture, we used one simple and one complex network such that the number of hidden units of the simpler network is half of the other one. Empirical results showed these modifications helped with both the convergence of the two networks in achieving more similar evaluation metrics and overall better performance across different synthetic datasets.

3 Experiments

3.1 Baseline Methods

The best performing methods from crowdsourcing studies (see Sect. 1.2) are chosen as comparison models. The original Co-teaching algorithm and Co-teaching using only uniformly perturbed input are also used to illustrate the advantage of certainty-aware perturbation. All methods employ the same base classifier, a neural network with one hidden layer of $\frac{|F_c|+|F_d|}{4}$ units. Sequential methods share the same truth inference method (D&S) and are marked with *.

– Naive baseline* (Base_clf) [3]: Base classifier trained with D&S labels.
– Simultaneous Expectation Maximization (S-EM) [1]: An algorithm that jointly learns the classifier and annotators' parameters using EM algorithm.
– Dr. Net [4]: An individual annotation based model that separately learns each annotator's labels and their weights.

- Crowdlayer (CL_MW and CL_VW) [11]: An algorithm that estimates ground truth first and replicates each annotator's labels via a simple final layer. This final layer is removed at test time. The number of parameters for the last layer determines the Crowdlayer variant. We evaluated the vector of weights (VW) and matrix of weights (MW) variants.
- Vanilla Co-teaching* (V_Coteach) [5]: The original Co-teaching algorithm trained with D&S labels.
- Co-teaching with uniform perturbation* (P_Coteach): The Co-teaching algorithm trained on D&S labels and synthetic samples.
- CrowdTeacher*: Our proposed method with the Co-teaching algorithm trained on D&S labels and sample-specific certainty-informed perturbed samples.

We conducted our experiments using these baseline models. Since S-EM and Dr. Net constantly performed poorly compared to the other baselines, we omitted them from the plots for better readability. The Python implementation for all our experiments is publicly available on GitHub[1].

3.2 Annotation Simulation

For our experiments, we set the number of annotators to be 5 ($R = 5$). To simulate the annotators' behavior, we consider two parameters: (1) mean reliability, or the average likelihood of the annotators to label a positive sample correctly and (2) variability in annotators' expertise or the difference in their qualities. We set the distribution of samples having 1 to 5 labels as $[\tau\,,\, 0.55(1-\tau),\, 0.27(1-\tau),\, 0.13(1-\tau),\, 0.05(1-\tau)]$ and vary the parameter τ for our experiments. Note that τ determines the average number of labels per sample.

Conventionally, the Beta distribution is used to generate each annotator's reliability. After determining each annotator's reliability, its labels are created by randomly choosing (100-reliability) percent of positive cases and switching their labels into negative 0. Flipping negative samples to positive occurs at 0.01 times this rate. Samples not assigned to specific annotators are marked with -1 in the answer matrix ($\mathbf{A}$). The exact parameters used for simulating annotations in each experiment are summarized in the GitHub repository.

3.3 Datasets

Synthetic Datasets: To test the performance of our framework on a non-specific dataset for which the ground truth is known, we generated synthetic data to mimic real-world features and a range of annotator reliabilities.

Statistical Distribution Families: Families of continuous and discrete distributions were used to generate the synthetic data. In particular, we used Normal, Beta, Wald, Laplace, Binomial, Multinomial, Geometric and Poisson distributions. The corresponding distribution parameters for a feature within each family

---

[1] https://github.com/manisci/CrowdTeacher.

are randomly chosen from a specified range. 5 features were chosen from each family for a total of 40 features.

Output: The ground truth labels are determined based on a polynomial combination of feature values. Each feature's coefficient value is chosen randomly. To assign labels and model class balance (% of positive samples), outputs falling in percentiles below the level of balancedness are assigned to the positive class.

Noise Level: Two versions of labels are generated. Labels for a specified percentage of samples are flipped to obtain the noisy truth used for annotation generation. However the true labels before flipping are used for evaluation purposes. This resembles the availability of noisy labels in practice.

PUI Dataset: Determining whether a patient has developed a pressure ulcer injury (bedsore) is a complex clinical decision that requires considerable nursing expertise. Early detection of PUI is extremely useful since it is preventable with proper care. However, even highly trained nurses do not agree on the existence or severity of PUI cases. Training a classifier that utilizes a limited set of annotated health records from multiple nurses can revolutionize nursing care through use in similar clinical settings. We use the MIMIC-III dataset [7], a publicly available dataset which holds information of patients admitted to intensive care units (ICU) of a populated tertiary care hospital from 2001 to 2012. We identified hospital stays of individuals over 20 years old with length of stays between 2 d and 120 d. A hospital stay was considered positive if there was a presence of the ICD-9 diagnosis code associated with pressure ulcer and there was a mention of PUI in the notes. A hospital stay was negative if there was no indication of PUI in both the ICD-9 codes or the notes. A total of 10518 samples were identified, 31% of which are positive.

4   Results

Since the datasets are imbalanced, we evaluate all the models based on the area under the precision recall curve (AUPRC). AUPRC offers a holistic picture of CrowdTeacher's predictive performance, independent of the classification threshold choice. We split each dataset into 80% training & 20% test. The AUPRCs in plots are averaged across multiple seeds. We also confirmed CrowdTeacher performance on AUROC metric, but omit the results due to limited space.

4.1   Synthetic Dataset

Sensitivity to Choice of Synthesizer: To analyze the effect of using different synthesizers on CrowdTeacher performance, we compared the average gain obtained by using CrowdTeacher with CTGAN, TVAE, and Gaussian copula synthesizers compared to using the next two top-performing baseline methods of P_Coteach and V_Coteach, respectively shown by circle and cross markers in Fig. 1b. Firstly, we can see that Gaussian copula has the greatest gain among the three synthesizers. However, employing the two other synthesizers for CrowdTeacher would still be beneficial in terms of predictive performance in many of the sparsity settings. Given the promising performance of Gaussian copula synthesizer, we use Gaussian copula for all the remaining experiments.

Sensitivity to Perturbation Fraction (α): To understand the impact of the perturbation fraction, α, we varied it between [0.01, 0.2] and evaluated the performance of CrowdTeacher and P_Coteach (the two perturbation-based methods). Figure 1a shows the average AUPRC of P_Coteach and CrowdTeacher as α increases with the average number of labels set to 2.34. It is observed that CrowdTeacher constantly outperforms P_Coteach regardless of the chosen perturbation fraction indicating its robustness. From the results, there is an optimal range of α to achieve the greatest benefit from CrowdTeacher and that either a very low ($\alpha \leq 0.05$) or very high ($\alpha \geq 0.2$) perturbation fraction decreases the usefulness of CrowdTeacher but does not diminish it. Given these results, the remainder of our experiments uses $\alpha = 0.11$.

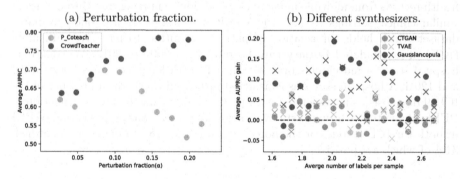

Fig. 1. CrowdTeacher Sensitivity to perturbation fraction and synthesizer choice (in Fig. 1b circles/crosses show gain w.r.t. P_Coteach/V_Coteach accordingly)

Predictive Performance: Figure 2a shows the performance of baseline crowdsourcing and Co-teaching variants against CrowdTeacher across various sparsity settings on the synthetic dataset. Confirming intuition, all methods experience an increase in AUPRC since the average number of labels per sample increases, which exposes methods to less noisy annotation. All Co-teaching based methods (CrowdTeacher, V_Coteach, and P_Coteach) constantly outperform both crowdlayer variants and also Dr.Net and S-EM. The last two always performed the worst and therefore were excluded from these plots. Even though the base classifier performance improves with more labels, its performance gap with Co-teaching based methods remains large in all sparsity settings. Across a wide range of label sparsities, using CrowdTeacher results in a significant boost in

AUPRC, compared to the other two Co-teaching based methods, even with as low as only 1.68 labels per sample. Also, we can observe that V_Coteach performs worse than P_Coteach in very sparse settings (average number of labels < 2.1), but as the number of labels increases it catches up with P_Coteach and even surpasses it at higher densities. Another interesting observation is that beyond an average of 2 labels per sample, all three methods reach a plateau and only improve negligibly in response to an increased number of labels.

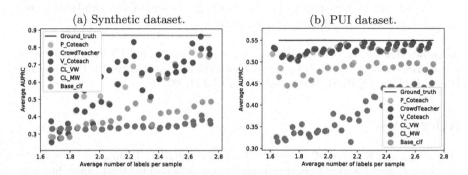

Fig. 2. CrowdTeacher Performance on Synthetic and PUI data as average number of labels per sample increases, averaged on 10 and 4 initializations respectively.

4.2   PUI Dataset

To challenge CrowdTeacher's performance under more chaotic distributions of real data, we tested it on the bedsore detection task with 10k samples. Figure 2b shows how the performance of the chosen methods changes as the average number of labels per sample goes up. We observed similar patterns to synthetic dataset here too in terms of Co-teaching variants' overall predictive advantage over other methods, however, the gap between Co-teaching variants and other methods is less substantial. The range of AUPRC of all models on this dataset proves that this is a much harder learning problem, yet CrowdTeacher is able to beat P_Coteach and V_Coteach at multiple points, especially at lower sparsities, which are actually more practical for obtaining labels for hospital-acquired bedsores, while at other sparsity points it has comparable performance to these methods.

5   Conclusion

We proposed CrowdTeacher, a novel Co-teaching based approach that leverages certainty of samples from truth inference algorithms to apply sample-specific perturbations on training points, and combines it with Co-teaching algorithm to further rectify noisy annotations and incorporate that knowledge in the training process. Our proposed approach bridges overarching themes and ideas from data augmentation, crowdsourcing, and learning with noisy labels and is agnostic to the truth inference method and the synthesizer used. To illustrate the predictive benefits of CrowdTeacher over similar methods, we conducted experiments on both synthetic and real dataset of different scales, and our results for both tasks (including a real-world medical classification task) confirmed CrowdTeacher's performance edge for learning with crowdsourced labels. We also successfully employed Co-teaching mechanism primarily tested on images, for tabular data. For our future work, we plan to propose new perturbation schemes to introduce more variety for perturbations of a given sample during training, and extend our current framework to semi-supervised learning.

Acknowledgements. This work was supported by the National Science Foundation, awards IIS-#1838200 and CNS-1952192, National Institutes of Health (NIH) awards 1R01LM013323, 5K01LM012924, and CTSA UL1TR002378.

References

1. Albarqouni, S., Baur, C., Achilles, F., Belagiannis, V., Demirci, S., Navab, N.: Aggnet: deep learning from crowds for mitosis detection in breast cancer histology images. IEEE Trans. Med. Imaging **35**(5), 1313–1321 (2016)
2. Berthelot, D., Carlini, N., Goodfellow, I., Papernot, N., Oliver, A., Raffel, C.A.: Mixmatch: a holistic approach to semi-supervised learning. In: Advances in Neural Information Processing Systems, pp. 5049–5059 (2019)
3. Dawid, A.P., Skene, A.M.: Maximum likelihood estimation of observer error-rates using the EM algorithm. Appl. Stat. **28**, 20–28 (1979)
4. Guan, M.Y., Gulshan, V., Dai, A.M., Hinton, G.E.: Who said what: modeling individual labelers improves classification. arXiv preprint arXiv:1703.08774 (2017)
5. Han, B., et al.: Co-teaching: robust training of deep neural networks with extremely noisy labels. In: Advances in Neural Information Processing Systems, pp. 8527–8537 (2018)
6. Hinton, G., Vinyals, O., Dean, J.: Distilling the knowledge in a neural network. arXiv preprint arXiv:1503.02531 (2015)
7. Johnson, A.E., et al.: Mimic-iii, a freely accessible critical care database. Sci. Data **3**, 1–9 (2016)
8. Mobadersany, P., et al.: Predicting cancer outcomes from histology and genomics using convolutional networks. Proc. Natl. Acad. Sci. **115**(13), E2970–E2979 (2018)
9. Nguyen, V.A., et al.: CLARA: confidence of labels and raters, pp. 2542–2552. Association for Computing Machinery, New York (2020). https://doi.org/10.1145/3394486.3403304
10. Patki, N., Wedge, R., Veeramachaneni, K.: The synthetic data vault. In: 2016 IEEE International Conference on Data Science and Advanced Analytics (DSAA), pp. 399–410 (2016). https://doi.org/10.1109/DSAA.2016.49
11. Rodrigues, F., Pereira, F.: Deep learning from crowds. In: Proceedings of the AAAI Conference on Artificial Intelligence, vol. 32, no. 1 (2018)
12. Soans, N., Asali, E., Hong, Y., Doshi, P.: Sa-net: robust state-action recognition for learning from observations. In: 2020 IEEE International Conference on Robotics and Automation (ICRA), pp. 2153–2159. IEEE (2020)

13. Tahmasebian, F., Xiong, L., Sotoodeh, M., Sunderam, V.: Edgeinfer: robust truth inference under data poisoning attack. In: 2020 IEEE International Conference on Smart Data Services (SMDS), pp. 45–52 (2020). https://doi.org/10.1109/SMDS49396.2020.00013

14. Tahmasebian, F., Xiong, L., Sotoodeh, M., Sunderam, V.: Crowdsourcing under data poisoning attacks: a comparative study. In: Singhal, A., Vaidya, J. (eds.) DBSec 2020. LNCS, vol. 12122, pp. 310–332. Springer, Cham (2020). https://doi.org/10.1007/978-3-030-49669-2_18

15. Waugh, S.M., Bergquist-Beringer, S.: Inter-rater agreement of pressure ulcer risk and prevention measures in the national database of nursing quality indicators (ndnqi). Res. Nurs. Health **39**(3), 164–174 (2016)

16. Xu, L., Skoularidou, M., Cuesta-Infante, A., Veeramachaneni, K.: Modeling tabular data using conditional GAN. In: Advances in Neural Information Processing Systems, pp. 7335–7345 (2019)

17. Zhang, Z., Zhang, H., Arik, S.O., Lee, H., Pfister, T.: Distilling effective supervision from severe label noise. In: Proceedings of the IEEE/CVF Conference on Computer Vision and Pattern Recognition, pp. 9294–9303 (2020)

Effective and Adaptive Refined Multi-metric Similarity Graph Fusion for Multi-view Clustering

Wentao Rong, Enhong Zhuo, Guihua Tao, and Hongmin Cai[✉]

School of Computer Science and Engineering, South China University of Technology,
Guangzhou 510006, China
hmcai@scut.edu.cn

Abstract. Multi-view graph-based clustering aims to partition samples via fusing similarity graphs from different views into a unified graph. The clustering performance relies on the accuracy of similarity measurement. However, most existing methods utilize a single metric whose similarity measurement can be easily corrupted by noises thus lacking high accuracy and generalization capability. We propose an effective multi-metric similarity graph refinement and fusion method for multi-view clustering. We construct multiple similarity graphs for each view by different metric, exploit a novel refined similarity through symmetric conditional probability to preserve the important similarity information and finally adaptively fuse multiple refined similarity graphs to an informative unified one. Extensive experiments on eight benchmark datasets have validated the effectiveness and superiority of our proposed method comparing to thirteen state-of-the-art methods.

Keywords: Multi-metric · Similarity graph fusion · Symmetric conditional probability · Multi-view clustering

1 Introduction

Clustering aims to partition objects into different groups such that objects in the same groups are similar. Many graph-based clustering methods partition the data based on the similarity matrix. The similarity matrix, similarity measurement among samples, plays a crucial role in affecting the clustering performance. Similarity can be constructed by various metrics. The kernel is one of the popular similarity measurements, which is wildly used in spectral clustering. However, the performance of spectral clustering highly dependent on the choice and parameter of the kernel matrix. For instance, how to select a proper standard deviation parameter for the Gaussian kernel is an open problem [21]. Then,

Electronic supplementary material The online version of this chapter (https://doi.org/10.1007/978-3-030-75765-6_16) contains supplementary material, which is available to authorized users.

© Springer Nature Switzerland AG 2021
K. Karlapalem et al. (Eds.): PAKDD 2021, LNAI 12713, pp. 194–206, 2021.
https://doi.org/10.1007/978-3-030-75765-6_16

multiple kernel learning (MKL) is developed to pick or combine the candidate kernels. In addition to the kernel matrix, the similarity can be constructed by subspace clustering based on self-representation.

Although these approaches are effective, the information provided by single-source data is limited or insufficient. In real-world applications, each object has a variety of relationship graphs as each object can be sampled in different views and the sampled data of each view can form a graph. Multi-view graph-based clustering [9,11,13,15,22] aim to partition data into different groups by making use of complementary information from multiple similarity graphs. They fuse multiple similarity graphs from all view into a unified similarity graph. The weights of these similarity graphs can be automatically learned, manually set, or without consideration. Some of these methods [4,15] perform similarity fusion and clustering simultaneously.

These methods have made significant progress in multi-view clustering. However, for most of them, the clustering performance is affected by similarity measurement which is easily corrupted by noises. Similarity refinement is in demand to attain accurate similarity. Besides, most of them tend to utilize a single metric to attain similarity matrix for each view. A single metric does not fit various feature type well and lacks generalization capability. To overcome these limitation, we propose an effective and adaptive multi-metric refined similarity fusion method. Firstly, we generate multiple similarity graphs with multiple metrics and exploit a novel symmetric conditional probability to attain refined similarity. Then, we fuse refined similarity graphs of all views under different metric into an informative unified similarity graph. Meanwhile, we directly learn the clustering membership. Our main contributions are as follows:

1 We exploit a novel similarity refinement and multiple metrics to improve the accuracy and generalization of measuring similarity.
2 We propose an effective and adaptive multi-metric similarity fusion method where graph fusion and clustering promote mutually.
3 Extensive experimental results demonstrate that our method outperforms several state-of-the-art multi-view clustering methods.

The remainder of the paper is organized as follows. Section 2 briefly reviews related works for multi-view clustering. Section 3 introduces the proposed model. Section 4 demonstrates the extensive experimental results. Section 5 presents the conclusion of this paper.

2   Related Work

Our method falls into multi-view graph-based clustering. The multi-view graph-based clustering method fuses multiple graphs constructed for each view into a unified graph. For example, similarity network fusion (SNF) [13] fuses the similarity networks, obtained from each of their respective data types, by propagating similarity through the common neighborhood. Neighborhood-based multi-omics clustering (NEMO) [11] fuses multiple graphs to a unified graph by average strategy, where relative similarity is defined based on the neighborhood. Multiview consensus graph clustering (MCGC) [22] learns a consensus graph by minimizing disagreement between different views and constraining the rank of the Laplacian matrix. Auto-weighted multiple graph learning (AMGL) [7] and graph-based system for multi-view clustering (GBS) [16] firstly learn the similarity matrix of each view from data and then performs graph fusion and data clustering. These methods divide the construction of graph and graph fusion into two independent processes without adaptive interaction. In contrast, graph-based multi-view clustering (GMC) [15] weights each view automatically, learns the graph of each view and the fusion graph jointly, and produces the final clusters directly after fusion.

In addition to multi-view graph-based clustering, there are three categories of multi-view clustering methods: 1) Co-training style clustering; 2) multi-kernel clustering; 3) and multi-view subspace clustering.

Co-training style clustering applies a co-training strategy to multi-view data. Co-regularized multiview spectral clustering [3] (Co-reg) utilizes the eigenvectors from one view to guide the graph constructions in the other views. Consequently, the clusterings of multiple views tend towards consensus. Co-training for multi-view spectral clustering [2] (Co-training) co-regularizes the clustering hypotheses to make the clusterings in different views agree with each other. The multi-kernel clustering method predefines a group of candidate kernels and then combines or picks these kernels. For example, cancer integration via multi-kernel learning (CIMLR) [10] learns a similarity matrix with block structure by combining multiple Gaussian kernels of each view, corresponding to the different and complementary representations of the data. The multi-view subspace clustering is based on self-representation where each data point can be expressed by a linear combination of the data points themselves [19]. The self-representation matrix with different regularizations is constructed from samples and then used to construct the similarity matrix. For example, Low-rank representation (LRR) [5] subspace clustering and sparse subspace clustering (SSC) [1] pursue a sparse and low rank representation, respectively. Low-rank and sparse subspace clustering (LRSSC) [17] takes the advantages of LRR and SSC in preserving the self-expressiveness property and graph connectivity at the same time.

3   Methodology

3.1   Construction of Multiple Similarity Graphs via Different Metric

Given a multi-view dataset $X = \{X^{(1)}, X^{(2)}, ..., X^{(n_v)}\}$ of n_v views, $X^{(i)} = \{X_j^{(i)\mathsf{T}} \in \mathbb{R}^{p^{(i)}}\}_{j=1}^N$ consists N samples with $p^{(i)}$ features in the i-th view. For each view, we use different metrics to measure the sample similarity, yielding multiple similarity graphs. Let $W^{(v)(q)}$ denote the similarity matrix in the v-th view measured by q-th metric, with each entry defined by

$$W^{(v)(q)}(i,j) = d(X_i^{(v)}, X_j^{(v)}) \tag{1}$$

3.2 Measurement of Sample Similarity via Symmetric Conditional Probability

Based on original similarity $\boldsymbol{W}^{(v)(q)}$, we propose a novel similarity refinement to retain only the highly proximal samples while filtering out the weak ones. Such operation is valuable to elucidate the sample-wised similarity by diminishing the distance deterioration caused by noises or outliers [8,13]. The similarity between the sample x_j and sample x_i is the conditional probability $\boldsymbol{P}(j|i)$ that x_i would pick x_j as its top $k\%$ neighbor if neighbors are picked in proportion to their probability density under a Gaussian distribution centered at x_i. Conversely, one can also compute the similarity between x_i and x_j via its conditional probability $\boldsymbol{P}(i|j)$. Then the overall refined similarity between x_i and x_j is calculated by their mean conditional probabilities

$$\boldsymbol{M}(i,j) = \frac{\boldsymbol{P}(i|j) + \boldsymbol{P}(j|i)}{2}, \tag{2}$$

where

$$\boldsymbol{P}(j|i) = \frac{\boldsymbol{W}(i,j)}{\sum_{Topk\%} \boldsymbol{W}(i,k)} \cdot \mathbb{1}(j \text{ rank to top k\%})$$

and

$$\boldsymbol{P}(i|j) = \frac{\boldsymbol{W}(j,i)}{\sum_{Topk\%} \boldsymbol{W}(j,k)} \cdot \mathbb{1}(i \text{ rank to top k\%}).$$

Here, $\mathbb{1}$ is the indicator function.

3.3 Fusion of Multiple Similarity Graphs Through Directly Learning Cluster Membership

We propose a multi-metric similarity graph fusion theme as follow:

$$\min_{S,H,w} \|S - \sum_{v=1}^{n_v} \sum_{q=1}^{n_q} w^{(v)(q)} M^{(v)(q)}\|_F^2 + \lambda\|S - HH^\top\|_F^2 \tag{3}$$

$$s.t. \ H \in \{0,1\}, H1 = 1, w^\top 1 = 1, w \geq 0,$$

where $\boldsymbol{w}^{(v)(q)}$ and $\boldsymbol{M}^{(v)(q)}$ are the weight and refined similarity matrix of the v-th view data under the q-th metric, respectively. $\boldsymbol{H} \in \mathbb{R}^{N \times C}$ is the cluster assignment matrix, where C is the number of clusters. λ is the tuning parameter. The first term is used to adaptively fuse multiple refined similarity matrices from different metric and view to a unified one $\boldsymbol{S}$. Our method can pick up or integrate different metrics and consider the differences of view through automatically learned weights. The second term is used to directly learn the clustering membership by minimizing the difference between the fused similarity matrix $\boldsymbol{S}$ and the pairwise similarity matrix of clustering result $\boldsymbol{H}$. Furthermore, $\boldsymbol{S}$ will be constrained as a low-rank block diagonal matrix because, in an ideal case, $\boldsymbol{H}\boldsymbol{H}^\top$ is strictly block diagonal matrix.

The first constraint in problem (3) can be relaxed from binary values to real values with $U = \frac{H}{\|H\|_2}$ and the second constraint is relaxed to $U^\mathsf{T}U = I_c$. Therefore, the problem (3) is relaxed to the following optimization problem:

$$\min_{S,U,w} \|S - \sum_{v=1}^{n_v}\sum_{q=1}^{n_q} w^{(v)(q)} M^{(v)(q)}\|_F^2 + \lambda\|S - UU^\mathsf{T}\|_F^2 \tag{4}$$

$$s.t.\ U^\mathsf{T}U = I_c, w^\mathsf{T}1 = 1, w \geq 0.$$

Once we have the clustering assignment matrix U, we apply k-means to cluster the samples into different groups. Since k-means is sensitive to the initialization, a discretization method [12] has been used to remedy this drawback.

3.4 Optimization Algorithm

We optimize three variables in Eq. (4) by alternating optimization strategy.

In the **first step**, by fixing both S and w, (4) is reduced to

$$\min_U \lambda\|S - UU^\mathsf{T}\|_F^2 \quad s.t.\ U^\mathsf{T}U = I_c. \tag{5}$$

The problem (5) is minimized when U is an orthogonal basis of the eigenspace associated with the C largest eigenvalues of S.

In the **second step**, by fixing both U and w, (4) is reduced to

$$\min_S \|S - \sum_{v=1}^{n_v}\sum_{q=1}^{n_q} w^{(v)(q)} M^{(v)(q)}\|_F^2 + \lambda\|S - UU^\mathsf{T}\|_F^2. \tag{6}$$

Setting the partial derivative of Eq. (6) with respect to S to zero. S is updated as follows:

$$S = \frac{\sum_{v=1}^{n_v}\sum_{q=1}^{n_q} w^{(v)(q)} M^{(v)(q)} + \lambda UU^\mathsf{T}}{1 + \lambda}. \tag{7}$$

In the **third step**, by fixing both U and S, (4) is reduced to

$$\min_w \|S - \sum_{v=1}^{n_v}\sum_{q=1}^{n_q} w^{(v)(q)} M^{(v)(q)}\|_F^2 \quad s.t.\ w^\mathsf{T}1 = 1, w \geq 0. \tag{8}$$

We vectorize each matrix $M^{(v)(q)}$ into $\hat{m}^{(v)(q)}$, i.e.,

$$\hat{m}^{(v)(q)} = [m_1^{(v)(q)}; m_2^{(v)(q)}; ...m_n^{(v)(q)}] \in \mathbb{R}^{NN \times 1}, \tag{9}$$

where $m_i^{(v)(q)}$ denotes the i-th column of $M^{(v)(q)}$. Therefore, the similarities of from all views and measure functions can be gathered into matrix $\hat{M} = [\hat{m}^{(1)(1)}; \hat{m}^{(1)(2)}; ...\hat{m}^{(v)(q)}] \in \mathbb{R}^{NN \times n_v n_q}$ and $\hat{s}$ denotes the vector of S. The problem (8) becomes:

$$\min_w \|\hat{s} - \hat{M}w\|_F^2 \quad s.t.\ w^\mathsf{T}1 = 1, w \geq 0, \tag{10}$$

and then transformed into:

$$\min_{w} w^{\mathsf{T}} A w - w^{\mathsf{T}} f \quad s.t. \ w^{\mathsf{T}} \mathbf{1} = 1, w \geq 0, \tag{11}$$

where $A = \hat{M}^{\mathsf{T}} \hat{M}$ and $f = 2\hat{M}^{\mathsf{T}} \hat{s}$. It is a constrained least square problem and can be efficiently solved by standard quadratic programming methods.

Algorithm 1. The algorithm for solving the proposed method

Require: $X = \{X^{(v)}\}_{v=1}^{n_v}$, $\{\{M^{(v)(q)}\}_{v=1}^{n_v}\}_{q=1}^{n_q}$, λ, the number of clusters C
1: Initialize: $w = \frac{1}{n_v n_q}$, $S = \sum_{v=1}^{n_v} \sum_{q=1}^{n_q} w^{(v)(q)} M^{(v)(q)}$, $U = 0$
2: **while** not converge **do**
3:     Fix S, w, and update U by solving (5)
4:     Fix U, w, and update S by solving (7)
5:     Fix U, S, and update w by solving (11)
6: **end while**
7: Apply k-means clustering to U
Ensure: The clustering result

The above three steps are iteratively solved and updated until convergence. The convergence condition is that relative change in consecutive rounds is lower than a threshold $(\frac{\|S_{t+1}-S_t\|}{\|S_t\|} + \frac{\|U_{t+1}-U_t\|}{\|U_t\|}) < 10^{-2}$. The complete algorithm is summarized in Algorithm 1. Given N is the number of samples, P is the total number of the feature of all views and n_q is the number of metric functions. Initializing all similarity matrices $M^{(v)(q)}$ requires $\mathcal{O}(N^2 \cdot P \cdot n_q)$. Updating U needs to calculate the eigenvectors of S. It takes $\mathcal{O}(C \cdot N^2)$. Updating S takes $\mathcal{O}(N^2)$. The update of weights w takes $\mathcal{O}((n_q \cdot n_v)^2)$. K-means clustering takes $\mathcal{O}(t \cdot C^2 \cdot N)$, where t is the number of iterations in k-means. The total computational complexity of our method is $\mathcal{O}(N^2 \cdot P \cdot n_q + T \cdot (C \cdot N^2 + N^2 + (n_q \cdot n_v)^2) + t \cdot C^2 \cdot N)$, where T is number of iterations.

4 Experiments

4.1 Experiment Setting

We use eight benchmark datasets to evaluate the performance of our method. These datasets are as follows: Hdigit[1], 100leaves[2], Caltech 101[3], Pascals [18], NGs[4], BBCSport[5], MSRCV1 [20] and 3-sources[6]. The statistics of these data sets are summarized in Table 1.

---

[1] https://cs.nyu.edu/roweis/data.html.
[2] https://archive.ics.uci.edu/ml/datasets/One-hundred+plant+species+leaves+data+set.
[3] http://www.vision.caltech.edu/archive.html.
[4] http://lig-membres.imag.fr/grimal/data.html.
[5] http://mlg.ucd.ie/datasets/bbc.html.
[6] http://mlg.ucd.ie/datasets/3sources.html.

To evaluate the performance of the proposed method, we compare it with thirteen state-of-the-art methods, including five single-view clustering methods and eight multi-view clustering methods. SP [6], SSC [1], LRR [5], LRSSC [17] and SIMLR [14] are the single view methods. These method are performed with the best single view. Also, we compare our method with eight state-of-the-art multi-view clustering methods that have been mentioned at the related works of Sect. 2: Co-reg [3], Co-training [2], AMGL [7], NEMO [11], GMC [15], MCGC [22], SNF [13] and CIMLR [10]. The comparative methods are searched gridwise to achieve the best performances. For our method, we use four different metrics, including Gaussian similarity, Pearson correlation, Spearman correlation and Cosine similarity. Parameters k and λ are tuned from the set $\{1, 3, 5, 7, 9\}$ and $\{1, 5, 10\}$, respectively. For evaluation metrics, we utilize the normalized mutual information (NMI), accuracy (ACC), and adjusted rand index (ARI) to comprehensively evaluate the clustering performance. For all of them, a higher value indicates better clustering performance. Throughout the experiments, we perform ten times for all methods. The means and standard deviations are computed and recorded for performance comparison. The Gaussian kernel is used to compute the sample similarity when needed. The standard deviation of the Gaussian kernel is set to be equal to the median of the pair-wise Euclidean distances between the samples.

4.2   Experiment Results

We report the performances of all methods on eight benchmark datasets in Tables 2 and 3. The best result is in bold to highlight. Overall, our method is superior to the state-of-art multi-view methods in most of datasets. Although our method presents a similar performance as GMC or CIMLR in Hdigit and 100leaves datasets, our method achieves the best performance in another six datasets. Especially, our method achieves significant improvements of approximately 5%, 9%, and 13% over the most competitive method GMC in Caltech 101, Pascals, and 3-sources, in terms of NMI, respectively. NEMO is similar to

Table 1. Statistical information on the datasets

Dataset	# of instances	# of views	# of classes	Feature type
Hdigit	2000	2	10	Continuous, sparse
100leaves	1600	3	100	Continuous, dense
Caltech 101	1474	6	7	Continuous, dense
Pascals	1000	2	20	Continuous, sparse
NGs	500	3	5	Continuous, sparse
BBCSport	282	3	5	Discrete, sparse
MSRCV1	210	3	7	Continuous, dense
3-sources	169	3	6	Continuous, sparse

Table 2. Clustering performances on benchmark datasets

Dataset	View	Method	NMI	ACC	ARI
Hdigit	Single	SP	0.480 (0.006)	0.555(0.007)	0.360 (0.008)
		SSC	0.481 (0.000)	0.444 (0.000)	0.300 (0.000)
		LRR	0.037 (0.003)	0.104 (0.001)	0.000 (0.000)
		LRSSC	0.376 (0.001)	0.444 (0.004)	0.251 (0.002)
		SIMLR	0.740 (0.017)	0.727 (0.025)	0.636 (0.026)
	Multiple	Co-reg	0.844 (0.001)	0.844 (0.001)	0.692(0.002)
		Co-training	0.820 (0.006)	0.899 (0.011)	0.806 (0.010)
		NEMO	0.655 (0.000)	0.561 (0.000)	0.477 (0.000)
		GMC	**0.985(0.000)**	**0.994(0.000)**	**0.987 (0.000)**
		MCGC	0.619 (0.000)	0.569 (0.000)	0.396 (0.000)
		SNF	0.979 (0.000)	0.992 (0.000)	0.981 (0.000)
		CIMLR	0.816 (0.009)	0.693 (0.020)	0.655 (0.027)
		AMGL	0.950 (0.042)	0.945 (0.093)	0.925 (0.106)
		Ours	0.982 (0.000)	0.993 (0.000)	0.984 (0.000)
100leaves	Single	SP	0.775 (0.004)	0.561 (0.013)	0.441 (0.009)
		SSC	0.742 (0.000)	0.509 (0.000)	0.374 (0.000)
		LRR	0.668 (0.003)	0.405 (0.011)	0.263 (0.007)
		LRSSC	0.515 (0.003)	0.213 (0.003)	0.077 (0.004)
		SIMLR	0.779 (0.018)	0.541 (0.036)	0.212 (0.057)
	Multiple	Co-reg	0.913(0.004)	0.783(0.016)	0.724(0.015)
		Co-training	0.920 (0.003)	0.786 (0.007)	0.741 (0.008)
		NEMO	0.748 (0.001)	0.471 (0.001)	0.348 (0.002)
		GMC	0.930 (0.000)	0.824 (0.000)	0.497 (0.000)
		MCGC	0.526 (0.013)	0.262 (0.012)	0.015 (0.002)
		SNF	0.969 (0.002)	0.935 (0.003)	0.909 (0.004)
		CIMLR	**0.993(0.002)**	**0.977(0.009)**	**0.968 (0.014)**
		AMGL	0.901 (0.019)	0.749 (0.046)	0.446 (0.131)
		Ours	0.972 (0.000)	0.913 (0.000)	0.894 (0.000)
Caltech 101	Single	SP	0.505 (0.001)	0.402 (0.001)	0.300 (0.000)
		SSC	0.428 (0.000)	0.560 (0.000)	0.258 (0.000)
		LRR	0.100 (0.003)	0.339 (0.0143)	0.083 (0.010)
		LRSSC	0.541 (0.001)	0.595 (0.0040)	0.401 (0.004)
		SIMLR	0.631 (0.000)	0.417 (0.000)	0.365 (0.000)
	Multiple	Co-reg	0.487(0.003)	0.394(0.002)	0.281(0.002)
		Co-training	0.512 (0.007)	0.422 (0.010)	0.322 (0.010)
		NEMO	0.509 (0.000)	0.523 (0.000)	0.342 (0.000)
		GMC	0.662 (0.000)	0.692 (0.000)	0.594 (0.000)
		MCGC	0.509 (0.000)	0.571 (0.000)	0.399 (0.000)
		SNF	0.637 (0.000)	0.647 (0.000)	0.504 (0.000)
		CIMLR	0.613 (0.000)	0.495 (0.000)	0.405 (0.000)
		AMGL	0.557 (0.033)	0.637 (0.047)	0.414 (0.038)
		Ours	**0.712(0.000)**	**0.701(0.000)**	**0.609 (0.000)**
Pascals	Single	SP	0.627(0.007)	0.598(0.014)	0.444(0.011)
		SSC	0.512 (0.000)	0.462 (0.000)	0.298 (0.000)
		LRR	0.470 (0.010)	0.409 (0.016)	0.264 (0.012)
		LRSSC	0.474 (0.006)	0.397 (0.011)	0.219 (0.012)
		SIMLR	0.557 (0.013)	0.522 (0.026)	0.331 (0.027)
	Multiple	Co-reg	0.650 (0.006)	0.620 (0.014)	0.475(0.007)
		Co-training	0.641 (0.002)	0.609 (0.007)	0.463 (0.004)
		NEMO	0.609 (0.000)	0.511 (0.000)	0.344 (0.000)
		GMC	0.578 (0.000)	0.464 (0.000)	0.204 (0.000)
		MCGC	0.500 (0.000)	0.398 (0.000)	0.177 (0.000)
		SNF	0.635 (0.002)	0.591 (0.007)	0.441 (0.006)
		CIMLR	0.571 (0.010)	0.516 (0.030)	0.366 (0.023)
		AMGL	0.565 (0.011)	0.467 (0.019)	0.258 (0.030)
		Ours	**0.669(0.000)**	**0.638(0.000)**	**0.495 (0.000)**

Table 3. Clustering performances on benchmark datasets

Dataset	View	Method	NMI	ACC	ARI
NGs	Single	SP	0.048 (0.010)	0.230 (0.034)	0.007 (0.009)
		SSC	0.130 (0.000)	0.350 (0.000)	0.056 (0.000)
		LRR	0.049 (0.011)	0.220 (0.016)	0.001 (0.003)
		LRSSC	0.704 (0.000)	0.880 (0.000)	0.728 (0.000)
		SIMLR	0.477 (0.000)	0.622 (0.000)	0.427 (0.000)
	Multiple	Co-reg	0.091 (0.01)	0.252 (0.009)	0.008 (0.003)
		Co-training	0.442 (0.014)	0.514 (0.025)	0.237 (0.012)
		NEMO	0.131 (0.000)	0.358 (0.000)	0.095 (0.000)
		GMC	0.939 (0.000)	0.982 (0.000)	0.955 (0.000)
		MCGC	0.064 (0.000)	0.220 (0.000)	0.001 (0.000)
		SNF	0.563 (0.000)	0.506 (0.000)	0.296 (0.000)
		CIMLR	0.119 (0.000)	0.354 (0.000)	0.076 (0.000)
		AMGL	0.417 (0.017)	0.526 (0.037)	0.251 (0.015)
		Ours	**0.960(0.000)**	**0.988(0.000)**	**0.970 (0.000)**
BBCSport	Single	SP	0.237(0.006)	0.451(0.016)	0.141(0.010)
		SSC	0.150 (0.000)	0.376 (0.000)	0.054 (0.000)
		LRR	0.048 (0.004)	0.351 (0.002)	0.009 (0.006)
		LRSSC	0.409 (0.002)	0.621 (0.000)	0.353 (0.001)
		SIMLR	0.588 (0.000)	0.794 (0.000)	0.629 (0.000)
	Multiple	Co-reg	0.288 (0.012)	0.520 (0.017)	0.216 (0.024)
		Co-training	0.424 (0.012)	0.577 (0.016)	0.336 (0.014)
		NEMO	0.060 (0.000)	0.408 (0.000)	0.039 (0.000)
		GMC	0.801 (0.000)	0.886 (0.000)	0.790 (0.000)
		MCGC	0.093 (0.000)	0.316 (0.000)	−0.018 (0.000)
		SNF	0.157 (0.000)	0.390 (0.000)	0.018 (0.000)
		CIMLR	0.448 (0.000)	0.716 (0.000)	0.499 (0.000)
		AMGL	0.133 (0.037)	0.376 (0.025)	0.020 (0.012)
		Ours	**0.812(0.000)**	**0.887(0.000)**	**0.826 (0.000)**
MSRCV1	Single	SP	0.544 (0.015)	0.700 (0.015)	0.460 (0.021)
		SSC	0.580 (0.000)	0.695 (0.000)	0.495 (0.000)
		LRR	0.506 (0.015)	0.569 (0.011)	0.403 (0.012)
		LRSSC	0.599 (0.010)	0.719 (0.007)	0.521 (0.012)
		SIMLR	0.703 (0.021)	0.794 (0.044)	0.614 (0.028)
	Multiple	Co-reg	0.722 (0.010)	**0.837(0.007)**	0.661(0.013)
		Co-training	0.681 (0.007)	0.764 (0.008)	0.606 (0.008)
		NEMO	0.632 (0.000)	0.676 (0.000)	0.520 (0.000)
		GMC	0.771 (0.000)	0.748 (0.000)	0.640 (0.000)
		MCGC	0.634 (0.002)	0.668 (0.002)	0.446 (0.004)
		SNF	0.718 (0.000)	0.757 (0.000)	0.629 (0.000)
		CIMLR	0.733 (0.010)	0.706 (0.018)	0.580 (0.006)
		AMGL	0.674 (0.038)	0.684 (0.088)	0.512(0.092)
		Ours	**0.793(0.000)**	0.819 (0.000)	**0.716(0.000)**
3-sources	Single	SP	0.473(0.036)	0.496(0.015)	0.240 (0.036)
		SSC	0.174 (0.000)	0.408 (0.000)	0.097 (0.000)
		LRR	0.124 (0.006)	0.381 (0.003)	0.038 (0.005)
		LRSSC	0.482 (0.015)	0.608 (0.021)	0.399 (0.017)
		SIMLR	0.462 (0.030)	0.466 (0.011)	0.298 (0.025)
	Multiple	Co-reg	0.528 (0.014)	0.556 (0.021)	0.315 (0.009)
		Co-training	0.569 (0.009)	0.576 (0.014)	0.388 (0.018)
		NEMO	0.210 (0.000)	0.325 (0.000)	0.054 (0.000)
		GMC	0.627 (0.000)	0.692 (0.000)	0.443 (0.000)
		MCGC	0.173 (0.000)	0.367 (0.000)	−0.012 (0.000)
		SNF	0.418 (0.000)	0.497 (0.000)	0.175 (0.000)
		CIMLR	0.468 (0.000)	0.521 (0.000)	0.284 (0.000)
		AMGL	0.121 (0.021)	0.336 (0.018)	−0.019 (0.013)
		Ours	**0.770(0.000)**	**0.793(0.000)**	**0.665 (0.000)**

our method but it only uses Gaussian kernel to constructs similarity. With the power of multiple metrics, our method performs better than NEMO with a wide margin. For example, it achieves average improvements of approximately 32%, 22%, 82%, 75%, and 56% over NEMO in Hdigit, 100leaves, NGs, BBCSport and 3-sources, respectively. The performance of our method using multiple views of features is better than that of only considering one single view of feature, indicating that it can effectively fuse useful information of multiple views to improve the clustering performance, as shown in Table 6.

The superior performances of our method lie in three aspects. Firstly, our method can automatically learn the weights of similarity graphs constructed by multiple metrics. Hence it is fit to the data of a variety of features, such as dense and sparse features. To verify the effectiveness of the multiple metrics, we compare the clustering performances between our methods using single metric and multiple metrics. Our method with single metric only uses the Gaussian similarity. As shown in Table 4, our method using multiple metrics outperforms that using a single metric. Especially, owing to complementary information provided by other metrics, our method achieves overwhelming performance in datasets with sparse features, such as BBCSport, 3-sources, and NGs. Secondly, the noise of the similarity graph, caused by weak similarities, is substantially reduced by our proposed similarity refinement through symmetric conditional probability. We compare the clustering performances between our methods with refined similarity and no-refined similarity to validate the necessity of the proposed similarity measurement, as shown in Table 5. From the results, our method achieves better clustering performance due to our proposed similarity refinement. After utilizing similarity refinement, the within-class similarity is strengthened and between-class noise is substantially reduced (see **Suppl.Table 1**, available at https://github.com/scutbioinformatic/MMRSGF). Thirdly, our method directly learns the clustering membership and enforces the final similarity matrix to be a block diagonal matrix simultaneously. It is clear that the final similarity matrix of our method reveals a clear diagonal block structure, which contributes to enhancing the clustering performance.

On all datasets, the algorithm reaches the convergence status within 5 iterations (see **Suppl.Fig. 1**). In our method, there are two free parameters, i.e., k, λ

Table 4. Clustering performances comparison between our method using single metric and multiple metrics

Dataset	Hdigit	100leaves	Caltech 101	Pascals
Single metric	0.971 (0.000)	0.961 (0.001)	0.646 (0.000)	0.637 (0.000)
Multiple metrics	**0.982(0.000)**	**0.972(0.000)**	**0.712(0.000)**	**0.669(0.001)**
Dataset	NGs	BBCSport	MSRCV1	3-sources
Single metric	0.367 (0.000)	0.484 (0.000)	0.706 (0.000)	0.403 (0.000)
Multiple metrics	**0.960(0.000)**	**0.812(0.000)**	**0.783(0.000)**	**0.770(0.000)**

Table 5. Clustering performances comparison between refined similarity and no-refined similarity of our method

Dataset	Hdigit	100leaves	Caltech 101	Pascals
No-refined similarity	0.481 (0.000)	0.940 (0.000)	0.316 (0.000)	0.575 (0.000)
Refined similarity	**0.982(0.000)**	**0.972(0.001)**	**0.712(0.000)**	**0.669(0.000)**
Dataset	NGs	BBCSport	MSRCV1	3-sources
No-refined similarity	0.891 (0.000)	0.700 (0.000)	0.486 (0.000)	0.610 (0.000)
Refined similarity	**0.960(0.000)**	**0.812(0.000)**	**0.793(0.000)**	**0.770(0.000)**

Table 6. Clustering performances comparison between our method using single view and multiple views

Dataset	Hdigit	100leaves	Caltech 101	Pascals
Single view	0.622 (0.000)	0.853 (0.000)	0.620 (0.000)	0.647 (0.000)
Multiple views	**0.982(0.000)**	**0.972(0.001)**	**0.712(0.000)**	**0.669(0.000)**
Dataset	NGs	BBCSport	MSRCV1	3-sources
Single view	0.612 (0.000)	0.640 (0.000)	0.648 (0.000)	0.715 (0.000)
Multiple views	**0.960(0.000)**	**0.812(0.000)**	**0.793(0.000)**	**0.770(0.000)**

in Eq. (3). **Suppl.Fig. 2** and **Suppl.Fig. 3** demonstrate the sensitivity of the parameters k and λ on eight datasets, respectively. Our method is robust with respect to the parameters λ and k.

5   Conclusions

We propose an effective and adaptive multi-metric refined similarity graph fusion method for multi-view clustering. Our main novelty is making use of different metric to construct similarity graphs, exploiting a novel similarity refinement to preserve the reliable important similarity information, and then fusing refined similarity graphs from all views and metrics to a unified one. The proposed method fuses useful information of multiple view and directly learns the cluster membership to improve the clustering performance. In addition, it has two free but insensitive parameter, which greatly relieves the burden of parameter tuning. The experimental results on eight datasets demonstrate the effectiveness and superiority of our proposed model, compared with thirteen state-of-the-art methods.

Acknowledgment. This work was partially supported by the National Natural Science Foundation of China (61771007), Key-Area Research and Development of Guangdong Province (2020B010166002, 2020B111119001), Science and Technology Planning Project of Guangdong Province (2017B020226004), and the Health & Medical Collaborative Innovation Project of Guangzhou City (202002020049).

References

1. Elhamifar, E., Vidal, R.: Sparse subspace clustering: algorithm, theory, and applications. IEEE Trans. Pattern Anal. Mach. Intell. **35**(11), 2765–2781 (2013)
2. Kumar, A., Daumé, H.: A co-training approach for multi-view spectral clustering. In: Proceedings of the 28th International Conference on Machine Learning (ICML-11), pp. 393–400 (2011)
3. Kumar, A., Rai, P., Daume, H.: Co-regularized multi-view spectral clustering. Adv. Neural Inf. Process. Syst. **24**, 1413–1421 (2011)
4. Li, X., Zhang, H., Wang, R., Nie, F.: Multi-view clustering: a scalable and parameter-free bipartite graph fusion method. IEEE Trans. Pattern Anal. Mach. Intell. (2020)
5. Liu, G., Lin, Z., Yan, S., Sun, J., Yu, Y., Ma, Y.: Robust recovery of subspace structures by low-rank representation. IEEE Trans. Pattern Anal. Mach. Intell. **35**(1), 171–184 (2012)
6. Ng, A.Y., Jordan, M.I., Weiss, Y.: On spectral clustering: analysis and an algorithm. Adv. Neural Inf. Process. Syst. **14**, 849–856 (2002)
7. Nie, F., Li, J., Li, X., et al.: Parameter-free auto-weighted multiple graph learning: a framework for multiview clustering and semi-supervised classification. In: IJCAI, pp. 1881–1887 (2016)
8. Olayan, R.S., Ashoor, H., Bajic, V.B.: DDR: efficient computational method to predict drug-target interactions using graph mining and machine learning approaches. Bioinformatics **34**(7), 1164–1173 (2018)
9. Peng, H., Hu, Y., Chen, J., Haiyan, W., Li, Y., Cai, H.: Integrating tensor similarity to enhance clustering performance. IEEE Trans. Pattern Anal. Mach. Intell. (2020)
10. Ramazzotti, D., Lal, A., Wang, B., Batzoglou, S., Sidow, A.: Multi-omic tumor data reveal diversity of molecular mechanisms that correlate with survival. Nat. Commun. **9**(1), 1–14 (2018)
11. Rappoport, N., Shamir, R.: Nemo: cancer subtyping by integration of partial multi-omic data. Bioinformatics **35**(18), 3348–3356 (2019)
12. Shi, J., Malik, J.: Normalized cuts and image segmentation. IEEE Trans. Pattern Anal. Mach. Intell. **22**(8), 888–905 (2000)
13. Wang, B., et al.: Similarity network fusion for aggregating data types on a genomic scale. Nat. Meth. **11**(3), 333 (2014)
14. Wang, B., Zhu, J., Pierson, E., Ramazzotti, D., Batzoglou, S.: Visualization and analysis of single-cell RNA-seq data by kernel-based similarity learning. Nat. Meth. **14**(4), 414–416 (2017)
15. Wang, H., Yang, Y., Liu, B.: GMC: graph-based multi-view clustering. IEEE Trans. Knowl. Data Eng. **32**(6), 1116–1129 (2019)
16. Wang, H., Yang, Y., Liu, B., Fujita, H.: A study of graph-based system for multiview clustering. Knowl.-Based Syst. **163**, 1009–1019 (2019)
17. Wang, Y.X., Xu, H., Leng, C.: Provable subspace clustering: When LRR meets SSC. IEEE Trans. Inf. Theory **65**(9), 5406–5432 (2019)
18. Wei, Y., et al.: Modality-dependent cross-media retrieval. ACM Trans. Intell. Syst. Technol. (TIST) **7**(4), 1–13 (2016)
19. Weng, W., Zhou, W., Chen, J., Peng, H., Cai, H.: Enhancing multi-view clustering through common subspace integration by considering both global similarities and local structures. Neurocomputing **378**, 375–386 (2020)

20. Winn, J., Jojic, N.: Locus: learning object classes with unsupervised segmentation. In: Tenth IEEE International Conference on Computer Vision (ICCV 2005) Volume 1, vol. 1, pp. 756–763. IEEE (2005)
21. Zelnik-Manor, L., Perona, P.: Self-tuning spectral clustering. Adv. Neural Inf. Process. Syst. **17**, 1601–1608 (2004)
22. Zhan, K., Nie, F., Wang, J., Yang, Y.: Multiview consensus graph clustering. IEEE Trans. Image Process. **28**(3), 1261–1270 (2018)

ahCQ: Adaptive Hierarchical Clustering Based Quantization Framework for Deep Neural Networks

Jiaxin Hu, Weixiong Rao$^{(\boxtimes)}$, and Qinpei Zhao$^{(\boxtimes)}$

School of Software Engineering, The Tongji University, Shanghai, China
{wxrao,qinpeizhao}@tongji.edu.cn

Abstract. For deep neural networks (DNNs), a high model accuracy is usually the main focus. However, millions of model parameters commonly lead to high space overheads, especially parameter redundancy. By maintaining network weights with less bit-widths, network quantization has been used to compress DNNs for lower space costs. However, existing quantization methods cannot well optimally balance the model size and the accuracy, thus they suffer from the accuracy loss more or less. Besides, though few of existing quantization techniques can adaptively determine layers quantization bit-widths, they either give little consideration on the relations of different DNN layers, or are designed for special hardware environment that are not universal in broad computer fields. To overcome these issues, we propose an adaptive Hierarchical Clustering based Quantization (aHCQ) framework. The aHCQ can find a largely compressed model from the quantization of each layer and take only little loss on the model accuracy. It is shown from the experiments that the aHCQ can achieve 11.4× and 8.2× model compression rates with only around 0.5% drop of the model accuracy.

Keywords: Deep neural network · Hierarchical clustering · Network quantization · Compression rate

1 Introduction

Nowadays deep neural networks (DNNs) are ubiquitous in many learning tasks, and particularly popular for image classification, where large images usually lead to large NN models. Due to millions of network parameters, DNNs unfortunately suffer from high model storage sizes.

Model quantization has been widely used to maintain network weights with shorter bit-widths [1,19]. One of the commonly used quantization approaches is *weights rounding*. The main idea of the approach is to round each weight into low bit-width. The most straightforward weights rounding in [2,3] simply rounds each float weight to 16 bits and 8 bits respectively. Ternary Neural Network [11] on the other hand represents each weight by either +1, 0 or −1, and the Binarized Neural Network [12] represents each weight by +1 or −1. The QIL

© Springer Nature Switzerland AG 2021
K. Karlapalem et al. (Eds.): PAKDD 2021, LNAI 12713, pp. 207–218, 2021.
https://doi.org/10.1007/978-3-030-75765-6_17

framework in [6] adjusts the $[min, max]$ weights range for weights rounding. Yang et al. [2] propose to round the weights into low bit-widths by sigmoid functions. These weight rounding approaches can lead to high compression rate and shorten running time. However, they inevitably damage the model structure through the simplification of the weights of models, leading to the drop of accuracy.

Compared to weights rounding, *weights sharing* methods can better keep the weights information so as to better preserve the model accuracy. The main idea of the weights sharing is to group weights into a few clusters so that each weight can be represented by its cluster index with lower bit-width. In the weights sharing, two data structures are obtained, which are the code book for storing the cluster indexes to which the weights belong, and the centroids for storing the mean of each cluster. The idea of weights sharing was first introduced by Song, et al. in [5], and was extended by plenty of works [4,9]. Basically, previous works used k-means clustering to share weights (namely k-means weights sharing), where they simply picked the initial centroids that evenly divide the range $[min, max]$ of original weights. The initialization issue and the local optimal problem lead to the loss of accuracy also.

Instead of quantizing layers by a fixed bit-width, an adaptive quantization framework that employs various bit-widths to different layers can adaptively keep the model accuracy with a relatively small model size. The quantization bit-width margin for each layer is mathematically determined by loss functions all at once in [10]. However, it is pointed out in [14] that if one layer is quantized, the other layers weights' optimal distribution would be changed, as well as their quantization bit-widths margins. The recent works [7,8] exploit reinforcement learning such as DDPG and DQN to learn an optimal quantization bit-width for each DNN's layer. However, these frameworks are designed for special hardware environments (e.g., FPGA) and heuristic metrics from weights (i.e., weights input/output channels number, weights change after high bit-widths quantization) to offer meaningful rewards, which are not universal quantization algorithms.

Nevertheless, all these quantization works suffer from the following issues.

Issue 1: Existing quantization techniques suffer from the accuracy loss more or less. The key point of the issue therefore is to find the optimal balance between the model size and the accuracy loss, i.e., largely compress the model while keeping the accuracy as high as possible.

Issue 2: Existing adaptive quantization methods cannot well determine the optimal bit-widths for DNN layers. They either give little consideration on the relations of different DNN layers (The change of the weights on one layer globally affects the other layers), or are designed for special hardware environment that are not universal in broad computer fields.

To tackle the two issues, we propose an *adaptive Hierarchical Clustering based Quantization* (aHCQ) framework. For each layer in the DNN, the aHCQ adaptively determines the quantized bit-width by monitoring the accuracy loss of DNN during quantization, where a hierarchical clustering quantization is performed. To solve **Issue 1**, compared with existing quantization techniques (e.g. k-means weights clustering), the aHCQ uses an improved weights sharing method to preserve the weights distribution so as to better maintain the model accuracy. To solve **Issue 2**, the aHCQ quantizes a DNN layer by layer and adaptively decides each layer's quantization bit-width by directly monitoring the accuracy loss of DNN during the quantization procedure, but not by heuristic metrics.

The experiments demonstrate that our proposed aHCQ framework guarantees model accuracy loss no more than the given acc_{loss}, as well as achieves higher accuracy with same model size compared with other quantizaton techniques. Experiments show that our aHCQ can achieves 11.4× and 8.2× model compression rates with only 0.5% cost on the model accuracy.

2   An Adaptive Hierarchical Clustering Based Quantization (aHCQ) Framework

We introduce the adaptive Hierarchical Clustering based Quantization (aHCQ) framework for DNNs in this section. The aHCQ intends to find a largely compressed model while keeping the model accuracy as high as possible. To achieve this goal, the aHCQ adaptively determines the quantization bit-width for each layer by globally considering the whole model. For each layer, the quantization is constrained by a threshold on the accuracy loss, which is determined by model accuracy obtained from the whole model on part of the training set and the pre-trained model accuracy. With the quantization bit-width determined, the hierarchical clustering is employed in the weights sharing method for each layer.

We firstly introduce the weights sharing method and the hierarchical agglomerative clustering in the following part of the section. Then, the details of the aHCQ framework are presented.

2.1   Weights Sharing and the Hierarchical Agglomerative Clustering

Weights sharing is a quantization technique [4,5]. In Fig. 1, we illustrate how the weights sharing technique quantizes a $3 \times 3 = 9$ weight-matrix from $b_t = 32$ bits to 2 bits.

The weights sharing method usually consists of two steps. The first step is the clustering quantization and the second step is the centroids re-training for fine-tuning the weights quantization.

Step 1. Weights Clustering. This step is to cluster the weights in W into several groups whose labels can be represented by lower bit-width integers. In this way the original weihts matrix can be quantized to a code book matrix B, whose shape is the same as the W and elements are lower bit-width labels of the corresponding weights, and an array of centroids O. The ith element of the O is the centroid of the ith group. In Fig. 1, the number of groups is 4 so all labels can be represented by a 2 bits integer. And O is composed of the centroids of the 4 groups. The clustering method in this step is usually the k-means clustering.

Step 2. Centroids Re-training. In order to fine tune the centroids O, the centroids re-training step is performed. After the clustering quantization, the original weight matrix W is approximated by W_q, which can be acquired by O

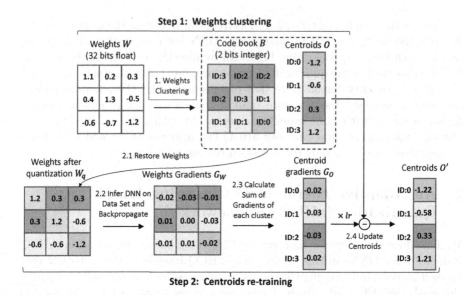

Fig. 1. The weights sharing method: How to quantize a weights matrix from 32 bits into 2 bits?

and B (*restore weights* in Step 2.1). To compensate the accuracy loss brought by the quantization, the centroids O are retrained. The weights on the corresponding DNN layer are updated by the W_q, and the DNN is inferred on the data set and a back-propagation approach (i.e., SGD) is exploited to find the gradients G_W of the W_q. The gradients of each group are summed up to have centroid gradients G_O (*Step 2.3*). Finally, with a given learning rate lr, the operation $O' = O - lr \times G_O$ (*Step 2.4*) is performed to update the centroids.

As a classic clustering algorithm, it is natural that k-means is chosen to cluster the weights in previous works [4,5,9]. The k-means weight sharing method is relatively fast. However, it suffers from centroids initialization problem, which could lead to high accuracy loss. Besides, the number of clusters (i.e., 2^{b_t}) in the k-means is set as a parameter, where the b_t is not adaptively determined. Unlike the k-means clustering, *Hierarchical Agglomerative Clustering* (HAC) has better ability to discover the data structure. We denote the size of the dataset as N. Starting from N clusters, the main idea of the HAC is to gradually merge the closest two in all clusters at a time, until all the clusters have been merged into a single cluster. The merge of two closest clusters is calculated by an average linkage in this paper. In the algorithm, the merge can be stopped at any number of clusters.

One of the advantages of the HAC compared with the k-means is that it has no initialization problem, which may lead to local optimal. Another benefit is that the clustering results with different number of clusters can be obtained from one run of the HAC. The cost of the two advantages is the high time complexity of the HAC. For a data set with N items, the time complexity of a usual implementation of the HAC can lead to $\mathcal{O}(N^3)$. In terms of keeping the advantage and overcoming the disadvantage of the HAC, we introduce the adaptive Hierarchical Clustering based Quantization (aHCQ) framework. In order to reduce the time complexity of the HAC, the weights are sorted firstly and the merge is between the neighbor clusters. Thereby, the time complexity is reduced to $O(N^2)$. Furthermore, the bit-width (corresponds to the number of clusters) for each layer in the DNN model is adaptively determined by considering the relationship with other layers. The bit-width is dynamically changed according to the accuracy change of the whole model during the quantization.

2.2   Details of the aHCQ Framework

The proposed aHCQ framework is designed based on the weights sharing method and adaptive quantization. Taking the *model weights* (W) of each layer in a network and a *target accuracy loss* (acc_{loss}) as inputs, the aHCQ framework outputs a quantized weights matrix, which is represented by a *code book B* and a *centroid list O*.

To overcome the high time complexity from the distance calculation on pairs of clusters, the aHCQ ensures each weights cluster only needs a limited number of linkage comparisons with other clusters in each merging loop by sorting the weights at the beginning. In this way, we can reduce the running time from $\mathcal{O}(N^3)$ into $\mathcal{O}(N^2)$. Besides, the input acc_{loss} is to help decide each layers' quantization bit-width by directly monitoring the accuracy loss in each merging loop. The adaptively determined bit-widths therefore promise the model accuracy.

An example on how to quantize one layer in a DNN is illustrated in Fig. 2. A 3×3 weights matrix W and a target accuracy loss acc_{loss} are the inputs. Besides, the total number of layers in the DNN is represented by n and the training data set for the model is denoted as D_{train}.

The aHCQ firstly sorts the weights in W ascendingly to get a sorted weights list W_r. At the beginning, each weight is considered as a cluster. The merge step is then performed on pairs of clusters. Since the clusters are ordered, the merge is conducted on their neighbors. To merge two neighbor clusters (say -0.02 and 0.08), we make sure that the distance between such clusters must be smaller than the one between each of such clusters (say -0.02) and its alternative neighbor (say -0.31), if any. That is, since both $||(-0.02) - (0.08)||_2 < ||(-0.02) - (-0.31)||_2$ and $||(-0.02) - (0.08)||_2 < ||(0.23) - (0.08)||_2$ hold, we then merge -0.02 and 0.08, but not -0.02 and -0.31. Those neighbor clusters marked by solid arrows are merged. One unique property of this improved algorithm is that these clusters, after merging, still preserve ascending order. In this way, we do not need to re-sort clusters in the next merging loop, thus leading to higher efficiency. The clustering results C_W contains the centroids O and the code book B.

The merge between pairs of clusters needs a stopping criterion. Note that there are totally n layers, and the overall accuracy loss is acc_{loss}. As a result, the average accuracy loss for each layer's weights is simply set as $\frac{acc_{loss}}{n}$. Therefore,

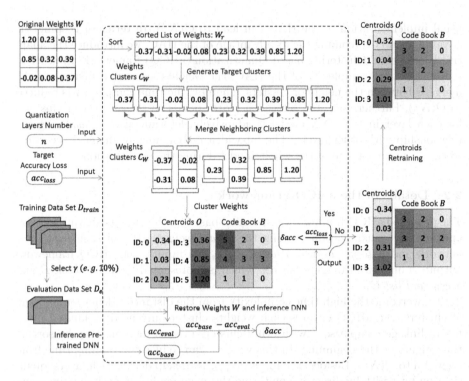

Fig. 2. The adaptive Hierarchical Clustering Quantization (aHCQ) framework. The quantization steps on an individual DNN layer are described.

the stopping criterion is set as the number of clusters (i.e., the bit-widths) that leads the accuracy loss on the layer δ_{acc} be larger than $\frac{acc_{loss}}{n}$.

As for the accuracy loss on the layer δ_{acc} that caused by the quantization, it is obtained from the difference of the acc_{base} and the acc_{eval}, which are the model accuracy trained from the training data set (D_{train}) and a small part of it (D_e). The D_e is randomly chosen from the training data set D_{train} with a proportion of γ (10% by default).

When the stopping criterion is met ($\delta_{acc} \geq \frac{acc_{loss}}{n}$), the clustering results O and B are obtained. The centroids O is re-trained to compensate the accuracy loss (see Fig. 1). Suppose there are c clusters of the O list, the quantization bit-width for the layer is $\lceil log_2(c) \rceil$. As shown in Fig. 2, the weights matrix W is clustered into four clusters, where 2-bits can represent code book B.

Considering the efficiency of the aHCQ on large data sets, a *pre-processing step* is added to speed up the aHCQ. The idea of the pre-processing step is to perform a rough compression on the original weights matrix. Generally, the bit-widths from 32 to 8 bits rarely reduce the model accuracy. Therefore, the pre-processing is to run the aHCQ once with a hard bit-widths setting. Given the target 8-bit-widths, the number of clusters is then $2^8 = 256$, which is set as the stopping criterion.

Table 1. The settings and parameters of the networks including the number of layers, the batch size, the momentum, the learning rate and the model size.

Network	Layers number n	Batch size	Momentum	Learning rate	Model size
LeNet [16]	5	128	0.9	0.05	243 KB
AlexNet [17]	8	128	0.9	0.05	217 MB
ResNet18 [18]	18	64	0.9	0.1	42.6 MB
ResNet34 [18]	34	64	0.9	0.1	81.2 MB

3 Experiments

3.1 Experiments Settings

The experiments are conducted on two datasets which are the CIFAR-10 and CIFAR-100 [15]. The two datasets both consist of 60,000 32×32 color images with 50,000 training images and 10,000 test images. The CIFAR-10 has 10 classes while the CIFAR-100 has 100 classes.

Four DNNs have been chosen to be quantized in the experiments, which are the LeNet [16], AlexNet [17], ResNet18 [18] and ResNet34 [18]. LeNet is a classic shallow neural network containing a small number of weights. AlexNet contains five convolutional (Conv) layers and three fully connected (FC) layers, where FC layers contain quite a large number of weights. Compared with the AlexNet, ResNet18/34 contains more Conv layers but less FC layers, thus we can deepen the depths of the models as well as reduce the model sizes. Except for the input and output layers, ResNet18/34 consist of several blocks which contain multiple sequential convolutional layers. Commonly, the quantization operation of DNNs do not include the first convolutional layer and the last fully connected layer [11]. The settings of the networks are shown in Table 1.

Besides, we choose top-1 and top-5 accuracy as evaluation metrics. Top-k accuracy refers to the accuracy rate at which the top k ranked categories include the actual result, and we use *accuracy* to represent top-1 accuracy for simplification. In Sect. 2.2, γ of the training data set are randomly chosen as the evaluation data set to help monitor the accuracy loss, which is set as 10% in the experiments. Because of the length of the article, this paper omits the comparative experiments with γ as 5%, 10% and 20% respectively. The experimental results show that the aHCQ can attain highest model compression rate under the same acc_{loss} settings on CIFAR-10 and 4 models in Table 1.

The experiments are conducted on the hardware with Ubuntu 16.04 LTS(x64) as the operating system, Intel(R) Core(TM) i7-7700 CPU @ 3.60 GHz, 32 GB memory and a 11 GB GeForce GTX 1080 Ti graphics card.

3.2 Comparison on the aHCQ and Other Weights Sharing

In this section, we compare the aHCQ with the k-means and HAC weights sharing. For a fair comparison, the quantization bit-width of the aHCQ has been

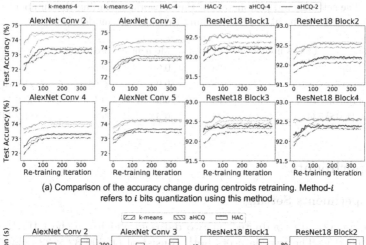

(a) Comparison of the accuracy change during centroids retraining. Method-i refers to i bits quantization using this method.

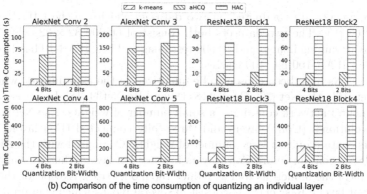

(b) Comparison of the time consumption of quantizing an individual layer

Fig. 3. Comparison of accuracy change during quantization and time consumption between our aHCQ, HAC and k-means weights sharing on CIFAR-10. Here ResNet18 Block i refers to first convolutional layer of ith block.

fixed as the same as that in the k-means and the HAC. We choose four layers of the AlexNet and the ResNet18, and we set the quantization bit-width b_t as 4 and 2 bits respectively. We choose the 2nd, 3rd, 4th and 5th convolutional layers in AlexNet as well as the first convolutional layers of four blocks in ResNet18 as target layers, on the dataset CIFAR-10. The model accuracy and the time consumption of the methods on different models are compared.

As shown in Fig. 3, the aHCQ has comparable performance with the HAC weights sharing on model accuracy, both of which are better than the k-means weights sharing. It further verifies that the hierarchical clustering can better discover the weights structure than the k-means. In general, the accuracy loss of 2-bits quantization is higher than that of 4-bits. Therefore, the bit-width has to be well determined for controlling the accuracy loss of the whole model.

Time consumption here refers to the running time on the weights clustering step (step 1 in Fig. 1) in the weights sharing method. The running time of the aHCQ is much less than the HAC with the improvements performed, e.g., the

Table 2. Experiments on the pre-processing step of the aHCQ on four DNNs, where the bit-width for each layer is 8. R refers to the results of the original model and Q refers to that of quantized model. The accuracy and compression rate are compared.

Dataset	Network	Top-1 acc (R/Q) (%)	Top-5 acc (R/Q) (%)	Compression rate
CIFAR-10	LeNet	65.92% / 66.96%	- / -	×3.5
	AlexNet	73.67% / 73.68%	- / -	×3.8
	ResNet18	92.60% / 92.63%	- / -	×3.9
	ResNet34	93.01% / 93.02%	- / -	×3.9
CIFAR-100	AlexNet	56.52% / 56.56%	79.07% / 80.12%	×3.8
	ResNet18	74.23% / 74.26%	92.13% / 92.22%	×3.9
	ResNet34	75.62% / 75.48%	92.41% / 92.37%	×3.9

sorting procedure. Theoretically, the time complexity of the k-means is $O(N)$, which is the most efficient among the three methods. However, the consumption time at this stage is very trivial compared to the quantization on the whole model. The running time of the k-means on the ResNet18 into 4-bits is larger than that into 2-bits. The higher bit-width indicates larger number of clusters and the time complexity of the k-means is proportional to the number of clusters.

3.3   Results for Preprocessing Step of aHCQ

In the aHCQ framework, a pre-processing step has been introduced to enhance the efficiency. The pre-processing step is to hardly compress each layer from 32-bits into 8-bits. We show that the pre-processing step brings little effect on the accuracy from Table 2. The experiments are performed on the four networks trained on the CIFAR-10 and CIFAR-100. The top-1 accuracy and top-5 accuracy on the original models (R) and quantized models (Q) are compared. Basically, top-5 accuracy is not commonly used to measure the accuracy of CIFAR-10. As a result, the top-5 accuracy of four models is omitted on CIFAR-10 in this table. It is shown that there is little accuracy loss of the quantized model. The accuracy even increases because the quantization has reduced the redundancies among the model. Therefore, with a 3.5–3.9 compression rate achieved, the pre-processing step brings little on the accuracy loss.

3.4   Results for Adaptability of aHCQ

As a parameter in the aHCQ, the acc_{loss} is tested in the experiment, where the acc_{loss} is set in the range of $[0.0\%, 1.8\%]$ with 0.2% as an interval. The experiment is performed on the ResNet18/34 on data CIFAR-10 and CIFAR-100. The actual accuracy loss is calculated from the accuracy difference of the quantized model and the original model. For each setting of the acc_{loss}, a compression rate is obtained after the quantization. It is shown from Fig. 4 that the aHCQ guarantees the actual accuracy loss is always less than the acc_{loss} while high compression rates can be achieved. It also shows that the aHCQ can adaptively quantize the networks.

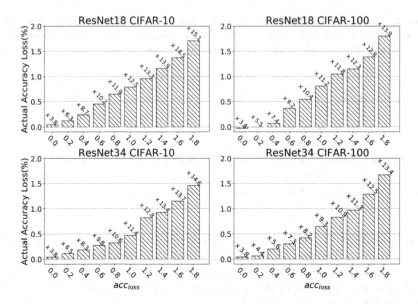

Fig. 4. The experiment on the setting of acc_{loss}. The compression rates and the actual accuracy loss of the DNNs after the aHCQ quantization are obtained at each setting of the acc_{loss}.

3.5   Results for aHCQ Compared with Benchmarks

We compare the aHCQ with the state-of-art DNN quantization methods in the experiment, where the Resnet18/34 are selected on dataset CIFAR-10 and CIFAR-100. The existing quantizatin methods can be categorized as non-adaptive and adaptive. For non-adaptive methods, the bit-width of each layer are the same. Here the non-adaptive methods include the SLQ/MLQ [9] (SLQ/MLQ-i means quantizing DNNs with i bit-width by improved k-means weights sharing), TWN [11] (rounding DNNs weights into 2 bits), QIL [6] (adjusting quantization intervals to improve the TWN) and Deep Compression [4] (DC, which quantizes convolutional layers into 8 bits and fully connected layers into 5 bits). For adaptive quantization methods, the Adaptive Quantization framework (AQ) [10] is compared. The AQ uses the loss function gradients to iteratively determine the quantization bit-width margin for each layer's weights.

The accuracy of the models that have been quantized with different compression rates are shown in Fig. 5. Compared with the non-adaptive methods (TWN, QIL, MLQ-2, SLQ-3 and DC), our aHCQ can preserve the model accuracy under basically same compression rate, as well as achieve adaptability. Besides, compared with the AQ, the aHCQ's compression-accuracy curves are all above these of AQ, which means our aHCQ's trade-off between accuracy and compression rate is better than that of AQ overall. Besides, the aHCQ method performing slightly better than the MLQ-2 when compression rate is around 15x is acceptable, because the aHCQ framework mainly focus on how to adaptively

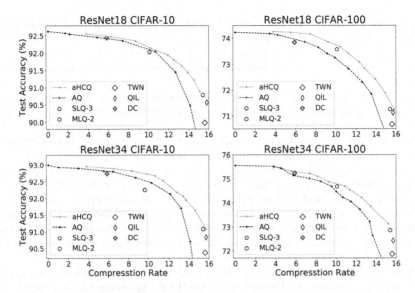

Fig. 5. The comparison on different DNN quantization methods. aHCQ compared with commonly used methods.

find proper bit-width for each layer. In conclusion, the aHCQ achieves higher accuracy with same model size compared with other quantizaton techniques.

4   Conclusion

In this paper, we propose an adaptive hierarchical clustering quantization (aHCQ) framework that can compress the weights of the network models while largely preserve the model accuracy. A hierarchical agglomerative clustering algorithm has been introduced on the weights quantization of each layer, which promises less accuracy loss happened during the quantization. Meanwhile, the quantized bit-width for each layer is determined adaptively according to the accuracy loss happened locally from each layer and globally at the whole network. The experiments demonstrate that the aHCQ achieves a high compression rate of the model with quite less model accuracy loss.

Acknowledgment. We would like to thank all reviewers for their comments. This work was partially supported by National Natural Science Foundation of China (Grant No. 61972286). And this work was supported by the Natural Science Foundation of Shanghai, China (No. 20ZR1460500).

References

1. Cheng, Y., Wang, D., Zhou, P., et al.: A survey of model compression and acceleration for deep neural networks. arXiv preprint arXiv:1710.09282 (2017)

2. Choi, Y., El-Khamy, M., Lee, J.: Towards the limit of network quantization. arXiv preprint arXiv:1612.01543 (2016)
3. Gupta, S., Agrawal, A., Gopalakrishnan, K., et al.: Deep learning with limited numerical precision. In: International Conference on Machine Learning, pp. 1737–1746 (2015)
4. Han, S., Mao, H., Dally, W.J.: Deep compression: compressing deep neural networks with pruning, trained quantization and huffman coding. arXiv preprint arXiv:1510.00149 (2015)
5. Han, S., Pool, J., Tran, J., et al.: Learning both weights and connections for efficient neural network. Advances in Neural Information Processing Systems (2015)
6. Jung, S., Son, C., Lee, S., et al.: Learning to quantize deep networks by optimizing quantization intervals with task loss. In: Proceedings of the IEEE Conference on Computer Vision and Pattern Recognition, pp. 4350–4359 (2019)
7. Liu, S., Lin, Y., Zhou, Z., et al.: On-demand deep model compression for mobile devices: a usage-driven model selection framework. In: Proceedings of the 16th Annual International Conference on Mobile Systems, Applications, and Services, pp. 389–400 (2018)
8. Wang, K., Liu, Z., Lin, Y., et al.: Haq: hardware-aware automated quantization with mixed precision. In: Proceedings of the IEEE Conference on Computer Vision and Pattern Recognition, pp. 8612–8620 (2019)
9. Xu, Y., Wang, Y., Zhou, A., et al.: Deep neural network compression with single and multiple level quantization. arXiv preprint arXiv:1803.03289 (2018)
10. Zhou, Y., Moosavi-Dezfooli, S.M., Cheung, N.M., et al.: Adaptive quantization for deep neural network. arXiv preprint arXiv:1712.01048 (2017)
11. Zhu, C., Han, S., Mao, H., et al.: Trained ternary quantization. arXiv preprint arXiv:1612.01064 (2016)
12. Courbariaux, M., Hubara, I., Soudry, D., et al.: Binarized neural networks: training deep neural networks with weights and activations constrained to + 1 or -1. arXiv preprint arXiv:1602.02830 (2016)
13. Wen, W., Wu, C., Wang, Y., et al.: Learning structured sparsity in deep neural networks. arXiv preprint arXiv:1608.03665 (2016)
14. Wu, J., Leng, C., Wang, Y., et al.: Quantized convolutional neural networks for mobile devices. In: On Computer Vision and Pattern Recognition, pp. 4820–4828 (2016)
15. Darlow, L.N., Crowley, E.J., Antoniou, A., et al.: CINIC-10 is not ImageNet or CIFAR-10. arXiv preprint arXiv:1810.03505 (2018)
16. LeCun, Y.: LeNet-5, convolutional neural networks, vol. 20, no. 5, p. 14 (2015). http://yann.lecun.com/exdb/lenet
17. Krizhevsky, A., Sutskever, I., Hinton, G.E.: Imagenet classification with deep convolutional neural networks. Commun. ACM 60(6), 84–90 (2017)
18. He, K., Zhang, X., Ren, S., et al.: Deep residual learning for image recognition. In: Proceedings of the IEEE Conference on Computer Vision and Pattern Recognition (2016)
19. Choudhary, T., Mishra, V., Goswami, A., Sarangapani, J.: A comprehensive survey on model compression and acceleration. Artif. Intell. Rev. 53(7), 5113–5155 (2020). https://doi.org/10.1007/s10462-020-09816-7

Maintaining Consistency with Constraints: A Constrained Deep Clustering Method

Yi Cui, Xianchao Zhang$^{(\boxtimes)}$, Linlin Zong, and Jie Mu

School of Software, Dalian University of Technology, Dalian 116620, China

Abstract. Constrained clustering has been intensively explored in the data mining. Popular clustering algorithms such as k-means and spectral clustering are combined with prior knowledge to guide the clustering process. Recently, constrained clustering with deep neural network gains superior performance by jointly learning cluster-oriented feature representations and cluster assignments simultaneously. However, these methods face a common issue that they have poor performance when only minimal constraints are available because of their single way to mine constraint information. In this paper, we propose an end-to-end clustering method that learns unsupervised information and constraint information in two consecutive modules: an unsupervised clustering module to obtain feature representations and cluster assignments followed by a constrained clustering module to tune them. The constrained clustering module is composed of a Siamese or triplet network to maintain consistency with constraints. To capture more information from minimal constraints, the consistency is maintained from two perspective simultaneously: embedding space distance and cluster assignments. Extensive experiments on both pairwise and triplet constrained clustering validate the effectiveness of the proposed algorithm.

Keywords: Constrained clustering · Semi-supervised clustering · Deep clustering · Metric learning

1 Introduction

Clustering with deep neural networks has extensively explored due to the inherent property of highly non-linear transformation of DNNs. These methods effectively combine the neural network with popular clustering algorithms, such as k-means [7,14,22], spectral clustering [17], subspace clustering [10], agglomerative clustering [23] to joint dimensionality reduction and clustering-oriented representation learning. These unsupervised methods refer to unlabeled data, however, some prior knowledge such as pairwise constraints or triplet constraints could be obtained automatically in many clustering tasks.

This work was supported by National Science Foundation of China (No.61632019; No.61876028; No.61972065; No.61806034).

© Springer Nature Switzerland AG 2021
K. Karlapalem et al. (Eds.): PAKDD 2021, LNAI 12713, pp. 219–230, 2021.
https://doi.org/10.1007/978-3-030-75765-6_18

Constrained clustering is a kind of task that few auxiliary information is provided to guide clustering. Some constrained clustering methods are explored with pairwise constraints (must-link and cannot-link) [8,16]. SDEC [16] decreases the embedding distance between must-link pairs and increases distance between cannot-link pairs. But the distance in the embedding space between cannot-link pairs have already been large at the beginning of training due to the good separation of the pre-trained network, which leads to the inefficiency of its objective. Hsu et al. [8] present their objective on softmax output with KL divergence but abandon the contribution of instances without constraints. Zhang et al. [25] explore more complex constraints. They enforce the must-link pairs with similar assignment probability and cannot-link pairs oppositely. But when the number of constraints is not enough to mitigate the negative effect of imbalance (which means very few must-link assignments can be referred to, e.g. approximately 10% in Fashion dataset), this method that only mines constraint information from the perspective of cluster assignments is sensitive to the reduction of the number of constraints. For these reasons, these methods face a common issue that they have poor performance when the number of constraints is small.

In this paper, we propose a Constrained Deep Clustering method (CDC) that aims to maintain consistency with constraints. To be effective even if minimal constraints are available, our method learns unsupervised information and constraint information in two consecutive modules: an unsupervised clustering module followed by a constrained clustering module. Inspired by the metric learning, we construct the network based on a Siamese network or triplet network in the constrained clustering module. For the purpose of capturing more information from minimal constraints, the consistency is maintained from two perspective simultaneously: embedding space distance and cluster assignments. The model is trained by cosine function as the similarity metric avoiding the inefficiency when embedding distance between cannot-link pairs is large and weighted cross entropy objective to tune cluster assignments. The main contributions of this paper are summarized as follows:

- We propose an end-to-end clustering method that learns unsupervised information and constraint information in two consecutive modules: an unsupervised clustering module to obtain feature representations and cluster assignments followed by a constrained clustering module to tune them.
- We propose effective objective function to maintain consistency with constraints from two perspective: embedding space distance and cluster assignments.
- Extensive experiments are conducted on both image and text datasets. The results show competitive performance on both pairwise and triplet constrained clustering, validating the effectiveness of CDC algorithm.

2   Related Work

Deep clustering is a category of clustering in recent years that combine deep neural network to learn cluster-friendly features. There are approaches [6,7,21, 22] obtaining feasible feature space based on autoencoder (AE). Other novel methods adopt deep generative model to perform clustering task, such as VAE-based [5,11] and GAN-based [3,15,24] methods. In addition, some clustering methods recently has shifted to handle high-dimensional data, including spectral clustering [9,17] and subspace clustering [10,26,27].

Constrained clustering has been widely studied to lead an auxiliary guidance to clustering. Some methods explore strategies for improving clustering performance with pairwise constraints [1,2,18,19]. Other methods with deep neural network gains better performance. Hsu et al. [8] view the outputs of the softmax layer as the distribution of possible clusters given a sample and evaluate the similarity with KL divergence. Zhang et al. [25] explore more complex constraints generated from new types of side information. Although these methods capture the point that similar samples should output similar assignment distribution, there is no work noticing consistency of embedding space distance and cluster assignments simultaneously.

3   Proposed Method

Consider a task about clustering a data set X containing n unlabeled instances, each sample $\{x_i \in \mathbb{R}^d\}_{i=1}^n$ should be assigned to one of k clusters. Except these unlabeled data, two types of user-specified prior information is also provided to guide the clustering process, including pairwise constraints and triplet constraints. A pairwise constraint indicates that a pair of samples $\{(x_i, x_j) : x_i, x_j \in X\}$ have a relationship of must-link (x_i and x_j belong to the same clusters) or cannot-link (x_i and x_j belong to different clusters). A triplet constraint consists of a triple of samples $\{(\widetilde{x}, x_p, x_n) : \widetilde{x}, x_p, x_n \in X\}$, where the positive sample x_p is closer to the anchor $\widetilde{x}$ than the negative sample x_n in the embedding space.

We propose to find a non-linear mapping $f_\theta : X \to Z$ that transforms the original data into latent space Z, in which the embedding distance is consistent with the original semantic distance and cluster assignments are consistent with constraints. The model contains two consecutive modules: the unsupervised clustering module followed by our constrained clustering module. The whole structure of CDC is illustrated in Fig. 1.

We introduce the referred method in unsupervised clustering module in Sect. 3.1. Then we propose two types of constrained clustering module with pairwise constraints and triplet constraints respectively in Sect. 3.2 and Sect. 3.3.

3.1   Unsupervised Clustering Module

The first module aims to learn cluster-oriented feature representations. We refer the DEC [21] to learn feature representations and cluster assignments.

The DEC method initializes the centroids $\{\mu_j\}_{j=1}^k$ through k-means on the embedding space of the autoencoder pre-trained by a stacked autoencoder (SAE), then computes the soft assignments q_{ij} as:

$$q_{ij} = \frac{(1 + \|z_i - \mu_j\|^2/\alpha)^{-\frac{\alpha+1}{2}}}{\sum_{j'=1}^k (1 + \|z_i - \mu_{j'}\|^2/\alpha)^{-\frac{\alpha+1}{2}}}, \tag{1}$$

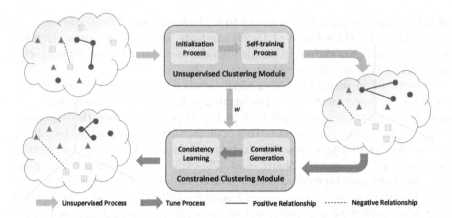

Fig. 1. The process of CDC algorithm. The method learns unsupervised information and constraint information in two consecutive modules: an unsupervised clustering module to obtain feature representations and cluster assignments followed by a constrained clustering module to tune them.

where q_{ij} measures the similarity between embedded data z_i and centroids μ_j with Student's t-distribution being the kernel, α is a constant, e.g. $\alpha = 1$.

The auxiliary distribution P is defined to refine the cluster assignments . By squaring the soft assignments q_{ij} and then normalizing it, p_{ij} is formulated as:

$$p_{ij} = \frac{q_{ij}^2/\sum_i q_{ij}}{\sum_{j'=1}^k (q_{ij'}^2/\sum_i q_{ij'})}. \tag{2}$$

The loss function is defined as the reconstruction loss added to the KL divergence between soft assignments Q and auxiliary distribution P as follows:

$$L = KL(P\|Q) + L_R = \sum_i \sum_j p_{ij} \log \frac{p_{ij}}{q_{ij}} + \sum_i \|x_i - x_i'\|^2. \tag{3}$$

The clusters are iteratively refined during this self-training process. Constrained clustering module inherits the parameters and centroids and then learn from pairwise constraints or triplet constraints.

3.2   Clustering with Pairwise Constraints

The pairwise constraints are learned in our constrained clustering module based on a Siamese architecture, which is a popular network in metric learning. Two samples with pairwise constraints are required as inputs at the same step. Each group of inputs can be expressed as a triad $((x_1, x_2), y)$, where y is an indicator that $y = 1$ when given x_1 and x_2 with must-link relationship while $y = 0$ with cannot-link constraint. The structure of pairwise constrained clustering module is illustrated in Fig. 2. For the purpose of maintaining consistency with constraints, we define the objective function in two parts: embedding space distance and cluster assignments.

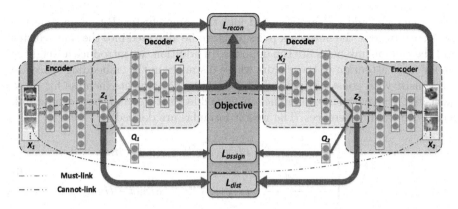

Fig. 2. The structure of constrained clustering module on pairwise constrained clustering based on a Siamese network. Constrained pairs are transformed into embedded features Z_1 and Z_2. Soft assignments Q_1 and Q_2 are normalized to compute assignment objective. The shared parameters are optimized by Eq. (7).

Consistency of Embedding Space Distance. The main idea of this part is to seek a mapping that transforms pairs of inputs into a embedding space, in which a similarity measure approximates the semantic information in the original space. To this end, the distance loss for all m groups of $((x_1, x_2), y)$ is defined as:

$$L_{dist} = -\frac{1}{m} \sum_{i=1}^{m} \left(y^{(i)} \lambda_1 \sigma(z_1^{(i)}, z_2^{(i)}) - (1 - y^{(i)}) \lambda_2 \sigma(z_1^{(i)}, z_2^{(i)}) \right), \quad (4)$$

where $z_1^{(i)}$ and $z_2^{(i)}$ are corresponding embedded features of the ith group of inputs, $\sigma(\cdot)$ is a similarity function, λ_1 and λ_2 are trade-off parameters. In summary, the embedded features with the same label prefer larger similarity, while points with different labels obtain smaller similarity by minimizing the objective function.

Consistency of Cluster Assignments. The main idea of this part is to tune cluster assignments with given constraints. Soft assignments are learned from its high confidence assignments in the unsupervised clustering module. We expect to tune cluster assignments to maintain the consistency with constraints. Specifically, must-link pairs are expected to have similar cluster assignments distribution, while assignment differences of cannot-link pairs are strengthened. The assignment loss is formulated as:

$$L_{assign} = -\frac{1}{m} \sum_{i=1}^{m} \left(y^{(i)} \lambda_3 w^{(i)} \log(q_1^{(i)} \cdot q_2^{(i)}) + (1 - y^{(i)}) w^{(i)} \log(1 - q_1^{(i)} \cdot q_2^{(i)}) \right). \quad (5)$$

This process is treated as a binary classification problem that whether or not two constrained samples belong to the same cluster. The inner product of corresponding normalized soft assignments $q_1^{(i)}$ and $q_2^{(i)}$ reflects the probability that two inputs $x_1^{(i)}$ and $x_2^{(i)}$ are assigned into the same cluster. By minimizing the cross entropy loss, the must-link pairs prefer to be allocated into the same cluster and the cannot-link pairs are the opposite. In addition, we introduce a weight w to pay more attention to those pairs whose distances in the embedding space are not consist with constraints. Precisely speaking, the weights increase for those must-link pairs with large differences in embedded features and those cannot-link pairs with small differences. The weight formulas are defined as:

$$
w^{(i)} = \begin{cases} \dfrac{1}{1 + e^{-d^{(i)}}}, & if (x_1, x_2)^{(i)} \in must - link, \\ \dfrac{3 + e^{d^{(i)}}}{2(1 + e^{d^{(i)}})}, & if (x_1, x_2)^{(i)} \in cannot - link, \end{cases} \tag{6}
$$

where $d^{(i)} = \alpha \| z_1^{(i)} - z_2^{(i)} \|_2$ reflects the difference between a pair of embedded features, α is an adjustment parameter to control the distance. We set $\alpha = 0.01$ in all experiments because the great masses of samples are well-separated. The weight w is a monotonically increasing function for must-link, while monotonically decreasing function in the opposite case.

In summary, we define the objective function in constrained clustering module for pairwise constraints as:

$$
L_{pair} = L_{dist} + L_{assign} + L_{recon}, \tag{7}
$$

$$
L_{recon} = \frac{1}{m} \sum_{i=1}^{m} y^{(i)} (\|x_1 - x_1'\|^2 + \|x_2 - x_2'\|^2)^{(i)}, \tag{8}
$$

where L_{recon} is the sum of reconstruction losses of two instances, which is added to the must-link cases to avoid a large scale cluster.

3.3   Clustering with Triplet Constraints

Triplet constraints are weaker constraints and easily accessible with only a trained embedding space. They could replace the stronger constraints in some constrained clustering tasks that lack ground truth labels or partition-based constraints, e.g. pairwise constraints. Different from these stronger constraints coming from specific partitions, triplet constraints convey the differences in distance level.

We construct a triplet network for training triplet constraints. As we can see in Fig. 3, a triple of samples $(\tilde{x}, x_p, x_n)$ are input to the network simultaneously. The similarities $\sigma(\tilde{z}, z_n)$ and $\sigma(\tilde{z}, z_p)$ are calculated in the embedding space output by the network with shared parameters. The objective function in constrained clustering module for triplet constraints is formulated as:

$$
L_{trip} = \max(\sigma(\tilde{z}, z_n) - \sigma(\tilde{z}, z_p) + m, 0), \tag{9}
$$

where $\sigma(\tilde{z}, z_n)$ and $\sigma(\tilde{z}, z_p)$ represent similarities between positive and negative samples against the anchor respectively. Those positive samples are pulled close

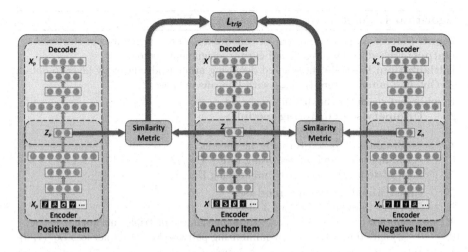

Fig. 3. The structure of constrained clustering module on triplet constrained clustering based on a triplet network. A triple of samples are input into the network at the same step. The similarities are obtained in the embedding space. Parameters are shared among the triplet network and are optimized by Eq. (9).

to their anchor and negative samples are separated from them. A hyperparameter margin m is introduced as a threshold that tries to widen the gap in $\sigma(\widetilde{z}, z_n)$ and $\sigma(\widetilde{z}, z_p)$. Due to the partition uncertainty of triplet constraints, some cases cannot be avoided that some positive samples and their anchors come from different classes, or some negative samples have the same labels with their anchors, which we call *imperfect triplet constraints*. The margin m also works by preventing x_p being too close or x_n being too separated from $\widetilde{x}$ in these cases. The parameter study about m is illustrated in Sect. 4.4.

In summary, our method learns feature representations and cluster assignments in the unsupervised clustering module and then tunes them in the constrained clustering module in one epoch. The procedure is summarized in Algorithm 1.

4   Experiments

4.1   Datasets

To verify the effectiveness and efficiency of the proposed CDC on constrained clustering tasks, we evaluate it on five benchmark datasets:

- **MNIST** [12]: A dataset composed of 70000 handwritten digits of 10 types. Each sample is a 28×28 gray image.
- **Fashion-MNIST** [20]: A dataset of Zalando's article images with the same size as MNIST. Each sample is a 28×28 gray image, divided into 10 classes.
- **USPS**: A handwritten digits dataset that contains 9298 images (7291 for training, 2007 for test) with size of 16×16 pixels.

Algorithm 1. Constrained Deep Clustering (CDC)

Input: Dataset X, pairwise or triplet constraint dataset $\widetilde{X}$, number of clusters k.
Output: Embedded features Z and cluster assignment vector s.
Initialization: Pre-train the stacked denoising autoencoder layer by layer to obtain Z. Obtain k initial centers $\{\mu_j\}_{j=1}^{k}$ with k-means in space Z.

1: **while** not reach the maximum epochs **do**
2:    **Unsupervised clustering module:**
3:    **for** every mini-batch data in X **do**
4:        Obtain $z_i = f_\theta(x_i)$ through the encoder.
5:        Compute q_{ij} and p_{ij} according to Eq. (1, 2).
6:        Update θ and $\{\mu_j\}_{j=1}^{k}$ by minimizing Eq. (3).
7:    **Constrained clustering module:**
8:    **for** every mini-batch data in $\widetilde{X}$ **do**
9:        Obtain (z_1, z_2) or $(\tilde{z}, z_p, z_n)$ through Siamese or triplet network.
10:       Update θ and $\{\mu_j\}_{j=1}^{k}$ by minimizing pairwise loss or triplet loss Eq. (7, 9).
11:   Obtain Z and $s_i = \arg\max_j q_{ij}$ for all instances.
12:   **if** stopping criterion is met **then**
13:       Stop training.

- **KMNIST** [4]: Kuzushiji-MNIST is a dataset which focuses on cursive Japanese, composed of 28×28 images of 10 types. Train and test set sizes are 6,000 and 1,000 per class.
- **Reuters10K** [13]: A subset consist of 10000 examples of Reuters. Each sample is composed of the 2000 most frequently occurring word stems in an English news story.

All datasets are preprocessed for each element before being fed into the algorithms. Precisely, we normalize all datasets to approach $\frac{1}{d}\|x_i\|_2^2$ to 1 for each $x_i \in \mathbb{R}^d$ in X.

4.2   Experimental Setting

The structure of the encoder network is set in the same way as DEC [21], SDEC [16] and FDCC [25] to be comparable with them. Concretely, we set the encoder network with dimensions of d - 500 - 500 - 2000 - 10 and the decoder with a symmetrical structure, where d is the dimension of input data. All layers are fully connected and activated by ReLU function except for the input, output, and embedding layers.

The parameters and centroids are initialized with a SAE and k-means in the same way as DEC [21]. Cosine similarity $\cos(a, b) = \frac{a \cdot b}{\|a\|\|b\|}$ is selected in Eq. (4, 9) for all experiments. In each iteration, we train the network with Adam optimizer. The learning rate and batch-size are set to 0.001 and 256 respectively. We investigate the influence of trade-off parameter in Eq. (5) with grid search and set it as 10. The whole training process will stop when breaks the threshold in stopping criterion $\delta = 0.001$ or reach the maximum epoch.

Table 1. Clustering performance of pairwise constraints in terms of accuracy (ACC %) and normalized mutual information (NMI %) over 5 datasets. The results of baseline models are obtained by running the released code except the ones marked by (*), which are reported from the corresponding papers. The mark (-) represents that the result is unavailable.

Dataset	MNIST		Fashion		USPS		KMNIST		Reuters10K	
	ACC	NMI	ACC	NMI	ACC	NMI	ACC	NMI	ACC	NMI
k-means	53.09	49.87	46.14	50.85	42.55	37.95	28.52	10.89	50.38	48.61
SAE-KM	85.23	80.76	58.03	60.57	68.75	65.99	47.16	39.10	76.53	56.61
DEC	86.59	83.73	56.62	62.21	75.81	76.91	48.64	40.79	72.17	53.08
IDEC	88.72	86.47	58.48	62.47	72.20	72.66	48.89	40.89	75.27	54.16
FCSP	62.80*	58.70*	41.70*	46.20*	-	-	-	-	-	-
COP-KM	81.60*	77.30*	54.80*	58.90*	71.85	70.24	46.78	38.53	70.42	51.83
MPC-KM	84.60*	80.80*	58.90*	61.30*	75.61	74.36	49.75	41.82	73.08	55.06
SDEC	85.02	81.69	59.62	63.89	75.84	76.96	50.05	42.18	75.31	55.24
FDCC	96.29	90.72	66.29	67.08	80.54	76.62	56.90	42.88	77.90	58.42
CDC	**96.69**	**91.92**	**76.88**	**72.13**	**82.71**	**77.26**	**71.78**	**55.38**	**88.20**	**69.88**

4.3 Experimental Results

Evaluation of Experiments on Pairwise Constraints. Our method is compared with both unsupervised clustering algorithms and constrained clustering methods. Unsupervised algorithms include k-means [14], k-means on latent feature space obtained by SAE (SAE-KM), DEC [21] and IDEC [6]. Constrained clustering algorithms include flexible CSP [19], COP-$k$means [18], MPC-$k$means [2], SDEC [16] and FDCC [25].

For the purpose of simulating human-guided constraints, we construct constraints from existing labeled data sets. We pick a set of randomly selected pairwise samples from training set and generate must-link or cannot-link constraints according to their ground truth labels. The number of constraints N is set to 3600 on MNIST, Fashion and KMNIST that accounts for merely 0.0002% of the number of possible constraints C_n^2, and 1000 on USPS and Reuters10K that accounts for 0.0038% and 0.002% respectively. Besides, transitive constraints are also added to the known constraints. For instance, given must-link $(a, b), (a, c)$ and cannot-link (a, d), we can easily deduce addable constraint: must-link (b, c) and cannot-link $(b, d), (c, d)$. This conduction may cause an explosion of the constraint quantity when N is large, but can be ignored with a small amount of constraints.

The evaluation of ACC and NMI are reported in Table 1. As we can see, the performance of CDC outperforms the unsupervised algorithms with just minimal pairwise constraints. This shows that our algorithm of maintaining consistency with constraints has a positive effect on clustering. The constrained methods below are set with the same ratio of number of constraints as ours for fair comparison. The results show obvious improvement, especially on Fashion, KMNIST and Reuters10K, validating the superiority of CDC algorithm.

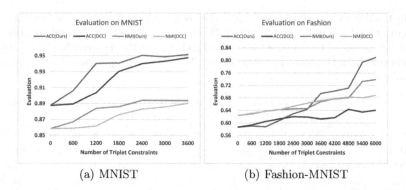

Fig. 4. Clustering ACC and NMI on MNIST and Fashion with different numbers of triplet constraints.

Evaluation of Experiments on Triplet Constraints. We evaluate the clustering performance of our method on triplet constraints by comparative experiment with FDCC [25] that put forwards triplet constraints first. To be comparable fairly with it, we introduce the same embedding space to compute Euclidean Metric among triples. Figure 4 plots the results of comparative experiment with different numbers of constraints. The results show clearly that the increase of constraint number reflects positive feedback in performance. On MNIST, minimal constraints bring about obvious improvement and then performance becomes stable, which means enough prior information has been captured. On Fashion-MNIST, the performance enhances continuously and leads to a sharp improvement in range [3000, 6000]. Comparing with FDCC, our method brings slight improvements on MNIST and obvious enhancement on Fashion-MNIST. The results validate the effectiveness of our algorithm for weak constraint information.

4.4   Parameter Analysis

We evaluate the performance with different settings of m in Eq. (9) by grid search in range $[0.3, 0.6]$. Figure 5 shows the parameter study results on Fashion-MNIST. Two interesting observations can be obtained: (1) The larger m produce better performance than a smaller one when given less constraints. (2) As the number of constraints increases, the results of larger m are not significantly improved or even decreased. The first observation can be explained that our objective tends to widen the difference in the similarity between positive and negative samples against the anchor, larger m enforces larger threshold to be broken down, which can promote the optimization when constraints are not enough. The second consequence occurs because our method learns enough information when more constraints are provided, a smaller m reduce the inefficiency of *imperfect triplet constraints*, which we illustrate in Sect. 3.3.

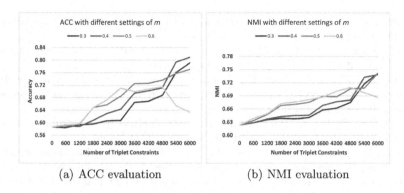

(a) ACC evaluation   (b) NMI evaluation

Fig. 5. The performance of our method across different settings of m on Fashion.

5 Conclusion

In this paper, we propose a Constrained Deep Clustering method (CDC) that aims to maintain consistency with constraints. The CDC method learns unsupervised information and constraint information in two consecutive modules. Effective objective function are proposed to maintain the consistency from two perspective simultaneously: embedding space distance and cluster assignments. Extensive experimental results on both pairwise and triplet constrained clustering validate the effectiveness of our method even if only minimal constraints are provided. Our future work will be explored from the perspective of exploring more complex similarity metric or addressing the imbalance of the constraints.

References

1. Basu, S., Banerjee, A., Mooney, R.J.: Active semi-supervision for pairwise constrained clustering. In: Proceedings of the 2004 SIAM, pp. 333–344 (2004)
2. Bilenko, M., Basu, S., Mooney, R.J.: Integrating constraints and metric learning in semi-supervised clustering. In: ICML, p. 11 (2004)
3. Chen, X., Duan, Y., Houthooft, R., Schulman, J., Sutskever, I., Abbeel, P.: Infogan: interpretable representation learning by information maximizing generative adversarial nets (2016)
4. Clanuwat, T., Bober-Irizar, M., Kitamoto, A., Lamb, A., Yamamoto, K., Ha, D.: Deep learning for classical japanese literature. arXiv preprint arXiv:1812.01718 (2018)
5. Dilokthanakul, N., et al.: Deep unsupervised clustering with gaussian mixture variational autoencoders. arXiv preprint arXiv:1611.02648 (2016)
6. Guo, X., Gao, L., Liu, X., Yin, J.: Improved deep embedded clustering with local structure preservation. In: IJCAI (2017)
7. Guo, X., et al.: Adaptive self-paced deep clustering with data augmentation. IEEE TKDE, p. 1 (2019)
8. Hsu, Y.C., Kira, Z.: Neural network-based clustering using pairwise constraints. CoRR abs/1511.06321 (2015)

9. Huang, Z., Zhou, J.T., Peng, X., Zhang, C., Lv, J.: Multi-view spectral clustering network. In: IJCAI (2019)
10. Ji, P., Zhang, T., Li, H., Salzmann, M., Reid, I.: Deep subspace clustering networks. In: NIPS (2017)
11. Jiang, Z., Zheng, Y., Tan, H., Tang, B., Zhou, H.: Variational deep embedding: an unsupervised and generative approach to clustering. arXiv preprint arXiv:1611.05148 (2016)
12. LeCun, Y., Bottou, L., Bengio, Y., Haffner, P.: Gradient-based learning applied to document recognition. Proc. IEEE **86**(11), 2278–2324 (1998)
13. Lewis, D.D., Yang, Y., Rose, T.G., Li, F.: Rcv1: a new benchmark collection for text categorization research. J. Mach. Learn. Res. **5**(4), 361–397 (2004)
14. MacQueen, J., et al.: Some methods for classification and analysis of multivariate observations. In: Proceedings of the Fifth Berkeley Symposium on Mathematical Statistics and Probability, vol. 1, pp. 281–297. Oakland, CA, USA (1967)
15. Mukherjee, S., Asnani, H., Lin, E., Kannan, S.: Clustergan: latent space clustering in generative adversarial networks. Proc. AAAI Conf. Artif. Intell. **33**, 4610–4617 (2019)
16. Ren, Y., Hu, K., Dai, X., Pan, L., Hoi, S.C., Xu, Z.: Semi-supervised deep embedded clustering. Neurocomputing **325**, 121–130 (2019)
17. Shaham, U., Stanton, K., Li, H., Nadler, B., Basri, R., Kluger, Y.: Spectralnet: spectral clustering using deep neural networks (2018)
18. Wagstaff, K., Cardie, C., Rogers, S., Schrödl, S., et al.: Constrained k-means clustering with background knowledge. ICML **1**, 577–584 (2001)
19. Wang, X., Davidson, I.: Flexible constrained spectral clustering. In: SIGKDD, pp. 563–572 (2010)
20. Xiao, H., Rasul, K., Vollgraf, R.: Fashion-mnist: a novel image dataset for benchmarking machine learning algorithms. arXiv preprint arXiv:1708.07747 (2017)
21. Xie, J., Girshick, R., Farhadi, A.: Unsupervised deep embedding for clustering analysis (2015)
22. Yang, B., Fu, X., Sidiropoulos, N.D., Hong, M.: Towards k-means-friendly spaces: simultaneous deep learning and clustering (2017)
23. Yang, J., Parikh, D., Batra, D.: Joint unsupervised learning of deep representations and image clusters. In: Proceedings of the IEEE Conference on Computer Vision and Pattern Recognition, pp. 5147–5156 (2016)
24. Yu, Y., Zhou, W.J.: Mixture of gans for clustering. In: IJCAI (2018)
25. Zhang, H., Basu, S., Davidson, I.: A framework for deep constrained clustering - algorithms and advances. In: Brefeld, U., Fromont, E., Hotho, A., Knobbe, A., Maathuis, M., Robardet, C. (eds.) ECML PKDD 2019. LNCS (LNAI), vol. 11906, pp. 57–72. Springer, Cham (2020). https://doi.org/10.1007/978-3-030-46150-8_4
26. Zhang, T., Ji, P., Harandi, M., Huang, W., Li, H.: Neural collaborative subspace clustering (2019)
27. Zhou, L., Xiao, B., Liu, X., Zhou, J., Hancock, E.R., et al.: Latent distribution preserving deep subspace clustering. In: IJCAI. York (2019)

Data Mining Theory and Principles

Towards Multi-label Feature Selection by Instance and Label Selections

Dou El Kefel Mansouri[1(✉)] and Khalid Benabdeslem[2]

[1] University Ibn Khaldoun, BP P 78 Zaâroura, 14000 Tiaret, Algeria
`douelkefel.mansouri@univ-tiaret.dz`
[2] University Lyon1, 43 Bd. du 11 Novembre, 69622 Villeurbanne, France
`khalid.benabdeslem@univ-lyon1.fr`

Abstract. In multi-label learning, feature and instance selection represent two effective dimensionality reduction techniques, which remove noise, irrelevant and redundant entries from original data for easy later analysis, such as clustering and classification. Label selection also plays a fundamental role in the pre-processing step since label-noises could negatively affect the performance of the underlying learning algorithms. The literature has been mainly limited to feature and/or instance selection, but has somewhat overlooked label selection. In this paper, we introduce, for the first time, a combination of the three selection techniques (feature, instance and label) for multi-label learning. We propose an efficient convex optimization based algorithm that evaluates the usefulness of features, instances and labels in order to select the most relevant ones, simultaneously. Experimental results on some known benchmark datasets are presented to demonstrate the performance of the proposed method.

Keywords: Multi-label learning · Feature selection · Instance selection · Label selection · Optimization

1 Introduction

In multi-label learning, data might be determined by multiple features and instances, and simultaneously associated with multiple labels. For example, in image annotation, images are usually represented by multiple features and, at the same time, associated with multiple semantic labels [13]. In text categorization, each document can be represented by a set of instances and is assigned to multiple categories [25, 30]. In bio informatics, a gene may have many functions, simultaneously [20].

Due to the curse of the large dimensionality of such data, which are only likely to grow further both in terms of the sample size as well as the number of classes, the performance of multi-label learning algorithms would be strongly influenced [17]. Hence, selecting the most meaningful features or instances become a crucial pre-processing steps for these algorithms [22]. In fact, feature selection (FS) aims

© Springer Nature Switzerland AG 2021
K. Karlapalem et al. (Eds.): PAKDD 2021, LNAI 12713, pp. 233–244, 2021.
https://doi.org/10.1007/978-3-030-75765-6_19

to select the most informative feature subsets from the original set, whereas instance selection (IS) is a procedure that reduces noise or outlier data points.

Many works have been carried out in this context, for example Huang *et al.* [12] proposed JFSC, a method which can perform joint feature selection and classification for multi-label learning . Zhang *et al.* [33] proposed MSFS, a multi-view multi-label sparse feature selection that exploits both label correlations and view relations for hierarchical multi-view multi-label feature selection. Jian *et al.* [15] introduced MIFS, a novel multi-label informed feature selection framework that exploits label correlations to select discriminative features across multiple labels. In [1], authors applied two new instance selection methods, based on the adaptation of single-label classification algorithms to multi-label learning: LSBo and LSSm. It should be noted that feature selection and instance selection are often addressed separately, while few works combine both tasks in single-label scenario [5,6,16,26], and to our knowledge no work has been proposed in multi-label scenario. In addition, all works cited evaluate the correlation between features and labels associated with for each instance in order to remove only unnecessary features or instances. Unfortunately, labeled data are often noisy and as it often exhibit dependencies, the performance of the underlying learning algorithms could be negatively affected [14]. For that reason, it seems evident that label selection step may greatly contribute to improving performance. To the best of our knowledge, the literature was mainly limited to feature and/or instance selection, but there is no work that directly selects the best labels from the original labelset, while considering feature and instance selection simultaneously.

In this paper, we propose a novel unified framework called mFILS that combines the three selection tasks (features, instances and labels) for multi-label learning. The framework is based on $l_{2,1}$-norm regularization which is performed to evaluate the usefulness of features, instances and labels in order to select the most relevant ones, simultaneously.

We summarize the technical contributions of this paper as follows:

1. We propose a novel framework mFILS for multi-label triple selection of features instances and labels, simultaneously.
2. We apply $l_{2,1}$-norm regularization to promote sparsity and remove irrelevant information.
3. We conduct experiments on some known benchmark datasets to validate our proposal with different scenarios.

2   Proposed Method: mFILS

In a multi-labeled dataset, we have n instances $\{\mathbf{x}_1, \mathbf{x}_2, ..., \mathbf{x}_n\}$ and k different labels $\{c_1, c_2, ..., c_k\}$. We assume that $\mathbf{X} = [\mathbf{x}_1, \mathbf{x}_2, ..., \mathbf{x}_n] \in \mathbb{R}^{n \times m}$ be the instance matrix and $\mathbf{Y} = [\mathbf{y}_1, \mathbf{y}_2, ..., \mathbf{y}_n] \in \{0, 1\}^{n \times k}$ be the label matrix. m and k represent the size of feature vectors and the number of class labels, respectively. $\mathbf{y}_i = [y_{i1}, y_{i2}, ..., y_{ik}] \in \{0, 1\}^k$ is a binary vector, where $y_{ij} = 1$ if $\mathbf{x}_i$ is associated with the label c_j and $y_{ij} = 0$, otherwise. The Frobenius norm of a matrix $\mathbf{X}$ is denoted as $\parallel \mathbf{X} \parallel_F = \sqrt{\sum_{i=1}^n \sum_{j=1}^m x_{ij}^2}$, and its $l_{2,1}$-norm is denoted as $\parallel \mathbf{X} \parallel_{2,1} = \sum_{i=1}^n \sqrt{\sum_{j=1}^m x_{ij}^2}$.

According to [10], the multi-labeled output space $\mathbf{Y}$ can be decomposed to a product of two low-dimensional nonnegative matrices $\mathbf{V}$ and $\mathbf{B}$. The nonnegative constraint is imposed on the decomposition phase since the latent semantic matrix obtained later will be more physically interpretable [7,18].

Let $\mathbf{V} \in \mathbb{R}^{n \times l}$ be the low-dimensional latent semantics matrix and $\mathbf{B} \in \mathbb{R}^{l \times k}$ be the coefficient matrix of latent semantics. Mathematically, the decomposition is done by minimizing the following reconstruction error:

$$\min_{\mathbf{V},\mathbf{B}} \parallel \mathbf{Y} - \mathbf{VB} \parallel_F^2 \tag{1}$$

In addition to the Eq. (1) that will guide the feature selection process, our goal is to select the most effective labels from the original label-set in order to reduce its size (matrix $\mathbf{Y}$) and facilitate the learning task. We use the coefficient matrix $\mathbf{B}$ to weight the labels. Thus, the Eq. (1) can be formulated as follows:

$$\min_{\mathbf{V},\mathbf{B}} \parallel \mathbf{Y} - \mathbf{VB} \parallel_F^2 + \delta \parallel \mathbf{B} \parallel_{2,1} \tag{2}$$

δ is a regularization parameter, used to control the sparsity of $\mathbf{B}$ and $\parallel \mathbf{B} \parallel_{2,1}$ is the $l_{2,1}$-norm of $\mathbf{B}$. Then, we employ the Eq. (3) to ensure that local geometry structures are consistent between the input space $\mathbf{X}$ and the reduced low-dimensional semantics $\mathbf{V}$. To be specific, if two instances are close to each other in $\mathbf{X}$, they should also show the similar characteristic in $\mathbf{V}$.

$$\frac{1}{2} \sum_{i=1}^n \sum_{j=1}^n \mathbf{S}_{ij} (\mathbf{V}_{i:} - \mathbf{V}_{j:})^2 = Tr(\mathbf{V}^T (\mathbf{Z} - \mathbf{S})\mathbf{V}) = Tr(\mathbf{V}^T \mathbf{LV}) \tag{3}$$

where $\mathbf{S}_{ij}$ denotes the similarity matrix. $\mathbf{V}_i$ is the latent semantics of $\mathbf{y}_i$. $\mathbf{Z}$ is a diagonal matrix with $\mathbf{Z}_{ii} = \sum_{j=1}^n \mathbf{S}_{ij}$. $\mathbf{L} = \mathbf{Z} - \mathbf{S}$ is the graph laplacian matrix. We model the affinity graph $\mathbf{S}$ by Eq. (4) according to [4],

$$\mathbf{S}_{ij} = \begin{cases} e^{-\frac{\parallel \mathbf{x}_i - \mathbf{x}_j \parallel^2}{\xi^2}} & \text{if } \mathbf{x}_i \in N_p(x_j) \text{ or } \mathbf{x}_j \in N_p(x_i) \\ 0 & otherwise, \end{cases} \tag{4}$$

where $N_p(\mathbf{x})$ denotes the p-nearest neighbors of instance $\mathbf{x}$. By integrating the local geometric structure of the data, the Eq. (2) becomes:

$$\min_{\mathbf{V},\mathbf{B}} \parallel \mathbf{Y} - \mathbf{VB} \parallel_F^2 + \alpha Tr(\mathbf{V}^T \mathbf{LV}) + \delta \parallel \mathbf{B} \parallel_{2,1} \tag{5}$$

where α represents a regularization parameter, used to control local geometry structures.

Our second main goal in this paper is to incorporate instance selection with feature and label selection. Therefore, we evaluate the usefulness of the features, instances and labels at the same time and we select the most relevant ones simultaneously.

First, feature selection term based on $l_{2,1}$-norm regularization can be given by Eq. (6) [21]. Note that the latent semantics matrix $\mathbf{V}$ replaces $\mathbf{Y}$ since it is more able to reflect the label information.

$$\min_{\mathbf{W}} \| \mathbf{XW} - \mathbf{V} \|_F^2 + \lambda \| \mathbf{W} \|_{2,1} \tag{6}$$

where $\mathbf{W} \in \mathbb{R}^{m \times l}$ and $\| \mathbf{W} \|_{2,1}$ are the feature coefficient matrix and the $l_{2,1}$-norm of $\mathbf{W}$, respectively. λ is a regularization parameter, used to control the sparsity of $\mathbf{W}$.

Afterwards, we incorporate a new unknown variable $\mathbf{A}$ into the Eq. (6) for weighting the instances, in addition to $\mathbf{W}$ (associated with features). This new variable is a strong indicator of anomalies in a dataset [27].

Let $\mathbf{A} = \mathbf{W}^T \mathbf{X}^T - \mathbf{V}^T - \mathbf{E}$, be a residual matrix where $\mathbf{E}$ is a random matrix, generally assumed to be a multi-dimensional normal distribution [27]. Each column of $\mathbf{A}$ corresponds to a data instance, and a large norm of $\mathbf{A}(:, i)$ indicates an important deviation of the ith data instance, potentially to be an irrelevant instance [26]. Therefore, the residual matrix $\mathbf{A}$ can be used to realize instance selection.

Note that the residual matrix idea is inspired by the works in [24,27].

By incorporating the instance selection, the Eq. (6) becomes:

$$\min_{\mathbf{W},\mathbf{A}} \| \mathbf{XW} - \mathbf{A}^T - \mathbf{V} \|_F^2 + \lambda \| \mathbf{W} \|_{2,1} + \gamma \| \mathbf{A} \|_{2,1} \tag{7}$$

$\| \mathbf{A} \|_{2,1}$ is the $l_{2,1}$-norm of $\mathbf{A}$, and γ is introduced to control the sparsity of $\mathbf{A}$.

Based on the different aforementioned equations, the objective function of mFILS can be finally defined as follows (Eq. (8)):

$$\min_{\mathbf{W},\mathbf{A},\mathbf{V},\mathbf{B}} \| \mathbf{XW} - \mathbf{A}^T - \mathbf{V} \|_F^2 + \alpha Tr(\mathbf{V}^T \mathbf{LV}) + \beta \| \mathbf{Y} - \mathbf{VB} \|_F^2$$
$$+ \lambda \| \mathbf{W} \|_{2,1} + \gamma \| \mathbf{A} \|_{2,1} + \delta \| \mathbf{B} \|_{2,1} \tag{8}$$

where β is used to balance the contribution of feature learning and label decomposition.

Our mFILS framework is now suitable for the simultaneous triple selection of features instances and labels.

Since the objective function of mFILS is not convex with respect to $\mathbf{W}$, $\mathbf{A}$, $\mathbf{V}$ and $\mathbf{B}$, jointly, and not smooth due to the $l_{2,1}$-norm regularization term, it is therefore difficult to resolve it. To settle this problem, we rely on the work of Nie et $al.$ [21]. We relax the terms $\| \mathbf{W} \|_{2,1}$, $\| \mathbf{A} \|_{2,1}$ and $\| \mathbf{B} \|_{2,1}$ by $2Tr(\mathbf{W}^T \mathbf{DW})$, $2Tr(\mathbf{ATA}^T)$ and $2Tr(\mathbf{B}^T \mathbf{JB})$, respectively. $\mathbf{D}$, $\mathbf{T}$ and $\mathbf{J}$ are a diagonal matrices with its diagonal elements $dd_{jj} = \frac{1}{2\|\mathbf{W}(j,:)\|_2}$, $tt_{ii} = \frac{1}{2\|\mathbf{A}^T(:,i)\|_2}$ and $jj_{ll} = \frac{1}{2\|\mathbf{B}(:,l)\|_2}$ respectively.

Thus, we can rewrite the objective function shown in Eq. (8) as follows:

$$\min_{\mathbf{W},\mathbf{A},\mathbf{V},\mathbf{B}} \| \mathbf{XW} - \mathbf{A}^T - \mathbf{V} \|_F^2 + \alpha Tr(\mathbf{V}^T \mathbf{LV}) + \beta \| \mathbf{Y} - \mathbf{VB} \|_F^2$$
$$+ 2\lambda Tr(\mathbf{W}^T \mathbf{DW}) + 2\gamma Tr(\mathbf{ATA}^T) + 2\delta Tr(\mathbf{B}^T \mathbf{JB}) \tag{9}$$

For minimizing Eq. (9), we adopt an alternating optimization over $\mathbf{W}$, $\mathbf{A}$, $\mathbf{V}$ and $\mathbf{B}$, by solving the following problems:

Problem 1: *Derivative w.r.t $\mathbf{W}$* by fixing $\mathbf{A}$, $\mathbf{V}$ and $\mathbf{B}$ to find the solution for $\mathbf{W}$ (for feature selection). The optimization problem for updating $\mathbf{W}$ becomes:

$$\min_{\mathbf{W}} \| \mathbf{XW} - \mathbf{A}^T - \mathbf{V} \|_F^2 + 2\lambda Tr(\mathbf{W}^T \mathbf{DW}) \tag{10}$$

The derivative w.r.t $\mathbf{W}$ is given as:

$$\frac{\partial \mathcal{L}}{\partial \mathbf{W}} = 2[\mathbf{X}^T(\mathbf{XW}) - \mathbf{X}^T(\mathbf{A}^T + \mathbf{V}) + \lambda \mathbf{DW}]. \tag{11}$$

Problem 2: *Derivative w.r.t $\mathbf{A}$* by fixing $\mathbf{W}$, $\mathbf{V}$ and $\mathbf{B}$ to find the solution for $\mathbf{A}$ (for instance selection). The optimization problem for updating $\mathbf{A}$ becomes:

$$\min_{\mathbf{A}} \| \mathbf{XW} - \mathbf{A}^T - \mathbf{V} \|_F^2 + 2\gamma Tr(\mathbf{ATA}^T) \tag{12}$$

The derivative w.r.t $\mathbf{A}$ is given as:

$$\frac{\partial \mathcal{L}}{\partial \mathbf{A}} = 2[\mathbf{A}^T - (\mathbf{XW} - \mathbf{V}) + \gamma \mathbf{TA}^T]. \tag{13}$$

Problem 3: *Derivative w.r.t $\mathbf{V}$* by fixing $\mathbf{W}$, $\mathbf{A}$ and $\mathbf{B}$ to find the solution for $\mathbf{V}$ (for latent label space). The optimization problem for updating $\mathbf{V}$ becomes:

$$\min_{\mathbf{V}} \| \mathbf{XW} - \mathbf{A}^T - \mathbf{V} \|_F^2 + \alpha Tr(\mathbf{V}^T \mathbf{LV}) + \beta \| \mathbf{Y} - \mathbf{VB} \|_F^2 \tag{14}$$

The derivative w.r.t $\mathbf{V}$ is given as:

$$\frac{\partial \mathcal{L}}{\partial \mathbf{V}} = 2[(\mathbf{A}^T + \mathbf{V} - \mathbf{XW}) + \alpha \mathbf{LV} + \beta(\mathbf{VB} - \mathbf{Y})\mathbf{B}^T]. \tag{15}$$

Problem 4: *Derivative w.r.t $\mathbf{B}$* by fixing $\mathbf{W}$, $\mathbf{A}$ and $\mathbf{V}$ to find the solution for $\mathbf{B}$ (for label selection). The optimization problem for updating $\mathbf{B}$ becomes:

$$\min_{\mathbf{B}} \beta \| \mathbf{Y} - \mathbf{VB} \|_F^2 + 2\delta Tr(\mathbf{B}^T \mathbf{JB}) \tag{16}$$

The derivative w.r.t $\mathbf{B}$ is given as:

$$\frac{\partial \mathcal{L}}{\partial \mathbf{B}} = 2[\beta \mathbf{V}^T(\mathbf{VB} - \mathbf{Y}) + \delta \mathbf{JB}]. \tag{17}$$

To ensure the nonnegative constraints of matrices $\mathbf{V}$ and $\mathbf{B}$, we use the projected gradient descent method [19] to project the updated solution of the gradient descent to a bounded region. Depending on these, the update rule of the alternating algorithm for mFILS can be summarized as follows:

$$\begin{cases} \mathbf{W} := \mathbf{W} - \phi_W \frac{\partial \mathcal{L}}{\partial \mathbf{W}} \\[2mm] \mathbf{A} := \mathbf{A} - \phi_A (\frac{\partial \mathcal{L}}{\partial \mathbf{A}})^T \\[2mm] \mathbf{V} := P[\mathbf{V} - \phi_V \frac{\partial \mathcal{L}}{\partial \mathbf{V}}] \\[2mm] \mathbf{B} := P[\mathbf{B} - \phi_B \frac{\partial \mathcal{L}}{\partial \mathbf{B}}] \end{cases} \tag{18}$$

where $P[\mathbf{H}]$ represents a box projection operator that maps the update $\mathbf{H}$ to a bounded region in order to ensure the nonnegativity:

$$P[\mathbf{H}]_{ij} = \begin{cases} \mathbf{H}_{ij} & \text{if } \mathbf{H}_{ij} \geq 0 \\ 0 & otherwise, \end{cases} \tag{19}$$

and ϕ_W, ϕ_A, ϕ_V and ϕ_B are stepsizes for the different rules in Eq. (18). It is crucial to choose suitable stepsizes for the gradient descent update rules in Eq. (18), to accelerate the convergence rate and to reduce the running time of mFILS. In this paper, we employ Armijo rule [15] to adaptively determine stepsizes ϕ_W, ϕ_A, ϕ_V and ϕ_B in each iteration. We summarize all the above mathematical developments on Algorithm (1).

Algorithm 1. mFILS

Input: Data matrix $\mathbf{X} \in \mathbb{R}^{n \times m}$; Label matrix $\mathbf{Y} \in \{0,1\}^{n \times k}$; Parameters: $\alpha, \beta, \lambda, \gamma, \delta, \xi$.
Output: Top ranked features, instances and labels.
1: Initialize $\mathbf{W}$, $\mathbf{V}$ and $\mathbf{B}$ randomly ($\mathbf{V}$ and $\mathbf{B}$ are initialized to be nonnegative);
2: Initialize $\mathbf{A}$ to zero-matrix; initialize $\mathbf{D}$, $\mathbf{T}$ and $\mathbf{J}$ as identity matrices;
3: **repeat**
4: determine step sizes ϕ_W, ϕ_A, ϕ_V and ϕ_B with Armijo rule;
5: Update the matrices $\mathbf{W}$, $\mathbf{A}$, $\mathbf{V}$ and $\mathbf{B}$ according to Eq. 18)
6: Update the matrices $\mathbf{D}$, $\mathbf{T}$ and $\mathbf{J}$ as $dd_{jj} = \frac{1}{2\|\mathbf{W}(j,:)\|_2}$, $tt_{ii} = \frac{1}{2\|\mathbf{A}^T(:,i)\|_2}$, $jj_{ll} = \frac{1}{2\|\mathbf{B}(:,l)\|_2}$, respectively.
7: **until** Convergence
8: Rank the features according to $\| \mathbf{W}(j,:) \|_2$ in descending order ($j = 1..m$).
9: Rank the instances according to $\| \mathbf{A}(:,i) \|_2$ in ascending order ($i = 1..n$).
10: Rank the labels according to $\| \mathbf{B}(:,l) \|_2$ in descending order ($l = 1..k$).

---

3   Experiments

3.1   Datasets and Compared Methods

Experiments are performed on six benchmark datasets, including: birds [3], CAL500 [29], enron [11], genbase [8], medical [23] and scene [2], to validate the performance of mFILS. All datasets are available in MULAN Project[1].

As long as there is no method that makes the triple and simultaneous selection of instances, features and labels in multi-label setting, we compare our mFILS with the six competitive state-of-the-art feature selection/extraction methods for multi-label classification, including: Fisher Score (F-score) [9], CoSelect [26], Robust Feature Selection (RFS) [21], Multilabel Dimensionality Reduction via Dependence Maximization (MDDM) [32], Multi-label Informed Feature Selection (MIFS) [15] and (MDFS) Embedded multi-label feature selection technique with manifold regularization [31].

3.2   Experimental Setting

The necessary parameters for implementing mFILS include $\alpha, \beta, \lambda, \gamma$ and δ. We use a grid search strategy to adjust these parameters from $\{10^{-3}, 10^{-2}, 10^{-1}, 1, 10, 10^2\}$. To model the local geometric structures, ξ and p are set to 1 and 5, respectively. Five-fold cross-validation is performed to split of training and testing sets. The number of selected features is varied from 5% to 30% of the total number of features. As for the numbers of selected instances and labels, we set them at 70% and 30%, respectively. The performance of the selected feature, instance and label subsets were evaluated using Binary Relevance (BR) with Ridge classifier [28]. We employ four evaluation metrics widely used in multi-label learning for comparison, including: Area Under the Receiver Operating Characteristic curve metric (AUC), Macro-average, Micro-average and Hamming loss [28]. Note that, the higher the AUC, Macro-Average, and Micro-Average values are, the better the classification performance is. For Hamming loss, a lower value indicates a better classification performance.

3.3   Results

In this section, we present and discuss the obtained results. We evaluate mFILS by incorporating the instance and label selections into the feature selection process. As a reminder, the numbers of selected instances and labels are set at 70% and 30%, respectively. Table 1 and Figs. (1, 2, 3) show the results of the classification performance comparison of mFILS in terms of AUC, Macro-average, Micro-average and Hamming on six aforementioned datasets. We can make the following observations.

- In terms of average rank, across all datasets and with different numbers of selected features, our mFILS ranks first followed by MIFS. It means that the

---

[1]   http://mulan.sourceforge.net/datasets.html.

idea of decomposing the label information into a low-dimensional semantic space places mFILS and MIFS in the foreground. The superior performance of mFILS compared to MIFS is explained by the fact of modifying the feature selection term in Eq. (6) and the latent semantics term of multi-label information in Eq. (1), by adding the functions of instance and label importance (see Eq. (8)).

– In terms of most evaluation metrics, and on at least five out of six of datasets, mFILS consistently outperforms other methods. Some degradation in performance are reported with "scene" dataset where mFILS is ranked second after CoSelect.

In summary, in view of the very favorable results of the mFILS method, we can safely conclude that our framework is competitive with the other compared methods.

Table 1. Performance comparison in terms of AUC of different methods on six datasets. The last row illustrates the average ranking of each method. The best results are bold face.

Datasets	F-score	CoSelect	RFS	MDDM	MIFS	MDFS	mFILS
Birds	78.95 ±0.00	58.31 ±0.03	79.13 ±0.01	77.19 ±0.01	80.46 ±0.02	68.41 ±0.01	**81.89 ±0.00**
CAL500	80.51 ±0.00	50.19 ±0.09	80.56 ±0.00	80.81 ±0.00	80.36 ±0.00	59.00 ±0.07	**81.12 ±0.00**
Enron	84.73 ±0.02	78.75 ±0.06	83.57 ±0.01	83.79 ±0.01	86.01 ±0.00	61.08 ±0.02	**87.99 ±0.00**
Genbase	87.72 ±0.02	81.84 ±0.03	90.42 ±0.00	48.55 ±0.23	90.36 ±0.03	93.07 ±0.09	**94.24 ±0.04**
Medical	89.80 ±0.00	74.01 ±0.05	81.30 ±0.02	77.60 ±0.07	90.50 ±0.00	84.95 ±0.03	**91.94 ±0.02**
Scene	68.55 ±0.08	**92.43 ±0.03**	86.87 ±0.00	71.55 ±0.05	88.92 ±0.04	83.33 ±0.01	90.10 ±0.03
Average rank	4.33	5.66	3.83	5	3	5	**1.16**

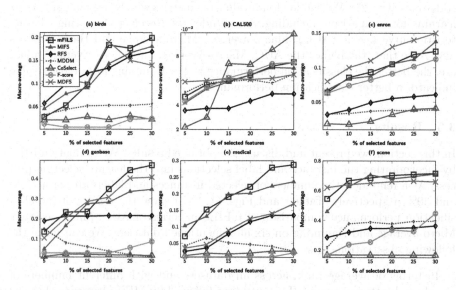

Fig. 1. Macro-average ($\nearrow$) v.s. percentage of selected features.

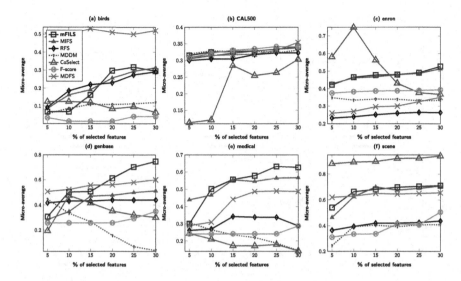

Fig. 2. Micro-average ($\nearrow$) v.s. percentage of selected features.

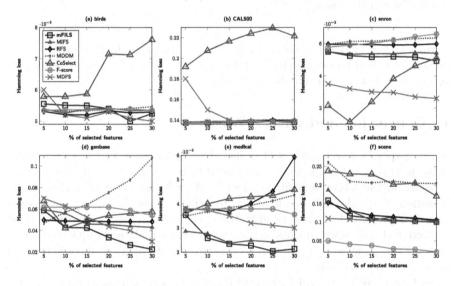

Fig. 3. Hamming loss ($\searrow$) v.s. percentage of selected features.

In the following, we study the impact of changing the number of selected labels on the performance of our proposed method. We vary the number of selected labels from 20% to 100% of the total number of labels, and we set the number of selected features and instances at 30% and 70%, respectively. Recall that in previous experiments, we varied the number of selected features from 5% to 30% of the total number of features and set the number of selected instances and labels to 70% and 30%, respectively. Based on Fig. 4, we can conclude that

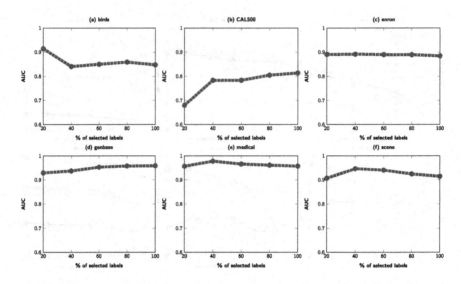

Fig. 4. Impact of label selection on the performance of mFILS with 30% of best features and 70% of best instances.

as the number of selected labels increases, the corresponding accuracy of our proposed method keeps practically stable. i.e., we can easily achieve better performance with a reduced number of labels.

4   Conclusion and Future Works

In this paper, a novel method that includes the instance and label selections in the feature selection process, called mFILS, has been proposed. The method is based on the latent semantics principle of multi-labels and $l_{2,1}$-norm regularization. With the help of these two principles, noise, irrelevant and redundant data presented at the level of features, instances or labels are considerably reduced. Extensive experiments on different benchmark datasets up to date show that, mFILS achieves significant and competitive performance compared to other state-of-the-art methods.

In future works, we will extend mFILS to consider regression problems. We will also consider the triple selection with multi-view data that can help handle noisy and partial data for single-view triple selection.

References

1. Arnaiz-González, Á., Díez-Pastor, J.F., Rodríguez, J.J., García-Osorio, C.: Local sets for multi-label instance selection. Appl. Soft Comput. **68**, 651–666 (2018)
2. Boutell, M.R., Luo, J., Shen, X., Brown, C.M.: Learning multi-label scene classification. Pattern Recogn. **37**(9), 1757–1771 (2004)

3. Briggs, F., et al.: Acoustic classification of multiple simultaneous bird species: a multi-instance multi-label approach. J. Acoust. Soc. Am. **131**(6), 4640–4650 (2012)
4. Cai, D., Zhang, C., He, X.: Unsupervised feature selection for multi-cluster data. In: Proceedings of the 16th ACM SIGKDD International Conference on Knowledge Discovery and Data Mining, pp. 333–342 (2010)
5. Derrac, J., García, S., Herrera, F.: Ifs-coco: instance and feature selection based on cooperative coevolution with nearest neighbor rule. Pattern Recogn. **43**(6), 2082–2105 (2010)
6. Derrac, J., Triguero, I., García, S., Herrera, F.: Integrating instance selection, instance weighting, and feature weighting for nearest neighbor classifiers by coevolutionary algorithms. IEEE Trans. Syst. Man Cybern. Part B (Cybern.) **42**(5), 1383–1397 (2012)
7. Ding, C., Li, T., Peng, W., Park, H.: Orthogonal nonnegative matrix t-factorizations for clustering. In: Proceedings of the 12th ACM SIGKDD International Conference on Knowledge Discovery and Data Mining, pp. 126–135 (2006)
8. Diplaris, S., Tsoumakas, G., Mitkas, P.A., Vlahavas, I.: Protein classification with multiple algorithms. In: Bozanis, P., Houstis, E.N. (eds.) PCI 2005. LNCS, vol. 3746, pp. 448–456. Springer, Heidelberg (2005). https://doi.org/10.1007/11573036_42
9. Duda, R.O., Hart, P.E., Stork, D.G.: Pattern Classification. Wiley, New Jersey (2012)
10. Dumais, S.T.: Latent semantic analysis. Ann. Rev. Inform. Sci. Technol. **38**(1), 188–230 (2004)
11. Goldstein, J., Kwasinksi, A., Kingsbury, P., Sabin, R.E., McDowell, A.: Annotating subsets of the enron email corpus. In: CEAS (2006)
12. Huang, J., Li, G., Huang, Q., Wu, X.: Joint feature selection and classification for multilabel learning. IEEE Trans. Cybern. **48**(3), 876–889 (2017)
13. Huang, S.J., Gao, W., Zhou, Z.H.: Fast multi-instance multi-label learning. In: Twenty-Eighth AAAI Conference on Artificial Intelligence (2014)
14. Jian, L., Li, J., Liu, H.: Exploiting multilabel information for noise-resilient feature selection. ACM Trans. Intell. Syst. Technol. (TIST) **9**(5), 1–23 (2018)
15. Jian, L., Li, J., Shu, K., Liu, H.: Multi-label informed feature selection. In: IJCAI, pp. 1627–1633 (2016)
16. Kuncheva, L.I., Jain, L.C.: Nearest neighbor classifier: simultaneous editing and feature selection. Pattern Recogn. Lett. **20**(11–13), 1149–1156 (1999)
17. Lapin, M., Hein, M., Schiele, B.: Analysis and optimization of loss functions for multiclass, top-k, and multilabel classification. IEEE Trans. Pattern Anal. Mach. Intell. **40**(7), 1533–1554 (2017)
18. Lee, D.D., Seung, H.S.: Algorithms for non-negative matrix factorization. In: Advances in Neural Information Processing Systems, pp. 556–562 (2001)
19. Lin, C.J.: Projected gradient methods for nonnegative matrix factorization. Neural Comput. **19**(10), 2756–2779 (2007)
20. Lin, Y., Hu, Q., Liu, J., Duan, J.: Multi-label feature selection based on max-dependency and min-redundancy. Neurocomputing **168**, 92–103 (2015)
21. Nie, F., Huang, H., Cai, X., Ding, C.H.: Efficient and robust feature selection via joint $l2$, 1-norms minimization. In: Advances in Neural Information Processing Systems, pp. 1813–1821 (2010)
22. Paniri, M., Dowlatshahi, M.B., Nezamabadi-pour, H.: Mlaco: A multi-label feature selection algorithm based on ant colony optimization. Knowl.-Based Syst. **192**, 105285 (2020)

23. Pestian, J., et al.: A shared task involving multi-label classification of clinical free text. In: Biological, Translational, and Clinical Language Processing, pp. 97–104 (2007)
24. She, Y., Owen, A.B.: Outlier detection using nonconvex penalized regression. J. Am. Stat. Assoc. **106**(494), 626–639 (2011)
25. Shen, X., Liu, W., Tsang, I.W., Sun, Q.S., Ong, Y.S.: Multilabel prediction via cross-view search. IEEE Trans. Neural Netw. Learn. Syst. **29**(9), 4324–4338 (2017)
26. Tang, J., Liu, H.: Coselect: feature selection with instance selection for social media data. In: Proceedings of the 2013 SIAM International Conference on Data Mining, pp. 695–703. SIAM (2013)
27. Tong, H., Lin, C.Y.: Non-negative residual matrix factorization with application to graph anomaly detection. In: Proceedings of the 2011 SIAM International Conference on Data Mining, pp. 143–153. SIAM (2011)
28. Tsoumakas, G., Katakis, I.: Multi-label classification: an overview. Int. J. Data Warehouse. Min. (IJDWM) **3**(3), 1–13 (2007)
29. Turnbull, D., Barrington, L., Torres, D., Lanckriet, G.: Semantic annotation and retrieval of music and sound effects. IEEE Trans. Audio Speech Lang. Process. **16**(2), 467–476 (2008)
30. Yang, S.H., Zha, H., Hu, B.G.: Dirichlet-bernoulli alignment: a generative model for multi-class multi-label multi-instance corpora. In: Advances in Neural Information Processing Systems, pp. 2143–2150 (2009)
31. Zhang, J., Luo, Z., Li, C., Zhou, C., Li, S.: Manifold regularized discriminative feature selection for multi-label learning. Pattern Recogn. **95**, 136–150 (2019)
32. Zhang, Y., Zhou, Z.H.: Multilabel dimensionality reduction via dependence maximization. ACM Trans. Knowl. Discovery Data (TKDD) **4**(3), 1–21 (2010)
33. Zhang, Y., Wu, J., Cai, Z., Philip, S.Y.: Multi-view multi-label learning with sparse feature selection for image annotation. IEEE Trans. Multimedia **22**(11), 2844–2857 (2020)

FARF: A Fair and Adaptive Random Forests Classifier

Wenbin Zhang[1]([✉]), Albert Bifet[2,3], Xiangliang Zhang[4], Jeremy C. Weiss[5], and Wolfgang Nejdl[6]

[1] University of Maryland, Baltimore County, MD 21250, USA
wenbinzhang@umbc.edu
[2] University of Waikato, Hamilton 3216, New Zealand
abifet@waikato.ac.nz
[3] Télécom Paris, Institut Polytechnique de Paris, Palaiseau 91764, France
[4] King Abdullah University of Science and Technology, Thuwal 23955, Saudi Arabia
xiangliang.zhang@kaust.edu.sa
[5] Carnegie Mellon University, Pittsburgh, PA 15213, USA
jeremyweiss@cmu.edu
[6] L3S Research Center and Leibniz University Hannover, 30167 Hannover, Germany
nejdl@L3S.de

Abstract. As Artificial Intelligence (AI) is used in more applications, the need to consider and mitigate biases from the learned models has followed. Most works in developing fair learning algorithms focus on the offline setting. However, in many real-world applications data comes in an online fashion and needs to be processed on the fly. Moreover, in practical application, there is a trade-off between accuracy and fairness that needs to be accounted for, but current methods often have multiple hyper-parameters with non-trivial interaction to achieve fairness. In this paper, we propose a flexible ensemble algorithm for fair decision-making in the more challenging context of evolving online settings. This algorithm, called FARF (Fair and Adaptive Random Forests), is based on using online component classifiers and updating them according to the current distribution, that also accounts for fairness and a single hyper-parameters that alters fairness-accuracy balance. Experiments on real-world discriminated data streams demonstrate the utility of FARF.

1 Introduction

AI-based decision-making systems are routinely being used across a wide plethora of online (e.g., the targeting of products, the setting of insurance rates) as well as offline services (e.g., the issuing of mortgage approval, the allocation of health resource). As AI becomes integrated into more systems, various AI-based discriminatory incidents have also been observed and reported [3,18,24].

A large number of methods have been proposed to address this issue, ranging from discrimination discovery to discrimination elimination and interpretation in order to provide ethical and accurate decisions [28,30]. These studies have

© Springer Nature Switzerland AG 2021
K. Karlapalem et al. (Eds.): PAKDD 2021, LNAI 12713, pp. 245–256, 2021.
https://doi.org/10.1007/978-3-030-75765-6_20

typically adopted one or more of the three following strategies: i) *Pre-processing solutions* aim to eliminate discrimination at the data level, including the most popular ones massaging [21] and reweighting [9]. ii) *In-processing approaches* mitigate bias by modifying the algorithm design [4,22]. As a recent example, the Bayesian probabilistic modeling is leveraged to account for fairness [15]. iii) *Post-processing techniques* consist of a-posteriori adjusting the output of the model [18,19]. For instance, the decision boundary for the protected group is shifted based on the theory of margins for boosting [14].

However, most of these methods tackle fairness as a static problem, i.e., that all the data is available at training time. This does not satisfy situations that may require online learning due to a continuously drifting data distribution, or can not computationally afford to process all of their data in memory [29]. There is very little work in the area of online learning that includes any definition of fairness as a goal of the method [20,27]. Our work seeks to fill this void.

Current methods also lack a mechanism for easily adjusting the trade-off that exists between accuracy and fairness [23]. For instance, the "business necessity" clause [2] states that a certain degree of disparate impact discrimination can be allowed for the sake of meeting certain performance-related business constrains, on the condition that such decision-making causes the least disparate impact when fulfilling the current business needs. If an initial model fails to meet the discrimination or accuracy requirement for practical use, we would prefer there exist a single parameter with a direct and predictable impact on this trade-off. However, current studies solely focus on preserving prediction performance while minimizing discrimination, and do not allow for fine-grained control between fairness and accuracy [3,30].

To overcome these issues we propose FARF, an online statistical parity aware Random Forest (RF) model. Like prior online RF algorithms, it is built from a sampling approach for the ensemble creation. In creating this fair variant of RF, we develop a number of contributions: i) We study a new research direction of fairness-aware learning considering concept and fairness drift. We then propose FARF, a fairness-aware and fairness-updated ensemble method to tackle online fairness. ii) We study another research direction of fairness-aware learning with customized control, and design a clear mechanism for fine-grained fairness control, providing more flexibility than state of the art. iii) We theoretically analyze the inadequacy of current sampling approaches in fairness studies and introduce a new effective sampling direction with experimental verification. iv) Extensive experimental evaluation on real-world datasets demonstrates the capability of the proposed model in online settings.

2   Problem Definition

An online stream D consists of a sequence of instances arriving over time, potentially infinite. One instance x_t at time step t in D is described in a feature space $A = \{A_1, ..., A_n\}$ within respective domains $dom(A_i)$ and its class label C_t. An online classifier is trained incrementally by taking instances up to time t to predict C_{t+1} for the unlabeled instance arriving at time step $t + 1$. Once C_{t+1} is predicted, the actual class label of x_{t+1} becomes available and can be used for model update, known as prequential evaluation [16].

We assume one of the attributes A is a special attribute S, referred to as *sensitive attribute* (e.g., gender) with a special value $s \in dom(S)$ referred to as *sensitive value* (e.g., female), from which the discriminated group is defined. For simplicity, we consider binary classification tasks assuming $dom(C) \in \{+, -\}$ and S also is binary with $dom(S) \in \{p, u\}$ (i.e., protected and unprotected respectively). Four fairness related groups can therefore be distinguished combining S and C. These groups are p^+, p^- and u^+, u^- representing protected group (e.g., female) receiving positive and negative classification and unprotected group (e.g., male) receiving positive and negative classification, respectively.

Although more than twenty notions have been proposed to measure the discriminative behavior of AI models [26], formalizing fairness is a hard topic per se, and there is no consensus which measure is more versatile than others [3]. In addition, what constitutes "fair" or "discriminative" is dependent on many factors and context, as well as philosophical questions that have been researched long before the AI communities' interest [7]. In this work, we adopt the *statistical parity* because American user studies have found that it is a measure compatible with many users' intuition of what constitutes a "fair" decision [25], expecting a wide spectrum of applications of our method. Briefly, statistical parity examines whether the probability of being granted for a positive benefit (e.g., the provision of health care) is the same for both protected and unprotected groups. While statistical parity is designed for offline fairness, the discriminative behavior of the AI model up to time t in the online setting, which we term as *accumulated statistical parity*, can be analogically defined as:

$$Disc(D_t) = \frac{u_t^+}{u_t^+ + u_t^-} - \frac{p_t^+}{p_t^+ + p_t^-} \tag{1}$$

where u_t^+, u_t^-, p_t^+ and p_t^+ are up to time t the number of individuals from respective groups.

People from the protected group can claim they are discriminated up to time t when more of them are rejected a benefit comparing to the people of the unprotected group. The aim of online fairness-aware learning is therefore to provide real time accurate but also fair predictions from the massive data streams, where D needs to be processed on the fly without the need for storage and reprocessing, and data distribution including $Disc(D_t)$ could also evolve over time.

3   The Fair and Adaptive Random Forests

Ensemble learning combines multiple base learners to generate more robust descriptions. Three common strategies are bagging, boosting and random forests. Specific to online learning, there are multiple versions of bagging and boosting that are part of the state of the art ensemble methods for evolving online learning [6,11], while random forests for non-stationary data stream are currently represented by [1,17], which also show random forests approaches have a superior performance comparing to bagging and boosting methods. One possible reason is that training on sampled data and selected features for splitting generalize more than adding more random weights to instances by bagging and adding weights to incorrectly classified instances by boosting. In this paper, we follow the idea of online random forests [1,17] as a powerful tool to increase the generalization and fairness when constructing an ensemble of classifiers.

Specifically, the proposed Fair and Adaptive Random Forests (FARF) is an adaptation of the classical random forest algorithm [8], and can also be viewed as an updated and fairness-aware version of the previous attempts to perform this adaptation [1,17]. In comparison to these attempts, FARF proposes a theoretically sound and fairness-oriented sampling (Sect. 3.2), an updated adaptive strategy (Sect. 3.3) as well as employing a fairness-aware base learner also for ensemble diversity (Sect. 3.1) to cope with discriminatory evolving data streams collectively. The following subsections elaborate these three improvements one by one.

3.1   Diversified Fairness-Aware Base Learner

Most of the existing online ensemble approaches [1,17] induce their base learners based on the Hoeffding Tree (HT) algorithm [13], which exploits the fact that an optimal splitting attribute can be determined by a small sample and the learned model is asymptotically nearly identical to that of a conventional non-incremental learner. However, such induction is based on the *information gain (IG)* aiming to optimize for predictive performance and does not account for fairness. In our previous work [27], the *fair information gain (FIG)* is proposed as an alternative tree splitting criterion to address the discrimination issue of *IG*, formally put,

$$FIG(D, A) = \begin{cases} IG(D, A), & \text{if } FG(D, A) = 0 \\ IG(D, A) \times FG(D, A), & \text{otherwise} \end{cases} \tag{2}$$

where *fairness gain (FG)* measures the discrimination difference due to the splitting and is formulated as:

$$FG(D, A) = |Disc(D)| - \sum_{v \in dom(A)} |Disc(D_v)| \tag{3}$$

where D is the collection of instances and A represents the attribute that under evaluation, $D_v, v \in dom(A)$ are the partitions induced by A, and the resultant discrimination value is assessed according to Eq. (1). In FIG, multiplication is favoured, when combining IG and FG as a conjunctive objective, over other operations for example addition as the values of these two metrics could be in different scales, and in order to promote fair splitting which results in a reduction in the discrimination after split, i.e., FG is a positive value.

In FARF, other than the discrimination reduction merit similar to the previous fairness-driven IG reformulation efforts [22,27], such splitting criterion also detects local discrimination to increase diversity for the sake of maximizing the accumulated fairness. Specifically, each partition induced by the attribute A contributes equally to the accumulated fairness of A regardless the number and size of branches. In the context of ensemble learning, diversity of the each individual classifier plays a key role. Increasing diversity by eyeing on local discrimination, i.e., identifying certain attribute values with a high discrimination rate but small in representation size, could therefore induce diversified base classifiers, reflecting different discrimination representation and improving the final ensemble capability. Such emphasis can also be regarded as selecting those attributes that otherwise would not be used for splitting thus adding more randomization for the construction of the tree.

This diversified fairness-aware learner therefore learns different attribute value level discrimination during the tree construction to maximize the accumulated fairness, and is used as the base learner of FARF. To align with such diversity-promoting strategy, different from the base learner of the previous ensemble approaches [1,17], FARF also does not perform early tree pruning for its base learners, and a random subset of fair features are selected for new split attempts to further encourage diversity.

3.2 Fairness-Aware Sampling

In batch random forests, each base classifier is trained on a bootstrap of the entire training set. However, such bootstrap replicates sampling strategy is infeasible in online setting as each training instance needs to be processed once "on arrival" without reprocessing. Oza et al. [6] simulate the construction of bootstrap replicates in online context by sending K copies of each training instance to update the base classifier accordingly, where K is a suitable Poisson random variable. Considering the arbitrary length of online stream, we follow [6] that found setting

$$K = Poisson(6) \tag{4}$$

to have the best accuracy by increasing diversity of the base learners. Others have consistently found this approach effective in accuracy and computing requirements [17]. Then the latest arriving instances can be classified by voting of the base learners, the same way in online and batch random forests. We will propose two different methods of altering the sampling of K to encourage fair tree induction.

Sampling techniques have been studied in recent fairness-aware learning approaches to alleviate discrimination [4,19]. In these studies, they exclusively concentrate on **over-sampling the protected positive group** through different heuristics. However, we argue that such interventions are insufficient especially in online setting for two reasons. First, the protected positive group is normally the under-represented minority. Solely focusing on sparse representation might not have significant bias mitigation effect. Such ineffectiveness is further exacerbated in online setting as instances from the protected positive group could discontinue for a certain period of time. Second, over-sampling protected positive group in random forest can be regarded as **minority over-sampling with replacement**. Previous research has noted that it does not significantly improve minority class recognition [10]. We interpret the underlying effect in terms of spreading the decision regions of protected positive group to mitigate biases. Essentially, as protected positive group is over-sampled by increasing amounts, the effect is to learn qualitatively similar but more specific regions that overfit the protected positive group rather than spreading its decision boundary into the unprotected positive group region.

Therefore, instead of over-sampling protected positive group, our ensemble learning method **under-samples the unprotected positive group** to mitigate the discrimination. We design the update rule for instance weight for sampling as:

$$fairK(x_t) = \begin{cases} Disc(D_t) * K, \text{if } x_t \in u^+ \& Disc(D_t) > 0 \\ K, \qquad\qquad\quad \text{otherwise} \end{cases} \tag{5}$$

where $Disc(D_t)$ measures the accumulated discrimination up to the current instance at time t in the stream and K is the Poisson weight defined in Eq. (4). When the current accumulated discrimination is positive ($Disc(D_t) > 0$), i.e., protected group has been discriminated, and the current instance is a member of unprotected positive group, the sampling weight $fairK(x_t)$ is down-scaled for the current instance x_t, making it to be $Disc(D_t)$ proportional of Poisson weight K. When there is no membership discrimination against the protected group or the current instance belongs to unprotected group, $fairK(x_t)$ is equivalent to the Poisson weight K. This allows our models to learn a more effective decision surface for the unprotected group, while avoiding prior shortcomings to sampling based fairness.

Other than exclusively focusing on over-sampling the protected positive group, the previous fair sampling studies also require additional neighborhood information through KNN [4] and clustering [19]. On the contrary, sampling in our work is directly defined in terms of the targeting discrimination. While enjoying simplicity, this also opens the door to flexible control on the degree of fairness. Specifically, we present a second method of altering the sampling ratio K that allows the user to control a trade off between model accuracy and fairness by manually customizing the re-scaling ratio in $fairK$ to manage the trade-off. This is done with a fixed under-sampling weight α that is incorporated into an alternative equation $customK$ as:

$$customK(x_t) = \begin{cases} \alpha * K, & \text{if } x_t \in u^+ \\ K, & \text{otherwise} \end{cases} \tag{6}$$

where α is the tunable parameter adjusting the sampling ratio. Note that like $fairK$, the under-sampling only occurs for positive instances of the unprotected group. Such flexible control on the degree of fairness instantiates application-wise fairness-aware learning to accommodate scenarios such as the "business necessity" clause [2].

3.3   FARF Algorithm

Online fairness additionally requires learning algorithms process each instance upon arrival as well as dealing with non-stationary data distribution indicating concept drifts and fairness implications. That is to say, the relationship between sensitive attribute and class variable might also change over time. A stream classifier pays attention to the boundary evolution but ignores fairness drift. To this end, FARF encapsulates the capability of fairness drift detection and adaptation as well as standby trees and weighted voting to address online fairness comprehensively.

Ensemble learning has been used as a powerful tool by resetting under-performing base learners to adapt to change quickly. The conventional approach resets base learners the moment a drift is detected [6]. However, such reseting could be ineffective since the reseted learner cannot have a positive impact on the ensemble process as it has not been well trained. To this end, FARF employs a more permissive threshold to detect potential drifts and builds standby trees for ensemble members who detect such drifts. The standby trees are trained along the ensemble without intervening the ensemble prediction, and appear on the stage when they outperform their respective ensemble members.

The ensemble design of FARF also offers space for different change detectors being incorporated. One possible detector is ADWIN [5], which recomputes online whether two "large enough" subwindows of the most recent data exhibit "distinct enough" averages, and the older portion of the data is dropped when such distinction is detected. Different from the previous non-stationary studies [11,17], FARF employs ADWIN to detect changes in accuracy but also fairness, reflecting both concept and fairness drifts. That is to say drift is detected when either of them evolves.

FARF also weights the prediction of each base learner in proportion to their prequential evaluation [16] fairness since its last reset, reflecting the tree performance on the current fairness distribution. Such weighting scheme enjoys the merit of free of predefined window or fading factor to estimate fairness as in other stream ensembles [1,17] (their estimation focus is accuracy to reflect concept drift though). Note that FARF prioritizes fairness over accuracy by weighting and replacing ensemble members according to fairness. Algorithm 1 shows the sketch of FARF.

For each new instance (line 2), FARF first decides its weight according to fairness-aware sampling based on its fairness information and the accumulated discrimination up to the current instance (line 5–7). When customizable fairness is deployed, the weight is set according to customized sampling ratio (line 3–4). FARF then trains each ensemble member (line 9) with this weight (line 10). When a change is detected (line 11) in one ensemble member who does not have a standby tree (line 12), a respective standby tree is created (line 13), otherwise performances between the ensemble member and its respective standby tree are compared (line 15) to decide ensemble membership replacement if needed (line 16). All standby trees are also trained along the ensemble (line 21–22). The weighted vote can be performed at anytime to predict the class of an instance

---

Algorithm 1: FARF Leaning Algorithm

Input: a discriminated data stream D, the number of base models M, optional sampling ratio α

1 Init base models h_m for all m $\in \{1, 2, ..., M\}$
2 **for** *each instance x_t in D* **do**
3 $\quad$ **if** α *specified* **then**
4 $\quad\quad$ | $\quad w_t \leftarrow customK(x_t)$ according to Equation (6);
5 $\quad$ **else**
6 $\quad\quad$ | $\quad$ Calculate $Disc(D_t)$ according to Equation (1);
7 $\quad\quad$ | $\quad w_t \leftarrow fairK(x_t)$ according to Equation (5);
8 $\quad$ **end**
9 $\quad$ **for** *m= 1, 2, ..., M* **do**
10 $\quad\quad$ Update h_m with x_t with weight w_t;
11 $\quad\quad$ **if** *ADWIN detects a change in fairness or accuracy in h_m* **then**
12 $\quad\quad\quad$ **if** *standby learner $h'_m = \emptyset$* **then**
13 $\quad\quad\quad\quad$ | Build a new diversified fair standby learner h'_m;
14 $\quad\quad\quad$ **else**
15 $\quad\quad\quad\quad$ **if** $|Disc(h_m)| > |Disc(h'_m)|$ **then**
16 $\quad\quad\quad\quad\quad$ | Replace h_m with h'_m;
17 $\quad\quad\quad\quad$ **end**
18 $\quad\quad\quad$ **end**
19 $\quad\quad$ **end**
20 $\quad$ **end**
21 $\quad$ **for** *all h'_m* **do**
22 $\quad\quad$ | Update h'_m with x_t with weight w_t;
23 $\quad$ **end**
24 **end**
25 **anytime output:** $h(x_t) = argmax_{c \in C} \sum_{m=1}^{M} W(h_m(x_t) = \mu_m(c))$

(line 25). Note that the replacement and voting could also be performed from the accuracy perspective, i.e., replacing the ensemble member when its error is higher and weighted vote on accuracy instead. FARF does fairness replacement and voting in order to prioritize fairness at these steps.

4   Experimental Evaluation

In the case of static datasets and evaluation, accepted benchmarks for evaluating fairness mitigating approaches are limited in number [3]. With respect to the highly under-explored online fairness, this challenge is further magnified by the drift and the demanding requirement of the number of instances contained therein. We evaluate our approach on the datasets used in the recent works of this research direction [20,27], the *Adult* and the *Census* datasets [12] both targeting the learning task of determining whether a person earns more than 50K dollars per annum. We follow the same options in our experiments for fair comparison including the selection of sensitive attribute "gender" with female being the sensitive value and processing them in sequence. One difference is that instead of randomizing the order, we order the datasets by the "race" attribute for both datasets to better simulate concept drift and possibly increase the learning bias. The previous discussed prequential evaluation is employed for evaluation.

4.1 Benchmark Performance

This section first investigates the theoretically designed fairness-aware and fairness-updated capabilities of FARF. For comparison, we implemented two recently proposed fair online learners, FEI [20] and FAHT [27]. While the paper of FEI did not compare with any baselines, FAHT studied two. We compare with these two baselines therein as well, namely the Hoeffding Tree (HT) and KHT in which the fairness-aware splitting criterion proposed in [22] is embedded into HT. We also trained the state of the art concept-adapting ensemble learner ARF [17] as another baseline. Other competing fairness methods, including recent proposed fairness ensemble methods which require multiple full data scan, are not considered as none of them can be transferred to online settings. All methods are trained the same way for fair comparison. Relevant results on all datasets are shown in Table 1. Note that since accuracy can be misleading for imbalanced class distributions, we also report Kappa statistics [16].

Table 1. The predictive performance-vs-discrimination between FARF and baseline models. Best results in **bold**, second best in *italics*.

Metric Methods	Adult dataset			Census dataset		
	Disc%	Acc%	Kappa%	Disc%	Acc%	Kappa%
HT	24.14	82.16	68.15	6.61	93.11	87.54
KHT	24.24	82.43	67.2	6.74	93.26	87.12
FAHT	*17.20*	81.62	70.48	*3.63*	93.06	88.14
ARF	24.17	**84.51**	**78.15**	6.64	*94.18*	**90.41**
FEI	23.06	74.27	54.27	6.64	80.06	84.27
FARF	**8.89**	*84.19*	*77.54*	**0.07**	**94.83**	*90.33*

As shown in Table 1 our new FARF method dominates all other baselines in terms of minimizing discrimination, and is best of second-best by both Accuracy and Kappa scores in all other cases. We note that when second best FARF is still highly competitive, being at most 0.78% within the top performer. This is a desirable trade-off since FARF reduced the discrimination score by a factor of 1.9× and 51.8× for Adult and Census dataset, respectively.

4.2 Accuracy-Fairness Control

The design of FARF provides a clear mechanism to manage the trade-off between fairness and accuracy. This can be necessary when an initial model does not meet one of these requirements, allowing the end-user to make adjustments. FARF controls thus with the α parameter. As α is in proportion to accuracy, increasing its value leads to a higher accuracy at the expense of a higher discrimination. Such expected trend is clear from the results visualized in Fig. 1. Clients can therefore accommodate their needs according to their respective constraints.

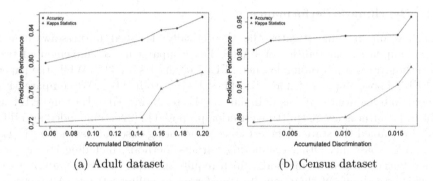

(a) Adult dataset   (b) Census dataset

Fig. 1. The predictive performance and accumulated discrimination trade-off fine grained by the tunable parameter α ranging from 0.3 to 1.5 with step size 0.3.

The x-axis of the above figure is with respect to the amount of discrimination that is present (larger values indicate more discrimination), and the y-axis is the predictive accuracy (larger is more accurate). With respect to both accuracy and Kappa scores we see a monotonic behavior with respect to the α parameter. This means it behaves as we desire: a simple and direct relationship controlling the trade-off between accuracy and statistical parity. This makes it easy to use, compared to most methods that have multiple parameters that all need to be adjusted to achieve a satisficing trade-off [23].

4.3   Justification of Sampling Component in FARF

Recent fairness-aware learning approaches employ sampling techniques to mitigate bias, which exclusively focus on over-sampling protected positive group through different heuristics. We theoretically discussed the drawbacks of these methods (c.f., Sect. 3.2). This section provides experimental justification and verifies our choice to instead under sample the protected positive group and that it is critical to our results. We perform two ablations to confirm this by replacing our sampling with: 1) over-sampling protected positive group, and 2) over-sampling protected positive group and under-sampling unprotected positive group. All other components of our approach remain the same so that we can isolate our sampling approach as the critical factor in results. These two types of ensemble are denoted as **FARFS⁻** and **FARFS⁻⁺** respectively in comparison with **RF**, which refers to random forests without sampling intervention, and our proposed FARF. The results are shown in Table 2.

Table 2. The predictive performance-vs-discrimination comparison between different sampling strategies. Best results in **bold** second best in *italics*.

Metric / Methods	Adult dataset			Census dataset		
	Disc%	Acc%	Kappa%	Dis%	Acc%	Kappa%
RF	16.32	**84.31**	**78.05**	1.34	*94.13*	**90.37**
FARFS^-	19.36	83.26	73.47	1.10	94.17	90.24
FARFS^{-+}	*10.53*	81.64	72.49	*0.45*	93.95	89.15
FARF	**8.89**	*84.19*	*77.54*	**0.07**	**94.83**	*90.33*

As can be seen FARF is the only method that consistently obtains accuracy near that of an unconstrained Random Forest. At the same time, neither approach is able to reach discrimination rates as low as FARF. This shows that over-sampling approaches of prior fairness studies are not as effective as our under-sampling based approach.

5 Conclusions

Our work has proposed the first online version of Random Forests with fairness constraints. Our design includes a mechanism for altering the trade off between accuracy and fairness so that users can adjust it easily toward their specific applications. In doing so we have show positive results compared to alternative methods available, without compromising on the desirable properties of online Random Forests.

References

1. Abdulsalam, H., Skillicorn, D.B., Martin, P.: Classifying evolving data streams using dynamic streaming random forests. In: Bhowmick, S.S., Küng, J., Wagner, R. (eds.) DEXA 2008. LNCS, vol. 5181, pp. 643–651. Springer, Heidelberg (2008). https://doi.org/10.1007/978-3-540-85654-2_54
2. Barocas, S., Selbst, A.D.: Big data's disparate impact. Calif. Law Rev. **104**(3), 671 (2016)
3. Beutel, A. et al.: Putting fairness principles into practice: challenges, metrics, and improvements. In: AIES (2019)
4. Bhaskaruni, D., Hu, H., Lan, C.: Improving prediction fairness via model ensemble. In: ICTAI, pp. 1810–1814 (2019)
5. Bifet, A., Gavalda, R.: Learning from time-changing data with adaptive windowing. In: SDM, pp. 443–448 (2007)
6. Bifet, A., Holmes, G., Pfahringer, B.: Leveraging bagging for evolving data streams. In: Balcázar, J.L., Bonchi, F., Gionis, A., Sebag, M. (eds.) ECML PKDD 2010. LNCS (LNAI), vol. 6321, pp. 135–150. Springer, Heidelberg (2010). https://doi.org/10.1007/978-3-642-15880-3_15
7. Binns, R.: Fairness in machine learning: Lessons from political philosophy. In Conference on Fairness, Accountability and Transparency, pp. 149–159 (2018)

8. Breiman, L.: Random forests. Mach. Learn. **45**(1), 5–32 (2001)
9. Calders, T., Kamiran, F., Pechenizkiy, M.: Building classifiers with independency constraints. In: ICDMW, pp. 13–18 (2009)
10. Chawla, N.V., Bowyer, K.W., Hall, L.O., Kegelmeyer, W.P.: Smote: synthetic minority over-sampling technique. JAIR **16**, 321–357 (2002)
11. Chen, S.-T., Lin, H.-T., Lu, C.-J.: An online boosting algorithm with theoretical justifications. In: ICML, pp. 1873–1880 (2012)
12. Dheeru, D., Karra Taniskidou, E.: UCI machine learning repository (2017)
13. Domingos, P., Hulten, G.: Mining high-speed data streams. In: KDD, pp. 71–80. ACM (2000)
14. Fish, B., Kun, J., Lelkes, Á.D.: A confidence-based approach for balancing fairness and accuracy. In: SDM, pp. 144–152 (2016)
15. Foulds, J.R., Islam, R., Keya, K.N., Pan, S.: Bayesian modeling of intersectional fairness: the variance of bias. In: SDM, pp. 424–432 (2020)
16. Gama, J.: Knowledge discovery from data streams. Chapman and Hall/CRC, Boca Raton (2010)
17. Gomes, H.M., et al.: Adaptive random forests for evolving data stream classification. Mach. Learn. **106**(9), 1469–1495 (2017). https://doi.org/10.1007/s10994-017-5642-8
18. Hardt, M., Price, E., Srebro, N., et al.: Equality of opportunity in supervised learning. In: Advances in Neural Information Processing Systems, pp. 3315–3323 (2016)
19. Iosifidis, V., Fetahu, B., Ntoutsi, E.: Fae: a fairness-aware ensemble framework. In: IEEE International Conference on Big Data (Big Data), pp. 1375–1380 (2019)
20. Iosifidis, V., Tran, T.N.H., Ntoutsi, E.: Fairness-enhancing interventions in stream classification. In: Hartmann, S., Küng, J., Chakravarthy, S., Anderst-Kotsis, G., Tjoa, A.M., Khalil, I. (eds.) DEXA 2019. LNCS, vol. 11706, pp. 261–276. Springer, Cham (2019). https://doi.org/10.1007/978-3-030-27615-7_20
21. Kamiran, F., Calders, T.: Classifying without discriminating. In: 2nd International Conference on Computer, Control and Communication, pp. 1–6 (2009)
22. Kamiran, F., Calders, T., Pechenizkiy, M.: Discrimination aware decision tree learning. In: ICDM, pp. 869–874 (2010)
23. Kleinberg, J., Mullainathan, S., Raghavan, M.: Inherent trade-offs in the fair determination of risk scores. In: FAT ML Workshop (2016)
24. Meyer, D.: Amazon reportedly killed an AI recruitment system because it couldn't stop the tool from discriminating against women. fortune (10 October 2018)
25. Srivastava, M., Heidari, H., Krause, A.: Mathematical notions vs. human perception of fairness: a descriptive approach to fairness for machine learning. In: KDD, pp. 2459–2468 (2019)
26. Verma, S., Rubin, J.: Fairness definitions explained. In: 2018 IEEE/ACM International Workshop on Software Fairness (FairWare), pp. 1–7. IEEE (2018)
27. Zhang, W., Ntoutsi, E.: Faht: an adaptive fairness-aware decision tree classifier. In: IJCAI, pp. 1480–1486 (2019)
28. Zhang, W., Tang, X., Wang, J.: On fairness-aware learning for non-discriminative decision-making. In: ICDMW, pp. 1072–1079. IEEE (2019)
29. Zhang, W., Wang, J.: A hybrid learning framework for imbalanced stream classification. In: 2017 IEEE International Congress on Big Data (BigData Congress), pp. 480–487. IEEE (2017)
30. Zliobaite, I.: A survey on measuring indirect discrimination in machine learning. arXiv preprint arXiv:1511.00148 (2015)

Sparse Spectrum Gaussian Process for Bayesian Optimization

Ang Yang$^{(\boxtimes)}$, Cheng Li, Santu Rana, Sunil Gupta, and Svetha Venkatesh

Deakin University, Geelong, Australia

Abstract. We propose a novel sparse spectrum approximation of Gaussian process (GP) tailored for Bayesian optimization (BO). Whilst the current sparse spectrum methods provide desired approximations for regression problems, it is observed that this particular form of sparse approximations generates an overconfident GP, i.e., it produces less epistemic uncertainty than the original GP. Since the balance between the predictive mean and variance is the key determinant to the success of BO, the current methods are less suitable for BO. We derive a new regularized marginal likelihood for finding the optimal frequencies to fix this overconfidence issue, particularly for BO. The regularizer trades off the accuracy in the model fitting with targeted increase in the predictive variance of the resultant GP. Specifically, we use the entropy of the global maximum distribution (GMD) from the posterior GP as the regularizer that needs to be maximized. Since the GMD cannot be calculated analytically, we first propose a Thompson sampling based approach and then a more efficient sequential Monte Carlo based approach to estimate it. Later, we also show that the Expected Improvement acquisition function can be used as a proxy for it, thus making the process further efficient.

1 Introduction

Bayesian optimization (BO) is a leading method for global optimization for expensive black-box functions [1–3]. It is widely used in hyperparameter tuning of massive neural networks [4], some of which can take days to train. It has also been used for optimization of physical products and processes [5] where one experiment can cost days, and experiments can also be expensive in terms of material cost. However, there could be scenarios when a large number of observations is available from priors or during the experiments. For example, in transfer learning, where many algorithms [6,7] pool existing observations from source tasks together for use in the optimization of a target task. Then even though the target function is expensive, the number of observations can be large if the number of source tasks is large and/or the number of observations from each source is large. Another scenario where we may have a large number of observations is when we deal with optimization of objective functions which are not very costly. For example, consider the cases when BO is performed using simulation software. They are often used in the early stage of a product design

© Springer Nature Switzerland AG 2021
K. Karlapalem et al. (Eds.): PAKDD 2021, LNAI 12713, pp. 257–268, 2021.
https://doi.org/10.1007/978-3-030-75765-6_21

process to reduce a massive search space to a manageable one before real products are made. Whilst evaluation, a few thousands may be feasible, but millions are not because each evaluation can still take from several minutes to hours. We term this problem as a semi-expensive optimization problem. Such a problem cannot be handled by the traditional global optimizers which often require more than thousands of evaluations. Bayesian optimization will also struggle, because its main ingredient, Gaussian process (GP) does not scale well beyond few hundreds of observations. In this paper, we address the scalability issue of GP for BO in such scenarios where a large number of observations appear naturally.

The scalability issue for Bayesian optimization has been previously addressed in two main ways: 1) by replacing GP with a more scalable Bayesian model, *e.g.* using Bayesian neural network [8] or random forest [9], or 2) by making sparse approximation of the full GP. The latter is often desirable as it still maintains the principled Bayesian formalism of GP. There are many sparse models in the literature, such as fully independent training conditional (FITC) [10,11] which induces pseudo inputs to approximate the full GP, and variational approximation (VFE) [12] which learns inducing inputs and hyperparameters by minimizing the KL divergence between the true posterior GP and an approximate one. Another line of work involves approximating a stationary kernel function using a sparse set of frequencies in its spectrum domain representation, e.g., sparse spectrum Gaussian process (SSGP) [13]. These methods suffer from either variance underestimation (i.e. overconfidence) [10,13] or overestimation [12] and thus may hamper BO as the balance between predictive mean and variance is important to the success of BO. Recently, [14] has proposed variational Fourier features (VFF), which combines variational approximation and spectral representation of GP together and plausibly can approximate both mean and variance well. However, it is difficult to extend VFF to multiple dimensional problems, since a) the number of inducing variables grows exponentially with dimensions if the Kronecker kernel is used, or b) the correlation between dimensions would be ignored if an additive kernel is used. We also note that there has been a push to scale GP inference to millions of data points using modern hardware [15]. However, it remains computationally demanding and vulnerable to kernel matrix ill-conditioning, thus infeasible for practical use.

In this paper, we aim to develop a sparse GP model tailored for Bayesian optimization. The main intuition that drives our solutions is that while being overconfident at some regions is not very critical to BO when those regions have both low predictive value and low predictive variance. However, being overconfident in the regions where either predictive mean or predictive variance is high would be quite detrimental to BO. Hence, a targeted fixing may be enough to make the sparse models suitable for BO. An overall measure of goodness of GP approximation for BO would be to look at the global maximum distribution (GMD) [16,17] from the posterior GP and check its difference to that of the full GP. Fixing overconfidence in the important regions may be enough to make the GMD of the sparse GP closer to that of the full GP. The base method in our work (SSGP) is known to underestimate variance, which is why we need maximizing the entropy of GMD. Following this idea, we add entropy of the GMD as a new regularizer that is to be maximized in conjunction with the marginal likelihood so the optimal sparse set of the frequencies are not only benefit for model fitting, but also fixes the overconfidence issue from the perspectives of the Bayesian optimization.

We first provide a Thompson sampling approach to estimate the maximum distribution for the sparse GP, and then propose a more efficient sequential Monte Carlo based approach. The latter approach provides efficiency as many Monte Carlo samples can be reused during the optimization for the optimal frequencies. Later, we empirically show that expected improvement acquisition function can be used as a proxy of the maximum distribution, significantly improving the computational efficiency. We demonstrate our method on two synthetic functions and two real world problems, one involving alloy design using a thermodynamic simulator and another involving hyperparameter optimization in a transfer learning setting. In all the experiments our method provides superior convergence rate over standard sparse spectrum methods. Additionally, our methods also performs better than the full GP when the covariance matrix faces ill-conditioning due to large number of observations placed close to each other.

2 Background

We consider the maximization problem $x^* = \text{argmax}_{x \in \mathcal{X}} f(x)$, where $f : x \rightarrow \mathbb{R}$, $\mathcal{X}$ is a compact subspace in $\mathbb{R}^d$, and x^* is the global maximizer.

2.1 Bayesian Optimization

Bayesian optimization includes two main components. It first uses a probabilistic model, typically a GP, to model the latent function and then constructs an acquisition function that determines the next sample point.

Gaussian process [18] provides a distribution over the space of functions and it can be specified by a mean function $\mu(x)$ and a covariance function $k(x, x')$. A sample from a GP is a function $f(x) \sim \mathcal{GP}(\mu(x), k(x, x'))$. Without loss of generality, we often assume that the prior mean function is zero function and thus GP can be fully defined by $k(x, x')$. The squared exponential kernel and the Matérn kernel are popular choices of k.

In GP, the joint distribution for any finite set of random variables are multivariate Gaussian distribution. Given a set of noisy observations $\mathcal{D}_t = \{x_i, y_i\}_{i=1}^t$, where $y_i = f_i + \varepsilon_i$ with $\varepsilon_i \sim \mathcal{N}(0, \sigma_n^2)$, the predictive distribution of y_{t+1} in GP follows a normal distribution $p(f_{t+1} | \mathcal{D}_t, x_{t+1}) = \mathcal{N}(\mu(x_{t+1}), \sigma^2(x_{t+1}))$ with $\mu(x_{t+1}) = \mathbf{k}^T [\mathbf{K} + \sigma_n^2 \mathbf{I}]^{-1} Y$ and $\sigma^2(x_{t+1}) = k(x_{t+1}, x_{t+1}) - \mathbf{k}^T [\mathbf{K} + \sigma_n^2 \mathbf{I}]^{-1} \mathbf{k}$, where $\mathbf{k} = [k(x_{t+1}, x_1), \cdots, k(x_{t+1}, x_t)]$, $\mathbf{K}$ is the Gram matrix, and $Y = \{y_i\}_{i=1}^t$.

The posterior computation of GP involves the inversion of the Gram matrix and it is very costly for a large number of observations. Sparse approximation is the usual way to reduce the computational cost with slight reduction in modeling accuracy. We focus on the SSGP for optimization purpose due to its simplification and scalability, details of which is discussed in the following subsection.

Once the GP has been built to model the latent function, we can construct acquisition functions by combining the predictive mean and variance of the posterior GP to find the next query. Some popular acquisition functions include Expected Improvement (EI) [1], and GP-UCB [19]. We use EI function since it can work well without human efforts.

2.2 Sparse Spectrum Gaussian Process

Sparse Gaussian process often introduce inducing points to approximate the posterior mean and variance of full GP whilst sparse spectrum Gaussian process uses optimal spectrum frequencies to approximate the kernel function. Briefly, according to the Bochner's theorem [20], any stationary covariance function can be represented as the Fourier transform of some finite measure $\sigma_f^2 p(\mathbf{s})$ with $p(\mathbf{s})$ a probability density as

$$k(\boldsymbol{x}_i, \boldsymbol{x}_j) = \int_{\mathbb{R}^D} e^{2\pi i \mathbf{s}^T(\boldsymbol{x}_i - \boldsymbol{x}_j)} \sigma_f^2 p(\mathbf{s}) d\mathbf{s}, \tag{1}$$

where the frequency vector $\mathbf{s}$ has the same length D as the input vector $\boldsymbol{x}$. In other words, a spectral density entirely determines the properties of a stationary kernel. Furthermore, Eq. (1) can be computed and approximated as

$$k(\boldsymbol{x}_i, \boldsymbol{x}_j) = \sigma_f^2 \mathbb{E}_{p(\mathbf{s})} \left[e^{2\pi i \mathbf{s}^T \boldsymbol{x}_i} (e^{2\pi i \mathbf{s}^T \boldsymbol{x}_j})^* \right] \simeq \frac{\sigma_f^2}{m} \sum_{r=1}^{m} \cos \left[2\pi \mathbf{s}_r^T (\boldsymbol{x}_i - \boldsymbol{x}_j) \right] \tag{2}$$

$$= \frac{\sigma_f^2}{m} \phi(\boldsymbol{x}_i)^T \phi(\boldsymbol{x}_j). \tag{3}$$

The Eq. (2) can be obtained by Monte Carlo approximation with symmetric sets $\{\mathbf{s}_r, -\mathbf{s}_r\}_{r=1}^{m}$ sampled from $\mathbf{s}_r \sim p(\mathbf{s})$, where m is the number of spectral frequencies (Fourier features). Equation (3) holds with the setting

$$\phi(\boldsymbol{x}) = [\cos(2\pi \mathbf{s}_1^T \boldsymbol{x}), \sin(2\pi \mathbf{s}_1^T \boldsymbol{x}), \cdots, \cos(2\pi \mathbf{s}_m^T \boldsymbol{x}), \sin(2\pi \mathbf{s}_m^T \boldsymbol{x})]^T, \tag{4}$$

which is a column vector of length $2m$ containing the evaluation of the m pairs of trigonometric functions at $\boldsymbol{x}$. The posterior mean and variance are derived as

$$\mu(\boldsymbol{x}_{t+1}) = \phi(\boldsymbol{x}_{t+1})^T \mathbf{A}^{-1} \boldsymbol{\Phi} \boldsymbol{Y}, \quad \sigma^2(\boldsymbol{x}_{t+1}) = \sigma_n^2 + \sigma_n^2 \phi(\boldsymbol{x}_{t+1})^T \mathbf{A}^{-1} \phi(\boldsymbol{x}_{t+1}), \tag{5}$$

where $\boldsymbol{\Phi} = [\phi(\boldsymbol{x}_1), \dots, \phi(\boldsymbol{x}_t)] \in \mathbb{R}^{2m \times t}$ and $\mathbf{A} = \boldsymbol{\Phi}\boldsymbol{\Phi}^T + \frac{m\sigma_n^2}{\sigma_f^2} \mathbf{I}_{2m}$. We maximize the log marginal likelihood $\log p(\boldsymbol{Y}|\Theta) =$

$$-\frac{1}{2\sigma_n^2}[\boldsymbol{Y}^T \boldsymbol{Y} - \boldsymbol{Y}^T \boldsymbol{\Phi}^T \mathbf{A}^{-1} \boldsymbol{\Phi} \boldsymbol{Y}] - \frac{1}{2}\log|\mathbf{A}| + m\log\frac{m\sigma_n^2}{\sigma_f^2} - \frac{t}{2}\log 2\pi\sigma_n^2 \tag{6}$$

to select the optimal frequencies, where Θ is the set of all hyperparameters in the kernel function and the frequencies. By using m optimal frequencies to approximate the full GP, SSGP holds the computational complexity $\mathcal{O}(tm^2)$, and provides computational efficiency if $m \ll t$.

3   Bayesian Optimization Using Regularized Sparse Spectrum Gaussian process

The naive SSGP can be directly used for Bayesian optimization by replacing the full GP. However, it leads to overconfidence on the GMD of interest in BO. We illustrate the overconfidence of SSGP in Fig. 1a and b, where we compared the GMD of SSGP to that of full GP and found the GMD of SSGP (the lower graph of 1b) is narrower and sharper than that of full GP (the lower graph of 1a).

To overcome this overconfidence on GMD, we propose a novel sparse spectrum Gaussian process model tailoring for BO. Our approach involves maximizing a new loss function to select the optimal spectrum frequencies. We design the loss function to include the marginal likelihood in the SSGP and a regularization term, which has the goal of minimizing the difference between the GMD of the full GP and that of the proposed sparse spectrum model. We denote our proposed model as the regularized SSGP (RSSGP). For the sake of convenience, we denote the GMD of the full GP as $p(x^*)$ and that of RSSGP as $q(x^*)$.

We first discuss the choice for our regularizer. Whilst the KL divergence $D_{KL}(q \| p)$ seems to be the solution to measure difference between two distributions, it is not feasible in our cases as we cannot access $p(x^*)$. Nevertheless, the property that the SSGP tends to be over-fitting implies that the entropy of the GMD in SSGP would be smaller than that of the full GP. Therefore, we can use the entropy of $q(x^*)$, or $\mathbb{H}[q(x^*)]$ as the regularization term in the loss function that needs to be maximized. In this way, the resultant sparse GP would minimize the difference between $q(x^*)$ and $p(x^*)$. Formally, the loss function in RSSGP is defined as

$$\mathcal{L} = \log p(Y|\Theta) + \lambda \log \mathbb{H}[q(x^*)], \tag{7}$$

where the first term is the log marginal likelihood as Eq. (6) in the SSGP, the second term is the entropy of $q(x^*)$ and λ is the trade-off parameter. Now we can obtain Θ by maximizing the loss function

$$\Theta = \operatorname{argmax} \log p(Y|\Theta) + \lambda \log \mathbb{H}[q(x^*)]. \tag{8}$$

The questions break down to that how $q(x^*)$ can be computed and how $q(x^*)$ is relevant to spectrum frequencies. Next, knowing there is no analytical form for $q(x^*)$, we propose two methods to estimate $q(x^*)$. One is Thompson sampling and the other is a sequential Monte Carlo approach that takes less computation. We also propose a significantly computationally-efficient approximation by treating the EI acquisition function as a proxy of $q(x^*)$.

3.1   Thompson Sampling Based Approach

We show how to approximate $q(x^*)$ by following the work of [17]. In Thompson sampling (TS), we use a linear model to approximate the function $f(x) = \phi(x)^T \bar{\theta}$, where $\bar{\theta} \sim \mathcal{N}(0, I)$ is a standard Gaussian. Giving observed data $\mathcal{D}_t$,

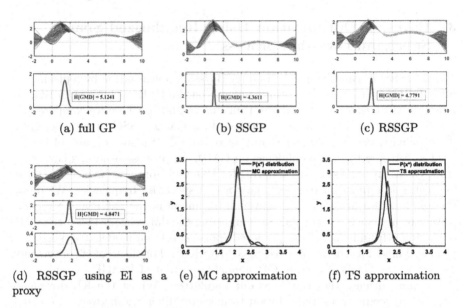

(a) full GP   (b) SSGP   (c) RSSGP

(d) RSSGP using EI as a   (e) MC approximation   (f) TS approximation
proxy

Fig. 1. (a)–(c) The visualization of overconfidence of SSGP on the GMD. The *upper* graphs show 200 posterior samples of Sinc function, modeled by (a) full GP, (b) SSGP with 30 optimal frequencies, and (c) RSSGP with 30 optimal frequencies. The red circle denotes observation and the blue circle denotes the maximum location of a posterior sample. The *lower* graphs illustrate the resultant GMD respectively. The $\mathbb{H}$[GMD] is the entropy of the GMD. We can see the GMD of RSSGP is closer to that of full GP than SSGP. (d) RSSGP with 30 optimal frequencies by using the EI function as a proxy to the regularization. Its GMD is at the middle and the EI function is at the bottom. (e) MC approach and (f) TS approach to approximate the reference $p(\boldsymbol{x}^*)$ distribution within the same running time. (Color figure online)

the posterior of $\bar{\boldsymbol{\theta}}$ conditioning $\mathcal{D}_t$ is a normal $\mathcal{N}(\mathbf{A}^{-1}\boldsymbol{\Phi}^T\mathbf{Y}, \mathbf{A}^{-1}\sigma_n^2)$, where $\mathbf{A}$ and $\boldsymbol{\Phi}$ have already been defined in Eq. (5). Note that $\phi(\boldsymbol{x})$ is a set of random Fourier features in the original TS while it is a set of m pairs of symmetric Fourier features (Eq. (4)) in our framework.

To estimate the GMD in RSSGP, we let ϕ_i and $\bar{\boldsymbol{\theta}}_i$ be a random set of m pairs of features and corresponding posterior weights. Both are sampled according to the generative process above and they can be used to construct a sampled function $f_i(\boldsymbol{x}) = \phi_i(\boldsymbol{x})^T\bar{\boldsymbol{\theta}}_i$. We can maximize this function to obtain a sample $\boldsymbol{x}_i^*$. Once we have acquired sufficient samples, we use histogram based method to obtain the probability mass function (PMF) over all $\boldsymbol{x}^*$, denoted as $F(\boldsymbol{x}^*)$. Then we estimate the entropy via $\mathbb{H}[q(\boldsymbol{x}^*)] = -\sum_{i=1}^{L} F(\boldsymbol{x}_i^*) \log F(\boldsymbol{x}_i^*)$, where L is the number of samples. Since our RSSGP uses Fourier features $\phi(\boldsymbol{x})$ to approximate a stationary kernel function, and $q(\boldsymbol{x}^*)$ also changes with applying different Fourier features, therefore we can obtain the optimal features by maximizing the combined term $\mathcal{L}$ in Eq. (7). As a result, the selected optimal features in RSSGP are not only take care of posterior mean approximation, but also maximize the entropy of $q(\boldsymbol{x}^*)$. This is the key why we choose SSGP as our base sparse method. Sparse models like FITC and VFE are not capable with this idea since we cannot relate their sparse sets to their GMDs due to insufficient research in this area.

We illustrate the GMD of RSSGP in Fig. 1c. We can see that it is closer to the GMD of the full GP than that of SSGP. The GMDs in Fig. 1a –d are estimated via TS.

3.2   Monte Carlo Based Approach

The estimation of $q(\boldsymbol{x}^*)$ by TS often requires thousands of samples, one of which involves the inversion of a $m \times m$ matrix. Inspired by a recent work [21] employing sequential Monte Carlo algorithm to approximate the GMD, we develop an significant efficient approach to estimate $q(\boldsymbol{x}^*)$ in our RSSGP.

We start with n_p particles at positions $\bar{\boldsymbol{x}}^1, \ldots, \bar{\boldsymbol{x}}^{n_p}$. Then we assign each particle a corresponding weight $\omega_1, \ldots, \omega_{n_p}$. Ultimately, these particles are supposed to converge to the GMD. At each iteration, we can approximate the $q(\boldsymbol{x}^*)$ through kernel density estimation

$$q(\boldsymbol{x}^* = \boldsymbol{x}) \approx \frac{\sum_{i=1}^{n_p} \omega_i k(\boldsymbol{x}, \bar{\boldsymbol{x}}^i)}{\sum_{i=1}^{n_p} \omega_i}, \tag{9}$$

where $k(\boldsymbol{x}, \bar{\boldsymbol{x}}^i)$ is the approximated kernel function using m features as in Eq. (3).

All the particles are sampled from the flat density distribution $v(\boldsymbol{x}) = \beta$ at the beginning, so that they are randomly distributed across the input space and the constant β is nonzero. To obtain the maximum position, we will challenge existing particles. We first sample a number of n_c challenger particles from a proposal distribution $v'(\boldsymbol{x})$ and denote them as $\bar{\boldsymbol{x}}_{C_1}, \ldots, \bar{\boldsymbol{x}}_{C_{n_c}}$. To challenge an existing particle e.g. $\bar{\boldsymbol{x}}^i$, we need to set up the joint distribution over $\bar{\boldsymbol{x}}^i$ and all challenger particles, which is a multivariate Gaussian distribution. We can subsequently generate a sample $[\bar{f}_i, \bar{f}_{C_1}, \cdots, \bar{f}_{C_{n_c}}]^T$ from the joint distribution. If the maximum value in the sample is greater than $\bar{f}_i$, we replace $\bar{\boldsymbol{x}}^i$ with the corresponding challenger particle. Otherwise, we retain $\bar{\boldsymbol{x}}^i$.

The challenger particle has an associated weight, which is often set as the ratio of the initial distribution over the proposal distribution. To speed up converge, we use the proposal distribution $v'(\boldsymbol{x})$ that is the mixture of the initial distribution and the current particle distribution as

$$v'(\boldsymbol{x}) = (1 - \alpha)v(\boldsymbol{x}) + \alpha q(\boldsymbol{x}^* = \boldsymbol{x}), \tag{10}$$

where $q(\boldsymbol{x}^* = \boldsymbol{x})$ is estimated through Eq. (9) and α is trade-off parameter (e.g., 0.5 in our experiments). To generate a challenger particle $\bar{\boldsymbol{x}}_{C_1}^i$, we first select one of the existing particles e.g. $\bar{\boldsymbol{x}}^i$ according to the particle weights. Based on Eq. (10), we then can sample $\bar{\boldsymbol{x}}_{C_1}^i$ from $k(\boldsymbol{x}, \bar{\boldsymbol{x}}^i)$ with the probability α or from the flat density distribution $v(\boldsymbol{x})$ with the probability $1-\alpha$. Hence, the challenger particle has a weight as

$$\omega_{C_j}^i = \frac{v(\bar{\boldsymbol{x}}_{C_j}^i)}{\alpha k(\bar{\boldsymbol{x}}_{C_j}^i, \bar{\boldsymbol{x}}^k) + (1 - \alpha)v(\bar{\boldsymbol{x}}_{C_j}^i)}. \tag{11}$$

Algorithm 1. Sparse spectrum Gaussian process for Bayesian optimization

---

1:**for** $n = 1, 2,...t$ **do**
2:    Optimize Eq.(8) to obtain hyerpararameters and optimal features,
3:    Fit the data $\mathcal{D}_t$ with RSSGP,
4:    Suggest the next point x_{t+1} by maximising $x_{t+1} = \text{argmax}\alpha_{EI}(x|\mathcal{D}_t)$,
5:    Evaluate the function value y_{t+1},
6:    Augment the observations$\mathcal{D}_t = \mathcal{D}_t \cup (x_{t+1}, y_{t+1})$.
7: **end for**

Based on this, we will challenge every particle once. After each round, the systematic re-sampling [22] will be employed to make sure that all particles have the same weight for the next round. This process stops till sufficient rounds. Thereafter, we calculate the PMF of the particles and then estimate its entropy.

The Monte Carlo (MC) approach does not require a large matrix inversion or nonlinear function optimization for the purpose of $q(x^*)$ approximation. Moreover, during the optimization process, $q(x^*)$ does not vary a lot with the change of Θ. Therefore, most of the particles can be reused in the process, significantly reducing computation cost.

We demonstrate the superiority in Fig. 1. We denote the GMD estimated from 50,000 TS samples of a full GP posterior on a $1d$ function as our reference $p(x^*)$, showing as blue lines in Fig. 1e and f. We give the same running time (0.5 s) to TS and MC approaches to approximate the reference $p(x^*)$ respectively, showing as red lines in the figures. We can see that our MC approach successfully approximate the reference $p(x^*)$ while TS is not desirable.

3.3 Expected Improvement Acquisition Function as a Proxy

To further reduce the computation, we propose to use EI function as a proxy for $q(x^*)$. This choice is reasonable in sense that they both measure the belief about the location of the global maximum, It can be seen from Fig. 1d that the GMD of full GP and the EI resembles closely. We can expect that this approximation setting has a similar performance of capturing $q(x^*)$ information as RSSGP with TS does, which is justified in Fig. 1c–d. Since EI is a function, we firstly use histogram based method to acquire the PMF of EI and then calculate the entropy. In most of the cases we find the approximation works well.

We use stochastic gradient descent to optimize Eq. (8) although alternatives are available. The proposed method is described in Algorithm 1.

4   Experiments

In this section, we evaluate our methods on optimizing benchmark functions, an alloy design problem and hyperparameter tuning of machine learning problems by transfer learning. We compare the following probabilistic models used for Bayesian optimization: 1. Full Gaussian process (**Full GP**), 2. Sparse spectrum Gaussian process (**SSGP**), 3. Our method 1: RSSGP using MC estimation for

$q(\boldsymbol{x}^*)$ (**RSSGP-MC**), 4. Our method 2: RSSGP using EI approximation for $q(\boldsymbol{x}^*)$ (**RSSGP-EI**), 5. VFF using additive kernel (**VFF-AK**), 6. VFF using Kronecker kernel (**VFF-KK**)

In all settings, we use EI as the acquisition function in BO and use the optimiser DIRECT [23] to maximize the EI function. We include both RSSGP-MC and RSSGP-EI in synthetic experiments. We later only use RSSGP-EI due to its computational advantage and the similar performance with RSSGP-MC. Given d-dimensional optimization problems and m frequencies, the size of inducing variables would be $(2m) * d$ for VFF-AK and $(2m)^d$ for VFF-KK [14]. Thus, VFF-KK becomes almost prohibitively expensive for $d > 2$ and a large m.

4.1   Optimizing Benchmark Functions

We test on the following two benchmark functions:

- $2d$ Ackley function. The search space is $[-10, 10]^2$;
- $6d$ Hartmann function. The search space is $[0, 1]^6$.

We run each method for 50 trials with different initializations and report the average simple regret along with its standard error. The simple regret is defined as $r_t = f(\boldsymbol{x}^*) - f(\boldsymbol{x}^+)$, where $f(\boldsymbol{x}^*)$ is the global maximum and $f(\boldsymbol{x}^+) = \max_{\boldsymbol{x} \in \{\boldsymbol{x}_{1:t}\}} f(\boldsymbol{x})$ is the best value till iteration t. We use the squared exponential kernel in our experiments. In terms of kernel parameters, we use the isotropic length scale, $\rho_l = 0.5, \forall l$, signal variance $\sigma_f^2 = 2$, and noise variance $\sigma_n^2 = (0.01)^2$. We empirically find that the proposed algorithms perform well when the regularization term has the more or less scale with the log marginal likelihood. Hence, we set the trade-off parameter $\lambda = 10$ for all of our methods.

For the $2d$ Ackley function, we start with 20 initial observations and use 20 frequencies in all sparse GP models. The experimental result is shown in Fig. 2a. The Full GP setting performs the best, and both of our approaches (e.g., RSSGP-MC and RSSGP-EI) perform better than SSGP. RSSGP-EI performs slightly worse than RSSGP-MC since it only provides a rough approximation to the true global maximum distribution but holds simplicity. VFF-KK performs well in a low dimensional problem whilst VFF-AK performs worst. The use of additive kernel which does not capture the correlation between dimensions may result in a bad performance.

For the $6d$ Hartmann function, we start with 150 initial observations and use 50 frequencies in all spectrum GP models. Similar results as the $2d$ Ackley function can be seen in Fig. 2b. We did not run VFF-KK on this case due to a huge size of inducing variables mentioned before.

4.2   Alloy Optimization

In the joint project with our metallurgist collaborators, we aim to design an alloy with a micro-structure that contains as much fraction of FCC phase as possible. We use a thermodynamic simulator called ThermoCalc [24]. Given a composition of an alloy, the simulator can compute thermodynamic equilibrium and

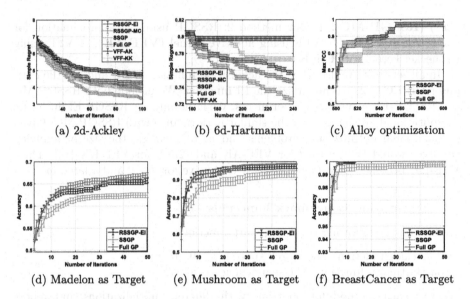

(a) 2d-Ackley   (b) 6d-Hartmann   (c) Alloy optimization

(d) Madelon as Target   (e) Mushroom as Target   (f) BreastCancer as Target

Fig. 2. (a)–(b) Simple regret vs iterations for the optimization of benchmark functions. The plots show the mean of minimum reached and its standard error at each iteration. (c) Alloy optimization at 15 dimensions. The plot shows the mean of maximal FCC reached and its standard error at each iteration. (d)–(f) Hyperparameter tuning for the SVM by transfer learning. We use 2700 observations from source tasks and 3 observations from target task. The plots show the mean of maximal accuracy reached till the current iteration and its standard error.

predict the micro-structure of the resultant alloy using CALPHAD [25] methodology. In this experiment, the search space is a 15 dimensional combination of the elements: Fe, Ni, Cr, Ti, Co, Al, Mn, Cu, Si, Nb, Mo, W, Ta, C, N. For each composition, ThermoCalc provides the amount of FCC in terms of volume fraction. The best value of volume fraction is 1. Since ThermoCalc takes around 10 min per composition to compute volume fraction, it fits perfectly in our notion of semi-expensive functions. We use 500 initial points and 50 frequencies and run 5 different trials with different initial points. The results in Fig. 2c shows BO with RSSGP-EI performs the best over all three methods. We found that the covariance matrix of the full GP quickly became ill-conditioned in the presence of a large number of observations, and hence, fails to be inverted properly, being ended up harming the BO.

4.3 Hyperparameter Tuning by Transfer Learning

Transfer learning in the context of Bayesian optimization pools together observations from the sources and the target to build a combined covariance matrix in the GP. In this case when the number of sources is large or/and the number of existing observations per source is large, the resultant covariance matrix can be quite huge, demanding a sparse approximation. We conduct experiments for tuning hyperparameters of support vector machine (SVM) classifier in a transfer learning setting. We use the datasets: LiverDisorders, Madelon, Mushroom and BreastCancer from UCI repository [26] and construct three transfer learning scenarios. For each scenario, we use 3 out of 4 datasets as the source tasks, and the rest one as the target task. We randomly generate 900 samples of hyperparameters and the corresponding accuracy from each source task. We also randomly generate 3 initial samples from the target task. As a result, we have 2703 initial observations to build the combined covariance matrix. Following the framework [27], where the source points are considered as noisy observations for the target function, we add a higher noise variance (3 times of that in target observations) to 2700 source observations. This allows us to use the same covariance function to capture the similarity between the observations from both source and target tasks. We optimize two hyperparameters in SVM which are the cost parameter (C) and the width of the RBF kernel (γ). The search bounds for the two hyperparameters are $C = 10^\lambda$ where $\lambda \in [-3, 3]$, and $\gamma = 10^\omega$ with $\omega \in [-3, 0]$, respectively, and we optimize λ and ω. We run each scenario 30 trials with different initializations. The results are showed in Fig. 2d–f. We can see that in all scenarios BO with RSSGP-EI outperforms the naive SSGP. We note that the covariance matrix of full GP does not suffer from ill-conditioning since the source observations have a higher noise. Therefore, we can see the Full GP case works well from the results.

5   Conclusion

In this paper we propose a new regularized sparse spectrum Gaussian process method for Bayesian optimization applications. The original SSGP formulation results in an overconfident GP. BO using such GP may fare poorly as the correct uncertainty prediction is crucial for the success of Bayesian optimization. We propose a modification to the marginal likelihood in the original SSGP by adding the entropy of the GMD induced by the posterior GP as a regularizer. By maximizing the entropy of the GMD along with the marginal likelihood, we aim to obtain a sparse approximation which is more aligned with the goal of BO. We show that an efficient formulation can be obtained by using a sequential Monte Carlo approach to approximate the GMD. We also experimented with the expected improvement acquisition function as a proxy for the GMD. Experiments on benchmark functions and two real world problems show superiority of our approach over the vanilla SSGP method at all times and even better than the usual full GP based approach at certain scenarios.

Acknowledgment. This research was partially funded by the Australian Government through the Australian Research Council (ARC). Prof Venkatesh is the recipient of an ARC Australian Laureate Fellowship (FL170100006).

References

1. Jones, D.R., Schonlau, M., Welch, W.J.: Efficient global optimization of expensive black-box functions. J. Global Optim. **13**(4), 455–492 (1998)

2. Shahriari, B., et al.: Taking the human out of the loop: a review of Bayesian optimization. Proc. IEEE **104**(1), 148–175 (2015)
3. Yang, A., Li, C., Rana, S., Gupta, S., Venkatesh, S.: Efficient Bayesian optimisation using derivative meta-model. In: Geng, X., Kang, B.-H. (eds.) PRICAI 2018. LNCS (LNAI), vol. 11013, pp. 256–264. Springer, Cham (2018). https://doi.org/10.1007/978-3-319-97310-4_29
4. Snoek, J., Larochelle, H., Adams, R.P.: Practical Bayesian optimization of machine learning algorithms. In: NeurIPS, pp. 2951–2959 (2012)
5. Li, C., et al.: Rapid Bayesian optimisation for synthesis of short polymer fiber materials. Sci. Rep. **7**, 5683 (2017)
6. Pan, S.J., Yang, Q.: A survey on transfer learning. IEEE Trans. Knowl. Data Eng. **22**(10), 1345–1359 (2009)
7. Long, M., et al.: Transfer feature learning with joint distribution adaptation. In: Proceedings of the IEEE International Conference on Computer Vision (2013)
8. Jasper, S., et al.: Scalable Bayesian using deep neural networks. In: ICML (2015)
9. Hutter, F., Hoos, H.H., Leyton-Brown, K.: Sequential model-based optimization for general algorithm configuration. In: Coello, C.A.C. (ed.) LION 2011. LNCS, vol. 6683, pp. 507–523. Springer, Heidelberg (2011). https://doi.org/10.1007/978-3-642-25566-3_40
10. Snelson, E., et al.: Sparse GP using pseudo-inputs. In: NeurIPS (2006)
11. Yang, A., Li, C., Rana, S., Gupta, S., Venkatesh, S.: Sparse approximation for Gaussian process with derivative observations. In: Mitrovic, T., Xue, B., Li, X. (eds.) AI 2018. LNCS (LNAI), vol. 11320, pp. 507–518. Springer, Cham (2018). https://doi.org/10.1007/978-3-030-03991-2_46
12. Titsias, M.: Variational learning of inducing variables in SGP. In: AISTATS (2009)
13. Lazaro, G., et al.: Sparse spectrum gaussian process regression. J. Mach. Learn. Res. **11**, 1865–1881 (2010)
14. Hensman, J., Durrande, N., Solin, A., et al.: Variational Fourier features for Gaussian processes. J. Mach. Learn. Res. **18**(151), 1–151 (2017)
15. Wang, K., et al.: Exact GP on a million data points. In: NeurIPS (2019)
16. Hennig, P., Schuler, C.J.: Entropy search for information-efficient global optimization. J. Mach. Learn. Res. **13**, 1809–1837 (2012)
17. Hernández, J.M., Hoffman, M.W., Ghahramani, Z.: Predictive entropy search for efficient global optimization of black-box functions. In: NeurIPS, pp. 918–926 (2014)
18. Rasmussen, C.E., et al.: Gaussian Processes for Machine Learning, vol. 1 (2006)
19. Srinivas, N., et al.: Gaussian process optimization in the bandit setting: no regret and experimental design. arXiv preprint arXiv:0912.3995 (2009)
20. Bochner, S.: Lectures on Fourier Integrals. Princeton University Press, Princeton (1959)
21. Bijl, H., et al.: A sequential Monte Carlo approach to Thompson sampling for Bayesian optimization. arXiv preprint arXiv:1604.00169 (2016)
22. Kitagawa, G.: Monte Carlo filter and smoother for non-gaussian nonlinear state space models. J. Comput. Graph. Stat. **5**(1), 1–25 (1996)
23. Finkel, D.E.: DIRECT Optimization Algorithm User Guide. CRSC (2003)
24. Andersson, J.O., Helander, T., Höglund, L., Shi, P., Sundman, B.: Thermo-Calc & DICTRA, computational tools for materials science. Calphad **26**(2), 273–312 (2002)
25. Saunders, N., et al.: CALPHAD: A Comprehensive Guide. Elsevier (1998)
26. Dheeru, D., Karra Taniskidou, E.: UCI Machine Learning Repository (2017)
27. Joy, T.T., et al.: A flexible transfer learning framework for Bayesian optimization with convergence guarantee. Exp. Syst. Appl. **115**, 656–672 (2019)

Densely Connected Graph Attention Network Based on Iterative Path Reasoning for Document-Level Relation Extraction

Hongya Zhang, Zhen Huang$^{(\boxtimes)}$, Zhenzhen Li, Dongsheng Li, and Feng Liu

School of Computer Science, National University of Defense Technology,
Changsha, China
{zhanghongya_0727,huangzhen,lizhenzhen,dsli,richardlf}@nudt.edu.cn

Abstract. Document-level relation extraction is a challenging task in Natural Language Processing, which extracts relations expressed with one or multiple sentences. It plays an important role in data mining and information retrieval. The key challenge comes from the indirect relations expressed across sentences. Graph-based neural networks have been proved effective for modeling structural information among the document. Existing methods enhance the graph models by using either the attention mechanism or the iterative path reasoning, which is not enough to capture all the effective structural information. In this paper, we propose a densely connected graph attention network based on iterative path reasoning (IPR-DCGAT) for document-level relation extraction. Our approach uses densely connected graph attention network to model the local and global information among the document. In addition, we propose to learn dynamic path weights for reasoning relations across sentences. Extensive experiments on three datasets demonstrate the effectiveness of our approach. Our model achieves 84% F1 score on CDR, which is about 16.3%–22.5% higher than previous models with a significant margin. Meanwhile, the results of our approach are also comparably superior to the state-of-the-art results on the GDA and DocRED dataset.

Keywords: Relation extraction · Densely connected graph attention network · Iterative path reasoning

1 Introduction

Relation extraction (RE) aims to identify the relations of entities from the plain text. It is important for many downstream NLP tasks, such as data mining and information retrieval [21]. Most previous RE approaches [11,19,26] extract relations within one sentence. However, it is also common that two entities may express some relation across sentences [2]. Recently, document-level RE [2,25] that requires intra- and inter-sentence RE has gained increasing attention. The key challenge is to extract relations indirectly expressed across several sentences.

© Springer Nature Switzerland AG 2021
K. Karlapalem et al. (Eds.): PAKDD 2021, LNAI 12713, pp. 269–281, 2021.
https://doi.org/10.1007/978-3-030-75765-6_22

Input:	
[1]Washington Place **(William Washington House)** is one of the first homes built by freed slaves after the Emancipation Proclamation **of 1863 in Hampshire County, West Virginia,** United States.	
[2]Washington Place **was built by William and Annie Washington in north Romney between 1863 and 1874 on land given to Annie by her former owner,** Susan Blue Parsons **of Wappocomo plantation.**	
Intra-sentence RE:	Inter-sentence RE:
Entity: Emancipation Proclamation , United States **Relation:** country **Supporting sentences:** [1]	**Entity:** Susan Blue Parsons , United States **Relation:** country of citizenship **Supporting sentences:** [1], [2]

Fig. 1. Example of document-level RE from DocRED [25].

We further illustrate the challenge of inferring the different types of relations by giving an example in Fig. 1. There are two sentences in this excerpt, in which entities are represented with different colors. The relation between *Emancipation Proclamation* and *United States* can be identified through the first sentence, which is an example of intra-sentence RE. However, we need to consider two sentences together to infer the relation between entities *Susan Blue Parsons* and *United States*. These two entities are connected through entity *Washington Place*. By considering the relatedness of *Susan Blue Parsons* and *Washington Place* in the first sentence and the connection of *United States* and *Washington Place* in the second sentence, our approach can infer the indirect relation expressed between *Susan Blue Parsons* and *United States*.

Previous approaches tackle the document-level RE with sequential methods [4,10] or graph-based neural network models [17,20]. The graph-based neural networks are capable of modeling structural information between sentences over long distances [6,17], so that they can perform better than sequential methods. Recent approaches further enhance the graph-based models by using convolution network [28], attention mechanism [13] or iterative path reasoning algorithms [2]. However, they only capture the structural information from one aspect and fail to model all effective connections within the graph. In addition, the methods described above either rely on an external parser to learn the attention among different entities, which suffer errors from the parser [13] or regard the weights of different rounds in iterative path reasoning as the same, which should be considered contextually [2]. Intuitively, the more distant path information should have less impact when performing path reasoning.

To address above challenges, we propose a novel approach - IPR-DCGAT: an iterative-path-reasoning based densely connected graph attention network model, for document-level RE. We construct the heterogeneous graph for each document based on three types of nodes, i.e., entities, mentions and sentences. To model the local and global information of the graph, we propose the densely connected graph attention network (DCGAT) to compute attention weights of adjacent nodes when updating node representations. Besides, our approach further captures the structural information across sentences through a multiround iterative path reasoning algorithm. We also empirically find that including the entity type and co-reference information is essential for inter-sentence RE.

We conduct extensive experiments on three datasets for document-level RE. Our approach achieves new state-of-the-art results on two public biomedical-domain datasets - CDR [9] and GDA [24] as well as the result of our method is comparably superior to other current state-of-the-art methods in a general-domain dataset DocRED [23]. Our contributions are summarized as follows:

- We propose IPR-DCGAT - a novel approach for document-level RE, which combines the advantages of both attention mechanism and path reasoning for capturing structural information of the document graph.
- We innovatively apply dense connectivity to graph attention network in heterogeneous graph for better modeling useful information. Meanwhile, we investigate some other related structures such as GCN to verify the validity of our structure.
- Our iterative path reasoning algorithm with varied path weights further enhance relation inferring across sentences. Experiments show that using different weights in multiple iterations is effective.

2 Related Work

Previous researches on RE mainly focus on the extraction at the intra-sentence RE. Researchers have proposed a series of supervised approaches such as CNN [11], CNN with max-pooling [27]. In recent years, graph neural network attracts tremendous attention and has been applied in various NLP applications such as RE. Miwa et al.(2016)'s proposed model [12] depends on external grammar tools to construct the shortest dependency path (SDP) between two entities in a sentence. Then Christopoulou et al.(2018) [3] further improve performance by a walk-based graph independent of external grammar tools.

However, such kind of methods are hard to be performed well in inter-sentence RE, because this task requires better extraction of structure feature [2,13]. Recently, many methods based on graph have also been developed to address it. The original models [6,17] consider words as nodes and the connections between them as edges while updating node representations during training. Then Christopoulou et al.(2019) [2] propose an edge-oriented neural network model. The model constructs heterogeneous types of nodes and edges to generate graph of the document, so as to infer the relation between entity pairs through updating edge representations. The researchers [13] then integrate the meta dependency paths using external tools to improve performance. Meanwhile, Zeng et al.(2020) [28] also innovatively propose the double graph based reasoning architecture from another perspective of heterogeneous graph structure. There are also some models [15,29] that take two different submodels to improve performance according to the characteristics of different types of RE.

The existing works have some limitations. Some approaches [2,13] extract structured information from only one aspect such as structured attention or iterative algorithm. Some other models [10,29] use different models for inter- and intra-sentence RE with external knowledge and tools. Combining the surrounding information from the two perspectives by DCGAT and iterative path reasoning algorithm, our model architecture has a stronger expression ability to collect and synthesize inter-sentence information.

3   Proposed Model

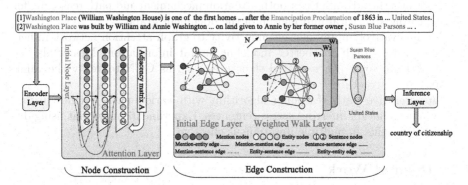

Fig. 2. The overall model architecture. The model consists of four modules, i.e., *Encoder Layer* for encoding tokens by each sentence, *Node Construction* for constructing the nodes of graphs, *Edge Construction* for edges similarly and *Inference Layer*.

Figure 2 shows the overall framework of our model. We will elaborate on the details of each module later. Significantly, the key to document-level RE is how to extract structured information. *Attention Layer* and *Weighted Walk Layer* in our model can enhance information extraction from two aspects.

3.1   Task Modeling

Formally, we define the task as follows. Given a document, it consists of n sentences $D = \{s_1, s_2, ..., s_n\}$, each sentence contains different numbers of words $s_i = \{w_1, w_2, ..., w_d | i \in [1, n]\}$. Meanwhile, the document contains multiple entities $E = \{e_1, e_2, ..., e_j\}$, each entity e_i has k mentions $e_i = \{m_1, m_2, ..., m_k | i \in [1, j]\}$. A relation list $R = \{r_1, r_2, ..., r_l\}$ is also provided. We should infer the relation of specified entity pair (e_i, e_j) in the relation list R. In order to express the difference between entities and mentions, we give an example that as "Obama" is a unique concept-level entity, it can be mentioned in different ways, such as "President of the United States", "Obama", "Michelle's husband", and etc.

3.2   Encoder Layer

Firstly, we encode the sentences in the document via a encoder to obtain each word vector $\mathbf{w}_i$ combined with the context. In this paper, we adopt BiLSTM [18] as the encoder. The inputs of the encoder respectively are word embedding

$\mathbf{d}_{w_i}$, co-reference embedding $\mathbf{d}_{p_i}$, entity type embedding $\mathbf{d}_{e_i}$. $\mathbf{d}_{p_i}$ marks different mentions to the same entity while $\mathbf{d}_{e_i}$ maps the entity categories (e.g. PER, LOC) of the words. We concatenate these three kinds of embeddings, denote the intermediate variable as $\gamma_i = [\mathbf{d}_{w_i}; \mathbf{d}_{p_i}; \mathbf{d}_{e_i}]$ where the square bracket [;] shows the concatenation of vectors. Then γ_i is fed into BiLSTM to get the final representation $\mathbf{w}_i$ for each word as the following equation:

$$\mathbf{h}_{i\_left} = \text{LSTM}_{left}(\mathbf{h}_{(i+1)\_left}, \gamma_i)$$
$$\mathbf{h}_{i\_right} = \text{LSTM}_{right}(\mathbf{h}_{(i-1)\_right}, \gamma_i) \qquad (1)$$
$$\mathbf{w}_i = [\mathbf{h}_{i\_left}; \mathbf{h}_{i\_right}]$$

It's worth noting that we directly fixed them after initialization in this work.

3.3 Node Construction

After the word vectors $\mathbf{W} = [\mathbf{w}_1, \mathbf{w}_2, ..., \mathbf{w}_n]$ of the document are obtained, we construct the heterogeneous graph [2] with different kinds of nodes and edges of the document. Firstly, we conduct *Node Construction*.

Initial Node Layer. There are three types of nodes in our heterogeneous network, i.e., sentence nodes s, mention nodes m, and entity nodes e, while the corresponding representations are denoted as $\mathbf{n}_s$, $\mathbf{n}_m$, $\mathbf{n}_e$, respectively. The representation of a mention node is the average of the words that form the mention. Sentence nodes are in the same way. The representation of an entity node is computed as the mean of the representations of mentions which belong to the specified entity. To distinguish between the three node types, we concatenate type embedding $\mathbf{t}_e$, $\mathbf{t}_m$, $\mathbf{t}_s$ at the end of the original representation. Thus we give the final representations for the three types of nodes:

$$\mathbf{n}_m = [\text{avg}_{w_i \in m}(\mathbf{w}_i); \mathbf{t}_m], \quad \mathbf{n}_e = [\text{avg}_{m_i \in e}(\mathbf{n}_m); \mathbf{t}_e], \quad \mathbf{n}_s = [\text{avg}_{w_i \in s}(\mathbf{w}_i); \mathbf{t}_s] \quad (2)$$

Attention Layer. For document-level RE, especially inter-sentence RE, the association between nodes is particularly important. Inspired by DCGCN [5], we introduce an *Attention Layer* to update the node representation such that it contains more information about its neighbors.

The inputs of *Attention Layer* are adjacency matrix $\mathbf{A} \in \mathbb{R}^{n \times n}$ and the initial node representations $\mathbf{N}' = \{\mathbf{n}'_1, \mathbf{n}'_2, ..., \mathbf{n}'_n | \mathbf{n}'_i \in \mathbb{R}^d\}$. The outputs are the updated values $\mathbf{N} = \{\mathbf{n}_1, \mathbf{n}_2, ..., \mathbf{n}_n | \mathbf{n}_i \in \mathbb{R}^d\}$. The principle of adjacency matrix is as follows [2]: any two sentence nodes; any two mention nodes in the same sentence; the mention node and entity node when the former is an instance of the latter; the mention node and sentence node when the words of mention are contained in the sentence; the entity node and sentence node when an instance of the entity appears in the sentence. The information can be obtained directly or indirectly from the data set. We consider that these node pairs are related and concatenate to one at the corresponding position of adjacency matrix $\mathbf{A}$.

Dense connectivity allows nodes to receive information not only from the latest layer, but also from all the preceding layers. Meanwhile, each intermediate layer is specified to a very small size for learning different sets of feature maps at different locations [5]. Thus, assume that *Attention layer* has t sub_layers, let $\mathbf{h}_i^k \in \mathbb{R}^{d_{temp}}$ be the output and $\mathbf{g}_i^k \in \mathbb{R}^{d+(k-1)\times d_{temp}}$ be the input for the ith node in the kth sub_layer where $d_{temp} = d/t$. Particularly, $\mathbf{g}_i^1$ is the initial node representation. $\mathbf{g}_i^k$ is the concatenation of initial node representation and the outputs of the previous hidden layers $\{\mathbf{h}_i^1, \mathbf{h}_i^2, ..., \mathbf{h}_i^{k-1}\}$ as shown below:

$$\mathbf{g}_i^k = [\mathbf{n}_i'; \mathbf{h}_i^1; ...; \mathbf{h}_i^{k-1}], k \in [2, t] \tag{3}$$

Then vector $\mathbf{a}^k \in \mathbb{R}^{2d_{temp}}$ and weight matrix $\mathbf{W}^k \in \mathbb{R}^{d_{temp}\times[d+(k-1)\times d_{temp}]}$ are introduced for implementing self-attention mechanism. We compute the coefficient e_{ij}^k to represent the importance of the jth node to the ith node as follows:

$$e_{ij}^k = \mathbf{a}^k[\mathbf{W}^k\mathbf{g}_i^k; \mathbf{W}^k\mathbf{g}_j^k] \tag{4}$$

It is worth noting that if A_{ij} is 0, the coefficient e_{ij}^k should be set to 0. The resulting coefficient is then nonlinearly activated by LeakyRelu and normalized by softmax to get the final coefficient α_{ij}^k between the ith and j^{th} node. The specific equation is as follows:

$$\alpha_{ij}^k = \frac{\exp(\text{LeakyRelu}(e_{ij}^k))}{\Sigma_{m\in\mathscr{N}}\exp(\text{LeakyRelu}(e_{im}^k))} \tag{5}$$

where $\mathscr{N}$ expresses the node set.

Thus we can get the new node representations $\mathbf{h}_i^k \in \mathbb{R}^{d_{temp}}$ for the ith node:

$$\mathbf{h}_i^k = \sigma(\Sigma_{j\in\mathscr{N}}\alpha_{ij}^k\mathbf{W}^k\mathbf{g}_i^k) \tag{6}$$

where σ expresses the activation function.

Finally, we add the concatenation of all outputs of the sub_layers and the initial node representation together, then take a linear conversion to obtain the updated node representation. $\mathbf{W}^o$ is the learned weight for linear conversion.

$$\mathbf{n}_i = \mathbf{W}^o([\mathbf{h}_i^1; \mathbf{h}_i^2; ...; \mathbf{h}_i^t] + \mathbf{n}_i') \tag{7}$$

3.4   Edge Construction

Next, we build edge construction with the updated node representations.

Initial Edge Layer. We construct the edges according to heuristic rules for constructing adjacency matrix. An edge is added between adjoining nodes in adjacency matrix $\mathbf{A}$. Edge representation is the concatenation of the representations of the corresponding node pair. Our edges are divided into five types based on their node types, i.e., Mention-Mention edge $\mathbf{E}_{mm}$, Mention-Sentence edge $\mathbf{E}_{ms}$, Mention-Entity edge $\mathbf{E}_{me}$, Sentence-Sentence edge $\mathbf{E}_{ss}$ and Entity-Sentence edge $\mathbf{E}_{es}$. The Entity-Entity edge $\mathbf{E}_{ee}$ will be generated in the next subsection *Weighted Walk Layer*. Distance between different mentions in the same sentence or different sentences plays a role in RE, so the corresponding edge adds embedding $\mathbf{d}_{mm}$ or $\mathbf{d}_{ss}$. The edge representations are as follows:

$$\mathbf{E}_{es} = [\mathbf{n}_e; \mathbf{n}_s]; \quad \mathbf{E}_{ms} = [\mathbf{n}_m; \mathbf{n}_s]; \quad \mathbf{E}_{me} = [\mathbf{n}_m; \mathbf{n}_e];$$
$$\mathbf{E}_{mm} = [\mathbf{n}_m; \mathbf{n}_m; \mathbf{d}_{mm}]; \quad \mathbf{E}_{ss} = [\mathbf{n}_s; \mathbf{n}_s; \mathbf{d}_{ss}] \tag{8}$$

Weighted Walk Layer. *Attention Layer* is mainly responsible for fusion of information between node and its first-order neighbor nodes, however, it is necessary to extract further information for inter-sentence RE at the document level. Therefore, we obtain more information in *Weighted Walk Layer* inspired by Christopoulou et al.(2019) [2]. We divide it into two stages, generating stage and aggregating stage.

- **Generating Stage** Denote the intermediate nodes between of the ith and j^{th} node as $\mathbf{N}_{temp} = \{\mathbf{n}_1, \mathbf{n}_2, ...\mathbf{n}_m\}$. We utilize edge $\mathbf{E}_{ik}$ and $\mathbf{E}_{kj}$ to generate the new representation of edge $\mathbf{E}_{ij}^{new}$. It is implemented by einsum operation $\odot$ and a learned matrix $\mathbf{W}$ according to the equation below:

$$\mathbf{E}_{ij}^{new} = \Sigma_{\mathbf{n}_k \in \mathbf{N}_{temp}} \sigma((\mathbf{W}\mathbf{E}_{ik}) \odot \mathbf{E}_{kj}) \tag{9}$$

- **Aggregating Stage** After obtaining new representation, we take linear interpolation between old and new representation using coefficient β to control the contribution of old one. The final representation is computed as follows:

$$\mathbf{E}_{ij} = \beta\mathbf{E}_{ij} + (1 - \beta)\mathbf{E}_{ij}^{new} \tag{10}$$

Intuitively, we analyse the relation of an entity pair usually starting with content that is close to the entity pair. The information obtained from a long distance is relatively insignificant in the final generated edge representation. That is to say, the weight $\mathbf{W}$ of different iteration rounds should be different, whereas the previous work [2] was handled with the same weight.

3.5 Inference Layer

We incorporate a softmax classifier to predict relation between entity pair (e_i, e_j) using the generated edge $\mathbf{E}_{n_{e_i}, n_{e_j}}$ by the following equation:

$$y = \text{softmax}(\mathbf{W}\mathbf{E}_{n_{e_i}, n_{e_j}} + \mathbf{b}) \tag{11}$$

where $\mathbf{W}$ is the weight and $\mathbf{b}$ is the bias. We adopt the cross entropy loss function.

4   Experiment

Dataset.   Our experiment employs two datasets in biology spheres. One is a human annotated dataset CDR [9] while another is a distantly supervised dataset GDA [24]. We also apply one generic dataset DocRED [25] built by Wikipedia and Wikidata. The statistics for these datasets are shown in Table 1.

Implementation Details.   Firstly, we utilize the GENIA Sentence Splitter4 and GENIA tagger to get the processed data following the paper [2]. During training, we use early stopping to identify the best training epoch and employ Adam [7] to optimize our model with $\beta_1 = 0.9$, $\beta_2 = 0.999$. Learning_rate is 0.001, weight deacy is 0.0001 and gradient clipping is 10. CDR, GDA, DocRED employ PubMed pre-trained embeddings [1], randomly initialized word embeddings, and GloVe embeddings [16] respectively. In *Weighted Walk Layer*, the value of the coefficient β is different for CDR, GDA and DocRED. The first two are 0.8, while DocRED is 0.9. Finally, due to the uneven distribution of DoCRED, we utilize weighted cross entropy. Table 2 shows some other hyperparameters.

Table 1. Statistics for datasets.

	CDR	GDA	DocRED
Documents	1,500	30,192	5,053
Relations	2	2	97
Entities	10,225	146,198	98,610
Mentions	28,848	557,128	132,375
Facts	3,116	46,343	63,427

Table 2. Hyper-parameters list.

Hyperparameters name	Value
Batch size	3
DCGAT/DCGCN dropout	0.5
Classifier dropout	0.3
Co-reference/distance dimension	10
Node/Entity type dimension	10
Inference iterations	3
DCGAT/DCGCN layers	2

Evaluation Metrics.   We evaluate the performance of CDR and GDA on the overall, intra- and inter-sentence RE in terms of F1, precision, recall values which are marked as $F1$, P and R, respectively. For DocRED, we report the F1 excluding those relational facts shared by the training and dev/test sets [25], denoted as Ign F1. Different metrics are adopted to facilitate direct comparison with previous experimental results of these data sets. For different datasets, we also list current state-of-the-art results and the baselines when the datasets are presented. The experimental results fluctuate within a small range. We repeat each experiment five times and report the highest value. The results of the test set in DocRED are submitted online[1]. We also make the source code available[2].

---

[1] https://competitions.codalab.org/competitions/20717.
[2] https://github.com/zhanghongya0727/IPR-DCGAT.

5   Results

Overall Comparison

Table 3 depicts the performance of our proposed model (IPR-DCGAT) on various datasets. In Table 3(a), our model can achieve *84.0%* F1 on test set, outperform all available models by a wide margin of *16.3%–22.5%* on the whole. F1 on Intra- and inter-sentence improve *17.6%* and *24.7%* respectively which proves that our model is not only effective for intra-, but also more effective for inter-sentence RE. We also report the results on GDA and DocRED. Compared with CDR, GDA is larger but the proportion of inter-sentence RE is smaller [2]. Thus, the effect of *Attention Layer* and the iterative algorithm for inter-sentence RE will be compromised. However, it still exceeds the best results available by *1.1%* as shown in Table 3(b). Table 3(c) shows the comparisons with baseline and state-of-the-art models on DocRED. Significantly, it is a new relation(*NA*) if entities express no specific relation, and *NA* accounts for up to 97%. In such a complex situation, our model obtains a *4.4%/3.9%* F1 improvement compared with the best baseline(Contex Aware). Even our model exceeds the performance of the model using Bert by *1.3%/1.4%*, which shows strong capturing capability.

Table 3. Main results on various datasets

(a) Results on the test set of CDR

model	Overall{%}			Intra {%}			Inter{%}		
	P	R	F1	P	R	F1	P	R	F1
Zheng et al.[29] *	56.2	67.9	61.5	-	-	-	-	-	-
Nguyen et al.[14]	57.0	68.6	62.3	-	-	-	-	-	-
Peng et al.[15] *	62.1	64.2	63.1	-	-	-	-	-	-
Christopoulou et al. [2]	62.1	65.2	63.6	64.0	73.0	68.2	56.0	46.7	50.9
Nan et al. [13]	-	-	64.8	-	-	**68.9**	-	-	**53.1**
Li et al.[10] *	60.8	76.4	**67.7**	67.3	52.4	58.9	-	-	-
IPR-DCGAT	89.6	79.0	**84.0**	91.2	82.2	86.5	85.4	71.5	**77.8**

The methods with * utilize additional training data or tools.

(b) Results on the test set of GDA

Model	F1{%}		
	Overall	Intra	Inter
EoG [2]	81.5	85.2	50.0
EoG(Full) [2]	80.8	84.1	**54.7**
EoG(NoInf) [2]	74.6	79.1	49.3
LSR [13]	**82.2**	**85.4**	51.1
IPR-DCGAT	**82.6**	**85.9**	52.9

(c) Results on DocRED

Model	Dev / Test{%}	
	F1	IngF1
CNN [25][†]	43.5/42.3	41.6/40.3
BiLSTM [25][†]	50.9/**51.1**	48.9/**48.8**
Contex Aware [25][†]	**51.1**/50.7	**48.9**/48.4
BERT [23]	54.2/53.2	-
HIN-GloVe [21]	53.0/53.3	51.1/51.2
LSR-GloVe [13]	55.2/54.2	48.8/52.2
GAIN-GloVe [28]	**55.3/55.1**	**53.1**/52.7
IPR-DCGAT	**55.5**/54.6	52.1/**52.8**

The results with [†] are baselines from [25].

Analysis on *Attention Layer*.   Firstly, we report the performances of several contrastive settings in Table 4, i.e., IPR-BASELINE, IPR-GCN, IPR-GAT, IPR-DCGCN. They do not include *Attention Layer* or realize it separately through

GCN [8], GAT [22] and DCGCN [5]. The performances of IPR-GCN and IPR-DCGCN are *0.9%* and *0.7%* lower than IPR-GAT and IPR-DCGAT. This indicates that assigning different weights to each node based on the features of its neighbors is effective for that the strength of association between different nodes is generally not the same empirically. Meanwhile, almost all results are better than BASELINE, which proves that the effectiveness of *Attention Layer*. IPR-DCGAT is *0.6%* higher than IPR-GAT and IPR-DCGCN is *0.8%* higher than GCN. It shows dense connectivity can learn a better structural representation [5].

Table 4. Analysis on *attention layer*

Model	Overall{%}			Intra {%}			Inter{%}		
	P	R	F1	P	R	F1	P	R	F1
IPR-DCGAT	89.6	79.0	**84.0**	91.2	82.2	86.5	85.4	71.5	**77.8**
IPR-BASELINE	89.2	77.9	83.1	90.0	83.0	86.4	86.8	65.8	74.9
IPR-GCN	86.2	79.2	82.5	87.8	84.0	85.8	81.9	68.0	74.3
IPR-DCGCN	90.0	77.5	83.3	91.5	82.5	86.8	85.7	65.8	74.5
IPR-GAT	89.5	78.1	83.4	91.3	83.1	**87.0**	84.4	66.1	74.2

Analysis on *Weighted Walk Layer*. The impact of *Weighted Walk Layer* is shown in Fig. 3. We do not add *Attention Layer* here to avoid confusing effects. Adding *Weighted Walk Layer* can improve the performance by *3.3%*. Compared with the inspired method [2] which used the same learnable parameter , we believe that the contents learned in different iterations are diverse. It has been proved effective that the improved model has a *0.9%* higher F1 and the result of inter-sentence RE is improved more than that of inter-sentence RE.

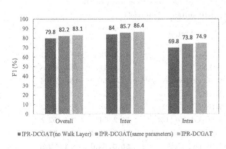

Fig. 3. Analysis on *weighted walk layer*

Table 5. Ablation analysis on CDR

Model	F1{%}		
	Overall	Intra	Inter
IPR-DCGAT	**84.0**	**86.5**	**77.8**
- distance	83.3	86.4	75.5
- entity type	82.4	86.0	73.2
- co-reference	68.8	73.0	57.8
- all	67.3	72.4	54.3

Ablation Study. For ablation experiments, *weighted Walk Layer* and *Attention Layer* have been discussed in detail above. For other components, it can be seen from Table 5 that removing the distance, entity type and co-reference embedding will lead the worse results. Each component plays a greater role in the inter- than intra-sentence RE. Entity type embeddings can cause a *0.5%* drop in intra- while a *4.6%* drop in inter-sentence. The effect of co-reference embeddings surprisingly brings *13.5%/20.0%* improvements. This phenomenon only appears in CDR, while other datasets are not so obvious in the same experimental configuration. It also leads to the most significant improvement in CDR. We consider the reason is that CDR is a smaller, manually annotated data set with fewer types of relations and a balanced distribution. The above aspects cause the effect brought by the addition of co-reference embeddings will be relatively obvious. For GDA, the large size makes the impact of data scale on the result more important. Distant supervision also introduces some noise. While the co-reference information has already been applied in previous papers referencing DocRED. The performance degradation caused by removing all components is less than the sum of removing one of them separately, indicating that there may be overfitting.

---

[1]Neuropsychiatric behaviors in the **MPTP** marmoset model of Parkinson's disease.
[5]The levodopa - treated **MPTP** - lesioned marmoset was used as a model of neuropsychiatric symptoms in PD patients.
[7] METHODS : Marmosets were administered 1 - **methyl - 4 - phenyl - 1 , 2 , 3 , 6** - tetrahydropyridine for five days , resulting in stable parkinsonism.
[8]Animals were evaluated for **parkinsonian disability** (...).

[1]A case of **isotretinoin embryopathy** with bilateral anotia and Taussig - Bing malformation .
[2]We report a newborn infant with multiple congenital anomalies (...) due to exposure to **isotretinoin** within the first trimester .

[1]Cardiovascular dysfunction and hypersensitivity to sodium pentobarbital induced by chronic **barium chloride** ingestion .
[11]Overall, (...)suggest the existence of a heretofore undescribed **cardiomyopathic disorder** induced by chronic barium exposure

Fig. 4. Some errors in CDR

Case Study.   Finally, we summarize several typical errors in Fig. 4. From the first one, entity *parkinsonian disability* does not appear in a single sentence with any other entity, making it difficult to capture the connection between them. The second is the confusion between entities. Entity *isotretinoin embryopathy* and *isotretinoin* are two completely different entities whose words are similar. The last type is that the distance between entity pair is too long. The ability to capture structured information will be weakened with the increase of distance.

6 Conclusion

We introduce a novel heterogeneous graph network (IPR-DCGAT) for better document-level RE. It not only adopts DCGAT to update representations of nodes, but also update the representations of edges with a two-step iterative algorithm. This model outperforms new state-of-the-art results in various datasets. We will further improve the model to solve some problems mentioned above.

Acknowledgment. This work was supported by the National Key R&D Program of China (Grant No.2018YFB0204300).

References

1. Chiu, B., Crichton, G., Korhonen, A., Pyysalo, S.: How to train good word embeddings for biomedical NLP. In: Proceedings of the BioNLP 2016 Workshop
2. Christopoulou, F., Miwa, M., Ananiadou, S.: Connecting the dots: document-level neural relation extraction with edge-oriented graphs. In: EMNLP-IJCNLP(2019)
3. Christopoulou, F., Miwa, M., Ananiadou, S.: A walk-based model on entity graphs for relation extraction. In: ACL (2018)
4. Gu, J., Sun, F., Qian, L., Zhou, G.: Chemical-induced disease relation extraction via convolutional neural network. Database (2017)
5. Guo, Z., Zhang, Y., Teng, Z., Lu, W.: Densely connected graph convolutional networks for graph-to-sequence learning. TACL **7**, 297–312 (2019)
6. Gupta, P., Rajaram, S., Schütze, H., Runkler, T.: Neural relation extraction within and across sentence boundaries. In: AAAI (2019)
7. Kingma, D.P., Ba, J.: Adam: a method for stochastic optimization. arXiv preprint arXiv:1412.6980 (2014)
8. Kipf, T.N., Welling, M.: Semi-supervised classification with graph convolutional networks. arXiv preprint arXiv:1609.02907 (2016)
9. Li, J., et al.: Biocreative V CDR task corpus: a resource for chemical disease relation extraction. Database (2016)
10. Li, Z., et al.: CIDExtractor: a chemical-induced disease relation extraction system for biomedical literature. In: BIBM (2016)
11. Liu, C.Y., Sun, W.B., Chao, W.H., Che, W.X.: Convolution neural network for relation extraction. In: Motoda, H., Wu, Z., Cao, L., Zaiane, O., Yao, M., Wang, W. (eds.) ADMA 2013, Part II. LNCS (LNAI), vol. 8347, pp. 231–242. Springer, Heidelberg (2013). https://doi.org/10.1007/978-3-642-53917-6_21
12. Miwa, M., Bansal, M.: End-to-end relation extraction using LSTMs on sequences and tree structures. In: ACL (2016)
13. Nan, G., Guo, Z., Sekulić, I., Lu, W.: Reasoning with latent structure refinement for document-level relation extraction. In: ACL (2020)
14. Nguyen, D.Q., Verspoor, K.: Convolutional neural networks for chemical-disease relation extraction are improved with character-based word embeddings. In: Proceedings of the BioNLP 2018 Workshop (2018)
15. Peng, Y., Wei, C.H., Lu, Z.: Improving chemical disease relation extraction with rich features and weakly labeled data. J. Cheminf. (2016). https://doi.org/10.1186/s13321-016-0165-z
16. Pennington, J., Socher, R., Manning, C.D.: Glove: global vectors for word representation. In: EMNLP (2014)
17. Quirk, C., Poon, H.: Distant supervision for relation extraction beyond the sentence boundary. In: EACL (2017)
18. Schuster, M., Paliwal, K.K.: Bidirectional recurrent neural networks. TSP **45**(11), 2673–2681 (1997)
19. Soares, L.B., FitzGerald, N., Ling, J., Kwiatkowski, T.: Matching the blanks: distributional similarity for relation learning. In: ACL (2019)
20. Song, L., Zhang, Y., Wang, Z., Gildea, D.: N-ary relation extraction using graph-state LSTM. In: EMNLP (2018)
21. Tang, H., et al.: HIN: hierarchical inference network for document-level relation extraction. In: Lauw, H.W., Wong, R.C.-W., Ntoulas, A., Lim, E.-P., Ng, S.-K., Pan, S.J. (eds.) PAKDD 2020, Part I. LNCS (LNAI), vol. 12084, pp. 197–209. Springer, Cham (2020). https://doi.org/10.1007/978-3-030-47426-3_16

22. Veličković, P., Cucurull, G., Casanova, A., Romero, A., Liò, P., Bengio, Y.: Graph attention networks. In: ICLR (2018)
23. Wang, H., Focke, C., Sylvester, R., Mishra, N., Wang, W.: Fine-tune bert for DocRED with two-step process. arXiv preprint arXiv:1909.11898 (2019)
24. Wu, Y., Luo, R., Leung, H.C.M., Ting, H.-F., Lam, T.-W.: RENET: a deep learning approach for extracting gene-disease associations from literature. In: Cowen, L.J. (ed.) RECOMB 2019. LNCS, vol. 11467, pp. 272–284. Springer, Cham (2019). https://doi.org/10.1007/978-3-030-17083-7_17
25. Yao, Y., et al.: DocRED: a large-scale document-level relation extraction dataset. In: ACL (2019)
26. Zeng, D., Liu, K., Chen, Y., Zhao, J.: Distant supervision for relation extraction via piecewise convolutional neural networks. In: EMNLP (2015)
27. Zeng, D., Liu, K., Lai, S., Zhou, G., Zhao, J.: Relation classification via convolutional deep neural network. In: COLING (2014)
28. Zeng, S., Xu, R., Chang, B., Li, L.: Double graph based reasoning for document-level relation extraction. In: EMNLP (2020)
29. Zheng, W., et al.: An effective neural model extracting document level chemical-induced disease relations from biomedical literature. JBI **83**, 1–9 (2018)

Causal Inference Using Global Forecasting Models for Counterfactual Prediction

Priscila Grecov[1]([⊠]), Kasun Bandara[1]([⊠])[iD], Christoph Bergmeir[1]([⊠])[iD],
Klaus Ackermann[2]([⊠])[iD], Sam Campbell[3]([⊠]), Deborah Scott[3]([⊠]),
and Dan Lubman[3]([⊠])

[1] Department of Data Science and Artificial Intelligence, Monash University,
Melbourne, Australia
{priscila.grecov,herath.bandara,christoph.bergmeir}@monash.edu
[2] Department of Econometrics and Business Statistics, Monash University,
Melbourne, Australia
klaus.ackermann@monash.edu
[3] Turning Point, Eastern Health Clinical School, Monash University,
Melbourne, Australia
{sam.campbell,debbie.scott,dan.lubman}@monash.edu

Abstract. This research proposes a global forecasting and inference method based on recurrent neural networks (RNN) to predict policy interventions' causal effects on an outcome over time through the counterfactual approach. The traditional univariate methods that operate within the well-established synthetic control method have strong linearity assumptions in the covariates. This has recently been addressed by successfully using univariate RNNs for this task. We use an RNN trained not univariately per series but globally across all time series, which allows us to model treated and control time series simultaneously over the pre-treatment period. Therewith, we do not need to make equivalence assumptions between distributions of the control and treated outcomes in the pre-treatment period. This allows us to achieve better accuracy and precisely isolate the effect of an intervention. We compare our novel approach with local univariate approaches on two real-world datasets on 1) how policy changes in Alcohol outlet licensing affect emergency service calls, and 2) how COVID19 lockdown measures affect emergency services use. Our results show that our novel method can outperform the accuracy of state-of-the-art predictions, thereby estimating the size of a causal effect more accurately. The experimental results are statistically significant, indicating our framework generates better counterfactual predictions.

Keywords: Global forecasting · Causal inference · Counterfactual

Acknowledgments to Turning Point researchers who code the NASS data and ambulance services and paramedics who create and provide that data.

© Springer Nature Switzerland AG 2021
K. Karlapalem et al. (Eds.): PAKDD 2021, LNAI 12713, pp. 282–294, 2021.
https://doi.org/10.1007/978-3-030-75765-6_23

1   Introduction

Causal inference determines causal relationships of interventions and effects, and measures the impact of interventions. It is important in situations where fully randomized control trials (A/B testing) are too costly, ethically questionable, or otherwise not possible. The insights drawn from causal inference analysis are useful to understand why and how effects happen, and enable targeted interventions and robust predictions. Causal inference has important applications in policy-making, as well as in marketing, advertisement targeting, and other areas.

The base idea is that an *intervention* affects only part of the overall amount of observable instances, known as the treated instances, so that the remaining instances can be used as the control group that is not impacted by the intervention. For example, a policy change (e.g., about COVID19 lockdowns, Alcohol licenses issued, or others), could have affected only certain counties, not others. This is the base idea behind the Rubin Causal model [24] and is called the "potential outcome" approach. In this approach, the difference between the counterfactual prediction and the true values is considered as an estimation of the causal effect. Here, the counterfactual prediction refers to the prediction under the assumption of absence of intervention, for treated instances in the post-intervention period.

Using the Rubin Causal model premise, numerous strategies have been developed in the literature to conduct causal inference analysis. This includes the regression discontinuity methods [17], the differences-in-differences methods [3], the synthetic control methods [1], the network settings methods [9], and the observational combined methods [2]. In these methods, to compute the counterfactual prediction, usually a time series forecasting model is trained on parts of the dataset that have not been affected by the intervention (pre-intervention period), and is then applied to parts that have been affected (post-intervention period). Recently, deep neural network based counterfactual prediction methods have been introduced [12,14,20,21,25]. These studies argue that the nonparametric nature of deep learning models obviate the nonlinear, non-convex limitations of the traditional counterfactual prediction methods.

Nonetheless, the underlying forecasting methods used in the current counterfactual prediction frameworks are mostly univariate models. In contrast, the state of the art in time series forecasting has moved from such local, per-series univariate modelling to global forecasting models (GFM) that learn across many time series [4,19]. Compared to univariate forecasting models that treat each time series separately, GFMs are unified forecasting models that are trained across sets of many time series. This allows the GFMs to exploit the cross-series information available in a set of time series. The application of GFMs to conduct causal analysis, using the notion of Granger Causality [13], has already proven useful [5]. We say that a variable Y_t "Granger causes" X_{t+1} if making Y_t available as an input to the forecasting of X_{t+1} yields a more accurate forecast. It indicates that Y contains useful information, not found in the other inputs to the forecasting procedure, that helps to explain the behaviour of X. However, when using Granger Causality analysis, in practice it is usually not possible to include all the relevant external variables for model training [22]. Therefore, we focus our work on the application of the counterfactual prediction approach to perform causal impact analysis.

In this work, we propose Deep Counterfactual Prediction Net (DeepCPNet), a GFM-based counterfactual prediction method that performs causal analysis. To the best of our knowledge, this is the first study that employs a GFM-based methodology to conduct causal inference using the counterfactual approach. Compared to univariate approaches [23,26], GFMs are better suited for making counterfactual prediction, as they learn across multiple time series simultaneously. In univariate approaches, training during the pre-treatment period takes into consideration only the combination of control unit time series as covariates, having then to transfer the learned parameters (e.g., network weights) to the treated time series in the post-intervention period to predict the counterfactual. With a global approach, when we add the treated unit before the intervention effect to the training phase, we are able to add more information to the modelling and therewith the forecasting without the effects of the intervention and therewith the subsequent causal inference becomes more accurate. Furthermore, we do not need to make an assumption of equivalence between distributions of the control and treated outcomes in the pre-treatment period, and do not need to search for or limit ourselves to similar control units (therewith also not having to define a notion of similarity). With a global approach, we are in addition reducing the risk to bias the results by pre-splitting our data in control and treated group. Forgoing cross-series dependence between the groups could otherwise dramatically decrease the overall forecasting performance. To model the nonlinear, non-convex, and dynamic interactions between the treated and controlled time series groups, we use Long Short-Term Memory networks (LSTM) that are naturally suited for time series forecasting.

We evaluate the proposed DeepCPNet using two real-world datasets. The first dataset is an Emergency Medical Services (EMS) demand dataset, which consists of attendances related to alcohol intoxication reported in Australia. The second dataset is related to 911 emergency call demand in the Montgomery County, Pennsylvania, United States. In our framework, we first validate the externally given policy variable for the potential causal factors that can influence the time series. In the first dataset, we identify the number of alcohol licenses issued (ALI) as a potential causal influence towards the alcohol intoxication related EMS demand. Here, ALI is a factor that policymakers can control and is therefore of interest [5]. We consider the effect of COVID19 lockdown measures as a potential causal factor in the second dataset. As the second step of our DeepCPNet framework, we classify each time series into treated and control groups, based on the effect of the causal factor. As the third step, we define the time periods for the pre-intervention and the post-intervention process. For the second and the third steps, we perform a comprehensive exploratory analysis to validate our exogenous given policy variable and the intervention starting time. Next, we use the GFM forecast architecture in DeepCPNet to train across all the treated and the controlled time series for the pre-treatment period. Then, the DeepCPNet estimates the counterfactual outcome for the treated unit in the post-intervention period, which is considered as the estimated treated unit trajectory without the effect of the intervention. Finally, we perform Wilcoxon signed-rank test to assess whether the difference between the gaps of errors from the control units and the treats units are statistically significant. The source code of our DeepCPNet framework and the experiments is available at https:// bit.ly/3mWFbEO.

The rest of this research paper is organised as follows. In Sect. 2, we formally define the counterfactual prediction task and describe the methodology used in the DeepCPnet framework. In Sect. 3, we apply DeepCPnet to the benchmark datasets. In Sect. 4, we analyse the results obtained, and discuss the main insights from our experiments. Finally, Sect. 5 concludes the paper.

2   Methodology

In the following, we first define the counterfactual prediction task. Then, we explain the forecast engine used to generate the counterfactual prediction in the DeepCPNet framework, and detail the placebo testing framework.

2.1   Counterfactual Prediction

The problem of counterfactual output prediction is formulated as follows. Let N be the number of time series of each unit $i = 1, ..., N$, and T be the time $t = 1, ..., T_0, ..., T$, where T_0 is the beginning of the intervention. We denote Y as the matrix $N \times T$. Among the units i, the control units are represented by $Y_{i,t}^C$, and the treated units are represented by $Y_{i,t}^I$. Thus, $Y_{i,t \leq T_0}^{C,I}$ is the pre-intervention matrix and $Y_{i,t>T_0}^{C,I}$ the post-intervention matrix.

The counterfactual outcome for the treated units is their forecasting output $\hat{Y}_{i,t>T_0}^I$ from the model fitted over the whole pre-intervention matrix $Y_{i,t \leq T_0}^{C,I}$ of observed values, assuming that treated units are exposed to the intervention at time T_0 and forward. There is an implicit assumption that the treatment is well-defined, i.e., each unit presenting the same number of potential outcomes [18]. Finally, the causal effect estimation of this intervention over the treated units $\hat{\phi}_{i,t>T_0}^I$, will be the difference between their observed values in the post-intervention period and the counterfactual prediction, for each treated unit $i = 1, ..., N$, as follows [8]:

$$\hat{\phi}_{i,t>T_0}^I = Y_{i,t>T_0}^I - \hat{Y}_{i,t>T_0}^I, \tag{1}$$

$$Causal\ Effect_i = \sum_{t=T_0+1}^{T} \hat{\phi}_{i,t}^I, \tag{2}$$

2.2   DeepCPNet Forecast Engine

We implement the DeepCPNet framework using the open-source deep-learning toolkit TensorFlow [15]. The forecasting engine of DeepCPNet consists of three layers, namely: 1) the preprocessing layer, 2) the DeepCPNet training layer, and 3) the post-processing layer.

In the pre-processing layer, the time series are first normalised using the mean-scale transformation strategy. Then, we apply the log transformation to stabilise the variance of the time series, which also assures seasonality and trend in the series to be additive. As the last step of the pre-processing phase, we use a decomposition technique to extract the seasonal components of the time series. These extracted components are later used as teacher inputs to the DeepCPNet training layer. In our experiments, we use the Seasonal and Trend Decomposition using Loess (STL) [10] method as our primary time series decomposition technique.

The DeepCPNet training layer uses an LSTM, which is naturally suited for modelling time series data, and has been heavily used in the time series forecasting literature [4, 7]. To train the DeepCPNet, we use the past observations of time series in the form of input and output windows, following the Moving Window transformation strategy recommended by Hewamalage et al. [15]. Furthermore, we use the Seasonal Exogenous (SE) training approach proposed by Bandara et al. [6] to train our framework. In the SE training approach, the seasonal components which are extracted in the pre-processing phase are used as exogenous variables to the original time series observations. This supplements the Deep-CPNet to learn the seasonality present across multiple related time series. Furthermore, we use the stacked architecture as the primary training architecture of DeepCPNet. Again following the recommendations of Hewamalage et al. [15], we use COntinuous COin Betting (COCOB) as the primary learning algorithm to learn DeepCPNet.

The third layer of DeepCPNet, the post-processing layer, reverts back the transformations applied in the pre-processing phase. Finally, to calculate the counterfactual predictions, the DeepCPNet is applied to the pre-intervention matrix $Y_{i,t \leq T_0}^{C,I}$ (as defined in Sect. 2.1) to obtain the counterfactual outcome for each treated unit $\hat{Y}_{i,t > T_0}^{I}$, where the training window is $[1, T_0]$ and the forecasting window is $(T_0, T]$.

Our method has different hyper-parameters such as LSTM-cell-dimension, Mini-batch-size, Epoch-size, Hidden Layers, etc. We reserve the last output window of each time series for automatic hyper-parameter tuning. Here, we use the sequential model-based configuration (SMAC) algorithm that implements a Bayesian hyper-parameter optimisation process [16].

2.3   Placebo Tests

In the literature, studies often conduct a placebo test to benchmark the accuracy of the model estimators used for counterfactual predictions [1, 8, 23]. The placebo method evaluates the performance of the predictor only over the forecasting accuracy of the control units. That is, it removes the actual treated units from the training phase and evaluates the models on their ability to produce lower error on the control units. Good accuracy in the placebo tests indicates that the counterfactual forecasts are accurate, and the predictor is able to successfully generalise.

Also, if the placebo tests generate error gaps that are similar to the one estimated in the treated units, the analysis does not provide significant evidence of a null effect of the treatment over-analysis. This shows that the counterfactual predictions are not accurate enough. On the other hand, if the placebo tests demonstrate the error gap for treated units is unusually large relative to the ones for the control units, then the results indicate the quality of the counterfactual predictions.

To ensure that the difference between these error gap magnitudes are statistically significant, we apply a non-parametric paired Wilcoxon signed-rank exact test. We use the default implementation of this statistical test available in R, with a significance level of $\alpha = 0.05$.

3 Experimental Setup

In this section, we present the experimental setup used to evaluate the Deep-CPNet on two real-world datasets, including a discussion of the datasets, error metrics, and benchmarks.

3.1 Datasets

The National Ambulance Surveillance System (NASS) Dataset. The national dataset of coded ambulance clinical records held by Turning Point, an Australian addiction research and education centre. This dataset [11] holds surveillance data on alcohol and other drug, self-harm and mental health-related ambulance attendances across 5 of the 6 Australian states and 2 territories. In our experiments, we only use the monthly EMS demand data relevant to the alcohol intoxication category for 79 local government areas (LGAs) in Australia. In this dataset, we investigate how the number of alcohol licenses issued (ALI) impacts the alcohol intoxication calls demand. The ALI variable is used to separate the time series into control and treated units, and it is also used as an exogenous variable to train the DeepCPNet. The entire time period for both alcohol intoxication and ALI time series is from January-15 to May-19. The observations from June-18 to May-19 are used as the test set because they correspond to the intervention period. This intervention period is determined by the abnormal increase of ALI observed for some local jurisdictions during July-18 to November-18; then, the pre-intervention time period is set to January-15 to May-18. When training the DeepCPNet, the training output window size is set to 12, as the intended forecast horizon is 12 months. Also, the corresponding input window size is set to 15 (1.25*12), following the recommendations of Hewamalage et al.[15].

911 Emergency Calls Dataset. This dataset contains emergency calls relevant to EMS, traffic, and fire, specified in detail in 88 distinct types of codes. The data is available for 62 municipalities of Montgomery County in the United States for the time period of December-2015 to July-2020. We aggregate the original daily observations to monthly level to overcome the data sparsity, and categorise the 88 codes into EMS, traffic, and fire. In this dataset, we investigate the impact of COVID19 lockdown measures on the 911 emergency calls demand. The COVID19 lockdown restriction measures were put into place from the beginning of January 2020. Therefore, the post-intervention period is set to January-2020 to July-2020, whereas the pre-intervention period is set to December-2015 to December-2019. Following the same heuristic used for the NASS dataset, here we set the training output window size of the DeepCPNet to 7, and the corresponding training input window size to 15.

3.2   Error Metrics for Performance Measuring

To evaluate the forecast accuracy of the DeepCPNet, we report two scale-independent error metrics that are commonly used in time series forecasting research. These are the symmetric Mean Absolute Percentage Error (sMAPE) and the Mean Absolute Scaled Error (MASE), defined as follows:

$$sMAPE = \frac{2}{h} \sum_{t=n+1}^{n+h} \frac{|F_t - Y_t|}{|Y_t| + |F_t|}, \quad MASE = \frac{1}{h} \frac{\sum_{t=n+1}^{n+h} |F_t - Y_t|}{\frac{1}{n-S} \sum_{t=S+1}^{n} |Y_t - Y_{t-S}|} \quad (3)$$

Here, h indicates the number of data points in the test set (the forecasting horizon), n is the number of observations in the training set, F_t represents the forecasts generated by DeepCPNet, and Y_t the actual observation at time t. Also, S refers to the frequency of the seasonality in a given time series. The mean and median of these error measures across series are reported in our evaluation.

3.3   Benchmarks and DeepCPNet Variants

We benchmark the GFM-based forecasting engine used in the DeepCPNet against some univariate state-of-the-art forecasting algorithms, namely ETS and ARIMA. Both these methods are used with their default parameters from the forecast package in R. We also compare the results with a univariate LSTM method, which is identical to DeepCPNet but trained on each series separately. Furthermore, we define DeepCPNet-ALI as a variant of the DeepCPNet model that adds a time series of the amount of ALI as an external variable to the original ambulance calls time series when training the DeepCPNet.

4   Results and Discussion

Table 1 shows the evaluation summary of the DeepCPNet variants and benchmarks for the NASS dataset. According to Table 1, we can see that overall the proposed DeepCPNet-ALI variant achieves the best results for both treated and control groups. We see that after incorporating ALI as an exogenous variable (DeepCPNet-ALI), the accuracy of DeepCPNet has improved, outperforming

Table 1. Results for the 79 monthly series of NASS.

Method	Mean sMAPE	Median sMAPE	Mean MASE	Median MASE
DeepCPNet				
- All LGAs	0.1527	0.1425	1.0628	0.9818
- Treated Group	0.1547	0.1477	1.0731	0.9790
- Control Group	0.1388	0.1375	0.9917	1.0117
DeepCPNet-ALI				
- All LGAs	0.1396	0.1341	0.9786	0.9467
- Treated Group	0.1405	0.1341	0.9812	0.9413
- Control Group	0.1332	0.1357	0.9604	0.9733
LSTM-univariate				
- All LGAs	0.1557	0.1537	1.0828	1.0205
- Treated Group	0.1570	0.1560	1.0900	1.0205
- Control Group	0.1464	0.1323	1.0331	0.9716
ARIMA				
- All LGAs	0.1560	0.1458	1.0888	0.9853
- Treated Group	0.1572	0.1427	1.0973	0.9643
- Control Group	0.1476	0.1490	1.0300	1.0069
ETS				
- All LGAs	0.1507	0.1441	1.0647	1.0078
- Treated Group	0.1515	0.1427	1.0705	0.9981
- Control Group	0.1450	0.1555	1.0244	1.0876

the original DeepCPNet and the rest of the statistical benchmarks, LSTM univariate, ARIMA, and ETS.

Afterwards, we confirm the causal influence of ALI over the alcohol intoxication calls demand using the counterfactual modelling approach. To achieve this, we first investigate the trend of the ALI to capture a possible anomaly trajectory. Here, we normalise the 79 ALI time series by the population of the respective LGA, and then use the STL decomposition through the overall ALI time series. In Fig. 1, we see that there exists a non-seasonal and abnormal growth in the issuing of alcohol licenses from June 2018 to November 2018. Therefore, we take this event as our intervention event and set the post-intervention period from June 2018. Our aim is to predict the counterfactual outcome for the treated units (LGAs that presented this same outlier trajectory of abnormally high ALI increase) from June 2018 onwards.

Based on the above grouping criteria, we split the ALI time series into control and treated groups. The control group represents the LGAs with no increase/decrease of ALI during the post-intervention period, while the treated group represents the LGAs with growth at the number of ALI during this period. We identify 69 LGAs for the treated group, and 10 LGAs for the control group.

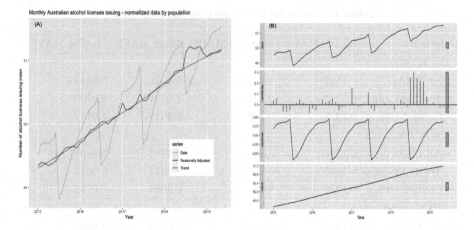

Fig. 1. (A) The STL Decomposition of the ALI time series. The blue line indicates a non-seasonal and abnormally high increase in the amount of alcohol licenses (ALI) issued between July 2018 and November 2018. (B) STL Decomposition of the ALI time series. This plot displays each decomposition component in the time series. In the remainder component, it clearly shows the non-seasonal event that occurred between July 2018 and November 2018, which is considered as the intervention event for this dataset. (Color figure online)

In Table 1, we see that in both DeepCPNet and DeepCPNet-ALI variants the errors for the control group are smaller than those of the treated group. To confirm the quality of the counterfactual outcome prediction, two factors need to be confirmed: (1) the forecast for the control group outcome should be at least as accurate as that for the alternative benchmark methods and (2) the null effect of the intervention over the control units (the placebo test proceedings). Concerning the first point, Table 1 shows that DeepCPNet and DeepCPNet-ALI for the control groups perform better, compared to LSTM univariate, ARIMA, and ETS. To validate the second point, as described in Sect. 2.3, we perform statistical significance tests of the differences between the gaps of errors from the control units and the treated units. The results are statistically significant with a *p-value* of 0.012 and 0.021 for the DeepCPNet and the DeepCPNet-ALI, respectively. These results show supporting evidence that the variable ALI has a causal effect on the alcohol intoxication related EMS demand. Here, the causal effect can be considered as the difference between the observed trajectory of the treated units and its counterfactual trend (see Fig. 2-A).

Table 2 summarises the results of the DeepCPNet and benchmarks for the 911 emergency calls. To estimate the counterfactual outcome for the townships that were affected by the COVID19 lockdown, we train the DeepCPNet up to December 2019 (pre-intervention period), and forecast from January 2020 to July 2020 (post-intervention period). The control group for this dataset is the set of townships that implemented lighter (or none) lockdown restriction measures. Following a similar procedure to Fig. 2-A, we identify 12 municipalities from

Table 2. Results for the 62 monthly series of 911 emergency calls.

	Methods							
	Control group				Treated group			
Error metric	DeepCPNet	LSTM-uni	ARIMA	ETS	DeepCPNet	LSTM-uni	ARIMA	ETS
Mean sMAPE	0.1899	0.1945	0.1847	0.1920	0.2525	0.2525	0.2508	0.2624
Median sMAPE	0.1740	0.1783	0.1717	0.1746	0.2290	0.2256	0.2250	0.2336
Mean MASE	0.8521	0.8698	0.8288	0.8616	1.3939	1.3926	1.3857	1.4498
Median MASE	0.9176	0.9370	0.9272	0.9430	1.3100	1.2842	1.2848	1.3334

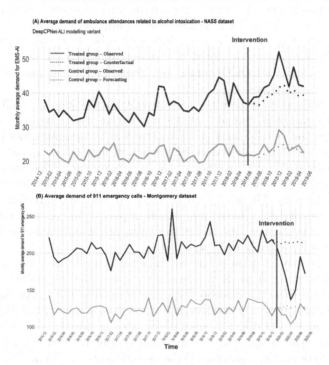

Fig. 2. The full lines denote the observed data and the dashed lines represent the forecasts. The dashed blue line indicates the counterfactual prediction for the treated group, where its trajectory is free from the intervention effect. We can see that the error gap from the control group is smaller than the error gap for the treated group. The difference between the blue lines indicate the causal effect of the variable ALI over the alcohol intoxication related EMS demand - graphic (A); and the causal effect of the COVID19 lockdown measures over the 911 emergency callouts - graphic (B). (Color figure online)

a total of 62 townships, as the control group. According to Table 2, we observe that the performance of DeepCPNet in the control group time series is at least as accurate as the benchmarks, LSTM univariate, ETS, and ARIMA. Furthermore, the results are statistically significant with a *p-value* of 0.005.

Therefore, we conclude that the COVID19-lockdown has affected the number of 911 emergency calls. Here, the counterfactual prediction can be considered as a good estimation for the trend of 911 emergency calls, in the absence of the COVID19 lockdown measures. Hence, the effect of the lockdown measures over the number of 911 emergency calls can be estimated as the difference between the observed trajectory and the projected counterfactual trend (see Fig. 2-B).

5   Conclusions

We have proposed a novel counterfactual framework based on global forecasting models. By incorporating the global forecasting approach, the proposed method offers more complex and realistic modelling to predict reliable counterfactual outcomes. In particular, our global RNN-based approach uses a stacked architecture, LSTM cells, a COCOB optimizer, deseasonalisation, and some further pre-processing techniques.

Our method not only handles non-convexity limitations of traditional synthetic control methods, but also allows us to relax the assumption of equivalence between the distributions of the control and treated outcomes in the pre-treatment period. Our counterfactual prediction method is trained over both control and treated units together in the pre-treatment period to predict the counterfactual of treated units, by applying the forecasting model to the post-intervention periods. Though we do not need to assume equal distribution for control and treated series in the pre-treatment period, we assume an equivalent distribution between the pre- and post-treatment-period outcomes for control units, which is more likely to be satisfied.

Our results show that the proposed framework outperforms univariate state-of-the-art forecasting methods in terms of accuracy. The statistically significant results obtained from the placebo testing indicate that the causal factors have affected the emergency services demand. These results show the ability of Deep-CPNet to estimate the size of a causal effect more accurately. Moreover, we have demonstrated that DeepCPNet is capable of conducting causal analysis in the events of two treatment scenarios: (1) the one-off treatment event depicted in the case of COVID-19 lockdown measures and (2) the across-time treatment event depicted in the case of liquor licensing policies.

Some limitations of the counterfactual approach remain in our method, such as the assumption that intervention effects keep constant in the post-treatment period. Also, RNN-based estimators continue to require sufficient pre-treatment period observations, thus being more appropriate in contexts of higher frequency and higher dimensional datasets of sufficient size.

A future direction of our research is the framework's use on simulated data where the causality relationships can be added to the variables for the simulation of causal effects. The inclusion of more than one external factor to study the effects of more than one intervention also is a possible future direction.

References

1. Abadie, A., Diamond, A., Hainmueller, J.: Synthetic control methods for comparative case studies: estimating the effect of California's tobacco control program. J. Am. Stat. Assoc. **105**(490), 493–505 (2010)
2. Athey, S., Chetty, R., Imbens, G., Kang, H.: Estimating treatment effects using multiple surrogates: The role of the surrogate score and the surrogate index. arXiv preprint arXiv:1603.09326 (2016)
3. Athey, S., Imbens, G.W.: Identification and inference in nonlinear difference-in-differences models. Econometrica **74**(2), 431–497 (2006)
4. Bandara, K., Bergmeir, C., Smyl, S.: Forecasting across time series databases using recurrent neural networks on groups of similar series: a clustering approach. Expert Syst. Appl. **140**, 112896 (2020)
5. Bandara, K., Bergmeir, C., Campbell, S., Scott, D., Lubman, D.: Towards accurate predictions and causal 'what-if' analyses for planning and policy-making: a case study in emergency medical services demand. In: IJCNN, pp. 1–10. IEEE (2020)
6. Bandara, K., Bergmeir, C., Hewamalage, H.: LSTM-MSNet: leveraging forecasts on sets of related time series with multiple seasonal patterns. IEEE TNNLS (2020)
7. Bandara, K., Shi, P., Bergmeir, C., Hewamalage, H., Tran, Q., Seaman, B.: Sales demand forecast in e-commerce using a long short-term memory neural network methodology. In: Gedeon, T., Wong, K.W., Lee, M. (eds.) ICONIP 2019, Part III. LNCS, vol. 11955, pp. 462–474. Springer, Cham (2019). https://doi.org/10.1007/978-3-030-36718-3_39
8. Brodersen, K.H., Gallusser, F., Koehler, J., Remy, N., Scott, S.L.: Inferring causal impact using Bayesian structural time-series models. Ann. Appl. Stat. **9**(1), 247–274 (2015)
9. Chandrasekhar, A.: Econometrics of network formation. In: The Oxford Handbook of the Economics of Networks, pp. 303–357 (2016)
10. Cleveland, R., Cleveland, W., McRae, J., Terpenning, I.: STL: a seasonal-trend decomposition procedure based on loess. J. Off. Stat. **6**(1), 3–33 (1990)
11. Lubman, D.I., et al.: The national ambulance surveillance system. PLoS One **15**, e0228316 (2020)
12. Farrell, M.H., Liang, T., Misra, S.: Deep neural networks for estimation and inference. arXiv preprint arXiv:1809.09953 (2018)
13. Granger, C.W.: Testing for causality: a personal viewpoint. J. Econ. Dyn. Control **2**, 329–352 (1980)
14. Hartford, J., Lewis, G., Leyton-Brown, K., Taddy, M.: Deep IV: a flexible approach for counterfactual prediction. In: ICML, pp. 1414–1423 (2017)
15. Hewamalage, H., Bergmeir, C., Bandara, K.: Recurrent neural networks for time series forecasting: current status and future directions. Int. J. Forecast. **37**(1), 388–427 (2020)
16. Hutter, F., Hoos, H.H., Leyton-Brown, K.: Sequential model-based optimization for general algorithm configuration. In: Coello, C.A.C. (ed.) LION 2011. LNCS, vol. 6683, pp. 507–523. Springer, Heidelberg (2011). https://doi.org/10.1007/978-3-642-25566-3_40
17. Imbens, G.W., Lemieux, T.: Regression discontinuity designs: a guide to practice. J. Econ. **142**(2), 615–635 (2008)
18. Imbens, G.W., Rubin, D.B.: Causal Inference in Statistics, Social, and Biomedical Sciences. Cambridge University Press, Cambridge (2015)

19. Januschowski, T., et al.: Criteria for classifying forecasting methods. Int. J. Forecast. **36**(1), 167–177 (2020)
20. Johansson, F., Shalit, U., Sontag, D.: Learning representations for counterfactual inference. In: International Conference on Machine Learning, pp. 3020–3029 (2016)
21. Lim, B.: Forecasting treatment responses over time using recurrent marginal structural networks. NeurIPS **18**, 7483–7493 (2018)
22. Nauta, M., Bucur, D., Seifert, C.: Causal discovery with attention-based convolutional neural networks. ML Knowl. Extr. **1**(1), 312–340 (2019)
23. Poulos, J.: RNN-based counterfactual prediction. arXiv preprint arXiv:1712.03553 (2017)
24. Rubin, D.B.: Estimating causal effects of treatments in randomized and nonrandomized studies. J. Educ. Psycho. **66**(5), 688 (1974)
25. Shi, C., Blei, D., Veitch, V.: Adapting neural networks for the estimation of treatment effects. In: NeurIPS. pp. 2507–2517 (2019)
26. Steinkraus, A.: Estimating treatment effects with artificial neural nets: a comparison to synthetic control method. Econ. Bull. **39**(4), 2778–2791 (2019)

CED-BGFN: Chinese Event Detection via Bidirectional Glyph-Aware Dynamic Fusion Network

Qi Zhai, Zhigang Kan, Sen Yang, Linbo Qiao[(⊠)], Feng Liu[(⊠)], and Dongsheng Li[(⊠)]

College of Computer, National University of Defense Technology, Changsha, China
{zhaiqi18,qiao.linbo,richardlf,dsli}@nudt.edu.cn

Abstract. Event Detection is an essential task in information extraction. However, most existing studies on event detection are designed for English text. There is still a lack of efficient algorithm for Chinese event detection, which is expected to be greatly improved. Recent work has shown that enhanced text representation, such as introducing glyph information, can significantly improve downstream tasks in natural language processing. In this paper, we propose a novel method for Chinese Event Detection via Bidirectional Glyph-aware Dynamic Fusion Network, called CED-BGFN. We use two representations: glyph-aware information and pre-trained language model. To integrate the heterogeneous representation modules, we propose a creative fusion network Bidirectional Glyph-aware Fusion Network, named BGFN. Considering the dynamic interaction of the two expressions, BGFN adaptively learns the fusion weights for the downstream event detection task. We conduct extensive experiments to investigate the validity of the proposed method on the ACE 2005 Chinese corpus. Results demonstrate that compared with the previous state-of-the-art methods, our approach obtains transcendent performance in both event trigger identification task and classification task, with an increase of 5.48 (7.46%) and 5.03 (7.1%) in F1-score, respectively.

Keywords: Chinese event detection · Interactive fusion network · Glyph

1 Introduction

As a complex natural language processing (NLP) task, event detection is a vital step of event extraction. It aims to automatically extract trigger words from unstructured text and identify event types by trigger words. For example, *"The militants attacked the town and injured three people"* illustrates an *"Attack"*

The work was partially supported by the National Key Research & Development Program of China under Grant No. 2018YFB0204300, and the National Natural Science Foundation of China under Grant No. 61806216, 62025208 and 61932001.

© Springer Nature Switzerland AG 2021
K. Karlapalem et al. (Eds.): PAKDD 2021, LNAI 12713, pp. 295–307, 2021.
https://doi.org/10.1007/978-3-030-75765-6_24

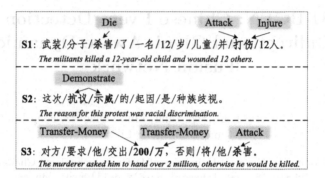

Fig. 1. An example of word-triggers mismatch and character-triggers ambiguity.

event triggered by the word *"attacked"* and an *"Injure"* event triggered by the word *"injured"*. Due to the characteristics of Chinese itself, Chinese event detection (CED) still has the following two challenges: (1) Since there is no obvious segmentation in Chinese, the word-wise method may cause mismatches in the stage of trigger words identification stage. (2) The same trigger words may express different semantics in various contexts. As shown in Fig. 1, in the S1 "打" (hit) and "伤" (wounded) in the word "打伤" (wounded) represent the trigger words *"Attack"* and *"Injure"*, respectively. On the contrary, in the S2 "抗议\示威" (protest\demonstration) is a trigger but contains two words. What's more, in the S1 the trigger word "杀" (kill) represents the event *"Die"*, but denotes *"Attack"* in the S3.

Currently, several studies have attempted to address these issues utilizing various methods. Traditional methods are almost feature-based, which may be restricted by hand-crafted features, leading to error accumulation, ambiguity, and portability problems [2,12,19]. Nowadays, as neural networks evolve, their strengths in automatically extracting and learning features offer exciting new opportunities for researchers to alleviate these troubles [6,14,23–25,30]. However, these methods directly and simply concatenate information in the acquisition of language structure information, without considering the interactions between diverse representations. Simultaneously, as a fresh NLP paradigm, pre-trained language models (PLMs) have the profit of providing better model initialization methods and general language representations, but glyphs are not taken into account in the processes of pre-training [5]. Notably, Glyce [16] scanned 13 Chinese natural language task records and experimentally showed that glyphs provided effective support for the acquisition of structural information in Chinese.

In this paper, we propose a new CED method via BGFN. Instead of directly encoding Chinese glyph images, we adopt multiple CNN encoding methods which model the fine-grained representation of characters in different kernels to gain more comprehensive glyph information. We apply BiLSTM for glyph characters to learn position information implicitly and to reduce the generation gap between the context-aware representations of PLMs and glyph, which is beneficial to couple heterogeneous networks. Besides, BGFN uses cross-coding two expressions and obtains interactive attentional dynamic weights to fuse the two representations. In summary, our contributions in this paper are:

- To our knowledge, this is the first attempt to fuse glyph information with PLMs for CED. Our proposed bidirectional glyph-aware method further increases sequence information and reduces the generation gap with the context-aware representation of PLMs.
- We design the BGFN to integrate heterogeneous representations, thus enriching the language structure information.
- We conduct extensive experiments on the ACE 2005 Chinese corpus. The results not only show that our approach outperforms the previous state-of-the-art methods, but also demonstrate the effectiveness of glyphs in CED.

2   Related Works

Event Detection (ED). ED is a key link in the field of information extraction. The traditional methods [2,12,19] use existing natural language processing toolkits (e.g., part of speech tagging, entity information, etc.) to obtain feature representations. Wu et al. [23] proposed to incorporate part of speech, dependency grammar, distance from the HEAD information. These approaches may lead to error accumulation, ambiguity, and portability problems. Recently, deep learning methods [9,10,27] have been extensively used in the ED task. Ding et al. [6] introduced the Trigger-aware Lattice Neural Network to enhance the understanding of polysemous trigger words through an external language knowledge base (HowNet). However, it didn't consider the complete context and required the construction of a large number of external features. Xi et al. [25] first used the language model representation to obtain contextual semantic information in CED. Based on character-wise models, it also incorporated word embeddings to aid structural pattern learning.

Pre-trained Language Models (PLMs). PLMs use different tasks to pre-train on the large-scale unlabeled text and then fine-tune the model or representation for a specific task. Early PLMs like ELMo [18] used the deep bidirectional language model that consists of a forward and a backward LSTM. GPT [20] adopted a left-to-right Transformer decoder to generate context word vectors. But they only use one-way information. In terms of this issue, BERT [5] proposed to use the bidirectional Transformer encoder. ERNIE [22] added the prior knowledge of phrases and entities, BERT-wwm [4] utilized the whole word masking in Chinese text, RoBERTa [15] improved the BERT training method and optimized the training process, and XLNet [28] introduced the permutation language model and Transformer-XL. To obtain a more fine-grained internal semantic representation of Chinese characters, researchers proposed some methods: radicals [13], strokes [1], wubi [17], glyphs [16], characters [3], etc.

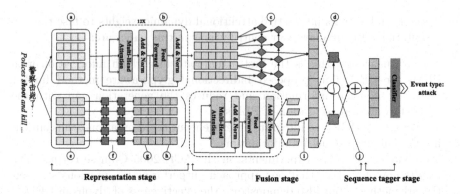

Fig. 2. Illustration of the CED-BGFN architecture. It shows the processing of the event instance triggered by the word "击" (shoot). The labels are (a) BERT input representation, (b) bidirectional Transformer encoder, (c) BiLSTM, (d) scalar multiplication, (e) glyph representation, (f) two-layer BiLSTM, (g,h) final forward and backward hidden states, respectively, (i) context encoder output, (j) PReLU(·).

Meta-embeddings. Recently, some researches combine multiple word embeddings in the text representation stage. CharWNN [7] combined character-based and word-based embeddings. Glyce [16] concatenated glyph representation with BERT. Yin and Schütze [21] first proposed the meta-embeddings through neural networks. However, word embedding fusion was considered as a pre-processing step. It did not dynamically adapt to specific tasks. DME [11] dynamically obtained the weight value of each word embedding based on sentence-level self-attention. The interaction between the elements inside the word embeddings were not considered. Based on DME, DTFME [26] increased the internal relations of word embeddings through factorization and pooling operations.

3   Methodology

We regard the event detection task as a sequence labeling task to identify and classify each character in the input sentence. The architecture of our model is shown in Fig. 2, which includes the following three stages:

(1) **Representation stage**, this module is mainly to obtain the word embeddings that need to be fused. One is the glyph-aware representation, the other is context-aware representation by BERT.
(2) **Fusion stage**, this module is to merge heterogeneous representations and construct new independent representation from them.
(3) **Sequence tagger stage**, this module mainly uses multi-layer nonlinear perception to project the fusion representation of each character into 35 (add pad and null types) event type space.

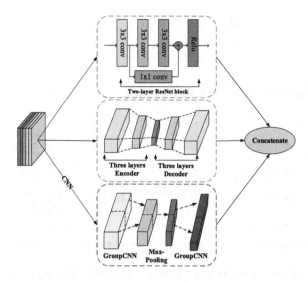

Fig. 3. Three encoding methods of the glyph character images. The gray box represents ResNet, the yellow box denotes AutoEncoder, and the purple box is GroupCNN. (Color figure online)

3.1 Representation Stage

Given a sentence, CED-BGFN will first learn a representation for each character. The embeddings consist of glyph-aware and context-aware representations.

Glyph-Aware Representation. In this module, we convert the input characters into font images to form the glyph-level embedding. The specific realization is shown in Fig. 3. Given an input sequence $S = \{c_1, c_2, ..., c_s\}$, where c_i represents the ith character in the sequence. For c_i, firstly we use GroupCNN, ResNet, AutoEncoder three encoding methods to obtain glyph information from different perspectives. GroupCNN [16] uses two-layer group convolutions with the 2 * 2 kernel. ResNet is composed of two residual blocks with the 3 * 3 kernel. AutoEncoder contains the three-layer encoder and decoder. At each layer of AutoEncoder's encoder, the input channels are twice as large as the output channels, and conversely, at the decoder layer, the output channels are twice as much as the input channels. Then they are concatenated, which can be formulated by Eq. (1):

$$G_i = [\text{Emb}_{Group}; \text{Emb}_{Res}; \text{Emb}_{AE}; \text{Emb}_{Char}] \tag{1}$$

where Emb_{Group}, Emb_{Res}, Emb_{AE}, Emb_{Char} denote GroupCNN, ResNet, AutoEncoder, and Character embedding, respectively. When encoding glyph images, we add an image classification loss L_{img} given as follows:

$$L_{img} = -\log \text{softmax}(W \times G + b) \tag{2}$$

where W, b are parameters, G refers to the glyph image representations of the input sentence. Then we apply a two-layer bidirectional LSTM to construct the contextual glyph embedding, which can be formulated by Eq. (3):

$$\overrightarrow{G}_i = \overrightarrow{LSTM}(G_1, G_2, ..., G_i)$$
$$\overleftarrow{G}_i = \overleftarrow{LSTM}(G_i, G_{i+1}, ..., G_s) \tag{3}$$
$$G'_i = [\overrightarrow{G}_i; \overleftarrow{G}_i]$$

where G'_i is the c_i glyph-aware representation.

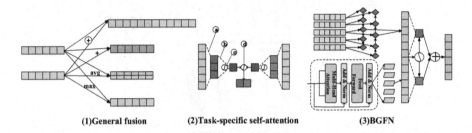

Fig. 4. Three fusion representation learning methods. The purple block and the orange block represent the context-aware representation and glyph-aware representation, respectively. The labels are (a,b) fully connected layer, (c) ReLU($\cdot$), (d) softmax($\cdot$). (Color figure online)

Context-Aware Representation. Context-aware representation relies on the PLMs BERT. The architecture of BERT is a multi-layer bidirectional Transformer encoder. The bidirectional Transformer encoder is composed of multi-head attention and feed-forward neural network. Multi-head attention consists of multiple self-attention structures. For c_i, we use B'_i to denote its context-aware representation, B denotes the context-aware representation of the sentence.

3.2 Fusion Stage

This section describes how we fuse them up to get a representation with rich language structure information. We design three different paradigms to integrate them: General fusion, Task-specific self-attention, and BGFN. As illustrated in Fig. 4, general fusion includes simply concatenation, summation, max-pooling, and avg-pooling. Task-specific self-attention directly captures the sentence-level self-attention of each representation and learns the weights of different embeddings by softmax($\cdot$). BGFN first couples two heterogeneous encoding methods:

$$G_i^T = \text{Encoder}(G'_i) \tag{4}$$

where *Encoder* is a layer bidirectional Transformer encoder.

$$\overrightarrow{B}'_i = \overrightarrow{LSTM}(B'_1, B'_2, ..., B'_i)$$
$$\overleftarrow{B}'_i = \overleftarrow{LSTM}(B'_i, B'_{i+1}, ..., B'_s) \tag{5}$$
$$B_i^L = [\overrightarrow{B}'_i; \overleftarrow{B}'_i]$$

where G_i^T and B_i^L are c_i interactive representations, respectively. To better measure two heterogeneous encoding interaction, we add the similarity calculation loss function, as shown in Eq. (6):

$$L_{sim}(G^T, B^L) = \frac{1}{s} \sum_{i=1}^{s} \begin{cases} 0.5(G^T - B^L)^2, & |G^T - B^L| < 1 \\ |G^T - B^L| - 0.5, & \text{otherwise.} \end{cases} \tag{6}$$

For fusion embedding, we dynamically acquire the weights of each character by using the interaction between the two representations:

$$\text{Emb}_{fusion} = \alpha_G G^T \times \alpha_B B^L \tag{7}$$

where $\alpha_G, \alpha_B = f(\{c_i\}_{j=1}^s)$ is a self-attention mechanism in Eq. (8):

$$\alpha_G, \alpha_B = f(\{c_i\}_{j=1}^s) = \text{softmax}(W\sigma(G^T, B^L)) \tag{8}$$

where Emb_{fusion} is the fusion representation, σ is the PReLU activation function, W is the linear weight initialized through Xavier.

3.3 Sequence Tagger Stage

The goal of sequence tagger stage is to calculate the event category of each character in the event mention. We input the fusion representation Emb_{fusion} into the classifier $P(F)$:

$$P(F) = \max(0, \text{Emb}_{fusion} W_1 + b_1)W_2 + b_2 = Y \tag{9}$$

where W, b are learnable parameters. We train the output results through the cross entropy error function Eq. (10):

$$\text{Loss}(Y, P) = -\sum_{j=1}^{s} \sum_{c=1}^{C} p_{jc} \cdot \log(\frac{e^{Y_j c}}{\sum_{c=1}^{C} e^{Y_j c}}) \tag{10}$$

where C is all event types. p_{jc} is 1 if the sample j belongs to class c. Besides calculating the task loss function, we add the classification accuracy loss of the glyph encoding and encoding similarity calculation loss function. The final loss function is obtained, namely:

$$\text{Loss}_{final} = \text{Loss}(Y, P) + \beta \text{L}_{img} + \text{L}_{sim}(G^T, B^L) \tag{11}$$

where β is a hyperparameter, and set to 0.1 in the experiment. To optimize the parameters, we use Adam for the optimizer.

4   Experiments

4.1   Experiment Setup

We conduct massive experiments on the ACE 2005 Chinese corpus for CED. The dataset contains 633 documents in total. We follow our previous work and divide the data into 569/64/64, using 569 training set, 64 validation set, 64 test set. The dimensions of GroupCNN embedding, ResNet embedding, AutoEncoder embedding, and Character embedding are 128/64/64/50, respectively. To be consistent with the dimension of BERT, the hidden state of BiLSTM is set to 384. In addition, we set the learning rate of the glyph encoder to 0.002 and BERT to 1e-5. Furthermore, we set the batch size to 16 and the epoch to 100. Finally, we follow the evaluation methods in the previous works [2,14,25], using precision (P), recall (R), and F1-score (F1) as the evaluation values. And only when the trigger word offset and type are exactly the same as the label, the trigger word can be correctly matched.

4.2 Baselines

We propose a novel fusion network that specifically fuses the information of the glyph and the pre-trained language model BERT. We compare CED-BGFN with previous state-of-the-art methods as follows:

C-BiLSTM. [29] proposed to input the text into BiLSTM and CNN separately, and concatenated the hidden state of BiLSTM with feature extracted by CNN.

HNN. [8] developed a hybrid neural network to capture both sequence and chunk information from specific contexts.

NPN. [14] proposed entire trigger nuggets centered at each character regardless of word boundaries and divided trigger words identification and classification tasks into different models.

TLNN. [6] used HowNet as an external knowledge base to obtain sense-level information. Trigger-aware lattice LSTM was designed as the feature extractor.

Hybrid Character Representation. [25] formed character embedding, word embedding, segmentation embedding, and language model embedding concatenate into character representation.

4.3 Overall Results

The results are depicted in Table 1. It displays that: (1) CED-BGFN yields significant improvements on the ACE 2005 Chinese corpus. It achieves 5.48 (7.46%) and 5.03 (7.1%) F1-score improvements on trigger identification and classification, respectively, which demonstrates its effectiveness on glyph information and fusion network. (2) Glyph information plays an important role in the semantic representations. Compared with the model $BiLSTM+CRF$ ($char+lm$), which takes character embedding and BERT as input, CED-BGFN achieves at least 6.18 (8.49%) and 5.33 (7.55%) F1-score improvements, respectively.

Table 1. Comparison with existing Chinese event detection methods (%).

Model	Trigger identification			Trigger classification		
	P	R	F1	P	R	F1
Char-based C-BiLSTM	65.6	66.7	66.1	60.0	60.9	60. 4
Word-based C-BiLSTM	75.8	59.0	66.4	69.8	54.2	61.0
HNN	74.2	63.1	68.2	**77.1**	53.1	63.0
NPN	64.8	73.8	69.0	60.9	69.3	64.8
TLNN	67.34	74.68	70.82	64.45	71.47	67.78
BiLSTM+CRF (char+lm) *	69.5	76.6	72.8	67.4	74.2	70.6
BiLSTM+CRF (char+lm+seg+word) *	68.9	78.8	73.5	66.4	76.0	70.9
CED-BGFN (ours)	**77.41**	**80.62**	**78.98**	74.42	**77.51**	**75.93**

The methods with * are from the *Hybrid Character Representation.*

Table 2. Effect of different text representations on CED task. Group, Res, AE and Char denote GroupCNN, ResNet, AutoEncoder, Character embeddings, respectively.

Model	Trigger identification			Trigger classification		
	P	R	F1	P	R	F1
Group+Res+AE+Char	73.76	67.13	70.29	**71.10**	64.71	67.75
Only Char	69.86	68.17	69.00	67.02	65.40	66.20
Group+Res+AE	70.67	69.20	69.93	67.84	66.44	67.13
Group+AE+Char	**74.46**	**71.63**	**73.02**	69.78	67.13	68.43
Res+AE+ Char	70.77	69.55	70.16	68.66	67.47	68.06
Group+Res	67.81	68.51	68.16	65.75	66.44	66.09
Char+Res	68.97	69.20	69.08	67.24	67.47	67.36
Char+Group	71.75	66.78	69.18	69.89	65.05	67.38
Group+Res+Char	71.53	71.28	71.40	69.10	**68.86**	**68.98**

4.4   Effect of Glyph Embedding

To further investigate the effects of the glyph embedding, we carry out supplementary experiments by only using glyph encoding for text representation. Glyph encoding consists of two parts: one is character embedding, the other is glyph information encoded by GroupCNN, ResNet, and AutoEncoder. In the experiments, BiLSTM is used as the context encoding, and only the text representation is changed to test the effect of different glyph representation components.

Through Table 2, we can observe *Group + Res + Char* clearly outperforms other methods in trigger classification. (1) Compared top five models with *Group + Res + Char*, we notice that while the first model *Group + Res + AE + Char* has more information, it is still inferior to *Group + Res + Char* in performance. We analyze that this may be due to the focus of information obtained by different encoding methods is different, and the effect after the fusion is different. Therefore, the usefulness of information can't be achieved simply by accumulating multiple types of information, but based on specific downstream tasks analysis and selection. (2) Compared $Group + Res$, $Char + Res$, $Char + Group$ with $Group + Res + Char$, we can see that the trigger word classification is improved 2.89 (4.37%), 1.62 (2.4%) and 1.6 (2.37%), respectively. It shows the effectiveness of three encoding methods.

4.5 Effect of Context Encoding

Glyph embedding obtains glyph and character information. To further obtain contextual semantic information, we compare two classical semantic encoding structures: LSTM and Transformer. As Table 3 shows, the effect of LSTM is far better than the encoding of the Transformer. Our explanations for the inferior performance of the Transformer encoding are as follows: on the one hand, the input representation of the glyph is different from BERT, which may cause the performance of Transformer not to perform well; on the other hand, the length of the text in the corpus is not very long, so LSTM can obtain richer the semantic information of the context.

Table 3. Effect of context encoding methods.

Model	Trigger identification			Trigger classification		
	P	R	F1	P	R	F1
No-context	35.74	29.07	32.06	35.32	28.72	31.68
Transformer	41.19	52.60	46.20	39.30	50.17	44.07
LSTM	71.53	71.28	71.40	69.10	68.86	68.98
CED-BGFN *	75.08	**83.39**	**79.02**	71.65	**79.58**	75.41
CED-BGFN	**77.41**	80.62	78.98	**74.42**	77.51	**75.93**

* denotes CED-BGFN without glyph context encoding during the fusion.

Table 4. Effect of different fusion methods.

Model	Trigger identification			Trigger classification		
	P	R	F1	P	R	F1
BERT	73.52	81.66	77.38	70.72	78.55	74.43
Glyph	71.53	71.28	71.40	69.10	68.86	68.98
Concatenate	74.14	**82.35**	78.03	71.03	**78.89**	74.75
Max_pooling	74.44	80.62	77.41	70.93	76.82	73.75
Avg_pooling	74.76	82.01	78.22	71.29	78.20	74.59
Sum	74.28	79.93	77.00	71.38	76.82	74.00
Liner_attention	73.75	81.66	77.50	71.25	**78.89**	74.88
CED-BGFN #	74.92	80.62	77.67	71.70	77.16	74.33
CED-BGFN	**77.41**	80.62	**78.98**	**74.42**	77.51	**75.93**

# denotes CED-BGFN without interacting with two heterogeneous semantic encoding methods during the fusion.

4.6   Effect of Fusion Methods

This part is to study the importance of fusion networks. Different word embeddings are encoded in different ways and the information obtained is complementary. Therefore, we propose BGFN to acquire richer semantic information.

We conduct a mass of ablation experiments to verify the effectiveness of the fusion network. Table 4 shows the performance of the fused word vectors outperforms the independent representations of the first block. Moreover, from different fusion methods: max-pooling, avg-pooling, summation, concatenate, and liner attention, the performance of concatenating and liner attention that dynamically allocates weights are better. Our explanation for the superior performance of the these two strategy is as follows: the dimension of these methods is twice as much as max-pooling, avg-pooling, summation, which can obtain more information while avoiding the problem of information loss in the other methods. From the last two lines we can obviously see the importance of the interaction of the two heterogeneous encoding methods. The trigger word identification and classification are improved by 1.32 (1.69%) and 1.6 (2.15%), respectively.

4.7   Effect of Auxiliary Task Training Objectives

When encoding the glyph representation, to better fit the encoded glyph image information, we add an image classification loss. In the fusion stage, in order to better fit the similarity of the two encoding methods, we propose to employ a similarity calculation loss function. It can be seen from Table 5: By adding the above two losses simultaneously, the F1-score of the trigger classification is increased by 0.8 (1.07%). The two auxiliary tasks play an essential role in the loss function calculation, avoiding overfitting.

Table 5. Effect of auxiliary task training objectives

Model	Trigger identification			Trigger classification		
	P	R	F1	P	R	F1
Task_loss	76.49	79.93	78.17	73.51	76.82	75.13
Task_loss+fusion_loss	74.52	80.97	77.61	71.97	**78.20**	74.96
Task_loss+ image_loss	74.60	**81.31**	77.81	71.75	**78.20**	74.83
Task_loss+fusion_loss+image_loss	**77.41**	80.62	**78.98**	**74.42**	77.51	**75.93**

5   Conclusion

In this paper, we propose a novel method for Chinese Event Detection via Bidirectional Glyph-aware Dynamic Fusion Network (CED-BGFN) to integrate glyph information with a pre-trained language model. Moreover, to better fuse these information, we propose the BGFN. It dynamically obtains the weights of each representation through the interaction between the two representations. The experimental results indicate that the proposed CED-BGFN model yields substantial improvements in the Chinese event detection task compared to the state-of-the-art methods. In the further, we will integrate other types of knowledge into representation models, such as entity types, whole word information, etc. In addition, we will also validate this idea in other NLP tasks.

References

1. Cao, S., Lu, W., Zhou, J., Li, X.: cw2vec: learning Chinese word embeddings with stroke n-gram information. In: AAAI (2018)
2. Chen, Z., Ji, H.: Language specific issue and feature exploration in Chinese event extraction. In: NAACL (2009)
3. Collobert, R., Weston, J.: A unified architecture for natural language processing: deep neural networks with multitask learning. In: ICML (2008)
4. Cui, Y., et al.: Pre-training with whole word masking for Chinese bert. arXiv preprint arXiv:1906.08101 (2019)
5. Devlin, J., Chang, M.W., Lee, K., Toutanova, K.: Bert: pre-training of deep bidirectional transformers for language understanding. In: NAACL (2019)
6. Ding, N., Li, Z., Liu, Z., Zheng, H., Lin, Z.: Event detection with trigger-aware lattice neural network. In: EMNLP-IJCNLP (2019)
7. Dos Santos, C., Zadrozny, B.: Learning character-level representations for part-of-speech tagging. In: ICML (2014)
8. Feng, X., Qin, B., Liu, T.: A language-independent neural network for event detection. Sci. China Inf. Sci. **61**(9), 1–12 (2018). https://doi.org/10.1007/s11432-017-9359-x
9. Han, Z., Jiang, J., Qiao, L., Dou, Y., Xu, J., Kan, Z.: Accelerating event detection with DGCNN and FPGAS. Electronics **9**(10), 1666 (2020)
10. Kan, Z., Qiao, L., Yang, S., Liu, F., Huang, F.: Event arguments extraction via dilate gated convolutional neural network with enhanced local features. IEEE Access **8**, 123483–123491 (2020)
11. Kiela, D., Wang, C., Cho, K.: Dynamic meta-embeddings for improved sentence representations. In: EMNLP (2018)
12. Li, P., Zhou, G.: Employing morphological structures and sememes for Chinese event extraction. In: COLING (2012)
13. Li, Y., Li, W., Sun, F., Li, S.: Component-enhanced Chinese character embeddings. In: EMNLP (2015)
14. Lin, H., Lu, Y., Han, X., Sun, L.: Nugget proposal networks for Chinese event detection. In: ACL (2018)
15. Liu, Y., et al.: Roberta: A robustly optimized bert pretraining approach. arXiv preprint arXiv:1907.11692 (2019)
16. Meng, Y., et al.: Glyce: glyph-vectors for Chinese character representations. In: NIPS (2019)
17. Nikolov, N.I., Hu, Y., Tan, M.X., Hahnloser, R.H.R.: Character-level Chinese-English translation through ASCII encoding. In: Proceedings of the Third Conference on Machine Translation: Research Papers (2018)
18. Peters, M.E., et al.: Deep contextualized word representations. In: NAACL (2018)
19. Qin, B., Zhao, Y., Ding, X., Liu, T., Zhai, G.: Event type recognition based on trigger expansion. Tsinghua Sci. Technol. **15**(3), 251–258 (2010)

20. Radford, A., Narasimhan, K., Salimans, T., Sutskever, I.: Improving language understanding by generative pre-training. Technical report, OpenAI (2018)
21. Santos, C.N.D., Guimaraes, V.: Boosting named entity recognition with neural character embeddings. In: Proceedings of the Fifth Named Entity Workshop, NEWS@ACL (2015)
22. Sun, Y., et al.: Ernie: enhanced representation through knowledge integration. arXiv preprint arXiv:1904.09223 (2019)
23. Wu, Y., Zhang, J.: Chinese event extraction based on attention and semantic features: a bidirectional circular neural network. Future Internet **10**(10), 95 (2018)
24. Xia, Y., Liu, Y.: Chinese event extraction using deepneural network with word embedding. arXiv preprint arXiv:1610.00842 (2016)
25. Xiangyu, X., Tong, Z., Wei, Y., Jinglei, Z., Rui, X., Shikun, Z.: A hybrid character representation for Chinese event detection. In: IJCNN (2019)
26. Xie, Y., Hu, Y., Xing, L., Wei, X.: Dynamic task-specific factors for meta-embedding. In: Douligeris, C., Karagiannis, D., Apostolou, D. (eds.) KSEM 2019. LNCS (LNAI), vol. 11776, pp. 63–74. Springer, Cham (2019). https://doi.org/10.1007/978-3-030-29563-9_7
27. Yang, S., Feng, D., Qiao, L., Kan, Z., Li, D.: Exploring pre-trained language models for event extraction and generation. In: ACL (2019)
28. Yang, Z., Dai, Z., Yang, Y., Carbonell, J., Salakhutdinov, R.R., Le, Q.V.: Xlnet: generalized autoregressive pretraining for language understanding. In: NIPS (2019)
29. Zeng, Y., Yang, H., Feng, Y., Wang, Z., Zhao, D.: A convolution BiLSTM neural network model for Chinese event extraction. In: Lin, C.-Y., Xue, N., Zhao, D., Huang, X., Feng, Y. (eds.) ICCPOL/NLPCC -2016. LNCS (LNAI), vol. 10102, pp. 275–287. Springer, Cham (2016). https://doi.org/10.1007/978-3-319-50496-4_23
30. Zhang, W., Ding, X., Liu, T.: Learning target-dependent sentence representations for chinese event detection. In: Zhang, S., Liu, T.-Y., Li, X., Guo, J., Li, C. (eds.) CCIR 2018. LNCS, vol. 11168, pp. 251–262. Springer, Cham (2018). https://doi.org/10.1007/978-3-030-01012-6_20

Learning Finite Automata with Shuffle

Xiaofan Wang[1,2(✉)]

[1] State Key Laboratory of Computer Science, Institute of Software,
Chinese Academy of Sciences, Beijing 100190, China
[2] University of Chinese Academy of Sciences, Beijing, China
wangxf@ios.ac.cn

Abstract. Learning finite automata has been a popular topic. Shuffle has been applied in information systems. Since shuffle introduced into finite automata makes the membership problem NP-hard, and there are no learning algorithms for finite automata supporting shuffle so far, it is an essential work to devise effective and precise algorithms for learning finite automata supporting shuffle. In this paper, finite automata are learned from sets of positive samples. First, we define *finite automata with shuffle* (FA(&)s), for which both the uniform and the non-uniform membership problem are decidable in polynomial time. Then, we learn an FA(&) from a given finite sample step by step. Our algorithm can ensure that the learned FA(&) is a precise representation of the given finite sample. Experimental results demonstrate that, FA(&) is more efficient in membership checking, and our algorithm can obtain a more concise automaton.

1 Introduction

Automata are the fundamental computation models widely used in various applications, including information processing systems. Learning finite automata has been a popular topic in machine learning, artificial intelligence and automated verification. Learning finite automata from sets of positive samples also become common works in information processing tasks, such as validating XML documents against schema languages [1], schemata inference [4,5], mining workflows from business processes [13,15,16], etc. In this paper, we focus on the automata supporting shuffle, and study the corresponding learning algorithms.

Shuffle (&) [11] has been applied in information systems, such as XML database systems for schema definitions [8,10,17] and workflow management systems [13,14,16]. Shuffle applied to any two strings returns the set of all possible interleavings of the symbols in the two strings. For example, the shuffle of ab and cd is $ab\&cd = \{abcd, acbd, acdb, cdab, cadb, cabd\}$. There are some finite automata supporting shuffle [2,3,7,10,12,19], which recognize the languages defined by regular expressions with shuffle, and are also applied in XML database systems

Work supported by National Natural Science Foundation of China under Grant Nos. 61872339, 61472405.

ⓒ Springer Nature Switzerland AG 2021
K. Karlapalem et al. (Eds.): PAKDD 2021, LNAI 12713, pp. 308–320, 2021.
https://doi.org/10.1007/978-3-030-75765-6_25

and workflow management systems. The above finite automata supporting shuffle are as follows: parallel finite automaton (PFA) [19], shuffle automaton (SA) [12], non-deterministic finite automaton supporting shuffle (NFA(&)) [10], concurrent finite-state automaton (CFSA) [2,3] and partial derivative automaton (PDA) [7]. However, for each one of the following automata: PFAs, SAs, CFSAs and PDAs, the uniform membership problem[1] is NP-complete [2,3,7,12,19]. The uniform membership problem for NFA(&)s is PSPACE-complete [10]. The non-uniform membership problem for CFSAs is also NP-complete [2]. For PFAs, SAs, NFA(&)s and PDAs, although the non-uniform membership problems for them can be decided in polynomial time [7,10,12,19], for PFAs, SAs and NFA(&)s, each one of them has many ε-transitions, which can lead to unnecessarily non-deterministic recognitions, and a PDA is a plain deterministic finite automaton (DFA), which can result in an exponential blow up of the size of automaton [7]. This results in some challenges to infer schema languages by learning automata supporting shuffle or validate XML documents (against schema languages supporting shuffle [8]) by membership checking. Additionally, for mining workflow from interleaved traces [13,16], the workflow model mentioned in [13] is just plain finite-state automaton. Although the workflow model proposed in [16] can be respected as an automaton supporting shuffle, the workflow model is mined from interleaved traces by using statistical inference, which leads to that the obtained result is over-generalized [16], and so far, there are no learning algorithms for the above finite automata supporting shuffle.

Therefore, for solving above problems, it is an essential work to devise more effective and precise algorithms for learning finite automata supporting shuffle from sets of positive samples. Different from existing works, we propose more succinct and polynomial decidable (for membership problem) finite automata: finite automata with shuffle (FA(&)s). For a given finite sample, an FA(&) is learned from the given finite sample step by step. We can ensure that the learned FA(&) is a precise representation (see Definition 4) of the given finite sample.

The main contributions of this paper are as follows.

- We introduce a new class of automata supporting shuffle: FA(&)s, for which both the uniform and the non-uniform membership problem are decidable in polynomial time. An FA(&) recognizes the language defined by a regular expression with shuffle, where each alphabet symbol occurs at most once.
- We devise an algorithm for learning FA(&)s. Our algorithm can ensure that the learned FA(&) is a precise representation of the given finite sample.
- We provide evaluations on FA(&)s in terms of conciseness and the time performance for membership checking. Experimental results demonstrate that, FA(&) is more efficient in membership checking, and our algorithm can obtain a more concise automaton.

The rest of this paper is organized as follows. Section 2 gives the basic definitions. Section 3 describes the FA(&) and provides an example of such an automa-

---

[1] For membership problem, in the uniform version, both the string and a representation of the language are given as inputs. In the non-uniform version, the language is fixed, only the string to be tested is considered as input.

ton. Section 4 presents the algorithm of learning an FA(&) from a given finite sample. Section 5 presents experiments. Section 6 concludes the paper.

2   Preliminaries

Let Σ be a finite alphabet of symbols. A standard regular expression over Σ is inductively defined as follows: ε and $a \in \Sigma$ are regular expressions, for any regular expressions r_1, r_2 and r_3, the disjunction $(r_1|r_2)$, the concatenation $(r_1 \cdot r_2)$, and the Kleene-star r_1^* are also regular expressions. Usually, we omit writing the concatenation operator in examples. The regular expressions with shuffle, which are denoted by RE(&)s, are extended from standard regular expressions by adding the shuffle operator: $r_1 \& r_2$. Note that, r^+ and $r?$ are used as abbreviations of rr^* and $r|\varepsilon$, respectively. The language $\mathcal{L}(r)$ is defined in the following inductive way: $\mathcal{L}(\varepsilon) = \{\varepsilon\}$; $\mathcal{L}(a) = \{a\}$; $\mathcal{L}(r_1|r_2) = \mathcal{L}(r_1) \cup \mathcal{L}(r_2)$; $\mathcal{L}(r_1 r_2) = \mathcal{L}(r_1)\mathcal{L}(r_2)$; $\mathcal{L}(r_1^*) = \mathcal{L}(r_1)^*$; $\mathcal{L}(r_1 \& r_2) = \mathcal{L}(r_1) \& \mathcal{L}(r_2) = \bigcup_{s_1 \in \mathcal{L}(r_1), s_2 \in \mathcal{L}(r_2)} s_1 \& s_2$. The shuffle operation & is defined inductively as follows: $u \& \varepsilon = \varepsilon \& u = \{u\}$, for $u \in \Sigma^*$; and $au \& bv = \{az | z \in u \& bv\} \cup \{bz | z \in au \& v\}$, for $u, v \in \Sigma^*$ and $a, b \in \Sigma$. & also obeys the associative law, that is $r_1 \& (r_2 \& r_3) - (r_1 \& r_2) \& r_3 - r_1 \& r_2 \& r_3$.

For a finite sample S, N denotes the sum of the length of strings in S. Let $\mathbb{N} = \{1, 2, 3, \cdots\}$. Let Σ_s ($s \in S$) denote the set of all symbols from Σ that appear in s. A string $s \in \Sigma^+$ is a shuffled string if $s \in u \& v$ for $u, v \in \Sigma^+$. For a directed graph (digraph) $G(V, E)$, $G. \succ (v)$ ($v \in G.V$) denotes the set of all direct successors of v in G. $G. \prec (v)$ denotes the set of all direct predecessors of v in G. For space consideration, all omitted proofs can be found at https://github.com/GraceFun/LearnFAS.

2.1   SOA, Shuffle Unit and Precise Representation of Sample

SOA is defined as follows.

Definition 1 (single-occurrence automaton (SOA) [6,9]). *Let Σ be a finite alphabet, and let q_0 and q_f be distinct symbols that do not occur in Σ. A single-occurrence automaton (SOA) over Σ is a finite directed graph $G = (V, E)$ such that (1) $q_0, q_f \in V$, and $V = \Sigma \cup \{q_0, q_f\}$; (2) q_0 has only outgoing edges, q_f has only incoming edges, and any string $a_1 \cdots a_n$ ($n \geq 1$) is accepted by an SOA G, if and only if there is a path $q_0 \to a_1 \to \cdots \to a_n \to q_f$ in G.*

Let $P(s, a, b) \in \{0, 1\}$ for $s \in S$ and $a, b \in \Sigma$ ($a \neq b$). $P(s, a, b) = 1$ if and only if a symbol b occurs in s and there exists a symbol a ($a \in \Sigma_s$) occurring before b. a can be interleaved with b if there exists $s_1, s_2 \in S$ such that $P(s_1, a, b) = P(s_2, b, a) = 1$. Let $w, z, x_i, y_j \in \Sigma \cup \{\varepsilon\}$, where $1 \leq i \leq m$, $1 \leq j \leq n$ and $m, n \in \mathbb{N}$. Let pattern $MutexStr(a, b) = wx_1 \cdots x_m a^k y_1 \cdots y_n z$ ($w \neq b, z \neq b, x_i \neq b, y_j \neq b, k \geq 2$), where a can be respectively interleaved with x_i and y_j (for each i, j) if $x_i, y_j \in \Sigma$, but neither w nor z can be interleaved with a if $w, z \in \Sigma$. A string described by $MutexStr(a, b)$ comprises a but not b.

Definition 2 (necessary interleaving). *For a given finite sample S, $a, b \in \Sigma$ ($a \neq b$), a is necessarily interleaved with b for S if and only if a can be interleaved with b and there does not exist the two distinct strings or substrings s_1 and s_2 occurring in S such that s_1 and s_2 can be described by $MutexStr(a, b)$ and $MutexStr(b, a)$, respectively.*

Example 1. Let $S = \{cd, dc, cc, dd\}$, $P(cd, c, d) = P(dc, d, c) = 1$, c can be interleaved with d, however, $s_1 = cc$ ($d \notin \Sigma_{s_1}$) and $s_2 = dd$ ($c \notin \Sigma_{s_2}$) are in S such that s_1 and s_2 can be described by $MutexStr(c, d)$ and $MutexStr(d, c)$, respectively. c is unnecessarily interleaved with d. Note that, $\mathcal{L}(c^* \& d^*) \supset \mathcal{L}((c|d)^+) \supseteq S$.

Shuffle unit is defined as follows.

Definition 3 (shuffle unit). *For a given finite sample S, a shuffle unit is a list $[e_1, e_2, \cdots, e_k]$ ($k \geq 2$), where $e_i \subset \Sigma$ and $e_i \cap e_j = \emptyset$ ($1 \leq i, j \leq k, i \neq j$). If a symbol $u \in e_i$, there is at least one symbol $v \in e_j$ such that u is necessarily interleaved with v for S, and there is at least one symbol $u' \in e_i$ ($u' \neq u$) such that u is unnecessarily interleaved with u' for S.*

Example 2. For sample $S = \{abcd, dcab, cc, dd\}$, a is necessary interleaved with c and d, respectively. b is also necessary interleaved with c and d, respectively. But a (resp. c) is unnecessary interleaved with b (resp. d). Then, $[\{a, b\}, \{c, d\}]$ can be a shuffle unit.

A shuffle unit can be used to discover the substructure of an FA($\&$) recognizing shuffled strings. Such as $[\{a, b\}, \{c, d\}]$, the corresponding substructure is just the FA($\&$) shown in Fig. 1(a), which recognizes the shuffled string $acbd$.

Definition 4 (Precise Representation of Sample [9]). *Let $\mathcal{D}$ denote a class of finite automata. $\alpha \in \mathcal{D}$ is a precise representation of a finite sample S if $\mathcal{L}(\alpha) \supseteq S$ and there does not exist $\beta \in \mathcal{D}$ such that $\mathcal{L}(\alpha) \supset \mathcal{L}(\beta) \supseteq S$.*

3   Finite Automata with Shuffle

An FA($\&$) is defined to recognize the language defined by a regular expression with shuffle, where each alphabet symbol occurs at most once. For a regular expression r, if there is an FA($\&$) recognizing the language $\mathcal{L}(r)$, then for the ith subexpression of the form $r_i = r_{i_1} \& r_{i_2} \& \cdots \& r_{i_k}$ ($i \in \mathbb{N}, k \geq 2$) in r, there are start marker $\&_i$ and end marker $\&_i^+$ in the FA($\&$) for recognizing the strings derived by r_i. For each subexpression r_{i_j} ($1 \leq j \leq k$) in r_i, there is a concurrent marker $\|_{ij}$ in the FA($\&$) for recognizing the symbols or strings derived by r_{i_j}. There are at most $\lceil \frac{|\Sigma|-1}{2} \rceil$ start markers (resp. end markers) in an FA($\&$), and there are at most $|\Sigma|$ concurrent markers in an FA($\&$) (see Theorem 1). Let $\mathbb{D}_\Sigma = \{1, 2, \cdots, \lceil \frac{|\Sigma|-1}{2} \rceil\}$ and $\mathbb{P}_\Sigma = \{1, 2, \cdots, |\Sigma|\}$. Then, the definition of an FA($\&$) is as follows.

Definition 5 (Finite Automata with Shuffle). *A finite automaton with shuffle (FA(&)) is a tuple $\mathcal{A} = (V, Q, \Sigma, q_0, q_f, H, \delta)$. The members of the tuple are described as follows:*

- Σ *is a finite and non-empty alphabet.*
- q_0 *and* q_f: q_0 *is the initial state,* q_f *is the unique final state.*
- V *is a finite set of nodes.* $V = \Sigma \cup V'$, *where* $V' \subseteq \{\&_i, \&_i^+\}_{i \in \mathbb{D}_\Sigma} \cup \{||_{ij} | i \in \mathbb{D}_\Sigma, j \in \mathbb{P}_\Sigma\}$.
- Q *is a finite set of states.* $Q = Q' \cup \{q_0, q_f\}$, $Q' \subset 2^V$. *For a state* $q \in Q$, q *is a set of the nodes in V if* $q \notin \{q_0, q_f\}$.
- $H(V, E, R)$ *is a node transition graph (a directed graph), where* $H.V = \mathcal{A}.V \cup \{q_0, q_f\}$ *and* $H.R$: $\{\&_i | i \in \mathbb{D}_\Sigma\} \mapsto 2^\Sigma$. $H.R(\&_i)$ *is a set of alphabet symbols, where a symbol is the first letter of the shuffled string that can be recognized by an (FA(&)) starting from the state including the node $\&amp_i$. q_0 has only outgoing edges, q_f has only incoming edges.*
- δ *is the state transition function.* $\delta : Q_1 \times (\Sigma \cup \{\dashv\}) \mapsto 2^{Q_2}$, *where* $Q_1 = Q \setminus \{q_f\}$, $Q_2 = Q \setminus \{q_0\}$ *and* $\dashv$ *denotes the end symbol of a string.*
  (1) $q = q_0$ *or q is a set, where* $q = \{a\}$ *or* $\{\&_i^+\}$ ($a \in \Sigma, i \in \mathbb{D}_\Sigma$):
  - $y \in \Sigma$: $\delta(q, y) = \{\{y\} | y \in H.\succ (x), x \in \{q_0, a, \&_i^+\}\} \cup \{\{\&_j\} | \&_j \in H.\succ (x), y \notin H.\succ (x) \wedge y \in H.R(\&_j), x \in \{q_0, a, \&_i^+\}, j \in \mathbb{D}_\Sigma\}$;
  - $y = \dashv$: $\delta(q, y) = \{p | p \in H.\succ (x) \wedge p = q_f, x \in \{q_0, a, \&_i^+\}\}$.
  (2) $q = \{\&_i\}$ ($i \in \mathbb{D}_\Sigma$) *and* $y \in \Sigma$: $\delta(q, y) = \{H.\succ (\&_i) | y \in H.R(\&_i)\}$.
  (3) q *is a set and* $|q| \geq 2$:
  - $y \in \Sigma$: $\delta(q, y) = \bigcup_{1 \leq t \leq 3} \delta_t(q, y)$, *where:*
    * $\delta_1(q, y) = \{(q \setminus \{x\}) \cup \{z\} | z \in H.\succ (x), z = y \vee y \in H.R(z), z \in \{y, \&_i\}, i \in \mathbb{D}_\Sigma, x \in q\}$;
    * $\delta_2(q, y) = \{(q \setminus \{\&_i\}) \cup H.\succ (\&_i) | \exists i \in \mathbb{D}_\Sigma : \&_i \in q \wedge y \in H.R(\&_i))\}$;
    * $\delta_3(q, y) = \{(q \setminus W) \cup \{\&_i^+\} | \exists i \in \mathbb{D}_\Sigma \forall x \in W : x \in H.\prec (\&_i^+) \wedge y \notin H.\succ (x), W \subseteq q \wedge |W| = |H.\succ (\&_i)|\}$.
  - $y = \dashv$: $\delta(q, y) = \{(q \setminus W) \cup \{\&_i^+\} | \exists i \in \mathbb{D}_\Sigma \forall x \in W : x \in H.\prec (\&_i^+), W \subseteq q \wedge |W| = |H.\succ (\&_i)|\}$.

Since the digraph H is a parameter implied in the state transition function δ of an FA(&), and a state (excluding q_0 and q_f) in an FA(&) is a set of the nodes in $H.V$, an FA(&) can be intuitively denoted by the corresponding node transition graph. Additionally, we can learn an FA(&) from a given finite sample by constructing the node transition graph of the FA(&).

For recognizing a string $s \in S$ in an FA(&), the current symbol y ($y \in \Sigma_s$) is consumed if and only if the state (a set of nodes) including node y is reached. $\dashv$ is consumed if and only if the final state q_f is reached. If y (resp. $\dashv$) is not consumed, then y (resp. $\dashv$) will be still read as the current symbol to be recognized. The next state p' is specified by the state transition function of an FA(&) such that the current state q transits to state p', from which the state including node y (resp. the final state q_f) can be reached. A string is not recognized by an FA(&) if there is a symbol occurring in the string that has not been consumed and the next state is an empty set.

Example 3. Let $V = \Sigma \cup \{\&_1, \&_1^+, ||_{11}, ||_{12}\}$, where $\Sigma = \{a, b, c, d\}$. Let $Q = \{q_0, q_f, \{\&_1\}, \{||_{11}, ||_{12}\}, \{a, ||_{12}\}, \{b, ||_{12}\}, \{||_{11}, c\}, \{||_{11}, d\}, \{a, c\}, \{a, d\}, \{b, c\}, \{b, d\}, \{\&_1^+\}\}$. Figure 1(a) shows the FA($\&$) $\mathcal{A} = (V, Q, \Sigma, q_0, q_f, H, \delta)$, where $H.R(\&_1) = \{a, c, d\}$. $\mathcal{A}$ is denoted by the node transition graph (digraph H) and recognizes the language $\mathcal{L}(((ab)?\&(c|d)^+)^+)$. Figure 1(b) is a state transition table, which demonstrates how the FA($\&$) $\mathcal{A}$ recognizes the string *acbd*.

Theorem 1. *An FA($\&$) recognizes the language defined by a regular expression with shuffle, where each alphabet symbol occurs at most once. For a regular expression r, if an FA($\&$) recognizes the language $\mathcal{L}(r)$, then the FA($\&$) has at most $\lceil \frac{|\Sigma|-1}{2} \rceil$ start markers, at most $\lceil \frac{|\Sigma|-1}{2} \rceil$ end markers and at most $|\Sigma|$ concurrent markers.*

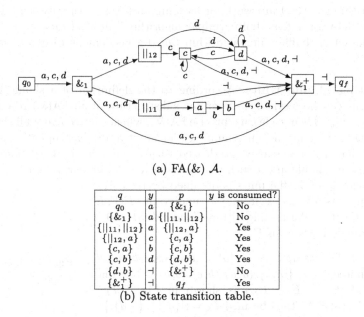

(a) FA($\&$) $\mathcal{A}$.

q	y	p	y is consumed?
q_0	a	$\{\&_1\}$	No
$\{\&_1\}$	a	$\{||_{11}, ||_{12}\}$	No
$\{||_{11}, ||_{12}\}$	a	$\{||_{12}, a\}$	Yes
$\{||_{12}, a\}$	c	$\{c, a\}$	Yes
$\{c, a\}$	b	$\{c, b\}$	Yes
$\{c, b\}$	d	$\{d, b\}$	Yes
$\{d, b\}$	$\dashv$	$\{\&_1^+\}$	No
$\{\&_1^+\}$	$\dashv$	q_f	Yes

(b) State transition table.

Fig. 1. (a) is the FA($\&$) $\mathcal{A}$ for recognizing the language $\mathcal{L}(((ab)?\&(c|d)^+)^+)$. (b) is the state transition table for the FA($\&$) $\mathcal{A}$ recognizing the string *acbd*. $q \in Q \setminus \{q_f\}$ is the current state, $y \in \Sigma \cup \{\dashv\}$ is the current symbol, $p \in Q \setminus \{q_0\}$ is the next state.

Theorem 2. *Both the uniform and the non-uniform membership problem for FA($\&$)s are solvable in polynomial time.*

4   Learning FA($\&$)

The learning algorithm is based on the learning style defined in Definition 4.

For a given finite sample S, to learn an FA(&), first, any two distinct symbols $u, v \in \Sigma$ that u is necessarily interleaved with v are identified from S. We obtain the set $U_{\&}$ of all such tuples (u, v) from S (if $(u, v) \in U_{\&}$, then $(v, u) \notin U_{\&}$). Then, we obtain the set $P_{\&}$ of shuffle units from the undirected graph (undigraph) $F(V, E)$, where $F.E = U_{\&}$.

Algorithm 1. *LearnFAS*

Input: A finite sample S;
Output: An FA(&) $\mathcal{A}$;
1: SOA G=2T-INF(S); $P_{\&} = \emptyset$;
2: Compute $U_{\&}$ from S;;
3: Construct undigraph $F(V, E) : F.E = U_{\&}$;
4: $P_{\&} = UnorderUnits(F, P_{\&})$;
5: FA(&) $\mathcal{A} = ConsFAS(G, P_{\&})$;
6: **return** $\mathcal{A}$;

Finally, we convert the SOA built for S to an FA(&) by traversing the shuffle units in $P_{\&}$. Our algorithm can ensure that the learned FA(&) is a precise representation of S (see Theorem 4).

Algorithm 1 is the framework for learning an FA(&). Algorithm 2T-INF [6] builds an SOA for a given finite sample; algorithm *UnorderUnits* [20] is used to obtain the set of shuffle units; algorithm *ConsFAS* is demonstrated to construct an FA(&).

Computing Shuffle Units. According to the definition of a shuffle unit, a shuffle unit can be used to discover the substructure of an FA(&) recognizing shuffled strings. Then, to learn a precise FA(&), which can recognize all the shuffled strings from a given finite sample S, for any two distinct alphabet symbols u and v that u is necessarily interleaved with v (i.e., $(u, v) \in U_{\&}$), there must exist a unique shuffle unit l such that u and v are in different sets in l.

The set $P_{\&}$ of shuffle units is obtained by recursively extracting sets of nodes from the undigraph $F(V, E)$, where $F.E = U_{\&}$. We use algorithm *UnorderUnits* [20] to extract shuffle units from F.

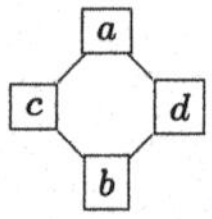

Example 4. For sample $S = \{abcd, dcab, abcacb, cc, dd\}$, the computed $U_{\&} = \{(a, c), (a, d), (b, c), (b, d)\}$. The undigraph $F(V, E)$ ($F.E = U_{\&}$) is shown in Fig. 2. $P_{\&} = UnorderUnits(F, \emptyset)$, the obtained $P_{\&} = \{[\{a, b\}, \{c, d\}]\}$.

Fig. 2. The undigraph F.

Theorem 3. *Let* $P_{\&} = UnorderUnits(F(V, E), \emptyset)$ *where* $F.E = U_{\&}$, *then for any tuple* $(u, v) \in U_{\&}$, *there exists a unique shuffle unit* $l \in P_{\&}$ *such that* u *and* v *are in different sets in* l.

Constructing FA(&). We construct an FA(&) by building the node transition graph (a finite directed graph) of an FA(&). Since an SOA built for S is also a precise representation of S [9], and a shuffle unit in $P_{\&}$ can be used to discover the substructure of an FA(&) recognizing the shuffled strings from S, we first convert the SOA G built for S to the node transition graph of an FA(&) by traversing the shuffle units in $P_{\&}$. The detailed descriptions of the FA(&) are then presented.

Algorithm 2 is presented to construct an FA(&). First, we remove the directed edges in G, where tails and heads are in two disjoint sets of a shuffle unit in $P_\&$, respectively (line 2). Then, for the ith shuffle unit in $P_\&$ ($P_\&(i)$), we identify the corresponding set of nodes from G (by using $extract$) which is the union of the all sets of nodes in $P_\&(i)$ to add the start marker ($\&_i$) and the end marker ($\&_i^+$) in G (lines 4 $\sim$ 6). Additionally, for the jth set in $P_\&(i)$ ($P_\&(i)(j)$, initially, $i, j = 1$), we

Algorithm 2. *ConsFAS*

Input: A digraph $G(V, E)$, a set $P_\&$ of shuffle units;
Output: An FA(&) $\mathcal{A}$;
1: **for** $i = 1$ to $|P_\&|$ **do**
2:    Delete edges $\{(v_1, v_2)|v_1 \in e_1, v_2 \in e_2, e_1, e_2 \in P_\&(i), e_1 \neq e_2\}$ in G;
3: **for** $i = 1$ to $|P_\&|$ **do**
4:    Let $T = \bigcup_k P_\&(i)(k)$; $G_1 = G.extract(T)$;
5:    $G.addnode_1(\&_i, G_1 . \succ (q_0))$; $\mathcal{R}(\&_i) = G . \succ (\&_i)$;
6:    $G.addnode_2(\&_i^+, G_1 . \prec (q_f))$;
7:    **if** $Loop(S, G, P_\&(i))$ **then** add edge $(\&_i^+, \&_i)$ in G;
8:    **for** $j = 1$ to $|P_\&(i)|$ **do**
9:       $G_1 = G.extract(P_\&(i)(j))$;
10:       $G.addnode_1(||_{ij}, G_1 . \succ (q_0))$;
11:       **if** $NO(S, P_\&(i)(j), P_\&(i))$ **then**
12:          Add edge $(||_{ij}, \&_i^+)$ in G;
13: FA(&) $\mathcal{A} = (V', Q, \Sigma, G.q_0, G.q_f, H(G.V, G.E, \mathcal{R}), \delta)$;
14: **return** $\mathcal{A}$;

---

identify the corresponding set of nodes from G (by using $extract$) to add concurrent marker $||_{ij}$ in G (line 10). Note that, the edge $(\&_i^+, \&_i)$ (resp. edge $(||_{ij}, \&_i^+)$) is possibly added into G (lines 7,12). The finally obtained G is the node transition graph of an FA(&), then the FA(&) $\mathcal{A}$ is obtained (line 13). The constructed FA(&) $\mathcal{A}$ is described as follows.

$\mathcal{A} = (V', Q, \Sigma, G.q_0, G.q_f, H, \delta)$, where $V' = G.V \setminus \{q_0, q_f\}$, $H.V = G.V$, $H.E = G.E$, $Q = Q' \cup \{G.q_0, G.q_f\}$ and $Q' = \bigcup_q \bigcup_y \delta(q, y)$ ($q \in \{G.q_0\} \cup Q'$ and $y \in \Sigma \cup \{\dashv\}$). δ can be derived from the node transition graph H, which is a parameter implied in δ. Note that, $\mathcal{R} : \{\&_i | i \in \mathbb{D}_\Sigma\} \mapsto 2^\Sigma$, $\mathcal{R}(\&_i)$ (obtained in line 5) ensures that, starting from the state including the node $\&_i$, an FA(&) can begin to recognize the shuffled strings, where the first letters are in $\mathcal{R}(\&_i)$. Thus, $H.R = \mathcal{R}$. Theorem 4 illustrates that, for any given finite sample, the learned FA(&) is a precise representation of the given finite sample.

Some subroutines in Algorithm 2 are described as follows.

$extract$ on a digraph G takes a set of nodes U (of G) as input, it extracts a new digraph G_1 ($G_1.V = \{q_0, q_f\} \cup U$) from G, G_1 reserves the directed edges (in G) between any two nodes in U. All nodes in U, which have not incoming edges or have incoming edges from outside of U in G, have incoming edges from q_0 in G_1. Moreover, all nodes in U, which have not outgoing edges or have outgoing edges to outside of U in G, have outgoing edges to q_f in G_1.

$addnode_1$ and $addnode_2$ work on a digraph G, both of them take a node v and a set of nodes U (of G) as inputs. $addnode_1$ works on G as follows. Add a node v in G; add edges $\{(v_1, v)|v_1 \in G . \prec (v_2), v_2 \in U\}$; remove edges $\{(v_1, v_2)|v_1 \in G . \prec (v_2), v_2 \in U\}$; add edges $\{(v, v_2)|v_2 \in U\}$. $addnode_2$ works on G as follows. Add a node v in G; add edges $\{(v, v_1)|v_1 \in G . \succ (v_2), v_2 \in U\}$; remove edges $\{(v_2, v_1)|v_1 \in G . \succ (v_2), v_2 \in U\}$; add edges $\{(v_2, v)|v_2 \in U\}$.

$Loop(S, G, P_\&(i))$ and $NO(S, P_\&(i)(j), P_\&(i))$ are bool functions. $Loop$ returns $true$ if there exists k ($1 \leq k \leq |P_\&(i)|$), $l \in P_\&(i)(k)$ and a string $s \in S$ such that there are two nodes that are labelled by the symbols from $P_\&(i)(k)$

but not strongly connected in G, and $l \in \mathcal{R}(\&_i)$ occurs in s more than once but does not consecutively appears in s. NO returns $true$ if there exists the substring s_b of $s \in S$ (which consists of at least one symbol from the set $T = \bigcup_k P_\&(i)(k)$.) such that s_b does not contain any symbols from $P_\&(i)(j)$ and neither $t s_b$ nor $s_b t$ ($t \in T$) are substrings of s.

The SOA $G(V, E)$ and $P_\&$ are as inputs of Algorithm 2. It takes $\mathcal{O}(|V|^2)$ time to delete the specified edges in G (line 2). For each shuffle unit $l \in P_\&$, the average time complexity of $extract$ in line 4 (resp. in line 9) is $\mathcal{O}(\frac{|V||\Sigma|}{|P_\&|})$ (resp. $\mathcal{O}(\frac{|V||\Sigma|}{|P_\&||l|})$). For $addnode_1$ and $addnode_2$, the time complexity of them are both $\mathcal{O}(|V|)$. Both $Loop$ (line 7) and NO (line 12) take $\mathcal{O}(|\Sigma|N)$ time for judgments. There are $|\Sigma|$ symbols at most that are used to form a shuffle unit, and $P_\&$ includes $\lceil \frac{|\Sigma|-1}{2} \rceil$ shuffle units at most. Thus, the average time complexity of algorithm $ConsFAS$ is $\mathcal{O}(|V||\Sigma| + |\Sigma|\lceil \frac{|\Sigma|-1}{2} \rceil N) = \mathcal{O}(|\Sigma|^2 N)$ ($|V| = |\Sigma| + 2, N > |\Sigma|$).

For a given finite sample S, it takes $\mathcal{O}(|\Sigma|N)$ time to compute $U_\&$. The time complexity of algorithm $UnorderUnits$ is $\mathcal{O}(|\Sigma|^3)$ [20]. I.e., the set $P_\&$ of shuffle units can be obtained in $\mathcal{O}(|\Sigma|^3)$ time. An SOA can be built for S in $\mathcal{O}(N)$ time. Thus, the time complexity of algorithm $LearnFAS$ is $\mathcal{O}(|\Sigma|^2 N)$.

Example 5. For $S = \{abcd, dcab, abcacb, cc, dd\}$, the SOA recognizing S is shown in Fig. 3(a). The set of shuffle units $P_\& = \{[\{a, b\}, \{c, d\}]\}$. Figure 3 illustrates the main steps to convert the SOA to the node transition graph H of the FA(&) $\mathcal{A}$ by traversing shuffle units in $P_\&$. $H.\mathcal{R}(\&_1) = \{a, c, d\}$. The labels on the edges of H can be seen in Fig. 1(a), which illustrates the finally obtained FA(&) $\mathcal{A}$.

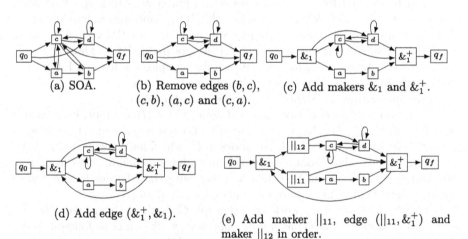

(a) SOA.

(b) Remove edges (b, c), (c, b), (a, c) and (c, a).

(c) Add makers $\&_1$ and $\&_1^+$.

(d) Add edge $(\&_1^+, \&_1)$.

(e) Add marker $||_{11}$, edge $(||_{11}, \&_1^+)$ and maker $||_{12}$ in order.

Fig. 3. The procedures converting the SOA (in (a)) to the node transition graph (in (e)) of the FA(&) $\mathcal{A}$ by traversing shuffle units in $\{[\{a, b\}, \{c, d\}]\}$. For $S = \{abcd, dcab, abcacb, cc, dd\}$, G' is the digraph in (c), $Loop(S, G', [\{a, b\}, \{c, d\}]) = true$, for a and b are not strongly connected in G' and a ($a \in \mathcal{R}(\&_1)$) does not consecutively occur in string $abcacb$. $NO(S, \{a, b\}, [\{a, b\}, \{c, d\}]) = true$, for neither a nor b occur in string cc. In (d) (resp. in (e)), the edge $(\&_1^+, \&_1)$ (resp. $(||_{11}, \&_1^+)$) is added.

Theorem 4. *For any given finite sample S, let $\mathcal{A} = LearnFAS(S)$, then $\mathcal{A}$ is a precise representation of S.*

5   Evaluation

In this section, we provide evaluations on FA(&)s in terms of conciseness and the time performance of membership checking. We evaluate our results on XML data, which are collected from Maven[2] and GitHub[3].

We searched Relax NG files from above repositories, and then extracted 1000 diverse RE(&)s from Relax NG files with corresponding XML data for each alphabet size $(10, 20, \cdots, 100)$. Let Q_1 denote the set of the 1000 RE(&)s of alphabet size 20. Let Q_2 $(Q_2 \supset Q_1)$ denote the set of 10000 RE(&)s of the alphabet size ranging from 10 to 100. For each target expression (such as the one in Q_2), the random sample in experiments, which is a finite set of strings, is extracted from the corresponding XML data. The size of sample is the number of the strings in sample. FA(&)s are mainly compared with the other automata supporting shuffle (excluding CFSA), which can be equivalently transformed from the target expressions in Q_2, and where states are also denoted by the sets of nodes in the corresponding node transition graphs. Since a state in a CFSA is not denoted by a set of nodes, CFSA is not considered.

Conciseness. Since the complexity of automata algorithms is usually more sensitive to the number of states than the number of transitions [12,18,19], the conciseness of the learned FA(&) can be measured by the corresponding number of states. However, for the learned FA(&), which can be denoted by a directed graph, a state (excluding q_0 and q_f) is denoted by a set of the nodes in the directed graph. Figure 4(a) shows that how the alphabet size affects the number of nodes (denoted by M). Figure 4(b) presents that how the number of nodes affects the number of states (denoted by $|Q|$).

We evaluate the conciseness of the learned FA(&) by using the data in Q_2 and the corresponding XML data. For each expression in Q_2, we randomly extracted the corresponding sample, of which the size is 2000. We compute the number of nodes for the corresponding learned FA(&). In Fig. 4(a), the value for a given alphabet size is the logarithm of the average of the 1000 computed numbers of nodes. In Fig. 4(b), for the learned FA(&)s, we partitioned them into 10 groups according to the numbers of nodes ranging from 15 to 100 (listed in Fig. 4(b)). For each group and each learned FA(&), we compute the corresponding number of states. The value for a given number of nodes is the logarithm of the average of the numbers of states computed for the corresponding group.

Figure 4(a) shows that, for a give alphabet size, although the numbers of nodes are close for SA, NFA(&), PFA and FA(&), FA(&) has minimum number of nodes[4]. Figure 4(b) illustrates that, as the number of nodes increases, only for

---

[2] https://mvnrepository.com/.

[3] https://github.com/topics/.

[4] Note that, for the learned FA(&) in Sect. 4, the corresponding number of nodes is no more than $3|\Sigma|$ (see Sect. 3).

the learned FA(&), the number of states does not grow exponentially. Especially, the number of states is about 181 ($\approx 2^{7.5}$) when the number of nodes is 100. The number of states for FA(&) is more less than that for each other automaton. In general, a more concise FA(&) can be learned from a given finite sample.

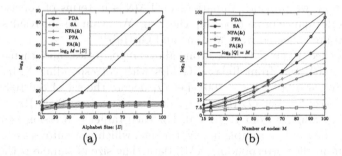

Fig. 4. (a) is the logarithm of number of nodes as the function of alphabet size for each automaton. (b) is the logarithm of number of states as the function of number of nodes for each automaton.

Time Performance of Membership Checking. We provide the statistics about running time in different length of strings and different size of alphabets for membership checking. For each automaton recognizing each string, we record the corresponding running time. For each one of 1000 target expressions in Q_1, we extracted the corresponding 1000 strings with fixed length, which ranges from 10^3 to 10^4 such that all the strings can be recognized by each automaton. In Fig. 5(a), the running time for a given length of string is the average of the corresponding recorded 10^6 (1000*1000) running times. For each alphabet size in $\{10, 20, \cdots, 100\}$, and for each one of 1000 target expressions with that alphabet size in Q_2, we also extracted the 1000 strings with fixed lengths of 5000 such that all the strings can be recognized by each automaton. In Fig. 5(b), the running time for a given alphabet size is the average of the corresponding recorded 10^6 running times. Note that, for each target expression $r \in Q_1$ or $r \in Q_2$, FA(&) is equivalently transformed from r. We also evaluate the time performance of membership checking for brick automaton utilities[5] (BAU), which can be extremely fast to deal with shuffle currently.

Figure 5(a) presents that the running time for FA(&) is less than 0.15 s, when the length of string is not over 10^4. Figure 5(b) illustrates that the running time for FA(&) is less than 0.35 s, when the alphabet size is not over 100. Thus, the time performance of membership checking for FA(&), which is compared with that for other automata or utilities, demonstrates that FA(&) is more efficient in membership checking.

---

[5] https://www.brics.dk/automaton/.

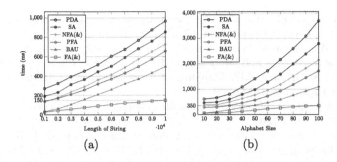

(a)   (b)

Fig. 5. (a) and (b) are running times in seconds for each automaton as the functions of length of string and alphabet size, respectively.

6   Conclusion

This paper proposed automata model: FA(&)s, for which both the uniform and non-uniform membership problem are decidable in polynomial time, and a learning algorithm for FA(&)s. We learn an FA(&) from a given finite sample step by step, our algorithm can ensure that the learned FA(&) is a precise representation of the given finite sample. Experimental results demonstrate that, FA(&) is efficient in membership checking, and our algorithm can obtain a concise automaton. For future works, we focus on the applications of FA(&) and its learning algorithm. Such as learning FA(&) from interleaved traces, which facilitates mining precise workflows for efficient workflow management [14,16].

References

1. Balmin, A., Papakonstantinou, Y., Vianu, V.: Incremental validation of XML documents. ACM Trans. Database Syst. (TODS) **29**(4), 710–751 (2004)
2. Berglund, M., Björklund, H., Björklund, J.: Shuffled languages representation and recognition. Theor. Comput. Sci. **489**, 1–20 (2013)
3. Berglund, M., Björklund, H., Högberg, J.: Recognizing shuffled languages. In: Dediu, A.-H., Inenaga, S., Martín-Vide, C. (eds.) LATA 2011. LNCS, vol. 6638, pp. 142–154. Springer, Heidelberg (2011). https://doi.org/10.1007/978-3-642-21254-3_10
4. Bex, G.J., Gelade, W., Neven, F., Vansummeren, S.: Learning deterministic regular expressions for the inference of schemas from XML data. ACM Trans. Web **4**(4), 1–32 (2010)
5. Bex, G.J., Neven, F., Schwentick, T., Tuyls, K.: Inference of concise DTDs from XML data. In: International Conference on Very Large Data Bases, Seoul, Korea, September, pp. 115–126 (2006)
6. Bex, G.J., Neven, F., Schwentick, T., Vansummeren, S.: Inference of concise regular expressions and DTDs. ACM Trans. Database Syst. **35**(2), 1–47 (2010)
7. Broda, S., Machiavelo, A., Moreira, N., Reis, R.: Automata for regular expressions with shuffle. Inf. Comput. **259**, 162–173 (2018)
8. Clark, J., Makoto, M.: Relax NG Tutorial. OASIS Committee Specification (2001). http://www.oasis-open.org/committees/relax-ng/tutorial-20011203.html

 9. Freydenberger, D.D., Kötzing, T.: Fast learning of restricted regular expressions and DTDs. Theor. Comput. Syst. **57**(4), 1114–1158 (2015)
10. Gelade, W., Martens, W., Neven, F.: Optimizing schema languages for XML: numerical constraints and interleaving. SIAM J. Comput. **38**(5), 2021–2043 (2009)
11. Ginsburg, S., Spanier, E.H.: Mappings of languages by two-tape devices. J. ACM (JACM) **12**(3), 423–434 (1965)
12. Jedrzejowicz, J., Szepietowski, A.: Shuffle languages are in P. Theor. Comput. Sci. **250**(1–2), 31–53 (2001)
13. Jones, J., Oates, T.: Learning deterministic finite automata from interleaved strings. In: Sempere, J.M., García, P. (eds.) ICGI 2010. LNCS (LNAI), vol. 6339, pp. 80–93. Springer, Heidelberg (2010). https://doi.org/10.1007/978-3-642-15488-1_8
14. Kougka, G., Gounaris, A., Simitsis, A.: The many faces of data-centric workflow optimization: a survey. Int. J. Data Sci. Anal. **6**(2), 81–107 (2018). https://doi.org/10.1007/s41060-018-0107-0
15. Liu, X., Alshangiti, M., Ding, C., Yu, Q.: Log sequence clustering for workflow mining in multi-workflow systems. Data Knowl. Eng. **117**, 1–17 (2018)
16. Lou, J.G., Fu, Q., Yang, S., Li, J., Wu, B.: Mining program workflow from interleaved traces. In: Proceedings of the 16th ACM SIGKDD International Conference on Knowledge Discovery and Data Mining, pp. 613–622 (2010)
17. Martens, W., Neven, F., Niewerth, M., Schwentick, T.: Bonxai: combining the simplicity of DTD with the expressiveness of XML schema. ACM Trans. Database Syst. (TODS) **42**(3), 15 (2017)
18. Pitt, L.: Inductive inference, DFAs, and computational complexity. In: Jantke, K.P. (ed.) AII 1989. LNCS, vol. 397, pp. 18–44. Springer, Heidelberg (1989). https://doi.org/10.1007/3-540-51734-0_50
19. Stotts, P.D., Pugh, W.: Parallel finite automata for modeling concurrent software systems. J. Syst. Softw. **27**(1), 27–43 (1994)
20. Wang, X., Chen, H.: Inferring deterministic regular expression with unorder and counting. In: International Conference on Database Systems for Advanced Applications. Springer, Cham (2021)

Active Learning Based Similarity Filtering for Efficient and Effective Record Linkage

Charini Nanayakkara[(⊠)], Peter Christen, and Thilina Ranbaduge

School of Computing, The Australian National University,
Canberra, ACT 2600, Australia
charini.nanayakkara@anu.edu.au

Abstract. The limited analytical value of using individual databases on their own increasingly requires the integration of large and complex databases for advanced data analytics. Linking personal medical records with travel and immigration data, for example, will allow the effective management of pandemics such as the current COVID-19 outbreak by tracking potentially infected individuals and their contacts. One major challenge for accurate linkage of large databases is the quadratic or even higher computational complexities of many advanced linkage algorithms. In this paper we present a novel approach that, based on the expected number of true matches between two databases, applies active learning to remove compared record pairs that are likely non-matches before a computationally expensive classification or clustering algorithm is employed to classify record pairs. Unlike blocking and indexing techniques that are used to reduce the number of record pairs to be compared, using recursive binning on a data dimension such as time or space, our approach removes likely non-matching record pairs in each bin after their comparison. Experiments on two real-world databases show that similarity filtering can substantially reduce run time and improve precision, at the costs of a small reduction in recall, of the final linkage results.

Keywords: Entity resolution · Efficiency enhancement · Binning

1 Introduction

Record linkage, as outlined in Fig. 1, is the process of identifying pairs of records that correspond to the same entity in one or across two or more databases [3]. Due to the quadratic time complexity of comparing every possible pair of records across two databases to be linked, the comparison step in record linkage is often preceded by a *blocking* or *indexing* step [16], where similar records are grouped into blocks such that only pairs of records within a block are compared. Additional *meta-blocking* [7] methods can be applied to further reduce the number of record pairs that need to be compared by analysing records within and across blocks to prevent redundant and superfluous record pair comparisons [16].

This work was partially funded by the ARC under grant DP160101934.

© Springer Nature Switzerland AG 2021
K. Karlapalem et al. (Eds.): PAKDD 2021, LNAI 12713, pp. 321–333, 2021.
https://doi.org/10.1007/978-3-030-75765-6_26

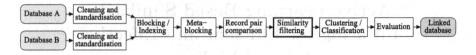

Fig. 1. The steps of the record linkage process, with our contribution highlighted.

The pairwise comparison step of record linkage then consists of the calculation of similarities between two records, generally using string comparison functions applied on attributes such as names and addresses [3]. A *similarity graph* can then be generated where nodes correspond to records and edges to the calculated similarities between them. However, even with blocking, indexing, and meta-blocking applied, many of these similarities will be low, and furthermore they do not correspond to true matches [3,16]. In the classification step all compared record pairs are then classified as *matches* (records assumed to correspond to the same entity) or *non-matches* (records assumed to correspond to different entities) using a decision model that can be as simple as a similarity threshold, that can take match and error probabilities into account, or that uses training data to learn a supervised classification model [3]. Given training data are often not available in real-world linkage applications, unsupervised techniques need to be used that exploit the structure of a similarity graph [2,6,10,20].

While blocking, indexing, and meta-blocking can significantly reduce the number of record pairs that need to be compared in the comparison step, the similarity graph generated from pair-wise comparisons can still be very large. For example, using a Min-hash LSH [13] based blocking on the data sets used in the evaluation in Sect. 4 that contain 17,613 and 3,007,153 records, resulted in similarity graphs containing over 4 and 34 million edges, respectively. Such large graphs are commonly required to ensure that the vast majority of true matches are included in order to obtain a high recall of the final linkage results [3].

Large similarity graphs can, however, challenge any algorithm used to classify record pairs because these graphs are likely very imbalanced and contain many non-matching record pairs. The size of these graphs can also result in the classification step to become the bottleneck of the record linkage process [6].

In our work we remove record pairs from a similarity graph that are unlikely true matches before this graph is being used for clustering or classification. We assume that for a given linkage problem an approximate number of expected true matches can be obtained from a domain expert. For example, when linking product databases from two online stores (where one-to-one links are expected), then the number of true matches is limited by the number of records in the smaller of two databases being linked. On the other hand, when linking birth records of families, then the known distribution of family sizes in a population can be used to estimate an expected number of true matches [19].

We develop an active learning process where we bin the record pairs in a similarity graph according to a suitable data dimension, such as time or space. For example, work on temporal linkage [11] has shown that people will move over time and possibly even change their names, resulting in lower similarities for true matches. Similarly, if people move longer distances then a larger number of their address details will change (such as state or even country). Our approach recursively splits a similarity graph into bins, where we then obtain, via active learning, information from a domain expert about the distribution of matches and non-matches in these bins. We finally select a desired number of record pairs with the highest similarities from each bin, resulting in a much reduced similarity graph that still has a high recall of true matches, and that facilitates accurate clustering or classification with substantially reduced run times.

2   Related Work

The need for linking databases has ensured research for over fifty years and led to a diverse range of methods being developed [4,5,14]. Research into how to improve the scalability of record linkage has concentrated on blocking and indexing, and more recently meta-blocking [16]. The former aim to limit comparisons to only record pairs that are likely true matches, while meta-blocking aims to prevent redundant record pair comparisons, or superfluous comparisons between pairs already classified as non-matches [7]. Any good blocking, indexing, and meta-blocking method needs to be able to group true matches into the same block while records of different entities are grouped into different blocks [3].

Even though blocking, indexing, and meta-blocking help to improve the efficiency of the comparison step, the classification step may still be inefficient due to the presence of a large number of record pairs where many of them are likely not matches. Apart from the parallelisation of linkage algorithms [7], limited research has so far investigated how to improve the efficiency of the classification step without compromising the final linkage quality.

For many real-world record linkage applications, obtaining complete ground truth data (all true matching record pairs) is challenging due to large database sizes [3]. Even though crowdsourcing has been explored for record linkage [23] to mitigate the lack of ground truth data, allowing the public to classify record pairs is not applicable in many domains due to privacy concerns [4]. Active learning approaches, where a small number of selected record pairs are manually classified by trusted domain experts, have therefore been adopted for record linkage to generate ground truth data suitable to train supervised classifiers [17, 18,24], or to generate high quality blocking results [21]. Active learning based on domain expertise, while being able to generate high quality ground truth data, can however only generate small numbers of labelled record pairs. Therefore, approaches that consider a limited labelling budget are crucial [24]. To the best of our knowledge, our approach is a first to explore how active learning can be employed to conduct filtering of record pairs after their comparison to improve the overall efficiency and effectiveness of the linkage process.

3   Active Learning Based Similarity Filtering

We now describe our record pair similarity filtering approach based on domain knowledge. Domain experts often have a good understanding about what the number of true matches in their databases might be, depending upon the linkage situation (such as one-to-one or many-to-many links) and application [3]. As shown in Fig. 1, similarity filtering is an additional step applied between the comparison and classification steps in the record linkage process [3]. The aim of filtering is to improve effectiveness and run time of the classification step by reducing the number of non-matching record pairs (represented by their similarities) that are given to a classification or clustering algorithm [2,6,10,20].

3.1   Problem Definition

Without loss of generality, we assume two databases, $\mathbf{D}_A$ and $\mathbf{D}_B$, are to be linked. A blocking method [16] has generated a set of candidate record pairs (r_i, r_j), with $r_i \in \mathbf{D}_A$ and $r_j \in \mathbf{D}_B$. These pairs have been compared using comparison functions, such as approximate string comparators [3], applied on a set of attributes, A, that generally includes names, addresses, and so on. Each compared record pair is represented by a similarity vector, $\mathbf{s}_{i,j}$, where $|\mathbf{s}_{i,j}|$ corresponds to the number of compared attributes, $|A|$. Assuming all similarities are in $[0, 1]$ (with a similarity of 0 for totally different values and 1 for an exact match), an overall normalised similarity for a pair can be calculated as $s_{i,j} = \sum_{k=1}^{|A|} \mathbf{s}_{i,j}[k]/|A|$. Each record pair is either a true match or a true non-match, where we assume the true match status is unknown for all pairs. We denote the sets of true matches and non-matches by M and N, respectively.

We also assume each record pair has a distance, $d_{i,j}$, in a specific data dimension, such as time and/or space. For example, records about people often contain addresses, and using geocoding [12] these can be used to calculate geographical distances between records. Similarly, for records that contain timestamps (such as publication records, birth, marriage or death certificates, or census records) temporal distances can be calculated between record pairs [11].

The set of compared record pairs can be represented as an undirected similarity graph, $G = (V, E)$, where each node (vertex) in V represents a record, r_i or r_j, and an edge $(r_i, r_j) \in E$ connects two records r_i and r_j if their overall similarity $s_{i,j}$ is at least a certain similarity threshold t, $s_{i,j} \geq t$, with $0 \leq t \leq 1$. The problem we aim to solve can now be defined as follows.

Definition 1 (Similarity Graph Filtering). *Given a similarity graph $G = (V, E)$, a budget β_t of the number of manual classifications of record pairs that can be conducted by an oracle, the expected number of true matches m in G, and a multiplier ϵ for the number of links to select. The aim of similarity filtering is to select a subset of record pairs $(r_i, r_j) \in E$ into a similarity graph $G_s = (V_s, E_s)$, with $V_s \subseteq V$ and $E_s \subset E$, based on manual classification of β_t record pairs in E, such that the number of matches in E_s is maximised while $|E_s| = m \cdot \epsilon$.*

Our similarity filtering approach is based on the assumption that record pairs that have a higher similarity are generally more likely to be true matches, i.e. $P((r_a, r_b) \in M | s_{a,b}) > P((r_e, r_f) \in M | s_{e,f})$ if $s_{a,b} > s_{e,f}$. While this assumption does not necessarily hold for every record pair in G, it is a common assumption

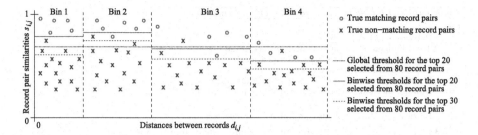

Fig. 2. Filtering of record pairs (links) with the highest similarities. Compared to using all 80 links, with $m = 20$ and $\epsilon = 1$, the filtered similarity graph contains a much smaller number of true non-matches at the cost of losing only few true matches. If the top 20 links are chosen globally (no binning), then the recall of the filtered graph is only 0.8 (4 out of 20 true matches are missed), whereas when links are chosen locally using bin specific thresholds, then recall would be 0.9 (only 2 true matches are removed by the filtering process). If we set $\epsilon = 1.5$ and select 30 record pairs then recall will be 1.

used in record linkage [1,22]. We also assume that the distances, $d_{i,j}$, of record pairs affect the values in their corresponding similarity vectors, $\mathbf{s}_{i,j}$, as is illustrated in Fig. 2. For example, the further people move the more details in their addresses will likely change. While a local move will result in a changed street address only, a move further away can also lead to changed city, zipcode, and even state values. As we discuss next, we employ a binning based active learning approach to identify different similarity thresholds for filtering on different subsets (bins) of record pairs in E using the distances $d_{i,j}$ of record pairs.

3.2 Binning Based Filtering

After initialising the main data structures, in line 3 of Algorithm 1 we generate the first bin $\mathbf{b}_1$ with the full similarity graph G, and set the level of this bin to $\mathbf{b}_1.l = 1$. The budget β_1, of how many record pairs are manually classified (labelled) by the human oracle in this first bin is calculated with the $CalcBudget()$ function. Due to the recursive process of splitting a bin into two in each iteration, we allocate a labelling budget that depends on the level of a bin. With a total budget of β_t, for a bin at level l we allocate a budget of $\beta_l = \beta_t/(2^{2l-1})$, such that a budget of $\beta_t/2^l$ is allocated across all bins at level l. For example, with $\beta_t = 1,000$, we will manually label $\beta_1 = 500$ record pairs in $\mathbf{b}_1$ (with level $l = 1$), $\beta_2 = 125$ in each of the two bins at level $l = 2$, $\beta_3 = 31$ in each of the four bins at level $l = 3$, and so on. Note that the set of manually labelled (classified) record pairs in a bin $\mathbf{b}$, denoted by $\mathbf{b}.\mathbf{c}$, is propagated from a parent bin to its two child bins in the recursive bin splitting process.

In line 5 of Algorithm 1 we calculate the optimal similarity threshold $\mathbf{b}_1.t$ corresponding to the $m \cdot \epsilon$ record pairs with the highest similarities in $\mathbf{b}_1$. In line 6 the oracle then manually classifies β_1 record pairs in bin $\mathbf{b}_1$ as $\mathbf{b}_1.\mathbf{c}$ using the $GetOracleLabels()$ function. This function conducts labelling such that both the child bins of $\mathbf{b}_1$ inherit labelled record pairs from $\mathbf{b}_1$ based on the binning method

---

Algorithm 1: *Binning based similarity graph filtering using active learning*

Input:
- G: Pairwise similarity graph
- β_t: Total budget (maximum number of record pairs the oracle can manually classify)
- β_m: Minimum number of manual classifications a bin must contain
- m: Expected number of true matches
- ϵ: Multiplier for number of record pairs (links) to select
- γ: Binning method (either equal width or equal depth)

Output:
- G_s: Pairwise similarity graph containing $m \cdot \epsilon$ selected links

1:   $\mathbf{B} = [\,]$ // Initialise an empty list to store the final bins
2:   $\mathbf{Q} = [\,]$ // Initialise a queue to hold bins to be processed further
3:   $\mathbf{b}_1 = InitBin(G)$; $\mathbf{b}_1.l = 1$ // Initialise first bin with all links in G and set bin level to 1
4:   $\beta_1 = CalcBudget(\beta_t, 1)$ // Get budget for the first bin
5:   $\mathbf{b}_1.t = GetTopPairsThresh(\mathbf{b}_1, m \cdot \epsilon)$ // Get the threshold for the top $m \cdot \epsilon$ links
6:   $\mathbf{b}_1.c = GetOracleLabels(\mathbf{b}_1, \beta_1, \gamma)$ // Manual Classification of β_1 links in bin $\mathbf{b}_1$
7:   $\mathbf{b}_1.s = CalcScore(\mathbf{b}_1)$ // Calculate the score for bin $\mathbf{b}_1$
8:   $\mathbf{Q}.add(\mathbf{b}_1)$ // Add the first bin to the queue
9:   **while** $(\mathbf{Q} \neq [\,])$ **do:**   // Process queue sorted by bin scores
10:    $\mathbf{b}^p = \mathbf{Q}.pop()$ // Get the next (parent) bin to process based on its score
11:    $\mathbf{b}^l, \mathbf{b}^r = SplitBin(\mathbf{b}^p, \gamma)$ // Split parent bin into two based on binning method γ
12:    $\beta_c = CalcBudget(\beta_t, \mathbf{b}^p.l + 1)$ // Get the budget for the two child bins
13:    **if** $(((|\mathbf{b}^l.c| + \beta_c) \geq \beta_m)$ **and** $((|\mathbf{b}^r.c| + \beta_c) \geq \beta_m)$ **then:**   // Enough labels in both bins
14:      $\mathbf{b}^l.c = \mathbf{b}^l.c \cup GetOracleLabels(\mathbf{b}^l, \beta_c, \gamma)$; $\mathbf{b}^r.c = \mathbf{b}^r.c \cup GetOracleLabels(\mathbf{b}^r, \beta_c, \gamma)$
15:      $t^l, t^r = CalcBestThresh(\mathbf{b}^l, \mathbf{b}^r)$ // Run Algorithm 2 to get optimal bin thresholds
16:      **if** $(t^l == \mathbf{b}^p.t)$ **and** $(t^r == \mathbf{b}^p.t)$ **then:** // Best thresholds are same as for parent bin
17:        $\mathbf{B}.add(\mathbf{b}^p)$; **go to line 9**   // Add parent bin to final bin list and process next bin
18:      $\mathbf{b}^l.t = t^l$; $\mathbf{b}^l.s = CalcScore(\mathbf{b}^l)$; $\mathbf{Q}.add(\mathbf{b}^l)$ // Add both child bins to queue
19:      $\mathbf{b}^r.t = t^r$; $\mathbf{b}^r.s = CalcScore(\mathbf{b}^r)$; $\mathbf{Q}.add(\mathbf{b}^r)$
20:    **else if** $(|\mathbf{b}^l.c| + \beta_c) \geq \beta_m)$ **then:**   // Only the left child bin has enough labels
21:      $\mathbf{b}^l.c = \mathbf{b}^l.c \cup GetOracleLabels(\mathbf{b}^l, \beta_c, \gamma)$; $\mathbf{b}^l.s = CalcScore(\mathbf{b}^l)$; $\mathbf{Q}.add(\mathbf{b}^l)$
22:      $\mathbf{B}.add(\mathbf{b}^r)$ // Add right child bin to final bin list
23:    **else if** $(|\mathbf{b}^r.c| + \beta_c) \geq \beta_m)$ **then:**   // Only the right child bin has enough labels
24:      $\mathbf{b}^r.c = \mathbf{b}^r.c \cup GetOracleLabels(\mathbf{b}^r, \beta_c, \gamma)$; $\mathbf{b}^r.s = CalcScore(\mathbf{b}^r)$; $\mathbf{Q}.add(\mathbf{b}^r)$
25:      $\mathbf{B}.add(\mathbf{b}^l)$ // Add left child bin to final bin list
26:    **else:** $\mathbf{B}.add(\mathbf{b}^p)$ // Add parent bin to the final bin list
27:   $G_s = (V_s = \emptyset, E_s = \emptyset)$ // Initialise empty similarity graph of selected links
28:   **for** $\mathbf{b} \in \mathbf{B}$ **do:**   // Iterate through the bins in the final bin list
29:    $G_s.insert(GetLinks(\mathbf{b}, \mathbf{b}.t))$ // Generate the final similarity graph with selected links
30:   **return** G_s // Return the final similarity graph

γ (which we describe below). The function selects record pairs for labelling that are close to the bin threshold $\mathbf{b}_1.t$, with $\beta_1/2$ pairs selected above and $\beta_1/2$ pairs below the threshold. This helps to effectively shift the bin threshold depending upon the manual labels obtained, as we discuss below. We then calculate the score $\mathbf{b}_1.s$ of bin $\mathbf{b}_1$ in line 7, where we describe four score functions in Sect. 3.4. These scores are used to order the queue $\mathbf{Q}$ and determine which bin to process next in the iterative phase of our approach.

We iteratively process bins in $\mathbf{Q}$ starting in line 9 as long as the queue is not empty. In line 10 we select the next (parent) bin, $\mathbf{b}^p$, with the highest score, which we then split into two child bins, $\mathbf{b}^l$ and $\mathbf{b}^r$, using the binning method γ. The function $SplitBin()$ performs either equal width or equal depth binning [8] on the parent bin $\mathbf{b}^p$ as specified by γ, using the distances $d_{i,j}$ of each record pair in $\mathbf{b}^p$. $SplitBin()$ also increases the level of the child bins as $\mathbf{b}^l.l = \mathbf{b}^p.l + 1$ and $\mathbf{b}^r.l = \mathbf{b}^p.l + 1$, propagates the optimal threshold ($\mathbf{b}^l.t = \mathbf{b}^p.t$ and $\mathbf{b}^r.t = \mathbf{b}^p.t$), and splits the set of manual classifications in $\mathbf{b}^p$ according to the binning method such that $\mathbf{b}^l.c \cup \mathbf{b}^r.c = \mathbf{b}^p.c$.

In line 12 we calculate the oracle budget β_c for the child bins based on their level, and in line 13 we check if both child bins will contain enough manual classifications (based on their allocated budgets as well as the labels inherited from their parent). The reason for checking if a bin can have at least β_m labels is to avoid underfitting (where not enough manual labels are available in a bin to calculate an optional similarity threshold). If both bins can have β_m labels, then in line 14 we obtain new manual classifications ($\mathbf{b}^l.\mathbf{c}$ and $\mathbf{b}^r.\mathbf{c}$) for them, and in line 15 we calculate the new optimal similarity thresholds for the child bins using the function $CalcBestThres()$, as we describe in Sect. 3.3. If it turns out that the optimal threshold of the parent, $\mathbf{b}^p.t$ cannot be improved (in line 16) because the distribution of the similarities of links in both child bins is homogeneous (highly similar), then we add the parent bin $\mathbf{b}^p$ to the final list of bins $\mathbf{B}$ in line 17, and go back to line 9 to process the next bin in $\mathbf{Q}$.

Otherwise, in lines 18 and 19, for each child bin $\mathbf{b}^l$ and $\mathbf{b}^r$, the threshold is set to its calculated optimal value, its bin score is calculated, and then both child bins are added to the queue $\mathbf{Q}$. On the other hand, if only one of the two child bins can have at least β_m labels, in lines 20 to 25 we obtain manual classifications for that bin, update the remaining budget and the score of that bin, and add it to $\mathbf{Q}$, while the other child bin (the one not having enough labels) is added to the final list of bins $\mathbf{B}$. If neither child bin can have at least β_m labels then in line 26 we add the parent bin $\mathbf{b}^p$ to the final list of bins $\mathbf{B}$.

Subsequent to processing all bins in $\mathbf{Q}$, we generate the filtered similarity graph of selected links (record pairs), G_s, in lines 27 to 29 by looping over all bins in $\mathbf{b} \in \mathbf{B}$, and adding all record pairs with a pairwise similarity of at least the bin threshold $\mathbf{b}.t$ into the graph G_s.

3.3   Calculating Optimal Bin Similarity Thresholds

We now describe the functionality of the $CalcBestThresh()$ function (used in line 15 in Algorithm 1), as outlined in Algorithm 2. The input to Algorithm 2 is a bin pair $\mathbf{b}^l$ and $\mathbf{b}^r$, and the function calculates a pair of optimal thresholds, t^l and t^r, which minimise the total number of false negatives across both bins. The algorithm starts with obtaining the lists of false negatives, $\mathbf{fn}_l$ and $\mathbf{fn}_r$, in the two bins, where true matching records pairs (as manually classified by the oracle) that have a similarity below the thresholds $\mathbf{b}^l.t$ and $\mathbf{b}^r.t$ are considered as false negatives. We assume that record pairs in a bin are sorted based on their similarities. In lines 2 and 3, we then calculate the initial total number of false negatives, f_t, and initialise a list $\mathbf{S}$ with a tuple made of f_t and the initial thresholds.

The loop starting in line 4 (with $\oplus$ representing list concatenation) then shifts thresholds for each false negative record pair fn in both child bins, where the function $ShiftThresh()$ sets the threshold of one of the bins ($\mathbf{b}^l$ or $\mathbf{b}^r$) to the similarity value of fn. The threshold of the other child bin is adjusted such that the total number of record pairs with a similarity greater than the thresholds is unchanged. This ensures that we select $m \cdot \epsilon$ links at any time, despite the changing thresholds. The new thresholds t^l and t^r are returned by

---

Algorithm 2: *Calculate optimal bin similarity thresholds, function CalcBestThres()*

Input: Output:
- $\mathbf{b}^l, \mathbf{b}^r$: Left and right child bins   - t^l, t^r: Optimal bin threshold pair

1:   $\mathbf{fn}_l = GetFalseNeg(\mathbf{b}^l, \mathbf{b}^l.t)$; $\mathbf{fn}_r = GetFalseNeg(\mathbf{b}^r, \mathbf{b}^r.t)$ // Get list of false negatives
2:   $f_t = |\mathbf{fn}_l| + |\mathbf{fn}_r|$ // Get the initial total false negative count
3:   $\mathbf{S} = [(f_t, \mathbf{b}^l.t, \mathbf{b}^r.t)]$ // Initialise a list with bin thresholds and total false negative count
4:   **for** $fn \in \mathbf{fn}_l \oplus \mathbf{fn}_r$ **do:**   // Iterate through list of all false negative record pairs
5:       $t^l, t^r = ShiftThresh(\mathbf{b}^l, \mathbf{b}^r, fn)$ // Shift thresholds in child bins
6:       $\mathbf{fn}_l = GetFalseNeg(\mathbf{b}^l, t^l)$; $\mathbf{fn}_r = GetFalseNeg(\mathbf{b}^r, t^r)$ // Get new false negatives lists
7:       **if** $(|\mathbf{fn}_l| > f_t)$ **or** $(|\mathbf{fn}_r| > f_t)$ **then:**   // One bin exceeds the false negative total
8:           **break**   // Stop shifting threshold in a given direction
9:       **else:** $\mathbf{S}.add((|\mathbf{fn}_l| + |\mathbf{fn}_r|, t^l, t^r))$:   // Add thresholds and total false negative count
10:   $t^l, t^r = GetMinFalseNegThres(\mathbf{S})$ // Get thresholds with minimum total false negatives
11: **return** t^l, t^r // Return the optimal thresholds

$ShiftThresh()$, and we then obtain the lists of false negatives $\mathbf{fn}_l$ and $\mathbf{fn}_r$ for t^l and t^r. In lines 7 and 8 we check if at least one of the bins has more false negatives than the original total false negative count, f_t, and if so we end further shifting of thresholds because no more improvement can be gained (a threshold combination that results in one of the bins having more false negatives compared to the original cannot be improved). If the condition in line 7 is not met, in line 9 we add the new total false negative count $|\mathbf{fn}_l| + |\mathbf{fn}_r|$ together with the new threshold pair t^l and t^r to the list $\mathbf{S}$. In line 10, we finally obtain the optimal bin threshold pair t^l and t^r that has a minimum total false negative count, and in line 11 we return this threshold pair.

3.4   Bin Scoring Functions

An important aspect of our recursive binning approach is the ordering of the queue $\mathbf{Q}$ based on the bin scores, $\mathbf{b}.s$, which determine how bins are being processed. Our aim is to calculate an optimal threshold for each bin such that the total number of false negatives is minimised before the budget is used up. We describe four variations of the function $CalcScore()$. In all variations we only consider the record pairs manually classified by the oracle in a given bin, $\mathbf{b}.c$.

1. **False negative count (score$_{\mathbf{fn}}$):** With this approach we calculate the number of false negative record pairs contained in a bin $\mathbf{b}$, where a false negative is a pair that has been classified as a true match by the oracle and that has a similarity below the bin threshold $\mathbf{b}.t$. Using this scoring function means bins that contain more false negatives will be at the top of the queue $\mathbf{Q}$, and processed first.
2. **Bin recall (score$_{\mathbf{r}}$):** With this approach we calculate the recall of bin $\mathbf{b}$ as the proportion of manually classified true matches with a similarity above $\mathbf{b}.t$ over all manually classified true matches in $\mathbf{b}$. With this scoring function we process bins in $\mathbf{Q}$ such that those bin with lowest recall are processed first. This allows us to further explore bins that have fewer true positives and adjust their thresholds to improve their recall.

3. **Normalised false negative count ($score_{nfn}$):** This approach is similar to the $score_{fn}$ approach, except that we divide the score $score_{nfn}$ by the bin size $|b|$, to find the bins with the largest proportion of false negatives.
4. **Adjusted bin recall ($score_{ar}$):** This approach is similar to the $score_r$ function except that we adjust the original $score_r$ value by dividing it by the bin size $|b|$. With this approach, larger bins that have a lower bin recall value will be processed first, whereas with the $score_r$ approach we order bins independent of their sizes.

We next evaluate our active learning based similarity filtering approach.

4   Experimental Evaluation

The aim of our experiments is to evaluate how applying similarity filtering before classification, as shown in Fig. 1, can improve the overall record linkage process by reducing run time and memory consumption, while at the same time improving or at least retaining linkage quality as obtained without filtering.

We evaluated our novel filtering technique using two real world data sets for which ground truth data are available. The Isle of Skye (IoS) data set [19] contains 17,614 birth records from Scotland from 1861 to 1901, where the aim is to link (cluster) all birth records (siblings) by the same mother. The North Carolina voter (NCVR) data set (see: https://dl.ncsbe.gov) contains records with personal details (such as names and addresses) of US voters from the years 2011 to 2020, from where we selected around 3 million records of voters who were represented by multiple records across several years and where at least one (likely several) of their name and/or address values changed over time (as a voter moved and/or changed their name). The number of true matches for IoS is $m = 40,891$ while for NCVR it is $m = 6,978,001$. For the data dimensions used for binning, we calculated time distances as the number of days between two birth records in IoS and the number of months between two voter records in NCVR, while we calculated geographical (space) distances using address geocoding [12] for IoS and the distances between zipcodes for NCVR, respectively. We will make our programs and similarity graphs available to allow repeatability.

As evaluation metrics we use precision and recall as commonly used to evaluate record linkage algorithms [9], where recall is the proportion of true matches that were correctly included in a filtered similarity graph, while precision is the proportion of true matches in a filtered similarity graph. For the final clustering results, recall measures the proportion of correctly classified true matches and precision the proportion of true matches in the set of classified matches.

As illustrated in Fig. 2, as baseline we explore a simple filtering approach using a global threshold for selecting the m record pairs (links) with the highest similarity, assuming m was provided by a domain expert. We then investigate our active learning based filtering approach, where we explore if the binning of record pairs can help improve the quality of the filtered similarity graph.

In a set of initial experiments we found that equal depth binning [8] always produced better results than equal width binning on both data dimensions time

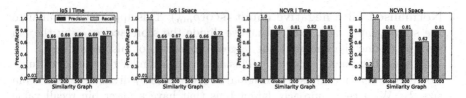

Fig. 3. Precision and recall results of the full similarity graph (unfiltered) compared with the quality of the graph filtered with a global threshold (top m links), as well as binwise thresholds for different total budgets and against different data dimensions.

and space, and that a value of $\beta_m = 25$ for the minimum number of manual classifications per bin always gave the best results. We therefore use these parameter settings in all our experiments. We then set the total budget as $\beta_t = [200, 500, 1000]$ (as well as to *unlimited* for the IoS data set), to investigate how different budgets influence the quality of the generated filtered similarity graphs. All of the four scoring functions discussed in Sect. 3.4 produced very similar results, with the false negative count score function, **score**$_{fn}$, obtaining slightly better results, and we therefore used this function in all our experiments.

In Fig. 3 we show the precision and recall results obtained for the original full similarity graph, as compared with the filtered graphs for the global threshold, as well as results for binning when using different total budgets. For all filtered graphs, both precision and recall values are the same because we limit the number of record pairs in the filtered graph to m, the number of true matches as estimated by a domain expert. We can see that the precision of the filtered graphs are far better compared to the original graph, since our filtering approach was able to remove a large proportion of the true non-matching record pairs.

Our aim of capturing more true matches with binning, compared to using a global threshold, has been successful mostly for the IoS data set with the time data dimension with a 4.5% maximum improvement even with a limited budget. The maximum recall improvement we can obtain with a fully supervised method (unlimited budget) is nine percent and therefore obtaining an improvement of 4.5% with a limited total budget of $\beta_t \leq 1000$ shows that our approach of using active learning can lead to improved similarity filtering. The fact that recall can be improved using bin-wise thresholds indicates that linked records in different bins do have different similarity distributions of true matching record pairs.

Our binning approach has worked well for the IoS data set on the time dimension, since for birth record pairs we find patterns such as no true matches between zero to nine months (an impossible age gap for siblings). For experiments on the space dimension on IoS, and time dimension on NCVR, the maximum recall improvement obtained is less, which indicates less distinct differences in the bins generated on these data dimensions. With NCVR in the space dimension, recall drops with $\beta_t = 500$. This indicates that certain numbers of manual classifications can lead to wrong binning due to incorrectly set classification thresholds that result in wrong selection of record pairs in some bins. Therefore, clear patterns across a data dimension are needed for our approach to work.

Table 1. Percentage changes for time (T), precision (P), and recall (R), of clustering the filtered similarity graphs (using the time data dimension) compared to clustering the full graphs. Significant reductions in time and graph sizes ($|G| = 4$ M and $|G_s| = 41$ K for **IoS**, while $|G| = 34.5$ M and $|G_s| = 6.9$ M for **NCVR**) and improvements in precision can be seen, at the costs of some reductions in recall.

		Global threshold T / P / R	$b_{tot} = 200$ T / P / R	$b_{tot} = 500$ T / P / R	$b_{tot} = 1,000$ T / P / R
	Robust [15]	−71/129/−12	−70/122/−10	−69/122/−9	−69/122/−9
IoS	Star [6]	−98/71/−17	−98/70/−16	−98/71/−15	−98/71/−15
	Conn [6]	−100/8154/−19	−99/6519/−17	−99/5996/−17	−99/5996/−17
NCVR	Star [6]	−65/12/−16	−65/12/−16	−63/16/−14	−66/13/−16
	Conn [6]	−97/1348/−7	−97/1302/−8	−97/1379/−8	−97/1155/−8

Table 1 shows the percentage difference in time, precision, and recall obtained with three clustering algorithms on the full similarity graphs compared to running these algorithms on the filtered graphs. We used three algorithms that have been used for record linkage; robust graph clustering [15], star clustering [6], and simple connected components clustering [6]. Robust graph clustering results are not shown for NCVR because we could not run this algorithm on the full NCVR graph in reasonable time. This highlights the advantage of similarity filtering to reduce the run times of computationally expensive algorithms used for linking large databases. For most experiments, precision has improved considerably with small losses in recall, while the time taken to run clustering was reduced quite significantly as well. The reduction in recall is justifiable especially for the IoS data set, where the results show the reduction in time and the improvement in precision to be more than five fold the reduction in recall. The percentage reductions in recall are slightly reduced when bin-wise thresholds are applied on the IoS data set compared to using a global threshold. Such improvements were obtained while reducing the similarity graph size from four million record pairs to only around forty thousand pairs for IoS, and a reduction from over 34 million to less than seven million record pairs for NCVR, as shown in the table.

5   Conclusions and Future Work

Record linkage is increasingly challenged by database sizes and the lack of ground truth data available in linkage applications. While blocking, indexing, and more recently meta-blocking, aim to reduce the number of record pairs that need to be compared, here we have presented a novel similarity filtering approach that removes compared pairs of records that have low similarities and are therefore unlikely true matches. Combining recursive binning of record pairs with active learning, we identify thresholds in bins that result in a substantially filtered set of record pairs while maintaining high recall of these pairs. Experiments on two real-world data sets have shown that even with a small manual labelling budget we can obtain filtered record pairs of high quality. As future work we aim to improve our method of how to select suitable record pairs for manual labelling, and we plan to incorporate the manually labelled matches and non-matches into the final clustering process using constraint clustering approaches.

References

1. Arasu, A., Götz, M., Kaushik, R.: On active learning of record matching packages. In: ACM SIGMOD. pp. 783–794. Indianapolis (2010)
2. Bhattacharya, I., Getoor, L.: Collective entity resolution in relational data. ACM TKDD **1**(1), 5-es (2007)
3. Christen, P.: Data Matching - Concepts and Rechniques for Record Linkage, Entity Resolution, and Duplicate Detection. Springer, Heidelberg (2012). https://doi.org/10.1007/978-3-642-31164-2
4. Christen, P., Ranbaduge, T., Schnell, R.: Linking Sensitive Data. Springer, Heidelberg (2020). https://doi.org/10.1007/978-3-030-59706-1
5. Dong, X.L., Srivastava, D.: Big Data Integration. Synthesis Lectures on Data Management, Morgan and Claypool Publishers, San Rafael (2015)
6. Draisbach, U., Christen, P., Naumann, F.: Transforming pairwise duplicates to entity clusters for high-quality duplicate detection. ACM JDIQ **12**(1), 1–30 (2019)
7. Efthymiou, V., Papadakis, G., Papastefanatos, G., Stefanidis, K., Palpanas, T.: Parallel meta-blocking for scaling entity resolution over big heterogeneous data. Inf. Syst. **65**, 137–157 (2017)
8. Han, J., Kamber, M., Pei, J.: Data Mining: Concepts and Techniques, 3rd edn. Morgan Kaufmann, Burlington (2012)
9. Hand, D., Christen, P.: A note on using the F-measure for evaluating record linkage algorithms. Stat. Comput. **28**(3), 539–547 (2017). https://doi.org/10.1007/s11222-017-9746-6
10. Hassanzadeh, O., Chiang, F., Lee, H., Miller, R.: Framework for evaluating clustering algorithms in duplicate detection. VLDB **2**(1), 1282–1293 (2009)
11. Hu, Y., Wang, Q., Vatsalan, D., Christen, P.: Improving temporal record linkage using regression classification. In: Kim, J., Shim, K., Cao, L., Lee, J.-G., Lin, X., Moon, Y.-S. (eds.) PAKDD 2017, Part I. LNCS (LNAI), vol. 10234, pp. 561–573. Springer, Cham (2017). https://doi.org/10.1007/978-3-319-57454-7_44
12. Kirielle, N., Christen, P., Ranbaduge, T.: Outlier detection based accurate geocoding of historical addresses. In: Le, T.D., et al. (eds.) AusDM 2019. CCIS, vol. 1127, pp. 41–53. Springer, Singapore (2019). https://doi.org/10.1007/978-981-15-1699-3_4
13. Leskovec, J., Rajaraman, A., Ullman, J.D.: Mining of Massive Datasets. CUP, Cambridge (2014)
14. Mudgal, S., Li, H., Rekatsinas, T., Doan, A., et al.: Deep learning for entity matching: a design space exploration. In: ACM SIGMOD, pp. 19–34. Houston (2018)
15. Nanayakkara, C., Christen, P., Ranbaduge, T.: Robust temporal graph clustering for group record linkage. In: Yang, Q., Zhou, Z.-H., Gong, Z., Zhang, M.-L., Huang, S.-J. (eds.) PAKDD 2019, Part II. LNCS (LNAI), vol. 11440, pp. 526–538. Springer, Cham (2019). https://doi.org/10.1007/978-3-030-16145-3_41
16. Papadakis, G., Skoutas, D., Thanos, E., Palpanas, T.: Blocking and filtering techniques for entity resolution: a survey. ACM Comput. Surv. **53**(2), 1–42 (2020)
17. Primpeli, A., Bizer, C., Keuper, M.: Unsupervised bootstrapping of active learning for entity resolution. In: Harth, A., et al. (eds.) ESWC 2020. LNCS, vol. 12123, pp. 215–231. Springer, Cham (2020). https://doi.org/10.1007/978-3-030-49461-2_13

18. Qian, K., Popa, L., Sen, P.: Active learning for large-scale entity resolution. In: ACM CIKM, pp. 1379–1388. Singapore (2017)
19. Reid, A., Davies, R., Garrett, E.: Nineteenth-century Scottish demography from linked censuses and civil registers: a 'sets of related individuals' approach. Hist. Comput. **14**(1–2), 61–86 (2002)
20. Saeedi, A., Peukert, E., Rahm, E.: Using link features for entity clustering in knowledge graphs. In: Gangemi, A., et al. (eds.) ESWC 2018. LNCS, vol. 10843, pp. 576–592. Springer, Cham (2018). https://doi.org/10.1007/978-3-319-93417-4_37
21. Shao, J., Wang, Q.: Active blocking scheme learning for entity resolution. In: Phung, D., Tseng, V.S., Webb, G.I., Ho, B., Ganji, M., Rashidi, L. (eds.) PAKDD 2018, Part II. LNCS (LNAI), vol. 10938, pp. 350–362. Springer, Cham (2018). https://doi.org/10.1007/978-3-319-93037-4_28
22. Tao, Y.: Entity matching with active monotone classification. In: ACM PODS, pp. 49–62. Houston (2018)
23. Vesdapunt, N., Bellare, K., Dalvi, N.: Crowdsourcing algorithms for entity resolution. PVLDB **7**(12), 1071–1082 (2014)
24. Wang, Q., Vatsalan, D., Christen, P.: Efficient interactive training selection for large-scale entity resolution. In: Cao, T., Lim, E.-P., Zhou, Z.-H., Ho, T.-B., Cheung, D., Motoda, H. (eds.) PAKDD 2015, Part II. LNCS (LNAI), vol. 9078, pp. 562–573. Springer, Cham (2015). https://doi.org/10.1007/978-3-319-18032-8_44

Stratified Sampling for Extreme Multi-label Data

Maximillian Merrillees and Lan Du[(⊠)]

Faculty of Information Technology, Monash University, Clayton, VIC 3800, Australia
lan.du@monash.edu

Abstract. Extreme multi-label classification (XML) is becoming increasingly relevant in the era of big data. Yet, there is no method for effectively generating stratified partitions of XML datasets. Instead, researchers typically rely on provided test-train splits that, 1) aren't always representative of the entire dataset, and 2) are missing many of the labels. This can lead to poor generalization ability and unreliable performance estimates, as has been established in the binary and multi-class settings. As such, this paper presents a new and simple algorithm that can efficiently generate stratified partitions of XML datasets with millions of unique labels. We also examine the label distributions of prevailing benchmark splits, and investigate the issues that arise from using unrepresentative subsets of data for model development. The results highlight the difficulty of stratifying XML data, and demonstrate the importance of using stratified partitions for training and evaluation.

Keywords: Extreme multi-label learning · XML · Stratified sampling

1 Introduction

The composition of data used for training and testing can have a big impact on the model development process. It can influence choices regarding training strategy and hyperparameter selection, and can also effect performance estimates. As such, for classification tasks, stratified sampling is commonly used to generate these subsets because they have been shown to result in performance estimates with lower bias and variance compared to random sampling [4].

Performing stratified sampling on binary and multi-class datasets is straightforward. Each data point is only associated with one label, so generating stratified splits can be achieved by simply sampling instances of each class based on its prevalence in the dataset. On the other hand, generating stratified subsets of multi-label data is more difficult because each instance can be associated with one or more labels. Assigning an instance to a subset based on one of its labels will impact all the other labels associated with that instance.

As such, to facilitate comparability between models, it's common for XML researchers to use benchmark datasets with provided test-train splits [7,8,13,16]. However, our investigation into these provided splits revealed that a number of

© Springer Nature Switzerland AG 2021
K. Karlapalem et al. (Eds.): PAKDD 2021, LNAI 12713, pp. 334–345, 2021.
https://doi.org/10.1007/978-3-030-75765-6_27

them have sub-optimal characteristics. Specifically, there are subsets where the distribution of labels is very dissimilar to that of the entire dataset. Also, there are test sets where a significant proportion of rare labels are missing.

This can be problematic since using unrepresentative data can lead to biased results or sub-optimal choices for a model's hyperparameters. Also, excluding a large proportion of rare labels from being evaluated implies that a model's performance on rare labels is not important. That's not always the case. In fact, the authors of PfastreXML argue that such situations are common [3]. They provide the example of tagging Wikipedia articles, where there would be less value in assigning a generic label like *Poem* than novel labels like *Epic poems in Italian* or *14th century Christian texts*. For another example, in the medical domain, some diseases are rare. Therefore, the corresponding ICD labels might not be observed as often as some other common diseases, like seasonal influenza. However, less frequent diseases do not mean they are not important.

These issues have been known for some time in multi-label classification (MLC) research. A paper from 2011 points out similar issues, and presented an iterative algorithm to perform stratified partitioning of MLC datasets [9]. Since then, one other method has been proposed [11]. A review of recent literature suggests that the iterative algorithm from 2011 remains the preferred stratification method [1,10,15]. However, our tests of the iterative algorithm revealed that it was unable to effectively generate stratified splits of XML data. This is possibly due to the difference in scale between MLC and XML data. In any case, there is currently no method, to our knowledge, for efficiently generating stratified test-train splits of XML datasets. Given the increasing prevalence of XML research, this gap needs to be addressed.

In this paper, we propose a new stratified sampling algorithm for XML data, which makes use of a simple sampling strategy that swaps instances between the train and the test sets based on scores that measure the dissimilarity between the current split state and the stratified state. Compared with random sampling and iterative sampling, the proposed algorithm: 1) achieves lower KL divergence between the label distribution of each test set against the distribution of their respective data set, and 2) is much faster than the iterative sampling method that is widely used in multi-label learning. Meanwhile, we also examine the label distributions of prevailing benchmark splits, and highlight the bias in performance estimates that can arise from using unrepresentative subsets of data.

This paper is structured as follows: Sect. 2 provides a summary of related works. Section 3 contains an overview of XML datasets. We present our algorithm in Sect. 4, and the resulting partitions in Sect. 5. In Sect. 6, we highlight the difference in performance estimates from using different splits. Finally, we provide our concluding remarks in Sect. 7.

2   Related Works

The first method for generating stratified partitions of MLC data was presented by Sechidis and Tsoumakas in 2011 [9]. Their iterative algorithm creates k-subsets of data by allocating data points to subsets one-by-one based on the suitability of its labels. Prior to that algorithm, MLC researchers typically performed random sampling or relied on the splits available through the MULAN repository [14].

The authors were motivated to develop such an algorithm because it had been established that using stratified partitions results in performance estimates with lower bias and variance compared to estimates obtained using randomly sampled data [4]. Yet, up to that point, no stratification method existed for MLC data. In their paper, they demonstrated that using stratified subsets resulted in more robust performance estimates. A python implementation of the algorithm is available from the scikit-multilearn package [12].

Since then, one other stratification method has been proposed for MLC datasets. In 2017, an extension of the iterative algorithm was presented that takes into account second-order relationships between labels [11]. That is, an algorithm that seeks to maintain the distribution of label-pairs during partitioning. In their paper, the authors demonstrated how doing so improves classification performance as measured by label-pair oriented metrics. Despite this newer method, a review of the recent literature suggests that the iterative algorithm from 2011 remains the preferred stratified partitioning method. Perhaps this is because second-order relationships are not typically considered in MLC research.

Despite the widespread use of the iterative algorithm, this study found it unsuitable for large-scale XML datasets. The algorithm is slow, and does not seem to be capable of generating well stratified partitions for XML datasets. This is not surprising given the method was developed and tested on relatively small MLC datasets. Indeed, the largest dataset they considered had just 983 labels and 16K data points - much smaller than XML data that can contain millions of labels and data points.

3   Overview of XML Datasets

XML is defined by datasets that contain thousands to millions of labels - this is what makes it *extreme*. Another notable characteristic is the high proportion of labels with few associated instances - typically referred to as tail labels[1]. Also, as with MLC datasets in general, each data point is associated with multiple labels. Table 1 summarizes the basic statistics of four datasets that are often used in XML research, the label size of which ranges from 4K to 670K, which often follows a power-law distribution [5].

Together, these properties make it challenging to create stratified partitions. Having multiple labels per data point means conventional stratification methods cannot be applied, and the high proportion of rare labels makes random sampling risky, since it's possible to generate subsets with missing labels. Finally, the large output space makes iterative partitioning slow. Currently, to our knowledge, there does not exist a stratification method that can overcome these problems.

---

[1] For this paper, tail labels are those with fewer than 10 instances in the dataset.

Table 1. Statistics for a selection of XML datasets [2]

	Num. labels	Num. train	Num. test	Avg. labels per sample	Avg. samples per label	% Tail labels
EURLex-4K	3,993	15,539	3,809	5.31	25.73	59%
Wiki10-31K	30,938	14,146	6,616	18.64	8.52	83%
Delicious-200K	205,443	196,606	100,095	75.54	72.29	51%
Amazon-670K	670,091	490,449	153,025	5.45	3.99	89%

Table 2. Percentage of labels missing from the provided test set

EURLex-4K	Wiki10-31K	Delicious-200K	Amazon-670K
32.4%	28.7%	10.4%	48.2%

Given the lack of a suitable sampling method, XML researchers typically use test-train splits provided by the XML repository [2]. Doing so negates the need to generate their own partitions, and ensures that performance estimates are comparable between papers. However, our examination of these splits reveals that they aren't always representative of their datasets, particularly, there exist many labels that do not have any testing instances. This is shown in Fig. 1, where each chart shows the proportion of labels that fall in each of the 10 bins, where each bin represents a range of the proportion of label instances that appears in the test set. For example, for EURLex-4K, 36% of the labels have between 0% and 10% (first bin) of their instances present in the test set - the remaining labels are spread out across the other 9 bins. The red vertical line represents the test size as a proportion of the entire dataset. In a perfectly stratified test set, all the labels would have this percentage of instances in the test set. Categorizing the labels as either a head- or tail- label reveals that it's mostly tail labels that fall within the first and final bins.

A closer examination reveals that almost all labels that fall within the first bin are actually completely missing from the test set. The proportion missing labels is provided in Table 2. This is problematic because it means that models trained on these splits aren't being adequately evaluated on their performance on rare labels. It is also known that models' performance can be largely impacted by those labels, known as few-shot learning [5]. This paper also points out the following conundrum: why train for labels that never get tested?

4   Stratified Sampling Algorithm

In this Section, we present our stratified sampling algorithm. The inputs to the algorithm are the set of documents, X, the set of associated labels, y, and the *target_test_size*. It generates *X_train*, *X_test*, *y_train*, and *y_test*, much in the same way as the train_test_split() function from scikit-learn [6]. Documentation for the python implementation of the stratified sampling algorithm is available

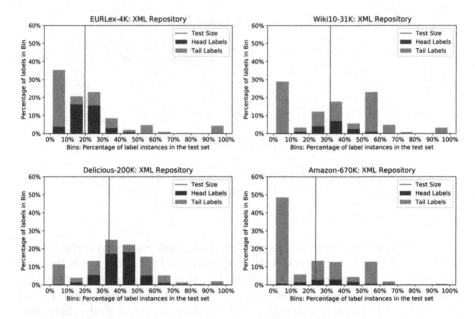

Fig. 1. Label distributions of provided splits from the XML repository

on GitHub[2]. The pseudo-code for the algorithm is outlined in Algorithm 1. Essentially, it seeks to minimize a score that measures how far the current state is from a well-stratified state. A high positive score indicates the partitions are far from stratified. Scores close to 0 indicate that the partitions are well stratified.

The algorithm starts by randomly allocating each data point to the train or test set so the *target_test_size* is achieved (line 1). Then, it performs stratified sampling for a number of epochs. First, it counts the instances of each label in each partition (lines 6 to 10) and calculates a score for each label based on the extent to which a label's *actual_test_proportion* diverges from the *target_test_size* (lines 12 to 17). Scores are normalized to be within the range of 0 and ±1. A positive score means too much of the label is in the test set, while a negative score means too much of the label is in the train set. For example, if a the *target_test_size* is 20%, and 60% of a label's instances are in the test set, the label score would be 0.5, since 60% is half-way between 20% and 100%. If a label's *actual_test_proportion* is 5%, the label score would be −0.75, since 5% is 75% of the way between 0% and 20%.

After calculating a score for each label, it calculates a score for each data point based on the scores of its labels (lines 19 to 27). A high data point score indicates that many of its labels have too many instances in the data point's current partition, and the datapoint should be swapped to the alternate partition.

Finally, a proportion of the data points with the highest scores are swapped from their current partition to the alternate partition (lines 32 to 36). At each

---

[2] https://github.com/maxitron93/stratified_sampling_for_XML.

Algorithm 1: Stratified sampling algorithm

---

1 // Start by randomly allocating each data point to either X_train or X_test so the test size is equal to $target\_test\_size$

2

3 // Perform stratified sampling for 50 epochs
4 **while** $epoch \leq 50$ **do**
5   │
6   │ // For each $label$, count the appearances in the train and test sets
7   │ **for** x in X **do**
8   │   │ **for** $label$ in $label\_set$ of x **do**
9   │   │   │ **if** x in X_train **then** $label\_train\_count \mathrel{+}= 1$;
10   │   │   │ **else** $label\_test\_count \mathrel{+}= 1$;
11   │
12   │ // Calculate the score for each $label$
13   │ **for** $label$ in y **do**
14   │   │ **if** $actual\_test\_proportion \geq target\_test\_size$ **then**
15   │   │   │ $label\_score = \frac{actual\_test\_proportion - target\_test\_size}{1 - target\_test\_size}$;
16   │   │ **else**
17   │   │   │ $label\_score = \frac{actual\_test\_proportion - target\_test\_size}{target\_test\_size}$;
18   │
19   │ // Calculate the score for each data point
20   │ **for** x in X **do**
21   │   │ **for** $label$ in $label\_set$ of x **do**
22   │   │   │ **if** $label\_score > 0$ **then**
23   │   │   │   │ **if** x in test **then** $data\_point\_score \mathrel{+}= label\_score$;
24   │   │   │   │ **else** $data\_point\_score \mathrel{-}= label\_score$;
25   │   │   │ **else**
26   │   │   │   │ **if** x in train **then** $data\_point\_score \mathrel{-}= label\_score$;
27   │   │   │   │ **else** $data\_point\_score \mathrel{+}= label\_score$;
28   │
29   │ // Calculate threshold score for swapping
30   │ $threshold\_score = \text{percentile}(scores, threshold\_proportion)$
31   │
32   │ // Swap proportion of data points with high scores to the alternate partition
33   │ **for** x in X **do**
34   │   │ **if** $data\_point\_score > threshold\_score$ **then**
35   │   │   │ **if** $rand(0,1) \geq swap\_probability$ **then**
36   │   │   │   │ swap data point to alternate partition;
37   │
38   │ // Decay threshold_proportion and swap_probability for next epoch
39   │ $threshold\_proportion, swap\_probability = \frac{0.1}{1.1^{epoch}}$
40   │ $epoch \mathrel{+}= 1$
41
42 // Return stratified splits
43 **return** $X\_train, X\_test, y\_train, y\_test$

---

epoch, only a proportion of the highest-scored instances get swapped. This proportion is based on the *threshold_proportion* and *swap_probability*, which decays with every epoch (lines 38 to 40). In our experiments, we found that constraining the number of instances that gets swapped is import to mitigate 'overshooting'.

The values for *epochs*, *swap_probability*, *threshold_proportion*, and *decay* are key parameters for the provided python implementation of the algorithm. During development, we found that the optimal values depended on the characteristics of each dataset, but very good results were obtained using certain default values. The default values were determined by testing different combinations for all 18 datasets on the XML repository [2]. The default value is 10% for the starting *swap_probability* and *threshold_proportion*. Higher values result in more aggressive stratification, but can result in 'overshoot'. *swap_probability* and *threshold_proportion* are *decayed* at a default rate of 10% per epoch, and the default number of *epochs* is 50. We found that these values worked well, and either matched or came very close to the partitions that were generated using tailored values. However, users of the algorithm can easily trial different values by passing in the desired parameter values when calling the function.

One notable behaviour of the algorithm is that it increases the test size as needed to achieve stratified partitions with few missing labels. It automatically finds this test size by balancing two competing priorities: 1) generating partitions where the proportion of label instances in the test set is equal to the *target_test_size*, and 2) reducing the number of missing labels from either set. Initially, the algorithm swaps more instances into the test set since the decrease in score achieved from reducing the number of missing labels is greater than the increase in score caused by deviating from the *target_test_size*. At some point, the respective changes to the score reaches equilibrium; this is the test size that the algorithm settles on. We believe this to be a desirable trait, since we consider generating stratified partitions with few missing labels to be more important than maintaining an arbitrary test size. However, we acknowledge that this may not be suitable for all applications.

5 Partitioning Results

In this section, we compare the test-train splits generated by random, iterative [9], and stratified sampling against the splits provided on the XML repository [2]. We generated splits for all 18 datasets and calculated two statistics for each test set: 1) KL-Divergence, and 2) Percentage of labels missing. The results are presented in Table 3. The lowest values for each dataset are bolded.

Following the work of Aguilar et al., we measured KL-Divergence of each test set against their respective dataset [1]. Also known as relative entropy, this metric measures the difference between two probability distributions. While not typically used for this purpose, this metric succinctly conveys the extent to which the label ratios are maintained after partitioning. A high number indicates that the label distributions are highly divergent, while values close to zero indicate they are very similar.

Table 3. Label distribution statistics of XML datasets - statistics are of the test set.

	Provided [2]		Random sampling		Iterative algorithm [9]			Stratified sampling		
	KL-Divergence	% labels missing	KL-Divergence	% labels missing	KL-Divergence	% labels missing	time (mins)	KL-Divergence	% labels missing	time (mins)
Mediamill	<0.001	0.0%	0.001	0.0%	<0.001	0.0%	0.8	<0.001	0.0%	0.1
Bibtex	0.009	0.0%	0.01	0.0%	<0.001	0.0%	0.03	<0.001	0.0%	0.02
Delicious	0.008	0.0%	0.006	0.0%	0.005	0.0%	2.4	0.001	0.0%	0.1
RCV1-2K	0.023	2.1%	0.003	0.6%	0.003	0.7%	110.7	<0.001	0.0%	1.4
EURLex-4K	0.602	32.4%	0.501	28.8%	0.444	29.2%	2.5	0.103	12.3%	0.03
EURLex-4.3K	0.474	40.0%	0.4	36.5%	0.29	33.5%	5.2	0.066	13.4%	0.1
AmazonCat-13K	0.004	0.4%	0.02	10.0%	0.007	6.0%	488.6	0.001	0.2%	3.6
AmazonCat-14K	0.001	0.0%	0.006	4.7%	–	–	>24H	<0.001	0.1%	11.0
Wiki10-31K	1.106	28.7%	0.681	18.0%	0.648	17.3%	117.1	0.264	7.2%	0.2
Delicious-200K	0.067	11.1%	0.065	10.4%	–	–	>24H	0.023	3.6%	16.1
WikiLSHTC-325K	0.157	12.8%	0.563	23.1%	–	–	>24H	0.103	9.6%	9.2
WikiSeeAlsoTitles-350K	0.772	5.5%	2.865	31.6%	–	–	>24H	0.582	8.5%	2.4
WikiTitles-500K	0.09	2.0%	0.43	12.7%	–	–	>24H	0.026	0.9%	12.4
Wikipedia-500K	0.036	0.0%	0.399	11.5%	–	–	>24H	0.018	0.1%	15.6
AmazonTitles-670K	5.757	48.6%	1.98	18.5%	–	–	>24H	0.198	1.9%	4.7
Amazon-670K	5.714	48.2%	1.96	18.1%	–	–	>24H	0.182	1.5%	4.8
AmazonTitles-3M	0.033	0.1%	0.215	7.7%	–	–	>24H	0.031	0.8%	85.4
Amazon-3M	0.03	0.0%	0.215	7.6%	–	–	>24H	0.031	0.7%	79.1

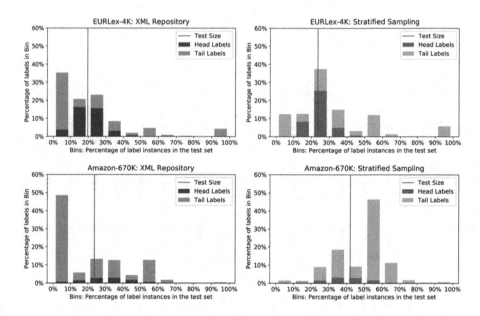

Fig. 2. Comparison of label distributions between provided and stratified splits.

Firstly, we observe that random sampling produced highly divergent parti- tions for many of the datasets. This is most apparent for the EURLex, Wiki, and very large Amazon datasets, where the KL-Divergences of their test sets are comparatively high. They are also missing a large proportion of labels. This highlights the risk of relying on random sampling for partitioning XML data - it can result in splits that are highly unrepresentative of the dataset. Based on the results, this risk appears to be greatest for very large datasets.

Interestingly, we see that the provided splits are sometimes more-, and some- times less-, stratified than what was generated from random sampling. For RCV1-2K, EURLex-4(.3)K, Wiki10-31K, and Amazon(Titles)-670K, the pro- vided partitions are materially more divergent. Based on the results, it appears that non-random partitioning methods were used to create the splits. It's not clear to us what they were, or the motivation behind them, since they pro- duced splits with higher KL-Divergence and more missing labels. On the other hand, the partitions for AmazonCat, very large Wiki, and Amazon(Titles)-3M are materially more representative of their dataset than what was produced through random sampling. In these cases, KL-Divergences are much lower, and significantly fewer labels are missing. The authors of the XML repository [2] do briefly mention that they used some method to ensure the test sets contain as many labels as possible, but what that method is remains unclear.

In any case, the stratified sampling algorithm produced the best results over- all. In all cases but one, it generated splits with the lowest KL-Divergence. It also produced splits with the fewest missing labels from the test set in a majority of cases. However, for the very large datasets, a number of the provided splits contain fewer missing labels. This suggests that the authors' partitioning method prioritised minimizing the amount of missing labels. Meanwhile, the stratified sampling algorithm prioritizes generating representative splits.

Finally, we note that the stratified sampling algorithm outperforms the iterative algorithm [9]. It produced better splits overall, and did so more efficiently. For example, for AmazonCat-13K, stratified sampling was completed in 3.6 min, while the iterative algorithm took over 8 h to generate a result. In fact, it was unable to generate a result within 24 h for the largest datasets.

The label distributions of two datasets are plotted in Fig. 2[3]. As in Sect. 3, each chart shows the proportion of labels that fall in each of the 10 bins, and the red line represents the test size. The charts show that the stratified sampling algorithm produced splits with a greater concentration of labels around the vertical red line, and fewer labels in the first and last bins. This provides visual confirmation of their lower KL-Divergence scores.

6   Bias in Estimated Performance

Here, we compare the performance estimates of three XML models trained on several provided and stratified splits. We selected Parabel [7], FastXML [8] and AnnexML [13] for testing since they are commonly used as benchmark models. Following prevailing literature, we used Precision@1 (P@1) to represent performance. Training and evaluation was carried out on datasets with a large difference in the amount of missing labels between the provided and stratified splits. We also included two datasets with very little difference between splits. The results are presented in Table 4.

As we can see, there are material deltas in estimated performance for datasets where there is a large difference between the provided and stratified data splits (EURLex-4(.3)K, Wiki10-31K, Delicious-200K and Amazon-670K). For these datasets, it appears that models trained and evaluated on the provided split achieves higher P@1 than if the stratified split was used. On the other hand, there is significantly less delta for RCV1-2K and AmazonCat-13K - datasets where there is little difference between the provided and stratified partitions.

These results highlight how training and testing models using unrepresentative splits can lead to biased performance estimates. It makes sense that excluding tail labels during evaluation results in higher P@1, since they are the hardest-to-train for labels. Conversely, including them would drag down overall performance. This is most apparent for Amazon-670K, where P@1s of the models trained with stratified splits are as much has 22% lower. This coincides with the very large proportion of labels missing from the provided test set: 48.2%.

In addition to generating biased performance estimates, using unrepresentative splits could also results in sub-optimal choices for hyperparameters - it's plausible to think that what's suitable for the specific split might not be the best choice for the entire dataset. Overall, these results lend more support to

---

[3] Remaining charts available at: https://github.com/maxitron93/stratified_sampling_for_XML/tree/master/label_distribution_charts.

Table 4. Difference in P@1 between models trained and tested using different partitions

	Parabel			FastXML			AnnexML		
	Provided	Stratified	%Δ	Provided	Stratified	%Δ	Provided	Stratified	%Δ
EURLex-4K	0.819	0.791	−3.5%	0.716	0.682	−4.8%	0.799	0.775	−3.0%
EURLex-4.3K	0.907	0.881	−2.9%	0.868	0.835	−3.8%	0.903	0.870	−3.7%
Wiki10-31K	0.842	0.830	−1.5%	0.828	0.815	−1.5%	0.865	0.857	−1.0%
Delicious-200K	0.466	0.425	−8.8%	0.432	0.390	−9.7%	0.465	0.429	−7.7%
Amazon-670K	0.447	0.373	−17%	0.370	0.288	−22%	0.420	0.336	−20%
RCV1-2K	0.904	0.911	+0.7%	0.912	0.916	+0.5%	0.906	0.911	+0.6%
AmazonCat-13K	0.934	0.933	−0.1%	0.931	0.932	+0.1%	0.935	0.935	0.0%

the already well established notion that using stratified splits during model development helps with ensuring the derivation of robust performance estimates [4, 9]. As such, stratified splits should be used where available.

7   Conclusion

In this paper, we examined the label distributions of test-train splits of XML data, generated using different partitioning methods. We also studied their impact on estimated performance. A summary of our findings is as follows:

– Many of the commonly used test-train splits provided by the XML repository are not representative of the entire dataset. Random sampling is not a suitable alternative since it produced partitions with label distributions that are highly divergent from the entire dataset.
– Stratified sampling is commonly used in the binary and multi-class settings, but those methods cannot be applied to multi-label data. Existing methods for MLC don't work well for XML-scale datasets: the commonly used iterative algorithm [9] is slow, and cannot produce well stratified splits.
– Our proposed stratified sampling method is capable of efficiently generating representative test-train splits of XML data that contain fewer missing labels compared to random sampling and most of the provided splits.
– Training and testing models with unrepresentative data can lead to optimistic performance estimates since, currently, many of the hardest-to-train-for tail labels aren't included in a number of the test sets.

Overall, our findings lend further support to the notion that it's apt to use stratified subsets of data during model development. As XML research becomes increasingly prevalent in this era of big data, we hope that future researchers will find our stratified sampling method useful in their endeavours.

References

1. Aguilar, G., Kar, S., Solorio, T.: LinCE: a centralized benchmark for linguistic code-switching evaluation. In: Proceedings of the 12th Language Resources and Evaluation Conference, pp. 1803–1813 (2020)

2. Bhatia, K., Dahiya, K., Jain, H., Mittal, A., Prabhu, Y., Varma, M.: The extreme classification repository: Multi-label datasets and code (2016). http://manikvarma. org/downloads/XC/XMLRepository.html
3. Jain, H., Prabhu, Y., Varma, M.: Extreme multi-label loss functions for recommendation, tagging, ranking; other missing label applications. In: Proceedings of the 22nd ACM SIGKDD International Conference on Knowledge Discovery and Data Mining, pp. 935–944 (2016)
4. Kohavi, R.: A study of cross-validation and bootstrap for accuracy estimation and model selection. In: Proceedings of the 14th International Joint Conference on Artificial Intelligence - Volume 2, pp. 1137–1143 (1995)
5. Lu, J., Du, L., Liu, M., Dipnall, J.: Multi-label few/zero-shot learning with knowledge aggregated from multiple label graphs. In: Proceedings of the 2020 Conference on Empirical Methods in Natural Language Processing, pp. 2935–2943 (2020)
6. Pedregosa, F., et al.: Scikit-learn: machine learning in python. J. Mach. Learn. Res. **12**, 2825–2830 (2011)
7. Prabhu, Y., Kag, A., Harsola, S., Agrawal, R., Varma, M.: Parabel: partitioned label trees for extreme classification with application to dynamic search advertising. In: Proceedings of the 2018 World Wide Web Conference, pp. 993–1002 (2018)
8. Prabhu, Y., Varma, M.: FastXML: a fast, accurate and stable tree-classifier for extreme multi-label learning. In: Proceedings of the 20th ACM SIGKDD International Conference on Knowledge Discovery and Data Mining, pp. 263–272 (2014)
9. Sechidis, K., Tsoumakas, G., Vlahavas, I.: On the stratification of multi-label data. In: Gunopulos, D., Hofmann, T., Malerba, D., Vazirgiannis, M. (eds.) ECML PKDD 2011, Part III. LNCS (LNAI), vol. 6913, pp. 145–158. Springer, Heidelberg (2011). https://doi.org/10.1007/978-3-642-23808-6_10
10. Shaheen, Z., Wohlgenannt, G., Filtz, E.: Large scale legal text classification using transformer models. arXiv preprint arXiv:2010.12871 (2020)
11. Szymański, P., Kajdanowicz, T.: A network perspective on stratification of multi-label data. In: First International Workshop on Learning with Imbalanced Domains: Theory and Applications, pp. 22–35 (2017)
12. Szymanski, P., Kajdanowicz, T.: Scikit-multilearn: a scikit-based python environment for performing multi-label classification. J. Mach. Learn. Res. **20**(1), 209–230 (2019)
13. Tagami, Y.: AnneXML: approximate nearest neighbor search for extreme multi-label classification. In: Proceedings of the 23rd ACM SIGKDD International Conference on Knowledge Discovery and Data Mining, pp. 455–464 (2017)
14. Tsoumakas, G., Spyromitros-Xioufis, E., Vilcek, J., Vlahavas, I.: Mulan: a Java library for multi-label learning. J. Mach. Learn. Res. **12**, 2411–2414 (2011)
15. Wagner, P., et al.: PTB-XL, a large publicly available electrocardiography dataset. Sci. Data **7**(1), 1–15 (2020)
16. You, R., Zhang, Z., Wang, Z., Dai, S., Mamitsuka, H., Zhu, S.: AttentionXML: label tree-based attention-aware deep model for high-performance extreme multi-label text classification. Adv. Neural Inf. Process. Syst. **32**, 5820–5830 (2019)

Vertical Federated Learning
for Higher-Order Factorization Machines

Kyohei Atarashi[1(✉)] and Masakazu Ishihata[2]

[1] Hokkaido University, Sapporo, Hokkaido, Japan
katarashi0305@gmail.com
[2] NTT Communication Science Laboratories, Kyoto, Japan
masakazu.ishihata.ze@hco.ntt.co.jp

Abstract. In the real world, multiple parties sometimes have different data of common instances, e.g., a customer of a supermarket can be a patient of a hospital. In other words, datasets are sometimes vertically partitioned into multiple parties. In such a situation, it is natural for those parties to collaborate to obtain more accurate prediction models; however, sharing their raw data should be prohibitive from the point of view of privacy-preservation. Federated learning has recently attracted the attention of machine learning researchers as a framework for efficiently collaborative learning of predictive models among multiple parties with privacy-preservation. In this paper, we propose a lossless vertical federated learning (VFL) method for higher-order factorization machines (HOFMs). HOFMs take into feature combinations efficiently and effectively and have succeeded in many tasks, especially recommender systems, link predictions, and natural language processing. Although it is intuitively difficult to evaluate and learn HOFMs without sharing raw feature vectors, our generalized recursion of ANOVA kernels enables us to do it. We also propose a more efficient and robust VFL method for HOFMs based on anonymization by clustering. Experimental results on three real-world datasets show the effectiveness of the proposed method.

1 Introduction

Machine learning techniques have become fundamental methods for the prediction and analysis of data, and as a result, various communities collect various types of data. Since the use of a larger dataset brings more accurate predictive models in general, it is reasonable for such parties to collaborate. However, sharing their raw data should be prohibitive for the following two reasons. The first one is about computational cost: the size of the centralized dataset can be too enormous to handle a single computer. The second one is about privacy-preservation [1,14]: some features include personal information that should not be shared with the different parties (e.g., a case history and a debt).

Federated learning (FL) [6,7,9,12,13,15,22,24–26] has attracted much attentions of the machine learning community as a framework to learn models from distributed datasets. FL can be categorized into horizontal FL (HFL), vertical

© Springer Nature Switzerland AG 2021
K. Karlapalem et al. (Eds.): PAKDD 2021, LNAI 12713, pp. 346–357, 2021.
https://doi.org/10.1007/978-3-030-75765-6_28

FL (VFL), and federated transfer learning [24]. In HFL, instances are partitioned into multiple parties, i.e., each party has the same features for different instances. In VFL, features are partitioned into multiple parties, i.e., each party has different features for the same instances. In federated transfer learning, both instances and features are partitioned into multiple parties. HFL corresponds to increasing the number of training instances and VFL corresponds to increasing the number of features. Thus, for predictive models considering the combinatorial effect of multiple features, introducing VFL exponentially increases the number of possible feature combinations.

The key idea of VFL is to share limited statistics that contain useful information for learning instead of sharing raw feature vectors. However, it sometimes happens that the raw feature vectors can be reproduced or accurately predicted from the limited statistics. To avoid such information leakage, techniques of secure multi-party computations, homomorphic encryption, and/or garbled circuits are used to share statistics securely [9,16,17]. The goal of VFL is to design secure statistics and constructing an efficient algorithm for learning predictive models that only refer to the designed statistics of other parties.

Higher-order factorization machines (HOFMs) [3] are machine learning predictive models that take into higher-order feature combinations. L-th order HOFMs consider from second to L-th order feature combinations and second-order HOFMs are equivalent to (vanilla) factorization machines (FMs) [19]. HOFMs have succeeded in many tasks, especially recommender systems [19], link predictions [3], and natural language processing [18]. The most important idea of HOFMs is a factorization of weight tensors for feature combinations: HOFMs can be regarded as polynomial models with low-rank (factorized) feature combination weight tensors. Due to this factorization, HOFMs can be represented as the sum of ANOVA kernels [21], which can be efficiently evaluated by dynamic programming [3]. Hence, HOFMs can be evaluated efficiently.

Increasing the number of features can make HOFMs more accurate because HOFMs take into higher-order feature combinations. Therefore, the development of a VFL method for HOFMs seems promising because the VFL setting is a simple way to increase the number of features; however, at the same time, it seems intuitively difficult to evaluate and learn HOFMs without sharing raw feature vectors because of considering feature combinations. Unfortunately, no VFL method for HOFMs has been proposed while Li et al. proposed a method for learning FMs on horizontally distributed datasets [11] and there exists many VFL methods for much simpler models [6,7,23,26].

In this paper, we propose two VFL methods for HOFMs:

- The first method only refers to the values of *local* ANOVA kernels of each instance in each party and achieves the same results as fully collaborative learning: the model learned from the centralized dataset. This method is based on the generalized ANOVA kernel recursion derived in this paper.
- The second method is more robust than the first one from the point of view of privacy-preservation. This method only refers to the *anonymized* values of local ANOVA kernels that is the value of local ANOVA kernels for centroids

of clusters. As a result, the method no longer obtains the same model as fully corroborated learning; however, its computation cost can be lower and can achieve comparable or higher performance than the first method.

We also show the effectiveness of the proposed method on three multi-label classification tasks that simulate VFL for HOFMs.

2 Preliminary

2.1 Vertical Federated Learning

In this paper, we consider the supervised learning of *multiple* parties on vertically partitioned datasets, i.e., VFL.

The goal of *single* party supervised learning is finding an accurate model $f : \mathcal{X} \to \mathcal{Y}$ that predicts the label $y \in \mathcal{Y}$ of the input $x \in \mathcal{X}$ from a labeled training dataset $\mathcal{D} = \{(x_n, y_n) \mid x_n \in \mathcal{X}, \, y_n \in \mathcal{Y}, \, n \in [N]\}$, where $N \in \mathbb{N}_{>0}$ is the number of training instances.

The goal of M parties supervised learning is finding M predictive models in the following situation: each feature vector x_n is partitioned into M parties and each party has its own target labels $y_n^{(m)} \in \mathcal{Y}^{(m)}$ of x_n, $m \in [M]$. We use $x_n^{(m)} \in \mathcal{X}^{(m)}$ to denote a part of x_n stored by the m-th party and use $\mathcal{D}^{(m)} = \{(x_n^{(m)}, y_n^{(m)}) \mid n \in [N]\}$ to denote the training dataset of the m-th party. Furthermore, we assume that datasets are *name sorted*: the index of instances n is shared by those parties, and that $\mathcal{X} = \mathbb{R}^d$ and $\mathcal{X}^{(m)} = \mathbb{R}^{d_m}$ (namely, $\sum_{m=1}^{M} d_m = d$). Then, the objective of the m-th party is finding an accurate predictive model $f^{(m)}$ for their task.

In M parties supervised learning, it is reasonable for the parties to collaborate to obtain more accurate predictive models $f^{(m)}$ because they have different information on the common instances. The types of collaboration can mainly be categorized into the following three situations:

– **Fully collaborative learning (FCL):** The most straightforward and effective collaboration is integrating their datasets directly and learning their models using the integrated dataset. It is equivalent to performing single party supervised learning on $\mathcal{D}$ for each task. In this setting, $f^{(m)}$ is a predictive model from $\mathcal{X}$ to $\mathcal{Y}^{(m)}$. However, in many cases, this FCL is prohibitive from the point of view of privacy-preservation in the dataset, e.g., features include personal information that cannot be shared with other parties.
– **Fully independent learning (FIL):** If the parties do not collaborate to prevent leakage of personal information, they have to learn their own model $f^{(m)}$ only from their own datasets independently, namely, each party solves single party supervised learning problem independently on the partitioned dataset $\mathcal{D}^{(m)}$. In this case, $f^{(m)}$ is a predictive model from $\mathcal{X}^{(m)}$ to $\mathcal{Y}^{(m)}$.
– **Partially collaborative learning (PCL):** As a compromise of FCL and FIL, the parties may agree to *partially* collaborate: they do not share their raw data, but share some statistics that are useful for learning and do not violate

their privacy policy. Thus, in PCL, the parties share the limited statistics and learn their predictive models using their own datasets and the shared statistics.

Constructing a PCL method corresponds to designing (i) effective statistics that can be shared with other parties and (ii) an efficient learning algorithm such that the parties only refer to shared statistics and their own datasets. The goal of VFL is to construct PCL methods that can obtain (a) completely the same model as FCL, or (b) more accurate models than FIL.

2.2 Higher-Order Factorization Machines

Factorization machines (FMs) [19] are predictive models based on second-order feature combinations, and higher-order FMs (HOFMs) [3] are higher-order extension of FMs. The key insight for efficient evaluation and learning of HOFMs is the representation of the sum of feature combinations by the ANOVA kernel [3,21]. For any parameter vector $p \in \mathbb{R}^d$ and instance $x \in \mathbb{R}^d$, the L-th order ANOVA kernel $\mathcal{A}_L : \mathbb{R}^d \times \mathbb{R}^d \to \mathbb{R}$ is defined as

$$\mathcal{A}_L(p, x) := \sum_{d \geq j_1 > \cdots > j_L \geq 1} \prod_{l=1}^{L} p_{j_l} x_{j_l}. \tag{1}$$

Then, the L-th order HOFM is defined as

$$f(x; P) := \sum_{s=1}^{k} \sum_{l=2}^{L} \mathcal{A}_l(p_{l,s}, x), \tag{2}$$

where $P := \{P_l \mid P_l \in \mathbb{R}^{k \times d}, l = 2, \ldots, L\}$ are learnable parameters (we omit linear term for convenience) and $p_{l,s}$ is the s-th row vector of P_l.

At first glance, the evaluation of L-th order HOFMs seems to require $O(kd^L)$ computational cost. Fortunately, HOFMs can be evaluated in $O(kL^2 \mathrm{nnz}(x))$ time and $O(d)$ memory because the l-th order ANOVA kernel $\mathcal{A}_l(p, x)$ can be computed in $O(l \cdot \mathrm{nnz}(x))$ time and $O(l)$ memory by dynamic programming based on the following recursion [3,21]:

$$\mathcal{A}_l(p, x) = \mathcal{A}_l(p_{\neg j}, x_{\neg j}) + p_j x_j \mathcal{A}_{l-1}(p_{\neg j}, x_{\neg j}), \tag{3}$$

where $\mathrm{nnz}(x)$ is the number of non-zero elements in x and $p_{\neg j}$ and $x_{\neg j}$ ($j \in [d]$) is the $(d-1)$-dimensional vector with p_j and x_j removed, respectively.

The optimization problem of L-th order HOFMs is

$$\min_{P} \sum_{n=1}^{N} \ell(y_n, f(x_n; P)) + \frac{1}{2} \sum_{s=1}^{k} \sum_{l=2}^{L} \beta \|p_{l,s}\|_2^2, \tag{4}$$

where $\ell : \mathcal{Y} \times \mathcal{Y} \to \mathbb{R}_{\geq 0}$ is a μ-smooth ($\mu > 0$) convex loss function and $\beta > 0$ is a regularization hyper-parameter. Although HOFMs defined by Eq. (2) are non-linear w.r.t $p_{l,s}$, they are fortunately linear w.r.t each coordinate $p_{l,s,j}$ ($s \in [k]$

and $j \in [d]$). Thus, the optimization problem (4) is convex optimization problem w.r.t each $p_{l,s,j}$ and it can be solved efficiently by using the coordinate descent (CD) algorithm [3]. The update rule of the CD algorithm is

$$
p_{l,s,j} \leftarrow p_{l,s,j} - \eta^{-1} \left(\sum_{n=1}^{N} \ell'(y_n, f(\boldsymbol{x}_n)) a'_{n,l,s,j} + \beta p_{l,s,j} \right), \tag{5}
$$

where $a'_{n,l,s,j} = \partial \mathcal{A}_l(\boldsymbol{p}_{l,s}, \boldsymbol{x}_n)/\partial p_{l,s,j}$ and $\eta = \mu \sum_{n=1}^{N} (a'_{n,l,s,j})^2 + \beta$. Given the values of ANOVA kernels $\mathcal{A}_1(\boldsymbol{p}, \boldsymbol{x}), \ldots, \mathcal{A}_L(\boldsymbol{p}, \boldsymbol{x})$, the gradient of the ANOVA kernel $\partial \mathcal{A}_L(\boldsymbol{p}, \boldsymbol{x})/\partial p_j$ actually can be computed in $O(L)$ time and memory by the dynamic programming based on the following recursion [2]:

$$
\frac{\partial \mathcal{A}_l(\boldsymbol{p}, \boldsymbol{x})}{\partial p_j} = x_j \mathcal{A}_{l-1}(\boldsymbol{p}_{\neg j}, \boldsymbol{x}_{\neg j}) \tag{6}
$$

$$
= x_j (\mathcal{A}_{l-1}(\boldsymbol{p}, \boldsymbol{x}) - p_j x_j \mathcal{A}_{l-2}(\boldsymbol{p}_{\neg j}, \boldsymbol{x}_{\neg j})) \tag{7}
$$

$$
= x_j \left(\mathcal{A}_{l-1}(\boldsymbol{p}, \boldsymbol{x}) - p_j \frac{\partial \mathcal{A}_{l-1}(\boldsymbol{p}, \boldsymbol{x})}{\partial p_j} \right). \tag{8}
$$

The j-th column of $\boldsymbol{P}_l$ is the parameter for the j-th feature. In the VFL setting, we assume that $\boldsymbol{P}_l$ is also partitioned into M parties similarly for the datasets: if the m-th party stores j-th feature $x_{n,j}$, the party also stores the corresponding parameters $p_{l,s,j}$. We use $\boldsymbol{P}_l^{(m)}$ and $\boldsymbol{p}_{l,s}^{(m)}$ to denote a part of $\boldsymbol{P}_l$ and $\boldsymbol{p}_{l,s}$ stored by the m-th party, and let $\boldsymbol{P}^{(m)} := \{\boldsymbol{P}_l^{(m)} \mid l = 2, \ldots, L\}$.

Strictly speaking, we need M HOFMs to solve M tasks of M parties: we have to introduce M suits of parameters $\boldsymbol{P}^{(t)}$ $(t \in [M])$ and we have to learn $f(\boldsymbol{x}; \boldsymbol{P}^{(t)})$ for the t-th task at the same time. Of course, we can employ a multi-task learning method to learn those M HOFMs; however, for simplifying notation, we hereinafter assume that we independently learn these M HOFMs and especially focus on the t-th task: namely, we omit the task index t. We call the t-th party *target party* and the c-th party $(c \in [M] \setminus \{t\})$ *collaborating party*.

3 Vertical Federated Learning for HOFMs

In this section, we propose two types of VFL methods for HOFMs (VFL-HOFMs). We firstly generalize the well-known recursion of the ANOVA kernel of Eq. (3). Next, we propose two VFL methods for HOFMs that do not share their raw data. The first method only shares the values of local ANOVA kernels but it can achieve the same learning results as FCL. The second method shares *anonymized* local ANOVA kernels, which is the value of local ANOVA kernel of *centoroids of clusters*, instead of raw feature vectors. Note that the second method does NOT achieve the same learning results with FCL; however, this method is robust from the point of view of privacy-preservation.

3.1   VFL-HOFMs by Local ANOVA Kernel Aggregation

Local ANOVA Kernel Aggregation: We firstly generalize the recursion of the ANOVA kernel of Eq. (3). For simplicity, we start by the case $M = 2$.

Corollary 1 (A generalized ANOVA kernel recursion). *Let $p^{(1)} \in \mathbb{R}^{d_1}$ and $p^{(2)} \in \mathbb{R}^{d_2}$ be sub-vectors of $p = (p^{(1)}; p^{(2)}) \in \mathbb{R}^d$ and similarly for $x^{(1)} \in \mathbb{R}^{d_1}$, $x^{(2)} \in \mathbb{R}^{d_2}$ and $x = (x^{(1)}; x^{(2)})$. Then, $\mathcal{A}_L(p, x)$ can be written as the sum of the product of ANOVA kernels:*

$$\mathcal{A}_L(p, x) = \sum_{l=0}^{L} \mathcal{A}_{L-l}(p^{(1)}, x^{(1)}) \mathcal{A}_l(p^{(2)}, x^{(2)}). \tag{9}$$

Proof. Let $a_l := \mathcal{A}_l(p, x)$ and $a_l^{(m)} := \mathcal{A}_l(p^{(m)}, x^{(m)})$ ($m \in [2]$). By the definition of the ANOVA kernel, a_l and $a_l^{(m)}$ are sum of all possible l-th order feature combinations between $\{p, x\}$ and $\{p^{(m)}, x^{(m)}\}$, respectively. First, for each possible L-th order feature combination between $\{p, x\}$, there exists a unique l such that $(L - l)$ features out of L come from $p^{(1)}$ and $x^{(1)}$, and the rest l features come from $p^{(2)}$ and $x^{(2)}$. Second, a product $a_{L-l}^{(1)} a_l^{(2)}$ is the sum of all possible products of an $(L - l)$-th order feature combination between $\{p^{(1)}, x^{(1)}\}$ and an L-th order feature combination between $\{p^{(2)}, x^{(2)}\}$. From the above two facts, $\sum_{l=0}^{L} a_{L-l}^{(1)} a_l^{(2)}$ must be the sum of all possible L-th order feature combinations: namely, $a_L = \sum_{l=0}^{L} a_{L-l}^{(1)} a_l^{(2)}$ and this equation is certainly Eq. (9).

By recursively applying Eq. (9), we can easily extend the above corollary for the case $M > 2$ and Eq. (9) is equivalent to Eq. (3) if $d_1 = 1$ and/or $d_2 = 1$. Equation (9) deduces that the value of the *full* ANOVA kernel $\mathcal{A}_L(p, x)$ can be evaluated by integrating the values of *local* ANOVA kernels: $\mathcal{A}_l(p^{(1)}, x^{(1)})$ and $\mathcal{A}_l(p^{(2)}, x^{(2)})$ for $l \in [L]$. In the same manner, when p and x are partitioned into M parties, $\mathcal{A}_L(p, x)$ can be evaluated by integrating the value of $\mathcal{A}_l(p^{(m)}, x^{(m)})$ for $m \in [M]$ and $l \in [L]$.

Algorithm 1 shows the procedure of secure evaluation of the full ANOVA kernel $\mathcal{A}_L(p, x)$ by the target party. In Algorithm 1, each party computes the values of its own local ANOVA kernels and the target party gathers and integrates those values from the collaborating to obtain the value of its full ANOVA kernel. We call this algorithm *local ANOVA kernel aggregation* (LAKA). Using LAKA, the target party can evaluate HOFMs securely because $f(x_n; P)$ can be computed by the sum of the full ANOVA kernel as shown in Eq. (2). The complexity of LAKA is $O(\text{nnz}(x_n)L + L^2 M)$: each party firstly computes its own local ANOVA kernels $\mathcal{A}_l(p_{l,s}^{(m)}, x_n^{(m)})$ in $O(\text{nnz}(x_n^{(m)})L)$ time, and then, the target party aggregates them in $O(L^2 M)$ time.

Secure Learning of HOFMs Using LAKA: We present a secure CD algorithm for HOFMs on vertically partitioned datasets. Recall we assume that parameters P are also vertically partitioned into M parties and sub-parameter $P^{(m)}$ is updated by m-th party. From Eq. (5), (i) $\partial \mathcal{A}_l(p_{l,s}, x_n)/\partial p_{l,s,j}$ and

---

Algorithm 1. LAKA: Secure evaluation of the full ANOVA kernel $\mathcal{A}_l(\boldsymbol{p}_{l,s}, \boldsymbol{x}_n)$ on vertically partitioned datasets

---

Input: $\boldsymbol{p}_{l,s}^{(m)}$ and $\boldsymbol{x}_n^{(m)}$ for only the m-th party.
Output: $\mathcal{A}_l(\boldsymbol{p}_{l,s}, \boldsymbol{x}_n)$ for only the target party t.

1: Each party $m \in [M]$ locally computes the values of local ANOVA kernels $a_{n,h,s}^{(m)} = \mathcal{A}_h(\boldsymbol{p}_{l,s}^{(m)}, \boldsymbol{x}_n^{(m)})$ for each $h \in [l]$ only using its own $\boldsymbol{p}_{l,s}^{(m)}$ and $\boldsymbol{x}_n^{(m)}$.
2: Each collaborating party $c \in [M] \setminus \{t\}$ sends the computed values $\{a_{n,h,s}^{(c)} \mid h \in [l]\}$ to the target party t.
3: **for each** $h \in [l]$ and $c \in [M] \setminus \{t\}$ **do**
4:     The target party updates $a_{n,h,s}^{(t)}$ by integrating collected values: $a_{n,h,s}^{(t)} \leftarrow \sum_{h'=0}^{h} a_{n,h-h',s}^{(t)} a_{n,h',s}^{(c)}$.
5: **end for**
6: $a_{n,l,s}^{(t)}$ is the value of full ANOVA kernel $\mathcal{A}_l(\boldsymbol{p}_{l,s}, \boldsymbol{x}_n)$.

(ii) $\ell'(y_n, f(\boldsymbol{x}_n; \boldsymbol{P}))$ are required for updating $p_{l,s,j}$ by the CD algorithm, $s \in [k], j \in [d]$. Thus, a secure CD algorithm is accomplished if these values are computed securely. From Eq. (8), given the values of the *full* ANOVA kernels $\mathcal{A}_1(\boldsymbol{p}_{l,s}, \boldsymbol{x}_n), \ldots, \mathcal{A}_{l-1}(\boldsymbol{p}_{l,s}, \boldsymbol{x}_n)$, the m-th party storing the j-th feature can compute $\partial \mathcal{A}_l(\boldsymbol{p}_{l,s}, \boldsymbol{x}_n)/\partial p_{l,s,j}$ in $O(l)$ time. Using LAKA, the values of full ANOVA kernels can be computed securely and thus $\partial \mathcal{A}_l(\boldsymbol{p}_{l,s}^{(m)}, \boldsymbol{x}_n)/\partial p_{l,s,j}$ can also be computed securely. Similarly, the target party can compute $\ell'(y_n, f(\boldsymbol{x}_n; \boldsymbol{P}))$ without violation of privacy. As a result, each party can update stored parameters by the CD algorithm with privacy-preservation. Of course, we can employ LAKA with homomorphic encryption instead of vanilla LAKA to enrich its security. Algorithm 2 shows the procedure of a secure CD algorithm for HOFMs. In Algorithm 2, the m-th party storing the j-th feature updates $p_{l,s,j}$. We call this algorithm CD-LAKA. Given the values of $f(\boldsymbol{x}_n; \boldsymbol{P})$ and $\mathcal{A}_l(\boldsymbol{p}_{l,s}, \boldsymbol{x}_n)$ for $n \in [N]$, $l \in [L]$, and $s \in [k]$, the complexity of CD-LAKA for updating $p_{l,s,j}$ is $O(\text{nnz}(\boldsymbol{X}_{:,j})L)$, where $\boldsymbol{X}_{:,j}$ is the j-th column vector of $\boldsymbol{X}$, because the partial gradients of ANOVA kernels can be computed in $O(L)$.

Using CD-LAKA, the parties can evaluate and learn HOFMs without sharing the raw feature vectors. However, someone might suspect that it is not secure sufficiently to protect from the adversary. Unfortunately, in some cases, the target party can identify the value of the raw features of other parties. Assume that the parameters $\{\boldsymbol{P}^{(m)}\}_{m \in [M]}$ are shared (leaked) among parties at each CD-LAKA iteration and $p_{l,s,j}$ is updated as $p_{l,s,j} - \delta$ at current iteration. Then, the target party knows the values of δ (because $p_{l,s,j}$ and $p_{l,s,j} - \delta$ are shared) and first order ANOVA kernels $\langle \boldsymbol{p}_{l,s}, \boldsymbol{x}_n \rangle$ and $\langle \boldsymbol{p}_{l,s}, \boldsymbol{x}_n \rangle - \delta x_{n,j}$, so the target party can identify $x_{n,j}$ for all $n \in [N]$. Fortunately, the parties can evaluate and learn HOFMs more securely by employing LAKA/CD-LAKA with fully homomorphic encryption [10], which supports both multiplication and addition on ciphertexts, for the values of local ANOVA kernels guarantees the privacy-preservation: (1) the target party generates the public/private key of the fully homomorphic

---

Algorithm 2. CD-LAKA: Secure CD update for HOFMs by LAKA

Input: $\boldsymbol{x}_n^{(m)}$ and $\boldsymbol{P}_l^{(m)}$ for only the m-th party, and y_n for only the target party
Output: Updated $p_{l,s,j}$ for only the m-th party who stores the j-th feature
1: Each party obtains $a_{n,l,s} = \mathcal{A}_l(\boldsymbol{p}_{l,s}, \boldsymbol{x}_n)$ by LAKA.
2: The target party computes $f_n := f(\boldsymbol{x}_n; \boldsymbol{P})$ by Eq. (2): $f_n = \sum_{s=1}^{k} \sum_{l=2}^{L} a_{n,l,s}$.
3: The target party evaluates $\ell'(y_n, f_n)$ and sends them to the collaborating parties.
4: The m-th party computes $\partial \mathcal{A}_l(\boldsymbol{p}_{l,s}, \boldsymbol{x}_n)/\partial p_{l,s,j}$ by Eq. (8) using $a_{n,l,s}$ for each j-th
   feature that it stores.
5: The m-th party updates $p_{l,s,j}$ by Eq. (5) using $a_{n,l,s}$ and $\ell'(y_n, f_n)$.

---

encryption and sends the public key to the collaborating parties, (2) the target party encrypts the values of its local ANOVA kernels and sends them another party as messages, (3) the collaborating party who receives the encrypted values integrates messages and the encrypted values of its local ANOVA kernels, and sends integrated values to another party who has not received them yet, and (4) finally the target party receives the encrypted values of full ANOVA kernels and decrypts them. However, its computational cost becomes large because each party encrypts messages whose size is $O(NL^2)$. Mechanisms of differential privacy [8] provide us strong and robust guarantees of privacy-preservation but they might cause a decline in the performance of learned HOFMs. Therefore, we propose a more secure and efficient extension of LAKA in the next subsection.

The following is the summary of the VFL-HOFM by LAKA. In the VFL-HOFM by LAKA, the collaborating parties only share the values of local ANOVA kernels, and the target party computes the *exact* values of the full ANOVA kernels by integrating shared values and its own values, namely, the target party can compute completely same values that are computed in the FCL setting. However, if the parameters are leaked, CD-LAKA is not secure.

3.2 VFL-HOFMs by LAKA with Anonymization Using Clustering Techniques

Here, we propose anonymized LAKA (ALAKA) being an extension of LAKA based on anonymization using clustering techniques [4]. As preprocessing, each party $m \in [M]$ runs a clustering algorithm for its own dataset $\mathcal{D}^{(m)}$. Here we denote the cluster ID of $\boldsymbol{x}_n^{(m)}$ as $r_n^{(m)}$ and the centroid of its r-th cluster as $\boldsymbol{\mu}_r^{(m)}$, and use $\boldsymbol{\mu}_n^{(m)}$ as a shorthand of $\boldsymbol{\mu}_{r_n^{(m)}}^{(m)}$. The idea of ALAKA is to use the $\boldsymbol{\mu}_n^{(c)}$ instead of $\boldsymbol{x}_n^{(c)}$ in LAKA: each collaborating party $c \in [M] \setminus \{t\}$ computes values of $\mathcal{A}_h(\boldsymbol{p}_{l,s}^{(c)}, \boldsymbol{\mu}_n^{(c)})$ instead of $\mathcal{A}_h(\boldsymbol{p}_{l,s}^{(c)}, \boldsymbol{x}_n^{(c)})$ and sends these values as anonymized values of local ANOVA kernels to the target party. Then, the target party approximately evaluates the value of the full ANOVA kernel $\mathcal{A}_l(\boldsymbol{p}_{l,s}, \boldsymbol{x}_n)$ by integrating collected anonymized values. Algorithm 3 shows the procedure of ALAKA. ALAKA is more secure than LAKA because $\boldsymbol{x}_n^{(c)}$ is never used in ALAKA. In CD-ALAKA, even if the parameters are leaked at each iteration, the

---

Algorithm 3. ALAKA: LAKA with anonymization using clustering techniques

Input: $p_{l,s}^{(m)}$, $x_n^{(m)}$, and $\mu_n^{(m)}$ for only the m-th party.
Output: Anonymized $\mathcal{A}_l(p_{l,s}, x_n)$ for only the target party.
1: The target party t locally computes the values of local ANOVA kernels $a_{n,h,s}^{(t)} = \mathcal{A}_h(p_{l,s}^{(t)}, x_n^{(t)})$ for each $h \in [l]$ only using its own $p_{l,s}^{(t)}$ and $x_n^{(t)}$.
2: Each collaborating party $c \in [M] \setminus \{t\}$ locally computes $a_{n,h,s}^{(c)} = \mathcal{A}_h(p_{l,s}^{(c)}, \mu_n^{(c)})$ for each $h \in [l]$ only using its own $p_{l,s}^{(c)}$ and $\mu_n^{(c)}$.
3: Each collaborating party $c \in [M] \setminus \{t\}$ sends the computed values $\{a_{n,h,s}^{(c)} \mid h \in [l]\}$ to the target party.
4: **for each** $h \in [l]$ and $c \in [M] \setminus \{t\}$ **do**
5:    The target party updates $a_{n,h,s}^{(t)}$ by integrating collected values: $a_{n,h,s}^{(t)} \leftarrow \sum_{h'=0}^{h} a_{n,h-h',s}^{(t)} a_{n,h',s}^{(c)}$.
6: **end for**
7: $a_{n,h,s}^{(t)}$ is the anonymized value of the full ANOVA kernel $\mathcal{A}_l(p_{l,s}, x_n)$.

Table 1. Datasets used in experiments.

Dataset	#training	#test	#features	#parties
Yeast	1,500	917	103	3
SIAM	21,519	7,077	30,438	7
RCV1	23,149	781,265	47,236	7

target party can identify only the values of centroids vectors, not raw feature vectors. We call the CD algorithm with ALAKA as CD-ALAKA. The performance of the VFL-HOFM with CD-ALAKA will be worse than that of the HOFM with FCL (equivalent to VFL-HOFM with CD-LAKA) but better than that of the HOFM with FIL because ALAKA does not use the raw feature vectors but uses the centroids of clusters computed from raw feature vectors.

4   Experiments

In this section, we demonstrate the effectiveness of the proposed CD-ALAKA.

4.1   Settings

For simulating the learning problem on vertically partitioned datasets, we used three datasets for the multi-label classification: Yeast, SIAM, and RCV1 that are public and available in [5]. We assumed that each label corresponds to one task, and each party has its own task (thus the number of parties is equal to the number of tasks). Although there are 14, 22, and 101 multi-labels in the Yeast, SIAM, and RCV1 dataset respectively, we did not use all multi-labels because many of them are very imbalanced. We picked three, seven, and seven

Table 2. Comparison of HOFMs with **FCL**, **FIL**, and **ALAKA** on three datasets.

(a) Yeast dataset

	FCL	FIL	ALAKA
Task 1	**0.660**	0.655	0.653
Task 2	**0.696**	0.634	0.686
Task 3	**0.728**	0.670	0.687

(b) SIAM dataset

	FCL	FIL	ALAKA
Task 1	**0.844**	0.708	0.778
Task 2	**0.901**	0.813	0.880
Task 3	**0.945**	0.886	0.933
Task 4	**0.948**	0.862	0.912
Task 5	**0.908**	0.820	0.866
Task 6	**0.937**	0.862	0.887
Task 7	**0.826**	0.713	0.737

(c) RCV1 dataset

	FCL	FIL	ALAKA
Task 1	0.939	0.829	**0.946**
Task 2	0.968	0.897	**0.970**
Task 3	**0.916**	0.770	0.870
Task 4	**0.955**	0.830	0.940
Task 5	**0.976**	0.889	0.954
Task 6	**0.979**	0.923	0.961
Task 7	**0.970**	0.859	0.919

labels in the Yeast, SIAM, and RCV1 dataset respectively, which are top-three, -seven, and -seven balanced labels. For all datasets, we set $d_m = \text{floor}(d/M)$ for all $m \in [M-1]$ and $d_M = d - \sum_{m=1}^{M-1} d_m$, and we partitioned feature vectors randomly. Table 1 shows a summary of these three datasets.

We compared the following three methods: HOFMs with (i) FCL (it is equivalent to LAKA) using integrated full dataset $\mathcal{D}$ (**FCL**), (ii) FIL using only partial (their own) datasets $\mathcal{D}^{(m)}$ (**FIL**), and (iii) CD-ALAKA (**ALAKA**). We optimized all methods by using the CD algorithm with 100 iterations. For the **FCL** and **FIL**, we tuned hyper-parameters based on the validation datasets that are split from training datasets. After determining hyper-parameters, we re-fit these methods by using full training datasets including validation datasets used for tuning hyper-parameters. We tuned $L \in \{2,3\}$ and $\beta \in \{0.01, 0.1, 1, 10\}$. For the rank hyper-parameter, we followed Blondel et al. [3] and set it to 30 for all methods. For the **ALAKA**, we used the same hyper-parameters as for the **FIL**. We used the mini-batch k-means clustering algorithm [20] and set $C = 5$ for all parties. We evaluated these methods by the area under the receiver operating characteristic curve (ROC-AUC). Because the performance of HOFMs depends on the initial parameters, we ran experiments five times with different random seeds for all datasets. Moreover, we ran the experiments with different five partitions generated randomly because the performances of the **FIL** and **ALAKA** depend on the partition. We report the average ROC-AUC on test datasets.

4.2 Results

The experimental results are shown in Table 2. The performances of the **FCL** were always greater than those of the **FIL**. Thus, the collaboration among parties who have different features is effective for HOFMs. We emphasize that the HOFM learned by the proposed CD-LAKA is equivalent to that by **FCL**. Our **ALAKA** outperformed **FIL** for all settings and sometimes achieved comparable or higher predictive performance than **FCL**. The performance improvement brought by **ALAKA** for the SIAM and RCV1 datasets ($M = 7$) was larger than that for the Yeast dataset ($M = 3$). It seems reasonable because HOFMs use higher-order feature combinations and hence increasing the number of features was effective combinatorially. However, it is needed to investigate further when **ALAKA** is effective, especially, when **ALAKA** is better than **FCL**.

5 Conclusion

We have proposed two VFL methods for HOFMs. The first method shares values of local ANOVA kernels instead of raw feature vectors and achieves the same evaluation and learning results of the FCL setting. On the other hand, in the second method, the parties share the values of their ANOVA kernels of centroids of clusters and parameters, that is, parties use centroids of clusters instead of original feature vectors for other parties. Although this method is no longer equivalent to FCL, the performances of HOFMs learned by this method can outperform those of HOFMs with FIL and sometimes be comparable to those of HOFMs with FCL. In our experiments, CD-ALAKA outperformed those with FIL and was comparable to those with fully collaborative learning as expected. Our future work includes a theoretical investigation of the proposed ALAKA.

Acknowledgements. K.A. was supported by JSPS KAKENHI Grant Number JP20J13620 and by the Global Station for Big Data and Cybersecurity, a project of the Global Institution for Collaborative Research and Education at Hokkaido University.

References

1. Anderson, J.G.: Security of the distributed electronic patient record: a case-based approach to identifying policy issues. Int. J. Med. Inf. **60**(2), 111–118 (2000)
2. Atarashi, K., Oyama, S., Kurihara, M.: Link prediction using higher-order feature combinations across objects. IEICE Trans. Inf. Syst. **103**(8), 1833–1842 (2020)
3. Blondel, M., Fujino, A., Ueda, N., Ishihata, M.: Higher-order factorization machines. In: NeurIPS, pp. 3351–3359 (2016)
4. Byun, J.-W., Kamra, A., Bertino, E., Li, N.: Efficient k-anonymization using clustering techniques. In: Kotagiri, R., Krishna, P.R., Mohania, M., Nantajeewarawat, E. (eds.) DASFAA 2007. LNCS, vol. 4443, pp. 188–200. Springer, Heidelberg (2007). https://doi.org/10.1007/978-3-540-71703-4_18
5. Chang, C.C., Lin, C.J.: LIBSVM Data: Classification, Regression, and Multi-label. https://www.csie.ntu.edu.tw/~cjlin/libsvmtools/datasets/

6. Cheng, K., Fan, T., Jin, Y., Liu, Y., Chen, T., Yang, Q.: Secureboost: A lossless federated learning framework. arXiv preprint arXiv:1901.08755 (2019)
7. Du, W., Han, Y.S., Chen, S.: Privacy-preserving multivariate statistical analysis: linear regression and classification. In: SDM, pp. 222–233 (2004)
8. Dwork, C., Roth, A., et al.: The algorithmic foundations of differential privacy. Found. Trends Theor. Comput. Sci. **9**(3–4), 211–407 (2014)
9. Gascón, A., et al.: Privacy-preserving distributed linear regression on high-dimensional data. PETS **2017**(4), 345–364 (2017)
10. Gentry, C., et al.: Fully homomorphic encryption using ideal lattices. In: STOC, pp. 169–178 (2009)
11. Li, M., Liu, Z., Smola, A.J., Wang, Y.X.: Difacto: distributed factorization machines. In: WSDM, pp. 377–386 (2016)
12. Li, Q., Wen, Z., Wu, Z., Hu, S., Wang, N., He, B.: A survey on federated learning systems: vision, hype and reality for data privacy and protection. arXiv preprint arXiv:1907.09693 (2019)
13. Liu, Y., et al.: A communication efficient vertical federated learning framework. In: NeurIPS Workshop on Federated Learning for Data Privacy and Confidentiality (2019)
14. Malin, B., Sweeney, L.: How (not) to protect genomic data privacy in a distributed network: using trail re-identification to evaluate and design anonymity protection systems. J. Biomed. Inf. **37**(3), 179–192 (2004)
15. McMahan, B., Moore, E., Ramage, D., Hampson, S., y Arcas, B.A.: Communication-efficient learning of deep networks from decentralized data. In: AISTATS, pp. 1273–1282 (2017)
16. Mohassel, P., Zhang, Y.: Secureml: a system for scalable privacy-preserving machine learning. In: SP, pp. 19–38 (2017)
17. Nikolaenko, V., Weinsberg, U., Ioannidis, S., Joye, M., Boneh, D., Taft, N.: Privacy-preserving ridge regression on hundreds of millions of records. In: SP, pp. 334–348 (2013)
18. Petroni, F., Corro, L.D., Gemulla, R.: Core: context-aware open relation extraction with factorization machines. In: EMNLP, pp. 1763–1773 (2015)
19. Rendle, S.: Factorization machines. In: ICDM, pp. 995–1000 (2010)
20. Sculley, D.: Web-scale k-means clustering. In: WWW, pp. 1177–1178 (2010)
21. Shawe-Taylor, J., Cristianini, N., et al.: Kernel Methods for Pattern Analysis. Cambridge University Press, Cambridge (2004)
22. Shokri, R., Shmatikov, V.: Privacy-preserving deep learning. In: CCS, pp. 1310–1321 (2015)
23. Slavkovic, A.B., Nardi, Y., Tibbits, M.M.: Secure logistic regression of horizontally and vertically partitioned distributed databases. In: ICDM Workshops, pp. 723–728 (2007)
24. Yang, Q., Liu, Y., Chen, T., Tong, Y.: Federated machine learning: concept and applications. ACM Trans. Intell. Syst. Technol. **10**(2), 1–19 (2019)
25. Yu, H., Jiang, X., Vaidya, J.: Privacy-preserving SVM using nonlinear kernels on horizontally partitioned data. In: SIGAPP SAC, pp. 603–610 (2006)
26. Yu, H., Vaidya, J., Jiang, X.: Privacy-preserving SVM classification on vertically partitioned data. In: Ng, W.-K., Kitsuregawa, M., Li, J., Chang, K. (eds.) PAKDD 2006. LNCS (LNAI), vol. 3918, pp. 647–656. Springer, Heidelberg (2006). https://doi.org/10.1007/11731139_74

dK-Projection: Publishing Graph Joint Degree Distribution with Node Differential Privacy

Masooma Iftikhar[✉] and Qing Wang

The Australian National University, Canberra, Australia
{masooma.iftikhar,qing.wang}@anu.edu.au

Abstract. Network data has great significance for commercial and research purposes. However, most networks contain sensitive information about individuals, thereby requiring privacy-preserving mechanisms to publish network data while preserving data utility. In this paper, we study the problem of publishing higher-order network statistics, i.e., *joint degree distribution*, under strong mathematical guarantees of *node differential privacy*. This problem is known to be challenging, since even simple network statistics (e.g., edge count) can be highly sensitive to adding or removing a single node in a network. To address this challenge, we propose a general framework of publishing dK-distributions under node differential privacy, and develop a novel graph projection algorithm to transform graphs to θ-bounded graphs for controlled sensitivity. We have conducted experiments to verify the utility enhancement and privacy guarantee of our proposed framework on four real-world networks. To the best of our knowledge, this is the first study to publish higher-order network statistics under node differential privacy, while enhancing network data utility.

Keywords: Data publishing · Node differential privacy · dK-distributions

1 Introduction

Network analysis provides a rich source of insights for data science research and business purposes [22]. However, many networks such as social networks often contain sensitive relationships among individuals, (e.g., friendships and acquaintances) or sensitive attributes of individuals (e.g., age, location and race) [10]. Hence, releasing network data raises privacy concerns to individuals, requiring privacy preserving mechanisms for network analysis.

In recent years, differential privacy (DP) [6] has received increasing attention, since it offers a robust privacy guarantee while making no assumptions about the prior knowledge of an adversary. Early works [2,7,10,17,18,20,21] on differentially private network data focused on *edge-DP*, aiming to hide the presence and absence of a single edge in a network. A more desirable notion of

© Springer Nature Switzerland AG 2021
K. Karlapalem et al. (Eds.): PAKDD 2021, LNAI 12713, pp. 358–370, 2021.
https://doi.org/10.1007/978-3-030-75765-6_29

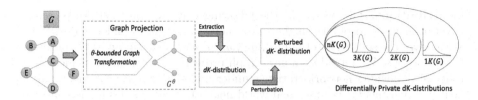

Fig. 1. A high-level overview of the proposed framework (*dK-Projection*).

privacy – the focus of this work – is *node-DP*, which aims to hide the presence and absence of a single node and the set of edges incident to that node [11]. It is acknowledged that, although node-DP can provide stronger privacy protection than edge-DP, it is more challenging to design and implement [1,3,11,19]. This is because changing a single node may potentially lead to changes on one or more edges, particularly in real-world networks (e.g. Twitter) that are often dense. Some recent studies [3,4,11,16] have attempted to tackle this challenge. However, these studies are limited to publishing only simple network statistics (e.g., edge count, triangle count, and degree distribution) in order to maintain relatively low sensitivity under node-DP.

In this paper we aim to develop a framework for publishing higher-order network statistics under node-DP. We observe that dK-distributions [13,14] can serve as a good basis for representing higher-order network statistics. Informally, dK-distributions [13,14] are a set of reproducible graph properties, which capture degree correlations within d-sized subgraphs of a network. As networks are structures of connections between nodes, dK-distributions provide rich information about network structures for analysis. To explore the sensitivity of higher-order network statistics under node-DP, we theoretically analyze the sensitivity of dK-distributions for $d = 2$, i.e., *joint degree distribution* [15]. It is known that joint degree distribution contains useful information about connectivity in a graph, i.e., given a joint degree distribution, one can always restore both the degree distribution and average degree [5,15].

To alleviate the challenge posed by high sensitivity of higher-order network statistics under node-DP, we further propose a "graph projection" technique that can transform a graph G into a θ-bounded graph G^θ such that the maximum degree in G^θ is no larger than a threshold θ. The motivation behind graph projection is to bound the sensitivity of publishing network statistics through a control on node degrees. In doing so, a query Q for higher-order network statistics with high sensitivity on a graph G is transformed to an approximate query $Q \circ \mathcal{P}$ which has lower sensitivity than Q, where $\mathcal{P}$ refers to a graph projection algorithm that transforms a graph G to a θ-bounded graph G^θ.

Figure 1 provides a high-level overview of our proposed framework. Given a graph G, a graph projection algorithm transforms G into a θ-bounded graph G^θ. Then higher-order network statistics such as dK-distributions [14] are extracted from G^θ, and finally extracted dK-distributions are perturbed yielding ε-differentially private dK-distributions.

Contributions. This work has the following contributions: (1) We present a novel framework to publish higher-order network statistics under node-DP. (2) We analyse the sensitivity of publishing *joint degree distribution* in the proposed framework. (3) We introduce a new graph projection algorithm to reduce sensitivity of publishing network statistics under node-DP. (4) We conduct comprehensive experiments over four real-world networks, and the results demonstrate that our proposed framework can effectively enhance the utility of differentially private network statistics.

2 Related Work

Privacy of network data has attracted much attention in recent years, due to the growing popularity of social network sites such as Facebook and Twitter. Recently, attention has shifted to applying more rigorous mathematical privacy guarantees of *differential privacy* (DP) [6] to analyse network data in a private manner. When applying DP to network data, there are two variants: *edge-DP* and *node-DP* [7]. Node-DP is known to be more challenging to achieve and can provide stronger privacy protection than edge-DP [3,11,19]. However, network data is highly sensitive to structural changes under node-DP, which thus requires a large amount of noise to be added into published network statistics and can significantly degrade the utility of published network statistics.

Recently, several studies [3,4,11,16] have suggested "graph projection" techniques which project an input graph to a graph whose maximum degree is below a certain threshold θ, i.e., a θ-bounded graph, in order to bound the sensitivity. The authors of [11] have proposed a graph project technique by truncating all nodes whose degrees are larger than θ and proven that publishing a degree histogram after truncation has a sensitivity of $2\theta S_T$, where S_T is the smooth upper bound on the number of nodes whose degrees may change because of truncation. Another graph projection technique was introduced in [1], which traverses the edges of a graph in a random order and removes all edges that are connected to a node with degree greater than θ. The sensitivity for publishing subgraph counting queries (i.e., number of triangles) after this edge-removal operation has been shown to be $p(2\theta)^{p-1}$, where p is the number of nodes in subgraphs. In the work [3], projection is performed by adding edges according to *stable edge ordering*. This edge-addition approach is similar to [1], except that it inserts edges while [1] deletes edges. While this difference is minor but it is shown in [3] that the edge-addition approach preserve more edges, and publishing a degree histogram of a projected graph has a sensitivity of $2\theta + 1$. In [16] another projection method was introduced by constructing a weighted graph, and publishing degree histograms has the sensitivity of 6θ in their work. Despite considerable progress being achieved in understanding node-DP, these works have only studied the release of simple statistical data of networks (i.e., edge count [11,19], counts of small subgraphs [1,4], and degree distribution [3,11,16]).

Different from existing work, we aim to release higher-order network statistics, i.e., *joint degree distribution*, using dK-distributions which not only capture

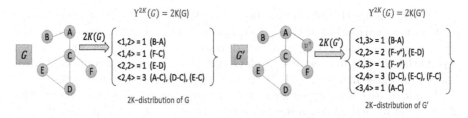

Fig. 2. An illustrative example of *dK-distribution* and its maximum change on two neighboring graphs $G \sim G'$, when $d = 2$.

connectivity of a network, but also contain useful information about subgraph-based and degree-based characteristics at multiple levels of granularity in a network [13,14]. Further, in order to effectively control sensitivity under node-DP, our work also presents a new graph projection technique which generates θ-bounded graphs by applying a two-level ordering strategy.

3   Problem Formulation

We consider a network as an undirected graph $G = (V, E)$, where V is the set of nodes and $E \subseteq V \times V$ is the set of edges. Let $N_G(v) = \{u \in V | (u, v) \in E\}$ denote the set of neighbors of a vertex v in G, $deg(v)$ the degree of a node v, and $deg(G) = max\{deg(v) | v \in V\}$ the maximum degree of G. Below, we define the notion of neighboring graphs under node-DP.

Definition 1. (NEIGHBORING GRAPHS) *Two graphs* $G = (V, E)$ *and* $G' = (V', E')$ *are said to be* neighboring graphs, *denoted as* $G \sim G'$, *iff* $V' = V \cup \{v^+\}$, $E' = E \cup E^+$, *and* E^+ *is the set of all edges incident to* v^+ *in* G'.

Given a graph, we represent its topology properties as dK-distributions [14].

Definition 2. (DK-DISTRIBUTION) *A dK-distribution over a graph* $G = (V, E)$, *denoted as* $dK(G)$, *is a probability distribution* $p : D^d \rightarrow \mathbb{N}$ *such that* $p(a_1, \ldots, a_d)$ *refers to the total number of connected subgraphs of size d in G with the nodes* $\{v_1, \ldots, v_d\}$ *and* $a_i = deg(v_i)$ *for* $i = 1, \ldots, d$.

For a graph, $1K$-distribution captures the degree distribution, $2K$-distribution captures the joint degree distribution, i.e. the number of edges between nodes of different degrees, and $3K$-distribution captures the clustering coefficient distribution, i.e. the number of triangles and wedges connecting nodes of different degrees. When $d = |V|$, a dK-distribution specifies the entire graph. To formulate queries on dK-distributions of a graph, we define the notion of dK-function.

Definition 3. (DK-FUNCTION) *Let* $\mathcal{D}$ *be the set of all possible dK-distributions over* G. *A dK function* $\gamma^{dK} : \mathcal{G}_n \rightarrow \mathcal{D}$ *mapping a graph* $G \in \mathcal{G}_n$ *to its dK-distribution in* $\mathcal{D}$ *s.t.* $\gamma^{dK}(G) = dK(G)$.

$\gamma^{dK}(G)$ queries the dK-distribution of G. When $d = 2$, $\gamma^{dK}(G)$ returns the joint degree distribution of G, i.e., $p(i, j)$ is a frequency value, referring to the number of edges connecting nodes of degrees i and j. Consider Fig. 2, which depicts the $2K$-distribution of a graph G. $p(2, 4) = 3$ because G contains 3 edges between 2 degree nodes (i.e., A, D, and E) and 4 degree node (i.e., C).

To release dK-distribution under the guarantees of node-DP, we perturb dK-distribution by adding controlled noise from Laplace stochastic process [6].

Definition 4. (PERTURBED DK-DISTRIBUTION) *Let $\varepsilon > 0$ be the privacy parameter (smaller values provide stronger privacy guarantees). The following Laplace mechanism is applied to produce a perturbed output of γ^{dK}:*

$$\mathcal{K}(G) = \gamma^{dK}(G) + Lap\left(\frac{\Delta\gamma}{\varepsilon}\right)^{|V|^d}$$

where $\Delta\gamma = \max_{G \sim G'}(\gamma^{dK}(G) - \gamma^{dK}(G'))$ and $\Pr[Lap(\beta) = x] = \frac{1}{2\beta}e^{-|x|/\beta}$.

$\Delta\gamma$ refers to the *sensitivity* of the dK-function γ^{dK}, which is the maximum variation in its output, i.e., dK-distribution, over two neighboring graphs $G \sim G'$. Below, the notion of ε-differentially private dK-distribution (i.e., an anonymized version of $\gamma^{dK}(G)$ satisfying differential privacy) is defined.

Definition 5. (DIFFERENTIALLY PRIVATE DK-DISTRIBUTION) *A randomized mechanism $\mathcal{K}$ is ε-differentially private, if for each pair of neighboring graphs $G \sim G'$ and all possible perturbed dK-distributions $\mathcal{D} \subseteq range(\mathcal{K})$, we have:*

$$Pr[\mathcal{K}(G) \in \mathcal{D}] \leq e^{\varepsilon} \times Pr[\mathcal{K}(G') \in \mathcal{D}]. \tag{1}$$

The challenge of releasing differentially private dK-distributions is to determine how much noise should be added to perturb dK-distributions. Adding more noise can better guarantee node-DP; however, data utility deteriorates. When ε is specified, the magnitude of noise depends on the sensitivity of dK-function.

4   Sensitivity Analysis

In this section, we analyze the sensitivity of dK-function $\gamma^{dK}(G)$ for $d = 2$, to publish joint degree distribution of a graph G. Our goal is to derive the minimum amount of noise needed to achieve node-DP.

Suppose that a node v^+ is added to G with a set E^+ of edges, each edge $(v^+, v_i) \in E^+$ may cause at most $2 \times deg(G) + 1$ entries of $\gamma^{2K}(G)$ being changed. Thus, for each $v_j \in N(v_i)$, $p(deg(v_i), deg(v_j))$ may decrease by one and $p(deg(v_i) + 1, deg(v_j))$ may increase by one, which amount to the number $2 \times deg(G)$ of entries being changed if each $v_j \in N(v_i)$ has the maximum degree, i.e., $deg(v_j) = deg(G)$. In addition to this, $p(deg(v^+), deg(v_i))$ increases by at least one. Thus, the total number of entries of $\gamma^{2K}(G)$ being changed by all edges in E^+ is upper bounded by $(2 \times deg(G) + 1) \times |E^+|$.

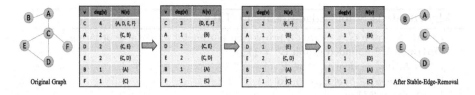

Fig. 3. An illustration of Stable-Edge-Removal with $\theta = 1$.

Lemma 1. *Let $G \sim G'$ be two neighboring graphs. We have $\Delta\gamma = (2 \times deg(G) + 1) \times |E^+|$ entries, where $|E^+|$ is the set of all edges incident to v^+.*

Prior studies [12,17] have shown that, in large social networks, $deg(G)$ is upper bounded by $O(\sqrt{|V|})$. Thus, for such networks, the sensitivity of $2K$-function is upper bounded by $O(2 \times |V|\sqrt{|V|} + |V|)$.

Consider Fig. 2 in which a node v^+ and two edges $\{(v^+, F), (v^+, A)\}$ are added into a graph G, resulting in the graph G'. There are 7 entries of $\gamma^{2K}(G)$ being changed: (1) (v^+, F) leads to changing 3 entries, i.e., $p(1,4)$ decrease by one, and $p(2,4)$ and $p(2,2)$ increase by one; (2) (v^+, A) leads to changing 5 entries, i.e., $p(1,2)$ and $p(2,4)$ decrease by one, and $p(1,3)$, $p(3,4)$ and $p(2,3)$ increase by one. Although $p(2,4) = 3$ in both G and G', it is changed twice by increasing one and decreasing one. If G is a complete graph with $deg(G) = 4$ and $|E^+| = 2$, 18 entries of $\gamma^{2K}(G)$ would be changed, which is the worst case.

5 Proposed Approach

In this section, we first introduce a novel graph projection technique and then incorporate it into a node-DP releasing mechanism.

5.1 Stable-Edge-Removal Graph Projection

Existing graph projection techniques generally fall into two categories: (1) vertex ordering methods such as truncation [11]; (2) edge ordering methods such as edge-removal [1] and edge-addition [3]. However, these methods have some limitations. Vertex ordering methods often truncate all nodes $v \in V$ with $deg(v) > \theta$ [11], which severely affects the topological structure of a graph. Indeed, up to θ edges incident to these nodes may be preserved in a θ-bounded graph. For edge ordering methods [1,3], they handle edges based on a random edge ordering, which may cause an excessive number of edges to be lost from an original graph.

To alleviate these limitations, we propose *Stable-Edge-Removal* (SER) that transform a graph G to a θ-bounded graph G^θ with $\theta < deg(G)$ based on a two-level ordering strategy on G.

Definition 6. *A two-level ordering over $G = (V, E)$ is a pair $\Gamma = (\succ_N, \succ_V)$ where $\succ_N$ is a local neighbour ordering such that, for each $v \in V$, there is a bijection: $N_G(v) \rightarrow \{1, \ldots, |N_G(v)|\}$; $\succ_V$ is a global node ordering such that there is a bijection: $V \rightarrow \{1, \ldots, |V|\}$.*

Algorithm 1: Stable-Edge-Removal (SER)

Input: A graph $G = (V, E)$; a projection parameter θ; a stable ordering Γ
Output: A θ-bounded graph $G^\theta = (V, E^\theta)$

1 $E^\theta := E$; $d[v] \leftarrow deg(v)$, $\forall v \in V$
2 **foreach** $(v, u) \in Seq(E, \succ_\Gamma)$ **do**
3 | **if** $d[v] > \theta$ **then**
4 | ⌊ $E^\theta \leftarrow E^\theta \setminus \{(u, v)\}$; $d[u] \leftarrow d[u] - 1$; $d[v] \leftarrow d[v] - 1$

5 **Return** $G^\theta = (V, E^\theta)$

The intuition behind such a two-level ordering is to provide the flexibility of ranking nodes from two aspects: (i) global importance in a graph, and (ii) local importance in neighbourhoods. Given a two-level ordering Γ, an edge ordering is defined. Specifically, for a graph $G = (V, E)$, there exists a total ordering $\succ_\Gamma$ on edges in E such that, for any two edges $e_1 = (v_1, u_1)$ and $e_2 = (v_2, u_2)$ (assume $v_i \succ_V u_i$ for simplicity), we have $e_1 \succ_\Gamma e_2$ if and only if $v_1 \succ_V v_2$, or $u_1 \succ_N u_2$ when $v_1 = v_2$.

For two neighboring graphs $G \sim G'$, one important property of a graph projection algorithm $\mathcal{P}$ is to ensure that θ-bounded graphs $\mathcal{P}(G)$ and $\mathcal{P}(G')$ are also neighboring graphs, i.e., $\mathcal{P}(G) \sim \mathcal{P}(G')$. To obtain this property, we require Γ, upon which $\mathcal{P}$ depends, to be stable on two neighboring graphs $G \sim G'$.

Definition 7. (STABLE ORDERING) *Given two neighboring graphs $G = (V, E)$ and $G' = (V', E')$, a two-level ordering $\Gamma = (\succ_N, \succ_V)$ is stable if and only if,*

- *for any node v in $V \cap V'$, the relative orderings of their common neighbors in $(N_G(v) \cap N_{G'}(v))$ are the same in $\succ_N (G)$ and $\succ_N (G')$, and*
- *for any two nodes in $V \cap V'$, their relative orderings are the same in $\succ_V (G)$ and $\succ_V (G')$.*

Algorithm 1 describes the main steps of our *SER* algorithm. Given an input graph $G = (V, E)$, a projection parameter θ, and a stable ordering Γ, we initialize E^θ with all edges in E and d with degrees of all nodes in V (Line 1). Let $Seq(E, \succ_\Gamma)$ denote the sequence of edges from E according to the edge order $\succ_\Gamma$. Then for each edge (v, u) in this sequence, if the degree of v is greater than θ, we remove (v, u) from E^θ and also decrease the degree count of v and u in d by 1 (Lines 2–4). Finally, the algorithm returns a θ-bounded graph G^θ (Line 5).

Example 1. Assume that a two-level ordering $\Gamma = (\succ_N, \succ_V)$ on a graph G in Fig. 3 is obtained by sorting nodes based on degrees from highest to lowest $(\succ_V)$, and for each node v sorting their neighbours in $N_G(v)$ in a similar manner $(\succ_N)$. Thus, we have a sequence of edges ordered by $\succ_\Gamma$, i.e., $\langle (C, A), (C, D), (C, E), (C, F), \ldots, (F, C) \rangle$. Then, following this sequence, by checking whether $deg(C) > \theta$, *SER* first removes edge (C, A) and decreases the degree counts of nodes C and A by 1. Similarly, *SER* removes edges (C, D) and then the other edges if their node degree counts is greater than θ until G^θ is obtained.

SER generates θ-bounded graphs that are maximal in the sense that no edge from $E - E^\theta$ can be added into such θ-bounded graphs without making their maximal node degree be above θ. However, *SER* does not guarantee that these θ-bounded graphs are optimal, i.e., keeping the largest possible number of edges, because *SER* depends on the ordering Γ which may be locally optimal.

5.2   Releasing *dK*-Distribution via Projection

Given a graph G, instead of extracting a *dK*-distribution from G directly, we extract a *dK*-distribution from a θ-bounded graph G^θ which is transformed from G by a graph projection algorithm $\mathcal{P}$. In this work, $\mathcal{P}$ refers to our *SER* algorithm. By Lemma 1 and the fact that the maximum degree in G^θ is no larger than θ, we have the following lemma about the sensitivity of $\gamma^{dK} \circ \mathcal{P}$.

Algorithm 2: $\theta - dK_\varepsilon$ *algorithm*

Input: A graph $G = (V, E)$;
      a privacy parameter ε
Output: A perturbed $\widehat{dK}$
1   $G^\theta \leftarrow$ Project G by Algorithm 1
2   $dK^\theta \leftarrow$ Query G^θ with γ^{2K}
3   $\widehat{dK} \leftarrow$ Perturb dK^θ w.r.t. Def. 4
4 **Return** $\widehat{dK}$

Lemma 2. *Let $G \sim G'$ be two neighboring graphs. Then the sensitivity of $\gamma^{dK} \circ \mathcal{P}$ is upper bounded by $(2\theta + 1) \times \theta$, where $d = 2$.*

Based on the sensitivity of $\gamma^{dK} \circ \mathcal{P}$, the perturbation is performed over the *dK*-distribution being extracted from G^θ to generate a ε-differentially private joint degree distribution. A high-level description of this algorithm of releasing differentially private joint degree distribution via projection, namely $\theta - dK_\varepsilon$, is presented in Algorithm 2. Since the perturbation in Algorithm 2 is conducted using the Laplace mechanism based on the sensitivity of $\gamma^{dK} \circ \mathcal{P}$, we have the following lemma regarding the privacy guarantee of $\theta - dK_\varepsilon$.

Lemma 3. *$\theta - dK_\varepsilon$ generates ε-node-differential private dK-distribution.*

6   Experiments

In this section, we conduct experiments to evaluate our proposed approach and discuss the experimental results.

6.1   Experimental Setup

Datasets. We use four network datasets in the experiments from different domains including social network and citation networks: (1) *Facebook*[1] is a network of social interactions and personal relationships, containing 4,039 nodes and

---
[1] Network datasets are available at http://snap.stanford.edu/data/index.html.

88,234 edges. (2) *Wiki-Vote*[1] is a voting network of Wikipedia users, containing 7,115 nodes and 103,689 edges.(3) *Ca-HepPh*[1] is a scientific collaborative networks between authors and papers, containing 12,008 nodes and 118,521 edges. (4) *Email-Enron*[1] is a Email communication network from Enron, containing 36,692 nodes and 183,831 edges.

Table 1. Comparison on the preserved edge ratio $|E^\theta|/|E|$ of *EAD* and our proposed *SER* graph projection approach under different values of θ.

Dataset	$\theta = 16$		$\theta = 32$		$\theta = 64$		$\theta = 128$		$\theta = 256$	
	EAD	SER	EAD	SER	EAD	SER	EAD	SER	EAD	SER
Facebook	0.27	0.61	0.44	0.71	0.66	0.84	0.88	0.96	0.97	0.98
Wiki-Vote	0.19	0.59	0.32	0.66	0.50	0.76	0.71	0.87	0.88	0.96
Ca-HepPh	0.16	0.61	0.24	0.68	0.31	0.77	0.39	0.84	0.46	0.96
Email-Enron	0.17	0.52	0.22	0.61	0.29	0.71	0.36	0.80	0.43	0.89

Baseline Methods. We first compare our projection method, *Stable-Edge-Removal (SER)*, with the state-of-the art graph project method *Edge-Addition (EAD)* [3]. Then, we compare the utility of the following methods for generating differentially private dK-distributions: (1) $SER - \theta - dK_\varepsilon$, which applies our proposed $\theta - dK_\varepsilon$ algorithm on projected graphs generated by SER; (2) $EAD - \theta - dK_\varepsilon$, which applies our proposed $\theta - dK_\varepsilon$ algorithm on projected graphs generated by EAD; (3) ε-DP, which is a standard ε-differential privacy algorithm in which noise is added on an original graph using the Laplace mechanism [6].

Utility Metrics. Following [3,11,16], we use three utility metrics: (1) *preserved edge ratio* $|E^\theta|/|E|$ measures the ratio of edges being preserved by graph projection, where $|E|$ and $|E^\theta|$ denote the number of edges before and after applying graph projection, respectively; (2) *L1 distance* (or *L1 error*) measures the network structural error between an original dK-distribution p and its perturbed dK-distribution p', i.e., $\|p - p'\|_1 = \sum_{j=1}^{deg(G)} \sum_{i=1}^{deg(G)} |p(i,j) - p'(i,j)|$, where we pad entries for degree pairs (i,j) with 0 if such degree pairs do not exist in p or p'; and (3) *Kolmogorov-Smirnov distance* (or *KS distance*) quantifies the closeness between an original dK-distribution p and its perturbed dK-distribution p', i.e., $KS(p,p') = max_i|CDF_{p(i,j)} - CDF_{p'(i,j)}|$, where $CDF_{p(i,j)}$ is the value of cumulative distribution function on degree pairs (i,j) from distribution p.

Parameter Settings and Others. For the privacy parameter ε, we choose $\varepsilon \in [0.01, 10.0]$ which cover the range of differential privacy levels widely used in the literature [8,9]. For the projection parameter θ, we follow [3,4,16] to choose $\theta \in \{1, 2, 4, \ldots, 2^{\lfloor 2log_2(|V|) \rfloor}\}$. We use *Orbis* [13] to generate 2K-distributions.

6.2 Results and Discussion

Evaluating Graph Projection. We first compare our method *SER* with the state-of-the-art graph projection method *EAD* [3].

(1) Preserved edge ratio. Table 1 shows the results for preserved edge ratio. For every value of θ, *SER* outperforms *EAD* by preserving more edges over all four datasets. This is consistent with the discussion in Sect. 5 that our two-level ordering can generally preserve more edges than a random edge ordering.

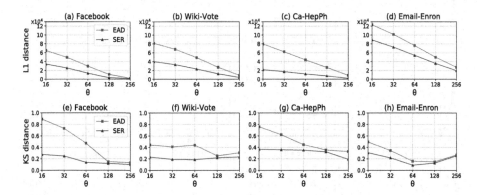

Fig. 4. Comparison of graph project methods under varying θ over four datasets: (a)–(d) L1 distance and (e)–(h) KS distance.

(2) L1 distance. Figure 4(a)–(d) presents the results for L1 distance. For all four datasets, our projection method *SER* leads to less network structural error for every value of θ as compared to *EAD*. This verifies that *SER* can better preserve topological structure of a graph than *EAD* and maintain the shape of distribution after projection. Thus, the utility of projected dK-distribution by *SER* is higher as compared to *EAD*.

(3) KS distance. Figure 4(e)–(h) presents the results for KS distance. We can see that, for every value of θ, our projection method *SER* outperforms *EAD* with smaller KS-distances over all four datasets. Thus, projected dK-distributions generated by *SER* are more similar to their original dK-distributions.

Evaluating Differentially Private dK-Distributions. We compare the overall utility of differentially private dK-distributions generated by our method $SER - \theta - dK_\varepsilon$ against the baseline methods. Figure 5 presents the results.

(1) L1 distance. For all four datasets, our method $SER - \theta - dK_\varepsilon$ yields less network structural error than ε-DP for every value of ε and θ. Compared to ε-DP, the results of $SER - \theta - dK_\varepsilon$ and $EAD - \theta - dK_\varepsilon$ are close and both much less. This is because, by approximating γ^{dK} to $\gamma^{dK} \circ \mathcal{P}$ via a graph projection $\mathcal{P}$, two kinds of errors are introduced: one is random noise to guarantee node-DP and the other one is due to projection. We notice that, the first kind of error,

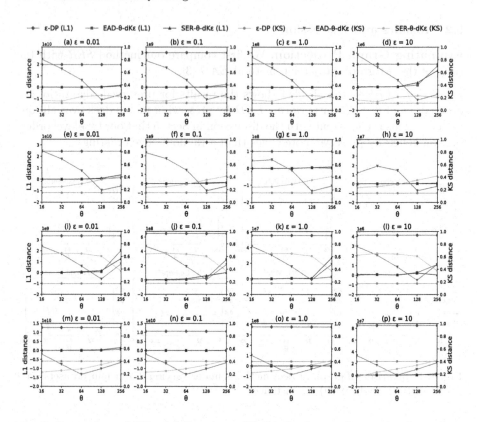

Fig. 5. Comparison of differentially private dK-distributions under varying θ over four datasets: (left) L1 distance and (right) KS distance.

which depends on the sensitivity of $\gamma^{dK} \circ \mathcal{P}$, dominates the impact on the utility of differentially private dK-distributions generated w.r.t. L1 distance. Thus, by reducing the sensitivity of a dK function via projection, the amount of random noise being added to achieve node-DP is reduced significantly and the L1 errors of differentially private dK-distributions are thus also reduced significantly.

(2) KS distance. We observe that ε-DP outperforms $SER-\theta-dK_\varepsilon$ and $EAD-\theta-dK_\varepsilon$ for smaller datasets, except for the largest network *Email-Enron*. This is because, a projection method may change the topological structure of an original graph. However, for large networks such as *Email-Enron*, due to their high sensitivity, $SER-\theta-dK_\varepsilon$ and $EAD-\theta-dK_\varepsilon$ generally perform better than ε-DP. In addition, for smaller values of θ, differentially private dK-distributions generated by $SER-\theta-dK_\varepsilon$ are more similar to their original dK-distributions than $EAD-\theta-dK_\varepsilon$. However, for larger θ values, the results of $SER-\theta-dK_\varepsilon$ and $EAD-\theta-dK_\varepsilon$ are close. This is because for larger θ values the amount of noise injected to achieve DP is high, and the fact that $SER-\theta-dK_\varepsilon$ preserves

more edges leads to more noise being added to frequency values of degree pairs in dK-distributions.

7 Conclusions and Future Work

In this paper, we have studied the problem of publishing higher-order network statistics such as *joint degree distribution* under node-DP. We have theoretically analyzed the sensitivity for publishing joint degree distribution and proposed a novel projection-based method in order to enhance the utility of released network statistics under node-DP. The effectiveness of our work has been empirically verified over four real-world networks. Future extensions to this work will consider personalized differential privacy to release statistics about social networks while protecting privacy of individuals based on individuals preferences.

References

1. Blocki, J., Blum, A., Datta, A., Sheffet, O.: Differentially private data analysis of social networks via restricted sensitivity. In: ITCS, pp. 87–96 (2013)
2. Clauset, A., Moore, C., Newman, M.E.: Hierarchical structure and the prediction of missing links in networks. Nature **453**(7191), 98 (2008)
3. Day, W.Y., Li, N., Lyu, M.: Publishing graph degree distribution with node differential privacy. In: SIGMOD, pp. 123–138 (2016)
4. Ding, X., Zhang, X., Bao, Z., Jin, H.: Privacy-preserving triangle counting in large graphs. In: CIKM, pp. 1283–1292 (2018)
5. Dorogovtsev, S., Mendes, J., et al.: Evolution of Networks: From Biological Nets to the Internet and www. OUP Catalogue, Oxford (2013)
6. Dwork, C., McSherry, F., Nissim, K., Smith, A.: Calibrating noise to sensitivity in private data analysis. In: Halevi, S., Rabin, T. (eds.) TCC 2006. LNCS, vol. 3876, pp. 265–284. Springer, Heidelberg (2006). https://doi.org/10.1007/11681878_14
7. Hay, M., Li, C., Miklau, G., Jensen, D.: Accurate estimation of the degree distribution of private networks. In: ICDM, pp. 169–178 (2009)
8. Iftikhar, M., Wang, Q., Lin, Y.: Publishing differentially private datasets via stable microaggregation. In: EDBT, pp. 662–665 (2019)
9. Iftikhar, M., Wang, Q., Lin, Yu.: dK-microaggregation: anonymizing graphs with differential privacy guarantees. In: Lauw, H.W., Wong, R.C.-W., Ntoulas, A., Lim, E.-P., Ng, S.-K., Pan, S.J. (eds.) PAKDD 2020, Part II. LNCS (LNAI), vol. 12085, pp. 191–203. Springer, Cham (2020). https://doi.org/10.1007/978-3-030-47436-2_15
10. Jorgensen, Z., Yu, T., Cormode, G.: Publishing attributed social graphs with formal privacy guarantees. In: SIGMOD, pp. 107–122 (2016)
11. Kasiviswanathan, S.P., Nissim, K., Raskhodnikova, S., Smith, A.: Analyzing graphs with node differential privacy. In: Sahai, A. (ed.) TCC 2013. LNCS, vol. 7785, pp. 457–476. Springer, Heidelberg (2013). https://doi.org/10.1007/978-3-642-36594-2_26
12. Kwak, H., Lee, C., Park, H., Moon, S.: What is Twitter, a social network or a news media? In: WWW, pp. 591–600 (2010)

13. Mahadevan, P., Hubble, C., Krioukov, D., Huffaker, B., Vahdat, A.: Orbis: rescaling degree correlations to generate annotated internet topologies. In: SIGCOMM, vol. 37, pp. 325–336 (2007)

14. Mahadevan, P., Krioukov, D., Fall, K., Vahdat, A.: Systematic topology analysis and generation using degree correlations. In: SIGCOMM, No. 4, pp. 135–146 (2006)

15. Mahadevan, P., Krioukov, D., Fomenkov, M., Dimitropoulos, X., Claffy, K., Vahdat, A.: The internet as-level topology: three data sources and one definitive metric. ACM SIGCOMM Comput. Commun. Rev. **36**(1), 17–26 (2006)

16. Raskhodnikova, S., Smith, A.: Efficient lipschitz extensions for high-dimensional graph statistics and node private degree distributions. CoRR/1504.07912 (2015)

17. Sala, A., Zhao, X., Wilson, C., Zheng, H., Zhao, B.Y.: Sharing graphs using differentially private graph models. In: SIGCOMM, pp. 81–98 (2011)

18. Shen, E., Yu, T.: Mining frequent graph patterns with differential privacy. In: SIGKDD, pp. 545–553 (2013)

19. Ullman, J., Sealfon, A.: Efficiently estimating erdos-renyi graphs with node differential privacy. In: NeurIPS, pp. 3765–3775 (2019)

20. Wang, Y., Wu, X.: Preserving differential privacy in degree-correlation based graph generation. Trans. Data Priv. **6**(2), 127–145 (2013)

21. Xiao, Q., Chen, R., Tan, K.L.: Differentially private network data release via structural inference. In: SIGKDD, pp. 911–920 (2014)

22. Zheleva, E., Getoor, L.: Privacy in social networks: a survey. In: Aggarwal, C. (ed.) Social Network Data Analytics, pp. 277–306. Springer, Boston (2011). https://doi.org/10.1007/978-1-4419-8462-3_10

Recommender Systems

Improving Sequential Recommendation with Attribute-Augmented Graph Neural Networks

Xinzhou Dong[1,2], Beihong Jin[1,2(⊠)], Wei Zhuo[3], Beibei Li[1,2], and Taofeng Xue[1,2]

[1] State Key Laboratory of Computer Science, Institute of Software, Chinese Academy of Sciences, Beijing, China
Beihong@iscas.ac.cn
[2] University of Chinese Academy of Sciences, Beijing, China
[3] MX Media Co., Ltd., Singapore, Singapore

Abstract. Many practical recommender systems provide item recommendation for different users only via mining user-item interactions but totally ignoring the rich attribute information of items that users interact with. In this paper, we propose an attribute-augmented graph neural network model named Murzim. Murzim takes as input the graphs constructed from the user-item interaction sequences and corresponding item attribute sequences. By combining the GNNs with node aggregation and an attention network, Murzim can capture user preference patterns, generate embeddings for user-item interaction sequences, and then generate recommendations through next-item prediction. We conduct extensive experiments on multiple datasets. Experimental results show that Murzim outperforms several state-of-the-art methods in terms of recall and MRR, which illustrates that Murzim can make use of item attribute information to produce better recommendations. At present, Murzim has been deployed in MX Player, one of India's largest streaming platforms, and is recommending videos for tens of thousands of users.

Keywords: Recommender system · Deep learning · Graph neural network · Sequential recommendation

1 Introduction

Sequential recommendation is to predict the next item that a user is most likely to interact with according to the user-item interaction sequence over a period of time in the past and then recommend the predicted item to the user. The target scenarios include but are not limited to e-commerce platforms where products are recommended based on the user click records in the recent period, and video streaming platforms where videos are recommended to users based on their historical watching records.

Since the records in a user-item interaction sequence are sorted in chronological order and the sequences are essentially time series, the early methods [1,4,16]

© Springer Nature Switzerland AG 2021
K. Karlapalem et al. (Eds.): PAKDD 2021, LNAI 12713, pp. 373–385, 2021.
https://doi.org/10.1007/978-3-030-75765-6_30

model these sequences as Markov chains and predict the next actions for users based on their previous actions, thereby generating recommendations. However, these methods require strong dependency assumptions over user behaviors, and in reality, for a user, his/her next action is likely to be unrelated to the previous one but related to earlier actions. With the progress of deep learning methods, RNNs (Recurrent Neural Networks) are adopted in recommender systems due to their capabilities of modeling sequences. RNN-based methods [5,7] can capture long-term dependencies in sequences, but they are also easy to generate fake dependencies. Recently, Graph Neural Networks (GNNs), which combine the flexible expressiveness of graph data and the strong learning capability of neural networks, have emerged as a promising way to achieve recommender tasks.

On the other hand, we notice that in many recommendation scenarios, besides user-item interaction sequences, the attribute information of the items is relatively complete. Moreover, attributes of the item have been gradually used for help modeling [7,18]. However, so far, there has been still a lack of in-depth research on the modeling and mining of multiple attributes and multi-valued attributes of the item.

To mine the potential of item attributes in learning the user preference patterns, in this paper, we treat the discrete attribute value of an item as a node on the graph. In this way, for a user-item interaction sequence, there are sequences of attributes of the item being interacted with. Next, we describe these attribute sequences with graphs, besides constructing an item graph from the user-item interaction sequence. Then, we construct a GNN model to generate next-item recommendations.

The main contributions of our work are summarized as follows.

1. We present a reasonable method to construct attribute sequences from user-item interaction sequences and attribute graphs from attribute sequences. Further, we propose a method to calculate attribute scores so as to quickly determine which attributes are valuable for modeling user preferences.
2. We propose the sequential recommendation model Murzim. Based on gated GNNs, Murzim adopts attention mechanisms to integrate information from the node level and the sequence level, and fuses the influence of item attributes on the semantics implied in user-item interaction sequences into the recommendation results.
3. We conduct extensive experiments on open datasets and the MX Player dataset. Murzim outperforms several methods in terms of Recall@20 and MRR@20. Moreover, we apply Murzim to the MX Player, one of India's largest streaming platforms, and the resulting business indicators such as CTR have been improved, which illustrates the effectiveness of Murzim.

The rest of the paper is organized as follows. Section 2 introduces the related work. Section 3 gives the formulation of the problem to be solved. Section 4 describes the Murzim model in detail. Section 5 gives the experimental evaluation. Finally, the paper is concluded in Sect. 6.

2   Related Work

Conventional recommendation methods, such as item-based neighborhood methods [12,15] and matrix factorization methods [9,14], do not integrate with the sequential information, thus for sequential recommendation scenarios, these methods can work but perform far from the desired level.

Some existing sequence modeling methods can be adapted for the sequential recommendation. For example, in [16], the recommendation task is regarded as a sequence optimization problem and an MDP (Markov Decision Process) is applied to solve it. In [4], a mixture variable memory Markov model is built for web query recommendation. Further, in [1], a Markov chain model and a matrix decomposition method are combined to build the personalized probability transfer matrix for each user. However, most Markov chain based methods have to face the problem brought by the strong assumption about dependency between user behaviors.

With the rapid development of deep learning methods, RNNs demonstrate their advantages in sequential data modeling. As a result, RNNs are also adopted and then improved for the sequential recommendation [5,6,17]. Besides sequential data, item features have been integrated into the RNN based models in [7,18], where the former employs 3D convolution operations to fuse item features, and the latter employs multiple parallel RNNs with item's image features, text features, etc. as input and gives several fusion strategies. The attention mechanisms are also applied in the sequential recommendation. For example, NARM [10] is a recommendation model based on an encoder-decoder structure, which designs an RNN with an attention mechanism in the encoder to capture the user's sequential behaviors and main purpose, and predicts the next item in the decoder. STAMP [13] uses simple MLP cells and an attention network to capture the user's general and current interests to predict the next item. However, the RNN-based models have some intrinsic weaknesses since they encode the interaction sequence into a hidden vector, and using only one vector may lose information. As a remedy, some methods [2,8] encode user states through the memory network, which has the larger capacity.

Recently, GNNs have received much attention, which are a kind of neural networks running on graph structure data. We note that applying the idea of CNN to the graph results in the GCN (Graph Convolution Network) methods. For example, GraphSage [3] is an inductive GCN model, which aggregates node neighbor information by training a set of aggregation functions and generate the node embeddings. Applying the idea of RNN to the graph is also feasible. GGS-NN [11] is such an example. Currently, there exist several GNN models for sequential recommendations. For example, the SR-GNN model [20] and its improved version [21] which borrows the self-attention structure from Transformer [19] and applies it to original SR-GNN.

Compared to the existing work, our work simultaneously models the user-item sequence and the corresponding attribute information in the form of directed graphs, and then build GNNs to generate the item sequence embeddings which capture the user preferences on items and attribute values.

3   Problem Formulation

For the sequence recommendation task, given the user-item interaction sequence set S, we use $V = \{v_1, v_2, \ldots, v_{|V|}\}$ to denote the set consisting of all unique items involved in all the sequences, $P = (p_{ij})_{|V| \times K}$ to denote the attribute matrix of the items, where $p_{ij} = f_j(v_i) \subseteq A_j$ denotes the set of values for the j-th attribute of the i-th item, $A_j = \{a_1^j, a_2^j, \ldots, a_m^j\}$ denotes the value set of the j-th attribute, f_j is the attribute mapping function which maps the item v_i into the value set $A_j, j = 1, 2, \ldots, K$.

We use $s_0 = [v_{s,1}, v_{s,2}, \ldots, v_{s,T}]$ to denote the sequence of a user's behavior over a period of time, where $v_{s,t} \in V$. At the same time, through the attribute matrix, we can get K attribute sequences, that is, $s_j = [f_j(v_{s,1}), f_j(v_{s,2}), \ldots, f_j(v_{s,T})]$. Our goal is to generate next-item prediction through the item sequence s_0 and K attribute sequences $s_1, s_2, \ldots, s_K$, that is to predict $v_{s,T+1}$.

4   The Murzim Model

In Murzim, we first construct the attribute sequences according to the item sequence and attribute mappings, and represent all the $1 + K$ sequences (i.e., a item sequence and K attribute sequences) as directed graphs. Then, we use gated GNN based on GRU to update the embeddings of nodes in the graphs. After obtaining the embeddings of nodes, we aggregate them to get the embeddings of the sequences. Finally, we gather all sequence embeddings through an attention network to predict the next item. The basic structure is shown in Fig. 1.

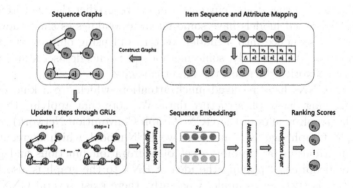

Fig. 1. Structure of Murzim

4.1   Constructing Item and Attribute Graphs

We use the attribute mapping functions(a total of K) to map the items in the user-item interaction sequence to their attribute values. In this way, we get K attribute sequences. Each sequence, i.e., $s_j, j = 0, 1, \ldots, K$, is represented by a directed graph $G_{s_j} = (V_{s_j}, E_{s_j}), V_{s_0} \subseteq V, V_{s_j} \subseteq A_j, j > 0$. If two items (or attribute values) are adjacent in the sequence, we add a directed edge between the corresponding nodes in the graph, that is $\langle v_{s,t}, v_{s,t+1} \rangle \in E_{s_0}$ (or $\langle f_j(v_{s,t}), f_j(v_{s,t+1}) \rangle \in E_{s_j}, j > 0$). If f_j maps an item $v_{s,t}$ to multiple attributes (for example, a movie to multiple actors), then we have a full connection between $f_j(v_{s,t})$ and $f_j(v_{s,t+1})$, where there is a directed edge between each attribute value in $f_j(v_{s,t})$ and each attribute value in $f_j(v_{s,t+1})$.

We use adjacency matrices to represent the item graph and attribute graphs. Specifically, we distinguish the forward and reverse of the sequence, build incoming matrix M^{in} and outgoing matrix M^{out} respectively, and normalize each row. An example is shown in Fig. 2.

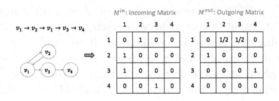

Fig. 2. An attribute graph example and its corresponding matrices

Since items often contain multiple attributes, it is necessary to assess the importance of these attributes in advance. We believe that a good attribute should reflect the user's preference on certain attribute values. To this end, we define a method to calculate the score $R(S, A_j)$ of the attribute A_j on the sequence set S according to the attribute map f_j:

$$R(S, A_j) = \frac{1}{|S|} \sum_{s \in S} \left(1 - \frac{|\bigcup_t f_j(v_{s,t})|}{\sum_t |f_j(v_{s,t})|} \right) \tag{1}$$

In formula (1), $f_j(v_{s,t})$ denotes the value set of item $v_{s,t}$ in sequence s on attribute j, $|\bigcup_t f_j(v_{s,t})|$ denotes the number of values of all items in sequence s on attribute j, and $\sum_t |f_j(v_{s,t})|$ denotes the sum of the number of values of each item in sequence s on attribute j. The greater the number of attribute values in a sequence, that is, the larger $\sum_t |f_j(v_{s,t})|$, and the more concentrated these attribute values, that is, the smaller $|\bigcup_t f_j(v_{s,t})|$, the higher the attribute score, which means the user's interest is focused on only a few attribute values. When we apply Murzim in a specific scenario, we first calculate the scores and then select the attributes with high scores for modeling.

4.2 Generating Node Embeddings

We get the initial item embeddings through the embedding look-up operations from a trainable matrix with dimension $d \times |V|$. The d-dimensional vector v_i is used to represent the embedding of the i-th item. As for attribute, we treat it as a partition of items, that is, different attribute values divide items into multiple intersecting or disjoint sets. Therefore, we use item embeddings to generate the initial embeddings of attribute values.

Let $s_0 = [v_{s,1}, v_{s,2}, \ldots, v_{s,T}]$ be the user-item interaction sequence, $s_j = [f_j(v_{s,1}), f_j(v_{s,2}), \ldots, f_j(v_{s,T})]$ be the sequence corresponding to attribute j, and $A_{s,j} = \cup_{i=1}^{T} f_j(v_{s,i})$ be the value set of attribute j on the item sequence s_0, $A_{s,j} \subseteq A_j$. For any $a^j \in A_{s,j}$, the calculation of its embedding $\boldsymbol{a}^j$ is:

$$a^j = \frac{1}{|V_{s_0}|} \sum_{i=1}^{|V_{s_0}|} I(a^j \in f_j(v_i)) \boldsymbol{W}_j \boldsymbol{v}_i \tag{2}$$

In formula (2), V_{s_0} is the set of items contained in the user-item interaction sequence s_0, $\boldsymbol{W}_j \in \mathbb{R}^{d \times d}$ is a model parameter, I is an indicator function that outputs 1 when its input is true, otherwise outputs 0.

After obtaining the initial embeddings of items and attribute values, we update them through graphs. Let $\boldsymbol{e}_i$ represent the embedding of node i on the graph (item graph or attribute graph), and then we propagate the information between nodes according to the matrices $\boldsymbol{M}^{in}$ and $\boldsymbol{M}^{out}$, as shown below.

$$m_i = \text{concat}(M_{i*}^{in}[\boldsymbol{e}_1, \ldots, \boldsymbol{e}_n]^T, M_{i*}^{out}[\boldsymbol{e}_1, \ldots, \boldsymbol{e}_n]^T) \tag{3}$$

In formula (3), $[\boldsymbol{e}_1, \ldots, \boldsymbol{e}_n]$ is a matrix of size $d \times n$ formed by the embeddings of all n nodes in the graph, $M_{i*}^{in}, M_{i*}^{out} \in \mathbb{R}^{1 \times n}$ denote the i-th row of the corresponding matrix. In the subsequent step, $\boldsymbol{m}_i \in \mathbb{R}^{2d \times 1}$ is used as the input of the GRU to updated the embedding of node i:

$$e_i = \text{GRU}(e_i, m_i) \tag{4}$$

The above process is iterated multiple times, so that each node can obtain information from nodes farther away.

4.3   Generating Sequence Embedding

The generation of sequence embeddings goes through two steps. We first aggregate the embeddings of the nodes in different graphs to get the embeddings of $1 + K$ sequences. There are many ways to aggregate, here we choose the method similar to [20]: calculate the attention coefficient of each node embedding with the last item embedding(or attribute value embedding) in the sequence, and sum all node embeddings according to the coefficients:

$$\alpha_i = \boldsymbol{q}^T \sigma(\boldsymbol{W}_1 \boldsymbol{e}_T + \boldsymbol{W}_2 \boldsymbol{e}_i + \boldsymbol{c}) \tag{5}$$

$$\tau = \sum_{i=1}^{n} \alpha_i \boldsymbol{e}_i \tag{6}$$

$$s_j = \boldsymbol{W}_3 \text{concat}(\boldsymbol{\tau}; \boldsymbol{e}_T) \tag{7}$$

In formulas (5)-(7), $W_1, W_2 \in \mathbb{R}^{d \times d}, W_3 \in \mathbb{R}^{d \times 2d}, q, c \in \mathbb{R}^d$ are model parameters, e_T is the embedding of the last item(or attribute value) in the sequence, the output s_j is the embedding of the sequence($j = 0$ for item sequence, $j = 1, \ldots, K$ for attribute sequences).

Then we use an attention network to aggregate all sequence embeddings, and finally get the embedding z containing both the user's item preference and attribute preference:

$$\alpha_j = \sigma(\frac{s_0 W_q s_j^T}{\sqrt{d}}), j = 0, 1, 2, \ldots K \tag{8}$$

$$z = s_0 + \sum_{j=0}^{K} \alpha_j s_j \tag{9}$$

In formula (8), the item sequence embedding s_0 is used as the query in the attention mechanism, $W_q \in \mathbb{R}^{d \times d}$ is a model parameter. We perform weighted summation in formula (9) to get z that integrates all sequence information.

4.4   Generating Prediction and Model Loss

We use cosine similarity to score all items according to z:

$$\hat{y}_i = softmax \left(\gamma \frac{z^T v_i}{||z||_2 ||v_i||_2} \right) \tag{10}$$

In formula (10), γ is a trainable factor, and item embedding v_i is obtained in Sect. 4.2. We adopt the cross entropy loss for predicting the next item:

$$L = -\sum_{i=1}^{|V|} y_i \log \hat{y}_i + \lambda ||\theta||^2 \tag{11}$$

In formula (11), $y \in \mathbb{R}^{|V|}$ is the one-hot encoding vector corresponding to the ground truth item. θ is the set of all trainable parameters of the model. We train the model by optimizing L through the gradient descent method.

5   Experiments and Analyses

To evaluate the performance of Murzim, we conduct performance comparison experiments on different datasets, comparing Murzim with several existing models. Next, we deploy Murzim to the MX player and observe its performance in the actual production environment.

5.1   Experimental Setup

Datasets: We adopt the Yoochoose dataset, the Diginetica dataset, and our own MX Player dataset.

The Yoochoose dataset is from RecSys Challenge 2015[1]. It provides the user click sequence data of an e-commerce website, and contains the category information for each item which is treated as an attribute in our model. In particular, we fetch recent 1/64 and 1/4 sequences of the total Yoochoose dataset to form two datasets. The Diginetica dataset is from CIKM Cup 2016[2], which provides more item attribute information, including: category, priceLog2 (log-transformed product price) and item name token (comma separated hashed product name tokens). We only use its transactional data.

As for the pre-processing of the two datasets, we keep the same as [20]. Further, the training and testing sets are divided in the same way as [20]: data in the last day in the Yoochoose dataset are used as the testing set, and data in the last week of the Diginetica dataset are used as the testing set.

Besides, we construct a dataset named MXPlayer_1W_1M from the MX Player log. We extract the interaction sequences on the movies from 2020-01-20 to 2020-01-26, and filter out items whose number of occurrences is less than 3 and sequences whose length is 1. We use the data in the first six days for training and the last day for testing. Here, the items, i.e., movies, contain rich attribute information. We select seven attributes of items: genre (G), publisher (P), country(C), language(L), release year(R), director(D), and actor(A). The details of the three datasets are shown in Table 1.

Table 1. Details of the three datasets.

Dataset	#Item	#Train	#Test	Avg. len.	#Attribute values						
Yoochoose 1/64	17745	369859	55898	6.16	Category 282						
Yoochoose 1/4	30470	5917745	55898	5.71	Category 322						
Diginetica	43097	719470	60858	4.85	Category 1217	priceLog2 13		Name token 164774			
MXPlayer_1W_1M	11386	1658463	69804	6.38	G 34	P 130	C 55	L 40	R 106	D 6806	A 16248

According to the attribute score calculation method defined previously, we obtain attribute scores on the training sets of different datasets, as shown in Table 2. For the Diginetica dataset, the category attribute has the highest score, which indicates that most users seem to only pay attention to a few categories of items during browsing. For the MXPlayer_1W_1M dataset, the language

---

attribute has the highest score, indicating that the values of language might play more important roles in the sequence.

Metrics: We adopt Recall@20 and MRR(Mean Reciprocal Rank)@20 to evaluate the recommendations. Recall@20 is the proportion of ground-truth items among the top-20 recommended items, and here is equivalent to Hit@20. MRR@20 is the average of the inverse of the ranking of ground truth in the recommendation results. If the ground truth does not appear in the top-20 of the recommendations, then MRR@20 is 0.

Implementation Details: In Murzim, the embedding dimension d is set to 64 and 128 on the public datasets and MXPlayer_1W_1M dataset, respectively, the L2 penalty and batch size are set to 1e-5 and 512, respectively. We implement Murzim with Tensorflow, using the Adam optimizer where the initial learning rate is set to 0.004 and decays by 0.1 after every 2 epochs.

Table 2. Attribute scores on the three datasets

Dataset	Attribute scores						
Yoochoose 1/64	Category 0.5962						
Yoochoose 1/4	Category 0.5974						
Diginetica	Category 0.6450	priceLog2 0.4971		Name token 0.2498			
MXPlayer_1W_1M	G 0.4218	P 0.4155	C 0.5385	L 0.6271	R 0.2648	D 0.1719	A 0.1833

Table 3. Performance comparison

	Yoochoose 1/64		Yoochoose 1/4		Diginetica		MXPlayer_1W_1M	
	Recall@20	MRR@20	Recall@20	MRR@20	Recall@20	MRR@20	Recall@20	MRR@20
POP	6.71	1.65	1.33	0.30	0.89	0.20	14.78	3.95
S-POP	30.44	18.35	27.08	17.75	21.06	13.68	29.14	13.67
Item-KNN	51.60	21.81	52.31	21.70	35.75	11.57	50.03	19.33
GRU4Rec	60.64	22.89	59.53	22.60	29.45	8.33	53.54	20.71
NARM	68.32	28.63	69.73	29.23	49.70	16.17	53.97	20.43
STAMP	68.74	29.67	70.44	30.00	45.64	14.32	53.80	20.56
SR-GNN	70.57	30.94	71.36	31.89	50.73	17.59	55.05	21.52
Murzim	**71.52**	**31.65**	**72.19**	**32.04**	**54.74**	**19.40**	**55.51**	**21.82**

5.2 Performance Comparison

First, we conduct a comparative experiment, comparing our model with the following six models:

1. POP/S-POP: They recommend the top-N popular items in the entire training set or the current sequence. In S-POP, if the number of recommended items is insufficient, we use top-N popular items in the entire training set for completion.
2. Item-KNN [15]: It recommends the top-N items that are most similar to the items in the sequence. The similarity between item i and item j is calculated based on the number of co-occurrences in the sequence.
3. GRU4Rec [6]: It models sequences with RNN to predict the next item.
4. NARM [10]: It adds an attention mechanism to RNN to capture user's sequence behavior and main interaction purpose in the current sequence.
5. STAMP [13]: It uses a new attention mechanism to capture general interest and short-term attention of users.
6. SR-GNN [20]: It uses a GNN to model sequences, while using an attention mechanism to fuse users' long-term and short-term interests in sequences.

The experimental results are shown in Table 3. We note that SR-GNN works best among the comparison methods, which shows the effectiveness of graph-based representation in the sequential recommendation. However, our model (i.e., the Murzim version with the category attribute for public datasets and language attribute for MX Player dataset) outperforms SR-GNN. The performance gain over SR-GNN should originate from the fact that Murzim mines user preferences implicit in the attributes of items that users interact with.

Table 4. Effects of different attribute combinations on the Diginetica dataset

Attribute Combination	Recall@20	MRR@20
Category	**54.74**	**19.40**
Pricelog2	54.29	19.19
Name token	54.27	19.20
Category + pricelog2	54.60	19.36
Pricelog2 + name token	54.60	19.40
Category + name token	54.32	19.24
Category + pricelog2 + name token	54.66	19.39

Table 5. Effects of different attribute combinations on the MXPlayer_1W_1M dataset

	G	P	C	L	R	D	A	L+C	L+G	C+G
Recall@20	55.44	55.45	55.43	55.51	55.27	55.31	55.16	55.50	55.47	**55.54**
MRR@20	21.71	21.74	21.76	**21.82**	21.70	21.73	21.61	21.77	21.80	21.75

Next, we observe how and to what degree Murzim exploits the attribute effects. Table 4 shows the performance of different versions of Murzim on the

Diginetica dataset, where the different versions adopt different attributes or attribute combinations. The results in the first three lines are consistent with the attribute scores we calculate above: the higher the score is, the greater the performance improvement is. The results in the subsequent lines show the effect of adding multiple attributes. We find that except for the combination of pricelog2+name token, the effects of other combinations are lower than just adding one attribute. It indicates that attributes might influence each other and the performance is not always improved with the increasing of attribute information.

Table 5 shows the performance of different versions of Murzim on the MXPlayer_1W_1M dataset. The experimental results in the first seven columns are generally consistent with the scores of attributes of the MXPlayer_1W_1M dataset in Table 2. For example, the language attribute score is the highest, and the corresponding version of Murzim works best in comparison with the other versions with a single attribute. This shows that our attribute score calculation method can measure the importance of attributes to a certain extent. Then, we select any two attributes from three attributes with the highest scores: language, country, and genre, and form the corresponding version of Murzim to conduct the experiment. The results are listed in the last three columns in Table 5. We find that the combination of any two attributes does not get further improvement on MRR@20. Meanwhile, although the combination of language and genre achieves the best result on Recall@20, the results of the other groups are close to that of adding a single attribute. This indicates again that attributes are useful in improving the recommendation but it is not necessarily the case that more attributes lead to better recommendations.

5.3   Online Test

We have deployed Murzim to the online production environment of the MX Player and generate recommendation for users based on their viewing sequences. In the online version of Murzim, we choose two attributes, i.e., language and genre. We compare the click-through rates (CTRs) on a group of users before and after using Murzim, as shown in Fig. 3. It can be seen that after Murzim is deployed, the CTR gradually increases. Compared with the previous values, it increases by about 60% on the average. This shows that Murzim generates better recommendations than before.

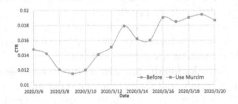

Fig. 3. CTRs before and after using Murzim

6   Conclusion

In this paper, we propose a GNN model Murzim for sequential recommendation. Murzim describes the user-item interaction sequences and attribute sequences by directed graphs, and then gathers information through node aggregation and the attention network, which not only inherits the advantages of GNNs but also excavates user preferences through attributes, thus improving the recommendation performance. Currently, Murzim is running in the online production environment of the MX player and mainly serving the people in India.

Acknowledgement. This work was supported by the National Natural Science Foundation of China under Grant No. 62072450 and the 2019 joint project with MX Media.

References

1. Factorizing personalized markov chains for next-basket recommendation (2010)
2. Chen, X., et al.: Sequential recommendation with user memory networks. In: Proceedings of the Eleventh ACM International Conference on Web Search and Data Mining, pp. 108–116 (2018)
3. Hamilton, W., Ying, Z., Leskovec, J.: Inductive representation learning on large graphs. In: Advances in Neural Information Processing Systems, pp. 1024–1034 (2017)
4. He, Q., et al.: Web query recommendation via sequential query prediction. In: 2009 IEEE 25th International Conference on Data Engineering, pp. 1443–1454. IEEE (2009)
5. Hidasi, B., Karatzoglou, A.: Recurrent neural networks with top-k gains for session-based recommendations. In: Proceedings of the 27th ACM International Conference on Information and Knowledge Management, pp. 843–852 (2018)
6. Hidasi, B., Karatzoglou, A., Baltrunas, L., Tikk, D.: Session-based recommendations with recurrent neural networks. arXiv preprint arXiv:1511.06939 (2015)
7. Hidasi, B., Quadrana, M., Karatzoglou, A., Tikk, D.: Parallel recurrent neural network architectures for feature-rich session-based recommendations. In: Proceedings of the 10th ACM Conference on Recommender Systems, pp. 241–248 (2016)
8. Huang, J., Zhao, W.X., Dou, H., Wen, J.R., Chang, E.Y.: Improving sequential recommendation with knowledge-enhanced memory networks. In: The 41st International ACM SIGIR Conference on Research & Development in Information Retrieval, pp. 505–514 (2018)
9. Koren, Y., Bell, R., Volinsky, C.: Matrix factorization techniques for recommender systems. Computer **42**(8), 30–37 (2009)
10. Li, J., Ren, P., Chen, Z., Ren, Z., Lian, T., Ma, J.: Neural attentive session-based recommendation. In: Proceedings of the 2017 ACM on Conference on Information and Knowledge Management, pp. 1419–1428 (2017)
11. Li, Y., Tarlow, D., Brockschmidt, M., Zemel, R.S.: Gated graph sequence neural networks. In: 4th International Conference on Learning Representations, ICLR 2016, San Juan, Puerto Rico, 2–4 May 2016, Conference Track Proceedings (2016)
12. Linden, G., Smith, B., York, J.: Amazon.com recommendations: item-to-item collaborative filtering. IEEE Internet Comput. **7**(1), 76–80 (2003)

13. Liu, Q., Zeng, Y., Mokhosi, R., Zhang, H.: STAMP: short-term attention/memory priority model for session-based recommendation. In: Proceedings of the 24th ACM SIGKDD International Conference on Knowledge Discovery & Data Mining, pp. 1831–1839 (2018)
14. Mnih, A., Salakhutdinov, R.R.: Probabilistic matrix factorization. In: Advances in Neural Information Processing Systems, pp. 1257–1264 (2008)
15. Sarwar, B., Karypis, G., Konstan, J., Riedl, J.: Item-based collaborative filtering recommendation algorithms. In: Proceedings of the 10th International Conference on World Wide Web, pp. 285–295 (2001)
16. Shani, G., Heckerman, D., Brafman, R.I.: An mdp-based recommender system. J. Mach. Learn. Res. **6**(Sep), 1265–1295 (2005)
17. Tan, Y.K., Xu, X., Liu, Y.: Improved recurrent neural networks for session-based recommendations. In: Proceedings of the 1st Workshop on Deep Learning for Recommender Systems, pp. 17–22 (2016)
18. Tuan, T.X., Phuong, T.M.: 3d convolutional networks for session-based recommendation with content features. In: Proceedings of the Eleventh ACM Conference on Recommender Systems, pp. 138–146 (2017)
19. Vaswani, A., et al.: Attention is all you need. In: Advances in Neural Information Processing Systems, pp. 5998–6008 (2017)
20. Wu, S., Tang, Y., Zhu, Y., Wang, L., Xie, X., Tan, T.: Session-based recommendation with graph neural networks. Proc. AAAI Conf. Artif. Intell. **33**, 346–353 (2019)
21. Xu, C., et al.: Graph contextualized self-attention network for session-based recommendation. In: Proceedings of 28th International Joint Conference Artificial Intelligence (IJCAI), pp. 3940–3946 (2019)

Exploring Implicit Relationships in Social Network for Recommendation Systems

Yunhe Wei[1], Huifang Ma[1,2,3($\boxtimes$)], Ruoyi Zhang[1], Zhixin Li[2], and Liang Chang[3]

[1] College of Computer Science and Engineering, Northwest Normal University,
Lanzhou Gansu 730070, China
mahuifang@yeah.net
[2] Guangxi Key Lab of Multi-source Information Mining and Security,
Guangxi Normal University, Guilin Guangxi 541004, China
[3] Guangxi Key Lab of Trusted Software, Guilin University of Electronic Technology,
Guilin Guangxi 541004, China

Abstract. Online social platforms have provided a large amount of available information to recommendation systems. With this intuition, social recommendation systems emerged and have attracted increasing attention over the past years. Most existing social recommendation methods only use explicit social relationships among users. However, implicit social relationships can effectively improve the quality of recommendation when users only have few social relationships. To this end, the discovery of implicit relations among users plays a central role in advancing social recommendation. In this paper, we propose a novel approach to fuse direct and indirect friends toward discovering more accurate social recommendation method. We learn users' preferences by carefully integrating users' direct and indirect friends. In particular, we construct item rankings based on the feedback from users' direct and indirect friends on the item. Furthermore, to distinguish the impact of users' direct friends and indirect friends, we also extend the ranking assumption in item domain to user domain, so that information from user rankings can be leveraged to further improve the recommendation performance. Extensive experiments on two real-world datasets demonstrate the effectiveness of the proposed method.

Keywords: Social information · Indirect friends · Item ranking · User ranking

1 Introduction

As an indispensable information filtering technique, recommendation system is nowadays ubiquitous in various domains, such as e-commerce, online news, and

Supported by the National Natural Science Foundation of China (61762078, 61363058, 61966004), Research Fund of Guangxi Key Lab of Multisource Information Mining and Security (MIMS1808), Northwest Normal University Young Teachers Research Capacity Promotion Plan (NWNU-LKQN2019-2) and Research Fund of Guangxi Key Laboratory of Trusted Software (kx202003).

© Springer Nature Switzerland AG 2021
K. Karlapalem et al. (Eds.): PAKDD 2021, LNAI 12713, pp. 386–397, 2021.
https://doi.org/10.1007/978-3-030-75765-6_31

social media. The most impactful theory behind recommendation system is to propose items that are most likely to be of interest to the user based on the user's interests, preferences, needs, and behaviors. For decades, one of the most popular ideas in recommendation research is the idea that the collaborative filtering. Even though a lot of collaborative filtering methods have been proposed and lead to promising results, they suffer from data sparsity and perform poorly on cold-start users who have no or few past behavior data. The explicitly observed additional information have been widely exploited to alleviate these problems in recommendation systems. Due to the explosive development of online social platforms, social relations provide the extra information about users.

To capture more information in the learned user embeddings, most social recommendation systems simultaneously use user-user social networks and user-item interaction information to thoroughly model user preferences. A user's preference for one item should be similar to his friends, which motivates us to probe into such social effect to improve recommendation performance. Existing methods for social recommendation attempt to exploit social information in various ways, such as by trust propagation, regularization loss, matrix factorization, network embedding, and causal inference. These methods have achieved certain success, but there are still the following limitations. On one hand, they only use the user's direct social information. However, social information also contains other complex relationships, such as heterogeneous relationships. As users have diverse interests, they seek different suggestions in different communities. On the other hand, they believe that users have the same level of trust in all social friends. However, the impact of direct and indirect friends is different when predicting user preferences.

To alleviate these problems, a social recommendation method EIRSN(short for **E**xplore **I**mplicit **R**elationships in **S**ocial **N**etwork) is proposed in this paper. First, we divide users into different communities according to their direct social relationships to capture users' indirect friends. Second, the item ranking is established based on the interactive information of the user's direct and indirect friends. Third, we build user ranking based on users' trust information. Finally, the item ranking and user ranking are combined to predict the user's preference for non-interactive items. In addition, an effective sampling strategy is used in the model training process to improve recommendation performance by reducing the negative sampling space.

2   Related Work

Social recommendation task is based on the theories that users and their friends often have similar preferences and influence each other in certain aspects, so considering users' social information can enhance recommendation performance. Recently, researchers have demonstrated that recommendation models with the aid of social relations can improve recommendation performance.

The social recommendation methods related to our work are divided into three types. The first type of methods consider social information as a regularization. TrustSVD [3] model proposed by Guo et al. , which treats users' explicit trust relationships as implicit feedback information. They use different penalty weights for different regularization parameters. Yang et al. propose a TrustPMF [11] model, which decomposes the social matrix into a trustee feature matrix and a trustee feature matrix. Lin et al. propose a regularization term for modeling variable social influence in CSR [5]. The second type of methods use different information to integrate the user's preferences. Tang et al. propose a fine-grained method in the mTrust [8] model to capture the user's multi-faceted trust information. Liu et al. propose a community-based social recommendation model InSRMF [6], which can fully explore the interdependence between social information and user behavior. The third type of methods divides items into different sets based on social relationships and then defines the item ranking. For example, Zhao et al. propose an SBPR model [14], assuming that each user's rating behavior should be at a certain level Similar to the scoring behavior of his friends, the item set is divided into positive items, social items, and negative items to build a ranking of items. Considering the different strengths of links in social networks, Wang et al. proposed the TBPR model [10]. This model uses Jaccard similarity to calculate the link strength in social networks and divides the social relationship into strong and weak links. Yu et al. propose a method IF-BPR [13], which uses the implicit friends for each user to find more reliable relationships. In addition, with the development of deep neural networks, several deep models are proposed to enhance social recommendation systems, such as GraphRec [2]. GraphRec can aggregate information from user-item graph and user social graph to learn better user representations.

Despite the success of these methods, most of them only consider explicitly model the relationships of user's direct friends. Besides, they do not model the impact of different social relationships, which leads to a suboptimal prediction.

3   Preliminaries

3.1   Notations and Problem Statement

Let $U = \{u_1, u_2, \ldots, u_n\}$ and $V = \{v_1, v_2, \ldots, v_m\}$ be the sets of users and items respectively, where n is the number of users, and m is the number of items. We assume that $\boldsymbol{R}_{n \times m}$ is the user-item feedback matrix, where $R_{ij} = 1$ if u_i gives a feedback to v_j and zero otherwise. We use $\boldsymbol{S}_{n \times n}$ to denote the user-user social matrix, where $S_{ij} = 1$ if u_j has a relation to u_i and zero otherwise. Given the social network $G(U, E)$, we use overlapping community detection methods to divide each user into different communities. Let the set of overlapping communities be $C = \{C_1, C_2, \ldots, C_D\}$, where $C_i \cap C_j \neq \emptyset$ and $C_1 \cup \cdots \cup C_D = U$. Let $V_u^P, V_u^D, V_u^I, V_u^N$ denote the positive feedback items set, direct social feedback items set, indirect social feedback items set and negative feedback items set of u. Let U_u^D, U_u^I, U_u^N respectively denote the direct social users set, indirect social users set and negative social users set of u. We use an embedding vector $\boldsymbol{U}_i$ to denote a user u_i and an embedding vector $\boldsymbol{V}_j$ to represent an item v_j. Given the size ratio γ of reduced sampling space, we randomly assign each user $\gamma \times N$

samples as the negative user sampling space R_U^- and negative item sampling space R_V^-.

Given a user-item rating matrix $\boldsymbol{R}_{n \times m}$ and a user-user social matrix $\boldsymbol{S}_{n \times n}$. We aim to predict the likelihood of $u_i's$ preference for v_j.

3.2 User Overlapping Community Detection Based on Social Information

In social network, implicit social information provides extra information for predicting users' preferences. A user can belong to multiple communities in a social network, and users have similar preferences in the same community. Hence, we can capture users' indirect social relationships through overlapping community detection method [12]. More specifically, let F be a nonnegative matrix where F_{ik} is a weight between user u_i and community C_k. Given F, the overlapping community detection method generates a graph $G(U, E)$ by creating edge (i, h) between a pair of nodes $u_i, u_h \in U$ with probability $P(i, h)$.

$$p(i, h) = 1 - \exp\left(-\boldsymbol{F}_i \cdot \boldsymbol{F}_h^T\right) \tag{1}$$

The likelihood function $l(F) = P(G|F)$ of G is calculated as follows:

$$l(F) = \prod_{(i,h) \in E} \left(1 - \exp\left(-\boldsymbol{F}_i \boldsymbol{F}_h^T\right)\right) \prod_{(i,h) \notin E} \exp\left(-\boldsymbol{F}_u \boldsymbol{F}_v^T\right) \tag{2}$$

We detect D communities by maximizing the log-likelihood function of G

$$\hat{F} = \underset{F \geq 0}{\arg\max} \sum_{(i,h) \in E} \ln\left(1 - \exp\left(-\boldsymbol{F}_i \boldsymbol{F}_h^T\right)\right) - \sum_{(i,h) \notin E} \boldsymbol{F}_i \boldsymbol{F}_h^T \tag{3}$$

Whether u_i belongs to the community C_k is determined by F_{ik}.

4 Bayesian Personalized Recommendation Method Fusing Social Information

4.1 Item Ranking Based on Social Feedback

To motivate this work, we first conduct a simple analysis of preference data from two sources that we will consider in this paper: Ciao and Epinions. Table 1 shows the detailed information of the used datasets, where Rdensity represents user-item interaction data density and Sdensity represents user social relationship density.

First, Fig. 1 shows the probability that an item selected by a user is also selected by their direct and indirect friends. More specifically, we compare the probability with the baseline setting: the probability that an item selected by a user is also selected by randomly sampled users. It is clear that the first probability and the second probability are higher than the baseline. Besides, Fig. 2

Table 1. Summary of the datasets used in the experiments

Dataset	Users	Items	Feedbacks	Social relations	Rdensity(%)	Sdensity(%)
Ciao	1,705	12,252	22,839	47,842	0.1093	1.6467
Epinions	49,289	139,738	664,824	487,183	0.0097	0.0201

shows that the probability that a user selects an item increases monotonically as a function of the number of direct friends and indirect friends who have selected the item. Based on this result, we build a model based on a simple assumption about item ranking:

(Rank of) items I've consumed $\succ$ items my direct friends have consumed $\succ$ items my indirect friends have consumed $\succ$ items neither me nor my friends have consumed.

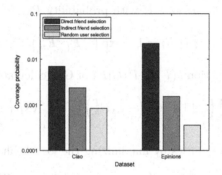

Fig. 1. Coverage probability analysis

For each user, we divide the item set into the following four sets:

Positive feedback item set V_u^P: the set of items selected by user u.

Direct social feedback item set V_u^D: this item set is that user u has not feedback but at least one of his direct friends has feedback.

Indirect social feedback item set V_u^I: this item set is that user u did not choose but at least one of his indirect friends selected.

Negative feedback item set V_u^N: V_u^N is the set of items that neither user u nor any of their friends selected.

One can easily find that $V_u^P \cap V_u^D \cap V_u^I \cap V_u^N = \emptyset$ and $V_u^P \cup V_u^D \cup V_u^I \cup V_u^N = V$.

The above assumption is stated as:

$$w_{ui} \geq w_{uq}, \ w_{uq} \geq w_{ug}, \ w_{ug} \geq w_{uj}, \quad i \in V_u^P, \ q \in V_u^D, \ g \in V_u^I, \ j \in V_u^N$$

where $w_{ui}, w_{uq}, w_{ug}, w_{uj}$ respectively represent the preference of user u on positive feedback items, direct social feedback items, indirect social feedback items and negative feedback items.

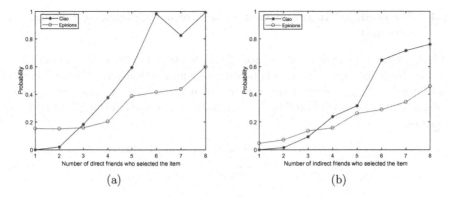

Fig. 2. Influence of the number of friends on selection probability

Based on this assumption, the optimization likelihood of each user's item ranking can be expressed as:

$$\prod_{i\in V_u^P, q\in V_u^D} P(w_{ui} \geq w_{uq}|\theta) \prod_{q\in V_u^D, g\in V_u^I} P(w_{uq} \geq w_{ug}|\theta) \prod_{g\in V_u^I, j\in V_u^N} P(w_{ug} \geq w_{uj}|\theta)$$

$$(4)$$

4.2   User Ranking Based on Social Information

We can capture users' direct friends and indirect friends from social networks. We assume that users trust direct friends more than indirect friends. Hence, we propose the following user ranking assumption:

User's direct friends $\succ$ User's indirect friends $\succ$ Other users

For each user, we divide the user set into the following three sets:

Direct friends U_u^D: the set of users who have a direct social relationship with u.

Indirect friends U_u^I: the set of users who do not have a direct social relationship with u but have an indirect social relationship.

Negative social user U_u^N: the set of users who have neither direct nor indirect social relationships with u.

The above assumption is stated as:

$$x_{ut} \geq x_{ul}, \quad x_{ul} \geq x_{uz}, \quad t \in U_u^D, \quad l \in U_u^I, \quad z \in U_u^N$$

where x_{ut}, x_{ul}, x_{uz} respectively represent the trust level of user u to direct social users, indirect social users and other users.

Based on this assumption, the optimization likelihood of each user's user ranking can be expressed as:

$$\prod_{t\in U_u^D, l\in U_u^I} P(x_{ut} \geq x_{ul}|\theta) \prod_{l\in U_u^I, z\in U_u^N} P(x_{ul} \geq x_{uz}|\theta) \qquad (5)$$

4.3 Personalized Ranking that Fuses Item Feedback and Social Information

When predicting the final preference of user u, we use both item ranking based on user feedback and user ranking based on social relationships. We combine the optimization likelihood of item ranking and user ranking to construct the final optimization likelihood function. We aim to minimize the following log likelihood function:

$$J = -\sum_u [\sum_{i,q,g,j} [\ln \sigma(w_{ui} - w_{uq}) + \ln \sigma(w_{uq} - w_{ug}) + \ln \sigma(w_{ug} - w_{uj})]$$
$$+\alpha_u \sum_{t,l,z} [\ln \sigma(x_{ut} - x_{ul}) + \ln \sigma(x_{ul} - x_{uz})]] + \alpha_\theta \parallel \theta \parallel_F^2 \tag{6}$$

We use the matrix factorization method. let $\theta = (U, V)$, the loss function is further rewritten as:

$$J = -\sum_u [\sum_{i,q,g,j} [\ln \sigma(U_u V_i^T - U_u V_q^T) + \ln \sigma(U_u V_q^T - U_u V_g^T) + \ln \sigma(U_u V_g^T - U_u V_j^T)]$$
$$+\alpha_u \sum_{t,l,z} [\ln \sigma(U_u U_t^T - U_u U_l^T) + \ln \sigma(U_u U_l^T - U_u U_z^T)]] + \alpha_\theta (\parallel U \parallel_F^2 + \parallel V \parallel_F^2)$$
$$\tag{7}$$

where a regularization term $\alpha_\theta(\parallel U \parallel_F^2 + \parallel V \parallel_F^2)$ is used to avoid overfitting in the learning process. We use stochastic gradient descent (SGD) algorithm to optimize the above objective function.

4.4 Sampling Strategy

Since the negative sampling space is quite large for each user, it will not only lead to low efficiency, but also reduce performance. In order to overcome this problem, the sampling strategy proposed in [1] is used to sample negative items, and design a negative user sampling strategy to further improve the recommendation performance. The specific sampling plan is as follows.

$$P(V = v) = \frac{1}{n} \sum_{u \notin U_v} \frac{1}{m - |V_u|} \tag{8}$$

$$P(U = u) = \frac{1}{n^*} \sum_{u' \notin S_u} \frac{1}{n - 1 - |S_{u'}|} \tag{9}$$

$$n^* = |\{u| \, |S_u| < n - 1\}| \tag{10}$$

Where U_v is the set of users who have interacted with item v. V_u is the set of items that u has interacted with and S_u is the set of users who have a social relationship with u. According to the sample space reduction rate γ (the ratio of the size of the reduced space to the original space) and the probability distributions $P(V)$ and $P(U)$, candidate sets V^- and U^- with sizes $R_V^-(\gamma \times m)$ and $R_U^-(\gamma \times n)$ can be obtained as negative sampling spaces. Thereby reducing the negative sampling space.

Algorithm 1: Personalized ranking that fuses item feedback and social information

---

Input: User-item feedback matrix $R_{n \times m}$; User-user social matrix $S_{n \times n}$
Output: User latent factor matrix $U_{n \times d}$; Item latent factor matrix $V_{m \times d}$
Initialization:
Initialize **for** $u = 1$; $u \leq n$ **do**
  | split $n - 1$ users into three parts: $U_u{}^D$, $U_u{}^I$, $U_u{}^N$;
  | split m items into four parts: $V_u{}^P$, $V_u{}^D$, $V_u{}^I$, $V_u{}^N$;
end
Training:
for *iterations* **do**
  | **for** *#training sample* **do**
  | | Sample a user $u \in U$;
  | | Sample an item i from $V_u{}^P$;
  | | Sample an item q from $V_u{}^D$;
  | | Sample an item g from $V_u{}^I$;
  | | Sample an item j from $V_u{}^N$;
  | | Sample a user t from $U_u{}^D$;
  | | Sample a user l from $U_u{}^I$;
  | | Sample a user z from $U_u{}^N$;
  | | Calculate $\frac{\partial \mathcal{O}(\Theta)}{\Theta}$;
  | | Update $\boldsymbol{U}_u, \boldsymbol{U}_t, \boldsymbol{U}_l, \boldsymbol{U}_z, \boldsymbol{V}_i, \boldsymbol{V}_q, \boldsymbol{V}_g, \boldsymbol{V}_j$ according to Eq.7;
  | **end**
end

---

5 Experiments and Results

In this section, We conduct experiments to answer the following research questions:

RQ1: How do different parameters in EIRSN impact social recommendation performance?

RQ2: Are the key components in EIRSN, such as implicit information and user rankings, necessary for improving performance?

RQ3: How does our proposed model EIRSN perform compared with state-of-the-art methods on the social recommendation task?

5.1 Experimental Settings

Evaluation Metrics. Two metrics - Recall and the Normalized Discounted Cumulative Gain (NDCG) are used to measure the recommendation performance of our proposed model and various baseline methods.

Baseline Methods. To verify the performance of our proposed method, we compare EIRSN with the most popular recommendation methods:BPR [7], NCF

[4], NGCF [9], SBPR[14], IF-BPR[13], TrustSVD [3], InSRMF [6], GraphRec [2]. Among these methods, BPR, NCF and NGCF do not use social information, and all the remaining methods are social recommendation methods. NCF, NGCF and GraphRec are all classic deep learning-based recommendation methods.

5.2   Recommendation Performance

Effect of Parameters. We investigate the influence of parameters on the performance of EIRSN. Figure 4 and Fig. 5 show the effect of user ranking weight, regularization parameter and the number of communities on two datasets in term of Recall.

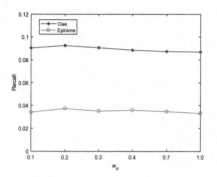

Fig. 3. Impact of parameter α_u **Fig. 4.** Impact of parameter α_θ

As shown in Figs. 3 and 4, when α_u and α_θ become extremely small, the importance of social user ranking and regularization terms will become ignorable. To study their impacts, we test how different values of α_u and α_θ affect the performance. From the results, we can conclude that the performance of EIRSN first increases with the increasing α_u and α_θ, and then begins to decrease. Our EIRSN achieves its best performances with $\alpha_u = 0.2$ and $\alpha_\theta = 0.05$.

From Fig. 5, we observe that EIRSN behaves inconsistently on different datasets when the number of user communities D is adjusted in 5,10,15,,45,50. For each dataset, EIRSN performs better as D increases, reaches the best value (around $D = 20$ for Ciao, and $D = 45$ for Epinions), and its performance is destroyed as D become much larger.

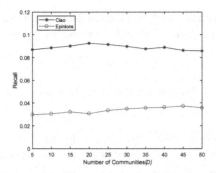

Fig. 5. Coverage probability analysis

Importance of Key Components. To understand the working of EIRSN, we compare EIRSN with its two variants: EIRSN-IF, and EIRSN-UR. These two variants are defined in the following:

EIRSN-IF: The user's indirect friend information of EIRSN is removed . This variant only uses the user's direct friends information. EIRSN-UR: The user ranking of EIRSN is removed . This variant only uses the item ranking.

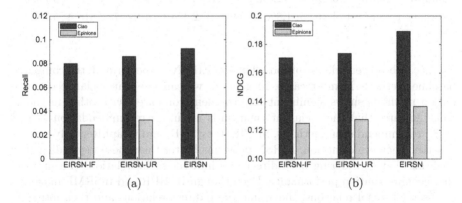

Fig. 6. Performance of indirect friend and user ranking

The indirect social information of users can more accurately construct their preferences. As shown in Fig. 6, EIRSN-IF performs worse than EIRSN. It verifies that the user's indirect friend information is important to learn user preferences and improve the recommendation performance.

Users trust direct friends rather than indirect friends in social networks. We can see that without user ranking, the performance of our model is deteriorated significantly. It justifies our assumption that user ranking can effectively distinguish the different influences of direct friends and indirect friends on users.

Performance Comparison of Recommender Systems. Table 2 shows the overall performance compared with different methods. One can draw the following conclusions.

Table 2. Experimental results on epinions and Ciao

Method	Epinions				Ciao			
	K = 10		K = 20		K=10		K = 20	
	Recall	NDCG	Recall	NDCG	Recall	NDCG	Recall	NDCG
BPR	0.0117	0.1391	0.0301	0.1426	0.0483	0.1857	0.0923	0.1885
NCF	0.0139	0.1407	0.0320	0.1438	0.0516	0.1879	0.0952	0.1902
NGCF	0.0153	0.1415	0.0355	0.1464	0.0532	0.1897	0.0985	0.1911
SBPR	0.0145	0.1412	0.0337	0.1451	0.0541	0.1904	0.1012	0.1938
IF-BPR	0.0157	0.1421	0.0350	0.1460	0.0557	0.1916	0.1036	0.1954
TrustSVD	0.0166	0.1426	0.0359	0.1468	0.0571	0.1925	0.1058	0.1971
InSRMF	0.0184	0.1439	0.0373	0.1474	0.0583	0.1936	0.1076	0.1985
GraphRec	0.0198	0.1453	**0.0385**	**0.1483**	0.0594	0.1949	0.1089	0.1990
EIRSN	**0.0205**	**0.1461**	0.0376	0.1476	**0.0617**	**0.1957**	**0.1105**	**0.2003**
Improv.	3.5%	0.6%	−2.3%	−0.5%	3.9%	0.4%	1.5%	0.7%
p-value	3.61e−4	4.81e−5	1.86e−5	4.98e−3	2.47e−6	6.16e−7	3.81e−4	5.76e−6

As can be observed, our proposed model EIRSN outperform all the compared baseline methods in most cases. In general, we can see that social recommendation methods shows significant improvement compared with other methods. This indicates that the social information is useful for recommendations. In all social recommendation methods, SBPR, TrustSVD, and GraphRec only use the observed social information. EIRSN performs better than these methods, which confirms that considering both direct and indirect social relations can improve the recommendation performance. Even though IF-BPR and InSRMF make use of observed social relations, they mine the indirect relations and then integrate them to user latent factors. However, our proposed EIRSN further incorporates the influence of different friends into user representation learning, which boosts the performance of the recommendation system.

6   Conclusion

In this work, we explore indirect social information and social influence for collaborative filtering. We devise a novel social recommendation framework EIRSN, which integrates the different social information of users to solve the data sparsity problem. The core of our model is to generate user embedding by performing embedding influence along direct and indirect social friends. Specifically, it enables us to find the indirect friends that are not necessarily connected with each other on the social network, and the obtained indirect friends are further exploited for the recommendation via an social Bayesian personalized ranking approach. We conduct extensive experiments on two real-world datasets, demonstrating that our proposed EIRSN could boost the social recommendation performance over existing methods.

References

1. Ding, J., Yu, G., He, X., Feng, F., Li, Y., Jin, D.: Sampler design for Bayesian personalized ranking by leveraging view data. IEEE Trans. Knowl. Data Eng. (2019)
2. Fan, W., Ma, Y., Li, Q., He, Y., Zhao, E., Tang, J., Yin, D.: Graph neural networks for social recommendation. In: The World Wide Web Conference, pp. 417–426 (2019)
3. Guo, G., Zhang, J., Yorke-Smith, N., et al.: Trustsvd: collaborative filtering with both the explicit and implicit influence of user trust and of item ratings. AAAI. **15**, 123–125 (2015)
4. He, X., Liao, L., Zhang, H., Nie, L., Hu, X., Chua, T.S.: Neural collaborative filtering. In: Proceedings of the 26th International Conference on World Wide Web, pp. 173–182 (2017)
5. Lin, T.H., Gao, C., Li, Y.: Recommender systems with characterized social regularization. In: Proceedings of the 27th ACM International Conference on Information and Knowledge Management, pp. 1767–1770 (2018)
6. Liu, H., Jing, L., Yu, J., Ng, M.K.P.: Social recommendation with learning personal and social latent factors. IEEE Trans. Knowl. Data Eng. (2019)
7. Rendle, S., Freudenthaler, C., Gantner, Z., Schmidt-Thieme, L.: BPR: Bayesian personalized ranking from implicit feedback. arXiv preprint arXiv:1205.2618 (2012)
8. Tang, J., Gao, H., Liu, H.: mtrust: discerning multi-faceted trust in a connected world. In: Proceedings of the Fifth ACM International Conference on Web Search and Data Mining, pp. 93–102 (2012)
9. Wang, X., He, X., Wang, M., Feng, F., Chua, T.S.: Neural graph collaborative filtering. In: Proceedings of the 42nd International ACM SIGIR Conference on Research and Development in Information Retrieval, pp. 165–174 (2019)
10. Wang, X., Lu, W., Ester, M., Wang, C., Chen, C.: Social recommendation with strong and weak ties. In: Proceedings of the 25th ACM International on Conference on Information and Knowledge Management, pp. 5–14 (2016)
11. Yang, B., Lei, Y., Liu, J., Li, W.: Social collaborative filtering by trust. IEEE Trans. Pattern Anal. Mach. Intell. **39**(8), 1633–1647 (2016)
12. Yang, J., Leskovec, J.: Overlapping community detection at scale: a nonnegative matrix factorization approach. In: Proceedings of the Sixth ACM International Conference on Web Search and Data Mining, pp. 587–596 (2013)
13. Yu, J., Gao, M., Li, J., Yin, H., Liu, H.: Adaptive implicit friends identification over heterogeneous network for social recommendation. In: Proceedings of the 27th ACM International Conference on Information and Knowledge Management, pp. 357–366 (2018)
14. Zhao, T., McAuley, J., King, I.: Leveraging social connections to improve personalized ranking for collaborative filtering. In: Proceedings of the 23rd ACM International Conference on Conference on Information and Knowledge Management, pp. 261–270 (2014)

Transferable Contextual Bandits with Prior Observations

Kevin Labille⑩, Wen Huang⑩, and Xintao Wu$^{(\boxtimes)}$⑩

University of Arkansas, Fayetteville, AR 72701, USA
{kclabill,wenhuang,xintaowu}@uark.edu

Abstract. Cross-domain recommendations have long been studied in traditional recommender systems, especially to solve the cold-start problem. Although recent approaches to dynamic personalized recommendation have leveraged the power of contextual bandits to benefit from the exploitation-exploration paradigm, very few works have been conducted on cross-domain recommendation in this setting. We propose a novel approach to solve the cold-start problem under the contextual bandit setting through the cross-domain approach. Our developed algorithm, T-LinUCB, takes advantage of prior recommendation observations from multiple domains to initialize the new arms' parameters so as to circumvent the lack of data arising from the cold-start problem. Our bandits therefore possess knowledge upon starting which yields better recommendation and faster convergence. We provide both a regret analysis and an experimental evaluation. Our approach outperforms the baseline, LinUCB, and experiment results demonstrate the benefits of our model.

Keywords: Contextual bandits · Cross-domain recommendation · Personalized recommendation

1 Introduction

Personalized recommendation has long been studied through traditional approaches such as content-based techniques and collaborative filtering techniques. Yet, in recent years, it has been tackled through a new approach known as the exploration-exploitation dilemma. Indeed, an efficient recommender system should be able to recommend items that are both diverse and accurate. Naturally, diversity can be achieved through the exploration of new horizon and unknown interests while accurate predictions can be achieved through the exploitation of historical and known user interests. The key factor of such an approach thus becomes to properly balance exploration and exploitation in order to optimize the recommendation. Early works to tackle this problem were formulated as the multi-armed bandit (MAB) problem [2].

Although multi-armed bandits directly tackle the exploration-exploitation dilemma, they would be ineffective to use for personalized recommendation purposes, since they do not incorporate user-side information. To circumvent such

© Springer Nature Switzerland AG 2021
K. Karlapalem et al. (Eds.): PAKDD 2021, LNAI 12713, pp. 398–410, 2021.
https://doi.org/10.1007/978-3-030-75765-6_32

limitations, contextual multi-armed bandits (or CMAB) [12] were introduced. Contextual bandits have the capability to observe, at each iteration, some features related to both the arm and the user. As opposed to regular multi-armed bandits which only use the rewards to update their model, contextual bandits use the rewards along with the contextual feature vector to update the arm-picking strategy. By exploring the relationship between the context and the observed reward, contextual bandits are able to improve upon multi-armed bandits by making personalized decisions.

Both the MAB and CMAB have been applied to recommendation systems [4]. However, these approaches still suffer from the cold-start problem. A common method is to leverage observations from another domain and transfer them to the new domain. We study the problem of cross-domain recommendations under the linear contextual bandit setting. Specifically, we focus on the task of using a bandit capable of recommending educational videos (i.e. the arms) across various topics. We make the following assumptions: (1) the set of users remain unchanged across topics, (2) the topic and the set of arms change over time, and (3) the topics or domains are homogeneous, that is, they have the same feature space. In such a setting, the challenge for the bandit is to maintain accurate recommendations across topics (or domains) without restarting its learning strategy from scratch. To address this problem, we develop a new algorithm, T-LinUCB, which leverages recommendation observations of similar arms from prior topics. Consequently, the learning process is sped up and the estimation of the true reward parameters is improved, which results in better recommendations.

2 Related Work

There exist many approaches to solve the contextual bandits problem. Langford and Zhang [10] introduced an epoch-greedy approach, Li et al. [12] used a UCB-based approach that assumes a linear payoff model, and Agrawal et al. [1] tackled the problem using a Thompson sampling approach. Bandits have been widely applied to recommendation systems. Zhou et al. [19] and Nguyen & Kofod-Petersen [14] leveraged the context-free bandit to solve the widely-known cold-start problem present in recommender systems. Li et al. [12] used a contextual bandit based on the UCB algorithm while Chapeller & Li [5] investigated a Thompson-sampling approach for news item recommendation purposes. Bouneffouf et al. [3] used contextual bandits for recommendations in mobile environments. Nguyen & Lauw [15] proposed to tackle recommendation with a large population by dynamically clustering users into several clusters that are each served by a contextual bandit. Huang et al. [9] studied how to achieve user-side group fairness in contextual bandits. Tang et al. [17] explored ensemble strategies of different contextual bandits to make a recommendation decision.

Cross-domain recommendation has long been studied and is still an active research topic [8]. However, very few works take advantage of the powerful contextual bandit framework. Azar et al. [11] introduced the transfer-UCB Bandit algorithm that uses a transfer learning approach wherein they leverage prior knowledge by transferring the estimated bandit parameters from one task to another. Zhang & Bareinboim [18] tackled the offline transfer problem between bandits using a causal inference approach named B-kl-UCB. Although these two works are related, they focus on the context-free multi-armed bandit (MAB) as opposed to the contextual bandit. More recently, Liu et al. [13] introduced TCB where they tackled the cross-domain problem in contextual bandit using a transfer learning approach. TCB relies on a source and a target domain, as well as a matrix of correspondence data that captures the relatedness of the source and the target observations. It uses a translation matrix to align feature spaces between both domains and to translate the contexts. Their approach successfully outperformed several single-domain bandits. However, their TCB algorithm is set in the uniform contextual bandit model wherein there exists a single unknown reward parameter vector shared between all arms. We consider the more common disjoint contextual bandit model wherein each arm has its own unknown reward parameter. Furthermore, their setting only considers the problem of cross-domain recommendations from a single source domain. We extend upon this limitation and consider the more general case of having multiple source domains. Indeed, in the event that the bandit has access to several past topics or domains, their TCB algorithm would have to choose a single one to be the source to learn from.

3   Background

Throughout this paper, we use bold letters to denote a vector, e.g., $\mathbf{x}$, and capital bold letters to denote a matrix, e.g., $\mathbf{A}$. We use $||\mathbf{x}||_2$ to define the ℓ_2-norm of a vector $\mathbf{x} \in \mathbb{R}^d$. For a positive definite matrix $\mathbf{A} \in \mathbb{R}^{d \times d}$, we define the weighted ℓ_2-norm of $\mathbf{x} \in \mathbb{R}^d$ to be $||\mathbf{x}||_\mathbf{A} = \sqrt{\mathbf{x}^\mathrm{T} \mathbf{A} \mathbf{x}}$. We define the operation $\mathbf{A} \oplus \mathbf{B}$ as the row concatenation of matrices $\mathbf{A}$ and $\mathbf{B}$ and $\mathbf{a} \oplus \mathbf{b}$ as the regular concatenation of vectors $\mathbf{a}$ and $\mathbf{b}$. The notation $|\mathbf{x}|$ represents the magnitude of a vector $\mathbf{x}$. Finally, we denote $diag(\mathbf{v})$ the operation of making a square diagonal matrix with the elements of vector $\mathbf{v}$ on the main diagonal.

We revisit the linear contextual bandit (LinUCB) [6]. Formally, there is a set of users u also known as "bandit players" and a set of arms $a \in \mathcal{A}$ that are the items to be recommended. At time t, a user u comes in with the set of arm $\mathcal{A}$, and the bandit observes the contextual feature vector $\mathbf{x}_{t,a} \in \mathbb{R}^d$ for arm a, that represents the information of both the user and the arm. LinUCB assumes that the expected reward for each action is linear in its d-dimensional features $\mathbf{x}_{t,a}$ with some unknown coefficient vector $\boldsymbol{\theta}_a^*$.

The algorithm chooses an arm $a_t \in \mathcal{A}$ to recommend, observes the reward $r_{t,a} = \langle \boldsymbol{\theta}_a^*, \mathbf{x}_{t,a} \rangle + \epsilon_t$ where ϵ_t is the noise term, and then updates its arm recommendation strategy with the new observation $(\mathbf{x}_{t,a_t}, a_t, r_{t,a_t})$. LinUCB applies ridge regression to estimate the true coefficients. Let $D_a \in \mathbb{R}^{m_a \times d}$ denote the context of the historical observations when arm a is selected and $\mathbf{b}_a \in \mathbb{R}^{m_a}$ denote the relative rewards. The regularised least-square estimator for $\boldsymbol{\theta}_a$ could be expressed as:

$$\hat{\boldsymbol{\theta}}_a = \arg\min_{\boldsymbol{\theta} \in \mathbb{R}^d} \left(\sum_{i=1}^{m_a} (r_{i,a} - \langle \boldsymbol{\theta}, D_a(i,:) \rangle)^2 + \lambda ||\boldsymbol{\theta}||_2^2 \right) \tag{1}$$

where λ is the penalty factor of the ridge regression. The solution to Eq. 1 is:

$$\hat{\boldsymbol{\theta}}_a = (D_a^T D_a + \lambda I_d)^{-1} D_a^T \mathbf{b}_a \tag{2}$$

Li et al. [12] derived a confidence interval that contains the true expected reward. Following the rule of optimism in the face of uncertainty for linear bandits (OFUL), this confidence bound leads to a reasonable arm-selection strategy:

$$a_t = argmax_{a \in \mathcal{A}_t} \left(\hat{\boldsymbol{\theta}}_a^T \mathbf{x}_{t,a} + \alpha \sqrt{\mathbf{x}_{t,a}^T A_a^{-1} \mathbf{x}_{t,a}} \right) \tag{3}$$

where $A_a = D_a^T D_a + \lambda I_d$.

Formally, the expected reward at time t with arm a is expressed as $\mathbb{E}[r_{t,a}|\mathbf{x}_{t,a}] = \boldsymbol{\theta}_a^{*T} \mathbf{x}_{t,a}$. During the learning process, the algorithm only observes the reward of the chosen arm. The total reward by round t is defined as $\sum_t r_{t,a_t}$ while the optimal expected reward is defined as $\mathbb{E}[\sum_t r_{t,a^*}]$, where a^* indicates the arm that can achieve the optimal reward at time t. We call T-trial regret $R(T)$, the difference between the optimal reward and the observed reward over T rounds: $R(T) = \mathbb{E}[\sum_t r_{t,a^*}] - \mathbb{E}[\sum_t r_{t,a_t}]$. The contextual bandit algorithm balances exploration and exploitation to maximize the expected total reward. Equivalently, the algorithm aims to minimize the total regret.

4   T-LinUCB

4.1   Problem Overview

Consider the problem of recommending educational videos to a class of students. Formally, we model the personalized video recommendation as a contextual bandit problem, where each student t is a bandit player and each video $a \in \mathcal{A}$ is an arm. The videos are divided into $\mathcal{L}$ topics where each topic $l \in \mathcal{L}$ has a pool $\mathcal{A}_l$ of videos. Each video belongs to one **single** topic. We assume that the set of students remain unchanged across the topics. Given a topic $l \in \mathcal{L}$ and a student t, the goal of the bandit is to choose an arm $a \in \mathcal{A}_l$ that maximizes the reward. We further assume that each video a has a true unknown coefficient vector $\boldsymbol{\theta}_a^*$ that remains unchanged for the entirety of the topic. Thus, similarly to a typical contextual bandit problem, the goal is to estimate the unknown coefficient vector $\boldsymbol{\theta}_a^*$ for each video of the current topic l. However, unlike a typical contextual bandit problem, the arm pool $\mathcal{A}$ changes from one topic to another, meaning that the unknown coefficient vectors $\boldsymbol{\theta}_a^*$ have to be re-estimated. LinUCB algorithm is not designed to handle changing coefficient vectors $\boldsymbol{\theta}_a^*$. Indeed, for each individual topic $l \in \mathcal{L}$, a new LinUCB algorithm has to be re-started, where it would have to learn the new estimates of $\boldsymbol{\theta}_a^*$ from scratch again. Such an approach would yield lower performances.

We intend to tackle the problem of cross-domain recommendations and to solve these limitations of LinUCB by utilizing observations acquired from past topics to initialize the parameters of the new arms. The bandit therefore possesses knowledge upon the start of a new topic which results in better performances and faster regret convergence when compared to a cold start situation.

4.2   Algorithm Design

Henceforth, we assume that we have $\mathcal{L}$ topics denoted by l ($l = 1, 2, ..., \mathcal{L}$) where each has a pool $\mathcal{A}_l$ of videos (or arms). We assume that the contextual feature vector of an arm a is denoted as $\mathbf{x}_a \in \mathbb{R}^n$. The contextual bandit algorithm runs in a sequential fashion for $t = 1, 2, ..., T$ given a particular topic $l \in \mathcal{L}$. At each time t, a student plays the bandit which reads the student's information and must choose an arm $a \in \mathcal{A}_l$ that maximizes the reward. We thus have the contextual feature vector $\mathbf{x}_{t,a} \in \mathbb{R}^d$ which encompasses both information from the user and the arm. We assume that the dimension of the vectors remains the same throughout and across all topics.

Algorithm 1. T-LinUCB

1: Input: $\alpha \in \mathbb{R}^+, k \in \mathbb{N}^+, l$
2: **for** $a \in \mathcal{A}_l$ **do**
3:     Observe contextual features of arm $a \in \mathcal{A}_l : \mathbf{x}_a \in \mathbb{R}^n$
4:     $\mathbf{A}_a, \mathbf{b}_a \leftarrow INIT(\mathbf{x}_a, k)$
5: **end for**
6: **for** $t = 1, 2, ..., T$ **do**
7:     **for** $a \in \mathcal{A}_l$ **do**
8:         Observe contextual features of arm $a \in \mathcal{A}_l : \mathbf{x}_{t,a} = (\mathbf{x}_t, \mathbf{x}_a) \in \mathbb{R}^d$
9:         $\hat{\boldsymbol{\theta}}_a \leftarrow (\mathbf{A}_a)^{-1} \mathbf{b}_a$
10:        $p_{t,a} \leftarrow \hat{\boldsymbol{\theta}}_a^{\mathrm{T}} \mathbf{x}_{t,a} + \alpha \sqrt{\mathbf{x}_{t,a}^{\mathrm{T}} (\mathbf{A}_a)^{-1} \mathbf{x}_{t,a}}$
11:    **end for**
12:    Choose arm $a_t = argmax_{a \in \mathcal{A}_l} p_{t,a}$ with ties broken arbitrarily, and observe a
       real-valued payoff r_{t,a_t}
13:    $\mathbf{A}_{a_t} \leftarrow \mathbf{A}_{a_t} + \mathbf{x}_{t,a_t} \mathbf{x}_{t,a_t}^{\mathrm{T}}$
14:    $\mathbf{b}_{a_t} \leftarrow \mathbf{b}_{a_t} + r_{t,a_t} \mathbf{x}_{t,a_t}$
15: **end for**

Algorithm 1 shows the main T-LinUCB algorithm. We first initialize all of the arms' parameters $(\mathbf{A}, \mathbf{b})$ of the current topic l using the historical observations from k historical topics (line 4). Once the arms are initialized, the algorithm runs as a traditional LinUCB. We show in Algorithm 2 the procedure that initializes the parameters $(\mathbf{A}, \mathbf{b})$ of an arm using historical observations. $\mathbf{D}_a$ represents a matrix of observations from k previous topic(s), $\mathbf{c}_a$ represents a vector of the corresponding historical responses, and $\mathbf{w}$ represents a vector of weights. We compute the similarity score between the current arm a of the current topic l

and every arms a_h in the k previous topics using the Euclidean distance between their respective contextual feature vector, i.e., $\mathbf{x}_a$ and $\mathbf{x}_{a_h}$ (line 6). Because we only make use of historical arms that share some degree of similarity in the feature space, we compare the resulting similarity scores to a threshold τ. The design matrix $\mathbf{D}_{a_h}$ and the corresponding response vector $\mathbf{c}_{a_h}$ of the most similar arms are then concatenated together to form the design matrix $\mathbf{D}_a$ and response vector $\mathbf{c}_a$ of the current arm (line 9–10).

Similarly, a weight vector $\mathbf{w}_{a_h}$ with values ranging from 0 to 1 stores the weight of all historical observations from arm a_h. The weight vector of arm a, $\mathbf{w}_a$, is the aggregation of the weight vector of all similar arms (line 11–12). We consider that the more recent an observation is, the more valuable it is and therefore the larger its weight should be. The impact of the observation in the previous topics will thus decay with the time interval according to the following formula (line 10) of Algorithm 2:

$$w = exp(-\frac{p||\mathbf{x}_a - \mathbf{x}_{a_h}||_2}{2\eta^2})$$

where η is a parameter that controls the decaying speed. We then create a diagonal matrix $\mathbf{W}_a$ with the elements of the vector $\mathbf{w}_a$ on the main diagonal. The weight matrix $\mathbf{W}_a$ along with the design matrix $\mathbf{D}_a$ and the corresponding response vector $\mathbf{c}_a$ are then used to initialize the arm's parameters $\mathbf{A}_a$ and $\mathbf{b}_a$ (line 17–18). Additionally, τ is computed from the average similarity scores and their standard deviation as follows: $\tau = \bar{s} + \gamma \, \sigma$ where $\bar{s}$ is the average of the similarity scores and σ is their standard deviation. The threshold τ has a parameter γ that controls the weight of the standard deviation. Specifically, the higher it is, the more restrictive the threshold becomes, and the smaller the number of similar arms we will make use of.

4.3   Regret Analysis

There are several works that give detailed regret analysis on the non-stationary environments. Among them, [16] has the most similar setting as ours. It assigns time-decaying weight to previous observations and obtains $O(d^{2/3}B_T^{1/3}T^{2/3})$ regret bound, where d represents the feature dimension, T represents time horizon, and $B_T = \sum_{s=1}^{T-1} ||\theta_s^* - \theta_{s+1}^*||_2$ denotes the variation budget of the coefficients.

In previous works, the change-points of the reward function are usually unknown in advance. However, in the recommendation process discussed in our paper each transformation of the topic will raise an abrupt change of the reward function, which means that we are able to know each changing time point beforehand. Thus T-LinUCB could be regarded as an oracle linear bandit algorithm that restarts LinUCB algorithm with historical observations as side information at each changing point. It helps us get rid of the variation budget of the coefficients and achieve a long-term regret bound of $\tilde{O}(d^{1/2}T^{1/2})$. From the experiment section we can see that in most cases the regret of T-LinUCB is significantly less

---

Algorithm 2. Initialize - Get the initialized matrix related to each arm

---

1: $INIT(\mathbf{x}_a, k)$
2: $\mathbf{D}_a \leftarrow \mathbf{0}_{0 \times d}, \mathbf{c}_a \leftarrow [\,], \mathbf{w}_a \leftarrow [\,]$
3: **for** $p = 1, ..., k$ **do**
4:      Observe contextual features of all arms $a_h \in \mathcal{A}_p : \mathbf{x}_{a_h} \in \mathbb{R}^n$
5:      **for** $a_h \in \mathcal{A}_{l-p}$ **do**
6:          $SIM(\mathbf{x}_a, \mathbf{x}_{a_h}) = ||\mathbf{x}_a - \mathbf{x}_{a_h}||_2$
7:          **if** $SIM(\mathbf{x}_a, \mathbf{x}_{a_h}) \geq \tau$ **then**
8:              $\mathbf{D}_a = \mathbf{D}_a \oplus \mathbf{D}_{a_h}$
9:              $\mathbf{c}_a = \mathbf{c}_a \oplus \mathbf{c}_{a_h}$
10:             $w = exp(-\frac{p||\mathbf{x}_a - \mathbf{x}_{a_h}||_2}{2\eta^2})$
11:             $\mathbf{w}_{a_h} \leftarrow w_{|\mathbf{c}_{a_h}| \times 1}$
12:             $\mathbf{w}_a = \mathbf{w}_a \oplus \mathbf{w}_{a_h}$
13:          **end if**
14:      **end for**
15:      $\mathbf{W}_a \leftarrow diag(\mathbf{w}_a)$
16: **end for**
17: $\mathbf{A}_a \leftarrow \mathbf{D}_a^T \mathbf{W}_a \mathbf{D}_a + \lambda \mathbf{I}_d$
18: $\mathbf{b}_a \leftarrow \mathbf{D}_a^T \mathbf{W}_a \mathbf{c}_a$
19: **return** $\mathbf{A}_a, \mathbf{b}_a$

---

than LinUCB algorithm for each topic and enjoys a faster convergence speed. One disadvantage for T-LinUCB is that the computational complexity might be higher since it needs to incorporate historical information when initializing observation matrices and conducting matrix multiplication.

5 Experimental Evaluation

5.1 Experiment Setup

Simulated Dataset. We evaluate the performances of our approach on a simulated dataset that fits our scenario and allows us to model a change of topic. Our simulated environment combines both of the following publicly available datasets.

- **Adult dataset:** The Adult dataset [7] is composed of 31,561 instances: 21,790 males and 10,771 females, each having 8 categorical variables (work class, education, marital status, occupation, relationship, race, sex, native-country) and 3 continuous variables (age, education number, hours per week), yielding an overall of 107 features after one-hot encoding.
- **YouTube dataset:** The Statistics and Social Network of YouTube Videos[1] is composed of 4,522 instances separated into four categories: Comedy (1,580),

---

[1] https://netsg.cs.sfu.ca/youtubedata/.

Music (1,819), Sports (932), and Travel & Places (191). Each instance has 6 categorical features (age of video, length of video, number of views, rate, ratings, number of comments), yielding a total of 25 features after one-hot encoding.

Our users (bandit players) are represented using the Adult dataset. For our experiments we use a subset of 10,000 instances drawn randomly and we assume that the set of users remain unchanged across topics. Similarly, our videos (or arms) are represented through the Youtube dataset. For our experiments we will be using several topics which are each represented by a Youtube category. For each topic we select a random subset as our pool of videos to recommend. In particular, topic 1 uses 30 videos from the Comedy category, topic 2 uses 20 videos from the Music category, topic 3 uses 20 videos from the Sports category, and topic 4 uses 30 videos from the Travel & Places category. We reduce the dimensionality of both the user and video feature vectors through Principal Component Analysis (PCA) by choosing a number of components that explains 80% of the variance. Thereafter, the dimensions of the user feature vectors are reduced to 19 while the dimensions of the video feature vectors are reduced to 7. Throughout the experiment, we use the concatenation of both the user feature vector and the video feature vector as our contextual feature vector $\mathbf{x}_{t,a}$, yielding a total of 26 features.

Reward Functions. The reward mechanism follows that of LinUCB where the reward of an arm a is assumed to be the noisy linear combination of its context vector and unknown coefficient vector (also called unknown reward parameters vector) $\boldsymbol{\theta}_a^*$. Specifically $r_{t,a} = \langle \mathbf{x}_{t,a}, \boldsymbol{\theta}_a^* \rangle + \epsilon$ where ϵ is a random Gaussian noise, i.e., $\epsilon \sim \mathcal{N}(0, 0.01)$. For each arm within a topic, we generate the unknown coefficient vectors $\boldsymbol{\theta}_a^*$ by randomly drawing each of the 26 dimensions from a Gaussian distribution, i.e., $\mathcal{N}(0.5, \sigma)$ where σ is drawn randomly from a normal distribution, i.e., $\sigma \sim \mathcal{U}(0, 1)$. We then normalize the reward parameters such that the Manhattan norm of the vector is equal to 1. As a consequence, the reward generated in our setting is bounded between 0 and 1.

Evaluation Metric. We use the regret to evaluate the performances of the algorithms. Since the true reward function is known in our simulated environment, it is possible to compute the regret over T rounds: $R(T) = \mathbb{E}[\sum_t r_{t,a^*}] - \mathbb{E}[\sum_t r_{t,a_t}]$ where the first term is the optimal reward, and the second term is the observed reward at time t.

5.2   Experimental Results

Our intuition is that using prior knowledge from multiple topics can help initializing the parameters of the bandit for a new topic thereby circumventing the cold-start problem. To confirm our intuition, we compare the performances of our T-LinUCB algorithm to the classic LinUCB algorithm.

Impact of the Decaying Factor η. We first investigate the impact of the decaying factor η introduced in Algorithm 2 (line 10) on our first two topics and report the cumulative regret at topic 2 on Fig. 1. For this experiment, γ is set to 1 since we have not investigated its effect yet. As introduced in Sect. 4.2, η is a decaying factor that allows to control the weight of the historical observations. Specifically, the more recent the observations are, the larger the weights are. Our intuition is that larger weights will speed up the learning process thereby decreasing the regret. As Fig. 1 shows, the higher η is, the lower the regret is at topic 2. Indeed, with an η close to 0, the weights of the historical observations are almost nil, T-LinUCB will thus behave as a regular LinUCB, achieving a regret of 362.45. The regret stabilizes when η reaches 2, with a regret oscillating between 106.13 and 101.33. These empirical results confirm our intuition that historical observations with larger weights provides the bandit with stronger knowledge and therefore accelerates the learning of the unknown coefficients θ_a^*.

Impact of the Parameter γ. As introduced in Sect. 4.2, γ is used in the computation of the threshold τ as a parameter to control the weight of the standard deviation. A higher γ yields a higher value of τ, which translates into making the algorithm more restrictive as to the inclusion of an arm into the historical data. Therefore, γ has a direct impact on the number of similar arms to consider. We aim at understanding the impact of γ on our algorithm. We run T-LinUCB with the first two topics with various values of γ ranging from 0.0 to 3, and compare their performances. We report the cumulative regret at topic 2 for various γ on Fig. 2. For this experiment, η is set to 5 as per the results achieved previously.

As shown on Fig. 2, a large regret is achieved when γ is either too small or too large (313.74 for $\gamma = 0$, 319.5 for $\gamma = 0.5$, 252.58 for $\gamma = 1.5$, 361 for $\gamma = 2$ and 3). Indeed, in the former case a large number of arms satisfy the threshold condition (Alg. 2 line 7), yielding too many arms to be deemed similar enough. Considering a large number of arms will introduce noisy observations and negatively impact the performances of T-LinUCB. Conversely, on the latter case, very few arms satisfy the threshold condition, yielding a lower number of arms to be considered. Consequently, T-LinUCB does not have sufficient information to initialize the arms in the current topic, and will behave similarly to a traditional LinUCB. Finally, the performances of T-LinUCB are drastically improved with γ being close to 1. Indeed, when $\gamma = 1.1$ the regret at topic 2 drops to 100.4 In such a case the bandit collects sufficient historical observations that help it initialize the parameters of the arms of the new topic by taking full advantage of the past. This experiment shows that γ, which controls the number of similar arms to use, plays an important role in the initialization process that can severely affect the performances of T-LinUCB. While a low value of γ brings noisy observations, a high value of γ allows not enough historical observations to be used for initialization.

Robustness to the Change of the Unknown Coefficient Vectors. We investigate the robustness of our T-LinUCB algorithm to the degree of change

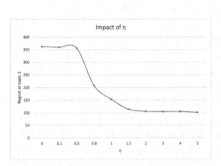

Fig. 1. Regret for various values of η

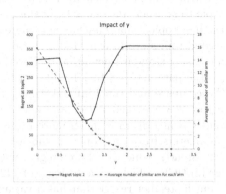

Fig. 2. Regret for various values of γ

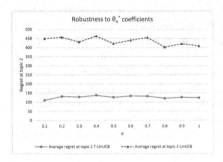

Fig. 3. Regret for various value of σ

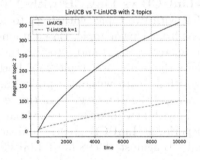

Fig. 4. Regret with two topics

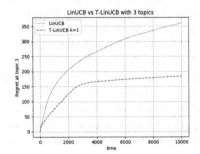

Fig. 5. Regret with three topics

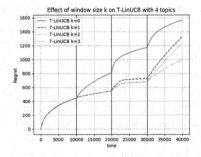

Fig. 6. Regret with various k size

of the unknown coefficient vectors (or unknown reward parameters), $\boldsymbol{\theta}_a^*$, from one topic to another. Particularly, in this setting, the unknown coefficient vectors of the first topic remain unchanged whereas the unknown coefficient vectors of the second topics are drawn randomly from a Gaussian distribution $\mathcal{N}(0.5, \sigma)$ with increasing standard deviation σ. Based upon our previous empirical results, we set the parameters η to 1.1 and γ to 5 as they achieved the best performances. We compare and run LinUCB versus T-LinUCB ten times per value of σ and report the averaged regret at topic 2 in Fig. 3. As depicted in Fig. 3, our T-LinUCB algorithm is much more robust to the degree of change of the reward parameters from one topic to another than LinUCB is. Indeed, our algorithm consistently achieves a lower regret with an average of 126.99 against 307.916 for LinUCB, which has a decrease of 142.45%. Furthermore, T-LinUCB achieves a much steadier regret that has a variance of 87.35 against 342.87 for LinUCB. These results confirm that our T-LinUCB is robust to the change of reward parameters and that it not only achieves a much lower regret than LinUCB but also maintains a consistent regret.

T-LinUCB vs LinUCB with 2 Topics. We compare our algorithm to Lin-UCB with two topics with k set to 1, that is, our algorithm only uses observations from 1 prior topic. Based upon our previous empirical results, we set the parameters η to 1.1 and γ to 5 as they achieved the best performances. Figure 4 shows the regret over topic 2 for both LinUCB and our T-LinUCB. Since both algorithms learn without a-priori knowledge during topic 1, they are expected to achieve the same regret. In the second topic, however, the arm pool changes along with new unknown reward parameters, $\boldsymbol{\theta}_a^*$. As Fig. 4 shows, our approach outperforms LinUCB greatly and achieves a much lower regret of 359.29 for LinUCB against 100.08 for T-LinUCB.

T-LinUCB Vs LinUCB with 3 Topics. We check the long-term benefit of our approach by running the same experiment using three topics instead of two. We report the regret at topic 3 for both LinUCB and our T-LinUCB on Fig. 5. Similarly to the previous scenario, LinUCB will start learning from scratch for all three topics while T-LinUCB will make use of historical observations from topic 1 when switching to topic 2, and from topic 2 when switching to topic 3. We notice on Fig. 5 that, as expected, T-LinUCB outperforms LinUCB. Indeed, the former achieves a regret of 361.87 at topic 3 against 184.02 for the latter. Moreover, we can see that LinUCB has not converged after $T = 10,000$ rounds, which indicates that it is still learning, as opposed to T-LinUCB which converges much faster, emphasizing yet another benefit of our approach. Our experiments demonstrate the benefits of using prior knowledge to avoid the cold-start problem. By initializing the parameters of the bandit in the new topic, the bandit already possesses knowledge that speeds up the estimation of the unknown reward parameters $\boldsymbol{\theta}_a^*$, yielding a much lower regret.

Impact of the Number of Historical Topic k. We investigate how k affects our T-LinUCB. k controls the number of prior topics to learn from (Algorithm 2, line 4). We run T-LinUCB with 4 topics with $k = 0, 1, 2, 3$. We report the cumulative regret over all four topics on Fig. 6 wherein a vertical blue line indicates the start of a new topic. Based upon our previous empirical results, we set the parameters η to 1.1 and γ to 5 as they achieved the best performances. Figure 6 shows that all T-LinUCB instances that learn from prior knowledge outperform the baseline LinUCB (i.e., T-LinUCB with k=0). A regular LinUCB learns from scratch at each new topic, yielding a very high regret of 1567.98 at topic 4. When k is set to 1, T-LinUCB achieves a regret of 1328.96 at topic 4. With a k set to 2, T-LinUCB greatly outperforms both LinUCB and T-LinUCB $k=1$, with a regret of 996.05 at topic 4. Surprisingly enough, with k set to 3, T-LinUCB achieves a regret of 1229.96 at topic 4, which outperforms both LinUCB and T-LinUCB $k = 1$, but performs slightly under T-LinUCB $k = 2$. This could be due to the fact that historical observations that are too obsolete can introduce noisy information. Figure 6 noticeably shows the advantage of using historical knowledge from multiple topics to circumvent the cold-start problem and speed up the learning of the bandit. Indeed, the regret difference between LinUCB and T-LinUCB $k = 2$ is substantial at topic 4. The knowledge acquired from topics 1 and 2 by T-LinUCB allows it to estimate the unknown reward parameters more rapidly, thereby decreasing the regret drastically. The experimental results confirm our intuition that learning from multiple topics not only overcome the cold-start problem, but also allows it to converge faster.

6   Conclusions

We have developed a new contextual bandit algorithm that leverages historical observations from prior domain(s) to overcome the cold-start problem of personalized recommendation. Through the use of prior observations from multiple source domain(s) for initalization of the new arm's parameters, our T-LinUCB algorithm speeds up the learning of the unknown reward parameters and greatly improves the regret of the algorithm. Furthermore, our regret analysis showed that our approach achieves the same regret bound as the oracle linear bandit algorithm under the changing environment. Finally, our experimental results showed that T-LinUCB achieves a much lower regret and benefit from a faster convergence speed than the traditional LinUCB algorithm.

Acknowledgments. This work was supported in part by NSF 1937010 and 1940093.

References

1. Agrawal, S., Goyal, N.: Thompson sampling for contextual bandits with linear payoffs. In: International Conference on Machine Learning, pp. 127–135 (2013)
2. Berry, D.A., Fristedt, B.: Bandit problems: sequential allocation of experiments (monographs on statistics and applied probability), vol. 5(71–87), p. 7. Chapman and Hall, London (1985)

3. Bouneffouf, D., Bouzeghoub, A., Gançarski, A.L.: A contextual-bandit algorithm for mobile context-aware recommender system. In: Huang, T., Zeng, Z., Li, C., Leung, C.S. (eds.) ICONIP 2012. LNCS, vol. 7665, pp. 324–331. Springer, Heidelberg (2012). https://doi.org/10.1007/978-3-642-34487-9_40

4. Bouneffouf, D., Rish, I., Aggarwal, C.: Survey on applications of multi-armed and contextual bandits. In: 2020 IEEE Congress on Evolutionary Computation (CEC), pp. 1–8. IEEE (2020)

5. Chapelle, O., Li, L.: An empirical evaluation of thompson sampling. In: Advances in Neural Information Processing Systems, pp. 2249–2257 (2011)

6. Chu, W., Li, L., Reyzin, L., Schapire, R.: Contextual bandits with linear payoff functions. In: Proceedings of the Fourteenth International Conference on Artificial Intelligence and Statistics pp. 208–214 (2011)

7. Dua, D., Graff, C.: UCI machine learning repository (2017). http://archive.ics.uci.edu/ml

8. Fernández-Tobías, I., Cantador, I., Kaminskas, M., Ricci, F.: Cross-domain recommender systems: A survey of the state of the art. In: Spanish Conference on Information Retrieval pp. 1–12. sn (2012)

9. Huang, W., Labille, K., Wu, X., Lee, D., Heffernan, N.: Achieving user-side fairness in contextual bandits. CoRR abs/2010.12102 (2020), https://arxiv.org/abs/2010.12102

10. Langford, J., Zhang, T.: The epoch-greedy algorithm for multi-armed bandits with side information. In: Advances in Neural Information Processing Systems, pp. 817–824 (2008)

11. Lazaric, A., Brunskill, E., et al.: Sequential transfer in multi-armed bandit with finite set of models. In: Advances in Neural Information Processing Systems pp. 2220–2228 (2013)

12. Li, L., Chu, W., Langford, J., Schapire, R.E.: A contextual-bandit approach to personalized news article recommendation. In: Proceedings of the 19th International Conference on World Wide Web, pp. 661–670 (2010)

13. Liu, B., Wei, Y., Zhang, Y., Yan, Z., Yang, Q.: Transferable contextual bandit for cross-domain recommendation. In: AAAI (2018)

14. Nguyen, H.T., Kofod-Petersen, A.: Using multi-armed bandit to solve cold-start problems in recommender systems at telco. In: Prasath, R., O'Reilly, P., Kathirvalavakumar, T. (eds.) MIKE 2014. LNCS (LNAI), vol. 8891, pp. 21–30. Springer, Cham (2014). https://doi.org/10.1007/978-3-319-13817-6_3

15. Nguyen, T.T., Lauw, H.W.: Dynamic clustering of contextual multi-armed bandits. In: Proceedings of the 23rd ACM International Conference on Conference on Information and Knowledge Management, pp. 1959–1962 (2014)

16. Russac, Y., Vernade, C., Cappé, O.: Weighted linear bandits for non-stationary environments. In: Advances in Neural Information Processing Systems. pp, 12040–12049 (2019)

17. Tang, L., Jiang, Y., Li, L., Li, T.: Ensemble contextual bandits for personalized recommendation. In: Proceedings of the 8th ACM Conference on Recommender Systems, pp. 73–80 (2014)

18. Zhang, J., Bareinboim, E.: Transfer learning in multi-armed bandit: a causal approach. In: Proceedings of the 16th Conference on Autonomous Agents and Multi-Agent Systems, pp. 1778–1780 (2017)

19. Zhou, Q., Zhang, X., Xu, J., Liang, B.: Large-scale bandit approaches for recommender systems. In: International Conference on Neural Information Processing. pp. 811–821. Springer (2017)

Modeling Hierarchical Intents and Selective Current Interest for Session-Based Recommendation

Mengfei Zhang[1,2], Cheng Guo[1,2], Jiaqi Jin[1,2], Mao Pan[1,2], and Jinyun Fang[1(✉)]

[1] Institute of Computing Technology, Chinese Academy of Sciences, Beijing, China
{zhangmengfei,guocheng18s,jinjiaqi19b,panmao17b,fangjy}@ict.ac.cn
[2] University of Chinese Academy of Sciences, Beijing, China

Abstract. Session-based recommendation is a challenging problem due to the limited session data. In the real scene, there are two insights in sessions: (1) **Hierarchical intents**: the implicit hierarchy in user preference is a common phenomenon, since users usually click a specific item with a general intent. (2) **The influence of the current interest**: the items that users click in order have sequence dependencies, and the next item is affected by the current operation. However, recent approaches are all inherently flat and neglect the hierarchical intents. Besides, they neglect the truly related subsequence for modeling the current interest. This can lead to inaccurate user intents, and fail when the user's next click tendency falls into the more general intent. In this paper, we propose a method modeling from both Hierarchical Intents and Selective Sequential Interests (HISSI). Methodologically, we design a general intent abstractor to extract the common features and transmit general intents through the hierarchy to form fine-to-coarse grained intents. In addition, a selector-GRU is proposed to model the user's subsequence behavior that is related to the last click without noises. Extensive experiments on three real-world datasets verify our model's effectiveness.

Keywords: Recommender system · Session-based recommendation · Hierarchical intent · General intent learning · Sequential tendency

1 Introduction

Session-based Recommender Systems (SRS) are becoming increasingly indispensable in helping anonymous users discover their interests. The SRS task is to predict the next item that the user is probably interested in solely based on the actions, i.e., clicks, of the current session. Existing studies have investigated various factors that might influence SRS performances, e.g., sequential patterns ch33hidasi2015session, item transitions/relations [19,20], local/global interests [7,9], etc. Despite the success of these methods, predicting the next action from the limited user behavior data is still a challenging task.

To illustrate, Fig. 1 depicts a session sequence from a real-world ecommence system (e.g. Taobao), where two insights are revealed: (1) **Hierarchical intent**,

© Springer Nature Switzerland AG 2021
K. Karlapalem et al. (Eds.): PAKDD 2021, LNAI 12713, pp. 411–422, 2021.
https://doi.org/10.1007/978-3-030-75765-6_33

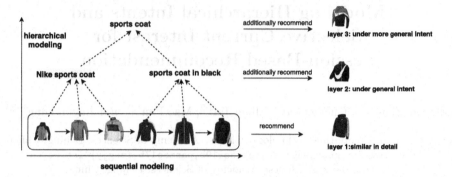

Fig. 1. A session sequence with several items sharing common features. For example, the user first clicks three Nike sport coats, and then clicks black sport coats with similar styles. We can model this implicit commonness, thus forming hierarchical preference. Then the method can recommend the next items that the user prefer, such as Nike sport coat in black and other styles coat.

In reality, the implicit hierarchy in user preference is a common phenomenon, since users usually click on a specific item with a general intention. For example, the overall goal of the user is to buy a sports coat, and the more fine-grained intents are a certain brand or style of sport coats. Finally, these purposes are reflected by several specific behaviors, which represent the user's personalized taste for items of different colors, styles or prices. (2) **The influence of the current interest**, the items that users click in order have sequence dependencies, and the next item is affected by the current operation. For instance, if the user has the intent to buy a sport coat and the current action is to click an Adidas coat in black, then the user is very likely to visit another brand or the same style of sport coats at the next timestep. Based on the above insights, it is important to learn both hierarchical intents and the accurate expression of current interest for better recommendation performance.

However, recent works ignore the hierarchical intent modeling and haven't accurately capture the current interest: (1) Although recent successful GNN-based methods [10,19,20] deploy multiple layers on the graph and capture complex transitions of items, the graph structure only helps make the items in a session tend to be homogeneous and smooth the item representations. CNN-based models [14,15] use convolutional filters to model sequential patterns instead of hierarchical intent. (2) STAMP [9] proposes to consider the last click as the current interest. However, it is insufficient since it ignores other items related to the last click in the sequence. RNN-based models [5,7] consider the last hidden state as the current interest, which probably introduces noise items. In essence, GNN and RNN based methods are all inherently flat in modeling SRS as they only propagate information across the edges of the graph or the time order of the sequence. These flat modeling methods can only recommend items with similar details, while they will fail when the user's next click falls into the second or even the third layer of more general intent. In summary, all of these methods are inherently flat and ignore the hierarchical intent. Besides, the existing methods are inaccurate to model the current interest and neglect the influence of other items that are truly associated with the last click item.

To address these problems, in this paper, we propose a method modeling from both Hierarchical Intents and Selective Sequential Interests (HISSI). The hierarchical intention is reflected in the gradual generalization of user intention from fine-grained to coarse-grained. Selective sequence interest carefully identifies the subset related to the last item to remove the noise items and represent the current interest more accurately. Specifically, we design a *General Intent Abstractor* (GIA) to extract the common features among items and transmit them through the hierarchy of layers. Furthermore, we propose a *Selector Gated Recurrent Unit* (SGRU) to model the session's current interest more accurately by employing a subset selector before the items are input into the GRU. Finally, HISSI fuses the output of GIA and SGRU to force the final session representation to consider both the intention of different granularities and the influence of current sequence preference. We conduct experiments and verify the effectiveness of our model, and make some detailed analysis.

To summarize, the major contributions of this paper are listed as follows: (1) We propose a Hierarchical Intents and Selective Sequential Interests (HISSI) modeling method for SRS. The method models the fine-to-coarse grained intents representation from the bottom up and identifies the current interest from accurate subsequence. (2) In HISSI, we design a general intent abstractor and a selector-GRU to address the hierarchical intention and inaccurate modeling of current interest problem, respectively. (3) Extensive experiments on three e-commerce datasets show that our method outperforms state-of-the-art baselines.

2   Related Work

In this section, we illustrate some related works about the proposed model, including conventional methods, deep learning-based methods.

Conventional studies on SRS can be classified into neighbor-based methods [1,12] and Markov chains (MC) based methods [11]. For example, Item-KNN [12] considers the item similarities to find the nearest neighbor. FPMC [11] combines MC and Matrix Factorization (MF) to capture both sequential behaviors and general interests.

In recent years, deep learning has achieved great success in many fields including recommender systems. Recent researches focus on leveraging RNN and consider the items as a sequence. GRU4Rec [5] firstly uses RNN to handle this problem. Improved-GRU4Rec [13] introduces four optimization methods for GRU4Rec, in which the data augmentation strategy has a great impact on later works. Later, NARM [7] proposes to integrate attention mechanism into RNN which can calculate the importance of each item and capture the main purpose. After that, MLP and attention based method STAMP [9] emphasizes the long-term interests and current interest. However, it simply takes the last click as the current interest, which is insufficient for accurate recommendation. Afterward, recent works highlight the item transitions and use graph neural networks

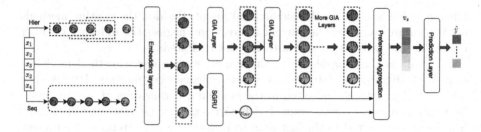

Fig. 2. The framework of HISSI.

(GNN) to learn the sessions [2,19,20]. For example, SR-GNN [19] proposes to use a gated graph neural network [8] to learn the item transitions. GC-SAN [20] extends the model by combining the self-attention network [16] and GNN to enhance the performance. LESSR [2] handles the lossy encoding problem and the ineffective long-range dependency capturing problem by preserving the edge-order and adding shortcut connections of the graph. Furthermore, some studies show neighborhood-based methods in neural networks can still provide compet-itive results. CSRM [17] exploits collaborative information to better predict the intent by investigating neighborhood sessions based on NARM.

3   Problem Formulation

Let $\mathcal{I} = \{i_1, i_2, ..., i_{|N|}\}$ denote the set of all unique items and $|N|$ be the total number of items. For an anonymous click session, the clicked sequence $X = [x_1, ..., x_t, ..., x_n]$ is ordered by timestamps, where $x_t \in \mathcal{I}$ is an item that a user clicks at timestep t. We build a model and output the probability $\hat{y}$ of all candidate items in $\mathcal{I}$. The items with top-k scores are the final recommendations.

4   Method

The architecture of HISSI is illustrated in Fig. 2. HISSI contains three main parts: (1) the GIA module which models the hierarchical session specific-to-general intents, and each level of intent is extracted by a GIA layer. (2) the *Selector GRU* (SGRU) models the current interest through selecting a subset of items from the session and applying GRU to learn the subsequence. (3) the *Preference Generation* (PG) aggregates the hierarchical intents, and takes current interest into account when making recommendations.

These three main modules work together to make the model have the abil-ity of learning hierarchical intents, and the user's intents also benefit from the influence of recent behavior tendency. Next, we introduce each part in detail.

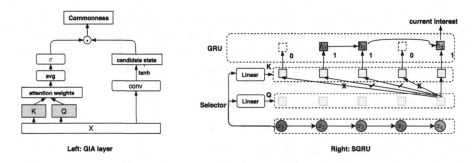

Fig. 3. The General Intent Abstractor (GIA) and the Selector-GRU (SGRU).

4.1 Embedding Layer

The embedding layer maps the item into low-dimensional dense vectors by matrix $\mathbf{E} \in \mathbb{R}^{|N| \times d}$, where d is the dimension. We first encode the item i ($i \in \mathcal{I}$) as a one-hot vector $\mathbf{e}_i \in \mathbb{R}^{|N|}$, then the embedding vector of item i is denoted by $\mathbf{x}_i = \mathbf{E}\mathbf{e}_i$. Afterwards, the item sequence are represented as $\mathbf{X} = [\mathbf{x}_1, \ldots \mathbf{x}_n] \in \mathbb{R}^{n \times d}$.

4.2 General Intent Abstractor

The General Intent Abstractor (GIA) in Fig. 3 (left) module aims to identify the fine-to-coarse grained intents successively. Technically, each GIA layer contains a commonness gate and a convolution operation. The commonness gate controls how many common features should be passed through the hierarchy of layers to form high-level intent. To calculate the importance of each item, we need to calculate the correlation between items. Inspired by the self-attention mechanism [16], we first calculate the pairwise similarity between each item and other items. Then we average the similarity matrix to get the distance between each item and other items. Intuitively, if an item has a relatively small similarity with other items, it indicates that the item is far from the main intent of the session. On the contrary, the item may have more in commonness with others. We apply the sigmoid function to get the commonness gate $\mathbf{g}_t$:

$$\mathbf{g}_t = \text{sigmoid}(\frac{1}{n-1} \sum_{j=1,j \neq t}^{n} \mathbf{M}_{tj}) \tag{1}$$
$$\mathbf{M} = \mathbf{Q}_s \mathbf{K}_s^T,$$

where $\mathbf{Q}_s \in \mathbb{R}^{n \times d}$ and $\mathbf{K}_s \in \mathbb{R}^{n \times d}$ are transformed from the session sequence $\mathbf{X}$ by two weight matrices. $\mathbf{M} \in \mathbb{R}^{n \times n}$ indicates the similarity matrix.

To capture the effective common features among items that affect user behaviors. We generate the current candidate state representation as follows:

$$\widetilde{\mathbf{H}_l} = \tanh(\mathbf{W}_f * \mathbf{Z}_{l-1} + \mathbf{b}_1), \tag{2}$$

where $*$ is the convolution operation, and $\mathbf{b}_1$ is a constant bias. $\mathbf{W}_f$ is a 1D convolutional filter with kernel size k. $\mathbf{Z}_{l-1}$ is the $(l-1)_{th}$ layer's item input, and we make $\mathbf{Z}_0 = \mathbf{X}$. We use a left $(k-1)$ zero-padding to make the sequence $\mathbf{Z}_{l-1}$ fixed length and prevent the kernels from seeing future items. $\widetilde{\mathbf{H}_l}$ is the extracted the common features of the items in each layer. We output the l_{th} layer by multiplying commonness gate with $\widetilde{\mathbf{H}_l}$:

$$\mathbf{Z}_l = \mathbf{g}_t \odot \widetilde{\mathbf{H}_l}, \tag{3}$$

where $\odot$ is element-wise multiply.

The user's intent in a session is generally concentrated. Related fine-grained intent will be further abstracted to more general intent. In the bottom layer of GIA, only local specific interests which are reflected by continuous clicks are captured within a small-scale span. With the layers upper, the receptive field is enlarged and intents among more wide context windows are extracted.

To generate certain-grained intent representation, a self attentive-pooling operation is performed by assigning different importance to each item. The attention score and the intent representation at layer l are defined as follows:

$$\alpha_i - \text{softmax}(\mathbf{q}^\top \tanh(\mathbf{W}_l \mathbf{z}_{l,i} + \mathbf{b}_2)),$$
$$\mathbf{v}_l = \sum_{i=1}^{n} \alpha_i \mathbf{z}_{l,t}, \tag{4}$$

where $\mathbf{q}, \mathbf{b}_2 \in \mathbb{R}^d$, and $\mathbf{W}_l \in \mathbb{R}^{d \times d}$ is a weight parameter. $\mathbf{z}_{l,t} \in \mathbb{R}^d$ is the item representation at timestep t in the l_{th} layer.

4.3   Selector-GRU

The Selector-GRU (SGRU) in Fig. 3 (right) aims to model current interest more accurately by removing noise items. Inspired by the selective mechanism [3], we implement a selector, which can select a subset of items related to the last click item. On top of the selector, we conduct a GRU to learn the subsequence, and generate the current interest representation. Technically, we calculate the correlation score between each item and the last item, and derive a selection action decision. The item will be selected as one element of the subset when the decision is 1. Otherwise, if the decision is 0, the item will be discarded. The similarity scores between the last item and other items are represented as $\mathbf{A}_n$:

$$\mathbf{A}_n = (\mathbf{X}\mathbf{W_q})(\mathbf{W_k}\mathbf{x_n}), \tag{5}$$

where $\mathbf{W_q} \in \mathbb{R}^{d \times d}$ and $\mathbf{W_k} \in \mathbb{R}^{d \times d}$ are transformation matrices. To get the two cases of discrete 0 or 1 probability $(\pi(\mathbf{A}_n))$ and address the non-differentiable problem which is caused by discrete variables. Similarly to Gumbel-Softmax [6] distribution, we adopt the Gumbel-Sigmoid to decide whether to select or discard actions.

$$\text{Gumbel-Sigmoid}(\mathbf{A}_n) = \text{sigmoid}((\mathbf{A}_n + \mathbf{G}_1 - \mathbf{G}_2)/\tau),$$
$$= \frac{\exp((\mathbf{A}_n + \mathbf{G}_1)/\tau)}{\exp((\mathbf{A}_n + \mathbf{G}_1)/\tau) + \exp(\mathbf{G}_2/\tau)}, \tag{6}$$

where $\mathbf{G}_1 \in \mathbb{R}^n$ and $\mathbf{G}_2 \in \mathbb{R}^n$ are two independent Gumbel noises, τ is the temperature parameter. Then we conduct a GRU to learn sequential behaviors of the subset items:

$$\text{SGRU}(\boldsymbol{h}_{t-1}, \boldsymbol{x}_t) = \begin{cases} \text{GRU}(\boldsymbol{h}_{t-1}, \boldsymbol{x}_t) & \text{if } \pi(\mathbf{A}_n) = 1 \\ \boldsymbol{h}_{t-1} & \text{if } \pi(\mathbf{A}_n) = 0, \end{cases} \tag{7}$$

We regard the last hidden state as the current interest representation $\mathbf{v_{cur}}$.

4.4   Preference Generation

The different level of intent is represented as $\mathbf{v}_1, \mathbf{v}_2 \ldots \mathbf{v}_l$. To make the recommender decision considers both the hierarchical intents and the current interest. We first perform a sum aggregation on the multi-granularity intents, then we output the session preference $\mathbf{v}_s$ by combining the hierarchical and sequential vectors:

$$\mathbf{v_{hier}} = \sum_{l=1}^{L} \mathbf{v}_l, \qquad \mathbf{v}_s = \mathbf{W}_s[\mathbf{v_{hier}}; \mathbf{v_{cur}}], \tag{8}$$

where L is the total layer number, matrix $\mathbf{W}_s \in \mathbb{R}^{d \times 2d}$ compresses two combined embedding vectors into the latent space $\mathbb{R}^d$.

4.5   Prediction Layer

We use a dot product operation to get the match score $\hat{c}_i$ for each candidate item $x \in \mathcal{I}$ between its embedding $\mathbf{x}_i$ and the session representation $\mathbf{v_s}$. Then we use a softmax function to compute the probabilities of all candidate items:

$$\hat{\mathbf{y}} = \text{softmax}(\hat{\mathbf{c}}), \qquad \hat{c}_i = \mathbf{v_s}^\top \mathbf{x}_i, \tag{9}$$

where $\hat{\mathbf{c}} \in \mathbb{R}^{|N|}$ and $\hat{\mathbf{y}} \in \mathbb{R}^{|N|}$ denote the recommendation scores and probabilities over all items, respectively. Finally, our model is trained by minimizing the cross-entropy loss computed with the prediction and ground truth:

$$\mathcal{L}(\hat{\mathbf{y}}) = -\sum_{i=1}^{|N|} \mathbf{y}_i \log(\hat{\mathbf{y}}_i) + (1 - \mathbf{y}_i) \log(1 - \hat{\mathbf{y}}_i), \tag{10}$$

where $\mathbf{y}$ denotes the one-hot encoding vector of the ground truth item and we use the back-propagation through time (BPTT) algorithm to train our model.

5   Experiments

5.1   Evaluation Setup

We use three real-world benchmark datasets for evaluation, i.e. **Diginetica**[1], **Taobao**[2], **Yiwugo**[3]. Diginetica and Taobao are two public datasets and Yiwugo is a private dataset formed by the click behavior of wholesale users.

---

[1] http://cikm2016.cs.iupui.edu/cikm-cup.
[2] https://tianchi.aliyun.com/dataset/dataDetail?dataId=46.
[3] https://www.yiwugo.com.

After preprocessing operations the statistics of three datasets are shown in Table 1. We follow the session and item filter preprocess rules in [18]. We use 27 days for training and the rest 3 d for testing for Taobao and Yiwugo, while the rest 7 d for testing for Diginetica. We generate sequences and corresponding labels by splitting the input of length n into n-1 partial sessions. For example, given an session $[x_1, x_2, \ldots, x_n]$, we generate the inputs and labels $([x_1], x_2), ([x_1, x_2], x_3), \ldots, ([x_1, x_2, \ldots, x_{n-1}], x_n)$, where x_n refers the label.

Table 1. Statistic details of datasets used in the experiments.

Statistics	Diginetica	Taobao	Yiwugo
Training sessions	719,470	2,396,322	4,478,158
Test sessions	60,858	376,234	636,740
All the items	43,097	60,834	69,914
Average length of sessions	4.85	12.48	8.08
Average categories of sessions	1.38	3.69	3.61

We compare and analyze our model with the following representative methods: (1) **S-POP** recommends the top-N popular items in the current session. (2) **Item-KNN** [12] recommends items similar to the last item in the session. (3) **GRU4REC** [5] applies RNN to model user sessions. (4) **NARM** [7] employs GRU with an attention mechanism to encode the sessions' sequential pattern and main purpose. (5) **CSRM** [17] is a memory augmented approach which applies collaborative neighborhood information to SRS. (6) **SR-GNN** [19] considers the session as a graph and utilizes GGNN [8] to update item embeddings. (7) **LESSR** [2] handles the lossy encoding problem by preserving the edge-order and adding shortcut connections. (8) **MCPRN** [18] proposes to route each item into a specific channel, then represent the multi-purpose of a session through multiple RNNs. (9) **HLN** [4] proposes to model users' multiple preferences with subsequent group learning.

We evaluate our model with the classical Recall@k and MRR@k metrics for recommendation accuracy evaluation. We employ k = 20 and train the model three times to report the average test scores in terms of accuracy in Table 2.

For all baseline models, the parameters and initialization strategies are consistent with the corresponding papers and then we optimize the models in our datasets to obtain the best performance for fairness. For HISSI, we use Adam optimizer with the initial learning rate of 0.001 and decays by 0.1 after every 3 epochs. Moreover, the batch size is 100. The hidden vector size and embedding size d are both set to 100. We select other hyper-parameters on a validation set, which is a 10% subset of the training set. We set the number of channels in GIA to 100 and kernel size k to 3. We set the layer L to 3 and dropout p to 0.3. The temperature τ is set to 0.01.

Table 2. The performance (%) of HISSI with other baseline methods over three datasets. The best results are highlighted in boldface and the best results among the baselines are underlined.

Method	Diginetica		Taobao		Yiwugo	
	Recall	MRR	Recall	MRR	Recall	MRR
S-POP	19.24	12.73	21.55	11.82	23.08	16.75
Item-KNN	34.61	10.82	37. 14	15.89	32.77	21.70
GRU4Rec	29.75	8.49	46.57	27.69	46.53	32.60
NARM	49.66	16.87	51.04	31.01	58.11	46.54
CSRM	50.56	17.32	51.64	31.89	58.73	46.50
SR-GNN	50.73	17.59	51.42	32.36	59.21	46.28
LESSR	<u>51.71</u>	<u>18.15</u>	54.03	34.49	60.02	46.91
MCPRN	50.24	16.92	54.28	35.42	59.98	47.33
HLN	49.97	17.24	<u>54.97</u>	<u>36.73</u>	<u>60.36</u>	<u>47.89</u>
HISSI	**53.62**	**18.78**	**61.24**	**39.05**	**63.14**	**48.75**

5.2   Performance Comparison with Baselines

Table 2 presents the detailed performance among baseline methods and our method on three datasets. Some observations can be made: (1) The neural approaches outperform the conventional methods. (2) RNN-based methods prove the effectiveness of RNN. GRU4Rec encodes the session ignoring the noise items. Later NARM and CSRM solve this problem by incorporating the attention mechanism into RNN to focus on important items. However, they may easily generate false dependencies, which can be avoided by SGRU's selector. GNN-based methods (SR-GNN, LESSR) outperform the single layer RNN-based methods overall, and prove the advantage of learning session graph. (3) The recent multi-interest based models MCPRN and HLN perform well and benefit from distinguishing different purposes. However, they manage purposes in a flat way and ignore the hierarchical intents. (4) Overall, our method HISSI outperforms both conventional methods and recent neural approaches and achieves state-of-the-art performance. Particularly, HISSI obtains improvements over the best baseline results of 3.69%, 11.41%, and 4.61% in Recall@20 on three datasets, respectively. In terms of MRR@20, the relative improvements are 3.47%, 6.32%, and 1.80%, respectively. Besides, the absolute improvement on Taobao and Yiwugo is more obvious than Diginetica. Since Taobao and Yiwugo datasets contain more categories in a session as shown in Table 1, and we assume that more categories represent more extensive intents, which is naturally suitable for modeling hierarchical interests than Diginetica (Table 3).

Table 3. The ablation analysis of HISSI on Diginetica and Taobao datasets. Best performance (%) is boldfaced.

Method	Diginetica		Taobao	
	Recall@20	MRR@20	Recall@20	MRR@20
HISSI	**53.62**	**18.78**	**61.24**	**39.05**
HISSI w/o GIA	50.32	17.21	53.11	36.85
HISSI w/o g_t	51.04	18.14	57.42	38.21
HISSI w/o SGRU	51.72	17.54	58.91	37.70
HISSI-GRU	52.12	17.92	59.22	38.64

5.3 Ablation Analysis

To investigate how different modules affect the performance, we consider the variants of HISSI that calculate the metric score after removing or replace each module. We introduce each module separately:

(1) **Impact of GIA.** Without GIA, HISSI ignores hierarchical modeling and only use SGRU for prediction. This is similar to RNN-based methods that capture sequential behaviors. We observe that the variation slightly outperforms NARM and CSRM, since it benefits from the accurate current interest modeling. However, the performance decrease proves that the hierarchical intents modeling plays a great role in our method. (2) **Impact of common feature gate.** Without common feature gate g_t, the input item sequence in each layer is directly encoded by a convolution operation. Interestingly, we observe an obvious decrease in model performance. This verifies the importance of g_t. (3) **Impact of SGRU.** Removing the current interest learning leading to obvious performance degradation on all datasets, especially in MRR@20. Compared with the removal of GIA module, it can be seen that GIA has a greater impact on performance improvement in this model. In addition, we also replace the SGRU with the original GRU to verify the advantage of our design SGRU, as shown in HISSI-GRU, the performance decrease is smaller than HISSI w/o SGRU.

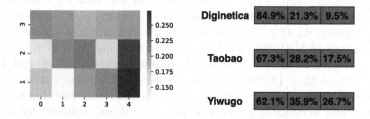

Fig. 4. Left: Visualization of attention weights from layer 1 to 3. The square scores represent the average attention score of the items at each position. Right: Recall of different layers.

5.4 Case Study

Visualize the Attention Weights. We randomly select a session from the Taobao dataset to visualize the attention distribution of each layer. From Fig. 4 (left) we have the following observations: (1) In the first layer, although the items share common features, there are many differences in details, and the difference of attention scores is relatively large. Besides, the last item is important for prediction. (2) As the number of layers increases, the difference of the attention scores becomes smaller, and the intents become more general, which proves our model captures multi-level user preferences from fine-to-coarse grained.

Recall of Different Level of Intents. We use the vectors of each layer v_l to make predictions and calculate the percentage of matching items of each layer in the total number of matching items in all layers to count the accuracy of different intent levels. Note that we only calculate the sessions that can successfully hit the target by multi-layer vectors. The result is shown in Fig. 4 (right). We can see that not only the first layer, but also the high layers can hit target items. The model increases the coverage of users' interest, and enhance the item hit probability, while other flat models may ignore the contribution of more general intents for matching items.

6 Conclusion

This paper proposes a hierarchical intent and selective subsequential interests learning model with general intent abstractor module extracting the coarse-grained intent progressively, and a selector-GRU module helping model the user's accurate subset items that are related to the last click. Empirical experiments show that our model achieves state-of-the-art performance on all datasets.

Acknowledgements. This work was supported by Beijing Municipal Science and Technology Project Z201100001820003.

References

1. Bonnin, G., Jannach, D.: Music playlists: Survey and experiments. ACM Comput. Surv. **47**(2), 26:1–26:35 (2014). https://doi.org/10.1145/2652481, https://doi.org/10.1145/2652481
2. Chen, T., Wong, R.C.W.: Handling information loss of graph neural networks for session-based recommendation. In: Proceedings of the 26th ACM SIGKDD International Conference on Knowledge Discovery & Data Mining, pp. 1172–1180 (2020)
3. Geng, X., Wang, L., Wang, X., Qin, B., Liu, T., Tu, Z.: How does selective mechanism improve self-attention networks? arXiv preprint arXiv:2005.00979 (2020)
4. Guo, C., Zhang, M., Fang, J., Jin, J., Pan, M.: Session-based recommendation with hierarchical leaping networks. In: Proceedings of the 43rd International ACM SIGIR Conference on Research and Development in Information Retrieval, pp. 1705–1708 (2020)

5. Hidasi, B., Karatzoglou, A., Baltrunas, L., Tikk, D.: Session-based recommendations with recurrent neural networks. arXiv preprint arXiv:1511.06939 (2015)
6. Jang, E., Gu, S., Poole, B.: Categorical reparameterization with gumbel-softmax. arXiv preprint arXiv:1611.01144 (2016)
7. Li, J., Ren, P., Chen, Z., Ren, Z., Lian, T., Ma, J.: Neural attentive session-based recommendation. In: Proceedings of the 2017 ACM on Conference on Information and Knowledge Management, pp. 1419–1428. ACM (2017)
8. Li, Y., Tarlow, D., Brockschmidt, M., Zemel, R.: Gated graph sequence neural networks. arXiv preprint arXiv:1511.05493 (2015)
9. Liu, Q., Zeng, Y., Mokhosi, R., Zhang, H.: Stamp: short-term attention/memory priority model for session-based recommendation. In: Proceedings of the 24th ACM SIGKDD International Conference on Knowledge Discovery & Data Mining, pp. 1831–1839. ACM (2018)
10. Qiu, R., Li, J., Huang, Z., Yin, H.: Rethinking the item order in session-based recommendation with graph neural networks. In: Proceedings of the 28th ACM International Conference on Information and Knowledge Management, pp. 579–588 (2019)
11. Rendle, S., Freudenthaler, C., Schmidt-Thieme, L.: Factorizing personalized Markov chains for next-basket recommendation. In: Proceedings of the 19th International Conference on World Wide Web, pp. 811–820. ACM (2010)
12. Sarwar, B., Karypis, G., Konstan, J., Riedl, J.: Item-based collaborative filtering recommendation algorithms. In: Proceedings of the 10th International Conference on World Wide Web, pp. 285–295 (2001)
13. Tan, Y.K., Xu, X., Liu, Y.: Improved recurrent neural networks for session-based recommendations. In: Proceedings of the 1st Workshop on Deep Learning for Recommender Systems, pp. 17–22. ACM (2016)
14. Tang, J., Wang, K.: Personalized top-n sequential recommendation via convolutional sequence embedding. In: Proceedings of the Eleventh ACM International Conference on Web Search and Data Mining pp. 565–573. ACM (2018)
15. Tuan, T.X., Phuong, T.M.: 3d convolutional networks for session-based recommendation with content features. In: Proceedings of the Eleventh ACM Conference on Recommender Systems, pp. 138–146 (2017)
16. Vaswani, A., et al.: Attention is all you need. In: Advances in Neural Information Processing Systems, pp. 5998–6008 (2017)
17. Wang, M., Ren, P., Mei, L., Chen, Z., Ma, J., de Rijke, M.: A collaborative session-based recommendation approach with parallel memory modules. In: Proceedings of the 42nd International ACM SIGIR Conference on Research and Development in Information Retrieval, pp. 345–354 (2019)
18. Wang, S., Hu, L., Wang, Y., Sheng, Q.Z., Orgun, M., Cao, L.: Modeling multi-purpose sessions for nextitem recommendations via mixture-channel purpose routing networks. In: Proceedings of the 28th International Joint Conference on Artificial Intelligence, pp. 1–7. AAAI Press (2019)
19. Wu, S., Tang, Y., Zhu, Y., Wang, L., Xie, X., Tan, T.: Session-based recommendation with graph neural networks. In: Proceedings of the AAAI Conference on Artificial Intelligence, vol. 33, pp. 346–353 (2019)
20. Xu, C., Zhao, P., Liu, Y., Sheng, V.S., Xu, J., Zhuang, F., Fang, J., Zhou, X.: Graph contextualized self-attention network for session-based recommendation. In: Proceedings of 28th International Joint Conferences on Artificial Intelligence (IJCAI), pp. 3940–3946 (2019)

A Finetuned Language Model for Recommending cQA-QAs for Enriching Textbooks

Shobhan Kumar$^{(\boxtimes)}$ ⓘ and Arun Chauhan ⓘ

IIIT Dharwad, Karnataka, India

Abstract. Textbooks play a vital role in any educational system, despite their clarity and information, students tend to use community question answers (cQA) forums to acquire more knowledge. Due to the high data volume, the quality of Question-Answers (QA) of cQA forums can differ greatly, so it takes additional effort to go through all possible QA pairs for a better insight. This paper proposes an "sentence-level text enrichment system" where the fine-tuned BERT (Bidirectional Encoder Representations from Transformers) summarizer understands the given text, picks out the important sentence, and then rearranged them to give the overall summary of the text document. For each important sentence, we recommend the relevant QA pairs from cQA to make the learning more effective. In this work, we fine-tuned the pre-trained BERT model to extract the relevant QA sets that are most relevant for enriching important sentences of the textbook. We notice that fine-tuning the BERT model significantly improves the performance for QA selection and find that it outperforms existing RNN-based models for such tasks. We also investigate the effectiveness of our fine-tuned BERT$_{Large}$ model on three cQA datasets for the QA selection task and observed a maximum improvement of 19.72% compared to the previous models. Experiments have been carried out on NCERT (Grade IX and X) Textbooks from India and "Pattern Recognition and Machine Learning" Textbook. The extensive evaluation methods demonstrate that the proposed model offers more precise and relevant recommendations in comparison to the state-of-the-art methods.

Keywords: cQA · BERT · QA · Precision · Text-enrichment

1 Introduction

The Community Question Answering (cQA) portals, including Quora[1], and Reddit[2] offers people to share their knowledge and learn from each other. In the past decade, these cQA forums have attracted the attention of a large number of users, it results in accumulating a massive amount of QA-comment threads

---

[1] –https://www.quora.com/.
[2] –https://www.reddit.com/.

© Springer Nature Switzerland AG 2021
K. Karlapalem et al. (Eds.): PAKDD 2021, LNAI 12713, pp. 423–435, 2021.
https://doi.org/10.1007/978-3-030-75765-6_34

by these users. Despite the fact that there is a great substance in the available textbooks, students prefer to use cQA forums to acquire more knowledge. There will be several responses in cQA that are attached to the same question, so it makes it difficult for any user to pick the right one. As a consequence, students spend more time gathering the requisite data from the web to get a better picture of a textbook concept. The productivity of students could be impaired by this process. The conventional models of information retrieval [1,15,16,24] can retrieve the QA sets from the old archived data. These existing methods have not addressed issues like how to use these large volumes of QAs from cQA forums to enrich textbook contents in a real-time manner to help the students fraternity with minimal effort. Therefore it would be very essential to automate the procedure of obtaining relevant QA from cQA for their textbooks for better insight.

Our contributions in this work include the following:

- Text summary generation: For the given text document our fine-tuned BERT summarizer select the important/informative sentence and rearranged them to give the precise summary.
- Text enrichment using QA: For each informative sentences of the textbook our fine-tuned BERT$_{Large}$ model extracts the relevant QA pairs from Quora (see Footnote 1) cQA forum.
- Experiments on cQA dataset: We conduct rigorous experiments in three cQA datasets by fine-tuning the BERT$_{Large}$ model for the QA selection task and observe that the fine-tuned BERT$_{Large}$ model outperforms state-of-the-art methods where pre-trained language models have not been used.

The rest of this paper has the following sections. Section 2 highlights the related work. Section 3 gives a detailed description of the proposed model. Section 4 reports the experimental results and discussion. Finally, we conclude the paper in Sect. 5.

2   Related Work

An important part of education is the student's learning. Good quality education is based mainly on how well the student attains the knowledge. Few attempt [9,10] has took place to enrich the textbook contents which makes the learning process more effective and joyful. The selection of best matched QA is intimate relation to the subjects such as semantic search (Jose et al.) [7], (Badri et al.) [16], QA recommendation (Dirk et al.) [24], and retrieval from cQA. The engagement of students in MOOCs absolutely relies upon the quality materials of the educational cQA systems. (Macina et al.) [13] Assigning the weight to the experts who can provide the quality answer for the asked questions can stabilized the quality of QA in cQA. (Nakov et al.) [15] the Semeval 2017 task 3 competition stresses the concepts like cosine distance that can be used to verify the lexical, syntactic, semantic relations. Tay et al. [21] describes the neural network models which have been used for learning word illustrations to make a faster QA system to retrieve the questions. The text enrichment model (Agrawal et al.) [1] augments the text documents with QAs from Wikipedia archives. A sentence-level text enrichment model(sk et al.)[8], fetches the relevant cQA-QA pairs for the given text sentences. The textbook contains a large number of sentences so identifying the important sentence and fetching the relevant cQA-QAs is a tiresome process. Therefore in this work, we select the important sentences from the textbook using the finetuned BERT summarizer and for these sentences, our model retrieves the relevant QA pairs from cQA.

Different sentence similarity models based on the neural network (Qin et al.) [4], (Chen et al.) [3], (Jinfeng et al.) [19] has been used in recent years to test the similarity between the question and the candidate's answer. At first, the word embedding (GloVe (Pennington et al.) [17] or Word2Vec (Mikolov et al.) [14]) representations of the question and the candidate's answer have been used as input to such neural models. Later on, the vector representations of these sentences generated by the neural models are used for the similarity calculation [3,4]. But, such word embedding can offer only a fixed representation of a word and does not capture its context. In recent years, the language model has shown to be effective for improving many natural language processing tasks. Pre-trained language models can provide contextual representations of each word in different sentences (Devlin et al.) [6], (Matthew et al.) [18]. Among the different pre-trained language models, the (BERT) [6] is an empirically powerful one and it performs a wide range of NLP tasks (Vaswani et al.) [23]. The pre-trained BERT model can be fine-tuned with additional architectures to perform specific tasks. However, the model is not deeply investigated for the answer selection task yet (Tahmid et al.) [11]. In this work, we fine-tuned the pre-trained BERT$_{Large}$ model for the QA selection task.

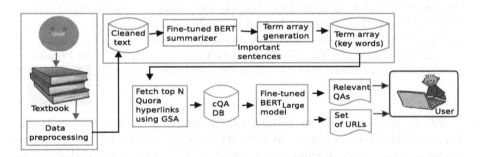

Fig. 1. The overall architecture of the proposed "Sentence Level Text Enrichment" system with cQA-QAs.

3   Methodology

In this section, we depict the working sequence of our text enrichment model with relevant QA from Quora (see Footnote 1). Figure 1 describes the overall architecture of the proposed enrichment model where the model takes text as an input and gives the required number of relevant QA pairs from Quora. The work in this paper has the following phases. i) Data preprocessing ii) Summary generation iii) The term array generation for the informative sentence. iv) Finding the relevant data for Text Enrichment.

3.1 Data Analysis and Preprocessing

The enrichment system will fetch the relevant QAs from Quora for a given text. The input text document requires a preprocessing task since these textbook copies may contain several special characters, HTML links, images, tables, etc., which is not relevant to the task. The enrichment method exploits various lexical and structural features to provide clean text and it becomes the facts for the succeeding information retrieval process.

3.2 Text Summary Generation

Text summarization keeps the relevant information from a large document while retaining the most important information. The pre-trained BERT model [6] is fine-tuned to perform the summarization tasks (ref. Fig. 2). For a set of sentences $\{s_1, s_2, s_3, ..., s_n\}$ we have two possibilities, that are, y_i $i = \{0,1\}$ which denotes whether a particular sentence will be picked or not. The complete process has multiple phases such as (i) Encoding-Multiple-Sentences. (ii) Embeddings. The input text document is encoded in the Encoding-Multiple-Sentences phase. Three types of embeddings are applied to the cleaned text prior to feeding it to the BERT layer. The token embeddings convert the words into a fixed dimension vector, and the sentence is preceded by a CLS tag and succeeded by a SEP tag, where the CLS tag aggregates the features of one or more sentences. The Interval-Segment-Embeddings phase distinguishes the sentences in a document. Sentences are assigned the labels such as E_x or E_y ($sent_i = E_x$ or E_y based on i. i.e. E_x for even i and E_y for odd i). Positional embedding is used because a word's position in a sentence may change the sentence's contextual meaning.

BERT Architecture: The pre-trained BERT model has 12 transformer layers along with 12 attention layers and 110 million parameters. In order to learn the summarization specific features, in this work an LSTM layer is added with the BERT model output. Where each LSTM cell is normalized. At time step i, the input to the LSTM layer is the BERT output T_i.

$$C_i = \sigma(A_i).D_i - 1 + \sigma(B_i).tanh(H_i - 1) \tag{1}$$

$$O_i = \sigma(C_i).tanh(NP_c(C_i)) \tag{2}$$

where A_i, B_i, C_i are forget gates, input gates, output gates. H_i represents the hidden vector and D_i is the memory vector, O_i is the output vector and NP_c is the normalization operations. The output layer is again the sigmoid layer.

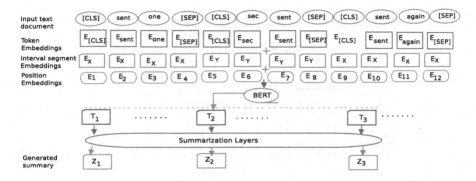

Fig. 2. The architecture of the BERT summarization model.

3.3 Term Array Generation

Algorithm 3 describes how the key phrases are selected for each important sentence of a given text document. These key phrases are excellent means for presenting a concise summary of a document. The key phrases with an added keyword "Quora" is given to **Google** Search API (GSA) which returns the relevant hyperlinks from which we fetch top N relevant hyperlinks.

Algorithm 1: Term array (key phrases) generation from text document

---

Input   : A set of important/informative sentences S for a given text document
Output: Term array (key phrases) S_i for each sentences

1 Identify the sentence list in the text document using sentence tokenizer
2 **for** each sentence i do
3   Use word tokeniser to compute the set S_i of keyphrases (tokens)
4   Use predefined stop word list to remove non-keywords in S_i
5   Prepare a final S_i list
6 **end for**

3.4 Text Enrichment - Finding the Enriched Data

There are several cQA forums are available, for this work we focused on the Quora cQA forum to retrieve relevant QA pairs. Relevant QA pairs help students to understand and learn in a variety of ways, in turn, it promotes their learning autonomy levels. Our sentence level enrichment process extracts the relevant QAs, corresponding URLs from Quora, and then present the same to the user in standard formats.

- [3]https://webscope.sandbox.yahoo.com/catalog.php?datatype=l&did=10.
- [4]https://huggingface.co/transformers/pretrained_models.html.

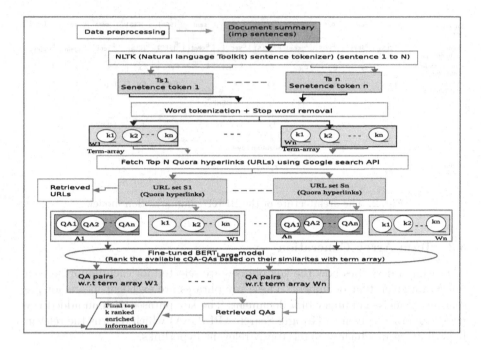

Fig. 3. Term (key-phrase) array generation for the informative sentences of the text.

3.4.1 Find Relevant QA from Quora

Figure 3 describes the sequence of operations that are required to generate the best matched QA sets for the given text document as proposed. First, the system generates a keyphrase array for the given input. Then each keyphrase array (W_1 to W_n) is given to GSA to extract relevant URLs from Quora. For each extracted URL there may be several answers for the question referred by URL which may or may not be relevant for the input text. We used our fine-tuned the BERT$_{Large}$ model to select the relevant QAs from cQA.

Fine-tuning BERT for Relevant QA Selection: Figure 4 demonstrates the fine-tuning phase of the pre-trained BERT$_{Large}$ model for the relevant QA selection task. For fine-tuning, parameters are added for the additional classification layer F to the pre-trained BERT model. In order to maximize the log-probability of the correct label, all parameters of the BERT model, and the additional parameters for the classifier F are jointly fine-tuned. The probability of each label $P \in R^j$ is determined as follows (where j is the total number of classifier labels).

$$P = softmax(CF^T) \tag{3}$$

In the QA selection task, there are two classifier labels (label 0: candidate answer is irrelevant to the question/term array, label 1: candidate answer is relevant). In the pre-trained BERT model [6], the sentence pair classification

Fig. 4. BERT Fine Tuning: The term array X and the candidate answer Y are combined to form an input to the BERT model (pre-trained) for fine-tuning.

task was carried out by determining the correct label. In this work, we alter the final layer and only consider the predicted P_r score for the similarity label to rank the available answers based on their similarities with the term array/question. After the similarity checking operation we selected the top k QA pairs and corresponding URLs

$$P_r = P(C = 1|X, Y) \qquad (4)$$

4   Experimental Results and Discussion

The proposed sentence-level text enrichment approach retrieves the relevant QAs and URLs from the Quora cQA forum to enrich the given text sentence. We verified our model with the following data sets.

Data Set 1 To validate the enrichment model, we have considered NCERT textbook (Science Grade X, Computers and Communication Technology part I&II, Grade XI) and graduate levels textbook Pattern Recognition and Machine Learning by Christopher M. Bishop [2]. Textbook contains a number of images, HTML links, etc. The data sets will be preprocessed as explained in Sect. 3.1. To validate our proposed model, we randomly chosen 25 text documents (pages)from the above-mentioned textbooks and then applied a preprocessing method to generate clean text. For this task, we processed approximately 625 sentences (25 * 25 = 625 sentences) from the above-mentioned textbook in which all sentences may not be informative. For incomplete or ambiguous sentences the retrieval model will not return any QA pairs from Quora, therefore we select the informative sentence using our fine-tuned BERT model as explained in Sect. 3.2. We have selected 315 informative sentences and it becomes the input data for the subsequent QA retrieval process.

Table 1 describes the statistics of the retrieved QA pairs from Quora for the above mentioned textbook (data set1). Table 2 to Table 4 shows the retrieved questions from Quora for important sentences of the sample text (heighlighted part in Fig. 5).

In our experiments, we have also used three cQA datasets. The overall statistics of the datasets are shown in Table 5.

1.2. Probability Theory

A key concept in the field of pattern recognition is that of uncertainty. It arises both through noise on measurements, as well as through the finite size of data sets. Probability theory provides a consistent framework for the quantification and manipulation of uncertainty and forms one of the central foundations for pattern recognition. When combined with decision theory, discussed in Section 1.5, it allows us to make optimal predictions given all the information available to us, even though that information may be incomplete or ambiguous.

We will introduce the basic concepts of probability theory by considering a simple example. Imagine we have two boxes, one red and one blue, and in the red box we have 2 apples and 6 oranges, and in the blue box we have 3 apples and 1 orange. This is illustrated in Figure 1.9. Now suppose we randomly pick one of the boxes and from that box we randomly select an item of fruit, and having observed which sort of fruit it is we replace it in the box from which it came. We could imagine repeating this process many times. Let us suppose that in so doing we pick the red box 40% of the time and we pick the blue box 60% of the time, and that when we remove an item of fruit from a box we are equally likely to select any of the pieces of fruit in the box.

Fig. 5. Sample of test data 1, text data (Sect. 1.2), taken from the textbook "Pattern Recognition and Machine Learning" by Christopher M Bishop [2]. (Chosen informative sentences using fine-tuned BERT summarizer are highlighted).

Table 1. The statistics of the retrieved QA pairs from Quora for the data set 1.

Retrieved QA pairs for the Text documents					
Threshold value K	01	02	03	04	05
QA pairs@text_document	315	618	904	1217	1486

Table 2. The retrieved cQA-Questions from Quora (see Footnote 1) for the input text (sentence 1 of the highlighted part in Fig. 5) (only questions from Quora cQA are presented here)

Sentence: "A key concept in the field of pattern recognition is that of uncertainty"
Retrieved cQA-Questions, when k=03
Q1: What is pattern recognition?
Q2: Why is Pattern Recognition important?
Q3: What is the difference between pattern recognition and machine learning?

Table 3. The retrieved cQA-Questions from Quora (see Footnote 1) for sentence 2 (ref. Fig. 5)

Sentence: "It arises both through noise on measurements, as well as through the finite size of data sets."
Retrieved cQA-Questions, when k = 03
Q1: How can you quantify the amount of noise in a data set?
Q2: What is noise in data science/machine learning?
Q3: Why is it good to have large data sets?

Table 4. The retrieved questions from Quora (see Footnote 1) for the (3rd sentence ref. Fig. 5)

Sentence: "Imagine we have two boxes, one red and one blue, and in the red box we have 2 apples and 6 oranges, and in the blue box we have 3 apples and 1 orange"
Q1: A blue box contains 30 oranges & 10 apples, and a red box contains 10 oranges and 20 apples. If I first choose randomly one of the boxes, and then randomly pick one fruit from that box, what is the probably that the fruit will be an Apple?
Q2: If 1 apple and 1 orange costs Rs. 2, how much will 3 apples and 2 oranges cost?
Q3: What is the number of ways to distribute 8 identical balls in 3 different boxes, none being empty?

The YahooCQA[3]: In this dataset at most one correct answer and four negative responses are associated with each question [22].

SemEval-2016CQA:. This dataset is developed by Qatar Living Forums. Some labels such as "Good", "Bad" or "Potentially Useful" is tagged for each candidate answers. In this work, we considered "Good" as positive and other tags as negative [12,20].

SemEval-2017CQA: The training and validation data in this dataset is the same as SemEval-2016CQA, but the test sets are different [15].

Table 5. An overview of the cQA dataset used in this work.

Dataset	# Questions			# Candidate Answers		
	Train	Valid	Test	Train	Valid	Test
YahooCQA	50112	6289	6283	253440	31680	31680
SemEval-2016CQA	4879	244	327	36198	2440	3270
SemEval-2017CQA	4879	244	293	36198	2440	2930

Training Parameters and Evaluation Metrics: In this work, we have used both the cased and uncased BERT[4] models (pre-trained) and fine-tuned them for relevant QA selection task[6]. The BERT$_{Large}$ model has 24 transformer layers and 16 attention layers (hidden size = 1024, feed-forward layer size = 4096, and 340 million parameters). For smoother implementation, we used the Transformer library of Huggingface [25]. For training the model, we used the cross-entropy loss function to measure the loss and used Adam as the optimizer. The model was trained for 10 epochs with batch size 16 and learning rate being set to 2 $\times$ 10^{-5}. We used the Mean Average Precision (MAP) and the Mean Reciprocal Rank (MRR) as the evaluation metrics to assess our models.

Table 6. Performance comparison of our fine-tuned BERT$_{Large}$ model with state-of-the-art work.

Model	cQA dataset					
	Yahoo cQA		SemEval'16		SemEval'17	
	MAP	MRR	MAP	MRR	MAP	MRR
Sha et al. [5]	–	–	0.801	0.872	–	–
Tay et al. [21]	-	0.801	–	–	–	–
Nakov et al. [15]	–	–	–	–	0.884	0.928
Fine-tuned BERT$_{Large}$ (cased)	0.949	0.951	0.853	0.899	0.908	0.946
Fine-tuned BERT$_{rmLarge}$ (uncased)	0.955	0.958	0.871	0.936	0.931	0.974

Table 6 describes the comparison results of our fine-tuned BERT model with the state-of-the-art model. In the cQA datasets, we observe that the fine-tuned BERT model (both cased and uncased) outperforms the state-of-the-art work. In terms of MRR, we find that the BERTLarge (uncased) model outperforms prior work [5,21], and [15] with an improvement of 19.72%, 7.34%, and 4.95% in the YahooCQA, SemEval-2016CQA, and SemEval-2017CQA datasets respectively.

Evaluation Metrics for QA Retrieval Task: We have used precision as an evaluation metric to validate the performance of our approach, where($P@k$) is defined as the proportion of the k results that are relevant. Where rQA is the number of relevant QA pairs retrieved up to rank k. The $P@k(QA)$ and represents the computed precision scores for the retrieved QA pairs at different values of k.

$$P@k(QA) = \frac{\sum_{i=1}^{n} rQA_i}{k} \tag{5}$$

Table 7 shows the statistics of the obtained precision at different values of k for QA. We asked 25 students who have taken "Machine Learning" courses for their undergraduate studies for evaluation purposes. An evaluator is asked to label the retrieved QAs with the flags like "relevant" or "irrelevant" based on the relevance of the retrieved QA for the input data. We took one-third of the total retrieved QA pairs corresponds to threshold values for a smoother evaluation process. During the evaluation, the evaluators have presented both text documents and retrieved QAs. The precision value reaches its peak rate (when k = 03), i.e. on average, we can have 2–3 relevant QAs for each informative sentence, in the rest of the case retrieval relevancy is quite less in manner.

We have conducted a quiz session to assess the effectiveness of our enrichment model. The quiz were prepared from the same text documents, a total of 25 undergraduate students took part in the quiz session. In the first week, the

Table 7. The obtained precision scores.

Threshold value k	1	2	3	4	5
QA sets	105	206	300	406	497
Precision@k	0.467	0.512	0.603	0.364	0.322

Table 8. Quiz session results.

Week	Quiz scores max:10 points	Avg time spent max:30 min
Week 1	6.93	27:13
Week 2	8.57	24:05

students have read the text documents (Chap. 1-PRML) [2] and then answered the first set of quiz questions. The students previewed both the retrieved QAs and text documents (Chap. 2-PRML) [2] and then answered the second set of quiz questions. Each week the average time spent by the students to answer the given quiz questions and their obtained scores were noted and analyzed. Table 8 describes the obtained results for short quiz questions and these results revealed that students who previewed the enriched data (cQA-QAs) finished quiz questions in a shorter time and obtained good scores compared to the first-week performance. Importantly, this finding indicates that the proposed method has a noticeable impact on the student's ability to preview and understand the material effectively.

5   Conclusion and Future Scope

The prime motive of this paper is to present a relevant QA pair from the cQA forum that becomes the enriched information for the given text document. This enrichment model is quite different from the general search engines, or retrieval models rather than focusing on concepts we augment textbooks at the sentence level for key concepts discussed in the section. We selected informative sentences of the text using our fine-tuned BERT summarizer and then selected important keywords in each sentence. Finally, we enriched the same by retrieving the relevant QA pairs from cQA using our fine-tuned $BERT_{Large}$ model for the given inputs. We evaluated our enrichment model using NCERT(Grade X, XI) & PRML textbook and infer that our model is effective in enriching textbooks on different subjects by providing the quality reference materials from cQA in real-time. The fine-tuned $BERT_{Large}$ model efficiency is evaluated using three cQA datasets, we compare its performance with different state-of-the-art models [5,15,21] and the results demonstrate that our model is competitive. Presently we are working on the development of a cross-language retrieval system using Natural Language Understanding (NLU) methods i.e. presenting the question in one language and obtaining the appropriate QAs from cross-language cQA platforms and plan to extend our enrichment model accordingly.

References

1. Agrawal, R., Gollapudi, S., Kenthapadi, K., Srivastava, N., Velu, R.: Enriching textbooks through data mining. In: Proceedings of the First ACM Symposium on Computing for Development, ACM DEV 2010, pp. 19:1–19:9 (2010)

2. Bishop, C.M.: Pattern Recognition and Machine Learning (Information Science and Statistics). Springer, Heidelberg (2006)

3. Chen, Q., Hu, Q., Huang, J.X., He, L.: Can: enhancing sentence similarity modeling with collaborative and adversarial network. In: The 41st International ACM SIGIR Conference on Research; Development in Information Retrieval. SIGIR 2018, pp. 815–824. NY, USA, New York (2018)

4. Chen, Q., Hu, Q., Huang, X., He, L.: Ca-rnn: using context-aligned recurrent neural networks for modeling sentence similarity. In: AAAI (2018)

5. Yang, D.: Multi-task learning with multi-view attention for answer selection and knowledge base question answering. In: Proceedings of the AAAI Conference on Artificial Intelligence, vol. 33(01), pp. 6318–6325, July 2019

6. Devlin, J., Chang, M.-W., Lee, K., Toutanova, K.: BERT: re-training of deep bidirectional transformers for language understanding. In: Proceedings of the 2019 ACL: Human Language Technologies, vol. 1, pp. 4171–4186, Minneapolis, Minnesota, June 2019

7. Herrera, J., Poblete, B., Parra, D.: Learning to leverage microblog information for QA retrieval. In: Pasi, G., Piwowarski, B., Azzopardi, L., Hanbury, A. (eds.) ECIR 2018. LNCS, vol. 10772, pp. 507–520. Springer, Cham (2018). https://doi.org/10.1007/978-3-319-76941-7_38

8. Kumar, S., Chauhan, A.: Enriching textbooks by question-answers using CQA. In: IEEE Region 10 Conference (TENCON), pp. 707–714 (2019)

9. Kumar, S., Chauhan, A.: Making kids learning joyful using artistic style transferred youtube vcs. In: IEEE Region 10 Conference (TENCON), pp. 1106–1111 (2020)

10. Kumar, S., Chauhan, A.: Recommending question-answers for enriching textbooks. In: Bellatreche, L., Goyal, V., Fujita, H., Mondal, A., Reddy, P.K. (eds.) BDA 2020. LNCS, vol. 12581, pp. 308–328. Springer, Cham (2020). https://doi.org/10.1007/978-3-030-66665-1_20

11. Laskar, Md.T.R., Hoque, E., Huang, J.X.: Utilizing bidirectional encoder representations from transformers for answer selection (2020)

12. Laskar, Md.T.R., Huang, J.X., Hoque, E.: Contextualized embeddings based transformer encoder for sentence similarity modeling in answer selection task. In: Proceedings of the 12th Language Resources and Evaluation Conference, pp. 5505–5514, May 2020

13. Macina, J., Srba, I., Williams, J.J., Bielikova, M.: Educational question routing in online student communities. In: Proceedings of the Eleventh ACM Conference on Recommender Systems, RecSys '17, pp. 47–55 (2017)

14. Mikolov, T., Chen, K., Corrado, G.S., Dean, J.: Efficient estimation of word representations in vector space (2013)

15. Nakov, P.: SemEval-2017 task 3: community question answering. In: Proceedings of the 11th International Workshop on (SemEval-2017), pp. 27–48, Vancouver, Canada, August 2017

16. Patro, B.N., Kurmi, V.K., Kumar, S., Namboodiri, V.P.: Learning semantic sentence embeddings using pair-wise discriminator. CoRR, abs/1806.00807 (2018)

17. Pennington, J., Socher, R., Manning, C.: GloVe: global vectors for word representation. In: Proceedings of the 2014 Conference on EMNLP, pp. 1532–1543, October 2014

18. Peters, M., et al.: Deep contextualized word representations. In: Proceedings of the 2018 Conference of ACL: Human Language Technologies, Volume 1 (Long Papers), pp. 2227–2237, New Orleans, Louisiana, June 2018

19. Rao, J., Liu, L., Tay, Y., Yang, W., Shi, P., Lin, J.: Bridging the gap between relevance matching and semantic matching for short text similarity modeling. In: Proceedings of EMNLP-IJCNLP, pp. 5370–5381, November 2019
20. Sha, L., Zhang, X., Qian, F., Chang, B., Sui, Z.: A multi-view fusion neural network for answer selection. In: AAAI (2018)
21. Tay, Y., Luu, A.T., Hui, S.: Hyperbolic representation learning for fast and efficient neural question answering. In: Proceedings of the Eleventh ACM International Conference on Web Search and Data Mining (2018)
22. Tay, Y., Phan, M.C., Tuan, L.A., Hui, S.C.: Learning to rank question answer pairs with holographic dual lstm architecture. In: Proceedings of the 40th International ACM SIGIR Conference on Research and Development in Information Retrieval, SIGIR 2017, pp. 695–704 (2017)
23. Ashish Vaswani, A., et al.: Attention is all you need. In: Guyon, I., et al. (eds.) Advances in Neural Information Processing Systems, vol. 30, pp. 5998–6008. Curran Associates Inc. (2017)
24. Weissenborn, D., Wiese, G., Seiffe, L.: Fastqa: a simple and efficient neural architecture for question answering. ArXiv, abs/1703.04816 (2017)
25. Wolf, T., et al.: Huggingface's transformers: state-of-the-art natural language processing. CoRR, abs/1910.03771 (2019)

XCrossNet: Feature Structure-Oriented Learning for Click-Through Rate Prediction

Runlong Yu[1], Yuyang Ye[2], Qi Liu[1(✉)], Zihan Wang[3], Chunfeng Yang[4], Yucheng Hu[4], and Enhong Chen[1]

[1] Anhui Province Key Laboratory of Big Data Analysis and Application, School of Computer Science and Technology, University of Science and Technology of China, Hefei, China
yrunl@mail.ustc.edu.cn, {qiliuql,cheneh}@ustc.edu.cn
[2] Management Science and Information Systems, Rutgers Business School, Rutgers University, Newark, USA
yuyang.ye@rutgers.edu
[3] MOE Key Laboratory of Computational Linguistics, School of Electronics Engineering and Computer Science, Peking University, Beijing, China
wzh@stu.pku.edu.cn
[4] Tencent Inc, Shenzhen, China
{yannisyang,nikohu}@tencent.com

Abstract. Click-Through Rate (CTR) prediction is a core task in nowadays commercial recommender systems. Feature crossing, as the mainline of research on CTR prediction, has shown a promising way to enhance predictive performance. Even though various models are able to learn feature interactions without manual feature engineering, they rarely attempt to individually learn representations for different feature structures. In particular, they mainly focus on the modeling of cross sparse features but neglect to specifically represent cross dense features. Motivated by this, we propose a novel Extreme Cross Network, abbreviated XCrossNet, which aims at learning dense and sparse feature interactions in an explicit manner. XCrossNet as a feature structure-oriented model leads to a more expressive representation and a more precise CTR prediction, which is not only explicit and interpretable, but also time-efficient and easy to implement. Experimental studies on Criteo Kaggle dataset show significant improvement of XCrossNet over state-of-the-art models on both effectiveness and efficiency.

1 Introduction

Accurate targeting of commercial recommender systems is of great importance, in which Click-Through Rate (CTR) prediction plays a key role. CTR prediction aims to estimate the ratio of clicks to the impression of a recommended item for a user. Therefore, we consider users have negative preferences instead of implicit feedbacks on those un-clicked items [25,26]. In common display advertising systems, advertisers expect lower costs to achieve a higher return on investment.

© Springer Nature Switzerland AG 2021
K. Karlapalem et al. (Eds.): PAKDD 2021, LNAI 12713, pp. 436–447, 2021.
https://doi.org/10.1007/978-3-030-75765-6_35

The ad exchange platforms usually trade with advertisers and publishers according to the generalized second price of the maximum effective Cost Per Mille (eCPM). If CTR is overestimated, advertisers could waste campaign budgets on the useless impression; On the other hand, if CTR is underestimated, advertisers would lose some valuable impressions and the campaigns may under deliver. With multi-billion dollar business on commercial recommendation today, CTR prediction has received growing interest from communities of both academia and industry [3,13,21].

In web-scale commercial recommender systems, the inputs of users' characteristics are in two kinds of structures. The first kind of structure is described by numerical or dense parameters, e.g., "Age_years=22, Height_cm=165". Each of such characteristics is formalized as a value associated with a numerical field, while the values are named as dense features. The second kind of structure is described by categorical or sparse parameters, e.g., "Gender=Female, Relationship=In love". Each of such characteristics is formalized as a vector of one-hot encoding associated with a categorical field, while the vectors are named as sparse features. Research shows an important property of recommendation datasets for industrial use cases is the availability of both dense features and sparse features [22]. Thus, Criteo Kaggle dataset[1] is usually regarded as representative of real production use cases. Moreover, the number of dense and sparse features for industrial use cases are often 100s to 1000 with a 50:50 split[2].

Data scientists usually spend much time on interactions of raw features to generate better predictive models. Among these feature interactions, cross features, previously focused more on the product of sparse features, show a promising way to enhance the performance of prediction [15]. Owing to the fact that correct cross features are mostly task-specific and difficult to identify a priori, the crucial challenge is in automatically extracting sophisticated cross features hidden in high-dimensional data. Research on feature crossing as the mainline of CTR prediction has attracted widespread attention in recent years. Shallow models are simple, interpretable, and easy to scale, but limited in expressive ability. Alternatively, deep learning has shown powerful expressive capabilities, nevertheless, deep neural networks (DNNs) require many more parameters than tensor factorization to approximate high-order cross features. Besides, almost all deep models leverage multilayer perceptron (MLP) to learn high-order feature interactions, however, whether plain DNNs indeed effectively represent right functions of cross features remains an open question [10,21].

In addition, most methods neglect to represent cross dense features. There are three major patterns for handling dense features. First, dense features are discarded when crossing features, that is, dense features only participate in the linear part of the model [20]. Second, dense features are directly concatenated with the embeddings of sparse features, which could cause an important feature dimensionality imbalance problem [21]. Third, dense features are converted into

---

[1] https://labs.criteo.com/2013/12/download-terabyte-click-logs/.

[2] The statistics for the dense and sparse features and proportion are based on the survey outcome conducted in December 2019 with the MLPerf Advisory Board.

sparse features through bucketing, which could introduce hyper-parameters and loss information of dense features [12].

Based on all these observations, we propose a novel **Extreme Cross Network (XCrossNet)**, to represent feature structure-oriented interactions. Modeling with XCrossNet consists of three stages. In the Feature Crossing stage, we separately propose a cross layer for crossing dense features and a product layer for crossing sparse features. In the Feature Concatenation stage, cross dense features and cross sparse features interact through a concatenate layer and a cross layer. Lastly, in the Feature Selection stage, we employ an MLP for capturing non-linear interactions and their relative importance. Experimental results on Criteo Kaggle dataset demonstrate the superior performance of XCrossNet over the state-of-the-art baselines.

2   Related Work

Studies on CTR prediction can be categorized into five classes which will be respectively introduced below.

Generalized Linear Models. Logistic Regression (LR) models such as FTRL are widely used in CTR prediction for their simplicity and efficiency [9,16]. Ling Yan et al. argue that LR cannot capture nonlinear feature interactions and propose Coupled Group Lasso (CGL) to solve it [24]. Human efforts are usually needed for LR models. Gradient Boosting Decision Tree (GBDT) is a method to automatically do feature engineering and search interactions [4], then the transformed feature interactions can be fed into LR. In practice, tree-based models are more suitable for dense features but not for sparse features.

Quadratic Polynomial Mappings and Factorization Machines. Poly2 enumerates all pairwise feature interactions to avoid feature engineering which works well on dense features [2]. For sparse features, Factorization Machine (FM) and its variants project each feature into a low-dimensional vector and model cross features by inner product [20]. SFM introduces Laplace distribution to model the parameters and better fit the sparse data with a higher ratio of zero elements [17]. FFM enables each feature to have multiple latent vectors to interact with features from different fields [8]. As FM and its variants can only model order-2nd cross features. An efficient algorithm Higher-Order FM (HOFM) for training arbitrary-order cross features was proposed by introducing the ANOVA kernel [1]. As reported in [23], HOFM achieves marginal improvement over FM whereas using many more parameters and only its low-order (usually less than 5) form can be practically used.

Implicit Deep Learning Models. As deep learning has shown promising representation capabilities, several models use deep learning to improve FM. Attention FM (AFM) enhances the importance of different order-2nd cross features via attention networks [23]. Neural FM (NFM) stacks deep neural networks on top of the output of the order-2nd cross features to model higher-order cross features [6]. FNN uses FM to pre-train low-order features and then feeds feature embeddings into an MLP [27]. In contrast, DSL uses MLP to pre-train high-order non-linear features and then feeds them with basis features into an FM layer [7]. Moreover, CCPM uses convolutional layers to explore local-global dependencies of cross features [14]. IPNN (also known as PNN) feeds the interaction results of the FM layer and feature embeddings into an MLP [18]. PIN introduces a micro-network for each pair of fields to model pairwise cross features [19]. FGCNN combines a CNN and MLP to generate new features for feature augmentation [11]. However, all these approaches learn the high-order cross features in an implicit manner, therefore lack good model explainability.

Wide&Deep Based Models. Jianxun Lian et al. argue that implicit deep learning models focus more on high-order cross features but capture little low-order cross features [10]. To overcome this problem, there has been proposing a hybrid network structure, namely Wide&Deep, which combines a shallow component and a deep component with the purpose of learning both memorization and generalization [3]. Wide&Deep framework revolutionizes the development of CTR prediction, and attracts industry partners a lot from the beginning. As for the first Wide&Deep model proposed by Google [3], it combines a linear model (wide part) and DNN, while the input of the wide part still relies on feature engineering. Later on, DeepFM uses an FM layer to replace the wide component. Deep&Cross [21] and xDeepFM [10] take outer product of features at the bit- and vector-wise level respectively. However, xDeepFM uses so many parameters that great challenges are posed to identify important cross features in the huge combination space.

AutoML Based Models. There exist some pre-trained approaches using AutoML techniques to deal with cross features. AutoCross is proposed to search over subsets of candidate features to identify effective interactions [15]. This requires training the whole model to evaluate the selected feature interactions, but the candidate sets are incredibly many. AutoGroup treats the selection process of high-order feature interactions as a structural optimization problem, and solves it with Neural Architecture Search [12]. It achieves state-of-the-art performance on various datasets, but is too complex to be applied in industrial applications.

3   Extreme Cross Network (XCrossNet)

In this section, we will introduce the problem statement and describe the details of Extreme Cross Network (XCrossNet) in the following three steps: Feature Crossing, Feature Concatenation, and Feature Selection. The complete XCrossNet model is depicted in Fig. 1.

3.1   Problem Statement

In web-scale commercial recommender systems, the inputs of users' characteristics are in two kinds of structures. The first kind of structure is described by numerical or dense parameters, denoted as D. The second kind of structure is described by categorical or sparse parameters, denoted as S.

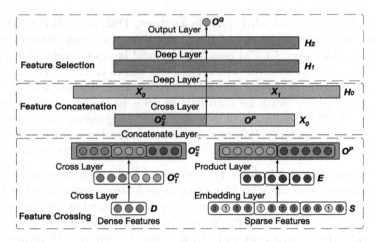

Fig. 1. The structure of XCrossNet.

Suppose that the dataset for training consists of n instances $([\boldsymbol{D}; \boldsymbol{S}], y)$, where $\boldsymbol{D} = [D_1, D_2, \cdots, D_M]$ indicates dense features including M numerical fields, and $\boldsymbol{S} = [S_1, S_2, \cdots, S_N]$ indicates sparse features including N categorical fields, and $y \in \{0, 1\}$ indicates the user's click behaviors ($y = 1$ means the user clicked the item, and $y = 0$ otherwise). The task of CTR prediction is to build a prediction model $\hat{y} = pCTR\_Model([\boldsymbol{D}; \boldsymbol{S}])$ to estimate the ratio of clicks to impressions of a given feature context.

3.2 Feature Crossing

A cross feature is defined as a synthetic feature formed by multiplying (crossing) two features. Crossing combinations of features can provide predictive abilities beyond what those features can provide individually. Based on the definition, cross features can be generalized to high-order cases. If we consider individual features as order-1st features, an order-kth cross feature is formed by multiplying k individual features.

Cross Layers on Dense Features. First we introduce a novel cross layer for crossing dense features (see in Fig. 2). Cross layers have the following formula:

$$
\begin{aligned}
C_1 &= \boldsymbol{D} \cdot \boldsymbol{D}^\mathsf{T} \cdot \boldsymbol{W}_{C,0} + b_{C,0}, \quad O_1^C = [\boldsymbol{D}; C_1], \\
C_{l+1} &= \boldsymbol{D} \cdot C_l^\mathsf{T} \cdot \boldsymbol{W}_{C,l} + b_{C,l}, \quad O_{l+1}^C = [O_l^C; C_{l+1}],
\end{aligned}
\tag{1}
$$

where $\boldsymbol{D} \in \mathbb{R}^M$ indicates the input dense features, and $C_l \in \mathbb{R}^M$ is a column vector denoting the order-$(l + 1)$th cross features. Later we prove how C_l expresses multivariate polynomials of degree $(l + 1)$ after weighted mapping. $\boldsymbol{W}_{C,l}, b_{C,l} \in \mathbb{R}^M$ are the weight and bias parameters respectively, and O_l^C, O_{l+1}^C denote the outputs from the l-th and the $(l + 1)$-th cross layers.

We denote $\boldsymbol{\alpha} = [\alpha_1, \cdots, \alpha_M]$. If our proposed cross layer expresses any cross features of order-$(l+1)$th, it could approximate to any multivariate polynomials

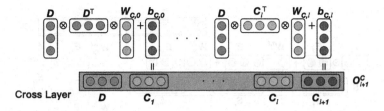

Fig. 2. The structure of cross layers.

of degree $(l+1)$, denoted as $P_{l+1}(\boldsymbol{D})$:

$$P_{l+1}(\boldsymbol{D}) = \left\{ \sum_{\alpha} W_\alpha D_1^{\alpha_1} D_2^{\alpha_2} \cdots D_M^{\alpha_M} \,\middle|\, |\boldsymbol{\alpha}| = l+1 \right\}, \qquad (2)$$

where $|\boldsymbol{\alpha}| = \sum_{i=1}^{M} \alpha_i$. For simplicity, here we use $\boldsymbol{W}^i = [W_1^i, W_2^i, \cdots, W_M^i]$ to denote the original subscript of $\boldsymbol{W}_{C,i}$. We study the coefficient $\hat{W}_\alpha$ given by $C_l^{\mathsf{T}} \cdot \boldsymbol{W}^l$ from cross layers, since it constitutes the output O_{l+1}^C from the $(l+1)$-th cross layer. Besides, the following derivations do not include bias terms. Then:

$$\begin{aligned} C_l^{\mathsf{T}} \cdot \boldsymbol{W}^l &= \left(C_{l-1}^{\mathsf{T}} \cdot \boldsymbol{W}^{l-1}\right) \cdot \left(\boldsymbol{D}^{\mathsf{T}} \cdot \boldsymbol{W}^l\right) = \prod_{i=0}^{l} \boldsymbol{D}^{\mathsf{T}} \cdot \boldsymbol{W}^i \\ &= \prod_{i=0}^{l} [D_1, D_2, \cdots, D_M]^{\mathsf{T}} \cdot [W_1^i, W_2^i, \cdots, W_M^i]. \end{aligned} \qquad (3)$$

Afterwards, let $\boldsymbol{I}$ denotes the multi-index vectors of orders $[0, 1, \cdots, l]$, and I_j denotes the order of field j. Clearly $C_l^{\mathsf{T}} \cdot \boldsymbol{W}^l$ from cross layers approaches the coefficient $\hat{W}_\alpha$ as:

$$\hat{W}_\alpha = \sum_{k=1}^{M} \sum_{|\boldsymbol{I}|=\alpha_k} \prod_{j=1}^{M} W_j^{I_j}. \qquad (4)$$

With $C_l^{\mathsf{T}} \cdot \boldsymbol{W}^l$ approximate to multivariate polynomials of degree $(l+1)$, the output O_{l+1}^C from the $(l+1)$-th cross layer that includes all cross features to order-$(l+1)$th could approximate polynomials in the following class:

$$P_{l+1}(\boldsymbol{D}) = \left\{ \sum_{\alpha} W_\alpha D_1^{\alpha_1} D_2^{\alpha_2} \cdots D_M^{\alpha_M} \,\middle|\, 0 \le |\boldsymbol{\alpha}| \le l+1 \right\}. \qquad (5)$$

Embedding and Product Layers on Sparse Features. Here we introduce the embedding layer and product layer for crossing sparse features (see in Fig. 3). As sparse features $\boldsymbol{S}$ are represented as vectors of one-hot encoding of high-dimensional spaces, we employ an embedding layer to transform these one-hot encoding vectors into dense vectors $\boldsymbol{E}$ as:

$$\begin{aligned} \boldsymbol{E} &= [\boldsymbol{E}_1, \cdots, \boldsymbol{E}_i, \cdots, \boldsymbol{E}_N], \\ \boldsymbol{E}_i &= \text{embed}(\boldsymbol{S}_i), \; \left(\boldsymbol{E}_i \in \mathbb{R}^K, i = 1, \cdots, N\right) \end{aligned} \qquad (6)$$

where $\boldsymbol{S}_i$ indicates the input sparse feature of field i, K denotes the embedding size, and $\boldsymbol{E}_i$ denotes the feature embedding of field i.

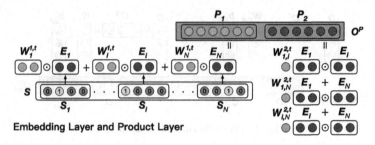

Fig. 3. The structure of embedding layer and product layer.

Afterwards, we can propose a product layer for cross sparse features. First, we donate order-2nd cross sparse features as P_2, and order-1st sparse features as P_1, thus the output of product layer is $O^P = [P_1; P_2]$.

The cross feature of two sparse features of field i and field j equals the inner product of two embedding vectors as $\langle E_i, E_j \rangle$. Intuitively, we expect cross features to be vectors, so we concatenate the weighted sums of inner products to formulate order-2nd cross features as:

$$P_2 = [P_2^1, \cdots, P_2^t, \cdots, P_2^T], \tag{7}$$

where T is the size of product layer, and P_2 is a T dimensional vector, of each dimension P_2^t denotes a weighted sum of inner products of two sparse features. Thus, we have $P_2^t = \sum_{i=1}^{N} \sum_{j=1}^{N} W_{i,j}^{2,t} \langle E_i, E_j \rangle$. We assume that the weighted parameter $W_{i,j}^{2,t} = \Theta_i^t \cdot \Theta_j^t$ for reduction, so P_2^t can be given as:

$$P_2^t = \sum_{i=1}^{N} \sum_{j=1}^{N} \Theta_i^t \cdot \Theta_j^t \langle E_i, E_j \rangle = \left\langle \sum_{i=1}^{N} \Theta_i^t \cdot E_i, \sum_{j=1}^{N} \Theta_j^t \cdot E_j \right\rangle. \tag{8}$$

The feature vector of order-1st features has a similar formula as follows:

$$P_1 = [P_1^1, \cdots, P_1^t, \cdots, P_1^T], \tag{9}$$

where P_1 is a T dimensional vector, of each dimension P_1^t denotes a weighted sum of sparse features. The weighted feature can be expressed as inner product $\langle W_i^{1,t}, E_i \rangle$. Thus, we have $P_1^t = \sum_{i=1}^{N} \langle W_i^{1,t}, E_i \rangle$.

3.3   Feature Concatenation

In the Feature Concatenation stage, in order to learn feature interactions of different structures, cross dense features O^C and cross sparse features O^P are concatenated as a vector through a concatenate layer, then the concatenated feature vector is fed into a cross layer, which can be expressed as:

$$
\begin{aligned}
X_0 &= [O^C; O^P], \\
X_1 &= X_0 \cdot X_0^\mathsf{T} \cdot W_{X,0} + b_{X,0}, \quad H_0 = [X_0; X_1],
\end{aligned} \tag{10}
$$

where X_0 denotes the concatenated feature of cross dense features and cross sparse features, X_1 denotes the cross features between two kinds of feature structures, H_0 denotes the output from this cross layer, and $W_{X,0}, b_{X,0}$ are the weight and bias parameters of this cross layer.

3.4 Feature Selection

In the Feature Selection stage, we employ an MLP to capture non-linear interactions and the relative importance of cross features. The deep layers and the output layer respectively have the following formula:

$$
\begin{aligned}
H_i &= \mathrm{ReLU}(W_{H,i-1} \cdot H_{i-1} + b_{H,i-1}), \\
O^G &= \mathrm{Sigmoid}(W_{H,i} \cdot H_i + b_{H,i}),
\end{aligned}
\tag{11}
$$

where H_i, H_{i-1} are hidden layers, ReLU$(\cdot)$ and Sigmoid$(\cdot)$ are activation functions, $W_{H,i}, W_{H,i-1}$ are weights, and $b_{H,i}, b_{H,i-1}$ are biases, and O^G is the output result.

For CTR prediction, the loss function is the Logloss as follows:

$$
\mathcal{L} = -\frac{1}{n} \sum_{i=1}^{n} y_i \log(O^G) + (1 - y_i) \log(1 - O^G),
\tag{12}
$$

where n is the total number of training instances. The optimization process is to minimize the following objective function:

$$
\mathcal{J} = \mathcal{L} + \lambda \|\Theta\|,
\tag{13}
$$

where λ denotes the regularization term, and Θ denotes the set of learning parameters, including cross layers, embedding layer, product layer, deep layers and output layer.

4 Experiments

In this section, extensive experiments are conducted to answer the following research questions[3]:

RQ1: How does XCrossNet perform compared with the state-of-the-art CTR prediction models?
RQ2: How does the feature dimensionality imbalance impact CTR prediction?
RQ3: How do hyper-parameter settings impact the performance of XCrossNet?

4.1 Experimental Setup

Dataset. Experiments are conducted on Criteo Kaggle dataset, which is from a world-wide famous Demand-Side Platforms. Criteo Kaggle dataset contains one month of $45,840,617$ ad click instances. It has 13 integer feature fields and 26 categorical feature fields. We select 7 consecutive days of samples as the training set while the next one day for evaluation.

---

[3] We release the source code at https://github.com/bigdata-ustc/XCrossNet/.

Table 1. Performance comparison of different CTR prediction models.

Model	AUC(%)	Logloss
LR	78.00	0.5631
GBDT	78.62	0.5560
FM	79.09	0.5500
AFM	79.13	0.5517
FFM	79.80	0.5438
CCPM	79.55	0.5469
Wide& Deep	79.77	0.5446
Cross	78.70	0.5550
Deep& Cross	79.76	0.5445
FNN	79.87	0.5428
DeepFM	79.91	0.5423
IPNN	80.13	0.5399
PIN	80.18	0.5394
CIN	78.81	0.5538
xDeepFM	80.06	0.5408
FGCNN	80.22	0.5389
AutoGroup	80.28	0.5384
XCrossNet	**80.68**	**0.5339**

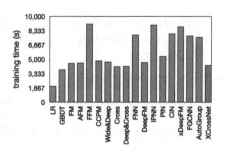

Fig. 4. Training time comparison of different CTR prediction models.

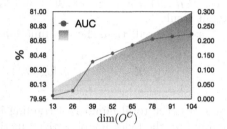

Fig. 5. Impact of feature dimensionality imbalance.

Baselines. As aforementioned, we use following highly related state-of-the-art models as baselines: **LR** [9], **GBDT** [4], **FM** [20], **AFM** [23], **FFM** [8], **CCPM** [14], **Wide&Deep** [3], **Deep&Cross** [21] and its shallow part **Cross** network, **FNN** [27], **DeepFM** [5], **IPNN** [18], **PIN** [19], **xDeepFM** [10] and its shallow part **CIN**, **FGCNN** [11], and **AutoGroup** [12].

Hyper-parameter Settings. For model optimization, we use Adam with a mini-batch size of 4096, and the learning rate is set as 0.001. We use the L2 regularization with $\lambda = 0.0001$ for all neural network models. For Wide&Deep, Deep&Cross, FNN, DeepFM, IPNN, PIN, xDeepFM, and XCrossNet, the numbers of neurons per deep layer are 400, and the depths of deep layers are set as 2. For our XCrossNet, the number of cross layers on dense features is set as $l=4$. In the main experiments, we set the embedding size for all models be a fixed value of 20.

4.2   Overall Performance (RQ1)

Table 1 summarizes the performance of all compared methods on Criteo Kaggle datasets, while the training time on Tesla K80 GPUs is shown in Fig. 4 for comparison of efficiency. From the experimental results, we have the following key observations: Firstly, most neural network models outperform linear models (i.e.,

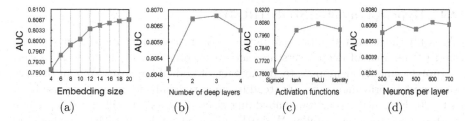

Fig. 6. Impact of network hyper-parameters on AUC performance.

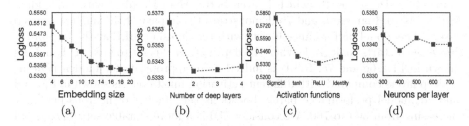

Fig. 7. Impact of network hyper-parameters on Logloss performance.

LR), tree-based models (i.e., GBDT), and FM variants (i.e., FM, FFM, AFM), which indicates MLP can learn non-linear feature interactions and endow better expressive ability. Meanwhile, comparing IPNN, PIN with FNN, Wide&Deep based models, we find that explicitly modeling low-order feature interactions can simplify the training of MLP and boost the performance. Secondly, XCrossNet achieves the best performance. Statistically, XCrossNet significantly outperforms the best baseline in terms of AUC and Logloss on p-value < 0.05 level, which indicates feature structure-oriented learning can provide better predictive abilities. Thirdly, from the training time comparison, we can observe XCrossNet is very efficient, especially compared to field-aware models, mainly because these models further allow each feature to learn several vectors where each vector is associated with a field, which leads to huge parameter consumption and time consumption.

4.3 Feature Dimensionality Imbalance Study (RQ2)

In XCrossNet, we denote $\frac{\dim(O^C)}{\dim(O^P)} \Big/ \frac{M}{N}$ as the balance index of dimensions of dense and sparse features. Noted that, the dimension of cross dense features O^C equals $M \cdot l$, increasing with the depth of cross layers. As for Criteo Kaggle dataset, $M = 13$ and $N = 26$, we set the depths of cross layers from 1 to 8, while the corresponding dimensions of cross dense features are from 13 to 104. Experimental results are shown in Fig. 5 in terms of AUC. We can observe that increasing the depth of cross layers benefits XCrossNet to achieve stable improvements on AUC performance, mainly because the higher dimensions of cross dense features are able to boost the balance index, which results in relatively balanced impacts of dense and sparse features on prediction.

4.4   Hyper-parameter Study (RQ3)

We study the impact of hyper-parameters of XCrossNet, including (1) embedding size; (2) number of deep layers; (3) activation function; (4) neurons per layer. Figures 6a and 7a demonstrate the impact of embedding size. We can observe that model performance boosts steadily when the embedding size increase from 4 to 20. Even with very low embedding sizes, XCrossNet still has comparable performance to some popular Wide&Deep based models with high embedding size. Specifically, XCrossNet achieves AUC> 0.800 and Logloss< 0.541 with embedding size set as 10, which is even better than DeepFM with embedding size set as 20. Figures 6b and 7b demonstrate the impact of the number of deep layers. The model performance boosts with the depth of MLP at the beginning. However, it starts to degrade when the depth of MLP is set to greater than 3. As shown in Figs. 6c and 7c, ReLU is indeed more appropriate for hidden neurons of deep layers compared with different activation functions. As shown in Figs. 6d and 7d, model performance barely boosts as the number of neurons per layer increasing from 300 to 700. We consider 400 is a more suitable setting to avoid the model being overfitting.

5   Conclusion

Due to the fact that previous work rarely attempts to individually learn representations for different feature structures, this paper presented a novel feature structure-oriented learning model, namely Extreme Cross Network (XCrossNet), for improving CTR prediction in recommender systems. A XCrossNet model starts with a Feature Crossing stage, followed by a Feature Concatenation stage and a Feature Selection stage. The main contribution of our approach is to represent dense and sparse feature interactions in an explicit and efficient way. Empirical studies verified the effectiveness of our model on Criteo Kaggle dataset.

Acknowledgements. This research was partially supported by grants from the National Key Research and Development Program of China (No. 2018YFC0832101), and the National Natural Science Foundation of China (Grants No. 61922073 and U20A20229). Qi Liu acknowledges the support of the Youth Innovation Promotion Association of CAS (No. 2014299).

References

1. Blondel, M., et al.: Higher-order factorization machines. In: NeurIPS, pp. 3351–3359 (2016)
2. Chang, Y., et al.: Training and testing low-degree polynomial data mappings via linear SVM. J. Mach. Learn. Res. (JMLR) **11**, 1471–1490 (2010)
3. Cheng, H.T., et al.: Wide & deep learning for recommender systems. In: 1st Workshop on Deep Learning for Recommender Systems, pp. 7–10 (2016)
4. Friedman, J.H.: Greedy function approximation: a gradient boosting machine. Annals of Statistics, pp. 1189–1232 (2001)

5. Guo, H., et al.: DeepFM: a factorization-machine based neural network for CTR prediction. In: IJCAI, pp. 1725–1731 (2017)
6. He, X., Chua, T.S.: Neural factorization machines for sparse predictive analytics. In: SIGIR, pp. 355–364 (2017)
7. Huang, Z., et al.: An ad CTR prediction method based on feature learning of deep and shallow layers. In: CIKM, pp. 2119–2122 (2017)
8. Juan, Y., et al.: Field-aware factorization machines for CTR prediction. In: RecSys, pp. 43–50 (2016)
9. Lee, K., et al.: Estimating conversion rate in display advertising from past performance data. In: SIGKDD pp. 768–776. ACM (2012)
10. Lian, J., et al.: XDeepFM: combining explicit and implicit feature interactions for recommender systems. In: SIGKDD, pp. 1754–1763 (2018)
11. Liu, B., et al.: Feature generation by convolutional neural network for click-through rate prediction. In: WWW, pp. 1119–1129 (2019)
12. Liu, B., et al.: Autogroup: automatic feature grouping for modelling explicit high-order feature interactions in CTR prediction. In: SIGIR, pp. 199–208. ACM (2020)
13. Liu, Q., et al.: Personalized travel package recommendation. In: ICDM, pp. 407–416. IEEE (2011)
14. Liu, Q., et al.: A convolutional click prediction model. In: CIKM, pp. 1743–1746 (2015)
15. Luo, Y., et al.: Autocross: automatic feature crossing for tabular data in real-world applications. In: SIGKDD, pp. 1936–1945 (2019)
16. McMahan, H.B., et al.: Ad click prediction: a view from the trenches. In: SIGKDD, pp. 1222–1230. ACM (2013)
17. Pan, Z., et al.: Sparse factorization machines for click-through rate prediction. In: ICDM, pp. 400–409. IEEE (2016)
18. Qu, Y., et al.: Product-based neural networks for user response prediction. In: ICDM pp. 1149–1154. IEEE (2016)
19. Qu, Y., et al.: Product-based neural networks for user response prediction over multi-field categorical data. ACM Trans. Inf. Syst. (ACM TOIS) 37(1), 1–35 (2018)
20. Rendle, S.: Factorization machines. In: ICDM pp. 995–1000. IEEE (2010)
21. Wang, R., et al.: Deep & cross network for ad click predictions. In: ADKDD, pp. 1–7 (2017)
22. Wu, C.J., et al.: Developing a recommendation benchmark for MLPerf training and inference. arXiv preprint arXiv:2003.07336 (2020)
23. Xiao, J., et al.: Attentional factorization machines: learning the weight of feature interactions via attention networks. In: IJCAI, pp. 3119–3125 (2017)
24. Yan, L., et al.: Coupled group lasso for web-scale CTR prediction in display advertising. ICML **32**, 802–810 (2014)
25. Yu, R., et al.: Collaborative list-and-pairwise filtering from implicit feedback. IEEE Trans. Know. Data Eng. (IEEE TKDE). https://doi.org/10.1109/TKDE.2020.3016732
26. Yu, R., et al.: Multiple pairwise ranking with implicit feedback. In: CIKM, pp. 1727–1730. ACM (2018)
27. Zhang, W., Du, T., Wang, J.: Deep learning over multi-field categorical data. In: Ferro, N., Crestani, F., Moens, M.-F., Mothe, J., Silvestri, F., Di Nunzio, G.M., Hauff, C., Silvello, G. (eds.) ECIR 2016. LNCS, vol. 9626, pp. 45–57. Springer, Cham (2016). https://doi.org/10.1007/978-3-319-30671-1_4

Learning Multiclass Classifier Under Noisy Bandit Feedback

Mudit Agarwal$^{(\boxtimes)}$ and Naresh Manwani

Machine Learning Lab, KCIS, International Institute of Information Technology
Hyderabad, Hyderabad, India
mudit.agarwal@research.iiit.ac.in, naresh.manwani@iiit.ac.in

Abstract. This paper addresses the problem of multiclass classification
with corrupted or noisy bandit feedback. In this setting, the learner may
not receive true feedback. Instead, it receives feedback that has been
flipped with some non-zero probability. We propose a novel approach to
deal with noisy bandit feedback based on the unbiased estimator technique. We further offer a method that can efficiently estimate the noise
rates, thus providing an end-to-end framework. The proposed algorithm
enjoys a mistake bound of the order of $O(\sqrt{T})$ in the high noise case
and of the order of $O(T^{2/3})$ in the worst case. We show our approach's
effectiveness using extensive experiments on several benchmark datasets.

Keywords: Online learning · Recommender system · Classification

1 Introduction

In machine learning, multiclass classification is of particular interest due to its
widespread application in several domains such as digit-recognition [17], text
classification [18] and recommender systems [14]. Some of the well-known batch
learning approaches for multiclass classification are discussed in [1,5,13,21]. An
extension of Perceptron [23] to the multiclass setting was first proposed in [11],
which was later modified by [14] to deal with bandit feedback setting. Unlike
the full information setting, the bandit setting's learner receives only partial
feedback, indicating whether the predicted label is correct or incorrect, popularly
known as bandit feedback. The learner's ability to learn a correct hypothesis
under bandit feedback finds several web-based applications, such as sponsored
advertising on web pages and recommender systems as mentioned by [14]. In the
typical setting of the recommender system, when a user makes a query to the
system, then the user is presented with a suggestion based on the past browsing
history; finally, the user responds to the suggestion, either positively (clicking it)

Electronic supplementary material The online version of this chapter (https://
doi.org/10.1007/978-3-030-75765-6_36) contains supplementary material, which is
available to authorized users.

© Springer Nature Switzerland AG 2021

K. Karlapalem et al. (Eds.): PAKDD 2021, LNAI 12713, pp. 448–460, 2021.
https://doi.org/10.1007/978-3-030-75765-6_36

(a)   **(b)**   **(c)**

Fig. 1. Three kinds of supervised learning (a) Full Information Setting: In this setting, the learner receives the actual class label. (b) Bandit Feedback Setting: A bandit feedback is revealed to the learner, indicating whether the predicted label is correct or not. (c) Noisy Bandit Setting: The learner receives noisy bandit feedback (noisy feedback is received by flipping the correct feedback with some small probability).

or negatively (not clicking it). However, the system does not know the behavior of the user if presented with other suggestions.

Banditron [14] uses an exploitation-exploration scheme proposed in [3]. When it updates, it replaces the gradient of the loss function with an unbiased estimator of the gradient. When the data is linearly separable, the expected number of mistakes made by Banditron is shown to be $O(\sqrt{T})$. In the general case, the expected number of mistakes of Banditron is $O\left(T^{2/3}\right)$. Another bandit algorithm, named Newtron [12], is based on the online Newton method. It uses a strongly convex objective function (adding regularization term with the loss function) and Follow-The-Regularized-Leader (FTRL) strategy to achieve $O(\log T)$ regret bound in the best case and $O\left(T^{2/3}\right)$ regret bound in the worst case. Second-order Perceptron is also extended in bandit feedback setting by Crammer, and Gentile [6]. It uses upper-confidence bounds (UCB) [2] based approach to handle exploration-exploitation and achieves regret bound of $O\left(\sqrt{T}\log(T)\right)$ Beygelzimer et al. [4] proposed efficient algorithms under bandit feedback when the data is linearly separable by a margin of γ. They show that their algorithm achieves a near-optimal bound of $O\left(K/\gamma\right)$ under strong linear separability condition [4].

In all the above approaches, it is assumed that the user has provided correct bandit feedback. There are many practical situations where the bandit feedback can become noisy too. In such a scenario, this means that the feedback that indicates that the predicted label is identical to the actual label may be incorrect with some non-zero probability. Consider the following examples of noisy bandit feedback. In the recommendation system, there are few cases in which a user may accidentally click (positive feedback) the recommended ad. In this case, the true feedback should be negative (no clicks). However, instead of negative, the recommender system receives positive feedback. Fake reviews and ratings are also posted using automated bots, which can boost the visibility of those products on recommendation platforms [15] (Fig. 1).

In this paper, we model the noisy bandit feedback by assuming an adversary between the learner and the environment. Whenever the learner asks a binary query, the environment releases the actual feedback. Then, the adversary flips the actual feedback with probability ρ and releases it to the learner. The problem of multiclass classification under noisy bandit feedback is as follows: on each round, the learner is given an instance vector $\mathbf{x}$; the learner predicts a label $\hat{y}$; then the learner receives the corrupted feedback f_ρ. The noisy version of this problem is more challenging because, besides bandit feedback, the learner also has to deal with noise or corruption present in the feedback. To learn a robust classifier in the presence of noisy bandit feedback, we propose an unbiased estimator $h(f_\rho)$ of the actual feedback f. The goal is to maximize the sum of $h(f_\rho^t)$, which in expectation, turns out to be the maximizing sum of actual feedbacks. Similar ideas have been explored to handle label noise in classification problems [20] under full information setting. This is the first work proposing a robust multiclass classifier under noisy bandit feedback to the best of our knowledge.

Key Contribution of The Paper:

1. We propose a robust algorithm for learning multiclass classifiers under noisy bandit feedbacks. The proposed algorithm enjoys a mistake bound of $O(\sqrt{T})$ in the high noise case and $O(T^{2/3})$ in the worst case.
2. We also propose an algorithm for noise rate estimation.
3. We validate our algorithms through experiments on benchmark datasets.

2   Multiclass Classification

In the multiclass classification, the goal is to learn a function which maps each example to one of the K categories. Let $g : \mathcal{X} \to [K]$ be the multiclass classifier where $\mathcal{X} \subseteq \mathbb{R}^d$ and $[K] = \{1, \ldots, K\}$. A multiclass classifier can be modeled using a weight matrix $W \in \mathbb{R}^{K \times d}$ as $g(\mathbf{x}) = \arg\max_{j \in [K]} \mathbf{w}_j \cdot \mathbf{x}$, where $\mathbf{w}_j$ is the jth row of matrix W and $\mathbf{x} \in \mathcal{X}$. We need to identify the weight matrix W to find the classifier. In order to identify the parameters in W of the underlying classifier, we use training data of the form $\{(\mathbf{x}^1, y^1), \ldots, (\mathbf{x}^T, y^T)\}$ where $(\mathbf{x}^t, y^t) \in \mathcal{X} \times \{1, \ldots, K\}$, $\forall t \in [T]$. The performance of the classifier f described by parameters W on example $\mathbf{x}^t$ is measured using 0–1 loss as $L_{0-1}(g(\mathbf{x}^t), y^t) = \mathbb{I}[g(\mathbf{x}^t) \neq y^t]$.[1] L_{0-1} is difficult to optimize. In practice, we use convex surrogates of L_{0-1}. L_H is one such surrogate [7] described as follows.

$$L_H(W, (\mathbf{x}^t, y^t)) = \max_{j \neq y^t} [1 - \mathbf{w}_{y^t} \cdot \mathbf{x}^t + \mathbf{w}_j \cdot \mathbf{x}^t]_+ \tag{1}$$

Here $[a]_+ = \max(0, a)$. Loss L_H becomes 0 when $\mathbf{w}_{y^t} \cdot \mathbf{x}^t - \mathbf{w}_j \cdot \mathbf{x}^t \geq 1$, $\forall j \neq y^t$.

---

[1] Here, $\mathbb{I}[A] = 1$ when the predicate A is true and 0 otherwise.

Online Multiclass Classification: Full Information Case

In the full information case, the learner receives the actual class label of examples in every trial. A large margin Perceptron algorithm for multiclass classification using L_H is proposed in [8]. The algorithm works as follows. The algorithm starts with W^1 as a zero matrix. Let W^t be the weight matrix, and $\mathbf{x}^t$ be the example presented at trial t, to algorithm. Then the algorithm predicts the labels $\hat{y}^t$ as $\hat{y}^t = \arg\max_{j \in [K]} \mathbf{w}_j^t \cdot \mathbf{x}^t$. Now it receives the true class label y^t of $\mathbf{x}^t$. Algorithm incurs a loss $L_H(W^t, (\mathbf{x}^t, y^t))$ and updates the parameters as $W^{t+1} = W^t + U^t$.

$$U_{r,j}^t = \Big[\mathbb{I}[y^t = r] - \mathbb{I}[\hat{y}^t = r]\Big] x_{t,j}. \tag{2}$$

This algorithm converges in finite iterations if the data is linearly separable [8].

Online Multiclass Classification: Bandit Feedback Case

In the bandit feedback setting [14], the learner can only know whether the predicted label is correct or not. Banditron [14] modifies the Perceptron algorithm to deal with the bandit feedback. Let W^t be the weight matrix in the beginning of trial t and $\mathbf{x}^t$ be the example presented at trial t. Let $\hat{y}^t = \arg\max_{j \in [K]} \mathbf{w}_j^t \cdot \mathbf{x}^t$. Banditron defines a probability distribution p^t on class labels as follows.

$$p^t(i) = (1 - \gamma)\mathbb{I}\,[i = \hat{y}^t] + \frac{\gamma}{K} \tag{3}$$

Here, $\gamma \in [0, 1)$ is the probability of exploration. The algorithm predicts the label $\tilde{y}^t$, which is randomly drawn from the distribution p^t. The algorithm then receives a feedback $f^t = \mathbb{I}[\tilde{y}^t = y^t]$. Banditron updates the weight matrix as $W^{t+1} = W^t + \tilde{U}^t$ where $\tilde{U}_{r,j}^t = x_{t,j} \left(\dfrac{\mathbb{I}[y^t = \tilde{y}^t]\mathbb{I}[\tilde{y}^t = r]}{p^t(r)} - \mathbb{I}[\hat{y}^t = r] \right).$

3   Learning Using Noisy Bandit Feedback

In the noisy feedback setting, an adversary is present between the learner and the feedback, which manipulates the feedback to confuse the learner. It is hypothetical to assume noise-free data [15] in the real world. So, one can find many real-world applications which are more appropriately modeled using a noisy feedback setting. For example, in a click-based recommendation system, we try to model the user behavior based on the clicks. These clicks are nothing but the bandit feedbacks, which are assumed to describe whether the user liked the recommended ad/product. Indeed, a user clicking the ad (or like the product) and likes it are two correlated events. However, the user may like the ad and does not click on it. On the other hand, the user may not like the ad but clicks on it (accidentally or in the absence of other exciting ads). These clicks are noisy as each user click does not necessarily mean that they agree with the recommended ad/product.

In this paper, we model the noisy bandit feedback as follows. Let there be an adversary which flips the true feedback, f, with a non-zero probability and generates noisy feedback. We denote the noisy bandit feedback by f_ρ. Let $P(f_\rho = 1|f = 0) = \rho_0$, $P(f_\rho = 0|f = 1) = \rho_1$ be the noise rates ($\rho_1 + \rho_0 < 1$).

Proposed Approach

Here, we propose a robust algorithm that can learn the true underlying classifier given noisy bandit feedback. To deal with the noisy or corrupted feedback, we propose a modified or proxy feedback $h(f_\rho)$, which is an unbiased estimator of true feedback f, as follows. Given the noisy feedback f_ρ, Lemma 1 shows how to construct an unbiased estimator of the true feedback f.[2]

Lemma 1. *Let* $f^t = \mathbb{I}[\tilde{y}^t = y^t]$ *be the true feedback. Let* $h(f_\rho^t)$ *be defined as,*

$$h(f_\rho) = \frac{(1 - \rho_{f'_\rho})f_\rho - \rho_{f_\rho}f'_\rho}{1 - \rho_0 - \rho_1} \tag{4}$$

where $f'_\rho = 1 - f_\rho$. *Then,* $\mathbb{E}_{f_\rho^t}[h(f_\rho^t)] = \mathbb{I}[\tilde{y}^t = y^t] = f^t$.

Instead of noisy feedback f_ρ, we use $h(f_\rho)$ (see Eq. (4)) which is an unbiased estimator of the true feedback f (Lemma 1). Similar ideas have been used to deal with the label noise in full information case [20]. We are now in a position to state a robust classifier for noisy bandit feedback. When there is no noise (*i.e.,* $\rho_0 = \rho_1 = 0$), we see that $h(f_\rho) = f_\rho = f$. Thus, under noise-free case, $h(f_\rho)$ becomes same as the noise-free bandit feedback f. At each round, the learner finds $\hat{y}^t = \arg\max_{j \in [K]} (\mathbf{w}_j^t \mathbf{x}^t)$ and defines a distribution P^t over the class labels as described in Eq. (3). Now, it samples a label $\tilde{y}^t$ randomly from P^t. It receives noisy bandit feedback f_ρ^t. We find $h(f_\rho^t)$ and update as $W^{t+1} = W^t + H^t$, where

$$H_{r,j}^t = x_j^t \left(\frac{h(f_\rho^t)\mathbb{I}[\tilde{y}^t = r]}{P^t(r)} - \mathbb{I}[\hat{y}^t = r] \right). \tag{5}$$

H^t has two sources of randomness, namely, $\tilde{y}^t$ (randomness used in the RCNBF algorithm) and f_ρ^t (randomness due to noise). Lemma 2 shows that the update matrix H^t used in RCNBF is an unbiased estimator of the matrix U^t (used in multiclass Perceptron), described in Eq. (2).

Lemma 2. *Suppose* H^t *be the update matrix as defined in Eq. (5) and let* U^t *be the matrix as defined in Eq. (2). Then,* $\mathbb{E}_{\tilde{y}^t, f_\rho^t}[H^t] = U^t$, *where* $\mathbb{E}_{\tilde{y}^t, f_\rho^t}[H^t]$ *is the expected value conditioned on* $y^1, \cdots, y^{t-1}$.

We keep repeating these steps for T trials. Complete details of the approach are given in Algorithm 1.

---

[2] All the omitted proofs can be found in the supplementary material.

Algorithm 1. Robust Classifier for Noisy Bandit Feedback (RCNBF)	**Algorithm 2.** RCNBF with Implicit Noise Estimation (RCINE)
Input: $\gamma \in (0, 0.5)$, $\rho_0, \rho_1 : \rho_0 + \rho_1 < 1$	**Input:** $\gamma \in (0, 0.5)$, N_s
Initialize: Set $W^1 = 0 \in \mathbb{R}^{K \times d}$	**Initialize:** $W^1 = 0 \in \mathbb{R}^{K \times d}, \hat{\rho}_0 = \hat{\rho}_1 = 0, \mathcal{S}$

Algorithm 1. Robust Classifier for Noisy Bandit Feedback (RCNBF)

for $t = 1, 2, \cdots, T$ **do**
  Receive $\mathbf{x}^t \in \mathbb{R}^d$.
  Set $\hat{y}^t = \arg\max_{r \in [K]}(\mathbf{w}_r^t \cdot \mathbf{x}^t)$
  Set $P^t(r) = (1 - \gamma)\mathbb{I}[r = \hat{y}^t] + \frac{\gamma}{K}, \forall r$

  Randomly sample $\tilde{y}^t$ according to P^t.

  Predict $\tilde{y}^t$ and receive feedback f_ρ^t
  Calculate $h(f_\rho^t)$ using

$$h(f_\rho^t) = \frac{(1 - \rho_{f_\rho^{t'}})f_\rho^t - \rho_{f_\rho^t}f_\rho^{t'}}{1 - \rho_0 - \rho_1}$$

  Compute $H^t \in \mathbb{R}^{K \times d}$ such that

$$H_{r,j}^t = x_j^t \left(\frac{h(f_\rho^t)\mathbb{I}[\tilde{y}^t = r]}{P^t(r)} - \mathbb{I}[\hat{y}^t = r] \right)$$

  Update: $W^{t+1} = W^t + H^t$
end for

Algorithm 2. RCNBF with Implicit Noise Estimation (RCINE)

for $t = 1, 2, \cdots, T$ **do**
  Receive $\mathbf{x}^t \in \mathbb{R}^d$.
  Set $\hat{y}^t = \arg\max_{r \in [K]}(\mathbf{w}_r^t \cdot \mathbf{x}^t)$
  Set $P^t(r) = (1 - \gamma)\mathbb{I}[r = \hat{y}^t] + \frac{\gamma}{K}, \forall r$
  Randomly sample $\tilde{y}^t$ according to P^t.
  Predict $\tilde{y}^t$ and receive feedback f_ρ^t
  Calulate $h(f_\rho^t)$ using

$$h(f_\rho^t) = \frac{(1 - \hat{\rho}_{f_\rho^{t'}})f_\rho^t - \hat{\rho}_{f_\rho^t}f_\rho^{t'}}{1 - \hat{\rho}_0 - \hat{\rho}_1}$$

  Define $H^t \in \mathbb{R}^{K \times d}$ such that

$$H_{r,j}^t = x_j^t \left(\frac{h(f_\rho^t)\mathbb{I}[\tilde{y}^t = r]}{P^t(r)} - \mathbb{I}[\hat{y}^t = r] \right)$$

  Update: $W^{t+1} = W^t + H^t$
  Data: Push $\{(\mathbf{x}^t, \tilde{y}^t), f_\rho^t\}$ in $\mathcal{S}$
  if $t \% N_s == 0$ **then**
    $\hat{\rho}_0, \hat{\rho}_1 = $ NREst$(\mathcal{S})$, Clear $\mathcal{S}$
  end if
end for

Mistake Bound Analysis of RCNBF

In this section, we derive the mistake bound for the RCNBF (Algorithm 1). To do that, we first show that the expected value of the norm of H^t is bounded.

Lemma 3. *Let H^t be defined as in Eq. (5) and $\beta = 1 - \rho_0 - \rho_1$. Then,*

$$\mathbb{E}_{\tilde{y}^t, f_\rho^t}[\|H^t\|^2] \leq \|\mathbf{x}^t\|^2 \left(A_1 \mathbb{I}[y^t \neq \hat{y}^t] + A_2 \mathbb{I}[y^t = \hat{y}^t] \right)$$

where $A_1 = \frac{2K}{\gamma} + \frac{2\rho_0(1-\rho_0)K}{\beta\gamma} + \frac{K\rho_1}{\beta^2\gamma} + \frac{\rho_0(1-\rho_0)K^2}{\beta^2\gamma^2}$, $A_2 = 2\gamma + \frac{\rho_1}{\beta^2(1-\gamma)} + \frac{\rho_0(1-\rho_0)K^2}{\beta^2\gamma}$.

Note that the norm of the matrix H^t is inversely proportional to $\beta = 1 - \rho_0 - \rho_1$. Thus, if the noise rate increases, the upper bound on the norm of H^t will increase. We now find the expected mistake bound of the RCNBF algorithm.

Theorem 1 (Mistake Bound). *Let $\mathbf{x}^1, \cdots, \mathbf{x}^T$ be the sequence of examples presented to the RCNBF in T trials. Let, $\|\mathbf{x}^t\| \leq 1, \forall t \in [T]$ and $y^t \in [K]$. Let $R_H = \sum_{t=1}^T L_H(W^*; (\mathbf{x}^t, y^t))$ and $D = \|W^*\|_F^2 = \sum_{r=1}^K \sum_{j=1}^d (W_{i,j}^*)^2$ be the*

Algorithm 3. Noise Rate Estimator (NREst)

Input: $\mathcal{S} = \{(\mathbf{x}^t, \tilde{y}^t), f_\rho^t) : t = 1 \ldots T\}$

    Train a network using $\mathcal{S}$ which approximates $q(\mathbf{x}, \tilde{y}) = \hat{p}(f_\rho = 1 | \mathbf{x}, \tilde{y})$

    Find $\mathbf{x}^j = \arg\max_{\mathbf{x} \in \mathcal{X}} \hat{p}(f_\rho = 1 | \mathbf{x}, \tilde{y} = j)$, $j \in [K]$

    Set $1 - \rho_1 = \hat{p}(f_\rho = 1 | \mathbf{x}^l, \tilde{y} = l)$ and $\rho_0 = \hat{p}(f_\rho = 1 | \mathbf{x}^k, \tilde{y} = l)$

Output: ρ_0, ρ_1

---

cumulative hinge loss and the complexity of any matrix, W^*. Let ρ_0 and ρ_1 be the noise parameters. Then the expected number of mistakes made by RCNBF is upper bounded as $\mathbb{E}[M] \leq R_H + \sqrt{A_1 D R_H} + 3 \max\{A_1 D, \sqrt{A_2 D T}\} + \gamma T$. Here, expectation is with respect to all the randomness of the algorithm.

Before moving, let us find the optimal value for the exploration-exploitation parameter γ and the corresponding mistake bound.

Corollary 1. *(Zero Noise Case, $\rho_0 = \rho_1 = 0$) In this case the mistake bound of RCNBF is of the order $O(\sqrt{T})$ which can be obtained by setting $\gamma = O(T^{-1/2})$.*

Corollary 2. *(High Noise Case, $\rho_0, \rho_1 \leq \min\{0.5, O(\sqrt{\frac{D}{T}})\}$) In this case, we obtain the bound $\mathbb{E}[M] \leq O(\sqrt{DT}\beta^{-1})$ for $\gamma = O(\sqrt{\frac{D}{\beta^2 T}})$.*

Corollary 3. *(Very High Noise Case, $\rho_0, \rho_1 \leq 1$) In this case the mistake bound of is $O(T^{2/3}\beta^{-1})$ for $\gamma = O(T^{-1/3}\beta^{-1})$.*

We see that the above mistake bound is inversely proportional to β, *i.e.*, as we increase the noise rate, the mistake bound will increase, which is as expected and also aligns with the batch mode algorithm in the presence of label noise [20].

Noise Rate Estimation

Here, we propose an approach for estimating ρ_0 and ρ_1 which uses ideas presented in [16,22]. The proposed approach is based on the following Theorem.

Theorem 2. *Assume that*

1. *There exist at least one "perfect example" for every class $j \in [K]$. Which means, there exists $\mathbf{x}_j^* \in \mathcal{X}$ (prefect example for class j) such that $p(\mathbf{x}_j^*) > 0$ and $p(y = \tilde{y} | \mathbf{x}_j^*, \tilde{y} = j) = p(y = j | \mathbf{x}_j^*) = 1$.*
2. *There exist sufficient corrupted examples to estimate $p(f_\rho | \mathbf{x}, \tilde{y} = l)$ accurately.*

Then it follows that $1 - \rho_1 = p(f_\rho = 1 | \mathbf{x}_l^*, \tilde{y} = l)$, $l \in [K]$ and $\rho_0 = p(f_\rho = 1 | \mathbf{x}_k^*, \tilde{y} = l)$, $l \neq k$, where $\mathbf{x}_l^*$ and $\mathbf{x}_k^*$ are perfect examples of class l and k.

Theorem 2 assumes that for every class $j \in [K]$, there exists a perfect example $\mathbf{x}_j^*$ such that $p(f = 1 | \mathbf{x}_j^*, \tilde{y} = j) = p(y = j | \mathbf{x}_j^*) = 1$. We use this idea to estimate the noise rates as follows. We use the data generated by RCNBF under noisy bandit feedback setting. Using this, we create a training set $\mathcal{S}$ with following sequence of examples $\{(\mathbf{x}^t, \tilde{y}^t), f_\rho^t\}$ for $t = 1 \ldots N_s$. Note that the input to the

Table 1. Estimated noise rates (rounded to 3 decimal digits)

Actual noise rates		Estimated noise rates					
		MNIST		USPS		Fashion-MNIST	
ρ_0	ρ_1	$\hat{\rho}_0$	$\hat{\rho}_1$	$\hat{\rho}_0$	$\hat{\rho}_1$	$\hat{\rho}_0$	$\hat{\rho}_1$
0.000	0.000	0.063	0.029	0.017	0.000	0.090	0.004
0.150	0.150	0.172	0.147	0.181	0.153	0.189	0.140
0.250	0.250	0.248	0.264	0.258	0.257	0.264	0.259
0.200	0.400	0.211	0.439	0.194	0.419	0.215	0.393
0.400	0.200	0.400	0.260	0.393	0.229	0.404	0.222
0.400	0.400	0.403	0.508	0.402	0.515	0.397	0.502

network is $\mathbf{x}^t$ concatenated with $\tilde{y}^t$. This is the major difference with the noise rate estimation presented in [22]. We use $\mathcal{S}$ to train a neural network with a output layer of size 2 and softmax as the activation function of the output layer. Our classification problem is binary however following [24], we prefer to use softmax with one-hot output instead of sigmoid as it allows the network to learn non-convex boundaries. This network approximates $q(\mathbf{x}, \tilde{y}) = \hat{p}(f_\rho = 1|\mathbf{x}, \tilde{y})$. Now we find perfect example for each class. A perfect example $\mathbf{x}_j^*$ for class j is the one for which $\hat{p}(y = j|\mathbf{x}_j^*) = \hat{p}(f_\rho = 1|\mathbf{x}_j^*, \tilde{y} = j) = 1$. We can find $\mathbf{x}_j^*$ as

$$\mathbf{x}_j^* = \arg\max_{\mathbf{x} \in \mathcal{S}} \hat{p}(f_\rho = 1|\mathbf{x}, \tilde{y} = j), \ j \in [K] \tag{6}$$

Now, we can approximate $\hat{\rho}_0$ and $\hat{\rho}_1$ as $1 - \hat{\rho}_1 = \hat{p}(f_\rho = 1|\mathbf{x}_l^*, \tilde{y} = l)$ and $\hat{\rho}_0 = \hat{p}(f_\rho = 1|\mathbf{x}_k^*, \tilde{y} = l)$. The noise estimation approach is described in Algorithm 3.

Learning Using Noisy Bandit Feedback with Implicit Noise Rate Estimation

RCNBF (Algorithm 1) runs under the online setting while NREst (Algorithm 3) is a batch algorithm. With the help of the above two algorithms, we are proposing a pseudo online mode algorithm, RCNBF with Implicit Noise Estimation(Algorithm 2), which runs under the online setting. The RCINE Algorithm[3] uses RCNBF to make predictions and generate dataset $\mathcal{S}$ for Noise Estimation. After every N_s trails, the algorithm updates the estimated noise rate parameters by running the NREst algorithm on the collected dataset $\mathcal{S}$. The crux of this setup is that the RCNBF will run in the online mode, while NREst, which is running parallelly at the same time, will estimate the noise rates parameter $\hat{\rho}_0$ and $\hat{\rho}_1$ and update them repetitively after a small interval of time.

4   Experimentation

We do experiments on various real-world as well as synthetic datasets. The synthetic dataset is called SynSep. SynSep is a 9-class, 400-dimensional synthetic

---

[3] The complete code for all the experiments can be found here.

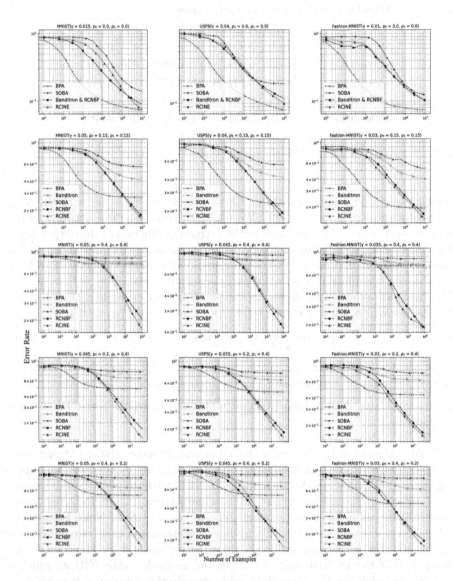

Fig. 2. Average error rates of RCNBF, RCINE and other benchmarking algorithms under noise-free case (first row; $\rho_0 = \rho_1 = 0$), low noise case (second row; $\rho_0 = \rho_1 = 0.15$), high noise case (third row; $\rho_0 = \rho_1 = 0.40$) and mixed noise case (fourth row; $\rho_0 = 0.2, \rho_1 = 0.4$ and fifth row; $\rho_0 = 0.4, \rho_1 = 0.2$). Three datasets are used (left to right): MNIST, USPS and Fashion-MNIST.

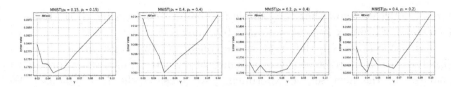

Fig. 3. Average error rates of RCINE against parameter's value γ under different noise rate setting on MNIST.

data set of size 10^5. While constructing SynSep, we ensure that the dataset is linearly separable. For more detail about the dataset, one can refer to [14]. We also perform experiments on MNIST and Iris datasets from UCI repository [9], USPS dataset[4] and Fashion-MNIST for image classification [25][5].

Feature Extraction for Fashion-MNIST Dataset: We first randomly sampled 35,000 images from the dataset for feature extraction and trained a four-layer convolutional neural network. The first layer is a convolutional layer with 32 feature maps having a size of 3×3 and a stride of 1. It takes an input of 28×28 grayscale images. The convolutional layer is followed by a max-pooling layer having 2×2 as pool size. The next layer is a fully-connected layer with 100 units and a dropout of the probability of 0.2. The last layer is a fully connected softmax layer. To extract features, we took the output of the fully connected layer of size 100. By experimenting on this dataset, we show that our approach can also be used for learning classifiers for complex datasets.

Benchmark Algorithms and Noise Rate Setting: We present experimental comparisons of our proposed algorithms (RCNBF and RCINE) with Banditron [14], Bandit Passive Aggressive [26] and Second Order Banditron Algorithm [4]. Five different settings of noise rate are used. These are (a) $\rho_0 = \rho_1 = 0.0$, (b) $\rho_0 = \rho_1 = 0.15$, (c) $\rho_0 = \rho_1 = 0.4$, (d) $\rho_0 = 0.2, \rho_1 = 0.4$ and (e) $\rho_0 = 0.4, \rho_1 = 0.2$. On each of the different noise setting, we ran our proposed algorithm, RCNBF (using original noise rates) and RCINE (with initial value of $\hat{\rho}_0 = \hat{\rho}_1 = 0$). For updating the noise rates parameter, the RCINE algorithm, runs the NREst algorithm after N_s trails on the collected dataset $\mathcal{S}$. NREst algorithm uses a neural network to estimate the noise rates. Table 1 shows the results of estimation of noise rates at an intermediate instance of RCINE algorithm.

In NREst algorithm, train-test ratio of 90:10 is taken. Cross-entropy loss is chosen for comparison. 10% of the training set is used for validation. The mini-batch size used for training is 128. The activation function for all the network is ReLU and optimizer is AdaGrad [10] with initial learning rate 0.01 and $\delta = 10^{-6}$. After training, we apply the estimator to find $\hat{\rho}_0, 1 - \hat{\rho}_0, \hat{\rho}_1$ and $1 - \hat{\rho}_1$ on $\mathcal{S}$. Then we normalize the values of $\hat{\rho}_0, 1 - \hat{\rho}_0$ and $\hat{\rho}_1, 1 - \hat{\rho}_1$ such that they sum up to 1.

---

[4] https://www.kaggle.com/bistaumanga/usps-dataset.

[5] The results and further discussion for SynSep and IRIS dataset are included in the supplementary file due to the space restrictions.

From [19, 22] we know that the sample maximum is susceptible to the outliers, so instead of argmax Eq. (6), we take 89%-percentile.

For *MNIST dataset*, the architecture consists of two dense hidden layers of size 128 with a dropout of the probability of 0.2. We train the network for 70 epochs. For the next set of experiments, we consider the *USPS dataset*. We trained an architecture with three dense hidden layers of 32, 256, and 32 respectively, with a dropout of probability 0.2 for 70 epochs. Lastly, for *Fashion-MNIST dataset*, the architecture consists of three dense layers of size 32, 128 and 32 respectively with a dropout of probability 0.2 and is trained for 70 epochs.

Parameter Selection: For each dataset and each different noise setting, simulations for RCINE are run for a wide range of values of the exploration parameter, γ.[6] For MNIST dataset, γ exploration results are shown in Fig. 3. We choose the γ value for which the minimum error rate is achieved.

Results: We ran our proposed algorithms (RCNBF and RCINE) and compared the average[7] error rate with other benchmark algorithms as shown in Fig. 2. For better visualization of the asymptotic bounds, we plotted the result on a log-log scale. It shows that in the presence of noise, the final error rate of RCINE and RCNBF is significantly better than SOBA, BPA, and Banditron. While all other algorithms converge, RCNBF and RCINE are still learning and yet to converge.

Analysis of Fig. 2 shows that as the number of examples grows, the slope of the error rate of RCNBF and RCINE under all different settings of noise rate is comparable to that of SOBA, BPA, and Banditron for the noise-free (0%) setting. The final error rate of RCNBF and RCINE under all different noise rate settings is also close to SOBA, BPA, and Banditron under the noise-free setting. RCINE performs comparably to RCNBF for all the datasets and noise settings. This happens as we can efficiently estimate the noise rates.

5   Conclusion and Future Work

In this paper, we proposed a noisy bandit feedback setting in online multiclass classification, which can effectively incorporate the noise present in real-world data. We proposed a novel algorithm based on the unbiased estimation technique, which enjoys a favorable bound (both theoretically and practically) under the proposed noisy bandit feedback setting. The proposed algorithm is robust to the noisy bandit feedback and can learn the true hypothesis in the presence of noise. We also propose a technique to estimate the noise rate, thus providing an end-to-end framework. Experimental comparisons on various datasets with benchmarking algorithms show that RCNBF and RCINE are comparable to other algorithms under noise-free bandit feedback settings but far better than others under noisy bandit feedback settings.

---

[6] The value of γ as shown in the figure are for RCINE. For other algorithms, the optimal value of γ is chosen.

[7] Note that here averaging is done over ten independent simulations of the algorithm.

References

1. Anthony, M., Bartlett, P.L.: Neural network learning: Theoretical foundations. Cambridge University Press (2009)
2. Auer, P.: Cesa-Bianchi, Nicolò, Fischer, Paul: Finite-time analysis of the multi-armed bandit problem. Mach. Learn. **47**(2–3), 235–256 (2002)
3. Auer, P., Cesa-Bianchi, N., Freund, Y., Schapire, R.E.: The nonstochastic multi-armed bandit problem. SIAM J. Comput. **32**(1), 48–77 (2003)
4. Beygelzimer, A., Pal, D., Szorenyi, B., Thiruvenkatachari, D., Wei, C.-Y., Zhang, C., (eds.) Bandit Multiclass Linear Classification: Efficient Algorithms for the Separable Case, Proceedings of the 36th International Conference on Machine Learning ICML, February 2019
5. Bishop, C.M., et al.: Neural networks for pattern recognition. Oxford University Press (1995)
6. Crammer, K., Gentile, C.: Multiclass classification with bandit feedback using adaptive regularization **90**, 273–280 (2011)
7. Crammer, K., Singer, Y.: On the algorithmic implementation of multiclass kernel-based vector machines. J. Mach. Learn. Res. **2**, 265–292 (2002)
8. Crammer, K., Singer, Y.: Ultraconservative online algorithms for multiclass problems. J. Mach. Learn. Res. **3**, 951–991 (2003)
9. Dua, D., Graff, C.: UCI machine learning repository (2017)
10. Duchi, J., Hazan, E., Singer, Y.: Adaptive subgradient methods for online learning and stochastic optimization. J. Mach. Learn. Res. **12**, 2121–2159 (2011)
11. Duda, R.O., Hart, P.E., et al.: Pattern classification and scene analysis, vol. 3. Wiley, New York (1973)
12. Hazan, E., Kale, S.: Newtron: an efficient bandit algorithm for online multiclass prediction. In: Shawe-Taylor, J., Zemel, R., Bartlett, P., Pereira, F., Weinberger, K.Q. (eds.) Advances in Neural Information Processing Systems, vol. 24, pp. 891–899. Curran Associates Inc. (2011)
13. Hsu, C.-W., Lin, C.-J.: A comparison of methods for multiclass support vector machines. IEEE Trans. Neural Networks **13**(2), 415–425 (2002)
14. Kakade, S.M., Shalev-Shwartz, S., Tewari, A.: Efficient bandit algorithms for online multiclass prediction. In: Proceedings of the 25th International Conference on Machine Learning, pp. 440–447 (2008)
15. Kapoor, S., Patel, K.K., Kar, P.: Corruption-tolerant bandit learning. Machine Learning **108**(4), 687–715 (2018). https://doi.org/10.1007/s10994-018-5758-5
16. Liu, T., Tao, D.: Classification with noisy labels by importance reweighting. IEEE Trans. Pattern Anal. Mach. Intell. **38**(3), 447–461 (2015)
17. Ma, C., Zhang, H.: Effective handwritten digit recognition based on multi-feature extraction and deep analysis. In: 2015 12th International Conference on Fuzzy Systems and Knowledge Discovery (FSKD), pp. 297–301. IEEE (2015)
18. McCallum, A.: Multi-label text classification with a mixture model trained by em. In: AAAI Workshop on Text Learning, pp. 1–7 (1999)
19. Menon, A., Van Rooyen, B., Ong, C.S., Williamson, B.: Learning from corrupted binary labels via class-probability estimation. In: International Conference on Machine Learning, pp. 125–134 (2015)
20. Natarajan, N., Dhillon, I.S., Ravikumar, P.K., Tewari, A.: Learning with noisy labels. In: Advances in Neural Information Processing Systems, pp. 1196–1204 (2013)

21. Ou, G., Murphey, Y.L.: Multi-class pattern classification using neural networks. Pattern Recogn. **40**(1), 4–18 (2007)
22. Patrini, G., Rozza, A., Menon, A.K., Nock, R., Qu, L.: Making deep neural networks robust to label noise: a loss correction approach. In: Proceedings of the IEEE Conference on Computer Vision and Pattern Recognition, pp. 1944–195 (2017)
23. Rosenblatt, F.: The perceptron: a probabilistic model for information storage and organization in the brain. Psychol. Rev. **65**(6), 386 (1958)
24. Sivaprasad, S., Manwani, N., Gandhi, V.: The curious case of convex networks. arXiv preprint arXiv:2006.05103 (2020)
25. Xiao, H., Rasul, K., Vollgraf, R.: Fashion-mnist: a novel image dataset for benchmarking machine learning algorithms. arXiv preprint arXiv:1708.07747 (2017)
26. Zhong, H., Daucé, E.: Passive-aggressive bounds in bandit feedback classification. In: Proceedings of the ECMLPKDD, pp. 255–264 (2015)

Diversify or Not: Dynamic Diversification for Personalized Recommendation

Bin Hao, Min Zhang$^{(\boxtimes)}$, Cheng Guo, Weizhi Ma, Yiqun Liu, and Shaoping Ma

Department of Computer Science and Technology, Institute for Artificial Intelligence,
Beijing National Research Center for Information Science and Technology,
Tsinghua University, Beijing 100084, China
haob15@mails.tsinghua.edu.cn, z-m@tsinghua.edu.cn

Abstract. Diversity is believed to be an essential factor in improving user satisfaction in recommender systems, while how to take advantage of it has long been a problem worth exploring. Existing work either ignores the influence of diversity or overlooks users' different diversity demands in recommendations. In this study, we analyze users' behaviors on a real-world dataset collected from an e-commerce website and find that the demand for diversity changes among different users, even the same user's demand varies among different shopping scenarios. There is also evidence that users' behaviors are affected by the diversity of impressions, which has been often ignored by traditional session-based recommendation models. Then, we propose a Dynamic Diversification Recommendation Model (DDRM) with the integration of both click and impression diversities to better make use of diversity for recommendations. Extensive experimental results demonstrate that DDRM outperforms all baseline methods significantly. Further studies show our model can provide more precise and reasonable recommendations.

Keywords: Recommender systems · Diversity · Recurrent neural networks

1 Introduction

Since the concept of "diversity in recommendation" was raised in 2000 s [8, 16], more and more researchers have realized that diversity is one of the fundamental metrics in recommender systems. From the user perspective, diversity provides opportunities for users to find his/her preference among a great extent of uncertainty; it is also a source of satisfaction by browsing rich and colorful products. Consequently, customer satisfaction indirectly benefits the business in increased activities, revenues, and customer loyalty.

This work is supported by the National Key Research and Development Program of China (2018YFC0831900), Natural Science Foundation of China (Grant No. 62002191, 61672311, 61532011) and Tsinghua University Guoqiang Research Institute. This project is also funded by China Postdoctoral Science Foundation (2020M670339) and Dr. Weizhi Ma has been supported by Shuimu Tsinghua Scholar Program.

© Springer Nature Switzerland AG 2021
K. Karlapalem et al. (Eds.): PAKDD 2021, LNAI 12713, pp. 461–472, 2021.
https://doi.org/10.1007/978-3-030-75765-6_37

What makes the idea of diversity attractive is the primary hypothesis: users' behaviors are affected not only by an individual item but also by the impression list presented. Diversity is defined as "relates to the internal difference within parts of an experience" [2], and previous studies have addressed the importance of diversity in recommendation. In this study, we focus on category-based diversity to measure user diversity as mentioned in [6], in which both click diversity and impression diversity are taken into consideration.

Fig. 1. Users' *diversity demands* vary in different scenarios.

Users may hold different demands of diversity. By analyzing real-world data, results show that user's requirements of diversity vary in different browsing/shopping scenarios. Figure 1 shows an example: a boy with the intention of "buying a cellphone for myself" may require a more straightforward recommendation. While the girl may get happier if the impression list is more diverse when thinking about what to buy for the summer holiday.

Besides users' different *diversity demands*, the other question is how to measure them and give further recommendations. It is widely recognized that a user's click/purchasing history could indicate his/her preference [10]. The "history" is limited to a relatively short period (when the user's intent is supposed to remain the same) in session-based recommendations [18], where the previous part of a click sequence is used to predict the rear one. The concept of context here includes two aspects: Firstly, the diversity of items clicked by a user could reflect his/her diversity demand to some extent. **Click diversity** is a dynamic factor: it changes as the user clicks on a new item. Secondly, user's behaviors (clicks) are affected not only by his/her preference but also by impressions [3]. Therefore, **impression diversity** is another context information that could be used to infer user preference.

To tackle the above problem, we propose a novel neural networks framework, named Dynamic Diversification Recommendation Model (DDRM), aiming at giving diversified recommendations based on both users' click and impression history. We first build a Recurrent Neural Network (RNN) to learn the encoding of the click sequence. Then two lists of clicked items and impression items are individually updated to calculate diversity at each time node. The two diversity sequences are further used for constraining the generation of sequential embeddings. For individual items, we train a Word2Vec model for item encoding.

In the last step, after a similarity layer and softmax layer, the model outputs the prediction scores of each item in the candidate list.

The main contributions of this work are summarized as follows:

- We make data analysis on a real-world dataset collected from the online-shopping website to explore how diversity affects users' behaviors. Results show that firstly diversity does affect users' click behavior. Secondly, there are significant differences between different user groups.
- We propose a model named DDRM to take into account both the click diversity and impression diversity and compute recommendation scores to give recommendations.
- Extensive experiments on a real-world dataset show that DDRM outperforms baseline methods in terms of main evaluation metrics. Moreover, real cases show how our model gives appropriate recommendations based on different diversity demands.

2   Related Work

Diversity Metric. Evaluation metric is one of the most important research questions of diversity. The intra-list diversity (ILD) has been used in a number of works [13,17,19], with the consideration of the influence of recommendation lists. The computation of ILD requires a distance measure between each item, which can be defined differently for specific problems. The distance is generally a function of item features or a function in terms of user interaction patterns. However, few previous studies compare different types of diversities, nor do they validate whether the diversities designed are consistent with the diversity perceived by users.

Diversity Enhancement. Re-ranking is the most straight-forward group of approaches for diversity enhancement, which exploits specific diversity measures to re-rank a recommendation result from a recommender system. Belém et al. [1] re-ranks the recommendations provided by any tag recommender in order to jointly promote relevance, novelty, and topic diversity, where topics are generated by Latent Dirichlet Allocation (LDA). Other groups of diversity enhancement approaches are cluster-based methods. Li et al. [7] propose a nearest-neighbor algorithm to improve aggregate diversity. Sar et al. [14] use Gradient Boosted Trees with item diversity features to predict CTR of the recommendation lists.

Deficiently, these methods are proposed to diversify recommendations for all users to the same degree, regardless of users' different requirements or diversity tolerance. They fail to consider the diversity demand varies in different scenarios even with the same user.

Sequence-based Recommendation. Sequence-based recommendation, or session-based recommendation [15] is proposed based on the assumption that the user's next behavior could be inferred from his/her previous behavior sequence. The sequence is believed to depict the user's preference within a certain time interval. Recurrent Neural Networks (RNN) have been successfully applied in sequential recommmendation recently. Hidasi et al. [5] first apply RNN to session-based recommendation and achieve significant improvement over traditional methods. Besides considering users' historical behaviors, Rakkappan et al. [11] propose a context-aware sequential recommendation, based on Stacked Recurrent Neural Networks, that model the dynamics of contexts and temporal gaps.

It's an interesting phenomenon that both diversity enhancement methods and sequence-based methods attempt to make use of context information to provide better recommendations. We design and implement a dynamic diversification recommender system, which to the best of our knowledge, is the first work to combine the two types of information in recommendation.

3   Diversity Measurement

As mentioned in Sect. 2, since we are trying to measure user perceived diversity by contextual information, we adopt the popular diversity metric, average intra-list distance (ILD):

$$ILD = \frac{1}{|R|(|R| - 1)} \sum_{i \in R} \sum_{j \in R, i! = j} d(i, j) \tag{1}$$

Where R is the recommendation list given to a user during a period of time, i and j are both items in it. The computation of ILD requires defining a distance measure $d(i, j)$. The concept of "category" is often considered in modern e-commerce as evidence to give recommendations. We adopt "category diversity" in this work.

Category Diversity. When a user views a list of recommended items, one of the most prominent factors is the category distribution of the list. Most people would find that a list with "dress, potato chips, earphones, computer chair, etc." is more diverse than another list of "shirt, jeans, polo, T-shirt, etc.", due to the number of categories included in the list. In many e-commerce websites, the category of items is a multi-level tree structure. Let i_{cm} be the m-level subcategory of item i, and P_k be a logical proposition that "$i_{ck} == j_{ck}$", then the category diversity is measured by the distance between items i and j, it is calculated by:

$$d(i, j) = \sum_{k=1}^{m} \phi_k \left(\frac{2m - 2(k - 1)}{2m} \right) = \sum_{k=1}^{m} \phi_k \left(\frac{m - k + 1}{m} \right) \tag{2}$$

where

$$\phi_k = \begin{cases} 1, & \text{if } P_1 \wedge P_2 \wedge \cdots \wedge P_{k-1} \wedge \neg P_k \\ 0, & \text{otherwise} \end{cases}$$

Here $P_0 \equiv true$ and m is the category levels. The molecules $(2m - 2(k - 1))$ are the shortest path length on a tree between two subcategories of the same level. Besides, $2m$ is the longest path length if the two items are with different 1-level category, used as normalization.

4 Large-Scale Log Based Diversity Analysis

4.1 Data Preparation

We collect data from an online-shopping website (www.jd.com), which has more than 360 million active users each year. Moreover, we sampled users whose purchase order is between 100 and 1,000 within a year and their behaviors recorded within one week (from $1_{st}, AUG, 2017$ to $7_{th}, AUG, 2017$). The sampled dataset consists of 90,331 users, 5,662,595 items, and 6,657,048 impressions.

In this paper, we focus on analyzing users' click behaviors due to the following reasons: first, "click" is a relatively frequent action, since a user may click more than 20 times before he/she buys a product. Second, click-through-rate (CTR) has long been an effective metric in information retrieval, which is also a vital recommendation metric in the industry. Thirdly, "click" is a direct reaction after shown impression lists, which reflects users' choices and preferences.

4.2 Analysis on Impression-Level Behaviors

Firstly, we want to verify whether there is a relation between users' click behavior and diversity within an impression. Heat maps in Fig. 2 show the correlation between CTR and impression-list level diversity.

We investigate CTR vs. diversity on different gender groups to see if there exists divergence between different people. Figure 2(a) and Fig. 2(b) show a comparison between different genders. We can see that more male users are attracted by diverse lists, for the CTR is relatively higher when diversity is high ($0.6 \sim 1.0$). In contrast the distribution of female users goes more dispersed. Next, Fig. 2(c) and Fig. 2(d) show the distributions on two age groups. High diversity ($0.6 \sim 1.0$) usually leads to a higher CTR ($0.10 \sim 0.18$) for young users (age $21 - 25$), while diversity seems not that attractive for middle-aged users (age $41 - 45$).

Conclusions can be drawn from the above analysis: firstly, diversity does affect a user's click behavior, indicating that diversity is an essential factor that should be considered in recommendation. Secondly, there are significant differences between different user groups. It indicates that diversification is a personalized task more than a generalized one: the decision of whether to diversify belongs to the user himself/herself. Due to it is not easy to get user personal information, we focus on adequately introducing diversity into recommendation methods in this study.

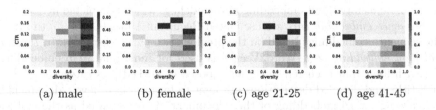

| (a) male | (b) female | (c) age 21-25 | (d) age 41-45 |

Fig. 2. Heat map of CTR and impression diversity of different gender and age groups.

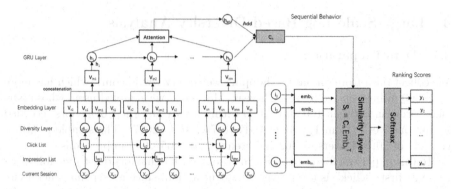

Fig. 3. Overview of the structure of DDRM

5   Dynamic Diversification Recommendation Model

5.1   Problem Formulation

We define the session-based recommendation task as follow. Given a time window size Δt, let $L = \{(l_1, t_1), (l_2, t_2), ..., (l_n, t_n)\}$ be the set of impression lists presented to the user, let $X = [(x_1, t_1), (x_2, t_2), ..., (x_n, t_n)]$ be a click session, where $t_n - t_1 \leq \Delta t, x_i \in l_i, 1 \leq i \leq n$. For any given prefix of the click sequence in the session, $\mathbf{x} = [x_1, x_2, ..., x_{t-1}, x_t], \mathbf{l} = [l_1, l_2, ..., l_{t-1}, l_t], 1 \leq t \leq n$, a session-based recommender system RS should output $\mathbf{y} = RS(\mathbf{x})$, where $\mathbf{y} = [y_1, y_2, ..., y_{d-1}, y_d]$ and $y_j(1 \leq j \leq d)$ corresponds to the recommendation score of item j. In the task of top-$k(1 \leq k \leq d)$ recommendation, k items with the highest scores in $\mathbf{y}$ are recommended.

5.2   Model Overview

Figure 3 gives an overview of the structure of Dynamic Diversification Recommendation Model (DDRM). The model mainly includes five parts: *diversity integrated sequence modeling part, time gap integrated sequence modeling part, sequence embedding part, individual item embedding part*, and *dynamic diversification prediction part*.

Diversity integrated sequence modeling part integrates click diversity and impression diversity into input embedding; the detail will be introduced in Sect. 5.3. *Time gap integrated sequence modeling part* takes the time gaps between items into input embedding into modeling, which is depicted in Sect. 5.4. In *Sequence embedding part*, we use Gated Recurrent Units (GRU) [5] to model the sequence embeddings based on the previous two parts (Sect. 5.5). In *Individual item embedding part*, Word2Vec [9] is used for individual item embedding. For each item that occurred (whether exposed or clicked), its categories (3 levels), title, and detailed descriptions are joint to form an item-level "document". The average word embedding of the "document" is represented as the embedding of each item. At last, *Dynamic diversification prediction part* is used to make predictions for each candidate item and give the final recommendation. The detail is introduced in Sect. 5.6.

5.3   Diversity Integrated Sequence Modeling Part

Click Diversity Integration. The diversity of clicked item list in a session is a variable, which changes with the user's click action as new items are added into the list. $x_i(1 \leq i \leq n)$ is the item clicked at time t_i, and l_{ci} is the clicked item set until time t_i. Then, if a user clicks item x_{i+1}, this process is linear according to chronological order:

$$l_{ci+1} = l_{ci} \cup \{x_{i+1}\} \tag{3}$$

and the value of "click diversity" $d_{ci}(1 \leq i \leq n)$, which is calculated by Eq. 1, updates when a new item is added. We assume that part of the embeddings from the temporal sequence should be constrained (or presented) by the corresponding "click diversity", as a result, the input of a GRU unit at time n is given by:

$$\mathbf{v}_{Inn} = \mathbf{v}_{xn} \odot \mathbf{v}_{cn} \tag{4}$$

where $\mathbf{v}_{xn} \in R^{1*d_1}$, $\odot$ denotes concatenation.

Impression Diversity Integration. Similar to "click diversity", l_{Imi} indicates the impression list presented to the user before time t_i, which is also expanded with time order:

$$l_{Imi+1} = l_{Imi} \cup l_i \tag{5}$$

Correspondingly, the impression diversity d_{Imi} (which is also calculated by Eq. 1), together with the click diversity, form the embedding layer:

$$\mathbf{v}_{Inn} = \mathbf{v}_{xn} \odot \mathbf{v}_{cn} \odot \mathbf{v}_{Imn} \tag{6}$$

where $\mathbf{v}_{xn} \in R^{1*d_1}$, $\mathbf{v}_{cn} \in R^{1*d_2}$, $\mathbf{v}_{Imn} \in R^{1*d_3}$.

5.4   Time Gap Integrated Sequence Modeling Part

Time gap between two clicks can capture the duration of each click behavior. X_{ti} indicates the time gap between t_i and t_{i-1}.

$$\begin{cases} X_{ti} = t_i - t_{i-1} \\ X_{t1} = 0 \end{cases} \tag{7}$$

the time gap X_{ti}, together with the click diversity and impression diversity, form the embedding layer:

$$\mathbf{v}_{Inn} = \mathbf{v}_{xn} \odot \mathbf{v}_{cn} \odot \mathbf{v}_{Imn} \odot \mathbf{v}_{tn} \tag{8}$$

where $\mathbf{v}_{xn} \in R^{1*d_1}$, $\mathbf{v}_{cn} \in R^{1*d_2}$, $\mathbf{v}_{Imn} \in R^{1*d_3}$, $\mathbf{v}_{tn} \in R^{1*d_4}$.

5.5   Sequence Modeling Part

Gated Recurrent Units (GRU) [5] is used for sequence modeling.

$$h_n = GRU\left(v_{Inn}, h_{n-1}\right) \tag{9}$$

Besides the final GRU output, we also adopt attention to combine the whole sequence and each hidden state to enhance the sequence embedding :

$$h_{att} = \sum_{i=1}^{n} a_i h_i \tag{10}$$

where a_i is the attention weight of h_i calculated in [4]. The final representation of the sequence c_t is given by:

$$c_t = h_n + h_{att} \tag{11}$$

5.6   Dynamic Diversification Prediction Part

As depicted in Fig. 3, c_t is the embedding of the sessional sequence with diversity integration, and emb_i is the embedding of item i in the candidate list. For most previous work in top-k recommendation, the candidate list is exactly $\mathcal{I}$ itself. However, the method ignores the real situation perceived by the user; in other words, item impressions exposed to a user may affect his/her decisions and behaviors. More importantly, diversity is a list-level concept that calls for consideration of how a recommendation list is presented. The impression lists "pushed" to the user at every time point are made use of as candidate lists. Similarity between c_t and emb_i is calculated as:

$$S_i = \mathbf{c}_t \mathbf{B} emb_i^T \tag{12}$$

where $\mathbf{B}$ is a parameter matrix. The prediction score of item i is the output of a softmax layer:

$$y_i = \sigma(S_i) \tag{13}$$

The model is trained by using a mini-batch gradient descent on cross-entropy loss, where q is the prediction distribution and p is the true one:

$$L(p, q) = -\sum_{i=1}^{d} p_i log(q_i) \tag{14}$$

For negative cases, we randomly sample items exposed while not clicked by users with a ratio 5 : 1 of negative and positive ones.

6   Experiment

6.1   Experimental Settings

Dataset. The dataset we use is the same as in Sect. 4.1. Since some of the users' behaviors are extremely sparse, we filter some active users as follows: based on the task definition and general meaning of "diversity". As there should be at least 3 items to talk about "diversity", users who perform 4 clicks during a period of time are selected. Table 1 gives some statistics. We randomly sampled 70% of the dataset for training, 10% for validation, and the rest for test.

Table 1. Statistics of the experiment dataset

	Users	Items	Impressions
Meta-data	90,331	5,662,595	6,657,048
≥ 1 click	33,347	943,817	132,498
≥ 4 clicks	9,994	750,513	95,315

Table 2. Performance comparison of DDRM with baseline methods

Type	Methods	Recall@5	Recall@10	MRR@5	MRR@10	NDCG@5	NDCG@10
Without diversity	POP	0.1094	0.1113	0.0856	0.0859	0.0917	0.0924
	BPRMF	0.0996	0.0996	0.0685	0.0685	0.0764	0.0764
	GRU-Rec	0.2051	0.4609	0.0899	0.1239	0.1180	0.2006
With diversity	XTReD	0.2188	0.4656	0.0922	0.1249	0.1231	0.2047
Our model	DDRM-noD	0.2246	0.4670	0.0944	0.1272	0.1285	0.2024
	DDRM-clkDo	0.2311	0.4720	0.0973	0.1298	0.1309	0.2046
	DDRM	**0.2383****	**0.4767****	**0.0996****	**0.1325****	**0.1328****	**0.2071****

**. Significantly better than the best baseline with $p < 0.05$

Baselines. The methods used as baselines in the recommendation task are as follows. **POP** always recommends the most popular items (clicked by users) in the training set. **BPRMF** [12], which optimizes a pairwise ranking objective function via stochastic gradient descent. **GRU-Rec** [5], which utilizes session-parallel mini-batch training process and employing ranking-based loss functions for learning. **xTReD** is short for "Explicit Tag Recommendation Diversifier" [1]. This baseline seeks to explicitly maximize the set of categories covered by the recommended tags as well as relevance.

All these methods above are widely used in modern e-commerce scenarios. GRU-Rec is the main comparison partner as an effective RNN-based recommendation method. xTReD is another main competitor as the state-of-the-art diversification methods.

Evaluation Metrics. Recall@K, MRR (Mean Reciprocal Rank)@K, and NDCG (Normalized Discounted Cumulative Gain)@K are chosen as the evaluation metrics in our task. K is set to 5, 10 respectively for each metric listed above. The reason we set K no more than 10 is that the length of most impression lists is less than 10.

6.2   Results and Analysis.

Table 2 gives a performance overview of all the models considered. We split each session with time window of 6 hours. **DDRM-noD** is the model without any diversity information, **DDRM-CDo** is the model with *click diversity* only, and **DDRM** is the final model with both *impression diversity* and *click diversity*. The parameters of different models are as follows. For BPRMF, the dimension of latent factors is set to 50. Models based on RNN, including Gru-Rec, DRRM-noD, DRRM-CDo and DRRM all use one GRU layer, which is set at 100 hidden units. The embedding dimensions input to GRU layer are 128 (Gru-Rec and DRRM-noD), 128 + 32 (DRRM-CDo) and 128 + 32 + 32 (DRRM) respectively. We use 100−dimensional embeddings for the presentation of both sequences and items. For all methods, we select the best hyper-parameters using the validation set and report the corresponding performance on the test set.

We have the following observations from the results:

For baseline models, BPRMF gives the worst performance and the reasons are as follows: the data is very sparse for Matrix Factorization, and there are too many "cold" items that are incapable for CF methods to handle. Besides, POP also gives a poor performance as it does not provide personalization results. Methods based on neural networks consistently outperform the traditional baselines, demonstrating that RNN-based models are good at dealing with sequence information. At last, as a diversification method that jointly optimizes relevance and diversity, xTReD shows a better performance.

For the proposed DDRM, DDRM-noD shows a little promotion over xTReD and GRU-Rec, indicating that embeddings from Word2Vec could better describe item features than CF methods. DDRM-CDo further improves from DDRM-noD. It indicates that *click diversity* can help model users' diversity demand within a session. With the further integration of *impression diversity*, DDRM significantly outperforms all the methods above ($p < 0.05$). It indicates that the joint action of *impression diversity* and *click diversity* can model users' preference more precisely.

6.3   Influence of Time Window

Figure 4 (a) and (b) shows Recall@5 and NDCG@5 of xTReD and DDRM as the time window changes. We have the following observations from the results: Firstly, DDRM outperforms XTReD in all time windows Then, the performance of both DDRM and XTReD improves from 3hs to 6hs. Besides, the performance of DDRM begins to decline after 6hs; we consider this the result of the change of user's diversity demand if the time duration is too long.

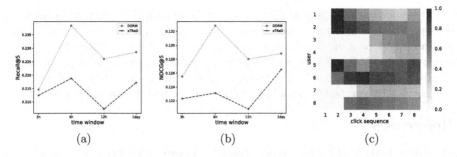

        (a)   (b)   (c)

Fig. 4. Comparison between DDRM and GRU-rec (a) Recall@5 and (b) MRR@5 with the change of the time window size, (c) Click diversity with sequence length 8

6.4   Case Study

This section shows some representative cases of how DDRM gives recommendations based on dynamic diversification. Figure 4 (c) shows the change of click diversity of 8 users with a sequence length of 8, where a darker color square means a higher diversity. Note that the previous 7 squares are the user clicking history, and the last one is the recommendation put forward by DDRM. As shown in Fig. 4, there are 4 types of users: (1) For user 1 and user 2, the click diversity gradually declines as they clicked on more items. For most users, online-shopping is a process to find what they really want. They may click on diverse items but finally become concentrated after they made a decision. (2) For user 3 and user 4, the diversity performs a slow rise. The two users might be those who "click for fun" and find satisfaction in diverse recommendations. (3) User 5 and user 6 shows a fluctuation of diversity but finally converge to a stable value. (4) User 7 and user 8 are "firm" users on the issue of diversity, where diversity keeps almost a constant value. However types of these users, DDRM recommends items similar to users' past preferences.

7   Conclusion and Future Work

In this paper, first, we collect user logs from a real-world e-commerce website, finding that users from different groups are with different diversity demands, and the demands vary in different scenarios. Real cases indicate that it is not enough to infer users' diversity demands only by items clicked, where impressions should also be considered. Second, we propose a Dynamic Diversification Recommendation Model (DDRM), integrating both click diversity and impression diversity with recurrent networks. Third, we conduct extensive experiments on the real-world dataset in terms of different evaluation metrics. Comparisons between our models and baseline methods demonstrate that DDRM outperforms all these baseline methods on providing accurate recommendations. Furthermore, we visualize the change of diversities to show in detail how DDRM gives recommendations.

The work initiated is a first step towards integrating diversity in recommendation. There is still much work to do: first, the user's personal profile information might be a vital source to infer his/her acceptance of diversity. Second, researches have shown that user's attention on items at different positions of the list varies, which inspires us to improve the calculation method of list-level diversity. All these factors should be taken into consideration in future work.

References

1. Belém, F.M., Batista, C.S., et al.: Beyond relevance: explicitly promoting novelty and diversity in tag recommendation. TIST **7**(3), 26 (2016)
2. Castells, P., Hurley, N.J., Vargas, S.: Novelty and diversity in recommender systems. In: Ricci, F., Rokach, L., Shapira, B. (eds.) Recommender Systems Handbook, pp. 881–918. Springer, Boston, MA (2015). https://doi.org/10.1007/978-1-4899-7637-6_26
3. Cen, R., Liu, Y., Zhang, M., Ru, L., Ma, S.: Study on the Click Context of Web Search Users for Reliability Analysis. Springer, Berlin (2009)
4. Chaudhari, S., Polatkan, G., Ramanath, R., Mithal, V.: An attentive survey of attention models. arXiv preprint arXiv:1904.02874 (2019)
5. Hidasi, B., Karatzoglou, A., Baltrunas, L., Tikk, D.: Session-based recommendations with recurrent neural networks. arXiv preprint arXiv:1511.06939 (2015)
6. Hu, R., Pu, P.: Enhancing recommendation diversity with organization interfaces. In: IUI, pp. 347–350. ACM (2011)
7. Li, X., Murata, T.: Multidimensional clustering based collaborative filtering approach for diversified recommendation. In: ICCSE, pp. 905–910. IEEE (2012)
8. McNee, S.M., Riedl, J., Konstan, J.A.: Being accurate is not enough: how accuracy metrics have hurt recommender systems. In: Proceeding CHI 2006 Extended Abstracts on Human Factors in Computing Systems, pp. 1097–1101. ACM (2006)
9. Mikolov, T., Chen, K., Corrado, G., Dean, J.: Efficient estimation of word representations in vector space. arXiv preprint arXiv:1301.3781 (2013)
10. Oard, D.W., Kim, J., et al.: Implicit feedback for recommender systems. In: AAAI, pp. 81–83. AAAI Press (1998)
11. Rakkappan, L., Rajan, V.: Context-aware sequential recommendations withstacked recurrent neural networks. In: WWW, pp. 3172–3178 (2019)
12. Rendle, S., Freudenthaler, C., et al.: BPR: Bayesian personalized ranking from implicit feedback. In: Proceedings of the Twenty-Fifth Conference on Uncertainty in Artificial Intelligence, pp. 452–461. AUAI Press (2009)
13. Ribeiro, M.T., Ziviani, N., Moura, E.S.D., Hata, I., Lacerda, A., Veloso, A.: Multiobjective pareto-efficient approaches for recommender systems. ACM Trans. Intell. Syst. Technol. (TIST) **5**(4), 53 (2015)
14. Sar Shalom, O., Koenigstein, N., Paquet, U., Vanchinathan, H.P.: Beyond collaborative filtering: the list recommendation problem. In: WWW, pp. 63–72 (2016)
15. Schafer, J.B., Konstan, J., Riedl, J.: Recommender systems in e-commerce. In: Proceedings of ACM Conference on Electronic Commerce, pp. 158–166. ACM (1999)
16. Smyth, B., McClave, P.: Similarity vs. diversity. In: ICCBR, pp. 347–361 (2001)
17. Vargas, S., Castells, P.: Rank and relevance in novelty and diversity metrics for recommender systems. In: Recsys, pp. 109–116. ACM (2011)
18. Wang, S., Cao, L., Wang, Y.: A survey on session-based recommender systems. arXiv preprint arXiv:1902.04864 (2019)
19. Zhang, M., Hurley, N.: Avoiding monotony: improving the diversity of recommendation lists. In: Recsys, pp. 123–130. ACM (2008)

Multi-criteria and Review-Based Overall Rating Prediction

Edgar Ceh-Varela$^{(\boxtimes)}$ ⓘ, Huiping Cao ⓘ, and Tuan Le ⓘ

Department of Computer Science, New Mexico State University, Las Cruces, USA
{eceh,tuanle}@nmsu.edu, hcao@cs.nmsu.edu

Abstract. An overall rating cannot reveal the details of user's preferences toward each feature of a product. One widespread practice of e-commerce websites is to provide ratings on predefined aspects of the product and user-generated reviews. Most recent multi-criteria works employ aspect preferences of users or user reviews to understand the opinions and behavior of users. However, these works fail to learn how users correlate these information sources when users express their opinion about an item. In this work, we present **Multi-task & Multi-Criteria Review-based Rating (MMCRR)**, a framework to predict the overall ratings of items by learning how users represent their preferences when using multi-criteria ratings and text reviews. We conduct extensive experiments with three real-life datasets and six baseline models. The results show that *MMCRR* can reduce prediction errors while learning features better from the data.

Keywords: Multi-criteria · Multi-task · Rating prediction

1 Introduction

Multi-criteria recommender systems (*MCRS*) have been developed to increase the recommender systems (*RS*) performance. Most recent multi-criteria works employ user prefernces [14,20] or reviews [2,11] to understand users'opinions and analyze their behaviors. However, these works fail to consider the analytical tasks users need to follow to express their opinion about an item in different forms and how these tasks are related (i.e., summarizing the textual reviews into criteria, and finally into an overall rating). This process is challenging, as users have different scales for their ratings and for the intensity of some of the opinion words used in their reviews [18]. For example, a user could write the sentence "This is a good hotel" and rate the hotel with five stars, while another user for the same sentence could use four stars.

Considering that these forms for expressing user preferences are related, this study proposes a new **Multi-task & Multi-Criteria Review-based Rating (MMCRR)** framework to predict the overall rating that a user would give to a new item. *MMCRR* uses a multi-task learning (MTL) approach to learn how users represent their preferences when using multi-criteria ratings and text

ⓒ Springer Nature Switzerland AG 2021
K. Karlapalem et al. (Eds.): PAKDD 2021, LNAI 12713, pp. 473–484, 2021.
https://doi.org/10.1007/978-3-030-75765-6_38

reviews and the relationship between these two. Furthermore, it can also predict each criterion rating because of the multi-task process, which can be presented to explain why a given overall rating.

This paper's contributions are as follows: (i) we present a model that takes advantage of MTL to use multi-criteria ratings and text reviews to learn the relationship between these types of evaluations. (ii) our approach can predict the overall and criterion ratings that a user would give to an item. Moreover, the model does not need the item's multi-criteria or individual review during the prediction phase. (iii) we evaluate the model's performance on three real-life datasets against baseline models from the most utilized types of *MCRS*.

The remainder of this paper is organized as follows: Sect. 2 presents the related literature. Section 3 details the proposed methodology. Section 4 outlines the experimental settings used to test our proposed model. The results showing the validity of our proposed method and its effectiveness are in Sect. 5. Finally, our conclusions are in Sect. 6.

2   Related Work

2.1   *MCRS* with User Preferences

Models in this category try to learn the relationships between the criteria ratings and the overall rating. User preferences are known directly from the user's explicit ratings on the items' features. Different works have extended existing single-criteria Collaborative Filtering (CF) techniques to work with multi-criteria ratings [1]. A method to learn and rank user preferences over each criterion and find each item's dominant criterion is presented in [14]. These ranks are used to predict the overall rating using CF techniques. In [10], multi-criteria ratings are decomposed into k separate single rating problems using matrix factorization techniques (e.g., SVD). An aggregation function is then extracted using different machine learning approaches. These works only exploit the user's preference from multi-criteria ratings, which can fail short on representing the user's whole opinion towards an item.

2.2   Multi-criteria Review-Based *RS*

Works from this category consider an implicit relationship between the user's overall rating and her expressed comment. The most widely used method is the extraction of aspects and their polarity scores (i.e., positive or negative sentiments) [11,12]. Aspects are extracted using different Natural Language Processing (NLP) techniques. Similarly, other works [2,17] generate latent feature representations from reviews. These representations are then used as an input for the overall rating prediction. These works only analyze user reviews without considering the explicit multi-criteria ratings.

Moreover, some *MCRS* works [5,7,9] jointly use reviews and ratings for the target item as additional input for the prediction. However, in real-life recommendations, we do not know at recommendation time what the user would write or how the user would rate the criteria. Our proposed solution does not have this problem as it uses historical reviews, and criteria ratings only for training.

2.3 Multi-Task Learning (MTL)

In many situations, we may have a task composed of related sub-tasks, and where each of them shares some features. MTL [3] allows solving all these sub-tasks, and consequently, the overall task, in an end-to-end learning model. In MTL, each task provides regularization to the other tasks, which is especially useful in scenarios where part of the data is not available at test time. Recently, different works [2,19] have started to use MTL in recommendation problems.

In this work, we exploit the multi-task learning paradigm. We consider two related tasks: (i) an associated task, used during training, which predicts the overall rating given the multi-criteria ratings, and (ii) a main task, composed of two subtasks, to predict the multi-criteria and overall ratings based on historical user and item reviews.

3   Proposed Approach

3.1   Problem Definitions

Let $U = \{u_1, \cdots, u_M\}$ and $I = \{i_1, \cdots, i_N\}$ be the set of users and set of items that users have rated respectively. We denote H_{UI} the set of reviews written by U about I.

Definition 1 (Reviews document). *A reviews document $H_u \subset H_{UI}$ is the set of reviews written by a user $u \in U$. Similarly, $H_i \subset H_{UI}$ is the set of reviews about an item $i \in I$.*

Each item $i \in I$ is described by a set of aspects (i.e., criteria) $K = \{k_0, k_1, \cdots, k_K\}$. A user $u \in U$ can rate a criterion k with a rating $r_{u,i,k}$, a non-negative real number. We consider the overall rating as one particular aspect, denoted as $r_{u,i,0}$.

Definition 2 (Multi-criteria ratings). *Is the set of ratings following the function $R : U \times I \to R_0 \times R_1 \times \cdots \times R_k$.*

Where R_0 represents the overall ratings, and R_1 to R_k is the rating values for each criterion. For the rest of the paper, when we mention the multi-criteria ratings, we will not consider R_0.

Definition 3 (Problem statement). *Having the set of reviews H_{UI}, the set of users U, the set of items I, and the set of multi-criteria ratings from R, the **problem** is to find a function $r_{u,i,0} = f(U, I)$, where $r_{u,i,0}$ is the overall rating that a user $u \in U$ would give to an item $i \in I$ which he/she has not interacted with before.*

3.2   MMCRR Model

Figure 1 shows the general architecture of the *MMCRR* model. It consists of two parts, one for each task of our MTL approach. During training, *MMCRR* uses the multi-criteria representation from the associated task to adjust the feature representation and to improve the accuracy in the main task. Moreover, user and item embeddings are shared between the two tasks allowing them to create better representations of users and items. For clarity, we use bold lowercase for vectors and bold uppercase for matrices.

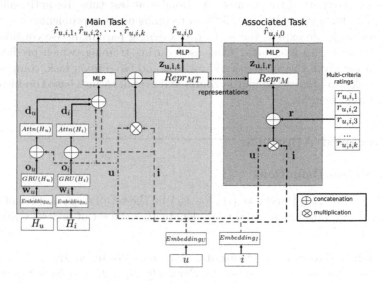

Fig. 1. MMCRR model components

3.3   Associated Task

This task is only used during the model training, given that the criteria ratings are not available for the final overall rating predictions. It aims to learn a representation of the user's preferences for each item's criterion. Figure 1 shows in blue the architecture of this task. The inputs for this task are the user u and item i IDs, and the ratings given by u to each of i's criterion. Each user u and item i is represented with an embedding vector. These vectors represent the intrinsic properties of u and i learned from the data. We use two embedding layers $Embedding_U \in \mathbb{R}^{U \times D_U}$ and $Embedding_I \in \mathbb{R}^{I \times D_I}$, where D_U and D_I are the vectors' dimensionalities. Then, $\mathbf{u} \in \mathbb{R}^{D_U}$ and $\mathbf{i} \in \mathbb{R}^{D_I}$ are the embedding vectors for each user and item, respectively.

Similarly, let $r_{u,i,k}$ be the rating of user u to item i in criterion k. We represent the criteria ratings given by a user u to an item i as $\mathbf{r}$. The interaction of embedding vectors $\mathbf{u}$ and $\mathbf{i}$ is obtained using an element-wise product, which has been demonstrated to be highly effective [6]. Finally, this interaction and $\mathbf{r}$, are passed to a neural network ($Repr_M$) to obtain the features representation as

$$\mathbf{z_{u,i,r}} = \sigma(\mathbf{W_r}[\mathbf{u} \times \mathbf{i}, \mathbf{r}] + \mathbf{b_r}) \tag{1}$$

where $\mathbf{W_r}$ and $\mathbf{b_r}$ denote the weight matrix and bias vector, respectively. σ is the activation function and $\mathbf{z_{u,i,r}}$ is the features representation. The representation is used to predict the overall rating as:

$$\hat{r}_{u,i,0} = \mathbf{w_r}^\top(\sigma(\mathbf{W_o}\mathbf{z_{u,i,r}} + \mathbf{b_o})) \tag{2}$$

where $\mathbf{w_r}$ denotes the weights of the prediction layer, $\mathbf{W_o}$ and $\mathbf{b_o}$ are the parameters, σ is the activation function, and $\hat{r}_{u,i,0}$ is the overall rating prediction for a user u and item i.

3.4   Main Task

This task aims to predict the overall rating and, in an auxiliary way, the multi-criteria ratings that a user u would give to an item i. This task consists of several steps: (i) word sequence encoding, (ii) word-level attention, (iii) multi-criteria rating prediction, and (iv) overall rating prediction. Figure 1 presents in green the architecture of this task. We detail this task in the following sections.

Word Sequence Encoding.   We rely on the GRU [4] gating mechanism. Assume that a document (i.e., H_u or H_i) contains T words. The words in this document are represented as w_t with $t \in [1, T]$. The main task transforms the raw document into a vector representation, on which we build a multi-criteria rating predictor. Without loss of generality, we present how we build the document level vector for H_u, the steps for H_i are similar. Each word is embedded as a vector $\mathbf{w} \in \mathbb{R}^{W_U}$, using an embedding layer $Embedding_{H_U} \in \mathbb{R}^{W_U \times D_W}$, where W_U is the size of the vocabulary for the users' documents, and D_W is the dimensionality of the embedding vector. The sequence of words embeddings $\mathbf{w_t}$ for each document is the GRU input to get the contextual information of each word. This step is represented as $\mathbf{o_u} = \text{GRU}(\mathbf{w_t}), t \in [1, T]$, where $\mathbf{o_u}$ contains the output features h_t for each t.

Word-Level Attention.   The same words may have a different intention for different users. Hence, we introduce an attention mechanism to extract those words that are important to the document's meaning, considering the user who wrote it. Then, we aggregate those informative words to form a document vector. Concretely,

$$e_t = \tanh(\mathbf{W}_w[\mathbf{o_u}, \mathbf{u}] + \mathbf{b}_w) \tag{3}$$

$$\alpha_t = \frac{\exp(e_t)}{\sum_t \exp(e_t)} \tag{4}$$

$$\mathbf{d_u} = \sum_t \alpha_t \mathbf{o_u} \tag{5}$$

where e_t is a hidden representation of $\mathbf{o_u}$ and $\mathbf{u}$, α_t is the normalized importance weight. Finally, we compute a user document vector $\mathbf{d_u}$ as a weighted sum of the weights α_t and $\mathbf{o_u}$.

Multi-criteria Rating Prediction.   After obtaining the document representations $\mathbf{d_u}$ and $\mathbf{d_i}$ ($\mathbf{d_i}$ is the item's document vector), we proceed to predict each criterion's rating. The embedding vectors $\mathbf{u}$ and $\mathbf{i}$, along with $\mathbf{d_u}$ and $\mathbf{d_i}$, are passed to a two-layer neural network to obtain the features representation.

$$\mathbf{z_{u,i,k}} = \sigma(\mathbf{W_{k1}}(\sigma(\mathbf{W_{k0}}\,[\mathbf{u, i, d_u, d_i}] + \mathbf{b_{k0}})) + \mathbf{b_{k1}}) \tag{6}$$

where $\mathbf{W_{k0}}$, $\mathbf{W_{k1}}$, $\mathbf{b_{k0}}$, and $\mathbf{b_{k1}}$ denote the weight matrices and bias vectors, respectively. σ is the activation function, and $\mathbf{z_{u,i,k}}$ is the feature representation. This representation is used to predict a vector with the multi-criteria ratings as follows:

$$\hat{\mathbf{r}}_{u,i,k} = \mathbf{w_k}^\top \mathbf{z_{u,i,k}} \tag{7}$$

where $\mathbf{w_k}$ denotes the weights of the prediction layer, and $\hat{r}_{u,i,k}$ is a vector with the multi-criteria rating predictions for a user u and an item i.

Overall Rating Prediction.   To predict the overall rating, the interaction of $\mathbf{u}$ and $\mathbf{i}$, along with $\hat{r}_{u,i,k}$, are passed to a simple neural network to get the features representation ($Repr_{MT}$).

$$\mathbf{z_{u,i,t}} = \sigma(\mathbf{W_t}\,[\mathbf{u} \times \mathbf{i}, \hat{r}_{u,i,k}] + \mathbf{b_t}) \tag{8}$$

where $\mathbf{W_t}$ and $\mathbf{b_t}$ denote the weight matrix and bias vector, respectively. σ is the activation function, and $\mathbf{z_{u,i,t}}$ is the features representation. Then, we get the overall rating as:

$$\hat{r}_{u,i,0} = \mathbf{w_t}^\top(\sigma(\mathbf{W_t z_{u,i,t}} + \mathbf{b_t})) \tag{9}$$

where $\mathbf{w_t}$ denotes the weights of the prediction layer, $\mathbf{W_t}$ and $\mathbf{b_t}$ are the parameters, σ is the activation function, and $\hat{r}_{u,i,0}$ is the overall rating prediction for a user u and item i.

3.5   Model Optimization

First, for the associated task, given the ground-truth overall rating of user u on item i, and the predicted overall rating calculated using Eq. 2, the loss of this rating prediction is defined as follows:

$$Loss_{AT} = (r_{u,i,0} - \hat{r}_{u,i,0})^2 \tag{10}$$

Second, the main task performs two additional tasks: predicting the aspect ratings and predicting the overall rating. First, given the ground-truth aspect ratings of user u on item i and the aspect rating predictions using Eq. 7, the loss of rating predictions is defined as:

$$Loss_A = \sum_{j=1}^{k} (r_{u,i,j} - \hat{r}_{u,i,j})^2 \tag{11}$$

Then, for the ground-truth overall rating and the predicted rating from Eq. 9, we have:

$$Loss_{MT} = (r_{u,i,0} - \hat{r}_{u,i,0})^2 \tag{12}$$

The associated and main tasks are closely related; therefore, their representations need to be close to each other. Hence, we add a representation loss as:

$$Loss_R = \|\mathbf{z_{u,i,r}} - \mathbf{z_{u,i,t}}\|_2 \tag{13}$$

Finally, to optimize all model parameters, we try to minimize the following loss function:

$$Loss = \frac{1}{|N|} \sum_{r_{ui} \in N} (\lambda(Loss_{MT} + Loss_A + Loss_R) + (1-\lambda)Loss_{AT}) + \alpha_\theta |\boldsymbol{\theta}|_F^2 \tag{14}$$

where N is the training set and λ determines the relative importance of the tasks. This optimization function considers $Loss_R$ when both tasks are trained (i.e., $0 < \lambda < 1$). We use the Frobenius norm regularization term $|\theta|_F^2 = \sum_i \theta_i^2$, where θ stands for the parameters to optimize, and α_θ is the penalty term.

4   Experimental Settings

4.1   Datasets

We use three real-life datasets to test our model. These datasets have rating values and written reviews for the items. The first two correspond to non-alcoholic (**NALC**) and regular beer (**BEER**) reviews collected from the *BeerAdvocate* website by [11]. They have ratings on four beer aspects (i.e., feel, look, smell, and taste) and an overall rating. The third dataset has hotel reviews from TripAdvisor (**TRIP**) collected by [16]. This dataset includes ratings on seven aspects in each review (i.e., value, room, location, cleanliness, check-in/front desk, service, business service), and an overall rating. For the three datasets, the rating range is from 1 to 5 stars. Table 1 shows the description of these datasets. We remove instances considered outliers. For example, an instance having all its aspects with ratings of 5 stars, but an overall rating of 1. Further, we remove users with less than five reviews. We transform each review to lowercase and remove all numbers and special characters. For BEER and TRIP, we randomly get a sample of 50,000 instances. We randomly split each dataset into 80% for training, 10% for evaluation, and 10% for testing. For each user, we concatenate the text from her reviews. We do the same for the reviews about each item. We specify a maximum text size of 10,000 words. We use "<UNK>" to replace those words with a frequency below 10.

Table 1. Dataset descriptions

	NALC	BEER	TRIP
Instances	1,201	1,585,887	67,155
Users	582	33,372	60,107
Items	162	66,051	1,850
Avg. words per review	110.24	123.84	177.70
Aspects	4	4	7
Avg. overall rating	2.58	3.82	4.07
Std. overall rating	1.01	0.72	1.16
Aut. Read. Index	8.06	9.09	11.73
Sparsity	∼ 0.91	∼ 0.99	∼ 0.97

4.2 Baselines

We choose baselines that only use user and item IDs as input for the prediction phase, given that additional input information (i.e., multi-criteria ratings and user's review) is not present in such a phase. We compare our proposed model with the following baselines:

1. Multi-criteria rating-based models:

   MultiDim [1]: This method extends the standard CF approach. It calculates similarity using multi-dimensional distance metrics to reflect multi-criteria information.

   PrefLearn [14]: This algorithm learns and ranks the user's preferences over different criteria. Similarly, it finds and ranks the dominant criterion of each item. Then, it uses these rankings with modified versions of *UBCF* and *IBCF* algorithms. The results of these algorithms are unified to obtain the final overall rating.

   AggFunc [10]: This model assumes that the overall rating and the multi-criteria ratings have a relationship. It decomposes the multi-criteria rating space into k single-rating recommendation problems. It uses *SVD* to predict each criterion's missing ratings and a two-layer Neural Network to learn an aggregation function for predicting the overall rating based on the known multi-criteria ratings.

2. Multi-criteria review-based models:

   AspectBased [12]: This model extracts relevant aspects and sentiment scores from the user's reviews. The sentiment scores associated with each extracted aspect are used as ratings. Then it uses a *Multi-criteria User-to-User* algorithm to predict the overall rating.

   GRURec: We implemented this baseline based on [2,8]; this model uses two bidirectional GRU RNN to get latent preference factors for H_u and H_i. Both vectors are then concatenated with the user and item embeddings. The resulting vector is then used as input for an MLP neural network to predict the overall rating.

3. Multi-criteria rating- & review-based models:

AggFunc+GRURec: We use an ensemble method to combine Multi-criteria rating-based models and Multi-criteria review-based models. This model calculates the overall rating using the average of the ratings predicted by **Agg-Func** and **GRURec**.

4.3 Hyperparameters

We use Pytorch on a Tesla P100 GPU with 16 GB of RAM. We use a hidden layer size of 128, an embedding dimension of 256 for users and items, a learning rate of 0.001 with a learning scheduler. The word embedding dimensions are set to 100 and initialize with pre-trained GloVe embeddings. The activation function is LeakyReLU. The model is trained with a batch size of 256 for NALC and 128 for BEER and TRIP. We use Adam as the optimizer. On the embedding layers, we use a dropout percentage of 0.2. For the loss, we initially set $\lambda = 0.5$, for the regularization, α_θ is set to 0.01, and for epochs, we use an early stopping strategy based on the validation loss.

5 Experimental Results

5.1 Model Performance

We use the standard metric, *Root Mean Square Error (RMSE)*. A smaller RMSE value indicates better performance. Table 2 shows the average performance of the six baselines and *MMCRR* after running the tests three times. From these results, we observe the following:

(1) For methods using criteria ratings, the *AggFunc* method has the best results for all datasets, indicating that using the preferences for each criterion is useful. (2) For methods using reviews, the *AspectBased* method results show that using only the sentiment of latent aspects extracted from the reviews as the multi-criteria ratings do not provide good results. These results happen because different user's words can have different sentiment strengths, which implies a different rating scale [15]. The results of *GRURec* are better, showing that it can find more useful representations of users and items based on the reviews. (3) Combining models for criteria ratings and reviews improves those models' results just using text.

We can see that *MMCRR* outperforms all baselines, which indicates that it can learn the analytical tasks that a user makes when expressing preferences about an item.

5.2 Effect of Parameter λ

Figure 2 shows the results of varying the parameter λ from Eq. 14. When λ increases, the contribution from the associated task decreases. For the NALC

Table 2. Performance results for all datasets ($\lambda = 0.5$)

Method	NALC	BEER	TRIP
MultiDim	1.0251	0.6059	1.171
PrefLearn	0.932	0.6045	1.1235
AggFunc	0.9314	0.5939	1.073
AspectBased	1.2958	0.8856	1.4238
GRURec	0.9726	0.6473	1.164
AggFunc+GRURec	0.9349	0.6974	1.081
MMCRR	**0.873**	**0.579**	**0.9751**

Table 3. Comparing different losses

Method	NALC	BEER	TRIP
MMCRR_NA	1.0346	0.6374	1.2314
MMCRR_NR	0.9003	**0.5778**	0.9881
MMCRR_NRA	1.0130	0.6398	1.2869
MMCRR	**0.873**	0.579	**0.9751**

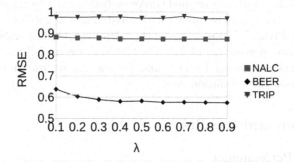

Fig. 2. MMCRR varying λ for each dataset (considering $Loss_R$)

and TRIP datasets, RMSE error is lower around the middle, meaning that there is a contribution from both tasks. RMSE starts with high values in the BEER dataset, and as λ increases, these values decrease and stabilize. The results obtained by these metrics are coherent with our definition of *MMCRR*.

5.3   Effect of Loss Functions

We create three different variations of Eq. 14. First, *MMCRR_NA*, which does not consider the loss from Eq. 11. Second, *MMCRR_NR*, which does not consider the loss from Eq. 13. Finally, *MMCRR_NRA* does not consider both losses. Table 3 shows the results. *MMCRR_NRA* has higher error values than *MMCRR*, showing that these losses allow the model to minimize the prediction errors and fit the data better. Only for BEER, *MMCRR_NR* has a lower value; we attribute it to the dataset sparsity (i.e., $\sim 99\%$).

5.4   Performance of the Main Task

We test the performance of using only the *Main* task (Sect. 3.4). Table 4 shows the results. The λ values are the ones where we get better results for *MMCRR*.

Table 4. Comparing performance of the *Main* task

Method	NALC $\lambda = 0.4$	BEER $\lambda = 0.9$	TRIP $\lambda = 0.5$
MMCRR_Main	0.8829	0.5717	0.9907
MMCRR	**0.8731**	**0.5702**	**0.977**

Table 5. RMSE median for the aspect predictions

Method	NALC	BEER	TRIP
AggFunc	0.7950	0.5382	**1.0015**
MMCRR	**0.7377**	**0.4027**	1.4372

We can see that *MMCRR* has better performance overall, as it uses the *Associated* task to learn the multi-criteria preference representations for the users. These representations, along with the shared user and item representations, help the *Main* task to improve its learning.

5.5   Metrics for Aspect Ratings

Although not the primary goal of *MMCRR*, we analyze how it predicts the aspect ratings. Only the *AggFunc* baseline predicts individual aspect ratings. Table 5 shows the RMSE medians for all item aspects. Only for TRIP does not show a better performance. Recall that these ratings are predicted based on item reviews and the user and item representations. Therefore, given that the TRIP dataset has seven aspects to predict and it has more complex text (i.e., Automatic Reading Index [13] is higher, see Table 1) than the other datasets, the model's job is more challenging.

6   Conclusions

We proposed *MMCRR*, a framework leveraging multi-task learning to address the problem of predicting at the same time the ratings for each item's criterion and its overall rating. We use three real-life datasets with six baseline models. Our results show that *MMCRR* makes predictions with a lower prediction error than these baselines. Moreover, our model can learn the users' rating profiles and predict ratings considering how users write their reviews. Similarly, we show how our approach also reduces the prediction error for the criteria ratings.

Acknowledgements. This work has been supported by the National Council of Science and Technology of Mexico (CONACYT) #602434/440684, and National Science Foundation of USA (NSF) #1633330, #1757207, and #1914635.

References

1. Adomavicius, G., Kwon, Y.: New recommendation techniques for multicriteria rating systems. IEEE Intell. Syst. **22**(3), 48–55 (2007)
2. Bansal, T., Belanger, D., McCallum, A.: Ask the GRU: multi-task learning for deep text recommendations. In: Proceedings of the 10th ACM Conference on Recommender Systems, pp. 107–114 (2016)

3. Caruana, R.: Multitask learning. Mach. Learn. **28**(1), 41–75 (1997)
4. Cho, K., et al.: Learning phrase representations using rnn encoder-decoder for statistical machine translation. arXiv preprint arXiv:1406.1078 (2014)
5. Ding, Y., Li, S., Yu, W., Wang, J., Liu, M.: A unified neural model for review-based rating prediction by leveraging multi-criteria ratings and review text. Cluster Comput. **22**(4), 9177–9185 (2019)
6. He, X., Chua, T.S.: Neural factorization machines for sparse predictive analytics. In: Proceedings of the 40th International ACM SIGIR Conference on Research and Development in Information Retrieval, pp. 355–364 (2017)
7. Jin, Z., et al.: Jointly modeling review content and aspect ratings for review rating prediction. In: Proceedings of the 39th International ACM SIGIR conference on Research and Development in Information Retrieval, pp. 893–896 (2016)
8. Li, P., Tuzhilin, A.: Latent multi-criteria ratings for recommendations. In: Proceedings of the 13th ACM Conference on Recommender Systems, pp. 428–431 (2019)
9. Li, P., Tuzhilin, A.: Learning latent multi-criteria ratings from user reviews for recommendations. IEEE Trans. Knowl. Data Eng. (2020)
10. Majumder, G.S., Dwivedi, P., Kant, V.: Matrix factorization and regression-based approach for multi-criteria recommender system. In: Satapathy, S.C., Joshi, A. (eds.) ICTIS 2017. SIST, vol. 83, pp. 103–110. Springer, Cham (2018). https://doi.org/10.1007/978-3-319-63673-3_13
11. McAuley, J., Leskovec, J., Jurafsky, D.: Learning attitudes and attributes from multi-aspect reviews. In: 2012 IEEE 12th International Conference on Data Mining, pp. 1020–1025. IEEE (2012)
12. Musto, C., de Gemmis, M., Semeraro, G., Lops, P.: A multi-criteria recommender system exploiting aspect-based sentiment analysis of users' reviews. In: Proceedings of the Eleventh ACM Conference on Recommender Systems, pp. 321–325 (2017)
13. Senter, R., Smith, E.A.: Automated readability index. CINCINNATI UNIV OH, Technical Report (1967)
14. Sreepada, R.S., Patra, B.K., Hernando, A.: Multi-criteria recommendations through preference learning. In: Proceedings of the Fourth ACM IKDD Conferences on Data Sciences, pp. 1–11 (2017)
15. Tang, D., Qin, B., Liu, T., Yang, Y.: User modeling with neural network for review rating prediction. In: Twenty-Fourth International Joint Conference on Artificial Intelligence (2015)
16. Wang, H., Lu, Y., Zhai, C.: Latent aspect rating analysis on review text data: a rating regression approach. In: Proceedings of the 16th ACM SIGKDD International Conference on Knowledge Discovery and Data Mining, pp. 783–792 (2010)
17. Wang, H., Lu, Y., Zhai, C.: Latent aspect rating analysis without aspect keyword supervision. In: Proceedings of the 17th ACM SIGKDD International Conference on Knowledge Discovery and Data Mining, pp. 618–626 (2011)
18. Wang, J., De Vries, A.P., Reinders, M.J.: Unifying user-based and item-based collaborative filtering approaches by similarity fusion. In: Proceedings of the 29th Annual International ACM SIGIR Conference on Research and Development in Information Retrieval, pp. 501–508 (2006)
19. Wang, N., Wang, H., Jia, Y., Yin, Y.: Explainable recommendation via multi-task learning in opinionated text data. In: The 41st International ACM SIGIR Conference on Research & Development in Information Retrieval, pp. 165–174 (2018)
20. Zheng, Y.: Utility-based multi-criteria recommender systems. In: Proceedings of the 34th ACM/SIGAPP Symposium on Applied Computing, pp. 2529–2531 (2019)

W2FM: The Doubly-Warped Factorization Machine

Mao-Lin Li[(✉)] and K. Selçuk Candan

Arizona State University, Tempe, AZ 85281, USA
{maolinli,candan}@asu.edu

Abstract. Factorization Machines (FMs) enhance an underlying linear regression or classification model by capturing feature interactions. Intuitively, FMs warp the feature space to help capture the underlying non-linear structure of the machine learning task. In this paper, we propose novel Doubly-Warped Factorization Machines (or W2FMs) that leverage multiple complementary space warping strategies to improve the representational ability of FMs. Our approach abstracts the feature interaction in FMs as additional affine transformations (thus warping the space), which can be learned efficiently without introducing large numbers of model parameters. We also explore alternative W2FM based approaches and conduct extensive experiments on real world data sets. These experiments show that W2FM achieves better performance in collaborative filtering task not only relative to vanilla FMs, but also against other state-of-the-art competitors, such as Attention FM (AFM), Holographic FM (HFM), and Neural FM (NFM).

Keywords: Factorization machine · Collaborative filtering

1 Introduction

The prediction task can be formulated as the problem of *estimating* a function that takes values for a set of input variables (features) and returns a target value (real value for regression and categorical value for classification).

1.1 Space Warping and Kernels

Linear models (such as linear regression [18] or support vector machines, SVMs [10]) make the assumption that features are independent (Fig. 1(a)) – and consequently, these may fail to learn when there are significant interactions among feature-value pairs. Another technique to warp space to obtain better

This work is supported by NSF (#1610282, #1633381, #1909555, #2026860, #1827757, #1629888), and EUH2020 Marie Sklodowska-Curie grant agreement #690817. Results were obtained using the ChameleonCloud resources supported by the NSF.

© Springer Nature Switzerland AG 2021
K. Karlapalem et al. (Eds.): PAKDD 2021, LNAI 12713, pp. 485–497, 2021.
https://doi.org/10.1007/978-3-030-75765-6_39

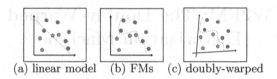

(a) linear model   (b) FMs   (c) doubly-warped

Fig. 1. While (a) regular SVMs learn a linear separator, FMs (b) warp the space through a polynomial kernel (itself represented using a low-rank linear transformation); (c) the proposed W2FM technique, on the other hand, doubly-warps the space (using low-rank linear transformations) to learn a more effective separator.

data representation has been studied to tackle crucial machine learning problems. [1,20], for example, authors have presented methodologies for automatically learning warping of the input space, using a beta distribution function, to help in Bayesian optimization. One commonly used mechanism to take into account feature interactions is to leverage the so-called kernel trick [10], for instance, by relying on a polynomial kernel. Intuitively, the kernel trick *warps* the vector space to capture the underlying non-linear structure of the machine learning model, without having to explicitly fit an expensive non-linear model (Fig. 1(b)).

1.2   Factorization Machines with Polynomial Kernels

One difficulty with the use of polynomial kernels is the increased number of parameters that need to be learned. In addition, to add to the overall computational cost, larger number of model parameters also make it difficult to accurately estimate these parameters in the presence of sparse data – which is a very common occurrence in collaborative filtering and recommendation tasks [8]. Factorization Machines (FMs) [16] address this challenge by assuming that the (linear) transformation needed to describe the necessary warping is low-rank and, thus, can be represented by a smaller number of latent parameters. Thus, FMs parameterize the weight of the *cross feature* interactions as the inner product of the embedding vectors of the corresponding features. Despite FMs success in model learning in various application domains, recent research [11] has shown that FMs' performance in capturing complex and non-linear structures in many real-world data sets may be hampered due to the limited expressive power of the kernel used for warping the space. Recent solutions proposed to alleviate this issue include Attentional FMs [24], Neural FMs [11], and Holographic FMs [23], many of which rely on neural network based non-linear learning.

1.3   Our Contributions: Doubly-Warped FMs

In this paper, we note that, recent techniques, such as AFM, NFM, and HFM, capture additional non-linearities to improve upon the conventional FMs, they primarily focus on space transformations that *shift* decision boundaries. However, we note that these lack sufficient input warping capabilities to discover additional types of non-linearities in the model structure. To tackle this challenge, we propose a novel *Doubly-Warped Factorization Machine (or* W2FM*)* that leverages *input warping* along with *boundary warping* to improve the representational ability of FMs. In addition to using the kernel trick to warp the decision boundary, W2FM abstracts additional feature interactions in terms of *low-rank* linear transformations of the input space (Fig. 1(c)).

2   Related Works

2.1   Factorization Machines and Variants

Recent researchers [6,19], proposed to leverage the feature interactions that explicitly augment a feature vector (cross features) with products of features. However, data sets in some critical machine learning applications (such as recommender systems) are very sparse, which negatively impacts these approaches since only few cross features can be observed in practice. To resolve this sparsity issue, factorization machines (FMs) combine search for feature interactions with matrix factorization [13,17] to eliminate the need to rely on detailed pair-wise feature interactions. Consequently, several variants to FMs have been proposed. SeqFM [4], which considers sequential dependencies within higher-order feature interactions, is applicable in temporal predictive analytics applications. RaFM [5] adopts pairwise interactions from embeddings with different ranks. Neural FM [11], which deepens FMs under the neural framework to learn high-order feature interactions, and field-aware FM [12], which associates multiple embedding vectors for each feature to differentiate its interaction with other features of different fields. [3] recovers polynomial networks [14] and FMs to obtain higher order feature interactions. For efficient training high-order FMs, HOFM [2] leverages a dynamic programming algorithm for evaluating the ANOVA kernel and computing its gradient. To further discriminate the importance of different feature interactions, attentional FM (AFM) [24] method utilizes a neural attention network to learn the importance of each feature interaction. The recent Holographic FM (HFM) [23] approach replaces the inner product in FMs with a holographic reduced representation.

2.2   Input Warping in Other Domains

Recent Bayesian optimization works adapt Gaussian processes (GPs) [15] to express flexible prior distribution over the objective function. However, a limitation from GPs is the assumption of stationarity [20], which reduces the ability of the GPs to model non-stationary functions and brings challenge for Bayesian optimization. Hence, several works [1,20] leverage *input warping* that transforming input space to remove major non-stationary effects.

3   Preliminaries

3.1   Domain Warping

Warping simply means that one distorts the domain of a given function with another function [1,20]. Formally, given an input x, instead of mapping x with a function $f(x)$, we replace $f(x)$ with $f(w(x))$. Note that this transformation $w(x)$ may or may not include *local* or *torsion type* distortions. As we describe in this section, vanilla FMs introduce a regularization term to warp the optimal separator and, as shown in [16], this is equivalent to a polynomial kernel (PK) transformation (or *warping*) of the input domain.

3.2   Factorization Machines

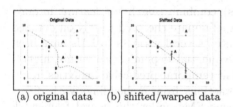

(a) original data   (b) shifted/warped data

Fig. 2. Domain warping in FMs: Adding a shifting term to the model can potentially account for non-linear separators by selectively shifting the effective position of the data relative to the linear separator.

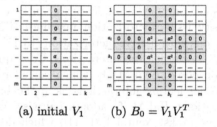

(a) initial V_1 (b) $B_0 = V_1 V_1^T$

Fig. 3. (a,b) Identity initialization: the initial configuration of the B matrix (i.e., B_0) is block diagonal and approximates the identity matrix, I.

Capturing Pairwise Interactions Through Domain Warping. Factorization Machines (FMs [16]) enhance a linear model learning by capturing pairwise interactions among features[1]. In this respect, they are similar to polynomial kernels (PKs):

$$\hat{F}_{PK}(X) = \underbrace{\rho_0 + wX^T}_{lin.\ predictor} + \underbrace{diag(XAX^T)}_{interaction\ term}, \qquad (1)$$

where $X \in \mathbb{R}^{n \times m}$ is a data matrix where the n rows are the (transpose of) m-dimensional data vectors, $\rho_0 \in \mathbb{R}^n$ is global bias where all entries have the same value, $w_0 \in \mathbb{R}$, $w \in \mathbb{R}^m$ is a weight vector, and $A \in \mathbb{R}^{m \times m}$ is a (symmetric)

---

[1] Note that FMs can be generalized to higher degrees of feature interactions. In this paper, without loss of generality, we focus on pairwise FMs, which have been shown to be generally effective and, thus, make up the most commonly used approach for FMs – details can be found in [16].

matrix that describes the degree of feature interaction, and $diag(X) \in \mathbb{R}^n$ represents the diagonal elements in matrix X: the first half of the model represents a linear predictor (Fig. 1(a)), consisting of a global bias and a linear transformation of the input data; the second term shifts the prediction for each individual data point by an amount representing the interactions between its features – the effective result is that the decision boundary gets *warped* in a non-linear manner as in Fig. 1(b). Figure 2 provides an example: adding a shifting term to the model can alter the *effective* positions of the data with respect to a linear separator (Fig. 2 (b)) enabling accurate classification. Note that, when considering each data vector individually, the above model can be written as

$$\hat{F}_{PK}(\boldsymbol{x}) = w_0 + \underbrace{\sum_{i=1}^{m} w_i x_i}_{lin.\ predictor} + \underbrace{\sum_{i=1}^{m} \sum_{j=i+1}^{m} A_{(i,j)} x_i x_j}_{warping\ term}. \tag{2}$$

Here x_i are the individual components of a real-valued input vector, $\boldsymbol{x} \in \mathbb{R}^m$; $x_i = 0$ when the i-th feature does not exist in the observation. The notation $\langle .,. \rangle$ denotes the dot product operation. w_0 is global bias and w_i is the weight for i-th feature. The output of $\hat{F}_{PK}(\boldsymbol{x})$ is a scalar, representing the estimated target.

Low-Rank Assumption. As we see in Eq. 2, the numbers of model parameters are quadratic in the number of dimensions of the feature space and, consequently, PK models may be ineffective when the data is sparse – in particular, when the data is sparse, only few cross feature observations may exist in the data. To address this sparsity issue, FMs assume that the $m \times m$ feature interaction matrix A is low-rank and can be decomposed into $A \simeq VV^T$, where $V \in \mathbb{R}^{m \times k}$. Relying on this assumption, factorize pair-wise feature interaction matrix to capture hidden interactions within features. This means that instead of representing the feature interactions as a single monolithic $m \times m$ matrix, FMs associate a k-dimensional vector $\boldsymbol{v}_i \in \mathbb{R}^k$ (where $k \ll m$) to each component i, such that $A_{(i,j)} \simeq \langle \boldsymbol{v}_i, \boldsymbol{v}_j \rangle$. In other words, each feature will be represented as a vector instead of a scalar value. This factorized feature vector allows FMs avoid the effect from sparse data. Hence, we can consider FMs provide the ability to *curve* separator to achieve better classification without side effect from sparse data.

$$\hat{F}_{FM}(\boldsymbol{x}) = w_0 + \underbrace{\sum_{i=1}^{m} w_i x_i}_{lin.\ predictor} + \underbrace{\sum_{i=1}^{m} \sum_{j=i+1}^{m} \langle \boldsymbol{v}_i, \boldsymbol{v}_j \rangle x_i x_j}_{low\ rank\ warping}. \tag{3}$$

As we see in Eq. 3, this significantly reduces the number of model parameters from quadratic to linear in the number of dimensions of the feature space and, thus, supports more effective learning when the data is sparse. Hence, existing FMs leverage *domain warping* in the form of a regularization term that alters the *effective* positions of the data with respect to a linear separator (Fig. 2). FMs couple this with a *low-rank assumption* to reduce cost and improve accuracy.

4   Doubly-Warped Factorization Machines

In this section, we introduce the proposed *Doubly-Warped Factorization Machines* (W2FM) model. We argue that through carefully constructed warping transformations that help change the way the model *views* the input data, we can significantly increase the expressive ability of the model to enhance the performance of factorization machines, especially in sparse settings.

4.1   Double Warping

The key strength of polynomial kernels and factorization machines comes from the term, $diag(XAX^T)$, where the prediction for each data point, x, is shifted by an additive term $x^T Ax$; i.e., the dot product of the vector x by itself in a space *warped* through an affine transformation, A, which can *rotate scale, and shear the underling space.*

While, as we have seen earlier, this warping can help uncover some of the non-linear structures in the underlying model, in this section, we note that this formulation misses more general (and potentially critical) warpings of the space that may uncover richer non-linear structures in the data.

Let us remember from Eq. 1 through 3 that, for a given data matrix X, factorization machines can be formulated as

$$\hat{F}_{FM}(X) = \underbrace{\rho_0 + wX^T}_{lin.\ predictor} + \underbrace{diag(XAX^T)}_{low\ rank\ warping}, \tag{4}$$

where $\rho_0 \in \mathbb{R}^n$ is a vector where all entries have the same value w_0, $w \in \mathbb{R}^m$ is a weight vector, and $A = \mathbb{R}^{m \times m}$ is a low-rank matrix that describes the degree of interaction among features (i.e., $A \simeq VV^T$, for some $V \in \mathbb{R}^{m \times k}$, where $k \ll m$). In this paper, we argue that a doubly warped FM, formulated as

$$\hat{F}_{W2FM}(X) = \underbrace{\rho_0 + w(XB)^T}_{warped\ lin.\ pred.} + \underbrace{diag((XB)A(XB)^T)}_{low\ rank\ warping}, \tag{5}$$

has the potential to uncover richer non-linear structures in the data. In particular, since the space is warped not only for the second term that recovers the amount of shifts in the predictions for the individual data elements (curve separator in Fig. 1(b)), but the entire feature space (i.e., the entire data set) is warped using the transformation B *before* the model learning step, this has the potential to emphasize distances between points along certain pairs of dimensions, while de-emphasizing distances along other pairs (as in Fig. 1(c)).

4.2   Low Rank Approximation

If we again make the assumption that the transformation B is low rank (i.e., $B = V_1 V_1^T$, for some $V_1 \in \mathbb{R}^{m \times k}$, where $k \ll m$), we can rewrite the above equation as

$$\hat{F}_{\text{W2FM}}(X) = \underbrace{\boldsymbol{\rho}_0 + \boldsymbol{w}(V_1 V_1^T) X^T}_{\text{warped lin. pred.}} + \underbrace{diag(X(V_1 V_1^T)^T (VV^T)(V_1 V_1^T) X^T)}_{\text{low rank warping}}, \quad (6)$$

which can be further simplified as

$$\hat{F}_{\text{W2FM}}(X) = \underbrace{\boldsymbol{\rho}_0 + \boldsymbol{w}(V_1 V_1^T) X^T}_{\text{warped lin. pred.}} + \underbrace{diag(X(V_2 V_2^T) X^T)}_{\text{low rank warping}}. \quad (7)$$

Considering an individual data vector $\boldsymbol{x}$, instead of the entire data set, we can restate this doubly-warped model as

$$\hat{F}_{\text{W2FM}}(\boldsymbol{x}) = \underbrace{w_0 + \sum_{i=1}^{m} \langle \boldsymbol{v}_{1,i}, \boldsymbol{v}_{1,j} \rangle w_i x_i}_{\text{warped lin. pred.}} + \underbrace{\sum_{i=1}^{m} \sum_{j=i+1}^{m} \langle \boldsymbol{v}_{2,i}, \boldsymbol{v}_{2,j} \rangle x_i x_j}_{\text{low rank warping}}, \quad (8)$$

where $V_{1,(i,j)} = \langle \boldsymbol{v}_{1,i}, \boldsymbol{v}_{1,j} \rangle$ and $V_{2,(i,j)} = \langle \boldsymbol{v}_{2,i}, \boldsymbol{v}_{2,j} \rangle$.

4.3   Model Parameters and the Learning Process

In W2FM, the machine learning process needs to recover the values of w_0, an m dimensional weight vector $\boldsymbol{w}$, $m \times k$ matrix V_1, and $m \times k$ matrix V_2; therefore, the number of model parameters that need to be recovered is $1 + (2k + 1) \times m$; i.e., linear in the data dimensionality, as in the original FM formulation.

To estimate these model parameters for a regression problem[2], we adopt a squared loss term $L = (\hat{F}_{\text{W2FM}}(\boldsymbol{x}) - y)^2$, where $\boldsymbol{x}$ is an observation and y is the corresponding ground truth target. To prevent overfitting, we further adopt L_2 regularization on the parameters: $L = (\hat{F}_{\text{W2FM}}(\boldsymbol{x}) - y)^2 + \lambda_W \|\boldsymbol{w}\|^2 + \lambda_V \left(\|V_1\|^2 + \|V_2\|^2 \right)$, where λ_W and λ_V control the regularization strength of different components of the model. In our implementation, we train this model using stochastic gradient descent, starting with a random configuration (parameters selected from a normal distribution) using Adam optimizer [7].

4.4   Summary: Double Warping in W2FM

The proposed W2FM algorithm introduces *double warping*, in the form of a second layer of warping to transform the input domain. This transformation is *linear, but not orthonormal*, thereby "stretching" the space as visualized in Fig. 1. Note that if this second warping matrix B is identity matrix, the result would be identical to the existing FM formulation. The proposed extension lets the model learn a low rank matrix $B = V_1 V_1^T$ different from the identify matrix, which provides accuracy gains as shown in the experiments.

---

[2] For other machine learning tasks, e.g. classification, log loss may be used.

5   Variants of W2FM

5.1   Identity Initialization (W2FM$_I$)

As we see in Eq. 7, the newly introduced *warped* linear predictor term involves a complex interaction, $W(V_1 V_1^T)$, between unknown parameters captured by W and V_1. This, however, may imply that the learning process for this term may get stuck at an undesirable local optimum, especially if the search starts from a random initial point. To avoid this, in the first W2FM variant, W2FM$_{B_0 \sim I}$ (or simply W2FM$_I$) we start training from a configuration where the initial values for V_1 are set such that $B_0 = V_1 V_1^T \simeq I$.

As illustrated in Fig. 3, this is achieved by setting the initial configuration of V_1 to a matrix, where[3] in the ith column, the entries $a_i = (i-1)\lfloor \frac{m}{k} \rfloor + 1$ to $b_i = i\lfloor \frac{m}{k} \rfloor$ are set to $\alpha_i = ((b_i - a_i) + 1)^{-1/2}$. This ensures that the resulting $V_1 V_1^T$ matrix is block-diagonal, with block entries equal to $\alpha^2 = ((b_i - a_i) + 1)^{-1}$; i.e., the initial configuration of the B matrix approximates the identity matrix, I. Note that, since $V_1 V_1^T \simeq I$, in its first epoch, W2FM$_I$ works similarly to vanilla FM, but $V_1 V_1^T$ is allowed to diverge from I from that point on.

5.2   Shared Warping (W2FM$_{SW}$, W2FM$_{ISW}$)

As discussed earlier, W2FM needs to recover roughly twice as many model parameters as vanilla FM. In the second variant, W2FM$_{SW}$, we reduce the number of model parameters through a parameter sharing constraint, $V_1 = V_2 = V_s$, which reflects the assumption that the same transformation can capture the warping needed by both terms of the model:

$$\hat{F}_{\text{W2FM}_{SW}}(X) = \underbrace{\rho_0 + w(V_s V_s^T) X^T}_{\text{warped lin. pred.}} + \underbrace{diag(X(V_s V_s^T) X^T)}_{\text{low rank warping}}. \tag{9}$$

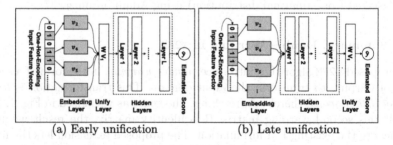

| (a) Early unification | (b) Late unification |

Fig. 4. Neural warping (a): the early unification replaces the bi-interaction pooling layer in [11] with a unification layer (b) the late unification delays the unification step until before score estimation. (the term w_0 for global bias is not shown for clarity)

---

[3] Note that for the very last column of V_1, we have $a_k = (k-1)\lfloor \frac{m}{k} \rfloor + 1$ to $b_k = m$.

5.3 Term Reduction ($\texttt{W2FM}_{TR}$, $\texttt{W2FM}_{ITR}$)

In the next variant, we reduce the number of model parameters by solely relying on space warping ability of the warped linear predictor. In other words, we reduce the number of terms of the model from two to one, by dropping the regularization term:

$$\hat{F}_{\texttt{W2FM}_{TR}}(X) = \underbrace{\rho_0 + \boldsymbol{w}(V_1 V_1^T)X^T}_{warped\ lin.\ pred.}. \qquad (10)$$

5.4 Neural Warping

In NFM [11], authors have argued that the feature interactions (which lead to non-linear models) can be learned by extending the original FM model with a neural network that help recover higher-order feature interactions:

$$\hat{F}_{NFM}(\boldsymbol{x}) = \underbrace{w_0 + \sum_{i=1}^{m} w_i x_i +}_{lin.\ predictor} \underbrace{N(\boldsymbol{x})}_{neural\ shift}. \qquad (11)$$

Although NFM can extract certain non-linear structures, the data source of this process is the unwarped input space. We therefore, argue that NFM can potentially miss critical interactions. Hence, we further introduce warping into NFM-based architectures. Formally speaking, in this case, the warped linear predictor term in $\texttt{W2FM}$ is expressed within a neural framework[4]:

$$\hat{F}_{\texttt{W2FM}_{NW}}(\boldsymbol{x}) = \underbrace{w_0 + N_1(\boldsymbol{x})}_{neural.\ warped\ pred.} \qquad (12)$$

where $N_1(\boldsymbol{x})$ represents a multi-layer feed-forward neural network visualized in Fig. 4 and described below. Here we propose two alternative ways to enhance NFM by merging warping ability.

Early-Unification ($\texttt{W2FM}_{NW-Early}$). In early unification, we replace the bi-interaction pooling layer in [11] with a unification layer that combines the embedding with the predictor and then apply the hidden layers after that (Fig. 4 (a)). Intuitively, this approach warps the space once and then finds a neurally-based complex (non-linear) separator on this warped space.

Embedding Layer. Given a sparse input feature vector with one-hot-encoding, the embedding layer projects each feature to a dense vector representation. Let $V_1 = \langle \boldsymbol{v}_i \rangle$, $i \le m$, where $\boldsymbol{v}_i \in \mathbb{R}^k$ is the embedding vector for the i-th feature. Given a data vector $\boldsymbol{x} = \langle x_i \rangle$, $i \le m$, the corresponding embedding can be computed as $\mathcal{V}(\boldsymbol{x}) = \{x_1 \boldsymbol{v}_1, \ldots, x_m \boldsymbol{v}_m\}$. And we only need to consider the embedding vector for non-zero features, which means $\mathcal{V}(\boldsymbol{x}) = \{x_i \boldsymbol{v}_i\}$, where $x_i \neq 0$.

---

[4] Here we use $\texttt{W2FM}_{TR}$ for clarity, other $\texttt{W2FM}$ variants can be seamlessly integrated.

Unification Layer. Intuitively, in the embedding layer computes the term $V_1^T X^T$ in Eq. 10; in the subsequent (so called "unification") layer, we further compute $\hat{F}_{Unify}(\mathcal{V}(x)) = wV_1(\mathcal{V}(x))$.

Hidden Layers. The unification layer, then, is connected to a stack of fully connected layers $z_l(x) = \sigma_l(\mathcal{W}_l z_{l-1}(x) + b_l)$, learning more complex interactions between features [19]: where l denotes the number of hidden layers and $z_1(x) = \sigma_1(\mathcal{W}_1 \hat{F}_{Unify}(\mathcal{V}(x)) + b_1)$. $\mathcal{W}_j$, σ_j and b_j denote the weight matrix, bias vector, and the activation function for the j-th hidden layer, respectively.

Prediction Layer. Finally, the output vector from z_l is transformed to compute estimated score: $N_1(x) = h^T z_l(x)$, where vector $h \in \mathbb{R}^m$ denotes the neuron weights of the prediction layer.

Late-Unification ($\texttt{W2FM}_{NW-Late}$). In late unification, on the other hand, we first apply hidden layers that recover higher order interactions among the features, and apply the unification layer at the end, before the predictions are generated (Fig. 4 (b)). Intuitively, this approach warps the space using a neural network and then finds a linear separator in the warped space.

6 Experiments

We compare W2FM and its variants as we introduced in Sect. 5 against the competitors[5]. With four publicly accessible data sets[6] , and we assume the feature interactions are row-rank and consider values of $k \in \{32, 64, 128\}$. For training, we randomly split each data set into three parts: 60% is used for training, 20% for validation, and 20% for testing. The batch size is set to 4096. The validation set was used for hyper-parameter tuning and the performance evaluation was conducted on the test data set. In particular, as in prior FM works [11,24], we train all methods for up to 100 epochs, but stop the training process if the RMSE for the validation data increases for 5 consecutive epochs. We then select the hyper-parameters of the best model identified up to that point for testing. All models are learned by optimizing the squared loss with L_2-regularization and learned by mini-batch Adagrad [7].

---

[5] Support Vector Machine (SVM) with linear kernel [10], Factorization Machine (FM, single warping baseline) [16], Attention FM (the attention factor: 256, activation function: ReLU, drop out rate: 0.5, the valid dimension:2 (*user id* and *item id*)) [24], Neural FM (drop out rate for bi-interaction layer: 0.5, 1 hidden layer with 64 neuron and drop out rate: 0.8, activation function: ReLU) [11] and Holographic FM [23].

[6] Ciao (# of instances: 284K, # of features: 107K, density: 0.0003) [21], Epinions (# of instances: 922K, # of features: 141K, density: 0.0003) [22], MovieLens-100K (# of instances: 100K, # of features: 2273, density: 0.041) [9] and MovieLens-1M (# of instances: 1M, # of features: 9746, density: 0.059) [9].

Table 1. RMSE for test data, and Per epoch training time (seconds) - each row is individually colored from the best/fastest (green) to the worst/slowest (red) accuracy/training times.

RMSE for Test Data

Data	k	SVM	FM	AFM	HFM	Base	SW	TR	I	ISW	ITR	NFM	Early	Late
		SVM	FM Variants			W2FM Variants						NFM	W2FM_NW	
Ciao	32	2.311	1.188	2.314	2.624	1.233	1.224	1.132	0.997	1.075	0.994	2.907	1.245	1.118
	64	2.311	1.065	2.405	2.682	1.251	1.277	1.280	1.076	1.076	1.029	3.035	1.215	1.107
	128	2.310	1.051	2.554	2.600	1.429	1.382	1.337	1.070	1.121	1.056	2.801	1.425	1.125
Epinions	32	1.511	1.174	1.562	1.484	1.144	1.140	1.138	1.128	1.133	1.122	1.390	1.170	1.162
	64	1.511	1.170	1.623	1.536	1.188	1.151	1.142	1.161	1.085	1.126	1.886	1.146	1.145
	128	1.506	1.175	1.724	1.516	1.180	1.204	1.167	1.135	1.131	1.098	2.330	1.179	1.152
ML-100K	32	2.098	2.028	1.160	1.158	1.164	1.153	1.154	1.144	1.149	1.143	1.780	1.146	1.225
	64	2.091	1.288	1.156	1.161	1.163	1.152	1.154	1.154	1.150	1.149	2.343	1.128	1.213
	128	2.098	1.123	1.154	1.174	1.174	1.155	1.153	1.158	1.148	1.151	1.971	1.170	1.190
ML-1M	32	1.108	1.067	1.040	1.044	1.048	1.040	1.040	1.044	1.041	1.042	1.590	1.084	1.092
	64	1.108	1.084	1.041	1.052	1.089	1.041	1.041	1.043	1.039	1.042	2.030	1.076	1.084
	128	1.112	1.095	1.042	1.062	1.051	1.040	1.043	1.051	1.042	1.040	1.722	1.055	1.078

Training Time Per Epoch (sec.)

Data	k	SVM	FM	AFM	HFM	Base	SW	TR	I	ISW	ITR	NFM	Early	Late
		SVM	FM Variants			W2FM Variants						NFM	W2FM_NW	
Ciao	32	2.16	3.79	1.37	4.84	4.16	4.05	4.39	4.64	4.14	4.16	1.27	3.76	3.46
	64	1.95	4.33	1.48	8.19	5.28	4.65	4.87	5.51	5.45	4.86	1.48	4.24	4.08
	128	2.34	5.72	2.15	15.37	6.45	6.60	6.45	7.75	7.79	6.40	1.62	5.51	5.02
Epinions	32	7.93	14.30	3.98	17.99	19.26	17.73	17.82	18.67	19.88	17.57	4.31	15.25	14.37
	64	7.79	17.35	5.18	29.26	21.10	18.48	19.55	31.05	26.56	26.21	4.74	17.81	16.98
	128	7.73	22.97	6.27	53.79	30.55	26.08	25.38	51.56	40.60	33.75	6.34	21.90	20.28
ML-100K	32	0.21	0.30	0.33	1.01	0.29	0.26	0.27	0.29	0.27	0.28	0.48	0.35	0.34
	64	0.24	0.35	0.41	2.03	0.29	0.28	0.29	0.30	0.31	0.28	0.42	0.37	0.38
	128	0.23	0.46	0.46	4.11	0.38	0.31	0.30	0.35	0.36	0.30	0.66	0.38	0.37
ML-1M	32	2.76	3.70	3.92	11.03	3.19	4.37	3.65	3.33	3.59	3.73	3.70	3.81	3.69
	64	3.13	4.44	3.98	23.54	6.07	3.58	3.49	3.47	3.97	3.71	4.27	5.25	3.77
	128	2.98	5.81	5.55	44.27	5.66	5.64	4.00	6.02	5.55	3.64	5.34	4.95	5.16

Table 2. Convergence patterns; each cell is of the form X/Y, where X is the index of the epoch with the lowest validation error, whereas Y is the number of training epochs – as in prior works [11,24], we train all methods for up to 100 epochs, but stop the training process if the RMSE for the validation data increases for 5 consecutive epochs.

(Epoch with Lowest Val. Error) / (# of Training Epochs)

Data	k	SVM	FM	AFM	HFM	Base	SW	TR	I	ISW	ITR	NFM	Early	Late
		SVM	FM Variants			W2FM Variants						NFM	W2FM_NW	
Ciao	32	100/100	4/8	100/100	100/100	52/100	66/70	70/76	18/26	14/100	95/100	95/100	30/100	61/100
	64	100/100	1/6	100/100	100/100	30/44	100/100	44/48	23/33	20/38	20/100	7/11	28/100	56/100
	128	100/100	1/6	100/100	78/100	7/100	58/62	85/100	32/36	62/100	58/87	5/100	99/100	97/100
Epinions	32	100/100	1/6	100/100	100/100	20/66	74/78	23/92	33/37	42/46	100/100	99/100	99/100	50/54
	64	100/100	1/6	100/100	35/47	14/100	96/100	92/100	16/25	64/68	92/96	100/100	17/27	73/100
	128	100/100	1/6	100/100	34/42	23/100	48/52	20/45	41/86	72/90	100/100	9/27	98/100	62/100
ML-100K	32	100/100	4/8	100/100	33/42	14/39	33/37	57/75	1/23	44/66	1/43	99/100	88/100	24/74
	64	100/100	2/6	98/100	18/34	13/27	72/93	38/42	10/30	52/56	56/100	73/100	67/97	22/34
	128	100/100	1/6	72/84	9/13	10/23	36/69	27/45	1/15	1/6	1/98	19/100	98/100	62/100
ML-1M	32	100/100	1/6	100/100	25/29	8/20	91/100	84/100	9/15	80/100	48/59	100/100	45/49	79/98
	64	100/100	1/6	87/91	8/22	6/22	84/100	90/100	6/14	54/58	99/100	8/16	99/100	84/88
	128	100/100	1/6	34/40	7/50	5/23	93/100	51/55	8/12	61/65	100/100	100/100	98/100	50/100

6.1 Results and Analysis

Accuracy. In Table 1, we report the testing RMSE for the various models trained on the four data sets we considered in this paper. The models are categorized into variants of FM and W2FM; we also present SVM baseline and neural FM variants (NFM and W2FM$_{nw}$). Each row is colored from the best (green) to the worst (red) accuracy. The proposed W2FM variants, overall, perform better than SVM and the FM variants – in fact, this is true both for non-neural and neural strategies. This is because, as also noted in [11], a more informative transformation at low-level layers (as W2FM is able to perform) has the potential to ease the burden of high-level layers in trying to extract useful information. And, the identity initialized, term reduced approach, W2FM_{ITR}, proves to be the most robust technique.

Per Epoch Training Time. Table 1 also presents per epoch training times (as before, each row is individually colored from fastest, green, to the slowest, red): For the sparser Ciao and Epinions data sets, aside from the naive SVM, AFM and NFM have the overall fastest per epoch training times and HFM trains very slowly. For the two relatively denser MovieLens data sets, on the other hand, the W2FM variants train (per epoch) faster than the all FM variants.

Convergence Patterns. In Table 2, we study the convergence patterns of the various models. As stated earlier, we train all methods for up to 100 epochs, but as in [11,24], we stop the training process if the RMSE for the validation data increases for 5 consecutive epochs. In Table 2, each cell is of the form X/Y, where (a) X is the index of the epoch with the best validation accuracy and (b) Y is the number of training epochs. As we can see, conventional FM stops very early, in 6–8 epochs, while it often returns its best results in the very first epoch. This indicates that the learning process gets stuck at an early solution (often the very first one) and is not able to improve on it. Unlike FM, the SVM, AFM, and NFM models require many more epochs (often 100) to converge and the training epoch with the best accuracy is or close to the maximum number of epochs ran. These together indicate that these models tend to converge slowly. In contrast, we see that base W2FM and W2FM_I are able to improve on their initial solutions, but nevertheless are able to locate their best solutions relatively early, indicating a faster convergence rate. In particular, the W2FM_I variant provide the best trade-off: (1) it is able to improve over the solution identified in the first few epochs ($X \not\sim 1$), (2) it converges relatively quickly to its best solution (X tends to be $\ll 100$), and (3) it is able to benefit from early stopping (Y tends to be $\ll 100$). The weight sharing and term reducing variants of W2FM and W2FM_I converge relatively slowly; however, considering the accuracy gains they are able to provide (Table 1) this is generally worthwhile.

7   Conclusions

In this paper, we presented a novel *Doubly-Warped Factorization Machines (W2FM)* model for enhancing factorization machines (FM) by leveraging additional low-rank *affine* linear transformations that warp the space to improve the expressiveness of the model. We further presented several variants which provide various trade-offs in terms of starting configuration and number of model parameters. We have also shown that W2FM can accommodate neural-based models. Experiments have shown that W2FM provides accuracy gains over competitors, including basic FM, AFM, HFM, and NFM, and that the *identity initialization* variant, W2FM_I, provides the overall best accuracy, and convergence trade-offs.

References

1. Binois, M., Ginsbourger, D., Roustant, O.: A warped kernel improving robustness in Bayesian optimization via random embeddings. In: International Conference on Learning and Intelligent Optimization (2015)
2. Blondel, M., Fujino, A., Ueda, N., Ishihata, M.: Higher-order factorization machines. In: NIPS 2016 (2016)
3. Blondel, M., Ishihata, M., Fujino, A., Ueda, N.: Polynomial networks and factorization machines: New insights and efficient training algorithms. In: PMLR (2016)
4. Chen, T., Yin, H., Nguyen, Q.V.H., Peng, W., Li, X., Zhou, X.: Sequence-aware factorization machines for temporal predictive analytics. In: ICDE 2020 (2020)
5. Chen, X., Zheng, Y., Wang, J., Ma, W., Huang, J.: RaFM: Rank-aware factorization machines. In: PMLR (2019)
6. Cheng, H.T., et al.: Wide & deep learning for recommender systems. In: DLRS, vol. 2016, (2016)
7. Duchi, J., Hazan, E., Singer, Y.: Adaptive subgradient methods for online learning and stochastic optimization. J. Mach. Learn. Res. **12**, 2121–2159 (2011)
8. Grčar, M., Mladenič, D., Fortuna, B., Grobelnik, M.: Data sparsity issues in the collaborative filtering framework. In: Advances in Web Mining and Web Usage Analysis (2006)
9. Harper, F.M., Konstan, J.A.: The movielens datasets: History and context. ACM Trans. Interact. Intell. Syst. **5**(4), 1–19 (Dec 2015)
10. Hastie, T., Tibshirani, R., Friedman, J.: The Elements of Statistical Learning: Data Mining, Inference and Prediction. Springer, New York (2009)
11. He, X., Chua, T.S.: Neural factorization machines for sparse predictive analytics. In: SIGIR 2017 (2017)
12. Juan, Y., Zhuang, Y., Chin, W.S., Lin, C.J.: Field-aware factorization machines for CTR prediction. In: RecSys 2016 (2016)
13. Koren, Y.: Factorization meets the neighborhood: a multifaceted collaborative filtering model. In: KDD 2008 (2008)
14. Livni, R., Shalev-Shwartz, S., Shamir, O.: On the computational efficiency of training neural networks. In: NIPS (2014)
15. Rasmussen, C.E., Williams, C.K.I.: Gaussian Processes for Machine Learning (Adaptive Computation and Machine Learning). The MIT Press (2005)
16. Rendle, S.: Factorization machines. In: ICDM 2010, IEEE Computer Society (2010)
17. Salakhutdinov, R., Mnih, A.: Probabilistic matrix factorization. In: NIPS 2007 (2007)
18. Seal, H.L.: Studies in the history of probability and statistics. xv: The historical development of the gauss linear model. Biometrika **54**(1–2), 1–24 (1967)
19. Shan, Y., Hoens, T.R., Jiao, J., Wang, H., Yu, D., Mao, J.: Deep crossing: web-scale modeling without manually crafted combinatorial features. In: KDD 2016 (2016)
20. Snoek, J., Swersky, K., Zemel, R., Adams, R.P.: Input warping for Bayesian optimization of non-stationary functions. In: ICML 2014 (2014)
21. Tang, J., Gao, H., Liu, H., Sarma, A.D.: eTrust: Understanding trust evolution in an online world. In: KDD (2012)
22. Tang, J., Hu, X., Gao, H., Liu, H.: Exploiting local and global social context for recommendation. In: IJCAI (2013)
23. Tay, Y., Zhang, S., Luu, A.T., Hui, S.C., Yao, L., Vinh, T.D.Q.: Holographic factorization machines for recommendation. In: AAAI (2019)
24. Xiao, J., Ye, H., He, X., Zhang, H., Wu, F., Chua, T.S.: Attentional factorization machines: Learning the weight of feature interactions via attention networks. In: IJCAI 2017 (2017)

Causal Combinatorial Factorization Machines for Set-Wise Recommendation

Akira Tanimoto[1,2,3]($\boxtimes$) [iD], Tomoya Sakai[1,3], Takashi Takenouchi[3,4], and Hisashi Kashima[2] [iD]

[1] NEC Corporation, Kawasaki, Japan
{a.tanimoto,tomoya_sakai}@nec.com
[2] Kyoto University, Kyoto, Japan
kashima@i.kyoto-u.ac.jp
[3] RIKEN, Tokyo, Japan
ttakashi@fun.ac.jp
[4] Future University Hakodate, Hakodate, Japan

Abstract. With set-wise (exact-k, slate, combinatorial) recommendation, we aim to optimize the whole set of items to recommend while taking the dependency among items into consideration. This enables us to model, for example, the substitution relationship of items, i.e., a customer tends to purchase only one item in the same category, in contrast to the top-k recommendation in which the independency of items is assumed. Recent efforts in this context have focused on the computational aspects of optimizing the set of items to recommend. However, they have not taken into account sample selection bias in datasets. Real-world datasets for recommendation have missing entries not completely at random due to biased exposure or user preferences. Addressing the selection bias is important for the set-wise recommendation since methods with larger hypothesis spaces are more likely to overfit biased training data. In light of recent top-k recommendation research that has addressed this issue by using causal inference techniques, we therefore propose a set-wise recommendation model with debiased training methods based on recent causal inference techniques. We demonstrate the advantage of our method using real-world recommendation datasets consisting of biased training sets and randomized test sets.

Keywords: Set-wise recommendation · Causal inference

1 Introduction

Recently, the importance of optimizing the combinations of items, i.e., set-wise (exact-k, slate, combinatorial) modeling, has received attention in the recommendation context [5,7,8,22]. Set-wise modeling aims to overcome the limitation inherent in the greedy top-k recommendations [4], such as the lack of diversity in the recommended items [23,27]. For example, recommending multiple TVs at

© Springer Nature Switzerland AG 2021
K. Karlapalem et al. (Eds.): PAKDD 2021, LNAI 12713, pp. 498–509, 2021.
https://doi.org/10.1007/978-3-030-75765-6_40

(a) CATE estimation

	$T=0$	$T=1$
x_1	1	
x_2		3
x_3		2
x_4	2	

(b) Top-k recommendation

	Item 1	Item 2	Item 3	Item 4
User 1	1			4
User 2			2	3
User 3	4	2		
User 4			5	2

(c) Set-wise recommendation

a	{Item 1, Item 2}		{Item 1, Item 3}		{Item 1, Item 4}		{Item 2, Item 3}		{Item 2, Item 4}		{Item 3, Item 4}	
a^i (Item 1)	2	1	3	1	4	2	3	2	4	3	4	
User 1					1	4						
User 2											2	3
User 3	4	2										
User 4											5	2

Fig. 1. Example data tables for existing and our problem settings. Potential outcome framework for CATE estimation (a) assumes two random variables of outcomes for each treatment $T \in \{0, 1\}$ and treats the counterfactual potential outcome as missing. Thus, potential outcome estimation and matrix completion for recommendation are both missing value completion under biased observations.

the same time is unlikely to result in the purchase conversion of both, while recommending a TV and a DVD player may increase the probability that both will be purchased. The former is called the substitute relation and the latter is called the complementary relation [12]. In this work, we train a set-wise model that captures such relationships to evaluate the whole set of items to recommend.

We should note here the difference between causation and association. Just because some items are often purchased at the same time does not necessarily mean that the probability of being purchased increases if they are recommended at the same time [12, 14]. We want to recommend a set of items that results in a larger expected total outcome (e.g., purchase conversion) through recommending simultaneously. That is, we have to consider the prediction under interventions (aka actions or treatments) by a recommender system, which is known as the causal effect inference problem [17]. As shown in Fig. 1, conditional average treatment effect (CATE) estimation in causal inference, as well as recommendation problems, can be viewed as learning from a biasedly missing dataset (missing not completely at random) [13, 17], as we see in Sect. 3.

Recently, in the context of the top-k recommendation, several methods have been proposed that address the missing entries not completely at random by using debiasing techniques in causal inference [19, 24]. As shown in Fig. 1(c), a dataset for the set-wise recommendation would be severely sparse, and thus it is quite important to avoid overfitting for biased training data. We therefore consider the problem of debiased inference for the set-wise recommendation.

In our approach, we train a set-wise evaluation (rate/click prediction) model for the recommendation. Considering that the final goal is to choose the action that is expected to maximize the outcome, a straightforward approach would be learning a policy that outputs the recommended set (as in [5, 7, 8, 22]) instead of making a prediction of outcomes. Even so, it is reasonable to make a prediction of the outcome when the predicted value itself is needed. In assortment optimization in retail stores, for example, store owners should also determine the ordering quantity on the basis of the demand forecast [12]. In such cases, the prediction of the outcome itself is essential for the decision-makers. We discuss how to optimize the set of items to recommend using a prediction model in Sect. 4.3.

2 Problem Setting

Our goal is to build an outcome (rate/click) prediction model under the feature x (typically the customer ID) and the action a (the set of recommended items) from biased data. Our training instance is $(x, a, y^{(a)}) \sim p\left(y^{(a)}|x\right) \mu(a|x) p(x)$, where $x \in \mathcal{X}$ is the feature of a user (typically the one-hot encoding of the user ID), $a \in \mathcal{A} \subset \{0,1\}^{|\mathcal{I}|}$ is the action (the recommended set) in a combinatorial action space $\mathcal{A}$ with the candidate set of items $\mathcal{I}$, $\mu(a|x)$ is the propensity (the policy of the past decision-makers or logging policy), and $y^{(a)} = \left(y_t^{(a)}\right)_{t \in a} = \left(y_{t_1}^{(a)}, \dots, y_{t_{|a_n|}}^{(a)}\right) \in \mathbb{R}^{|a|}$ is the outcome vector that consists of outcomes for each recommended item. Then, we train a model $f(x, a)$ to predict the outcomes $\left(y_t^{(a)}\right)_{t \in a}$.

The overall outcome of a set-wise recommendation a for a user can be evaluated by the summation of the rates of the recommended items, i.e., $y_a = \sum_{t \in a} y_t^{(a)}$. In that case, the difference from the simple outcome prediction on a combinatorial action space [21,28] is that we observe not only the overall outcome $y_a \in \mathbb{R}$ but all the rates for each recommended item $\left\{y_t^{(a)}\right\}_{t \in a}$. The challenge in this paper is how to obtain an outcome prediction model f sample-efficiently from observational data collected by a biased and possibly unknown policy (propensity) $\mu(a|x)$. Formally, we pursue the prediction accuracy on unbiased distribution as

$$L^u(f) := \underset{p(y_a|x) p^u(a) p(x)}{\mathbb{E}} [\ell(y_a, f(x, a))], \tag{1}$$

where y_a denotes the overall potential outcome, $p^u(a) = \mathrm{Unif}(\mathcal{A})$ is the discrete uniform distribution on the action space $\mathcal{A}$, and ℓ is the instance-wise loss. To evaluate (1) unbiasedly, we use unbiased datasets for testing. In addition to the prediction accuracy, we also evaluate the value of the recommendation, i.e., the estimated average clicks when we optimize the item set to recommend with the model. We will discuss this metric in Sect. 5.2.

3 Related Work

Treatment Effect Estimation. The goal of conditional average treatment effect (CATE) estimation is to estimate the average causal effect τ under the feature x specified. CATE is defined as $\tau(x) = \mathbb{E}[y^{(1)} - y^{(0)}|x]$, where $y^{(1)}, y^{(0)} \in \mathcal{Y} \subset \mathbb{R}$ are the potential outcomes for each action, namely, if we take an action $a = 1$, then we observe $y^{(1)}$, and if $a = 0$, we observe $y^{(0)}$. The challenges here are the missing values and the selection bias, i.e., true τ is never observed but either $y^{(0)}$ or $y^{(1)}$ is observed, and the logging policy $\mu(a|x)$ is not constant (biased) in x. A typical approach is to train a potential outcome prediction model $f : \mathcal{X} \times \{0,1\} \to \mathcal{Y}$ and estimate CATE by $\hat{\tau}(x) = f(x, a = 1) - f(x, a = 0)$. A typical performance measure is the expected precision in estimation of heterogeneous effect (PEHE) [6] $\epsilon_{\text{PEHE}}(\tau) := \mathbb{E}_x[(\tau(x) - \hat{\tau}(x))^2]$, or the MSE on the joint distribution with the uniform policy.

A well-known workaround called inverse probability weighting using the propensity score (IPW) [1] aims to debias by means of instance weighting using the propensity $\mu(a|x)$ as $L_{\text{IPW}}(f) := \mathbb{E}_{x,a}\left[\frac{1}{2\mu(a|x)}(y_a(x) - f(x,a))^2\right]$. Since the expected IPW risk matches the expected risk on the randomized controlled trials (RCTs), a good performance can be expected asymptotically. When the true propensity is not recorded, however, we have to estimate the propensity score and plug-in with a finite sample size, and then its performance might degrade [11]. A recent trend to improve non-asymptotic performance is to extract *balanced* representation by means of adversarial domain adaptation techniques [9,20,21]. We combine these two approaches as described in Sect. 4.2.

Modeling for Recommendation. In real-world recommendation systems, the sampling distribution for items is not uniform because popular items tend to be frequently recommended, among other reasons. To reduce such sample selection bias, treatment effects have been actively considered recently. [19] proposed a simple approach of utilizing propensity scores to weight the error of the matrix factorization method. A similar approach in [2] aims at debiasing by means of multi-task learning of a large (biased) observational dataset and a small randomized dataset. At the same time, the importance of selecting the combinations of items, i.e., set-wise modeling, has also received attention recently in the recommendation context [5,7,8,22]. [5] considered the exact-k recommendation problem, in which the task is to select k items to show to users in a limited area of a screen. In [5], the item interaction is expressed as a graph, and then a neural network with an attention mechanism learns a policy for selecting items one by one. While these methods [5,7,8] focus on generating the recommended set of items in a computationally efficient manner, the selection bias is not considered, and there is a risk of performance decay under strong selection biases in real-world problems. Therefore, we investigate the debiased modeling of the evaluator for set-wise modeling utilizing recent techniques in causal inference.

4   Causal Combinatorial Factorization Machines for Set-Wise Recommendation

4.1   Model: Combinatorial Factorization Machines

In recommendation tasks, the outcome, which we aim to maximize, would typically be the sum of the rates of recommended items to users. However, we can observe not only the sum but also the rates for each item. Therefore, we use the rates for each item as the supervision, with consideration of the other items recommended to (or rated by) each customer user. That is, our data consists of

$$D = \{y_n, x_n, a_n^i, a_n^{-i}\}_{n=1}^N,$$

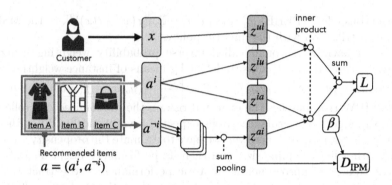

Fig. 2. Combinatorial FM structure.

where n is the sample index, x_n and a_n^i are the one-hot encoded user ID and the target item ID associated with the rate y_n, respectively, and $a_n^{-i} = (0, 1, 1, 0, \ldots)$ is the other items recommended to the user at the same time, where 1s correspond to the IDs of other recommended items. The final set-wise outcome for a user identified by x' is the summation of the outcomes of recommended items $\sum_{n:x_n=x'} y_n$ and the corresponding action is denoted as $a = a_n^i + a_n^{-i}$.

Factorization machines [16] enable us to learn the matrix factorization model by means of SGD with one-hot encoding of the user IDs and the item IDs. We extend the factorization machines to take the second-order interactions between the recommended items into account for the set-wise modeling. Specifically, we include the second-order interaction term of the target item and the other recommended items (or other items rated by the same user), as

$$f(x, a) = w_0 + \sum_j w_j^u x_j + \sum_j w_j^a a_j^i + \sum_{j,j'} \langle z_j^{ui}, z_{j'}^{iu} \rangle x_j a_{j'}^i + \sum_{j,j'} \langle z_j^{ia}, z_{j'}^{ai} \rangle a_j^i a_{j'}^{-i},$$

(2)

where $w_0, w^u, w^a, z^{ui}, z^{iu}, z^{ia}$, and z^{ai} are the model parameters. The resulting network structure is shown in Fig. 2. Let 1_j be the one-hot encoding of an integer j. When one recommends the t-th item to the s-th user, and at the same time the other item set recommended is $\mathcal{T}'$, prediction (2) is written as

$$f\left(x = 1_s, a = \left(1_t, \sum_{t' \in \mathcal{T}'} 1_{t'} \right) \right) = w_0 + w_s^u + w_t^a + \langle z_s^{ui}, z_t^{iu} \rangle + \left\langle z_t^{ia}, \sum_{t' \in \mathcal{T}'} z_{t'}^{ai} \right\rangle.$$

The final term handles the interaction between the target item t and other recommended items $\mathcal{T}'$, which represents the substitution or complementary relation between recommended items. A positive inner product value $\langle z_j^{ia}, z_{j'}^{ai} \rangle > 0$ means that the j-th target item has a complementary relation with respect to the j'-th item and the rate would be higher when recommended with the j'-th item. Since the interaction is considered to be invariant to the permutation of other recommended items, we utilize the sum-pooling as proposed in deep sets for permutation-invariant functions [25].

4.2 Debiased Loss with Causal Inference Techniques

To train our model (2) in a debiased manner from the biased observational data, we introduce two debiasing techniques: the weighting technique proposed in the top-k recommendation and the representation balancing technique proposed in causal inference for large treatment spaces.

Although the representation balancing approach in [21] is scalable to a huge set-wise action space both statistically and computationally, a limitation is that the balanced representation of inputs cannot capture the difference in the output distributions (i.e., when $p(y) \neq p^u(y)$), as shown in [10,26]. Especially in recommendation datasets with explicit-feedbacks, the rate prior shift is often observed because the users are likely to rate their favorite items among others. This difference is exactly what previous IPW-based methods for recommendation address (called naive-Bayes IPW) [19,24]. Therefore, we combine this weighting with the representation balancing approach.

Let us define the integral probability metric (the representation balancing regularizer) as

$$D_{\text{IPM}}(p_1, p_2) := \sup_{g \in G} \left| \int_{\mathcal{Z}} g(z)(p_1(z) - p_2(z)) \mathrm{d}z \right| \tag{3}$$

with a function class G. We utilize the 1-Lipschitz function class for G as in [20,21], after which D_{IPM} would be the Wasserstein distance D_{wass}. With any weighting function $\beta(z)$, assuming that the representation extractor $z = \phi(x, a)$ is invertible and $\frac{1}{B}\ell(z)$ is in the function class G for some $B > 0$ with respect to z, our target loss on the randomized distribution (1) can be bounded as

$$L^u(f) \leq L(f; \beta) + B \cdot D_{\text{IPM}}\left(p(z)\beta(z), p^u(z)\right),$$

where $L(f; \beta)$ is the weighted loss on the observational data. This bound justifies minimizing the empirical estimate of r.h.s. as a proxy of unobservable unbiased loss $L^u(f)$. The proof is given by replacing the source distribution $p(z)$ in the non-weighted version of the bound in [21] with the weighted distribution $p(z)\beta(z)$. Note that the weighted distribution must satisfy $\int p(z)\beta(z)\mathrm{d}z = 1$, otherwise a constant critic $g(z) = c$ for $c > 0$ gives a non-zero IPM value and the supremum in (3) does not exist when G is the 1-Lipschitz function class.

For the weights β, we can utilize the information obtained in each problem setting. Assuming there exists a true rating function $y = h^*(z)$, the naive-Bayes weighting can be reproduced as $\beta(z) := \mathbb{E}_{p^u(z)}[h^*(z)] \big/ \mathbb{E}_{p(z)}[h^*(z)] = p^u(y)/p(y) =: \beta(y)$. Thus, when we have no access to the true propensity μ but do have access to the rate prior shift $p^u(y)/p(y)$, as assumed in [19,24], we can utilize this weighting. If we have access to the true propensity, we can utilize it as $\beta(z = \phi(x, a)) = p^u(a)/\mu(a|x)$, after which D_{IPM} would be zero, which recovers the full IPW method.

Our resulting objective function is

$$\min_f \frac{1}{N} \sum_{n=1}^{N} \beta_n \ell(f(x_n, a_n), y_n) + \mathfrak{R}(f) + \alpha \cdot \hat{D}_{\text{wass}}\left(\{z_n, z_n^u, \beta_n\}_{n=1}^N\right), \tag{4}$$

where $\beta_n = \beta(y_n) = p^u(y_n)/p(y_n)$ if available, $\ell(y', y)$ is the instance-wise loss, namely, the weighted MSE or cross-entropy for rate and click prediction, respectively, $\mathfrak{R}$ is a regularizer, $z_n = \phi(x_n, a_n)$, $z_n^u = \phi(x_n, a_n^u)$, a_n^u is random actions sampled from $\mathrm{Unif}(\mathcal{A})$, $\alpha \geq 0$ is the regularization strength, and $\hat{D}_{\mathrm{wass}}$ is the balancing regularizer with weights, as

$$\hat{D}_{\mathrm{wass}}(\{z_n, z_n^u, \beta_n\}_{n=1}^N) := \sup_{g \in G} \left| \frac{1}{\sum_{n=1}^N \beta_n} \sum_{n=1}^N \beta_n g(z_n) - \frac{1}{N} \sum_{n=1}^N g(z_n^u) \right|, \quad (5)$$

where G is the 1-Lipschitz function class.

4.3   Optimizing the Item Set to Recommend Using a Model

We here explain how to obtain a set-wise recommendation from our prediction model. Recall that k is the number of items that we present to customers from $|\mathcal{I}|$ candidate items. One approach to finding a promising set-wise recommendation is to first prepare $|\mathcal{A}| = {}_{|\mathcal{I}|}C_k$ candidates of a set-wise recommendation and then choose the one that achieves the highest estimated outcome. Specifically, for a customer whose feature vector is x, we prepare a set of item-set vectors $\{a_j\}_{j=1}^{{}_{|\mathcal{I}|}C_k}$ with $|a| = k$ and then choose the combination by $\mathrm{argmax}_j \hat{f}(x, a_j)$, where $\hat{f}$ is the learned predictor. This approach is accurate, but it is intractable when ${}_{|\mathcal{I}|}C_k$ is large. When the number of item-sets is large, one can adopt a greedy approach to a set-wise recommendation. That is, we iteratively select one item to construct a set-wise recommendation. We initialize the selected item-set vector a' with zero vector. For a customer x, we select an item by $j' = \mathrm{argmax}_j \hat{f}\left(x, (a^i = 1_j, a^{\neg i} = a')\right)$. Let a'' be the vector of the current selected item-set, as $a'' = a' + 1_{j'}$. We again select an item by $j'' = \mathrm{argmax}_j \hat{f}\left(x, (a^i = 1_j, a^{\neg i} = a'')\right)$. We repeat the above procedure until the number of selected items becomes k. Since ${}_{|\mathcal{I}|}C_k$ increases quickly even for a small k, this greedy approach is effective in terms of computation.

5   Experiments

5.1   Sequential Display Setting

Datasets. As in [19], we first evaluated on two real-world datasets with explicit feedbacks, Yahoo!R3 [15] and Coat [19], to compare with existing causal-aware top-k recommendation methods [19,24]. Yahoo!R3 had 15,300 user IDs and 1,000 song IDs, and Coat had 290 user IDs and 300 item IDs, both of which contain missing not at random (MNAR) data for training and missing completely at random (MCAR) data for testing. For the combi-FM-based methods, we used the set of rated items for each user as a in each of the training and testing datasets without overlap, i.e., a in the test data did not contain the rated items in the training. We cannot completely reproduce the situation in which a user examines each item and rates it sequentially due to the lack of the order of items that the user rated, though the set of rated items contains the set of previously exposed items to the user, which can be captured by our set-wise modeling.

Table 1. Test MAE and MSE on the Yahoo and Coat datasets. (*) reported in [24]. The top methods for each metric are in bold and the second places are italicized and underlined.

Method	YAHOO		COAT	
	MAE	MSE	MAE	MSE
MF (*)	1.154	1.891	0.920	1.257
MF-IPS (*)	0.810	0.989	_0.860_	_1.093_
MF-DR-JL (*)	_0.747_	_0.966_	**0.778**	**0.990**
FM	0.803	1.170	1.187	2.534
FM-IPW	**0.736**	1.031	1.148	2.398
Combi-FM	0.959	1.259	0.930	1.290
Combi-FM-IPWnb	0.821	1.050	0.945	1.281
Combi-FM-Wass (proposed)	0.781	**0.958**	0.966	1.287

Compared Methods. We compared our proposed method with several existing methods and straightforward combinations of our model and existing training methods, namely, factorization machines (FM) [16], FM with IPW with weights estimated by naive Bayes (FM-IPW), combinatorial FM (2) without IPM regularization or IPW (Combi-FM), Combi-FM with naive-Bayes IPW (Combi-FM-IPWnb), Combi-FM with the Wasserstein with weights by naive-Bayes IPW (Combi-FM-Wass), and existing matrix factorization (MF) and its causal-aware extensions based on naive-Bayes IPW reported in [24]. For the FM-based methods, we used the width of 10 for the representation ϕ. For the combi-CFR (proposed), α in (4) was fixed to 0.5.

Results. Table 1 lists the overall results. The proposed method outperformed all other methods with respect to MSE on the Yahoo!R3 dataset. In contrast, an existing method (MF-DR-JL) performed best on the Coat dataset. The Coat dataset is relatively small, which might be why the SGD-based methods (FM-based and Combi-FM-based) did not achieve a good performance. On the Yahoo!R3 dataset, in contrast, the Combi-FM model worked well, which implies that the set of items rated by the user affected the user's rating to the target item and our model effectively extracted that information. Combi-FM-based methods suffered from their model complexity and tended to overfit the biased observational training data (e.g., vanilla Combi-FM performed worse than FM); however, with a proper regularization, as proposed (IPW and the Wasserstein-based), the generalization improved. This indicates that the combination of set-wise modeling and debiased training is important.

5.2 Simultaneous Display Setting

We investigated a CTR prediction for situations in which more realistic set-wise recommendations are made. In this scenario, a customer sees three items simultaneously in an impression and clicks for each item are recorded. Here, we evaluated not only the accuracy of the predictions but also the value of the recommendations made.

Dataset. We used Open Bandit Dataset (OBD) [18] taken from a fashion e-commerce platform (ZOZOTOWN). OBD contains two datasets taken with two (recorded) logging policies μ, namely, a random policy and a biased policy (Bernoulli Thompson sampling, BTS). We used the dataset with BTS for training and validation, and used the dataset with the random policy for testing. Half of the BTS dataset was used for validation. OBD contains three "campaigns", namely, "men's", "women's", and "all". We used only the dataset of the "all" campaign. The size of the candidate set of items was $|\mathcal{I}| = 80$, and the size of the action space would be $|\mathcal{A}| = {}_{80}C_3 = 82,160$.

We preprocessed the datasets as follows. OBD is anonymized, i.e., the customer ID is deleted, so we constructed pseudo-user IDs (PUIDs) from four hashed customer features. Only records tied to PUIDs that appeared in both training and test datasets were used, after which we had 397 unique PUIDs in total. The original data was not intended for set-wise recommendation, and the three items displayed at the same impression were divided into three (mostly consecutive) records, so we processed to combine them. Consecutive records with the same pseudo-user ID and with different display positions were treated as an impression. After these processes, we had $2,549,288$ combined records in the BTS training/validation set and had $293,871$ records in the random test set.

Compared Methods. We compared FM and our Combi-FM models with three losses, namely, the naive loss, weighted loss with the true propensity score, and the Wasserstein regularized loss without weights ($\beta_n = 1$). The regularization strength of the balancing regularizer was chosen from $\{0.1, 0.3, 1., 3.\}$ by validation.

Evaluation. We evaluated our method and baselines with two metrics. The first one is a conventional ranking-based metric for imbalanced classification, average precision (AP), which is the area under the precision-recall curve. While AP (or AUC, discounted cumulative gain, etc.) is a popular metric in recommendation and information retrieval, these global ranking-based metrics do not fit well with the recommendation problem on e-commerce platforms. A platform needs to choose a recommendation action for a customer rather than choosing a customer to recommend, and therefore it is preferable to use metrics based on local ranking of candidate actions for each customer. For this reason, the other metric we evaluated was the value of the policy with predictions $V(\pi_f)$, i.e., the expected clicks when determining the action using the model:

$$V(\pi_f) = \mathbb{E}_{\pi_f, p(x)}[y_a] = \mathbb{E}_{\mu(a|x), p(x)}\left[\frac{\pi_f(a|x)}{\mu(a|x)} y_a\right], \tag{6}$$

Table 2. Test policy value $V(\pi_f^{k=1\%})$ and average precision (AP) on the ZOZO dataset. The top methods for each metric are in bold. Mean and standard deviation under three runs with different training/validation splits are reported.

Method	ZOZOTOWN	
	Policy value ($k = 1\%$) ($\times 10^{-2}$)	AP ($\times 10^{-3}$)
FM	1.18 ± 0.05	4.05 ± 0.06
FM-IPW	0.93 ± 0.02	$\mathbf{4.64 \pm 0.09}$
FM-Wass	1.23 ± 0.07	3.81 ± 0.16
Combi-FM	1.18 ± 0.05	4.05 ± 0.06
Combi-FM-IPW (proposed)	$\mathbf{1.47 \pm 0.02}$	4.51 ± 0.08
Combi-FM-Wass (proposed)	1.43 ± 0.09	4.58 ± 0.42

where π_f is a plug-in policy distribution with a model f (defined below), μ is the propensity (logging policy) of the dataset, and y_a is the summation of clicks for each item shown at the same time. We use a policy of randomly performing an action from among the top $k\%$-predicted actions for evaluation:

$$\pi_f^k(a|x) = \begin{cases} k/100 & (\text{rank}(\tilde{f}(x,a); \{\tilde{f}(x,a')\}_{a' \in \mathcal{A}}) \le |\mathcal{A}|k/100) \\ 0 & (\text{otherwise}), \end{cases} \quad (7)$$

where $\text{rank}(v; S)$ denotes the ranking of a value v among a set of values S, $\tilde{f}(x,a) = \sum_{t \in \mathcal{T}_a} f(x, (a^i = 1_t, a^{-i} = \sum_{t' \in \mathcal{T}_a \setminus t} 1_{t'}))$ is the total predicted clicks, and $\mathcal{T}_a$ is the set of recommended items. Since the expectation in (6) is taken over the same distribution with the dataset, we can empirically estimate (6) with the test set, which is known as the inverse propensity score estimate [3]. This metric (with the plug-in policy (7)) is similar to the cumulative gain, where the outcomes of the top-k best-predicted items are counted, but the difference is that the ranking takes place for all candidate actions for each customer. To avoid heavy computation of $\{f(x,a')\}_{a' \in |\mathcal{A}|}$ for each customer, we subsampled $\mathcal{A}' \subset \mathcal{A}$ of cardinality $1,000$ to evaluate $\pi_f^{k=1\%}$.

In terms of off-line evaluation, it is difficult to evaluate only with respect to the best-predicted action (as described in Sect. 4.3) because it is very rare that a single action chosen among the $_{|\mathcal{I}|}C_k$ candidates matches exactly the recorded action, and the estimation variance of the metric would be too large. Therefore, we adopted a stochastic policy rather than the deterministic policy of performing the best-predicted action.

Results. As shown in Table 2, our proposed Combinatorial FM model with debiasing techniques achieved the best performances in policy value and comparable performances in AP. Notably, Combi-FM-Wass (without weights β) performed almost the best in both scores despite not using propensity score information. The chance rate that calculated from the click rate was $V(\text{Unif}(\mathcal{A})) = 1.05 \times 10^{-2}$. Thus, the proposed method achieved approximately 1.4 times more clicks compared to random, even though the action was not optimized but randomly chosen from the top 1% predicted actions.

6 Summary

In this paper, we have proposed an extended FM model to take into account the second-order interactions between recommended items and debiased learning method for set-wise recommendation. We utilize weighting and the representation balancing regularizer to alleviate the bias in observations and to achieve a better performance in terms of decision-making. Experiments on real-world recommendation datasets demonstrated the superior performance of the proposed methods, especially for large-scale datasets.

Acknowledgements. TT was partially supported by JSPS KAKENHI Grant Numbers 20K03753 and 19H04071. HK was supported by the JSPS KAKENHI Grant Number 20H04244.

References

1. Austin, P.C.: An introduction to propensity score methods for reducing the effects of confounding in observational studies. Multivar. Behav. Res. **46**(3), 399–424 (2011)
2. Bonner, S., Vasile, F.: Causal embeddings for recommendation. In: Proceedings of the 12th ACM Conference on Recommender Systems, RecSys 2018, pp. 104–112. ACM, New York (2018)
3. Bottou, L., et al.: Counterfactual reasoning and learning systems: the example of computational advertising. J. Mach. Learn. Res. **14**(1), 3207–3260 (2013)
4. Cremonesi, P., Koren, Y., Turrin, R.: Performance of recommender algorithms on top-n recommendation tasks. In: Proceedings of the Fourth ACM Conference on Recommender Systems, pp. 39–46. ACM (2010)
5. Gong, Y., et al.: Exact-k recommendation via maximal clique optimization. In: Proceedings of the 25th ACM SIGKDD International Conference on Knowledge Discovery & Data Mining, KDD 2019, pp. 617–626. ACM, New York (2019)
6. Hill, J.L.: Bayesian nonparametric modeling for causal inference. J. Comput. Graph. Stat. **20**(1), 217–240 (2011)
7. Ie, E., et al.: Slateq: A tractable decomposition for reinforcement learning with recommendation sets. In: IJCAI (2019)
8. Jiang, R., Gowal, S., Qian, Y., Mann, T.A., Rezende, D.J.: Beyond greedy ranking: Slate optimization via list-cvae. In: ICLR (2019)
9. Johansson, F., Shalit, U., Sontag, D.: Learning representations for counterfactual inference. In: International Conference on Machine Learning, pp. 3020–3029 (2016)
10. Johansson, F.D., Sontag, D., Ranganath, R.: Support and invertibility in domain-invariant representations. In: The 22nd International Conference on Artificial Intelligence and Statistics, pp. 527–536 (2019)
11. Kang, J.D., Schafer, J.L., et al.: Demystifying double robustness: a comparison of alternative strategies for estimating a population mean from incomplete data. Stat. Sci. **22**(4), 523–539 (2007)
12. Kök, A.G., Fisher, M.L., Vaidyanathan, R.: Assortment planning: Review of literature and industry practice. In: Agrawal, N., Smith, S. (eds.) Retail Supply Chain Management. International Series in Operations Research & Management Science, vol. 122, pp. 99–153. Springer, Boston (2008) https://doi.org/10.1007/978-0-387-78902-6_6

13. Little, R.J., Rubin, D.B.: Statistical Analysis with Missing Data, vol. 793. Wiley, Hoboken (2019)
14. Manchanda, P., Ansari, A., Gupta, S.: The "shopping basket": a model for multi-category purchase incidence decisions. Mark. Sci. **18**(2), 95–114 (1999)
15. Marlin, B.M., Zemel, R.S., Roweis, S., Slaney, M.: Collaborative filtering and the missing at random assumption. In: Proceedings of the Twenty-Third Conference on Uncertainty in Artificial Intelligence, pp. 267–275. AUAI Press (2007)
16. Rendle, S.: Factorization machines. In: 2010 IEEE International Conference on Data Mining. pp. 995–1000. IEEE (2010)
17. Rubin, D.B.: Causal inference using potential outcomes: design, modeling, decisions. J. Am. Stat. Assoc. **100**(469), 322–331 (2005)
18. Saito, Y., Aihara, S., Matsutani, M., Narita, Y.: A large-scale open dataset for bandit algorithms. arXiv preprint arXiv:2008.07146 (2020)
19. Schnabel, T., Swaminathan, A., Singh, A., Chandak, N., Joachims, T.: Recommendations as treatments: Debiasing learning and evaluation. In: Balcan, M.F., Weinberger, K.Q. (eds.) Proceedings of The 33rd International Conference on Machine Learning. Proceedings of Machine Learning Research, vol. 48, pp. 1670–1679. PMLR, New York, USA (20–22 June 2016)
20. Shalit, U., Johansson, F.D., Sontag, D.: Estimating individual treatment effect: generalization bounds and algorithms. In: Proceedings of the 34th International Conference on Machine Learning, vol. 70. pp. 3076–3085. JMLR. org (2017)
21. Tanimoto, A., Sakai, T., Takenouchi, T., Kashima, H.: Regret minimization for causal inference on large treatment space. In: AISTATS (2021)
22. Wang, F., et al.: Sequential evaluation and generation framework for combinatorial recommender system. arXiv preprint arXiv:1902.00245 (2019)
23. Wang, X., Qi, J., Ramamohanarao, K., Sun, Yu., Li, B., Zhang, R.: A joint optimization approach for personalized recommendation diversification. In: Phung, D., Tseng, V.S., Webb, G.I., Ho, B., Ganji, M., Rashidi, L. (eds.) PAKDD 2018. LNCS (LNAI), vol. 10939, pp. 597–609. Springer, Cham (2018). https://doi.org/10.1007/978-3-319-93040-4_47
24. Wang, X., Zhang, R., Sun, Y., Qi, J.: Doubly robust joint learning for recommendation on data missing not at random. In: International Conference on Machine Learning, pp. 6638–6647 (2019)
25. Zaheer, M., Kottur, S., Ravanbakhsh, S., Poczos, B., Salakhutdinov, R.R., Smola, A.J.: Deep sets. In: Advances in Neural Information Processing Systems, pp. 3391–3401 (2017)
26. Zhao, H., Combes, R.T.D., Zhang, K., Gordon, G.: On learning invariant representations for domain adaptation. In: Chaudhuri, K., Salakhutdinov, R. (eds.) Proceedings of the 36th International Conference on Machine Learning. Proceedings of Machine Learning Research, vol. 97, pp. 7523–7532. PMLR, Long Beach, California, USA (09–15 June 2019)
27. Ziegler, C.N., McNee, S.M., Konstan, J.A., Lausen, G.: Improving recommendation lists through topic diversification. In: Proceedings of the 14th International Conference on World Wide Web, pp. 22–32. ACM (2005)
28. Zou, H., et al.: Counterfactual prediction for bundle treatment. In: Larochelle, H., Ranzato, M., Hadsell, R., Balcan, M.F., Lin, H. (eds.) Advances in Neural Information Processing Systems, vol. 33, pp. 19705–19715. Curran Associates, Inc. (2020)

Transformer-Based Multi-task Learning for Queuing Time Aware Next POI Recommendation

Sajal Halder[1(✉)], Kwan Hui Lim[2], Jeffrey Chan[1], and Xiuzhen Zhang[1]

[1] School of Computing Technologies, RMIT University, Melbourne, Australia
{sajal.halder,jeffrey.chan,xiuzhen.zhang}@rmit.edu.au
[2] Singapore University of Technology and Design, Singapore, Singapore
kwanhui_lim@sutd.edu.sg

Abstract. Next point-of-interest (POI) recommendation is an important and challenging problem due to different contextual information and wide variety in human mobility patterns. Most of the prior studies incorporated user travel spatiotemporal andsequential patterns to recommend next POIs. However, few of these previous approaches considered the queuing time at POIs and its influence on user's mobility. The queuing time plays a significant role in affecting user mobility behaviour, e.g., having to queue a long time to enter a POI might reduce visitor's enjoyment. Recently, attention based recurrent neural networks-based approaches show promising performance in next POI recommendation but they are limited to single head attention which can have difficulty finding the appropriate complex connections between users, previous travel history and POI information. In this research, we present a problem of queuing time aware next POI recommendation and demonstrate how it is non-trivial to both recommend a next POI and simultaneously predict its queuing time. To solve this problem, we propose a multi-task, multi head attention transformer model called TLR-M. The model recommends next POIs to the target users and predicts queuing time to access the POIs simultaneously. By utilizing multi-head attention, the TLR-M model can integrate long range dependencies between any two POI visit efficiently and evaluate their contribution to select next POIs and to predict queuing time. Extensive experiments on eight real datasets show that the proposed model outperforms than the state-of-the-art baseline approaches in terms of precision, recall and F1 score evaluation metrics. The model also predicts and minimizes the queuing time effectively.

Keywords: Points of Interest (POI) · POI Recommendation · Transformer · Multi-tasking · Multi-head attention · Queuing time

1 Introduction

Travel and tourism are popular leisure activities and a trillion-dollar industry across the world. To improve the travel and tourism experience, appropriate next

© Springer Nature Switzerland AG 2021
K. Karlapalem et al. (Eds.): PAKDD 2021, LNAI 12713, pp. 510–523, 2021.
https://doi.org/10.1007/978-3-030-75765-6_41

point-of-interest (POI) recommendation based on tourist personalized interest has attracted much attention from the researchers in recent years [2,7,21]. These personalized next POI recommendations can be challenging because visitors can have multiple criteria and different preferences when choosing a POI to visit next. Some visitors may prefer the nearest available POI that they are mildly interested in, while other visitors might prefer one that they are very interested in despite travelling a longer distance. Others may have dynamic preferences and their previous visit history is not that important to consider. Most of the deep learning technique cannot handle multiple conflicting of near and long-distance preferences as well as recent and past visit influence simultaneously. LSTM or RNN based approaches focus on recent visits and nearest preferences based on spatiotemporal dependencies. Thus, learning spatiotemporal dependencies can be challenging. In addition, another factor that affects visitor's satisfaction is the length of queuing time. Figure 1 depicts an example showing the significance of queuing time. Assume at lunch time (1:00 PM), a visitor wants to go to a restaurant for lunch. If the next POI recommendation model does not consider queuing time of these POIs, it may recommend nearby restaurant A or B according to the distance and other users' sequential patterns. However, these two are crowded places and users have to wait a long time having their lunch which is generally undesirable. Thus, a queuing time aware next POI recommendation model, which takes POIs queuing information along with spatiotemporal dependencies and personalized interest is more likely to recommend restaurant C to the user as next move. These kinds of queuing related activities are significant in many other real-life applications, e.g., theme park and popular tourist attracts, restaurants, concerts and festivals. In addition, with the COVID-19 pandemic, there is a need to keep physical distance and queuing takes on a health dimension, making queuing influence even more significant. To the best of our knowledge, this is the first work to consider queuing time and its prediction for the next POI recommendation.

These challenges inspired us to build a model that can capture complex spatiotemporal dependencies along with queuing time influence in next POIs recommendation. The problems of POI recommendation and queue time predic-

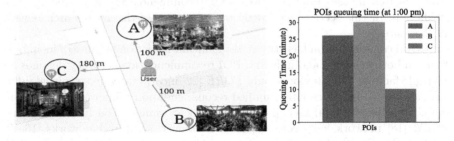

Fig. 1. Influence of queuing time along with spatiotemporal features in POI recommendation.

tion are inter-dependent. Thus, one single model that jointly recommends top-k POIs and predict queuing time simultaneously is necessary.

Existing studies on next POI recommendation have considered spatiotemporal preferences [11] but did not consider user preferences. In another group of prior research, user identification is considered and attention-based spatiotemporal influence based *ATST-LSTM* [7] and self-attentive network *SANST* [6] have been proposed. All these works are appropriate for next POI recommendation, but they are not capable of multi-tasking (recommend POIs and predict queuing time) simultaneously. Recently, attention-based transformer shows significant improvement to capture all dependencies at once using non-recurrent encoder-decoder model in volatility prediction [17,20] and natural language processing [4]. Transformer allows multi-tasking which uses an attention mechanism to compute the dependencies of its input and output. Therefore, in this work, we propose multi-attention layers-based transformer network leverages to complex spatiotemporal dependencies. After that, we use a multi-tasking approach to recommend POIs and predict queuing time simultaneously. The main contributions of the paper can be summarized as follows:

- This work discusses the significance of queuing time aware next POI recommendation model in which queuing time affects POI selection. More specifically, the model captures user behaviour along with spatiotemporal and queuing time influences.
- We develop a multi attention transformer-based multi-task learning model for next top-k POI recommendation and queue time prediction, simultaneously. The model can recommend appropriate next POIs because of the advantages of two parallel joint learning processes.
- Experiment results using eight real-life datasets show our proposed transformer model outperforms the state-of-the-art next personalized POI recommendation based on precision, recall, F1-score and is able to predict queuing time effectively.

2 Related Works

This research focuses on next top-k POI recommendation and queuing time prediction. In this section, we briefly describe state-of-the-art research related to these areas.

POI recommendation has attracted significant attention because of its importance in both academy and industry. POI recommendation accuracy depends on multiple factors. The previous study *LORE* [22] incorporates geographical influence and social influence into a unified recommendation framework for check-in data. To solve temporal and spatial dependencies simultaneously convolutional LSTM [18] network has been proposed. Moreover, some recent works [16,19] have employed convolutional neural network and multi-layer preceptors to POI recommendation. Huang et al. [7] proposed an attention-based spatiotemporal long and short-term memory (ATST-LSTM) network for the next POI recommendation. Zhou et al. [23] proposed generative and discriminator based POI recommendation model that maximize the learned probabilities distributions and optimize the differences between recommend POIs and true check-ins. Lim et al. [9] introduced queuing time as an important factor in itinerary recommendation. Therefore, in this work, we introduce the queuing time aware of top-k POI recommendation.

Transformer network-based model improves accuracy across a variety of NLP tasks. The model can capture all words dependencies in a sentence to predict next word. Recently, some research works in transformer-based model [17,20] show the significant improvements in volatility prediction and event forecasting using multi-head attention technique. It has been shown that the transformer model is faster than the recurrent and convolutional layers-based models and improved performance using the multi-headed self-attention technique [14]. Multi-task learning approach has been used for a variety of research areas i.e., sentence classification and tagging [15], entity recognition and semantic labelling [1], and two different financial forecasting [20]. Inspired by transformer multi-task learning, we use multi-head attention-based transformer model for next top-k POI recommendation and predict queue time simultaneously. The multi-head attention model can capture POIs relationships among other POIs in multiple ways and it is effective to handle users' dynamic behaviours. Our proposed TLR-M model differs from the state-of-the-art POI recommenders in various aspects. First, we introduce complex spatiotemporal dependencies along with POI sequence in transformer model. Second, we present multi-task learning in POI recommendation that can recommend top-k POI and predict queuing time simultaneously. Most importantly, the approach can set up the relationship among heterogeneous features (i.e. geographical, time and user identity features etc.) automatically using multi-head attention mechanism.

3 Preliminary and Problem Statement

In this section, we first describe key preliminary definitions and then describe the problem statement.

Definition 1. *Point of Interest (POI): A POI p is defined as a uniquely identified location (e.g., roller coaster, museum, hotel and etc.) that has longitude and latitude values. A sequence represents a set of POIs, $P = \{p_1, p_2, \cdots, p_n\}$ that user visits sequentially.*

Definition 2. *Visit Activity: User visit activity is a quadri-tuple $v_{t_k}^u = (p_{t_k}^u, l_{t_k}^u, t_k, u)$ which represents the user u visits POI $p_{t_k}^u$ with location $l_{t_k}^u$ at timestamp t_k.*

Definition 3. *Visit Sequence: A user visit sequence is a set of visit activities of the user, represented by $V_u = \{v_{t_1}^u, v_{t_2}^u, \cdots, v_{t_i}^u\}$. All users historical visit sequences in a dataset are defined by $V^U = \{V_{u_1}, V_{u_2}, \cdots, V_{u_{|U|}}\}$, here $|U|$ is the number of all users.*

Definition 4. *Visit Trajectory: A user's visit trajectory is a subset of user's visit sequence i.e.* $V_u = \cup_i S_i^u$, *represented by* $S_i^u = \left\{ v_{t_k}^u, v_{t_{k+1}}^u, \cdots, v_{t_{k+n-1}}^u \right\}$, *where sequence length is n. In the sequence if the time difference between two consecutive POI visits is more than six hours, we divided it into different trajectories, all the isolated POI visits are ignored.*

Definition 5. *Queuing Time Trajectory: The queuing time is a triplet* $q_{T_k}^p = (p_{T_k}^u, T_k, q_i)$ *represents the user u need to wait* q_i *time to access the POI* $p_{T_k}^u$ *at timestamps* T_k. *The queuing time sequence is a set of queuing time triplet* $S_q^{u_i} = \left\{ q_{T_k}^p, q_{T_{k+1}}^p, \cdots, q_{T_{k+n-1}}^p \right\}$. *All database queuing time trajectory indicates by* $Q^U = \cup_i S_q^{u_i}$, *where* $u_i \in U$. *The length of visit sequence and queuing time sequence will be same. The timestamps* T_k *may be hour based or half hour based time interval.*

Problem Statement: Given the input of all users' visit trajectories V^U and queuing time trajectories Q^U during past T timestamp, the output of our proposed multi-task learning model is to recommend next top-k POIs to the users and predict the prospective queuing time of recommended POIs, simultaneously. The model can recommend a fixed set of POIs (top-5 or top-10) and can optimize queuing time between original time and predicted queuing time.

4   Proposed TLR-M Model

In this section, we describe our proposed **T**ransformer based **L**earning **R**ecommendation using **M**ulti-tasking **TLR-M** model. We capture the global dependencies between users visit trajectories and POIs queuing influences using multi-head self-attention mechanism. The self-attention mechanism overcomes two limitations of RNN based top-k prediction tasks. Firstly, the RNN model is hard to support parallel work because of its recursive nature. Secondly, RNN can not capture the whole sequence information directly. The purpose of using self-attention is two-folds. It captures the whole sequence information flow directly and it permits parallel operations that join multiple learning objectives effectively.

Our proposed model uses multi-head self-attention based on two pairs of encoder and decoder. Figure 2(a) illustrates the architecture of TLR-M model. Some transformer based classifier used encoder only rather than encoder and decoder. Encoder based model can generate global attention based transition matrix but can not generate personalized attention based different recommendation appropriately. However, we use encoder and decoder together to capture personalize correlation between POIs visits whole sequence directly without sequential propagation. Here, the spatial, the temporal,user inter-dependencies among the time and geographical locations and queuing time influence are jointly considered which performed by the attentive learning. The model takes POIs visit trajectories as quadruplet $(p_{t_i}^u, l_{t_i}^u, t_i, u_{t_i})$ input in transformer *Encoder-1* and queuing time trajectories as triplet $(p_{t_i}^u, T_i, q_i)$ input in transformer *Encoder-2*. Thus, the inputs (x_t^1 and x_t^2) of the two transformer encoders are as follows:

$$x_t^1 = W_p p_{t_i}^u + W_l l_{t_i}^u + W_t t_i^u + W_u u_{t_i} \text{ and } x_t^2 = W_p p_{t_i}^u + W_T T_i + W_q q_{t_i} \quad (1)$$

where $p_{t_i}^u$, $l_{t_i}^u$, t_i^u and u_{t_i} represent POI IDs, spatial, temporal context and user vector respectively. W_p, W_l, W_t and W_u are transition matrices. Besides this, q_{t_i} is the queuing time and T_i is timestamps. W_T and W_q are transition matrices.

Unlike recurrent networks (LSTMs and GRUs), the transformer network can process the input sequentially, POI after POI (as token after token). The transformer uses positional encoding to keep a separate embedding table with input vectors. The model use POI position in the trajectory instead of POI index in the table. Thus, the positional embedding table is much smaller than the one-hot encoding table. Positional embeddings may train with the rest of the deep network or pre-computed by the following sinusoidal formula. Here, we use pre-computed positional embedding sinusoidal signal manner [14].

$$PE_{pos,2i} = \sin\left(\frac{pos}{10000^{2i/E_{size}}}\right) \text{ and } PE_{pos,2i+1} = \cos\left(\frac{pos}{10000^{2i/E_{size}}}\right) \quad (2)$$

where E_{size} and *pos* denotes the embedding size and relative position of POIs in trajectories, respectively. We define $2i$ and $2i+1$ to indicate the embedding element index with the even and odd position, respectively.

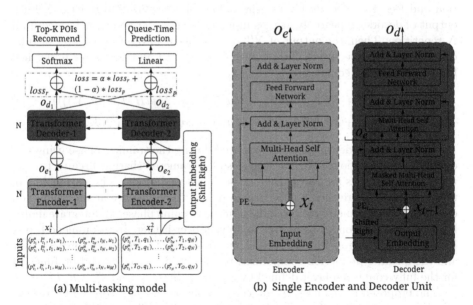

(a) Multi-tasking model   (b) Single Encoder and Decoder Unit

Fig. 2. The architecture of TLR-M model.

Encoder consists of N layers and each layer are composed of multi head self-attention, fully connected feed forward followed by layers normalization [14]

depicts in Fig. 2(b). In our model Fig. 2(a), the inputs of first encoder layers in *Encoder-1* and *Encoder-2* come from the element wise addition between inputs embedding latent vector and positional encoding represent by $x_e^1 = x_t^1 + PE$ and $x_e^2 = x_t^2 + PE$. The output of first encoder layer feeds as input embedding in the next layer. Thus, the Nth layer outputs of two encoders (Encoder-1 and Encoder-2) are o_{e_1} and o_{e_2}.

$$o_{e_1} = lNo(x_e^1 + FFN(lNo(x_e^1 + MulH(Q, K, V))))$$
$$o_{e_2} = lNo(x_e^2 + FFN(lNo(x_e^2 + MulH(Q, K, V))))$$

(3)

where *lNo(.)* is layer normalization, *FFN(.)* is fully connected feed-forward network and *MulH(.)* is multi-head attention mechanism.

These two encoder outputs are concatenated ($o_e = o_{e_1} + o_{e_2}$) and fed into the decoders that share the impact of top-k and queuing time together. The decoder unit in Fig. 2(b) consists of six layers, among them masked multi head attention uses to avoid the significance of padding token. We use padding token to construct the same length of visit trajectories and queuing time trajectories. Decoder takes same input as encoder input but in this case, information is shifted one position right, ensure that the prediction output of position t_{i+1} only depends on known outputs up to time t_i. Then, these embeddings added with positional embeddings and construct $x_d^1 = x_{t-1}^1 + PE$ and $x_d^2 = x_{t-1}^1 + PE$. This output embedding transforms through the mask layer, multi head attention and feed forward sub-layers using add and normalization functions. Each output of decoder repeatedly uses as input in the decoder and transformed until N repetition. Then, the output of Nth decoder feeds into soft-max layer or fully connected layer based on the target output. *Decoder-1* and *Decoder-2* performed based on following equation.

$$o_{d_1} = lNo(x_d^1 + FFN(lNo(x_d^1 + MulH(o_e, o_e, MulHM(Q, K, V)))))$$
$$o_{d_2} = lNo(x_d^2 + FFN(lNo(x_d^2 + MulH(o_e, o_e, MulHM(Q, K, V)))))$$

(4)

These two decoder outputs are updated during the training phase using two different loss functions. We have used soft parameter sharing architecture in which each task has its own parameter setting based model. The parameters of these two models are then regularized to reduce the difference among them and encourage the parameters to be similar. In the training phase, we integrate multi-layer perceptron dropout technique to prevent over-fitting. To recommend top-K POIs with higher probabilities, the outputs of *Decoder-1* feeds into softmax layer and the queuing prediction component, we use *ReLU* as the activation function for the fully connected layer defined by $\hat{y} = softmax(o_{d_1})$ and $\hat{y}_i^q = ReLU(o_{d_2})$.

The proposed model uses two objective functions for best top-K POI recommendation and appropriate queuing time prediction. Thus, the first objective function uses sparse-cross-entropy as a loss function for accurate top-k recommendation as follows.

$$loss_r = -\frac{1}{N} \sum_{i=1}^{N} [y_i log(\hat{y}_i) + (1 - y_i)log(1 - \hat{y}_i)]$$

(5)

where y_i is the original output and $\hat{y}_i$ is the predicted output.

In the *Decoder-2* output, we find the queuing probability corresponding POI distributions. Then, to reduce the difference between predicted probability and likelihood probability we use mean square error loss function as follows.

$$loss_p = -\sum\nolimits_{i=1}^{N}[(y_i^q - \hat{y}_i^q)^2] \tag{6}$$

where y_i^q and $\hat{y}_i^q$ represent original queuing time and predicted queuing time respectively. Therefore, our objective function is a weighted average of these two loss functions using weight parameter $\alpha \in [0,1]$.

$$loss = \alpha \times loss_r + (1-\alpha) \times loss_p \tag{7}$$

We use Adam-optimizer and applied the trick of decay learning rate with the steps until it reaches convergence. Finally, the *TLR-M* extract our two desire goals simultaneously that are to recommend top-k POIs and predict proceeding queuing time.

4.1 Algorithm

Algorithm 1 depicts an overview of our proposed TLR-M model. It takes two sets of inputs including POI sequence, spatiotemporal, users, and queue time features. First, we initialize all parameters in line 1. Then based on two minibatch inputs x_b^1 and x_b^2 we train our proposed model in lines 2–10. These inputs feed into the encoders and generate outputs using multi attention-based feed-forward network using Eq. 3 in line 4. The two encoder outputs fed as input into the decoders with right-shifted encoder inputs in line 5. After that, the output of

---

Algorithm 1: TLR-M Model

Data: (x^1, x^2)= Model inputs, PE = positional embedding, b_{size}: batch size

Result: TLR-M model $\{M\}_u$: [top-k POIs], [Queue time]

1 **TRAIN MODEL:** Initialize all parameters
2 **for** $(x_b^1, x_b^2) \leftarrow sample(x^1, x^2, b_{size})$ **do**
3 $\quad$ $x_e^1, x_e^2 = x_b^1 + PE, x_b^2 + PE$
4 $\quad$ Using equation 3 find o_e^1 and o_e^2
5 $\quad$ $x_d^1, x_d^2 = Input(RightShift(x_e^1, x_e^2), o_e^1, o_e^2)$
6 $\quad$ Using equation 4 fund decoder output o_d^1 and o_d^2
7 $\quad$ $\hat{y} = softmax(o_d^1)$ and $\hat{y}^q = Relu(o_d^2)$
8 $\quad$ Calculate loss J using equations 5, 6, 7
9 $\quad$ Build the learned TLR-M Model $\{M\}_u$
10 $\quad$ Update the parameters.
11 **end**
12 **TEST MODEL** : $\hat{y}_{test}, \hat{y}_{test}^q$ = Predict output based on Model $\{M\}_u$ and test data.
13 *Return* $\hat{y}_{test}, \hat{y}_{test}^q$;

---

the multi-head attention layer is normalized and passed fully connected feed-forward network. It generates two probabilities distributions as outputs in line 6. The outputs are passed with softmax and rectified linear unit to find top-k POIs recommendation and queuing time prediction probabilities in line 7. Using this probability, we applied two loss functions and achieved our goal in line 8. Furthermore, using the loss functions of Eqs. 5, 6 and 7 we train our proposed model $\{M\}_u$ and update all parameters in lines 10. After constructing the model, we predict the next top-k potential POIs $\hat{y}_{test}$ using our test data and predict queuing time $\hat{y}_{test}^q$ in line 12. Finally, we measure our evaluation matrices based on output $\hat{y}_{test}$ and $\hat{y}_{test}^q$ compare to original POI and queuing time.

5   Experiments

In this section, we present experimental setup, datasets, baseline algorithms and evaluation metrics. For these comparisons, our proposed *TLR-M* and the existing baseline methods are implemented in the Python language. Training and testing sets selection are important factors in the deep learning model. At first, we construct itinerary based on visiting POI where the first t steps used as a model design and $t+1$ step is used as a next target POI. Thus, we construct all the prefixes of the input trajectories and make sub-trajectories as per standard practice [13]. Then, among these itineraries, we select training set using 70% random itineraries and the testing set using remaining 30% itineraries. For baseline models, we used authors' publicly shared codes.

To analyse the significance of the proposed models, we have used *t-test* statistical method. Experimental results show that TLR-M significantly out-performs all baseline with at least 96.5% confidence interval ($p \leq 0.035$), based on t-test.

Table 1. Parameters description of various datasets.

Dataset	# Photos	POI Visits	# Users	# POIs	Dataset	# Chick-ins/ POI Visits	# Users	# POIs
Epcot	90,435	38,950	2,725	17	Edinburgh	82,060	33,944	1,454	29
Magic kingdom	133,221	73,994	3,342	27	Melbourne	17,087	5,871	911	242
California Adv	193,069	57,177	2,593	25	Foursquare	315,084	315,084	7,642	6,202
Budapest	36,000	18,513	935	39	Gowalla	407,894	407,894	5,628	7,283

5.1   Datasets and Baseline Algorithms

For our experiments, we use various datasets comprising three theme parks, three cities and two social networks [9,10,12]. The visit sequences of POIs are constructed based on photos taken or check-in times to these POIs. If the time gap between two consecutive photos taken time or check-in time is greater than 6 h, it is considered as a new visit sequence. Among these datasets Foursquare and Gowalla do not hold queuing time information, thus we describe the results differently. Foursquare and Gowalla datasets are sparse. Hence, we consider the users who have at least 20 records and the POIs that has been visited at least 20 times. All other datasets, we filter out those users and POIs with fewer than 3 visits and 3 visitors, respectively. The variation of eight datasets is shown in Table 1.

Several baselines are described to compare the performance of our proposed *TLR-M* model that plays a significant role in the next POI recommendation. Among a large number of existing works, we have considered several recent works as baselines that outperform than the other baselines [3,5,8]. To best evaluate the performance of our proposed *TLR-M* model, we compare our proposed models with four recent baselines which are ST-RNN [11], STACP [12], APOIR [23] and ATST-LSTM [7]. Queuing time information are not always present in dataset i.e. Gowalla and Foursquare datasets contain only check-in time. If there are check-out times information, we can define queuing time as the time difference between one check-in and previous check-out time. However, to show the transformer-based POI recommendation efficiency, we develop a single-tasking TLR model. It takes only visit trajectories information as input and uses single encoder and decoder instead of pair encoders and decoders. All parameters are same, and the objective function is $loss_r$ in Eq. 5. To predict queuing time prediction, we develop a single-tasking TLR_q model using queuing trajectories and $loss_p$ loss function.

5.2 Performance Evaluation

To compare the performance of our model against the various baselines, we use Precision@k, Recall@k, F1-Score@k and root mean square error (RMSE) metrics [11]. Theme parks and cites datasets are dense, thus we evaluate the sub-trajectories based recommendation accuracies. On the other hand, Gowalla and Foursquare datasets are very sparse datasets that case we consider users based accuracies. We combine test sub-trajectories target and predicted top-K POIs and find accuracy metrics as per research paper [7].

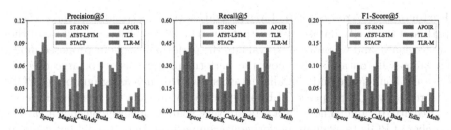

Fig. 3. Results comparison among proposed TLR, TLR-M and various baselines, in terms of Precision@5, Recall@5 and F1-Score@5 for six datasets.

5.3   Results and Discussion

The performance of *TLR* and *TLR-M* models with state-of-the-art POI recommendations are evaluated based on several experiments. The main evaluation process of POI recommendation is how accurately the recommended POIs reflect visitors real visit POIs. Figure 3 shows the results of proposed models against the various baselines for the datasets against the various evaluation metrics. The proposed *TLR* model performance against the existing POIs recommendation is the best in terms of all evaluation metrics. Three sub-figures in Fig. 3 show the precision@5, recall@5 and F1-score@5 results based on the six datasets.

It shows that our proposed multi-tasking model *TLR-M* outperforms all the baselines as well as our proposed single task *TLR* model. Because we have used multi-head attention-based transformer that can capture POI visit full trajectories relationship more efficiently than the RNN or CNN based approach. The transformer architecture can capture all inputs and outputs dependent relations efficiently. On the other hand, queuing time impact has been added at training time that also increases next POI recommendation efficiency. The results of evaluation metrics differ dataset to dataset because we consider top 5 POIs among all POIs. Thus, Melbourne dataset results show a lower score than the other datasets because of a comparatively larger number of POIs. Our results show the same output pattern for k values 3 and 10. In this experiment, we run each model 10 times and reported average values as a metric value.

The proposed *TLR-M* model not only outperforms in top-k POI recommendation but also predicts queuing time very well. To compare *TLR-M* model with single queuing time prediction model, we use single TLR_q model in which predicts target POIs queuing time as output. In this case, root mean square error loss function has been used. We have developed $ATST_q$ model applying the same input (queuing time and POI sequence) in $ATST\_LSTM$ model. The $ATST_q$ model is unable to predict the queuing time effectively, as shown by RMSE value that is at least 10 times higher than the *TLR-M* model. The table 2 shows that our multi-task model *TLR-M* outperforms single task LTR_q and $ATST_q$ models.

Performance Analysis for Larger Datasets. The results in three theme park and three city datasets show that our models outperform the state-of-the-art baselines, and we proceed to evaluate the performance of our proposed model on large-scale datasets. To show the performance, we use two large check-in datasets Foursquare and Gowalla datasets with the increasing number of POIs. Figure 4 shows the proposed TLR model outperforms than the baselines in terms of Recall@10 value. These data sets are very sparse, thus we consider a various number of POIs to evaluate performance comparison. Here, we did not compare our multi-tasking model TLR-M because the queuing time information is missing in these datasets. The results show that all algorithms values decrease with the increase of POIs number. Our proposed TLR model shows the best results because it can capture POI trajectories inter dependencies efficiently. Based on these results, it is obvious that our model outperforms on small and large datasets than the baselines.

Table 2. RMSE results between single and multi-task. Small value are better.

Dataset	$ATST_q$	TLR_q	TLR-M
Epcot	1319.9	173.1	**102.5**
MagicK	925.6	90.5	**84.7**
CaliAdv	1834.2	108.7	**101.5**
Buda	2157.5	147.3	**129.2**
Edin	1755.3	136.7	**113.2**
Melb	2602.5	132.4	**88.8**

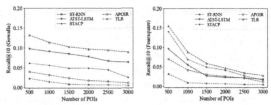

Fig. 4. Performance comparison based on two sparse datasets.

Effects of Parameters: We explore the effect of batch size and multi loss functions balancing factor (α). We consider learning rate = 0.001, dropout rate = 0.5, number of head = 4, training step = 200 and hidden size = 128. Our results show that the effect of batch size increases first then decreases with the value increases (due to page limit we could not show the figures). We find that batch size 32 is best for these algorithms. Besides this, we explore the effect of balancing factor α. We observe that the best value for the balance factor fluctuates between 0.50 to 0.75 in different datasets. Therefore, we set default value 0.5 to provide the equal significance of two-loss functions.

6 Conclusion

In this paper, we study the new research topic, queuing time aware next POI recommendation. By incorporating sequential, spatial, temporal and queuing time influences, we have proposed multi-head transformer-based multi-task learning recommendation model *TLR-M* that recommends top-k POIs and predicts queuing time simultaneously. By leveraging the attention technique instead of RNN architecture, the model can capture whole trajectory dependencies directly and efficiently. Experiment results based on eight datasets show that our proposed *TLR-M* model significantly outperforms the various state-of-the-art models.

In this work, we have studied the queuing time aware top-k POI recommendation problem. Our future research direction is to construct a full itinerary considering the budget time and social relationship influence that users get maximum entertainment.

References

1. Alonso, H.M., Plank, B.: When is multitask learning effective? Semantic sequence prediction under varying data conditions. In: EACL, pp. 1–10 (2017)
2. Chang, B., Park, Y., Park, D., Kim, S., Kang, J.: Content-aware hierarchical point-of-interest embedding model for successive poi recommendation. In: IJCAI, pp. 3301–3307 (2018)

3. Chen, X., et al.: Sequential recommendation with user memory networks. In: WSDM, pp. 108–116 (2018)
4. Devlin, J., Chang, M.W., Lee, K., Toutanova, K.: BERT: pre-training of deep bidirectional transformers for language understanding. arXiv preprint arXiv:1810.04805 (2018)
5. Feng, S., Li, X., Zeng, Y., Cong, G., Chee, Y.M., Yuan, Q.: Personalized ranking metric embedding for next new poi recommendation. In: IJCAI (2015)
6. Guo, Q., Qi, J.: SANST: a self-attentive network for next point-of-interest recommendation. arXiv preprint arXiv:2001.10379 (2020)
7. Huang, L., Ma, Y., Wang, S., Liu, Y.: An attention-based spatiotemporal LSTM network for next poi recommendation. IEEE Trans. Serv. Comput. (2019)
8. Li, X., Cong, G., Li, X.L., Pham, T.A.N., Krishnaswamy, S.: Rank-GeoFM: a ranking based geographical factorization method for point of interest recommendation. In: SIGIR, pp. 433–442. ACM (2015)
9. Lim, K.H., Chan, J., Karunasekera, S., Leckie, C.: Personalized itinerary recommendation with queuing time awareness. In: SIGIR, pp. 325–334. ACM (2017)
10. Lim, K.H., Chan, J., Leckie, C., Karunasekera, S.: Personalized trip recommendation for tourists based on user interests, points of interest visit durations and visit recency. Knowl. Inf. Syst. 54(2), 375–406 (2017). https://doi.org/10.1007/s10115-017-1056-y
11. Liu, Q., Wu, S., Wang, L., Tan, T.: Predicting the next location: a recurrent model with spatial and temporal contexts. In: AAAI (2016)
12. Rahmani, H.A., Aliannejadi, M., Baratchi, M., Crestani, F.: Joint geographical and temporal modeling based on matrix factorization for point-of-interest recommendation. In: Jose, J.M., Yilmaz, E., Magalhães, J., Castells, P., Ferro, N., Silva, M.J., Martins, F. (eds.) ECIR 2020. LNCS, vol. 12035, pp. 205–219. Springer, Cham (2020). https://doi.org/10.1007/978-3-030-45439-5_14
13. Tan, Y.K., Xu, X., Liu, Y.: Improved recurrent neural networks for session-based recommendations. In: Proceedings of the 1st Workshop on Deep Learning for Recommender Systems, pp. 17–22 (2016)
14. Vaswani, A., et al.: Attention is all you need. In: NIPS, pp. 5998–6008 (2017)
15. Wang, S., Che, W., Liu, Q., Qin, P., Liu, T., Wang, W.Y.: Multi-task self-supervised learning for disfluency detection. arXiv preprint arXiv:1908.05378 (2019)
16. Wang, S., Wang, Y., Tang, J., Shu, K., Ranganath, S., Liu, H.: What your images reveal: exploiting visual contents for point-of-interest recommendation. In: WWW, pp. 391–400 (2017)
17. Wu, X., Huang, C., Zhang, C., Chawla, N.V.: Hierarchically structured transformer networks for fine-grained spatial event forecasting. In: The Web Conference 2020, pp. 2320–2330. ACM (2020)
18. Xingjian, S., Chen, Z., Wang, H., Yeung, D.Y., Wong, W.K., Woo, W.C.: Convolutional LSTM network: a machine learning approach for precipitation nowcasting. In: NIPS, pp. 802–810 (2015)
19. Yang, C., Bai, L., Zhang, C., Yuan, Q., Han, J.: Bridging collaborative filtering and semi-supervised learning: a neural approach for poi recommendation. In: SIGKDD, pp. 1245–1254 (2017)
20. Yang, L., Ng, T.L.J., Smyth, B., Dong, R.: Html: Hierarchical transformer-based multi-task learning for volatility prediction. In: The Web Conference 2020, pp. 441–451 (2020)

21. Yin, H., Wang, W., Wang, H., Chen, L., Zhou, X.: Spatial-aware hierarchical collaborative deep learning for poi recommendation. TKDE **29**(11), 2537–2551 (2017)
22. Zhang, J.D., Chow, C.Y., Li, Y.: LORE: exploiting sequential influence for location recommendations. In: SIGSPATIAL, pp. 103–112. ACM (2014)
23. Zhou, F., Yin, R., Zhang, K., Trajcevski, G., Zhong, T., Wu, J.: Adversarial point-of-interest recommendation. In: WWW, pp. 3462–34618 (2019)

Joint Modeling Dynamic Preferences of Users and Items Using Reviews for Sequential Recommendation

Tianqi Shang[1], Xinxin Li[2], Xiaoyu Shi[3(✉)], and Qingxian Wang[2]

[1] College of Computer Science, Sichuan University, Chengdu 610207, China
[2] School of Information and Software Engineering, University of Electronic Science and Technology of China, Chengdu 610054, China
201921090312@std.uestc.edu.cn, qxwang@uestc.edu.cn
[3] Chongqing Key Laboratory of Big Data and Intelligent Computing, Chongqing Institute of Green and Intelligent Technology, Chinese Academy of Sciences, Chongqing 400714, China
xiaoyushi@cigit.ac.cn

Abstract. The emerging of sequential recommender (SR) has attracted increasing attention in recent years, which focuses on understanding and modeling the temporal dynamic of user behaviors hidden in the sequence of user-item interactions. However, with the tremendous increase of users and items, SR still faces several challenges: (1) the hardness of modeling user interests from spare explicit feedback; (2) the time and semantic irregularities hidden in the user's successive actions. In this study, we present a neural network-based sequential recommender model to learn the temporal-aware user preferences and item popularity jointly from reviews. The proposed model consists of the semantic extracting layer and the dynamic feature learning layer, besides the embedding layer and the output layer. To alleviate the data sparse issue, the semantic extracting layer focuses on exploiting the enriched semantic information hidden in reviews. To address the time and semantic irregularities hidden in user behaviors, the dynamic feature learning layer leverages convolutional filters with varying size, integrating with a time-ware controller to capture the temporal dynamic of user and item features from multiple temporal dimensions. The experimental results demonstrate that our proposed model outperforms several state-of-art methods consistently.

Keywords: Sequential recommendation · Preference modeling · Temporal dynamic · Semantic extracting · Deep learning

1 Introduction

In the era of information explosion, recommender systems (RS) are the essential enabler for online services and widely applied in a variety of fields, e.g., music/video recommendation, news push-delivery, online shopping. Up to now,

© Springer Nature Switzerland AG 2021
K. Karlapalem et al. (Eds.): PAKDD 2021, LNAI 12713, pp. 524–536, 2021.
https://doi.org/10.1007/978-3-030-75765-6_42

RS can be divided into two categories: general recommender system and sequential recommender system. The general recommender systems with representation of the content-based and collaborative filter (CF)-based solutions seek to capture users' long-term preference, presuming that the user-item interactions in a static way or change slowly over time. Among them, Factorization-based CF methods [5] are the most popular techniques in this era. However, the user preferences are drifting over time, rather than fixed. Different with the general recommender systems heavily focus on modeling users' long-term preference, sequential recommender system can capture the users' short-term preference for more accurate recommendation, with consideration of the sequential dependencies in the user-item interactions [6,11,16]. Hence, SR receives considerable attention due to its superiority in capturing item-to-item sequential relations.

Following this line, several solutions based on neural networks have been proposed to learn the users' short-term preferences. They can be divided into convolutional neural network (CNN)-based and recurrent neural network (RNN)-based methods. CNN-based methods [12] utilize the convolutional filters with different kernel sizes to learn the short-term contexts for recommendation. RNN-based methods include long short-term memory network (LSTM) [15,17] and gated recurrent network (GRU) [2]. They capture the short-term user preference via hidden state of RNN.

Although the previous solutions have achieved satisfactory results, there are still some challenges for sequential recommenders: (1) *the hardness of modeling the user interests from spare explicit feedback*. In most past studies, ratings are used as the only criterion of feedback information to measure the degree of user preference for the specified item. User reviews as another source of data usually contain more information than ratings. For example, *"I really like the style of this skirt and its length is just right. Although the white one is out of stock, I am also satisfied to buy the pink."* Through the above review, we find out the customer is satisfied with the style rather than the color. Meanwhile, we can also infer that the user is interested in white. However, the rating of "5" cannot show such plentiful information. Therefore, a review-based recommender system can capture more information about user preferences. (2) *the time and semantic irregularities are hidden in the user's successive actions*. The existing temporal-aware recommenders [6,16] always assume that the items in sequence can be considered as evenly spaced and semantically consistent when designing recommender. In practical, the sequence of user behavior is complex, the time intervals between two adjacent interactions can be various. For example, the historical interaction sequence of a user is: $H = \{(i_1, Apr\ 1st), (i_2, Apr\ 2nd), (i_3, May\ 2nd)\}$. It is more reasonable that the information hidden between (i_1, i_2) more than (i_2, i_3), because the user behaviors happen on (i_1, i_2) is just one day, while for the (i_2, i_3) is one month. Furthermore, the sequence of user behavior on items may not share the same semantic topic. For example, the items set of a user interaction is $\{iPhone, iPad, umbrella, dress\}$, the first two items indicate that the user is happy to buy electronic products, while the second two items have no such signal.

To track the above challenges, we present a novel neural network-based sequential recommendation model to learn both long- and short-term user preferences and item popularity jointly from reviews. To evaluate the performance of our proposed model, we conducted a large number of experiments on three datasets from Amazon. Experimental results show that our model is significantly better than the state-of-the-art methods. In summary, our contributions in this paper are as follows:

- We propose a neural network-based model sequential recommender to model the temporal dynamic of user preference and item popularity, which can learn the enrich semantic and temporal information hidden in users' reviews jointly;
- We introduce the dynamic feature learning layer with integrate of time-aware controller to solve the time and semantic irregularities hidden in the user behaviors. It leverages a couple of convolutional fitters with varying sizes to effectively learn the user and item features from multiple temporal dimensions;
- We implement our proposed model on the three datasets from Amazon, and experimental results show that our model is significantly better than state-of-the-art methods.

The remainder of this paper is organized as follows. Section 2 summaries the related work on related recommender methods. Section 3 describes the proposed neural network-based model in detail. The experimental setting and results are given in Sect. 4. In Sect. 5, we conclude our paper.

2   Related Work

2.1   Review-Based Recommender

User reviews, can potentially alleviate the data sparsity problem caused by rating-based methods. Bao et al. [1] proposed a novel matrix factorization model (called TopicMF) that simultaneously considers the ratings and accompanied review texts. Wu et al. [15] proposed a cyclic recommendation network to learn the implicit representation of users and items via traditional matrix factorization methods. Then these static hidden features are input into the RNN model to learn dynamic hidden features according to the order of time. Zheng et al. [19] presented a deep model to learn item properties and user behaviors from reviews. One of the networks is used to learn user behaviors, and the other one learns item properties. Lu et al. [7] proposes a multitasking learning framework that combines the probability matrix to decompose the PMF and the confrontational Seq2Seq model. Tay et al. [13] propose a review-by-review pointer-based learning scheme, named MPCN, to extract important reviews and match them in a word-by-word fashion. It enables the most informative reviews to be utilized for prediction and deeper word-level interaction. By introducing review information, these methods alleviate the data sparsity problem. However, they ignored the dynamic change of user preference and item properties over time.

2.2 Sequential Recommender

Sequential recommender considers the order of user interactions, which utilizes the previous interactions to predict the next one. Redle et al. [10] combines the Matrix Factorization and Markov Chains to learn a transition metric over time to predict the next action for a user. Hidasi et al. [3] employs the RNN-based model for sequential recommendation and proposes the session-based model. Pei et al. [8] and Wang et al. [4]. introduce attention mechanism into neural networks for the recommender. Based on [4], Li et al. [6] considers the timestamps of interactions to explore the influence of different time intervals on the next item prediction. Ying et al. [16] models the previous item and the long history item list of a user by the attention network to obtain the long and short-term preferences of the user. Usually, RNNs-based models perform well on dense datasets, but show poor performance on sparse datasets. The above sequential recommendation methods only focused on the combination of user long and short-term preferences without considering the time and semantic irregularities in user behavior.

3 Proposed Model

In this section, we first overview the architecture of our proposed model at a high-level. Then, we explain the implementation details of each layer and how the time-aware controller works in our model.

3.1 The Overview Architecture

Our proposed model consists of three important components: two parallel hybrid neural networks, and the Factorization Machine (FM)-based fusion module. One of the networks focuses on modeling user preferences, the other one captures item popularity. Specifically, the proposed neural network consists of four layers: the embedding layer, the semantic extracting layer, the dynamic feature learning layer, and the output layer. For the embedding layer, it encodes the review and time information into one-hot vectors. Then the semantic extracting layer focuses on exploiting the obtain plentiful sentiment with sequential dependencies information, by leveraging the Bi-directional Long Short-Term Memory (BiLSTM) network. After that the dynamic feature learning layer, integrating with a time-aware controller, utilizes several convolutional fitters with varying sizes, to capture the temporal dynamic of user preferences and item popularity from multiple temporal dimensions. In the output layer, the factorization machine technique is utilized to enable the user and item latent factors to interact with each other and obtain predictions. The overall architecture of the proposed model is shown in Fig. 1.

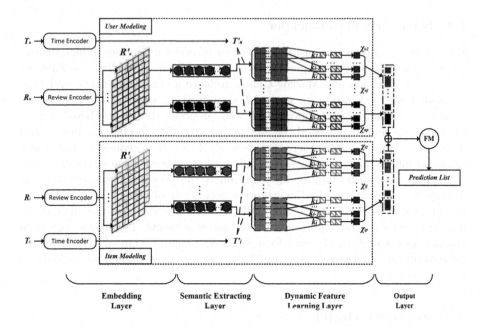

Fig. 1. Illustration of our proposed model.

3.2 The Embedding Layer

In our method, we consider reviews with time information as a strong supplementary to understand the user behavior. Therefore, review text and time from the input of the network are encoded in this layer. Let $R = \{r_1, r_2, \ldots, r_n\}$ denotes the set of n reviews of a user or an item. The i_{th} review is in the set represented as $r_i = \{w_1, w_2, \ldots, w_m\}$, where w_i represents the i_{th} word in review, and m is the number of words in this review. We type all reviews from a user or item into the embedding layer. Each review is converted into a word vector matrix through a table lookup operation from the pre-trained word matrix W_e. We use $w_i^{'} \in \mathbb{R}^d$ to represent the low-dimensional dense vectors of i_{th} word, where d is the dimension of the word vector in W_e. As a result, the $r_i^{'} \in \mathbb{R}^{m \times d}$ can be expressed as:

$$r_i^{'} = w_1^{'} \oplus w_2^{'} \oplus \cdots \oplus w_m^{'}, \tag{1}$$

where $\oplus$ denotes the concatenation operator. Therefore, the review set R is encoded as $R^{'} = [r_1^{'}, r_2^{'}, \ldots, r_n^{'}]$.

3.3 The Semantic Extracting Layer

In extraction layer, to obtain user preferences and item properties, user reviews set R_u and item reviews set R_i are input into two parallel neural networks respectively. Firstly, the words in each review are treated as sequential data. In recent, some studies have shown that Long Short-Term Memory (LSTM) performs well in processing text information. In particular, the Bi-directional LSTM (BiLSTM), an improved variant of LSTM, can capture both forward and backward contextual information. Motivated by it, we leverage the BiLSTM to obtain the sentiment information hidden in reviews.

The LSTM can change the flow of information through some gates: forgetting gate z^f , input gate z^i and output gate z^o, the equations of LSTM are as follows:

$$z^i = \sigma \left(W_i \times [h_{k-1}, x_k] + b_i \right), \tag{2}$$

$$z^f = \sigma \left(W_f \times [h_{k-1}, x_k] + b_f \right), \tag{3}$$

$$C_k = z^f \odot C_{k-1} + z^i \odot \phi \left(W_c \times [h_{k-1}, x_k] + b_c \right), \tag{4}$$

where C_k is the cell status of the k_{th} LSTM unit, h_{k-1} and x_k represent the previous hidden state and the current input respectively. Then, the output content z^o is determined based on the content saved by the cell state C_k, and the content stored in the cell state is selectively output:

$$z^o = \sigma \left(W_o \times [h_{k-1}, x_k] + b_o \right). \tag{5}$$

The hidden state of the k_{th} step is:

$$h_k = z^o \odot \phi(C_k), \tag{6}$$

where $W_i, W_f, W_o \in \mathbb{R}^{D \times D}$ are trainable parameters, and D is the dimension of input embedding and hidden layer in LSTM. In the above formulas, σ and ϕ represent the sigmoid function and tanh function, and $\odot$ denotes the elementwise product operation.

The BiLSTM contains forward and backward LSTM, which can capture the syntax and meaning of words respectively. The forward calculation of the forward layer and the inverse calculation of the backward layer are combined to obtain z_k^o:

$$\overrightarrow{h}_k = f(w_1 x_k + w_2 \overrightarrow{h}_{k-1}), \tag{7}$$

$$\overleftarrow{h}_k = f(w_3 x_k + w_4 \overleftarrow{h}_{k-1}), \tag{8}$$

$$z_k^o = g(w_5 \overrightarrow{h}_k + w_6 \overleftarrow{h}_k), \tag{9}$$

where $\overrightarrow{h}_k$ and $\overleftarrow{h}_k$ represent the hidden state of forward LSTM and backward LSTM at the k_{th} step, respectively. In the BiLSTM, the hidden state of the time step k is updated as:

$$h_k = \left[\overrightarrow{h}_k, \overleftarrow{h}_k \right]. \tag{10}$$

After the BiLSTM treatment, the massive reviews in R are turned into plentiful sentiment information set, denoted as $Y = [y_1, y_2, \ldots, y_n]$, $Y \in \mathbb{R}^{g \times p}$, where g is the length of the input review sequence from a user or item, p is the size of a review embedding. Then, we further extract the user preferences and item popularity from Y by leveraging CNN, which consists of a convolution layer and a pooling layer.

3.4   The Dynamic Feature Learning Layer

To address the time irregularity hidden in the sequence of user behaviors, we introduce the time-aware controller to make our model sensitive to time changes. We assume that the information hidden in two adjacent interactions with a short time interval is greater than two adjacent interactions with a large time interval. Hence, we employ time interval information to perceive dynamic changes in user and item characteristics. Let $T = \{t_1, t_2, \ldots, t_n\}$ denotes the set of review time in R. Furthermore, we also normalized the time interval between i_{th} review and $(i+1)_{th}$ review. Therefore, the time information of the i_{th} review is encoded as follows:

$$\tilde{t}_i = t_{i+1} - t_i, (i \in [1, n)), \tag{11}$$

$$t_i' = \frac{\tilde{t}_i - min(\tilde{T})}{max(\tilde{T}) - min(\tilde{T})}, \tag{12}$$

where $\tilde{T}$ is the set of intervals between two adjacent reviews, so $min(\tilde{T})$ and $max(\tilde{T})$ denote the minimum and maximum value of interaction time interval respectively.

Meanwhile, the review with longer time intervals is given less weight in our model. Hence, the y_i with time information can be represented as:

$$y_i' = y_i \times \frac{1}{t_i'}. \tag{13}$$

To address the semantic irregularity issue, we introduce several convolution kernels k_* to obtain user and item features from multiple temporal dimensions. Let X_i denotes the i_{th} review, and the result of the j_{th} convolution kernel operation for X_i is as:

$$l_i = \phi(k_j * X_i + b_j), \tag{14}$$

where k_j is a convolution kernel, b_j is a bias term, the $*$ represents the convolution operation, and ϕ is an activation function. For the i_{th} review, we can get a feature set $L_j = [l_1, l_2, \ldots, l_h]$ by k_j, where h is the count of a convolution kernel operation result. In our method, we employ multiple different sized kernels for feature acquisition. After the convolution operations, the max pooling layer is introduced to get the most meaningful feature. We can formalize it as follows:

$$z_j = \max(L_j), \tag{15}$$

$$Z_i = [z_1, z_2, \ldots, z_s], \tag{16}$$

where z_j is the result of max pooling from L_j, s is the number of convolutional kernels, and Z_i is the set of one review features. Multiple review feature vectors are connected to model the user or item, expressed as:

$$\Upsilon = Z_1 \oplus Z_2 \oplus \ldots \oplus Z_q. \tag{17}$$

Finally, we put the result of max pooling operation into a fully connected layer.

$$\chi = \delta\left(W \times \Upsilon + b\right),\tag{18}$$

where δ represents the *ReLU* function, W is a weight matrix, b is a bias term, and $\chi \in \mathbb{R}^{o \times 1}$ is a one-dimensional feature vector for a user or item. For easily distinguishing, the feature representation of a user and an item are identified as χ_u and χ_i respectively.

3.5 The Output Layer

We obtain user representation and item representation from the two above parallel neural networks. Motivated by the excellent performance of FM, we connect χ_u and χ_i into FM to obtain the corresponding prediction rating. Then, we select the top N as a list of recommendations for user. We formulate the process as follows:

$$\Psi = \chi_u \oplus \chi_i,\tag{19}$$

$$\langle v_n, v_m \rangle := \sum_{f=1}^{K} v_{n,f} \cdot v_{m,f},\tag{20}$$

$$\hat{y} := \omega_0 + \sum_{n=1}^{N} \omega_n \Psi_n + \sum_{n=1}^{N} \sum_{m=n+1}^{N} \langle v_n, v_m \rangle \Psi_n \Psi_m,\tag{21}$$

where ω_0 is the global bias, ω_n represents the n_{th} variable strength, $\langle v_n, v_m \rangle$ represents the interaction between the n_{th} and m_{th} variables. During the training process, we utilize the loss function as follows:

$$\zeta = \gamma + \eta \parallel \Theta \parallel_2,\tag{22}$$

$$\gamma = \frac{1}{2} \sum_{i=1}^{N} \left(\hat{y}_i - y_i\right)^2 + \xi,\tag{23}$$

where ξ is the regularization term to prevent over-fitting, η and Θ is the penalty coefficient and the set of trainable parameters, respectively. In (23) , N is the number of samples, $\hat{y}_i$ is the prediction and y_i is the truth.

4 Experiments

4.1 Experimental Settings

Datasets. In our experiments, we utilize the Amazon dataset for experimental analysis. Specifically, we select three different subcategories from Amazon as subset for experiment, i.e., Musical Instruments (MIs), Automotive (Auto) and Luxury Beauty (LB). The statistics of three datasets are shown in Table 1.

Table 1. The statistics of Amazon datasets.

Datasets	#users	#items	#reviews	Density
LB	19947	1798	23799	0.07%
Auto	2928	1835	20473	0.38%
MIs	1429	900	10261	0.80%

Baseline Models. To demonstrate the superiority in our proposed model, we compare it with the following baseline models:

- **BPR** [9]: The model optimizes for a pairwise ranking objective function. Matrix factorization is introduced as a recommender.
- **GRU4Rec** [3]: This model is a session-based recommendation and RNNs are introduced to model user interaction sequences.
- **CFKG** [18]: It considers various item relations and views interaction as another relation between users and items.
- **TiSASRec** [6]: Based on the SASRec, it considers the temporal information and the relative position of the interactions.
- **SLRC** [14]: It introduces Hawkes Process into Collaborative Filtering (CF), explicitly addresses two item-specific temporal dynamics: short-term effect and life-time effect.

Evaluation Metrics. To evaluate the performance of different methods, we adopted two well-known metrics in Top-N recommendation: Hit Ratio (HR) and Normalized Discounted Cumulative Gain (NDCG). In our experiments, we truncate the ranked list at 10 for two metrics. HR@10 counts the rates of the ground-truth items among the top 10 prediction items and NDCG@10 also considers the position. We select the latest interaction as the test set, the penultimate interaction as the validation set, and the remaining interactions are used for training. For each user, we randomly sample 100 negative items that are not interacted with by the user.

4.2   Results

Parameters Analysis. There are two deterministic parameters in our model worth exploring for optimal values: the size of latent factors ζ and the depth size d of the convolution layer. The performance of different values for two deterministic parameters is shown in Fig. 2. As we can see, the optimal values of ζ and d should be assigned to 50 and 3 respectively. We also test the dimension of word embedding κ with the range of [100, 200, 300, 400, 500], the batch size b in [32, 64, 128, 256], the learning rate λ in [0.0001, 0.0005, 0.001, 0.005]. According to the performance and efficiency of our proposed model, the κ, b and λ are set as 300, 128 and 0.001. The performance decreases when the batch size is below this optimal value because too little data does not have the characteristics of the overall sample. However, the batch size value is too large to increase memory usage and reduce efficiency. The value of learning rate mainly depends on the stability and time consuming of the model. We implement our proposed model with *PyTorch*.

Effectiveness of Time-Aware Controller. To verify the effect of time-aware controller on modeling user and item, we then conduct several experiments with three variants of our model:

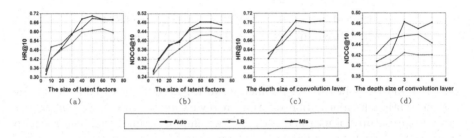

Fig. 2. Performance as a result of varying ζ shown in (a) and (b), and performance as a result of varying d shown in (c) and (d).

- **Ours-NoT:** Both timestamp information and time-aware controller are not used in this variant.
- **Ours-UT:** We introduce the time-aware controller in the users preferences net, which is equivalent to only considering the dynamic preferences of the user.
- **Ours-IT:** Similar to Ours-UT, instead of introducing a time-aware controller for item p, the variant utilizes it for modeling items to explore the dynamic properties over time.

The performance of our model and its three variants are shown in Table 2. As shown, the proposed model delivers the best results, and the Ours-UT and Ours-IT perform better than the Ours-NoT, which demonstrates the efficiency of time-aware controller for capturing dynamic preferences of users and items.

Comparison to Baselines. The performance of our model and all baselines are shown in Table 3. As shown, SLRC performs better compared with other baselines. Our model performs best on three datasets among all the recommendation models in our experiments, which indicates the proposed model can better capture dynamic characteristics of users and items. We can summarize the reasons as follows: (1) user reviews, as the complementary data source, contain more information than ratings. From all the historic reviews, we can extract user long-term preferences and static inherent properties of items. (2) we combine

Table 2. The performance of our proposed model and its variants.

Models	Ours-NoT	Ours-UT	Ours-IT	Ours
Luxury beauty				
HR@10	0.5331	0.5601	0.5877	**0.6075**
NDCG@10	0.3699	0.3720	**0.4261**	0.4251
Automotive				
HR@10	0.5964	0.6981	0.6653	**0.7039**
NDCG@10	0.4021	0.4762	0.4770	**0.4833**
Musical instruments				
HR@10	0.6003	0.6713	0.6621	**0.6874**
NDCG@10	0.3913	0.4231	0.4356	**0.4569**

BiLSTM and CNN in the two parallel networks. BiLSTM is capable of obtaining the sentiment information existing in review texts, and CNN can further extract the features of user and item. (3), we employ a time-aware controller to capture the short-term preferences of the user and item features.

Table 3. Models performance. The best result in each row is boldfaced, and the second best one in each row is underlined.

Models	Luxury beauty		Automotive		Musical instruments	
	HR@10	NDCG@10	HR@10	NDCG@10	HR@10	NDCG@10
BPR	0.4620	0.2917	0.4668	0.3102	0.4551	0.3007
GRU4Rec	0.4857	0.2811	0.4630	0.3095	0.4989	0.3336
CFKG	0.5021	0.3383	<u>0.5945</u>	0.3915	0.5548	0.3890
TiSASRec	0.5185	0.3318	0.5023	<u>0.4137</u>	0.5240	0.3906
SLRC	<u>0.5243</u>	<u>0.3907</u>	0.5662	0.3871	<u>0.5891</u>	<u>0.4038</u>
Ours	**0.6075**	**0.4251**	**0.7039**	**0.4833**	**0.6874**	**0.4569**

5   Conclusion

In this paper, we propose a novel neural network-based model for sequential recommendation, which can capture the dynamic preferences of users and items in the sequence of user-item interactions. We notice that the hardness of modeling user interests from the spare implicit feedback, thus we focus on exploiting plentiful semantic information from reviews via leveraging BiLSTM. Furthermore, we observe that user's behaviors are more complex in the field of recommender system than the sequences in NLP domain, thus we further propose the time-aware controller and integrate into the CNN-based dynamic feature learning layer, which learns the user and item feature from multiple temporal dimensions. Based on these methods, it makes the proposed model more suitable for modeling user behavior. Finally, we conduct a large number of experiments on the industrial dataset to explore the performance of our proposed model, the results demonstrate that our proposed model outperforms state-of-the-art models consistently.

Acknowledgments. This research is supported in part by the Chongqing Science and Technology Bureau under grant cstc2019jscx-zdztzxX0019 and cstc2018jszx-cyzdX0041, in supported by the National Natural Science Foundation of China (No. 61902370).

References

1. Bao, Y., Fang, H., Zhang, J.: TopicMF: simultaneously exploiting ratings and reviews for recommendation. In: Proceedings of the Twenty-Eighth AAAI Conference on Artificial Intelligence, p. 2C8. AAAI 2014, AAAI Press (2014)
2. Cho, K., et al.: Learning phrase representations using RNN encoder-decoder for statistical machine translation. Comput. Sci. (2014)
3. Hidasi, B., Karatzoglou, A., Baltrunas, L., Tikk, D.: Session-based recommendations with recurrent neural networks (2015)
4. Kang, W.C., McAuley, J.: Self-attentive sequential recommendation, pp. 197–206 (2018)
5. Koren, Y., Bell, R., Volinsky, C.: Matrix factorization techniques for recommender systems. Computer **42**(8), 30–37 (2009)
6. Li, J., Wang, Y., Mcauley, J.: Time interval aware self-attention for sequential recommendation. In: WSDM 2020: The Thirteenth ACM International Conference on Web Search and Data Mining (2020)
7. Lu, Y., Dong, R., Smyth, B.: Why I like it: multi-task learning for recommendation and explanation. In: the 12th ACM Conference (2018)
8. Pei, W., Yang, J., Sun, Z., Zhang, J., Bozzon, A., Tax, D.: Interacting attention-gated recurrent networks for recommendation, pp. 1459–1468 (2017)
9. Rendle, S., Freudenthaler, C., Gantner, Z., Schmidt-Thieme, L.: BPR: Bayesian personalized ranking from implicit feedback. In: Proceedings of the 25th Conference on Uncertainty in Artificial Intelligence, UAI 2009 (2012)
10. Rendle, S., Freudenthaler, C., Schmidt-Thieme, L.: Factorizing personalized Markov chains for next-basket recommendation, pp. 811–820 (2010)
11. Shi, X., Luo, X., Shang, M., Gu, L.: Long-term performance of collaborative filtering based recommenders in temporally evolving systems. Neurocomputing **267**, 635–643 (2017)
12. Tang, J., Wang, K.: Personalized top-n sequential recommendation via convolutional sequence embedding (2018)
13. Tay, Y., Tuan, L., Hui, S.: Multi-pointer co-attention networks for recommendation (2018)
14. Wang, C., Zhang, M., Ma, W., Liu, Y., Ma, S.: Modeling item-specific temporal dynamics of repeat consumption for recommender systems. In: The World Wide Web Conference (2019)
15. Wu, C.Y., Ahmed, A., Beutel, A., Smola, A., Jing, H.: Recurrent recommender networks, pp. 495–503 (2017)

16. Ying, H., Zhuang, F., Zhang, F., Liu, Y., Wu, J.: Sequential recommender system based on hierarchical attention networks. In: Twenty-Seventh International Joint Conference on Artificial Intelligence IJCAI-18 (2018)
17. Yu, Z., Lian, J., Mahmoody, A., Liu, G., Xie, X.: Adaptive user modeling with long and short-term preferences for personalized recommendation. In: Twenty-Eighth International Joint Conference on Artificial Intelligence IJCAI-19 (2019)
18. Zhang, Y., Ai, Q., Chen, X., Wang, P.: Learning over knowledge-base embeddings for recommendation (2018)
19. Zheng, L., Noroozi, V., Yu, P.S.: Joint deep modeling of users and items using reviews for recommendation. In: The Tenth ACM International Conference (2017)

Box4Rec: Box Embedding for Sequential Recommendation

Kai Deng[1], Jiajin Huang[2(✉)], and Jin Qin[1]

[1] Guizhou University, Guizhou, China
[2] Beijing University of Technology, Beijing, China
jhuang@bjut.edu.cn

Abstract. Sequential recommendation aims to predict a user's next behavior in near future by using the user's most recent behaviors. Most of the existing methods always embed a user or an item as a point in a vector space, and then model the user's recent behaviors as a sequence with a strict order to generate recommendations. However, both the point representation and strict order rule limit the capacity of sequential recommendation models as the diversity and uncertainty of a user's interests. In this paper, by relaxing the condition that a sequence must follow a strict order, we introduce the box embedding into the sequential recommendation and present a novel model called Box4Rec. Box4Rec embeds a user and the user's historical items as boxes instead of points to model the user's general preference and short-term preference, and then integrates the conjunction and disjunction operations on items to generate flexible recommendation strategies. Experiments on five real-world datasets show the proposed Box4Rec model outperforms the state-of-the-art methods consistently.

Keywords: Flexible order · Box embedding · Sequential recommendation

1 Introduction

The goal of sequential recommender systems is to predict sequential user actions based on users' historical activities, for example what items a user will consume in the next time [14]. Recently, some well-known models such as the markovchain (MC) recurrent neural network (RNN), self-attention mechanism-based transformer model, and convolutional Neural Networks (CNNs) have been used for sequential recommendations [4,11,13,15].

The above methods are essentially latent representation models. Specially, users and items are modeled points in the vector space in forms of fixed dimensional vectors. Items similar to a user's preference are embedded close (or similar) to the user vector. However, only modeling a user as a point in thevector space

Supported by organization Program of Guizhou Provincial Science and Technology Department (No. [2019]2502).

© Springer Nature Switzerland AG 2021

K. Karlapalem et al. (Eds.): PAKDD 2021, LNAI 12713, pp. 537–548, 2021.
https://doi.org/10.1007/978-3-030-75765-6_43

limits the capacities of existing methods because of the diversity and uncertainty of the user's preference.

In addition, to solve the flexible order problem for sequential recommendation [13,14], the existing methods also embed a historical item of a user into a single point in the vector space. The pooling operation (e.g. mean or sum) on historical item vectors is used to model the behavior. These pooling operations belong to a kind of direct methods of relaxing the condition that a sequence must be processed in order. However, such simple and crude pooling operations may bring more noises or lose information [6]. In fact, we need to refine common latent features of the items purchased together. These common information may determine items a user will consume in the next time. If we center on the point of the historical item to extend its range to a set, the intersection operation on these items could be naturally used to mine their common latent features.

Finally, items in the flexible order may lead to the user's next action with different rules. For example, there are three items p_1, p_2, and p_3 in a user's sequential action. We assume the user bought item v in the next time. This reason be the user bought all the three items, or the user bought p_1 or both p_2 and p_3, and so on. Due to the uncertainty of user actions, we need to use different recommendation rules to generate recommendations.

In order to satisfy the above requirements, inspired by the box model [9], this paper uses an axis-aligned rectangle structure to efficiently model users and historical items in the vector space. Essentially, the model, referred to as Box4Rec, assumes that users' actions are determined by their preferences and recent activities. Each user preference or each historical item is modeled as a box-like shape, instead of a point in the vector space. As a result, on the one hand, the target item whose embedding vector is a point inside the user preference box will have a higher probability of being recommended to the user; on the other hand, the learned box embeddings of historical items can also be combined in different ways according to different recommendation rules. For example, the intersection of historical item-boxes will be a smaller box which represents the common latent features of these historical items.

2 Related Work

2.1 Sequential Recommendation

The widely used recommendation methods usually embed users and items into a low-dimensional vector space. The well-known Matrix Factorization (MF) method [5] used the inner product of a user and an item's latent vector to generate recommendations. In the low-dimensional vector space, there are two kind of sequential recommendation methods.

One is based on Markov Chain (MC) assumption. The classical method is Factorized Personalized Markov Chains (FPMC) [11]. FPMC fused the MF and first-order MC for modeling global user preference and short-term interests. Furthermore, TransRec [1] learned a translation vector on the transition from an item to the next item. Fossil [2] adopted high-order MC that considers more previous items to predict the next item a user will consume.

The other is based on the neural network. GRU4REC [3] firstly introduced Gated Recurrent Units (GRU) to the session-based recommendation. Besides RNN, SASRec [4] applied the self-attention mechanism to the sequential recommendation problem. Caser [13] employed Convolutional Neural Networks (CNN) to explore flexible order problem of sequential recommendation.

2.2 Deep Set Learning

It is well known that the typical machine learning methods mainly process fixed dimensional data instances, while the machine learning methods defined on sets [16] focus on processing the permutation invariant problem. The permutation invariant problem means any permutation of the input can not change the output value of a model. [16] established the universal model of invariant networks named DeepSets. By using DeepSets, [9] extended query embedding vectors in knowledge graph (KG) to boxes. Using such box structure, conjunctions can be naturally represented as intersections of boxes. Inspired by the work of [9], we seek to build a new sequential recommendation model based upon the box structure. As the problem of sequential recommendation is quite different from the knowledge graph, this paper designs special model to use the box structure for improving the sequential recommendation performance.

3   Model

3.1   FPMC: A Basic Model

Let U and I represent the user and item set, respectively. The previous n items of user u at timestep t consist of a set S_t^u which can be modeled a list of d-dimensional item vectors $\{\overline{\mathbf{p}}_1, \overline{\mathbf{p}}_2, \cdots, \overline{\mathbf{p}}_n\}$ where $\overline{\mathbf{p}}_i \in \mathbb{R}^d$. We aim to predict which items the user will consume in next time $t+1$. In FPMC [11], given a user u and her previous n items S_t^u, the probability that u may like another item v in the next time is proportional to

$$x_{u,v} = \overline{\mathbf{u}} \cdot \mathbf{v} + f(\{\overline{\mathbf{p}}_i|_{i=1}^n\}) \cdot \mathbf{v}' \tag{1}$$

where $\overline{\mathbf{u}}$ is a user embedding, $\mathbf{v}$ and $\mathbf{v}'$ are target item embeddings for the MF in the user preference space and Factorized MC in the sequential space, respectively. $f(\{\overline{\mathbf{p}}_i|_{i=1}^n\})$ models the previous n items of user u at timestep t. For example, f could be an average pooling on $\{\overline{\mathbf{p}}_i|_{i=1}^n\}$. Specially, the FPMC model sets $n = 1$ which means it mainly uses the latent representation of last item of user u to generate recommendations.

Obviously, in FPMC, a user is represented by the single point (e.g. $\overline{\mathbf{u}}$), and an item is represented by three single points according to its different role (e.g. the role of target item as $\mathbf{v}$ and $\mathbf{v}'$, the role of historical item as $\overline{\mathbf{p}}_i$,). In this paper, we build our model on the top of FPMC by extending embeddings of users and items from the view of points to boxes. Next, we will introduce the details of such box's embedding style in context of the sequential recommendation task.

3.2   Box Block: A Basic Component

As shown in [9], let $\mathbf{q}^c \in \mathbb{R}^d$ be the center of the box, and $\mathbf{q}^o \in \mathbb{R}^d$ be the positive offset of the box, an embedding box $\mathbf{q} = (\mathbf{q}^c, \mathbf{q}^o) \in \mathbb{R}^{2d}$ models the box as:

$$Box_q = \{\mathbf{v} \in \mathbb{R}^d : \mathbf{q}_{min} \preceq \mathbf{v} \preceq \mathbf{q}_{max}\} \tag{2}$$

where $\preceq$ is dimension-wise inequality, and $\mathbf{q}_{min} = \mathbf{q}^c - \mathbf{q}^o$, $\mathbf{q}_{max} = \mathbf{q}^c + \mathbf{q}^o$ which can be used to model the size of the box. Each item v in the item pool I is assigned a single vector $\mathbf{v} \in \mathbb{R}^d$, and the box embedding $\mathbf{q}$ essentially models $\{v \in I : \mathbf{v} \in Box_q\}$, i.e. a set of items whose vectors are inside the box. For the rest of the paper, we use the bold face to denote the embedding, e.g., embedding of v is denoted by $\mathbf{v}$, the superscript c is the center part, and o is the offset part.

Given a query box $\mathbf{q} \in \mathbb{R}^{2d}$ and a target item vector $\mathbf{v} \in \mathbb{R}^d$, how to calculate the distance between the box and the target item depends on the target item is inside the box or not. Specially, if the target item is inside the box, the distance can be measured between the center of the box and the target item; If the target item is outside the box, the distance can be obtained by the distance between the target item and the box's corner which is closest to the target item plus the distance between this corner and the center of the box. Let dis_o be the distance between the target item and the box's corner which is closest to the target item, and dis_i be the distance between the center of the box and the box's corner which is closest to the target item. We have the distance as

$$dis_{box}(\mathbf{v}; \mathbf{q}) = dis_o(\mathbf{v}; \mathbf{q}) + \beta \cdot dis_i(\mathbf{v}; \mathbf{q}) \tag{3}$$

where
$$\begin{aligned} dis_o(\mathbf{v}; \mathbf{q}) &= ||Max(\mathbf{v} - \mathbf{q}_{max}, 0) + Max(\mathbf{q}_{min} - \mathbf{v}, 0)||_1 \\ dis_i(\mathbf{v}; \mathbf{q}) &= ||\mathbf{q}^c - Min(\mathbf{q}_{max}, Max(\mathbf{q}_{min}, \mathbf{v}))||_1 \end{aligned} \tag{4}$$

In Eq. 4, $||\cdot||_1$ is the $\mathcal{L}1$ distance. Max and Min are the dimension-wise maximum and minimum operator, respectively. For a target item vector which is inside the box, we can see that $dist_o$ is 0 and dis_i becomes the distance between the center of the box and the target item. Submitting them to Eq. 3, the contribution of dis_i is scaled by $\beta \in [0, 1]$. Obviously, β can be set to 0 if we consider that all target items inside the box should be recommended to the user, while β can also be set to 1 if we emphasize that a target item inside the box should be closer to the center of the box when the user is more interested in the target item. Furthermore, when $dist_o$ is not 0, as shown in Eq. 3, adding dis_o to dis_i is used to measure the distance between the box and the target item vectors which are outside the box.

3.3   Box4Rec: Prediction Method

Overall Structure. When we have the Box component, following the FPMC model as shown in Eq. 1, we need to calculate a score from both the user preference space and sequential space.

On the one hand, Box4Rec models the user preference as a box embedding $\mathbf{u} = (\mathbf{u}^c, \mathbf{u}^o)$. And then, Box4Rec captures the user's inherent preference by $dis_{box}(\mathbf{v}; \mathbf{u})$ which measures the distance between the user preference box and the target item in the user preference space.

On the other hand, Box4Rec needs to capture the short preference by modeling sequential dynamic behaviors of users. The previous n items of user u at timestep t can also be modeled as a set of box embeddings $\{\mathbf{p}_1, \mathbf{p}_2, \cdots, \mathbf{p}_n\}$ where $\mathbf{p}_j = (\mathbf{p}_j^c, \mathbf{p}_j^o)$. In order to extract the common latent features among these box embeddings, it is nature to model the intersection operation over these box embeddings. The intersection operation provides two important benefits:

- The output of the intersection operation can not change under any permutation of $\{\mathbf{p}_1, \mathbf{p}_2, \cdots, \mathbf{p}_n\}$, which has the benefit of handling a user-item interaction sequence with a flexible order.
- The intersection operation over these box embeddings is closed [9], which means we can generate a new box $\mathbf{p} = (\mathbf{p}^c, \mathbf{p}^o)$ by the intersection operation. Benefiting from the closed property, we can use $dis_{box}(\mathbf{v}'; \mathbf{p})$ to capture sequential dynamic by measuring the distance between the intersection box of the recent n historical items and the target item in the sequential space.

Finally, by combining the above two boxes $\mathbf{u}$ and $\mathbf{p}$, we have the score of user u on the target item v as

$$x_{u,v} = \alpha \cdot dis_{box}(\mathbf{v}; \mathbf{u}) + (1 - \alpha) \cdot dis_{box}(\mathbf{v}'; \mathbf{p}) \tag{5}$$

where α is a trade-off parameter to balance the contributions of the two parts. Obviously, if the target item is enough close to the two boxes, $x_{u,v}$ has an enough small value to show that the user may like the item.

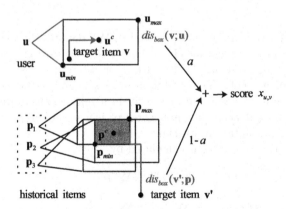

Fig. 1. An illustration of Box4Rec model (Color figure online)

Figure 1 gives an illustration example of Box4Rec model. The top of Fig. 1 is the part of general preference of Box4Rec. We take the target item $\mathbf{v}$ which is inside the user preference box $\mathbf{u}$ as the example. In such case, $dis_{box}(\mathbf{v}; \mathbf{u})$ depends on the $dis_i(\mathbf{v}; \mathbf{u})$ corresponding the distance between the center of the user preference box and the target item. The bottom of Fig. 1 is the part of sequential preference of Box4Rec. The previous three items of user u at timestep t are modeled three boxes, respectively. The shaded region represents the intersection of the three boxes as a new box $\mathbf{p}$. We take the target item which is outside the intersection box as the example. In such case, $dis_{box}(\mathbf{v}'; \mathbf{p})$ is the distance between the target item and the box's corner which is closest to the target item plus the distance between this corner and the center of the box. In Fig. 1, a red line represents the $\mathcal{L}1$ distance. Finally, the weighted sum of the two distances represents the score of user u on item v.

Totally, $dis_{box}(\mathbf{v}; \mathbf{u})$ can be directly obtained by substituting $\mathbf{q}$ with $\mathbf{u}$ in Eq. 3, where $dis_{box}(\mathbf{v}'; \mathbf{p})$ needs an additional embedding operation to generate $\mathbf{p}$. The next section will introduce intersection operation in the sequential part of Box4Rec.

Sequential Model. In the sequential part, we aim to model the intersection of a set of box embeddings $\{\mathbf{p}_1, \mathbf{p}_2, \cdots, \mathbf{p}_n\}$ as $\mathbf{p} = (\mathbf{p}^c, \mathbf{p}^o)$. As the system cost increases approximately linearly with the length of user behavior sequence and a longer sequential user behaviors may introduce more irrelevant noise data, there are more difficulties to deal with long sequential user behavior data [8]. So, usually in recommendation scenarios, three recent behaviors ($n = 3$) are preferable [11,12]. The average operation on the centers of historical item boxes can be considered as a simple operation of obtaining the common latent features of items purchased together. However, to represent the different contribution of historical item, we follow [9,16] to perform attention over the box centers as

$$f_i = \mathbf{H}^c(\cdots \sigma'(\mathbf{W}_2^c(\sigma'(\mathbf{W}_1^c \mathbf{p}_i^c))) \cdots), \quad a_i = \frac{exp(f_i)}{\sum_j exp(f_j)}, \quad \mathbf{p}^c = \sum_i a_i \mathbf{p}_i^c \quad (6)$$

where σ' is an activation function (e.g. Relu), $\mathbf{W}_x^c$ denotes the weight matrix for the x-th layer's perceptron, and $\mathbf{H}^c$ is the vector that projects the hidden layer into an 1-dimensional output f_i. The attention score a_i is a softmax over f_i to decide the importance of a historical item i to the center of the intersection box. Without confusion, we omit the bias term in a fully-connected neural network for notational convenience. The final center $\mathbf{p}^c$ is a sum of all $\mathbf{p}_i^c$ weighted by a_i. Obviously, $\mathbf{p}^c$ is permutation invariant.

In addition, the box offset is calculated by

$$\mathbf{g}_i = \mathbf{H}^o(\cdots \sigma'(\mathbf{W}_2^o(\sigma'(\mathbf{W}_1^o \mathbf{p}_i^o))) \cdots)$$

$$D(\mathbf{g}_i|_{i=1}^n) = \mathbf{W}_{L''}(\cdots (\mathbf{W}_1(\frac{1}{n} \sum_{i=1}^n \mathbf{g}_i)) \cdots) \quad (7)$$

$$\mathbf{p}^o = Min(\{\mathbf{p}_1^o, \cdots, \mathbf{p}_n^o\}) \odot \sigma(D(\mathbf{g}_i|_{i=1}^n))$$

In Eq. 7, $\mathbf{p}_i^o$ passes a fully-connected neural network where $\mathbf{W}_x^o$ denotes the weight matrix for the x-th layer's perceptron activated by function σ' (e.g.

Relu). $\mathbf{H}^o$ is the vector that projects the hidden layer into a d-dimensional output embedding vector $\mathbf{g}_i$. Then these vectors are aggregated by a sum operation. Following [9,16], the aggregated embedding vector is also transformed to a d-dimensional output by a fully connected neural network D stacked by L'' weight matrices. For simplification, we use the identity-function as the activation function in D. Obviously, the output value of $D(\cdot)$ is same for any permutation of the input. Finally, to generate a smaller box $\mathbf{p}$ that lies inside a set of boxes $\{\mathbf{p}_1, \cdots, \mathbf{p}_n\}$, the operation $Min(\cdot)$ not having strong order assumption is applied to get the minimization value in a dimension-wise manner of the offset parts of $\{\mathbf{p}_1, \cdots, \mathbf{p}_n\}$. The dimension-wise product $\odot$ combines $Min(\cdot)$ and $D(\cdot)$ activated by a sigmoid function σ, which means $\sigma(D(\cdot))$ is taken as the dimension-wise weight.

Training. To effectively learn the parameters of the proposed model, we define a pairwise ranking loss based on the assumption that an item which this user really visited at time $t + 1$ will have a relative smaller value than other items not in S_{t+1}^u that he/she has no interest in. We can get the parameters of the proposed model by minimizing the following BPR loss function [10]:

$$L(\Theta) = -\sum_u \sum_{i \in S_{t+1}^u - S_t^u} \sum_{j \notin S_{t+1}^u} \ln \sigma(y_{u,i,j}) + \lambda\Omega \tag{8}$$

where σ is a sigmoid function, $y_{u,i,j} = x_{u,j} - x_{u,i}$ and Ω is an $\mathcal{L}2$ regularizer scaled by λ. According to Eq. 5, smaller score means that the user like the item better. Following [10], we can minimize Eq. 8 to obtain $x_{u,i} < x_{u,j}$ for $i \in S_{t+1}^u - S_t^u, j \notin S_{t+1}^u$, which is consistent with Eq. 5.

4   Recommendation Strategies

In the previous sections, we learn the box representations of users, historical items and target items. Then we need to use the learned box representations to make recommendations. Specially, in the sequential space, we can take each user's behavior record as a logical implication rule. For example, when a user likes item v given the user's previous three items p_1, p_2, p_3, we can conclude a logical implication rule denoted by $p_1 \wedge p_2 \wedge p_3 \rightarrow v$ which means a user will like item v if the user bought p_1, p_2, p_3. In Box4Rex, the conjunction operation can be modeled by the the intersection of the box representation of historical items. In practice, we can also use other logical implication rule to make recommendations. These rules are summarized as follows:

- $p_1 \wedge p_2 \wedge p_3 \rightarrow v$ could be measured by $dis_{box}(\mathbf{v}'; \mathbf{p})$ as shown before. We can rank items in ascending order according to Eq. 5 to select top-K items to make recommendations.
- $p_1 \vee p_2 \vee p_3 \rightarrow v$ means a user likes item v because the user bought $p_1, p_2,$ or p_3 before. In the previous section, we focus on how to learn the box embedding based on the conjunction operation $\wedge$ on historical items. Now we need to

handle the new disjunction operation $\vee$ on historical items. Fortunately, we do not need to learn new box embeddings for the operation $\vee$ as the target item v only needs to locate in one of boxes under the $\vee$-based rule. So in Eq. 5, let $dis_{box}(\mathbf{v}';\mathbf{p})$ be $Min(dis_{box}(\mathbf{v}';\mathbf{p}_1), dis_{box}(\mathbf{v}';\mathbf{p}_2), dis_{box}(\mathbf{v}';\mathbf{p}_3))$, which can satisfy the rule $p_1 \vee p_2 \vee p_3 \rightarrow v$.

- $(p_1 \wedge p_2) \vee p_3 \rightarrow v$ means a user likes item v because the user brought both p_1 and p_2, or the user bought p_3. We can measure this rule by the minimum value between $dis_{box}(\mathbf{v}';\mathbf{p}')$ and $dis_{box}(\mathbf{v}';\mathbf{p}_3)$ where $\mathbf{p}'$ represents the intersection of a set of box embeddings $\{\mathbf{p}_1, \mathbf{p}_2\}$. As a result, $dis_{box}(\mathbf{v}';\mathbf{p})$ of Eq. 5 can be replaced by $Min(dis_{box}(\mathbf{v}';\mathbf{p}'), dis_{box}(\mathbf{v}';\mathbf{p}_3))$. Moreover, $p_1 \vee (p_2 \wedge p_3) \rightarrow v$ and $p_2 \vee (p_1 \wedge p_3) \rightarrow v$ could be measured by the similar method.

- $p_1 \wedge (p_2 \vee p_3) \rightarrow v$ means a user likes item v because the user bought either p_2 or p_3, but the user bought p_1 before. According to the disjunctive normal form that $p_1 \wedge (p_2 \vee p_3))$ is equivalent to $(p_1 \wedge p_2) \vee (p_1 \wedge p_3)$, this rule could be measured by the minimum value between $dis_{box}(\mathbf{v}';\mathbf{p}')$ and $dis_{box}(\mathbf{v}';\mathbf{p}'')$ where $\mathbf{p}'$ represents the intersection of a set of box embeddings $\{\mathbf{p}_1, \mathbf{p}_2\}$ and $\mathbf{p}''$ represents the intersection of a set of box embeddings $\{\mathbf{p}_1, \mathbf{p}_3\}$. As a result, we have $dis_{box}(\mathbf{v}';\mathbf{p}) = Min(dis_{box}(\mathbf{v}';\mathbf{p}'), dis_{box}(\mathbf{v}';\mathbf{p}''))$ in Eq. 5. Of course, so do $(p_1 \vee p_2) \wedge p_3 \rightarrow v$ and $p_2 \wedge (p_1 \vee p_3) \rightarrow v$.

In one word, we can use the learned box representations of historical items to model the above logical implication rules in the sequential space. The final recommendations can be generated by using Eq. 5 which combines the user preference space and sequential space.

5   Experiments

5.1   Experimental Details

Datasets: We evaluate our methods on five datasets from four real-world applications. The Amazon[1] dataset is crawled from Amazon.com which comprises reviews and ratings of products in the 'Beauty' category. The Douban[2] dataset is crawled from the Douban site on which users can review 'Book' and 'Movie' they previous consume. The Gowalla[3] dataset records locations which users checked in. Ml-1m[4] is a widely used benchmark dataset of MovieLens including users' ratings on movies.

For all datasets, we treat the presence of a review or rating as the interaction of a user with an item, and use timestamps to determine the sequence order of actions. We discard users and items with fewer than 10 interactions. Finally in the Beauty dataset, there are 29,215 interactions of 1,851 users on 2,434 items. In the Book dataset, there are 1,428,679 interactions of 23,986 users on 20,727

---

[1] https://jmcauley.ucsd.edu/data/amazon/.
[2] https://www.dropbox.com/s/u2ejjezjk08lz1o/Douban.tar.gz?dl=0.
[3] https://snap.stanford.edu/data/loc-gowalla.html.
[4] https://grouplens.org/datasets/movielens/.

items. In the Movie dataset, there are 11,071,957 interactions of 58,304 users on 28,789 items. In the Gowalla dataset, there are 2,985,833 interactions of 42,992 users on 122,694 items. In the Ml-1m dataset, there are 998,231 interactions of 6,309 users on 3,260 items.

For partitioning, we split the historical sequence for each user into three parts: we hold the first 90% of actions in each user's sequence as the training set and use the next 5% actions as the validation set. The remaining 5% actions in each user's sequence are used as the test set. Using the validation set, we search the optimal hyperparameter settings for all models, and terminate training process if the performance on the validation set does not improve for three successive epochs. At last, we evaluate a model's performance on the test set.

Metrics: We adopt two common Top-K metrics, $Recall@K$ and $NDCG@K$ [4], to evaluate the recommendation performance. The higher both metrics are, the better the recommendation performance is. By default, we set $K = 20$. For each user in the test set, we rank all items and then evaluate the $Recall$ and $NDCG$ with the ground-truth items. Finally, we report the average metrics for all users in the test set.

Implement Details: We use the Adam optimizer to optimize all models in which the batch size is 100 and the embedding size is 64. The learning rate is tuned amongst $\{0.0001, 0.0005, 0.001, 0.005\}$, the coefficient λ of $\mathcal{L}2$ normalization is searched in $\{0, 0.0001, 0.001, 0.01\}$. As for the initialization of deep neural networks, we use the default Xavier initializer to initialize the neural parameters. As for our model Box4Rec, without specification, we show the results of Box4Rec with the recommendation strategy just like the $p_1 \wedge p_2 \wedge p_3 \rightarrow v$ style. By fault, we use the Box4Rec with three layers, α of 0.8, and β of 0.3.

5.2   Performance Comparison

We compare our method Box4Rec with various state-of-the-art sequential recommendation methods, including two Markov chains-based models: FPMC [11] and Fossil [2], one translation-based model: TransRec [1], two neural network-based models: GRU4REC [3] and Caser [13], one self-attention based model: SASRec [4]. We exclude baselines utilizing additional information besides user-item sequential interaction information, and baselines not incorporating the sequential patterns (e.g. BPRMF [10]) because the existing research has shown that sequential patterns can improve upon methods which only use the user general interests. For fair comparison, all models are based on a public library of recommender systems[5] implemented by Python and TensorFlow, and run on a GPU with an NVIDIA Tesla P40 GPU and 20 GB GPU memory.

Table 1 shows results of Box4Rec on five datasets along with the baselines for $Recall$ and $NDCG$. We use the bold face and underlines to denote results of the best and second best method, respectively. From Table 1, we can see that the proposed model, Box4Rec, achieves the best performance on all five datasets

---

[5] https://github.com/DeepGraphLearning/RecommenderSystems.

Table 1. Comparison results

Method	Beauty		Book		Movie		Gowalla		Ml-1m	
	Recall	*NDCG*	*Recall*	*NDCG*	*Recall*	*NDCG*	*Recall*	*NDCG*	*Recall*	*NDCG*
FPMC	0.0642	0.0282	0.0644	0.0284	0.0356	0.0139	<u>0.3452</u>	<u>0.1911</u>	0.0677	0.0275
Fossil	0.1169	0.0450	0.1056	<u>0.0420</u>	0.0397	0.0157	0.2769	0.1563	0.0947	0.0337
TransRec	0.0703	0.0266	0.0530	0.0229	0.0340	0.0140	0.3040	0.1888	0.0650	0.0245
GRU4REC	0.0688	0.0286	0.0947	0.0407	0.0546	0.0209	0.1189	0.0539	0.1011	0.0393
Caser	0.0665	0.0367	0.0912	0.0398	0.0448	0.0173	0.1176	0.0595	0.1101	0.0365
SASRec	<u>0.1246</u>	<u>0.0471</u>	<u>0.1135</u>	<u>0.0420</u>	<u>0.0585</u>	<u>0.0267</u>	0.3014	0.1772	<u>0.1102</u>	<u>0.0397</u>
Box4Rec	**0.1330**	**0.0496**	**0.1224**	**0.0465**	**0.0755**	**0.0276**	**0.3867**	**0.2473**	**0.1219**	**0.0427**
Improvement	6.7%	5.3%	7.8%	10.7%	29.1%	3.37%	12.0%	29.4%	10.6%	7.6%

with all evaluation metrics, which illustrates the superiority of modeling users and historical items as boxes instead of points in the latent space.

Furthermore, FPMC, Fossil and TransRec also show competitive performance by using short sequential user behavior data. On the Gowalla data set, FPMC shows the most powerful performance among baselines. This is the reason that we select it as the basic model. Compared with the three methods, the $\mathcal{L}1$ distance between boxes makes Box4Rec satisfy the triangle inequality, and the intersection of boxes makes Box4Rec consider more historical user behaviors. With the above two important benefits, Box4Rec beats FPMC, Fossil and TransRec.

Box4Rec obtains better results than GRU4Rec and Caser. One possible reason is that Box4Rec explicitly defines the user general interests and the intersection operation on box embedding vectors to avoid the information loss problem caused by the simple pooling operation in GRU4Rec and Caser.

At last, in our experiments, SASRec obtains the best performances on all datasets but Gowalla. Although SASRec adopts the attention model to distinguish the items that users have visited, it neglects the common latent features among items, which is captured by Box4Rec's intersection operation on boxes.

5.3 Studies of Box4Rec

Effect of α and β. Figure 2 shows the parameter sensitivities of two crucial hyper-parameters in Rec4Box with respect to *Recall* and *NDCG*. α aims to balance the contributions of user preference and sequential preference in Eq. 5. From Fig. 2, we observe that the performance is not optimal if we only use one of the two preferences. The optimal results can be found when α is in [0.4, 0.8]. Hence, we set $\alpha = 0.8$ in our experiments. Furthermore, we observe that Box4Rec is insensitivity of β, which makes it be easily trained in practice.

Effect of the Different Rules. Using the $\vee$ and $\wedge$ operation on the learned box embedding vectors of the recent three items, we can have eight different recommendation rules. Figure 3 depicts the recommendation performance of the eight rules. We can see that $p_1 \wedge p_2 \wedge p_3$ achieves the best overall performance, while $p_1 \vee p_2 \vee p_3$ is worse. This may be due to the intersection operation. We observe that $(p_1 \vee p_2) \wedge p_3$ achieves the second best results on Beauty and Movie.

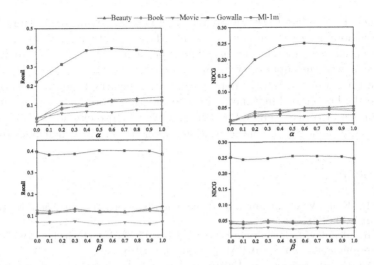

Fig. 2. Impact of α and β

As $(p_1 \vee p_2) \wedge p_3$ emphasizes the contribution of the last recent item, the observation is consistent with the assumption of other methods (e.g. TransRec). However, on Gowalla, the second best result is observed in $p_2 \wedge (p_1 \vee p_3)$ and $p_2 \vee (p_1 \wedge p_3)$ which emphasizes the contribution of the middle item. The observation suggests us that it may be insufficient to only consider the last recent item. Totally, these results show that we can use Box4Rec to drive some new rules which are unseen during training. Most of these new rules can achieve competitive recommendation performance. The problem arising from these rules is how to select appropriate rules to make recommendation be varied by users' different tastes. We leave this exploration as future work.

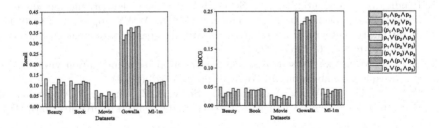

Fig. 3. Impact of the different rules

6 Conclusions

In this paper, we proposed the Box4Rec model to embed a user and items as a box instead of a point to model the user's general preference and short-term preference. By combining the box embedding with the conjunction and disjunction operations on items, different recommendation strategies have been used for the sequential recommendation task. The experimental results on five real-world datasets showed the superiority of our model.

In future, we will apply more permutation-invariant neural networks to enhance the box embedding method by considering more factors (e.g. the relevance among historical items). Furthermore, we will also extend the box embedding to more sequential recommendation models to improve their performance.

References

1. He, R., Kang, W.C., Mcauley, J.: Translation-based recommendation. In: RecSys, pp. 161–169 (2017)
2. He, R., Mcauley, J.: Fusing similarity models with Markov chains for sparse sequential recommendation. In: ICDM, pp. 191–200 (2016)
3. Hidasi, B, Karatzoglou, A., Baltrunas, L., Tikk, D.: Session-based recommendations with recurrent neural networks. In: ICLR (2016)
4. Kang, W., McAuley, J.J.: Self-attentive sequential recommendation. In: ICDM, pp. 197–206 (2018)
5. Koren, Y., Bell, R., Volinsky, C.: Matrix factorization techniques for recommender systems. IEEE Comput. **42**(8), 30–37 (2009)
6. Krizhevsky, A., Sutskever, I., Hinton.: ImageNet classification with deep convolutional neural networks. In: NIPS (2012)
7. Li, C., Niu, X., Luo, X., Chen, Z.: A review-driven neural model for sequential recommendation. In: IJCAI, pp. 2866–2872 (2019)
8. Pi, Q., Bian, W., Zhou, G., Zhu, X., Gai, K.: Practice on long sequential user behavior modeling for click-through rate prediction. In: KDD, pp. 2671–2679 (2019)
9. Ren, H., Hu, W., Leskovec, J.: Query2box: reasoning over knowledge graphs in vector space using box embeddings. In: ICLR, pp. 3391–3401 (2020)
10. Rendle, S., Freudenthaler, C., Gantner, Z., Schmidt-Thieme, L.: BPR: Bayesian personalized ranking from implicit feedback. In: UAI, pp. 452–461 (2009)
11. Rendle, S., Freudenthaler, C., Schmidt-Thieme, L.: Factorizing personalized Markov chains for next-basket recommendation. In: WWW, pp. 811–820 (2010)
12. Shani, G., Heckerman, D., Brafman, R.I.: An MDP-based recommender system. J. Mach. Learn. Res. **6**, 1265–1295 (2005)
13. Tang, J., Wang, k.: Personalized top-N sequential recommendation via convolutional sequence embedding. In: WSDM, pp. 565–573 (2018)
14. Wang, S., Hu, L., Wang, Y., Cao, L.L., Sheng, Q.Z., Orgun, M.A.: Sequential Recommender Systems: Challenges, Progress and Prospects, CoRRabs/2001.04830 (2020)
15. Wu, C., Ahmed, A., Beutel, A., Smoda, A.J., Jing, H.: Recurrent recommender networks. In: WSDM, pp. 495–503 (2017)
16. Zaheer, M., Kottur, S., Ravanbakhsh, S., Poczos, B., Salakhutdinov, R., Smola, A.J.: Deep sets. In: NeurIPS, pp. 3391–3401 (2017)

UKIRF: An Item Rejection Framework for Improving Negative Items Sampling in One-Class Collaborative Filtering

Antônio David Viniski[(✉)], Jean Paul Barddal, and Alceu de Souza Britto Jr.

Graduate Program in Informatics (PPGIa), Pontifícia Universidade Católica do Paraná (PUCPR), Rua Imaculada Conceição, 1155 Curitiba, Paraná, Brazil
{adviniski,jean.barddal,alceu}@ppgia.pucpr.br

Abstract. Collaborative Filtering (CF) is one of the most successful techniques in recommender systems. Most CF scenarios depict positive-only implicit feedback, which means that negative feedback is unavailable. Therefore, One-Class Collaborative Filtering (OCCF)techniques have been tailored to tackling these scenarios. Nonetheless, several OCCF models still require negative observations during training, and thus, a popular approach is to consider randomly selected unknown relationships as negative. This work brings forward a novel and non-random approach for selecting negative items called Unknown Item Rejection Framework (UKIRF). More specifically, we instantiate UKIRF using similarity approaches, i.e., TF-IDF and Cosine, to reject items similar to those a user interacted with. We apply UKIRF to different OCCF models in different datasets and show that it improves the recall rates up to 24% when compared to random sampling.

Keywords: Collaborative recommendations systems · Implicit feedback · Negative sampling · Similarity metrics

1 Introduction

In recent years, recommendation systems have become widely used by companies like Amazon, Netflix, and Spotify are have been proven to be effective in recommending personalized items to users, boosting businesses, and facilitating decision-making processes [5,17]. Collaborative filtering, which aims at predicting users' preferences towards items based on historical user feedback, is considered a central technique in recommender systems [13]. The users' feedback is expressed explicitly or implicitly to reflect the user's preferences for items. Explicit feedback is often represented by a numerical grade that describes different preference levels (such as a 1–5 scale) [6,7]. Nonetheless, collecting explicit feedback from users is difficult, complex, costly, and even unfeasible, depending on the scenario. Therefore, in many real situations, the feedback implicitly expressed by users' behavior (like clicks, bookmarks, and purchases) is easier to

© Springer Nature Switzerland AG 2021
K. Karlapalem et al. (Eds.): PAKDD 2021, LNAI 12713, pp. 549–560, 2021.
https://doi.org/10.1007/978-3-030-75765-6_44

obtain and attracted increasing interest from researchers and practitioners [7]. Despite the easiness of data acquisition, implicit feedback scenarios have specific problems, such as negative feedback's unavailability. The absence of user negative feedback is referred to as One-Class Collaborative Filtering (OCCF), or positive-only feedback [6]. Despite the lack of negative feedback, algorithms tailored for OCCF require strategies to assume the unknown relations between users and items as negative [15]. There are two ways to incorporate unknown inputs into the model's training: (i) consider that all missing interactions between users and items are negatives, or (ii) select a sub-sample of these missing interactions as negative. Following the former strategy is computationally prohibitive, and thus, several proposals follow the latter approach as interactions are randomly sampled and assumed as negative. We argue that there is a need for methods that perform negative interaction sampling, considering the data characteristics instead of randomly.

In this work, we propose two methods for rejection, i.e., removing items from the missing entries per user by calculating similarity measures between items in the training interactions. These methods use positive interactions to find patterns in user behavior and reject unlabeled interactions that are likely to be relevant. The first method uses Cosine similarity [4,14] in the interaction matrix, while the second combines Cosine similarity with a TF-IDF variant [1].

The paper is organized as follows. Section 2.1 introduces the one-class collaborative filtering task. Section 2.2 introduces related works that target improving the results obtained in OCCF scenarios. Section 3 presents the proposed framework for negative items rejection. Section 4 discusses the experiments performed alongside their analysis. Finally, Sect. 6 concludes this paper and states envisioned future works.

2   Related Work

This section introduces the research problem and reviews popular approaches designed for implicit positive-only scenarios that sample negative examples for training recommender models. In Sect. 2.1 we present the One-class collaborative filtering (OCCF) challenge and formalize the problem definition. Section 2.2 shows four popular recommender models that treat the unobserved interactions as negative ones.

2.1   One-Class Collaborative Filtering

One-class collaborative filtering (OCCF) predicts users' preferences given past positive feedback available in a dataset [5]. OCCF has characteristics that differentiate it from other tasks in recommendation systems. First, negative feedback lacks, as it is cumbersome to state with certainty which items a user dislikes. For instance, the lack of interaction is ambiguous as the user may indeed dislike an item or be unaware of it. Next, implicit datasets are highly sparse as few interactions are known, and most of the user-item relationship matrix corresponds to missing data. Furthermore, OCCF scenarios are noisy, as an interaction between a user and an item does not mean that the user prefers it. There is no explicit feedback from the user w.r.t. one's satisfaction after such interaction. Finally, implicit ratings expressed numerically indicate confidence and do not represent users' preferences as with explicit ratings, yet, it describes the frequency of interaction, e.g., how many times a user listens to a song, how frequently a user purchases an item, and so forth.

Existing solutions for OCCF differ in how they handle unobserved data. Although the one-class collaborative filtering is less visited than the multi-class setting, some approaches have been proposed in the literature to deal with missing (unknown) items [11]. According to how the unlabeled data is used, existing methods to OCCF can be classified into two categories [11], i.e., whole-data based approaches [6,15]; and sampling based approaches [3,8,15,18]. Both approaches share challenges. When considering all the missing entries as negative, two constraints are relevant. First, as most of the training instances are negative, the class imbalance problem reduces the positive class's predictive ability. Second, one must deal with the possibility of introducing false negative examples. Besides, suppose we randomly sample unobserved interactions. Consequently, it is challenging to identify representative negative examples as all of the negative and missing positive interactions are mixed and cannot be distinguished [6]. Conversely, if the sampling method considers the dataset characteristics during negative sampling, we have a smaller probability of selecting false negatives.

Notation-wise, we denote $R_{m \times n}$ to be an interaction matrix, where m and n represent the number of users and items, respectively. Therefore, OCCF methods assign a score $\hat{r}_{ui}$ for each u-th and i-th user-item pair in $R_{m \times n}$, such that $u \in U$ and $i \in I$. The value of $r_{ui} \in \{0, 1\}$ denotes the positive or unobserved interaction of the u-th user on i-th, where r_{ui} is an element of R. Consequently, $\omega_u^+ = \{i \in I \mid r_{ui} = 1\}$ and $\omega_u^- = \{i \in I \mid r_{ui} = 0\}$ denote the sets of positive and unobserved items for the u-th user. Our goal is to perform negative item sampling from ω_u^- so that items that tend to be irrelevant for the u-th user given the characteristics of the positive items ω_u^+ are dropped.

2.2   OCCF Techniques

We can categorize the approaches designed for OCCF scenarios according to how they learn the relevance order. Most algorithms exploiting OCCF focus on homogeneous positive feedback with point-wise [3], pair-wise [8], and list-wise [9] preference assumptions. Point-wise approaches regard user ratings as categorical labels or numerical values and learn the relevance scores of missing data directly [11]. The pair-wise approaches try to capture the preference order between missing data, correctly identifying the positive/negative item in each pair [11,18]. On the other hand, an individual training example is an entire list of items in a list-wise approach, rather than individual items or item pairs. However, due to their difficulty modeling the inter-list loss and inefficiency on large-scale datasets, list-wise CF approaches are not widely used compared to point-wise and pair-wise in ranking-oriented collaborative filtering [18]. Consequently, for further experimentation, we select the pair-wise model Bayesian Personalized Ranking for Matrix Factorization (BPRMF) [8], and the point-wise models proposed in the Neural Collaborative Framework (NCF): Generalized Matrix Factorization (GMF), Multi-layer Perceptron recommender (MLP) and Neural Matrix Factorization (NeuMF) [3].

Bayesian Personalized Ranking for Matrix Factorization (BPRMF).
BPRMF [8] is a popular familiar pair-wise method. Instead of only using the user-item interactions, for each interaction $(u; i)$, BPRMF selects a number of randomly selected items (j) to be used as negative items. BPR optimization decomposes triplets in the $(u; i; j)$ format using the difference of the predictions for the u-th user w.r.t. items i $(\hat{R}_{ui} = A_u \cdot B_i^T)$ and j $(\hat{R}_{uj} = A_u \cdot B_j^T)$, obtaining the instance prediction: $\hat{R}_{uij} = \hat{R}_{ui} - \hat{R}_{uj}$. The prediction error $e = |1 - \hat{R}_{uij}|$ is then used to update the u-th user (A_u), the i-th and j-th item $(B_i$ and $B_j)$ latent factors.

Neural Collaborative Framework (NCF). NCF is a deep neural network recommender framework composed of three recommender models: GMF, MLP, and NeuMF [3]. The NCF framework presents a probabilistic approach for learning the point-wise models that pay special attention to implicit data's binary property, i.e., training models using positive and negative examples. To endow the probabilistic explanation, NCF models constrain the output $\hat{r}_{ui}$ in the range of $[0, 1]$ using a probabilistic function in the output layer. Regarding negative instances, the authors suggest uniformly sampling them from unobserved interactions in each iteration.

Generalized Matrix Factorization (GMF). To represent the latent features of users and items, GMF uses embedding layers. Each embedding layer is a fully connected layer that projects users' sparse representation and items in a dense vector. Thus, projecting the vector to the output layer we obtained the probability prediction of user u interact with the item i: $\hat{r}_{ui} = a_{out}\left(h^T\left(A_u \odot B_i\right)\right)$, where a_{out} and h denote the output activation function and edge weights of the output layer, respectively.

Multi-layer Perceptron (MLP). Instead of the element-wise dot product between latent factors like in GMF, MLP concatenates the user and item latent features. The concatenated vector is fully connected with hidden layers to model the collaborative filtering effect and learn the interaction between latent features A_u and B_u. Therefore, the item prediction is achieved by $\hat{r}_{ui} = \sigma\left(h^T\phi_L\left(z_{L-1}\right)\right)$, where σ, z_{L-1}, and $h^T\phi_L$ denote the activation function, the last hidden layer, and the edge weights of the output layer, respectively.

Neural Matrix Factorization (NeuMF). NeuMF combines GMF and MLP architectures. More specifically, it combines the linear and non-linear kernels from GMF and MLP. Internally, NeuMF trains GMF and MLP with random initializers until convergence. To provide more flexibility to the combined model, NeuMF allows GMF and MLP to learn separated embedding and connects them by concatenating their last hidden layer.

3 Unknown Items Rejection Framework (UKIRF)

This section introduces the Unknown Items Rejection Framework (UKIRF) to improve OCCF models' performance. Our goal with this framework is to provide a pre-processing step of a collaborative filtering recommendation process, thus not requiring modifications in the recommender models.

Algorithm 1 describes UKIRF. To generate the items rejection, UKIRF uses the interaction matrix R, the set of all users U and items I. As input, UKIRF requires the number of items (N_r) for rejection per user. Line 1 denotes the rejection_method function call, which identifies item-item relationships using the interaction matrix R and stores these relationship data into the S similarity matrix. Details on the rejection methods proposed are given in Sect. 3.1. Line 2 instantiates ω_f^- as an empty dictionary-like structure responsible for storing the negative options for all users. The loop in lines 3 to 10 iterates over all users $u \in U$, in which the positive items ω_u^+ (line 4) are recovered, followed by the unobserved ω_u^- items per user. According to the number of positive observations to the u-th user, the framework decides (line 6) whether to apply the unobserved item rejection strategy or not. If $|\omega_u^+| = 0$ holds, i.e., the u-th user has no positive interactions yet; the set of unobserved items (ω_u^-) is maintained. On the other hand, if $|\omega_u^+| > 0$, UKIRF uses the apply_rejection function (line 7) to return the list of items (ω_u^r) that are the most similar w.r.t. to the items for which the u-th user interacted with. The apply_rejection has as parameters the positive items of user u-th (ω_u^+), the rejection data returned by the rejection_method function, and an integer N_r that denotes the number of items that shall be rejected. Thus, the UKIRF removes from ω_u^- the items stored in ω_u^r (line 8). Next, regardless of the rejection strategy chosen, the resulting ω_u^- is stored in ω_f^- $(\omega_f^-[u] = \omega_u^-)$, which corresponds to the negative options for all users (line 9).

Algorithm 1: Unknown Items Rejection Framework (UKIRF)

Data: Interaction Matrix R, set of all users U, set of all items I
Input: N_r: number of items to be rejected
Output: ω_f^-

1 $S \leftarrow$ rejection_method(R) ▷ Generating the item-item similarity data
2 $\omega_f^- \leftarrow \{\}$ ▷ Instantiate the dictionary to stores the negative options
3 **foreach** $u \in U$ **do**
4     $\omega_u^+ \leftarrow \{i \in I \mid r_{ui} = 1\}$ ▷ Recover all u-th user positive items
5     $\omega_u^- \leftarrow \{i \in I \mid r_{ui} = 0\}$ ▷ Recover all u-th user unobserved items
6   **if** $|\omega_u^+| \neq 0$ **then**
7        $\Omega_u^r \leftarrow$ apply_rejection(ω_u^+, S, N_r) ▷ Return the N_r most similar items
8        $\omega_u^- \leftarrow \omega_u^- \setminus \Omega_u^r$ ▷ Remove N_r items from ω_u^-
9     $\omega_f^-[u] \leftarrow \omega_u^-$
10 **end**
11 **return** ω_f^-

After rejecting unobserved items from the system's active users, the framework returns the dictionary containing all negative options per user in U (line 11).

3.1 Similarity-Based Rejection Strategies

This section presents two rejection strategies that can be used in UKIRF: Cosine-based rejection and UF-IIF rejection. These reflect the rejection_method function in UKIRF, which receives as input the interaction matrix R.

Cosine Similarity Approach: Among the existing similarity measures, the cosine function, which is defined as the inner product of two vectors divided by the product of their lengths [14], is the most popular and is widely used similarity measure. Its calculation is efficient, especially for sparse vectors, as only the non-zero dimensions are considered [4]. This characteristic is significant in the OCCF scenarios given the sparsity present in the interaction matrix R. Given two m-dimensional vectors $\vec{v}$ and $\vec{w}$, where m is the number of users, the Cosine similarity between them is calculated as follows:

$$\text{Cosine}(\vec{v}, \vec{w}) = \frac{\vec{v} \bullet \vec{w}}{\|\vec{v}\| \, \|\vec{w}\|} = \frac{\sum_{i=0}^{n} \vec{v}_i \times \vec{w}_i}{\sqrt{\sum_{i=0}^{n} \vec{v}_i^2} \sqrt{\sum_{i=0}^{n} \vec{w}_i^2}} \tag{1}$$

The Cosine approach applies the Cosine similarity function to all item-item ($\vec{v}$, $\vec{w}$) pairs. As a result, the rejection_method function returns the similarity matrix $S^{n \times n}$, where n is the number of items.

User Frequency-Inverse Item Frequency Approach (UF-IIF). The User frequency-inverse item frequency is a specialization of 'Term frequency-inverse document frequency' (TF-IDF), one of the most commonly used term weighting schemes in the information retrieval systems [1]. TF-IDF is a metric that multiplies the two quantities TF and IDF. TF provides the frequency of each term in the document from the document collection. On the other hand, IDF can be interpreted as the amount of information representing each term's weight in the document collection. Less frequent terms have higher IDF values. In this work, we use TF-IDF to calculate the similarity between items. First, we assume that the user is a "term" (UF), and the item is a "document" (IIF). Thus, instead of calculating the similarity between documents, we obtain the similarity of the items. In this sense, the formulation of UF and IIF measures are as follows:

$$\text{uf} = \frac{f_{u,i}}{\sum_m f_{u,i}}, \quad \text{iif} = log\left(\frac{n}{\text{if}_u}\right), \quad \text{uf-iif} = \text{uf} \times \text{iif}$$

where $f_{u,i}$ is the number of times the u-th user interacted with the i-th item, $\sum_m f_{u,i}$ is the total number of users who interacted with the i-item, n is the number of items present in the dataset, and if$_u$ is the number of items the u-th user interacted with. As the UF-IIF$^{m \times n}$ matrix stores the weights of each user-item pair, we use the *Cosine* function (Eq. 1) to calculate the similarity matrix S between all items.

Algorithm 2: Get a list of N_r similar items to items in ω_u^+

Input: ω_u^+: positive items for an user u, S: similarity matrix between items, N_r: number of items to be rejected

Output: ω_u^r: a list of N_r most similar items to items in ω_u^+

1 **Function** apply_rejection(ω_u^+,S,N_r):
2     $P \leftarrow D^{a \times b}$, such that $a \in \omega_u^+$ and $b \in I$, and $d_{a,b} = S_{a,b}$ ▷ get a partial similarity matrix with the weight vectors of items in ω_u^+
3     $V \leftarrow \sum_{k=0}^{a} P_{k,b}$ ▷ sum of similarities considering items in ω_u^+
4   Sort V in ascending order
5     $\omega_u^r \leftarrow V_k$, such that $(|V| - N_r \leq k \leq |V|)$
6   **return** ω_u^r
7 **End Function**

Both Cosine and UF-IIF techniques result in a similarity matrix S that stores the similarity between items in the recommender system. Therefore, both are used in the apply_rejection function given in Algorithm 2. It receives as input all the positive observations of the u-th user (ω_u^+), the S matrix returned by the rejection_method function, and the number of items N_r the rejection approach must reject. The first step (line 2) selects from the similarity matrix (S) a partial matrix P that denotes the similarity values $s_{a,b} = S_{a,b}$, such that $a \in \omega_u^+$ and $b \in I$. Next, line 3 generates a similarity vector V, which denotes the sum of rows (a) weights for all items in the columns (b) of the partial similarity matrix $\sum_{k=0}^{a} \leftarrow P_{k,b}$. Line 4 sorts the similarity vector V in ascending order. Finally, line 5 stores in ω_u^r such items with the highest similarity values (ω_u^r represents the return of the function apply_rejection).

4 Experimental Setup

4.1 Datasets

We test our proposed framework in three supermarket datasets (SMDI_original, SMDI_500E and SMDI_200UE) and in the Movie Lens 100k dataset [2], such that the last has been converted so that only ratings above 3.5 were considered positive. Table 1 presents the datasets characteristics. In this experimental setting, we also propose approaches to define the number of rejected items (N_r). Regarding that most real-world datasets have repeated interactions, we use the third quartile ($Q3$) and the superior limit (SL) on the number of interactions and on the number of unique interactions per user to obtain N_r values. Thus, we have four alternatives to define the N_r for each dataset, considering the unique interactions (SLU and $Q3U$) and repeated interactions (SLT and $Q3T$). Table 1 also shows the number of rejections (N_r) in each scenario.

4.2 Baselines

We compare our proposed rejection strategies with the most often used uniform random sampling and test the generated sets of unobserved items in four rec-

Table 1. Overview of the datasets used during experimentation.

Datasets	Interactions	Users	Items	Sparsity	N_r			
					SLT	SLU	Q3T	Q3U
SMDL_original	737893	9531	7141	99.57%	212	108	92	48
SMDL_500E	448791	9480	6933	99.59%	204	103	89	46
SMDL_200UE	447391	9472	6924	99.59%	204	103	89	46
Movie Lens 100k	21201	928	1172	98.05%	64	64	30	30

ommender models: BPRMF, GMF, MLP, and NeuMF. For the recommender algorithms, we tested the following hyper-parameter values: learning rate $\in$ [0.001,0.005,0.0001,0.0005], regularization rate $\in$ [0.01, 0.001, 0], latent factors $\in$ [5, 10, 15, 20, 25, 30, 35, 40, 45, 50, 55, 60, 65, 70, 75, 80, 85, 90, 95, 100]. After applying the rejection method, for each positive $\{u, i\}$ user-item interaction, we randomly sampled a number (from 1 to 10) of items from the previously filtered subset of unknown items to serve as negative ones.

4.3 Assessment

For each dataset, we made a temporal split, i.e., the first 50% of the time period were selected for training and the remaining 50% for testing. This temporal split is relevant as the dataset exhibits timestamps. From the training set, 20% of the instances were used for model validation. Thus, we use the validation loss to monitor the convergence of the models [10].

Following the protocol proposed in [12], we express the accuracy of the models using Recall@K, with $K \in \{1, 10\}$. The score, shown in Eq. 2, measures the average (on all users) of the proportion of recommended items that appear among the top K of the ranked list [16], where $|T|$ is the test set size.

$$\text{Recall@K} = \frac{1}{|T|} \sum_{u,i \in T} (\text{hit@K}(u, i)) \tag{2}$$

For each instance $((u, i))$ in the test set, we select a candidate list of 100 unknown items to user u, and the known item i is appended to this candidate list. The candidate list is randomly sampled from the set of unknown items of user u or from the optimized set of unknown items when considering the unknown items' rejection approaches. According to the recommender models' scores, we ranked and sorted the candidates in descending order. For each instance (u, i), hit@$K(u, i) = 1$ is said to happen when i is ranked amidst the top K items, and hit@$K(u, i) = 0$, otherwise.

We replicate each experiment 5 times in this work, so the results show the average and standard deviation of recall values. The source code and datasets used during experimentation are available at https://github.com/adviniski/ UKIRF.

5   Results and Analysis

Table 2 depicts the results obtained in the supermarket and Movie-Lens 100k datasets. We report the Recall@K (with $K = [1, 10]$) obtained by each model alongside the N_g and N_r values that achieved the best results, such that the former is the number of negative items per positive interaction, and the latter represents the strategy for rejecting items.

For BPRMF, which selects (positive, negative) pairs per positive instance, in the SDMI_original dataset (Table 2), the best results in comparison with the random sampling were obtained by the Cosine removal method, with ten negatives and SLT number of removals. We have an increase of 10.90% and 3.10% to the Recall@1 and Recall@10 values, respectively. Considering the Recall@10, the MLP model had superior performance, with a recall value of 73.4%, with ten negatives items per positive item in the training phase. The results with MLP increased 4.50% for Recall@10 in comparison to random sampling. The MLP and NeuMF models presented the best results for Recall@1 values in the original dataset, with an increase of 19.90% compared with the random sampling (from 32.9% to 52.8%), both with ten negative items. On the other hand, GMF presented inferior results when compared to MLP and NeuMF. GMF acquired results close to BPRMF, however, with lower recall values.

Despite being more straightforward than UF-IIF, the Cosine function obtained better results in all methods in the SDMI_original dataset, while the UF-IIF acquired close results to those obtained with random sampling. As UF-IIF also uses the Cosine similarity function, we expected close results to those obtained when using only the Cosine function in the interaction matrix. These results confirm the need for preprocessing approaches in the original supermarket dataset, showing that the datasets' noisy traits influence the models' results. Since UF-IIF generates weights to all user-item interactions before using the Consine function, we expected close or better results to those obtained by Cosine. The SLT approach rejects more items and provided the best results with the Cosine function.

In opposition to the previous dataset, in SDMI_500E, in which users with more than 500 interactions are removed, the model GMF outperformed BPRMF. However, the increase in recall values obtained by the Cosine removal compared to Random sampling for both methods was greater than those observed above. Here the Recall@1 and Recall@10 increased 16.70% and 3.80% for GMF and 14.30% and 2.10% for BPRMF. Besides, the MLP model presented better results for both recall measures. In this dataset, the UF-IIF rejection approach obtained close results to those presented by the Cosine method. Considering Recall@1, UF-IIF outperformed Cosine with recall values of 54.4% and 53.8%, respectively. Comparing the MLP with random sampling, the UF-IIF negative rejection approach provides an increase of 24.1% in the Recall@1 values (from 30.3% to 54.4%). Considering the number of negative items selected in the training phase, for UF-IIF, the best results were obtained with ten negative items in Recall@1, while for Cosine were eight negative items. On the other hand, for the Recall@10, the best results were found with 7 and 8 for Cosine and 6 and 5 for UF-IIF. For both

Table 2. Recall@K (%) values obtained by the recommender models with the different sampling strategies in the all tested datasets. N_g represents the number of negative items that yielded the best results, and N_r denotes the number of rejected items considering the approaches (SLT, SLU, Q3T, Q3U).

Model	Recall@K	Random		Cosine			UF-IIF		
		Recall (%)	N_g	Recall (%)	N_g	N_r	Recall (%)	N_g	N_r
Dataset: SMDI_original									
BPRMF	1	24.4 ± 0.0027	10	**35.3 ± 0.0020**	10	SLT	27.0 ± 0.0034	9	SLT
	10	48.6 ± 0.0055	10	**51.7 ± 0.0027**	10	SLT	48.6 ± 0.0030	10	SLU
GMF	1	22.5 ± 0.0030	3	**36.4 ± 0.0057**	1	SLT	25.9 ± 0.0034	2	SLT
	10	46.5 ± 0.0028	3	**50.4 ± 0.0060**	2	SLT	47.4 ± 0.0056	2	SLT
MLP	1	32.9 ± 0.0023	3	**52.8 ± 0.0004**	10	SLT	35.7 ± 0.0027	7	SLT
	10	68.9 ± 0.0021	10	**73.4 ± 0.0005**	10	SLT	69.0 ± 0.0029	10	Q3T
NeuMF	1	32.9 ± 0.0035	2	**52.8 ± 0.0004**	10	SLT	35.5 ± 0.0024	2	SLU
	10	68.6 ± 0.0037	10	**72.6 ± 0.0013**	4	SLT	68.7 ± 0.0048	9	SLU
Dataset: SMDI_500E									
BPRMF	1	21.5 ± 0.0038	10	35.8 ± 0.0028	9	SLT	**35.9 ± 0.0034**	8	SLT
	10	45.7 ± 0.0040	10	**48.6 ± 0.0034**	9	SLT	48.5 ± 0.0036	8	SLT
GMF	1	20.8 ± 0.0030	2	**37.5 ± 0.0027**	10	SLT	37.2 ± 0.0022	8	SLT
	10	46.6 ± 0.0026	6	**50.4 ± 0.0034**	10	SLT	50.2 ± 0.0033	8	SLT
MLP	1	30.3 ± 0.0033	10	53.8 ± 0.0023	8	SLT	**54.4 ± 0.0024**	10	SLT
	10	67.8 ± 0.0011	9	**72.2 ± 0.0015**	7	SLT	72.2 ± 0.0008	6	SLT
NeuMF	1	30.0 ± 0.0021	10	52.6 ± 0.0008	7	SLT	**52.8 ± 0.0008**	10	SLT
	10	67.1 ± 0.0018	10	**71.9 ± 0.0017**	8	SLT	71.9 ± 0.0026	10	SLT
Dataset: SMDI_200UE									
BPRMF	1	21.6 ± 0.0022	10	**36.3 ± 0.0030**	10	SLT	36.0 ± 0.0018	9	SLT
	10	46.0 ± 0.0051	9	**49.4 ± 0.0036**	10	SLT	48.9 ± 0.0023	9	SLT
GMF	1	20.8 ± 0.0037	10	**37.1 ± 0.0020**	10	SLT	37.1 ± 0.0021	10	SLT
	10	46.7 ± 0.0046	6	**50.3 ± 0.0073**	9	SLT	49.9 ± 0.0061	7	SLT
MLP	1	30.3 ± 0.0019	9	53.9 ± 0.0011	9	SLT	**54.3 ± 0.0016**	10	SLT
	10	67.8 ± 0.0013	10	72.3 ± 0.0011	5	SLT	**72.3 ± 0.0007**	6	SLT
NeuMF	1	30.2 ± 0.0022	3	53.9 ± 0.0016	10	SLT	**54.2 ± 0.0022**	10	SLT
	10	67.8 ± 0.0011	9	**72.3 ± 0.0008**	9	SLT	72.3 ± 0.0012	5	SLT
Dataset: Movie-Lens 100k									
BPRMF	1	2.6 ± 0.0066	10	3.6 ± 0.0070	8	SLU	**3.7 ± 0.0084**	8	SLU
	10	14.7 ± 0.0110	10	**15.5 ± 0.0130**	8	Q3T	15.4 ± 0.0128	8	SLU
GMF	1	5.0 ± 0.0000	10	**16.8 ± 0.0000**	10	SLU	16.2 ± 0.0068	9	SLT
	10	26.3 ± 0.0104	8	**33.7 ± 0.0000**	10	SLU	33.7 ± 0.0134	9	SLT
MLP	1	7.8 ± 0.0061	8	27.4 ± 0.0058	8	SLU	**28.2 ± 0.0054**	9	SLU
	10	43.3 ± 0.0022	9	**55.5 ± 0.0031**	8	SLT	55.5 ± 0.0038	10	SLT
NeuMF	1	6.8 ± 0.0079	7	**20.7 ± 0.0965**	10	SLT	19.2 ± 0.1171	10	SLU
	10	39.7 ± 0.0157	9	53.7 ± 0.0051	10	SLT	**54.2 ± 0.0039**	10	SLT

Cosine and UF-IIF, the SLT approach to select the number of rejected items was better than others in SDMI_500E.

The results of the two preprocessed datasets are very close. Still, if we had to choose one of the preprocessing approaches, we could see in the results Table 2 that for most of the recommender models, the SDMI_200UE dataset provided better results. In this dataset, we removed users with more than 200 unique (distinct items) interactions, which represented supermarket cashier operators.

In the three datasets analyzed, we found the most significant differences between the results of the rejection methods and the random sampling in the first top position (Recall@1). This means that the test dataset items were ranked in the top 1 position more effectively using the rejection methods than using random sampling without any rejection of unknown items. The MLP model presents the best increase in the Recall@1 value (24.1%) from the Random to the UF-IIF approach, considering the SDMI_500E dataset. For the SDMI_200UE dataset, both MLP and NeuMF increased Recall@1 values by 24% using the UF-IIF rejection method.

Finally, the results of the recommendation models obtained in the Movie Lens 100k dataset, also presented in Table 2, showed similar behavior to those obtained in supermarket datasets. We can see the effectiveness of the Cosine and UF-IIF methods compared to the Random approach, which showed an increase of 19.60% and 20.40% in Recall@1 values, respectively, for the MLP model.

6 Conclusion

This paper has shown how to increase the goodness of implicit recommendation models via the appropriate selection of negative items during the training phase. The motivation is that random sampling is insufficient and results in non-informative updates in the model's parameters. We propose a framework for rejecting potentially relevant items to users so that these are not assumed as negative. We used Cosine similarity to find similarity between items with that user interacted with either in the interaction matrix or in the user frequency-inverse item frequency (UF-IIF) matrix. We test our approaches in real-world datasets and provide the results obtained when it is coupled with four recommendation models (BPRMF, GMF, NeuMF, and MLP). Among the negative item rejection strategies, Cosine and UF-IIF obtained better results than random sampling, increasing Recall@1 values by up to 24.00%.

In future works, we plan to investigate other similarity metrics to quantify the relationship between items. Furthermore, we envision testing recommender models that are not built on matrix factorization to check how negative sampling affects their efficiency.

References

1. Aizawa, A.N.: An information-theoretic perspective of tf-idf measures. Inf. Process. Manage. **39**(1), 45–65 (2003)
2. Harper, F.M., Konstan, J.A.: The MovieLens datasets: history and context. TiiS **5**(4), 19:1–19:19 (2016)
3. He, X., Liao, L., Zhang, H., Nie, L., Hu, X., Chua, T.: Neural collaborative filtering. In: Proceedings of the 26th International Conference on World Wide Web, WWW 2017, 3–7 April 2017, Perth, Australia, pp. 173–182. ACM (2017)
4. Li, B., Han, L.: Distance weighted cosine similarity measure for text classification. In: Yin, H., Tang, K., Gao, Y., Klawonn, F., Lee, M., Weise, T., Li, B., Yao, X. (eds.) IDEAL 2013. LNCS, vol. 8206, pp. 611–618. Springer, Heidelberg (2013). https://doi.org/10.1007/978-3-642-41278-3_74

5. Li, G., Zhang, Z., Wang, L., Chen, Q., Pan, J.: One-class collaborative filtering based on rating prediction and ranking prediction. Knowl. Based Syst. **124**, 46–54 (2017)
6. Pan, R., et al: One-class collaborative filtering. In: Proceedings of the 8th IEEE International Conference on Data Mining (ICDM 2008), 15–19 December 2008, Pisa, Italy, pp. 502–511. IEEE Computer Society (2008)
7. Pan, W., Liu, M., Ming, Z.: Transfer learning for heterogeneous one-class collaborative filtering. IEEE Intell. Syst. **31**(4), 43–49 (2016)
8. Rendle, S., Freudenthaler, C., Gantner, Z., Schmidt-Thieme, L.: BPR: Bayesian personalized ranking from implicit feedback. CoRR abs/1205.2618 (2012)
9. Shi, Y., Larson, M.A., Hanjalic, A.: List-wise learning to rank with matrix factorization for collaborative filtering. In: Proceedings of the 2010 ACM Conference on Recommender Systems, RecSys 2010, 26–30 September 2010, Barcelona, Spain, pp. 269–272. ACM (2010)
10. Sidana, S., Laclau, C., Amini, M., Vandelle, G., Bois-Crettez, A.: KASANDR: a large-scale dataset with implicit feedback for recommendation. In: Proceedings of the 40th International ACM SIGIR Conference on Research and Development in Information Retrieval, 7–11 August 2017, Shinjuku, Tokyo, Japan, pp. 1245–1248. ACM (2017)
11. Song, B., Yang, X., Cao, Y., Xu, C.: Neural collaborative ranking. In: Proceedings of the 27th ACM International Conference on Information and Knowledge Management, CIKM 2018, 22–26 October 2018, Torino, Italy, pp. 1353–1362. ACM (2018)
12. Vinagre, J., Jorge, A.M., Gama, J.: Fast incremental matrix factorization for recommendation with positive-only feedback. In: Dimitrova, V., Kuflik, T., Chin, D., Ricci, F., Dolog, P., Houben, G.-J. (eds.) UMAP 2014. LNCS, vol. 8538, pp. 459–470. Springer, Cham (2014). https://doi.org/10.1007/978-3-319-08786-3_41
13. Volkovs, M., Yu, G.W.: Effective latent models for binary feedback in recommender systems. In: Proceedings of the 38th International ACM SIGIR Conference on Research and Development in Information Retrieval, 9–13 August 2015, Santiago, Chile, pp. 313–322. ACM (2015)
14. Ye, J.: Cosine similarity measures for intuitionistic fuzzy sets and their applications. Math. Comput. Model. **53**(1–2), 91–97 (2011)
15. Yu, H., Bilenko, M., Lin, C.: Selection of negative samples for one-class matrix factorization. In: Proceedings of the 2017 SIAM International Conference on Data Mining, 27–29 April 2017, Houston, Texas, USA, pp. 363–371. SIAM (2017)
16. Yuan, Q., Chen, L., Zhao, S.: Factorization vs. regularization: fusing heterogeneous social relationships in top-n recommendation. In: Proceedings of the 2011 ACM Conference on Recommender Systems, RecSys 2011, 23–27 October 2011, Chicago, IL, USA, pp. 245–252. ACM (2011)
17. Zhang, S., Yao, L., Sun, A., Tay, Y.: Deep learning based recommender system: a survey and new perspectives. ACM Comput. Surv. **52**(1), 5:1–5:38 (2019)
18. Zhang, W., Chen, T., Wang, J., Yu, Y.: Optimizing top-n collaborative filtering via dynamic negative item sampling. In: The 36th International ACM SIGIR Conference on Research and Development in Information Retrieval, SIGIR 2013, 28 July–01 August 2013, Dublin, Ireland, pp. 785–788. ACM (2013)

IACN: Influence-Aware and Attention-Based Co-evolutionary Network for Recommendation

Shalini Pandey[(✉)], George Karypis, and Jaideep Srivasatava

Department of Computer Science and Engineering, University of Minnesota,
Twin Cities, MN, USA
{pande103,karypis,srivasta}@umn.edu

Abstract. Recommending relevant items to users is a crucial task on online communities such as Reddit and Twitter. For recommendation system, representation learning presents a powerful technique that learns embeddings to represent user behaviors and capture item properties. However, learning embeddings on online communities is a challenging task because the user interest keep evolving. This evolution can be captured from 1) interaction between user and item, 2) influence from other users in the community. The existing dynamic embedding models only consider either of the factors to update user embeddings. However, at a given time, user interest evolves due to a combination of the two factors. To this end, we propose Influence-aware and Attention-based Co-evolutionary Network (IACN). Essentially, IACN consists of two key components: interaction modeling and influence modeling layer. The interaction modeling layer is responsible for updating the embedding of a user and an item when the user interacts with the item. The influence modeling layer captures the temporal excitation caused by interactions of other users. To integrate the signals obtained from the two layers, we design a novel fusion layer that effectively combines interaction-based and influence-based embeddings to predict final user embedding. Our model outperforms the existing state-of-the-art models from various domains.

Keywords: Co-evolutionary networks · Graph attention network · Recommendation system · Temporal embeddings

1 Introduction

Online communities such as Facebook, Twitter, and Reddit are a crucial part of today's online world. Recommendation of relevant information is essential for these platforms to improve users' experience and maintain their long-term engagement. However, the recommendation task involves various challenges. First, when a user interacts with an item both the user and item features are updated. Second, since users share information on online communities, they are

© Springer Nature Switzerland AG 2021
K. Karlapalem et al. (Eds.): PAKDD 2021, LNAI 12713, pp. 561–574, 2021.
https://doi.org/10.1007/978-3-030-75765-6_45

likely to influence each other. For instance, when a user posts a comment on a thread in Reddit, she influences other users to post comments on the thread. Further, the degree of influence of interaction is dependent on the relation between the users and the time elapsed since the interaction. Naturally, as more time elapses the degree of influence reduces [7]. Third, even when a user does not take any action, her interest keeps evolving [8]. It is important to determine user interest at any query time which can be predicted by the information from both her interactions and the influence of other users.

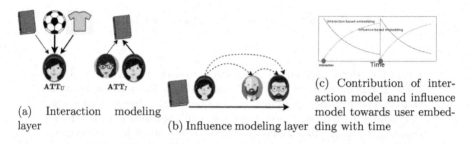

(a)   Interaction   modeling layer

(b) Influence modeling layer

(c) Contribution of interaction model and influence model towards user embedding with time

Fig. 1. A simplified diagram showing the main components of IACN.

The existing research has individually addressed either of the above-mentioned challenges. To capture the co-evolving nature of item properties and user interests, co-evolutionary models were proposed in [3,9]. These models update user embedding only when the user interacts with an item even when user interest keeps evolving with time. To capture the change in user's interest over time, JODIE [8] employs a projection operation that takes the user embeddings and time elapsed since the last user interaction to predict the user's embedding at any query time. Our model, instead, relies on the idea that users' interests at any future time can be predicted by the influence of other users on the user. To this front, several works have been done to augment the information from the influence of other users for predicting user interest [4,12]. However, in these methods the influence of other users is static [4] or context-dependent [12]. Furthermore, they generate static embeddings of items; thus, ignoring their evolving properties.

In this paper, we exploit both interaction and influence information for predicting temporal embeddings of users and items given the interaction sequence. The motivation is that when a user interacts with an item her interest at that time can be determined from the interaction features. However, as time elapses, the interest of the user drifts and tends to be more driven by the influence of other users. The key components in the IACN model are:

Interaction Modeling Layer: The interaction modeling layer is responsible for updating the embedding of corresponding users and items when they interact with each other. We leverage the attention mechanism to identify which interactions are important for determining the updated embedding of entities (users and items) involved in the interaction. As shown in Fig. 1a, when a user interacts with an item, ATT_U updates the embedding of the user by adaptively assigning weights to its previous interactions. Similarly, ATT_I updates the embedding of the item based on its past interaction.

Influence Modeling Layer: We design a "relation revealing" attention-based operation to capture the relation between users and then update the embedding of a user when any user who influences the user interacts with an item. As shown in Fig. 1b, when a user interacts with an item, it triggers a drift of interest of other users towards the item.

Fusion Layer: To learn future embedding of a user, we design a novel fusion layer that integrates the embedding from interaction and influence modeling layer. When an interaction occurs, the user embedding is determined solely by the interaction modeling layer because user interaction reveals the user's current interest [8]. As time progresses user embedding drifts further apart from the interaction embeddings. As shown in Fig. 1c, the future user embedding is computed by additively combining the influence-based embedding and the interaction-based embedding where the contribution of the interaction model decays while that of the influence model increases with time.

To recommend the next item which the user will interact with, IACN predicts an embedding for the next item and uses Locality Sensitive Hashing [5] to find the item whose embedding is most similar to the predicted item embedding. Extensive experimentation on real-world datasets shows that IACN outperforms six state-of-the-art models for the next item prediction task. Also, we conduct a comprehensive ablation study to show the effect of key components. Summary of our paper major contributions are:

- We study the contribution of both the interaction model and the influence model in predicting embeddings for the recommendation.
- We design a co-evolutionary network using two attention layers to update the embeddings of users and items. The attention layers help in improving the performance of our model along with providing insight into different user behaviors.
- We introduce a novel method to model the influence of other users on a user and integrate it with the interaction model to obtain the user embedding at query time
- We conduct experimentation on the real-world dataset and demonstrate the superiority of our model over state-of-the-art baselines over various domains.

2   Related Work

Dynamic Co-evolutionary Models. Joint modeling of users and items has been explored in recommendation systems. Models that concurrently learn both user and item embeddings have been developed in work such as [3,8,14]. Methods such as [3,14] use Recurrent Neural Nets (RNNs) to model the evolving features of items and users. They jointly learn representations of users and items with the idea that user and item embeddings influence each other whenever they interact. However, a user's interest changes with time even when he/she is not interacting with any item. JODIE [8] attempts to take into account the dynamic interest of users and update users' embedding by scaling their past embedding with a time context vector. Compared to other co-evolutionary models, we attempt to utilize self-attention mechanism to generate new embeddings since self-attention mechanism are more interpretable and have shown better performance at sequence modeling task [13] compared to the RNN-based method. In addition, we take into account the social influence of interaction by a user in evolving the interest of other users. This helps in predicting future embedding trajectory of users.

Recurrent Neural Networks Based Models. Several models employ recurrent neural networks (RNNs) or their variants (LSTMs and GRUs) to build recommender systems [6,14]. Models such as LSTM [6] consider item embedding to be static which does not change with time. Unlike these models, RRN [14] uses two RNN layers to generate dynamic user and item embeddings from ratings data. However RRN only considers static embedding of items and users as inputs. IACN, on the other hand, assigns each user and item both dynamic and static embedding. Also, IACN considers both the update of embedding caused by interactions between user and item and influence between users.

Social Recommendation Model. User's interest is affected by the neighboring members in social community. Some work [2,12] in social recommendation need information of social network structures to predict the social influence. However, such structural information is not always available. Even if the social structure exist, the degree of influence of a user on another is rarely explicitly declared. As a result, we can rely only on estimating influences and relations among users from their activities. These interactions are implicit in the sense that users interact with one another by expressing their preferences on shared items [15]. Modeling influence between users in the absence of knowledge of topology structure has been done in [7]. To incorporate dynamic user interaction, [7] uses a Poisson process for modeling the influence of one user over the other where the influence has an exponential time decaying factor. They model the social influence as a combination of features extracted from the users' behavior and features associated with their interactions with items. Finally, GraphRec [4] is a state-of-the-art model that utilizes both the interaction network and social network to predict user interest. Our model, however, differs from GraphRec as we consider the temporal dynamics involved in predicting embeddings of users by taking interactions of users and the influence from social network.

Temporal Network Embedding. Several models have recently been developed that generate embeddings for the nodes in temporal networks where nodes are continuously added and links between nodes keep changing. Such models have been employed for recommendation task as well constituting the time-aware recommendation models where the nodes comprise of users and items. Continuous-Time Dynamic Network Embeddings (CTDNE) [10] generates embeddings using temporally evolving random walks, but it generates one final static embedding of the nodes. HTNE [16] is the state-of-the-art model for generating the embeddings of nodes in temporal networks. It utilizes Hawkes Process and attention mechanism to predict future interaction. They model the likelihood of interaction between two nodes using Hawkes process to capture the influence of their historical neighbors on each other. IACN, also models the temporally evolving network and generates embeddings to represent the feature of nodes that evolves with time. However, IACN considers both the interaction and social network for predicting embeddings of entities.

3   Notations, Definitions, and Preliminaries

Notations. Given m users and n items, we denote the temporal list of N observed interactions as $\mathcal{O} = \{o_j = (u_j, i_j, t_j, \boldsymbol{q}_j) \forall j \in N\}$, where $u_j \in \{1, \ldots, m\}, i_j \in \{1, \ldots, n\}, t_j \in \mathbb{R}^+$ and $\boldsymbol{q}_j \in \mathbb{R}^F$ represent the interaction features. For simplicity, we define $\mathcal{O}^u = \{o_j^u = (i_j, t_j, \boldsymbol{q}_j)\}$ as the ordered listed of all interactions related to user u, and $\mathcal{O}^i = \{o_j^i = (u_j, t_j, \boldsymbol{q}_j)\}$ as the ordered list of all interactions related to item i.

In addition, users are influenced by other users in the social network. When we arrange different user's interaction with items as a sequence according to ascending time, we can find which users influence other users to interact with the item. These users form local user neighborhood for the user in consideration. As the user interacts with more items, its neighborhood keeps evolving. We can formally define the local user neighborhood of a user as follows:

Definition 1. *Local user neighborhood. Given a temporal interaction network $G = <V, E; \mathcal{O}>$ representing the observed user-item interactions, the local user neighborhood, $\mathcal{N}_u(t)$ of a user u are all those users $v \in U$ which are associated with at least one item before u interacted with it. Mathematically, when an interaction $o_j = (u_j, i_j, t_j, \boldsymbol{q}_j)$ is observed the local user neighborhood is updated as, $\mathcal{N}_u(t_j) = \mathcal{N}_u(t_j^-) \cup \mathcal{U}^i(t_j^-)$, where $\mathcal{U}^i(t_j^-)$ is the set of user who interacted with item i before time t_j and $\mathcal{N}_u(t_j^-)$ is the local neighborhood of user u right before time t_j.*

4   Proposed Method

In this section, we introduce our proposed model, Influence-aware and Attention-based Co-evolutionary Network (IACN), see Fig. 2 for a visual depiction of the architecture. To model the evolution of embeddings, IACN employs two layers to model the embedding update caused by interaction and influence and one layer to integrate the embeddings obtained from the modeling layers.

Interaction Modeling Layer: The interaction modeling layer consists of two attention functions, one to update user embedding (ATT_U) and the other to update item embedding (ATT_I). When an interaction $o = (u, i, t, \mathbf{q})$ is observed, ATT_U (resp., ATT_I) updates the embedding of u (resp., i).

Influence Modeling Layer: The influence modeling layer uses the local user neighborhood for predicting user future interest. When one of local user neighbor interacts with an item, it triggers the user to interact with the item. This results in update of the user embedding. The degree of influence is determined by the relation between the users and the time elapsed since the interaction.

Fusion Layer: This layer predicts the user embedding at a future time since its last interaction by integrating both its interaction-based embedding and influence-based embedding.

4.1   Model Details

We will now describe each layer in IACN in detail.

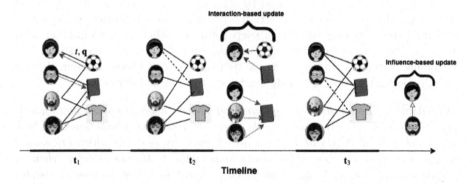

Fig. 2. Model Illustration: Temporal Interaction Network at different timestamps. Green dashed arrows and blue dashed arrows indicate the attention of items in computing user embedding and users in computing item embedding, respectively. Black dashed line refers to a new interaction and red arrow indicates the update in girl's embedding caused by an interaction by a user in her neighborhood at time t_3. (Color figure online)

Embedding Layer. We assign each user and item two embeddings: a static and a dynamic embedding. The static embedding encodes the long-term stationary properties while the dynamic embedding encodes the dynamic properties. This decision is made by following the setting in [8] such that static embeddings, for a user, u, $\bar{u} \in \mathbb{R}^m$ and item i, $\bar{i} \in \mathbb{R}^n$ represent the long-term properties of the entities. While dynamic embeddings $u(t) \in \mathbb{R}^d$ and $i(t) \in \mathbb{R}^d$ at time t, respectively model the time-varying behavior and features.

Interaction Modeling Layer. The interaction modeling layer updates the embedding of a user and an item when the user interacts with the item. In particular, when an interaction $o_j = (u_j, i_j, t_j, \mathbf{q}_j)$ is observed, the dynamic embedding of the involved user u and item i is updated. For simplicity of notations we drop the j subscript in the following section to represent static embeddings as $\bar{u}$ and $\bar{i}$ and dynamic embedding as $u(t)$ and $i(t)$.

To obtain interaction-based embedding of u and i, we consider their past interactions till time t $\mathcal{O}^u(t) = \{o_1^u, o_2^u, \ldots o_p^u\}$ such that $t_p \leq t$ and $\mathcal{O}^i(t) = \{o_1^i, o_2^i, \ldots o_q^i\}$ such that $t_q \leq t$, respectively. We use attention mechanism to compute the *importance* of past interactions in determining the updated embedding of u as:

$$e_k^u(t) = a(\mathbf{W}^i i_k(t_k^-), \mathbf{W}^u u(t^-)) + a(\mathbf{W}^q \mathbf{q}_k, \mathbf{W}^u u(t^-)) \tag{1}$$

where $i_k(t_k)$ represents the dynamic embedding of item occurring at kth interaction in $\mathcal{O}^u(t)$, t^- represents the time right before the time t, $\mathbf{W}^u, \mathbf{W}^i \in \mathbb{R}^{d \times d}$, $\mathbf{W}^q \in \mathbb{R}^{d \times F}$ are the weight matrices and d and F are the embedding size and the number of features associated with an interaction, respectively. The intuition is as follows, the first term computes importance of i's features at the time of interaction to predict u's future embedding. The second term introduces the level of contribution the interaction features have towards the evolution of u. In our experiments, we used a as the dot product between the two vectors (Fig. 3).

Having computed the attention coefficients, $e^u(t)$, corresponding to all historical interactions involving u, we compute the new embedding of u as:

$$u(t) = \sigma\left(\sum_{j, o_j \in \mathcal{O}^u(t)} \alpha_j^u(t) \mathbf{W}^i i_j(t_j)\right), \alpha_j^u(t) = \frac{exp(e_j^u(t))}{\sum_{k, o_k \in \mathcal{O}^u(t)} exp(e_k^u(t))}, \tag{2}$$

where σ is introduced for non-linearity. Here we have described an attention layer to update the embedding of user u. To update the embedding of i, we employ the same two operations with iteractions associated with the item.

Influence Modeling Layer. One of the major novelty of our method is that we introduce a time-varying self-attention based influence model for predicting user's future interest. The idea is to leverage the knowledge of evolution of a user's neighbors to predict future embedding of the user. Modeling neighborhood influence in temporal interaction network poses specific challenge as the influence

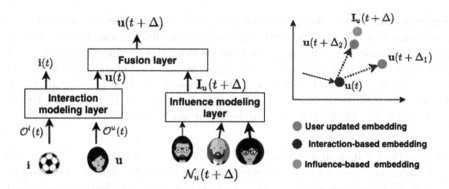

Fig. 3. The IACN model: After an interaction $(u, i, t, \mathbf{q})$, the dynamic embeddings of u and i are updated in the Interaction modeling layer. The Influence modeling layer predicts the user embedding at time $t+\Delta$, $\mathbf{u}(t+\Delta)$ by taking influence vector $\mathbf{I}_u(t+\Delta)$ into consideration. The figure on the right side shows how influence modeling layer updates user embedding. As more time elapses, $(\Delta_2 > \Delta_1)$, the user embedding tends to be closer to $\mathbf{I}_u(t)$.

of an interaction on a user is driven by both the relation between users and time elapsed since the interaction.

Our model captures the influence of u's local neighborhood on u's embedding by modeling a function that outputs a representation vector, influence embedding, $\mathbf{I}_u(t)$. This influence embedding is governed by an aggregation function parameterized by the temporal interaction sequence involving user neighborhood. Influence-based embedding at time $t + \Delta$ is computed as:

$$\mathbf{I}_u(t + \Delta) = \sum_{v \in \mathcal{N}_u(t) t < t_v < t+\Delta} \theta_{v,u} exp(-\delta_u(t + \Delta - t_v))\mathbf{v}(t_v), \qquad (3)$$

where $\theta_{v,u}$ models the influence user v has on u and $exp(-\delta_u(t+\Delta-t_v))$ models decay of the influence over time with user-specific parameter δ_u and $\mathcal{N}_u(t)$ is the local user neighborhood of u. To model the level of influence a user v has on the other u, we again utilize the attention mechanism, i.e.,

$$\theta_{v,u} = \begin{cases} a(\mathbf{W}_1^l \mathbf{v}(t_v), \mathbf{W}_2^l \mathbf{u}(t)) & \text{if } v \in \mathcal{N}_u(t), \\ 0 & \text{otherwise} \end{cases}, \qquad (4)$$

where $\mathbf{W}_1^l$ and $\mathbf{W}_2^l$ are the weight parameters of the attention mechanism. Due to peer engagement and affinity between users, θ is sparse as users tend to indulge in discussions with users of their community. For validating this, we computed the average length of local user neighborhood in 'Wikipedia' dataset (described in Sect. 5.1). We find that with 8227 users, the number of non-zero values in θ is 191,307. The average length of local user neighborhood is only 23.2.

Fusion Layer. To integrate the signals from interaction layer and influence layer, we introduce a fusion layer. This layer predicts embeddings of user at time t by taking into account the user embedding, the influence embedding, and the time elapsed since u's last interaction, Δ. The motivation behind constructing this layer is that a user interest keeps evolving even when it is not interacting with any item and as more time elapses the future embedding is farther from the user embedding. Furthermore, the interactions from the user local neighborhood influences the user interest which becomes more pronounced as more time elapses. To model this, we employ a kernel function such that the user embedding $u(t + \Delta)$ will continue to deterministically decay (at different rates for different users) from interaction-based embedding $u(t)$ towards influence-based embedding $I_u(t + \Delta)$. Thus, we extrapolate a user embedding at a future time as:

$$u(t + \Delta) = u(t) + (I_u(t + \Delta) - u(t))(1 - exp(-\beta_u \Delta)), \qquad (5)$$

where β_u is a parameter learned while training the model. On the interval $[t, t + \Delta)$, the u's embedding follows an exponential curve that begins at $u(t)$, when $\Delta \to 0$ and decays towards $I_u(t)$ (as $t \to \infty$, if extrapolated).

Recommendation Layer. Once we predict users' embeddings at time $t + \Delta$, we predict the embedding of the next item. For this we use the updated user embedding $u(t + \Delta)$ and the embedding of item that u last interacted with at time t, $i(t)$. The predicted item embedding is:

$$\hat{i}(t + \Delta) = W[u(t + \Delta), \bar{u}, i(t), \bar{i}] + B, \qquad (6)$$

where W is the weight matrix and B bias vector which make the linear layer. Then we recommend the items with the closest embedding with the predicted embedding. This step can be done in near-constant time by using LSH [5].

4.2   Network Training

We train our model to minimize the Euclidean distance between the predicted item embedding and the actual item embedding everytime a user interacts with an item. We calculate the total loss as,

$$\mathcal{L} = \sum_{(u,i,t,q) \in \mathcal{O}} ||\hat{i}(t) - [\bar{i}, i(t)]||_2 + \lambda_U ||u(t) - u(t^-)||_2 + \lambda_I ||i(t) - i(t^-)||_2,$$

where λ_U and λ_I are regularization parameters for temporal smoothness of user and item embeddings, respectively.

5   Experimental Settings

To comprehensively evaluate the performance of our proposed IACN model, we design different strategies to evaluate the effectiveness of the model. Our experiments are designed to answer the following research questions:

1. **RQ1:** How does IACN perform compared with other state-of-the-art recommendation models?
2. **RQ2:** What is the influence of various components in the IACN architecture?

Datasets. We used 4 public datasets and followed the same preprocessing steps as used in [8]. Thus, we selected 1000 most active items in each dataset.

- **Wikipedia dataset:** Public dataset consisting of one month of edits made on Wikipedia pages[1] obtained from [8]. This dataset contains 1000 items, 10,000 most active users, resulting in 672,447 interactions.
- **Reddit post dataset:** We processed reddit[2] forum dataset, which consists of one month of posts made by users. We first samples 1000 most active reddit post and the users who made at least 5 posts on the selected posts. This resulted in 13,840 users and a total of 121,258 interactions.
- **Yelp review dataset:** We obtained this dataset from the yelp dataset challenge[3]. We first selected top 1000 businesses with most number of reviews and users who made at least 5 reviews on the selected businesses. This resulted in 5325 users and 110,839 interactions.
- **StackOverFlow dataset:** We also gathered data from the popular question-answering website, StackOverFlow[4]. For this dataset also, we extracted users who made at least 5 posts. There are 4,125 users and 20,719 posts in this dataset.

These datasets, in addition to varying in size of users and density of interactions, also comprise of different users' behavior in terms of repetitive item consumption. In Wikipedia, Reddit, and StackOverFlow a user interacts with the same item consecutively in 79%, 77% and 62% interactions, respectively, while in Yelp it occurs only in 0.004% of interactions. Naturally, we expect that the Yelp dataset is the most challenging one to model.

Code available at https://github.com/shalini1194/IACN.

Metrics. We evaluate forum recommendation performance using the mean reciprocal rank (MRR) and recall@10. MRR is a standard ranking metric formulated as: $MRR = \frac{1}{\text{rank}_{pos}}$, where rank_{pos} denotes the rank of positive item. Recall@10 is the fraction of ground truth items ranked in the top 10 recommended items.

Comparison Approaches. To verify the performance gain of IACN, we compare its performance with various state-of-the-art models which can be categorized into four classes:

---

[1] https://meta.wikimedia.org/wiki/Data_dumps.
[2] http://files.pushshift.io/reddit/.
[3] https://www.kaggle.com/yelp-dataset/yelp-dataset.
[4] https://archive.org/details/stackexchange.

Table 1. Performance comparison on four datasets for all methods. The best and the second best results are highlighted by **boldface** and underlined respectively. Gain% denotes the performance improvement of IACN over the best baseline.

Methods	Wikipedia		Reddit		Yelp		StackOverFlow	
	MRR	Recall@10	MRR	Recall@10	MRR	Recall@10	MRR	Recall@10
LSTM [6]	0.329	0.455	0.205	0.251	0.007	0.009	0.014	0.017
RRN [14]	0.522	0.617	0.290	0.312	0.013	0.020	0.019	0.019
HTNE [16]	0.500	0.624	0.211	0.313	0.012	0.014	0.100	0.178
GrapRec [4]	0.634	0.823	0.621	0.815	0.006	0.009	0.012	0.041
DeepCo-evolve [3]	0.515	0.563	0.271	0.405	0.006	0.008	0.017	0.019
JODIE [8]	0.746	0.822	0.755	0.919	0.014	0.020	0.058	0.063
IACN	**0.796**	**0.861**	**0.869**	**0.922**	**0.015**	**0.026**	**0.106**	**0.280**
Gain %	6.702	4.617	15.099	0.326	7.143	30.000	6.000	57.303

1. RNN based models: This category comprises of RNN based models such as LSTM [6], RRN [14] among others. RNN uses only static embeddings to represent items and predicts users' embedding based on the items they have interacted with. RRN is widely used method and generates dynamic user and item embeddings based on the item and user interaction sequence independently. Both these models take one-hot vector of items as inputs.
2. Co-evolutionary models: These models update both user and item embedding when a user interacts with an item. We compare our model with JODIE [8] and Deep Co-evolve [3]. Both the models use RNN to learn representations of users and items. Deep-Coevolve uses the point process technique to predict the intensity of interaction between user and item, while JODIE uses Euclidean distance between the learned representation to predict the next item to recommend.
3. Temporal Network Embedding: Temporal Network Embedding models are used to generate embedding of nodes of a temporal network. HTNE [16] is a state-of-the-art model for temporal network embedding which integrates the Hawkes process into network embedding so as to capture the influence of historical neighbors on the current neighbors
4. Social Network: We compare our method with GraphRec [4] that combines the information from social network and interaction network to predict user embedding. However, it does not consider the temporal nature of the setting.

5.1 Performance Comparison (RQ1)

Table 1 compares the performance of IACN with the six state-of-the-art methods. We make the following observations from the results. IACN significantly outperforms all baselines in all datasets across both the metrics. GraphRec performs better than HTNE for Reddit and Wikipedia dataset. We believe that one of the reasons is the high volume of interactions in less timespan for these datasets. Due to this, the effect of time intervals between interactions is not observed here. HTNE models the impact of time intervals between interactions, which results in its better performance for Yelp and StackOverFlow compared to GraphRec. We find that for StackOverFlow dataset HTNE performs better than JODIE. This can be attributed to the idea that user-user affinity is more pronounced due to peer-engagement and depth of discussion on these platforms [11]. The fact that IACN outperforms co-evolutionary models confirms our hypothesis that it is important to consider both influence-based and interaction-based signals to predict embedding of user.

Table 2. Ablation analysis on four datasets.

Methods	Wikipedia		Reddit		Yelp		StackOverFlow	
	MRR	Recall@10	MRR	Recall@10	MRR	Recall@10	MRR	Recall@10
IACN - Influence	0.776	0.833	0.717	0.919	0.009	0.014	0.050	0.059
IACN-Attention+RNN	0.786	0.848	0.717	0.920	0.008	0.011	0.056	0.059
IACN-Fusion+LatentCross	0.612	0.776	0.702	0.918	0.011	0.018	0.072	0.012
IACN	0.796	0.861	0.869	0.922	0.015	0.026	0.106	0.280

5.2   Analysis of IACN (RQ2)

Table 2 shows the performance comparison of variation of IACN. We describe the variants and discuss the result drop caused by them:

IACN-Influence: Removing the influence modeling layer results in a co-evolutionary model with attention mechanism to update the embedding. We find that removing the influence modeling layer results in drop of IACN performance, revealing that it is useful to model the influence of other users on user interest evolution.

IACN-Attention+RNN: In this variant, we replace the attention in the interaction modeling layer with RNN. The drop in performance indicates that attention mechanism is better able to predict the embedding of user and item by adaptively assigning weights to the past interactions.

IACN-Fusion+LatentCross: In this variant of IACN, we replace our Fusion layer with LatentCross   [1]. Essentially, we take an element-wise product of user embedding $u(t)$ and the time context vector, $w_t = w * \Delta$, where, w is initialized by 0-mean Gaussian function and Δ is the elapsed time since user's last interaction. Then, we add the influence-based embedding to the resultant vector.

$$u(t + \Delta) = (1 + w_t) * u(t) + I_u(t + \Delta)$$

Using LatentCross instead of our fusion layer degrades performance of IACN showing that fusions layer is better then LatentCross.

6   Conclusion and Future Work

In this paper, we proposed a novel model to predict dynamic embedding of user and item which takes into account both reasons of evolution of user interest, namely, interaction with an item and influence from other users. IACN utilizes attention mechanism to update embedding of users and items when they interact. It also models the influence of activities by local user neighborhood on the user interest. For future work, instead of modeling the relation between each pair of users, one can model the group the users and use the embedding of local user group to predict the evolution of local neighborhood of user.

References

1. Beutel, A., et al.: Latent cross: making use of context in recurrent recommender systems. In: Proceedings of the Eleventh ACM International Conference on Web Search and Data Mining, pp. 46–54. ACM (2018)
2. Chen, C., Zhang, M., Liu, Y., Ma, S.: Social attentional memory network: modeling aspect-and friend-level differences in recommendation. In: Proceedings of the Twelfth ACM International Conference on Web Search and Data Mining, pp. 177–185. ACM (2019)
3. Dai, H., Wang, Y., Trivedi, R., Song, L.: Deep coevolutionary network: embedding user and item features for recommendation. arXiv preprint arXiv:1609.03675 (2016)
4. Fan, W., et al.: Graph neural networks for social recommendation. In: The World Wide Web Conference, pp. 417–426. ACM (2019)
5. Gionis, A., et al.: Similarity search in high dimensions via hashing
6. Hidasi, B., Karatzoglou, A., Baltrunas, L., Tikk, D.: Session-based recommendations with recurrent neural networks. arXiv preprint arXiv:1511.06939 (2015)
7. Iwata, T., Shah, A., Ghahramani, Z.: Discovering latent influence in online social activities via shared cascade Poisson processes. In: Proceedings of the 19th ACM SIGKDD International Conference on Knowledge Discovery and Data Mining, pp. 266–274. ACM (2013)
8. Kumar, S., Zhang, X., Leskovec, J.: Predicting dynamic embedding trajectory in temporal interaction networks. In: Proceedings of the 25th ACM SIGKDD International Conference on Knowledge Discovery & Data Mining, pp. 1269–1278 (2019)
9. Lu, Y., Dong, R., Smyth, B.: Coevolutionary recommendation model: mutual learning between ratings and reviews. In: Proceedings of the 2018 World Wide Web Conference, pp. 773–782 (2018)
10. Nguyen, G.H., Lee, J.B., Rossi, R.A., Ahmed, N.K., Koh, E., Kim, S.: Continuous-time dynamic network embeddings. In: Companion Proceedings of the The Web Conference 2018, pp. 969–976 (2018)
11. Paranjape, A., Benson, A.R., Leskovec, J.: Motifs in temporal networks. In: Proceedings of the Tenth ACM International Conference on Web Search and Data Mining, pp. 601–610 (2017)
12. Song, W., Xiao, Z., Wang, Y., Charlin, L., Zhang, M., Tang, J.: Session-based social recommendation via dynamic graph attention networks. In: Proceedings of the Twelfth ACM International Conference on Web Search and Data Mining, pp. 555–563. ACM (2019)

13. Vaswani, A., et al.: Attention is all you need. In: Advances in Neural Information Processing Systems, pp. 5998–6008 (2017)
14. Wu, C.Y., Ahmed, A., Beutel, A., Smola, A.J., Jing, H.: Recurrent recommender networks. In: Proceedings of the Tenth ACM International Conference on Web Search and Data Mining, pp. 495–503. ACM (2017)
15. Xia, M., Huang, Y., Duan, W., Whinston, A.B.: Ballot box communication in online communities. Commun. ACM **52**(9), 138–142 (2009)
16. Zuo, Y., Liu, G., Lin, H., Guo, J., Hu, X., Wu, J.: Embedding temporal network via neighborhood formation. In: Proceedings of the 24th ACM SIGKDD International Conference on Knowledge Discovery & Data Mining, pp. 2857–2866. ACM (2018)

Nonlinear Matrix Factorization via Neighbor Embedding

Xuan Li, Yunfeng Wu, and Li Zhang$^{(\boxtimes)}$

School of Software, Tsinghua University, Beijing 100084, China
{xuan-li15,wu-yf15}@mails.tsinghua.edu.cn, lizhang@tsinghua.edu.cn

Abstract. Matrix factorization plays a fundamental role in collaborative filtering. There are two basic disciplines among collaborative filtering approaches: neighborhood-based methods and latent factor models. Based on the neighbor-entity spatial relationships, neighborhood-based methods capture the local structure of the user-item rating matrix. Latent factor models capture the global structure of the matrix. Neither neighborhood-based methods nor latent factor models can capture both of them. The recently developed capsule network can capture the part-whole spatial relationships in the images. The basic matrix factorization model and its extensions are among the most successful latent factor models. Motivated by the need for capturing both the local structure and the global structure of the matrix, and inspired by the recently developed capsule network, we propose a new matrix factorization model called capsule matrix factorization, which attempts to capture the two structure of the matrix by propagating the neighbor-entity spatial relationships in the rating matrix into the latent factor vectors. Experimental results on real datasets demonstrate that the capsule matrix factorization model improves the basic matrix model in terms of recommendation accuracy greatly.

1 Introduction

Matrix factorization plays a basic role in collaborative filtering. Collaborative filtering is a common tool in recommender systems, which uncovers the patterns of the observed entries in the user-item rating matrix to approximate the unobserved entries. There are two basic strategies of collaborative filtering: neighborhood-based methods and latent factor models. With the assumption that similar users rate items similarly, or similar items are rated by users similarly, neighborhood-based methods are centering on capturing the neighbor-entity spatial relationships for users or, alternatively, items, which can capture the local structure of the rating matrix. With the assumption that there are only a small number of factors influencing the preferences, latent factor models map both users and items into a joint latent factor space, which can capture the global structure of the rating matrix. The basic matrix factorization model and

Supported by National Science and Technology Supporting Plan No. 2017YFC0804307.

© Springer Nature Switzerland AG 2021
K. Karlapalem et al. (Eds.): PAKDD 2021, LNAI 12713, pp. 575–587, 2021.
https://doi.org/10.1007/978-3-030-75765-6_46

its extensions are among the most successful latent factor models. However, neither neighborhood-based methods nor latent factor models can capture both the local structure and the global structure of the rating matrix [9]. It is important for better recommendation to capture both of them.

How to link neighborhood-based methods with latent factor models to capture both the local structure and the global structure of the rating matrix? A capsule is a group of neurons, which represents different properties of an entity. A capsule network consists of several layers. Each layer contains many capsules. Motivated by the need for routing between capsules in different layers, a dynamic routing algorithm is proposed in [21]: the higher-layer capsules can be represented by the weighed sum of many lower-layer capsules. The capsule network can capture part-whole spatial relationships in images. Therefore, the capsule architecture can be employed to link neighborhood-based methods to latent factor models.

In this paper, inspired by the capsule network (CapsNet) [21] and the ladder capsule network (L-CapsNet) [8], we propose a new matrix factorization model called **Capsule Matrix Factorization (CapsMF)**. Based on the neighbor-entity spatial relationships propagated into the latent factors, the CapsMF model improves the basic matrix factorization model through capturing both the local structure and the global structure of the matrix. Our contribution can be divided into the following three parts:

- We introduce the neighborhood layer and weight construction layer, and propose a modified dynamic routing algorithm. Based on these, our model can capture the neighbor-entity spatial relationships, which uncover the local structure of the user-item rating matrix.
- We introduce the propagation layer, which propagates the information of the local structure of the matrix into the latent factor vectors.
- Unlike the capsule network with reconstruction as a regularization, we incorporate the embedding cost function for latent factors into the basic matrix factorization model as a regularization, which makes that our model can capture both the local and the global structure of the user-item rating matrix.

Experimental results on real datasets show that CapsMF improves the basic matrix factorization model dramatically.

2   Related Work

2.1   Dynamic Routing of CapsNet

To compute the vector inputs and outputs of a capsule, a dynamic routing algorithm is proposed in [21], as shown in Algorithm 1.

Given the collection of output vectors of $\{u_i | i = 1, 2, ...N_l\}$ of capsule i in layer l. Let v_j be the output vector of capsule j in layer $(l+1)$. To construct v_j, the collection of prediction vectors $\{\hat{u}_{j|i} = W_{ij}u_i, i = 1, 2, ...N_l\}$ of capsule i in layer l are computed first, where W_{ij} is a transformation matrix that connects the capsule i in layer l to the capsule j in layer $(l+1)$. Let s_j be a weighted sum of prediction vectors $\{\hat{u}_{j|i} = W_{ij}u_i, i = 1,2,...N_l\}$: $s_j = \sum_i c_{ij}\hat{u}_{j|i}$, where c_{ij} is the weight coefficients between capsule i in layer l and capsule j in layer $(l+1)$, which is determined through Algorithm 1. The squashing function is applied to compute the vector output of capsule j in layer $l+1$: $l_j v_j = \dfrac{||s_j||^2}{||s_j||^2 + 1}\dfrac{s_j}{||s_j||}$, where $l_j = \dfrac{||s_j||^2}{||s_j||^2 + 1}$, $v_j = \dfrac{s_j}{||s_j||}$. The length of the vector output l_j represents the probability of existence of the entity represented by capsule j in the current layer.

Algorithm 1 . Dynamic Routing Algorithm

1: **for** all capsule i in layer l and capsule j in layer $(l+1)$: $b_{ij} = 0$
2: **for** iteration r **do**
3:    **for** all capsule i in l: $c_{ij} = \dfrac{exp(b_{ij})}{\sum_k exp(b_{ik})}$
4:    **for** all capsule j in $(l+1)$: $s_j = \sum_i c_{ij}\hat{u}_{j|i}$, $v_j = \dfrac{s_j}{||s_j||}$
5:    **for** all capsule i in layer l and capsule j in layer $(l+1)$: $b_{ij} = b_{ij} + l_j\hat{u}_{j|i} \cdot v_j$,
     where $l_j = \dfrac{||s_j||^2}{||s_j||^2 + 1}$
6: **end for**
7: **return** $l_j v_j$

Although the dynamic routing algorithm can capture the part-whole spatial relationships, too many unnecessary capsules in lower-level layer contribute to the constructions of the higher-level capsules [8]. Different from the dynamic routing algorithm in the CapsNet, L-CapsNet is proposed by introducing the pruning layer to remove irrelevant capsules and the ladder layer to capture the part-whole spatial relationships in images. It reconstructs the output of the lower-level capsules from the capsules in the higher-level layer with backpropagation from a loss function.

Our model introduces the neighborhood layer to search the nearest neighbors and uses the dynamic routing algorithm to capture the neighbor-entity spatial relationships in the rating matrix.

2.2 Collaborative Filtering

This paper develops a new architecture called capsule matrix factorization, which bridges the gap between the two primary areas of collaborative filtering: neighborhood methods and latent factor models.

There are two basic methods for neighborhood methods: user-based methods and item-based methods. We center on item-based methods, to which user-based methods are similar. Item-based methods rely on the ratings of similar items to approximate the unobserved ratings:

$$\hat{r}_{i,j} = \frac{\sum\limits_{k \in N_i(j)} w_{jk} r_{ik}}{\sum\limits_{j \in N_i(j)} |w_{jk}|} \tag{1}$$

where $N_i(j)$ represents the items that are the nearest neighbors of item j and rated by user i; r_{ij} is the rating given by user i on item j; w_{ij} represents the similarity between item i and item j. There are many ways to compute this similarity [16]. Item-based methods can capture the neighbor-entity spatial relationships for items.

Some of the most successful latent factor models are the basic matrix factorization model and its extension. With the assumption that the matrix is low-rank, the basic matrix factorization model factorizes the user-item rating matrix R into the user latent factor matrix $P = [p_1, p_2, ...p_M]$ and the item latent factor matrix $Q = [q_1, q_2, ...q_N]$: $R \approx PQ^T$. It uses the inner product of the latent factor vector of user i and the latent factor vector of item j to approximate the unobserved ratings:

$$\hat{r}_{ij} = p_i q_j^T. \tag{2}$$

Transforming users and items into a joint low-dimensional latent factor space is a challenging problem in collaborative filtering setting. There are too many unobserved ratings in the rating matrix. The result of factorizing the sparse matrix by the conventional SVD is undefined. Moreover, approximating the relatively few observed entries is highly prone to overfitting. The basic matrix factorization model [19] was proposed, which fits the observed rating directly and avoids overfitting through the regularizations

$$\min_{p^*, q^*} \sum_{(i,j) \in \mathcal{K}} [(r_{ij} - p_i q_j^T)^2 + \lambda(||p_i||^2 + ||q_j||^2)], \tag{3}$$

where $\mathcal{K}$ is the set of the (i, j) pairs that the rating on item j is given by user i in the training set. The magnitudes of latent factor vectors are penalized by regularization. The hyperparameter λ can be determined through cross-validation. The minimum problem can be solved by gradient descent methods. The basic matrix factorization model can uncover the global structure of the user-item rating matrix.

Adopting the advantages of both item-based methods and the basic matrix factorization model, the CapsMF model attempts to approximate the unobserved ratings by capturing both the local structure and the global structure of the rating matrix.

3   Capsule Matrix Factorization

As shown in Fig. 1, the CapsMF model consists of five components: input layer, neighborhood layer, weight construction layer, propagation layer, and embedding loss for latent factor.

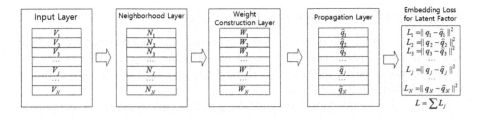

Fig. 1. Illustration of the CapsMF Layers.

3.1 Input Layer

In collaborative filtering, the observed ratings are very sparse. Given the user-item rating matrix R, we first construct the modified rating matrix X: $x_{ij} = r_{ij}$ if user i has rated item j, and 0 otherwise [16,17]. Note that $[R]_{ij} = r_{ij}$ and $[X]_{ij} = x_{ij}$. Subsequently, we construct item input matrix $V = [V_1, V_2, ..., V_N]$, where V_j is the jth column of X and represents the input vector of item j.

3.2 Neighborhood Layer

To capture the neighbor-entity spatial relationships in the item input matrix, we first need to find the neighborhood set for each item. Motivated by this need, we introduce the neighborhood layer, which uses the *BallTree* algorithm [18] to search nearest neighbors for items efficiently.

There are two basic ways to search nearest neighbors for each item: r-neighborhoods and K nearest neighbors [1]. According to r-neighborhoods, one can search all items k within the ball centered at item j of r radius, where $r \in R^+$. According to K nearest neighbors, one can search the K nearest neighbors k for item j. Although the r-neighborhoods approach has the geometric intuitions that the relationship between items is symmetric, the radius r is more difficult to determine than the neighbor number K. In this paper, we choose K nearest neighbors method to build the neighborhood set for each item.

One can search the K nearest neighbors for each user as measured by Cosine similarity or Euclidean distance. Empirically, Cosine similarity is better than Euclidean distance in collaborative filtering setting. We find the neighborhood set N_j for each item j as measured by Cosine similarity [16]. The similarity between two item j and item k can be calculated as

$$Cosine(j, k) = \frac{V_j V_k^T}{||V_j|| \cdot ||V_k||} = \frac{\sum\limits_{i \in I_{jk}} r_{ij} r_{ik}}{\sqrt{\sum\limits_{i \in I_j} r_{ij}^2 \sum\limits_{n \in I_k} r_{nk}^2}}. \tag{4}$$

where I_{jk} represents the users rating on both item j and item k, I_j denotes the users rating on item j, and I_k denotes the users rating on item k.

3.3   Weight Construction Layer

Based on the neighborhood set N_j found in the neighborhood layer for each item j, we introduce a new layer called weight construction layer, which captures the neighbor-entity spatial relationships through the dynamic routing algorithm as show in Algorithm 2.

The weight construction layer capsules j can be constructed as a linear combination of the selected capsules $k, k \in N_j$, from the neighborhood layer:

$$\hat{V}_j = \sum_{k \in N_j} w_{jk} V_k, \tag{5}$$

where N_j represents the neighborhood set produced from the neighborhood layer for the capsule j in the current layer, the weight coefficient w_{ik} determined by our routing algorithm represents the contribution to the construction of capsule j in current layer by the capsule k in the neighborhood layer, and V_k is the vector output of the capsule k in the neighborhood layer. The coupling coefficients w_{ik} between the weight construction layer capsule i and all the capsules k in the neighborhood layer sum to 1 and are calculated by a "routing softmax".

$$w_{jk} = \frac{exp(b_{jk})}{\sum\limits_{n \in N_j} exp(b_{jn})}, k \in N_j, otherwise, w_{jk} = 0 \tag{6}$$

where the initial logits b_{jk} represent the log prior probabilities that capsule k in the neighborhood layer should connect to capsule j in the weight construction layer. The initial weight coefficients are adjusted by measuring the agreement between capsule j in the weight construction layer and capsule k in the neighborhood layer iteratively. In this paper, we treat the Cosine distance, instead of Cosine similarity, between capsule j and capsule k as this agreement and add it to the initial logits b_{ik} before calculating the new values for all the weight coefficients connecting the neighbors represented by capsule k to the entity represented by capsule j. Experimental results demonstrate that Cosine distance $(1 - cos(\hat{V}_j, V_k))$ is more effective than Cosine similarity $cos(\hat{V}_j, V_k)$ which can be interpreted as the scaler product $\hat{V}_j \cdot V_k$ [21] when $||\hat{V}_j|| = 1$ and $||V_k|| = 1$.

The weight coefficient vector w_j returned by our routing algorithm capture the neighbor-entity spatial relationships in the item input matrix.

3.4   Propagation Layer

To propagate the neighbor-entity spatial relationships captured by weight coefficient vector w_j into the latent factor vectors, we introduce the propagation layer, which constructs the vector outputs $\hat{q}_j$ of the capsules j representing the latent factor vector for item j in the current layer by the weighted sum of the latent factor vectors q_k with the weight coefficient vector w_j:

$$\hat{q}_j = \sum_k w_{jk} q_k, \tag{7}$$

Algorithm 2 . Our Routing Algorithm

1: procedure UROUTING (V_k, t, l)

2: for all capsule k in layer l and capsule j in layer $(l + 1)$: $b_{jk} = 0$, where $k \in N_j$

3: for all capsule k in layer l and capsule j in layer $(l + 1)$: $w_{jk} = 0$

4: **for** t iterations **do**

5:    for all capsule k in layer l: $w_{jk} = \dfrac{exp(b_{jk})}{\sum\limits_{n \in N_j} exp(b_{jn})}$, where $k \in N_j$

6:    for all capsule j in $(l + 1)$: $\hat{V}_j = \sum\limits_k w_{jk} V_k$

7:    for all capsule k in layer l and capsule j in layer $(l+1)$: $b_{jk} = b_{jk} + (1 - cos(\hat{V}_j, V_k))$, where $k \in N_j$

8: **end for**

9: **return** w_j

---

where the vector outputs $\hat{q}_j$ contain the neighbor-entity spatial relationships in the item input matrix.

3.5 Embedding Loss for Latent Factor

Like the margin loss for classification[2, 4], we use a separate embedding loss, L_j for each item latent factor capsule j:

$$L_j = ||\hat{q}_j - q_j||^2, \tag{8}$$

where q_j is the latent factor vector for item j, and the vector output $\hat{q}_j$ of the propagation layer capsule j.

To capture both the local structure and the global structure of the rating matrix, the CapsMF model adds the embedding cost function for latent factors, $L = \sum_j L_j$, as regularization to the basic matrix factorization model to encourage the item latent factor vectors to preserve the neighborhood embedding of the matrix:

$$\min_{p^*, q^*} \sum_{(i,j) \in \mathcal{K}} (r_{ij} - p_i q_j^T)^2 + \lambda(||p_i||^2 + ||q_j||^2) + \lambda_I L \tag{9}$$

where $\mathcal{K}$ is the set of the (i, j) pairs that the rating on item j is given by user i in the training set.

4   Experiment

We conduct experiments on real-world recommendation systems data to evaluate the performance of CapsMF. We first compare the recommendation accuracy of CapsMF with the state-of-the-art methods. Then we analyze the sensitivity of our model from three aspects:the number of routing iterations, the neighborhood size and the latent factor rank.

4.1 Experiment Setup

We investigate our model on three popular datasets: MovieLens 100K, 1M and 10M. All of the three datasets are obtained from the MovieLens[1] research project which contains 10^5, 10^6 and 10^7 rating observations respectively. We treat ML-100K and ML-1M as smaller datasets and ML-10M as the larger dataset. We then split the data into random 9:1 train-test sets on ML-1M and ML-10M and 8:2 train-test sets on ML-100K for the fair comparison. For each of the three datasets, 5% of the training set are held out for validation.

We adopt the most popular metric—Root Mean Square Error (RMSE) to measure the quality of rating prediction in recommendation, which is defined as:

$$RMSE = \sqrt{\frac{\sum_{i=1}^{T}(r_i - \hat{r}_i)^2}{T}} \tag{10}$$

where r_i is the true rating, $\hat{r}_i$ is the predicted one and T is the total number of observed ratings in test set. All the results are reported by the average of RMSE over 5 different random splits.

We compare our model on the two small datasets with the following baseline methods: 1) RSVD [19]: a basic matrix factorization model [10]; 2) NNMF [6]: captures the interactions between users and items by multi-layer feed-forward neural network instead of inner product; 3) CF-NADE [24]: a neural autoregressive architecture which is inspired by the Neural Autoregressive Distribution Estimator (NADE); 4) GC-MC [2]: a graph auto-encoder framework based on a bipartite user-item graph; 5) Factorized-EAE [7]: a deep learning method; 6) STAR-GCN [23]: a stacked and reconstructed graph convolutional networks.

For the ML-10M dataset, we compare with all the newly proposed methods mentioned and two fundamental matrix factorization model in [20]: 1) LLORMA [11]: assumes the matrix is locally of low-rank; 2) WEMAREC [5]: a weighted and ensemble matrix approximation method for accurate and scalable recommendation; 3) MPMA [3]: a mixture models by weighting different base models across different user/items; 4) SMA [15]: a stable matrix approximation that can achieve better generalization performance; 5) GLOMA [4]: employs clustering techniques to capture global associations and local associations among users or items; 6) ERMMA [14]: gets better tradeoff between generalization error and optimization error; 7) AdaError [13]: an adaptive learning rate method by the proper learning rates; 8) MRMA [12]: a mixture of low-rank matrix approximation models with different ranks; 9) SGD MF [20]: same method as RSVD; 10) Bayesian MF [20]: same method as BPMF [22].

We implement our CapsMF model with TensorFlow. The models are trained by mini-batch gradient decent method with learning rate $lr = 0.001$. The training batch size is fixed to be 10K for ML-100K, 20K for ML-1M and ML-10M. The L_2 regularization parameter is set to 0.05 for ML-100K and 0.02 for ML-1M and ML-10M. The embedding regularization parameter is set to 5, 1, 0.1 respectively on 100K, 1M and 10M datasets.

Table 1. Performance comparison between CapsMF and six matrix approximation-based methods on two small datasets. Following NNMF, the number of latent factors is set to 60. In the neighborhood layer, the proposed CapsMF use 15 nearest neighbors by default. In the weight construction layer, the number of routing iterations is set to 5.

Method	ML-100K	ML-1M
RSVD	0.916	0.841
NNMF*	0.907	0.843
CF-NADE*	–	0.829
GC-MC*	0.910	0.832
Factorized EAE*	0.910	0.860
STAR-GCN*	0.895	0.832
CapsMF	**0.890**	**0.827**

*Taken from [23].

Table 2. Performance comparison between CapsMF and 11 matrix approximation-based methods on ML-10M dataset. Following SGD MF, the number of latent factors is set to 512. We set $K = 10$ and $T = 4$.

Method	RMSE
LLORMA	0.7815
WEMAREC	$0.7769_{\pm 0.0004}$
MPMA	$0.7712_{\pm 0.0002}$
STAR-GCN	0.777
SMA	$0.7682_{\pm 0.0003}$
GLOMA	$0.7672_{\pm 0.0001}$
ERMMA	$0.7670_{\pm 0.0007}$
AdaError	$0.7644_{\pm 0.0003}$
MRMA	$0.7634_{\pm 0.0009}$
SGD MF*	0.7720
Bayesian MF*	0.7633
CapsMF	$\mathbf{0.7627}_{\pm 0.0007}$

*Taken from [20].

4.2 Rate Prediction Accuracy

The rating prediction accuracy measured by RMSE on small and large datasets are reported in Table 1 and 2 respectively. The best results are highlighted in boldface. Except RSVD and the marked ones, other baseline results are all taken from the original papers.

We have the following observations: First, CapsMF improves the performance of RSVD by 2.8%, 1.7% and 1.2% on ML-100K, ML-1M and ML-10M. It shows that putting the neighbor-entity spatial relationships captured by capsules into

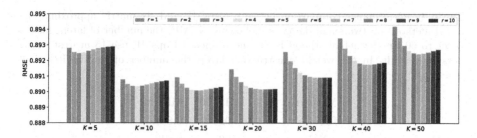

Fig. 2. Impact of neighborhood size for each routing iteration on ML-100K.

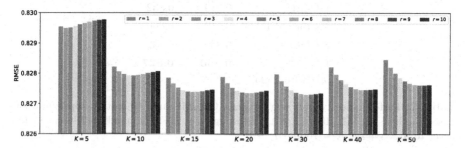

Fig. 3. Impact of neighborhood size for each routing iteration on ML-1M.

latent factors can improve the rating prediction accuracy of the basic matrix factorization model. Second, CapsMF outperforms all the state-of-the-art methods on all three datasets. Unlike the ensemble models like LLORMA or WEMAREC, our model is a single model that can achieve best performance. It has the room to improve when applying ensemble techniques to it. Third, SGD MF and Bayesian MF is newly reran by [20]. It shows that the basic matrix factorization has excellent performance. Our method adds the neighborhood regularization and then get more excellent results.

4.3 Parameter Analysis

In this set of experiments, we first evaluate the impact of three importance parameters: the neighborhood size K, the latent factor rank r, the number of maximum routing iterations T. Then, we compare the performance of cosine similarity and cosine distance as we mentioned in Sect. 3.3.

We first conduct experiments on varying the neighborhood size and keep records of each routing iteration. Figure 2 and 3 plot the RMSE of the CapsMF by varying the neighborhood size $K \in \{5, 10, 15, 20, 30, 40, 50\}$ for each routing iteration (up to 10) on ML-100K and ML-1M respectively.

The following observations can be seen from these figures: First, the neighborhood size K has a significant impact on the model. It should not be too small or too large and can get the best results when it is set to around 20–30. It can be explained that keeping smaller number of neighbors may lose some relevancy information while larger number can introduce noise information that harms the performance of matrix factorization. Second, the number of routing iterations has different impact on different datasets when the neighborhood size K is different. When K is set to be small, more routing iterations do not work on ML-100K and ML-1M. With K increasing, more routing iterations can improve the prediction quality. When K exceeds certain numbers such as 5 on ML-100k, it will in turn harm the prediction performance. This observation is similar to [21].

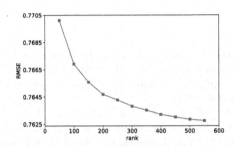

Fig. 4. mpact of latent rank on ML-10M.

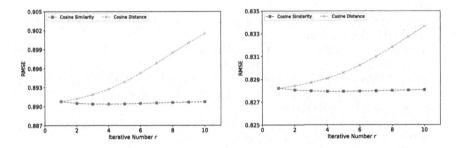

Fig. 5. Performance of cosine similarity vs cosine distance on ML-100K and ML-1M.

We then conduct experiments by varying latent factor rank r on ML-10M. The parameters are set as follows: $K = 10$ and $T = 1$. Results with rank varying in $\{50, 100, 150, 200, 250, 300, 350, 400, 450, 500, 550\}$ are shown in Fig. 4. As we can see from it, latent factor rank r has significantly impact on the performance of rating prediction. Larger r leads to better RMSE results. However, time consuming will increase at the same time. It is a tradeoff to determine the right rank between the time complexity and result accuracy.

Lastly, we compare the performance of Cosine Similarity and Cosine Distance in the weight construction layer. The parameters are set as follows: $K = 10$ and $T = 1$. Figure 5 shows that Cosine Distance outperforms Cosine Similarity on two datasets. With the iterative number increasing, the RMSE of Cosine Similarity increases gradually and forms a growing gap with Cosine Distance.

5   Conclusion

In this paper, we propose a novel matrix factorization model called Capsule Matrix Factorization (CapsMF), which is inspired by the recently developed capsule network. It can capture the very localized structure of a original rating matrix based on the neighbor-entity spatial relationships propagated into the latent factors. Experimental results confirm that CapsMF can indeed achieve better performance than such newly proposed clustering-based CF methods.

References

1. Belkin, M., Niyogi, P.: Laplacian eigenmaps for dimensionality reduction and data representation. Neural Comput. **15**, 1373–1396 (2002)
2. van den Berg, R., Kipf, T.N., Welling, M.: Graph convolutional matrix completion. arXiv abs/1706.02263 (2017)
3. Chen, C., Li, D., Lv, Q., Yan, J., Chu, S.M., Shang, L.: MPMA: mixture probabilistic matrix approximation for collaborative filtering. In: IJCAI (2016)
4. Chen, C., Li, D., Lv, Q., Yan, J., Shang, L., Chu, S.M.: GLOMA: embedding global information in local matrix approximation models for collaborative filtering. In: AAAI (2017)
5. Chen, C., Li, D., Zhao, Y., Lv, Q., Shang, L.: WEMAREC: accurate and scalable recommendation through weighted and ensemble matrix approximation. In: SIGIR (2015)
6. Dziugaite, G.K., Roy, D.M.: Neural network matrix factorization. arXiv preprint arXiv:1511.06443 (2015)
7. Hartford, J.S., Graham, D.R., Leyton-Brown, K., Ravanbakhsh, S.: Deep models of interactions across sets. In: ICML (2018)
8. Jeong, T., Lee, Y., Kim, H.: Ladder capsule network. In: ICML (2019)
9. Koren, Y.: Factorization meets the neighborhood: a multifaceted collaborative filtering model. In: KDD (2008)
10. Koren, Y., Bell, R., Volinsky, C.: Matrix factorization techniques for recommender systems. Computer **42**(8), 30–37 (2009)
11. Lee, J., Kim, S., Lebanon, G., Singer, Y.: Local low-rank matrix approximation. In: International Conference on Machine Learning, pp. 82–90 (2013)
12. sheng Li, D., Chen, C., Liu, W., Lu, T., Gu, N., Chu, S.M.: Mixture-rank matrix approximation for collaborative filtering. In: NIPS (2017)
13. sheng Li, D., et al.: AdaError: an adaptive learning rate method for matrix approximation-based collaborative filtering. In: WWW (2018)
14. sheng Li, D., Chen, C., Lv, Q., Shang, L., Chu, S.M., Zha, H.: ERMMA: expected risk minimization for matrix approximation-based recommender systems. In: AAAI (2017)
15. sheng Li, D., Chen, C., Lv, Q., Yan, J., Shang, L., Chu, S.M.: Low-rank matrix approximation with stability. In: ICML (2016)
16. Ning, X., Desrosiers, C., Karypis, G.: A comprehensive survey of neighborhood-based recommendation methods. In: Recommender Systems Handbook (2015)
17. Ning, X., Karypis, G.: SLIM: sparse linear methods for top-n recommender systems. In: 2011 IEEE 11th International Conference on Data Mining, pp. 497–506 (2011)

18. Omohundro, S.M.: Five balltree construction algorithms (1989)
19. Paterek, A.: Improving regularized singular value decomposition for collaborative filtering (2007)
20. Rendle, S., Zhang, L., Koren, Y.: On the difficulty of evaluating baselines: a study on recommender systems. arXiv abs/1905.01395 (2019)
21. Sabour, S., Frosst, N., Hinton, G.E.: Dynamic routing between capsules. arXiv abs/1710.09829 (2017)
22. Salakhutdinov, R., Mnih, A.: Bayesian probabilistic matrix factorization using Markov chain Monte Carlo. In: ICML 2008 (2008)
23. Zhang, J., Shi, X., Zhao, S., King, I.: STAR-GCN: stacked and reconstructed graph convolutional networks for recommender systems. In: Proceedings of the Twenty-Eighth International Joint Conference on Artificial Intelligence, IJCAI 2019, Macao, China, 10–16 August 2019 (2019)
24. Zheng, Y., Tang, B., Ding, W., Zhou, H.: A neural autoregressive approach to collaborative filtering. In: Proceedings of the 33nd International Conference on Machine Learning, ICML (2016)

Deconfounding Representation Learning Based on User Interactions in Recommendation Systems

Junruo Gao[1,2], Mengyue Yang[3], Yuyang Liu[1,2], and Jun Li[1,2(✉)]

[1] Computer Network Information Center, Chinese Academy of Sciences,
Beijing 100190, China
{gaojunruo,liuyuyang}@cnic.cn
[2] University of Chinese Academy of Sciences, Beijing 100049, China
jlee@cstnet.cn
[3] University College London, London, UK
mengyue.yang.20@ucl.ac.uk

Abstract. Representation learning provides an attractive solution to capture users' real intents by modeling user interactions in recommendation systems. However, there exist influencing factors called confounders in the process of user interactions. Most traditional methods might ignore these confounders, resulting in learning inaccurate users' intents. To address the issue, we take a new perspective to develop a deconfounding representation learning model named DRL. Concretely, we infer the unobserved confounders existing in the user-item interactions with an inference network. Then we leverage a generative network to generate users' personalized intents that contain no unobserved confounders. In order to learn comprehensive users' intents, we model the user-user interactions by adopting state-of-the-art GNN with a new aggregating strategy. Thus, the users' real intents we learn not only have their own personalized information but also imply the influence of their friends. The results of two real-world experiments demonstrate that our model can learn accurate and comprehensive representations.

Keywords: Representation learning · Causal inference · Graph neural networks

1 Introduction

Due to the rapid development of online services, including E-commerce platforms, online news, and social media sites, recommendation systems are widely used to facilitate the decision-making process and boost business [1]. For an efficient recommendation system, it is vital to mine users' real intents, and in turn to enhance user experience.

With the prevalence of representation learning, researchers pay attention to modeling user interactions that can reflect users' intents [2,3]. Due to the ability

© Springer Nature Switzerland AG 2021
K. Karlapalem et al. (Eds.): PAKDD 2021, LNAI 12713, pp. 588–599, 2021.
https://doi.org/10.1007/978-3-030-75765-6_47

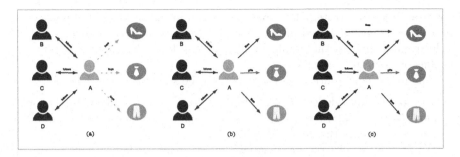

Fig. 1. Examples of buying behavior. The dotted lines demonstrate 'unkown' and the solid lines demonstrate 'known'. (a) buying behavior with confounders. (b) buying behavior without unobserved confounders. (c) buying behavior influenced by observed social influence

of modeling complex interactions of users, deep learning methods [4,5] allow incorporating more information into the learning process and generate more effective and expressive representations. Recently, graph-based approaches [6–8] achieve great success in recommendation systems, which can further model user interactions on the graph. The above methods have made substantial advances in representation learning for recommendation systems.

However, most of these methods fail to learn users' real intents because there exist observable and unobservable confounders that are behind user-item interactions when considering the concept of causality, which will lead Simpson's Paradox [9] and mislead model inference. For example, consider the example in Fig. 1(b) where we refer to the "follows" behaviors as the user-user interactions and the "buys" behaviors as user-item interactions. We can see that user A buys a Men's tie. Maybe she likes it or she just wants to give it to her new neighbor as a gift. We have no idea about the situation she is in when buying it, so we can not figure out user A's real intents. Such hidden factors are considered as unobserved confounders, which will influence user A's intent. Additionally, users' intents are also easily influenced by other users. This influence often happens among user-user interactions, such as social relationship. As Fig. 1(c) shows, user B is user A's friend, and thus, user B tends to buy the same high heels as user A does.

To this end, in order to capture users' real intents, we propose a deconfounding representation learning method(DGL) which can not only model user-item interactions and user-user interactions but also take into account the confounders among these interactions. Firstly, we take advantage of an inference network to infer the unobserved confounders behind the user-item interactions and identify the causal model. Based on the identified causal relationship between users and items, we design a generative network to generate users' personalized intents representations. Then, we will use the graph neural network (GNN) [10] to model the observed user-user interactions (manifested as "follows" interactions), which will help us to capture social influence on users' intents. Additionally, we propose a new aggregating strategy for GNN, which can incorporate social influence and prevent users' personalized intents from being indistinguishable because of the influence diffusion on the graph. Finally, we can learn deconfounding representations of users' real intents.

The major contributions of the paper can be summarized as follows:

- To our best knowledge, we are the first to consider the confounders when modeling user interactions. We not only infer the unobserved confounders but also consider the observed confounders.
- We propose a new random aggregating strategy for GNN, which can capture social influence on users meanwhile avoiding users' personal intents from converging to the same to a certain extent.
- We conduct empirical studies on two real-world datasets. And ablation studies are designed to demonstrate the effectiveness of our model.

2   Related Work

Unobserved Confounders Inference. Traditional causal inference requires strong assumptions, one of which is that all data is observable. However, there exist unobserved confounders that affect both the causes and the effect inevitably [11]. In order to infer the unobserved confounders, many notable methods have been proposed. In [12], Rajesh et al. develop an estimator to estimate the unobserved confounders, which works via information-based regularization and cross-validation. Mooij et al. [13] explicitly treat the "noise" as unobserved causes and depict it as a latent variable. They propose a Bayesian approach that can be used for inferring the latent variable. Louizos et al. [14] use variational autoencoders to infer unobserved confounders, and achieve great success. We will take advantage of this idea to infer the unobserved confounders behind the user-item interactions.

Graph-Based Recommendation. Generally speaking, graph-based methods for recommendation systems can achieve better performance than traditional methods, because they can incorporate both the topological structures of graph and node information into the learning process, which can alleviate the sparsity issue and learn rich representations. For example, GCMC [8] is a new attempt to complete the user-item rating matrix, which considers both side information and graph structure. Pinsage [7] is an inductive learning method based on GraphSAGE [15], which can be generalized to unseen nodes. Wu et al. [16] and Wang et al. [6] consider social influence between users, while they ignore the unobserved confounders behind user-item interactions, which may aggregate inaccurate users' intents representations during the propagation.

3   Method

3.1   Problem Formulation

We first build a heterogeneous graph $\mathcal{G} = \{\mathcal{V}, \mathcal{E}\}$ to describe user interactions in recommendation systems, where Nodes $\mathcal{V}$ are composed of users u and items i.

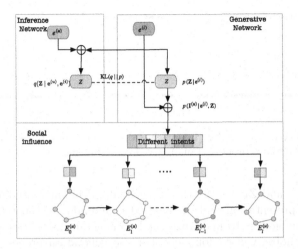

Fig. 2. The architecture of DGL. It contains three parts including Inference Network, Generative Network and Social Influence Model

Edge $\mathcal{E}$ represent all the interactions of users, including user-item interactions and user-user interactions. We denote the user and item attribute features by $\mathbf{e}^{(u)} \in \mathbb{R}^{D_1}$ and $\mathbf{e}^{(i)} \in \mathbb{R}^{D_2}$ correspondingly. The k-th user-item interaction can be represented as a tuple $S_k = (u_a, i_m)$, where $k \in \{1, 2, \cdots, K\}$, and K is the total number of interactions between users and interacted items. Our goal is to learn deconfounding representations $E^{(u)}$ of users' intents by considering the confounders existing in the process of user interactions. The architecture of the learning process is shown as Fig. 2. Analogously, the learning process of item representations $E^{(i)}$ is related to the users who have bought them. We won't introduce this part specifically.

3.2 User Intent Representation Generating

Unobserved Confounders Behind User-Item Interactions. The causal relationship between users and interacted items is formulated as a directed acyclic graph (DAG). In order to estimate the causal effect of interacted items on users' intents representations, we apply the rule of do-calculus [9] to the DAG, which can be considered as 'intervention'. In our case, buying behavior can be considered as an intervention on items, which will influence the generation of users' intents representations. Moreover, the unobserved confounders $\mathbf{Z}$ influence both the interacted items and users' intents representations generation process simultaneously, shown as Fig. 3(a). Pearl's back-door criterion [9] is introduced to identify the effect of interventions:

$$P(\mathbf{I}^{(u)} \mid do(\mathbf{e}^{(i)})) = \sum_{\mathbf{Z}_k} p_\theta(\mathbf{I}_k^{(u)} \mid \mathbf{e}_k^{(i)}, \mathbf{Z}_k) p_\theta(\mathbf{Z}_k \mid \mathbf{e}_k^{(i)}) \tag{1}$$

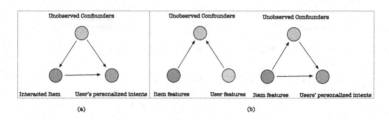

Fig. 3. Unobserved confounders inference. (a). causal model of user and interacted item. (b). the inference process of unobserved confounders.

where $\mathbf{I}_k^{(u)}$, $\mathbf{e}_k^{(i)}$ and $\mathbf{Z}_k$ are the user's personalized intent representation, interacted item representation and unobserved confounder in the k-th interaction separately. Our goal is to maximize Eq. 1 to generate users' intents $\mathbf{I}^{(u)}$ under the inferred unobserved confounders. For the generation process, we are supposed to sample $\mathbf{Z}$ from the prior network $p_\theta(\mathbf{Z} \mid \mathbf{e}^{(i)})$ and then generate users' intents representations through the generation network $p_\theta\left(\mathbf{I}^{(u)} \mid \mathbf{e}^{(i)}, \mathbf{Z}\right)$.

However, there exists an intractable marginalization over the unobserved confounders $\mathbf{Z}$. In order to infer unobserved confounders $\mathbf{Z}$, we resort to CVAE model [17] which can parametrize the causal effect as a latent variable model with neural net functions conditioned on observed information, like attribute features and buying behavior. The prior network is an approximate Gaussian with a mean and a diagonal covariance, written as:

$$p_\theta(\mathbf{Z} \mid \mathbf{e}^{(i)}) \sim \mathcal{N}\left(\mu = \hat{\mu}_0, \sigma^2 = \hat{\sigma}_0\right) \tag{2}$$

We model $\hat{\mu}_0$ and $\hat{\sigma}_0$ with neural networks of item attribute features. The variational parameter of neural networks is θ. We refer to posterior $q_\phi(\mathbf{Z} \mid \mathbf{e}^{(u)}, \mathbf{e}^{(i)})$ as an inference network which is dependent on the observed user and item attribute features. The variational approximate posterior q_ϕ is also assumed to follow multivariate Gaussian distribution with a mean and a diagonal covariance structure:

$$q_\phi\left(\mathbf{Z} \mid \mathbf{e}^{(i)}, \mathbf{e}^{(u)}\right) = \mathcal{N}\left(\mu = \hat{\mu}_1, \sigma^2 = \hat{\sigma}_1\right) \tag{3}$$

where $\hat{\mu}_1$ and $\hat{\sigma}_1$ can be modeled by neural networks with variational parameter ϕ. Finally, we can rewrite the objective function for the inference and generation networks which is also called variational lower bound:

$$\log P(\mathbf{I}^{(u)} | \mathbf{e}^{(i)}) \geq \mathcal{L}_{user}\left(\mathbf{e}^{(i)}, \mathbf{e}^{(u)}; \theta, \phi\right)$$
$$= \mathbb{E}_{q_\phi(\mathbf{z} | \mathbf{e}^{(i)}, \mathbf{e}^{(u)})}\left[\log p_\theta\left(\mathbf{I}^{(u)} | \mathbf{e}^{(i)}, \mathbf{Z}\right)\right] \tag{4}$$
$$- \mathrm{KL}\left(q_\phi\left(\mathbf{Z} | \mathbf{e}^{(u)}, \mathbf{e}^{(i)}\right) \| p_\theta\left(\mathbf{Z} | \mathbf{e}^{(i)}\right)\right)$$

where the first term is a reconstruction term and the KL-divergence term can be considered as a penalty term that ensures approximated density is close to the prior density. By maximizing Eq. 4, we can infer the unobserved confounders and generate users' personalized intents representations.

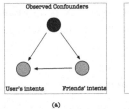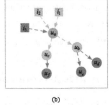

Fig. 4. observed social influence modeling. (a). causal model of user and friends. (b). aggregating and propagating information on the graph.

Observed Confounders Between User-User Interactions. In this subsection, we will consider the observed confounders between user-user interactions, aiming to generate users' real intents representations. We know that users' buying decisions will be easily influenced by their friends (such as mentioned in Section.1). In order to model such influence between users, we appeal to the Graph Neural Network [10] which can learn node representations as well as preserve the structural information of the graph. Traditional Graph Neural networks commonly aggregate and deliver the same information to different neighbors, which may make all the nodes on the graph indistinguishable. In our case, we would like to aggregate various personalized intents for each user randomly and generate various node representations for each user. Then, users can deliver different information to different neighbors, such as Fig. 4(b) shown. Suppose that we have generated user a's personalized intents representations $\{\mathbf{I}_{a,1}^{(u)}, \mathbf{I}_{a,2}^{(u)} \cdots\}$ conditioned on her interacted items. We then choose j of them randomly to aggregate during every layer-wise propagation. The intents representations of user a delivering to her l-th order neighbors can be written as follows:

$$Q_a^l = \text{AGGREGATE}\{rand_j(\mathbf{I}_{a,1}^{(u)}, \mathbf{I}_{a,2}^{(u)}, \cdots)\} \tag{5}$$

where AGGREGATE can be add or concatenation operation. Different personalized intents of user a will be delivered to her different-order neighbors during the layer-wise propagation. In the 0-th layer, the representation of user a is initialized by her personalized intents:

$$H_a^0 = Q_a^0 \tag{6}$$

During the propagation process, neighbors' intents will be aggregated as this process iterates. We denote user a's neighbors by set $\mathcal{N}_a^{(u)}$. The aggregation of neighbors' intents in the $l - 1$-th layer can be formulated as:

$$\mathbf{H}_{\mathcal{N}_a^{(u)}}^{(l-1)} = \text{MEAN}\left(\mathbf{H}_n^{(l-1)}, \forall n \in \mathcal{N}_a^{(u)}\right) \tag{7}$$

where MEAN refers to mean operation on neighbors' influence. Then we would like to combine neighbors' influence with user a's intents. We can obtain user a's representation in the l-th layer, as follows:

$$\mathbf{H}_a^{(l)} = \mathbf{f}\left(\mathbf{W} \cdot \left[\mathbf{H}_{\mathcal{N}_a^{(u)}}^{l-1}; \mathbf{Q}_a^l\right]\right) \tag{8}$$

where $\mathbf{f}$ is an activate function, such as RELU, $\mathbf{W}$ is a weight matrix, $[;]$ signifies concatenation. The representation of user a in the last layer is considered as the user a's real intent representation $\mathbf{E}_a^{(u)}$.

3.3   Item Representation Generating

Item Representation Inference. For an item, we would like to explore which kind of users prefer to buy it. Hence, we also need to identify the relationship between users and interacted items and infer the unobserved confounders behind every pair of user-item interaction by using an inference network. Similar to the learning process of users' personalized representations, we can learn item representations $\mathbf{I}^{(i)}$ for each user-item interaction by maximizing EBLO:

$$\log P(\mathbf{I}^{(i)}|\mathbf{e}^{(u)}) \geq \mathcal{L}_{item}\left(\mathbf{e}^{(u)}, \mathbf{e}^{(i)}; \eta, \gamma\right)$$
$$= \mathbb{E}_{q_\gamma\left(\mathbf{z}|\mathbf{e}^{(u)},\mathbf{e}^{(i)}\right)}\left[\log p_\eta\left(\mathbf{I}^{(i)}|\mathbf{e}^{(u)}, \mathbf{Z}\right)\right] \qquad (9)$$
$$- \mathrm{KL}\left(q_\gamma\left(\mathbf{Z}|\mathbf{e}^{(u)}, \mathbf{e}^{(i)}\right) \| p_\eta\left(\mathbf{Z}|\mathbf{e}^{(u)}\right)\right)$$

where p_η and q_γ are neural networks with variational parameter η and γ respectively.

Item Representation Aggregation. We denote the item m's representation after the k-th interaction by $\mathbf{I}_{m,k}^{(i)}$. We aggregate all the representations that are generated for item m. The the final representation of item m can be written as:

$$\mathbf{E}_m^{(i)} = \mathrm{AGGREGATE}\{\mathbf{I}_{m,1}^{(i)}, \cdots, \mathbf{I}_{m,k}^{(i)}, \cdots\} \qquad (10)$$

3.4   Learning Strategy

By considering the unobserved and observed confounders when modeling user interactions, we obtain the deconfounding representations for users and items. The deconfounding user representations contain user intents behind every interaction and the deconfounding item representations indicate that which kind of user prefer to buy them. We can then predict the preference score for a pair of user and item. The predicted rating is measured by the inner product between representations of user a and item m, which can be written as follows:

$$\hat{r}_{a,m} = \mathbf{E}_a^{(u)\top} \mathbf{E}_m^{(i)} \qquad (11)$$

Finally, similar to most ranking based methods [18,19], we use pair-wise loss function for optimization. The loss function of recommendation is designed as follows:

$$\mathcal{L}_{pair} = -\sum_{a=1}^{N} \sum_{m \in \mathcal{M}_a} \sum_{n \notin \mathcal{M}_a} \ln \sigma\left(\hat{r}_{a,m} - \hat{r}_{a,n}\right) + \lambda(\left\|\mathbf{E}^{(u)}\right\|^2 + \left\|\mathbf{E}^{(i)}\right\|^2) \qquad (12)$$

where σ is a sigmoid function, $\mathcal{M}_a$ is the positive instance set. The first term denotes that the probability of positive case is higher than negative ones. The second term is L2-regularizer and λ controls strength of regularization. Additionally, the EBLO of user and item representation learning process will be added to the final loss. We will minimize our following objective function for optimization:

$$\mathcal{L} = \delta\mathcal{L}_{pair} - \alpha\mathcal{L}_{user} - \beta\mathcal{L}_{item} \qquad (13)$$

4   Experiments

4.1   Experimental Settings

Datasets. In our evaluation experiments, we choose two famous datasets *Yelp* and *Flickr*, which both have buying behavior and social relationship of users. The dataset statistics after reprocessing is shown as table.1. We can get user and item embedding for *Yelp* with Word2vec [20], and for *Flickr* with a VGG16 convolutional neural network [21] following the work in [16]. For each dataset, we randomly select 80% of historical buying behavior of each user to constitute the training set, 10% as the validation set, and treat the remaining interactions as the test set. Since there are too many unrated items, in order to reduce the computational cost, we design our negative sampling strategy like the method in [16].

Table 1. The statistics of the two datasets.

Datasets	#Users	#Items	#Interaction	Sparsity
Yelp	17,237	3,8342	204,448	99.97%
Flickr	83587	82120	3148098	99.95%

Evaluation Metrics. For our top-N recommendation task, we adopt two metrics widely used in previous works: Normalized Discounted Cumulative Gain and Recall. NDCG@N denotes that the hit position by assigning higher scores should be at top-N ranks. Recall@N refers to the proportion of relevant items found in the top-N predictions. The higher the two values, the better performance we achieve.

Parameter Setting. Our model is trained with the RMSprop optimizer [22]. We empirically set the learning rate to 10^{-4} and batch size to 512. The depth of GNN layer is set to 4, since we consider that 4-order neighbors are enough to characterize the influence of neighbors for users. During the layer-wise propagation, we sample 20 neighbors and allow duplication in the samples for calculation convenience. The balance coefficients in the loss function Eq. 13 is set to 0.1 for α, 0.1 for β and 0.8 for δ. Additionally, L2-regularization coefficient λ in BPR loss set to 0.001, which can achieve the best performance. For comparison, the other hyper-parameters we use are mostly the same as the baseline methods. Our model has been implemented in PyTorch and trained on a single Tesla V100 GPU.

Baselines. We compare our method with various state-of-the-art baselines:

- **BPR** [23]: BPR is a classic pair-wise based personalized ranking model. It proposes a generic optimization which is the maximum posterior estimator derived from a Bayesian analysis of the problem. This optimization method is widely used in ranking based models as well as in our model.
- **NCF** [4]: Neural Collaborative Filtering (NCF) generalizes matrix factorization to a non-linear setting, where preferences are modeled through a simple multi-layer perception network that exploits latent factor transformations.
- **DiffNet** [16]: DiffNet leverages deep propagation model to stimulate the influence between users. The method can capture user behavior preference and user neighbor behavior preference at the same time for social recommendation.
- **NGCF** [6]:NGCF is a state-of-the-art graph-based model which exploits the user-item graph structure by propagating embeddings on it. It incorporates explicit user-item interaction into the embedding learning process and proves the rationality and effectiveness of the method.

Table 2. Top-N recommendation performance of different methods on two datasets

	Model	NDCG@10	Recall@10	NDCG@20	Recall@20
Yelp	BPR	0.1532	0.1829	0.1941	0.2104
	NCF	0.1421	0.1943	0.2067	0.2118
	NGCF	0.2023	0.2344	0.2395	0.2415
	Diffnet	0.2323	0.2491	0.2511	0.2673
	DGL	**0.2553**	**0.2623**	**0.2605**	**0.2808**
Flickr	BPR	0.0781	0.0812	0.0921	0.0911
	NCF	0.0823	0.0903	0.1021	0.1271
	NGCF	0.1114	0.1159	0.1239	0.1376
	Diffnet	0.1298	0.1379	0.1397	0.1589
	DGL	**0.1368**	**0.1384**	**0.1448**	**0.1667**

4.2 Overall Comparison

We represent all the experimental results on the two datasets in the table.2. We have the following observations:

- We note that BPR achieves poor performance on both of two datasets. This indicates that shallow model with only user-item rating information is not enough for recommendation.
- Though NCF applies deep learning method, it is still not enough for a complex recommendation scenario. It performs even worse than BPR on NDCG@10 in dataset *Yelp*.
- DiffNet and NGCF achieve good performance on the both datasets. Maybe aggregating node information, as well as graph structure, is helpful to the representation learning process.
- **DGL(Ours)** consistently outperforms all the baseline methods on the both two datasets. Our model performs better than the other two graph-based models, which demonstrates that the significance of identifying the causal relationship behind user-item interactions.

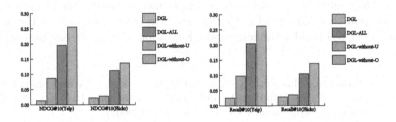

Fig. 5. Performances of different variants of DGL.

4.3 Ablation Study

We would like to demonstrate that it's essential to consider the unobserved confounders and observed confounders in the user interactions when learning users' real intents representations. Furthermore, we also want to prove that our new aggregating strategy can keep nodes distinguishable during the propagation process. For the two purposes, we compare our model with the following three variant:

- DGL-ALL: This variant uses the traditional aggregating strategy which aggregates all of the intents of a user as her fixed intent.
- DGL-without-U: Unobserved confounders are not considered in this variant. Users' intents are calculated as the concatenation of user and item features directly.
- DGL-without-O: Observed confounders are not considered in this variant. Only the user's personalized intents are used to predict.

Figure 5 illustrates the performances of all variants and our proposed method on the two datasets w.r.t. NDCG@10 and Recall @10. DGL-ALL performs a little bit worse than our DGL. The rationale behind may be that DGL-ALL aggregates and propagates the same information of nodes and lead to over-smoothing after several iterates. Both DGL-without-U and DGL-without-O perform poorly, which can prove that it's essential to consider the unobserved confounders and observed confounders in the meantime when modeling the user interactions. DGL consistently outperforms the other three variants, which further verifies that the effectiveness of our model.

5   Conclusions

In this paper, we propose a deconfounding representation learning method named DGL for recommendation systems. Concretely, we consider the unobserved and observed confounders at the same time when modeling user interactions. We introduce an inference network to identify the unobserved confounders and a generative network to generate users' personalized intents. Furthermore, we incorporate social influence into the learning process to learn users' real intents which contain no confounders. Experimental results on two real-world datasets show that our model outperforms all the other baselines. In the future, we would like to consider the temporal information when modeling user interactions.

Acknowledgments. This work is supported by the National Natural Science Foundation of China (No.61672490) and International Partnership Program of Chinese Academy of Sciences with Grant (No.241711KYSB20180002).

References

1. Adomavicius, G., Tuzhilin, A.: Toward the next generation of recommender systems: a survey of the state-of-the-art and possible extensions. IEEE Trans. Knowl. Data Eng. **17**(6), 734–749 (2005)
2. Su, X., Khoshgoftaar, T.M.: A survey of collaborative filtering techniques. Adv. Artif. Intell. **2009**(12), 4 (2012)
3. Koren, Y., Bell, R., Volinsky, C.: Matrix factorization techniques for recommender systems. Computer **42**(8), 30–37 (2009)
4. He, X., Liao, L., Zhang, H., Nie, L., Hu, X., Chua, T.S.: Neural collaborative filtering. In: Proceedings of the 26th International Conference on World Wide Web, pp. 173–182 (2017)
5. Wu, Y., DuBois, C., Zheng, A.X., Ester, M.: Collaborative denoising auto-encoders for top-n recommender systems. In: Proceedings of the Ninth ACM International Conference on Web Search and Data Mining, pp. 153–162 (2016)
6. Wang, X., He, X., Wang, M., Feng, F., Chua, T.S.: Neural graph collaborative filtering. In: Proceedings of the 42nd International ACM SIGIR Conference on Research and Development in Information Retrieval, pp. 165–174 (2019)
7. Ying, R., He, R., Chen, K., Eksombatchai, P., Hamilton, W.L., Leskovec, J.: Graph convolutional neural networks for web-scale recommender systems. In: Proceedings of the 24th ACM SIGKDD International Conference on Knowledge Discovery & Data Mining, pp. 974–983 (2018)
8. Wu, Y., Liu, H., Yang, Y.: Graph convolutional matrix completion for bipartite edge prediction. In: KDIR, pp. 49–58 (2018)

9. Pearl, J.: Causality. Cambridge University Press, Cambridge (2009)
10. Bruna, J., Zaremba, W., Szlam, A., LeCun, Y.: Spectral networks and locally connected networks on graphs. arXiv preprint arXiv:1312.6203 (2013)
11. Wang, Y., Blei, D.M.: The blessings of multiple causes. J. Am. Stat. Assoc. **114**(528), 1574–1596 (2019)
12. Ranganath, R., Perotte, A.: Multiple causal inference with latent confounding. arXiv preprint arXiv:1805.08273 (2018)
13. Stegle, O., Janzing, D., Zhang, K., Mooij, J.M., Schölkopf, B.: Probabilistic latent variable models for distinguishing between cause and effect. In: Advances in Neural Information Processing Systems, pp. 1687–1695 (2010)
14. Louizos, C., Shalit, U., Mooij, J., Sontag, D., Zemel, R., Welling, M.: Causal effect inference with deep latent-variable models. In: Advances in Neural Information Processing Systems, pp. 6446–6456 (2017)
15. Hamilton, W., Ying, Z., Leskovec, J.: Inductive representation learning on large graphs. In: Advances in Neural Information Processing Systems, pp. 1024–1034 (2017)
16. Wu, L., Sun, P., Fu, Y., Hong, R., Wang, X., Wang, M.: A neural influence diffusion model for social recommendation. In: Proceedings of the 42nd International ACM SIGIR Conference on Research and Development in Information Retrieval, pp. 235–244 (2019)
17. Sohn, K., Lee, H., Yan, X.: Learning structured output representation using deep conditional generative models. In: Advances in Neural Information Processing Systems, pp. 3483–3491 (2015)
18. Feng, S., Li, X., Zeng, Y., Cong, G., Chee, Y.M.: Personalized ranking metric embedding for next new poi recommendation. In: IJCAI 2015 Proceedings of the 24th International Conference on Artificial Intelligence, pp. 2069–2075. ACM (2015)
19. Huq, Z., Huq, F., Cutright, K.: BPR through ERP: avoiding change management pitfalls. J. Change Manage. **6**(1), 67–85 (2006)
20. Mikolov, T., Sutskever, I., Chen, K., Corrado, G., Dean, J.: Distributed representations of words and phrases and their compositionality. In: Advances in Neural Information Processing Systems, pp. 3111–3119 (2013)
21. Zeiler, M.D., Fergus, R.: Visualizing and understanding convolutional networks. In: European Conference on Computer Vision (2014)
22. McMahan, B., Streeter, M.: Delay-tolerant algorithms for asynchronous distributed online learning. In: Advances in Neural Information Processing Systems, pp. 2915–2923 (2014)
23. Rendle, S., Freudenthaler, C., Gantner, Z., Schmidt-Thieme, L.: BPR: Bayesian personalized ranking from implicit feedback. arXiv preprint arXiv:1205.2618 (2012)

Personalized Regularization Learning for Fairer Matrix Factorization

Sirui Yao[1](✉) and Bert Huang[2]

[1] Virginia Tech, Blacksburg, VA 24060, USA
ysirui@vt.edu
[2] Tufts University, Medford, MA 02155, USA
bert@cs.tufts.edu

Abstract. Matrix factorization is a canonical method for modeling user preferences for items. Regularization of matrix factorization models often uses a single hyperparameter tuned globally based on metrics evaluated on all data. However, due to the differences in the structure of per-user data, a globally optimal value may not be locally optimal for each individual user, leading to an unfair disparity in performance. Therefore, we propose to tune individual regularization parameters for each user. Our approach, *personalized regularization learning* (PRL), solves a secondary learning problem of finding the per-user regularization parameters by back-propagating through alternating least squares. Experiments on a benchmark dataset with different user group splits show that PRL outperforms existing methods in improving model performance for disadvantaged groups. We also analyze the learned parameters, finding insights into the effect of regularization on subpopulations with varying properties.

Keywords: Matrix factorization · Fairness · Error disparity ·
Personalized regularization

1 Introduction

Matrix factorization is an important and widely adapted collaborative filtering technique for training recommender systems to predict ratings. However, MF has been found to be easily influenced by data biases and becomes unfair [10,15]. For example, demographic groups for whom training data is less frequently available can suffer less accurate predictions of their preferences [15]. This phenomenon is a form of *error-based unfairness* where users may receive lower quality service because of a demographic attribute that ideally should not affect their experience. To make it worse, the group of users who receive less accurate recommendations are more likely to abandon the service, leading to an even more biased environment and more unfair models in the future [9].

Collecting more and better quality data for the disadvantaged groups will help a model better learn these users' preferences. However, this approach is usually expensive or even infeasible. For example, a recommender service provider

© Springer Nature Switzerland AG 2021
K. Karlapalem et al. (Eds.): PAKDD 2021, LNAI 12713, pp. 600–611, 2021.
https://doi.org/10.1007/978-3-030-75765-6_48

cannot request users to change how they interact with the service. Therefore, the more important questions is, can we handle these biases more appropriately to make better use of the available data, and build a model with improved accuracy for the ill-served users?

In this work, we first consider different types of data biases, which all refer to a certain form of divergence in the structure of per-user or per-group data. We verify on synthetic datasets that these biases can lead to one subgroup experiencing higher error than the others. We then consider the connection between prediction error and the role of regularization. If we acknowledge the difference in per-user data, then instead of tuning a global hyperparameter, a matrix factorization could benefit from personalized regularization, which better accommodates each individual user. This strategy not only directly addresses the cause of error disparity, but also provides more interpretability compared to directly manipulate the latent features since regularization is a comparatively well-understood concept.

Since personalized regularization drastically increases the number of hyperparameters, commonly used hyperparameter searching procedures—such as grid search and random search—become prohibitively expensive. It is also challenging to derive the parameters from heuristic because, in joint embedding models like matrix factorization, the effect of personalized regularization parameters are not independent of each other. Therefore, we propose a learning problem, *personalized regularization learning* (PRL), to learn the optimal set of hyperparameters that minimizes a secondary objective, in our case, the error of the disadvantage groups. We consider the secondary objective as a function of the personalized regularization parameters. To enable direct back-propagation and facilitate efficient learning, we leverage the closed-form solutions of *alternating least squares* (ALS) to solve MF.

The main contributions of this paper are as follows:

1. We identify the insufficiency of global regularization for matrix factorization in dealing with complexity or sparsity imbalance across users, and conduct validation on synthetic data with explicitly injected biases;
2. We propose *personalized regularization learning* (PRL), an interpretable algorithm for learning personalized regularization by back-propagating through the closed-form computation of ALS;
3. We demonstrate the effectiveness of the proposed approach with experiments on a benchmark dataset with different user group splits, comparing against three baseline models.

2   Related Work

In this section, we review literature related to the problem we aim to solve and our proposed approach.

Error Disparity. Error disparity is a form of error-based unfairness. Yao and Huang [15] discuss four variants of unfairness metrics computed based on the divergence between prediction and labels. [15] propose to reduce error disparity by adding the optimized metrics to the standard matrix factorization objective such that the model is incentivized to reduce disparity. Both [9] and [11] solve the error disparity problem by minimizing the maximum subgroup error, which is an upper bound on error disparity. In recommender systems, this phenomenon is also related to the cold-start problem [5,6], where the cause of high error is limited to insufficient data. Other notions of fairness such as statistical parity [16] is also studied in recommender systems but is not the focus of this paper.

Differentiated Regularization. Besides separating the regularization parameter of users and items, Beutel et al. [2] proposes to assign the advantaged and disadvantaged subpopulation to different sets, and regularize them differently. Chen et al. [5] take a step further by computing a set of per-user regularization parameter by linear or logarithm functions of user sparsity. Our work is closely related to [2] and [5] because we also seek to differentiate regularization but through an optimization-based approach.

Hyperparameter Search. In practice, grid search is often used when the space of hyperparameters is small. Random search [1] can be more efficient because it randomly samples hyperparameter values instead of trying all combinations of the candidate hyperparameters. Bayesian hyperparameter optimization [13] speeds up random search by taking into consideration the past evaluations to decide what areas of hyperparameter space to search next. For the task of optimizing a large number of hyperparameters, [12] devise a reversible learning method to compute hyperparameter gradients by reversing the dynamics of gradient descent. Our approach also uses gradient-based hyperparameter tuning, but we leverage the differentiability of closed-form updates in alternating least squares for matrix factorization to directly back-propagate to the hyperparameters.

3   Problem Definition

Given a dataset $\mathcal{D}$ that contains ratings by M users on N items. which can be represented as an $M \times N$ sparse matrix R where each observed entry r_{ui} represents the rating user u gives to item i. Suppose each user is associated with a set of properties S, based on one or more such properties $s \in S$, we can split users into a set of subgroups G.

A rating prediction model predicts the missing values in the sparse rating matrix. We randomly split all observed ratings into R^{Train} and R^{Test}. We train a model on R^{Train}, and use root mean squared error (RMSE) to measure prediction error on R^{Test} as

$$RMSE = \sqrt{\frac{1}{|R^{\text{Test}}|} \sum_{r_{ui} \in R^{\text{Test}}} (r_{ui} - \hat{r}_{ui})^2)} \tag{1}$$

where $\hat{r}_{ui}$ is the predicted value of r_{ui}. With a matrix factorization model, users and items are projected as matrices $P \in \mathbb{R}^{M \times d}$ and $Q \in \mathbb{R}^{N \times d}$. The uth row of P, denoted as p_u, is the latent feature of user u; the ith row of Q, denoted as q_i, is the latent feature of item i. The ratings are predicted as $\hat{r}_{ui} = p_u q_i^{\mathsf{T}}$.

Problem Formulation. Given a user subgroup of concern $\hat{g} \in G$, which has higher prediction error and is considered to be the disadvantage population. The goal is to find a model that reduces error for this subgroup. The error of a subgroup $\hat{g} \in G$ is denoted and measured as

$$RMSE_{\hat{g}} = \sqrt{\frac{1}{|R_{\hat{g}}^{\text{Test}}|} \sum_{r_{ui} \in R_{\hat{g}}^{\text{Test}}} (r_{ui} - \hat{r}_{ui})^2)} \tag{2}$$

where $R_{\hat{g}}^{\text{Train}}$ and $R_{\hat{g}}^{\text{Test}}$ denote the training and test data of $\hat{g}$ respectively.

4 Data Biases and Regularization

In this section, we discuss four types of data biases that contribute to higher prediction error in disadvantaged subgroups, and empirically show the consequences of these biases with synthetic datasets. We also discuss how these data biases are related to regularization and imply the need for personalized regularization.

4.1 Data Biases

We first consider a group-level bias called *population bias*, which refers to the discrepancy among the size of subgroups. The subgroups with smaller populations are more likely to be compromised in modeling, especially when the data of these minority groups have a very different structure from the other groups. We also consider three individual-level biases. The first one is *sparsity bias*, which refers to the difference in per-user data sparsity. A model with a particular complexity requires a corresponding amount of data to overcome the curse of dimensionality, which creates a disadvantage for users who are new or less active. The second one is *rank bias*, it refers to the situation that some users' preferences are more complicated than others. Therefore, a higher-dimensional model is required to capture their preferences. The third one is *noise bias*, which suggests different levels of data quality and the situation where some users' data is more noisy than the others. We believe these four types of data biases lead to increased prediction error for the subgroups that are being biased against.

4.2 Validation

We validate our heuristics on the effect of data bias on synthetic datasets where we explicitly inject two types of data bias among users. We create the synthetic data by first generating a twenty-dimensional user and item feature matrices for 100 users and 600 items. Then we compute the rating matrix as their dot product. To make the datasets more realistic, we also add Gaussian noise to these ratings and clamp them within the range of 1.0 to 5.0.

We assign users to two subgroups A and B. To inject data biases, without loss of generosity, we choose group B to be the disadvantaged group and the users from group B to be the disadvantaged users. For population bias, we lower the population of group B to be the minority group; for rank bias, we force some columns of the latent features of users from group A to be zero, so that group B has higher dimension than group A; for sparsity bias, we mask more ratings from group B than group A; for noise bias, we add a higher level of Gaussian noise to the rating of group B. Specifically, to create the biased settings, we set $|B| = 30, |A| = 70$; $d_A = 5, d_B = 20$; 5× amount of ratings are observed from group A than group B; 2× amount of noise is added to the ratings of group B[1].

We train matrix factorization models on these datasets and measure $RMSE_B$, the error of group B. The results are shown in Fig. 1. The blue bar represents a bias-free dataset; the orange bars represent datasets with each individual type of bias; the green, red, and purple bars represent datasets with 2, 3, and 4 types of biases respectively. R, N, P, S are short for rank bias, noise bias, population bias, and sparsity bias respectively. First, by comparing the fair setting (the blue bar) and the settings with each individual biases (the orange bars), we observe that, except population bias, each of the discussed biases alone directly leads to higher $RMSE_B$. Population bias is the exception because when the other three biases are not present, the two subpopulations have exactly the same data structure. Second, in general, $RMSE_B$ increases as more types of biases are injected, suggesting a compound impact of data biases. Third, the effect of these data biases are not independent but can enhance each other. For example, we observe a noticeable increase in $RMSE_B$ from setting "R, S, N" to "R, S, N, P" when population bias is added, which by itself does not have the same effect.

4.3 Relation to Regularization

The data biases discussed above are directly related to data properties that, if not carefully handled when building a model, will lead to overfitting or underfitting. Overfitting or underfitting are two forms of mistakes that a model could make to mishandle training data and increase error. Overfitting happens when a model attends to too much detail and noise, and is more likely to occur when data is insufficient due to increase variance; underfitting, on the other hand, happens when a model oversimplifies and fail to capture the underlying structure of the data.

An important component for balancing underfitting and overfitting in machine learning models is regularization. The strength of regularization needs

---

[1] Note that to avoid the effect of irrelevant factors, we normalize the ratings so that the ratings of group A and B follow the same distribution. We also keep the overall level of sparsity and noise unchanged by rescaling the configuration within each subgroup.

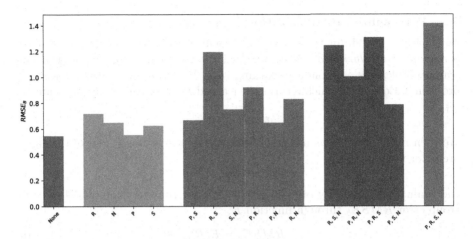

Fig. 1. The measured $RMSE_B$ of models trained on synthetic datasets with different data biases injected. Here we use R, N, P, S to indicate rank bias, noise bias, population bias, and sparsity bias respectively. The models are grouped based on the number of injected data biases and are presented in different colors. (Color figure online)

to be tuned to best fit the learning task and the data. Since we discussed that data properties such as quality, sparsity, and complexity may not be universal across all users, tuning a global regularization parameter λ^*, as is done in standard matrix factorization models, becomes insufficient to accommodate the important differences in per-user data, leading to poor model performance on certain user subgroups.

5   Personalized Regularization Learning

We have discussed that a globally tuned regularization parameter λ^* neglects the differences in per-user data. Therefore, we believe a model could benefit from a set of personalized regularization parameters. With this expanded set of hyperparameters, the objective function of training a matrix factorization model is modified by replacing the globally tuned regularization hyperparameter λ^* with user-personalized regularization parameters $\Lambda = \{\lambda_u\}_{u=1}^{M}$. The user and item latent features are learned as

$$P^*, Q^* = \min_{P,Q} \sum_{r_{ui} \in R^{\text{Train}}} (r_{ui} - P_u Q_i^{\mathsf{T}})^2 + \frac{1}{2} \left(\sum_{u=1}^{M} \lambda_u (P_u P_u^{\mathsf{T}}) + \sum_{i=1}^{N} \lambda^* (Q_i Q_i^{\mathsf{T}}) \right)$$
(3)

Since personalized regularization grows the space of hyperparameters from $\mathbb{R}$ to $\mathbb{R}^M$, traditional tuning procedures such as grid search become insufficient in such a high-dimensional space. Also, in joint embedding models like matrix factorization, the personalized regularization parameters are not independent of each other, therefore, it is challenging to derive the parameters from heuristics.

5.1   Personalized Regularization Learning

To efficiently search for the optimal personalized hyperparameters, we propose *personalized regularization learning* (PRL), which poses the hyperparameter search problem as a secondary learning task. We denote the primary learning problem in Eq. 3 as L, which returns the learned P, Q for a given hyperparameter set Λ

$$P, Q = L(\Lambda) \tag{4}$$

We then make predictions using the learned latent features P and Q through a predictor function H,

$$\hat{R} = H(P, Q) \tag{5}$$

and evaluate a secondary objective, which in our running example, is the subgroup error $RMSE_{\hat{g}}$ through function E,

$$RMSE_{\hat{g}} = E(\hat{R}) \tag{6}$$

Combining equation Eqs. (4) to (6), we get $RMSE_{\hat{g}} = E(H(L(\Lambda))) = F(\Lambda)$ where $F = E(H(L))$. The secondary learning problem is formulated as

$$\Lambda^* = \min_{\Lambda \in \mathbb{R}^M} F(\Lambda) \tag{7}$$

F is a differentiable function if E, H, and L are all differentiable. Then we can directly backpropagate through F to compute gradients of the secondary objective with respect to Λ.

5.2   Leveraging ALS

Solving the factorization problem L involves minimizing a non-convex regularized squared reconstruction error. One approach for optimizing this objective is through gradient descent [3], which has been made especially convenient with the advance of automatic differentiation tools [4]. However, the gradient of hyperparameters are usually unavailable [12]. Therefore, we instead use alternating least squares (ALS) [14] to solve L, which alternates between optimizing P and Q by iteratively applying a closed-form solution

$$P_u \leftarrow \left(\sum_{i:(u,i)\in\mathcal{D}} \tilde{q}_i \tilde{q}_i^T + \lambda^* I_d \right)^{-1} \sum_{i:(u,i)\in\mathcal{D}} r_{ui} \tilde{q}_i$$

$$Q_i \leftarrow \left(\sum_{u:(u,i)\in\mathcal{D}} \tilde{p}_u \tilde{p}_u^T + \lambda^* I_d \right)^{-1} \sum_{u:(u,i)\in\mathcal{D}} (r_{ui} - b_u) \tilde{p}_u \tag{8}$$

The closed-form updates are differentiable, so we can conveniently backpropagate through F to compute gradients of the secondary objective with respect to Λ and learn Λ with a standard gradient-based optimizer. Since the time complexity of computing partial derivative is the same as forward passing [7], the time it takes to back-propagate to Λ is the same as forward ALS, thus the time complexity of PRL is $\mathcal{O}(T)$, where T is the number of epochs ALS takes to converge. This is on par with the state-of-the-art hyperparameter optimization techniques [12].

5.3 Data Split

During learning, we must use different datasets for training the MF model and measuring subpopulation error. This is because our goal is to decrease generalization error, which needs to be evaluated on data unseen by the training algorithm. If we measure subpopulation error on the same data that the MF model is trained on, we may simply incentivize the learning optimization to overfit the data as much as possible.

Therefore, after we split data $\mathcal{R}$ into $\mathcal{R}^{\text{Train}}$ and $\mathcal{R}^{\text{Test}}$, we further split $\mathcal{R}^{\text{Train}}$ into $\mathcal{R}^{\text{Train-Primary}}$ and $\mathcal{R}^{\text{Train-Secondary}}$. In each PRL iteration, we train a matrix factorization model on $\mathcal{R}^{\text{Train-Primary}}$ and compute $RMSE_{\hat{g}}$ on $\mathcal{R}^{\text{Train-Secondary}}$, which is used to update Λ. After we obtained Λ^*, we apply it to train a final matrix factorization model on the full training set $\mathcal{R}^{\text{Train}}$. We then evaluate $RMSE_{\hat{g}}$ on $\mathcal{R}^{\text{Test}}$. The full algorithm is listed as Algorithm 1. In practice, we recommend creating multiple primary-secondary splits of $\mathcal{R}^{\text{Train}}$ so that the learned Λ^* is not overfitted to one particular split.

Algorithm 1: Personalized Regularization Learning

Given dataset $\mathcal{R}$, global optimal lambda λ^*, MF model L, error metric E, disadvantaged subpopulation $\hat{g}$. Split $\mathcal{R}$ into $\mathcal{R}^{\text{Train}}$ and $\mathcal{R}^{\text{Test}}$, further split $\mathcal{R}^{\text{Train}}$ into $\mathcal{R}^{\text{Train-Primary}}$ and $\mathcal{R}^{\text{Train-Secondary}}$.

Initialize $\Lambda \leftarrow \{\lambda_i = \lambda^*\}_{i=1}^{N}$, randomly initialize P and Q

while *not converged* **do**

$\quad P^*, Q^* \xleftarrow{\mathcal{R}^{\text{Train-Primary}}} L(\Lambda)$

$\quad \hat{R} \xleftarrow{\mathcal{R}^{\text{Train-Secondary}}} H(P^*, Q^*)$

$\quad RMSE_{\hat{g}} \xleftarrow{\mathcal{R}^{\text{Train-Secondary}}} E(\hat{R}_{\hat{g}})$

$\quad$ compute gradient $\nabla_\Lambda RMSE_{\hat{g}}$ through backpropagation

$\quad$ update Λ with $\nabla_\Lambda RMSE_{\hat{g}}$

end

Re-initialize P and Q

$P^*, Q^* \xleftarrow{\mathcal{R}^{\text{Train}}} L(\Lambda^*)$

5.4 Interpretability

A key advantage of PRL is that it provides interpretable feedback in the magnitude of the learned per-user regularization parameters. Compared to regularization-based methods that directly manipulate user and item latent representations, PRL's learned parameters indicate the level of regularization, which is comparatively well-understood and can help us understand how the model is improved. We can interpret them by comparing their values against the globally tuned value. If a user's parameter increases, it suggests that this user would have been overfitted. Conversely, if a user receives lower regularization from PRL, they were prone to underfit and needed a more complex model.

6   Experiments

6.1   Datasets

The choice of public real datasets that provide user demographic information is very limited. We use the benchmark MovieLens 100k dataset [8], which contains 100,000 ratings from 1,000 users on 1,700 movies, and conveniently provides multiple user demographic features. Specifically, we consider demographic information such as gender, age, zip code; we also consider user degree–the number of ratings each user has, and user error–the error of each user with a vanilla matrix factorization model. For gender, we split users by category and create two subgroups (female and male users); for zipcode, we split by the first digit of zip code and create 10 subgroups, representing users from different regions in the US; for age, degree, and error, we split by percentile and each split creates 10 equal size subgroups.

We randomly sample 10% of data as holdout set for testing and use the rest as training set. Then we do 10-fold cross-validation on the training set to select the best global regularization weight λ and the rank d. The optimal combination we found is $d^* = 30$ and $\lambda^* = 20.0$. We train a standard matrix factorization model and measure the subgroup errors under all user splits. For each split, we pick the subgroup with the highest error as the disadvantaged group, denoted as $\hat{g}$ and seek to reduce $RMSE_{\hat{g}}$. The disadvantaged subgroups are listed in the second row of Table 1.

6.2   Baselines

Focused Learning (FL). FL [2] assigns users to only two subgroups, a focused set, and an unfocused set. The two sets of users are regularized differently to optimize the model performance on the focused set of users. The optimal hyperparameter pair is searched via grid search.

Differentiated regularization (DR) DR [5] is motivated to alleviate the cold-start problem and regularize every user differently. The regularization parameters are computed from three functions (one linear and two logarithmic) of user degree. We denote the three formulas as DR-linear, DR-Log-1, and DR-Log-2.

Unfairness-Regularized Matrix Factorization (URMF). URMF [15] is designed to optimize a secondary fairness in matrix factorization models. The strategy is to add the optimized secondary objective as a penalty term to the standard matrix factorization objective, weighted by a weight parameter. URMF directly manipulates the fitted latent embeddings instead of through regularization.

6.3   Specifications and Results

For DR, we directly apply the three formula (Equation 5 in [5]) to compute personalized regularization parameters. For FL, we follow the same procedure as proposed by the authors and try a range of regularization values on the focused and unfocused set, $\{0.001, 0.01, 0.1, 1, 1, 10, 20, 30, 50, 100\}$, which gives 100 combinations. For URMF, we try 10 different unfairness penalty weights $\{1e-6, 1e-5, 1e-4, 1e-3, 1e-2, 1e-1, 1, 5, 10, 20\}$. For FL and UR, we identify the optimal setting or weight via cross-validation, then apply the same setting or weight to train a final model on the full training set. For all trained models, we measure $RMSE_{\hat{g}}$ on the holdout test set.

We show the results of all compared models on different user splits in Table 1. We first compare the performance of PRL against the standard matrix factorization model. We observed that PRL successfully reduces $RMSE_{\hat{g}}$ on all user splits, and achieves more than 10% improvement on subgroups split by Zip Code and Error. We also observe that PRL outperforms all baseline models by a convincing margin. Focused learning is the second-best method, this further suggests that fitting different regularization is effective in optimizing subpopulation error. We believe PRL wins over Focused learning due to the expanded set of hyperparameters and smart search through optimization. We observe a big fluctuation in the performance of URMF, it is possibly because URMF still can easily overfit to the training data since it measures both primary and secondary objectives on the same data. Lastly, DR performs the worst. It rarely reduces $RMSE_{\hat{g}}$ and even when it does, the improvements are trivial. This pattern aligns with the results and conclusion in the original paper that DR sometimes makes things worse and especially so on the MovieLens dataset. The poor performance of DR suggests it is challenging to find a one-fits-all heuristic for setting the personalized regularizations.

Table 1. Comparison of all model performance in reducing $RMSE_{\hat{g}}$. The rows are the $RMSE_{\hat{g}}$ of a standard matrix factorization model and all compared models, the lower the better. The columns are different user group splits. Bold values are the most significant improvement in each column.

User Split	Gender	Age	Zip Code	Degree	Error
$\hat{g}$	F	52–59	0	0%–10%	90%–100%
MF	1.029	1.045	1.062	1.118	1.612
PRL	**0.967 (−6.0%)**	**0.983 (−5.9%)**	**0.952 (−10.4%)**	**1.043 (−6.7%)**	**1.367 (−15.2%)**
FL	0.998 (−3.0%)	1.001 (−4.2%)	0.989 (−6.9%)	1.094 (−2.1%)	1.479 (−8.2%)
URMF	1.013 (−1.6%)	1.089 (+4.2%)	0.956 (−10.0%)	1.102 (−1.4%)	1.579 (−2.0%)
DR-Linear	1.041 (+1.2%)	1.127 (+7.8%)	1.047 (−1.4%)	1.114 (−0.4%)	1.601 (−0.7%)
DR-Log-1	1.067 (+3.7%)	1.113 (+6.5%)	1.082 (+1.9%)	1.109 (−0.8%)	1.641 (+1.7%)
DR-Log-2	1.059 (+2.9%)	1.114 (+6.6%)	1.098 (+3.9%)	1.112 (−0.5%)	1.632 (+1.2%)

We next examine the personalized regularization parameter fitted through PRL to understand how it reduces $RMSE_{\hat{g}}$. We compute the mean and standard deviation of the regularization parameters in each subgroup throughout PRL optimization. We show the plot in gender subgroups as an example in Fig. 2. In this case, female users is the disadvantaged subgroup. We observe that female users, on average, have been assigned lower regularization, and male users' regularization has been increased. This provides an interesting insight that the complexity of the originally tuned global model was lower than what is need for the disadvantaged group. PRL allows these users to enjoy a more complex model that better captures their preferences. We also noticed an increased variance in the regularization parameter, and surprisingly even more so in the advantaged group. As we discussed in Sect. 5, the personalized regularization parameters are not independent of each other in joint embedding models, therefore, the regularization of all users are shifted even though the objective is to only optimize the prediction error of the disadvantaged group. Further, we found the same direction of change in the pair of regularization parameters identified via focused learning ($\lambda_F = 10$ and $\lambda_M = 30$). This suggests an alignment between the two methods in reducing high subpopulation error through adjusted regularization.

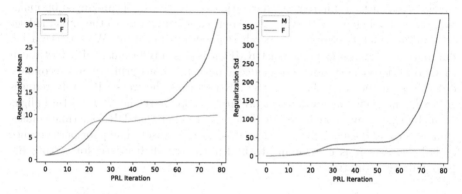

Fig. 2. The curve of mean and standard deviation of personalized regularization values during PRL. F means female users and M means male users.

7   Discussion

In this work, we address the problem of error disparity in matrix factorization models. We discuss four types of biases that contribute to higher subpopulation error and validate their effect on synthetic datasets. We presented *personalized regularization learning* (PRL), a method that learns to regularize users differently to improve prediction performance for disadvantaged subgroups of users. PRL solves a secondary learning problem to minimize validation unfairness by back-propagating through alternating least squares. In experiments, PRL outperforms existing methods for reducing error disparity in recommendations. Moreover, the learned per-user regularization parameters are interpretable and provide insight into how fairness is improved. For future work, we are interested in investigating the effectiveness of PRL in other variants of matrix factorization, such as SVD++, factorization machine. We are also interested in further exploring the learned regularization parameters to uncover richer group structures.

Acknowledgement. This work was partially supported by a Deloitte Data Analytics Fellowship and an Amazon Research Award.

References

1. Bergstra, J., Bengio, Y.: Random search for hyper-parameter optimization. J. Mach. Learn. Res. **13**, 281–305 (2012)
2. Beutel, A., Chi, E.H., Cheng, Z., Pham, H., Anderson, J.: Beyond globally optimal: focused learning for improved recommendations. In: Proceedings of the 26th International Conference on World Wide Web, pp. 203–212 (2017)
3. Bottou, L.: Large-scale machine learning with stochastic gradient descent. In: Lechevallier, Y., Saporta, G. (eds.) Proceedings of COMPSTAT 2010, pp. 177–186. Springer, Heidelberg (2010). https://doi.org/10.1007/978-3-7908-2604-3_16
4. Bücker, H.M., Corliss, G., Hovland, P., Naumann, U., Norris, B.: Automatic differentiation: applications, theory, and implementations. LNCSE, vol. 50. Springer, Heidelberg (2006). https://doi.org/10.1007/3-540-28438-9
5. Chen, H.H., Chen, P.: Differentiating regularization weights-a simple mechanism to alleviate cold start in recommender systems. ACM Trans. Knowl. Discov. Data (TKDD) **13**(1), 1–22 (2019)
6. Ferraro, A.: Music cold-start and long-tail recommendation: bias in deep representations. In: Proceedings of the 13th ACM Conference on Recommender Systems, pp. 586–590 (2019)
7. Griewank, A., Walther, A.: Evaluating derivatives: principles and techniques of algorithmic differentiation. SIAM (2008)
8. Harper, F.M., Konstan, J.A.: The movielens datasets: history and context. ACM Trans. Interact. Intell. Syst. **5**(4), 1–19 (2015)
9. Hashimoto, T.B., Srivastava, M., Namkoong, H., Liang, P.: Fairness without demographics in repeated loss minimization. arXiv preprint arXiv:1806.08010 (2018)
10. Kamishima, T., Akaho, S., Asoh, H., Sakuma, J.: Recommendation independence. In: Conference on Fairness, Accountability and Transparency, pp. 187–201 (2018)
11. Kim, M.P., Ghorbani, A., Zou, J.: Multiaccuracy: black-box post-processing for fairness in classification. In: Proceedings of the 2019 AAAI/ACM Conference on AI, Ethics, and Society, pp. 247–254 (2019)
12. Maclaurin, D., Duvenaud, D., Adams, R.: Gradient-based hyperparameter optimization through reversible learning. In: International Conference on Machine Learning, pp. 2113–2122 (2015)
13. Snoek, J., Larochelle, H., Adams, R.P.: Practical Bayesian optimization of machine learning algorithms. In: Advances in Neural Information Processing Systems, pp. 2951–2959 (2012)
14. Takács, G., Tikk, D.: Alternating least squares for personalized ranking. In: Proceedings of the ACM Conference on Recommender Systems, pp. 83–90 (2012)
15. Yao, S., Huang, B.: Beyond parity: fairness objectives for collaborative filtering. In: Advances in Neural Information Processing Systems, pp. 2921–2930 (2017)
16. Zhu, Z., Hu, X., Caverlee, J.: Fairness-aware tensor-based recommendation. In: Proceedings of the 27th ACM International Conference on Information and Knowledge Management, pp. 1153–1162 (2018)

Instance Selection for Online Updating in Dynamic Recommender Environments

Thilina Thanthriwatta[1]($\boxtimes$) and David S. Rosenblum[1,2]

[1] Department of Computer Science, National University of Singapore,
Singapore, Singapore
e0001932@u.nus.edu
[2] Department of Computer Science, George Mason University, Fairfax, VA, USA
dsr@gmu.edu

Abstract. Online recommender systems continuously learn from user interactions that occur in a streaming manner. A fundamental challenge of online recommendation is to select important instances (i.e., user interactions) for model updates to achieve higher prediction accuracy while omitting noisy instances. In this paper, we study (1) how to select the *best* instances and (2) how to effectively utilize the selected instances in dynamic recommender environments. We present two instance selection strategies based on Self-Paced Learning and rating profiles. We integrate them with Factorization Machines to perform online updates. Moreover, we study the impact of contextual information in online updating. We conducted experiments on a real-world check-in dataset, which contains temporal contextual features. Empirical results demonstrate that ox ur instance selection strategies effectively balance the trade-off between prediction accuracy and efficiency.

Keywords: Instance selection · Context-aware recommender systems · Online recommender systems

1 Introduction

Context-Aware Recommender Systems (CARSs) have gained significant interest with the rise of smart devices such as smartphones that employ physical sensors and applications to capture contextual information (e.g., location and time). Contrary to conventional Recommender Systems (RSs), which utilize information about users and items only, CARSs incorporate contextual information and make the recommendation problem multi-dimensional. In the real world, CARSs should be able to adapt to the dynamic nature of a recommender environment where a stream of user interactions (i.e., instances) happens over time. Note that an event of a user loggin in and searching for items is considered as a user interaction, and CARSs should provide recommendations for each incoming user. We assume that at a given moment of time only one user interaction occurs. Most of the developed CARSs rely on typical batch learning and evaluation (batch

© Springer Nature Switzerland AG 2021
K. Karlapalem et al. (Eds.): PAKDD 2021, LNAI 12713, pp. 612–624, 2021.
https://doi.org/10.1007/978-3-030-75765-6_49

setting). These models should be updated from scratch (re-trained) to provide quality recommendations over time. This introduces a significantly large computational overhead and makes these models impossible to use with a high-velocity stream of interactions.

An online RS should be able to provide recommendations to the incoming users and update the necessary model parameters based on user feedback without re-training the whole model. To satisfy these conditions, the online RS should be equipped with a minimal and efficient online updating mechanism. There are two questions to answer when devising an online updating mechanism: (1) how to select the *best* instances for online updating instead of using all the incoming instances? and (2) what is the *best* strategy that can be employed for online updating while minimizing the information loss that stems from the under-utilization of the incoming instances?

Forgetting obsolete instances has been commonly used to improve efficiency in dynamic recommender environments [11,14,18]. Al-Ghossein et al. proposed to use local models to track the changes in user preference over time [1], instead of using fixed parameters such as the size of a sliding window. Matuszyka et al. [13] presented a set of forgetting methods such as forgetting unpopular items and user factor fading.

However, the existing approaches do not study how the instance selection strategies affect the context-aware recommender task. Moreover, these methods identify the "best" instances either by the changes of components (e.g., latent vectors [13], local models [1], etc.) of users and items or by comparing a set of stored ratings [18]. In contrast to these methods, we use the loss that is incurred by an instance to determine its suitability for online updating. Accordingly, we use *Self-Paced Learning* (SPL) to devise a curriculum that gradually feeds "easy" to "hard" ("complex") instances to the learning process.

Existing studies suggest that biasing towards the users and items with small rating profiles is sufficient to achieve satisfactory performance while speeding up online updating [17]. In line with this observation, we present an instance selection method named as *Profile-based Selection* (PS) that selects incoming instances with the users, items, and contextual feature values that have small rating profiles. On the other hand, the practitioners in machine learning advocate not to introduce "complex" instances to a training process at its initial phase since those instances do not fit well with the existing model [10]. Usually, RSs incur relatively large losses when incorporating the users and items with small rating profiles since these RSs have not been sufficiently learned based on those user behaviors and item characteristics. We use the notion of SPL for online updates by changing its pace at regular intervals. Note that the SPL concept has been introduced for strategizing batch learning, which trains the model over a large number of epochs. However, in the online recommender task, a model is updated by each incoming instance over a small number of epochs (usually one or two epochs). Thus, it is not possible to employ SPL directly for online updating. We use it as a scoring function that determines the weight of an incoming instance, and this strategy is named as *SPL-based Selection* (SPS). In summary, the contributions of this study are as follows:

- We present two strategies, which are integrated with Factorization Machines (FMs), to select incoming instances for online updates based on the notion of SPL and the rating profiles of users, items, and contexts.
- To the best of our knowledge, this is the first study on how to use SPL with the online recommender task, which is evaluated by the *test-then-learn* method [1,19].
- We perform a comparative analysis of how different instance selection methods behave in the presence of contextual information. Moreover, the use of selected instances for online updating leads to information loss, and our instance selection strategies especially SPS balance the trade-off between prediction accuracy and efficiency while minimizing the impact of information loss.

2   Instance Selection in Online Recommendation

As prior work [17] highlighted, it is essential to perform online updating for an instance that relates to a new user and/or new item since the existing model does not have any (or limited) information of new users and new items. This approach makes the online updating of a recommender model biased towards new users (items). However, this leads to suboptimal performance due to the complete removal of the users and the items that have relatively large rating profiles. Furthermore, it is possible that the incorporation of new users (items) significantly changes the existing model. On the other hand, the SPL-based training process initiates training using *easy* instances, which do not lead to large errors, and gradually feeds more complex instances.

2.1   Profile-Based Selection

We begin by defining the *Profile-based Selection* (PS) which is based on the degree of newness. Assume that an incoming instance ρ consists of user u, item i and M number of contextual feature values $\{c_{m'}\}_1^M$ (e.g., "rainy", "weekend", "morning"). The selection of ρ is defined by the following indicator function:

$$\mathcal{D}_\rho := \mathbb{I}\left[\left(\delta(|u| + |i|) + (1 - \delta)\sum_{m'=1}^{M'} |c_{m'}|\right) < \theta\right], \tag{1}$$

where $|u|$ and $|i|$ represent the number of ratings given by user u and received by item i before the arrival of ρ, respectively. $|c_{m'}|$ denotes the number of ratings in which $c_{m'}$ had already appeared. In other words, $|u|$, $|i|$ and $|c_{m'}|$ correspond to the sizes of the rating profiles of u, i and $c_{m'}$, respectively. If the weighted combination of the rating profiles of ρ is less than θ, then it can be used to update the model in the online setting. We use δ to balance the rating profiles of users and items with the rating profiles of contextual values. Because they tend to be drastically different. In a real-world context-aware recommender setting, we can observe that the number of users and items are significantly larger than the number of contextual values. Due to this imbalance, the rating profile size of a user (an item) grow slowly compared to that of a contextual feature value over time.

2.2 SPL-Based Selection

The aim of SPL is to select easy to complex training instances for robust model learning [10]. In contrast to curriculum learning [3], where the model learning is regulated by gradually including easy to complex samples based on different types of heuristics, SPL incorporates parameters into model learning to support the selection process. Zhang et al. [20] used the notion of SPL with the recommender task to improve the optimization by avoiding bad local minima. Their evaluation method is similar to the evaluation in the batch learning setting. Moreover, they used the SPL concept to improve the overall optimization while we use it to select "best" instances for online updates. Hence, the problem that was addressed by them is different from ours.

Let r_{uic} be the actual rating given by user u for item i under context c. Assume that context c corresponds to d number of contextual feature values, and j-th contextual feature value is denoted by c_j. The dataset Ω contains instances (e.g., $< u, i, c_1, ..., c_d >$), for which ratings are known. We represent feature vectors using the one-hot encoding [16]. The SPL-integrated optimization function is defined as follows:

$$\min_{\mathbf{w},\mathbf{V},\mathbf{p}} \sum_{(u,i,c)\in\Omega} p_{uic}\ell_{uic} + \lambda R(.) + \sum_{(u,i,c)\in\Omega} f(p_{uic},\alpha) \quad \text{s.t. } \mathbf{p} \in [0,1]^{|\Omega|}. \quad (2)$$

We use the log loss to compute the error ℓ_{uic} between the predicted rating $\hat{r}_{uic}$ and the actual rating r_{uic}. It is defined as $\ell_{uic} = -(r_{uic}\log(\hat{r}_{uic}) + (1 - r_{uic})\log(1 - \hat{r}_{uic}))$. Based on FMs, $\hat{r}_{uic}$ is computed as follows:

$$\hat{r}_{uic} = \sum_{i=1}^{n} w_i x_i + \sum_{i=1}^{n} \sum_{j=i+1}^{n} \langle \mathbf{v}_i, \mathbf{v}_j \rangle x_i x_j, \quad (3)$$

where w_i models the weight of x_i, the i-th variable of the one-hot encoded feature vector that corresponds to instance uic. The weight of the pairwise interaction of i-th and j-th variables is modeled by the dot product of $\mathbf{v}_i$ and $\mathbf{v}_j$. The k-dimensional vector that corresponds to variable i is denoted as $\mathbf{v}_i$. λ is a non-negative regularization parameter, and $\mathbf{p}$ is used to store the weights assigned to the instances in Ω. In order to prevent over-fitting, $\mathbf{L_2}$ regularization function $R(.)$ is used. Self-paced function or self-paced regularizer $f(\mathbf{p}, \alpha)$ is used to select instances based on weights. Kumar et al. [10] proposed a simple self-paced regularizer $f(\mathbf{p}, \alpha) = -\frac{1}{\alpha}\mathbf{p}$. When all model parameters except $\mathbf{p}$ are fixed, the optimal p_{uic} value which is denoted by p_{uic}^*, is calculated as follows:

$$p_{uic}^*(\alpha, \ell_{uic}) = \begin{cases} 1 \text{ if } \ell_{uic} < 1/\alpha \\ 0 \text{ otherwise.} \end{cases} \tag{4}$$

For the sake of simplicity, we denote an instance by uic. Instance uic is considered as *easy* and selected if $p_{uic}^* = 1$. The parameter α regulates the pace at which the model learns from new instances. As $\frac{1}{\alpha}$ increases gradually, more *complex* instances will be used for model learning. SPL regularizer can be seen as a scoring function for training instances. Usually in the use of SPL with batch learning, the model is trained over a large number of epochs, and in each epoch, only a few selected instances are used for training. At the end of an epoch, $\frac{1}{\alpha}$ value is increased, and it allows the training process to use another set of *complex* instances for the training along with the used *easy* instances. Subsequently, all the instances are fed to the model as the number of epochs grows. In other words, during the first few epochs, an immature predictive model will be trained using easy instances, and it is gradually exposed to complex instances as the model becomes mature.

It may not be possible to directly use the concept of SPL for online updating of the recommender task since SPL is defined for batch learning. However, it is possible to conceptually consider performing online updates for all incoming instances as a training process. The main difference is that in the traditional use of SPL each instance is used for training a model in multiple epochs. However, in the online recommender task, we use each incoming instance for model updating with one epoch. We thus use the SPL regularizer as a scoring function to determine whether an incoming instance is suitable for online updating based on its fit to the existing recommender model.

In contrast to the use of rating profiles, the loss that is incurred by an incoming instance is used to define how suitable the instance is. We use two SPL regularizers to devise an *easy-to-hard* curriculum. In this case, more easy instances, which do not incur a large error, are fed to the model and hard (complex) instances will be fed gradually over time. The SPL regularizers are defined as follows [9,10]:

$$f(\mathbf{p}, \alpha) = -\frac{1}{\alpha}\mathbf{p} \tag{5}$$

$$f(\mathbf{p}, \alpha) = \frac{1}{\alpha}(\frac{1}{2}\|\mathbf{p}\|^2 - \mathbf{p}) \tag{6}$$

Equation 6 leads to the following closed-form solution for the optimal p_{uic}^*.

$$p_{uic}^*(\alpha, \ell_{uic}) = \begin{cases} -\alpha\ell_{uic} + 1 \text{ if } \ell_{uic} < 1/\alpha \\ 0 \text{ if } \ell_{uic} \geq 1/\alpha. \end{cases} \tag{7}$$

Optimizing p with other variables (w, V) fixed. This can be easily achieved by

$$\min_{\mathbf{p} \in [0,1]^\Omega} \sum_{(u,i,c) \in \Omega} p_{uic}\ell_{uic} - \frac{1}{\alpha}p_{uic}. \tag{8}$$

Note that here we choose the SPL regularizer defined in Eq. 5 for clarity.

Optimizing (w, V) with p fixed. In this case, the optimization problem in Eq. (2) for solving these variables becomes

$$\min_{\mathbf{w},\mathbf{V}} \sum_{(u,i,c)\in\Omega} p_{uic}\ell_{uic} + \lambda R(.)\,. \tag{9}$$

Based on previous work [10], we use an alternating strategy for the optimization. Once an incoming instance uic arrives, the RS determines the weight p_{uic} by minimizing Eq. 8. The closed-form solution for p_{uic} can be computed by either Eq. 4 or Eq. 7. Recall that Eq. 8 is formulated based on the SPL regularizer defined in Eq. 5, and it should be changed accordingly when other SPL regularizers are used. Based on p_{uic}, the optimization Eq. 9 is done using Adagrad optimizer [6]. We monotonically decrease α value by $\mu > 1$ (i.e., $\alpha \leftarrow \alpha/\mu$) in regular time interval (e.g., after observing 10,000 instances in the dynamic setting). Note that μ is set to 1.1. When using PS, the model is updated by minimizing the optimization function defined in Eq. 9 by ignoring p_{uic} (i.e., setting $p_{uic} = 1$).

3   Experiments

We conducted experiments with a real-world dataset—*Gowalla* [5]. We extracted check-ins made in the New York City area ($40.5 \leq$ latitude ≤ 41.0, $-74.5 \leq$ longitude ≤ -73.5) between 2009-04-23 and 2010-04-02 (inclusive). Based on check-in timestamps, three temporal contextual features were extracted as follows: *Times of the day* contains five values-Wee hours (00.00–05.59), Morning (6.00–10.59), Noon (11.00–13.59), Afternoon (14.00–17.59) and Evening (18.00–23.59). The contextual factor *Days of the week* contains seven days as values. *WorkdayEnd* indicates whether check-ins are made during a weekend or not. Since the Gowalla dataset contains only positive implicit ratings (i.e. a user checked-in to a point-of-interest (POI)), a uniform negative sampling method was used to ensure robust model training. We leave the study of the Effects of sampling approaches to the online recommender task as a future work.

For each positive instance with the target value as 1, we randomly created two negative instances with POIs which had not been checked-in by the user and assigned 0 as target values. In total, the Gowalla dataset contains 121,299 positive and negative ratings given by 2,482 users for 10,919 POIs. A one-hot encoded feature vector of the Gowalla dataset contains 13,415 feature values.

As per the common practices in online recommendations [1], the model is initialized using a small dataset. Note that the Gowalla dataset is chronologically ordered. We first split our dataset into train and test subsets. We used the first 30,000 ratings as the train set, and the rest of the data is used as a stream of incoming instances for testing. A validation set with 5000 ratings is also extracted from the train set for tuning hyperparameters. A large test set ($\approx 75\%$ of the dataset) has been used to simulate real-world dynamic recommender environments. For this simulation, we adopt the *test-then-learn* evaluation method.

The recommender models have to first provide recommendations for each incoming instance (i.e., user interaction). Based on user feedback (i.e., test) on the produced recommendations, the models are updated (i.e., learn) to keep parameters refreshed. Note that we produce recommendations only for the incoming positive instances since the negative instances do not represent an actual user interaction. However, the negative instances in the test set are used for the online updating process to avoid the learning bias towards the positive instances.

On the arrival of an incoming instance, we truncate a rank list at 100 items by following the work of He et al. [8]. The rank list includes the item that appeared in the instance and 99 items that had not been rated/checked-in by the user (i.e., the user of the instance) previously. *Hit Ratio* (HR) and *Normalized Discounted Cumulative Gain* (NDCG) [7] are used as the evaluation metrics. For both metrics, we report the average result considering all the positive test instances. Both are positive-oriented metrics, meaning that higher values for these metrics indicate better performance.

Baselines. PS and SPS are compared against the following baselines. Note that, for SPS, we use the SPL regularizer defined in Eq. 5: (a) RKMF: This is an online update mechanism integrated with Matrix Factorization (MF) [17]. Incoming instances were selected based on the profile sizes of users and items by favoring new users and new items for online updating. We use the linear kernel and set m of RKMF to the default value of 50; (b) ISGD: ISGD is an incremental MF approach that uses only positive feedback (instances) to update the model [19]; (c) UFF: User factor fading is one of the latent factor forgetting methods proposed by [13]. A constant has been used to regulate the effect of forgetting. As the name implies, latent vectors of users are penalized over time; (d) UnPOP: In this baseline, the latent vectors of unpopular items are penalized [13]; (e) POP: This strategy is the contradiction of UnPOP [13]. The popularity of an item is determined based on the number of ratings that the item had received; and (f) OD: Outlier discarding filters "outlier" of instances based on error values [4]. The authors used this idea to filter out historical ratings in the training, and we adopt this method in the recommender task where each instance is utilized for online updating only if the following condition holds: $|\hat{r}_{uic} - r_{uic}| > \beta.sd_U(u)$, where $\hat{r}_{uic}$ and r_{uic} denote the predicted rating and the ground truth of the instance, and $sd_U(U)$ is the standard deviation of the prediction errors for all previous ratings given by u, and β is the controlling parameter of the forgetting method.

Parameter Setting. For all baselines, we set the learning rate and L_2 regularization parameter to 0.001 and 0.1, respectively. The hyperparameter embedding size k was searched in $\{16, 32, 64, 128\}$, and k was set to 16 and 32 in PS and SPS, respectively. As presented by the authors, the forgetting factors of UFF, UnPOP and POP were set as 0.5, 2 and 1.00001, respectively. β of OD was set to 1.5. We empirically set α to 1.8, δ to 0.98, and θ to 1600. During the initial batch training, all models, except ISGD, were trained for 10 epochs, and PS and SPS used mini-batches (size of 512). Note that, in online updating, we considered the test instances individually and updated all the model using a single epoch.

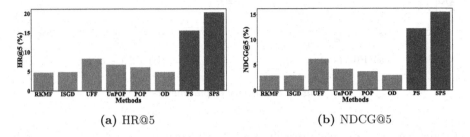

(a) HR@5   (b) NDCG@5

Fig. 1. Prediction accuracy.

3.1 Performance Comparison

Figure 1a and 1b show the comparisons between all methods when generating top-5 recommendations. SPS outperforms all methods by achieving 23.6% and 27.1% relative improvements over the best competitor PS w.r.t. HR and NDCG values, respectively. The improvements over the best competitor are statistically significant with $p < 0.05$ (two-tailed paired t-test). Compared to the MF-based methods which do not use contextual information, the FM-based methods (SPS and PS) show superior performance on the sparse Gowalla dataset. We argue that this improvement is attributed to (1) the use of temporal contextual information and (2) the ability to lead to a better model within a limited number of epochs during the initial training.

Out of all MF-based models, UFF shows better performance. In UFF, during the online update of a user latent vector, the current user vector is computed by multiplying the previous vector by a forgetting factor. Note that UFF does not completely ignore user interactions as proposed in RKMF. The performance improvement of UFF over RKMF indicates the adverse effect of neglecting the interactions of users who have higher rating profiles in online updates. We believe that the performance decline of PS against SPS is also caused by significant information loss that happens especially due to the disregard of short-term preferences of the users who have large rating profiles. On the contrary, SPS assigns 0 weights for the interactions that induce higher losses to the already learned model. The decision to incorporate a user interaction does not depend on the rating profile of the user (or the item or the contextual feature values). Irrespective of the size of a user's rating profile, SPS utilizes an interaction made by that specific user for online updating if it does not deteriorate the already learned model.

Impact of Testing Data. The performance of SPS boosts when the test data size decreases (or the train data size increases). This is an expected observation because the use of more data for initial training improves prediction accuracy.

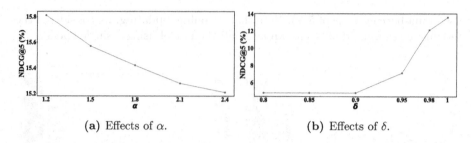

(a) Effects of α.   (b) Effects of δ.

Fig. 2. Sensitivity of parameters.

Decreasing the train set drastically leads to suboptimal performance in general, mainly due to the poorly trained models that are highly sensitive to the users, items, and contextual feature values with small rating profiles. We thus highlight the importance of utilizing a sufficient amount of train data, without overly reducing.

Efficiency. Ignoring instances in PS and SPS is the main reason for the improvements of efficiency. In FMs, the time complexity for updating an instance is $\mathcal{O}(k\bar{m})$ [16], where k is the dimension of a latent vector which corresponds to a feature value, and $\bar{m}$ is the number of non-zero feature values (i.e., variables) presented in the instance. Let $\mathcal{F}$ be the number of test instances in a recommender environment. Thus, updating all instances takes $\mathcal{O}(k\bar{m}\mathcal{F})$ time.

However, due to the instance selection in online updating, we deliberately reduce $\mathcal{F}$, and it leads to gaining efficiency. For example, $\mathcal{F}$ can be approximately reduced to $\frac{\mathcal{F}}{2}$ by setting δ to 0.98 and θ to 1600 in PS or by setting α to 2.1 in SPS. We thus define the time of complexity of the online updating process integrated with our instance selection strategies as $\mathcal{O}(k\bar{m}\mathcal{F}')$, where $\mathcal{F}' < \mathcal{F}$.

3.2   Sensitivity of Parameters

As can be seen in Fig. 2a, the performance of SPS slightly decreases with the increase of α. We conducted a micro-level analysis on this phenomenon. We observe that the increase of α discourages online updating especially at the initial stage of the testing process. For example, when α is set to 2.4, the RS does not update the model during the arrivals of the first 50,000 test instances since the instances are set p^*_{uic} (of Eq. 4) to 0. Moreover, in that setting, the model disregards 61% of instances in total. Omitting a high percentage of testing instances hinders prediction accuracy.

On the contrary, we observe that all the test instances, without selecting, were utilized when α is 1.2; however, this setting is computationally inefficient. Setting α to 1.8 shows a better balance between prediction accuracy and efficiency. If we compare the two settings where α is set to 1.2 and 1.8, when α is 1.8, the online updating declines accuracy only by 2.5% while utilizing 71.8% of testing instances. When α is 2.1, only 52.6% of testing instances are used, and the performance declines against the setting where α is 1.2 just by 3.4%. We thus argue that the use of SPL is important to improve the overall efficiency of the online updating process while achieving comparable prediction accuracy.

Figure 2b plots how NDCG@5 values obtained by PS change with different settings of δ. It is clearly visible that the use of higher values of δ improves the prediction accuracy. In fact, setting δ to 0.8, 0.85, and 0.9 shows similar performance since those settings ignore testing instances similarly. We can observe that setting δ to 1 (i.e., disregard the impact of the profile ratings of contextual feature values) slightly increases the performance. However, the setting where δ to 0.98 declines performance by 12.1% while utilizing only 46.3% of testing instances. Note that the setting where δ is 1 utilizes 93.7% of testing instances.

Based on this effect, we can conclude that the use of contextual information with PS filters out a large number of testing instances, which makes the online updating method efficient, with a decline of prediction accuracy. These observations along with the performance comparison illustrated in Fig. 1b show the superior performance of SPS in the online updating process in terms of balancing the trade-off between prediction accuracy and efficiency compared to PS.

3.3   Case Study

Baltrunas et al. released the *Frappe* dataset[1] that consists of 96,203 usage logs as implicit ratings of 957 users on 4,082 mobile applications under different contexts [2]. We use seven contextual factors (e.g., weather) excluding the attribute "cost". If a user has used an app less than 5 times under a context, we considered those events (i.e., app usages) as negative instances and assigned 0 as their target values. The remaining instances are assigned 1. Due to the unavailability of timestamps in the Frappe dataset, the default order of ratings is used for split data, and the split ratio is similar to that of the Gowalla dataset. It is evident that the use of contextual features generally improves prediction accuracy as shown in Fig. 1a and 1b.

We further analyse this phenomenon by comparing SPS, with SPS\C. SPS\C, which is a variant of SPS, considers users and items to construct feature vectors by ignoring contextual feature values. Both approaches show comparable performance on the Gowalla dataset. However, on the Frappe dataset, SPS outperforms SPS\C by 1.2% and 3.3% in terms of HR@5 and NDCG@5 values, respectively. This result indicates that the effectiveness of SPL for instance selection in the presence of a large number of contextual feature values.

4   Related Work

Most of the early attempts of handling streams of user interactions and updating user-user similarities are based on neighborhood models [15,18]. Vinagre and

---

[1] http://web.archive.org/web/20180422190150/http://baltrunas.info/research-menu/frappe.

Jorge presented a forgetting approach to gradually forget older instances using sliding windows and "fading factors" [18]. In 2014, Matuszyk and Spiliopoulou proposed two forgetting techniques and integrated those with MF [11]. They kept ratings of each user as a list, and once a new rating is provided by a user, the outdated rating was removed from her list of ratings while adding the newly arrived rating. After that, following the *test-then-learn* approach, the latent vector of the incoming user is updated by utilizing the ratings in the incoming user's list. Matuszyka et al. proposed a novel forgetting method in which they obtained a new latent vector of an incoming user by incremental training and compared it with the previously learned user vector [12,13]. Furthermore, the authors have discussed several other forgetting strategies based on item popularity and change detection.

Rendle and Schmidt-Thieme [17] proposed a filtering mechanism to select incoming user instances based on their profile sizes. If a user (item) of an incoming instance has a small profile, then the model incorporates such instances for online updating. Moreover, they proposed to consider the error between the predicted and true values of a user interaction. Devooght et al. also utilized Rendle's work [17] for online updating. Al-Ghossein et al. used local models to track changes in user preferences over time [1]. They argued that changes in user preferences do not occur uniformly. Their approach is based on the Item-based KNN method, and for each incoming instance, their model compares a set of local models to detect changes.

5   Conclusion

We provide an exploratory study on how instance selection mechanisms affect online updating, which is an essential component of the online recommender task. In addition to defining rating profile-based instance selection with the use of contextual feature values, we show how to utilize *Self-Paced Learning*, which has been traditionally used in the batch-learning setting, with online updating. To the best of our knowledge, this is the first attempt to integrate the notion of SPL with online recommendations. Our results indicate the impact of contexts on balancing the trade-off between prediction accuracy and efficiency. Moreover, we discuss how different usages of SPL affect overall performance. In the future, we believe that it is important to study different types of data manipulation mechanisms with online updating to further minimize the impact of information loss that is caused due to the disregard of instances, while improving efficiency.

References

1. Al-Ghossein, M., Abdessalem, T., Barré, A.: Dynamic local models for online recommendation. In: Companion Proceedings of the the Web Conference 2018, pp. 1419–1423 (2018)
2. Baltrunas, L., Church, K., Karatzoglou, A., Oliver, N.: Frappe: understanding the usage and perception of mobile app recommendations in-the-wild. CoRR abs/1505.03014 (2015). http://arxiv.org/abs/1505.03014

3. Bengio, Y., Louradour, J., Collobert, R., Weston, J.: Curriculum learning. In: Proceedings of the 26th Annual International Conference on Machine Learning, pp. 41–48 (2009)
4. Chen, J., Li, H., Xie, Q., Li, L., Liu, Y.: Streaming recommendation algorithm with user interest drift analysis. In: Shao, J., Yiu, M.L., Toyoda, M., Zhang, D., Wang, W., Cui, B. (eds.) APWeb-WAIM 2019. LNCS, vol. 11642, pp. 121–136. Springer, Cham (2019). https://doi.org/10.1007/978-3-030-26075-0_10
5. Cho, E., Myers, S.A., Leskovec, J.: Friendship and mobility: user movement in location-based social networks. In: Proceedings of the 17th ACM SIGKDD International Conference on Knowledge Discovery and Data Mining, pp. 1082–1090 (2011)
6. Duchi, J., Hazan, E., Singer, Y.: Adaptive subgradient methods for online learning and stochastic optimization. J. Mach. Learn. Res. **12**, 2121–2159 (2011)
7. He, X., Chen, T., Kan, M.Y., Chen, X.: TriRank: review-aware explainable recommendation by modeling aspects. In: Proceedings of the 24th ACM International on Conference on Information and Knowledge Management, pp. 1661–1670. ACM (2015)
8. He, X., Zhang, H., Kan, M.Y., Chua, T.S.: Fast matrix factorization for online recommendation with implicit feedback. In: Proceedings of the 39th International ACM SIGIR Conference on Research and Development in Information Retrieval, pp. 549–558 (2016)
9. Jiang, L., Meng, D., Mitamura, T., Hauptmann, A.G.: Easy samples first: self-paced reranking for zero-example multimedia search. In: Proceedings of the 22nd ACM International Conference on Multimedia, pp. 547–556 (2014)
10. Kumar, M.P., Packer, B., Koller, D.: Self-paced learning for latent variable models. In: Advances in Neural Information Processing Systems, pp. 1189–1197 (2010)
11. Matuszyk, P., Spiliopoulou, M.: Selective forgetting for incremental matrix factorization in recommender systems. In: Džeroski, S., Panov, P., Kocev, D., Todorovski, L. (eds.) DS 2014. LNCS (LNAI), vol. 8777, pp. 204–215. Springer, Cham (2014). https://doi.org/10.1007/978-3-319-11812-3_18
12. Matuszyk, P., Vinagre, J., Spiliopoulou, M., Jorge, A.M., Gama, J.: Forgetting methods for incremental matrix factorization in recommender systems. In: Proceedings of the 30th Annual ACM Symposium on Applied Computing, pp. 947–953 (2015)
13. Matuszyk, P., Vinagre, J., Spiliopoulou, M., Jorge, A.M., Gama, J.: Forgetting techniques for stream-based matrix factorization in recommender systems. Knowl. Inf. Syst. **55**(2), 275–304 (2018)
14. Nasraoui, O., Cerwinske, J., Rojas, C., Gonzalez, F.: Performance of recommendation systems in dynamic streaming environments. In: Proceedings of the 2007 SIAM International Conference on Data Mining, pp. 569–574. SIAM (2007)
15. Papagelis, M., Rousidis, I., Plexousakis, D., Theoharopoulos, E.: Incremental collaborative filtering for highly-scalable recommendation algorithms. In: Hacid, M.-S., Murray, N.V., Raś, Z.W., Tsumoto, S. (eds.) ISMIS 2005. LNCS (LNAI), vol. 3488, pp. 553–561. Springer, Heidelberg (2005). https://doi.org/10.1007/11425274_57
16. Rendle, S.: Factorization machines. In: 2010 IEEE International Conference on Data Mining, pp. 995–1000. IEEE (2010)
17. Rendle, S., Schmidt-Thieme, L.: Online-updating regularized kernel matrix factorization models for large-scale recommender systems. In: Proceedings of the 2008 ACM Conference on Recommender Systems, pp. 251–258 (2008)

18. Vinagre, J., Jorge, A.M.: Forgetting mechanisms for scalable collaborative filtering. J. Braz. Comput. Soc. **18**(4), 271–282 (2012)
19. Vinagre, J., Jorge, A.M., Gama, J.: Fast incremental matrix factorization for recommendation with positive-only feedback. In: Dimitrova, V., Kuflik, T., Chin, D., Ricci, F., Dolog, P., Houben, G.-J. (eds.) UMAP 2014. LNCS, vol. 8538, pp. 459–470. Springer, Cham (2014). https://doi.org/10.1007/978-3-319-08786-3_41
20. Zhang, Y., Wang, H., Lian, D., Tsang, I.W., Yin, H., Yang, G.: Discrete ranking-based matrix factorization with self-paced learning. In: Proceedings of the 24th ACM SIGKDD International Conference on Knowledge Discovery & Data Mining, pp. 2758–2767 (2018)

Text Analytics

Fusing Essential Knowledge
for Text-Based Open-Domain
Question Answering

Xiao Su[1], Ying Li[2(✉)], and Zhonghai Wu[2]

[1] Center for Data Science, Peking University, Beijing, China
`sugarshaw951018@pku.edu.cn`
[2] National Engineering Research Center of Software Engineering,
Peking University, Beijing, China
{`li.ying,wuzh`}`@pku.edu.cn`

Abstract. Question answering (QA) systems can be classified as either text-based QA systems or knowledge base QA (KBQA) systems, depending on the used knowledge source. KBQA systems are generally domain-specific and can't deal with a variety of questions in the open-domain QA setting, while text-based systems can. However, text-based systems' performance is far from satisfactory. This paper focuses on the text-based open-domain QA setting. We argue that text-based approaches' poor performance is largely caused by the lack of knowledge, which is often essential for answering the question and can be easily found in knowledge base (KB), in plain text. So in this paper, we propose a new text-based open-domain QA system called KF (Knowledge Fusion)-QA, which uses KB as a second knowledge source to incorporate essential knowledge into text to help answer the question. Our system has a Knowledge-Aware Encoder which extracts essential knowledge from KB and performs knowledge fusion to output knowledge-aware (KA) text representations. With this KA representations, the system first re-rank the retrieved documents, then read the re-ranked top-N documents to give the answer. Our system significantly outperforms existing text-based QA systems on multiple open-domain QA datasets, demonstrating the effectiveness of fusing essential knowledge.

Keywords: Question answering · Knowledge base · Document retrieval · Graph attention neural network

1 Introduction

Open-domain question answering (QA) has broad application prospects. Open-domain literally means the questions can be of any type, and an ideal open-domain QA system should be able to answer any question. Depending on the main knowledge source used to answer the questions, there are two kinds of QA systems: text-based QA and Knowledge Base QA (KBQA). Using text can

© Springer Nature Switzerland AG 2021
K. Karlapalem et al. (Eds.): PAKDD 2021, LNAI 12713, pp. 627–639, 2021.
https://doi.org/10.1007/978-3-030-75765-6_50

handle most types of questions by extracting text spans as answers from a large-scale corpus such as Wikipedia, which covers various domains. KBs more directly support inferences, which is often needed in answering a question, hence KBQA generally performs better on questions whose answers can be found in KBs. However, KBQA systems can't deal with descriptive questions like "How to correctly wear a mask?" or "What is COVID-19?", and under the open-domain QA setting, questions can be of any type. For open-domain QA, text-based QA is a better choice. But text-based QA systems' performance is far from satisfactory, an effective way for improving text-based QA systems is needed.

Existing text-based open-domain QA systems generally follow a 2-stage framework proposed by DrQA [5], which consists of a Retriever that retrieves relevant documents from a large-scale corpus and a Reader which reads the retrieved documents to give the answer. This process is quite similar to how human answer an unfamiliar question, we will also look for documents in the library or on the web, then read them to find the answer. However the difference is, human is aware of a large amount of knowledge in this whole process, while machine is not. This difference greatly limits the performance of existing systems, as knowledge is often quite essential for answering the question. Moreover, due to time efficiency and computational complexity considerations, retrievers in previous works are designed too simple, thus can't accurately find the relevant documents of the question.

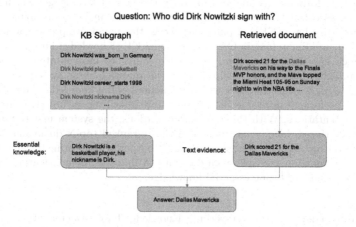

Fig. 1. An example of questions that are hard to answer only using surface text, but much easier with common sense knowledge in KB. In this example, it's hard to conclude that "sign with" means signing with a team, and "Dirk" means Dirk Nowitzki only reading the document. But with the knowledge that KB provides, it's easy to draw such conclusions and get the answer.

Knowledge bases (KBs) contain rich knowledge information which is helpful for QA, as shown in Fig. 1. Also, they are specially designed for machines to read and have been widely applied in NLP research in the recent years. Thus we believe KB can be a second knowledge source for text-based QA system. We argue that the problems mentioned before can be solved by introducing KB. By adding knowledge into text and getting the knowledge-aware text representations, it's certainly easier to understand the document and find the answer. In addition, with the text representations that contain not only semantic information, but also useful knowledge, we can more accurately find the relevant documents by re-ranking.

In this paper, we present a new text-based open-domain QA system that is capable of selectively extracting knowledge that is essential for QA and incorporating it into text. With the enhanced knowledge-aware text representations, our system first re-ranks the documents, then reads the selected documents to give the answer. Compared to several other famous text-based open-domain QA systems, ours achieves consistent improvements on 4 popular open-domain QA datasets. We name our system KF (Knowledge Fusion)-QA.

2   Related Work

2.1   Text-Based Question Answering

Text-based open-domain QA is a long studied problem. Recent work has focused on a "Retriever-Reader" 2-stage framework that combines information retrieval with machine reading comprehension (MRC) [5]. A lot of efforts have been made to improve this 2-stage framework. For example, R3 [17] uses a Ranker-Reader framework, in which Ranker and Reader shares an encoder, and uses reinforcement learning to train the Ranker, hoping to improve the retrieval accuracy by re-ranking. Multi-step reasoner [6] is also a new framework aiming at improving retrieval accuracy, but does it by training the Retriever with Retriever-Reader interactions. As pre-trained language models are widely used in NLP, there are also works that apply BERT-based dense retriever like ORQA [11] and DPR [10].

However, these works still only use the surface text, hence they have not achieved a notable performance improvement. Our system also has an encoder that provides inputs for both ranker and reader. However, unlike R3, our encoder is knowledge-aware, which means we can incorporate knowledge into the text representations, thus achieving a much better performance.

2.2   Knowledge Base Question Answering

Early works on question answering over knowledge bases do not use any external text, however recently, several works have succeeded in combining KBs with text from a large-scale corpus to increase factual coverage. These works can be classified as either early-fusion approaches or late-fusion approaches. Early-fusion approaches like Graft-Net [15] take text as special graph nodes to construct a heterogeneous graph containing both text and KB facts in the early stage. While late-fusion approaches [18] will get text-related representations and KB-related representations for entities, then aggregate them in the final answer prediction stage. Our goal is to incorporate knowledge into text, not text into KB. However late fusion approaches can still be inspiring to our work, as it combine KB and knowledge in the form of embedding rather than graph data.

3 Our System: KF-QA

3.1 Overview

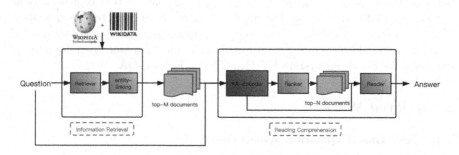

Fig. 2. Overview of our open-domain QA system KF-QA.

KF-QA follows the classic "Retriever-Reader" 2-stage framework, as shown in Fig. 2.

In the information retrieval stage, we use the same TF-IDF based Retriever of DrQA to find top-M relevant documents from a large corpus. As we introduce KB into the system, we have to annotate entities in the questions and documents with an entity linking tool, we use tagme [8] in practice.

In the reading comprehension stage, we incorporate knowledge into text and encode text using Knowledge-Aware Encoder, the core component of our system, which will be explained in detail later in Sect. 3.2, and get the question representation q_{ka} and document representations $\{p_1, p_2...p_n\}$. With the enhanced text representations, we first re-rank the top-M documents using a Ranker to select the final top-N documents as evidence. Then the Reader will read the selected documents and output the final answer. Details about Ranker and Reader will be explained in Sect. 3.3.

3.2 Knowledge-Aware Encoder

As shown in Fig. 3, the Knowledge-Aware (KA) Encoder consists of a SubGraph Encoder, which extracts KB entity knowledge by encoding the entities on a question-related KB subgraph, and a text Encoder which encodes text and incorporates knowledge extracted by SubGraph Encoder in the encoding process.

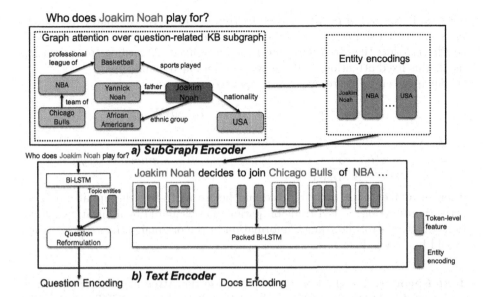

Fig. 3. Architecture of KA Encoder. a) shows part of the KB subgraph related to question "Who does Joakim Noah play for?", the entity encodings in SubGraph Encoder are passed to Text Encoder for knowledge fusion.

SubGraph Encoder. The SubGraph Encoder aims at extracting KB entity knowledge that is essential for answering the questions, and does it by encoding the entities. To make sure the knowledge we extract is useful for answering the question, we first retrieve a small question-related KB subgraph using the topic entities in the question as seed nodes, and only consider this subgraph. Also, we need to pay more attention to important entities, so we apply graph-attention technique (GAT) [16] to encode the entities. Instead of using standard GAT, we specifically modify it for the QA task setting. Under the QA task setting, important entities are defined like this: they are either mentioned in the question, or their neighbor relations are relevant to the question. The first factor can be simply described by a binary feature, while for the second, we have to evaluate how relevant a relation is to the question. To do this, we first tokenize the relations, then encode questions and relations to calculate a matching score s_r for relation r. This is similar to measuring semantic similarity, so we apply a fixed Universal Sentence Encoder (USE) [3], which is trained on a large corpus including semantic similarity corpus, and calculate the score by simple dot product.

For central entity e and neighbor (r_i, e_i), with the the binary feature $I[e_i \in \varepsilon_q]$ (ε_q is the set of topic entities of the question) and matching score s_{r_i}, we combine them with the original GAT attention coefficient co_{e,e_i} (with sigmoid to align with the first two factors) to calculate the attention score as:

$$\alpha_{e,e_i} \propto \exp(I[e_i \in \varepsilon_q] + s_{r_i} + sigmoid(co_{e,e_i}))$$

This modified GAT is partly inspired by [18], however [18] calculates the matching score with a simple LSTM and does not consider the original GAT attention coefficient, thus the attention score is actually fixed. According to our experiment, this fixed attention performs worse than our dynamic one.

Then the entity representation is updated as:

$$\acute{e} = \gamma_e e + (1 - \gamma_e) \sum_{(e_i, r_i) \in N_e} \alpha_{e,e_i} \sigma(\mathbf{W_e} e_i)$$

$$\gamma_e = g(e, \sum_{(e_i, r_i) \in N_e} \alpha_{e,e_i} \sigma(\mathbf{W_e} e_i)), g(x, y) = sigmoid(\mathbf{W}[x; y])$$

where e and $\acute{e}$ is the entity embedding before and after the update, σ is an activation function. γ_e is a trade-off parameter calculated by a linear gate function, which controls how much information in the original entity representation should be retained.

Text Encoder. For the text encoder, we use the Attentive Reader [4], which is also used in DrQA, and improve it by knowledge fusion. BERT-based model is not used because we believe pre-trained models already contain some type of knowledge in the pre-training process, using it may not be convincing enough to show the effectiveness of bringing in KB knowledge. We explain question encoding and document encoding separately, as the encoding strategy is different.

Question Encoding
For question encoding, we encode the question as a single vector. First we apply a Bi-LSTM to encode each token and get $\{q_1, ..., q_n\}$ for each question token. Then encode the whole question with a self-attentive encoder as: $q = \sum_i \alpha_i q_i, \alpha_i \propto w \cdot q_i$

However, this representation we get does not contain knowledge yet. We need to reformulate the question with knowledge of its topic entities. Here we apply a gating mechanism to do this reformulation as follows and get the final question representation q_{ka}:

$$q_{ka} = \beta_q q + (1 - \beta_q) \tanh(\mathbf{W}[q; e_q; q - e_q]), e_q = (\sum_{e \in \varepsilon_q} e)/|\varepsilon_q|$$

ε_q is the set of topic entities of the question, and β_q is a linear gate: $\beta_q = \sigma(\mathbf{W_{gate}}[q; e_q; q - e_q])$.

Document Encoding
For document encoding, since we need to get each token's knowledge-aware representation, knowledge fusion has to be done in a more fine-grained way. Specifically, we first add knowledge into each token's feature, then feed token features that contain knowledge into the Packed Bi-LSTM encoder to get the knowledge-aware representations. With the KB entity annotations, we fuse entity knowledge and the original token features in a similar gating mechanism to the question reformulation:

$$f_i^{ka} = \beta f_i + (1 - \beta)e_{f_i}$$

$$\beta = \sigma(\mathbf{W_{gate}}[\boldsymbol{f_i}; \boldsymbol{e_{f_i}}])$$

where $\boldsymbol{f_i}$ is the original token-level feature, and $\boldsymbol{e_{f_i}}$ is the embedding of the entity linked to token i. While for those tokens who don't link to any KB entity, we just keep their feature the way it is. Finally, we get the output token-level encodings $\{\boldsymbol{p_1}, \boldsymbol{p_2}...\boldsymbol{p_n}\}$ as the document representations.

3.3 Ranker and Reader

Ranker. The Ranker re-ranks the top-M documents with the knowledge-aware representations of document tokens $\{\boldsymbol{p_1}, \boldsymbol{p_2}...\boldsymbol{p_n}\}$ and question $\boldsymbol{q_{ka}}$. We first compute the representation of the whole document as: $\boldsymbol{d} = \sum_i \alpha_i \boldsymbol{p_i}$, the importance of each token α_i is computed by question-document attention: $\alpha_i \propto exp(\boldsymbol{q_{ka}} \cdot \boldsymbol{p_i})$. Then we compute the probability of the current document being relevant to the question with a bilinear classifier as:

$$P = sigmoid(\boldsymbol{d}\mathbf{W}\boldsymbol{q_{ka}})$$

and selects top-N ($N \ll M$) documents with the highest probabilities.

Reader. Our Reader takes the representations from the Knowledge-Aware Encoder as inputs, and computes the probability of each token being the start and end of the answer span in a way similar to the Ranker:

$$P_{start} = Softmax(\boldsymbol{p_i}\mathbf{W_{start}}\boldsymbol{q_{ka}}), P_{end} = Softmax(\boldsymbol{p_i}\mathbf{W_{end}}\boldsymbol{q_{ka}})$$

During prediction, we set a length limit of the answer span and choose the span that maximizes $P_{start} * P_{end}$.

3.4 Training

We train the whole system using multi-task learning. We regard Ranker and Reader as two models sharing the same Encoder, which is the KA-Encoder. Ranker's task is a binary classification task that decides whether the given document contains answer of the question. Loss for Ranker is defined as:

$$L_{ranker} = BCE(P_{ranker}, P_{truth})$$

P_{ranker} is the probabilities returned by Ranker, P_{truth} is the ground truth, and BCE is the Binary Cross Entropy loss function.

Reader's task is to find the answer's start and end positions in the given document. Its loss is defined as:

$$L_{reader} = CE(start_{predict}, start_{truth}) + CE(end_{predict}, end_{truth})$$

$start_{predict}$ and $start_{truth}$ is the prediction and ground truth of start indexs, the same for $end_{predict}$ and end_{truth}. CE is the Cross Entropy loss function.

Loss of the entire system is defined as:

$$L = L_{ranker} + \beta L_{reader}$$

β is a balancing parameter, we set it to 1.0 in our experiments .

Training data is provided by the Pre-Retriever. For one question, we retrieve top-M documents, all M documents will be used to train the Ranker, while only those who contain answers will be used to train the Reader.

4   Experiments

4.1   Setup

Datasets

We conduct experiments on 4 public open-domain QA datasets:

WebQuestions [1] is created to answer questions from the Freebase KB. It was built by crawling questions through the Google Suggest API, and then obtaining answers using Amazon Mechanical Turk.

WikiMovies [13] is originally built from the OMDb and MovieLens databases. The questions are all movie-related, and can be answered using a subset of Wikipedia. A small corpus and a movie-specific KB is constructed from Wikipedia and released with the dataset, so we use the given corpus and KB in the experiments.

SquAD [14] is the Stanford QA dataset. In the original dataset, relevant documents are already given for each question. So we take only the question-answer pairs and discard the given documents to form an open-domain QA setting.

Quasar-T [7] contains question-answer pairs from various Internet sources. For each QA pair, documents retrieved by their IR model from the ClueWeb09 data source is also given (100 short documents and 5 long documents). So instead of using our Pre-Retriever to retrieve from a corpus, we use the given documents.

The first two datasets are KBQA datasets, which means their answers are all KB entities, and we convert them to text form. While for the rest two, answer form is originally text. The question related KB subgraphs are retrieved by running Personalized PageRank (PPR) [9] around the topic entities annotated by tagme [8]. We choose Wikipedia as corpus for WebQuestions and SquAD as the rest two have their own corpus. And Freebase [2] is used as KB for all datasets except WikiMovies.

Evaluation Metrics

For evaluating the system's overall performance, Exact Match (EM) is certainly used, F1 score is also considered as there are situations where the predicted answer and the ground truth are partly overlapped. We also conduct experiments on Ranker, and retrieval precision is used for evaluating Ranker's performance.

Baselines

We compare our system with 6 text-based systems: DrQA [5], R3 [17], DS-QA [12], Multi-Step Reasoner [6], ORQA [11] and DPR [10]. We also use GraftNet [15], a state-of-the-art KBQA system, as a baseline on the first 2 datasets to see how close our system can get to KBQA systems.

4.2   Overall Performance

Table 1. Overall performance results.

Dataset	WebQuestions		Wikimovies		SquAD		Quasar-T	
	F1	EM	F1	EM	F1	EM	F1	EM
KF-QA (Ours)	43.4	41.9	80.5	79.6	**43.2**	**38.2**	**51.2**	**43.6**
DrQA [5]	–	19.5	–	34.3	–	28.4	–	–
R3 [17]	24.6	17.1	39.9	38.8	37.5	29.1	40.9	34.2
Multi-step reasoner [6]	–	–	–	–	39.2	31.9	46.7	35.9
DS-QA [12]	25.6	18.5	–	–	–	–	49.3	42.2
ORQA [11]	–	36.4	–	–	–	20.2	–	–
DPR [10]	–	34.6*	–	–	–	29.8	–	–
GraftNet [15]	**62.3**	**68.7**	**97.3**	**96.8**	–	–	–	–

* DPR achieves 42.4 EM on WebQuestions when jointly trained with other datasets. For fair comparison, we show the result when trained with only WebQuestions itself.

We use F1 score and Exact Match (EM) to evaluate the system's overall performance. In practice, we retrieve 50 documents with the Retriever ($M = 50$), and for fair comparison, only read top-1 document to give the answer ($N = 1$).

The overall performance results are shown in Table 1. As we can see, our system significantly outperforms other text-based systems on all datasets. Among the four datasets, improvement on the first two datasets is more significant compared to the rest two. As the first two datasets are KBQA datasets, whose questions are all KB-related, and our system mainly improves the performance by bringing in KB knowledge, this actually makes sense.

Although our system performs best among all text-based QA systems, there is still a certain gap compared to KBQA systems on KBQA datasets. But as mentioned before, KBQA can't handle various types of questions under the open-domain QA setting, while our system can. We believe this gap is partly due to the different task setting: KBQA's answer search space is much smaller than text-based QA . However this gap still indicates that there's much room for improvement, and we plan to work on finding a more subtle way of fusing knowledge to further improve our system in the future.

4.3   Ablation Study: Ranker Performance

We also investigate the performance of our Ranker to validate our hypothesis that re-ranking does help. We compare the retrieval precision with/without Ranker's re-ranking. In practice, we retrieve 50 documents for a single question in the pre-retrieving step, and evaluate precision of top-K ranked documents for K = 1,3,5.

Table 2. Ranker performance results.

Dataset	WebQuestions			Wikimovies		
	P@1	P@3	P@5	P@1	P@3	P@5
Without re-ranking	10.43	22.45	28.37	42.38	62.32	69.6
After re-ranking	**42.77**	**50.88**	**53.93**	**85.31**	**88.49**	**89.04**

Since this is just for qualitative analysis, we only conduct experiments on 2 datasets. From the results in Table 2, we can tell that re-ranking can largely improve retrieval precision, which demonstrates its effectiveness as a mechanism. We can also tell that this improvement, in terms of P@K, is more significant when K is smaller, which is quite satisfying because in practice, K is normally 1.

4.4   Case Study

Table 3 shows two examples of our system. For comparison, we also show the retrieved document and predicted answer of DrQA. From the table we find that:

(1) For question "What jersey did the Broncos wear for Super Bowl 50?", DrQA retrieves a document about "Super Bowl", which actually does not contain the right answer. So it gives a random answer like "Los Angeles Rams". While KF-QA correctly returns a document about "Super Bowl 50" and gives the right answer. That's because "Super Bowl 50" as a whole, is an entity in the KB. Knowing this knowledge, it's easy to retrieve documents about it. But DrQA is not aware of it, hence retrieves a document in which the word "Super Bowl" appears a lot.

(2) For question "Who does Jordan Palmer play for?", the 2 systems retrieve the same document about "Jordan Palmer", which contains the right answer "Jacksonville Jaguars", but DrQA mistakenly take the first team name appeared in this document, "UTEP", which is Jordan Palmer's college team, as the answer. With the help of KB, KF-QA is aware that Jordan Palmer is a professional player, and "UTEP" is a college team, thus can easily distinguish it from the right answer.

Table 3. Case study examples. **Doc-topic** means topic of the document. The first example illustrates that our system can find more relevant document. The second one shows that with the same document, our system can easily find the right answer with KB's help.

Question	What jersey did the Broncos wear for Super Bowl 50?
Answer	"road white jerseys", "matching white", "white"
KF-QA	**Doc**: Super Bowl 50 **content**: As the designated home team in the annual rotation between AFC and NFC teams, the Broncos elected to wear their **road white jerseys** with matching white pants. Elway stated, "We've had Super Bowl success in our white uniforms." The Broncos last wore matching white jerseys and pants in the Super Bowl in Super Bowl XXXIII, ...
DrQA	**Doc**: Super Bowl **content**: No team has ever played the Super Bowl in its home stadium. Two teams have played the Super Bowl in their home market: the San Francisco 49ers, who played Super Bowl XIX in Stanford Stadium instead of Candlestick Park; and the **Los Angeles Rams**, who played Super Bowl XIV in the Rose Bowl ... Besides those two, the only other Super Bowl venue that was not the home stadium to an NFL team at the time was Rice Stadium in Houston: the Houston Oilers had played there previously, but moved to the Astrodome several years prior to Super Bowl VIII. ...
Question	Who does Jordan Palmer play for?
Answer	"Jacksonville Jaguars"
KF-QA	**Doc**: Jordan Palmer **content**: ... During his freshman year at UTEP, Palmer threw seven touchdowns and 13 interceptions while completing 49.5% of his passes for 1,168 yards ... He was drafted by the Washington Redskins in the sixth round of the 2007 NFL Draft. He is the younger brother of the Arizona Cardinals quarterback Carson Palmer, who was the first overall pick in the 2003 NFL Draft by the Cincinnati Bengals. ... Palmer signed with the **Jacksonville Jaguars** on May 7, 2012. ...
DrQA	**Doc**: Jordan Palmer **content**: ... During his freshman year at **UTEP**, Palmer threw seven touchdowns and 13 interceptions while completing 49.5% of his passes for 1,168 yards ... He was drafted by the Washington Redskins in the sixth round of the 2007 NFL Draft. He is the younger brother of the Arizona Cardinals quarterback Carson Palmer, who was the first overall pick in the 2003 NFL Draft by the Cincinnati Bengals. ... Palmer signed with the Jacksonville Jaguars on May 7, 2012. ...

5   Conclusion

We propose a new text-based QA system that uses knowledge base (KB) as a second knowledge source, namely KF-QA. KF-QA first incorporates knowledge that is essential for QA into text representations with the KA-Encoder, then re-ranks the documents with a Ranker, finally outputs the answer by reading the documents selected by the Ranker. KF-QA significantly outperforms previous text-based QA systems on several QA datasets, demonstrating the effectiveness of introducing KB into text-based QA. Our ablation study on Ranker performance also demonstrates the effectiveness of re-ranking mechanism. However, we believe there is still much room for improvement, our future work will aim at finding a more subtle way for knowledge fusion, as the current way is still kind of rough.

References

1. Berant, J., Chou, A., Frostig, R., Liang, P.: Semantic parsing on freebase from question-answer pairs. In: Proceedings of the 2013 Conference on Empirical Methods in Natural Language Processing, pp. 1533–1544 (2013)
2. Bollacker, K., Evans, C., Paritosh, P., Sturge, T., Taylor, J.: Freebase: a collaboratively created graph database for structuring human knowledge. In: Proceedings of the 2008 ACM SIGMOD International Conference on Management of Data, pp. 1247–1250 (2008)
3. Cer, D., et al.: Universal sentence encoder. arXiv preprint arXiv:1803.11175 (2018)
4. Chen, D., Bolton, J., Manning, C.D.: A thorough examination of the CNN/daily mail reading comprehension task. arXiv preprint arXiv:1606.02858 (2016)
5. Chen, D., Fisch, A., Weston, J., Bordes, A.: Reading Wikipedia to answer open-domain questions. arXiv preprint arXiv:1704.00051 (2017)
6. Das, R., Dhuliawala, S., Zaheer, M., McCallum, A.: Multi-step retriever-reader interaction for scalable open-domain question answering. arXiv preprint arXiv:1905.05733 (2019)
7. Dhingra, B., Mazaitis, K., Cohen, W.W.: Quasar: datasets for question answering by search and reading. arXiv preprint arXiv:1707.03904 (2017)
8. Ferragina, P., Scaiella, U.: TAGME: on-the-fly annotation of short text fragments (by Wikipedia entities). In: Proceedings of the 19th ACM International Conference on Information and Knowledge Management, pp. 1625–1628 (2010)
9. Haveliwala, T.H.: Topic-sensitive PageRank: a context-sensitive ranking algorithm for web search. IEEE Trans. Knowl. Data Eng. **15**(4), 784–796 (2003)
10. Karpukhin, V., et al.: Dense passage retrieval for open-domain question answering. arXiv preprint arXiv:2004.04906 (2020)
11. Lee, K., Chang, M.W., Toutanova, K.: Latent retrieval for weakly supervised open domain question answering. arXiv preprint arXiv:1906.00300 (2019)
12. Lin, Y., Ji, H., Liu, Z., Sun, M.: Denoising distantly supervised open-domain question answering. In: Proceedings of the 56th Annual Meeting of the Association for Computational Linguistics (Long Papers), vol. 1, pp. 1736–1745 (2018)
13. Miller, A., Fisch, A., Dodge, J., Karimi, A.H., Bordes, A., Weston, J.: Key-value memory networks for directly reading documents. arXiv preprint arXiv:1606.03126 (2016)

14. Rajpurkar, P., Zhang, J., Lopyrev, K., Liang, P.: SQuAD: 100,000+ questions for machine comprehension of text. arXiv preprint arXiv:1606.05250 (2016)
15. Sun, H., Dhingra, B., Zaheer, M., Mazaitis, K., Salakhutdinov, R., Cohen, W.W.: Open domain question answering using early fusion of knowledge bases and text. arXiv preprint arXiv:1809.00782 (2018)
16. Veličković, P., Cucurull, G., Casanova, A., Romero, A., Lio, P., Bengio, Y.: Graph attention networks. arXiv preprint arXiv:1710.10903 (2017)
17. Wang, S., et al.: R 3: Reinforced ranker-reader for open-domain question answering. In: Thirty-Second AAAI Conference on Artificial Intelligence (2018)
18. Xiong, W., Yu, M., Chang, S., Guo, X., Wang, W.Y.: Improving question answering over incomplete KBs with knowledge-aware reader. arXiv preprint arXiv:1905.07098 (2019)

TSSE-DMM: Topic Modeling for Short Texts Based on Topic Subdivision and Semantic Enhancement

Chengcheng Mai, Xueming Qiu, Kaiwen Luo, Min Chen, Bo Zhao,
and Yihua Huang[(✉)]

Department of Computer Science and Technology, State Key Laboratory for Novel
Software Technology, Nanjing University, Nanjing, China
{maicc,xuemingqiu,mf1933070}@smail.nju.edu.cn, yhuang@nju.edu.cn

Abstract. Short texts have been prevalent in Web sites and the emerging social media for several years, which makes it a critical task to identify intelligible topics from online data sources. However, the existing topic models over short texts cannot analyze the internal components of the learned topics, which is significant for improving the coherence and interpretability of topics. In this paper, we propose a novel topic model for short texts, named TSSE-DMM, for improving the coherence and interpretability of topics by the topic subdivision and alleviating the problem of text sparsity by the semantic enhancement strategy. Firstly, we subdivide each topic into 4 detailed aspects, namely the location aspect, the people & organization aspect, the core word aspect, and the background word aspect, to obtain the different and interpretable components of topics. Then, we combine the Generalized Polya Urn model and the joint word embedding to solve the problem of data sparsity. The extensive experimental results carried on three real-world text collections in two languages show that our model achieves better topic representations than the baseline methods. Moreover, our method has been adopted by the public service hotline platform of Jiangsu province in China.

Keywords: Topic model · Topic subdivision · Semantic enhancement

1 Introduction

Short texts have become a fashionable form of Information on social media. Effective models to generate topics become critical to support downstream applications, such as bursty event detection [17], knowledge graph constructing [15], and information summarization [6].

Suffering from the severe data sparsity problem, conventional topic models, like pLSA [3] and LDA [1] experience a large performance degradation when directly applied to short texts. To solve the problem, Quan et al. [13] aggregate short texts into lengthy pseudo-documents before training a conventional topic model. Another solution is to enhance the word co-occurrence patterns by the

© Springer Nature Switzerland AG 2021
K. Karlapalem et al. (Eds.): PAKDD 2021, LNAI 12713, pp. 640–651, 2021.
https://doi.org/10.1007/978-3-030-75765-6_51

Generalized Poly Urn (GPU) model [4]. The overall idea of the GPU model is that we not only increase the counts of word w assigned to topic k but also increase the counts of other words with similar semantics to word w.

In addition, these above methods are unable to analyze the internal components of the topics because they do not exploit the following important observation: A topic is composed of many different aspects, like the related location, people's name, organization, core words, and background words. For example, as shown in Fig. 1, this record is a real complaint sample from the public service hotline platform of Jiangsu province in China that highly related to the topic of *'Noise during the College Entrance Examination'*. The word *'Gulou District'* can be recognized as named entities about the related locations. Likewise, the word *'examination venues'* can be considered as the core words of topic. The topic subdivision method is feasible for improving the coherence and interpretability of this topic because these core words are highly related to one certain topic.

Record:

The illegal construction is prohibited during the college entrance examination. A waterproofing construction in | No. 6 District of Doucai Bridge | in | Gulou District | was stopped which is adjacent to the Jinling Middle School Examination Venues.

Fig. 1. A complaint record about the prohibition of illegal construction during the college entrance examination. The square denotes the related location, the wavy underline denotes the organization, the double underline denotes the core words of the record, and the dotted underline denotes the background words (i.e. the noisy data).

Based on the analysis above, we propose a novel TSSM-DMM model. Firstly, we subdivide each topic into 4 topic aspects, namely the location aspect, people & organization aspect, core words aspect, and background word aspect. Each word in the corpus would be generated by its related topic-aspect-word distribution. Then, we propose a semantic enhancement strategy to alleviate the problem of data sparsity and Out-Of-Vocabulary (OOV). Compared with other baseline methods, significant improvements are achieved in the experiments. The code for our method is available online: https://github.com/PasaLab/TSSE.

The paper is organized as follows. Section 2 describes our model. Section 3 gives the experimental results and analyses. Section 4 introduces the related work. Conclusions are given in Sect. 5.

2 Our TSSE-DMM Model

2.1 Topic Subdivision

The Conception of the Topic Subdivision. Intuitively, the short texts from websites or social media consist of many named entities, like people's names, locations, and organizations. The existing topic models do not consider this characteristic and all the words belonging to different named entities are mixed up, which brings a huge challenge for improving the coherence of topics. Therefore, we propose a topic model for short texts named TSSE-DMM that could further subdivide each topic into 4 aspects, namely the location aspect, people & organization aspect, core word aspect and the background word aspect, according to the POS tags of the words in document d. As its name suggests, the TSSE-DMM model is built upon the Dirichlet Mixture Model (DMM) model that assumes that each document d is generated from a single topic k [9,12].

Table 1. The 863 POS tag set

POS	Meaning	Example	POS	Meaning	Example
a	Adjective	Beautiful	ni	Organization name	WTO
i	Idiom	A hundred flowers blossom	nl	Position	Suburb
j	Abbreviation	U.S.A.	ns	Place name	Shanghai
n	The common noun	Apple	nz	Proper noun	The Noble prize
nh	People's name	Tom	v	Verb	Run

As shown in Table 1, we select some named entities according to the POS tags in the 863 POS tag set[1] for the topic subdivision based on the expert knowledge and the practical requirements from the real applications. The aspect set of the topic can be denoted as $Q = \{q|q = 0, 1, 2\}$. The symbol q is used to denote the different aspects of the topic. For the word w with the POS tag in $\{ns, nl\}$, it would be identified as the location aspect of the topic, denoted as $q_w = 0$; The word w with the POS tag in $\{ni, nh, j\}$ would be identified as people & organization aspect of the topic, denoted as $q_w = 1$. For the word w with the POS tag in $\{n, nz, v, a, i\}$, we additionally need to introduce another switch variable s_w to determine whether the word w is the core word or background word of the topic. If $s_w = 1$, the word w would be identified as the core word aspect of the topic, also denoted as $q_w = 2$. If $s_w = 0$, the word would be considered as the background word aspect of the topic. The switch variable $s_w \in \{0, 1\}$ is sampled from the $Bernoulli(\lambda_{w,k})$ distribution. The $\lambda_{w,k}$ represents the similarity between word w and its topic k and its formula is given in Eq. 1.

The Generative Process of TSSE-DMM. Given a short text corpus of D documents, with K pre-defined topics and a vocabulary of size V, we assume that each document d only belongs to one specific topic k. For N_d words, $\{w_{d_1}, w_{d_2}, \ldots, w_{d_{N_d}}\}$, in document d, we recognize their POS tags, and then these words are generated by the topic-aspect-word multinomial distribution $p(w|z = k, q) = \phi_{k,q}$. The symbols are explained as follows: θ indicates the global topic distribution, $\phi_{k,q}$ denotes the word distribution under topic k in aspect q, and η is the global background word distribution. α, β_α and σ are the

---

[1] http://corpus.zhonghuayuwen.org/.

prior parameters of θ, $\phi_{k,q}$ and η. z_d represents the topic in document d. The definition of the generative process is described as follows:

Process 1: Generative process of TSSE-DMM

1:   Sample $\theta \sim Dirichlet(\alpha)$;
2:   **For** each topic $k \in [1, K]$:
3:     **For** each aspect $q \in \{0, 1, 2\}$:
4:       Draw $\phi_{k,q} \sim Dirichlet(\beta_q)$;
5:   Sample $\eta \sim Dirichlet(\sigma)$;
6:   **For** each document $d \in [1, D]$:
7:     Sample a topic $z_d \sim Multinomial(\theta)$;
8:     **For** each word $w \in \{w_{d_1}, w_{d_2}, \ldots, w_{d_{N_d}}\}$:
9:       **if** $q_w \in \{0, 1\}$ **then**
10:        Sample $w \sim Multinomial(\phi_{k=z_d, q=q_w})$;
11:       **else**
12:        Sample $s_w \sim Bernoulli(\lambda_{w,k})$;   /* determine the switch variable s_w */
13:        **if** $s_w == 1$ **then**
14:         Sample $w \sim Multinomial(\phi_{k=z_d, q_w=2})$;
15:        **else**
16:         Sample $w \sim Multinomial(\eta)$;

For word w whose $q_w \notin \{0, 1\}$, the calculating formula of $\lambda_{w,k}$ is given as:

$$\lambda_{w,k} = \frac{v(w) \cdot v(k)}{\|v(w)\| \cdot \|v(k)\|} \tag{1}$$

where $v(w)$ is the word embedding of word w, $v(k)$ is the average value of the word embeddings of the top N words with the highest probability in the topic-aspect-word distribution of topic k.

2.2   Semantic Enhancement

According to [9], the words with a high semantic relevance should appear under the same topic. On this basis, our semantic enhancement strategy increases the counts of core word w assigned to topic k and the words with similar semantics to core word w appearing in topic k at the same time while sampling. The similarity between each word is calculated based on the joint word embedding.

The joint word embedding, denoted as $u(w)$ in Eq. 2, is defined as the weighted average of the external word embeddings, denoted as $g(w)$, and the local word embeddings denoted as $l(w)$:

$$u(w) = \gamma g(w) + (1 - \gamma)l(w) \tag{2}$$

where the weight ratio of the external word embedding is denoted as γ. The semantic similarity $sim(w, w')$ between w and w' is calculated by the cosine distance of the two word embeddings.

For each word pair (w, w'), we consider the word pair is semantically related only when the threshold of it is greater than τ. The semantic similarity matrix M_w of word w is:

$$M_w = \{m_{ww'}|w, w' \in V\}; m_{ww'} = \begin{cases} sim\,(w, w')\,, & sim\,(w, w') > \tau \\ 0, & other \end{cases} \quad (3)$$

We also set the threshold χ in this paper. If the number of words that are semantically related to word w is greater than χ, the values of the rows and columns in M where word w is located are all set to 0.

2.3   Model Inference

In TSSE-DMM, the latent variables that we need to sample are $z, \theta, \phi_{k,q}$ and η. With the help of collapsed Gibbs sampling, we only have to sample the topic assignment and the aspect of them for each word from the conditional distribution $p(z_d = k|z_{\neg d}, d, \alpha, \beta_q, \sigma)$. The symbol $\neg d$ means that document d is excluded from the counting. The full conditional probability is given as:

$$p(z_d = k|z_{\neg d}, d, \alpha, \beta_q, \sigma) \propto \frac{p(d|z, \beta_q, \sigma)p(z|\alpha)}{p(d_{\neg d}, z_{\neg d}|\alpha, \beta_q, \sigma)} \quad (4)$$

For the numerator in the Eq. 4, by integrating out $\phi_{k,q}$, η, and θ, we obtain:

$$p(d|z, \beta_q, \sigma) = \underbrace{\int p(w|z, \phi)p(\phi|\beta_q)d\phi}_{s_w=1} \cdot \underbrace{\int p(w|\eta)p(\eta|\sigma)d\eta}_{s_w=0} \int p(z|\theta)p(\theta|\alpha)d\theta$$

$$= \frac{\Delta(m + \alpha)}{\Delta(\alpha)} \cdot \prod_{k=1}^{K} \prod_{q=0}^{|Q|-1} \frac{\Delta(n_{k,q} + \beta_q)}{\Delta(\beta_q)} \cdot \frac{\Delta(n_b + \sigma)}{\Delta(\sigma)} \quad (5)$$

where $n_{k,q}$ is the number of words assigned to topic k in aspect q. The denominator of the Eq. 4 can be worked out in the same way:

$$p\left(d_{\neg d}, z_{\neg d}|\alpha, \beta_q, \sigma\right) = \frac{\Delta(m_{\neg d} + \alpha)}{\Delta(\alpha)} \cdot \prod_{k=1}^{K} \prod_{q=0}^{|Q|-1} \frac{\Delta(n_{k,q,\neg d} + \beta_q)}{\Delta(\beta_q)} \cdot \frac{\Delta(n_{b,\neg d} + \sigma)}{\Delta(\sigma)} \quad (6)$$

By replacing terms in Eq. 4 with those in Eq. 5 and 6, we would have the conditional distribution probability in each iteration of Gibbs sampling:

$$p(z_d = k|z_{\neg d}, d, \alpha, \beta_q, \sigma) \propto \frac{m_{k,\neg d} + \alpha}{D - 1 + K\alpha} \cdot \prod_{q=0}^{|Q|-1} \frac{\prod_{w \in d} \prod_{i=1}^{N_{k,q,d}} (n_{k,q,\neg d}^w + \beta_q + i - 1)}{\prod_{i=1}^{N_{k,q,d}} (n_{k,q,\neg d} + V\beta_q + i - 1)}$$

$$\cdot \frac{\prod_{w \in d} \prod_{i=1}^{N_{b,d}} (n_{b,\neg d}^w + \sigma + i - 1)}{\prod_{i=1}^{N_{b,d}} (n_{b,\neg d} + V\sigma + i - 1)} \quad (7)$$

where m_k is the number of documents associated with topic k, $\tilde{n}_{k,q,\neg d}^w$ is the number of word w and other semantically related words that are identified as aspect q and associated with topic k, $\tilde{n}_{k,q,\neg d}$ is the number of words associated with topic k, $n_{b,\neg d}$ is the number of words that sampled as the background words, and $n_{b,\neg d}^w$ is the number of the word w that sampled as the background word. With the counters of the topic assignments of documents and semantically related words, we can estimate θ, $\phi_{k,q}$, and η as:

$$\theta_k = \frac{m_k + \alpha}{\sum_{k=1}^{K} m_k + K\alpha}, \quad \phi_{k,q,w} = \frac{\tilde{n}_{k,q}^w + \beta_q}{\sum_{w=1}^{V} \tilde{n}_{k,q}^w + V\beta_q}, \quad \eta_w = \frac{n_b^w + \sigma}{\sum_{w=1}^{V} n_b^w + V\sigma} \quad (8)$$

3   Experiments

3.1   Datasets and Experiment Setup

Datasets. We use three datasets in the experiments to demonstrate the effectiveness and generality of our proposed approach. **ServiceRecord** dataset is a real-world data set from the public service hotline platform of Jiangsu province in China, which contains 19,411 Chinese records of public complaints. **SogouCA** dataset is a collection of 30,000 Chinese news crawled from popular websites. Each news is annotated with a category label and the whole dataset is divided into 10 categories. **SearchSnippet** dataset contains 12,340 English Web search snippets and each snippet belongs to 1 of 8 categories. The dataset is previously used in a few studies [2,14].

Data Preprocessing. We perform the following preprocessing on the dataset: (1) segmenting Chinese texts into words; (2) removing stop words, and the punctuation. (3) retaining some certain words according to their POS tags. We use the NLTK toolkit[2] to identify the POS tags of the words.

Methods and Parameters Setting. We compare our TSSE-DMM model against the following five state-of-the-art topic models specific to short texts, namely SATM, BTM, DMM, LF-DMM, and GPU-DMM. The hyper-parameters of each model are set to the recommended values in their papers. The parameter γ, τ, and χ are set to 0.5, 0.5, and 20 respectively in our TSSE-DMM. The Chinese and English external word embeddings are provided by [5] and [8], respectively. The local word embedding is learned from the local dataset by the word2vec[3] tool. The dimensions of the above word embeddings are all set to 300.

3.2   Qualitative Analysis

To investigate the quality of topics generated by all the models, we sample a topic about *China's Shenzhou Manned Space Program* for visualization from the SogouCA dataset. The result is given in Fig. 2.

---

[2] http://www.nltk.org/.

[3] https://code.google.com/archive/p/word2vec.

Methods		Top 10 words of the topic ordered by $p(w|z)$
SATM		new poetry, Shenzhou 9, critic, Wei Minglun, Internet, virus, vaccine, signal, excessive, AIDS
BTM		Shenzhou 9, China, astronaut, spaceflight, Shenzhou 9, manned, launch, flight, docking, success
DMM		Shenzhou 9, China, astronaut, spaceflight, manned, Japan, launch, docking, expert
LF-DMM		Shenzhou 9, astronaut, Liu Yang, pictures, private photos, lotus, mistress, sister, younger Lu, support
GPU-DMM		Shenzhou 9, astronaut, spaceflight, China, manned, system, Beijing, spacecraft, launch, project
TSSE-DMM	Core word Aspect	spacecraft, astronaut, Shenzhou, manned, spacecraft, Tiangong, Shenzhou 9, manual control, astronaut, launching site
	Location Aspect	China, North China, Inner Mongolia, Beijing, Jiuquan, Taiyuan, Han River, Denmark, Shanghai, Gansu
	People & Organization Aspect	Liu Yang, Huang-Huai area, Shenzhou 9, Liu Wang, Jing Haipeng, Yang Liwei, Zhang Yu, assanation, Wuping, Margaret
	Background word Aspect	pictures, exposure, expert, uncover secrets, world, nationwide, response, issue, life, check

Fig. 2. Qualitative analysis of the learned topic related to the Shenzhou spacecraft

In Fig. 2, we can see that all the top 10 words in the core word aspect of TSSE-DMM are highly related to the topic. However, in SATM and LF-DMM, some other words, like '***private photos***', and '***lotus***' are completely irrelevant to the topic of the Shenzhou spacecraft. The results in BTM, DMM, and GPU-DMM seem better than SATM and LF-DMM, but still include a few words about locations, like '***China***' and '***Beijing***', which has been subdivided into the location aspect in our TSSE-DMM model. The words in the background word aspect are of low relevance to the topic and can be filtered out as noisy data. The visualization result demonstrated that the topic discovered by our method is more coherent than other compared methods, which benefits from our strategy of subdividing topics into multiple aspects.

3.3   Quantitative Analysis

In the following experiments, we use only the words in the core word aspect of the topic to represent documents, for filtering out noisy data based on the subdivided topic aspects.

Evaluation by Topic Coherence. Following [10], we use the PMI-Score to calculate topic coherence, which has been proved to be a better metric to assess topic quality by [9]. Given a topic k and its top T words, $\{w_1, w_2, \ldots, w_T\}$, with highest probabilities, the definition of the PMI score of topic k is:

$$PMI(k) = \frac{2}{T \cdot (T-1)} \cdot \sum_{1 \leq i < j \leq T} \log \frac{p(w_i, w_j)}{p(w_i)p(w_j)} \qquad (9)$$

where $p(w_i)$ denotes the probability of word w_i that appears in a document, and $p(w_i, w_j)$ is the probability that word w_i and w_j appear in the same document. A higher PMI score indicates a better topic. Also, we use the news dataset crawled from the Sohu Network[4] and Wikipedia[5] as the external corpora which are necessary for calculating the PMI-Score in Eq. 9.

---

[4] http://www.sohu.com/.

[5] https://www.wikipedia.org/.

Table 2. Topic coherence comparison when $T = 10$

Dataset	ServiceRecord			SogouCA			SearchSnippet		
K	40	60	80	40	60	80	40	60	80
SATM	0.73	0.63	0.57	−0.15	−0.04	0.04	0.33	0.25	0.26
BTM	1.14	1.06	1.16	1.18	1.16	1.23	1.04	1.02	1.09
DMM	1.17	1.18	1.13	0.97	0.93	0.80	1.03	1.12	1.09
LF-DMM	0.64	0.65	0.63	0.31	0.26	0.25	0.57	0.62	0.71
GPU-DMM	1.25	1.22	1.19	1.16	1.08	1.05	1.13	1.09	1.15
TSSE-DMM	**2.17**	**2.06**	**2.03**	**1.78**	**1.50**	**1.77**	**1.14**	**1.20**	**1.17**

Table 3. Topic coherence comparison when $T = 20$

Dataset	ServiceRecord			SogouCA			SearchSnippet		
K	40	60	80	40	60	80	40	60	80
SATM	0.44	0.36	0.31	−0.20	−0.21	−0.18	0.15	0.09	0.08
BTM	0.75	0.73	0.78	0.84	0.76	0.82	0.72	0.74	0.78
DMM	0.80	0.79	0.77	0.57	0.46	0.38	0.79	0.77	0.79
LF-DMM	0.36	0.38	0.33	0.06	0.02	0.05	0.42	0.40	0.43
GPU-DMM	0.91	0.86	0.83	0.74	0.71	0.62	**0.83**	**0.84**	**0.83**
TSSE-DMM	**1.54**	**1.38**	**1.41**	**1.27**	**1.07**	**1.25**	**0.83**	**0.84**	**0.83**

Table 2 and 3 display the topic coherence of all compared models on the three datasets with the number of top words per topic $T = \{10, 20\}$ and the number of topics $K = \{40, 60, 80\}$, respectively.

On the ServiceRecord dataset, our TSSE-DMM method achieves the best performance. On the SogouCA dataset, the TSSE-DMM model also achieves the best coherence score in all the settings. BTM receives the second-best performance. On the SearchSnippet dataset, when $T = 10$, TSSE-DMM is the best model compared to other baseline methods and GPU-DMM becomes the second-best model. When $T = 20$, TSSE-DMM, and GPU-DMM tied for first place in coherence scores. This phenomenon can be explained by two facts. Firstly, we only keep the words from the core word aspect from the refined aspects of the learned topics to evaluate the topic coherence, which can better reflect the concepts closely related to the topics. Secondly, the SearchSnippets dataset is not a raw corpus, which reduces the accuracy of recognizing the POS tags for each word and results in the performance degradation of TSSE-DMM. This phenomenon also further indicates that our TSSE-DMM model could still outperforms other existing methods, even if these are not sufficient named entities in the corpus.

Evaluation by Short Text Classification. Considering topic models as a dimension reduction method, we can present each document with posterior topic distribution $p(z|d)$. Based on the conclusions of [4], the way to infer $p(z|d)$ is:

$$p(z|d) \propto \sum_w p(z|w)p(w|d); p(z|w) = \frac{p(z)p(w|z)}{\sum_z p(z)p(w|z)} \tag{10}$$

where $p(z|d)$ denotes the frequency of word w appears in document d. we employ an SVM classifier in scikit-learn[6] to evaluate the classification accuracy through 5-fold cross validation on both datasets with the number of topics $K = \{40, 60, 80\}$ respectively.

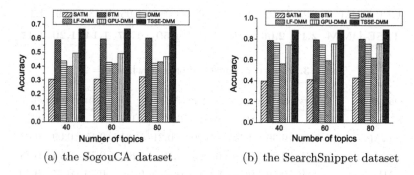

(a) the SogouCA dataset   (b) the SearchSnippet dataset

Fig. 3. Classification accuracy on two datasets

From Fig. 3, it can be observed that TSSE-DMM, as a form of document representation, outperforms other compared methods on both datasets across all the settings. This demonstrates that the words subdivided into the core word aspect by the TSSE-DMM model can effectively achieve more coherent and discriminative topic representations of documents and the joint word embeddings also alleviate the problem of data sparsity. The GPU-DMM model outperforms other DMM-based methods that further verified that the word embedding technology is more appropriate for topic-focused downstream applications like text classification over short texts.

Evaluation by Short Text Clustering. To further evaluate the clustering performance of TSSE-DMM, we regard each topic as a category label and assign each document d to topic k which has the highest value of $p(z|d)$ to form different clusters. Purity and Normalized Mutual Information (*herein after called the* NMI) are used to evaluate the clustering results.

Purity. Supposing the set $L = \{L_1, L_2, \ldots, L_{|K|}\}$ represents the clusters labeled by the topic model and set $C = \{C_1, C_2, \ldots, C_{|P|}\}$ is the P labeled classes of the documents, Purity is defined as the ratio of the number of documents allocated correctly to the number of documents in the dataset. Purity ranges from 0 to 1, and a higher Purity indicates a better clustering result.

---

[6] https://scikit-learn.org/stable/.

$$Purity(L, C) = \frac{1}{|K|} \cdot \sum_{i \in \{1, \cdots, |K|\}} \max_{j \in \{1, \dots, P\}} |L_i \cap C_j| \tag{11}$$

NMI. The calculation formula of NMI is: $NMI(L, C) = \frac{2 \cdot I(L,C)}{H(L) + H(C)}$, where $H(L)$ and $H(C)$ represent the entropy of set L and set C, respectively, and $I(L, C)$ denotes the mutual information between the two sets. Similarly, NMI ranges from 0 to 1, and a higher Purity indicates better a clustering result.

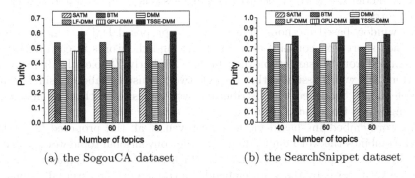

(a) the SogouCA dataset   (b) the SearchSnippet dataset

Fig. 4. Clustering results measured by Purity on two datasets

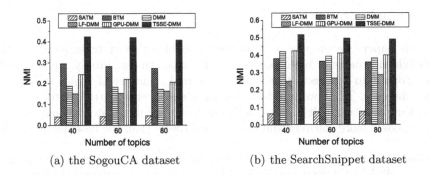

(a) the SogouCA dataset   (b) the SearchSnippet dataset

Fig. 5. Clustering results measured by NMI on two datasets

Figure 4 and Fig. 5 show the clustering results measured by Purity and NMI with the number of topics $K = \{40, 60, 80\}$, respectively. Our TSSE-DMM achieves the best performance on both the two datasets in all the settings, which is because that the joint word embeddings can capture more semantic relatedness in the dataset. On the SogouCA dataset, BTM is the second best model on both evaluation indexes. On the SearchSnippet dataset, GPU-DMM is the second best model in most cases and has a similar performance with DMM in Purity and NMI. The relative performance between these models in this experiment is basically consistent with the experimental results in the two previous experimental results that verified the effectiveness and stability of our method.

4   Related Work

The existing topic models for short texts can be divided into 3 categories: aggregation-based, window-based, and word-embedding-based methods.

In aggregation-based methods, Mehrotra et al. [7] used some auxiliary meta information to aggregate the tweets before applying conventional topic models. Zuo et al. [20] proposed PTM that sampled words from topic distribution of the aggregated long pseudo-text. Yan et al. [16] proposed the BTM model, which directly model the word co-occurrence patterns based on the biterms over the whole corpus.

In window-based methods, Yin et al. [18] proposed DMM, which assumes that each short text contains only one topic, and the words in each document are sampled from the same topic distribution. Similarly, Zhao et al. [19] proposed Twitter-LDA which assumed that a single tweet is usually about a single topic. Zuo et al. [21] modelled the distribution over topics for each word instead of learning topics from each document.

In word-embedding-based methods, Nguyen et al. [11] proposed LF-DMM, which combines the word embedding with the conventional topic-word distribution. Li et al. [4] proposed GPU-DMM, which calculates the semantic relatedness between words by the word embeddings trained on the external corpus for semantic enhancement.

5   Conclusions

In this paper, we propose a novel topic model for short texts based on the subdivided aspects of topics and semantic enhancement. Firstly, we subdivide each topic into 4 aspects to reveal the internal structure of topics to improve the coherence. Then, we propose a semantic enhancement strategy to solve the problem of data sparsity. The experiment results demonstrate that our method can discover more coherent and fine-grained topics than the baseline methods.

Acknowledgments. This work is support by the National Key R&D Program of China (2019YFC1711000), the National Natural Science Foundation of China (NO. U1811461, 61572250,) the Jiangsu Province Science & Technology Research Grant (BE2017155), and the Collaborative Innovation Center of Novel Software Technology and Industrialization, Jiangsu, China.

References

1. Blei, D.M., Ng, A.Y., Jordan, M.I.: Latent Dirichlet allocation. In: JMLR pp. 993–1022 (2003)
2. Chen, M., Jin, X., Shen, D.: Short text classification improved by learning multi-granularity topics. In: IJCAI, pp. 1776–1781 (2011)
3. Hofmann, T.: Probabilistic latent semantic indexing. In: SIGIR, pp. 50–57 (1999)
4. Li, C., Wang, H., Zhang, Z., Sun, A., Ma, Z.: Topic modeling for short texts with auxiliary word embeddings. In: SIGIR, pp. 165–174 (2016)

5. Li, S., Zhao, Z., Hu, R., Li, W., Liu, T., Du, X.: Analogical reasoning on Chinese morphological and semantic relations. In: ACL, pp. 138–143 (2018)
6. Liu, H., Zheng, H.T., Wang, W.: Topic attentional neural network for abstractive document summarization. In: PAKDD, pp. 70–81 (2019)
7. Mehrotra, R., Sanner, S., Buntine, W., Xie, L.: Improving lda topic models for microblogs via tweet pooling and automatic labeling. In: SIGIR, pp. 889–892 (2013)
8. Mikolov, T., Grave, E., Bojanowski, P., Puhrsch, C., Joulin, A.: Advances in pre-training distributed word representations. In: LREC, pp. 52–55 (2017)
9. Mimno, D., Wallach, H., Talley, E., Leenders, M., McCallum, A.: Optimizing semantic coherence in topic models. In: EMNLP, pp. 262–272 (2011)
10. Newman, D., Lau, J.H., Grieser, K., Baldwin, T.: Automatic evaluation of topic coherence. In: NAACL, pp. 100–108 (2010)
11. Nguyen, D.Q., Billingsley, R., Du, L., Johnson, M.: Improving topic models with latent feature word representations. In: TACL, pp. 299–313 (2015)
12. Nigam, K., McCallum, A.K., Thrun, S., Mitchell, T.: Text classification from labeled and unlabeled documents using EM. Mach. Learn. **39**, 103–134 (2000). https://doi.org/10.1023/A:1007692713085
13. Quan, X., Kit, C., Ge, Y., Pan, S.J.: Short and sparse text topic modeling via self-aggregation. In: IJCAI, pp. 2270–2276 (2015)
14. Sun, A.: Short text classification using very few words. In: SIGIR, pp. 1145–1146 (2012)
15. Wang, X., Zhang, Y., Wang, X., Chen, J.: A knowledge graph enhanced topic modeling approach for herb recommendation. In: Li, G., Yang, J., Gama, J., Natwichai, J., Tong, Y. (eds.) DASFAA 2019. LNCS, vol. 11446, pp. 709–724. Springer, Cham (2019). https://doi.org/10.1007/978-3-030-18576-3_42
16. Yan, X., Guo, J., Lan, Y., Cheng, X.: A biterm topic model for short texts. In: WWW, pp. 1445–1456 (2013)
17. Yang, Z., Li, Q., Liu, W., Lv, J.: Shared multi-view data representation for multi-domain event detection. In: TPAMI, pp. 1243–1256 (2019)
18. Yin, J., Wang, J.: A dirichlet multinomial mixture model-based approach for short text clustering. In: SIGKDD, pp. 233–242 (2014)
19. Zhao, W.X., et al.: Comparing Twitter and traditional media using topic models. In: Clough, P., et al. (eds.) ECIR 2011. LNCS, vol. 6611, pp. 338–349. Springer, Heidelberg (2011). https://doi.org/10.1007/978-3-642-20161-5_34
20. Zuo, Y., et al.: Topic modeling of short texts: a pseudo-document view. In: SIGKDD, pp. 2105–2114 (2016)
21. Zuo, Y., Zhao, J., Xu, K.: Word network topic model: a simple but general solution for short and imbalanced texts. Knowl. Inf. Syst. **48**(2), 379–398 (2015). https://doi.org/10.1007/s10115-015-0882-z

SILVER: Generating Persuasive Chinese Product Pitch

Yunsen Hong[1], Hui Li[1], Yanghua Xiao[2], Ryan McBride[3], and Chen Lin[1(✉)]

[1] School of Informatics, Xiamen University, Xiamen, China
chenlin@xmu.edu.cn
[2] School of Computer Science, Fudan University, Shanghai, China
[3] School of Computing, Simon Fraser University, Burnaby, BC, Canada

Abstract. Building a silver-tongued salesbot is attractive and profitable. The first and pivotal step is to generate a product pitch, which is a short piece of persuasive text which both convey product information and deliver persuasive explanations related to customer demand. Recent advances in deep neural networks have empowered text generation systems to produce natural language descriptions of products. However, to produce persuasive product pitches, deep neural networks need to be fed with massive amounts of persuasive samples, which are not available due to huge labelling cost. This paper proposes SILVER, a persuasive Chinese product pitch generator, which addresses the issue of insufficient labeled data with data-level, knowledge-level and model-level solutions. At the data level, SILVER employs statistic analysis to automatically derive weak supervision rules that correlate with persuasive texts. At the model level, SILVER apply the weak supervision rules to re-rank outputs from an ensemble of models to enhance pitch generation performance. Finally, at the knowledge level, SILVER incorporates attribute hierarchy to embed product information in the pitch. Both automatic and human-involved evaluations on real data demonstrate that SILVER is able to produce more fluent, catchy and informative snippets than state-of-the-art text generation approaches.

Keywords: Persuasive product pitch · Text generation · Creative text generation

1 Introduction

No behavior is more human than selling. The statement comes from the fact that selling is not only unique to the human species but also a very common social behavior. According to [14], an incredible 40% of our daily time is spent on selling, not only objects, but also ideas and techniques. When we are taking efforts to make machines more human, the large expenditure of selling time we spend and the human nature of the selling behavior bring us an interesting yet challenging question: *Can a machine function like a salesperson?*

© Springer Nature Switzerland AG 2021
K. Karlapalem et al. (Eds.): PAKDD 2021, LNAI 12713, pp. 652–663, 2021.
https://doi.org/10.1007/978-3-030-75765-6_52

Table 1. An example of persuasive snippets for a bookcase under different consumption contexts.

		书架, 木质, 自然 bookcase, wooden	
Input	Product Attributes	书架, 木质, 自然 bookcase, wooden	
	Consumption Context	现代家居 modern house decor	奢华家居 luxury house decor
Output	Regular Pitch	木质书架, 适合现代风格。 Wood bookshelf, suitable for modern style.	木质书架, 适合奢华风格。 Wood bookshelf, suitable for luxurious style.
	Persuasive Pitch	一款现代简约木质书架, 采用经典的原木材质, 成就充满风格的都市生活。 A modern wooden bookcase that speaks to your style, simple and classic log materials designed for urban living.	自然原木制造的书架, 设计典雅富贵, 创造舒适奢华的家居环境, 感受尊崇。 The bookshelf is made of natural logs. Its design has incorporated the elements of fortune, grace and fashion, making the of luxurious and comfortable living environment, which will surely make you feel esteemed.

Successful selling is complex. In selling technique, a sales *pitch* (i.e. a product snippet) is the most important step that initiates a sale. To help our industrial partner (i.e., an online E-commerce platform in China) to build a salesbot, we study the problem of generating persuasive Chinese product pitches. Planning the pitch requires powerful insights into the customer needs, great wisdom to connect client demands with product attributes, and conversational talents to convince the customer. Thus, we formalize the problem of persuasive pitch generator as follows: *Given a consumption context keyword that describes the customer needs, a set of product attributes, generate a persuasive snippet in natural language that relates the consumption context to the product.* Table 1 illustrates the difference between a regular pitch and a persuasive pitch. In general, the desirable pitch must be (1) informative: the product attributes are selected from the input to convey product information; (2) relevant: product attributes are expressed in a manner that achieves maximal relevance to the consumption context; (3) persuasive: the power of persuasion is enhanced by a catchy sentence that is enjoyable to read.

The problem falls in the broad class of language generation. Recently, end-to-end deep neural frameworks (DNN) [6,8,23,24], i.e., models that directly transform input of product attributes and consumption context to output of product pitch, have shown promising progress in this field. End-to-end frameworks have the advantage that errors do not accumulate across separate stages, i.e., in choosing the appropriate attributes and expressing the attributes. However, the success of neural frameworks is based on massive training data. In the problem of product pitch generation, it is difficult to obtain large amounts of training samples that pair the input of product attributes and consumption context with the output of informative, relevant and persuasive product pitch. The challenges include (1) human labeling is not only labor-costly but also subjective. Different people may have inconsistent opinions about which product snippets are persuasive. (2) the almost infinite space of product attributes lead to many out-of-vocabulary tokens which will affect the quality of the generated snippets. This problem is more severe for cold start products, i.e., products without enough training samples.

In this paper, we propose a persuasive product snippet generator **SILVER** (snippet loading via interest relevance) which functions as the pivotal component in a silver-tongued salesbot. SILVER addresses the challenges by data-level, model-level and knowledge-level solutions. As it is easy to obtain conventional product description data set (which is *not* persuasive) either publicly or from our industry partner, a practical and easy-to-implement alternative is to train DNNs on the conventional data set and post-process the outputs based on some persuasion rules. The contributions of our work are as follows:

- **At the data level** (Sect. 2), SILVER proposes a strategy to derive weak persuasion rules and avoid bias and subjectivity. The rules are automatically derived from comparative statistic analysis on two different data source regarding rhetoric, syntactic and vocabulary features.
- **At the model level** (Sect. 3), SILVER presents an ensemble-rerank framework to apply the automatically derived rules to enhance snippet generation performance.
- **At the knowledge level** (Sect. 3), SILVER incorporates knowledge of product attribute hierarchy to understand structural associations among product attributes and tackle the out-of-vocabulary product attributes.

Experiments on real data demonstrate the competency of SILVER. Our work not only brings economic benefits but also sheds insights on other efforts that make machines more human, e.g., creative text generation. Furthermore, the solutions we provide are practical to solve data scarcity problems that many other AI systems face.

The organization of this paper is as follows: Section 2 illustrates the method used for persuasion rule derivation in SILVER. Section 3 depicts the ensemble-rerank architecture used in SILVER. Section 4 presents the experimental study which shows the competency of our method. Section 5 briefly surveys related work and Sect. 6 concludes our work.

2   Persuasion Rule Derivation

Though our understanding of the art of persuasion in Chinese goes back at least as far as the *Ming school* (名学, 250 BCE) [7], we have not seen a fair and objective study of what linguistic factors contribute to successful persuasion in E-commerce. Toward this end, SILVER performs a comparative study on persuasive and non-persuasive product snippets and derives several labeling rules.

Persuasive Product Snippets: The PH Data Set. We crawl 48,320 headlines from blogs in the *"shopaholic's choice"* section on the largest E-commerce platform in China. This section collects purchase recommendations from the leading bloggers on the platform. It is reported[1] that bloggers in this section are regularly accessed based on content quality, numbers of views/followers/ hot blogs, Click-Through-Rates, trending topics and numerous other metrics. Therefore, its persuasiveness is verified to be effective in marketing. Product snippet

---

[1] http://news.mydrivers.com/1/596/596411.htm.

can be extracted from the body and the headlines of these blogs. Compared to the body of blogs, headlines tend to be more catchy and convey the most important information. Furthermore, the body usually consists of multimedia elements such as pictures while our focus in this work is purely textual. Consequently, we extract the headlines to learn essential language patterns. This collection is called Persuasive Headline (PH) data set hereafter.

Non-Persuasive Product Snippets: The Review Data Set. We compare the PH data set with regular product descriptions (i.e., they are not persuasive) obtained from a public Chinese online review data set[2]. As these reviews are not intended for advertising, we consider them as non-persuasive. This collection is called the review data set.

2.1 Features

Table 2. Binary (B) and numerical (N) features. Significant features that pass Bonferroni correction and their derived rules are highlighted.

Feature	Type	Value $f(s)$	Rule $l(s)$
		Rhetoric Features	
Simile 比喻	B	If s uses connecting words such as "仿佛/好像" (i.e., "like"), then $f(s) = 1$	$f(s) = 1 \rightarrow l(s) = 1$
Antithesis 对偶	B	If s contains two clauses with equal lengths, then $f(s) = 1$	-
Anadiplosis 顶真	B	If one clause's last word appears at the beginning of the succeeding clause, then $f(s) = 1$	$f(s) = 1 \rightarrow l(s) = 1$
Rhetorical repetition 排比	B	$f(s) = 1$ if s contains three clauses, which have at least one common word, and their positional indexes within three clauses are similar (±1 offset).	$f(s) = 1 \rightarrow l(s) = 1$
Repetition 反复	B	If one clause in s is followed by an identical cluase, then $f(s) = 1$	-
Rhetoric question 设问	B	If s contains at least a question clause, then $f(s) = 1$	-
Answer question 反问	B	If a question clause contains words such as "难道" (i.e.isn't)",then $f(s) = 1$	-
Regression 回环	B	If s follows a pattern "ABA,ABCBA," then $f(s) = 1$	-
Rhetorical exchanging 互文	B	If s contains two cluases with equal lengths and their POS tag sequences are identical, then $f(s) = 1$	-
Enumeration 枚举	B	If the words in s seperated by commas are with identical POS tags, then $f(s) = 1$	-
		Syntatic Features	
Normalized tree depth	N	$f(s) = d(s)/\max_s d(s)$, where $d(s)$ is the depth of the syntax tree of s	-
#clauses	N	$f(s) = c(s)/\max_s c(s)$, where $c(s)$ is the number of clauses in s	$c(s) \in [3,9] \rightarrow l(s) = 1$
#tokens	N	$f(s) = |s|/\max_s |s|$, where $|s|$ is the number of tokens in s	$|s| \in [9,51] \rightarrow l(s) = 1$
Causative verb 使动词	B	If a comma in s is followed by a causative verb such as "让/使/为/给" (i.e., "make/let/have/get"), then $f(s) = 1$	$f(s) = 1 \rightarrow l(s) = 1$
Sentence Entropy	N	$f(s) = \sum_{w \in s} \frac{n_s(w)}{|s|} \log \frac{n_s(w)}{|s|}$, where $w \in s$ is a word in s, $n_s(w)$ is the term frequency of w in s	-
Maximal tfidf	N	$f(s) = \max_{w \in s} n_s(w)/df(w)$, where $w \in s$ is a word in s, $n_s(w)$ is frequency of w in s, $df(w)$ is the document frequency of w	-
Position tfidf	N	$f(s) = 1/pos(w)$ where w is the word in s with maximal tfidf value	-
		Volcaburary Features	
Chinese modal particle 语气词	B	If s's POS tag consequence has at least one modal particle, then $f(s) = 1$	-
Passive verb 被动词	B	If s's POS tag consequence has at least one passive verb, then $f(s) = 1$	-
Chinese auxiliary wor 助词	B	If s's POS tag consequence has at least one auxiliary word, then $f(s) = 1$	-
Chinese auxiliary wor 助词	B	If s contains at least one conjunction word, then $f(s) = 1$	-
4-word phrases 成语	B	$f(s) = 1$, if s contains at least a four-word Chinese phrase	-
Numerals	B	If s contains at least one numeral, then $f(s) = 1$	-
Book title mark	B	If s contains at least one book title mark, then $f(s) = 1$	-
Time words	B	If s's POS tag consequence has at least one time word, then $f(s) = 1$	-
Misused marks	B	If two punctuation marks are adjacent in s, then $f(s) = 1$	$f(s) = 1 \rightarrow l(s) = 0$
Quote	B	If s contains at least one phrase quoted with """, then $f(s) = 1$	-
Without adj. adv.	B	If s does not contain any adjective or adverb, then $f(s) = 1$	$f(s) = 1 \rightarrow l(s) = 0$
Exclamation	B	If s contains at least one exclamation mark, then $f(s) = 1$	$f(s) = 1 \rightarrow l(s) = 1$
#Adverbs	N	$f(s) = v(s)/\max_s v(s)$, where $v(s)$ is the number of adverbs in s	$v(s) \in [1,2] \rightarrow l(s) = 1$
#Adjective	N	$f(s) = j(s)/\max_s j(s)$, where $j(s) = \sum_{w \text{is an adjective}_s(w)}$ is the number of adjectives	

Inspired by [16], we firstly pair the PH headlines with regular reviews under similar products. We filter trivial cases, i.e., products that have less than 300 snip-

---

[2] https://github.com/SophonPlus/ChineseNlpCorpus/blob/master/datasets/yf_amazon/intro.ipynb.

pets in any data set. We then explore 33 linguistic features, including rhetoric, syntactic and vocabulary features.

Many think that effective persuasion involves rhetorical skills, hence, we conduct a comprehensive study on traditional Chinese rhetorical skills according to [7], such as *Simile* (比喻), *Antithesis* (对偶), *Repetition* (反复), *Rhetoric Question* (设问), *Answer a question with a question* (反问), *Regression* (回环), *Rhetorical Exchanging* (互文), etc. For syntactic features, we include normalized syntax tree depth, sentence entropy, distribution of the word TFIDF, and so on. For vocabulary features, we use binary and numerical measures of the appearance of different POS tags in a snippet. We use a Chinese processing tool[3] for POS tagging. The features and their definitions are provided in Table 2.

2.2   Labeling Rules

We first compute the feature value $f(s)$ for each snippet s under each product, as defined in Table 2. Then, for binary features, we perform a two-tailed test of population proportion under each product. For numerical features, we perform Welch's t-test under each product, as it is more reliable when the numbers of headlines and reviews are generally not equivalent. Finally, for each feature, we perform Bonferroni correction to adjust significance level among all products. In this manner, we identify ten features that are statistically different in headlines and reviews with p-value less than 0.05.

Based on the statistic analysis, we derive a set $L = \{l\}$ of ten labeling rules, each of which consists of a precedent conditioned on a feature that passes Bonferroni corrected significance test, and a labeling rule $l(s) \in \{0, 1\}$. The precedent condition of the labeling rule is related to the feature value. For binary features, the precedent condition is $f(s) = 1$. For numeral features, we make the feature value fall in the range of $[\mu(f) \pm \sigma(f)]$, where $\mu(f)$ and $\sigma(f)$ are the mean value and variance of the feature on PH. A labeling rules $l(s)$ assigns either a positive label 1 to a persuasive snippet s, or a negative label 0 to a non-persuasive snippet. The sign of the label is determined by the z-score of the hypothesis test, i.e., more $f(s) = 1$ for binary feature or higher $f(s)$ for numerical feature in PH results in a positive labeling rule.

3   SILVER: Ensemble-Rerank

The overall architecture of SILVER, which is shown in Fig. 1, follows an encoder-decoder framework [2].

Input. Each training sample $\langle x^i, y^i \rangle$, where i indicates the index of the sample, contains a set of input segments $x^i = \{x_1^i, \cdots, x_J^i\}$ and an output sequence $y^i = \langle y_1^i, \cdots, y_T^i \rangle$. Let $1 \leq j \leq J$ and $1 \leq t \leq T$. Each x_j^i of the the input segments represents a consumption context or a product attribute. All tokens in the input and output are from the vocabulary $\mathcal{V}$, i.e., $x_j^i, y_t^i \in \mathcal{V}$.

---

[3] https://github.com/fxsjy/jieba.

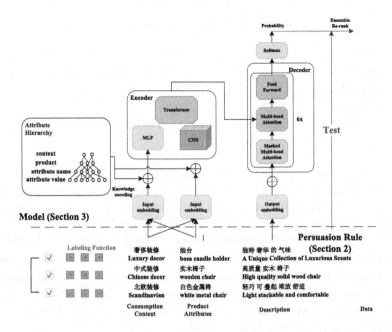

Fig. 1. Framework of SILVER

Knowledge. We construct a four-layer attribute hierarchy for each consumption, which we call *"knowledge"*, using users' search logs on our industrial partner's E-commerce platform. The node in the first layer of each hierarchy is the consumption context, the nodes of the second layer are products, the nodes of the third layer are product attributes associated with each product in the second layer, and the leaf nodes in the forth layer indicate the attribute values of the corresponding product attribute in the third layer. Different consumption contexts have their own hierarchical structure, but some nodes are shared among different hierarchies as the same products, attribute names and attribute values may exist in multiple consumption contexts. Therefore, all the hierarchies can be globally viewed as a graph.

To leverage the knowledge, we use DeepWalk [13], a graph embedding method, to learn the representations (i.e., embeddings) of each word for context (e.g., "北欧装修"/"Scandinavian house decor"), product (e.g., "书柜"/"bookcase"), attribute, (e.g., "风格"/"style") or attribute value (e.g., "现代"/"modern") from the structural associations contained in the graph. Then, SILVER used the learned word embedding as the *knowledge enhanced* input embedding. Note that many other graph embedding learning approaches [3] can be employed for this step. We choose DeepWalk, since its robust performance makes it a standard method used in many tasks [3].

Ensemble and Rerank. The overall architecture of SILVER follows an encoder-decoder framework [23,24] and the idea of *ensemble-rerank*. We create

Table 3. Statistics of data

Context	Modern	Luxury	Scandinavian
#snippets	15,294	6,306	12,725
#product categories	66	24	6
#attributes	168	158	168
#unique tokens (segmented words)	17,014	10,154	15,237

several neural networks with different encoder blocks including Multi-Layer Perception (MLP), CNN and Transformer [19], and identical Transformer [19] decoder blocks. We train each model individually with early stopping, i.e., a network stops when the loss does not decrease on a validation set. We accumulate the top-k predicted candidates from each model and assign each candidate a persuasive score $g(i) = \frac{\sum_{l \in L} l(y^i)}{|L|} + \frac{\sum_j I(x_j^i = y_j^i)}{|x^i|}$ where $l(y^i)$ is the output of each labeling rule, $|L|$ is the number of rules, $\sum_j I(x_j^i = y_j^i)$ is the number of attributes in input x^i which appear in the output snippet y^i, $|x^i|$ is the number of input attributes. We then rerank all candidates together by $g(i)$ and return the global top-k candidates as the output.

4   Experiments

In this section, we provide an experimental study to demonstrate the effectiveness of SILVER.

4.1   Experimental Setup

The data we use contains a set of product descriptions collected from online house decoration stores on the E-commerce platform of our industrial partner. Before weak-supervised labeling, it contains approximately 0.2 million descriptions for 91 different products. After labeling, 82% positive descriptions remain and each description is associated with 1 product and 3.52 product attributes on average. The average length of description before and after labeling is 103 tokens and 76 tokens, respectively. After labeling, 94.65% of the remaining descriptions do not contain any consumption context keywords. Statistics of the data are shown in Table 3.

We focus on four consumption contexts: modern house decor, luxury house decor, Chinese house decor, and Scandinavian house decor. For each consumption context, we randomly select approximate 80% descriptions (including instances without any context keyword) as the training set, the remaining 20% is used for testing.

4.2   Competitors

We compare SILVER with several state-of-the-art methods:

Table 4. Objective evaluations of all methods with best results shown in bold

Context	Model	BLEU-1	BLEU-2	BLEU-3	ROUGE-1	ROUGE-2	ROUGE-3	ROUGE-L	ROUGE-S	CRF
Modern	NPLM	0.0528	0.0232	0.0087	0.1188	0.0209	0.0020	0.1077	0.0338	39.9970
	SC-LSTM	0.2344	0.1370	0.0676	0.2232	0.0395	0.0064	0.1770	0.0609	76.1197
	MLP	0.2299	0.1737	0.1063	0.3232	0.0618	0.0106	0.2383	0.0839	75.3715
	MLP+K	0.1926	0.1480	0.0978	0.2867	0.0709	0.0144	0.2262	0.0839	77.1888
	ResCNN	0.2055	0.1524	0.0967	0.2605	0.0584	0.0090	0.1940	0.0565	73.0549
	Transformer	0.1024	0.0759	0.0380	0.1741	0.0255	0.0036	0.1315	0.0314	75.4345
	Transformer+K	0.1714	0.1215	0.0566	0.2606	0.0287	0.0033	0.1886	0.0459	75.5515
	SILVER-1	**0.2550**	**0.1917**	**0.1245**	**0.3482**	**0.0798**	**0.0155**	**0.2565**	**0.0950**	**77.2031**
	SILVER-2	0.2412	0.1813	0.1171	0.3326	0.0758	0.0145	0.2477	0.0899	76.9532
Luxury	NPLM	0.0622	0.0283	0.0105	0.1068	0.0182	0.0006	0.0963	0.0264	31.3454
	SC-LSTM	0.2208	0.1245	0.0584	0.2117	0.0344	0.0055	0.1686	0.0561	76.0965
	MLP	0.2239	0.1688	0.1020	0.3266	0.0640	0.0133	0.2455	0.0827	73.7697
	MLP+K	0.1853	0.1407	0.0882	0.2768	0.0594	0.0122	0.2214	0.0758	**76.2510**
	ResCNN	0.1967	0.1435	0.0833	0.2622	0.0499	0.0069	0.2050	0.0543	72.4910
	Transformer	0.0977	0.0725	0.0358	0.1642	0.0217	0.0036	0.1283	0.0292	74.9017
	Transformer+K	0.1633	0.1148	0.0487	0.2529	0.0252	0.0028	0.1847	0.0421	74.9978
	SILVER-1	**0.2515**	**0.1885**	**0.1174**	**0.3521**	**0.0767**	**0.0164**	**0.2641**	**0.0939**	75.6342
	SILVER-2	0.2382	0.1783	0.1099	0.3326	0.0723	0.0154	0.2523	0.0876	75.5868
Scandinavian	NPLM	0.0608	0.0284	0.0110	0.1004	0.0162	0.0010	0.0901	0.0244	29.7617
	SC-LSTM	0.2208	0.1257	0.0646	0.2018	0.0358	0.0055	0.1598	0.0557	76.6598
	MLP	0.2000	0.1510	0.0927	0.2952	0.0572	0.0106	0.2191	0.0691	73.9286
	MLP+K	0.1633	0.1239	0.0786	0.2591	0.0551	0.0113	0.2028	0.0635	**76.3754**
	ResCNN	0.2090	0.1497	0.0916	0.2663	0.0566	0.0085	0.2013	0.0611	72.2239
	Transformer	0.0712	0.0528	0.0286	0.1488	0.0201	0.0026	0.1145	0.0233	75.3881
	Transformer+K	0.1497	0.1066	0.0531	0.2428	0.0243	0.0027	0.1750	0.0395	74.8781
	SILVER-1	**0.2454**	**0.1818**	**0.1161**	**0.3291**	**0.0729**	**0.0140**	**0.2428**	**0.0841**	75.6040
	SILVER-2	0.2283	0.1683	0.1059	0.3127	0.0656	0.0117	0.2336	0.0772	75.5444

1. NPLM [10]: an unsupervised framework that expands a set of keywords to creative product descriptions.
2. SC-LSTM [22]: a supervised framework which is based on a semantically controlled LSTM structure. SC-LSTM has the advantage of scaling sentence generation to cover multiple domains (e.g.,, the consumption contexts in our problem).
3. Transformer [19]: a supervised text generation framework which is purely based on attention mechanism.
4. ResCNN [5]: text generation framework consists of CNN encoder with residual learning and transformer decoder.
5. MLP: text generation framework with MLP encoder and transformer decoder.

For transformer and MLP, we also test their performance with knowledge (denoted as K) incorporated. If knowledge is not leveraged, the input embedding will be randomly initialized.

We set the dimensions of the embedding and hidden units to be 128. The size of mini-batch is set to be 32. We use 1000 descriptions as validation for early stopping. Codes and data are available at https://shorturl.at/suvxI.

4.3   Objective Evaluation

We evaluate the snippets generated by the best result output by competitors and the top-2 results output by SILVER. We use two metrics for objective evaluation, i.e., BLEU [12] and ROUGE [9]. BLEU is a standard metric for machine translation task. ROUGE is a commonly adopted metric for multi-document summarization task. For each training instance (i.e., a pair of input and output $\langle x^i, y^i \rangle$), BLEU and ROUGE calculate a score based on how close the system output is to the ground truth. We exclude BLEU-4, because BLEU-4 is based on 4-gram match and is only meaningful in the corpus level. We also adopt a Chinese Readability Formula (CRF) [20] as a compensatory evaluation metric.

We report the evaluations on the first candidate and the second candidate from the top-2 results of SILVER as SILVER-1 and SILVER-2, respectively. From the results in Table 4, we can observe that:

1. Supervised methods are better than the unsupervised method.
2. SILVER constantly produces the best performances in terms of all BLEU and ROUGE measures. Furthermore, the second result output by SILVER achieves the second best performances. This shows that, the labeling rules and the rerank scoring functions which are based on them, are effective.
3. SILVER produces comparable results in CRF. In fact, the CRF values are close to each other, indicating that the results output by different methods are of the same difficulty level.

4.4   Evaluation by Human

Previous study has acknowledged that automatic metrics do not consistently agree with human perceptions [22], especially when they are not designed for assessing the persuasiveness. To gain better insights into how and why SILVER produces more persuasive snippets, we conduct an evaluation involving human participants to assess the performance of SILVER.

Evaluation Protocol. Five judges are recruited to evaluate the quality of 30 randomly selected snippets generated by different methods on five metrics. For a fair evaluation, the method name (i.e., the instance is generated by which approach) is invisible to judges. Furthermore, the judges do not directly give an overall score of the corresponding method. Instead, they are asked to score on three aspects of each method. The range of the score is between 0 and 5. The three criteria are as follows:

- **Fluency** [21] measures whether the snippet is smooth. The judge is asked to focus on repeated terms and grammar mistakes. A score of 5 stands for zero mistakes, while 0 will be given if there are more than five mistakes.
- **Catchyness** [10] measures whether the snippet is attractive. The judge is asked to find attractive words. The score is given based on the ratio of attractive words, i.e., the number of attractive words divided by the number of total tokens.
- **Informative** measures whether the snippet is informative. The judge is asked to look at product attributes which are distinguishing. The score is given based on the number of distinguishing attributes. A score of 5 will be given if more than five distinguishing attributes exist. If the product is not mentioned, the snippet is assigned with a score of zero.

Table 5. Evaluation results from human judges. "Trans" indicates Transformer. Best results are shown in bold.

Metrics	MLP	MLP+K	ResCNN	Trans	Trans+K	SILVER
Fluency	1.96	2.79	1.37	3.02	3.03	**3.05**
Catchyness	2.20	2.71	1.55	2.66	2.72	**2.76**
Informative	4.07	4.11	3.89	2.18	3.11	**4.33**

Results. We report the evaluation results, which are average scores from all judges, for the basic SILVER and three other supervised methods in Table 5. From Table 5, we can conclude that SILVER produces more fluent, catchy, and informative snippets than state-of-the-art text generation approaches.

5 Related Work

We briefly survey two lines of research related to our work, i.e., language generation and learning with weak supervision.

Natural Language Generation (NLG) task is one of the most widely studied problems in the area of natural language processing. We identify two types of NLG tasks: data-to-document generation and creative text generation.

Data-to-document generation (DDG) is a classic NLG task. Given some structured data (e.g., a table), DDG produces text, such as a sentence or a paragraph, that adequately and fluently describes the input data. Early DDG systems typically consist of two separate stages: a content selection stage to decide "what to say", and a surface realization stage to decide "how to say". The recent success of Deep Neural Network (DNN) models [15] has motivated research on end-to-end systems that blur the distinction between the two stages. Most of the DNN-based systems employ an encoder-decoder framework. Frequently adopted encoders include Multi-Level Perception (MLP) [1,23] or a hierarchical form of LSTM [24]. In the decoder layers, RNN [23] and LSTM [24] are common choices.

Creative text generation (CTG) has received considerably more attention, from a commercial point of view. In CTG, the generated text must reveal more human characteristics. DNN-based methods are also appealing in CTG when supervision is accessible. For example, most state-of-the-art research on poetry generation is based on the encoder-decoder framework [4,21,25]. However, training collections are difficult to obtain for other types of creative text, due to the inherent complexity of the cognitive process. In this case, unsupervised methods are the mainstream solution. Most of them are heavily dependent on syntactic templates, e.g., word substitution [11,17,18], and can only generate short headline style sentences or slogans. A recent work [10] explores the possibility of generating a complete persuasive sentence by an unsupervised approach.

Our work is different from existing NLG work on the following two aspects: (1) While most NLG tasks focus on the output's fluency and fidelity to references, we emphasize on the persuasiveness and relevance of the output. (2) End-to-end DNN-based models require a tremendous amount of training data in order to obtain promising results. When it is impossible to generate labeled corpus, CTG systems often resort to unsupervised approaches. On the contrary, our work attempts to exploit the superior learning power of DNNs by utilizing weak supervisions.

Recently, a surge of works has been proposed that aims to address the data scarcity issue using weak supervision [26], which is the opposite of strong supervision [26]. The collection of weak supervision can be obtained by either an unsupervised model (with possibly worse performance) or a set of manually constructed heuristics. As weak supervisions are often incomplete (i.e., only a small fraction of training set is labeled), inaccurate (i.e., only coarse-grained labels are given) and/or inexact (i.e., given labels are not always correct), an adaption of the model is necessary for optimizing performance. However, this is not fully explored in the literature of DNN, especially for NLG. Most previous works simply treat weak supervision signals as normal labels.

6 Conclusion

In this paper, we propose a persuasive product snippet generator SILVER. SILVER leverages data-level, model-level and knowledge-level solutions to overcome the data scarcity problem and generate persuasive product snippets. The evaluations on real data from our industrial partner demonstrate that SILVER is able to produce persuasive snippets like a persuasive salesman. In the future, we plan to employ more sophisticated graph embedding approaches to improve SILVER.

Acknowledgment. Chen Lin is supported by the Natural Science Foundation of China (No. 61972328), Joint Innovation Research Program of Fujian Province China (No. 2020R0130). Hui Li is supported by the Natural Science Foundation of China (No. 62002303), Natural Science Foundation of Fujian Province China (No. 2020J05001). Yanghua Xiao is supported by NSFC (No. 61732004, No. 61472085, No. U1509213, No. U1636207), National Key R&D Program of China (No. 2017YFC0803700, No. 2017YFC1201200), Shanghai Municipal Science and Technology project (No. 16JC1420401), Shanghai STCSMs R&D Program (No. 16JC1420400).

References

1. Bao, J., Tang, D., Duan, N., Yan, Z., Zhou, M., Zhao, T.: Text generation from tables. IEEE/ACM Trans. Audio Speech Lang. Process. **27**(2), 311–320 (2019)
2. Cho, K., et al.: Learning phrase representations using RNN encoder-decoder for statistical machine translation. In: EMNLP, pp. 1724–1734 (2014)
3. Cui, P., Wang, X., Pei, J., Zhu, W.: A survey on network embedding. IEEE Trans. Knowl. Data Eng. **31**(5), 833–852 (2019)
4. Ghazvininejad, M., Shi, X., Choi, Y., Knight, K.: Generating topical poetry. In: EMNLP, pp. 1183–1191 (2016)

5. Huang, Y.Y., Wang, W.Y.: Deep residual learning for weakly-supervised relation extraction. In: EMNLP, pp. 1803–1807 (2017)
6. Karpathy, A., Li, F.: Deep visual-semantic alignments for generating image descriptions. In: CVPR, pp. 3128–3137 (2015)
7. Kirapatrick, A., Xu, Z.: Chinese Rhetoric and Writing: An Introduction for Language Teachers. Parlor Press, South Carolina (2012)
8. Lebret, R., Grangier, D., Auli, M.: Neural text generation from structured data with application to the biography domain. In: EMNLP, pp. 1203–1213 (2016)
9. Lin, C.Y.: Rouge: a package for automatic evaluation of summaries. In: Text Summarization Branches Out (2004)
10. Munigala, V., Mishra, A., Tamilselvam, S.G., Khare, S., Dasgupta, R., Sankaran, A.: Persuaide! an adaptive persuasive text generation system for fashion domain. In: WWW, pp. 335–342 (2018)
11. Özbal, G., Pighin, D., Strapparava, C.: BRAINSUP: brainstorming support for creative sentence generation. In: ACL (1), pp. 1446–1455 (2013)
12. Papineni, K., Roukos, S., Ward, T., Zhu, W.: Bleu: a method for automatic evaluation of machine translation. In: ACL, pp. 311–318 (2002)
13. Perozzi, B., Al-Rfou, R., Skiena, S.: DeepWalk: online learning of social representations. In: KDD, pp. 701–710 (2014)
14. Pink, D.H.: To Sell is Human: The Surprising Truth About Persuading, Convincing, and Influencing Others. Canongate Books, New York (2013)
15. Sutskever, I., Martens, J., Hinton, G.E.: Generating text with recurrent neural networks. In: ICML, pp. 1017–1024 (2011)
16. Tan, C., Niculae, V., Danescu-Niculescu-Mizil, C., Lee, L.: Winning arguments: interaction dynamics and persuasion strategies in good-faith online discussions. In: WWW, pp. 613–624 (2016)
17. Thomaidou, S., Lourentzou, I., Katsivelis-Perakis, P., Vazirgiannis, M.: Automated snippet generation for online advertising. In: CIKM, pp. 1841–1844 (2013)
18. Valitutti, A., Toivonen, H., Doucet, A., Toivanen, J.M.: Let everything turn well in your wife: generation of adult humor using lexical constraints. In: ACL (2), pp. 243–248 (2013)
19. Vaswani, A., et al.: Attention is all you need. In: NIPS, pp. 6000–6010 (2017)
20. Wang, L.: Research on Chinese readability formula of texts for elementary and intermediate South Korean and Japanese learners. Lang. Teach. Linguist. Stud. 5(2017), 15–25 (2017)
21. Wang, Z., et al.: Chinese poetry generation with planning based neural network. In: COLING, pp. 1051–1060 (2016)
22. Wen, T., Gasic, M., Mrksic, N., Su, P., Vandyke, D., Young, S.J.: Semantically conditioned LSTM-based natural language generation for spoken dialogue systems. In: EMNLP, pp. 1711–1721 (2015)
23. Wiseman, S., Shieber, S.M., Rush, A.M.: Challenges in data-to-document generation. In: EMNLP, pp. 2253–2263 (2017)
24. Yang, Z., Blunsom, P., Dyer, C., Ling, W.: Reference-aware language models. In: EMNLP, pp. 1850–1859 (2017)
25. Zhang, X., Lapata, M.: Chinese poetry generation with recurrent neural networks. In: EMNLP, pp. 670–680 (2014)
26. Zhou, Z.H.: A brief introduction to weakly supervised learning. Nat. Sci. Rev. 5(1), 44–53 (2017)

Capturing SQL Query Overlapping via Subtree Copy for Cross-Domain Context-Dependent SQL Generation

Ruizhuo Zhao[1,2], Jinhua Gao[1(✉)], Huawei Shen[1,2], and Xueqi Cheng[1,2]

[1] CAS Key Lab of Network Data Science and Technology, Institute of Computing Technology, Chinese Academy of Sciences, Beijing 100190, China
{zhaoruizhuo,gaojinhua,shenhuawei,cxq}@ict.ac.cn
[2] School of Computer and Control Engineering, University of Chinese Academy of Sciences, Beijing 100049, China

Abstract. The key challenge of cross-domain context-dependent text-to-SQL generation tasks lies in capturing the relation of natural language utterance and SQL queries in different turns. A line of works attempt to combat this challenge by capturing the overlaps among consecutively generated SQL queries. Existing models sequentially generate the SQL query for a single turn and model the SQL overlaps via copying tokens or segments generated in previous turns. However, they are not flexible enough to capture various overlapping granularities, e.g., columns, filters, or even the whole query, as they neglect the intrinsic structures inhabited in SQL queries. In this paper, we employ tree-structured intermediate representations of SQL queries, i.e., SemQL, for SQL generation and propose a novel subtree-copy mechanism to characterize the SQL overlaps. At each turn, we encode the interaction questions and previously generated trees as context and decode the SemQL tree in a top-down fashion. Each node is either generated according to SemQL grammar or copied from previously generated SemQL subtrees. Our model can capture various overlapping granularities by copying nodes at different levels of SemQL trees. We evaluate our approach on the SParC dataset and the experimental results show the superior performance of our model compared with state-of-the-art baselines.

Keywords: Context-dependent · Text-to-SQL · Subtree-copy

1 Introduction

SQL query generation aims to map natural language utterances into executable SQL queries, which can ease information acquisition from databases. In the real-world scenario, users tend to interact with database in a multi-turn manner, i.e., asking a series of related questions to achieve their goals, making the interaction strongly context-dependent. The context-dependency comes at two-folds. Firstly, natural language questions are linguistically dependent, as users might

© Springer Nature Switzerland AG 2021
K. Karlapalem et al. (Eds.): PAKDD 2021, LNAI 12713, pp. 664–675, 2021.
https://doi.org/10.1007/978-3-030-75765-6_53

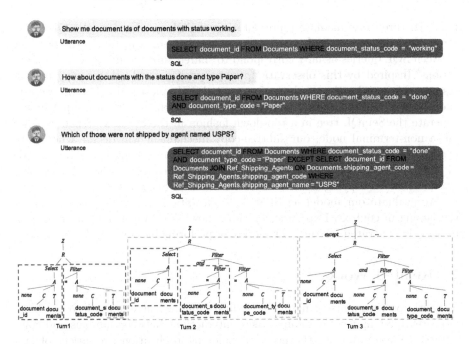

Fig. 1. An example of user interaction which consists of three turns. The bottom is the SemQL tree of each SQL query in the above turns. The subtrees in the same color dashed line are shared across different turns.

omit previously mentioned constraints and entities. Considering the example shown in Fig. 1, the user adopts "those" to refer to the document sets selected in the previous turns. Secondly, the generated SQL queries tend to overlap. As shown in Fig. 1, most parts of SQL queries of different turns are shared. Such context-dependency poses a great challenge for SQL query generation. Moreover, practical systems need to accommodate queries towards different domains, making this task even more challenging.

Existing models for context-dependent SQL query generation usually adopt the encoder-decoder framework. The encoder typically encodes the entire history of interaction to capture linguistical dependency. To characterize the overlaps of SQL queries, the decoder usually works in a copy manner. Suhr et al. [18] proposes to copy predefined segments extracted by rules, while Zhang et al. [30] proposes a sequence editing mechanism to model token-level changes between consecutively generated SQL queries. However, both methods are not flexible enough to capture various overlapping granularities. SQL queries tend to overlap at different levels, e.g., querying the same column, sharing the same filters, or reusing the whole query, making either token-level or segment-level copy less effective.

In this paper, we argue that different overlapping granularities of SQL queries are highly correlated to the intrinsic structures of SQL queries and empoly a tree-structured intermediate representation of SQL queries, i.e., SemQL in [8], for context-dependent SQL query generation. As shown in Fig. 1, the overlaps between SQL queries usually correspond to shared subtrees in SemQL representations. Inspired by this observation, we propose a novel subtree-copy mechanism to characterize the overlaps of generated SQL queries. To this end, we first encode the generated SemQL queries in previous turns in a bottom-up way and generate the SemQL tree in a top-down fashion in the decoder. When expanding a non-terminal node, our subtree-copy mechanism will decide whether to generate a new node based on SemQL grammars or to copy a generated node in previous turns. Our subtree-copy mechanism can capture various overlapping granularities by copying nodes at different levels of SemQL trees.

We evaluate our model on SParC [26], a dataset for cross-domain semantic parsing in context. Experiment results show that by copying subtrees from previously generated queries, our model outperforms baseline.

2   Related Work

Semantic parsing aims at mapping natural language utterances into machine-interpretable languages, enabling easier interactions between humans and computers. To accommodate the needs of different applications, a variety of languages have also been explored, including logical forms [5,27], lambda calculus [14,29], dependency-based compositional semantics [1], SQL queries [24,31] and other general-purpose programming languages [11,22]. Among them, SQL queries generation has attracted a lot of attention due to the large text-to-SQL dataset such as WikiSQL [31] and Spider [25]. Most of the methods adopt encoder-decoder model and perform well on WikiSQL [4,6,19,21,23]. Recently, some methods [2,20] are proposed for the cross-domain dataset Spider. IRNet [8] proposes to use SemQL as an intermediate representation to tackle the mismatch problem and the lexical problem of dataset Spider. In our work, we also use SemQL as intermediate representation because of its tree-structured form.

Recently, recovering context-dependent representations has been receiving increasing attention. Recovering context-dependent meaning was studied by methods [16,18,28] focusing on context-dependent semantic parsing with datasets such as ATIS [3,9], SCONE [7,10,15,17], SequentialQA [12] and SParC [30]. The ATIS and SParC are text-to-SQL datasets and the neural methods [18,30] on them are most related to our work. Suhr et al. [18] incorporates history turn with an interaction-level encoder and copying segments from previous SQL queries. Zhang et al. [30] propose query generation by editing the query in the previous turn on token-level. Both of them focus on what part of interaction history is useful and how history is used.

3   Task Formulation

Let I be an interaction and it has a sequence of n utterance-query pairs. A user utterance X is a sequence $\langle x_1, \ldots, x_{|X|} \rangle$ and each x_i is a natural language token. A SQL query is denoted as Y and its SemQL S is tree-structured. So an interaction I consisting of n turns is denoted as $I = [(X_i, Y_i, S_i)]_{i=1}^{n}$. At turn i, we denote the interaction history as $I[: i-1] = \langle (X_1, Y_1, S_1), \ldots, (X_{i-1}, Y_{i-1}, S_{i-1}) \rangle$. All types of nodes in SemQL except columns and tables (e.g., Z, R, *Select*, ...) make up a set $\mathcal{N}$ and we denote node type as N. Given $I[: i-1]$ and utterance X_i, our goal is to generate S_i and convert it to Y_i.

The database schema is also given to the model as input. Let $D = (\mathcal{C}, \mathcal{T})$ be a database schema, where $\mathcal{T}$ is the set of multiple tables and each table $T \in \mathcal{T}$ has a sequence of words $\langle t_1, \ldots, t_{|T|} \rangle$. The $\mathcal{C}$ is the set of columns and each table T contain multiple column names:

$$T = \langle C_1, \ldots, C_{|m|} \rangle$$

where m is the number of column numbers and $C_i \in \mathcal{C}$. Each C has a sequence of words $\langle c_1, \ldots, c_{|C|} \rangle$.

4   Model

4.1   Model Architecture

We use the encoder-decoder architecture and the decoder is designed as tree-structured. The framework is illustrated in Fig. 2, it consists of: (1) an utterance encoder and an interaction encoder to encode the interaction history, (2) a schema encoder to incorporate database schema, (3) a bottom-up tree-structured encoder to encode previously generated SemQL trees, (4) a top-down tree-structured decoder which generates tokens by either choosing from the SemQL grammar or copying nodes from previously generated trees.

The tree encoder and decoder lie at the core of our model. Our tree encoder works bottom-up to encode the generated SemQL trees at different granularities. Accordingly, our tree decoder works top-down and can copy nodes from different levels of generated trees, thus capturing various overlapping granularities of the SQL queries.

4.2   Utterance and Interaction Encoder

Utterance Encoder. Each word $x_{i,j}$ of utterance $X_i = \langle x_{i,1}, \ldots, x_{i,|X_i|} \rangle$ is converted into its embedding vector .Then the encoder use a bi-LSTM to encode the user utterance embedding vector and the hidden state for each token $x_{i,j}$ $\mathbf{h_{i,j}^U} = [h_{i,j}^{\overrightarrow{U}}, h_{i,j}^{\overleftarrow{U}}]$ where $h_{i,j}^{\overrightarrow{U}}$ is the forward embedding and $h_{i,j}^{\overleftarrow{U}}$ is the backward embedding.

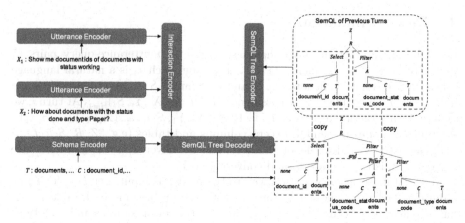

Fig. 2. The overall framework of our model.

Interaction Encoder. The interaction encoder aggregates the interaction history up to the current turn for SQL generation and is implemented via a uni-directional LSTM. The i-th input of LSTM is the hidden state at the last time step of the i-th turn utterance-encoder, i.e.,

$$\mathbf{h}^I_{i+1}, \mathbf{c}^I_{i+1} = \text{LSTM}^I(\mathbf{h}^U_{i,|\mathbf{X}_i|}, (\mathbf{h}^I_i, \mathbf{c}^I_i)) \tag{1}$$

where $\mathbf{h}^U_{i,|\mathbf{X}_i|}$ is the hidden state of the last time step of the i-th turn. The obtained hidden state $\mathbf{h}^I_i$ is fed into the decoder to predict the SemQL of i-th turn.

4.3   Schema Embedding

We use the pre-trained Glove word embedding and each column name embedding $\mathbf{e}^C_i$ is obtained by averaging the embeddings of words that appear in the column name. Besides the pre-trained Glove word embedding, we also adopt the contextualized word embedding based on BERT. Considering the linguistic dependency within multi-turn utterances and the connection between utterances and schemas, we concatenate the user utterances in $I[: i-1]$ together with X_i and all the column names as the input of BERT at the i-th turn. The input sequence for I_i is as follows:

$$[CLS], X_1, \ldots, X_i, [SEP], C_1, \ldots, C_m, [SEP]$$

The generated word embeddings in each X_i serve as the inputs for the utterance encoder. We take the average embeddings of words in C_i's name as its column representation. The construction of table representations follows the same way.

4.4   SemQL Tree Encoder

We propose two principles for designing the SemQL tree encoder: (1) the embedding of a node should represent the entire subtree rooted at it; (2) the embeddings for nodes at the same level should be independent to each other. Considering the hierarchical structure of SQL queries, we treat each subtree rooted at a nonterminal node as our copying block. When copying a nonterminal node, we need to copy the entire subtree rooted at that node. The first principle can guarantees that the learned representations of each non-terminal node can well represent the subtree, while the second principle keeps the representation of a node independent from its sibling nodes, allowing our model to capture SQL overlaps at different granularities.

Following the principles, we propose to encode the entire SemQL bottom-up with two LSTMs, i.e., the parent LSTM(P-LSTM) and the children LSTM(C-LSTM). For each node, the C-LSTM aggregates the representations of its direct children, while the P-LSTM generates its own representation based on the output of the C-LSTM. The C-LSTM satisfies the first principle while the P-LSTM guarantees the second.

To get the node embedding $\mathbf{h}_{j,i}^{PL}$ of the i-th node at the j-th level of the SemQL tree, the C-LSTM first aggregates the representations of all its children nodes at the $(j + 1)$-th level. Assuming it has K children nodes numbered 1 to K from left to right, the k-th time step of the C-LSTM is calculated as follows:

$$\mathbf{h}_{j+1,k}^{CL} = \mathrm{LSTM}^C(\mathbf{h}_{j+1,k}^{PL}, \mathbf{h}_{j+1,k-1}^{CL}) \tag{2}$$

After aggregating its children nodes, the P-LSTM generates its node embedding $\mathbf{h}_{j,i}^{PL}$ based on its node type (e.g., Z, R, $intersect$, ...) and the output of the last time step of the C-LSTM, i.e., $\mathbf{h}_{j+1,K}^{CL}$. The node type is converted into its embedding $\mathbf{e}_{j,i}^{N}$ to serve as the input. If the node corresponds to a table or a column, we adopt the corresponding table embedding $\mathbf{e}_{j,i}^{T}$ or column embedding $\mathbf{e}_{j,i}^{C}$ instead. Finally, the P-LSTM generates the node embedding $\mathbf{h}_{j,i}^{PL}$ as follows:

$$\mathbf{h}_{j,i}^{PL} = \mathrm{LSTM}^P(\mathbf{e}_{j,i}^{N}, (\mathbf{h}_{j+1,K}^{CL}, \mathbf{c}_{j+1,K}^{CL})) \tag{3}$$

This encoding process works bottom-up until the entire SemQL tree is encoded.

4.5 SemQL Tree Decoder

Our SemQL tree decoder works in a top-down manner. At the i-th turn, the output of the interaction encoder for the current turn, i.e., $(\mathbf{h}_i^I, \mathbf{c}_i^I)$, is fed into the decoder. We append an auxiliary root node to denote the start of the decoding process. A queue is adopted to store the nonterminal nodes to be expanded, which is initialized with the root node. Our decoder loops the queue and pops one node each time to expand it by generating its children nodes. The decoding process ends when the queue is empty.

To expand a nonterminal node, we adopt a list to record its generated children nodes, which is initialized empty. The expanding process works as follows:

(1) Candidate generation: We first restrict the candidate set based on SemQL grammar and its generated children nodes list. Take the expansion of the node with type Z as an example. The allowed expanding grammar is:

$$\{intersect\ R\ R\ |\ union\ R\ R\ |\ except\ R\ R\ |\ R\}$$

If the children node list is empty, the next possible node will be: {*intersect*, *union*, *except*, R}, which makes up the candidate set; If the child node *intersect* is already selected in the previous step, the candidate set will be restricted to R. To allow for copy, for each nonterminal node N in the candidate set, previously generated nodes with the same node type as node N will be appended to the candidate set.

(2) Node generation: We compute the generation likelihood for each candidate node and pick the most likely node as our generated node. If the picked node is a previously generated node, the corresponding subtree rooted at this node will be copied to the final SemQL tree of the current turn.

(3) Decoder queue update: If the generated node in step (2) is a newly generated nonterminal node, we will append to the decoder queue. Otherwise, the queue remains unchanged.

(4) Children node list update: The generated node, either copied or newly generated, will be appended to the children node list of the current expanding node. Then the expanding process will go back to step (1). This process of expanding a node iterates until the candidate set is empty or a node with type $<eos>$ is generated in step (2).

The core part of our decoder lies at node generation. Node generation first computes the node representation and then calculates the generation probability for each candidate. We provide the detailed implementation of node generation module as follows.

We adopt the LSTM to expand a given node. When expanding the k-th child of node N, the input of the LSTM unit consists of two parts: the node embedding e_{k-1}^N of the generated $(k-1)$-th child, and the hidden state h_{ep}^D when output the current expanding node N, which is also known as the parent-feeding mechanism. The node embedding of the generated $(k-1)$-th child depends on whether it is copied or generated. If it is copied from previously generated trees, we take its embedding obtained by the SemQL tree encoder; Otherwise, it is node type embedding at $(k-1)$-th time step. Finally, the output of the decoder for expanding the k-th child is:

$$h_k^D = \text{LSTM}^D([e_{k-1}^N; h_{ep}^D], h_{k-1}^D) \tag{4}$$

We use softmax to calculate the generation probability of the nodes in the candidate set. For each node in the candidate set, its embedding depends on its node type. If it is a symbol in SemQL grammar, its embedding is taken from an embedding matrix; If it is a column or a table, its embedding is taken from column embedding matrix or table embedding matrix; If it is a copied node, its embedding is denoted by the hidden state generated by the SemQL tree encoder.

We denote the embedding matrix for the candidate set as $\mathbf{e}^{\mathbf{Can}}$ and calculate the generation probability as follows:

$$\mathbf{o_k} = tanh(\mathbf{h_k^D W_o})$$

$$\mathbf{s_k} = \mathbf{o_k} \mathbf{e}^{\mathbf{Can}} \qquad (5)$$

$$P_{types \bigcup subtrees} = \text{softmax}(\mathbf{s_k})$$

where $\mathbf{W_o}$ is the parameter matrix. Our scores are distributed on the candidate node types and candidate subtrees.

4.6 Model Learning

Ground Truth Generation. The subtrees are deterministically extracted from SemQL that are coverted by the annotated SQL queries. But the dataset doesn't indicate what parts of SemQL subtrees are copied from previous turn. To generate ground truth copied subtrees for training, we use a subtree match approach to identify subtrees. The subtrees generated in previous turns make up a candidate set. For a SemQL tree in training data, we check whether its subtree matches a subtree in the candidate set from top to down. Once a subtrees match is identified, we replace the whole subtree with a placeholder and skip checking subtree match for all its descendant nodes. The copying subtrees appear to the learning algorithm as a single generation decision. We adopt the recursive algorithm to realize our subtree match approach. We check if the roots node of the subtrees are equal and then check their children recursively. Two nodes are equal if they have the same node type and their children are equal. Two subtrees are equal if their root nodes are equal and the children nodes of the two root nodes are equal too.

Training Objective. The training set of N interactions is denoted as $\{I_l\}_{l=1}^{N}$. Given an interaction I_l, each utterance X_i^l where $i \leq |I_l|$ is paired with an annotated query Y_i^l and the SemQL tree S_i^l. Given the subtree copy decisions, we minimize the interaction cross-entropy loss:

$$L = \sum_{i=1}^{|I_l|} \sum_{k=1}^{|S_i^l|} -\log P(S_{i,k}^l | X_i^l, S_{i,1:k-1}^l, I_l[: i-1])$$

where l is the index of the interaction, i is the index of turn and k is the index of the token or copied the subtree. The $P(S_{i,k}^l | X_i^l, S_{i,1:k-1}^l, I_l[: i-1])$ is the probability of generating the token or copying the subtree. We update the model parameters for each interaction.

5 Experiment

5.1 Dataset and Experimental Settings

We use SParC [26] which is a large-scale cross-domain context-dependent semantic parsing dataset with SQL labels as our evaluation benchmark. It consists of

Table 1. The results on SParC dataset without BERT.

Methods without BERT	Question match		Interaction match	
	Dev	Test	Dev	Test
SyntaxSQL-con [26]	18.5	20.2	4.3	5.2
CD-Seq2Seq [26]	21.9	23.2	8.1	7.5
EditSQL [30]	33.0	–	16.4	–
EditSQL(w/gold query) [30]	40.6	–	17.3	–
Ours(w/o subtree copy)	36.3	–	17.6	–
Ours(w/predicted tree)	**38.7**	–	**21.4**	–
Ours(w/gold tree)	**47.8**	–	**22.1**	–

Table 2. The results on SParC dataset with BERT.

Methods with BERT	Question match		Interaction match	
	Dev	Test	Dev	Test
EditSQL+BERT [30]	47.2	**47.9**	29.5	25.3
EditSQL+BERT(w/gold query) [30]	53.4	54.5	29.2	25.0
Ours+BERT(w/o subtree copy)	48.3	–	29.5	–
Ours+BERT(w/predicted tree)	**49.5**	47.4	**32.5**	**25.5**
Ours+BERT(w/gold tree)	**56.4**	–	**32.8**	–

4,298 coherent question sequences over 200 databases and each database appears only in one of train, dev and test sets.

We implement our model with PyTorch. Word embeddings, node type embeddings, and hidden vector are set to 300. Word embeddings are initialized with Glove and shared among the utterance encoder, schema encoder, and SemQL tree encoder. They are fixed during training. Model parameters are randomly initialized from a uniform distribution $U[-0.1, 0.1]$. We use Adam optimizer [13] to minimize the cross-entropy loss with the batch size 1. The learning rate of the model is 0.001. We use the pre-trained small uncased BERT model with 768 hidden size and we fine-tune it with a learning rate of 0.00001.

5.2   Baselines

We compare our model with the three baseline models: (1) CD-Seq2Seq: This model is originated from [18] and [26] use it on context-dependent SQL generation in multiple domains; (2) SyntaxSQL-con: This model is originated from [24] by using bi-LSTMs to encode the interaction history; (3) EditSQL: This model is proposed by [30] and they use sequence editing mechanism to model token-level changes.

Table 3. The results of token copy and ours

Methods	Question	Interaction
EditSemQL	37.2	19.4
Ours	**38.7**	**21.4**
EditSemQL+BERT	48.5	30.0
Ours+BERT	**49.5**	**32.5**

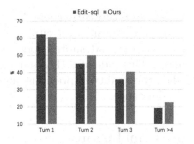

Fig. 3. Turn accuracy

5.3 Main Results

Metrics. We adopt the exact set match accuracy between the gold and the predicted queries as our evaluaton metric, which is proposed by [25]. The predicted queries are decomposed into different SQL clauses such as SELECT, WHERE, GROUP BY, and ORDER BY and the scores are calculated for each clause using set matching separately in case of ordering issues.

Overall Accuracy. Table 1 and Table 2 presents the question match accuracy and interaction match accuracy of our model and various baselines on the development set and the test set. Our model outperforms all the baselines without BERT by a large margin on the dev set. The performance is obviously improved when incorporating BERT. We compared our model and EditSQL with BERT and the interaction accuracy of our model exceed EditSQL both on dev set and test.

Turn Accuracy. To further show the effectiveness of our model, we show the performance split by turns on the dev set with BERT in Fig. 3. The SQL queries in later turns are more difficult to generate due to the complex context history. As is shown in Fig. 3, our model outperforms baseline after the first turn though our accuracy of the first turn is slightly lower. This further demonstrates that our subtree copy mechanism is more effective than edit mechanism for the later turns despite its hardness.

5.4 Ablation Study

Effects of Subtree Copy. We conduct ablation studies on our model to analyze the contribution of the subtree copy mechanism. As shown in Table 1, our model improves largely on interaction match accuracy with the use of subtree copying with or without the utterance-table BERT embedding. To eliminate the effect of employing SemQL grammar, the token copying proposed in EditSQL is also implemented with SemQL grammar by copying generated nodes in previous turns and the embedding of the nodes are obtained by SemQL tree encoder. As shown in Table 3, our model still outperforms EditSemQL when both of them use SemQL grammar.

Copying Gold Subtrees. And with copying gold subtrees, our model improves both question match accuracy and interaction match accuracy on dev set. Our model with gold subtree performs much better than EditSQL with the gold query. This indicates that our model can improve generation performance more when the quality of previous query is better and the oracle query is the extreme circumstance.

6 Conclusion

We propose a subtree copy mechanism for context-dependent cross-domain text-to-SQL. Our subtree-copy mechanism can capture various overlapping granularities by copying nodes at different levels of SemQL trees. Experimental results demonstrate the benefits of our subtree copy mechanism.

Acknowledgments. This paper is funded by the National Natural Science Foundation of China under Grant Nos. 91746301, 62002347 and 61902380. Huawei Shen is also funded by Beijing Academy of Artificial Intelligence (BAAI) and K.C. Wong Education Foundation.

References

1. Berant, J., Chou, A., Frostig, R., Liang, P.: Semantic parsing on freebase from question-answer pairs. In: Proceedings of EMNLP 2013
2. Bogin, B., Gardner, M., Berant, J.: Global reasoning over database structures for text-to-sql parsing. In: Proceedings of EMNLP-IJCNLP (2019)
3. Dahl, D.A., et al.: Expanding the scope of the ATIS task: The ATIS-3 corpus. In: Proceedings of Human Language Technology (1994)
4. Dong, L., Lapata, M.: Coarse-to-fine decoding for neural semantic parsing. In: Proceedings of ACL (2018)
5. Dong, L., Lapata, M.: Language to logical form with neural attention. In: Proceedings of ACL (2016)
6. Finegan-Dollak, C., et al.: Improving text-to-SQL evaluation methodology. In: Proceedings of the ACL (2018)
7. Fried, D., Andreas, J., Klein, D.: Unified pragmatic models for generating and following instructions. In: Proceedings of NAACL-HLT (2018)
8. Guo, J., et al.: Towards complex text-to-sql in cross-domain database with intermediate representation. In: Proceedings of ACL (2019)
9. Hemphill, C.T., Godfrey, J.J., Doddington, G.R.: The ATIS spoken language systems pilot corpus. In: Proceedings of Speech and Natural Language (1990)
10. Huang, H., Choi, E., Yih, W.: Flowqa: grasping flow in history for conversational machine comprehension. In: Proceedings of ICLR (2019)
11. Iyer, S., Konstas, I., Cheung, A., Zettlemoyer, L.: Mapping language to code in programmatic context. In: Proceedings of EMNLP (2018)
12. Iyyer, M., Yih, W., Chang, M.: Search-based neural structured learning for sequential question answering. In: Proceedings of ACL (2017)
13. Kingma, D.P., Ba, J.: Adam: a method for stochastic optimization. In: Proceedings of ICLR (2015)

14. Kwiatkowski, T., Zettlemoyer, L.S., Goldwater, S., Steedman, M.: Lexical generalization in CCG grammar induction for semantic parsing. In: Proceedings of EMNLP (2011)
15. Long, R., Pasupat, P., Liang, P.: Simpler context-dependent logical forms via model projections. In: Proceedings of ACL (2016)
16. Miller, S., Stallard, D., Bobrow, R.J., Schwartz, R.M.: A fully statistical approach to natural language interfaces. In: Proceedings of ACL (1996)
17. Suhr, A., Artzi, Y.: Situated mapping of sequential instructions to actions with single-step reward observation. In: Proceedings of ACL (2018)
18. Suhr, A., Iyer, S., Artzi, Y.: Learning to map context-dependent sentences to executable formal queries. In: Proceedings of NAACL-HLT (2018)
19. Sun, Y., et al.: Semantic parsing with syntax- and table-aware SQL generation. In: Proceedings of ACL (2018)
20. Wang, B., Shin, R., Liu, X., Polozov, O., Richardson, M.: RAT-SQL: relation-aware schema encoding and linking for text-to-sql parsers. CoRR abs/1911.04942
21. Yavuz, S., Gur, I., Su, Y., Yan, X.: What it takes to achieve 100 percent condition accuracy on wikisql. In: Proceedings of EMNLP (2018)
22. Yin, P., Neubig, G.: A syntactic neural model for general-purpose code generation. In: Proceedings of ACL (2017)
23. Yu, T., Li, Z., Zhang, Z., Zhang, R., Radev, D.: TypeSQL: Knowledge-based type-aware neural text-to-SQL generation. In: Proceedings of NAACL (2018)
24. Yu, T., et al.: SyntaxSQLNet: Syntax tree networks for complex and cross-domain text-to-SQL task. In: Proceedings of EMNLP (2018)
25. Yu, T., et al.: Spider: A large-scale human-labeled dataset for complex and cross-domain semantic parsing and text-to-SQL task. In: Proceedings of EMNLP (2018)
26. Yu, T., et al.: Sparc: Cross-domain semantic parsing in context. In: Proceedings of ACL (2019)
27. Zelle, J.M., Mooney, R.J.: Learning to parse database queries using inductive logic programming. In: Proceedings of AAAI (1996)
28. Zettlemoyer, L.S., Collins, M.: Learning context-dependent mappings from sentences to logical form. In: Proceedings of ACL (2009)
29. Zettlemoyer, L.S., Collins, M.: Learning to map sentences to logical form: Structured classification with probabilistic categorial grammars. In: Proceedings of UAI (2005)
30. Zhang, R., et al.: Editing-based SQL query generation for cross-domain context-dependent questions. In: Proceedings of EMNLP-IJCNLP (2019)
31. Zhong, V., Xiong, C., Socher, R.: Seq2sql: Generating structured queries from natural language using reinforcement learning. CoRR abs/1709.00103 (2017)

HScodeNet: Combining Hierarchical Sequential and Global Spatial Information of Text for Commodity HS Code Classification

Shaohua Du[1,2], Zhihao Wu[1,2,3], Huaiyu Wan[1,2,3(✉)], and YouFang Lin[1,2,3]

[1] School of Computer and Information Technology, Beijing Jiaotong University, Beijing, China
{shaohua_du,zhwu,hywan,yflin}@bjtu.edu.cn
[2] Beijing Key Laboratory of Traffic Data Analysis and Mining, Beijing, China
[3] CAAC Key Laboratory of Intelligent Passenger Service of Civil Aviation, Beijing, China

Abstract. Commodity Harmonization System (HS) code classification is an important customs procedure in cross-border trade. HS code classification is to identify the category (i.e., HS code) of a commodity according to its description information. In fact, HS code classification is essentially a text classification task. However, compared with general text classification, the challenge of this task is that commodity description texts are organized in special hierarchical structures and contain multiple independent semantic segments. What's more, the label space (i.e., the HS code system) has hierarchical correlation. In this paper, we propose a HS code classification neural network (HScodeNet) by incorporating the hierarchical sequential and global spatial information of texts, in which a hierarchical sequence learning module is designed to capture the sequential information and a text graph learning module is designed to capture the spatial information of commodity description texts. In addition, a label correlation loss function is presented to train the model. Extensive experiments on several real-world customs commodity datasets show the superiority of our HScodeNet model.

Keywords: HS code · Text classification · Hierarchical · Text graph

1 Introduction

The global daily import and export trade has exceeded 100 billion dollars in 2019. All cross-border commodities are subject to customs duties, which are determined by the categorization of commodities. So, it is crucial for enterprises and customs that commodities are efficiently classified into accurate categories. The World Customs Organization (WCO) has established the Harmonization System (HS) Codes to represent the categories of cross-border trade commodities in the form of 6-digit codes. China has appended extra 4 digits to form a

© Springer Nature Switzerland AG 2021
K. Karlapalem et al. (Eds.): PAKDD 2021, LNAI 12713, pp. 676–689, 2021.
https://doi.org/10.1007/978-3-030-75765-6_54

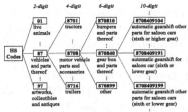

Fig. 1. An example of commodity description.

Fig. 2. Hierarchical structure of HS.

10-digit HS code system. Thus, HS code classification is to find the most proper 10-digit HS code for a commodity according to its description information. The description information is usually a text composed of a series of elements, called declaration elements. As shown in Fig. 1, the commodity description text consists of a series of declaration elements, such as commodity name, adaptable automobile mode and principle. And the corresponding HS code is 8708409199, which means the commodity is an automatic gearshift part for saloon cars.

HS code classification can be regarded as a text classification task. However, compared with general text classification, it faces the following challenges:

1) Commodity description texts are organized in special hierarchical structures. As shown in Fig. 1, a commodity description text is composed of several declaration elements, and a declaration element consists of many words.

2) A commodity description text contains several independent semantic segments (i.e., declaration elements) rather than one uniform semantic topic. Each declaration element has its own local short-range word-level sequential semantics, while in the element-level there is an order information defined by industry regulations. This is very different from the global continuous semantics in common texts such as news and comments.

3) The label space of HS codes is represented by a large 5-layer tree structure. As shown in Fig. 2, the labels (codes) are not independent, but have a hierarchical correlation. For example, "8708409191" and "8708409199" in the figure both belong to "870840", and the difference between them is if a commodity is a transmission or just a part, so they are highly correlated.

Recently, a surge of methods have been developed for text classification, which can be broadly divided into two categories: Sequence-based Methods are able to capture continuous context dependencies, but lose the global word co-occurrence information in the entire corpus and ignore the correlations between non-adjacent words in sentences; while, Graph-based Methods can effectively exploit the global word co-occurrence information to capture the correlations between non-adjacent words. However, to solve HS code classification task, these general methods will face the following problems: 1) they do not simultaneously consider the local sequential and global spatial information of the texts; 2) they cannot effectively deal with the unique hierarchical structure of commodity description texts; 3) they ignore the hierarchical correlation in the label space.

To address the above challenges, we propose a novel HS code classification neural network (HScodeNet) model by incorporating the hierarchical sequential and global spatial information of commodity description texts. First, a hierarchical sequence learning (HSL) module is designed to capture the multi-level sequential information. Then, we construct a global corpus-level graph based on the word co-occurrence information of the entire corpus and extract a subgraph for each commodity, and then design a text graph learning (TGL) module to capture the spatial information among non-adjacent words. Besides, a label correlation loss (LCL) function is proposed to capture the hierarchical correlations in the label space to further improve the classification accuracy.

The main contributions of this paper can be summarized as follows:

1) We have an insight into the commodity HS code classification problem and thoroughly analyze its differences and challenges compared with the widely studied text classification problem.
2) We propose a novel HScodeNet model for HS code classification, in which a hierarchical sequence learning module and a text graph learning module are designed to capture the multi-level sequential and global spatial information.
3) A label correlation loss function is proposed to utilize the hierarchical structure of the label space to improve the classification performance.
4) Extensive experiments are conducted on four real-world customs datasets, which verify the superiority of our proposed model.

2   Related Work

HS code classification is usually performed manually by domain experts. Machine learning methods are currently being integrated into this field [1,3]. However, traditional methods have limited modeling abilities, and deep learning methods have not yet been well explored in this field. In fact, HS code classification is essentially a text classification task with special text structure and label hierarchy, so we can refer to techniques on text classification and hierarchical classification.

Text Classification. Text classification methods can be divided into sequence-based models and graph-based models. Sequence-based models mainly capture text sequence features for classification. The most commonly used sequence-based models include convolutional neural networks (CNN) [2,7,19] which capture local n-gram semantics and recurrent neural networks (RNN) [9,20] which learn sequential information and context dependence in text. [4,17] employed attention mechanism to improve the model's ability to learn the representations of documents. [16] used capsule networks based on dynamic routing to explore text classification. Graph-based text classification models exploit the spatial features of texts from the constructed graphs by using the global co-occurrence information of corpus. [18] used a heterogeneous text graph to describe the local co-occurring constraint, and then used graph convolution networks (GCN) [8] to learn on the graph. [10] constructed a text graph tensor and then performed the jointly learning of multi-graphs.

Hierarchical Classification. Hierarchical classification methods are mainly divided into local classification methods and global classification methods. Local methods train a classifier for each local module [12], so they are much more computationally expensive. Global methods are usually cheaper because they consider the overall label hierarchy and train a unified classifier [5], but they are less likely to capture local information from the hierarchy. Recently, [15] used a cascaded neural network to simultaneously optimize the local and global loss. However, such special network structure can't consider the fact that the number of categories at different levels are very different, which limits its application.

3   Preliminaries

Definition 1. *Declaration Element. A declare element is a piece of text that reflects some aspect of a commodity's objective attributes. E_n^m denotes the m-th declaration element of commodity n, which consists of a sequence of T words:*

$$E_n^m = \left\{ w_{n,m}^1, w_{n,m}^2, \ldots, w_{n,m}^t, \ldots, w_{n,m}^T \right\}. \tag{1}$$

Definition 2. *Commodity Description. A commodity description is a sequence of declaration elements used for the HS code classification of a commodity n, denoted as D_n, in which the declaration elements are separated by "|":*

$$D_n = \left\{ E_n^1 | E_n^2 | \ldots | E_n^m | \ldots | E_n^M \right\}. \tag{2}$$

Definition 3. *HS Code. A HS code is a 10-digit code that can represent the class label of a commodity. Let $Y = \{y^{(1)}, y^{(2)}, \ldots, y^{(C)}\}$ be a set of HS codes, i.e., label space, where C is the total number of labels. Y is organized as a hierarchical tree structure like Fig. 2, in which each y_i is a leaf node, and an inner node is an ancestor (i.e., prefix) of the corresponding 10-digit code.*

Definition 4. *Commodity HS Code Classification. Given the commodity description D_n of a certain commodity n, the goal is to identify the correct code (label) of n from the label space Y.*

4   The HScodeNet Model

Figure 3 illustrates the architecture of our HScodeNet model. It is mainly composed of two modules: Hierarchical Sequence Learning (HSL) module, which captures multi-level sequential features; and Text Graph Learning (TGL) module, which captures global spatial features. Finally, we fuse these two features and use a label correlation loss function to optimize the model.

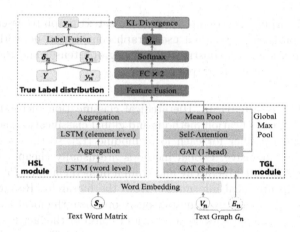

Fig. 3. Overall architecture of HScodeNet.

4.1 Hierarchical Sequence Learning (HSL) Module

The commodity description texts exhibit sequential features at two levels: 1) words within one declaration element are semantically positioned in order; 2) multiple declaration elements of one commodity description text are positioned in order of industry regulations. So, we use a hierarchical LSTM network to capture the two-level sequential information.

We first organize the description text of commodity n into a word matrix $S_n = \{E_n^m\}_{m=1}^M \in \mathbb{R}^{M \times T}$, where M is the number of declaration elements and T is the number of words in each declaration element. Then we use an embedding layer to fine-tune the pre-trained vector of each word, and a 3-dimensional word embedding tensor $X_S^n \in \mathbb{R}^{M \times T \times d}$ is obtained. As shown in Fig. 4, matrix X_S^n is spliced by M word embedding matrices $\{X_S^{n,m}\}_{m=1}^M$, where $X_S^{n,m} = [x_{n,m}^1, \ldots, x_{n,m}^t, \ldots, x_{n,m}^T] \in \mathbb{R}^{T \times d}$ is the word embedding matrix obtained after declaration element E_n^m is transformed through the embedding layer.

As shown in Fig. 4, each word embedding matrix $X_S^{n,m}$ in X_S^n is treated as a word sequence and fed to the first LSTM layer to capture the word-level sequential semantics, then we obtain the new representation of each word:

$$h_{n,m}^t = \text{LSTM}\left(x_{n,m}^t, h_{n,m}^{t-1}\right). \tag{3}$$

Then we aggregate the new embeddings of all the words in $X_S^{n,m}$ to get the initial embedding of declaration element m:

$$\eta_n^m = \text{concat}\left(\underset{t \in [1,T]}{\text{avg}}(h_{n,m}^t), \underset{t \in [1,T]}{\max}(h_{n,m}^t)\right). \tag{4}$$

Then, η_n^m obtained from the first LSTM layer is used to form a declaration element embedding matrix $H_n = [\eta_n^1, \ldots, \eta_n^m, \ldots, \eta_n^M]$. And we feed H_n to the

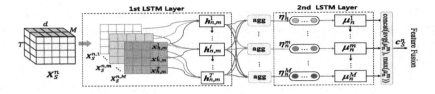

Fig. 4. Hierarchical sequence learning (HSL) module.

second LSTM layer to capture element-level sequential information, and obtain a deep-level representation of each declaration element:

$$\mu_n^m = \text{LSTM}\left(\eta_n^m, \mu_n^{m-1}\right), \tag{5}$$

where μ_n^{m-1} is the hidden state of the previous time step.

Finally, we aggregate the embeddings of all the declaration elements to obtain the hierarchical sequential feature vector of commodity description D_n:

$$c_S^n = \text{concat}\left(\underset{m\in[1,M]}{\text{avg}}\left(\mu_n^m\right), \underset{m\in[1,M]}{\max}\left(\mu_n^m\right)\right). \tag{6}$$

4.2 Text Graph Learning (TGL) Module

In this module, we first construct a text graph for each commodity description, and then learn the spatial information from the graph.

Text Graph Construction. The structure of text graph will greatly affect the learning performance. In text graph construction, different co-occurrence window choices and edge-weight calculation methods result in completely different text graph structures. In this work we combine the hierarchical structure of texts to build text graphs, mainly containing two steps: first construct a global corpus graph based on the word co-occurrence information in the entire corpus, and then extract a subgraph for each commodity from the global corpus graph. With regard to the edge-weights, we use graph attention networks (GAT) [14] to adaptively learn them.

1) Global Corpus Graph Construction: Let $G=(V,E)$ be the constructed global corpus text graph, where V is the vocabulary of the entire corpus, each node $v_i \in V$ corresponds to a word. We use declaration elements $\{E_n^m\}$ as windows to generate the word co-occurrence relations set E. Specifically, for any two words $v_i, v_j \in V$, if they co-occur in the same window, we add an edge $e_{i,j}$ into E. In addition, we agree that for any v_i, $e_{i,i} \in E$ is satisfied.

2) Commodity Text Graph Extraction: Let $G_n=(V_n, E_n)$ be the text graph of commodity n extracted from G, where $V_n \subset V$ and $E_n \subset E$. Specifically, we first extract all the words contained in D_n from V to form V_n and then extract all the edges between V_n from E to form E_n.

After constructing commodity text graph based on the global co-occurrence information, the spatial correlations between non-adjacent words are constructed, then we can use the following network to capture the spatial information.

Text Graph Learning. Before the TGL module, we also first use the embedding layer mentioned above to fine-tune the pre-trained word vectors of V_n to get a word vector set $\boldsymbol{X}_G^n = \left\{ \boldsymbol{x}_n^i \,\middle|\, \boldsymbol{x}_n^i \in \mathbb{R}^d, 1 \le i \le |V_n| \right\}$.

The structure of the TGL module is shown in Fig. 5. In this module, we first use GAT to learn the edge-weights in G_n to capture local spatial information (i.e., correlations between neighboring nodes), then we employ self-attention mechanism to capture long-range spatial information all over the graph.

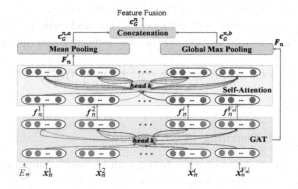

Fig. 5. Text graph learning (TGL) module.

The GAT layer first performs a learnable linear transformation $\boldsymbol{z}_n^i = \boldsymbol{\omega} \boldsymbol{x}_n^i$ on every node, where $\boldsymbol{\omega} \in \mathbb{R}^{d' \times d}$ is the weight matrix shared by each node. Then, it performs a shared attention mechanism $\boldsymbol{a} : \mathbb{R}^{2d'} \times \mathbb{R}^{2d'} \to \mathbb{R}$ and applies the LeakyReLU nonlinearity to compute the attention coefficient for each edge $e_{i,j}$:

$$\gamma_n^{i,j} = \text{LeakyReLU}\left(\boldsymbol{a}^{\mathrm{T}} \left[\boldsymbol{z}_n^i || \boldsymbol{z}_n^j \right] \right), \tag{7}$$

where $||$ is the concatenation operation. Then, we normalize these coefficients:

$$\alpha_n^{i,j} = \frac{\exp\left(\gamma_n^{i,j}\right)}{\sum_{k=1}^{|\Gamma_n^i|} \exp\left(\gamma_n^{i,k}\right)}, \tag{8}$$

where Γ_n^i is the set of neighbors of node v_i in graph G_n. Finally, we update the features of each node v_i by using the normalized attention coefficients to compute a linear combination of its neighbors' features:

$$\boldsymbol{x}_n^{i\prime} = \sum_{j=1}^{|\Gamma_n^i|} \alpha_n^{i,j} \boldsymbol{z}_n^j. \tag{9}$$

We use multi-head attention in the GAT layer, and the feature vector of a node obtained by using K-head attention is:

$$x_n^{i\prime} = \text{ELU}\left(\underset{k\in[1,K]}{\|} \left(x_{n,k}^{i\prime}\right) + b \right), \tag{10}$$

where $b \in \mathbb{R}^{(K\times d')}$ is a learnable bias vector, $\|$ is the concatenation operation, and K is a hyperparameter.

After the GAT layer captures the local spatial features in the commodity text graph, we further employ a self-attention layer to model the long-range spatial information. Suppose $F_n = (f_n^1, f_n^2, \ldots, f_n^i, \ldots, f_n^{|V_n|}) \in \mathbb{R}^{|V_n|\times d'}$ is the word embedding matrix after the GAT layer, where $f_n^i \in \mathbb{R}^{d'}$ is the feature vector of word node v_i, we calculate the normalized attention coefficient vector of v_i with all other word nodes in the graph as follows:

$$\beta_n^i = \text{softmax}\left(f_n^i W F_n^\mathrm{T}\right), \tag{11}$$

where $W \in \mathbb{R}^{d'\times d'}$, $\beta_n^i \in \mathbb{R}^{|V_n|}$, and the j-th element in β_n^i indicates the importance of word v_j's features to word v_i. Finally, the attention coefficient vector is used to compute a linear combination of all other nodes' features, to serve as the final output features of the TGL module for word v_i:

$$f_n^{i\prime} = \beta_n^i F_n. \tag{12}$$

Here $f_n^{i\prime}$ represents one word v_i's spatial features in text graph G_n, and $F_n' = (f_n^{1\prime}, f_n^{2\prime}, \ldots, f_n^{i\prime}, \ldots, f_n^{|V_n|\prime}) \in \mathbb{R}^{|V_n|\times d'}$. Then we need to aggregate the spatial features of all the words to obtain an embedding of the whole graph. We perform a max-k (k is a hyperparameter) pooling operation on all the word vectors in the graph, and then use an average pooling to aggregate them into one vector $c_G^{n,a}$. At the same time, after the GAT layer, a global max pooling is adopted to pool all the word features into a vector $c_G^{n,b}$. Then a residual structure is used to concatenate $c_G^{n,a}$ and $c_G^{n,b}$ into the final text graph embedding c_G^n.

4.3 Feature Fusion and Classification

We fuse the local sequential features c_S^n obtained from the HSL module and the global spatial features c_G^n obtained from the TGL module to form the final feature representation of commodity description D_n:

$$c_n = W_S \circ c_S^n + W_G \circ c_G^n, \tag{13}$$

where W_S and W_G are learnable parameters, and $\circ$ is the Hadamard product.

Then the final representation c_n is fed into two fully connected layers and a softmax layer to predict the normalized label probability distribution $\hat{y}_n$ of D_n:

$$\hat{y}_n = \text{softmax}(W_2(\text{ELU}(W_1 c_n + b_1)) + b_2), \tag{14}$$

where W_1, W_2, b_1 and b_2 are learnable parameters.

4.4   Label Correlation Loss (LCL) Function

In the multi-class classification problem, for a sample n, we usually use its true label distribution $\boldsymbol{y}_n = [y_n^{(1)}, y_n^{(2)}, \ldots, y_n^{(C)}]$ for model training, where $y_n^{(i)}$ represents the probability of label $y^{(i)}$ on sample n, $\sum_{i=1}^{C} y_n^{(i)} = 1$, and C is the total number of labels. We assume that the true label of sample n is y_n^*. In the situation that the labels are independent with each other, we can use $\boldsymbol{\delta}_n = [\delta_n^{(1)}, \delta_n^{(2)}, \ldots, \delta_n^{(C)}]$ to be the true label distribution of sample n, where

$$\delta_n^{(i)} = \begin{cases} 1, & y_n^* = y^{(i)}, \\ 0, & \text{otherwise.} \end{cases} \tag{15}$$

However, in the HS code classification scenario, as analyzed before and shown in Fig. 2, the labels are not independent but have a hierarchical correlation, so we cannot directly use $\boldsymbol{\delta}_n$ for model training. Therefore, based on the hierarchical structure of HS codes, we propose a method for calculating the correlation between any label $y^{(i)}$ and sample n when the true label of n is y_n^*:

$$r_n^{(i)} = e^{count(Ancestor(y_n^*) \cap Ancestor(y^{(i)}))}, \tag{16}$$

where $count$ is the counting operation and $Ancestor(y^{(i)})$ represents the set of ancestor labels of label $y^{(i)}$ in the entire label space Y. Then we normalize $r_n^{(i)}$ to get a new correlation-based label distribution $\boldsymbol{\xi}_n = [\xi_n^{(1)}, \xi_n^{(2)}, \ldots, \xi_n^{(C)}]$, where

$$\xi_n^{(i)} = r_n^{(i)} \Big/ \sum_{i=1}^{C} r_n^{(i)}. \tag{17}$$

According to Eq. 16, the greater the number of common ancestors between label $y^{(i)}$ and true label y_n^*, the stronger correlation between label $y^{(i)}$ and sample n, and thus the higher the probability of label $y^{(i)}$ on sample n.

Then, we perform a weighted summation operation on the above two kinds of label distributions to obtain the final true label distribution of sample n:

$$\boldsymbol{y}_n = \lambda \boldsymbol{\delta}_n + (1 - \lambda) \boldsymbol{\xi}_n, \tag{18}$$

where λ is a hyperparameter.

Finally, we use KL divergence to measure the distance between the true label distribution $\boldsymbol{y}_n$ and the predicted label distribution $\hat{\boldsymbol{y}}_n$, and minimize the following loss function:

$$D_{KL}(\boldsymbol{y}_n, \hat{\boldsymbol{y}}_n) = \sum_{i=1}^{C} y_n^{(i)} \log \left(y_n^{(i)} / \hat{y}_n^{(i)} \right). \tag{19}$$

5   Experiments

5.1   Datasets

We collected four real-world customs datasets from a customs agency in China. The datasets are all in Chinese and belong to vehicle industry, chemical industry, textile manufacturing and electrical industry, respectively. Specifically, the vehicle industry dataset (VID) contains commodities such as vehicles, aircrafts, ships and other transportation equipment; the chemical industry dataset (CID) contains commodities such as chemical products, plastic products and rubber products; the textile manufacturing dataset (TMD) contains commodities such as textile raw materials and textile products; and the mechanical electrical dataset (MED) contains commodities such as machinery appliances and electrical equipment. All commodities in the datasets are labeled by domain experts and have been verified by the customs agency. Table 1 shows the statistics of the datasets.

5.2 Settings

We set the dimension of the initial word embeddings to be 300 and use Word2Vec [11] for pre-training. Each layer in the HSL module adopts a 2-layer unidirectional LSTM. In the TGL module, the GAT layer includes two graph attention layers in which the first layer adopts an 8-head attention and the second layer a single-head attention, the self-attention layer adopts an 8-head attention. When generating the graph embedding, we use a max-10 pooling operation. The hyperparameter λ in Eq. 18 is set to 0.9. The batch-size is set to 64. The initial learning rate is 0.0004, which decays according to the step interval [2, 10, 30, 50] and the decay rate is 0.5. Accuracy and macro-F1 score are used to evaluate.

5.3 Baselines

We compare our proposed model with classic classifiers, transformer, hierarchical classifiers, and state-of-the-art text classifiers. ①TF+LR, ②TF+DT and ③TF+XGBoost are the logistic regression, decision tree and ensemble methods based on term frequency. ④Transformer [13] uses a multi-head self-attention to generate embeddings for words in sequence. We use the encoder structure in it. ⑤TextCNN [7] uses CNN and max-pooling to capture local semantics features. ⑥TextRNN [9] uses the last hidden state of RNN as the representation of the whole text. ⑦DeepMoji [4] is a hybrid neural network combining bidirectional LSTM and attention and performs well in text classification tasks. ⑧fastText [6] uses a position-independent fully connected neural network to learn document embeddings. We evaluate it with and without bigrams respectively. ⑨HMCN-F [15] is a hierarchical classifiers which fits the neural network layers to the label hierarchy. ⑩TextGCN [18] models the whole corpus as a heterogeneous graph and learns word and document embeddings with graph neural networks jointly.

Table 1. Statistics of datasets.

Dataset	#Samples	#Train	#Validation	#Test	#Words	Average length	Declare elements	Labels (HS codes)
VID	31,600	22,752	2,528	6,320	40,282	30	82	158
CID	165,600	119,232	13,248	33,120	115,920	31	200	828
TMD	179,800	129,456	14,384	35,960	98,823	22	228	899
MED	117,000	84,240	9,360	23,400	154,163	24	119	585

5.4   Experimental Results and Analyses

Classification Performance Comparison. Table 2 gives the comparison result of each model. HScodeNet achieves the best performance on all the four datasets. For more in-depth analysis, we note that the results of traditional machine learning methods are usually not good, demonstrating those methods' limited abilities of modeling complex data. By comparison, the methods which focus on sequential information, such as TextCNN and TextRNN perform much better. This is because word orders are important in text classification. We notice that the strong baseline TextGCN which focuses on the global co-occurrence information does not perform a significant advantage over CNN and LSTM-based models. This is because GCN ignores the sequential information in texts, while CNN and LSTM model consecutive word sequences explicitly. Another reason is that the edge-weights in TextGCN are calculated based on static statistics information, which limits the message passing among the nodes. Besides, the result of hierarchical classification method HMCN-F performs well, which showcases the effectiveness of capturing hierarchical information in label space.

Our model captures the special sequential and spatial information in the commodity description texts simultaneously, and designs a label correlation loss function to utilize the label hierarchy. Therefore, our HScodeNet achieves the best results against all the baselines, which demonstrates its advantages in representing sequential and spatial features of commodity description texts.

Ablation Study. We prove the effectiveness of each component of our HScodeNet model, and the results are shown in Fig. 6. "-HSL" means removing the HSL module, "-TGL" means removing the TGL module, and "-LCL" indicates using the common cross entropy loss to replace LCL function.

From the Fig. 6 we can find that removing any of the three components will make the classification accuracy drop obviously, which demonstrates the effectiveness of each component. And we can further observe that, among the three components, the TGL module has the greatest impact on the classification performance, the HSL module takes the second place, and the LCL function has

Table 2. Classification performance of different methods.

Model	VID		CID		TMD		MED	
	Acc (%)	F1 (%)	Acc (%)	F1 (%)	Acc (%)	F1 (%)	Acc (%)	F1 (%)
TF+LR	74.35 ± 2.01	75.63 ± 1.26	38.18 ± 1.60	40.50 ± 1.29	27.06 ± 1.53	25.10 ± 1.31	58.99 ± 2.65	57.86 ± 1.15
TF+DT	79.66 ± 0.28	79.64 ± 0.31	71.11 ± 0.08	71.45 ± 0.05	60.33 ± 0.14	59.32 ± 0.16	64.54 ± 0.10	64.89 ± 0.07
TF+XGBoost	84.95 ± 0.00	83.10 ± 0.00	74.05 ± 0.00	74.24 ± 0.00	65.36 ± 0.00	63.30 ± 0.00	67.88 ± 0.00	68.14 ± 0.00
Transformer	89.68 ± 0.27	87.45 ± 0.22	85.63 ± 0.35	84.53 ± 0.41	70.73 ± 0.12	69.76 ± 0.29	77.48 ± 0.37	75.39 ± 0.59
TextCNN	89.51 ± 0.37	88.08 ± 0.39	86.38 ± 0.35	86.69 ± 0.29	70.68 ± 0.54	67.79 ± 0.61	77.94 ± 0.97	74.26 ± 0.83
TextRNN	84.88 ± 0.14	81.72 ± 0.29	83.72 ± 0.38	83.30 ± 0.41	68.25 ± 0.26	65.83 ± 0.33	69.81 ± 0.14	65.64 ± 0.04
DeepMoji	86.00 ± 0.21	83.99 ± 0.19	84.03 ± 0.38	83.61 ± 0.35	68.63 ± 0.34	66.17 ± 0.42	71.64 ± 0.50	68.97 ± 0.47
fastText	89.52 ± 0.62	87.12 ± 0.75	86.32 ± 0.33	85.54 ± 0.27	67.70 ± 0.48	65.35 ± 0.46	77.50 ± 0.31	74.01 ± 0.36
fastText (bigram)	89.88 ± 0.55	88.03 ± 0.67	87.10 ± 0.60	86.94 ± 0.36	71.15 ± 1.07	69.49 ± 0.95	79.08 ± 0.43	76.47 ± 0.57
HMCN-F	88.13 ± 0.12	86.94 ± 0.16	86.02 ± 0.13	85.70 ± 0.10	71.33 ± 0.05	70.14 ± 0.09	77.38 ± 0.21	75.72 ± 0.29
TextGCN	88.80 ± 0.07	87.09 ± 0.11	86.11 ± 0.13	85.97 ± 0.19	70.87 ± 0.06	69.24 ± 0.08	78.72 ± 0.17	76.14 ± 0.24
HScodeNet (ours)	**93.10 ± 0.15**	**91.78 ± 0.23**	**90.89 ± 0.07**	**89.62 ± 0.09**	**77.18 ± 0.22**	**75.82 ± 0.19**	**85.12 ± 0.08**	**82.98 ± 0.14**

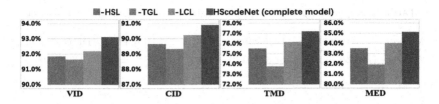

Fig. 6. Ablation experiments of each component.

the lowest influence. Even so, removing LCL causes the accuracy decrease by 0.92%, 0.66%, 1.03% and 1.09% on the four datasets respectively, which proves the effectiveness of modeling the hierarchical information in the label space.

Comparison of Text Graph Construction Methods. We compare the performances of the following text graph construction methods by experiments:

1) *DOC-PMI*: Each document (DOC) is taken as a co-occurrence window, and point-wise mutual information (PMI) is used to calculate edge-weight $ew_{i,j}$:

$$ew_{i,j} = \max \Big(\log \big(p(v_i, v_j) / (p(v_i)p(v_j)) \big), 0 \Big), \tag{20}$$

where $p(v_i, v_j)$ is the probability that a window contains both words v_i and v_j in the corpus, and $p(v_i)$ is the probability that a window contains v_i.

2) *DOC-CP*: Each document is treated as a co-occurrence window, and conditional probability (CP) is employed to calculate the edge-weight $ew'_{i,j}$:

$$ew'_{i,j} = (p(v_i|v_j) + p(v_j|v_i))/2. \tag{21}$$

3) *SLI-CP*: A sliding (SLI) window with a fixed size of 10 is utilized on all documents in the corpus, and the edge-weight calculation method is CP.

4) *DE-CP*: Each declaration element (DE) is taken as a co-occurrence window, and the edge-weight calculation method is CP.

5) *DE-GAT* (used in our model): Each declaration element is taken as a co-occurrence window, and edge-weights are adaptively learned by GAT.

The first four methods adopt word co-occurrence statistics information to calculate the edge-weights of text graphs, and then use a 2-layer GCN to aggregate information. Differently, the DE-GAT method employs GAT to learn the edge-weights adaptively. For fair comparison, we use 2-layer single-head GAT in experiments. As Table 3 shows, both the choice of co-occurrence window and the edge-weight calculation methods have an obvious influence on the results. Specifically, SLI window is better than DOC window, and DE window is the best, which demonstrates that taking declaration elements as co-occurrence windows conform the structure characteristics of commodity description texts. Similarly, the GAT method is far better than the CP and PMI method, which demonstrates the superiority of adaptively learning the edge-weights against using static statistics information. Therefore, DE-GAT achieves the best performance.

Table 3. Experiments of text graph construction methods on VID dataset.

Method	DOC-PMI	DOC-CP	SLI-CP	DE-CP	DE-GAT (ours)
Accuracy (%)	86.43 ± 0.14	87.32 ± 0.13	87.60 ± 0.09	88.84 ± 0.05	90.30 ± 0.06

6   Conclusion

In this paper, we present the HS code classification problem and propose HScodeNet model to incorporate the hierarchical sequential and global spatial information of texts. Besides, a label correlation loss function is designed to utilize the label hierarchy. The experimental results prove the superiority of our model.

References

1. Altaheri, F., Shaalan, K.: Exploring machine learning models to predict harmonized system code. In: EMCIS, pp. 291–303 (2019)
2. Conneau, A., Schwenk, H., Barrault, L., LeCun, Y.: Very deep convolutional networks for text classification. In: EACL, pp. 1107–1116 (2017)
3. Ding, L., Fan, Z., Chen, D.: Auto-categorization of HS code using background net approach. In: KES, pp. 1462–1471 (2015)
4. Felbo, B., Mislove, A., Søgaard, A., Rahwan, I., Lehmann, S.: Using millions of emoji occurrences to learn any-domain representations for detecting sentiment, emotion and sarcasm. In: EMNLP, pp. 1615–1625 (2017)
5. Gopal, S., Yang, Y.: Recursive regularization for large-scale classification with hierarchical and graphical dependencies. In: KDD, pp. 257–265 (2013)
6. Joulin, A., Grave, E., Bojanowski, P., Mikolov, T.: Bag of tricks for efficient text classification. In: EACL, pp. 427–431 (2017)
7. Kim, Y.: Convolutional neural networks for sentence classification. In: EMNLP, pp. 1746–1751 (2014)
8. Kipf, T.N., Welling, M.: Semi-supervised classification with graph convolutional networks. In: ICLR (2017)
9. Liu, P., Qiu, X., Huang, X.: Recurrent neural network for text classification with multi-task learning. In: IJCAI, pp. 2873–2879 (2016)
10. Liu, X., You, X., Zhang, X., Wu, J., Lv, P.: Tensor graph convolutional networks for text classification. In: AAAI, pp. 8409–8416 (2020)
11. Mikolov, T., Chen, K., Corrado, G., Dean, J.: Efficient estimation of word representations in vector space. In: ICLR (2013)
12. Sun, Z., Zhao, Y., Cao, D., Hao, H.: Hierarchical multilabel classification with optimal path prediction. Neural Process. Lett. **45**(1), 263–277 (2017)
13. Vaswani, A., et al.: Attention is all you need. In: NeurIPS, pp. 5998–6008 (2017)
14. Velickovic, P., Cucurull, G., Casanova, A., Romero, A., Liò, P., Bengio, Y.: Graph attention networks. In: ICLR (2018)
15. Wehrmann, J., Cerri, R., Barros, R.C.: Hierarchical multi-label classification networks. In: ICML, pp. 5225–5234 (2018)
16. Yang, M., Zhao, W., Ye, J., Lei, Z., Zhao, Z., Zhang, S.: Investigating capsule networks with dynamic routing for text classification. In: EMNLP, pp. 3110–3119 (2018)

17. Yang, Z., Yang, D., Dyer, C., He, X., Smola, A.J., Hovy, E.H.: Hierarchical attention networks for document classification. In: NAACL, pp. 1480–1489 (2016)
18. Yao, L., Mao, C., Luo, Y.: Graph convolutional networks for text classification. In: AAAI, pp. 7370–7377 (2019)
19. Zhang, X., Zhao, J.J., LeCun, Y.: Character-level convolutional networks for text classification. In: NeurIPS, pp. 649–657 (2015)
20. Zhang, Y., Liu, Q., Song, L.: Sentence-state LSTM for text representation. In: ACL, pp. 317–327 (2018)

PLVCG: A Pretraining Based Model for Live Video Comment Generation

Zehua Zeng[1,2,3(✉)], Neng Gao[1,3], Cong Xue[3], and Chenyang Tu[1,3]

[1] State Key Laboratory of Information Security, Institute of Information Engineering, CAS, Beijing, China
cengzehua@iie.ac.cn
[2] School of Cyber Security, University of Chinese Academy of Sciences, Beijing, China
[3] Institute of Information Engineering, Chinese Academy of Sciences, Beijing, China

Abstract. Live video comment generating task aims to automatically generate real-time viewer comments on videos like real viewers do. Like providing search suggestions by search engines, this task can help viewers find comments they want to post by providing generated comments. Previous works ignore the interactivity and diversity of comments and can only generate general and popular comments. In this paper, we incorporate post time of the comments to deal with the real-time related comment interactions. We also take the video type labels into consideration to handle the diversity of comments and generate more related and informative comments. To this end, we propose a pre-training based encoder-decoder joint model called PLVCG model. This model is composed of a bidirectional encoder to encode context comments and visual frames jointly as well as an auto-regressive decoder to generate real-time comments and classify the type of the video. We evaluate our model in a large-scale real-world live comment dataset. The experiment results present that our model outperforms the state-of-the-art on live video comment ranking and generating task significantly.

Keywords: Live video comment · Natural Language Generation · Auto-regressive generation

1 Introduction

Live comment video, which is also called time-sync comment video, is a new type of video that viewers can interact with each other by commenting on videos [2]. When a video is playing, the comments are shown at the right side of the video or fly crossing the video. Thus viewers can comment what they are watching in real-time, and even reply others comments. Like search suggestions provided by

Electronic supplementary material The online version of this chapter (https://doi.org/10.1007/978-3-030-75765-6_55) contains supplementary material, which is available to authorized users.

© Springer Nature Switzerland AG 2021
K. Karlapalem et al. (Eds.): PAKDD 2021, LNAI 12713, pp. 690–702, 2021.
https://doi.org/10.1007/978-3-030-75765-6_55

search engines, some viewers want to select comments from automatically generated comments. To promote the user experiences, there have been some live comment video service providers use random candidate comments for users to select. However, these comments are too common and uninformative for users to post. As a result, a new challenging task called live video comment generating is proposed [9]. This task aims to automatically generate natural language comments of videos like real viewers do. Therefore, the model is required to comprehend not only multi-modality, but also the interactions between viewers and videos.

Table 1. Different comments posted at different time. All comments are translated from Chinese into English by the authors.

Posted time	Comment
2016.04.16	I'm supervised that you upload this video!
2016.04.16	The uploader comes back.
2016.04.16	I'm the top 1000 watching this video.
2020.04.30	Archaeological study on this video from 2020.
2020.07.22	Episode 22 still hasn't been uploaded today

To deal with the multi-modality property, the proposed models need to consider not only visual information, but also natural language comments. This kind of challenge have been learned in field such as image captioning [18], video captioning [11,15] and visual question answering [7]. Some works [4,9]? have been proposed to solve the live video comment generating task by considering multi-modality property.

However, other properties, such as interactivity and diversity, are ignored. As viewers can post comments on videos and other viewers can see these comments, their comments often contain interactivity. The interactions are various such as replying others comments, posting video type related memes, talking to the uploaders, etc. These kinds of interaction make the live video comment generating task different from aforementioned traditional multi-modality tasks. As the large group of viewers makes comments crowd-sourced, it is also challenging to handle this task due to the diversity of comments. Table 1 shows some diverse comments and reveals the differences between interactive comments posted at different time in a live comment video[1]. The first three comments are posted when the video is just uploaded and viewers are celebrating the upload of this video. However, the last two are posted in years later and viewers are talking about the sequels of this video. It is obvious that viewers are more likely to celebrate the upload when the video is just uploaded than years later.

To handle these properties, some aspects must be taken into consideration. In live comment videos, each comment has two different time attributes, the

---

[1] https://www.bilibili.com/video/BV1Cs411z7fx.

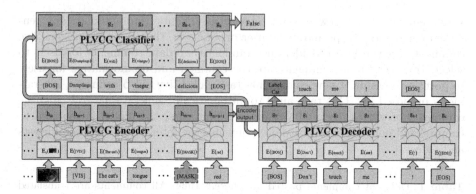

Fig. 1. PLVCG model. The lower left is the encoder module. The green boxes denote the input of the encoder and the purple box denotes the transformation of inputs. **E()** denotes embedding layer. The right is the PLVCG decoder module for pretraining and generation task. The red arrow denotes the video type classification layer. The upper left is the PLVCG decoder module for comment discrimination. (Color figure online)

post time and video time. The post time is the real world time denote when the viewer posted this comment in the video. And the video time is the time when comment is shown in the video timeline. Previous works [4,9]? use all surrounding comments regardless of these attributes. However, most of the viewers often post comments without knowing the succeeding content and it is also impossible for them to get future comments. As mentioned above, people in different real-world time may interact differently. As a result, using all surrounding comments like pervious works do may generate comments with wrong interaction. Thus, it is important to take post time of comment into consideration.

Another attribute that can influence the interaction of comments is the video type label, which is also ignored by pervious works. Video type label is important side information about the video. Different types of videos often have different comments and different interactions, yet comments in same video type diverse less. For example, videos labeled with "food" are more likely to talk about cooking and memes about foods than videos labeled with "piano". By incorporating the prediction of video type labels, models can generate more informative and content related comments rather than general and popular comments.

In this paper, we propose a pre-training based encoder-decoder joint model called PLVCG (Pretraining based Live Video Comments Generating) model to solve live video comment generating task. Our model is composed of a bidirectional encoder and an auto-regressive left-to-right decoder. The PLVCG model first uses a pretraining method to jointly learn the diverse context comments and the relationship between comments and video types. Then we propose two fine-tuning tasks to learn both comment generating and discriminate if the given context and comments are corresponded. By introducing a video classification objective in decoder, we incorporate video type labels and learn the diversity related to video types. And by only considering comments that posted before target comment, our model learns the interactions related to time. Finally, our PLVCG model generates real-time comments by introducing a prompt token which helps the model to generate more diverse comments.

We evaluate our model on a large-scale real-world dataset [9,13] and the results show that the proposed PLVCG model outperforms the state-of-the-art methods with a significant improvement. The main contributions of this paper are threefold:

- We take the challenge of interactivity and diversity into consideration and introduce the post time and video type labels to deal with these challenges in the live video comment generating task.
- We propose a pretraining based live video comment generation model to capture the correlation between video context and comments as well as generate comments with a bidirectional encoder and an auto-regressive decoder.
- Experiments on a large scale dataset show our model outperforms the state-of-the-art methods on live video comment ranking and generating tasks significantly and achieves real-time live video comment generating by introducing prompt tokens.

2 Related Work

Live Video Comment Learning. There have been some efforts in live video comment learning. [1] recommends personalized key frames using both comments and video frames. [5] leverages live video comments to predict the popularity of videos. In video shots annotating task, [14] proposes a summarization model using key sentences to annotate video shots. On the other hand, [8] proposes a supervised model to annotate video shots with labels. [16] annotates videos with both genre labels and keywords by combining video labels and comments. Most of these works focus on annotating and classifying video shots using live video comment and can't learn the natural language structure and interactivity of comments.

Live Video Comment Generating. There have been some efforts focus on live video comment generating. [9] implements a transformer based encoder-decoder model to generate live video comments, using both visual frames and surrounding context comments. [17] solves comments matching task with co-attention mechanism. [13] points out the discrepancies in [9] and proposes an alternative baseline implementation in solving this task. [4] introduces audio modality into the task. Their multimodal matching transformer model first learns representations of each modality iteratively as well as the relationships among them and then gets matching scores of comments. However, as a matching model, it can't generate comments auto-regressively. These approaches mainly focus on the multi-modality of the task and ignore the interactivity and diversity of comments, which makes them hard to generate video content related real-time comments.

3 PLVCG Model

3.1 Problem Formulation

Given a live comment video V, a video time stamp t, a comment post time p and some context comments set C, the model is required to generate a comment y that posted in real-world time p and video time t. Different from [4,9,17] that use all surrounding comments in the video as context, to ensure the generation of real-time comments, we only use a part of comments that posted earlier than p and at video time earlier than t. As a result, we denote $C = \{c_1, ..., c_n\}$, $c_{ip} < p$ and $c_{it} < t$ for $i = 1...n$, where c_p denotes the post time of comment c and c_t denotes the video time of comment c. As the videos are always too long to take the whole video into account, we reserve m frames and n comments which are closest to video time stamp t as the input. The m frames are denoted as $I = \{I_1, ...I_m\}$. By feeding these m frames and n comments into PLVCG encoder, our model aims to generate a new comment $y = \{y_1, ..., y_k\}$, where k is the number of tokens in comment that generated by PLVCG decoder.

3.2 PLVCG Encoder Module

The lower left part of Fig. 1 illustrates the architecture of our PLVCG encoder module. We follow the standard bidirectional sequence-to-sequence Transformer architecture in [12] and we also follow [6] to change ReLU activation functions to GeLUs. To incorporate visual frames into our encoder, we first apply a convolution layer to encode each frame I_i into vector v_i. These visual vectors are treated as "visual tokens" sequence. For the text comment, our encoder module concatenates each token in every comment sentence as the textual sequence. Then we concatenate "visual tokens" sequence with the textual sequence and introduce a special token [VIS] to separate these two sequences. We also leverage special token [SEP] to separate sentences in context comments sequence.

After the concatenation, we feed the token sequence into our encoder module and the textual tokens are embed to vectors by an embedding layer. We use the last hidden state h of the encoder module as the final representation of visual and textual context:

$$v_i = CNN(I_i) \tag{1}$$

$$h = Transformer(v_1, ..., v_m, [VIS], c_1, ..., c_n) \tag{2}$$

3.3 PLVCG Decoder Module

For the decoder module, we introduce two objectives to learn live video comments, the generation objective and the classification objective. The basic architecture of decoder uses the left-to-right auto-regressive transformer, which is based on BART model [6]. We also introduce two special tokens [BOS] and [EOS] to denote the beginning and ending of the target ground-truth comment sentence. The target ground-truth comment sequence can be denoted as

$T = \{t_0, t_1, ..., t_d, t_{d+1}\}$, where d denotes the length of target comment, t_0 denotes the [BOS] token and t_{d+1} denotes the [EOS] token. The differences between our model and BART model are: (1) The first token of the target ground-truth comment is provided for the decoder module as the prompt token to generate target comment. The output of the first token is not used to predict this token and other generated tokens are used in the generation objective. (2) As the first token is given, we utilize the output of the first token ([BOS] token) to predict the type label of current video as the classification objective.

The structure of our decoder module is shown in Fig. 1. Due to the strong interactivity and huge diversity of live video comments, a large amount of comments can be suitable for the context comments and visual frames. Some popular and general comments can appear in most of the video clips without anomaly. As a result, the decoder module tends to generate popular and general comments and this makes the generated comments uninformative. To deal with this challenge, the first method let the generation process prompted by a meaningful token rather than a [BOS] token. This guarantees the decoder to generate more informative comments.

Different types of video always have different topics as well as interactions and videos in same type are more likely to have similar comments. Follow this intuition, we introduce the second objective. It forces the decoder module to learn the type of video by the encoder outputs. This also helps the rest of the module improve the prediction of generating tokens by the classification information.

To achieve these objectives, we introduce a classification layer after the output of first token g_0 to get the classified video type label l. The rest of the outputs $\{g_1, ...g_k\}$ in decoder module are followed by a linear module to generate tokens $\{y_1, ...y_k\}$ as the generated comment:

$$g_0, g_1, ..., g_{k-1} = Transformer(h, t_0, t_1, ..., t_d, t_{d+1}) \qquad (3)$$

$$l = Classfication(g_0) \qquad (4)$$

$$y_1 = t_1 \qquad (5)$$

$$y_2, ..., y_k = Linear(g_1, ..., g_{k-1}) \qquad (6)$$

where t_0 and t_{d+1} denotes [BOS] and [EOS] token respectively. The final generated comment sequence y is the concentration of the prompt token t_1 and generated tokens $y_2, ..., y_k$.

4   Training PLVCG

4.1   Pre-training PLVCG

To learn the diversity of comments, we introduce a pretraining step follows the implement in [6]. The transformation of the context in this step can increase the diversity of context and is helpful for learning the diversity of comments. We choose the text infilling transformation as our implementation. In this transformation, our pre-training model first samples a number of text spans in the context comments and the span length is sampled by a Poisson distribution. For each span, words in the span are replaced with a special token [MASK]. 0-length spans are also acceptable and replacing these spans means the insertion of [MASK] token. Figure 1 also shows the transformed context of the encoder module. For the input of decoder module, the target comment is not transformed and follows the description of the decoder module to train with both video type classification objective and comment generation objective.

4.2 Comment Generation Task

On account of the decoder of PLVCG model is an auto-regressive decoder, the fine-tuning in comment generation task can be done directly. The input of encoder module is the concentration of visual tokens and textual comment tokens without transformation. The decoder objectives are also same as what is described in Decoder Module Section. For testing, we adopt beam search method and generate comments auto-regressively. A prompt token is given as the first token to handle the diversity of comments as mentioned above.

4.3 Comment Discrimination Task

Previous works [9,13,17] use the generation losses of candidate comments to rank them. In this work, we further introduce a downstream fine-tuning application after the generating step to learn whether the candidate comments correspond to the given context.

The structure of decoder in this task is shown in the right part of Fig. 1. The input of the encoder is also the concentration of visual tokens and textual comment tokens. Given the output of the encoder and a candidate comment, the decoder module should discriminate if the given candidate comment corresponds to the context. As shown in upper left part of Fig. 1, different from the generation task, the output of the [EOS] token is followed by a binary classification layer and we do not use the video type classification objective.

To train a ground-truth comment, we also sample 4 comments randomly from other videos as the negative samples. As for the candidate comment ranking task, rather than using generation loss, we calculate the logit of each candidate comment from the classification layer as its ranking score. In our model, this task is trained after the aforementioned comment generation task to get a better performance.

5   Experiment

5.1   Dataset

We evaluate our model on Live Comment Dataset provided by [9]. However, it is found that there are overlapped comments across the training and testing set in the original Live Comment Dataset [13]. Thus we follow the new dataset built by

[13] which removes redundant videos from the raw dataset. And we also follow the same partition as in [9]. Finally the fixed dataset contains 2118 videos and 882056 comments.

We present the influence of post time and video time on similarities. For each video, we first sort comments by post time and video time separately. Then we equally split the sorted comments into 10 clusters. We calculate the average similarity of each cluster in train dataset. The comments clustered by post time, video time and randomly are 0.175, 0.134 and 0.120. It is obvious that comments clustered by post time and video time are more similar than those clustered randomly. Therefore, taking post time into account is helpful for model to learn time related interactions. To incorporate post time into our dataset, we only pick comments posted before target comment as the context. We also measure the diversity of the live video comments in supplementary material.

5.2 Evaluation Metrics

The interactivity and diversity of video comments make it hard to find out all possible references. In this paper, we follow the previous works [3,9] to formulate the task into a ranking task. Consequently, we adopt **Recall@k (R@k)**, **Mean Recall (MR)** and **Mean Reciprocal Rank (MRR)** to evaluate the performance of our model. In this task, the model is given both visual and textual context sequence and asked to rank 100 candidate comments to find the most related comments. The candidate set consists of four kinds of comments: (1) **Ground-truth**: 5 ground-truth comments that are posted by human viewers from corresponding video. (2) **Plausible**: 20 comments that are most similar to the title of the corresponding video. (3) **Popular**: 20 most popular comments in the training dataset. (4) **Random**: randomly selected comments from training set.

Another task of the experiment is the generation task. We use **Bilingual Evaluation Understudy (BLEU)** [10] to evaluate this task. It is one of the most important metrics in Natural Language Generation task, and evaluates the correspondence between generated and reference sentences. To show the real effectiveness, we skip the prompt token and use following generated tokens to calculate these metrics.

5.3 Baseline Models

- **LiveBot** [9] applies a unified transformer model that uses linear structure to capture the dependency on visual clips, context comments and target comments.
- **LiveBot-reimp** [13] provides a reproducible implementation of the Livebot model and fixes some issues in the implement of Livebot model.
- **Match T-CFA** [4] incorporates not only visual and textual modalities, but also audio modality. This model matches video contexts and candidate comment to pick related comments and can not generate comments.

– **Random** get a random rank for 100 candidate comments for rank task and random comment begin with prompt token for generation task.

Table 2. The comparison of modality and performance of different models on the Live Comment Dataset. Tx, Vi, Au and Ty refer to textual, visual, audio, and type **R@k**, **BLEU** and **MMR**: higher is better; **MR**: lower is better.

Model	Tx	Vi	Au	Ty	R@1	R@5	R@10	MR	MRR	BLEU	BLEU2	BLEU4
Random					4.85	22.03	38.73	17.88	0.157	1.42%	1.49%	0.51%
LiveBot	✓	✓			18.01	38.12	55.78	16.01	0.275	–	–	–
LiveBot-reimp	✓	✓			14.79	33.45	48.93	17.45	0.257	2.37%	2.69%	0.82%
Match T-CF	✓	✓			22.77	46.71	62.87	11.19	0.3519	–	–	–
Match T-CFA	✓	✓	✓		23.52	46.99	64.24	11.05	0.360	–	–	–
PLVCG-NT	✓	✓			15.80	48.60	66.65	9.57	0.318	1.83%	2.69%	0.38%
PLVCG	✓	✓		✓	21.69	52.91	72.55	8.37	0.349	2.79%	2.81%	1.20%
PLVCG-Large	✓	✓		✓	**26.77**	**59.58**	**75.27**	**7.19**	**0.422**	**2.85%**	**2.82%**	**1.28%**

5.4   Experiment Settings

Follow [9], the vocabulary of all the models are set to 30000 and the visual frames are preprocessed by a pretrained resnet with 18 layers. For the textual context, each comment is related to at most $n = 8$ comments whose post time and video time are both earlier than the target comment rather than 8 surrounding comments as previous works do [9,13]. As for visual frames, we follow previous works to use $m = 5$ frames. The dimension of the model as well as the embedding size is set to 512 for both textual and visual tokens in our base model and 1024 in our PLVCG-Large model. For the encoder and decoder, both of them have 6 layers and 8 heads. We use AdamW optimizer to train all the pretraining and fine-tuning process and the hyper-parameters are default. We set the learning rate $\alpha = 1 \times 10^{-5}$ and the dropout rate $p = 0.1$. In the pretraining transformation, we set the $\lambda = 3$ for the Poisson distribution. Finally, the beam size is set to 5 for the beam search generation. The pretraning and generation tasks are trained in 10 epochs and the discrimination task is trained in 2 epochs.

5.5   Experiment Results

Table 2 shows the overall results of baseline models and our models. For LiveBot [9] and LiveBot-reimp model [13], they only use visual and textual contexts and ignore the post time and video types. This makes their models hard to rank diverse comments and their R@10 and MR metrics are close to random method. For the generation task, this model gets comparable result in BLEU2 but get worse in BLEU4. Matching T-CFA model [13] considers not only visual and textual contexts but also audio information. However, their Match T-CF model which only uses visual and textual modalities performs as good as well. This means that the contribution of audio information is weak. In addition, their model can only match comments and don't have the ability to generate comments auto-regressively. As for our models, the PLVCG-NT model does not incorporate video type data and classification objective into training steps, but also achieves a better performance in some rank metrics. As for the PLVCG base and PLVCG-Large model, they leverage both video type labels and post time and outperforms the state-of-the-art models significantly. The PLVCG-Large model achieves $+3.25$ on R@1, $+12.59$ on R@5, $+11.03$ on R@10 and -3.86 on MR. For the generation task, our PLVCG-Large model also performs better than LiveBot-reimp model especially on BLEU4, which means our model captures more long-term information. The PLVCG-Large model performs better than the PLVCG model because our model jointly process visual and textual contexts and 512 dimension encoder output vector leads to the loss of information.

Table 3. Result of human evaluation.

Model	Fluency	Relevance	Informativeness
LiveBot-reimp	4.03	3.63	3.28
PLVCG-Large	4.28	3.89	3.34
Ground-Truth	4.75	4.42	3.71

5.6 Human Evaluation

To represent the performance of the generation task, we follow the LiveBot model to evaluate the outputs by humans. We choose three aspects to evaluate the generated comments: **Fluency** measures how fluent the comments are. The more fluent the comments are, the more possible they are commented by a human. **Relevance** measures the relevance between generated comments and the videos. **Informativeness** is designed to judge how much information the generated comments carry, general and popular comments always have less information. We randomly pick 100 instances from test set and three human annotators are asked to score both generated and ground-truth comments. A 0–5 number is used to denote the score, the higher the better. Table 3 shows the results and our model outperforms the LiveBot model in all three metrics. Both scores of fluency are over 4 for two models which means the generated comments are fairly fluent for human viewers. However the relevance scores of two models are much lower than the ground-truth score. This is because the model sometimes predicts the type of the videos wrongly and generate comments about other comments. The scores of informativeness are all lower than 4 which denotes there are often general and popular comments in both generated and ground-truth comments.

Table 4. Examples of the generated comments, the first bold words of the ground-truth comments are given to both models as the prompt token. The prompt tokens and comments are translated to English by the authors.

Model	Generated Comments
G-T	**(top/first/ago)**: (I'm at the top)
LiveBot	(World records for the first two years)
	(I went few days ago)
PVLCG	400 (I'm at the top 400!!) (I'm at the top one hundred!)
G-T	**(this)**: ...... (What's this...)
LiveBot	?(Isn't this a buffet?) (This terrible color)
PVLCG	?(Isn't this egg soup?) ?(What is this?)
G-T	**(A basin)**: (A basin of cats)
LiveBot	(A basin of water) ? (A basin of water?)
PVLCG	(A basin of cats) (A basin of cat food)

5.7   Case Study

To further represent the performance of our PLVCG model, we compare some comments generated by our model and baseline models as a case study in Table 4. On account of the Matching Transformer-CFA model can only match comments rather than generating comments auto-regressively, we only compare with the LiveBot-reimp model. Both of the two models are given a token as a prompt token and use a beam search method with beam size 5 to generate comments.

For the first example, the given video clip is at the very beginning of the video and the ground-truth comment says "I'm at the top" which means he is the very first viewer. The LiveBot model generates some irrelevant comments after the prompt tokens. But our model generates "I'm at the top 400!!", which means he is the first 400 viewers to watch this video. This is more reasonable and closer to the ground-truth comment. In the second example, our model successfully generates the question which has the same meaning of the ground-truth comment. And both of the model capture the video content is about type "food". The last example shows the importance of video type labels. The ground-truth comment is "A basin of cats" which means the cats are so soft that can just fit the basin. By learning the video type is "cat" from context, our model successfully generate "A basin of cats", however the LiveBot model can only generate "A basin of water" without consideration of video types.

6   Conclusion

In this paper, we proposed a pretraining based live video comment generation model for real-time live video comment generating task. Our model combines a bidirectional encoder module to extract context information and a left-to-right auto-regressive decoder module to classify the video types and generate comments. In addition, our model also considers the post time of comments to deal with comments interaction and achieves real-time comment generating. The introduce of the video type labels also helps in generating more video related comments. We evaluate our PLVCG model in a large-scale live video comment dataset. The results show that our model outperforms the state-of-the-art methods significantly. However, as the data amount of live comments is too huge, the index to present the popularity of each comment from live video comment service providers is unavailable. So how to evaluate the popularity of the generated comments is still a problem to be solved in the future.

References

1. Chen, X., Zhang, Y., Ai, Q., Xu, H., Yan, J., Qin, Z.: Personalized key frame recommendation. In: Proceedings of the 40th International ACM SIGIR Conference on Research and Development in Information Retrieval, pp. 315–324 (2017)
2. Chen, Y., Gao, Q., Rau, P.L.P.: Watching a movie alone yet together: understanding reasons for watching Danmaku videos. Int. J. Hum.-Comput. Interact. **33**(9), 731–743 (2017)
3. Das, A., et al.: Visual dialog. In: Proceedings of the IEEE Conference on Computer Vision and Pattern Recognition, pp. 326–335 (2017)
4. Duan, C., Cui, L., Ma, S., Wei, F., Zhu, C., Zhao, T.: Multimodal matching transformer for live commenting. arXiv preprint arXiv:2002.02649 (2020)
5. He, M., Ge, Y., Wu, L., Chen, E., Tan, C.: Predicting the popularity of *DanMu*-enabled videos: a multi-factor view. In: Navathe, S.B., Wu, W., Shekhar, S., Du, X., Wang, X.S., Xiong, H. (eds.) DASFAA 2016. LNCS, vol. 9643, pp. 351–366. Springer, Cham (2016). https://doi.org/10.1007/978-3-319-32049-6_22
6. Lewis, M., et al.: BART: denoising sequence-to-sequence pre-training for natural language generation, translation, and comprehension. arXiv preprint arXiv:1910.13461 (2019)
7. Li, X., Song, J., Gao, L., Liu, X., Huang, W., He, X., Gan, C.: Beyond RNNs: positional self-attention with co-attention for video question answering. In: Proceedings of the AAAI Conference on Artificial Intelligence, vol. 33, pp. 8658–8665 (2019)
8. Lv, G., Xu, T., Chen, E., Liu, Q., Zheng, Y.: Reading the videos: temporal labeling for crowdsourced time-sync videos based on semantic embedding. In: Proceedings of the AAAI Conference on Artificial Intelligence, vol. 30 (2016)
9. Ma, S., Cui, L., Dai, D., Wei, F., Sun, X.: LiveBot: generating live video comments based on visual and textual contexts. In: Proceedings of the AAAI Conference on Artificial Intelligence, vol. 33, pp. 6810–6817 (2019)
10. Papineni, K., Roukos, S., Ward, T., Zhu, W.J.: BLEU: a method for automatic evaluation of machine translation. In: Proceedings of the 40th Annual Meeting of the Association for Computational Linguistics, pp. 311–318 (2002)
11. Sun, C., Myers, A., Vondrick, C., Murphy, K., Schmid, C.: VideoBERT: a joint model for video and language representation learning. In: Proceedings of the IEEE International Conference on Computer Vision, pp. 7464–7473 (2019)
12. Vaswani, A., et al.: Attention is all you need. In: Advances in Neural Information Processing Systems, pp. 5998–6008 (2017)
13. Wu, H., Jones, G.J., Pitie, F.: Response to LiveBot: generating live video comments based on visual and textual contexts. arXiv preprint arXiv:2006.03022 (2020)

14. Xu, L., Zhang, C.: Bridging video content and comments: Synchronized video description with temporal summarization of crowdsourced time-sync comments. In: Proceedings of the AAAI Conference on Artificial Intelligence, vol. 31 (2017)
15. Yu, Y., Kim, J., Kim, G.: A joint sequence fusion model for video question answering and retrieval. In: Ferrari, V., Hebert, M., Sminchisescu, C., Weiss, Y. (eds.) ECCV 2018. LNCS, vol. 11211, pp. 487–503. Springer, Cham (2018). https://doi.org/10.1007/978-3-030-01234-2_29
16. Zeng, Z., Xue, C., Gao, N., Wang, L., Liu, Z.: Learning from audience intelligence: dynamic labeled LDA model for time-sync commented video tagging. In: Cheng, L., Leung, A.C.S., Ozawa, S. (eds.) ICONIP 2018. LNCS, vol. 11303, pp. 546–559. Springer, Cham (2018). https://doi.org/10.1007/978-3-030-04182-3_48
17. Zhang, Z., Yin, Z., Ren, S., Li, X., Li, S.: DCA: diversified co-attention towards informative live video commenting. In: Zhu, X., Zhang, M., Hong, Yu., He, R. (eds.) NLPCC 2020. LNCS (LNAI), vol. 12431, pp. 3–15. Springer, Cham (2020). https://doi.org/10.1007/978-3-030-60457-8_1
18. Zhou, L., Palangi, H., Zhang, L., Hu, H., Corso, J.J., Gao, J.: Unified vision-language pre-training for image captioning and VQA. In: AAAI, pp. 13041–13049 (2020)

Inducing Rich Interaction Structures Between Words for Document-Level Event Argument Extraction

Amir Pouran Ben Veyseh[1], Franck Dernoncourt[2], Quan Tran[2],
Varun Manjunatha[2], Lidan Wang[2], Rajiv Jain[2], Doo Soon Kim[2],
Walter Chang[2], and Thien Huu Nguyen[1(✉)]

[1] Department of Computer and Information Science,
University of Oregon, Eugene, OR, USA
{apouranb,thien}@cs.uoregon.edu
[2] Adobe Research, San Jose, CA, USA
{franck.dernoncourt,qtran,vmanjuna,lidwang,rajijain,dkim,
wachang}@adobe.com

Abstract. Event Argument Extraction (EAE) is the task of identifying roles of entity mentions/arguments in events evoked by trigger words. Most existing works have focused on sentence-level EAE, leaving document-level EAE (i.e., event triggers and arguments belong to different sentences in documents) an under-studied problem in the literature. This paper introduces a new deep learning model for document-level EAE where document structures/graphs are utilized to represent input documents and aid the representation learning. Our model employs different types of interactions between important context words in documents (i.e., syntax, semantic, and discourse) to enhance document representations. Extensive experiments are conducted to demonstratethe effectiveness of the proposed model, leading to the state-of-the-art performance for document-level EAE.

Keywords: Event Argument Extraction · Document structures

1 Introduction

Event Extraction (EE) is an important and challenging task in Information Exaction (IE) that aims to identify instances of events (i.e., change of states of real-world entities) in text. To this end, two subtasks should be solved: (1) Event Detection (ED) to recognize event-triggering expressions (verbal predicates or nominalizations, called event triggers/mentions), and (2) Event Argument Extraction (EAE) to identify entity mentions that are involved in events (event participants and spatio-temporalattributes, collectively known as event arguments). This work focuses on EAE, a relatively less-explored task for EE (compared to ED). Technically speaking, our EAE task takes as inputs an event trigger and an argument candidate (entity mention), seeking to predict the role

© Springer Nature Switzerland AG 2021
K. Karlapalem et al. (Eds.): PAKDD 2021, LNAI 12713, pp. 703–715, 2021.
https://doi.org/10.1007/978-3-030-75765-6_56

that the argument candidate plays in the event mention associated with the trigger. A well performing EAE system will benefit various downstream applications such as Knowledge Base Construction and Question Answering.

Most of the recent work on EAE employs deep learning models to achieve state-of-the-art performance [17]. Unfortunately, these models are often restricted to sentence-level EAE where event triggers and arguments appear in the same sentence. In real world scenarios, arguments of an event might have been presented in sentences other than the sentence that hosts the event trigger in the input document. For instance, in the EE dataset of the DARPA AIDA program (phase 1)[1], 38% of arguments has been shown to be outside the sentences containing the corresponding triggers, i.e., in the document-level context [3]. As such, it is of paramount importance to develop models that can extract arguments of event mentions over the entire documents to provide a more complete view of information for events in documents.

A major challenge in document-level EAE involves long document context that hinders the ability of models to effectively identify important context words (among long word sequences) and link them to event triggers and arguments for role prediction. Recently, a promising approach to address this document context modeling issue has been explored for other related tasks in IE [10,14,15] where document structures (i.e., direct interactions between parts of documents) are employed to facilitate the connections and reasoning between important context words for a prediction problem.

Thus, one simple solution towards utilizing document structures for EAE is to exert one of the existing document-level models that has been designed for other related tasks. However, in this work, we show that such prior models have critical constraints that should be addressed to better serve EAE. As such, the existing document-level models have only exploited some (typically one) specific types of information/heuristics to form the edges in document structures, thus failing to leverage a diversity of useful information to enrich document structures in EAE. This is unfortunate as multiple information sources are often required simultaneously to capture necessary interaction information between nodes/words and improve the coverage/performance for EAE models. For instance, consider the following document: *"The foundation said that immediately following the Haitian earthquake, the Embassy of Algeria provided an unsolicited lump-sum fund to the foundation's relief plan. This was a one-time, specific donation to help Haiti and it had **donated** twice to the Clinton Foundation before"*. In this two-sentence document, an EAE system needs to recognize the entity mention *"Embassy of Algeria"* as an argument (of role *Giver*) for the event mention associated with the trigger word *"donated"*. To perform this reasoning, the models can utilize the coreference link between *"Embassy of Algeria"* and the pronoun *"it"* (i.e., discourse information) that can be directly connected with the trigger word *"donated"* via an edge in the syntactic dependency tree of the second sentence. Alternatively, if the coreference link cannot be obtained (e.g., due to errors in the coreference resolution systems), EAE models can rely on the close

---

[1] https://tac.nist.gov/2019/SM-KBP/data.html.

semantic similarity between *"donated"* and *"provided an unsolicited lump-sum fund"* that can be further linked to *"Embassy of Algeria"* via a dependency edge in the first sentence. As such, document-level models might need to jointly capture the information from syntax, semantic, and discourse structures to sufficiently encode necessary interactions between words for EAE.

Motivated by this intuition, we propose to combine different information sources to generate effective document structures for our EAE problem, focusing on the knowledge from syntax (i.e., dependency trees), discourse (i.e., coreference links), and semantic similarity. Importantly, for the semantic similarity, in addition to using contextualized representation vectors to compute interaction scores between words as in prior work [10], we propose to further leverage external knowledge bases to enrich document structures for EAE. As such, we link the words in the documents to the entries in some external knowledge bases and exploit the entry similarity in such knowledge bases to obtain word similarity scores for the structures. To our knowledge, this is the first work to employ external knowledge bases to compute document structures for an IE task in the literature.

Given various document structures, how can we effectively combine these structures for EAE? Our main principle for this goal is motivated from the running example where the role reasoning process for the event trigger and argument candidate involves a sequence of interactions with multiple other words, possibly using different types of information at each interaction step, e.g., syntax, discourse or semantic information (called heterogeneous interaction types). To this end, we propose to employ Graph Transformer Networks (GTN) [18] to facilitate the implementation of this multi-hop heterogeneous reasoning idea. More specifically, GTNs fulfill the multi-hop heterogeneous reasoning by multiplying weighted sums of different initial document structures to generate rich combined structures. Finally, the resulting combined structures will be used to learn representation vectors for EAE based on graph convolutional networks (GCN). To our knowledge, this is also the first work that introduces GTN and GCN for document structure computation and representation learning in document-level EAE.

We evaluate the proposed model on two benchmark datasets; one for document-level EAE [3] and one for the closely related task of implicit semantic role labeling. Our experiments demonstrate the effectiveness of the proposed model, establishing new state-of-the-art results on both benchmark datasets.

2 Model

We formulate document-level EAE as a multi-class classification problem. The input to the models is a document $D = w_1, w_2, \ldots, w_N$ which consists of multiple sentences, i.e., S_i's. To be comparable with previous work [3], we also use a golden event trigger, i.e., the t-th word of D (w_t), and an argument candidate, i.e., the a-th word of D (w_a), as the inputs (w_t and w_a can occur in different sentences). The goal of EAE is to predict the role of the argument candidate

w_a in the event evoked by w_t. Here, the role might be *None*, indicating that w_a is not a participant in the event mention w_t. Our model for EAE involve three major components: (i) Document Encoder to transform the words in D into high dimensional vectors, (ii) Structure Generation to generate initial document structures for EAE, and (iii) Structure Combination to combine the structures and learn representation vectors for role prediction. We provide details for these components below.

2.1   Document Encoder

In the first step, we transform each word $w_i \in D$ into a representation vector x_i that is the concatenation of the following two vectors:

(i) The pre-trained word embedding of w_i: Here, we consider both non-contextualized embeddings, i.e., GloVe and contextualized embeddings, i.e., BERT in the experiments. In particular, for BERT, as w_i might be split into multiple word-pieces, we use the average of the hidden vectors for the word-pieces of w_i in the last layer as the word embedding vector for w_i. Following [3], we employ the BERT$_{base}$ version that divides D into segments of 512 word-pieces to be encoded separately. In our experiments, we fix the parameters of the BERT$_{base}$.

(ii) The position embeddings of w_i: These vectors are obtained by looking up the relative distances between w_i and the trigger and argument words (i.e., $i-t$ and $i-a$ respectively) in a position embedding table. This table is initialized randomly and updated in the training process. Position embedding vectors are important as they notify the model about the positions of the trigger and argument words.

Given the vector sequence $X = x_1, x_2, \ldots, x_N$ to represent the words in D, we further send it to a bidirectional long short-term memory network (LSTM) to generate a more abstract vector sequence $H = h_1, h_2, \ldots, h_N$. Here, h_i is the hidden vector for w_i that is obtained by concatenating the corresponding forward and backward hidden vectors from the bidirectional LSTM. We will use the hidden vectors in H as the inputs for the next computation. Note that we do not include the sentence boundary information of D into the hidden vectors H so far as it will be addressed in our document structures later.

2.2   Structure Generation

The goal of this section is to generate initial document structures that will be combined to learn representation vectors for document-level EAE in the next step. Formally, a document structure in our work involves an interaction graph $\mathcal{G} = \{\mathcal{N}, \mathcal{E}\}$ between the words in D, i.e., $\mathcal{N} = \{w_i | w_i \in D\}$. As such, the document structure $\mathcal{G}$ can be represented via a real-valued adjacency matrix $A = \{a_{ij}\}_{i,j=1..N}$ where the value/score a_{ij} reflects the importance (or the level of interaction) of w_j for the representation computation of w_i for EAE. As presented in the introduction, we simultaneously consider three types of information to form the edges $\mathcal{E}$ (or compute the interaction scores a_{ij}) in this work, including syntax, semantics, and discourse. We describe initial document structures based on these information types in the following.

Syntax-Based Structures: The motivation for this type of document structures is based on sentence-level EAE where dependency parsing trees of input sentences have been used to reveal important context, i.e., via shortest dependency paths to connect event triggers and arguments, and guide the interaction modeling between words for argument role prediction. As such, we expect dependency trees for sentences in D can also be exploited to provide useful information for document structures for EAE. In particular, we propose to leverage dependency relations/connections between pairs of words in D to compute the interaction scores a_{ij}^{dep} in the syntax-based document structure $A^{dep} = \{a_{ij}^{dep}\}_{i,j=1..N}$ for D. Here, two words are more important to each other for representation learning if they are connected in dependency tress. To this end, we first obtain the dependency tree T_i for each sentence S_i in D using an off-the-shelf dependency parser[2]. Afterward, to connect the dependency trees T_i for the sentences, following [5], we create a link between the root node of a tree T_i for S_i with the root node of the tree T_{i+1} for the subsequent sentence S_{i+1}. The resulting graph with linked trees T_i is denoted by T^D. In the next step, motivated by shortest dependency paths in sentence-level EAE, we retrieve the shortest path P^D between the nodes for w_t and w_a in T^D. Finally, we compute the interaction score a_{ij}^{dep} by setting it to 1 if (w_i, w_j) or (w_j, w_i) is an edge in P^D, and 0 otherwise.

Semantic-Based Structures: These document structures aim to evaluate the interaction scores in the structures based on the semantic similarity between words (i.e., two words are more important for the representation learning of each other if they are more semantically related). As such, we consider two complementary approaches to capture the semantics of the words in D for semantic-based structure generation, i.e., contextual semantics and knowledge-based semantics.

First, in contextual semantics, we seek to reveal the semantic of a word via the context in which it appears. This suggests the use of the contextualized representation vectors $h_i \in H$ (obtained from the LSTM model) to capture contextual semantics for the words $w_i \in D$ and produce the contextual semantic-based document structure $A^{context} = \{a_{ij}^{context}\}_{i,j=1..N}$ for D. Accordingly, to compute the semantic-based interaction score $a_{ij}^{context}$ for w_i and w_j, we employ the normalized similarity score between their contextualized representation vectors:

$$k_i = U_k h_i, q_i = U_q h_i$$
$$a_{ij}^{context} = \exp(k_i q_j) / \sum_{v=1..N} \exp(k_i q_v) \tag{1}$$

where U_k and U_q are trainable weight matrices, and the biases are omitted in this work for brevity.

---

[2] We use the Stanford Core NLP Toolkit to parse the sentences in this work.

Second, in knowledge-based semantics, our goal is to employ the external knowledge of the words from knowledge bases to capture their semantics. We expect that such external knowledge can provide a complementary source of information for the contextual semantics of the words (i.e., external knowledge vs internal context), thereby enriching the document structures for D. To this end, we propose to utilize WordNet, a rich knowledge base for word meanings, to obtain external knowledge for the words in D. Essentially, WordNet involves a network that connects word meanings (i.e., synsets) according to various semantic relations (e.g., synonyms, hyponyms). Each node/synset in WordNet is associated with a textual glossary to provide expert definition about the corresponding meaning.

Our first step to generate knowledge-based document structures for D is to map each word $w_i \in D$ to a synset node M_i in WordNet that can be done with a Word Sense Disambiguation (WSD) tool. In this work, we use WordNet 3.0 and the state-of-the-art BERT-based WSD tool in [1] to perform such word-synset mapping. Afterward, to determine knowledge-based interaction scores between two words w_i and w_j in D, we can leverage the similarity scores between the two linked synset nodes M_i and M_j in WordNet. As such, to leverage the rich information embedded in the synset nodes M_i, we introduce two versions of knowledge-based document structures for D based on the glossaries of the synset nodes and the hierarchy structure in WordNet:

(1) The glossary-based structure $A^{gloss} = \{a_{ij}^{gloss}\}_{i,j=1..N}$: Here, for each word $w_i \in D$, we first retrieve the glossary GM_i from the corresponding linked node M_i in WordNet (GM_i can be seen as a sequence of words). A representation vector VM_i is then computed to capture the semantic information in GM_i, by applying the max-pooling operation over the pre-trained GloVe embeddings of the words in GM_i. Finally, the glossary-based interaction score a_{ij}^{gloss} for w_i and w_j is estimated via the similarity between the glossary representations VM_i and VM_j (with the consine similarity): $a_{ij}^{gloss} = cosine(VM_i, VM_j)$.

(2) The WordNet hierarchy-based structure $A^{struct} = \{a_{ij}^{struct}\}_{i,j=1..N}$: The interaction score a_{ij}^{struct} for w_i and w_j in this case relies on the structure-based similarity of the linked synset nodes M_i and M_j in WordNet. Accordingly, we employ the Lin similarity measure for the synset nodes in WordNet for this purpose: $a_{ij}^{struct} = \frac{2*IC(LCS(M_i,M_j))}{IC(M_i)+IC(M_j)}$ where IC and LCS represent the information content of the synset nodes and the least common subsumer of the two synsets in the WordNet hierarchy (most specific ancestor node), respectively.

Discourse-Based Structures: Besides the typical lengths of the input texts, a key difference between document-level and sentence-level EAE involves the presence of multiple sentences in document-level EAE where discourse information (i.e., where the sentences span and how they relate to each other) is helpful to understand the input documents. The goal of this part is to leverage such discourse structures to provide complementary information for the syntax- and semantic-based document structures for EAE. To this end, we propose to exploit two following types of discourse information to generate discourse-based document structures for EAE: (1) the sentence boundary-based document structure $A^{sent} = \{a_{ij}^{sent}\}_{i,j=1..N}$: This document structure concerns the same sentence information of the words in D. The intuition is that two words in the same sentence would involve more useful information for the representation computation of each other than those in different sentences. To implement this intuition, we compute A^{sent} by setting the sentence boundary-based score a_{ij}^{sent} to 1 if w_i and w_j appear in the same sentence in D and 0 otherwise; and (2) the coreference-based document structure $A^{coref} = \{a_{ij}^{coref}\}_{i,j=1..N}$: Instead of considering within-sentence information as in A^{sent}, this document structure exploits relations/connections between sentences (cross-sentence information) in D. To this end, we consider two sentences in D as being related if they contain entity mentions that refer to the same entity in D (coreference information)[3]. Given such a relation between sentences, we consider two words in D to be more relevant to each other if they appear in related sentences. To this end, for the coreference-based structure, a_{ij}^{coref} is set to 1 if w_i and w_j appear in different, but related sentences; and 0 otherwise.

2.3   Structure Combination

Up to this point, we have generated six different document structures for D (i.e., $\mathcal{A} = [A^{dep}, A^{context}, A^{gloss}, A^{struct}, A^{sent}, A^{coref}]$). As these document structures are based on complementary types of information (called structure types), this section aims to combine them to generate richer document structures for EAE. Our key intuition to achieve such a combination is to note that each importance score a_{ij}^v in one of the structures A_{ij}^v ($v \in V = \{dep, context, gloss, struct, sent, coref\}$) only considers the direct interaction between the two involving words w_i and w_j (i.e., not including any other words) according to one specific information type v. As motivated in the introduction, we expect each importance score in the combined structures to further condition on interactions with other important context words in D (i.e., in addition to the two involving words) where each interaction between a pair of words can flexibly use any of the six structure types (multi-hop and heterogeneous-type reasoning). To this end, we propose to use Graph Transformer Networks (GTN) [18] to enable such a multi-hop and heterogeneous-type reasoning in the structure combination for EAE.

In particular, to enable multi-hop reasoning paths at different lengths, we first add the identity matrix I (of size $N \times N$) into the set of initial document structures $\mathcal{A} = [A^{dep}, A^{context}, A^{gloss}, A^{struct}, A^{sent}, A^{coref}, I] = [\mathcal{A}_1, \ldots, \mathcal{A}_7]$. The GTN model is then organized into C channels for structure combination, where the k-th channel contains M intermediate document structures $Q_1^k, Q_2^k, \ldots, Q_M^k$ of size $N \times N$. As such, each intermediate structure Q_i^k is computed by a

---

[3] We use the Stanford Core NLP Toolkit to determine the coreference of entity mentions.

linear combination of the initial structures in $\mathcal{A}$ using learnable weights α_{ij}^k: $Q_i^k = \sum_{j=1..7} \alpha_{ij}^k \mathcal{A}_j$. Here, due to the linear combination, the interaction scores in Q_i^k are able to reason with any of the six initial structure types in V (although such scores still consider the direct interactions of the involving words only). Afterward, the intermediate structures $Q_1^k, Q_2^k, \ldots, Q_M^k$ in each channel k are multiplied to generate the final document structure $Q^k = Q_1^k \times Q_2^k \times \ldots \times Q_M^k$ of size $N \times N$ (for the k-the channel). As shown in [18], the matrix multiplication enables the importance score between a pair of words w_i and w_j in Q^k to condition on the multi-hop interactions/reasoning between the two words and other words in D (up to $M - 1$ hops due to the inclusion of I in $\mathcal{A}$). The interactions involved in one importance score in Q^k can also realize any of the initial structure types in V (heterogeneous reasoning) due to the flexibility of the intermediate structure Q_i^k.

Given the rich document structures $Q^1, Q^2, \ldots, Q^C$ from the C channels, GTN then feed them into C graph convolutional networks (GCN) [6] to induce document structure-enriched representation vectors for argument role prediction in EAE (one GCN for each $Q^k = \{Q_{ij}^k\}_{i,j=1..N}$). As such, each of these GCN models involve G layers that produces the hidden vectors $\bar{h}_1^{k,t}, \ldots, \bar{h}_N^{k,t}$ at the t-th layer of the k-th GCN model for the words in D ($1 \le k \le C$, $1 \le t < G$):

$$\bar{h}_i^{k,t} = ReLU(U^{k,t} \sum_{j=1..N} \frac{Q_{ij}^k \bar{h}_j^{k,t-1}}{\sum_{u=1..N} Q_{iu}^k}) \tag{2}$$

where $U^{k,t}$ is the weight matrix for the t-th layer of the k-th GCN model and the input vectors $\bar{h}_i^{k,0}$ for the GCN models are obtained from the contextualized representation vectors H (i.e., $\bar{h}_i^{k,0} = h_i$ for all $1 \le k \le C$, $1 \le i \le N$).

In the next step, the hidden vectors in the last layers of all the GCN models (at the G-th layers) for w_i (i.e., $\bar{h}_i^{1,G}, \bar{h}_i^{2,G}, \ldots, \bar{h}_i^{C,G}$) are concatenated form the final representation vector h_i' for w_i in the proposed GTN model: $h_i' = [\bar{h}_i^{1,G}, \bar{h}_i^{2,G}, \ldots, \bar{h}_i^{C,G}]$.

Finally, to predict the argument role for w_a and w_t in D, we assemble a representation vector R based on the hidden vectors for w_a and w_t from the GTN model via: $R = [h_a', h_t', MaxPool(h_1', h_2', \ldots, h_N')]$. This vector is then sent to a two-layer feed-forward network with softmax in the end to produce a probability distribution $P(.|D, a, t)$ over the possible argument roles. We then optimize the negative log-likelihood L_{pred} to train the model: $\mathcal{L} = -\log P(y|D, a, t)$ where y is the golden argument role for the input example. We call the proposed model the Multi-hop Reasoning for Event Argument extractor with heterogeneous Document structure types (MREAD) for convenience.

3   Experiments

Dataset and Parameters: We evaluate the document-level EAE models in this work on RAMS, a recent dataset introduced in [3] for document-level EAE.

RAMS contains 9,124 annotated event mentions across 139 types for 65 argument roles, serving as the largest available dataset for document-level EAE. We use the official train/dev/test split and evaluation script for RAMS provided by [3] to achieve a fair comparison. In addition, we evaluate the models on the BNB dataset [4] for implicit semantic role labelling (iSRL), a closely related task to document-level EAE where the models need to predict roles of argument candidates for a given predicate (arguments and predicates can appear in different sentences in iSRL). In our experiments, we use the version of BNB prepared by [3] (with the same data split and pre-processing script) for a fair comparison. This dataset annotates 2,603 argument mentions for a total of 12 argument roles (for 1,247 predicates/triggers). We use the development set of the RAMS dataset to fine-tune the hyper-parameters of the proposed model MREAD.

Results: We compare our model MREAD with two categories of baselines on RAMS:

(1) Structure-free: These baselines do not exploit document structures for EAE. In particular, we compare MREAD with the RAMS$_{model}$ model in [3] and the **Head-based** model in [19]. Here, RAMS$_{model}$ currently has the state-of-the-art (SOTA) performance for document-level EAE on RAMS.

(2) Structure-based: These baselines employ some forms of document structures (mostly based on syntax and semantic information) to learn representation vectors for input documents. Note that as none of the prior work has explored document structure-based models for document-level EAE, we compare MREAD with the existing document structure-based models for a related task of document-level relation extraction (DRE) in IE. As such, the following SOTA models for DRE are considered in this category: (i) **iDepNN** [5]; (ii) **GCNN** [14]: This baseline generates document structures based on both syntax and discourse information (e.g., dependency trees, coreference links). Note that although GCNN also considers more than one source of information for document structures as we do, it fails to exploit semantic-based document structures (for both contextual and knowledge-based semantics) and lacks effective mechanisms for structure combination (i.e., not using GTN); (iii) **LSR** [10]; and (iv) **EoG** [2].

In addition to the standard decoding (i.e., using `argmax` with $P(.|D, a, t)$ to obtain the predicted roles), following [3], we also consider the decoding setting where the models' predictions are constrained to the permissible roles for the event type e evoked by the trigger w_t. Tables 1 and 2 show the the models' performance on the RAMS test set using BERT and GloVe embeddings, respectively. There are several observations from these tables. First, the proposed model MREAD significantly outperforms all the baselines in both the standard and type constrained decoding regardless of the used embeddings (BERT or GloVe). This consistent performance improvement is significant with $p < 0.01$ and clearly demonstrates the effectiveness of MREAD for document-level EAE. Second, except for iDepNN, all the structure-based models significantly outperform the structure-free baselines. This finding is significant especially considering

Table 1. Performance on the RAMS test set using BERT.

Model	Standard decoding			Type constrained		
	P	R	F1	P	R	F1
RAMS	62.8	74.9	68.3	78.1	69.2	73.3
Head-based	71.5	66.2	68.8	81.1	66.2	73.0
iDepNN	65.8	68.0	66.9	77.1	67.7	72.1
EoG	71.0	71.7	71.4	82.4	69.2	75.2
GCNN	72.2	72.8	72.5	85.1	69.4	76.5
LSR	72.6	73.6	73.1	83.9	71.4	77.2
MREAD (ours)	75.7	75.3	**75.5**	88.2	72.1	**79.3**

Table 2. Performance on the RAMS test set using GloVe.

Model	Standard decoding			Type constrained		
	P	R	F1	P	R	F1
RAMS	66.3	69.8	68.0	77.4	68.8	72.9
Head-based	70.2	63.4	66.6	74.6	65.3	69.6
iDepNN	65.7	65.4	65.5	75.7	63.2	68.9
EoG	69.2	69.0	69.1	81.3	68.0	74.1
GCNN	71.1	70.9	71.0	83.7	68.1	75.1
LSR	72.5	72.0	72.2	82.9	70.3	76.1
MREAD (ours)	73.6	73.5	**73.5**	86.7	71.0	**78.1**

that the structure-based models are not originally designed for document-level EAE, thereby clearly showing the benefits of document structures for document-level EAE. Finally, compared to GCNN and EoG that also consider multiple sources of information as our model, MREAD achieves substantially better performance, suggesting the advantages of contextual and knowledge-based structures along with multi-hop heterogeneous reasoning in our EAE problem.

Finally, we evaluate the performance of MREAD on the BNB dataset for iSRL. As we use the data version prepared by [3] that involves a different train/dev/test split from the original BNB dataset in [4], we directly use the RAMS$_{model}$ model in [3] as our baseline for a fair comparison. In addition, we report the performance of the structure-based baselines (iDepNN, GCNN, LSR, and EoG) for a complete view. Table 3 shows the performance of the models on the BNB test dataset (using BERT embeddings). As can be seen, MREAD is also better than all the baseline models substantially and significantly ($p < 0.01$), further confirming the benefits of our proposed model in this work.

Table 3. Performance on the BNB test set for iSRL.

Model	P	R	F1
RAMS	–	–	76.6
iDepNN	80.0	75.1	77.5
EoG	78.5	74.4	76.4
GCNN	81.0	73.9	77.3
LSR	80.3	74.1	77.1
MREAD (ours)	82.9	75.0	**78.8**

Ablation Study: Our proposed model combines different types of document structures (i.e., six types in $\mathcal{A}$) using GTN to enable multi-hop and heterogeneous reasoning for document-level EAE. This section studies the contribution of the proposed document structures and structure combination in MREAD by evaluating the performance of the ablated versions of the model on the development set of the RAMS dataset. In particular, the following ablated models are examined: (i) **MREAD-A^v**: In this group of ablated models, we eliminate each of the document structures in $\mathcal{A}$ from MREAD and evaluate the performance of the model with the remaining structures (e.g., **MREAD-A^{dep}**, **MREAD-A^{sent}**, etc.), (ii) **MREAD-GTN**: In this ablated model, the GTN architecture is excluded from MREAD, so the GCN models are directly and separately applied to each document structure in $\mathcal{A}$. (iii) **MREAD-Multi-hop:** This ablated model is to show the effectiveness of multi-hop heterogeneous reasoning/interaction for EAE. As such, this model avoids the multiplication of the intermediate structures Q_i^k in each channel of GTN, and directly runs the GCN models over the intermediate document structures Q_i^k (i.e., the final structures Q^k are not produced).

Table 4. Performance of the models on the RAMS development set using BERT embeddings and standard decoding.

Model	P	R	F1
MREAD	75.5	76.5	**76.0**
MREAD-A^{def}	73.5	74.9	74.2
MREAD-$A^{context}$	72.7	73.5	73.1
MREAD-A^{gloss}	74.6	73.4	74.0
MREAD-A^{struct}	74.1	74.3	74.2
MREAD-A^{sent}	72.8	73.2	73.0
MREAD-A^{coref}	73.2	74.9	74.1
MREAD-GTN	72.1	73.7	72.9
MREAD-Multi-Hop	73.2	74.6	73.9

Table 4 presents the performance of the models on the RAMS development set. As can be seen from the table, the removal of any document structures in $\mathcal{A}$ would significantly hurt the performance of MREAD, thus confirming the effectiveness of the introduced document structures for EAE. Also, the significantly better performance of MREAD over MREAD-Multi-hop suggests that the multiplication of the intermediate structures in the channels of GTN is helpful to generate richer structures for EAE (i.e., by enabling multi-hop heterogeneous reasoning/interactions of words).

4   Related Work

Most of prior work on EE has focused on sentence-level EAE [7–9,11–13]. Recently, some work has considered document-level EAE, featuring [3] as the most related work to our problem. However, the model proposed by [3] (i.e., RAMS$_{model}$) does not consider document structures to improve the performance for document-level EAE as we do in this work. Our work is also related to the recent document structure-based models for other NLP tasks [2,15,16]. However, compared to our proposed model, these prior works on document structures fail to exploit external knowledge to generate the structures and do not involve mechanisms to combine multiple structures for multi-hop heterogeneous reasoning.

5   Conclusion

This work presents a novel deep learning model for document-level EAE. To facilitate the interaction of important context words in the documents for EAE, our model leverages multiple sources of information, including the novel employment of external knowledge bases, to generate document structures to provide effective knowledge for representation learning in EAE. Also, for the first time in EAE, graph transformer networks are employed to produce richer document structures. The experiments confirm the benefits of the proposed model, yielding to SOTA performance on benchamrk datasets.

Acknowledgments. This research has been supported by Vingroup Innovation Foundation (VINIF) in project VINIF.2019.DA18 and Army Research Office (ARO) grant W911NF-17-S-0002. This research is also based upon work supported by the Office of the Director of National Intelligence (ODNI), Intelligence Advanced Research Projects Activity (IARPA), via IARPA Contract No. 2019-19051600006 under the Better Extraction from Text Towards Enhanced Retrieval (BETTER) Program. The views contained herein are those of the authors and should not be interpreted as necessarily representing the official policies, either expressed or implied, of ARO, ODNI, IARPA, the Department of Defense, or the U.S. Government.

References

1. Blevins, T., Zettlemoyer, L.: Moving down the long tail of word sense disambiguation with gloss informed bi-encoders. In: ACL (2020)
2. Christopoulou, F., Miwa, M., Ananiadou, S.: Connecting the dots: document-level neural relation extraction with edge-oriented graphs. In: EMNLP (2019)
3. Ebner, S., Xia, P., Culkin, R., Rawlins, K., Van Durme, B.: Multi-sentence argument linking. In: ACL (2020)
4. Gerber, M., Chai, J.Y.: Semantic role labeling of implicit arguments for nominal predicates. In: Computational Linguistics (2012)
5. Gupta, P., Rajaram, S., Schütze, H., Runkler, T.: Neural relation extraction within and across sentence boundaries. In: AAAI (2019)
6. Kipf, T.N., Welling, M.: Semi-supervised classification with graph convolutional networks. In: ICLR (2017)
7. Lai, V.D., Nguyen, T.N., Nguyen, T.H.: Event detection: gate diversity and syntactic importance scores for graph convolution neural networks. In: EMNLP (2020)
8. Le, D.M., Nguyen, T.H.: Fine-grained event trigger detection. In: EACL (2021)
9. Li, Q., Ji, H., Huang, L.: Joint event extraction via structured prediction with global features. In: ACL (2013)
10. Nan, G., Guo, Z., Sekulic, I., Lu, W.: Reasoning with latent structure refinement for document-level relation extraction. In: ACL (2020)
11. Nguyen, T.H., Cho, K., Grishman, R.: Joint event extraction via recurrent neural networks. In: NAACL-HLT (2016)
12. Nguyen, T.M., Nguyen, T.H.: One for all: neural joint modeling of entities and events. In: AAAI (2019)
13. Ben Veyseh, A.P., Nguyen, T.N., Nguyen, T.H.: Graph transformer networks with syntactic and semantic structures for event argument extraction. In: EMNLP Findings (2020)
14. Sahu, S.K., Christopoulou, F., Miwa, M., Ananiadou, S.: Inter-sentence relation extraction with document-level graph convolutional neural network. In: ACL (2019)
15. Thayaparan, M., Valentino, M., Schlegel, V., Freitas, A.: Identifying supporting facts for multi-hop question answering with document graph networks. In: The Thirteenth Workshop on Graph-Based Methods for Natural Language Processing at EMNLP (2019)
16. Tran, H.M., Nguyen, M.T., Nguyen, T.H.: The dots have their values: exploiting the node-edge connections in graph-based neural models for document-level relation extraction. In: EMNLP Findings (2020)
17. Wang, X., et al.: HMEAE: hierarchical modular event argument extraction. In: EMNLP-IJCNLP (2019)
18. Yun, S., Jeong, M., Kim, R., Kang, J., Kim, H.J.: Graph transformer networks. In: NeurIPS (2019)
19. Zhang, Z., Kong, X., Liu, Z., Ma, X., Hovy, E.: A two-step approach for implicit event argument detection. In: ACL (2020)

Exploiting Relevant Hyperlinks in Knowledge Base for Entity Linking

Szu-Yuan Cheng[1,2], Yi-Ling Chen[1(✉)], Mi-Yen Yeh[2], and Bo-Tao Lin[1,2]

[1] National Taiwan University of Science and Technology, Taipei, Taiwan
{M10715090,yiling,M10815065}@mail.ntust.edu.tw
[2] Institute of Information Science, Academia Sinica, Taipei, Taiwan
miyen@iis.sinica.edu.tw

Abstract. In this study, we propose a new model aiming to enhance the quality of entity linking by exploiting highly relevant hyperlinks in knowledge base for entity disambiguation. We find that most existing studies do not filter the corresponding hyperlinks for each entity, where using the irrelevant ones may introduce noises and lower the linking accuracy. To address this issue, we design and combine the hyperlink extraction stage and the hyperlink attention stage to learn more suitable hyperlinks in the document-level disambiguation. In addition, we also enhance the context-level disambiguation by utilizing additional entity descriptions and work on retrieving high-quality candidate set for entities at the beginning of our model. Experimental results show that our proposed model outperforms the state-of-the-arts on various benchmark datasets, and even being competitive to the models that rely on additional information.

Keywords: Entity linking · Entity disambiguation · Hyperlink extraction · Knowledge base

1 Introduction

Entity Linking (EL) is the task of aligning textual mentions of entities with a unique identity in a given knowledge base (KB), which plays an important role in natural language understanding such as information extraction [1], semantic parsing [12], and question answering [25]. Such a task is challenging due to the mentions are usually ambiguous because different named entities may have the same surface form. For example, a mention "Brazil" can represent the *Federative Republic of Brazil* or *Brazil national football team* due to the different context "Rio is the second-most populous municipality in Brazil" and "Brazil has the best performance in the World Cup."

Usually, the process of entity disambiguation may contain three parts: candidate selection, context-level disambiguation, and document-level disambiguation. The candidate selection process aims to find the most relevant candidate entities of mentions for the model to make further inferences. The context-level

© Springer Nature Switzerland AG 2021
K. Karlapalem et al. (Eds.): PAKDD 2021, LNAI 12713, pp. 716–729, 2021.
https://doi.org/10.1007/978-3-030-75765-6_57

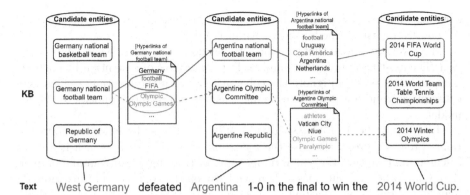

Text   West Germany defeated Argentina 1-0 in the final to win the 2014 World Cup.

Fig. 1. An illustrating example of EL using hyperlinks. Candidate entities list (in the cylinder) contains the candidates for a mention. Red rounded rectangles are the target entities. The rectangle connected to a certain entity contains the hyperlinks in the KB corresponding to that entity. The solid red path shows the correct entity linking result, while the dashed orange path indicates the wrong one. (Color figure online)

disambiguation aims to extract the information based on words that surround the mentions. However, such disambiguation may not perform well when the context does not have enough information. The document-level disambiguation tries to find out the topical coherence between all mentions in the same document. Most of the previous works [6,7,15,24] use entity embeddings, which are compact semantic meanings of entities from the KB information, to calculate the pairwise scores between all candidate entities and predict answers.

Since a KB may contain numerous entities, hyperlinks of entities in the KB provide additional help for the entity linking model to understand the semantic meaning of entities. However, we find that most existing EL models cannot utilize the KB information precisely when trying to find the topical coherence between mentions in the document-level disambiguation. Using irrelevant hyperlink information may increase noises and hurt the accuracy of EL models.

Figure 1 is an illustrating example, and suppose we want to link the three entities in the given text (i.e., the three red-colored phrases in the example sentence) to their corresponding identities. The mention "West Germany" may link to *Republic of Germany*, *Germany national football team*, and *Germany national basketball team*. We can find that *Germany national football team* has many hyperlinks in the KB, including "Germany", "football", "Olympic", "FIFA", and "Olympic Games". Using the relevant hyperlinks[1] "football" and "FIFA" can help the model accurately refer *Argentina* to *Argentina national football team* by the strong coherence between *Germany national football team* and *Argentina national football team*. However, when using irrelevant hyperlinks such as "Olympic" and "Olympic Games", the model may be misled and make

---

[1] The number of relevant hyperlinks can be different in different situations.

a wrong inference by aligning the mention "Argentina" to *Argentine Olympic Committee* (as the dashed orange path in Fig. 1).

Moreover, we notice that previous studies do not emphasize candidate selection. The existing approaches simply select candidates of a mention by context-independent scores and ignore the coherence between the mentions, which may cause more irrelevant candidates being selected and introduce noises to the EL model.

To address these problems, in this study, we make the following contributions. First, we propose to use the *hyperlink extraction stage*, which is able to calculate and capture the semantic meaning of the context surrounding a mention. Our model computes the coherence between the context and the candidate hyperlinks, and using an attention mechanism to choose the relevant hyperlinks for an entity.

Second, since different mentions in a document may not all have the same topical coherence, we propose to use a *hyperlink attention stage* to let our document-level disambiguation choose the most relevant linked entities and enhance the linking accuracy. In contrast to [24], which simply uses all of the hyperlinks for each entity to compute the coherence between entities, our model can figure out the most relevant hyperlinks to decrease the noises and categorize the semantic meaning of different domain entities more accurately.

Last but not least, for the candidate selection of each mention, we consider the topical coherence between candidate entities and the mention by computing their cosine similarity. Such a strategy produces better candidate sets and further boosts the linking accuracy.

We evaluate our model on various benchmark datasets. The experimental results show that by well leveraging the diverse domain expertise from the hyperlinks in KB, our model is able to precisely categorize the entities and learn the knowledge across different domains, leading to better linking quality on datasets of various domains. When compared with baselines, our model has 3%–21% higher F1 score on average, and our model even outperforms the models that rely on additional information.

2   Preliminaries and Related Works

Given a set of mentions $M = \{m_1, m_2, ..., m_K\}$ in document $\mathcal{D}$, where each mention $m_k \in \mathcal{D}$ has a candidate entity set $C_k = \{e_k^1, e_k^2, ..., e_k^T\}$ selected from the KB, the task of Entity Linking (EL) aims to link each mention m_k to its corresponding entity e_k^* or predict "NIL" if there is no target entity in the KB. Previous solutions of the EL task usually involve three parts: candidate selection, context-level disambiguation, and document-level disambiguation. In the following, We will introduce the main concept of each part and show the potential problems encountered by the existing solutions.

A mention may have a lot of candidate entities in the given KB. To increase both the efficiency and accuracy of the EL model for aligning mentions to correct entities, **candidate selection** is required. Specifically, candidate selection is to

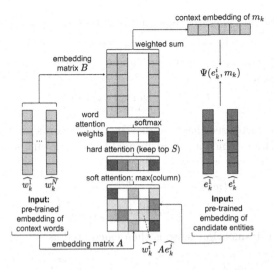

Fig. 2. Neural attention mechanism for context-level disambiguation.

find a proper reduced candidate set $\Delta(m_k)$ of a given mention m_k. A common and heuristic way for previous studies [7,15,24] is to select the top 30 candidates based on the context-independent scores $\hat{p}(e_k^i|m_k)$, which is generated by averaging the probabilities from Wikipedia, a large Web corpus [22], and YAGO dictionary [11]. Then, it further selects 7 candidates, including the top 4 entities based on $\hat{p}(e_k^i|m_k)$ and the top 3 entities based on the local context-entity similarity function

$$s(e_k^i) = \sum_{w_k^j \in c_k} \widehat{w_k^j}^{\mathsf{T}} \widehat{e_k^i}, \tag{1}$$

where $\widehat{w_k^j}$ and $\widehat{e_k^i}$ are the word and entity embeddings, and w_k^j is the local context around m_k.

On the other hand, **_context-level disambiguation_** aims to use the local contexts surrounding the mentions and ignore the coherence between mentions to link decisions. For each mention m_k and its corresponding local context c_k, the context-level disambiguation calculates the score function $\Psi(e_k^i, m_k)$ by finding

$$e_n^* = \arg\max_{e_n^i \in C_n} \Psi(e_n^i, c_n), \tag{2}$$

for each $n \in \{1, ..., K\}$ and $i \in \{1, ..., T\}$. The previous work [18] uses binary classification to disambiguate entities into commonness and relatedness, while [2] uses several ranking algorithms to order the entities. Other works like [23] and [8] use entity embeddings to compute the coherence scores between mention and entities, and [7] proposes a neural attention mechanism (as shown in Fig. 2) to compute the score, and this mechanism is used in many related studies [15,24]. Mention m_k is surrounded by context $c_k = \{w_k^1, w_k^2, ..., w_k^N\}$ and has a reduced candidate set $\Delta(m_k)$ generated by candidate selection. Each word $w_k^i \in c_k$ and candidate entity $e_k^i \in \Delta(m_k)$ are mapping to their pre-trained embeddings $\widehat{w_k^i}$ and $\widehat{e_k^i}$. The relevance score between candidate entities and context words is calculated as follows:

$$r(\widehat{w_k^i}) = \max_{e_k^j \in \Delta(m_k)} \widehat{w_k^i}^\mathsf{T} A \widehat{e_k^j}, \tag{3}$$

where A is a parameterized diagonal matrix. Top S words are the related words to candidate entities, which are transformed to the relevant scores as below:

$$a(\widehat{w_k^i}) = \frac{\exp[r(\widehat{w_k^i})]}{\sum_{\widehat{w_k^j} \in topS(c_k)} \exp[r(\widehat{w_k^j})]}. \tag{4}$$

The weighted entity-mention score is then calculated as

$$\Psi(e_k^i, m_k) = \sum_{\widehat{w_k^j} \in topS(c_k)} a(\widehat{w_k^j}) \widehat{w_k^j}^\mathsf{T} B \widehat{e_k^i}, \tag{5}$$

where B is another learnable diagonal matrix. However, this disambiguation may highly depend on the performance of entity embeddings and hence become unstable.

Document-level disambiguation aims to capture the coherence score between entities, which can be denoted by $\Phi(\mathcal{E}, \mathcal{D})$, where $\mathcal{E} = \{e_1, e_2, ..., e_k\}$. The previous studies [7–9,21,23] and [15] use the coherence score function that sums up the scores of all entity pairs. The disadvantage of this kind of methods is its NP-hard complexity. However, [7] and [15] use loopy belief propagation (LBP) to compute an approximate inference answer to overcome this problem. The related study [6] is the first one to consider EL as a sequential decision problem, and the authors implement a reinforcement learning algorithm to learn the relation between mentions. There is another study [24] lets the proposed model only require one pass through all mentions to reduce the computational efficiency. However, this model requires an additional pre-trained NER type system that may cause an over-fitting problem in the in-domain datasets. The EL model then tackles the problem as follows:

$$\mathcal{E}^* = \underset{\mathcal{E} \in C_1 \times ... \times C_K}{\arg\max} \sum_{n=1}^{K} \Psi(e_n^i, c_n) + \Phi(\mathcal{E}, \mathcal{D}). \tag{6}$$

In order to compute the score functions between mention and entities, previous studies employ a variety of techniques. Some of the approaches use feature engineering to define useful features. The previous work [21] exploits TF-IDF summary to compute the cosine similarity between the Wikipedia title and surrounding hyperlinks of context as their context-level features. For their document-level features, they use link information between Wikipedia pages to measure semantic relatedness. Other work [3] extracts high precision textual relations from the text and determines the semantic relation weights by combining type and confidence of the relation with the confidence in relations retrieved from an external KB by using the mention pairs as a query. Others use representation learning to replace feature engineering. These approaches often do not use any handcrafted features and compute their score functions with pre-trained embeddings of words (e.g., [17,19]) and entities (e.g., [7,10,13,16,20,23]). The previous study [10] learns representations by leveraging large scale annotations of Wikipedia. Some related works like [13,23], and [16] pre-train the entity embeddings based on the skip-gram model and directly model the semantic relatedness between KB entities. The related study [7] develops an effective method to bootstrap entity embeddings from entity pages and the local context of their hyperlink annotations. Another study [20] enhances the embeddings of entities and words in a common vector space with web corpus co-occurrence statistics.

3   Methodology

The structure of our model is shown in Fig. 3. We first introduce how we leverage the entity description to help the context-level disambiguation. Second, we introduce our proposed hyperlink extraction stage and hyperlink attention stage to extract relevant hyperlinks for entities and choose the coherent entities in the document-level disambiguation. Furthermore, we show how we improve the candidate entity selection for a mention by using cosine similarity. Finally, we illustrate how to combine these main components and produce the results of our proposed EL model.

3.1   Context-Level Disambiguation

Different from the previous work [7], our context-level disambiguation uses not only the entity embeddings but the entity description. Apart from the entity embeddings, there are many other valuable information in the KB. To let our model learn more about entities, we use the entity embeddings and the entity description to enrich our context-level disambiguation. Each entity has description words in the KB $d_{e_k^i} = \{s_{e_k^i}^1, s_{e_k^i}^2, ..., s_{e_k^i}^N\}$. We use the first R words and average their embeddings as the entity description embeddings $\widehat{d_{e_k^i}}$ and then calculate the weighted description-mention score $\Psi(d_{e_k^i}, m_k)$. Our context-level disambiguation score is then calculated as

$$\Psi_{CL}(e_k^i, m_k) = \alpha\Psi(d_{e_k^i}, m_k) + \beta\Psi(e_k^i, m_k), \tag{7}$$

where α and β are learnable linear weights.

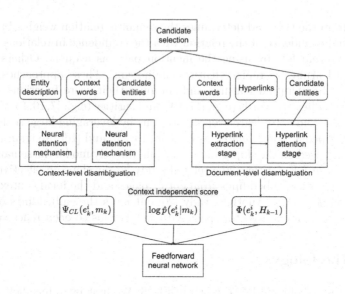

Fig. 3. The structure of our EL model.

3.2 Document-Level Disambiguation

In document-level disambiguation, we consider EL as a sequential decision problem, and our basic idea is to use the relevant hyperlinks to empower the decision. Formally, we denote the entity hyperlinks by $h_{k-1} = \{\widehat{l^1_{k-1}}, \widehat{l^2_{k-1}}, ..., \widehat{l^Q_{k-1}}\}$, where each $\widehat{l^i_{k-1}}$ represents a hyperlink embedding vector. Intuitively, some hyperlinks in h_{k-1} are irrelevant to mention m_k.[2] As illustrated in the Hyperlink Extraction Stage of Fig. 4, a single-layer neural network f computes the context embedding vector for mention m_k, where x_k is a concatenation of the left and right average embeddings of words of the mention. We then calculate the score between a context embedding vector and a hyperlink as follows:

$$w(\widehat{l^i_{k-1}}) = \widehat{l^i_{k-1}} \cdot f(m_k, x_k). \tag{8}$$

Hyperlink extraction stage then chooses top q relevant hyperlinks and uses softmax function to transform the scores as

$$b(\widehat{l^i_{k-1}}) = \frac{\exp\left[w(\widehat{l^i_{k-1}})\right]}{\sum_{\widehat{l^j_{k-1}} \in topq(h_{k-1})} \exp\left[w(\widehat{l^j_{k-1}})\right]}, \tag{9}$$

and the final weighted hyperlink embedding is

$$\widehat{h_{k-1}} = \sum_{\widehat{l^i_{k-1}} \in topq(h_{k-1})} b(\widehat{l^i_{k-1}}) \cdot \widehat{l^i_{k-1}}. \tag{10}$$

---

[2] For example, in Fig. 1, h_{k-1} can be (*Germany, football ,FIFA*, etc.), and m_k can be "Argentina".

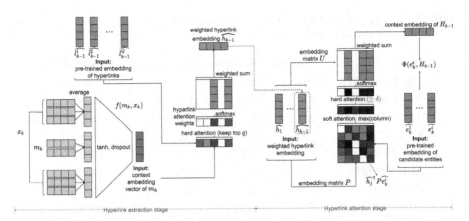

Fig. 4. The architecture of our document-level disambiguation. We compute the weighted hyperlink embeddings in the Hyperlink Extraction Stage and then use the attention mechanism in the Hyperlink Attention Stage to choose the relevant hyperlinks (the red words show the differences from the context-level disambiguation). (Color figure online)

Next, our document-level disambiguation uses the neural attention mechanism to highlight the important entities between previously linked entities' hyperlink set $H_{k-1} = \{\widehat{h_1}, \widehat{h_2}, ..., \widehat{h_k - 1}\}$ and candidate entities e_k^i (see the Hyperlink Attention Stage in Fig. 4). The calculation of relevance score for each $\widehat{h_i}$ is

$$v(\widehat{h_i}) = \max_{e_k^j \in \Delta(m_k)} \widehat{h_i}^{\mathsf{T}} P \widehat{e_k^j}, \tag{11}$$

where P is a learnable diagonal matrix. The weight of linked entity hyperlink is high if it is strongly related to candidate entities. We apply a threshold δ to select the relevant linked entity hyperlinks and use softmax function on these weights. We then define the reduced linked entity hyperlinks as

$$\overline{H_{k-1}} = \{\widehat{h_i} \in H_{k-1} | v(\widehat{h_i}) \geqslant \delta\}. \tag{12}$$

After that, the final attention weights are calculated as

$$d(\widehat{h_i}) = \frac{\exp[v(\widehat{h_i}]}{\sum_{\widehat{h_j} \in \overline{H_{k-1}}} \exp[v(\widehat{h_j})]}. \tag{13}$$

Finally, the document-level disambiguation score is explicitly

$$\Phi(e_k^i, H_{k-1}) = \sum_{\widehat{h_i} \in \overline{H_{K-1}}} d(\widehat{h_i}) \widehat{h_i}^{\mathsf{T}} U \widehat{e_k^i}, \tag{14}$$

where U is another parameterized diagonal matrix.

Table 1. Statistics of the datasets used in the experiments. *Gold recall* is the percentage of ground truth entities contained in candidate set of mentions.

Dataset	# docs	# mentions	Mentions per doc	Gold recall
AIDA-Train [11]	946	18448	19.5	–
AIDA-A(valid) [11]	216	4791	22.1	96.8%
AIDA-B(test) [11]	231	4485	19.4	98.7%
MSNBC [5]	20	656	32.8	98.5%
AQUAINT [18]	50	727	14.5	94.5%
ACE2004 [21]	36	257	7.1	91.4%
CWEB [9]	320	11154	34.8	91.3%
WIKI [9]	320	6821	21.3	92.9%

3.3 Candidate Selection

Before the context-level disambiguation and document-level disambiguation, we aim to prepare a better set of candidate entities from all possible candidates in the KB. For each candidate e_k^i of mention m_k, we first compute the candidate score as

$$R(e_k^i) = \sum_{\substack{m \neq k \\ m \in D}} \sum_{\widehat{e_m^j} \in C_m} sim(\widehat{e_k^i}, \widehat{e_m^j}),$$ (15)

where sim is cosine similarity.

To construct the reduced candidate set $\Delta(m_k)$, we first select the top 10 entities based on $\hat{p}(e_k^i|m_k)$ and the top 20 entities based on the candidate score $R(e_k^i)$. Then, in order to optimize for model's memory and decrease the noises for the model, we measure the local context-entity similarity (Eq. (1)) and keep only 7 of these entities, including the top 4 entities based on $\hat{p}(e_k^i|m_k)$ and the top 3 entities based on $s(e_k^i)$.

3.4 Result Generation

After introducing the main components in our model, in the following, we will describe how to combine the aforementioned components and produce the results. For a given mention-candidate pair (m_k, e_k^i), our model first generates context-level disambiguation score $\Psi_{CL}(e_k^i, m_k)$, document-level disambiguation score $\Phi(e_k^i, H_{k-1})$, and context-independent score $\log \hat{p}(e_k^i|m_k)$. Then, as shown in Fig. 3, the model combines these scores and outputs the probability $O_\theta(e_k^i|m_k)$. Specifically, the model uses a two-layer feedforward neural network to rank the model and minimize the max-margin loss defined as

$$L(\theta) = \sum_{D \in \mathcal{D}} \sum_{m_k \in D} \sum_{e_k^i \in \Delta(m_k)} g(m_k, e_k^i),$$ (16)

$$g(m_k, e_k^i) = \max(0, \gamma - O_\theta(e_k^*|m_k) + O_\theta(e_k^i|m_k)),$$

where θ includes the model parameters and e_k^* is the ground-truth entity.

4   Experiments

4.1   Experiment Setup

We conduct experiments on the commonly-used open benchmark datasets, of which the origins and statistics are available in Table 1. The parameter settings in our experiments are as follows. We set the dimensions of both word and entity embeddings to 300. For the word embeddings, we use Word2vec by [17] and GloVe by [19]. For the entity embeddings, we adopt the one developed by [7]. Word2vec is used in context-level disambiguation and candidate selection. GloVe is used in document-level disambiguation for computing f in Eq. (6). Hyper-parameters of the context-level disambiguation are: $N = 50$, $R = 50$, $S = 5$. For the document-level disambiguation, the length of words used in function f is set to 4 and the probability of dropout is set to 0.3, $q = 20$, $\delta = 0.5$, and $\gamma = 0.01$. For the candidate selection, the length of words $N = 40$. When training the model, we use the Adam [14] optimizer with the learning rate equal to 5e−5 and apply early stopping (i.e., we stop learning if validation accuracy does no increase after 200 epochs). Validation accuracy is computed after every 3 epochs. After the F1 score on the validation set reaches 90.8%, the learning rate is reduced to 1e−5. Furthermore, in order to avoid providing biased results, we run our model for multiple times and show the 95% confidence interval of the standard micro F1 score.

4.2   Results

We compare our model with the following existing EL systems, including the rank model in [21] and probability graph models in [7,9,11], and [15]. Table 2 shows the F1 scores of all the methods on the in-domain dataset AIDA-B. Note that the methods in [6] and [24] both use additional information: the former uses additional Wiki training data crawled by themselves, and the latter uses a NER-type system to enhance their performance. Therefore, their performances are mainly provided as references, since our model and the models in [7,9,11,21], and [15] do not use these kinds of additional information.

In Table 3, we show micro F1 scores on 5 out-domain test sets. Our model achieves the highest F1 scores on AQUAINT and CWEB. Please note that, although we do not use additional information as some previous studies (i.e., [6] and [24]), we still have the highest average F1 scores (88.49) among all the baselines on the five out-domain datasets.

Table 2. F1 scores of all methods on AIDA-B dataset for the in-domain KB. The overall best score is underlined and the score of the best result only using AIDA-Train as the training set is in bold face.

Methods	AIDA-B
AIDA-Train	
Chisholm and Hachey (2015) [4]	88.7
Guo and Barbosa (2018) [9]	89.0
Globerson et al. (2016) [8]	91.0
Yamada et al. (2016) [23]	91.5
Ganea and Hofmann (2017) [7]	92.2
Le and Titov (2018) [15]	**93.1**
Our model	93.01 ± 0.15
AIDA-Train + extra Wiki [6]	94.3
AIDA-Train + NER [24]	<u>94.6</u>

Table 3. F1 scores of all methods on out-domain datasets. The best results only using AIDA-Train as the training set are in bold face.

Methods	MSNBC	AQUAINT	ACE2004	CWEB	WIKI	Average
AIDA-Train						
Hoffart et al. (2011) [11]	79	56	80	58.6	63	67.32
Ratinov et al. (2011) [21]	75	83	82	56.2	67.2	72.68
Cheng and Roth (2013) [3]	90	90	86	67.5	73.4	81.38
Guo and Barbosa (2018) [9]	92	88	87	77	**84.5**	85.7
Ganea and Hofmann (2017) [7]	93.7	88.5	88.5	77.9	77.5	85.22
Le and Titov (2018) [15]	**93.9**	88.3	89.9	77.5	78.0	85.51
Our model	93.86 ± 0.2	**93.09** ± 0.2	**90.87** ± 0.5	**82.11** ± 0.1	82.51 ± 0.0	**88.49**
AIDA-Train + extra Wiki						
[6]	92.8	87.5	<u>91.2</u>	78.5	82.8	86.56
AIDA-Train + NER						
[24]	<u>94.6</u>	87.4	89.4	73.5	78.1	84.6

4.3 Discussions

Here we further analyze how our method can outperform others from three aspects: the effect of entity description, the impact of different mention linking orders, and the impact of different entity candidate selections.

Different from previous methods for context-level disambiguation that use only the entity embeddings to capture the information from the surrounding context, we additionally consider the entity description in the KB. To evaluate whether the entity description contributes to disambiguation, we compare the performance between the model with and without adding the entity description. As shown in Fig. 5(a), if we use entity description in our context-level disambiguation, the performance has more improvements on the datasets with lower accuracy, which means if entity embeddings are not well-trained, entity

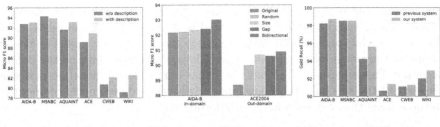

(a) Analysis on the effectiveness of entity description.

(b) Comparisons of different linking orders.

(c) Comparisons of different candidate selection strategies.

Fig. 5. Comparative analysis of different model components.

description can bring useful information and effectively improve the model performance. However, our context-level disambiguation shows a relatively low performance on MSNBC with entity description. The main reason is that the mentions in MSNBC have well-trained entity embeddings. Thus, the entity description might introduce some noise information to the model, which leads to a lower performance.

Since we consider EL as a sequential decision problem, the linking order also plays an important role in the prediction. In our study, we have evaluated five different linking orders, which are described as follows: *Original* links all of the mentions with their original orders in the document; *Random* links mentions with random orders; *Size* links the mentions with smaller candidate sizes first (if their candidate sizes are the same, *Size* links the one with the highest context-level disambiguation score); *Gap* links the mentions with context-level disambiguation score gap between the highest score and the second highest score; *Bidirectional* links the mentions with the average scores of normal orders and reverse orders. Figure 5(b) shows the performance comparison on the AIDA-B and the ACE2004 datasets. Overall, *Bidirectional* contains information for both sides, which leads to the best performance among all the linking orders.

In previous studies [7,15,24], they select the top 30 entities as the initial candidates for entity linking using the context-independent score $\hat{p}(e_k^i|m_k)$. However, such score ignores the same mention that may come from documents of different topics and thus selects the wrong entities. By contrast, our model uses cosine similarity to choose the relevant candidates by Eq. (15). Figure 5(c) shows that our method of selecting candidates outperforms the previous one on all the datasets, except on MSNBC having the same *gold recall*. This is because both of the methods already achieve the highest gold recall on MSNBC.

5   Conclusions

In this paper, we propose a model that adopts a new design of candidate selection and effectively utilizes highly relevant entity hyperlinks in the KB. Our model combines the hyperlink extraction stage and the hyperlink attention stage in the document-level disambiguation, in order to precisely extract the coherence between entities and hyperlinks. Compared to other existing EL systems which do not filter the corresponding hyperlinks for each entity, our model is able to locate and leverage more suitable hyperlinks and thereby enhance the linking accuracy. The experimental results show that our proposed model outperforms the state-of-the-arts on various benchmark datasets, and even being competitive to the models that rely on additional information.

References

1. Berant, J., Liang, P.: Semantic parsing via paraphrasing. In: Proceedings of the 52nd Annual Meeting of the Association for Computational Linguistics (Long Papers), vol. 1, pp. 1415–1425 (2014)
2. Chen, Z., Ji, H.: Collaborative ranking: a case study on entity linking. In: Proceedings of the 2011 Conference on Empirical Methods in Natural Language Processing, pp. 771–781. Association for Computational Linguistics, Edinburgh, Scotland, UK, July 2011. https://www.aclweb.org/anthology/D11-1071
3. Cheng, X., Roth, D.: Relational inference for wikification. In: Proceedings of the 2013 Conference on Empirical Methods in Natural Language Processing, pp. 1787–1796 (2013)
4. Chisholm, A., Hachey, B.: Entity disambiguation with web links. Trans. Assoc. Comput. Linguist. **3**, 145–156 (2015)
5. Cucerzan, S.: Large-scale named entity disambiguation based on Wikipedia data. In: Proceedings of the 2007 Joint Conference on Empirical Methods in Natural Language Processing and Computational Natural Language Learning (EMNLP-CoNLL), pp. 708–716. Association for Computational Linguistics, Prague, Czech Republic, June 2007. https://www.aclweb.org/anthology/D07-1074
6. Fang, Z., Cao, Y., Li, Q., Zhang, D., Zhang, Z., Liu, Y.: Joint entity linking with deep reinforcement learning. In: The World Wide Web Conference, pp. 438–447. ACM (2019)
7. Ganea, O.E., Hofmann, T.: Deep joint entity disambiguation with local neural attention. In: Proceedings of the 2017 Conference on Empirical Methods in Natural Language Processing, pp. 2619–2629 (2017)
8. Globerson, A., Lazic, N., Chakrabarti, S., Subramanya, A., Ringgaard, M., Pereira, F.: Collective entity resolution with multi-focal attention. In: Proceedings of the 54th Annual Meeting of the Association for Computational Linguistics (Long Papers), vol. 1, pp. 621–631 (2016)
9. Guo, Z., Barbosa, D.: Robust named entity disambiguation with random walks. Semant. Web **9**(4), 459–479 (2018)
10. He, Z., Liu, S., Li, M., Zhou, M., Zhang, L., Wang, H.: Learning entity representation for entity disambiguation. In: Proceedings of the 51st Annual Meeting of the Association for Computational Linguistics (Short Papers), vol. 2, pp. 30–34 (2013)
11. Hoffart, J., et al.: Robust disambiguation of named entities in text. In: Proceedings of the 2011 Conference on Empirical Methods in Natural Language Processing, pp. 782–792 (2011)
12. Hoffmann, R., Zhang, C., Ling, X., Zettlemoyer, L., Weld, D.S.: Knowledge-based weak supervision for information extraction of overlapping relations. In: Proceedings of the 49th Annual Meeting of the Association for Computational Linguistics: Human Language Technologies, vol. 1, pp. 541–550. Association for Computational Linguistics (2011)

13. Hu, Z., Huang, P., Deng, Y., Gao, Y., Xing, E.: Entity hierarchy embedding. In: Proceedings of the 53rd Annual Meeting of the Association for Computational Linguistics and the 7th International Joint Conference on Natural Language Processing (Long Papers), vol. 1, pp. 1292–1300 (2015)

14. Kingma, D.P., Ba, J.: Adam: a method for stochastic optimization. arXiv preprint arXiv:1412.6980 (2014)

15. Le, P., Titov, I.: Improving entity linking by modeling latent relations between mentions. In: Proceedings of the 56th Annual Meeting of the Association for Computational Linguistics (Long Papers), vol. 1, pp. 1595–1604 (2018)

16. Li, Y., Zheng, R., Tian, T., Hu, Z., Iyer, R., Sycara, K.: Joint embedding of hierarchical categories and entities for concept categorization and dataless classification. In: Proceedings of COLING 2016, the 26th International Conference on Computational Linguistics: Technical Papers, pp. 2678–2688 (2016)

17. Mikolov, T., Sutskever, I., Chen, K., Corrado, G.S., Dean, J.: Distributed representations of words and phrases and their compositionality. In: Advances in Neural Information Processing Systems, pp. 3111–3119 (2013)

18. Milne, D., Witten, I.H.: Learning to link with wikipedia. In: Proceedings of the 17th ACM Conference on Information and Knowledge Management, pp. 509–518 (2008)

19. Pennington, J., Socher, R., Manning, C.D.: GloVe: global vectors for word representation. In: Proceedings of the 2014 Conference on Empirical Methods in Natural Language Processing (EMNLP), pp. 1532–1543 (2014)

20. Radhakrishnan, P., Talukdar, P., Varma, V.: ELDEN: improved entity linking using densified knowledge graphs. In: Proceedings of the 2018 Conference of the North American Chapter of the Association for Computational Linguistics: Human Language Technologies, vol. 1 (Long Papers), pp. 1844–1853 (2018)

21. Ratinov, L., Roth, D., Downey, D., Anderson, M.: Local and global algorithms for disambiguation to wikipedia. In: Proceedings of the 49th Annual Meeting of the Association for Computational Linguistics: Human Language Technologies, vol. 1, pp. 1375–1384. Association for Computational Linguistics (2011)

22. Spitkovsky, V.I., Chang, A.: A cross-lingual dictionary for English wikipedia concepts. In: Proceedings of the Eighth International Conference on Language Resources and Evaluation (LREC 2012), pp. 3168–3175 (2012)

23. Yamada, I., Shindo, H., Takeda, H., Takefuji, Y.: Joint learning of the embedding of words and entities for named entity disambiguation. In: Proceedings of The 20th SIGNLL Conference on Computational Natural Language Learning, pp. 250–259 (2016)

24. Yang, X., et al.: Learning dynamic context augmentation for global entity linking. In: Proceedings of the 2019 Conference on Empirical Methods in Natural Language Processing and the 9th International Joint Conference on Natural Language Processing (EMNLP-IJCNLP), pp. 271–281 (2019)

25. Yih, W.T., Chang, M.W., He, X., Gao, J.: Semantic parsing via staged query graph generation: question answering with knowledge base. In: Proceedings of the 53rd Annual Meeting of the Association for Computational Linguistics and the 7th International Joint Conference on Natural Language Processing (Long Papers), vol. 1, pp. 1321–1331 (2015)

TANTP: Conversational Emotion Recognition Using Tree-Based Attention Networks with Transformer Pre-training

Haozhe Liu, Hongzhan Lin, and Guang Chen[✉]

School of Artificial Intelligence, Beijing University of Posts and Telecommunications,
Beijing, China
{liuhaozhe,linhongzhan,chenguang}@bupt.edu.cn

Abstract. Conversational emotion recognition has gained significant attention in data mining and text mining recently. Most existing methods only consider the utterance in conversations as a temporal sequence and ignore the fine-grained emotional clues in the compositional structure, where the non-ignorable semantic transitions and tone enhancement are implied. Consequently, such models hardly capture accurate semantic features of the utterance, which results in the accumulation of incorrect emotional features in the memory bank. To address this problem, we propose a novel framework, Tree-based Attention Networks with Transformer Pre-training (TANTP), which incorporates contextual representations and recursive constituency tree structure into the model architecture. Different from merely modeling the utterance in light of the time order, TANTP could effectively capture compositional emotion semantics of utterance features for the memory bank, where complex semantic transitions and emotional progression are difficult to be revealed by previous conventional sequential methods. Experimental results conducted on two public benchmark datasets demonstrate that TANTP could achieve superior performance compared with other state-of-the-art models.

Keywords: Conversational emotion recognition · Tree-based attention networks · Transformer · Compositional emotion semantics

1 Introduction

With the increasing popularity of conversational AI research, emotion recognition in the conversation has become indispensable in the field of data mining. It can be used to study financial volatility and develop emotional human–computer chatting systems. Text conversation is one of the important ways for humans to portray complex emotions. So in this paper, we center on the emotion recognition task in textual conversations. Emotion recognition in the conversation aims to detect the exact emotion states of speakers from their conversation. It is natural for humans to recognize underlying emotions in their verbal interactions. But machines have a hard time to recognize complex emotions within text features.

© Springer Nature Switzerland AG 2021
K. Karlapalem et al. (Eds.): PAKDD 2021, LNAI 12713, pp. 730–742, 2021.
https://doi.org/10.1007/978-3-030-75765-6_58

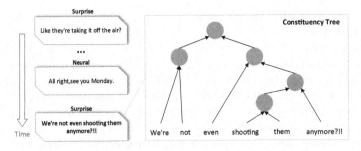

Fig. 1. The emotional clues of the utterance "We're not even shooting them anymore?!!" can be deeply explored through learning sentiment semantic compositionality.

One of the key challenges is how to extract the correct state referring to previous text information like utterance in the on-going and real-time regimes.

In conversational emotion recognition (CER), the semantic extraction of historical discourse is crucial since there is no future semantic environment. Thus, it is often necessary to construct a memory bank for identifying emotions, which is usually constructed hierarchically and depends on the representations of the token and utterance level. For CER, although most pioneering works [1–4] have earned remarkable performance, there are still two limitations. (1) At the token level, such models do not consider how to catch interactions between tokens so that it loses contextual information. (2) At the utterance level, these methods solely utilize convolutional neural networks (CNNs) [5] or gated recurrent units (GRUs) [6] to model the utterance according to the time order, largely ignoring or oversimplifying the structural information linked with constituency structure. These limitations will lead to the accumulation of incorrect semantic features in the memory bank. As a result, it is almost impossible for us to exploit the precise interactive information of the historical features from the memory bank. Therefore, it is vitally important to exactly derive emotion semantics at the token and utterance level, which determines the result of the CER task at the source.

To address these limitations, we present a new approach TANTP via tree-based attention networks with Transformer pre-training. At the token level, we obtain context-sensitive and emotionally rich embeddings by the Transformer [7–9] that is fine-tuned in the emotion recognition task. Context-sensitive embeddings can disambiguate homonyms, express semantic and syntactic patterns. More importantly, at the utterance level, our approach focuses more on capturing compositional semantic features of the utterance for the memory bank by the tree-based attention networks. We found the tree-based attention networks based on the structure of the binary constituency parse tree [10,11], which has been shown conducive to provide useful clues for modeling compositional emotion semantics. The utterance structure that expresses negations or emphases can be discovered straightforwardly by the binary constituency parse tree. As illustrated in Fig. 1, we can see the utterance "We're not even shooting them anymore?!!" consists of two parts which are connected by "not", and it reveals the semantic transition. Besides, the phrase "not even...anymore" that often appears in daily discourses has great effects on enhancing the emotional tone. It makes the inference that the emotion of the utterance is "surprise" more reasonable, while previous methods usually neglect it due to the certain distance among the phrase in time order. On the whole, TANTP can dig up semantic transitions and tone enhancement from more fine-grained compositional structures, which is hard to manipulate merely with traditional encoders like CNNs or GRUs. With the contextual information obtained by the fine-tuned Transformer and the binary constituency parse tree, we can better learn the composition meaning of the utterance and provide more accurate emotional representation for the memories-summarizing stage. Then, we can adopt self-attention networks to derive accurate interactive information of the historical features from the memory bank. To summarize, this paper makes the following contributions:

- We propose a novel framework towards conversational emotion recognition, which can exactly catch context-sensitive representations and compositional emotion semantics of utterances to improve the token-level and utterance-level features for the memory bank.
- We build the tree-based attention networks on top of Transformer to excavate more fine-grained emotional features like semantic transitions and emotional progression from the compositional structure. To our best knowledge, this is the first paper reflecting on the compositional structure of the utterance in conversational emotion recognition.
- Our experimental results on two public benchmark datasets outperform other state-of-the-art baselines on the conversational emotion recognition task.

2   Related Works

This section firstly reviews the recent progress of CER. Earlier research [12] is conducted to engineer new features, which annotated and detected emotions in call center dialogues using unigram topic modeling. Most previous automatic methods [13,14] intend to detect emotions by employing a range of features crafted from call center dialogues, like lexicon-based methods and audio features. These methods typically require heavy preprocessing and feature engineering.

In recent years, deep learning methods [1,15–17] have demonstrated state-of-the-art performances on emotion detection in conversational videos and multi-turn Tweets. DialogueRNN [2] is built on RNNs that keeps track of the individual party states throughout the conversation and uses this information for the emotion recognition task. AGHMN [4] uses Hi-GRU [18] and Attention GRU to produce utterance features and summarize the memories, respectively. HiTransformer-s [19] proposes a hierarchical transformer to refine the representations of tokens and utterances. KET [3] and COSMIC [20] incorporate knowledge into emotion detection in textual conversations.

Tree-based attention is proposed to integrate tree structures into self-attention [21,22]. Our proposed method is a substantial extension of tree-based attention to combine the syntactic structure with contextualized representation [19] for the semantic composition [23] in CER.

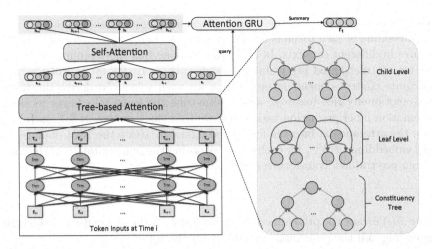

Fig. 2. The overall architecture of TANTP, including the submodules: Embedding Layer, Tree-Based Attention Layer, Self-attention Layer and Attention GRU. TANTP captures the compositional semantic features s_i of the utterance by the tree-based attention networks on top of the Transformer. Then, a memory bank B_t that contains K historical utterances is built up for more precise contextual information of the query utterance s_t. Furthermore, $h_i, i \in [t-K, t-1]$ which contains the interactive information between historical utterances is acquired by the self-attention mechanism. Finally, the vector representation r_t of the query utterance is reconstructed by Attention GRU based on the memory bank and itself, which is used to predict the emotion label of the query utterance.

3 Methodology

3.1 Task Definition

A conversation consists of different utterances spoken by different speakers. Suppose that $C_t = \{x_1, x_2, \cdots, x_t\}$ represents a t-turn conversation, which is made up of t utterances. An utterance is composed of a sequence of tokens, $x_i = \{e_1^i, e_2^i, \ldots, e_n^i\}$, where e_l^i represents the l-th token of the i-th utterance and n is the length of the utterance, $i \in [1, t]$ and $l \in [1, n]$. The CER task is to identify the emotion label of the query utterance x_t taking care of the utterances before x_t to a certain degree. Our model can recognize the emotion label of the query utterance based on the historical information in a conversation.

3.2 Architecture

Our core idea is to enhance representation learning of utterance indicative features by selectively attending over the corresponding semantic composition, which deeply explores speaker opinions and refines representation of the current utterance following the propagation conversation structure. In this section, we will introduce the architecture of the model as illustrated in Fig. 2 in detail.

Embedding Layer. As aforementioned, most traditional CER approaches usually get static word embedding like GloVe or Word2Vec for each token. However, it did not perform better in the word-level embedding phase due to the fact that the embedding of each token is fixed and does not change with different semantic features in different contexts. In order to overcome this shortcoming, our model uses transformer-based pre-training models such as BERT [8] or RoBERTa [9] to acquire context-dependent embedding for each token. To derive the token-level emotionally rich features, we can fine-tune the RoBERTa Large model in the emotion label prediction task. Then we feed the sequence of tokens $\{e_l^i\}_{l=1}^n$ given the utterance x_i into the fine-tuned model to attain the 1024-dimensional word embedding $\{T_l^i\}_{l=1}^n$ for each token, denoting the representation of the token e_l^i from pre-trained Transformers as T_l^i:

$$T_l^i = \mathcal{F}(E_l^i), \tag{1}$$

where $\mathcal{F}(\cdot)$ means the pre-trained Transformer, E_l^i is the summation of the token embedding and the positional embedding for the token e_l^i.

Tree-Based Attention Layer. As shown in Fig. 1, an utterance can be modeled in the form of a tree structure according to its constituencies. All the leaf nodes of the binary constituency parse tree represent the tokens in the utterance. In this module, we aim to attain the root node representation, which contains the compositional semantic features of the utterance, through the tree-based attention at the leaf and child level.

Leaf Level. For the current utterance $x_i = \{e_l^i\}_{l=1}^n$, we can get the representation of the l-th leaf (token) node, denoted as $\mathbf{f}_l^i = T_l^i$ from previous section. Each parent node that only has two child nodes could be related to two or more leaf nodes directly or indirectly. The representation of each parent node could be initialized by the leaf nodes covered by the node itself. For clarity's sake, we take the root node as an example, which is related to all leaf nodes. We could simply compute the vector representation $\mathbf{v}_i$ of the root node by summing up all the representations of leaf nodes and taking the average:

$$\mathbf{v}_i = \frac{1}{n} \sum_{l=1}^n \mathbf{f}_l^i. \tag{2}$$

However, the compositional information gained in such a way is not sufficient. Therefore, we generate the representation $\mathbf{q}_i$ of the root node by summing up representations of all leaf nodes according to the attention weights allocated to them based on their impact on the average representation. The calculation of the attention weight allocated to the l-th leaf node is thus:

$$\mathbf{c}_l^i = Atten(\mathbf{v}_i, \mathbf{f}_l^i)$$
$$= \tanh\left(\frac{1}{\alpha} \operatorname{SeLU}\left((W_1 \times \mathbf{v}_i)^T \times W_3 \times \operatorname{SeLU}\left(W_2 \times \mathbf{f}_l^i\right)\right)\right), \tag{3}$$

$$a_l^i = \frac{\exp\left(c_l^i\right)}{\sum_{k=1}^n \exp\left(c_k^i\right)}, \tag{4}$$

where W_1, W_2 and W_3 are trainable weight matrices and α is a hyper-parameter. Then we can compute the weighted sum representation of the root node:

$$\mathbf{q}_i = \sum_{l=1}^{n} a_l^i \cdot \mathbf{f}_l^i. \tag{5}$$

The initial representation $\mathbf{p}_i$ of the root node could be acquired by concatenating the weighted sum $\mathbf{q}_i$ and the averaged sum $\mathbf{v}_i$. Similarly, the representations $\mathbf{p}_{left}$ and $\mathbf{p}_{right}$, which are the two child nodes of the root node in the binary constituency parse tree, can be initialized in the same manner based on the representations of the leaf nodes covered by each node itself respectively.

Child Level. At the leaf level, we have initialized the representations of the root node and its child nodes. And the representation of the root node can be further enhanced by pondering the relationship between the child nodes of the root node and itself:

$$\mathbf{u}_i = a_{left} \cdot \mathbf{p}_{left} + a_{right} \cdot \mathbf{p}_{right} + a_{root} \cdot \mathbf{p}_{root}, \tag{6}$$

where a_{left}, a_{right} and a_{root} are the attention weights as followed:

$$a_{left}, a_{right}, a_{root} = \text{Softmax}\left(c_{left}, c_{right}, c_{root}\right), \tag{7}$$

in which c_{left}, c_{right} and c_{root} are computed following Eq. 3:

$$\begin{aligned} c_{left} &= Atten(\mathbf{p}_{root}, \mathbf{p}_{left}), \\ c_{right} &= Atten(\mathbf{p}_{root}, \mathbf{p}_{right}), \\ c_{root} &= Atten(\mathbf{p}_{root}, \mathbf{p}_{root}). \end{aligned} \tag{8}$$

The representation s_i of the utterance x_i can be refined by concatenating the weighted sum representation $\mathbf{u}_i$ and $\mathbf{p}_i$.

Self-attention Layer. In a conversation, the emotion label of a query largely depends on its historical utterances. To make full use of the historical information, it is crucial to build a memory bank B_t for the query. Suppose that s_t is the refined representation of the query utterance from the tree-based attention layer, which has a memory bank containing K utterances. Since these K utterances are extracted from a conversation in order, there are implicative emotion clues under them. We propose to use the self-attention mechanism [7] to gain interactive information of the historical features and update the memory bank. The fusion representations $h_i, i \in [t-K, t-1]$ of these utterances in the memory bank are generated by the following:

$$g\left(s_i, s_j\right) = s_i s_j^T, \tag{9}$$

$$a_{ij} = \frac{\exp\left(g\left(s_i, s_j\right)\right)}{\sum_{j'=t-K}^{t-1} \exp\left(g\left(s_i, s_{j'}\right)\right)}, \tag{10}$$

$$o_i = \sum_{j=t-K}^{t-1} a_{ij} s_j, \tag{11}$$

$$h_i = o_i + s_i, \tag{12}$$

where $j \in [t - K, t - 1]$, $B_t = \{h_{t-k}, \ldots, h_{t-1}\}$ is the memory bank of s_t with interactive information of K utterances.

Attention GRU for Final Prediction. The fusion representations from the self-attention layer are fed into an Attention GRU network [4] to take the memory bank into consideration for the final prediction of the query utterance. An attention weight of each historical utterance in the memory bank to the query need to be allocated as follows:

$$a_k = \frac{\exp\left(s_t^\top \mathbf{B}_{t,k}\right)}{\sum_{k'=1}^{K} \exp\left(s_t^\top \mathbf{B}_{t,k'}\right)}. \tag{13}$$

These attention weights are used to update the internal state $\tilde{\mathbf{h}}_t$ of a normal GRU by the following:

$$\mathbf{h}_k = a_k \circ \tilde{\mathbf{h}}_k + (1 - a_k) \circ \mathbf{h}_{k-1}. \tag{14}$$

The final hidden state of AGRU $c_t = h_K$ which considers not only the impact of different utterances in the memory bank on the query, but also the positional information of these utterances is the contextual representation of the query. We generate the query's final representation r_t by fusing its contextual representation and the representation of itself:

$$\mathbf{r}_t = \mathbf{s}_t + \mathbf{c}_t. \tag{15}$$

Finally, we feed the representation r_t of the query to the softmax layer to predict the emotion label:

$$\hat{\mathbf{y}}_t = \text{softmax}\left(\mathbf{W}_r \mathbf{r}_t + \mathbf{b}_r\right). \tag{16}$$

To solve the imbalance problem of different kinds of emotion labels, we optimize the model parameters by using a weighted categorical cross-entropy. Thus the loss function is defined as:

$$\text{loss} = -\frac{1}{\sum_{i=1}^{L} N_i} \sum_{i=1}^{L} \sum_{j=1}^{N_i} \omega\left(c_j\right) \sum_{c=1}^{|\mathcal{C}|} y_j^c \log_2\left(\hat{y}_j^c\right), \tag{17}$$

$$\frac{1}{\omega(c)} = \frac{I_c^\beta}{\sum_{c'=1}^{|c|} I_{c'}^\beta}, \tag{18}$$

where I_c denotes the total number of utterances with emotion label c, β is a hyper-parameter.

4   Experiments

4.1   Datasets

We experiment on two benchmark datasets: EmoryNLP [15] and MELD [24] which are both multi-party datasets and annotated from the TV show Friends.

Table 1. Statistics of EmoryNLP and MELD datasets.

Dataset	#Utter. (Train/Val/Test)	#Conv. (Train/Val/Test)	#Classes
EmoryNLP	7551/954/984	659/89/79	7
MELD	9989/1109/2610	1038/114/280	7

But their annotation principles and emotion label types are not the same. Both datasets are split into three parts: "train", "test", and "val". We show the full statistics of EmoryNLP and MELD in Table 1.

- EmoryNLP [15] is a dataset based on the show Friends. Utterances are labelled on seven emotion types including neutral, sad, mad, scared, powerful, peaceful, and joyful.
- MELD [24] is a dataset that comes from the Friends TV series with numerous speakers in a conversation. Each utterance has one of the seven emotion labels. They are anger, disgust, sadness, joy, neutral, surprise, and fear.

4.2 Implementation Details

Adam [25] is adopted as the optimizer, and the initial learning rate is 5×10^{-4}. We clip the gradients of model parameters and set the clipping threshold to 5. The hyper-parameters α and β equal 4 and 0.5, respectively. The window size K equals 10 that is the average length of a conversation in the dataset. And the number of training epochs is 20. Our model uses transformer-based pre-training models such as BERT[1] or RoBERTa[2] to obtain context-sensitive embedding for each token. To better capture the emotion features of the token, we fine-tune the RoBERTa Large model[3] in the emotion label prediction task.

4.3 Results and Discussion

Baselines. We compare our model with the following baselines:

- CNN [5] is a single-layer convolutional neural network model that is trained on the utterances for the emotion class prediction.
- DialogueRNN [2] uses separate GRUs to model context, speakers, and emotion features to track the states of various parties throughout the conversation.
- KET [3] learns structured conversation representations via hierarchical self-attention and leverages external, context-aware, and emotion-related knowledge entities from knowledge bases.

---

[1] https://github.com/hanxiao/bert-as-service.
[2] https://github.com/pytorch/fairseq/tree/master/examples/roberta.
[3] https://github.com/declare-lab/conv-emotion.

- AGHMN [4] proposes to use Hi-GRU and attention GRU to produce utterance features and summarize the memories appropriately to retrieve relevant information for emotion detection in textual conversations.
- HiTransformer-s [19] proposes a hierarchical transformer framework to extract features of tokens and utterances for the contexts of the utterance.
- COSMIC [20] is the state-of-the-art model for conversational emotion detection, which models various aspects of commonsense knowledge by considering mental states, events, actions, and cause-effect relations.

Main Results. In the experiment, weighted accuracy (WA) and weighted F1 (WF1) are evaluation metrics that take the imbalance proportion of emotion labels into account. From Table 2, compared with other baseline methods, we can see our model earns remarkable performance on both EmoryNLP and MELD. For EmoryNLP, our model obtains a 1.73% improvement on WA compared with RoBERTa AGHMN and 1.06% higher than COSMIC on WF1. We argue that the tree-based attention networks can accurately unearth the emotion venation from the more fine-grained structure information that concentrates on negations and emphases in the utterance as shown in Fig. 1. We can regard this fine-grained structure information as syntactic guidance that leads our model to capture the emotion kernel of the utterance. For MELD, our model obtains a 1.96% improvement compared with RoBERTa AGHMN on WA and is almost comparable but slightly worse than COSMIC in terms of WF1. It is probably because COSMIC explicitly introduces external commonsense knowledge from the knowledge base. Exploring emotional clues from the conversation itself is intrinsically more difficult for models to implicitly catch some of the complex interactions towards a better understanding of the emotional dynamics and other aspects of a conversation.

Ablation Study. To illustrate the reliability of the tree-based attention networks, we conduct the ablation study on both datasets. The result is shown in Table 3. TANTP w/o Tree is the model without tree-based attention networks, TANTP w/o Child level is the model without child-level attention networks and TANTP w/Att replaces tree-based attention networks with self-attention networks. We suppose the reasons for the outcome are that (1) TANTP w/o Child level is harder to grasp the semantic transitions than TANTP because it ignores the contrast between the two child leaves. (2) For TANTP w/Att, self-attention networks consider the interactive information between the tokens that make up an utterance compared with TANTP w/o Tree, and TANTP focuses more on compositional semantic features of the utterance which take an important part in conversational emotion recognition. FR-TANTP w/Att is slightly higher than FR-TANTP in terms of WA on EmoryNLP, but in general tree-based attention networks perform better and more robust than self-attention networks.

Table 2. Experimental results on EmoryNLP and MELD. The best results are highlighted in bold.

Methods	EmoryNLP		MELD	
	WF1	WA	WF1	WA
CNN	32.59	–	55.02	–
Dialogue RNN	31.70	–	57.03	–
AGHMN	33.57	39.84	58.10	60.30
KET	34.39	–	58.18	–
HiTransformer-s	–	37.98	–	–
RoBERTa	37.29	–	62.02	–
RoBERTa Dialogue RNN	37.44	–	63.61	–
RoBERTa AGHMN	38.25	40.85	63.53	63.52
COSMIC	38.11	–	**65.21**	–
TANTP	**39.17**	**42.58**	64.69	**65.48**

Table 3. Ablation study on TANTP model. "B/R/FR-" means the model is BERT/RoBERTa/Fine-tuned RoBERTa-based, respectively.

Methods	EmoryNLP		MELD	
	WF1	WA	WF1	WA
B-TANTP w/o Tree	32.86	40.04	57.79	61.80
B-TANTP w/o Child level	35.47	37.6	59.72	60.58
B-TANTP w/Att	33.09	39.13	56.82	57.32
B-TANTP	**36.68**	**39.43**	**60.91**	**61.87**
R-TANTP w/o Tree	34.25	39.84	58.44	60.80
R-TANTP w/o Child level	36.35	37.09	59.44	59.73
R-TANTP w/Att	34.81	39.63	58.29	61.19
R-TANTP	**36.69**	**40.45**	**61.5**	**62.76**
FR-TANTP w/o Tree	37.60	39.94	64.20	64.64
FR-TANTP w/o Child level	39.01	42.07	63.45	63.29
FR-TANTP w/Att	38.50	**42.78**	64.03	64.21
FR-TANTP	**39.17**	42.58	**64.69**	**65.48**

Effect of Pre-trained Transformers. Different pre-trained Transformers are adopted to attain context-dependent features for each token. BERT Large and RoBERTa Large are pre-trained models, and Fine-tuned RoBERTa Large has been fine-tuned in emotion label prediction tasks. Table 3 shows that Fine-tuned RoBERTa Large model extracts more accurate emotion-rich features than the other two pre-trained Transformers. It also depicts the effectiveness of tree-based attention networks regardless of embedding methods.

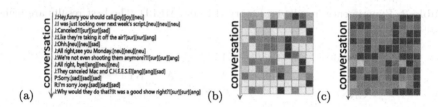

Fig. 3. The attention weights of memories to the queries in a conversation from MELD. (a) is the part of a conversation. There are three emotion labels after an utterance: the first is gold truth, the second is predicted from FR-TANTP and the last is from FR-TANTP w/o Tree. R: Rachel, J: Joey, P: Phoebe. (b) and (c) are attention wights maps learned from FR-TANTP and FR-TANTP w/o Tree, respectively. The darker the color, the greater the weight. The height is the number of utterances in (a). The width is the context window size K.

Case Study. In Fig. 3, we visualize the attention weights of memory banks to the queries in a conversation. Each row represents the attention weights of a memory bank to the query. Take the last utterance as an example, the true emotion label is "surprise", and our model FR-TANTP gives the correct prediction, but FR-TANTP w/o Tree makes a mistake. We can find the reason from (b) and (c) in Fig. 3 where FR-TANTP pays more attention to the utterances that promote Joey to be surprised step by step. However, FR-TANTP w/o Tree only takes note of the utterances closer to the query in time and could not seize the emotional shift for "surprise". Besides, FR-TANTP w/o Tree allocates indistinguishable attention weight to each utterance which cannot take full advantage of important utterances. Therefore, our model can better capture the compositional emotion semantics of the utterance for the memory bank so that it can better mine the clues between the discourse itself and historical information.

5   Conclusion

In this work, to improve the utterance-level and token-level features and avoid the accumulation of the incorrect emotion semantics in the memory bank, we propose a novel framework (TANTP) using tree-based attention networks with Transformer pre-training for conversational emotion recognition. The tree-based attention networks can better tap the compositional semantic features of an utterance and the context-dependent features can be extracted with pre-trained Transformers. Experiments on two public benchmarks have shown that our model could outperform other state-of-the-art baseline approaches.

References

1. Hazarika, D., Poria, S., Zadeh, A., Cambria, E., Morency, L.-P., Zimmermann, R.: Conversational memory network for emotion recognition in dyadic dialogue videos. In: Proceedings of NAACL-HLT, pp. 2122–2132 (2018)

2. Majumder, N., Poria, S., Hazarika, D., Mihalcea, R., Gelbukh, A., Cambria, E.: DialogueRNN: an attentive rnn for emotion detection in conversations. In: Proceedings of the AAAI Conference on Artificial Intelligence (2019)

3. Zhong, P., Wang, D., Miao, C.: Knowledge-enriched transformer for emotion detection in textual conversations. arXiv preprint arXiv:1909.10681 (2019)

4. Jiao, W., Lyu, M.R., King, I.: Real-time emotion recognition via attention gated hierarchical memory network (2020)

5. Kim, Y.: Convolutional neural networks for sentence classification. arXiv preprint arXiv:1408.5882 (2014)

6. Cho, K., et al.: Learning phrase representations using rnn encoder-decoder for statistical machine translation. In: EMNLP, pp. 1724–1734

7. Vaswani, A., et al.: Attention is all you need. In: Advances in neural information processing systems (2017)

8. Devlin, J., Chang, M.-W., Lee, K., Toutanova, K.: BERT: Pre-training of deep bidirectional transformers for language understanding. arXiv preprint arXiv:1810.04805 (2018)

9. Liu, Y., et al.: RoBERTa: a robustly optimized bert pretraining approach. arXiv preprint arXiv:1907.11692 (2019)

10. Gildea, D.: Dependencies vs. constituents for tree-based alignment. In: Proceedings of the 2004 Conference on EMNLP, pp. 214–221 (2004)

11. Wang, W., Knight, K., Marcu, D.: Binarizing syntax trees to improve syntax-based machine translation accuracy. In: Proceedings of the 2007 Joint Conference on EMNLP-CoNLL, pp. 746–754 (2007)

12. Devillers, L., Vasilescu, I., Lamel, L.: Annotation and detection of emotion in a task-oriented human-human dialog corpus. In: Proceedings of ISLE Workshop (2002)

13. Lee, C.M., Narayanan, S.S.: Toward detecting emotions in spoken dialogs. IEEE Trans. Speech Audio Process. 13(2), 293–303 (2005)

14. Devillers, L., Vidrascu, L.: Real-life emotions detection with lexical and paralinguistic cues on human-human call center dialogs. In: Ninth International Conference on Spoken Language Processing (2006)

15. Zahiri, S.M., Choi, J.D.: Emotion detection on tv show transcripts with sequence-based convolutional neural networks. arXiv preprint arXiv:1708.04299 (2017)

16. Chatterjee, A., Gupta, U., Chinnakotla, M.K., Srikanth, R., Galley, M., Agrawal, P.: Understanding emotions in text using deep learning and big data. Comput. Hum. Behav. 93, 309–317 (2019)

17. Poria, S., Majumder, N., Mihalcea, R., Hovy, E.: Emotion recognition in conversation: research challenges, datasets, and recent advances. IEEE Access 7, 100943–100953 (2019)

18. Jiao, W., Yang, H., King, I., Lyu, M.R.: HiGRU: hierarchical gated recurrent units for utterance-level emotion recognition. arXiv preprint arXiv:1904.04446 (2019)

19. Li, Q., Chunhua, W., Wang, Z., Zheng, K.: Hierarchical transformer network for utterance-level emotion recognition. Appl. Ences 10(13), 4447 (2020)

20. Ghosal, D., Majumder, N., Gelbukh, A., Mihalcea, R., Poria, S.: COSMIC: commonsense knowledge for emotion identification in conversations. arXiv preprint arXiv:2010.02795 (2020)

21. Wang, Y.-S., Lee, H.-Y., Chen, Y.-N.: Tree transformer: Integrating tree structures into self-attention. arXiv preprint arXiv:1909.06639 (2019)

22. Yin, D., Meng, T., Chang, K.-W.: SentiBERT: A transferable transformer-based architecture for compositional sentiment semantics. arXiv preprint arXiv:2005.04114 (2020)

23. Pelletier, F.J.: The principle of semantic compositionality. Topoi **13**(1), 11–24 (1994)
24. Poria, F., Hazarika, D., Majumder, N., Naik, G., Cambria, E., Mihalcea, R.: MELD: a multimodal multi-party dataset for emotion recognition in conversations. In ACL, pp. 527–536 (2019)
25. Kingma, D., Ba J.: ADAM: A method for stochastic optimization. Computer Ence (2014)

Semantic-Syntax Cascade Injection Model for Aspect Sentiment Triple Extraction

Wenjun Ke[1,2], Jinhua Gao[1(✉)], Huawei Shen[1,2], and Xueqi Cheng[1]

[1] CAS Key Laboratory of Network Data Science and Technology,
Institute of Computing Technology, Chinese Academy of Sciences,
Beijing 100190, China
{gaojinhua,shenhuawei,cxq}@ict.ac.cn
[2] University of Chinese Academy of Sciences, Beijing 100049, China

Abstract. Aspect sentiment triple extraction aims to extract all aspects, opinions, and sentiments in a sentence and pair them into triples. The main challenge lies at mining the dependency between the aspect and corresponding opinion with the specific sentiment. Existing methods capture the dependency via either pipeline framework or collapsed sequence labeling model. However, the pipeline framework may suffer from error propagation, while collapsed tags cannot deal with complex pairing situations where the overlap or long dependency exists. In this paper, we propose a novel semantic-syntax cascade injection model (SSCIM) to address above issues. SSCIM adopts a cascade framework with joint training schema, where its lower layer extracts the aspects and injects those aspects into the upper layer to extract opinion and sentiment simultaneously. Such design is inspired by the fact that the sentiment is often conveyed in opinions, and the joint training schema alleviates error propagation effectively. Moreover, a novel semantic-syntax information injection gate (IIG) is designed to bridge the upper and lower layers of our model, enabling SSCIM to better capture the dependency between aspects and opinions. Experimental results on four benchmark datasets demonstrate the superior performance of the proposed model over state-of-the-art baselines.

Keywords: Aspect sentiment triple extraction · Cascade pointer network · Semantic-syntax information injection gate

1 Introduction

Aspect-based sentiment analysis (ABSA) is capable of mining the fine-grained sentiment towards the specific aspect. The aspect extraction (AE), opinion extraction (OE), and sentiment classification (SC) are the three fundamental subtasks of ABSA. For example, given a review sentence, "The sauce is delicious and the crust is bad." AE and OE aim at extracting the aspect ("sauce" and "crust") and opinion ("delicious" and "bad"), respectively, while SC infers the polarity of each aspect as "positive" and "negative".

© Springer Nature Switzerland AG 2021
K. Karlapalem et al. (Eds.): PAKDD 2021, LNAI 12713, pp. 743–755, 2021.
https://doi.org/10.1007/978-3-030-75765-6_59

Considering the interaction among AE, OE and SC tasks, some multi-task learning schemas of ABSA have been adopted. Specifically, as shown in Fig. 1, these techniques can be grouped into three categories: aspect extraction alone (AE) [9,10], aspect and opinion co-extraction (AE+OE) [2,13,19] and aspect sentiment triple extraction (AE+OE+SC) [11,15]. This paper focuses on the aspect sentiment triple extraction task, which is a newly proposed task [11]. This task aims to extract not only the aspects and the corresponding sentiments, but also the opinion spans that convey the sentiment, enabling more fine-grained aspect sentiment analysis.

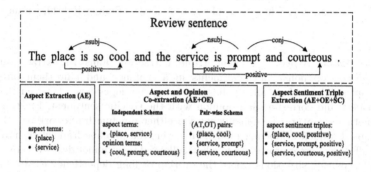

Fig. 1. An application example of aspect extraction methods.

Recently, two representative techniques, i.e., the pipeline framework [11] and the collapsed labeling model [15], have been applied for this task. The pipeline framework extracts aspects, opinions, and sentiments independently in the first stage and pairs them into triples in the second stage. **However, error propagation might emerge due to inaccurate extraction of aspect and opinion spans in the first stage.** On the other hand, the collapsed labeling model formalizes the task into a sequence tagging problem based on a designed collapsed-tagging schema. For example, the aspect "place" in Fig. 1 is labeled as $B_{3,3}^{+}$, where the superscript and subscript denote the polarity and offset of the corresponding opinion, respectively. **However, this model cannot handle complex pairing situations, e.g. overlaps or long offsets between aspects and opinions.** As shown in Fig. 1, a single collapsed-label cannot handle overlapping relations between one aspect ("service") and two corresponding opinions ("prompt" and "courteous"). Moreover, a longer offset between aspect and opinion could increase the number of collapsed labels, resulting in sparse labels.

To alleviate the disadvantages of above representative techniques, we propose a novel semantic-syntax cascade injection model (SSCIM) for aspect sentiment triple extraction. SSCIM adopts a cascade framework to extract aspects and opinions jointly, thus reducing the error propagation. Specifically, the lower layer of the cascade network is designed for extracting aspects, while the upper layer aims to extract opinions and sentiment (OE+SC), considering the sentiment is often conveyed in opinions. Moreover, we design a semantic-syntax information injection gate (IIG) to bridge the lower and upper layers. IIG can capture the interaction between aspects and opinions, and inject the aspect feature effectively into corresponding opinions. Experiments on four benchmark datasets demonstrate the superior performance of our approach. Further analysis also shows that our approach can explicitly encode semantic-syntax correlation between aspects and opinions, assisting in handling complex paring situations.

2   Related Work

Related work can be grouped into three categories: aspect extraction alone, aspect and opinion co-extraction, and aspect sentiment triple extraction.

Recent models for aspect extraction have widely adopted deep neural networks as building blocks, including recurrent neural networks (RNN) [6], convolutional neural networks (CNN) [16], graph neural networks (GNN) [18], sequence-to-sequence models [10], and pre-training language models [5]. Katiyar et al. [6] adopted deep bidirectional LSTMs for aspect extraction. Ye et al. [16] introduced dependency tree-based convolution to obtain syntax information for aspect extraction. Zhang et al. [18] adopted the graph neural network to model the dependency relationship between words. Ma et al. [10] formalized the aspect extraction task as a sequence-to-sequence learning task. Besides, to alleviate the lack of labeled data, some scholars proposed methods such as sample generation [7] and semi-supervised learning [8] for data enhancement.

Inspired by the fact that opinions can act as clues for aspect extraction, some methods [2,13,19] have been proposed to extract aspects and opinions simultaneously. On the one hand, some methods extract aspects and opinions independently without pairing them. Wang et al. [13] proposed a multi-layer attention network to propagate information between aspects and opinions. On the other hand, some other methods perform pair-wise extraction of aspects and opinions. Chen et al. [2] applied an opinion entity extraction unit and relation detection unit to extract aspects and opinions synchronously. Zhao et al. [19] proposed a multi-task learning framework to identify aspects and opinions from the perspective of relation extraction jointly.

Aims to provide a nearly complete solution, the aspect sentiment triple extraction task has been proposed recently [11,15]. Two major frameworks are the pipeline model [11] and the sequence tagging model with collapsed labels [15]. However, the pipeline-based model might propagate the error of the previous stage to the next one, while collapsed label approaches suffer from sparse label problem and can not solve overlapping cases. Therefore, the aspect sentiment triple extraction task needs further research.

Different from these works, which often neglect dependencies between opinions and aspects, we propose a cascade framework to extract aspects and opinions jointly. Moreover, a novel semantic-syntax information injection gate can strengthen the ability to capture interactions between aspects and opinions.

3   Method

The task of aspect sentiment triple extraction can be formalized as follows: given a review sentence $S = \{w_i\}_{i=1}^{n}$ of length n, the goal is to extract all m groups aspect sentiment triples $T = \{< a_j, o_j, s_j >\}_{j=1}^{m}$, where a_j, o_j, s_j represent the jth aspect, opinion and sentiment, respectively. Note that both aspect a_j and opinion o_j can be either a word or a phrase in the sentence, thus we can have $a_j \subset S$ and $o_j \subset S$. Generally, the sentiment polarity s_i can be categorized into three types: negative, neutral and positive.

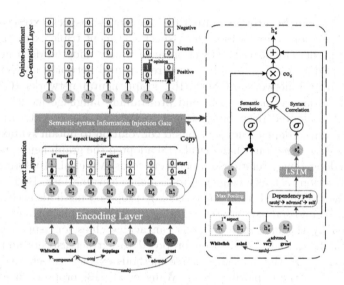

Fig. 2. The overview of SSCIM.

The overall architecture of SSCIM is shown in Fig. 2. SSCIM adopts the cascade pointer network architecture that consists of two layers. The lower layer and the higher layer are designed to extract aspects and opinion-sentiments pairs, respectively. Especially, the connection between two layers of the cascade pointer network is controlled by a semantic-syntax information injection gate (IIG), which can adjust the proportion of aspect information injected into each token. Furthermore, the training process of SSCIM exploits a joint learning paradigm to avoid error propagation. The inference process employs a two-stage strategy which first predicts all the aspects and then feeds each aspect into the model to obtain the corresponding opinions and sentiments.

3.1   Cascade Pointer Network

One of the most challenging subtasks of aspect sentiment triple extraction is to pair the aspect and opinion effectively.

To this end, a cascade framework, which is composed of encoding layer, aspect extraction layer and opinion-sentiment co-extraction layer, is proposed to model the probability of aspect sentiment triple $p(a, o, s)$ as $p(a, o, s) = p(a) * p(o, s \mid a)$. $p(a)$ represents the probability of aspect a, and $p(o, s \mid a)$ represents the conditional probability of opinions and sentiments for the given aspect a.

Encoding Layer. For each token w_i, the word embedding $e_i \in \mathbb{R}^{d_w}$ can be obtained from embedding lookup matrix $M_w \in \mathbb{R}^{|V_w| \times d_w}$, where d_w is the embedding dimension and $|V_w|$ denotes the vocabulary size. The context features of the sentence S can be denoted as $h^a = \{h_i^a | i = 1, 2, \ldots, n\}$. Bi-LSTM is used for encoding the context features $h_i^a \in \mathbb{R}^{d_h}$ as follows:

$$h_i^a = \overrightarrow{\text{LSTM}_w}\left(e_i, h_{i-1}^a\right) \oplus \overleftarrow{\text{LSTM}_w}\left(e_i, h_{i+1}^a\right) \tag{1}$$

where $\overrightarrow{\text{LSTM}_w}(\cdot)$ and $\overleftarrow{\text{LSTM}_w}(\cdot)$ represent the forward LSTM unit and backward LSTM unit, respectively. $\oplus$ denotes the concatenate operation and d_h is the dimension of the hidden state of LSTM. Note that the pre-trained language model BERT can also be applied to encode the context feature.

Aspect Extraction Layer. We formalize the aspect extraction task into a sequence labeling task, which aims to extract all aspects in the form of span. Compared to CRF, pointer network can reduce the search space via labeling only the head and tail position of aspect. Specifically, each token feature h_i^a is fed into the softmax function to obtain the distribution $p_i^a \in \mathbb{R}^2$, indicating the probability of being the head or tail aspect pointer. The cross-entropy is used to generate the loss of aspect extraction, which can be formalized as:

$$\text{Loss}_a = -\frac{1}{n} \sum_{i=1}^{n} y_i^a \cdot \log p_i^a \tag{2}$$

where $y_i^a \in \mathbb{R}^2$ stands for the one-hot ground truth distribution. Note that, to deal with sentences with different length, the result is divided by the sentence length n to calculate the average loss.

Opinion-Sentiment Co-Extraction Layer. We design three tagging modules to extract opinion spans with positive, neutral and negative polarities, respectively. Formally, the aspect-specific feature $h^a = \{h_1^a, h_2^a, \ldots, h_n^a\}$ would be injected into its context to produce the aspect-aware context representation $h^o = \{h_1^o, h_2^o, \ldots, h_n^o\}$. Then, each aspect-aware context token feature $h_i^o \in \mathbb{R}^{d_h}$ is fed into the linear transformation layer with three binary sequence labeling layers to predict the polarity distributions of positive $p_i^{o,+} \in \mathbb{R}^2$, neutral $p_i^{o,\sim} \in \mathbb{R}^2$, and negative $p_i^{o,-} \in \mathbb{R}^2$. Similar to the aspect extraction layer, the loss could be calculated as the sum of three polarities:

$$\text{Loss}_{o\text{-s}} = -\frac{1}{n}\left(\sum_{i=1}^{n} y_i^{o,+} \cdot \log p_i^{o,+} + \sum_{i=1}^{n} y_i^{o,\sim} \cdot \log p_i^{o,\sim} + \sum_{i=1}^{n} y_i^{o,-} \cdot \log p_i^{o,-}\right)$$

$$(3)$$

where $y_i^{o,*} \in \mathbb{R}^2$ presents the one-hot ground truth distribution for a polarity.

3.2 Semantic-Syntax Information Injection Gate

We design a novel semantic-syntax information injection gate (IIG) to inject aspect feature into each token of the sentence for opinion-sentiment co-extraction. The key motivation of IIG is that the aspect information can help infer opinion spans, both semantically and syntactically. On one hand, semantic similarity should be taken into consideration. For example, "food" is more likely to be modified by "delicious", while "restaurant" is more likely to be modified by "comfortable". On the other hand, the syntactic relation generated by dependency parsing, e.g. "nsubj", "amod", have proved to be an effective clue to explore the pairing of aspect and opinion [20]. Thus our proposed IIG captures both semantic and syntax correlation to weight the portion of aspect information that should be injected.

Semantic Correlation. A max pooling layer is used to extract the most significant features $q^a \in \mathbb{R}^{d_h}$ of the aspect span. Due to the proven powerful expressive ability of biaffine scorer [4], it is employed to capture the semantic correlation $co_i^{semantic} \in \mathbb{R}$ between the aspect and each token as follows:

$$co_i^{semantic} = \sigma\left((W_{sem}h_i^a + b_{sem})^T q^a\right) = \sigma\left((W_{sem}h_i^a)^T q^a + (b_{sem})^T q^a\right) \quad (4)$$

where $W_{sem} \in \mathbb{R}^{d_h \times d_h}$ and $b_{sem} \in \mathbb{R}^{d_h}$ are linear transformation parameters that should be learned. σ is the sigmoid function.

Syntax Correlation. The Stanford neural parser [1] is applied to obtain the dependency tree of input sentence to model the propagation chain from context to aspect. As a result, the dependency path, like "cool $\xrightarrow{nsubj}$ place" in Fig. 2, is used to characterize the syntax correlation between token and aspect.

The dependency path $path_i^a$ is composed of m dependency relationships $r_{i,k}$. For example, the path between the token "very" and the aspect "salad" in Fig. 2 can be expressed as "nsubj$^-$ $\rightarrow$ advmod$^+$ $\rightarrow$ self", where "+" and "−" represent the direction between token and aspect. Besides, the relation "self" is to introduced modify the aspect itself. To model the dependency path $path_i^a$, we first embed each dependency relation $r_{i,k}$ into a d_r-dimension vector. Then a unidirectional $\overrightarrow{\text{LSTM}}_p(\cdot)$ is utilized to encode the features $s_i^a \in \mathbb{R}^{d_h}$, which can be transformed into the syntax correlation $co_i^{syntax} \in \mathbb{R}$ between token and aspect.

$$co_i^{syntax} = \sigma\left(W_{syn}s_i^a + b_{syn}\right) \quad (5)$$

Information Injection Gate. The information injection gate is developed to obtain the correlation $co_i \in \mathbb{R}$:

$$co_i = \lambda_c co_i^{semantic} + (1 - \lambda_c) co_i^{syntax} \tag{6}$$

where $\lambda_c \in [0, 1]$ is a given parameter that controls the weight of the semantic and syntactic correlation. Finally, the injected proportion of aspect feature conveyed in co_i can be used to produce the aspect-aware context feature $h_i^o \in \mathbb{R}^{d_h}$:

$$h_i^o = co_i * q^a + h_i^a \tag{7}$$

3.3 Training and Inference

Joint Training. SSCIM adopts the cascade network [14], which extracts all aspects firstly, and feeds each aspect into the opinion-sentiment co-extraction layer to obtain opinions and sentiments. Accordingly, to ensure that all aspect sentiment triples can be trained, we extract multiple training samples for sentences with multiple aspects, where each sample x contains only one aspect and its corresponding opinion and sentiment. The ground truth y of the sample x is the result of sequence labeling in accordance with the requirements of Sect. 3.1. Finally, SSCIM is trained jointly with the L2-regularization:

$$\text{Loss} = \sum_{(x,y) \in D} [\text{Loss}_a(x, y) + \lambda_1 \text{Loss}_{o-p}(x, y)] + \lambda_2 \|\theta\|^2 \tag{8}$$

where D denotes the constructed dataset. The loss function is composed of three parts: the loss of aspect extraction, the loss of opinion-sentiment joint extraction, and the regularization term of parameters. The coefficients λ_1 and λ_2 need to be set manually.

Model Inference. The inference adopts a two-stage strategy. When processing a review sentence, the inference extracts all aspects in the first stage. Then, each aspect is fed to the second stage to obtain its opinions and sentiments. Moreover, the margin of the pointer network can be located only if the corresponding predicted value is higher than a given threshold $\hat{\xi}$.

4   Experiment

4.1   Datasets and Settings

Since the aspect sentiment triple extraction is a relatively new task, Peng et al. [11] labeled the pairing relationship between aspects and opinions based on the original datasets from SemEval 2014 task 4, SemEval 2015 task 12, and SemEval 2016 task 5, and constructed the aspect sentiment triples. However, Xu et al. [15] pointed out that the dataset provided by Peng et al. [11] eliminates the overlap of opinions; that is, multiple aspects are modified by one opinion.

Table 1. The dataset statistics

Dataset	Rest14				Lap14				Rest15				Rest16			
	#S	pos	neu	neg	#S	pos	neu	neg	#S	pos	neu	neg	#S	pos	neu	neg
Train	1266	1692	166	480	906	817	126	517	605	783	25	205	857	1015	50	329
Dev	310	404	54	119	219	169	36	141	148	185	11	53	210	252	11	76
Test	492	773	66	155	328	364	63	116	322	317	25	143	326	407	29	78

Therefore, we choose datasets provided by Xu et al. [15] as our benchmarks. The dataset statistics is shown in Table 1.

The proposed SSCIM model is implemented with Pytorch 1.6.0 of NVIDIA TESLA T4 platform and uses the Stanford neural parser to generate the dependency tree. Two types of word embeddings are used: GloVe [12] and BERT [3], i.e., $SSCIM_{GloVe}$, $SSCIM_{BERT}$. Dependency relations, e.g. *nsubj* and *amod*, are randomly initialized and updated during training. The model is trained by the Adam optimizer with the learning rate 2e−5. The batch size of $SSCIM_{GloVe}$ and $SSCIM_{BERT}$ are set into 32 and 8 respectively. The maximum epoch number is set into 100 and 30 towards $SSCIM_{GloVe}$ and $SSCIM_{BERT}$.

In the experiment, the dimension of the $\overrightarrow{LSTM_w}(\cdot)$ and $\overleftarrow{LSTM_w}(\cdot)$ hidden state is set to 200, and the dimension of the $\overrightarrow{LSTM_p}(\cdot)$ is set to 100. The dimension of dependency relation d_r is 300. The parameter λ_c that controls the weight of the semantic and syntax is set as $\lambda_c = 0.5$ and the inference threshold $\hat{\xi}$ is 0.5. In the Loss calculation, we set $\lambda_1 = 1$, $\lambda_2 = 0.01$.

4.2 Our Model and Baselines

To evaluate the performance of SSCIM, representative neural models are chosen as our baselines. The following baseline models consist of three folds: pipeline models with two-stage strategy, joint models with joint learning strategy, and variant models of our approach SSCIM for ablation studies.

Pipeline Models. We choose the four widely-used model with pipeline structure in the experiment. **CMLA+** [15] applies attention mechanism to obtain the dependencies between words at its first stage; **REINANTE+** [15] is designed with weak supervision; **Li-unified-R+** [15] applies the unified tagging scheme and two-stage framework; **Peng et al.** [11] adopts the two-stage framework with the fused feature by GCN and RNN.

Joint Models. We employ seven joint models that are designed with various strategies as baselines. **CMLA-MTL** [17] extends the original CMLA [13] model in a joint manner; **HAST-MTL** [17] extends the aspect-opinion co-extraction system HAST [9] by multi-task learning schema; **OTE-MTL** [17] extracts aspects and opinions independently, and mined the sentiment by modeling the interaction between aspects and opinions with a combined loss; $\textbf{JET}^t_{\textbf{GloVe}}$ [15]

applies a position-aware tagging scheme to decode the aspect with correspond-ing opinions and sentiments; $\text{JET}^{o}_{\text{GloVe}}$ [15] employs a tagging scheme on the opinion span to indicate its aspects and sentiments; $\text{JET}^{t}_{\text{BERT}}$ [15] applies the pre-trained language model BERT for contextualized word representation based on $\text{JET}^{t}_{\text{GloVe}}$; $\text{JET}^{o}_{\text{BERT}}$ [15] adopts the model BERT on the basis of $\text{JET}^{o}_{\text{GloVe}}$.

Our Model and Variants. To investigate the performance of our medel com-prehensively, we adopt our model with GloVe and BERT. Thus, we have the fol-lowing variant models: **SSCIM$_{\text{GloVe}}$** is our model with the GloVe embeddings; **SSCIM$_{\text{BERT}}$** is our model with the pre-training model BERT; **SSCIM$_{\text{BERT}}$ w/o IIG** is the model removing semantic-syntax information injection gate and injecting the aspect feature into each token with the same weight based on **SSCIM$_{\text{BERT}}$**. **SSCIM$_{\text{BERT}}$ w/o Semantic** adjusts the IIG on the base model **SSCIM$_{\text{BERT}}$**, which removes the use of semantic information while only remaining the syntax information. **SSCIM$_{\text{BERT}}$ w/o Syntax** abandons the use of syntactic information to weight the correlation between the aspect and its corresponding context, while retaining only semantic information.

We leverage precision (P), recall (R) and F1 score to assess the performance of models. Note that a correct triple means that its aspect range, opinion range and sentiment polarity are all correct at the same time.

4.3 Main Result

Table 2. The experiment results (%). The results with * are retrieved from Xu et al.'s work [15], with # are from the execution of our implementation based on [17], with † are from the execution of author provided code [17].

Model	Rest14			Lap14			Rest15			Rest16		
	P	R	F1	P	R	F1	P	R	F1	P	R	F1
CMLA+*	39.18	47.13	42.79	30.09	36.92	33.16	34.56	39.84	37.01	41.34	42.10	41.72
RINANTE+*	31.42	39.38	34.95	21.71	18.66	20.07	29.88	30.06	29.97	25.68	22.30	23.87
Li-unified-R*	41.04	67.35	51.00	40.56	44.28	42.34	44.72	51.39	47.82	37.33	54.51	44.31
Peng et al.*	43.24	63.66	51.46	37.38	50.38	42.87	48.07	57.51	52.32	46.96	64.24	54.21
CMLA-MTL#	45.34	44.45	44.89	34.93	36.64	35.76	37.87	40.19	39.00	45.21	47.90	46.52
HAST-MTL#	55.05	48.12	51.35	49.10	28.10	35.74	40.48	39.15	39.80	49.01	48.12	48.56
OTE-MTL†	65.13	54.19	59.16	47.91	41.12	44.26	55.01	46.83	50.59	57.58	52.40	54.87
$\text{JET}^{t*}_{\text{GloVe}}$	66.76	49.09	56.58	52.00	35.91	42.48	59.77	42.27	49.52	63.59	50.97	56.59
$\text{JET}^{o*}_{\text{GloVe}}$	61.50	55.13	58.14	53.03	33.89	41.35	64.37	44.33	52.50	70.94	57.00	63.21
$\text{JET}^{t*}_{\text{BERT}}$	63.44	54.12	58.41	53.53	43.28	47.86	68.20	42.89	52.66	65.28	51.95	57.85
$\text{JET}^{o*}_{\text{BERT}}$	70.56	55.94	62.40	55.39	47.33	51.04	64.45	51.96	57.53	70.42	58.37	63.83
SSCIM$_{\text{GloVe}}$ (ours)	61.55	68.11	64.66	48.56	62.29	54.57	50.31	66.80	57.40	66.87	64.01	65.41
SSCIM$_{\text{BERT}}$ (ours)	67.56	73.74	**70.51**	59.44	62.29	**60.83**	54.78	64.95	**59.43**	69.92	68.29	**69.09**

Table 2 shows that our model SSCIM$_{\text{BERT}}$ significantly outperforms the baseline models in all datasets while SSCIM$_{\text{GloVe}}$ also achieves considerable performance.

Specifically, for F1 score, SSCIM$_{BERT}$ exceeds the strongest baseline model JET$^O_{BERT}$ by 8.11%, 9.79%, 1.90%, 5.26% on Rest14, Lap14, Rest15, Rest16 datasets respectively, which fully demonstrates the superiority of our model. In addition, in comparison with baselines, our model performs better in the recall, because semantic-syntax information injection gate (IIG) can enhance the pairing relationship between aspects and opinions explicitly, and extract more triples with overlapping aspects or opinions.

4.4 Ablation Experiments

The results of ablation experiments are shown in Table 3. First of all, SSCIM$_{BERT}$ w/o IIG achieves the worst performance by injecting aspect feature to each context token in the same weight. This shows that semantic-syntax correlation can provide important clues for the dependency between aspects and opinions. Even so, SSCIM$_{BERT}$ w/o IIG still achieves better results than pipeline baselines, which also verifies the advantages of joint learning paradigm. Another observation is that SSCIM$_{BERT}$ w/o Semantic achieves better performance than SSCIM$_{BERT}$ w/o Syntax in most datasets (except Rest14), which indicates that syntax information is a key element of IIG. However, the language expressions of Rest14 may be somehow informal, reducing the effect of dependency parsing and affecting the performance of SSCIM$_{BERT}$ w/o Semantic.

Table 3. Results of the ablation experiments (%).

Model	Rest14			Lap14			Rest15			Rest16		
	P	R	F1	P	R	F1	P	R	F1	P	R	F1
SSCIM$_{BERT}$ w/o Semantic	61.44	65.23	63.28	60.98	55.45	58.08	53.16	58.45	55.68	64.66	69.07	66.79
SSCIM$_{BERT}$ w/o Syntax	65.77	73.64	69.48	55.08	52.83	53.93	50.82	57.53	53.97	55.84	59.53	57.63
SSCIM$_{BERT}$ w/o IIG	49.28	61.97	54.9	44.63	59.89	51.14	44.64	63.51	52.43	56.38	66.15	60.88
SSCIM$_{BERT}$ (ours)	67.56	73.74	**70.51**	59.44	62.29	**60.83**	54.78	64.95	**59.43**	69.92	68.29	**69.09**

4.5 Further Analysis

Overlapping Triples Analysis. Statistics show that there is a large amount (more than 30%) of overlap in all datasets, which brings great challenges. Compared with the baselines, the performance of our model keeps ahead and achieves a relatively stable and decent F1 score in Fig. 3a when processing overlap triples.

Offset Between Aspect and Opinion. We conduct experiments with different offsets on Rest14. It can be seen from Fig. 3b that the performance of all models decreases with the increase of offset, which demonstrates that it is hard to pair the triples with a long distance between aspect and corresponding opinion. Even so, SSCIM$_{BERT}$ still outperforms other baselines with all offsets, and the overall performance decline trend is relatively stable. This may benefit from the use of semantic-syntax correlation, helping identify longer dependency.

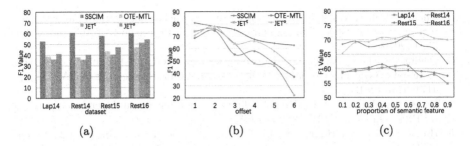

(a)   (b)   (c)

Fig. 3. The performance of SSCIM$_{BERT}$, OTE-MTL, JET^t and JET^o under different settings. (a) shows the performance of overlapping cases; (b) shows the performance of different offsets; and (c) shows the performance with different proportion of semantic feature.

Analysis of IIG. To verify the effect of semantic-syntax information injection gate, we adjust the proportion of semantic feature λ_c from 0.1 to 0.9. Accordingly, the corresponding proportion of syntax is from 0.9 to 0.1 on four datasets. As shown in Fig. 3c, our approach SSCIM$_{BERT}$ achieves the highest F1 value with a ratio between 0.3 and 0.7, verifying the effectiveness of fusing syntactic and semantic information. The model especially achieves the best performance on Rest14 with a semantic feature proportion of 0.7, which is higher than the other datasets. As mentioned in Sect. 4.3, the possible reason is that the syntax feature of Rest14 is less important because of its arbitrary expression.

5   Conclusion

We analyze the major challenges of the aspect sentiment triple extraction task and propose a novel semantic-syntax cascade injection model (SSCIM). On one hand, our work devotes to alleviate the propagation error by adopting the joint learning schema within a cascade framework. On the other hand, we design a novel semantic-syntax information injection gate (IIG) to capture the dependency between aspects and opinions. Experimental results show that SSCIM can extract triple with effective paring ability, thus achieving better performance than state-of-the-art baselines.

Acknowledgments. This paper is funded by the National Natural Science Foundation of China under Grant Nos. 91746301 and 62002347. Huawei Shen is also funded by Beijing Academy of Artificial Intelligence (BAAI) and K.C. Wong Education Foundation.

References

1. Chen, D., Manning, C.D.: A fast and accurate dependency parser using neural networks. In: Proceedings of EMNLP, pp. 740–750 (2014)

2. Chen, S., Liu, J., Wang, Y., Zhang, W., Chi, Z.: Synchronous double-channel recurrent network for aspect-opinion pair extraction. In: Proceedings of ACL, pp. 6515–6524 (2020)
3. Devlin, J., Chang, M.W., Lee, K., Toutanova, K.: Bert: pre-training of deep bidirectional transformers for language understanding. In: Proceedings of NAACL, pp. 4171–4186 (2019)
4. Dozat, T., Manning, C.D.: Deep biaffine attention for neural dependency parsing. In: Proceedings of ICLR (Poster) (2017)
5. Hu, M., Peng, Y., Huang, Z., Li, D., Lv, Y.: Open-domain targeted sentiment analysis via span-based extraction and classification. In: Proceedings of ACL, pp. 537–546 (2019)
6. Katiyar, A., Cardie, C.: Investigating LSTMS for joint extraction of opinion entities and relations. In: Proceedings of ACL, pp. 919–929 (2016)
7. Li, K., Chen, C., Quan, X., Ling, Q., Song, Y.: Conditional augmentation for aspect term extraction via masked sequence-to-sequence generation. In: Proceedings of ACL, pp. 7056–7066 (2020)
8. Li, N., Chow, C.-Y., Zhang, J.-D.: EMOVA: a semi-supervised end-to-end moving-window attentive framework for aspect mining. In: Lauw, H.W., Wong, R.C.-W., Ntoulas, A., Lim, E.-P., Ng, S.-K., Pan, S.J. (eds.) PAKDD 2020. LNCS (LNAI), vol. 12085, pp. 811–823. Springer, Cham (2020). https://doi.org/10.1007/978-3-030-47436-2_61
9. Li, X., Bing, L., Li, P., Lam, W., Yang, Z.: Aspect term extraction with history attention and selective transformation. In: Proceedings of IJCAI, pp. 4194–4200 (2018)
10. Ma, D., Li, S., Wu, F., Xie, X., Wang, H.: Exploring sequence-to-sequence learning in aspect term extraction. In: Proceedings of ACL, pp. 3538–3547 (2019)
11. Peng, H., Xu, L., Bing, L., Huang, F., Lu, W., Si, L.: Knowing what, how and why: a near complete solution for aspect-based sentiment analysis. In: Proceedings of AAAI, pp. 8600–8607 (2020)
12. Pennington, J., Socher, R., Manning, C.D.: Glove: global vectors for word representation. In: Proceedings of EMNLP, pp. 1532–1543 (2014)
13. Wang, W., Pan, S.J., Dahlmeier, D., Xiao, X.: Coupled multi-layer attentions for co-extraction of aspect and opinion terms. In: Proceedings of AAAI (2017)
14. Wei, Z., Su, J., Wang, Y., Tian, Y., Chang, Y.: A novel cascade binary tagging framework for relational triple extraction. In: Proceedings of ACL, pp. 1476–1488 (2020)
15. Xu, L., Li, H., Lu, W., Bing, L.: Position-aware tagging for aspect sentiment triplet extraction. In: Proceedings of EMNLP, pp. 2339–2349 (2020)
16. Ye, H., Yan, Z., Luo, Z., Chao, W.: Dependency-tree based convolutional neural networks for aspect term extraction. In: Kim, J., Shim, K., Cao, L., Lee, J.-G., Lin, X., Moon, Y.-S. (eds.) PAKDD 2017. LNCS (LNAI), vol. 10235, pp. 350–362. Springer, Cham (2017). https://doi.org/10.1007/978-3-319-57529-2_28
17. Zhang, C., Li, Q., Song, D., Wang, B.: A multi-task learning framework for opinion triplet extraction. In: Proceedings of EMNLP, pp. 819–828 (2020)
18. Zhang, J., Xu, G., Wang, X., Sun, X., Huang, T.: Syntax-Aware Representation for Aspect Term Extraction. In: Yang, Q., Zhou, Z.-H., Gong, Z., Zhang, M.-L., Huang, S.-J. (eds.) PAKDD 2019. LNCS (LNAI), vol. 11439, pp. 123–134. Springer, Cham (2019). https://doi.org/10.1007/978-3-030-16148-4_10

19. Zhao, H., Huang, L., Zhang, R., Lu, Q., et al.: Spanmlt: a span-based multi-task learning framework for pair-wise aspect and opinion terms extraction. In: Proceedings of ACL, pp. 3239–3248 (2020)
20. Zheng, Y., Zhang, R., Mensah, S., Mao, Y.: Replicate, walk, and stop on syntax: An effective neural network model for aspect-level sentiment classification. Proceedings of AAAI **34**, 9685–9692 (2020)

Modeling Inter-aspect Relationship with Conjunction for Aspect-Based Sentiment Analysis

Haoliang Zhao, Yun Xue$^{(\boxtimes)}$, Donghong Gu, Jianying Chen, and Luwei Xiao

Guangdong Provincial Key Laboratory of Quantum Engineering and Quantum
Materials, School of Physics and Telecommunication Engineering, South China
Normal University, Guangzhou 510006, China
xueyun@scnu.edu.cn, {gu_dh105,gochenjianying}@m.scnu.edu.cn

Abstract. Aspect-based sentiment analysis is currently a main focus within the domain of sentiment analysis, whose target is to identify the sentiment polarities of specific aspect terms. The ongoing research is absent of exploiting the inter-aspect relationship while mainly focus on modeling the aspect terms and its context independently. To address this problem, we propose a model integrating the conjunction information and the sentiment of the preceding aspect term. As such, the inter-aspect relation between adjacent aspect terms can be precisely modeled and applied to sentiment classification. Experimental results on SemEval 2014 and MAMS show that our model outperform the baseline methods, especially dealing with the multi-aspect terms, which establishes a strong evidence of the effectiveness of the proposed method.

Keywords: Aspect-based sentiment analysis · Conjunction · Inter-aspect relationship

1 Introduction

Aspect-based sentiment analysis (ABSA), yields fine-grained sentiment information which is useful for applications in various domains [13]. In general, sentiment polarity classification is a most significant and challenging issue in ABSA tasks. Basically, an aspect term can be a word or a phrase which delivers attributes of the target entity in the sentence. On the tasks of ABSA, it is often the case that multiple aspects are performed within one single sentence (Table 1). For instance, in the sentence "*Definitely try their Pizzas and Wines–although their desserts are not-to-shabby either.*", the sentiment polarities for aspects "*pizzas*", "*wines*" and "*desserts*" are positive, positive and negative, respectively.

Encouragingly, the advancing in ABSA tasks are largely promoted by the flourish of deep neural networks, specifically due to its use end-to-end training without any prior knowledge. To the best of our knowledge, recurrent neural networks (RNNs), specifically integrating with attention mechanisms, are currently widespread in dealing with such issues, with recent publications report

© Springer Nature Switzerland AG 2021
K. Karlapalem et al. (Eds.): PAKDD 2021, LNAI 12713, pp. 756–767, 2021.
https://doi.org/10.1007/978-3-030-75765-6_60

Table 1. Reviews from MAMS dataset [3], containing aspect term, polarity and conjunction

Additive conjunction		
S1: I love the complementary <u>hot salsa</u> and fresh <u>chips</u> that they put on the table.		
Term : hot salsa Polarity : positive	Conjunction : and	Term : chips Polarity : positive
S2: The <u>atmosphere</u> is cheesy as well as the <u>crowd</u>.		
Term : atmosphere Polarity : negative	Conjunction : as well as	Term : crowd Polarity : negative
Contrasting conjunction		
S3: The <u>decor</u> isn't quite like Shun Lee but the <u>service</u> will definitely make up for any shortcoming.		
Term : decor Polarity : negative	Conjunction : but	Term : service Polarity : positive
S4: Definitely try their <u>Pizzas</u> and <u>Wines</u> - - although their <u>desserts</u> are not-to-shabby either.		
Term : Pizzas, Wines Polarity : positive	Conjunction : although	Term : desserts Polarity : negative

the superiority [8,16]. As a most commonly used RNN method, long short-term memory (LSTM) layer aims to capture the semantic information as well as the sentiment in sequence. The attention weights of the contexts is assigned by using the attention mechanism. Notwithstanding, the sequential processing manner is characterized by large numbers of parameters and computational resources.

In contrast, since the sentiment of aspect term is conditioned by the specific opinion words, convolutional neural networks (CNNs) is more capable to extract the informative n-gram features as aspect sentential representations. A notably example is the Gated Convolutional network with Aspect Embedding (GCAE) established by Xue and Li [18]. The integration of CNN and gating mechanisms results in a far less training time and lower computational cost than LSTM based networks but a higher accuracy. Despite the innovation of GCAE, a fine-grained analysis of the contexts for each aspect term is absent. In line with the state-of-arts, the employment of position information [1], as well as attention mechanisms [16] can cater to the demand of maintaining more related information.

In most cases, because of more than aspect terms in one sentence, the effects of sentiment information on each other is inevitable. Previous work is absent of focusing on the sentiment relation among adjacent aspect terms. [1,8,16,18] On this occasion, the inter-aspect sentiment relation is pronounced. According to [1], the adjacent aspects have to be given more attention than others. That is, this important relationship is performed from one aspect term to the subsequent. Even though LSTM models are taken to process the inter-relation between aspects for sentiment classification [2,9], a more delicate analysis for the conjunction of aspect terms is desired for aspect sentiment identification. In NLP domain, conjunctions play a pivot role in identifying the sentiment information, based on which the prediction of aspect term sentiment is effectively facilitated. Theoretically, two different kinds of conjunctions, i.e. additive conjunctions and contrasting conjunctions are highlighted [10]. The former contain conjunctions like "and", "as well as", "also" and etc. While the latter contain those like "but", "however", "although" and etc. More concretely, the additive conjunction always comes with aspect terms of similar sentiment polarities (S1 in Table 1) while contrasting conjunction with the opposite ones (S3 in Table 1). As a result, the conjunctive words, in the sentence of one aspect conjunct another, can be employed to facilitate the sentiment classification.

In this work, we propose an inter-aspect relationship with conjunction (IARC) model, targeting at address the inter-aspects relationship in ABSA tasks. The aspect terms from one sentence are transformed into aspect-specific sentential representations. The improved GCAE model, by integrating attention mechanism and position information, is applied to obtain the representation of aspect and its contexts. Both the sentiment of the former aspect and the conjunction between them are taken to further predicting the sentiment of the target aspect term, thus to improve the model efficiency and improving the working accuracy. Specifically, the contribution of this work is threefold:

1. Revising GCAE model: The integration of attention mechanism and position information into GCAE optimize the capturing of aspect representation, especially for multi-aspect terms within one sentence.
2. Conjunction information fusion: The inter-aspect relation is modeled by using the sentiment of the adjacent aspect terms and the conjunctive word. In such manner, the sentiment of the target aspect term is presented.
3. Working performance evaluation: Experimental results on three datasets verify the effectiveness of IARC, indicating that our model is a competitive alternative to the state-of-arts.

2 Related Work

Compared to document level and sentence level, ABSA tasks refer to the sentiment associated with aspects of the entity, which allows for a more detailed analysis that utilizes more information provided by the text. Previous research combining deep-learning methods and attention mechanisms has primarily focused on obtaining the representation of specific aspect [8, 16]. As reported in [1], the position embedding, converted from the position information, is concatenated to the word embedding as the input of the Bi-GRU based network. In such work the relation between aspect term and its context is enhanced. Sixing Wua et al. apply information of conjunctions to capture the relations between clauses for the purpose of representation establishing [17]. Notably, a substantial number of RNN-based algorithms receive great attention [1,14]. Despite this, CNN-based models also show the effectiveness. Xue and Li [18] employ CNN for modeling the aspect and sentiment information and the gating unit for selecting the sentiment information. Similarly, Li et al. propose a CNN layer to extract salient features from word representations [6].

More recently, the inter-aspect relation is studied extensively. Researchers tend to generate more accurate sentential representations relative to each aspect for sentiment classification [2,9]. The RNN-based approaches, however, merely concentrate on capturing the sequence information of different aspect terms in one sentence, together with the attention mechanism modeling their relation. Besides, Jiang et al. develop a capsule network to model the complicated relationship between aspects and contexts, in which each sentence contains multiple aspects of different sentiment polarities [3]. Based on the memory network, Lin et al. [7] integrate aspect semantic parsing information into it and apply the attention mechanism to exploit inter-aspect information of target aspect. In comparison to the aforementioned methods, graph convolutional network (GCN) is both creative and practical in dealing with graph data containing rich relation information [19,20]. For instance, Zhao et al. [20] construct GCN-based model to effectively capture the sentiment dependencies between multi-aspects in one sentence.

3   Methodology

We describe the proposed approach IARC for aspect-level sentiment analysis in this section. The architecture of IARC model is presented in Fig. 1. The details of each part are described as follows.

3.1   Problem Definition and Notations

For a given sentence $S = [w_1, w_2, ..., w_L] \in \mathbb{R}^{d_m \times L}$, each word embedding w_i indicates a d_{em}-dimensional vector by looking up in a pretrained word embedding matrix of GloVe [11]. Within the sentence, there are M aspect terms, which are $A_1, A_2, ..., A_M$. Each aspect term $A_i = [w_{k_i}, ..., w_{k_i + m_i - 1}]$ ($1 \leq k_i \leq L$ and $0 \leqslant m_i \leqslant L - k_i + 1$) contains one or more consecutive words from the sentence. The task is to classify the sentiment polarity of aspect term in the sentence.

3.2   Input Layer

The sentence embeddings, as well as the aspect embeddings within it, are sent to the model as the inputs. As shown in Fig. 1, the attention mechanism and the position information are carried out on word embeddings, respectively. Multi-worded aspect terms are computed by the CNN layer, which results in aspect representation $a_i \in \mathbb{R}^{d_{em}}$ of ith aspect term A_i.

The attention mechanism aims at computing the interaction between the aspect term and its context, and thus to determine the contribution of different words to the aspect. In line with the sentence S and the ith aspect representation a_i, the attention weight of each word is presented as:

$$f(w_j, a_i) = tanh(w_j W_m a_i + b_m) \tag{1}$$

$$\alpha_{ij} = \frac{exp(f(w_j, a_i))}{\sum_{k=1}^{L} exp(f(w_k, a_i))} \tag{2}$$

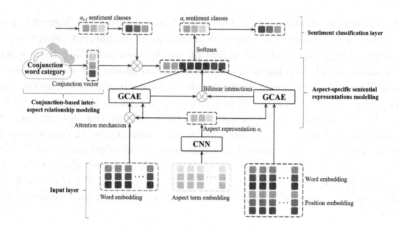

Fig. 1. Architecture of IARC. Our model firstly maps context and target words into continuous low dimensional word vectors as the input embeddings. Then the GCAE model is operated on these word embeddings to extract the aspect-specific sentential representation (for more details of GCAE see for example [18]). Specifically, attention mechanism and position information are also employed to obtain a more accurate representation. The inter-aspect relationship is determined with the integration of conjunction information. Finally, sentiment polarity is predicted through softmax layer.

together with

$$v_{ij}^{att} = \alpha_{ij}w_j \tag{3}$$

where α_{ij} is the attention weight of jth word to aspect term in the sentence, W_m and b_m are weight matrix and bias respectively. Thus the embeddings with more related information is transformed to $V_i^{att} = [v_{i1}^{att}, v_{i2}^{att}, \cdots, v_{iL}^{att}] \in \mathbb{R}^{d_{em} \times L}$.

On the other hand, the position embeddings, based on the each word's relative distance to the aspect term, is concatenated to the word embeddings. We shall define the position index as the relative distance of each word in the sentence to the aspect term. Subsequently, a position matrix $P \in \mathbb{R}^{d_p \times L}$ for position embedding establishing is randomly initialized and updated during training. According to Eq. (4), by calculating the position index of every other word, the position embedding matrix $P_i = (p_{i1}, p_{i2}, \cdots, p_{iL}) \in \mathbb{R}^{d_p \times L}$ is obtained based on the position index sequence from P.

$$o_j = \begin{cases} |j - t_s|, & j < t_s \\ 0, & t_s \leq j \leq t_e \\ |j - t_e|, & j > t_e \end{cases} \tag{4}$$

where o_j is the position index of the jth word in sentence while t_s and t_e indicate the starting and ending indices of the aspect term, respectively. Let $v_{ij}^{pos} = w_j \oplus p_{ij}$ be the position representation. Then the embeddings, with position information integrated, can be written as $V_i^{pos} = [v_{i1}^{pos}, v_{i2}^{pos}, \cdots, v_{iL}^{pos}] \in \mathbb{R}^{(d_{em}+d_p) \times L}$.

3.3   Aspect-Specific Sentential Representations Modeling

The outcomes from the input layer are taken to model the aspect-specific sentential representation of each aspect term in sentence order. At this stage, two GCAE models are employed to separately deal with V_i^{att} and V_i^{pos}. It is clear however that the matrices V_i^{att} and V_i^{pos} represent distinguishing information in the sentence. Thereby, the corresponding feature vectors x_i^{att} and x_i^{pos} can be:

$$x_i^{att} = GCAE\left(V_i^{att}, a_i\right) \tag{5}$$

$$x_i^{pos} = GCAE\left(V_i^{pos}, a_i\right) \tag{6}$$

Note that both $x_i^{att} \in \mathbb{R}^{d_n}$ and $x_i^{pos} \in \mathbb{R}^{d_n}$ denote the feature vector of aspect term a_i. The former contains more semantic and sentiment information in relation to the context while the latter incorporates the semantic information from the neighboring words.

Notwithstanding, there still exist some defects in the representations: the attention network tends to assign more attention weights to the domain-specific words rather than the sentiment-related words [15]; merely depending on the position information is absent of reliability while dealing with multiple aspect terms. On this occasion, considering the defects from both parts, we shall thus generate the hidden representation of the contexts, which is:

$$x_i^{co} = tanh\left(x_i^{att}W_{co1} + x_i^{pos}W_{co2} + b_{co}\right) \tag{7}$$

where $W_{co1} \in \mathbb{R}^{d_n \times d_{co}}$ and $W_{co2} \in \mathbb{R}^{d_n \times d_{co}}$ stand for the projection parameter matrices updated during training and $b_{co} \in \mathbb{R}^{d_{co}}$ is the bias.

Accordingly, the aspect-specific sentential representation X_i of the specific aspect term is obtained, i.e.

$$X_i = \left[x_i^{att}; x_i^{pos}; x_i^{co}\right] \in \mathbb{R}^{2d_n + d_{co}} \tag{8}$$

So is each aspect term in the sentence with the same manner.

3.4   Conjunction-Based Inter-aspect Relationship Modeling

After the aspect-specific sentential representation derived, the interaction of adjacent aspect terms is also considered. As such, the conjunctions are between two aspect terms are analyzed for sentiment identification. As pointed out in [15], both additive conjunction information and contrasting conjunction information has to be taken into account whilst specific conjunction words of these two categories are presented in Table 2.

A conjunction matrix, derived from the average initialization of conjunction word vectors in Table 2, is defined as $E \in \mathbb{R}^{c \times d_c}$ where c denotes the category and d_c is the word vector dimension. Furthermore, the sentiment information of the adjacent aspect term is incorporated as well because the sentiment of an aspect influences the succeeding one in line with the presence of conjunction [2]. We then construct a randomly initialized sentiment matrix $G \in \mathbb{R}^{k \times d_k}$ with k indicating

Table 2. Conjunction classification

S.no.	Conjunction class	Examples
1	Additive conjunction	And, or, as well as, also, further, moreover
2	Contrasting conjunction	But, however, instead, except, while, though, although, yet

the number of sentiment polarities and d_k representing the sentiment vector dimension. Instead of directly using the aspect-specific sentential representation, the preceding aspect term is employed for its sentiment polarity predicting, which is delivered as the sentiment vector in $G \in \mathbb{R}^{k \times d_k}$. Therefore, the inter-aspect representation r_i^{conj}, with both conjunction information and adjacent aspect term sentiment integrated, is given by

$$r_i^{conj} = \begin{cases} relu\left(W_a g_i + W_{ad} e_{ad}\right), c = 1 \\ relu\left(W_a g_i + W_{co} e_{co}\right), c = 2 \end{cases} \tag{9}$$

where $W_u \in \mathbb{R}^{d_k \times d_t}$, $W_{ad} \in \mathbb{R}^{d_c \times d_t}$ and $W_{co} \in \mathbb{R}^{d_c \times d_t}$ is the parameter matrix, $g_i \in \mathbb{R}^{d_k}$ is the sentiment vector of the preceding aspect term, $e_{ad} \in \mathbb{R}^{d_c}$ and $e_{co} \in \mathbb{R}^{d_c}$ represent the additive conjunction and contrasting conjunction, respectively. That is, c=1 is applied to the condition of additive conjunction between two aspect terms while c=2 to that of contrasting conjunction.

3.5   Final Classification

In this layer, the aforementioned aspect-specific sentential representation X_i and the inter-aspect representation r_i^{conj} are concatenated and fed into softmax classifier for sentiment polarity distribution identification, which is

$$\hat{y}_i = softmax\left(W_s \left[X_i; r_i^{conj}\right] + b_s\right) \tag{10}$$

where W_s and b_s are parameters to be learned in the softmax layer.

3.6   Model Training

The training process is conducted on by using the categorical cross-entropy, which is expressed as:

$$loss = -\frac{1}{m} \sum_{i=1}^{m} \sum_{j=1}^{n} y_{i,j} log\left(\hat{y}_{i,j}\right) + \lambda \|\theta\|^2 \tag{11}$$

where m is the number of aspect terms in the sentence, n is the number of sentiment polarities. The parameter y_i stands for the real sentiment distribution of ith aspect term and $\hat{y}_{i,j}$ is the predicted one on j^{th} sentiment polarity. Besides, λ is the weight of L_2 regularization term.

Table 3. Samples of SemEval 2014 Dataset and MAMS.

Datasets	Positive		Negative		Neutral	
	Train	Test	Train	Test	Train	Test
Restaurant	2164	728	807	196	637	196
Laptop	994	341	870	128	464	169
MAMS	3380	400	2764	329	5042	607

4 Experiments

4.1 Experimental Setting

We carry out our experiments on two publicly available datasets: SemEval-2014 ABSA dataset [12] and Multi-Aspect Multi-Sentiment (MAMS) dataset [3]. The SemEval-2014 ABSA dataset can be subdivided into user reviews on both laptop and restaurant domains with each review having a list of aspect terms and corresponding polarities. For the MAMS dataset, there exist over two aspect terms of distinguishing sentiment, together with their sentiment polarities as well. Details of each dataset is exhibited in Table 3.

The initialization of word embeddings in all datasets is performed using 300-dimensional word vectors pretrained by Glove [11]. All the parameter matrices involved are generated within the distribution $U(-0.1, 0.1)$ randomly and the bias set as 0. The position embedding, whose dimension is set as 150, is randomly initialized. The batch size for the three datasets is 32 and the kernel sizes are 3, 4 and 5 for the convolution layer. The learning rate is 0.001. Besides, the Adam optimizer is adopted [5]. The L_2 regularization weight is set as 10^{-5}. All the models are run 5 times on the test datasets with their average results reported.

4.2 Model Comparisons

In order to evaluate the performance of IARC, we compare our model against several baseline models. Concretely, the baselines can be categorized into two classes, namely single-aspect models and inter-aspect models. The former (including TextCNN [4], ATAE-LSTM [16], GCAE [18], IAN [8], MemNet [14], PBAN [1] and CapsNet [3]) deals with aspect term and the latter (including IARM [9] and SDGCN [20])also has the capability of tackling the inter-aspect relation. Concretely, among all the RNN-attention models, PBAN exploits the position information of the aspect terms while IARM addresses inter-aspect relation using recurrent memory networks with multihop attention mechanism. In terms of CNN-based models (i.e. TextCNN and GCAE), GCAE specifically employ gating mechanisms to capture the aspect related features. By contrast, CapsNet is an instance of capsule network whilst SDGCN tackles inter-aspect relation with the integration of GCN and bidirectional attention mechanism.

The accuracy of each dataset is presented in Table 4. Our model is competitive in all evaluation settings and outperforms baselines in laptop and MAMS.

Table 4. Experimental results on semEval-2014 restaurant and laptop review dataset and MAMS datasets. Best scores are in bold.

	Method	Restaurant	Laptop	MAMS
Single-aspect models	TextCNN	75.93	–	52.69
	ATAE-LSTM	77.28	68.70	77.05
	GCAE	75.93	72.56	77.59
	IAN	78.60	72.10	76.60
	MemNet	80.95	72.21	64.57
	PBAN	81.16	74.12	78.74
	CapsNet	80.79	–	79.78
Inter-aspect models	IARM	80.0	73.80	–
	SDGCN	**82.95**	75.55	79.19
	IARC	81.16	**76.33**	**80.76**

For single-aspect models, TextCNN has the worst performance due to its failing to utilize the aspect term information. Among all the attention-based networks, i.e. ATAE-LSTM, MemNet, IAN and PBAN, PBAN is the best-performing method in this group. One possible explanation is that the position information is also taken in PBAN, which facilitates the capture of semantic information of aspect terms. Besides, the CapsNet also gets a comparable outcome to PBAN. The main reason is that the capsule network is effective in capturing the relation between aspect term and its contexts. As a CNN-based model, GCAE performs better than TextCNN to a large extent, since the gate mechanism can be applied to select aspect-related sentiment features. Clearly, since our model is built on convolutional layers and gating units, with the integration of position information, attention mechanism and the inter-aspect relationship, it is reasonable to expect a better result, as it is the case. One can see that, for most baseline models, the classification accuracy on MAMS is less competitive than that on SemEval-2014. In order to resolve more aspect terms with various sentiment polarities in MAMS, the analysis of relation between adjacent aspect terms is of great significance. In contrast with the inter-aspect models, IARC is a competitive alternative in modeling the inter-aspect relationship. Current inter-aspect models mainly concentrate on the aspect-specific sentential representation within the context. Neither IARM nor SDGCN makes use of the conjunction words and the sentiment of the preceding aspect term.

Table 5. Result of ablation study for dataset.

Datasets	Restaurant	Laptop	MAMS
GCAE	77.28	72.56	77.588
IARC/inter+conj	79.91	74.99	79.27
IARC/conj	80.89	75.21	80.09
IARC	81.16	76.33	80.76

Table 6. Statistics of single aspect and multi-aspect in semEval 2014 datasets; n = 1: single aspect, n > 1: multi-aspect.

Domain	Train		Test	
	N = 1	N > 1	N = 1	N > 1
Restaurant	1009	2599	285	835
Laptop	918	1396	259	379

Table 7. Performance of different methods for single aspect and multi-aspect; n=1: single aspect, n>1: multi-aspect.

Model	Restaurant		Laptop	
	N=1	N>1	N=1	N>1
IARC/inter+conj	80.00	79.64	75.68	74.41
IARC	79.85	81.58	76.06	75.73

4.3 Ablation Study

An ablation study is performed to determine the significance of the different components in IARC. The classical GCAE is taken as the base model. According to Table 5, the removal of conjunction information (labeled as "IARC/conj") as well as conjunction information and inter-aspect sentiment (labeled as "IARC/inter+ conj") still results in a better performance than GCAE, which indicates the importance of attention mechanism and position information in interpreting the relation between aspect and the contexts. The "IARC/conj" model has a higher testing accuracy than the "IARC/inter+conj" model to confirm the effectiveness of inter-aspect sentiment. In contrast, our model performs notably better than the others. That is, the employment of both conjunction words and the adjacent aspect term sentiment is practical in sentiment prediction of the aspect term.

4.4 Effect on Single Aspect and Multi-aspect

To further verify the working performance of IARC, we divide the SemEval-2014 dataset into single-aspect samples and multi-aspect samples; see Table 6. The IARC model and "IARC/inter+conj" model are implemented on the four datasets, respectively, whose testing accuracy is presented in Table 7.

It can be observed that the outcomes of the two methods on single aspect samples are comparative. However, there is a considerable performance gap between IARC model and "IARC/inter+conj" model on multi-aspect samples sentiment classification. In comparison with the laptop reviews, a greater improvement appears in the restaurant dataset. For one thing, the multi-aspect samples account for a higher proportion in the restaurant dataset; for another, the sentences containing conjunctions in multi-aspect samples occupy 77.13% in restaurant reviews, which is higher than that of 72.82% in laptop reviews. Accordingly, it is beneficial to utilize inter-aspect relationship and conjunction information in multi-aspect term sentiment analysis (Table 8).

Table 8. Examples of aspect term sentiment prediction. Each aspect term is highlighted with different colors to indicate the sentiment where yellow stands for the positive, green for neutral and blue for negative.

ID	sentence	GCAE	PBAN	SDGCN	IARC
1	The [food]^{a1} was definitely good, but when all was said and done, I just couldn't justify it for the [price]^{a2} (including 2 [drinks]^{a3}, \$100/person)	a_1 ; a_2 ; a_3	a_1 ; a_2 ; a_3	a_1 ; a_2 ; a_3	a_1 ; a_2 ; a_3
2	The [food]^{a1} and [service]^{a2} was top notch, only the complain is that this place is so small that some [seats]^{a3} are not made for a big [guy]^{a4}	a_1 ; a_2 ; a_3 ; a_4	a_1 ; a_2 ; a_3 ; a_4	a_1 ; a_2 ; a_3 ; a_4	a_1 ; a_2 ; a_3 ; a_4
3	got the [guac]^{a1} but no [drinks]^{a2} until it was all gone (approximately 20 minutes later).	a_1 ; a_2	a_1 ; a_2	a_1 ; a_2	a_1 ; a_2
4	I'm not a fan of any of their [appetizers]^{a1} or [Thai food]^{a2}, but their [Japanese food]^{a3} is great.	a_1 ; a_2 ; a_3	a_1 ; a_2 ; a_3	a_1 ; a_2 ; a_3	a_1 ; a_2 ; a_3

4.5 Case Study

In this section, we give some instances and visualize their working principle on how to predict the sentiment polarities of aspect terms. The actual sentiment and predicted outcomes of the four models are exhibited, respectively. For the first sentence, the aspect "drink" is mis-identified by GCAE and PBAN due to its lack of context. By adopting the multi-aspects terms relationship, IARC, as well as SDGCN, achieves a decent outcome. In sentence 2, the sentiment of aspect "service" is identified by that of its adjacent aspect "food" within the same context, which is the same case for "guy" and "seats".

On the other hand, IARC obtains the best and most consistent results in multi-aspect terms with conjunctions. The contrasting conjunction "but" in sentence 3 and the additive conjunction "or" in sentence 4 are taken to improve the predicting accuracy. Specifically, as presented in sentence 4, it is more clear to identify the sentiment of aspect "Thai food" based on the sentiment of aspect "appetizers" and the conjunction information from conjunctive word "or".

5 Conclusion

In this work, we propose a CNN-based model with the integration of inter-aspect relationship and conjunction information for aspect-level sentiment analysis. By improving the current GCAE model, attention mechanism and position information are employed to deal with multi-aspects, and thus to obtain a more precise aspect-specific sentential representation. Furthermore, the inter-aspect relationship between adjacent aspect terms is considered. Both conjunction information and the sentiment of the preceding aspect term are integrated and exploited for aspect term modeling and sentiment prediction. As a result, the sentiment classification accuracy, especially for multi-aspect-sentences, is improved significantly. Experiments on SemEval2014 and MAMS verify that the proposed model is the best alternative comparing to the state-of-arts.

References

1. Gu, S., Zhang, L., Hou, Y., Song, Y.: A position-aware bidirectional attention network for aspect-level sentiment analysis. Proc. COLING **2018**, 774–784 (2018)
2. Hazarika, D., Poria, S., Vij, P., Krishnamurthy, G., Cambria, E., Zimmermann, R.: Modeling inter-aspect dependencies for aspect-based sentiment analysis. Proc. NAACL **2018**, 266–270 (2018)
3. Jiang, Q., Chen, L., Xu, R., Ao, X., Yang, M.: A challenge dataset and effective models for aspect-based sentiment analysis. Proc. EMNLP-IJCNLP **2019**, 6281–6286 (2019)
4. Kim, Y.: Convolutional neural networks for sentence classification. arXiv preprint arXiv:1408.5882 (2014)
5. Kingma, D.P., Ba, J.: Adam: A method for stochastic optimization. arXiv preprint arXiv:1412.6980 (2014)
6. Li, X., Bing, L., Lam, W., Shi, B.: Transformation networks for target-oriented sentiment classification. arXiv preprint arXiv:1805.01086 (2018)
7. Lin, P., Yang, M., Lai, J.: Deep mask memory network with semantic dependency and context moment for aspect level sentiment classification. In: IJCAI (2019)
8. Ma, D., Li, S., Zhang, X., Wang, H.: Interactive attention networks for aspect-level sentiment classification. arXiv preprint arXiv:1709.00893 (2017)
9. Majumder, N., Poria, S., Gelbukh, A., Akhtar, M.S., Cambria, E., Ekbal, A.: Iarm: inter-aspect relation modeling with memory networks in aspect-based sentiment analysis. Proc. EMNLP **2018**, 3402–3411 (2018)
10. Mukherjee, S., Bhattacharyya, P.: Sentiment analysis in twitter with lightweight discourse analysis. Proc. COLING **2012**, 1847–1864 (2012)
11. Pennington, J., Socher, R., Manning, C.D.: Glove: global vectors for word representation. Proc. EMNLP **2014**, 1532–1543 (2014)
12. Pontiki, M., Galanis, D., Pavlopoulos, J., Papageorgiou, H., Androutsopoulos, I., Manandhar, S.: Semeval-2014 task 4: aspect based sentiment analysis. In: Proceedings of the 8th International Workshop on Semantic Evaluation (SemEval 2014), pp. 27–35 (2014)
13. Schouten, K., Frasincar, F.: Survey on aspect-level sentiment analysis. IEEE Trans. Knowl. Data Eng. **28**(3), 813–830 (2015)
14. Tang, D., Qin, B., Liu, T.: Aspect level sentiment classification with deep memory network. arXiv preprint arXiv:1605.08900 (2016)
15. Wang, J., et al.: Human-like decision making: Document-level aspect sentiment classification via hierarchical reinforcement learning. arXiv preprint arXiv:1910.09260 (2019)
16. Wang, Y., Huang, M., Zhu, X., Zhao, L.: Attention-based lstm for aspect-level sentiment classification. Proc. EMNLP **2016**, 606–615 (2016)
17. Wu, S., Xu, Y., Wu, F., Yuan, Z., Huang, Y., Li, X.: Aspect-based sentiment analysis via fusing multiple sources of textual knowledge. Knowl.-Based Syst. **183**, 104868 (2019)
18. Xue, W., Li, T.: Aspect based sentiment analysis with gated convolutional networks. arXiv preprint arXiv:1805.07043 (2018)
19. Zhang, C., Li, Q., Song, D.: Aspect-based sentiment classification with aspect-specific graph convolutional networks. arXiv preprint arXiv:1909.03477 (2019)
20. Zhao, P., Hou, L., Wu, O.: Modeling sentiment dependencies with graph convolutional networks for aspect-level sentiment classification. Knowl.-Based Syst. **193**, 105443 (2020)

Author Index

Printed in the United States
by Baker & Taylor Publisher Services

Printed in the United States
by Baker & Taylor Publisher Services